WORD BIBLICAL COMMENTARY

WORD BIBLICAL COMMENTARY

Volume 52B

Revelation 6–16

DAVID E. AUNE

Publishers Since 1798

THOMAS NELSON PUBLISHERS
Nashville

Word Biblical Commentary
Revelation 6–16

Library of Congress Cataloging-in-Publication Data
Main entry under title:

Word biblical commentary.

Includes bibliographies.
1. Bible—Commentaries—Collected works.
BS491.2.W67 22.2'7 81-71768
ISBN 0-8499-0786-1 (v. 52B) AACR2

Printed in Colombia

The author's own translation of the Scripture text appears in italic type under the heading *Translation*.

4 5 6 7 8 QPV 03 02

To
Peder and Inger Borgen
and
Martin and Marianne Hengel

Contents

Editorial Preface

The launching of the *Word Biblical Commentary* brings to fulfillment an enterprise of several years' planning. The publishers and the members of the editorial board met in 1977 to explore the possibility of a new commentary on the books of the Bible that would incorporate several distinctive features. Prospective readers of these volumes are entitled to know what such features were intended to be; whether the aims of the commentary have been fully achieved time alone will tell.

First, we have tried to cast a wide net to include as contributors a number of scholars from around the world who not only share our aims but are in the main engaged in the ministry of teaching in university, college, and seminary. They represent a rich diversity of denominational allegiance. The broad stance of our contributors can rightly be called evangelical, and this term is to be understood in its positive, historic sense of a commitment to Scripture as divine revelation and the truth and power of the Christian gospel.

Then, the commentaries in our series are all commissioned and written for the purpose of inclusion in the *Word Biblical Commentary*. Unlike several of our distinguished counterparts in the field of commentary writing, there are no translated works, originally written in a non-English language. Also, our commentators were asked to prepare their own rendering of the original biblical text and to use those languages as the basis of their own comments and exegesis. What may be claimed as distinctive with this series is that it is based on the biblical languages, yet it seeks to make the technical and scholarly approach to the theological understanding of Scripture understandable by—and useful to—the fledgling student, the working minister, and colleagues in the guild of professional scholars and teachers as well.

Finally, a word must be said about the format of the series. The layout, in clearly defined sections, has been consciously devised to assist readers at different levels. Those wishing to learn about the textual witnesses on which the translation is offered are invited to consult the section headed *Notes*. If the readers' concern is with the state of modern scholarship on any given portion of Scripture, they should turn to the sections on *Bbiliography* and *Form/Structure/Setting*. For a clear exposition of the passage's meaning and its relevance to the ongoing biblical revelation, the *Comment* and concluding *Explanation* are designed expressly to meet that need. There is therefore something for everyone who may pick up and use these volumes.

If these aims come anywhere near realization, the intention of the editors will have been met, and the labor of our team of contributors rewarded.

General Editors: *Bruce Metzger,*
David A. Hubbard†
Glenn W. Barker†
Old Testament: *John D. W. Watts*
New Testament: *Ralph P. Martin*

Author's Preface

Serious research on this commentary began in 1982–83, when I spent the academic year at the University of Trondheim, as a Fulbright guest professor in the Department of Religious Studies. Professor Peder Borgen was my host, and I am grateful to him and his wife, Inger, for the kindness, hospitality, and friendship shown to my family and me during that exciting year. Work on the commentary was all but completed some twelve years later in 1994–95 at the University of Tübingen, where I continued my research as the recipient of an Alexander von Humboldt Forschungspreis. Professor Martin Hengel (whom I first met when he gave a lecture at the University of Trondheim in the spring of 1983) was my host, and my wife and I experienced the gracious hospitality of the Hengels and Professor and Mrs. Peter Stuhlmacher on many occasions. I must also express my appreciation to Dr. Jörg Frey, Professor Hengel's research assistant, for his ready help in dealing with many practical details at the Theologicum in Tübingen. Since the years at Trondheim and Tübingen were critical for the commencement and completion of this commentary, I have dedicated it in gratitude to the Borgens and the Hengels. I am, of course, profoundly grateful both to the Council for International Exchange of Scholars for the Fulbright award and to the Alexander von Humboldt Stiftung for the award of a Forschungspreis, as well as to Loyola University Chicago for providing me with a subsidized leave of absence during the 1994–95 academic year.

A number of colleagues and students have made important contributions to this commentary. Colleagues who have read and offered critiques of portions of the commentary include Professors Lee Levine of Hebrew University, Jan Willem van Henten of the University of Amsterdam, and Bruce Metzger of Princeton Theological Seminary. Some of the material that found its way into the commentary was originally formulated and delivered as lectures at the University of Aberdeen (February 1983), the University of Oslo and the Baptist Theological Seminary in Oslo (March 1983), Washington University (February 1990), and the University of Utrecht (March 1995). I also profited greatly by participating in various seminars on Revelation, including the Seminar on Early Christian Apocalypticism (1983–87), chaired by Professor Adela Yarbro Collins, the Seminar on Reading the Apocalypse (1991–97), chaired by Professor David Barr, both under the auspices of the Society of Biblical Literature, and the Seminar on Apocalyptic in the New Testament, chaired by a succession of scholars including Professors Traugott Holtz, Elizabeth Schüssler Fiorenza, Charles H. Giblin, and Jens Taeger, under the auspices of the Studiorum Novi Testamenti Societas. Three graduate research assistants, Peter Sibilio (spring 1994), Paul Hartog (fall 1995), and Kevin McCruden (Spring 1997), have waded through countless pages of text and saved me from hundreds of errors.

My own interest in Revelation began in connection with earlier work on issues relating to early Christiain prophecy that came to fruition in a book entitled *Proph-*

ecy in Early Christianity and the Ancient Mediterranean World (Grand Rapids, MI: Eerdmans, 1983). It seemed a natural continuation of that interest to focus on a detailed study of the Revelation of John. I am grateful for the confidence that Professor Ralph Martin had in my work, which led to the issuing of the contract that made this commentary part of the Word Biblical Commentary series.

The writing of a commentary on any book of the Bible is a daunting task, particularly so in the case of the Revelation of John. Though the bibliography of books and articles on Revelation is enormous (extensive as the bibliographies in this commentary are, they are far from exhaustive), I am particularly indebted to the rich and creative commentaries of Wilhelm Bousset and R. H. Charles, and to the very detailed and painstaking textual work of H. C. Hoskier and Josef Schmid. In the words of J. W. v. Goethe:

> Seh ich die Werke der Meister an,
> So seh ich das, was sie getan;
> Betracht ich meine Siebensachen,
> Seh ich, was ich hätt sollen machen.

The *Notes* sections in this commentary contain discussions of the grammar and text of Revelation. Readers who have a special interest in the text of Revelation are urged to read Section 6 of the *Introduction,* where a full explanation of the many abbreviations of manuscripts and families of manuscripts can be found.

DAVID E. AUNE

April 1997
Loyola University Chicago

Abbreviations

A. General Abbreviations

abs.	absolute
acc.	accusative
adj.	adjective, adjectival
adv.	adverb, adverbial
aor.	aorist
Aram.	Aramaic
ca.	*circa,* about
cent.	century
cf.	*confer,* compare
chap(s).	chapter(s)
d.	deceased
dat.	dative
DSS	Dead Sea Scrolls
ed.	editor, edited by
e.g.	*exempli gratia,* for example
ET	English translation
et. al.	*et alii,* and others
fem.	feminine
fig.	figure
fl.	*floruit,* flourished
fol.	folio
FS	*Festschrift,* volume written in honor of
fut.	future
gen.	genitive
Gk.	Greek
hap. leg.	*hapax legomenon,* sole occurrence
Heb.	Hebrew
id.	*idem,* the same
i.e.	*id est,* that is
imper.	imperative
impf.	imperfect
ind.	indicative
inf.	infinitive
lit.	literally
LXX	Septuagint
masc.	masculine
MS(S)	manuscript(s)
MT	Masoretic Text
n.	note
n.d.	no date
neut.	neuter
no.	number
nom.	nominative
n.s.	new series
NT	New Testament
obj.	object, objective
OL	Old Latin
OT	Old Testament
par.	parallel
pass.	passive
PEnteux	*Enteuxeis* Papyri (Cairo)
pf.	perfect
PGiss	Giessen Papyri
PKöln	Kölner Papyri
pl.	plural
plupf.	pluperfect
PLond	London Papyri
poss.	possessive
POxy	Oxyrhynchus Papyri
prep.	preposition
PRoss	Papyri russischer und georgischer Sammlungen
ptcp.	participle
PWash	Washington University Papyri
repr.	reprint
rev.	revised, reviser, revision
sc.	*scilicet,* namely
ser.	series
sing.	singular
s.v.	*sub verbo,* under the word
Sync	Syncellus
Theod	Theodotion
tr.	translator, translated by, translation
UP	University Press
v, vv	verse, verses
var. lect.	*varia(e) lectio(nes),* "variant reading(s)"
vol.	volume
x	times (2x = two times)

B. Abbreviations for Translations and Paraphrases

ASV American Standard Version, American Revised Version (1901)
AV Authorized Version = KJV
KJV King James Version (1611) = AV
NASB New American Standard Bible
NEB New English Bible
NIV New International Version
NRSV New Revised Standard Version
REB Revised English Bible
RSV Revised Standard Version

C. Abbreviations of Commonly Used Periodicals, Reference Works, and Serials

AAA R. A. Lipsius and M. Bonnet (eds.), *Acta Apostolorum Apocrypha*
AB Anchor Bible
ABD D. N. Freedman (ed.), *Anchor Bible Dictionary*, 6 vols.
AC *Antike und Christentum*
AcCl *Acta Classica*
AD I. J. Gelb et al. (eds), *The Assyrian Dictionary of the Oriental Institute of the University of Chicago*, 21 vols.
AHI G. I. Davies (ed.), *Ancient Hebrew Inscriptions: Corpus and Concordance*
AJA *American Journal of Archaeology*
AJAH *American Journal of Ancient History*
AJBI Annual of the Japanese Biblical Institute
AJP *American Journal of Philology*
ALUOS Annual of Leeds University Oriental Society
AnBib Analecta biblica
AnBoll Analecta Bollandiana
ANEP J. B. Pritchard (ed.), *The Ancient Near East in Pictures*
ANET J. B. Pritchard (ed.), *Ancient Near Eastern Texts*
ANRW *Aufsteig und Niedergang der römischen Welt*
ANTF Arbeiten zur neutestamentlichen Textforschung
AOB Acta Orientalia Beligica
AOT H. F. D. Sparks (ed.), *The Apocryphal Old Testament*
AramBib Aramaic Bible (Wilmington, DE: Glazier)
ARW *Archiv für Religionswissenschaft*
AsSeign *Assemblées du Seigneur*
ASTI *Annual of the Swedish Theological Institute*
ATANT Abhandlung zur Theologie des Alten und Neuen Testaments
ATR *Anglican Theological Review*
Aug *Augustinianum*
AUSDDS Andrews University Seminary Doctoral Dissertation Series
AUSS *Andrews University Seminary Studies*
BA *Biblical Archaeologist*
BAGD W. Bauer, W. F. Arndt, F. W. Gingrich, and F. W. Danker, *A Greek-English Lexicon of the NT*, 2nd ed.
BAR *Biblical Archaeologist Reader*
BARev *Biblical Archaeology Review*
BARevSup *BARev* Supplementary Series
BASOR *Bulletin of the American Schools of Oriental Research*
BASORSup *BASOR* Supplementary Studies
Bauer-Aland W. Bauer, *Griechisch-deutsches Wörterbuch zum den Schriften des Neuen Testaments und der frühchristlichen Literatur*, 6th ed., rev. K. and B. Aland

BCH	*Bulletin de Correspondance Hellénique*
BDB	F. Brown, S. R. Driver, and C. A. Briggs, *Hebrew and English Lexicon of the OT*
BDF	F. Blass, A. Debrunner, and R. W. Funk, *A Greek Grammar of the NT*
BDR	F. Blass, A. Debrunner, and F. Rehkopf, *Grammatik des neutestamentlichen Griechisch* (1984)
BETL	Bibliotheca ephemeridum theologicarum lovaniensium
BEvT	Beiträge zur Evangelischen Theologie
BG	W. C. Till (ed.), *Die gnostischen Schriften des koptischen Papyrus Berolinensis 8502*
BGBE	Beiträge zur Geschichte der biblischen Exegese
BHS	*Biblia hebraica stuttgartensia*
BHT	Beiträge zur historischen Theologie
Bib	*Biblica*
BibLeb	*Bibel und Leben*
BibReal	K. Galling (ed.), *Biblisches Reallexikon,* 2nd ed.
BJRL	*Bulletin of the John Rylands University Library of Manchester*
BJS	Brown Judaic Studies
BK	*Bibel und Kirche*
BMC	H. Mattingly, *Coins of the Roman Empire in the British Museum*
BMI	*British Museum Inscriptions*
BN	*Biblische Notizen*
BR	*Biblical Research*
BSac	*Bibliotheca Sacra*
BT	*The Bible Translator*
BTB	*Biblical Theology Bulletin*
BurH	*Buried History*
BVC	*Bible et vie chrétienne*
BWANT	Beiträge zur Wissenschaft vom Alten und Neuen Testament
ByzNeugrJb	*Byzantinisch-neugriechische Jahrbücher*
BZ	*Biblische Zeitschrift*
BZAW	Beihefte zur *ZAW*
BZNW	Beihefte zur *ZNW*
CA	*Classical Antiquity*
CAH	*Cambridge Ancient History*
CBQ	*Catholic Biblical Quarterly*
CBQMS	Catholic Biblical Quarterly—Monograph Series
CCL	Corpus Christianorum, Series Latina
CH	*Church History*
Checklist	J. F. Oates, R. S. Bagnall, W. H. Willis, and K. A. Worp, *Checklist of Editions of Greek Papyri and Ostraca,* 3rd ed.
CIG	*Corpus Inscriptionum Graecarum,* 4 vols.
CIJ	*Corpus Inscriptionum Judaicarum*
CIL	*Corpus Inscriptionum Latinarum*
CIMRM	M. J. Vermaseren (ed.), *Corpus Inscriptionum et Monumentorum Religionis Mithraicae,* 2 vols.
CJ	*Classical Journal*
CMIR	J. R. Cayón, *Compendio de las Monedas del Imperio Romano,* 2 vols.
ConBNT	Coniectanea biblica, NT series
ConBOT	Coniectanea biblica, Old Testament
ConNT	Coniectanea neotestamentica
CP	*Classical Philology*
CPJ	V. A. Tcherikover, A. Fuks, and M. Stern (eds.), *Corpus Papyrorum Judaicorum,* 3 vols.
CQ	*Classical Quarterly*
CQR	*Church Quarterly Review*
CREBM	H. Mattingly and R. A. G. Carson, *Coins of the Roman Empire in the*

British Museum, 6 vols.

CRINT Compendia Rerum Iudaicarum ad Novum Testamentum

CSCA *California Studies in Classical Antiquity*

CSCO Corpus scriptorum christianorum orientalium

CSEL Corpus scriptorum ecclesiasticorum latinorum

CTA A. Herdner, *Corpus des tablettes en cunéiformes alphabétiques*

CTM *Concordia Theological Monthly*

CTQ *Concordia Theological Quarterly*

CTR *Criswell Theological Review*

DACL F. Cabrol (ed.), *Dictionnaire d'archéologie chrétienne et la liturgie,* 15 vols.

DBSup *Dictionnaire de la Bible, Supplément*

DCH D. J. A. Clines (ed.), *The Dictionary of Classical Hebrew*

DDD K. van der Toorn, B. Becking, and P. W. van der Horst (eds.), *Dictionary of Deities and Demons in the Bible*

DJD Discoveries in the Judaean Desert

DJPA M. Sokoloff, *A Dictionary of Jewish Palestinian Aramaic of the Byzantine Period*

DSD *Dead Sea Discoveries*

DTT *Dansk teologisk tidsskrift*

EDNT H. Balz and G. Schneider (eds.), *Exegetical Dictionary of the New Testament,* 3 vols.

EEC Angelo Di Berardino (ed.), *Encyclopedia of the Early Church,* 2 vols.

EncJud *Encyclopedia Judaica,* 16 vols.

EncRel M. Eliade (ed.), *The Encyclopedia of Religion*

EPRO Études préliminaires aux religions orientales dans l'empire romain

ERE J. Hastings (ed.), *Encyclopedia of Religion and Ethics*

ErFor Erträge der Forschung

ESAR T. Frank (ed.), *An Economic Survey of Ancient Rome,* 5 vols.

ETL *Ephemerides theologicae lovanienses*

ETR *Études théologiques et religieuses*

EvQ *Evangelical Quarterly*

EvT *Evangelische Theologie*

EWNT H. Balz and G. Schneider (eds.), *Exegetisches Wörterbuch zum Neuen Testament,* 3 vols.

ExpTim *Expository Times*

FHJA C. R. Holladay (ed.), *Fragments from Hellenistic Jewish Authors,* 4 vols.

FNT *Filologia Neotestamentaria*

FOTL The Forms of the Old Testament Literature

FrGrHist F. Jacoby (ed.), *Die Fragmente der griechischen Historiker*

FRLANT Forschungen zur Religion und Literatur des Alten und Neuen Testaments

FuF *Forschungen und Fortschritte*

FVS H. Diels and W. Kranz, *Die Fragmente der Vorsokratiker,* 3 vols.

GCS Griechischen christlichen Schriftsteller

GELS J. Lust, E. Eynikel, and K. Hauspie, *A Greek-English Lexicon of the Septuagint*

GGR M. P. Nilsson, *Geschichte der griechischen Religion,* vol. 1, 3rd ed. (1967); vol. 2, 2nd ed. (1961)

GHÅ *Göteborgs Högskolas Årsskrift*

GKC *Gesenius' Hebrew Grammar,* ed. E. Kautzsch, tr. A. E. Cowley

GL *Geist und Leben*

GNS Good News Studies
GR *Greece and Rome*
GRBS *Greek, Roman, and Byzantine Studies*
GTJ *Grace Theological Journal*

HAT Handbuch zum Alten Testament
HCNT M. E. Boring, K. Berger, and C. Colpe, *Hellenistic Commentary to the NT*
HDA H. Bächtold-Stäubli with E. Hoffmann-Krayer (eds.), *Handwörterbuch des deutschen Aberglaubens*
HDR Harvard Dissertations in Religion
HeyJ *Heythrop Journal*
HibJ *Hibbert Journal*
HNT Handbuch zum Neuen Testament
HSCP *Harvard Studies in Classical Philology*
HSM Harvard Semitic Monographs
HSS Harvard Semitic Studies
HTR *Harvard Theological Review*
HTS Harvard Theological Studies
HUCA *Hebrew Union College Annual*
HUT Hermeneutische Untersuchungen zur Theologie

IBM *Ancient Greek Inscriptions in the British Museum,* 4 vols.
IDB G. A. Buttrick (ed.), *Interpreter's Dictionary of the Bible,* 4 vols.
IDBSup Supplementary Volume to *IDB*
IEJ *Israel Exploration Journal*
I. Eph. H. Wankel (ed.), *Die Inschriften von Ephesos,* IGSK, 8 vols.
IGRom R. Cagnat et al., *Inscriptiones Graecae ad res Romanas pertinentes,* 4 vols.
IGSK Inschriften griechischer Städte aus Kleinasien
IM *Istanbuler Mitteilungen*
Int *Interpretation*
ISBE G. W. Bromiley (ed.), *International Standard Bible Encyclopedia,* rev., 4 vols.
ITQ *Irish Theological Quarterly*

JAAR *Journal of the American Academy of Religion*
JAC Jahrbuch für Antike und Christentum
JAF *Journal of American Folklore*
JAOS *Journal of the American Oriental Society*
JBL *Journal of Biblical Literature*
JBR *Journal of Bible and Religion*
JE *Jewish Encyclopedia*
JES *Journal of Ecumenical Studies*
JETS *Journal of the Evangelical Theological Society*
JHS *Journal of Hellenic Studies*
JIGRE W. Horbury and D. Noy (eds.), *Jewish Inscriptions of Graeco-Roman Egypt*
JJS *Journal of Jewish Studies*
JMS *Journal of Mithraic Studies*
JNES *Journal of Near Eastern Studies*
JP *Journal of Philology*
JPOS *Journal of Palestine Oriental Society*
JQR *Jewish Quarterly Review*
JR *Journal of Religion*
JRS *Journal of Roman Studies*
JSJ *Journal for the Study of Judaism in the Persian, Hellenistic and Roman Period*
JSNT *Journal for the Study of the New Testament*
JSNTSup Journal for the Study of the New Testament—Supplement Series
JSOT *Journal for the Study of the Old Testament*
JSOTSup Journal for the Study of the Old Testament—Supplement Series
JSP *Journal for the Study of the Pseudepigrapha*
JSPSup Supplement to *JSP*

JSS *Journal of Semitic Studies*
JTC *Journal for Theology and the Church*
JTS *Journal of Theological Studies*
KAT Kommentar zum Alten Testament
KAV Kommentar zu den Apostolischen Vätern
KB³ L. Koehler and W. Baumgartner, *Hebräisches und Aramäisches Lexikon zum Alten Testament,* 3rd ed., 4 vols.
KD *Kerygma und Dogma*
Kleine Pauly K. Ziegler and W. Sontheimer, *Der Kleine Pauly: Lexikon der Antike,* 5 vols.

LB *Linguistica Biblica*
LCL Loeb Classical Library
LexÄgypt W. Helck and E. Otto (eds.), *Lexikon der Ägyptologie*
LIMC *Lexicon Iconographicum Mythologiae Classicae*
Louw-Nida J. P. Louw and E. A. Nida, *Greek-English Lexicon of the New Testament Based on Semantic Domains,* 2 vols.
LQHR *London Quarterly and Holburn Review*
LR *Lutherische Rundschau*
LSJ H. G. Liddell, R. Scott, H. S. Jones, and R. McKenzie, *A Greek-English Lexicon,* 9th ed.

MAMA W. M. Calder and J. M. R. Cormack (eds.), *Monumenta Asiae Minoris Antiqua*
MDAIRA *Mitteilungen des deutschen archaeologischen Instituts, Römische Abteilung*
MeyerK H. A. W. Meyer, Kritischexegetischer Kommentar über das Neue Testament
MGWJ *Monatsschrift für Geschichte und Wissenschaft des Judentums*
MIR I. G. Mazzini, *Monete Imperiale Romane,* 4 vols.
MM J. H. Moulton and G. Milligan, *The Vocabulary of the Greek Testament*
MQ *McCormick Quarterly*
Mus *Le Muséon*

NCB New Century Bible
NEAEHL E. Stern (ed.), *The New Encyclopedia of Archaeological Excavations in the Holy Land,* 4 vols.
NedTTs *Nederlands theologisch tijdschrift*
Neot *Neotestamentica*
Nestle-Aland²⁶ E. Nestle, K. Aland, et al. (eds.), *Novum Testamentum Graece,* 26th ed.
Nestle-Aland²⁷ E. Nestle, K. Aland, et al. (eds.), *Novum Testamentum Graece,* 27th ed.
Neuer Wettstein G. Strecker and U. Schnelle (eds.), *Neuer Wettstein: Texte zum Neuen Testament aus Griechentum und Hellenismus:* vol. 2/2. *Texte zur Briefliteratur und zur Johannes-apokalypse*
New Docs G. H. R. Horsley and S. R. Llewelyn (eds.), *New Documents Illustrating Early Christianity*
NGM *National Geographic Magazine*
NHS Nag Hammadi Studies
NICNT New International Commentary on the New Testament
NIDNTT C. Brown (ed.), *The New International Dictionary of New Testament Theology*
NKZ *Neue kirchliche Zeitschrift*
NorTT *Norsk Teologisk Tidsskrift*
NovT *Novum Testamentum*
NovTSup Novum Testamentum, Supplements
NRT *La nouvelle revue théologique*

NTA E. Hennecke and W. Schneemelcher (eds.), *New Testament Apocrypha*, rev. ed.
NTAbh Neutestamentliche Abhandlungen
NTOA Novum Testamentum et Orbis Antiquus
NTS *New Testament Studies*
NumenSup Supplements to *Numen*
NumZ *Numismatische Zeitschrift*

OBO Orbis biblicus et orientalis
OCD[2] *Oxford Classical Dictionary*, 2nd ed. (1975)
OGIS W. Dittenberger, *Orientis Graeci Inscriptiones Selectae*, 2 vols.
OLD P. G. W. Glare (ed.), *Oxford Latin Dictionary*
OrChr *Oriens christianus*
ORPB *Oberrheinisches Pastoralblat*
OTL Old Testament Library
OTP J. H. Charlesworth (ed.), *The Old Testament Pseudepigrapha*
OTS *Oudtestamentische Studiën*
OTS Old Testament Studies

PAAJR *Proceedings of the American Academy of Jewish Research*
PBA *Proceedings of the British Academy*
PDM H. D. Betz (ed.), *The Greek Magical Papyri in Translation, including the Demotic Spells*
PEQ *Palestine Exploration Quarterly*
PG J.-P. Migne, *Patrologia graeca*
PGL G. H. W. Lampe (ed.), *A Patristic Greek Lexicon*
PGM K. Preisendanz (ed.), *Papyri graecae magicae*, 2nd ed., 2 vols.
PL J.-P. Migne, *Patrologia latina*
PW Pauly-Wissowa, *Real-Encyclopädie der classischen Altertumswissenschaft*
PWSup Supplement to PW

RAC *Reallexikon für Antike und Christentum*
RArch *Revue archéologique*
RÄRG H. Bonnet (ed.), *Reallexikon der ägyptischen Religionsgeschichte*, 2nd ed.
RB *Revue biblique*
RBén *Revue bénédictine*
RCT *Revista Catalana de Teologia*
RE *Realencyklopädie für protestantische Theologie und Kirche*
REA *Revue des études anciennes*
REG *Revue des études grecques*
REJ *Revue des études juives*
ResQ *Restoration Quarterly*
RevExp *Review and Expositor*
RevistB *Revista bíblica*
RevQ *Revue de Qumran*
RevThom *Revue thomiste*
RF *Rivista di Filologia*
RGG *Religion in Geschichte und Gegenwart*
RGRW Religions in the Graeco-Roman World (formerly EPRO)
RHPR *Revue d'histoire et de philosophie religieuses*
RHR *Revue de l'histoire des religions*
RIC H. Mattingly, E. A. Sydenham, et al., *Roman Imperial Coinage*, 8 vols.
RivB *Rivista biblica*
RMP *Rheinisches Museum für Philologie*
RQ *Römische Quartalschrift für christliche Altertumskunde und Kirchengeschichte*
RQSup Supplement to *RQ*
RSR *Recherches de science religieuse*
RVV *Religionsgeschichtliche Versuche und Vorarbeiten*

SB F. Preisigke et al. (eds.), *Sammelbuch griechischer Urkunden aus Ägypten*
SBFLA *Studii Biblici Franciscani Liber Annuus*
SBL Society of Biblical Literature

SBLDS	SBL Dissertation Series
SBLMS	SBL Monograph Series
SBM	Stuttgarter biblische Monographien
SBS	Stuttgarter Bibelstudien
SBT	Studies in Biblical Theology
SC	Sources chrétiennes
SCHNT	Studia ad corpus hellenisticum Novi Testamenti
ScrT	*Scripta Theologica*
SEÅ	*Svensk exegetisk årsbok*
SE	*Studia Evangelica* 1, 2, 3 (= TU 73 [1959], 87 [1964], 88 [1964], 102 [1968], 103 [1968], 112 [1973])
SD	Studies and Documents
SEG	*Supplementum Epigraphicum Graecum*
SGU	Studia Graeca Upsaliensia
SIG	W. Dittenberger (ed.), *Sylloge Inscriptionum Graecarum*, 3rd ed., 4 vols.
SJLA	Studies in Judaism in Late Antiquity
SJT	*Scottish Journal of Theology*
SKI	Studien zu Kirche und Israel
SNT	Studien zum Neuen Testament
SNTSMS	Society for New Testament Studies Monograph Series
SNTU	*Studien zum Neuen Testament und seiner Umwelt*
SO	*Symbolae osloenses*
SPA	*Studia Philonica Annual*
SPap	*Studia papyrologica*
SPB	Studia postbiblica
SR	*Studies in Religion/Sciences religieuses*
ST	*Studia theologica*
STDJ	Studies on the Texts of the Desert of Judah
Str-B	[H. Strack and] P. Billerbeck, *Kommentar zum Neuen Testament aus Talmud und Midrash*
StudP	*Studia Patristica*
SUNT	Studien zur Umwelt des Neuen Testaments
SVF	J. von Arnim, *Stoicorum Veterum Fragmenta*, 4 vols.
SVTG	Septuaginta: Vetus Testamentum Graecum
TAPA	*Transactions of the American Philological Association*
TBA	*Tübinger Beiträge zur Altertumswissenschaft*
TBei	*Theologische Beiträge*
TBl	*Theologische Blätter*
TCGNT[1]	B. M. Metzger, *A Textual Commentary on the Greek New Testament*
TCGNT[2]	B. M. Metzger, *A Textual Commentary on the Greek New Testament*, 2nd ed.
TDNT	G. Kittel and G. Friedrich (eds.), *Theological Dictionary of the New Testament*, 10 vols.
TDOT	G. J. Botterweck and H. Ringgren (eds.), *Theological Dictionary of the Old Testament*
TextsS	Texts and Studies
TGl	*Theologie und Glaube*
TGL	H. Stephanus, *Thesaurus Graecae Linguae*
THAT	E. Jenni and C. Westermann (eds.), *Theologisches Handwörterbuch zum Alten Testament*
THKNT	Theologischer Handkommentar zum Neuen Testament
TLNT	C. Spicq, *Theological Lexicon of the New Testament*, tr. J. D. Ernst, 3 vols.
TLZ	*Theologische Literaturzeitung*
TPQ	*Theologisch-praktische Quartalschrift*
TQ	*Theologische Quartalschrift*
TRE	*Theologische Realenzyklopädie*
TRu	*Theologische Rundschau*
TS	*Theological Studies*

TSK	*Theologische Studien und Kritiken*
TT	*Theologisk Tijdskrift*
TThQ	*Tübinger theologische Quartalschrift*
TTZ	*Trierer theologische Zeitschrift*
TU	Texte und Untersuchungen
TWAT	G. J. Botterweck, H. Ringgren, and H.-J. Fabry (eds.), *Theologisches Wörterbuch zum Alten Testament*
TWNT	G. Kittel and G. Friedrich (eds.), *Theologisches Wörterbuch zum Neuen Testament*
TynBul	*Tyndale Bulletin*
TZ	*Theologische Zeitschrift*
UBSGNT[3]	K. Aland et al. (eds.), United Bible Societies *Greek New Testament,* 3rd ed.
UBSGNT[4]	K. Aland et al. (eds.), United Bible Societies *Greek New Testament,* 4th ed.
VC	*Vigiliae Christianae*
VCaro	*Verbum caro*
VD	*Verbum domini*
VoxEv	*Vox Evangelica*
VT	*Vetus Testamentum*
VTG	Vetus Testamentum Graecum
VTSup	Supplements to *Vetus Testamentum*
WBC	Word Biblical Commentary
WHort	B. F. Westcott and F. J. A. Hort, *The New Testament in the Original Greek*
WMANT	Wissenschaftliche Monographien zum Alten und Neuen Testament
WO	*Die Welt des Orients*
WTJ	*Westminster Theological Journal*
WUNT	Wissenschaftliche Untersuchungen zum Neuen Testament
ZASA	*Zeitschrift für Ägyptische Sprache und Altertumskunde*
ZAW	*Zeitschrift für die alttestamentliche Wissenschaft*
ZKT	*Zeitschrift für katholische Theologie*
ZNW	*Zeitschrift für die neutestamentliche Wissenschaft*
ZPE	*Zeitschrift für Papyrologie und Epigraphie*
ZRGG	*Zeitschrift für Religions- und Geistesgeschichte*
ZST	*Zeitschrift für systematische Theologie*
ZTK	*Zeitschrift für Theologie und Kirche*
ZVS	*Zeitschrift für vergleichende Sprachforschung*
ZWT	*Zeitschrift für wissenschaftliche Theologie*
ZZ	*Zeichen der Zeit*

D. Abbreviations for Books of the Bible with Aprocrypha

OLD TESTAMENT

Gen	1–2 Kgs	Cant	Obad
Exod	1–2 Chr	Isa	Jonah
Lev	Ezra	Jer	Mic
Num	Neh	Lam	Nah
Deut	Esth	Ezek	Hab
Josh	Job	Dan	Zeph
Judg	Ps(s)	Hos	Hag
Ruth	Prov	Joel	Zech
1–2 Sam	Eccl	Amos	Mal

NEW TESTAMENT

Mark	1–2 Cor	1–2 Thess	Jas
Luke	Gal	1–2 Tim	1–2 Pet
John	Eph	Titus	1–2–3 John
Acts	Phil	Philem	Jude
Rom	Col	Heb	Rev

APOCRYPHA

1 Kgdms	1 Kingdoms
2 Kgdms	2 Kingdoms
3 Kgdms	3 Kingdoms
4 Kgdms	4 Kingdoms
1–2 Esdr	1–2 Esdras
Tob	Tobit
Jdt	Judith
Add Esth	Additions to Esther
4 Ezra	4 Ezra
Wis	Wisdom of Solomon
Sir	Ecclesiasticus (Wisdom of Jesus the son of Sirach)
Bar	Baruch
Ep Jer	Epistle of Jeremiah
S Th Ch	Song of the Three Children (or Young Men)
Sus	Susanna
Bel	Bel and the Dragon
Pr Azar	Prayer of Azariah
1 Macc	1 Maccabees
2 Macc	2 Maccabees
3 Macc	3 Maccabees
4 Macc	4 Maccabees

E. Abbreviations of Pseudepigrapha and Early Jewish Literature

Adam and Eve	*Books of Adam and Eve* or *Vita Adae et Evae*
Apoc. Abr.	*Apocalypse of Abraham*
2–3 Apoc. Bar.	Syriac, Greek *Apocalypse of Baruch*
Apoc. Sedr.	*Apocalypse of Sedrach*
Apoc. Zeph.	*Apocalypse of Zephaniah*
Bib. Ant.	Ps.-Philo, *Biblical Antiquities*
1–2–3 Enoch	Ethiopic, Slavonic, Hebrew *Enoch*
Ep. Arist.	*Epistle of Aristeas*
Jos. *Ag. Ap.*	Josephus *Against Apion*
Ant.	*The Jewish Antiquities*
J. W.	*The Jewish War*
Life	*The Life*
Jos. As.	*Joseph and Aseneth*
Jub.	*Jubilees*
Mart. Isa.	*Martyrdom of Isaiah*
Par. Jer.	*Paraleipomena Jeremiou* or *4 Baruch*
Pr. Man.	*Prayer of Manassis*
Pss. Sol.	*Psalms of Solomon*
Sib. Or.	*Sibylline Oracles*
T. Job	*Testament of Job*
T. Mos.	*Testament of Moses (Assumption of Moses)*
T. 12 Patr.	*Testaments of the Twelve Patriarchs*
T. Levi	*Testament of Levi*
T. Benj.	*Testament of Benjamin*
T. Reub.	*Testament of Reuben*, etc.

F. Abbreviations of Dead Sea Scrolls

CD	Cairo (Genizah text of the) *Damascus* (*Document*)
Ḥev	Naḥal Ḥever texts
8 Ḥev XIIgr	Greek Scroll of the Minor Prophets from Naḥal Ḥever
Mas	Masada texts
MasShirShabb	*Songs of Sabbath Sacrifice,* or *Angelic Liturgy* from Masada
Mird	Khirbet Mird texts
Mur	Wadi Murabbaʿat texts

p	pesher (commentary)
Q	Qumran
1Q, 2Q, 3Q, etc.	Numbered caves of Qumran
QL	Qumran literature
1QapGen	*Genesis Apocryphon* of Qumran Cave 1
1QH	*Hôdāyôt* (*Thanksgiving Hymns*) from Qumran Cave 1
1QpHab	*Pesher on Habakkuk* from Qumran Cave 1
1QM	*Milḥāmāh* (*War Scroll*)
1QS	*Serek hayyaḥad* (*Rule of the Community, Manual of Discipline*)
1QSa	Appendix A (*Rule of the Congregation*) to 1QS
1QSb	Appendix B (*Blessings*) to 1QS
3Q*15*	*Copper Scroll* from Qumran Cave 3
4QFlor	*Florilegium* (or *Eschatological Midrashim*) from Qumran Cave 4
4QMess ar	Aramaic "Messianic" text from Qumran Cave 4
4QMMT	*Miqsat Maʿaseh Torah* from Qumran Cave 4
4QPhyl	Phylacteries from Qumran Cave 4
4QPrNab	*Prayer of Nabonidus* from Qumran Cave 4
4QPssJosh	*Psalms of Joshua* from Qumran Cave 4
4QShirShabb	*Songs of Sabbath Sacrifice*, or *Angelic Liturgy* from Qumran Cave 4
4QTestim	*Testimonia* text from Qumran Cave 4
4QTLevi	*Testament of Levi* from Qumran Cave 4
11QMelch	*Melchizedek* text from Qumran Cave 11
11QShirShabb	*Songs of Sabbath Sacrifice*, or *Angelic Liturgy* from Qumran Cave 11
11QTemple	*Temple Scroll* from Qumran Cave 11
11QpaleoLev	Copy of Leviticus in paleo-Hebrew script from Qumran Cave 11
11QtgJob	*Targum of Job* from Qumran Cave 11

G. Philo

Abr.	*De Abrahamo*
Aet.	*De aeternitate mundi*
Agr.	*De agricultura*
Cher.	*De cherubim*
Conf.	*De confusione linguarum*
Congr.	*De congressu eruditionis gratia*
Decal.	*De decalogo*
Det.	*Quod deterius potiori insidiari solet*
Ebr.	*De ebrietate*
Flacc.	*In Flaccum*
Fug.	*De fuga et inventione*
Gig.	*De gigantibus*
Hyp.	*Hypothetica/Apologia pro Iudaeis*
Jos.	*De Josepho*
Leg.	*De legatione ad Gaium*
Leg. All.	*Legum allegoriarum*
Mig.	*De migratione Abrahami*
Mos.	*De vita Mosis*
Mut.	*De mutatione nominum*
Op.	*De opificio mundi*
Plant.	*De plantatione*
Post.	*De posteritate Caini*
Praem.	*De praemiis et poenis*
Prov.	*De providentia*
Quaest. in Gn.	*Questiones et solutiones in Genesin*
Quaest. in Ex.	*Questiones et solutiones in Exodum*
Quis Her.	*Quis rerum divinarum heres sit*
Quod Deus	*Quod Deus sit immutabilis*
Quod Omn.	*Quod omnis Probus Prob. Liber sit*
Sac.	*De Sacrificiis Abelis et Caini*
Sob.	*De sobrietate*
Som.	*De somniis*
Spec. Leg.	*De specialibus legibus*
Virt.	*De virtute*
Vit. Cont.	*De vita contemplativa*

H. Abbreviations of Early Christian Literature

Acts Pil.	*Acts of Pilate*
Acts Scill.	*Acts of the Scillitan Martyrs*
Apoc. Pet.	*Apocalypse of Peter*
Apost. Const.	*Apostolic Constitutions*
Asc. Isa.	*Ascension of Isaiah*
Barn.	*Barnabas*
1–2 Clem.	*1–2 Clement*
Corp. Herm.	*Corpus Hermeticum*
Did.	*Didache*
Diogn.	*Diognetus*
Ep. Lugd.	*Epistula ecclesiarum apud Lugdunum et Viennam = Letter of the Churches of Lyons*
Eusebius *Hist. ecc.*	Eusebius *Historia Ecclesiastica*
Praep.	*Praeparatio evangelica*
Gos. Eb.	*Gospel of the Ebionites*
Gos. Heb.	*Gospel of the Hebrews*
Gos. Naass.	*Gospel of the Naassenes*
Gos. Pet.	*Gospel of Peter*
Herm. *Mand.*	Hermas *Mandate(s)*
Sim.	*Similitude(s)*
Vis.	*Vision(s)*
Ign. *Eph.*	Ignatius *Letter to the Ephesians*
Magn.	*Letter to the Magnesians*
Phld.	*Letter to the Philadelphians*
Pol.	*Letter to Polycarp*
Rom.	*Letter to the Romans*
Smyrn.	*Letter to the Smyrnaeans*
Trall.	*Letter to the Trallians*
Iren. *Adv. Haer.*	Irenaeus *Against All Heresies*
Jos. *Ag. Ap.*	Josephus *Against Apion*
Ant.	*The Jewish Antiquities*
J.W.	*The Jewish War*
Life	*The Life*
Justin *Apol.*	Justin *1 Apology*
2 Apol.	*2 Apology*
Dial.	*Dialogue with Trypho*
Mart. Agape	*The Martyrdom of Agape, Irene, Chione, Companions*
Mart. Apollonius	*The Martyrdom of Apollonius*
Mart. Carpus	*Martyrdom of Saints Carpus, Papylus, and Agathonice*
Mart. Dasius	*The Martyrdom of Dasius*
Mart. Fruct.	*The Martyrdom of Bishop Fructuosus and his Deacons, Augurius and Eulogius*
Mart. Julius	*The Martyrdom of Julius the Veteran*
Mart. Justin	*The Martyrdom of Saints Justin, Chariton, Charito, Evelpistus, Hierax, Paeon, Liberian, and Their Community*
Mart. Mont.	*Martyrdom of Saints Montanus and Lucius*
Mart. Perpetua	*The Martyrdom of Perpetua and Felicitas*
Mart. Pionius	*The Martyrdom of Pionius*
Mart. Pol.	*The Martyrdom of Polycarp*
Odes Sol.	*Odes of Solomon*
Pol. *Phil.*	Polycarp, *Letter to the Philippians*
Prot. Jas.	*Protevangelium of James*
Tert. *De Praesc, Haer.*	Tertullian, *On the Proscribing of Heretics*
Test. Forty Martyrs	*The Testament of the Forty Martyrs of Sebaste*

I. Abbreviations of Targumic Material

Tg. Onq.	*Targum Onqelos*
Tg. Neb.	*Targum of the Prophets*
Tg. Ket.	*Targum of the Writings*
Tg. Isa.	*Targum of Isaiah*
Tg. Neof.	*Targum Neofiti I*
Tg. Ps.-J.	*Targum Pseudo-Jonathan*
Tg. Esth. I, II	*First or Second Targum of Esther*
Tg. Ezek.	*Targum of Ezekiel*

J. Abbreviations of Nag Hammadi Tractates

Acts Pet. 12 Apost.	*Acts of Peter and the Twelve Apostles*
Allogenes	*Allogenes*
Ap. Jas.	*Apocryphon of James*
Ap. John	*Apocryphon of John*
Apoc. Adam	*Apocalypse of Adam*
1–2 Apoc. Jas.	*1–2 Apocalypse of James*
Apoc. Paul	*Apocalypse of Paul*
Apoc. Pet.	*Apocalypse of Peter*
Asclepius	*Asclepius 21–29*
Auth. Teach.	*Authoritative Teaching*
Dial. Sav.	*Dialogues of the Savior*
Disc. 8–9	*Discourse on the Eighth and Ninth*
Ep. Pet. Phil.	*Letter of Peter to Philip*
Eugnostos	*Eugnostos the Blessed*
Exeg. Soul	*Exegesis on the Soul*
Gos. Eg.	*Gospel of the Egyptians*
Gos. Phil.	*Gospel of Philip*
Gos. Thom.	*Gospel of Thomas*
Gos. Truth	*Gospel of Truth*
Great Pow.	*Concept of Our Great Power*
Hyp. Arch.	*Hypostasis of the Archons*
Hypsiph.	*Hypsiphrone*
Interp. Know.	*Interpretation of Knowledge*
Marsanes	*Marsanes*
Melch.	*Melchizedek*
Norea	*Thought of Norea*
On Bap. A–B–C	*On Baptism A–B–C*
On Euch A–B	*On Eucharist A–B*
Orig. World	*On the Origin of the World*
Paraph. Shem	*Paraphrase of Shem*
Pr. Paul	*Prayer of the Apostle Paul*
Pr. Thanks.	*Prayer of Thanksgiving*
Sent. Sextus	*Sentences of Sextus*
Soph. Jes. Chr.	*Sophia of Jesus Christ*
Steles Seth	*Three Steles of Seth*
Teach. Silv.	*Teachings of Silvanus*
Testim. Truth	*Testimony of Truth*
Thom. Cont.	*Book of Thomas the Contender*
Thund.	*Thunder, Perfect Mind*
Treat. Res.	*Treatise on Resurrection*
Treat. Seth	*Second Treatise of the Great Seth*
Tri. Trac.	*Tripartite Tractate*
Trim. Prot.	*Trimorphic Protennoia*
Val. Exp.	*A Valentinian Exposition*
Zost.	*Zostrianos*

K. Manuscripts of Revelation

Andr or Andreas — Andreas, or Andrew, a bishop of Caesarea in Cappadocia, wrote a commentary on Revelation, ca. A.D. 600 (J. Schmid, ed., *Studien,* part 1: *Der Apokalypse-Kommentar des Andreas von Kaisareia*). "Andreas" means that the reading is in the text of Schmid. "Andr," when followed by a letter, e.g., "a," refers to a group of Andreas MSS (listed in the *Introduction,* Section 6: Text); when a letter is followed by a superscript number, e.g., Andreas f^{051}, only that MS in the group has the reading; when a letter is followed by a super script prefixed with a minus sign, e.g., f^{-2023}, only that MS in the group lacks the reading.

Apringius — Apringius of Beja, a Spanish biblical interpreter (mid-sixth century A.D.) who wrote a commentary on Revelation; portions on Rev 1:5–7; 18:7–22:20 survive.

Arethas — Arethas (ca. 850–944), a native of the Peloponnesus who became the bishop of Caesarea in 902, wrote a commentary on Revelation that was a revision of the commentary of Andreas of Caesarea.

arm	Armenian version of the NT; F. C. Conybeare, *Armenian Version.* arm^{1} = Bodleian Codex (Conybeare, 115–134, appendix 1–189); arm^{2} = British Museum Codex (Conybeare, 135–37); arm^{3} = Bibliotheque Nationale (Conybeare, 135–37)); arm^{4} = Armenian Convent Codex (Conybeare, 95–114).
Beatus	Beatus of Liebana, d. 798, was a Spanish abbot who compiled a commentary on Revelation, chiefly from the now lost commentary of Tyconius. The Tyconian text of Beatus is printed in Vogels, *Untersuchungen,* 194–208. For the modern critical edition of Beatus, *Commentarius in Apocalypsin,* see Romero-Pose, *Sancti Beati.*
bo	Bohairic version of Coptic NT.
Byz	Byzantine family of MSS. When followed by an arabic numeral and superscript arabic numbers, e.g., Byz 1$^{920\ 1859}$, this refers to family 1 of the Byzantine recension (as described by Schmid, *Studien*), and specifically to MSS 920 and 1859 within that family.
Byzantine	When most MSS in the Byzantine, or Koine, recension support a reading, the designation is spelled out in full.
Compl.	Complutensian group of MSS.
cop	Coptic version of the NT; used when the Sahidic (sa) and Bohairic (bo) agree.
eth	Variants discussed by J. Hofmann, *Die äthiopische Johannes-Apokalypse.*
eth^{comm}	Commentaries on the Ethiopic version of Revelation published by R. W. Cowley, *Ethiopian Orthodox.*
Fulgentius	Bishop of Ruspe in North Africa (A.D. 468–533); Latin text of Revelation in Vogels, *Untersuchungen,* 217–19.
Irenaeus^{Lat}	Irenaeus, bishop of Lyons, died ca. A.D. 200; evidence for his use of the Old Latin version is collected in Sanday-Turner, *Nouum Testamentum.*
Oecumenius	Greek bishop of Tricca (early seventh century) and author of a commentary on Revelation; see in H. C. Hoskier, ed., *Oecumenius.* As used in the *Notes,* Oecumenius refers to the reading in Hoskier's text, while the citation of a particular MS with a superlinear number, e.g., Oecumenius^{2053}, refers to a specific MS.
Prom	*De promissionibus et praedictionibus dei,* anonymous composition with Latin quotations from Revelation (in Vogels, *Untersuchungen,* 215–17).
sa	Sahidic version of the NT.

syr — Syriac version of the NT.

TR — The so-called *Textus Receptus*, "Received Text," of the NT, consisting of Erasmus' edition of the Greek NT of 1516 based largely on minuscule codex 1 (twelfth–thirteenth century) of the NT.

Tyc — Tyconius, died ca. A.D. 400, was a Donatist who wrote a commentary on Revelation, which exists only in fragments and excerpts. Tyc^1 = Turin fragments of Tyconius (first edited by the Benedictines of Monte Cassino in the third volume of the *Spicilegium Casinense* [reproduced in Vogels, *Untersuchungen*, 179–82] but more recently edited by F. Lo Bue, *Tyconius*), containing only Rev 2:18–4:1; 7:16–12:6; Tyc^2 = Tyconius text of the Ps.-Augustine Homily (Vogels, *Untersuchungen*, 182–90); Tyc^3 = Tyconius text of the *Summa Dicendorum* of Beatus (Vogels, *Untersuchungen*, 190–93).

Victorinus — Victorinus of Petovium (died ca. 304 B.C.) wrote the first commentary on Revelation; see in J. Haussleiter, ed., *Victorinus*.

vg — Vulgate: *Biblia sacra iuxta Vulgatam versionem*, ed. R. Weber.

Note: Some textual notes and numbers are drawn from the apparatus criticus of *Novum Testamentum Graece*, ed. E. Nestle, K. Aland, et al., 26th ed. (Stuttgart: Deutsche Bibelgesellschaft, 1979); from *Novum Testamentum Graece*, ed. E. Nestle, K. Aland, et al., 27th ed. (Stuttgart: Deutsche Bibelgesellschaft, 1994), designated Nestle-Aland^{26} and Nestle-Aland^{27}; and from *The Greek New Testament*, ed. K. Aland, M. Black, C. Martini, B. M. Metzger, and A. Wikgren. 4th ed. (New York: United Bible Societies, 1994), designated UBSGNT^4. These three identical editions of the Greek New Testament are the bases for the *Translation* sections.

Commentary Bibliography

Alford, H. "Apocalypse of John." In *The Greek Testament.* Chicago: Moody, 1958. 4:544–750. **Allo, E. B.** *L'Apocalypse du Saint Jean.* Paris: Gabalda, 1933. **Beasley-Murray, G. R.** *Revelation.* Rev. ed. NCB. London: Marshall, Morgan & Scott, 1978. **Beckwith, I. T.** *The Apocalypse of John.* New York: Macmillan, 1919. **Behm, J.** *Die Offenbarung des Johannes.* Göttingen: Vandenhoeck & Ruprecht, 1935. **Böcher, O.** *Die Johannesapokalypse.* 2nd ed. ErFor 41. Darmstadt: Wissenschaftliche Buchgesellschaft, 1980. **Boring, M. E.** *Revelation.* Interpretation. Louisville: John Knox, 1989. **Bousset, W.** *Die Offenbarung Johannis.* 6th ed. Kritisch-exegetischer Kommentar zum Neuen Testament 16. Göttingen: Vandenhoeck & Ruprecht, 1906. ———. *Die Offenbarung Johannis.* 5th ed. Kritisch-exegetischer Kommentar zum Neuen Testament 16. Göttingen: Vandenhoeck & Ruprecht, 1896. **Brütsch, C.** *Die Offenbarung Jesu Christi: Johannes-Apokalypse.* 2nd ed. 3 vols. Zürcher Bibelkommentare. Zürich: Zwingli, 1970. **Buchanan, G. W.** *The Book of Revelation: Its Introduction and Prophecy.* Mellen Biblical Commentary, NT Series 22. Lewiston, NY: Mellen Biblical, 1993. **Caird, G. B.** *A Commentary on the Revelation of St. John the Divine.* Harper's/Black's New Testament Commentaries. New York: Harper & Row, 1966. **Charles, R. H.** *A Critical and Exegetical Commentary on the Revelation of St. John.* 2 vols. Edinburgh: T. & T. Clark, 1920. **Delebecque, É.** *L'Apocalypse de Jean.* Paris: Mame, 1992. **Eichhorn, J. G.** *Commentarius in Apocalypsin Joannis.* 2 vols. Göttingen: Dieterich, 1791. **Ford, J. M.** *Revelation: Introduction, Translation and Commentary.* AB 38. Garden City, NY: Doubleday, 1965. **Giblin, C. H.** *The Book of Revelation: The Open Book of Prophecy.* GNS 34. Collegeville, MN: Liturgical, 1991. **Giesen, H.** *Johannes-Apokalypse.* 2nd ed. Stuttgarter kleiner Kommentar NT 18. Stuttgart: Katholisches Bibelwerk, 1989. ———. *Die Offenbarung des Johannes.* Regensburger Neues Testament. Regensburg: Pustet, 1997. **Glasson, T. F.** *The Revelation of John.* CBC. Cambridge: Cambridge UP, 1965. **Hadorn, D. W.** *Die Offenbarung des Johannes.* THKNT 18. Leipzig: Deichert, 1928. **Harrington, W. J.** *Revelation.* Sacra Pagina 16. Collegeville: Liturgical, 1993. **Hendricksen, W.** *More Than Conquerors.* Grand Rapids, MI: Baker, 1944. **Hengstenberg, E. W.** *The Revelation of St. John.* Edinburgh: T. & T. Clark, 1851. **Hort, F. J. A.** *The Apocalypse of St John I–III.* London: Macmillan, 1908. **Kiddle, M.,** and **Ross, M. K.** *The Revelation of St. John.* London: Hodder & Stoughton, 1946. **Kraft, H.** *Die Offenbarung des Johannes.* HNT 16a. Tübingen: Mohr-Siebeck, 1974. **Krodel, G. A.** *Revelation.* Augsburg Commentary on the New Testament. Minneapolis: Augsburg, 1989. **Ladd, G. E.** *A Commentary on the Revelation of John.* Grand Rapids, MI: Eerdmans, 1972. **Lange, J. P.** *Die Offenbarung des Johannes.* 2nd ed. Bielefield/Leipzig:Velhagen und Klasing, 1878. **Lohmeyer, E.** *Die Offenbarung des Johannes.* 3rd ed. HNT 16. Tübingen: Mohr-Siebeck, 1970. **Lohse, E.** *Die Offenbarung des Johannes.* Göttingen: Vandenhoeck & Ruprecht, 1976. **Loisy, A.** *L'Apocalypse de Jean.* Paris: Nourry, 1923. **Moffatt, J.** "The Revelation of St. John the Divine." In *The Expositor's Greek Testament,* ed. W. R. Nicoll. London: Hodder & Stoughton, 1910. 5:297–494. **Mounce, R. H.** *The Book of Revelation.* NICNT. Grand Rapids, MI: Eerdmans, 1977. **Müller, U. B.** *Die Offenbarung des Johannes.* Gütersloh: Mohn, 1984. **Prigent, P.** *L'Apocalypse de Saint Jean.* 2nd ed. Geneva: Labor et Fides, 1988. **Rissi, M.** "The Revelation of St. John the Divine: Introduction and Exegesis." In *The Interpreter's Bible,* ed. G. A. Buttrick et al. New York; Nashville: Abingdon, 1957. 12:345–613. **Roloff, J.** *Die Offenbarung des Johannes.* Zürcher Bibelkommentare NT 18. Zürich: Theologischer, 1984. ———. *The Revelation of John.* Tr. J. E. Alsup. Continental Commentaries. Minneapolis: Fortress, 1993 (hereafter Roloff, ET). **Romero-Pose, E.** *Sancti Beati a Liebana Commentarius in Apocalypsin.* 2 vols. Rome: Typis Officinae Polygraphicae, 1985. **Rowland, C.** *Revelation.* Epworth Commentaries. London:

Epworth, 1993. **Spitta, F.** *Die Offenbarung des Johannes.* Halle: Waisenhaus, 1889. **Stuart, M.** *Commentary on the Apocalypse.* 2 vols. Andover: Allen, Morrill and Wardwell, 1845. **Sweet, J. P. M.** *Revelation.* Philadelphia: Westminster, 1979. **Swete, H. B.** *The Apocalypse of John.* 3rd ed. London: Macmillan, 1908. **Talbert, C. H.** *The Apocalypse: A Reading of the Revelation of John.* Louisville: Westminster John Knox, 1994. **Völter, D.** *Die Offenbarung Johannis neu untersucht und erläutert.* 2nd ed. Strassburg: Heitz & Mundel, 1911. **Weiss, J.**, and **Heitmüller, W.** "Die Offenbarung des Johannes." In *Die Schriften des Neuen Testaments.* 3rd ed. Göttingen: Vandenhoeck & Ruprecht, 1920. 4:229–319. **Wikenhauser, A.** *Die Offenbarung Johannes.* 3rd. ed. Das Neue Testament 9. Regensburg: Pustet, 1959. **Zahn, T.** *Die Offenbarung des Johannes.* 1st to 3rd ed. 2 vols. Kommentar zum Neuen Testament 18. Leipzig; Erlangen: Deichert, 1924.

General Bibliography

Abbott, E. A. *Johannine Grammar.* London: Adam & Charles Black, 1906. **Aberbach, M.,** and **Grossfeld, B.** *Targum Onkelos to Genesis.* New York: Ktav, 1982. **Abrahams, I.** *Studies in Pharisaism and the Gospels.* 1924. Repr. New York: Ktav, 1967. **Achelis, H.** *Hippolyt's kleinere exegetische und homiletische Shriften.* GCS 1.2. Leipzig: Hinrichs, 1897. **Adler, A.,** ed., *Suidae Lexicon.* Leipzig: Teubner, 1928–38. **Aejmelaeus, A.** *Parataxis in the Septuagint: A Study of the Renderings of the Hebrew Coordinate Clauses in the Greek Pentateuch.* Helsinki: Suomalainen Tiedeakatemia, 1982. **Albright, W. F.** *Archaeology and the Religion of Israel.* Baltimore: Johns Hopkins UP, 1956. ———. *Yahweh and the Gods of Canaan.* Garden City, NY: Doubleday, 1969. **Alföldi, A.** "Die Ausgestaltung des monarchischen Zeremoniells am römischen Kaiserhofe." *MDAIRA* 49 (1934) 1–118. ———. *Die monarchische Repräsentation im römischen Kaiserreiche.* Darmstadt: Wissenschaftliche Buchgesellschaft, 1970. **Allen, J. H.,** and **Greenough, J. B.** *A Latin Grammar: Founded on Comparative Grammar.* Rev. ed. Boston: Ginn and Heath, 1884. **Andersen, F. I.** *The Sentence in Biblical Hebrew.* The Hague: Mouton, 1974. ——— and **Freedman, D. N.** *Amos.* New York: Doubleday, 1989. **Attridge, H. W.** *The Epistle to the Hebrews.* Philadelphia: Fortress, 1989. ———. *First-Century Cynicism in the Epistles of Heraclitus.* HTS 29. Missoula, MT: Scholars, 1976. ———, ed. *Nag Hammadi Codex I (The Jung Codex).* NHS 22. Leiden: Brill, 1985. ———, ed. *Nag Hammadi Codex I (The Jung Codex) Notes.* NHS 23. Leiden: Brill, 1985. ——— and **Oden, R. A.** *Philo of Byblos: The Phoenician History.* CBQMS 9. Washington, DC: The Catholic Biblical Association, 1981. ——— and **Oden, R. A.** *The Syrian Goddess (De Dea Syria).* Missoula, MT: Scholars, 1976. **Audet, J.-P.** *La Didachè: Instructions des Apôtres.* Paris: Gabalda, 1958. **Aune, D. E.** "The Apocalypse of John and Graeco-Roman Revelatory Magic." *NTS* 33 (1987) 481–501. ———. "Charismatic Exegesis in Early Judaism and Early Christianity." In *The Pseudepigrapha and Early Biblical Interpretation,* ed. J. H. Charlesworth and C. A. Evans. Sheffield: JSOT, 1993. 126–50. ———. *The New Testament in Its Literary Environment.* Philadelphia: Westminster, 1987. ———. "The Odes of Solomon and Early Christian Prophecy." *NTS* 28 (1982) 435–60. ———. "Prolegomena to the Study of Oral Tradition in the Hellenistic World." In *Jesus and the Oral Gospel Tradition,* ed. H. Wansbrough. JSNTSup 64. Sheffield: Sheffield Academic, 1991. 59–106. ———. *Prophecy in Early Christianity and the Ancient Mediterranean World.* Grand Rapids, MI: Eerdmans, 1983. **Avigad, N.** *Beth She'arim: Report on the Excavations during 1953–1958.* Vol. 3. New Brunswick, NJ: Rutgers UP, 1976. **Bailey, C.** *Titi Lucreti Cari De Rerum Natura Libri Sex.* 3 vols. Oxford: Clarendon, 1947. **Baillet, M.** *Qumran Grotte 4.* Vol. 3. DJD 7. Oxford: Clarendon, 1982. **Bakker, W. F.** *The Greek Imperative: An Investigation into the Aspectual Differences between the Present and Aorist Imperatives in Greek Prayer from Homer up to the Present Day.* Amsterdam: Hakkert, 1966. ———. *Pronomen Abundans and Pronomen Coniunctum: A Contribution to the History of the Resumptive Pronoun with the Relative Clause in Greek.* Amsterdam: North-Holland, 1974. **Balsdon, J. P. V. D.** *Romans and Aliens.* Chapel Hill: University of North Carolina, 1979. **Barr, J.** *The Semantics of Biblical Language.* Oxford: Oxford UP, 1961. **Barrett, C. K.** *The Gospel According to St. John.* 2nd ed. London: SPCK, 1978. **Barton, J.** *Oracles of God: Perceptions of Ancient Prophecy in Israel after the Exile.* New York: Oxford UP, 1988. **Bauckham, R. J.** *The Climax of Prophecy: Studies on the Book of Revelation.* Edinburgh: T. & T. Clark, 1993. ———. *Jude, 2 Peter.* WBC 50. Waco, TX: Word, 1983. ———. *The Theology of the Book of Revelation.* Cambridge: Cambridge UP, 1993. **Bauer, W.,** and **Paulsen, H.** *Die Briefe des Ignatius von Antiochia und des Polykarp von Smyrna.* 2nd ed. HNT 18. Tübingen: Mohr-Siebeck, 1985. **Baumgarten, A. I.** *The Phoenician History of Philo of Byblos: A Commentary.* Leiden: Brill, 1981. **Beale, G. K.** *The Use of Daniel in Jewish Apocalyptic Literature and in the Revelation of John.* Lanham: University Press of America, 1984.

Beck, R. *Planetary Gods and Planetary Orders in the Mysteries of Mithras.* EPRO 109. Leiden: Brill, 1988. **Bell, A. A.** "The Date of John's Apocalypse." *NTS* 25 (1978) 98–99. **Benoit, P., Milik, J. T.,** and **Vaux, R. de.** *Les Grottes de Muraba'at.* DJD 2. Oxford: Clarendon, 1961. **Berger, A.** *Encyclopedic Dictionary of Roman Law.* Philadelphia: American Philosophical Society, 1953. **Berger, K.** *Die Amen-Worte Jesu: Eine Untersuchung zum Problem der Legitimation in apokalyptischer Rede.* BZNW 39. Berlin: de Gruyter, 1970. ———. *Formgeschichte des Neuen Testaments.* Heidelberg: Quelle & Meyer, 1984. ———. *Die griechische Daniel-Diegese: Eine altkirchliche Apokalypse: Text, Übersetzung und Kommentar.* SPB 27. Leiden: Brill, 1976. ———, **Boring, M. E.,** and **Colpe, C.** *Hellenistic Commentary to the New Testament.* Minneapolis: Fortress, 1995. **Bergman, J.** *Ich bin Isis: Studien zum memphitischen Hintergrund der griechischen Isisaretalogien.* Lund: Berlingska Boktryckeriet, 1968. **Bergmeier, R.** "'Jerusalem, du hochgebaute Stadt." *ZNW* 75 (1984) 86–106. **Berlin, A.** *Zephaniah.* AB 25A. New York: Doubleday, 1994. **Beskow, P.** *Rex Gloriae: The Kingship of Christ in the Early Church.* Stockholm: Almqvist & Wiksell, 1962. **Betz, H. D.** *Galatians: A Commentary on Paul's Letter to the Churches in Galatia.* Philadelphia: Fortress, 1979. ———. *Lukian von Samosata und das Neue Testament: Relgionsgeschichtliche und Paränetische Parallelen.* Berlin: Akademie, 1961. ———, ed. *The Greek Magical Papyri in Translation Including the Demotic Spells.* 2nd ed. Chicago: University of Chicago, 1992. ———, ed. *Plutarch's Ethical Writings and Early Christian Literature.* Leiden: Brill, 1978. ———, ed. *Plutarch's Theological Writings and Early Christian Literature.* Leiden: Brill, 1975. **Beyer, K.** *Die aramäischen Texte vom Toten Meer.* Göttingen: Vandenhoeck & Ruprecht, 1984. ———. *Die aramäischen Texte vom Toten Meer: Ergänzungsband.* Göttingen: Vandenhoeck & Ruprecht, 1994. ———. *Semitische Syntax im Neuen Testament.* Göttingen: Vandenhoeck & Ruprecht, 1962. **Beyerlin, J.** *Near Eastern Religious Texts Relating to the Old Testament.* Philadelphia: Westminster, 1978. **Bidez, J.,** and **Cumont, F.** *Les mages hellenises: Zoroastre, Ostanes et Hystaspe d'après la tradition grecque.* 1938. Repr. New York: Arno, 1975. **Bietenhard, H.** *Die himmlische Welt im Urchristentum und Spätjudentum.* Tübingen: Mohr-Siebeck, 1951. ———. *Der Tosefta-Traktat Soṭa: Hebräischer Text mit kritischem Apparat, Übersetzung, Kommentar.* Bern; Frankfurt am Main; New York: Lang, 1986. **Bihlmeyer, K.** *Die apostolischen Väter.* 2nd ed. Part 1. Tübingen: Mohr-Siebeck, 1956. ———. *Die apostolischen Väter: Neubearbeitung der funkschen Ausgabe.* 2nd ed. Ed. W. Schneemelcher. Tübingen: Mohr-Siebeck, 1956. **Birt, T.** *Das antike Buchwesen in seinem Verhältnis zur Literatur.* Berlin: W. Hertz, 1882. **Black, M.** *An Aramaic Approach to the Gospels and Acts.* 3rd ed. Oxford: Clarendon, 1967. ———. *The Book of Enoch or 1 Enoch: A New English Edition with Commentary and Textual Notes.* Leiden: Brill, 1985. ———. *The Scrolls and Christian Origins.* London: Thomas Nelson, 1961. ———, ed. *Apocalypsis Henochi Graeci.* Leiden: Brill, 1970. **Blakeney, E. H.,** ed. and tr. Laetantius, *Epitome institutionem divinarum.* London: S.P.C.K., 1950. **Blomqvist, J.** *Das sogennante KAI adversitivum: Zur Semantik einer griechischen Partikel.* SGU 13. Stockholm, 1979. **Blümner, H.** *The Home Life of the Ancient Greeks.* Tr. A. Zimmern. New York: Cooper Square, 1966. **Böcher, O.** "Johanneisches in der Apokalypse des Johannes." *NTS* 27 (1981) 310–21. ———. *Kirche in Zeit und Endzeit: Aufsätze zur Offenbarung des Johannes.* Neukirchen: Neukirchener, 1983. **Bodenmann, R.** *Naissance d'une Exégèse: Daniel dans l'Église ancienne de trois premiers siècles.* BGBE 28. Tübingen: Mohr-Siebeck, 1986. **Böhlig, A., Wisse, F.,** and **Labib, P.** *Nag Hammadi Codices II,2 and IV,2: The Gospel of the Egyptians.* NHS 4. Leiden: Brill, 1975. **Boll, F.** *Aus der Offenbarung Johannis: Hellenistische Studien zum Weltbild der Apokalypse.* Leipzig; Berlin: Teubner, 1914. **Bömer, F.** *Untersuchungen über die Religion der Sklaven in Griechenland und Rom.* 4 vols. Wiesbaden: Steiner, 1958–63. ———. *Untersuchungen über die Religion der Sklaven in Griechenland und Rom.* Dritter Teil: *Die wichtigsten Kulte der Griechischen Welt.* 2nd ed. with P. Herz. Stuttgart: Steiner, 1990. **Bonner, C.** *Studies in Magical Amulets Chiefly Graeco-Egyptian.* Ann Arbor: University of Michigan, 1950. **Boring, M. E.** *Sayings of the Risen Jesus: Christian Prophecy in the Synoptic Tradition.* SNTSMS 46. Cambridge: Cambridge UP, 1982. **Bornkamm, G.** "Die Komposition der apocalyptischen Visionen in der Offenbarung Johannis." *ZNW* 36 (1937) 132–49.

Borsch, F. H. *The Christian and Gnostic Son of Man.* SBT 2nd ser. 14. London: SCM, 1970. **Bouché-Leclerq, A.** *Histoire de la divination dans l'antiquité.* 4 vols. 1879–82. Repr. Aalen: Scientia, 1978. **Boulluec, A. Le,** and **Sandevoir, P.** *L'Exode.* Vol. 2 of *La Bible d'Alexandrie.* Paris: Cerf, 1980. **Bousset, W.** *Textkritische Studien zum Neuen Testament.* TU 11/4. Leipzig: Hinrichs, 1894. ——— and **Gressmann, H.** *Die Religion des Judentums im späthellenistischen Zeitalter.* 4th ed. Tübingen: Mohr-Siebeck, 1966. **Bowersock, G.** *Augustus and the Greek World.* Oxford: Clarendon, 1965. **Bowker, J.** *The Targums and Rabbinic Literature.* Cambridge: Cambridge UP, 1969. **Bratcher, R. G.,** and **Hatton, H. A.** *A Handbook on the Revelation to John.* New York: United Bible Societies, 1993. **Braude, W. G.** *The Midrash on Psalms.* 2 vols. New Haven, CT: Yale UP, 1959. **Brenk, F. E.** *In Mist Apparelled: Religious Themes in Plutarch's Moralia and Lives.* Leiden: Brill, 1977. **Brettler, M. Z.** *God Is King: Understanding an Israelite Metaphor.* JSOTSup 76. Sheffield: JSOT, 1989. **Briscoe, J.** *A Commentary on Livy, Books XXXIV–XXXVI.* Oxford: Clarendon, 1981. **Brown, R. E.** *The Epistles of John: A New Translation with Introduction and Commentary.* AB 30. Garden City, NY: Doubleday, 1982. ———. *The Gospel according to John.* 2 vols. Garden City, NY: Doubleday, 1966–70. **Brownlee, W. H.** *Ezekiel.* WBC 28. Waco, TX: Word, 1986. **Bruce, F. F.** "The Spirit in the Apocalypse." In *Christ and Spirit in the New Testament.* FS C. F. D. Moule, ed. B. Lindars and S. Smalley. Cambridge: Cambridge UP, 1973. 333–44. **Bultmann, R.** *Die Geschichte der synoptischen Tradition.* 8th ed. Göttingen: Vandenhoeck & Ruprecht, 1970. ———. *Die Geschichte der synoptischen Tradition: Ergänzungsheft.* Rev. G. Theissen and P. Vielhauer. 4th ed. Göttingen: Vandenhoeck & Ruprecht, 1971. ———. *The History of the Synoptic Tradition.* Tr. J. Marsh. New York: Harper & Row, 1963. **Burkert, W.** *Ancient Mystery Cults.* Cambridge: Harvard UP, 1987. ———. *Greek Religion.* Tr. J. Raffan. Cambridge: Harvard UP, 1985. ———. *Homo Necans: The Anthropology of Ancient Greek Sacrificial Ritual and Myth.* Tr. P. Bing. Berkeley; Los Angeles: University of California Press, 1983. ———. *Structure and History in Greek Mythology and Ritual.* Berkeley: University of California, 1979. **Burney, C. F.** *The Aramaic Origin of the Fourth Gospel.* Oxford: Clarendon, 1922. **Burton, E. DeW.** *Syntax of the Moods and Tenses in New Testament Greek.* 3rd ed. Edinburgh: T. & T. Clark, 1898. **Buttmann, A.** *A Grammar of the New Testament Greek.* Andover: Warren F. Draper, 1878. **Cadbury, H. J.** *The Making of Luke-Acts.* London: SPCK, 1958. **Caley, E. R.** *Orichalcum and Related Ancient Alloys: Origin, Composition and Manufacture, with Special Reference to the Coinage of the Roman Empire.* New York: American Numismatic Society, 1964. **Carr, W.** *Angels and Principalities.* SNTSMS 42. Cambridge: Cambridge UP, 1981. **Casson, L.** *The Periplus Maris Erythraei Text: with Introduction, Translation and Commentary.* Princeton: Princeton UP, 1989. **Cathcart, K. J.,** and **Gordon, R. P.** *The Targum of the Minor Prophets: Translated, with a Critical Introduction, Apparatus, and Notes.* AramBib 14. Wilmington, DE: Glazier, 1989. **Charles, R. H.** *The Book of Enoch.* 2nd ed. Oxford: Clarendon, 1912. ———. *The Greek Versions of the Testaments of the Twelve Patriarchs.* Oxford: Clarendon, 1908. ———. *Studies in the Apocalypse: Being Lectures Delivered before the University of London.* Edinburgh: T. & T. Clark, 1913. **Chilton, B. D.** *The Isaiah Targum: Introduction, Translation, Apparatus, Notes.* AramBib. Wilmington, DE: Glazier, 1987. **Chilver, G. E. F.** *A Historical Commentary on Tacitus' Histories I and II.* Oxford: Clarendon, 1979. **Clemen, C. C.** *Religionsgeschichtliche Erklärung des Neuen Testaments.* Giessen: Töpelmann, 1924. **Collins, J. J.** *The Apocalyptic Vision of the Book of Daniel.* Missoula, MT: Scholars, 1977. ———. *Daniel: A Commentary on the Book of Daniel.* Minneapolis: Fortress, 1993. ———. *The Sibylline Oracles of Egyptian Judaism.* Missoula, MT: Scholars, 1972. **Comblin, J.** *Le Christ dans l'Apocalypse.* Paris; Tournai: Desclée, 1965. **Conybeare, F. C.** *The Armenian Version of Revelation.* London: The Text and Translation Society, 1907. ——— and **Stock, St. G.** *Grammar of Septuagint Greek.* 1905. Repr. Peabody, MA: Hendrickson, 1988. **Conzelmann, H.** *1 Corinthians: A Commentary on the First Epistle to the Corinthians.* Tr. J. W. Leitch; ed. G. W. MacRae. Philadelphia: Fortress, 1975. ———. *An Outline of the Theology of the New Testament.* Tr. J. Bowden. New York; Evanston, IL: Harper & Row, 1969. **Copely, F. O.** *Vergil, The Aeneid.* 2nd ed. Indianapolis: Bobbs-Merrill, 1975. **Copenhaver, B. P.**

Hermetica: The Greek Corpus Hermeticum and the Latin Asclepius in a New English Translation with Notes and Introduction. Cambridge: Cambridge UP, 1992. **Court, J.** *Myth and History in the Book of Revelation.* Atlanta: John Knox, 1979. **Cousar, C. B.** *A Theology of the Cross: The Death of Jesus in the Pauline Letters.* Minneapolis: Fortress, 1990. **Cowley, A.** *Aramaic Papyri of the Fifth Century* B.C. Oxford: Clarendon, 1923. **Cowley, R. W.** *The Traditional Interpretation of the Apocalypse of St John in the Ethiopian Orthodox Church.* Cambridge: Cambridge UP, 1983. **Cranfield, C. E. B.** *Romans.* 2 vols. Edinburgh: T. & T. Clark, 1975–79. **Cross, F. M.** *Canaanite Myth and Hebrew Epic.* Cambridge, MA: Harvard UP, 1973. **Crossan, J. D.** *In Fragments: The Aphorisms of Jesus.* San Francisco: Harper & Row, 1983. **Cullmann, O.** *Early Christian Worship.* Tr. A. S. Todd and J. B. Torrance. London: SCM, 1953. **Cumont, F.** *The Mysteries of Mithra.* New York: Dover, 1956. ———. *Oriental Religions in Roman Paganism.* New York: Dover, 1956. ———. *Recherches sur le Symbolisme Funéraire des Romains.* Paris: Geuthner, 1942. **Cuss, D.** *Imperial Cult and Honorary Terms in the New Testament.* Fribourg: The University Press, 1974. **Dalman, G.** *Aramäisch-Neuhebräisches Handwörterbuch zu Targum, Talmud und Midrasch.* 2nd ed. Göttingen: Vandenhoeck & Ruprecht, 1938. ———. *Grammatik des jüdisch-palästinischen Aramäisch.* Leipzig: Hinrichs, 1905. ———. *Die Worte Jesu mit Berücksichtigung des nachkanonischen jüdischen Schrifttums und der Aramäischen Sprache.* 2nd ed. 1930. Repr. Darmstadt: Wissenschaftliche Buchgesellschaft, 1965. **Danby, H.** *The Mishnah.* London: Oxford UP, 1933. **Daniel, R. W.**, and **Maltomini, F.** *Supplementum Magicum.* Vol. 1. Papyrologica Coloniensia 16.1. Oppladen: Westdeutscher, 1990. Vol. 2. Papyrologica Coloniensia 16.2. Oppladen: Westdeutscher, 1992. **Daniélou, J.** *The Theology of Jewish Christianity.* Tr. J. A. Baker. London: Darton, Longman & Todd, 1964. **Danker, F. W.** *Benefactor: Epigraphic Study of a Graeco-Roman and New Testament Semantic Field.* St. Louis: Clayton, 1982. **Davies, P. R.** *1QM, the War Scroll from Qumran: Its Structure and History.* Rome: Biblical Institute, 1977. ———. *The Damascus Covenant.* JSOTSup 25. Sheffield: JSOT, 1983. **Davies, W. D.** *Paul and Rabbinic Judaism: Some Rabbinic Elements in Pauline Theology.* Rev. ed. New York; Evanston: Harper & Row, 1955. ——— and **Allison, D. C., Jr.** *A Critical and Exegetical Commentary on the Gospel according to Saint Matthew.* 2 vols. ICC. Edinburgh: T. & T. Clark, 1988, 1991. **Day, J.** *God's Conflict with the Dragon and the Sea.* Cambridge: Cambridge UP, 1985. **Debord, P.** *Aspects Sociaux et économiques de la vie religieuse dans l'Anatolie greco-romaine.* Leiden: Brill, 1982. **Deichgräber, R.** *Gotteshymnus und Christushymnus in der frühen Christenheit: Untersuchungen zu Form, Sprache und Stil der frühchristlichen Hymnen.* Göttingen: Vandenhoeck & Ruprecht, 1967. **Deissmann, A.** *Bible Studies.* Edinburgh: T. & T. Clark, 1901. ———. *Light from the Ancient East.* New York; London: Hodder & Stoughton, 1910. **Delatte, A.** *Anecdota Atheniensia.* Paris, Champion, 1927. ——— and **Derchain, Ph.** *Les intailles magiques gréco-égyptiennes.* Paris: Bibliothèque Nationale, 1964. **Delling, G.** *Jüdische Lehre und Frömmigkeit in den Paralipomena Jeremiae.* BZAW 100. Berlin: Töpelmann, 1967. ———. *Worship in the New Testament.* Tr. P. Scott. Philadelphia: Westminster,1962. **Delobel, J.** "Le texte de l'Apocalypse: Problemes de méthode." In *L'Apocalypse,* ed. J. Lambrecht. 151–66. **Denis, A.-M.** *Concordance Grecque des Pseudépigraphes d'ancien Testament: Concordance, Corpus des textes, Indices.* Louvain-la-Neuve: Université Catholique de Louvain, 1987. ———. *Fragmenta Pseudepigraphorum quae supersunt Graeca.* Leiden: Brill, 1970. **Deniston, J. D.** *The Greek Particles.* 2nd ed. Oxford: Clarendon, 1954. ———. *Greek Prose Style.* Oxford: Clarendon, 1952. **Dexinger, F.** *Henochs Zehnwochenapokalypse und offene Probleme der Apokalyptikforschung.* SPB 29. Leiden: Brill, 1977. **Dibelius, M.**, and **Greeven, H.** *James: A Commentary on the Epistle of James.* Tr. M. A. Williams. Philadelphia: Fortress, 1976. **Dick, K.** *Der schriftstellerische Plural bei Paulus.* Halle: Niemeyer, 1900. **Dieterich, A.** *Abraxas: Studien zur Religionsgeschichte.* Leipzig: Teubner, 1891. ———. *Eine Mithrasliturgie.* 2nd ed. Leipzig; Berlin: Teubner, 1910. **Diobouniotis, C.**, and **Harnack, A.** *Der Scholien-Kommentar des Origenes zur Apokalypse-Johannis.* TU 38/3. Leipzig: Hinrichs, 1911. **Dodd, C. H.** *According to the Scriptures.* Digswell Place: James Nisbet, 1952. ———. *The Interpretation of the Fourth Gospel.* Cambridge: Cambridge UP, 1965. **Dogniez, C.**, and **Harl, M.** *Le Deutéronome.* La Bible d'Alexandrie 5. Paris: Cerf,

1992. **Doran, R.** *Temple Propaganda: The Purpose and Character of 2 Maccabees.* CBQMS 12. Washington DC: Catholic Biblical Association, 1981. **Dornseiff, F.** *Das Alphabet in Mystik und Magie.* 2nd ed. Leipzig; Berlin: Teubner, 1925. **Dothan, M.** *Hammath Tiberias: Early Synagogues and the Hellenistic and Roman Remains.* Jerusalem: Israel Exploration Society, 1983. **Doudna, J. C.** *The Greek of the Gospel of Mark.* Philadelphia: Society of Biblical Literature, 1961. **Dover, K. J.** *Greek Popular Morality.* Berkeley; Los Angeles: University of California, 1974. **Dunn, J. D. G.** *Romans.* 2 vols. WBC 38A–B. Waco, TX: Word, 1988. **Durham, J. I.** *Exodus.* WBC 3. Waco, TX: Word, 1987. **Durling, R. J.** *A Dictionary of Medical Terms in Galen.* SAM 5. Leiden: Brill, 1993. **Eckhardt, K. A.** *Der Tod des Johannes.* Berlin: de Gruyter, 1961. **Ehrenberg, V.**, and **Jones, A. H. M.** *Documents Illustrating the Reigns of Augustus and Tiberius.* 2nd ed. Oxford: Clarendon, 1976. **Eisenman, R. H.**, and **Wise, M.** *The Dead Sea Scrolls Uncovered.* Rockport: Element, 1992. **Eissfeldt, O.** *The Old Testament: An Introduction.* Tr. P. R. Ackroyd. New York; Evanston, IL: Harper & Row, 1965. **Eitrem, S.** *Papyri Osloenses.* Fasc. 1: *Magical Papyri.* Oslo: Dybwad, 1925. ———. *Some Notes on the Demonology in the New Testament.* 2nd ed. Oslo: Universitetsforlaget, 1966. **Eliade, M.** *The Sacred and the Profane: The Nature of Religion.* Tr. W. R. Trask. New York: Harper & Row, 1959. **Elliott, J. H.** *A Home for the Homeless: A Sociological Exegesis of I Peter.* Philadelphia: Fortress, 1981. **Engelmann, H.** *The Delian Aretalogy of Sarapis.* Leiden: Brill, 1975. **Enslin, M. S.**, and **Zeitlin, S.** *The Book of Judith.* Leiden: Brill, 1972. **Epstein, I.**, ed. *Babylonian Talmud.* 35 vols. London: Soncino, 1935–52. **Ernst, J.** *Die eschatologischen Gegenspieler in den Schriften des Neuen Testaments.* Regensburg: Pustet, 1967. **Evans, C. A, Webb, R. L.**, and **Wiebe, R. A.** *Nag Hammadi Texts and the Bible: A Synopsis and Index.* Leiden: Brill, 1993. **Fanning, B. M.** *Verbal Aspect in New Testament Greek.* Oxford: Clarendon, 1990. **Farrer, A.** *A Rebirth of Images: The Making of St John's Apocalypse.* Albany: State University of New York, 1986. **Fee, G.** *The First Epistle to the Corinthians.* Grand Rapids, MI: Eerdmans, 1987. **Fekkes, J.** *Isaiah and Prophetic Traditions in the Book of Revelation.* JSNTSup 93. Sheffield: JSOT, 1994. **Ferrar, W. J.**, ed. and tr. *Eusebius, The Proof of the Gospel.* 2 vols. New York: Macmillan, 1920. **Festugière, A.-J.** *La révélation d'Hermès Trismégiste.* 4 vols. Paris: J. Gabalda, 1950–54. **Fiedler, P.** *Die Formel "Und Siehe" im Neuen Testament.* Munich: Kosel, 1969. **Field, F.** *Origenis Hexaplorum quae supersunt; sive Veterum Interpretum Graecorum in totus Veius Testamentum Fragmenta.* 2 vols. Oxford: Clarendon, 1875. **Finegan, J.** *The Archaeology of the New Testament.* Princeton: Princeton UP, 1969. **Finley, M. I.** *The Ancient Economy.* Berkeley; Los Angeles: University of California, 1985. ———. *The World of Odysseus.* Rev. ed. New York: Penguin, 1979. **Fitzmyer, J. A.** *The Gospel according to Luke.* 2 vols. Garden City, NY: Doubleday, 1979–83. **Fontenrose, J.** *The Delphic Oracle: Its Responses and Operations with a Catalogue of Responses.* Berkeley; Los Angeles: University of California, 1978. ———. *Didyma: Apollo's Oracle, Cult, and Companions.* Berkeley: University of California, 1988. **Forestell, J. T.** *Targumic Traditions and the New Testament.* Chico, CA: Scholars, 1979. **Fraenkel, E.** *Aeschylus, Agamemnon.* Oxford: Clarendon, 1950. ———. *Horace.* Oxford: Clarendon, 1957. **Frank, T.**, ed. *An Economic Survey of Ancient Rome.* 6 vols. Baltimore: Johns Hopkins, 1933–40. **Fraser, P. M.**, and **Matthews, E.** *A Lexicon of Greek Personal Names.* Vol. 1: *The Aegean Islands, Cyprus, Cyrenaica.* Oxford: Clarendon, 1987. **Freedman, H.**, and **Simon, M.**, eds. *Midrash Rabbah.* 3rd ed. 10 vols. London; New York: Soncino, 1983. **Friesen, S. J.** *Twice Neokoros: Ephesus, Asia and the Cult of the Flavian Imperial Family.* Leiden: Brill, 1993. **Frisk, H.** *Griechisches Etymologisches Wörterbuch.* 3 vols. Heidelberg: Winter, 1960. ———. *Le Périple de la Mer Érythrée suivi d'une étude sur la tradition et la langue.* Göteborg: Elander, 1927. **Frost, S. B.** *Old Testament Apocalyptic.* London: Epworth, 1952. **Fustel de Coulanges, N. D.** *The Ancient City.* Baltimore: Johns Hopkins UP, 1980. **Gallop, D.** *Plato, Phaedo: Translated with Notes.* Oxford: Clarendon, 1975. **García Martínez, F.** *The Dead Sea Scrolls Translated.* Leiden: Brill, 1994. ———. *Qumran and Apocalyptic: Studies on the Aramaic Texts from Qumran.* Leiden: Brill, 1994. **Geissen, A.** *Der Septuaginta-Text des Buches Daniel nach dem Kölner Teil des Papyrus 967: Kap. V-XII.* Bonn: Habelt, 1968. **Georgi, D.** *Die Gegner des Paulus im 2. Korintherbrief.* WMANT 11. Neukirchen:

Neukirchener, 1964. **Gibson, J. C. L.** *Canaanite Myths and Legends.* 2nd ed. Edinburgh: T. & T. Clark, 1978. ———. *Hebrew and Moabite Inscriptions.* Vol. 1 of *Textbook of Syrian Semitic Inscriptions.* Oxford: Clarendon, 1973. **Giet, S.** *L'Apocalypse et l'Histoire.* Paris: Presses universitaires de France, 1957. **Gignac, F. T.** *A Grammar of the Greek Papyri of the Roman and Byzantine Periods.* 2 vols. Milan: Cisalpino-Goliardica, 1976–81. **Ginzberg, L.** *The Legends of the Jews.* Philadelphia: Jewish Publication Society of America, 1909. **Goldin, J.** *The Fathers according to Rabbi Nathan.* 1955. Repr. New York: Schocken, 1974. **Goldingay, J. E.** *Daniel.* WBC 30. Dallas: Word, 1989. **Gollinger, H.** *Die Kirche in der Bewährung: Eine Einführung in die Offenbarung des Johannes.* Aschaffenburg: Pattloch, 1973. **Goodenough, E. R.** *Jewish Symbols in the Greco-Roman Period.* 12 vols. New York: Bollingen Foundation, 1953–65. ———. "The Menorah among Jews of the Roman World." *HUCA* 23 (1950–51) 449–92. **Goodspeed, E. J.** *Problems of New Testament Translation.* Chicago: University of Chicago, 1945. **Gow, A. S. F.**, and **Page, D. L.** *The Greek Anthology: The Garland of Philip and Some Contemporary Epigrams.* Vol. 1. Cambridge: Cambridge UP, 1968. **Grant F. C.**, ed. *Hellenistic Religions: The Age of Syncretism.* New York: Liberal Arts, 1953. **Grant, R. M.** *Early Christianity and Society.* New York: Harper & Row, 1977. **Grese, W. C.** *Corpus Hermeticum XII and Early Christian Literature.* SCHNT 5. Leiden: Brill, 1979. **Gressmann, H.** *Altorientalische Texte zum Alten Testament.* 2nd ed. Berlin; Leipzig: de Gruyter, 1926. **Griffiths, J. G.** *Apuleius of Madauros, The Isis-Book (Metamorphoses, Book XI).* Leiden: Brill, 1975. **Gross, W.** *Die Pendenskonstruktion im biblischen Hebräisch.* St. Ottilien: EOS, 1987. **Grossfeld, B.** *The First Targum to Esther.* New York: Sepher-Hermon, 1983. ———. *The Targum Sheni to the Book of Esther.* New York: Sepher-Hermon, 1994. ———. *The Two Targums of Esther.* AramBib 18. Wilmington, DE: Glazier, 1991. ———, tr. *The Targum Onqelos to Leviticus and The Targum Onqelos to Numbers.* AramBib 8. Wilmington, DE: Glazier, 1988. **Grotius, H.** *Annotationes in Novum Testamentum.* 8 vols. Groningen: Zuidema, 1830. **Gruenwald, I.** *Apocalyptic and Merkavah Mysticism.* Leiden: Brill, 1980. **Guelich, R. A.** *Mark 1–8:26.* WBC 34A. Dallas: Word, 1989. **Gunkel, H.** *Schöpfung und Chaos in Urzeit und Endzeit: Eine religionsgeschichtliche Untersuchung über Gen 1 und Ap Joh 12.* Göttingen: Vandenhoeck & Ruprecht, 1921. ———. *Zum religionsgeschichtlichen Verständnis des Neuen Testaments.* Göttingen: Vandenhoeck & Ruprecht, 1903. **Guthrie, D.** *New Testament Introduction.* Downers Grove, IL: Inter-Varsity Press, 1970. **Gwynn, J.** *The Apocalypse of St. John, in a Syriac Version Hitherto Unknown.* 1897. Repr. Amsterdam: APA-Philo, 1981. **Hachlili, R.** *Ancient Jewish Art and Archaeology in the Land of Israel.* Leiden: Brill, 1988. **Hadas, M.** *The Third and Fourth Books of Maccabees.* New York: Harper & Brothers, 1953. **Hadas-Lebel, M.** *Jérusalem contre Rome.* Paris: Cerf, 1990. **Haelst, J. van.** *Catalogue des papyrus littéraires Juifs et Chrétiens.* Paris: Publications de la Sorbonne, 1976. **Haenchen, E.** *A Commentary on the Gospel of John.* 2 vols. Hermeneia. Philadelphia: Fortress, 1984. **Hafemann, S. J.** *Paul, Moses, and the History of Israel.* WUNT 81. Tübingen: Mohr-Siebeck, 1995. ———. *Suffering and the Spirit: An Exegetical Study of II Cor. 2:14–3:3 within the Context of the Corinthian Correspondence.* WUNT 2/19. Tübingen: Mohr-Siebeck, 1986. **Hahn, F.** "Die Rede von der Parusie des Men-schensohnes Markus 13." In *Jesus und der Menschensohn,* ed. R. Pesch and R. Schnackenburg. Freiburg: Herder & Herder, 1975. ———. *Mission in the New Testament.* London: SCM, 1965. **Hals, R. M.** *Ezekiel.* FOTL 19. Grand Rapids, MI: Eerdmans, 1989. **Hands, A. R.** *Charities and Social Aid in Greece and Rome.* Ithaca, NY: Cornell UP, 1968. **Hannestad, N.** *Roman Art and Imperial Policy.* Aarhus: Aarhus UP, 1988. **Hanson, A. T.** *The Wrath of the Lamb.* London: S.P.C.K., 1957. **Hanson, P. D.** *The Dawn of Apocalyptic.* Philadelphia: Fortress, 1975. **Haran, M.** *Temples and Temple-Service in Ancient Israel.* Oxford: Clarendon, 1978. **Hare, D. R. A.** *The Son of Man Tradition.* Minneapolis: Fortress, 1990. **Harnisch, W.** *Verhängnis und Verheißung der Geschichte: Untersuchungen zum Zeit- und Geschichtsverständnis im 4. Buch Esra und in der syr. Baruchapokalypse.* FRLANT 97. Göttingen: Vandenhoeck & Ruprecht, 1969. **Harrington, D. J.**, and **Saldarini, A. J.** *Targum Jonathan of the Former Prophets: Introduction, Translation and Notes.* AramBib 10. Wilmington, DE: Glazier, 1987. **Harrington, W. J.** *Understanding the Apocalypse.* Washington, DC; Cleveland:

Corpus Books, 1969. **Harvey, W. W.** *Sanci Irenaei Episcopi Lugdunensis Libros quinque adversus Haereses.* 2 vols. Cambridge: Typis Academicis, 1857. **Hatch, E.** *Essays in Biblical Greek.* Oxford: Oxford UP, 1889. **Haussleiter, J.** *Victorinus Episcopi Petavionensis Opera.* Leipzig: Freytag, 1916. **Hay, D. M.** *Glory at the Right Hand: Psalm 110 in Early Christianity.* Nashville: Abingdon, 1973. **Hayward, R.** *The Targum of Jeremiah: Translated, with a Critical Introduction, Apparatus, and Notes.* AramBib 12. Wilmington, DE: Glazier, 1987. **Heidel, A.** *The Gilgamesh Epic and Old Testament Parallels.* 2nd ed. Chicago: University of Chicago, 1949. **Heiler, F.** *Prayer: A Study in the History and Psychology of Religion.* Tr. S. McComb. London; New York: Oxford UP, 1932. **Heinemann, J.** *Prayer in the Talmud.* Berlin; New York: de Gruyter, 1977. **Helbing, R.** *Die Kasussyntax der Verba bei den Septuaginta: Ein Beitrag zur Hebraismenfrage und zur Syntax der* Κοινή. Göttingen: Vandenhoeck & Ruprecht, 1928. **Hellholm, D.** "The Problem of Apocalyptic Genre and the Apocalypse of John." In *Early Christian Apocalypticism: Genre and Social Setting,* ed. A. Yarbro Collins. *Semeia* 36 (1986) 13–64. ———, ed. *Apocalypticism in the Mediterranean World and the Near East.* Tübingen: Mohr-Siebeck, 1983. **Hemer, C. J.** *The Letters to the Seven Churches of Asia in Their Local Setting.* JSNTSup 11. Sheffield: JSOT, 1986. **Hengel, M.** *The Charismatic Leader and His Followers.* New York: Crossroad, 1981. ———. *Judaism and Hellenism.* Philadelphia: Fortress, 1974. ———. *The Zealots: Investigations into the Jewish Freedom Movement in the Period from Herod I until 70 A.D.* Tr. D. Smith. Edinburgh: T. & T. Clark, 1989. **Hercher, R.** *Epistolographi graeci.* 1873. Repr. Amsterdam: Hocker, 1965. **Heubeck, A., West, S.,** and **Hainsworth, J. B.** *A Commentary on Homer's Odyssey.* Vol. 1. Oxford: Clarendon, 1988. **Hilhorst, A.** *Sémitismes et Latinismes dans le Pasteur d'Hermas.* Nijmegen: Dekker and Van de Vegt, 1976. **Hill, D.** *New Testament Prophecy.* Atlanta: John Knox, 1979. ———. "Prophecy and Prophets in the Revelation of St. John." *NTS* 18 (1971–72) 401–18. **Hillers, D.** *Treaty-Curses and the Old Testament Prophets.* Rome: Pontifical Biblical Institute, 1964. **Himmelfarb, M.** *Ascent to Heaven in Jewish and Christian Apocalypses.* New York; Oxford: Oxford UP, 1993. ———. *Tours of Hell: An Apocalyptic Form in Jewish and Christian Literature.* Philadelphia: University of Pennsylvania, 1983. **Hobbs, T. R.** *2 Kings.* WBC 13. Waco, TX: Word, 1985. **Hofmann, J.** *Die äthiopische Johannes-Apokalypse kritisch Untersucht.* CSCO 297. Louvain: Secrétariat du CorpusSCO, 1969. **Holladay, W. L.** *Jeremiah 1.* Philadelphia: Fortress, 1986. **Hollander, H. W.,** and **Jonge, M. de.** *The Testaments of the Twelve Patriarchs: A Commentary.* Leiden: Brill, 1985. **Holmberg, B.** *Sociology and the New Testament.* Minneapolis: Fortress, 1990. **Holtz, T.** *Die Christologie der Apokalypse des Johannes.* 2nd ed. Berlin: Akademie, 1971. **Hopfner, T.** *Griechisch-Ägyptischer Offenbarungszauber.* 2 vols. Leipzig: Haessel, 1921–24. **Horgan, M. P.** *Pesharim: Qumran Interpretations of Biblical Books.* CBQMS 8. Washington, DC: Catholic Biblical Association of America, 1979. **Horst, J.** *Proskynein: Zur Anbetung im Urchristentum nach ihrer religionsgeschichtlichen Eigenart.* Gütersloh: Bertelsmann, 1932. **Horst, P. W. van der.** *Ancient Jewish Epitaphs.* Kampen: Kok Pharos, 1991. **Hoskier, H. C.** *The Complete Commentary of Oecumenius on the Apocalypse.* Ann Arbor: University of Michigan, 1928. ———. *Concerning the Date of the Bohairic Version Covering a Detailed Examination of the Text of the Apocalypse.* London: Quaritch, 1911. ———. *Concerning the Text of the Apocalypse.* 2 vols. London: Quaritch, 1929. **Houtman, C.** *Der Himmel im Alten Testament: Israels Weltbild und Weltanschauung.* Oudtestamentische Studiën 30. Leiden: Brill, 1993. **Hurtado, L.** *One God, One Lord: Early Christian Devotion and Ancient Jewish Monotheism.* London: SCM, 1988. **Hvalvik, R.** *The Struggle for Scripture and Covenant: The Purpose of the Epistle of Barnabas and Jewish-Christian Competition in the Second Century.* WUNT 2/82. Tübingen: Mohr-Siebeck, 1996. **Isbell, C. D.** *Corpus of the Aramaic Incantation Bowls.* SBLDS 17. Missoula, MT: Scholars, 1975. **Jacobson, H.** *The Exagoge of Ezekiel.* Cambridge: Cambridge UP, 1983. **James, M. R.** *The Psalms of Solomon.* Cambridge: Cambridge UP, 1891. **Jastrow, M.** *A Dictionary of the Targumim, the Talmud Babli and Yerushalmi and the Midrashic Literature.* 2 vols. New York: Ktav, 1950. **Jellicoe, S.** *The Septuagint and Modern Study.* 1968. Repr. Winona Lake, IN: Eisenbrauns, 1989. **Jellinek, A.,** ed. *Bet Ha-Midrasch.* 3rd ed. 6 vols. Jerusalem: Sifre Vahrman, 1967. **Jeremias,**

A. *Babylonisches im Neuen Testament.* Leipzig: Hinrichs, 1905. **Jeremias, C.** *Die Nachtgeschichte des Sacharja.* FRLANT 117. Göttingen: Vandenhoeck & Ruprecht, 1977. **Jeremias, Joachim.** *The Eucharistic Words of Jesus.* New York: Scribner's Sons, 1966. ———. *Jerusalem in the Time of Jesus.* Tr. F. H. and C. H. Cave. Philadelphia: Fortress, 1969. ———. *The Parables of Jesus.* Rev. ed. New York: Scribner, 1964. ———. *The Prayers of Jesus.* Philadelphia: Fortress, 1978. ———. *New Testament Theology.* New York: Scribner's Sons, 1971. ——— and **Strobel, A.** *Die Briefe an Timotheus und Titus, Der Brief an die Hebräer.* 12th ed. Göttingen: Vandenhoeck & Ruprecht, 1981. **Jeremias, Jörg.** *Theophanie: Die Geschichte einer alttestamentlichen Gattung.* WMANT 10. 2nd ed. Neukirchen: Neukirchener, 1977. **Johannessohn, J.** *Der Gebrauch der Kasus und der Präpositionen in der Septuaginta.* Berlin: Friedrich-Wilhelms-Universität, 1910. **Jones, A. H. M.** *The Cities of the Eastern Roman Provinces.* Oxford: Clarendon, 1937. ———. *The Greek City from Alexander to Justinian.* Oxford: Clarendon, 1940. **Jones, C. P.** *The Roman World of Dio Chrysostom.* Cambridge: Harvard UP, 1978. **Jonge, M. de.** *The Testaments of the Twelve Patriarchs: A Critical Edition of the Greek Text.* Leiden: Brill, 1978. **Jörns, K.-P.** *Das hymnische Evangelium: Untersuchungen zu Aufbau, Funktion und Herkunft der hymnischen Stücke in der Johannesoffenbarung.* Gütersloh: Mohn, 1971. **Joüon, P.** *A Grammar of Biblical Hebrew.* 3 vols. Rome: Pontifical Biblical Institute, 1991. **Kahn, C. H.** *The Art and Thought of Heraclitus: An Edition of the Fragments with Translation and Commentary.* Cambridge: Cambridge UP, 1979. **Karrer, M.** *Die Johannesoffenbarung als Brief: Studien zu ihrem literarischen, historischen und theologischen Ort.* Göttingen: Vandenhoeck & Ruprecht, 1986. **Kaufmann, Y.** *The Religion of Israel: From Its Beginnings to the Babylonian Exile.* Tr. M. Greenberg. Chicago: University of Chicago, 1960. **Kavanagh, M. A.** *Apocalypse 22:6–21 as Concluding Liturgical Dialogue.* Rome: Pontifical Gregorian University, 1984. **Keel, O.** *Die Welt der altorientalischen Bildsymbolik und das Alte Testament.* Zürich: Benziger; Neukirchen: Neukirchener, 1972. **Kees, H.** *Der Götterglaube im alten Aegypten.* Leipzig: Hinrichs, 1941. **Kilmer, A. D., Crocker, R. L.,** and **Brown, R. R.** *Sounds from Silence: Recent Discoveries in Ancient Near Eastern Music.* Berkeley: Bit Enki, 1976. **Klein, M. L.** *The Fragment-Targums of the Pentateuch according to their Extant Sources.* AnBib 76. 2 vols. Rome: Biblical Institute, 1980. **Klein, R.** *1 Samuel.* WBC 10. Waco, TX: Word, 1983. **Kloppenborg, J. S.** *The Formation of Q: Trajectories in Ancient Wisdom Collections.* Philadelphia: Fortress, 1987. **Knibb, M. A.** *The Ethiopic Book of Enoch: A New Edition in the Light of the Aramaic Dead Sea Fragments.* 2 vols. Oxford: Clarendon Press, 1978. ———. *The Qumran Community.* Cambridge: Cambridge UP, 1987. **Koch, G.,** and **Sichtermann, H.** *Römische Sarkophage.* Munich: Beck, 1982. **Koch, K.** *The Growth of the Biblical Tradition.* New York: Scribner's Sons, 1969. **Koep, L.** *Das himmlische Buch in Antike und Christentum: Eine religionsgeschichtliche Untersuchung zur altchristlichen Bildersprache.* Bonn: Hanstein, 1952. **Koester, H.** *Introduction to the New Testament.* 2 vols. Philadelphia: Fortress, 1982. **Korpel, M. C. A.** *A Rift in the Clouds: Ugaritic and Hebrew Descriptions of the Divine.* Münster: UGARIT-Verlag, 1990. **Kraabel, A. T.** "Judaism in Western Asia Minor under the Roman Empire, with a Preliminary Study of the Jewish Community at Sardis, Lydia." Diss., Harvard, 1968. **Kraeling, C. H.** *The Synagogue.* The Excavations at Dura Europas 8/1. New Haven, CT: Yale UP, 1956. **Kraus, H.-J.** *Theology of the Psalms.* Tr. K. Crim. Minneapolis: Augsburg, 1986. ———. *Worship in Israel: A Cultic History of the Old Testament.* Richmond: John Knox, 1966. **Krause, M.,** and **Labib, P.** *Die drei Versionen des Apokryphon des Johannes.* Wiesbaden: Harrassowitz, 1962. **Krauss, F. B.** *An Interpretation of the Omens, Portents, and Prodigies Recorded by Livy, Tacitus, Suetonius.* Philadelphia: University of Pennsylvania, 1930. **Krauss, S.** *Talmudische Archäologie.* Leipzig: Fock, 1910–12. **Kreitzer, L. J.** *Jesus and God in Paul's Eschatology.* Sheffield: JSOT, 1987. **Kroll, J.** *Die Lehren des Hermes Trismegistos.* 2nd ed. Münster: Aschendorff, 1928. **Kropp, A. M.** *Ausgewählte Koptische Zaubertexte.* 3 vols. Bruxelles: Égyptologique Reine Élisabeth, 1930–31. **Krüger, G.,** and **Ruhbach, G.** *Ausgewählte Märtyrerakten.* 4th ed. Tübingen: Mohr-Siebeck, 1965. **Kuhn, P.** *Offenbarungsstimmen im Antiken Judentum: Untersuchungen zur Bat Qol und verwandten Phänomenen.* Texte und Studien zum Antiken Judentum 20. Tübingen: Mohr-Siebeck, 1989.

Kuhnen, H.-P. *Nordwest-Palästina in hellenistisch-römischer Zeit: Bauten und Gräber im Karmelgebiet.* Weinheim: VCH Verlagsgesellschaft, 1987. **Kühner, R.** and **Gerth, B.** *Ausführliche Grammatik der griechischen Sprache: Satzlehre.* 2 vols. 3rd ed. Hannover: Hahsche, 1898–1904. **Kümmel, W. G.** *Introduction to the New Testament.* Rev. ed. Tr. H. C. Kee. Nashville: Abingdon, 1975. **Lambrecht, J.**, ed. *L'Apocalypse johannique et l'Apocalyptique dans le Nouveau Testament.* Leuven: Leuven UP, 1980. **Lancellotti, A.** *Uso delle forme verbali nell'Apocalisse alla luce ella sintassi ebraica.* Assisi: Studio Teologico "Porziuncola," 1964. **Lange, N. M. R. de.** *Origen and the Jews.* Cambridge: Cambridge UP, 1976. **Lattimore, R.** *Themes in Greek and Latin Epitaphs.* Urbana: University of Illinois, 1962. **Laughlin, T. C.** *Solecisms of the Apocalypse.* Princeton: C. S. Robinson, 1902. **Lauterbach, J. Z.** *Mekilta De-Rabbi Ishmael.* 3 vols. Philadelphia: Jewish Publication Society of America, 1935. **Leaney, A. R. C.** *The Rule of Qumran and Its Meaning.* Philadelphia: Westminster, 1966. **Lee, D.** "The Narrative Asides in the Book of Revelation." Diss., Chicago Theological Seminary, 1990. **Levey, S. H.** *The Targum of Ezekiel: Translated, with a Critical Introduction, Apparatus, and Notes.* AramBib 13. Wilmington, DE: Glazier, 1987. **Levy, J.** *Wörterbuch über die Talmudim und Midraschim.* 4 vols. Darmstadt: Wissenschaftliche Buchgesellschaft, 1963. **Lieberman, S.** *Hellenism in Jewish Palestine.* New York: The Jewish Theological Seminary of America, 1962. **Liebeschuetz, J. H. W. G.** *Antioch: City and Imperial Administration in the Later Roman Empire.* Oxford: Clarendon, 1972. ———. *Continuity and Change in Roman Religion.* Oxford: Clarendon, 1979. **Lifshitz, B.** *Donateurs et fondateurs dans les synagogues juives.* Paris: Gabalda, 1967. **Lightfoot, J.** *Horae Hebraicae et Talmudicae.* 4 vols. Oxford UP, 1959. **Lightfoot, J. B.** *The Apostolic Fathers: Clement, Ignatius, and Polycarp.* Two parts in 5 vols. London: Macmillan, 1889–90. **Lindars, B.** *Jesus Son of Man: A Fresh Examination of the Son of Man Sayings in the Gospels in the Light of Recent Research.* Grand Rapids, MI: Eerdmans, 1983. ———. *New Testament Apologetic: The Doctrinal Significance of the Old Testament Quotations.* London: SCM, 1961. **Lindblom, J.** *Gesichte und Offenbarungen: Vorstellungen von göttlichen Weisungen und übernatürlichen Erscheinungen im ältesten Christentum.* Lund: Gleerup, 1968. **Lindemann, A.** *Die Clemensbriefe.* HNT 17. Tübingen: Mohr-Siebeck, 1992. ———. *Paulus im ältesten Christentum.* BHT 58. Tübingen: Mohr-Siebeck, 1979. **Ljungvik, H.** *Beiträge zur Syntax der spätgriechischen Volkssprache.* Uppsala: Almqvist & Wiksell; Leipzig: Harrassowitz, 1932. **Lo Bue, F.** *The Turin Fragments of Tyconius' Commentary on Revelation,* ed. G. G. Willis. Cambridge: Cambridge UP, 1963. **Lohse, E.** *Colossians and Philemon.* Philadelphia: Fortress, 1971. **Louw, J. P.** "On Greek Prohibitions." *AcCl* 2 (1959) 43–57. **Lücke, F.** *Versuch einer vollständigen Einleitung in die Offenbarung des Johannes oder Allgemeine Untersuchungen über die apokalyptischen Literatur überhaupt und die Apokalypse des Johannes insbesondere.* 2nd ed. Bonn, 1852. **Luterbacher, F.** *Der Prodigienglaube und Prodigienstil der Römer.* Burgdorf: Langlois, 1880. **MacDonald, D. R.**, ed. *The Acts of Andrew and The Acts of Andrew and Matthias in the City of the Cannibals.* Atlanta: Scholars, 1990. **Mach, M.** *Entwicklungsstadien des jüdischen Engelglaubens in vorrabbinischer Zeit.* Tübingen: Mohr-Siebeck, 1992. **Macho, A. D.** *Neophyti: Targum Palestinense Ms de la Biblioteca Vaticana.* Vol. 1. Madrid; Barcelona: Consejo Superior de Investigaciones Científicas, 1968. **MacMullen, R.** *Paganism in the Roman Empire.* New Haven, CT: Yale UP, 1981. **Magie, D.** *Roman Rule in Asia Minor to the End of the Third Century after Christ.* 2 vols. Princeton: Princeton UP, 1950. **Maher, M.** *Targum Pseudo-Jonathan: Genesis.* AramBib 1b. Wilmington, DE: Glazier, 1992. **Maier, J.** *The Temple Scroll.* JSOTSup 34. Sheffield: JSOT, 1985. **Malherbe, A. J.** *Moral Exhortation: A Greco-Roman Sourcebook.* Library of Early Christianity. Philadelphia: Westminster, 1986. ———. *Social Aspects of Early Christianity.* 2nd ed. Philadelphia: Fortress, 1983. **Malina, B. J.** *On the Genre and Message of Revelation: Star Visions and Sky Journeys.* Peabody, MA: Hendrickson, 1995. **Maloney, E. C.** *Semitic Interference in Marcan Syntax.* Chico, CA: Scholars, 1981. **Marcovich, M.**, ed. *Hippolytus Refutatio Omnium Haeresium.* Patristische Texte und Studien 25. Berlin; New York: de Gruyter, 1986. **Martin, J.** *Commodiani Carmina.* CCL 128. Turnholti: Typographi Brepols Editores Pontificii, 1960. **Martin, R. H.** *Tacitus.* Berkeley: University of California, 1981.

Mason, H. J. *Greek Terms for Roman Institutions: A Lexicon and Analysis.* Toronto: Hakkert, 1974. **Mateos, J.** *El Aspecta Verbal en el Neuevo Testamento.* Madrid: Ediciones Cristiandad, 1977. **Matthiae, K.**, and **Schönert-Geiss, E.** *Münzen aus der urchristlichen Umwelt.* Berlin: Evangelische, 1981. **Maurer, C.** *Ignatius von Antiochien und das Johannesevangelium.* Zürich: Zwingli, 1949. **Mayser, E.** *Satzlehre.* Vol. 2/3 of *Grammatick der griechischen Papyri aus der Ptolemäerzeit.* Berlin; Leipzig: de Gruyter, 1934. **Mazzaferri, F. D.** *The Genre of the Book of Revelation from a Source-critical Perspective.* BZNW 54. Berlin; New York: de Gruyter, 1989. **McDonald, M. F.**, tr. *Lactantius: The Divine Institutes.* Washington, DC: The Catholic University of America, 1964. **McKay, K. L.** *Greek Grammar for Students: A Concise Grammar of Classical Attic with Special Reference to Aspect in the Verb.* Canberra: Australian National University, 1974. **McNamara, M.** *The New Testament and the Palestinian Targum to the Pentateuch.* Rome: Pontifical Biblical Institute, 1966. ———. *Targum and Testament.* Grand Rapids, MI: Eerdmans, 1972. ———. *Targum Neofiti 1: Leviticus.* Collegeville: Liturgical, 1994. ——— and **Clarke, E. G.** *Targum Neofiti 1: Numbers.* AramBib 4. Wilmington, DE: Glazier, 1995. ———, **Hayward, R.**, and **Maher, M.** *Targum Neofiti 1: Exodus and Targum Pseudo-Jonathan: Exodus.* AramBib 2. Wilmington, DE: Glazier, 1984. ———, **Hayward, R.**, and **Maher, M.** *Targum Neofiti 1: Leviticus and Targum Pseudo-Jonathan: Leviticus.* AramBib 3. Wilmington, DE: Glazier, 1994. **Meiggs, R.**, and **Lewis, D.** *A Selection of Greek Historical Inscriptions to the End of the Fifth Century B.C.* Oxford: Clarendon, 1969. **Mellor, R.** ΘΕΑ ῬΩΜΗ: *The Worship of the Goddess Roma in the Greek World.* Göttingen: Vandenhoeck & Ruprecht, 1975. **Ménard, J. E.** *L'Évangile de Vérité: Rétroversion Grecque et Commentaire.* Paris: Letouzey & Ané, 1962. ———. *L'Évangile selon Thomas.* Montélimar: Marsanne, 1974. **Merk, A.**, ed. *Novum Testament: Graece et Latine.* 10th ed. Rome: Pontifical Biblical Institute, 1984. **Meshorer, Y.** *Jewish Coins of the Second Temple Period.* Tr. I. H. Levine. Tel-Aviv: Am Hassefer, 1967. **Metzger, B. M.** *Breaking the Code: Understanding the Book of Revelation.* Nashville: Abingdon, 1993. ———. *Manuscripts of the Greek Bible.* New York; Oxford: Oxford UP, 1981. ———. *The Text of the New Testament: Its Transmission, Corruption and Restoration.* 2nd. ed. New York: Oxford UP, 1968. ———. *A Textual Commentary on the Greek New Testament:* Stuttgart: United Bible Societies, 1975. **Meyer, E.** *Ursprung und Anfänge des Christentums.* 3 vols. 1923. Repr. Darmstadt: Wissenschaftliche Buchgesellschaft, 1962. **Michaels, J. R.** *1 Peter.* WBC 49. Waco, TX: Word, 1988. ———. *Interpreting the Book of Revelation.* Grand Rapids, MI: Baker, 1992. **Michl, J.** *Die Engelvorstellung in der Apokalypse.* Munich: Hueber, 1937. **Milik, J. T.** *The Books of Enoch: Aramaic Fragments of Qumran Cave 4.* Oxford: Clarendon, 1976. **Millar, F.** *The Emperor in the Roman World (31 B.C.–A.D. 337).* Ithaca, NY: Cornell UP, 1977. ———. *The Roman Near East 31 B.C.–A.D. 337.* Cambridge: Harvard UP, 1993. **Miller, A. M.** *From Delos to Delphi: A Literary Study of the Homeric Hymn to Apollo.* Leiden: Brill, 1986. **Minear, P. S.** *I Saw a New Earth: An Introduction to the Visions of the Apocalypse.* Washington DC; Cleveland: Corpus, 1968. **Mitchell, S.** *Anatolia: Land, Men, and Gods in Asia Minor.* 2 vols. Oxford: Clarendon, 1993. **Mommsen, T.** *Römisches Staatsrecht.* 3rd ed. Graz: Akademische Druck- und Verlagsanstalt, 1952. ——— and **Krueger, P.** *The Digest of Justinian.* Tr. and ed. Alan Watson. 4 vols. Philadelphia: University of Pennsylvania, 1985. **Montgomery, J. A.** *Aramaic Incantation Texts from Nippur.* Philadelphia: The University Museum, 1909. ———. *A Critical and Exegetical Commentary on the Book of Daniel.* Edinburgh: T. & T. Clark, 1927. **Moore, C. A.** *Judith: A New Translation with Introduction and Commentary.* AB 40. Garden City, NY: Doubleday, 1985. **Moore, G. F.** *Judaism in the First Centuries of the Christian Era: The Age of the Tannaim.* 3 vols. Cambridge: Harvard UP, 1927. **Moran, H. E.** *The Consolations of Death in Ancient Greek Literature.* Washington, DC: The Catholic University of America, 1917. **Morenz, S.** *Egyptian Religion.* Tr. A. E. Keep. Ithaca, NY: Cornell UP, 1973. **Morgan, M. A.**, tr. *Sepher ha-Razim: The Book of the Mysteries.* Chico, CA: Scholars, 1983. **Moule, C. F. D.** *An Idiom-Book of New Testament Greek.* 2nd ed. Cambridge: Cambridge UP, 1959. **Moulton, J. H.** *A Grammar of New Testament Greek.* 3 vols. Edinburgh: T. & T. Clark, 1908–76. ———. *Prolegomena.* Vol. 1 of *A Grammar of New Testament Greek.* 3rd ed. Edinburgh: T. & T. Clark, 1908. ——— and

Howard, W. F. *Accidence and Word-Formation.* Vol. 2 of *A Grammar of New Testament Greek.* Edinburgh: T. & T. Clark, 1928. **Mowinckel, S.** *Offersang og Sangoffer.* Oslo: Universitetsforlaget, 1951. ———. *The Psalms in Israel's Worship.* 2 vols. New York; Nashville: Abingdon, 1967. **Müller, U. B.** "Literarische und formgeschichtliche Bestimmung der Apokalypse des Johannes als einem Zeugnis frühchristlicher Apokalyptic." In *Apocalypticism,* ed. D. Hellholm. 599–620. ———. *Messias und Menschensohn in jüdischen Apokalypsen und in der Offenbarung des Johannes.* SNT 6. Gütersloh: Mohn, 1972. ———. *Prophetie und Predigt im Neuen Testament: Formgeschichtliche Untersuchungen zur urchristlichen Prophetie.* Gütersloh: Mohn, 1975. ———. *Zur frühchristlichen Theologiegeschichte: Judenchristentum und Paulinismus in Kleinasien an der Wende vom ersten zum zweiten Jahrhundert n. Chr.* Gütersloh: Mohn, 1976. **Muraoka, T.** *A Greek-English Lexicon of the Septuagint (Twelve Prophets).* Louvain: Peeters, 1993. **Mussies, G.** *Dio Chrysostom and the New Testament.* Leiden: Brill, 1972. ———. "Identification and Self-Identification of Gods in Classical and Hellenistic Times." In *Knowledge of God in the Graeco-Roman World,* ed. R. van den Broek, T. Baarda, and J. Mansfeld. EPRO 112. Leiden: Brill, 1988. 1–18. ———. *The Morphology of Koine Greek as Used in the Apocalypse of John: A Study in Bilingualism.* Leiden: Brill, 1971. **Musurillo, H.** *The Acts of the Christian Martyrs.* Oxford: Clarendon, 1972. **Myers, J. M.** *I and II Esdras.* AB 42. Garden City, NY: Doubleday, 1974. **Nachmanson, E.** *Partitives Subjekt im Griechischen.* Göteborg: Elanders Boktryckeri, 1942. **Nauck, A.** *Tragicorum graecorum fragmenta.* Leipzig: Teubner, 1856. **Naveh, J.**, and **Shaked, S.** *Amulets and Magic Bowls: Aramaic Incantations of Late Antiquity.* Jerusalem: Magnes; Leiden: Brill, 1985. **Neusner, J.**, ed. *Pesiqta de Rab Kahana.* 2 vols. BJS 122–23. Atlanta: Scholars, 1987. **Newsom, C.** *Songs of the Sabbath Sacrifice: A Critical Edition.* Atlanta: Scholars, 1985. **Nickelsburg, G. W. E.** *Jewish Literature between the Bible and the Mishnah.* Philadephia: Fortress, 1981. **Niederwimmer, K.** *Die Didache.* KAV 1. Göttingen: Vandenhoeck & Ruprecht, 1989. **Niggemeyer, J.-H.** *Beschwörungsformeln aus dem 'Buch der Geheimnisse' (Sefär ha-razîm).* Hildesheim; New York: Olms, 1975. **Nock, A. D.** *Essays on Religion and the Ancient World,* ed. Z. Stewart. 2 vols. Oxford: Clarendon, 1972. ——— and **Festugière, A.-J.**, eds. *Corpus Hermeticum.* 6th ed. Paris: Société d'édition "Les belles lettres," 1983. ——— and **Festugière, A.-J.** *Hermès Trismégiste.* 4 vols. Paris: Société d'édition 'Les belles lettres,' 1954–60. **Norden, E.** *Agnostos Theos: Untersuchungen zur Formengeschichte religiöser Rede.* Darmstadt: Wissenschaftliche Buchgesellschaft, 1956. **Nussbaum, M.** *The Therapy of Desire: Theory and Practice in Hellenistic Ethics.* Princeton: Princeton UP, 1994. **Odelain, O.**, and **Séguineau, R.** *Lexikon der Biblischen Eigennamen.* Düsseldorf: Patmos; Neukirchen: Neukirchener, 1981. **Olyan, S. M.** *A Thousand Thousands Served Him: Exegesis and the Naming of Angels in Ancient Judaism.* Tübingen: Mohr-Siebeck, 1993. **Palmer, L. R.** *The Greek Language.* Atlantic Highlands, NJ: Humanities, 1980. **Parker, R.** *Miasma: Pollution and Purification in Early Greek Religion.* Oxford: Clarendon, 1983. **Pax, E.** *Epiphaneia: Ein religionsgeschichtlier Beitrag zur biblischen Theologie.* Munich: Münchener Theologische Studien, 1955. **Peerbolte, L. J. L.** *The Antecedents of Antichrist: A Traditio-Historical Study of the Earliest Christian Views on Eschatological Opponents.* Leiden: Peerbolte, 1995. **Perrin, M.**, ed. *Épitomé des institutions divines, [par] Lactance.* SC 335. Paris: Cerf, 1987. **Perrin, N.** *Rediscovering the Teaching of Jesus.* New York; Evanston, IL: Harper & Row, 1967. **Pesch, R.** *Das Markus-evangelium.* 2 vols. Freiburg: Herder, 1977. ———. *Naherwartungen: Tradition und Redaktion in Mk 13.* Düsseldorf: Patmos, 1968. **Peterson, E.** *Εἷς Θεός: Epigraphische, formgeschichtliche und religionsgeschichtliche Untersuchungen.* Göttingen: Vandenhoeck & Ruprecht, 1926. **Pétrement, S.** *A Separate God: The Christian Origins of Gnosticism.* San Francisco: Harper & Row, 1990. **Petzl, G.** *Die Inschriften von Smyrna.* Part 1: *Grabinschriften, postume Ehrungen, Grabepigramme. Inschriften griechischer Städte aus Kleinasien,* vol. 23. Bonn: Habelt, 1982. ———. *Die Inschriften von Smyrna.* Part 2, vol. 2. Bonn: Habelt, 1990. **Philipp, H.** *Mira et Magica: Gemmen im ägyptischen Museum der staatlichen Museen, preussischer Kulturbesitz Berlin-Charlottenburg.* Mainz am Rhein: von Zabern, 1986. **Philonenko, M.** *Joseph et Aséneth.* Leiden: Brill, 1968. **Pietersma, A.** *The Apocryphon of James and James the*

Magician. RGRW 119. Leiden: Brill, 1994. ——— et al., eds. and trs. *The Apocalypse of Elijah: Based on P. Chester Beatty 2018.* Atlanta: Scholars, 1981. **Ploeg, J. P. M. van der,** and **Woude, A. S. van der,** eds. *Le Targum de Job de la grotte XI de Qumran.* Leiden: Brill, 1971. **Pohlenz, M.** *Vom Zorne Gottes: Eine Studie über den Einfluss der griechischen Philosophie auf das alte Christentum.* FRLANT 12. Göttingen: Vandenhoeck & Ruprecht, 1909. **Pollitt, J. J.** *Art in the Hellenistic Age.* Cambridge: Cambridge UP, 1986. **Porten, B.** *Archives from Elephantine: The Life of an Ancient Jewish Military Colony.* Berkeley; Los Angeles: University of California, 1968. ——— and **Yardeni, A.** *Textbook of Aramaic Documents from Ancient Egypt.* 3 vols. Jerusalem: Hebrew University, 1986–93. **Porter, S. E.** *Verbal Aspect in the Greek of the New Testament with Reference to Tense and Mood.* Frankfurt/M.; Berne; New York: Lang, 1978. **Qimron, E.,** and **Strugnell, J.** *Qumran Cave 4.* Vol. V: *Miqsat Ma'ase ha-Torah.* DJD 10. Oxford: Clarendon, 1994. **Rad, G. von.** *Old Testament Theology.* 2 vols. New York; Evanston, IL: Harper & Row, 1962–65. ———. *Wisdom in Israel.* Nashville; New York: Abingdon, 1972. **Radermacher, L.** *Neutestamentliche Grammatik.* 2nd ed. Tübingen: Mohr-Siebeck, 1925. **Rahlfs, A.** *Septuaginta: Id est Vetus Testamentum graece iuxta LXX interpretes.* 8th ed. 2 vols. Stuttgart: Würtembergische Bibelanstalt, 1935. **Ramsay, W. M.** *The Cities of St. Paul: Their Influence on His Life and Thought.* London: Hodder and Stoughton, 1907. ———. *The Letters to the Seven Churches.* London: Hodder & Stoughton, 1904. **Reader, W. W.** "Die Stadt Gottes in der Johannesapokalypse." Diss., Göttingen, 1971. **Rehm, B.** *Die Pseudoklementinen.* Vol. 1: *Homilien.* GCS. Berlin: Akademie, 1953. **Reichelt, G.** *Das Buch mit den sieben Siegeln in der Apokalypse des Johannes.* Göttingen: Georg-August-Universität zu Göttingen, 1975. **Reichelt, H.** *Angelus Interpres-Texte in der Johannes-Apokalypse.* Frankfurt am Main: Lang, 1994. **Reicke, B.** *The New Testament Era: The World of the Bible from 500 B.C. to A.D. 100.* Philadelphia: Fortress, 1968. ———. *Die zehn Worte in Geschichte und Gegenwart.* BGBE 13. Tübingen: Mohr-Siebeck, 1973. **Rendtorff, R.** *Studien zur Geschichte des Opfers im alten Israel.* Neukirchen: Neukirchener, 1967. **Reynolds, J.** *Aphrodisias and Rome.* London: Society for the Promotion of Roman Studies, 1982. ——— and **Tannenbaum, R.** *Jews and Godfearers at Aphrodisias.* Cambridge: Cambridge Philological Society, 1987. **Rijksbaron, A.** *The Syntax and Semantics of the Verb in Classical Greek: An Introduction.* Amsterdam: Gieben, 1984. **Rissi, M.** *The Future of the World: An Exegetical Study of Revelation 19.11–22.15.* SBT 23. Naperville, IL: Allenson, n.d. ———. *Die Hure Babylon und die Verführung der Heiligen: Eine Studie zur Apokalypse des Johannes.* BWANT 136. Stuttgart: Kohlhammer, 1995. ———. "The Kerygma of the Revelation to John." *Int* 22 (1968) 3–17. ———. *Zeit und Geschichte.* Zürich: Zwingli, 1952. ———. *Time and History: A Study on the Revelation.* Tr. G. C. Winsor. Richmond, VA: Knox, 1966. **Robert, L.** *Hellenica: Recueil d'epigraphie de numismatique et d'antiquities grecques.* 13 vols. Limoges: Bontemps, 1940–65. ———. *Nouvelles inscriptions de Sardes.* Paris: Librairie d'Amérique et d'Orient, 1964. **Robertson, A. T.** *A Grammar of the Greek New Testament in the Light of Historical Research.* Nashville: Broadman, 1934. **Robinson, J. A. T.** *Redating the New Testament.* Philadelphia: Westminster, 1976. **Robinson, J. M.,** ed. *The Nag Hammadi Library.* Rev. ed. San Francisco: Harper & Row, 1988. **Roloff, J.** *Das Kerygma und der irdische Jesus: Historische Motive in den Jesus-Erzählungen der Evangelien.* Göttingen: Vandenhoeck & Ruprecht, 1970. **Romero-Pose, E.,** ed. *Sancti Beati a Liebana Commentarius in Apocalipsin.* Rome: Typis officinae polygraphicae, 1985. **Rordorf, W.,** and **Tuilier, A.** *La Doctrine des douze Apôtres (Didachè).* SC 248. Paris: Cerf, 1978. **Roscher, W. H.** *Ausführliches Lexikon der griechischen und römischen Mythologie.* 6 vols. Leipzig: Teubner, 1884–1937. **Rosenstiehl, J.-M.** *L'Apocalypse d'Elie.* Paris: Geuthner, 1972. **Rosenthal, F.** *A Grammar of Biblical Aramaic.* Wiesbaden: Harrassowitz, 1963. **Rostovtzeff, M.** *The Social and Economic History of the Roman Empire.* 2nd ed. by P. M. Fraser. 2 vols. Oxford: Clarendon, 1957. **Roueché, C.** *Aphrodisias in Antiquity.* London: Society for the Promotion of Roman Studies, 1989. **Ruckstuhl, E.,** and **Dschulnigg, P.** *Stilkritik und Verfasserfrage im Johannesevangelium.* Göttingen: Vandenhoeck & Ruprecht; Freiburg: Universitätsverlag, 1991. **Rudolf, K.** *Gnosis: The Nature and History of Gnosticism.* Tr. R. McL. Wilson. San Francisco: Harper & Row,

1983. **Rusam, F.** "Hymnische Formeln in Apokalypse 1." Diss., Christian-Albrechts-Universität zu Kiel, 1970. **Russell, D. S.** *The Method and Message of Jewish Apocalyptic.* Philadelphia: Westminster, 1964. **Rydbeck, L.** *Fachprosa, Vermeintliche Volkssprache und Neues Testament.* Uppsala: Berlingska Boktryckeriet, 1967. **Sanday, W.**, and **Headlam, A. C.** *Romans.* 5th ed. Edinburgh: T. & T. Clark, 1902. ——— and **Turner, C. H.** *Nouum Testamentum Sancti Irenaei Episcopi Lugdunensis.* Old-Latin Biblical Texts 7. Oxford: Clarendon, 1923. **Sanders, E. P.** *Jesus and Judaism.* Philadelphia: Fortress, 1985. **Sanders, J. T.** *The New Testament Christological Hymns: Their Historical Religious Background.* SNTSMS 15. Cambridge: Cambridge UP, 1971. **Sandnes, K. O.** *Paul—One of the Prophets? A Contribution to the Apostle's Self-Understanding.* WUNT 2/43. Tübingen: Mohr-Siebeck, 1991. **Satake, A.** *Die Gemeindeordnung in der Johannesapokalypse.* WMANT 21. Neukirchen: Neukirchener, 1966. **Sattler, W.** "Das Buch mit sieben Siegeln: Studien zum literarischen Aufbau der Offenbarung Johannis." *ZNW* 20 (1921) 231–40. **Sauter, F.** *Der römische Kaiserkult bei Martial und Statius.* Stuttgart; Berlin: Kohlhammer, 1934. **Schäfer, P.** *Synopse zur Hekhalot-Literatur.* Tübingen: Mohr-Siebeck, 1981. **Schiffman, L. H.**, and **Swartz, M. D.** *Hebrew and Aramaic Incantation Texts from the Cairo Genizah: Selected Texts from Taylor-Schechter Box K1.* Sheffield: Sheffield Academic, 1992. **Schlatter, A.** *Das Alte Testament in der johanneischen Apokalypse.* Gütersloh: Bertelsmann, 1912. **Schlier, H.** *Der Brief an die Galater.* 12th ed. Göttingen: Vandenhoeck & Ruprecht, 1962. **Schmid, J.** *Studien zur Geschichte des griechischen Apokalypse-Textes.* 2 vols. Munich: Zink, 1955. **Schmidt, C.**, and **MacDermot, V.** *The Books of Jeu and the Untitled Text in the Bruce Codex.* NHS 13. Leiden: Brill, 1978. ——— and **MacDermot, V.** *Pistis Sophia.* NHS 9. Leiden: Brill, 1978. ——— and **Till, W.** *Koptisch-gnostische Schriften.* Vol. 1: *Die Pistis Sophia, Die beiden Bücher des Jeu, Unbekanntes altgnostisches Werk.* GCS 13. 3rd ed. Berlin: Akademie, 1962. **Schmidt, F.** *Le Testament grec d'Abraham.* Tübingen: Mohr-Siebeck, 1986. **Schnackenburg, R.** *The Gospel according to St. John.* 3 vols. Vol. 1: New York: Herder & Herder, 1968; Vol. 2: New York: Seabury, 1980; Vol. 3: New York: Crossroad, 1982. **Schoedel, W. R.** *Ignatius of Antioch: A Commentary on the Letters of Ignatius of Antioch.* Philadelphia: Fortress, 1985. **Schowalter, D. N.** *The Emperor and the Gods: Images from the Time of Trajan.* HDR 28. Minneapolis: Fortress, 1993. **Schrenk, G.** *Die Weissagung über Israel im Neuen Testament.* Zürich: Gotthelf, 1951. **Schröder, S.** *Plutarchs Schrift De Pythiae oraculis. Text, Einleitung und Kommentar.* Stuttgart: Teubner, 1990. **Schürer, E.** *The History of the Jewish People in the Age of Jesus Christ.* 4 vols. Ed. G. Vermes, F. Millar, and M. Goodman. Edinburgh: T. & T. Clark, 1973–87. **Schüssler Fiorenza, E.** "Apokalypsis and Propheteia: The Book of Revelation in the Context of Early Christian Prophecy." In *L'Apocalypse johannique et l'Apocalyptique dans le Nouveau Testament,* ed. J. Lambrecht. Leuven: Leuven UP, 1980. 105–28. ———. *The Book of Revelation: Justice and Judgment.* Philadelphia: Fortress, 1985. ———. "Composition and Structure of the Book of Revelation." *CBQ* 39 (1977) 344–66. ———. "The Eschatology and Composition of the Apocalypse." *CBQ* 30 (1968) 564. ———. *Priester für Gott: Studien zum Herrschafts- und Priestermotiv in der Apokalypse.* NTAbh 7. Münster: Aschendorf, 1972. ———. "The Quest for the Johannine School: The Apocalypse and the Fourth Gospel." *NTS* 23 (1976–77) 402–27. **Schwemer, A. M.** "Studien zu den frühjüdischen Prophetenlegenden: Vitae Prophetarum." 2 vols. Diss., Tübingen, 1993. **Scott, W.** *Hermetica: The Ancient Greek and Latin Writings Which Contain Religious or Philosophic Teachings Ascribed to Hermes Trismegistus.* 4 vols. 1924–36. Repr. Boston: Shambhala, 1985. **Scullard, H. H.** *Festivals and Ceremonies of the Roman Republic.* Ithaca, NY: Cornell UP, 1981. **Sellin, E.**, and **Fohrer, G.** *Introduction to the Old Testament.* Tr. D. E. Green. Nashville: Abingdon, 1968. **Shepherd, M. H.** *The Paschal Liturgy and the Apocalypse.* Richmond: John Knox, 1960. **Sherk, R. K.** *Roman Documents from the Greek East: Senatus Consulta and Epistulae to the Age of Augustus.* Baltimore: Johns Hopkins UP, 1969. **Sherwin-White, A. N.** *The Letters of Pliny: A Historical and Social Commentary.* Oxford: Clarendon, 1966. **Sickenberger, J. B.** *Erklärung der Johannesapokalypse.* Bonn: Hanstein, 1940. **Simon, M.** *Verus Israel: A Study of the Relations between Christians and Jews in the Roman Empire (A.D. 135–425).*

Oxford: Oxford UP, 1986. **Simpson, M.,** tr. *Gods and Heroes of the Greeks: The Library of Apollodorus.* Amherst: University of Massachusetts, 1976. **Skarsaune, O.** *The Proof from Prophecy: A Study in Justin Martyr's Proof-Text Tradition: Text-Type, Provenance, Theological Profile.* NovTSup 56. Leiden: Brill, 1987. **Skehan, W., Ulrich, E.,** and **Sanderson, J. E.** *Qumran Cave 4.* Vol. 4: *Palaeo-Hebrew and Greek Biblical Manuscripts.* DJD 9. Oxford: Clarendon, 1992. **Skutsch, O.** *The Annals of Quintus Ennius.* Oxford: Clarendon, 1985. **Smalley, S. S.** *Thunder and Love: John's Revelation and John's Community.* Milton Keynes: Nelson Word, 1994. **Smith, J. Z.** "The Prayer of Joseph." In *Religions in Antiquity,* ed. J. Neusner. NumenSup 14. Leiden: Brill, 1968. 253–94. **Smith, K. F.** *The Elegies of Albius Tibullus.* New York: American Book Company, 1913. **Smith, M.** *Tannaitic Parallels to the Gospels.* SBLMS 6. 2nd ed. Philadelphia: Society of Biblical Literature, 1968. **Smyth, H. W.** *Greek Grammar.* Rev. G. M. Messing. Cambridge: Harvard UP, 1956. **Soden, H. F. von.** *Text mit Apparat.* Part 2 of *Die Schriften des Neuen Testaments in ihrer ältesten erreichbaren Textgestalt.* Göttingen: Vandenhoeck & Ruprecht, 1913. **Söder, R.** *Die apokryphen Apostelgeschichten und die romanhafte Literatur der Antike.* Stuttgart: Kohlhammer, 1932. **Soisalon-Soininen, I.** *Die Infinitive in der Septuagints.* Helsinki: Suomalainen Tiedeakatemia, 1965. **Sokolowski, F.** *Lois sacrées de l'Asie Mineure.* Paris: de Boccard, 1955. **Sollamo, R.** *Renderings of Hebrew Semiprepositions in the Septuagint.* Helsinki: Suomalainen Tiedeakatemia, 1979. **Souza Nogueira, P. A. de.** "Der Widerstand gegen Rom in der Apokalypse des Johannes: Eine Untersuchung zur Tradition des Falls von Babylon in Apokalypse 18." Diss., Heidelberg, 1991. **Spengel, L.** *Rhetores Graeci.* 3 vols. Leipzig: Teubner, 1853–56. **Sperber, A.** *The Bible in Aramaic.* 4 vols. Leiden: Brill, 1959–73. **Spicq, C.** *Notes de lexicographie Néo-testamentaire.* 3 vols. Göttingen: Vandenhoeck & Ruprecht, 1978–82. **Stegemann, W.** *Zwischen Synagoge und Obrigkeit: Zur historischen Situation der lukanischen Christen.* Göttingen: Vandenhoeck & Ruprecht, 1991. **Stengel, P.** *Die griechischen Kultusaltertümer.* 3rd ed. Munich: Beck, 1920. **Stone, M. E.** *Fourth Ezra: A Commentary on the Book of Fourth Ezra.* Minneapolis: Fortress, 1990. **Stoneman, R.** *Palmyra and Its Empire: Zenobia's Revolt against Rome.* Ann Arbor: University of Michigan, 1992. **Strobel, A.** "Apokalypse des Johannes." In *Theologische Realenzyklopädie.* Vol. 3. New York; Berlin: de Gruyter, 1978. **Stroker, W. D.** *Extracanonical Sayings of Jesus.* Atlanta: Scholars, 1989. **Stuckenbruck, L. T.** *Angel Veneration and Christology: A Study in Early Judaism and the Apocalypse of John.* Tübingen: Mohr-Siebeck, 1995. **Stuhlmann, R.** *Das eschatologische Maß im Neuen Testament.* Göttingen: Vandenhoeck & Ruprecht, 1983. **Swartz, M. D.** *Mystical Prayer in Ancient Judaism: An Analysis of Maʿaseh Merkavah.* Tübingen: Mohr-Siebeck, 1992. **Swete, H. B.** *Introduction to the Old Testament in Greek.* Cambridge: Cambridge UP, 1914. **Syme, R.** *Tacitus.* 2 vols. Oxford: Clarendon, 1958. **Tagawa, K.** *Miracles et Évangile: la pensée personelle de l'évangeliste Marc.* Paris: Presses universitaires de France, 1966. **Tajra, H. W.** *The Martyrdom of St. Paul: Historical and Judicial Context, Traditions and Legends.* WUNT 2/67. Tübingen: Mohr-Siebeck, 1994. **Taylor, L. R.** *The Divinity of the Roman Emperor.* Middletown: American Philological Association, 1931. **Tcherikover, V.** *Hellenistic Civilisation and the Jews.* Philadelphia: Jewish Publication Society of America, 1961. **Thackeray, H. St. J.** *A Grammar of the Old Testament in Greek.* Cambridge: Cambridge UP, 1909. ———. *Josephus the Man and the Historian.* New York: Ktav, 1967. **Thayer, J. H.** *A Greek-English Lexicon of the New Testament.* Grand Rapids, MI: Zondervan, n.d. **Theisohn, J.** *Der auserwählte Richter: Untersuchungen zur traditionsgeschichtlicher Ort der Menschensohngestalt der Bilderreden des Äthiopisch Henoch.* Göttingen: Vandenhoeck & Ruprecht, 1976. **Theissen, G.** *The Gospels in Context: Social and Political History in the Synoptic Tradition.* Minneapolis: Fortress, 1991. ———. *The Miracle Stories of the Early Christian Tradition.* Philadelphia: Fortress, 1983. **Theodor, J.,** and **Albeck, Ch.** *Midrash Bereshit Rabba: Critical Edition with Notes and Commentary.* 3 vols. Jerusalem: Vahrman, 1965. **Thompson, L. L.** *The Book of Revelation: Apocalypse and Empire.* New York: Oxford UP, 1990. **Thompson, S.** *The Apocalypse and Semitic Syntax.* SNTSMS 52. Cambridge: Cambridge UP, 1985. ———. *Motif-Index of Folk-Literature.* 6 vols. 1932–34. Repr. Bloomington: Indiana UP, 1983. **Tischendorf, C.** *Novum Testamentum Graece.* 8th ed. 2 vols.

Leipzig: Giesecke & Devrient, 1872. **Tödt, H. E.** *The Son of Man in the Synoptic Tradition.* Tr. D. M. Barton. Philadelphia: Westminster, 1965. **Toit, A. du.** "Vilification as a Pragmatic Device in Early Christian Epistolography." *Bib* 75 (1994) 403–12. **Torrey, C. C.** *The Apocalypse of John.* New Haven: Yale UP, 1958. **Touilleux, P.** *L'Apocalypse et les cultes de Domitien et de Cybèle.* Paris: Librairie Orientaliste Paul Geuthner, 1935. **Tov, E.** *The Greek Minor Prophets Scroll from Nahal Ḥever (8ḤevXIIgr, The Seiyal Collection I).* DJD 8. Oxford: Clarendon, 1990. **Trebilco, P.** *Jewish Communities in Asia Minor.* SNTSMS 69. Cambridge: Cambridge UP, 1991. **Trites, A. A.** *The New Testament Concept of Witness.* Cambridge: Cambridge UP, 1977. **Tromp, J.** *The Assumption of Moses: A Critical Edition with Commentary.* Leiden: Brill, 1992. **Turner, N.** *Grammatical Insights into the New Testament.* Edinburgh: T. & T. Clark, 1965. ———. *Style.* Vol. 4 of *A Grammar of New Testament Greek,* ed. J. H. Moulton. Edinburgh: T. & T. Clark, 1976. ———. *Syntax.* Vol. 3 of *A Grammar of New Testament Greek,* ed. J. H. Moulton. Edinburgh: T. & T. Clark, 1963. **Ulrichsen, J. H.** *Die Grundschrift der Testamente der zwölf Patriarchen: Eine Untersuchung zu Umfang, Inhalt und Eigenart der ursprünglichen Schrift.* Uppsala: Almqvist & Wiksel, 1991. **Urbach, E. E.** *The Sages: Their Concepts and Beliefs.* Cambridge: Harvard UP, 1987. **VanderKam, J. C.** *The Book of Jubilees: A Critical Text.* CSCO 510; Scriptores Aethiopici 87. Louvain: Peeters, 1989. ———. *Enoch and the Growth of an Apocalyptic Tradition.* CBQMS 16. Washington, DC: Catholic Biblical Society of America, 1984. **Vanhoye, A.** "L'utilisation du livre d'Ézéchiel dans l'Apocalypse. *Bib* 43 (1962) 436–76. **Vanni, U.** *L'Apocalisse: Ermeneutica, Esegesi, Teologia.* Bologna: Editzioni Dehoniane, 1988. ———. *La struttura letteraria dell'Apocalisse.* 2nd ed. Napoli: Morcelliana, 1980. **Vaux, R. de.** *Ancient Israel: Its Life and Institutions.* Tr. J. McHugh. New York: McGraw-Hill, 1961. **Vermaseren, M. J.** *Mithraica III: The Mithraeum at Marino.* EPRO 16. Leiden: Brill, 1982. ———. *Mithras the Secret God.* London: Chatto & Windus, 1963. **Vermes, G.** *The Dead Sea Scrolls in English.* 3rd rev. and aug. ed. London: Penguin, 1987. ———. *Jesus the Jew.* New York: Macmillan, 1973. **Vermeule, C. C.** *Roman Imperial Art in Greece and Asia Minor.* Cambridge: Harvard UP, 1968. **Vermeule, E.** *Aspects of Death in Early Greek Art and Poetry.* Berkeley: University of California, 1979. **Versnel, H. S.** "Religious Mentality in Ancient Prayer." In *Faith, Hope and Worship: Aspects of Religious Mentality in the Ancient World.* Leiden: Brill, 1981. 1–64. ———. *Triumphus: An Inquiry into the Origin, Development and Meaning of the Roman Triumph.* Leiden: Brill, 1970. **Vielhauer, P.** *Geschichte der urchristlichen Literatur.* Berlin; New York: de Gruyter, 1975. **Vischer, E.** *Die Offenbarung Johannis: eine jüdische Apokalypse in christlicher Bearbeitung.* TU 2/3. Leipzig: Hinrichs, 1886. **Vlastos, G.** *Socrates: Ironist and Moral Reformer.* Cambridge: Cambridge UP, 1991. **Vogels, H. J.** *Untersuchungen zur Geschichte der lateinischen Apokalypse-Übersetzung.* Düsseldorf: Schwann, 1920. **Vögtle, A.** *Das Neue Testament und die Zukunft des Kosmos.* Düsseldorf: Patmos, 1970. ———. *Die Tugend- und Lasterkataloge im Neuen Testament.* NTAbh 16. Münster: Aschendorff, 1936. **Völter, D.** *Die Entstehung der Apokalypse.* 2nd ed. Freiburg: Mohr-Siebeck, 1882. **Volz, P.** *Die Eschatologie der jüdischen Gemeinde.* Tübingen: Mohr-Siebeck, 1934. **Vos, L. A.** *The Synoptic Traditions in the Apocalypse.* Kampen: Kok, 1965. **Votaw, C. W.** *The Use of the Infinitive in Biblical Greek.* Chicago: Votaw, 1896. **Vuyst, J. de.** *De structuur van de apokalyps.* Kampen: Kok, 1968. **Walbank, F. W.** *A Historical Commentary on Polybius.* 3 vols. Oxford: Clarendon, 1957–79. **Watson, A.,** ed. *The Digest of Justinian.* Philadelphia: University of Pennsylvania, 1985. **Weber, R.** ed., *Biblia sacra iuxta Vulgatam versionem.* 2 vols. Stuttgart: Deutsche Bibelgesellschaft, 1969. **Wehr, L.** *Arznei der Unsterblichkeit: Die Eucharistie bei Ignatius von Antiochien und im Johannesevangelium.* NTAbh 18. Münster: Aschendorff, 1987. **Weiser, A.** *The Psalms: A Commentary.* Philadelphia: Westminster, 1962. **Weiss, B.** *Die Johannes-Apokalypse: Textkritische Untersuchungen und Textherstellung.* TU 7.1. Leipzig: Hinrichs, 1892. **Weiss, H.-F.** *Untersuchungen zur Kosmologie des hellenistischen und palästinischen Judentums.* TU 97. Berlin: Akademie, 1966. **Weiss, J.** *Der erste Korintherbrief.* 8th ed. Göttingen: Vandenhoeck & Ruprecht, 1910. ———. *Die Offenbarung des Johannes: Ein Beitrag zur Literatur- und Religionsgeschichte.* Göttingen: Vandenhoeck & Ruprecht, 1904. **Wellhausen, J.** *Analyse der*

Offenbarung Johannis. Berlin: Weidmann, 1907. ———. *Skizzen und Vorarbeiten.* 6 vols. 1884–99. Repr. Berlin; New York: de Gruyter, 1985. **Wellmann, M.**, ed. *Pedanii Dioscurides Anazarbei, De material medica libri quinque.* 3 vols. Berlin: Weidmann, 1958. **Wengst, K.** *Schriften des Urchristentums: Didache (Apostellehre), Barnabasbrief, Zweiter Klemensbrief, Schrift an Diognet.* Munich: Kösel, 1984. **Werner, E.** *The Sacred Bridge: Liturgical Parallels in Synagogue and Early Church.* New York: Columbia UP, 1959. **West, M. L.** *Hesiod, Theogony: Edited with Prolegomena and Commentary.* Oxford: Clarendon, 1966. **Westcott, B. F.** *A General Survey of the History of the Canon of the New Testament.* 6th ed. Grand Rapids, MI: Baker, 1980. ——— and **Hort, F. J. A.** *Introduction to the New Testament in the Original Greek.* New York: Harper, 1882 (*indicates pages in the Appendix). **Westermann, C.** *Genesis: A Commentary.* Tr. J. J. Scullion. 3 vols. Minneapolis: Augsburg, 1984–86. ———. *The Praise of God in the Psalms.* Tr. K. R. Crim. Richmond: John Knox, 1965. **Wettstein, J. J.** *Novum Testamentum Graecum.* 2 vols. 1752. Repr. Graz: Akademische Druck- und Verlaganstalt, 1962. **Weyland, W. G. J.** *Omwerkings en Compilatie-Hypothesen toegepast op de Apokalypse van Johannes.* Groningen: Wolters, 1888. **White, R. J.** *The Interpretation of Dreams: Oneirocritica by Artemidorus.* Park Ridge, NJ: Noyes, 1975. **Wilken, R. L.** *The Christians as the Romans Saw Them.* New Haven; London: Yale UP, 1984. **Williams, F.** *Callimachus, Hymn to Apollo: A Commentary.* Oxford: Clarendon, 1978. **Wilson, W. T.** *The Mysteries of Righteousness: The Literary Composition and Genre of the Sentences of Pseudo-Phocylides.* Tübingen: Mohr-Siebeck, 1994. **Winer, G. B.** *A Treatise on the Grammar of New Testament Greek.* Tr. W. F. Moulton. 3rd ed. rev. Edinburgh: T. & T. Clark, 1882. **Winston, D.** *The Wisdom of Solomon.* Garden City, NY: Doubleday, 1979. **Wissowa, G.** *Religion und Kultus der Römer.* 2nd ed. Munich: Beck, 1912. **Witt, R. E.** *Isis in the Graeco-Roman World.* Ithaca, NY: Cornell UP, 1971. **Wolff, C.** *Jeremia im frühjudentum und Urchristentum.* TU 118. Berlin: Akademie, 1976. **Wolff, H. W.** *Joel and Amos.* Hermeneia. Philadelphia: Fortress, 1977. **Wülker, L.** *Die geschichtliche Entwicklung des Prodigienswesens bei den Römern: Studien zur Geschichte und Überlieferung der Staatsprodigien.* Leipzig: Glausch, 1903. **Yarbro Collins, A.** *The Combat Myth in the Book of Revelation.* Missoula, MT: Scholars, 1975. ———. *Crisis and Catharsis: The Power of the Apocalypse.* Philadelphia: Westminster, 1984. ———. "The Political Perspective of the Revelation to John." *JBL* 96 (1977) 241–56. ———. "The 'Son of Man' Tradition and the Book of Revelation." In *The Messiah: Developments in Earliest Judaism and Christianity,* ed. J. H. Charlesworth. Minneapolis: Fortress, 1992. 536–68. **Ysebaert, J.** *Die Amtsterminologie im Neuen Testament und in der Alten Kirche: Eine lexicographische Untersuchung.* Breda: Eureia, 1994. **Zahn, T.** *Ignatii et Polycarpi Epistolae Marytia Fragmenta.* Vol. 2 of *Patrum Apostolicorum Opera.* Leipzig: Hinrichs, 1876. ———. *Introduction to the New Testament.* 3 vols. Grand Rapids, MI: Kregel, 1953. ———, ed. *Forschungen zur Geschichte des neutestamentlichen Kanons und der altkirchlichen Literatur.* Erlangen: Deichert, 1891. **Zazoff, P.** *Die antike Gemmen.* Munich: Beck, 1983. **Zerwick, M.** *Biblical Greek.* Tr. J. Smith, S.J. Rome: Pontifical Biblical Institute, 1963. ——— and **Grosvenor, M.** *A Grammatical Analysis of the Greek New Testament.* 2 vols. Rome: Biblical Institute, 1974. **Ziegler, J.**, ed. *Duodecim prophetae.* VTG 13. Göttingen: Vandenhoeck & Ruprecht, 1943. ———, ed. *Ezechiel.* Septuaginta: VTG 16/1. Göttingen: Vandenhoeck & Ruprecht, 1952. ———, ed. *Susanna, Daniel, Bel et Draco.* VTG 16/2. Göttingen: Vandenhoeck & Ruprecht, 1954. **Ziegler, K.-H.** *Die Beziehungen zwischen Rom und dem Partherreich.* Wiesbaden: Steiner, 1964. **Zimmerli, W.** *Ezekiel.* Tr. R. E. Clements. 2 vols. Philadelphia: Fortress, 1979–83.

Revelation 6:1–16:21

2. *The Lamb Breaks the First Six Seals (6:1–17)*

Bibliography

Bachmann, M. "Der erste apokalyptische Reiter und die Anlage des letzten Buches der Bible." *Bib* 67 (1986) 240–75. **Baldensperger, W.** "Les cavaliers de l'Apocalypse." *RHPR* 4 (1924) 1–31. **Bauckham, R.** "The Eschatological Earthquake." In R. Bauckham, *Climax.* 199–209. ———. "The Use of Apocalyptic Traditions." In R. Bauckham, *Climax.* 38–91. **Björck, B.** *Der Fluch des Christen Sabinus.* Uppsala: Almqvist & Wiksell, 1938. **Black, M.** "Some Greek Words with Hebrew Meanings in the Epistles and Apocalypse." In *Biblical Studies in Honour of William Barclay,* ed. J. R. McKay and J. F. Miller. London: Collins, 1976. 135–46. **Cerny, L.** *The Day of Yahweh and Some Relevant Problems.* Prague: University of Karlovy, 1948. **Considine, J. S.** "The Rider on the White Horse: Apocalypse 6:1–8." *CBQ* 6 (1944) 406–22. **Dornseiff, F.** "Die apokalyptischen Reiter." *ZNW* 38 (1939) 196–97. **Everson, A. J.** "The Days of Yahweh." *JBL* 93 (1974) 329–37. **Eynde, P. van den.** "Le Dieu du désordre: Commentaire synthétique d'Apocalypse 6,9–11." *BVC* 74 (1967) 39–51. **Feuillet, A.** "Les martyrs de l'humanité et l'agneau égorgé: Une interprêtation nouvelle de la prière des égorgés en Ap 6,9–11." *NRT* 99 (1977) 189–207. ———. "Le premier cavalier de l'Apocalypse." *ZNW* 57 (1966) 229–59. **Gsell, S.** *Essai sur le regne de l'empereur Domitien.* Paris: Thorin & Fils, 1894. **Haapa, E.** "Farben und Funktionen bei den apokalyptischen Reitern (Apoc 6,1–8; Zach 1,7–17)." *Teologinen Aikakauskirja* 73 (1968) 216–25. **Heil, J. P.** "The Fifth Seal (Rev 6,9–11) as a Key to the Book of Revelation." *Bib* 74 (1993) 220–43. **Hillers, D.** *Treaty-Curses and the Old Testament Prophets.* Rome: Pontifical Biblical Institute, 1964. **Hodges, Z. C.** "The First Horseman of the Apocalypse." *BSac* 119 (1962) 324–34. **Johnston, S. I.** "Riders in the Sky: Cavalier Gods and Theurgic Salvation in the Second Century A.D." *CP* 87 (1992) 303–21. **Kerkeslager, A.** "Apollo, Greco-Roman Prophecy, and the Rider on the White Horse in Rev 6:2." *JBL* 112 (1993) 116–21. **Klasse, W.** "Vengeance in the Apocalypse." *CBQ* 28 (1966) 300–311. **Klauck, H.-J.** "θυσιαστήριον: Eine Berichtigung." *ZNW* 71 (1980) 274–77. **Krause, M. S.** "The Finite Verb with Cognate Participle in the New Testament." In *Biblical Greek Language and Linguistics: Open Questions in Current Research,* ed. S. E. Porter and D. A. Carson. JSNTSup 80. Sheffield: Sheffield Academic, 1993. 187–206. **Krauss, S.** "Die Schonung von Öl und Wein in der Apokalypse." *ZNW* 10 (1909) 81–89. **Levick, B.** "Domitian and the Provinces." *Latomus* 41 (1982) 50–73. **Licht, J.** "Taxo, or the Apocalyptic Doctrine of Vengeance." *JJS* 12 (1961) 95–103. **Maiberger, P.** "Zur Problem und Herkunft der sogennanten Fluchpsalmen." *TTZ* 97 (1988) 183–216. **Mendenhall, G. E.** "The Vengeance of Yahweh." In *The Tenth Generation.* Baltimore: Johns Hopkins UP, 1973. 69–104. **Merz, E.** *Die Blutrache bei den Israeliten.* BWANT 20. Leipzig: Heinrichs, 1916. **Michael, J. H.** "The Position of the Wild Beasts in Revelation 6:8b." *ExpTim* 58 (1946–47) 166. **Moffatt, J.** "'Hurt Not the Oil and the Wine.'" *The Expositor* 6 (1908) 359–69. **Moule, C. F. D.** "Fulfilment Words in the New Testament." *NTS* 14 (1968) 293–320. **Mowinckel, S.** "Jahves Dag." *NorTT* 59 (1958) 1–56, 209–29. **Muscovi, J. N.** *Vengeance in the Apocalypse.* AUSDDS 17. Berrien Springs: Andrews UP, 1993. **Peels, H. G. L.** *The Vengeance of God: The Meaning of the Root NQM and the Function of the NQM-Texts in the Context of Divine Revelation in the Old Testament.* OTS 31. Leiden: Brill, 1995. **Rad, G. von.** "The Origin of the Concept of the Day of Yahweh." *JSS* 4 (1959) 97–108. **Räisänen, H.** *The Idea of Divine Hardening.* Helsinki: The Finnish Exegetical Society, 1976. **Reinach, S.** "La mévente des vins sous le Haut-Empire romain." *RArch* 39 (1901) 350–74 (= "La date de l'Apocalypse et la mévente des vins sous l'Empire." In *Cultes, Mythes et Religions.* Paris: Leroux, 1906. 2:356–80). **Rissi, M.** "The Rider on the White Horse: A Study of Revelation 6:1–8." *Int* 18 (1964) 407–18. **Robinson, D. M.** "A New Latin Economic Edict from Pisidian Antioch." *TAPA* 55 (1924) 5–20. **Rowley, H. H.** *The Faith of Ancient Israel.* London: SCM, 1956. **Scholem, G.** "Über eine Formel in den koptisch-gnostischen Schriften und ihren jüdischen Ursprung." *ZNW* 30 (1931) 170–76. **Smith, M. S.** *The Early History of God.* San Francisco: Harper & Row, 1990. **Stolle, F.** *Der römische Legionar und sein Gepäck.* Strassburg: Trübner, 1914. **Stuhlmann, R.** *Das eschatologische Maß Neuen Testament.* Göttingen: Vandenhoeck & Ruprecht, 1983. **Taylor, F. W.** "The Seven Seals in the Revelation of John." *JTS* 31 (1929–30) 266–71. **Thomas, R. L.** "Imprecatory Prayers in the Apocalypse." *BSac* 126 (1969) 123–31. **Tromp, N. J.** *Primitive Conceptions of Death and the Nether World in the Old Testament.* Rome: Pontifical Biblical Institute, 1969. **Unnik, W. C. van.** "Die 'Zahl der vollkommenen Seelen' in der 'Pistis Sophia.'" In *Abraham unser Vater.* FS O. Michel, ed. O. Betz, M. Hengel, and P. Schmidt. Leiden: Brill, 1963. 467–77. ———. "Le nombre des élus dans le première épître de Clément." *RHPR* 42 (1962) 237–46. **Ulfgard, H.** *Feast and Future: Revelation 7:9–17 and the Feast of Tabernacles.* ConNT 22. Stockholm: Almqvist & Wiksell, 1989. **Vanni, U.** "Il terzo 'sigillo' dell'Apocalisse (Ap 6,5–6): simbols dell'ingiustizia sociale?" *Gregorianum Roma* 59 (1978) 691–719 (= *L'Apocalisse,* 193–213). **Watson, L.** *Arae: The Curse Poetry of Antiquity.* Leeds: Cairns, 1991. **Weiss, M.** "The Origin of the 'Day of the Lord'—Reconsidered." *HUCA* 37 (1966) 29–60. **Westermann, C.** "Struktur und Geschichte der Klage im Alten Testament." *ZAW* 66 (1954) 44–80. **Yarbro Collins, A.** "Persecution and Vengeance in the Book of Revelation." In *Apocalypticism,* ed. D. Hellholm. 729–49.

Translation

1 *Then [a]I saw[a] when[b] the Lamb broke the [c]first[d] of the seven seals, and I heard[e] one*
of the four cherubim[f] saying,[g] as though with a voice[h] of thunder, [i]"Come!"[j] 2 *[a]Then I*
looked,[a] and behold, there was a white horse, and the cavalier[b] had a bow. A[c] crown
was given to him, and [d]the conqueror went out[e] in order to conquer even more. 3 *When[a]*
he broke [b]the second seal,[b] I heard the second cherub saying, "Come!"[c] 4 *Then [a]another*
horse, a fiery red one,[b] rode out, and the cavalier[c] was given[d] the power to remove peace
from[e] the earth so that[f] people[g] might slaughter[h] each other. He was given a large
sword. 5 *When he broke the third seal, I heard the third cherub saying, "Come!"[a] [b]Then I*
looked,[b] and behold, there was a black horse, and the cavalier held a balance scale in his
hand. 6 *Then I heard, as it were,[a] a voice in the middle of the four cherubim saying, "A*
liter of wheat [b]for a denarius,[b] and three liters of barley[c] [b]for a denarius,[b] but[d] do not
harm[e] the oil and the[f] wine!" 7 *When he broke[a] the fourth seal, I heard the voice[b] of the*
fourth cherub saying, "Come!"[c] 8 *[a]I saw,[a] and behold, there was a pale-colored[b] horse,*
and [c]as for the[d] cavalier,[ec] [f]his name[f] was [g]Death, and Hades was following after him.[h]
[i]They[j] were given authority over a fourth part of the earth to kill with[k] the sword[l] and
with[k] famine and with[k] plague[m] and by[n] the wild animals of the earth.

9 *When he broke [a]the fifth seal,[a] [b]I saw[c] underneath the altar the souls of[d] [e]those*
slain[e] because of the word of God and because of the witness [f]which they bore.[g] 10 *They[a]*
[b]cried out[b] loudly saying, "O Master,[c] holy and true, how long will it be until you judge
and avenge our deaths[d] [e]caused by[e] [f]those who dwell on the earth?"[f] 11 *Then each[a] of*
them was given a white robe,[b] and [c]they were told[c] that they should rest[d] [e]a while longer[e]
until the number of their fellow servants, [f]that is,[f] their brothers who were [g]to be killed[g]
as they were, [h]would be complete.[h]

12 *Then [a]I saw,[a] when[b] he broke[c] the sixth seal, that[d] [e]a [f]great earthquake occurred,[f]*
and the sun [g]became dark[g] as haircloth,[h]
and [i]the entire moon[i] became red as blood,
13 *and the stars of the heaven fell to earth as a fig tree drops[a] its unripe figs[b] when*
shaken by a strong wind.
14 *Heaven disappeared from sight[a] like a scroll rolled up.*

Every mountain and island was shaken from its place.
15 *The kings of the earth and the important people and the generals* [a] *and the wealthy and the powerful and every slave and free person hid themselves in the caves and in the mountain rocks.* 16 *They said to the mountains and the cliffs,*[a] *"Fall on us and hide us from*[b] *the One who sits on the throne and from the wrath of the Lamb,* 17 *because the great day of his* [a] *wrath has come, and who is able to withstand it?"*

Notes

1.a-a. Variant: omit εἶδον] Andr h Primasius. Harmonistic omission to conform to the phraseology of 6:3, 5, 7, 9.

1.b. Variants: (1) ὅτε] ℵ A C Andreas. (2) ὅτι] Oecumenius^{2053} (καὶ ὅτε φησὶν εἶδον ὅτι); 2351 Andr d e f^{-2073} i n 1773 Byzantine vg. Because of the difficulty of the ὅτε clause following εἶδον, it was changed to a ὅτι clause that functions as an obj. clause. The phrase καὶ εἶδον ὅτε occurs in v 12, which indicates that it reflects the author's style.

1.c. Variants: (1) omit μίαν] Andr a$^{1\ 2186}$ b^{2059} l$^{1678\ 1778}$ arab. (2) ἕν] copies of printed TR: 296 2049. (3) πρώτην] eth. The fact that no Gk. MS substitutes πρώτην for μίαν suggests that the latter is *not* a Semitism but is perfectly comprehensible Gk. (see *Note* 1.d.).

1.d. Here μίαν is equivalent to πρώτην (see also Rev 9:12: ἡ οὐαὶ ἡ μία, "the first woe"), and many scholars regard this as a Semitism (BDF § 247; BAGD, 231–32; Mussies, *Morphology*, 216), though on the basis of the evidence presented below, the use of εἷς in both Rev 6:1 and 9:12 appears to be acceptable Gk. usage (see Moulton, *Prolegomena*, 95–96; MM, 187). The most discriminating discussion of this issue is found in Maloney, *Marcan Syntax*, 144–52. In Gk., cardinal and ordinal numbers are usually distinguished, except when the cardinal number εἷς is used to enumerate the first in a series of things when the subsequent items in the series are named (examples: Herodotus 4.161, μία . . . ἄλλη . . . τρίτη, "a first . . . another . . . a third"; Galen *De comp. med.* 4, μιᾶς καὶ δευτέρας ἡμέρας, "a first and a second day"; Aelius Aristides *Or.* 36.40, ἕν . . . δεύτεραν . . . τρίτον . . . τέταρτον, "first . . . second . . . third . . . fourth"; see BAGD, 231–32; Maloney, *Marcan Syntax*, 145). The same is true in Heb. and Aram. where the cardinal number אֶחָד *'eḥād*, "one," is sometimes used as an ordinal number meaning "first" (Gen 1:5; 2:11–14; 4:19; 8:5, 13; Exod 1:15; 25:12; Num 11:26; 1 Sam 1:2; Ruth 1:4; Ezra 10:16; Dan 9:1; see KB^3, 30; GKC § 98a; in all these passages Heb. אֶחָד *'eḥād* is translated by Gk. εἷς, while the Heb. ordinals are translated by Gk. ordinals), particularly in numbering the days of the month and years (GKC § 134p). In Gen 1:5 the phrase יוֹם אֶחָד *yôm 'eḥād*, lit. "day one" (LXX ἡμέρα μία), is a cardinal used as an ordinal (Josephus *Ant.* 1.26 comments, "This then should be the first day [πρώτη ἡμέρα] but Moses spoke of it as 'one' day [μίαν]," and Philo also comments on why Moses used μία here rather than πρώτη in *Op.* 35). In continuing the narrative of the creative days in Gen 1:8, the MT uses an ordinal number: יוֹם שֵׁנִי *yôm šēnî*, lit. "day second" (LXX ἡμέρα δευτέρα). The Heb. ordinals continue to be used throughout the rest of this narrative (Gen 1:13, 19, 23, 31; 2:2). There is therefore little difference between the Gk. and Heb./Aram. system of beginning an enumerated series with a cardinal number and continuing with ordinal numbers. It is only in the enumeration of dates that Gk. would use ordinal numbers and Heb./Aram. would use cardinal numbers. A number of scholars have regarded the analogous expression μία σαββάτων (Mark 16:2; Matt 28:1; Luke 24:1; John 20:1, 19; Acts 20:7) or μία σαββάτου (1 Cor 16:2) as a Semitism (Black, *Aramaic*, 124; Zerwick, *Greek*, § 154; Maloney, *Marcan Syntax*, 144–50), and this is probably correct (note that the phrase πρώτη σαββάτου does occur in Mark 16:9). With the exception of the seals and the woes, all other enumerated series in Revelation begin with the ordinal number πρῶτος: the four cherubim (4:7–8), the seven bowls (8:7), the seven trumpets (16:2), and the twelve foundations (21:19).

1.e. ἀκούειν + gen. + gen. ptcp. from λέγειν occurs eight times in Revelation: 6:1, 3, 5; 8:13; 16:1, 5, 7; 21:3. The same construction occurs occasionally in the LXX (Gen 27:5, 6; 37:17; Exod 19:9; 1 Kgdms 24:10; Isa 6:8; Jer 33:7; Ezek 2:2; Dan 8:13) and in the NT (Mark 12:28; 14:58; Luke 18:36; Acts 2:11; 6:11, 14; 8:30; 10:46; 11:7; 14:8; 15:12; 22:7).

1.f. For this translation, see *Comment* on 4:6.

1.g. The masc. and neut. gen. sing. ptcp. λέγοντος, "saying," is congruent with its antecedent noun ἑνός, "one." John's normal practice is to use the nom. masc. sing. ptcp. as an anacolouthon; see 4:1, 8.

1.h. Variants: (1) φωνή] A C 046 Andr c e^{2026} f^{-2056} g i^{-2042} l^{-1778} Byzantine; Bousset (1906) 264; Charles, 2:272. (2) φωνήν] ℵ fam 1611^{1854} Oecumenius^{2053} Andr i^{2042} l^{1778} n^{-2429} 2019. (3) φωνῇ] fam 1611^{2329} (φωνῆ);

Andr/Byz 3^{2196} (φωνῇ); WHort; B. Weiss, *Johannes-Apokalypse,* 172; [Bousset (1906) 264]; von Soden, *Text;* [Charles, 1:36]. (4) φωνῆς] 025 Andreas. Since the case following ὡς used in a comparison is normally the same as the case preceding ὡς, the form should be φωνῆς, modifying ἑνός; reading (4) is therefore a grammatical correction. According to Charles (1:161), the author had כקול *kĕqôl* in mind, which he rendered lit. by ὡς φωνή, though כקול can also be translated as ὡς φωνῇ.

1.i. The Gk. term ἔρχεσθαι can mean "go" as well as "come" (Metzger, *Code,* 57), and there are arguments for both translations. "Come!" suggests that the cherub summons the cavalier, while "Go!" implies that the cherub sends the cavalier on a mission. In this context the former seems more appropriate.

1.j. Variants affecting punctuation: (1) ἔρχου. καὶ εἶδον καὶ ἰδού] A C 025 Oecumenius^{2053} fam 1006^{1006} fam $1611^{1854\ 2329}$ Andreas cop; Nestle-Aland^{27}; UBSGNT^{4}; *TCGNT*^{2}, 667. (2) ἔρχου καὶ ἴδε. καὶ ἰδού] Byzantine. (3) ἔρχου καὶ ἴδε. καὶ εἶδον καὶ ἰδού] ℵ 046 it^{gig} syr$^{h\ ph}$ eth. The Byzantine tradition has altered εἶδον, "I saw," to ἴδε, "see," evident since the phrase καὶ ἴδε does not occur in any textually certain passage in Revelation (Charles, 1:clxii), a second-person imper. form apparently addressed to John (cf. the identical phrase in John 1:46). This constitutes evidence that ℵ has conflated the original reading with a distinctively Byzantine reading (Bousset [1906] 264 n. 2; Charles, 1:clxii; Schmid, *Studien* 2:129). A similar pattern of variants occurs in 6:3–8:

6:3–4	ἔρχου. καὶ εἶδον καὶ ἰδού] A C Andreas
	ἔρχου καὶ ἴδε. καὶ ἰδού] Byzantine
	ἔρχου καὶ ἴδε. καὶ εἶδον καὶ ἰδού] ℵ 046
6:5–6	ἔρχου. καὶ εἶδον καὶ ἰδού] A C Andreas
	ἔρχου καὶ ἴδε. καὶ ἰδού] Byzantine
	ἔρχου καὶ ἴδε. καὶ εἶδον καὶ ἰδού] ℵ 046
6:7–8	ἔρχου. καὶ εἶδον καὶ ἰδού] A C Andreas
	ἔρχου καὶ ἴδε. καὶ ἰδού] Byzantine
	ἔρχου καὶ ἴδε. καὶ εἶδον καὶ ἰδού] ℵ 046

Just as in 6:1–2, the Byzantine tradition has altered εἶδον to ἴδε, and the tradition represented by ℵ and 046 has conflated the two readings (Schmid, *Studien* 2:129).

2.a-a. Variants: (1) καὶ εἶδον] ℵ A (ἴδον); C (ἴδον); 025 fam $1006^{1006\ 1841}$ fam $1611^{1611\ 2344}$ Oecumenius^{2053} Andreas it^{gig} vg syr^{h} cop^{bo} arm; Nestle-Aland^{27}; UBSGNT^{4}; *TCGNT*^{2}, 667–68. (2) omit καὶ εἶδον] 046 fam $1611^{1854\ 2329}$ 2351 Andr c i^{2042} Byzantine Victorinus (Haussleiter, *Victorinus,* 69); Primasius Beatus Tyc^{2} it^{ar}. See *Note* 6:1.i. (3) καὶ ἤκουσα καὶ εἶδον] syr^{ph}.

2.b. ὁ καθήμενος ἐπ' αὐτόν, lit. "the one sitting upon it [i.e., 'the horse']," is here translated "cavalier."

2.c. Though this sentence begins with καί, "and," the word is left untranslated since it functions as a discourse marker indicating the beginning of a new sentence.

2.d. Variant: ὁ before νικῶν] A Oecumenius^{2053comm} 2048 arm^{2} arm^{4} syr^{s}. The article with νικῶν, forming a substantival ptcp., does not accord with the following clause, ἵνα νικήσῃ. Two readings are preserved in Oecumenius, νικῶν without the article and νικῶν with the article. The reading with the article, however, appears to have been formed for grammatical as well as christological reasons (see *Comment* on v 2). The comment of Oecumenius ad loc. is as follows: ἐξῆλθε δέ φησιν ἵνα ὁ νικῶν νικήσῃ. Χριστὸς δὲ ἦν ὁ νικῶν, "But he went out, he says, that the conqueror might conquer. And Christ was the conqueror."

2.e. Variant: omit καί] fam 1006 fam 1611^{1611} Oecumenius^{2053} latt syr^{h} Irenaeus. This omission was probably a grammatical correction.

3.a. The καί with which this sentence begins is left untranslated since it is simply a marker for a new clause or sentence and lacks independent semantic value.

3.b-b. Variants: (1) τὴν σφραγῖδα τὴν δευτέραν] ℵ A C 025 Oecumenius^{2053} fam 1006^{1841} fam $1611^{1611\ 1854\ 2329}$ Victorinus Primasius syr cop^{bo} arm. (2) τὴν δευτέραν σφραγῖδα] fam 1006^{1006} Oecumenius^{2062} 2351.

3.c. Variant: (1) ἔρχου] A C 025 046 fam 1006^{1006} fam $1611^{1611\ 1854}$ Oecumenius^{2053} vg syr^{ph} Nestle-Aland^{27}; UBSGNT^{4}; *TCGNT*^{2}, 668. (2) ἔρχου καὶ ἴδε] ℵ fam 1611^{2344} Andr d f^{2073} g it vg cop^{bo} syr^{h} Primasius Beatus. (3) ἔρχου καὶ βλέπε] fam 1611^{2050} Oecumenius^{2062}. Variants (2) and (3) construe the original ἔρχου, "come," as addressed to the seer, so that the phrases ἔρχου καὶ βλέπε and ἔρχου καὶ ἴδε mean "come and see" (see *Note* 6:1.i.).

4.a. Variant: insert καὶ εἶδον, καὶ ἰδού] ℵ Andr d. Addition to the text based on its presence in vv 2a, 5b, 8a.

4.b. Louw-Nida, § 79.31. Since horses are not normally "fiery red" in color, the problem is whether the term πυρρός should be translated with a color appropriate to horses, such as "chestnut" or "bay" (both reddish-brown) or "sorrel" (light reddish-brown). However, "apocalyptic" horses can presumably come in glaring colors. The phrase ἵππος πυρρός is derived from Zech 1:8, where the prophet sees a man on a ἵππος πυρρός, "red horse," while the MT lists only three horses behind him, "red, sorrel, and white"; the LXX has four: ἵπποι πυρροὶ καὶ ψαροὶ καὶ ποικίλοι καὶ λευκοί, "red and dapple-gray and roan [or dappled] and white." In Zech 6:2 the prophet saw four chariots drawn by red, black, white, and dapple-gray horses, respectively. Variant: πυρός] 2351.

4.c. The phrase τῷ καθημένῳ ἐπ' αὐτόν, lit. "to the one seated upon him," is here translated "cavalier."

4.d. Variants: (1) αὐτῷ before λαβεῖν] Tischendorf, *NT Graece;* bracketed in WHort; Bousset ([1906] 266); Charles (2:273); Nestle-Aland^{27}; UBSGNT^{4}. (2) omit αὐτῷ] א^{1corr} A fam 1611^{2344} Victorinus Primasius Tyc^{2} Beatus it^{gig}. (3) ἐξουσία before λαβεῖν] Oecumenius^{2053comm}.

4.e. Variants: (1) ἐκ before τῆς] א* C 025 fam 1006^{1006} fam 1611$^{1611\ 1854}$ Andr d f$^{2023\ 2073}$ i n^{-2429} 94 it^{gig} Byzantine; Tischendorf, *NT Graece;* bracketed in WHort; Bousset ([1906] 266); bracketed in Charles (2:273); Merk, *NT;* Nestle-Aland^{27}; UBSGNT^{4}; *TCGNT*^{1}, 738. (2) omit ἐκ before τῆς] A Andreas. (3) ἀπό before τῆς] Oecumenius^{2053} Andr a c n^{2429} 2019 TR. (4) ἐπί before τῆς] fam 1611^{2344}. The omission of ἐκ in variant (2) is either a correction (Schmid, *Studien* 2:99) or an accident of transcription (*TCGNT*^{1}, 738).

4.f. This purpose clause is introduced with καὶ ἵνα, lit. "and that," a peculiar combination found twice elsewhere in Revelation (6:2 and 13:17; cf. 13:15, ἵνα καί; see John 7:3; 11:37, 52; 12:9, 10; 13:34; 17:21; 19:35). The καί is redundant because it functions here to express purpose (Aejmelaeus, *Parataxis,* 18–20), and therefore it is left untranslated.

4.g. The verb σφάξουσιν is an indefinite pl., so I have translated the subject of the verb as "people."

4.h. Variants: (1) σφάξουσιν] A C 792 2019 2329; Tischendorf, *NT Graece;* Bousset ([1906] 266); Merk, *NT;* Nestle-Aland^{27}; UBSGNT^{4}. (2) σφάξωσιν] א Oecumenius^{2053} Andreas Byzantine 2351. (3) κατασφάξωσι] Andr e^{2026} i^{-2042}. σφάξουσιν in reading (1) is a fut. ind. literally meaning "they will slaughter" (see *Note* 4.g.) and ἵνα + fut. ind. is used eleven times in Revelation to express result or purpose (2:10; 3:9 [two fut. inds.]; 6:4, 11; 8:3; 9:4, 5, 20; 13:12; 14:13; 22:14). This is quite distinctive, since only seven other ἵνα clauses using the fut. ind. are found in the NT (Luke 14:10; 20:10; John 7:3; Acts 21:24; 1 Cor 9:18; Gal 2:4; Eph 6:3). There are a few examples in the LXX: Gen 16:2; 3 Kgdms 2:3; Sus 28; Dan 3:96 (Conybeare-Stock, *Septuagint,* 93). The originality of reading (1) is strengthened in view of the fact that Revelation frequently uses ἵνα + fut. ind. as a substitute for an inf. (3:9; 6:11; 8:3; 9:4, 5, 20; 13:12; 14:13; 22:14; see Schmid, *Studien* 2:220).

5.a. Variant: ἔρχου] see *Notes* 1.j. and 3.c.

5.b-b. Variant: καὶ εἶδον] see *Note* 2.a-a.

6.a. Variants: (1) ὡς] A C א 025 fam 1611^{2329} it^{gig} vg. (2) omit ὡς] Oecumenius^{2053} fam 1006$^{1006\ 1841}$ fam 1611^{1611} Byzantine Primasius Beatus syr cop. The use of ὡς here is unusual in that the first term of the comparison is missing (see also 4:6; 8:8; 9:7; 14:3; 19:1, 6[3x]). The term φωνήν, which follows, is an acc. because the omitted term of comparison would have been in the acc. as the obj. of the preceding ἤκουσα.

6.b-b. δηναρίου, "denarius," is a gen. of price or value (BDR § 179) and occurs twice as the predicate in two nominal clauses in v 6 (τοῦ θεοῦ similarly functions as a predicate in the nominal clause in 19:1). A verb such as πωλεῖται, "costs," is understood (BDR § 480.8). A denarius was the equivalent to a day's wages, and the term can be translated in monetary terms specific to a given culture.

6.c. Variants: (1) κριθῶν] *lectio originalis.* (2) κριθῆς] fam 1611^{2344} 2351 Byzantine syr^{ph}.

6.d. Since καί links two clauses, the second of which is antithetical to the first (see *Comment* on 6:6), it is a καί *adversativum* and can be translated "but."

6.e. The prohibition μὴ ἀδικήσῃς, "do not harm," using the aor. subjunctive, may be an attempt to prevent what has not yet taken place, with an *ingressive* emphasis, i.e., with a focus on the starting point (i.e., "Do not start harming the oil and the wine"), or may emphasize urgently the necessity of terminating an action; i.e., the terminating point should be reached at once (i.e., "Quit harming the oil and the wine"). Cf. J. P. Louw, "On Greek Prohibitions," *AcCl* 2 (1959) 43–57.

6.f. Variant: τό instead of τόν] 𝔓^{24} Andr/Byz 4a^{616} Byz 2^{2138} Byz 11^{368}.

7.a. Variant: ἤνεωξεν] 𝔓^{24} is a singular reading described by the editors of POxy 1230 (= 𝔓^{24}) as the result of the confusion of two forms, ἀνέῳξεν and ἤνοιξεν (both aor. ind. 3rd sing.); ἤνεωξα is a *var. lect.* for ἀνέῳξα in John 9:14.

7.b. Variants: (1) φωνήν] 𝔓^{24} א A fam 1006$^{1006\ 1841}$ fam 1611^{2344} Andreas lat syr^{ph} cop^{sa}. (2) τὴν φωνήν] Andr g l n. (3) φωνῆς] Andr d e^{2057} f$^{2031\ 2056}$ h. (4) omit φωνήν] C 025 fam 1611$^{1611\ 1854\ 2329}$ Oecumenius^{2053} 2351 Andr c e^{2026} i^{2042} 94 Byzantine it^{gig} syr^{h} cop^{bo} Primasius Beatus.

7.c. Variant: ἔρχου] see *Notes* 1.j. and 3.c.

8.a-a. Variant: καὶ εἶδον] see *Note* 2.a-a.

8.b. χλωρός, meaning "pale greenish gray," is a color typical of corpses and therefore is associated with death (Louw-Nida, § 79.35).

8.c-c. ὁ καθήμενος is a pendent nom., which is conveyed in the translation "as for the cavalier." Other pendent noms. or abs. noms. occur in Rev 2–3 (2:26; 3:12, 21; see Charles, 1:cxlix).

8.d. Variant: omit ὁ before καθήμενος] C. The entire phrase ὁ καθήμενος ἐπάνω αὐτοῦ I have translated simply as "the cavalier."

8.e. Variants: (1) ἐπάνω αὐτοῦ] א A 046 Victorinus (Haussleiter, *Victorinus,* 73); it^{gig} (*in illo*); Tischendorf, *NT Graece;* Nestle-Aland^{27}; UBSGNT^{4}; *TCGNT*^{1}, 738–39. (2) ἐπάνω] C 025 fam 1611^{1611} Oecumenius^{2053} Andreas vg. (3) ἐπ' αὐτόν] fam 1611^{1854} vg^{ADFIOUW} (*super eum*); Victorinus (Haussleiter, *Victorinus,* 72) (*super illum*). Reading (3) is the result of assimilation to the expression used in vv 2, 4, and 5 (*TCGNT*^{1}, 738). The omission of αὐτοῦ in reading (2) should be understood as an accidental omission (Schmid, *Studien* 2:100), not as a correction.

8.f-f. In the phrase ὄνομα αὐτῷ, ὄνομα is in apposition to ὁ καθήμενος and can be considered a parenthetical nom. (BDR § 144), while αὐτῷ is a dat. of possession, so that the phrase means "his name [is]," since the verb ἐστίν or ἦν is understood but nearly always omitted; the same idiom occurs in Rev 9:11. In 9:11 ὄνομα is also a parenthetical nom., though the construction is different; see *Note* 9:11.c. This idiom is found in the NT twice outside of Revelation, only in the Fourth Gospel (John 1:6; 3:1; Burney, *Aramaic Origin,* 150–52, regards this as one of several Semitisms proving common authorship for John and Revelation), as well as in the LXX, where ὄνομα αὐτῷ or ὄνομα αὐτῇ usually translates the word שְׁמוֹ *šĕmô,* "his name," or שְׁמָהּ *šĕmah,* "her name," indicating that the Gk. phrase is idiomatic and not a slavish rendering of a Heb. idiom (Exod 15:3; Judg 13:2; 16:4; 17:1; Ruth 2:1; 1 Kgdms 1:1; 9:1, 2; 2 Kgdms 4:4; 20:1; Isa 47:4), and in Eupolemus frag. 30.5: αὐτῷ ὄνομα (Denis, *Fragmenta,* 180; Eusebius *Praep. evang.* 9.30.5). More common is the phrase ᾧ [ᾗ] ὄνομα, i.e., a dat. of possession followed by a parenthetical nom., in which the verb ἐστίν or ἦν is nearly always omitted; see BDF § 128.3 (Luke 1:26, 27; 2:25; 8:41; 23:14; Acts 13:6; *T. Levi* 11:1; *Mart. Isa.* 2:12 [Denis, *Fragmenta,* 110]; Demetrius frag. 21.5 [Denis, *Fragmenta,* 176]; Eupolemus frag. 39.2: ᾧ εἶναι ὄνομα [Denis, *Fragmenta,* 185]). ᾧ [ᾗ] ὄνομα also occurs in the LXX, where it is also usually a translation of שְׁמוֹ or שְׁמָהּ (Gen 16:1; 22:24; 24:29; 25:1; 38:1; Theod Sus 1:2, 45).

8.g. Variants: (1) ὁ before θάνατος] Andreas Byzantine 2351 TR; B. Weiss, *Johannes-Apokalypse;* Merk, *NT;* Bousset (1906) 268; bracketed as possible by WHort; Nestle-Aland^{27}; UBSGNT^{4}. (2) omit ὁ before θάνατος] א C fam 1006$^{1006\ 1841}$ fam 1611$^{1611\ 1854}$ Oecumenius^{2053} Andr f n^{2065} Byz 1$^{911\ 920\ 1859\ 2256}$ Byz 4^{1719} Byz 16^{61} Andr/Byz 3 (thirty of the thirty-six MSS in this group) Andr/Byz 4c$^{2070\ 2305}$; Tischendorf, *NT Graece;* Charles, 2:274. (3) ὁ ἀθάνατος] A Byz 2^{2258}. Bousset ([1906] 175) argues correctly in favor of reading (1) that John tends to use the definite article with proper names in the predicate (see 6:8; 8:11; 12:9; 19:13; 20:2). Schmid, *Studien* 2:199, similarly observes that the addition of the *predicate* article with words used perhaps for the first time as proper names is a peculiarity of the style of Revelation, which contradicts the normal absence of the definite article before proper names. Further, the error in (3) confirms the originality of (1).

8.h. The Old Nubian version inserts "they came" (G. M. Browne, "An Old Nubian Fragment of Revelation," *SPap* 20 [1981] 76).

8.i. The καί with which this sentence begins is left untranslated since it is without semantic content but functions as a discourse marker indicating the beginning of a new sentence.

8.j. Variants: (1) αὐτοῖς] א A C 025 Oecumenius^{2053} Andreas. (2) αὐτῷ] fam 1611$^{1611\ 1854\ 2329}$ 2351 Andr c g n^{-2429} 94 2019 Byzantine lat syr cop.

8.k. ἐν + dat. of *instrument,* i.e., when the means used is an inanimate object (see Bousset [1906] 268–69).

8.l. ἐν ῥομφαίᾳ, lit. "with the sword," can be understood as a metaphor for war and therefore translated "by war" (Louw-Nida, § 55.6).

8.m. In the prep. phrase ἐν θανάτῳ, lit. "with death," θάνατος means "plague" or "pestilence" (see *Note* 2:23.b.). The LXX translates the Heb. term דבר *deber,* "plague, pestilence," with θάνατος thirty-one times (e.g., LXX Exod 5:3; 9:3, 15; Lev 26:25; 1 Chr 21:12 [ῥομφαίαν κυρίου καὶ θάνατον]; 2 Chr 7:13; Amos 4:10; Jer 24:10). In the OT מות *mawet* means "pestilence" only in Jer 15:2; 18:21; 43:11, though this meaning occurs elsewhere in northwest Semitic (Holladay, *Jeremiah 1,* 440). In the Targumim, דבר *deber* is frequently translated מותא *môtāʾ,* "death." θάνατος means "pestilence" also in a number of early Jewish texts in which the term is usually incorrectly translated "death" (*Pss. Sol.* 13:2; 15:7; *Sib. Or.* 3.317, 335).

8.n. ὑπό + gen. of agent, i.e., used when the means is an animate being; for a contrast see *Note* 8.e. (see Bousset [1906] 269).

9.a-a. Variants: (1) τὴν σφραγῖδα τὴν πέμπτην] א^{1} (τὴν σφραγίδα τὴν εἶδον); fam 1611$^{1611\ 1854\ 2344}$ Andr e[2026] syr[h ph] cop[bo] arm[1]. (2) τὴν σφραγίδα τὴν εἶδον (-πέμπτην)] ℵ*. The variant described in *Note* 9.c. is closely related to this variant; see below.

9.b. A peculiar variant version of vv 9–11 is found in Hippolytus *Comm. in Dan.* 4.22 (ed. Bonwetsch-Achelis, GCS 1:240), which exhibits a basic focus on the text though it uses alternate expressions: [1]καὶ εἶδον[1] [2]τὰς ψυχὰς τῶν πεπελεκισμένων[2] διὰ [3]τὸ ὄνομα Ἰησοῦ[3] [4]ὑποκάτω τοῦ θυσιαστηρίου[4] καὶ ἐβόησαν[5] [6]καὶ εἶδον πρὸς τὸν θεόν·[6] ἕως πότε, [7]κύριε ὁ θεὸς ἡμῶν,[7] οὐ κρίνεις καὶ ἐκδικεῖς τὸ αἷμα ἡμῶν ἀπὸ[8] τῶν κατοικούντων ἐπὶ τῆς γῆς; καὶ ἐδόθησαν αὐτοῖς [9,10]στολαὶ λευκαὶ[10] καὶ ἐρρέθη αὐτοῖς, ἵνα περιμείνωσιν[11] [12]χρόνον ἔτι[12] μικρόν, [13]ὅπως [καὶ] οἱ σύνδουλοι αὐτῶν πληρώσωσιν τὴν μαρτυρίαν[13] αὐτῶν οἱ μέλλοντες ἀποκτείνεσθαι ὡς καὶ αὐτοί.

[1-1]Perhaps from Rev 20:4, though εἶδον occurs in 6:9, and MS A of *Comm. in Dan.* omits καί.

[2-2]Rev 20:4. Rev 6:9 has τὰς ψυχὰς τῶν ἐσφαγμένων.

[3-3]6:9 has τὴν μαρτυρίαν. The phrase διὰ τὸ ὄνομα Ἰησοῦ occurs nowhere in Revelation, though διὰ τὸ ὄνομά μου does occur in 2:3.

[4-4]This phrase occurs immediately after εἶδον in 6:9.

[5]6:10: ἔκραξαν. βοᾶν occurs nowhere else in Revelation, though it is used twelve times in the NT.

[6-6]6:10: φωνῇ μεγάλῃ λέγοντες.

[7-7]6:10: ὁ δεσπότης ὁ ἅγιος καὶ ἀληθινός. The phrase κύριε ὁ θεός occurs three times in Revelation (11:17; 15:3; 16:7).

[8]6:11: ἐκ. ἀπό occurs in Andreas.

[9]6:11 inserts ἑκάστῳ, which is omitted in 046 1854 2351.

[10-10]6:11: στολὴ λευκή.

[11]6:11: ἀναπαύσονται. περιμένειν occurs in NT only in Acts 1:4.

[12-12]6:11: ἔτι χρόνον. χρόνον ἔτι attested by A 1006 1841 2344.

[13-13]6:11: ἕως πληρωθῶσιν καὶ οἱ σύνδουλοι αὐτῶν καὶ οἱ ἀδελφοί.

9.c. Variant: ἶδον for εἶδον] A C 046 fam 1611[1854 2329] 2351 Andr h[2060 2286] Andr Ø [-598] 792 2019 2038 Andr/Byz 2a[104 680] Andr/Byz 2b[336] Andr/Byz 3[757] Byz 6[218] Byz 10[935] Byz 16[61] Byz 17[69 2017] Byz 18[153]. The fact that ϵ was often used to represent πέμπτος caused confusion here, where ℵ* reads τὴν σφραγῖδα τὴν εἶδον instead of τὴν σφραγῖδα τὴν ϵ [πέμπτην] ἶδον.

9.d. Variant: insert τῶν ἀνθρώπων] ℵ 025 fam 1006[1841] fam 1611[2344] Andreas cop.

9.e-e. Variants: (1) τῶν ἐσφαγμένων] *lectio originalis.* (2) τῶν ἐσφραγισμένων] Andr c d[2051 2067] f [2031] g[2045*] n[2429] 2351.

9.f. Variant: add τοῦ ἀρνίου after μαρτυρίαν] fam 1611[1611corr] 2351 Byzantine syr[h]. The addition was motivated by the presence of the term μαρτυρία several times in Revelation followed by the name "Jesus" in the gen. (1:2, 9; 12:17; 19:10[2x]; 20:4).

9.g. The impf. verb εἶχον is used here in a narrative setting dominated by aors. to emphasize a process occurring in the past that provides the background for a present activity, which is indicated by the aor. verb ἔκραξαν, "they cried," in v 10 (McKay, *Grammar,* 142–43). The impf. εἶχον indicates action in progress but antecedent to the complete action indicated by ἔκραξαν.

10.a. Here the conjunction καί functions as a discourse marker, which indicates the beginning of a new sentence and is therefore not translated.

10.b-b. Variant: ἔκραζον] 2351.

10.c. The translation reflects the fact that ὁ δεσπότης, "master," is an articular nom. that functions as a vocative, even though the vocative form δέσποτα was in use (e.g., δέσποτα βασιλεῦ, addressed to the pharaoh, *Vita Aesopi* 107). There are twelve other occurrences of the articular nom. functioning as a vocative; see *Note* 4:11.a. Though Semitic influence cannot be demonstrated, this construction is similar to the Heb. vocative, which usually (but not always) consists of a substantive with an article (GKC § 126e).

10.d. The term αἷμα, "blood," is used here figuratively for violent death (*TDOT* 3:241–43), and therefore the phrase τὸ αἷμα ἡμῶν, "our blood," can be translated "our deaths," as here, or even "for killing us" (see Louw-Nida, §§ 23.107; 56.20).

10.e-e. Variants: (1) ἐκ] ℵ A C 046 fam 1006 fam 1611[-2050 -2344] Oecumenius[2053] 209 Andr f[2023] l[6787] 94 Andr/Byz 4a[424]. (2) ἀπό] Andreas.

10.f. The direct obj. of the present verb κρίνεις, "judge," is regularly placed in the acc. (in this context the verb refers to the final eschatological judgment). However, κρίνεις is then linked with the present ἐκδικεῖς (from ἐκδικεῖν, "to punish, avenge"), the direct obj. of which is τὸ αἷμα ἡμῶν, "our blood." Since τὸ αἷμα cannot be the obj. of κρίνεις, the following construction is now determined by ἐκδικεῖς, and while κρίνεις is general, ἐκδικεῖς is a specific aspect of eschatological judgment, namely, divine vengeance for Christians who have been martyred; the καί linking the two verbs therefore functions in an epexegetical or explanatory way, despite the awkwardness of the English translation:

"How long will you delay judging, that is, delay avenging . . . ." The chief grammatical difficulty is how to understand the syntactical role of the prep. phrase ἐκ τῶν κατοικούντων ἐπὶ τῆς γῆς, which can be construed in two quite different ways: (1) The phrase is usually understood by commentators and translators as an appeal to God by the Christian martyrs to take vengeance "*on* those who dwell on the earth" (G. Schrenk, *TDNT* 2:443; BAGD, 238). (2) The alternate way, proposed in the translation above, is to construe the phrase as an appeal to God to avenge the blood of the martyrs "*shed by*" (or, their deaths, "*caused by*") those who dwell on the earth.

(1) The first way of understanding the phrase is found in many commentaries (Charles, 2:405; Caird, 83; Mounce, 157; Roloff, 82; Sweet, 141). Arguing for this interpretation, Charles (1:175) understands ἐκδικεῖς τὸ αἷμα ἡμῶν as a literal rendering of a Heb. idiom: תקם את דמנו מן *tiqqom 'et dāmēnû min,* "avenge our blood from," meaning "avenge our blood *on* such-and-such"; i.e., the prep. מן *min* following the verb נקם *nāqam* indicates the person *from* whom revenge is taken (e.g., 1 Sam 24:13, ונקמני יהוה ממך *ûnĕqāmanî YHWH mimmekā,* "And may Yahweh avenge me from [i.e., 'upon'] you"; see LXX καὶ ἐκδικήσαι με κύριος ἐκ σοῦ). This passage constitutes perhaps the closest parallel to this syntactical Hebraism (Bousset [1906] 270). Another parallel occurs in Luke 18:3, ἐκδίκησόν με ἀπὸ τοῦ ἀντιδίκου μου, which means "vindicate me from my adversary," i.e., see that I get justice over my opponent; the woman seeks justice from her adversary, not his punishment (Fitzmyer, *Luke* 2:1179). Also relevant is *T. Levi* 2:2, ὅτε ἐποίησα μετὰ Συμεὼν τὴν ἐκδίκησιν τῆς ἀδελφῆς ἡμῶν Δίνας ἀπὸ τοῦ Ἐμμώρ, "when, with Simeon, I took revenge for our sister Dinah on Hamor."

(2) The second understanding of ἐκ τῶν κατοικούντων ἐπὶ τῆς γῆς (deaths "caused by those who dwell on the earth," or blood "shed by those who dwell on the earth") is based on the view that ἐκ + gen. here indicates the source of an event or activity. The parallel to which Charles calls particular attention in connection with the first interpretation, discussed above, is 4 Kgdms 9:7 (2:119–20), which, however, does not contain the idiom: καὶ ἐκδικήσεις τὰ αἵματα τῶν δούλων μου τῶν προφητῶν καὶ τὰ αἵματα πάντων τῶν δούλων κυρίου ἐκ χειρὸς Ἰεζάβελ, "And you will avenge the deaths of my servants the prophets and the deaths of all the servants of the Lord at the hand of Jezebel." The LXX phrase ἐκ χειρὸς Ἰεζάβελ clearly means that blood was shed "by [the hand of] Jezebel," not that vengeance would be taken upon her. This is confirmed by the paraphrase of 4 Kgdms 9:7 found in Jos. *Ant.* 9.108, καὶ ὅπως ἐκδικήσῃ τὸ αἷμα τῶν προφητῶν τῶν ὑπὸ Ἰεζαβέλας παρανόμως ἀποθανόντων, "that he might avenge the blood of the prophets illegally slain by Jezebel." The underlying Heb. phrase in 2 Kgs 9:7 is ונקמתי דמי עבדי הנביאים . . . מיד איזבל *wĕniqqamtî dĕmê 'ăbāday hannĕbî'îm . . . miyyad 'îzabel,* which seems just as clear: "and I will avenge the blood of my servants the prophets . . . shed by Jezebel" (NIV). This way of understanding the Heb. text is supported by BDB, 668; T. R. Hobbs, *2 Kings,* WBC 13 (Waco: Word Books, 1985) 107: "and avenge the blood of my servants the prophets . . . who suffered at the hand of Jezebel." These passages are important since 2 Kgs 9:7 is clearly alluded to in the parallel found in Rev 19:2, καὶ ἐξεδίκησεν τὸ αἷμα τῶν δούλων αὐτοῦ ἐκ χειρὸς αὐτῆς, "And he avenged the blood of his servants slain by her hand." The RSV translation of 2 Kgs 9:7, however, reflects a different understanding of the text: "that I may avenge on Jezebel the blood of my servants the prophets" (see REB: "And I shall take vengeance on Jezebel for the blood of my servants the prophets"). This is the perspective reflected in M. Cogan and H. Tadmor, *II Kings: A New Translation with Introduction and Commentary,* AB (Garden City, NY: Doubleday, 1988) 100: "thus will I avenge on Jezebel the blood of my servants, the prophets, the blood of all the servants of YHWH."

While either way of construing this sentence is grammatically correct, the fact that in Rev 19:2 the phrase ἐκ χειρὸς αὐτῆς means "by her hand," i.e., "caused by her," suggests that such an interpretation is also preferable here. On the translation of the Heb. semiprep. מיד *miyyad,* "from the hand of," in the LXX, which is rendered several times by ἐκ + gen. and three times with ἀπό + gen., see Sollamo, *Semiprepositions,* 191–204.

11.a. Variants: (1) αὐτοῖς ἑκάστῳ] ℵ A C 025 Oecumenius^{2053} fam 1006 fam 1611^{1611} Andreas. (2) αὐτοῖς] 046 fam 1611^{1854} 2351. (3) ἑκάστῳ] Byzantine. (4) ἑκάστῳ αὐτῶν] Andr i^{-2042}.

11.b. στολή is a distributive sing. (cf. Eng. word "clothing"); BDF § 140. The pl. form στολαί is used in the TR, just as the pl. form *stolae* is used in Primasius Victorinus Beatus Fulgentius vg.

11.c-c. The phrase καὶ ἐρρέθη αὐτοῖς (ἐρρέθη is an aor. pass. from λέγω) means lit. "and it was told to them." The subject of the verb, "it," refers to the ἵνα clause that follows, and therefore has been translated "and they were told."

11.d. Variants: (1) ἵνα ἀναπαύσονται] A 025 046 fam 1611^{2329} Oecumenius^{2053}. (2) ἀναπαύσασθαι] 2351. (3) ἵνα ἀναπαύσωνται] ℵ C Byzantine TR. (4) ἀναπαύσασθε] Oecumenius^{2053text}.

11.e-e. Variants: (1) ἔτι χρόνον μικρόν] C 025 (ℵ; see below under [9]); Andreas vg; WHort; B. Weiss, *Johannes-Apokalypse,* 174; Nestle-Aland^{27}; UBSGNT^{4}. (2) χρόνον ἔτι μικρόν] A fam 1006$^{1006\ 1841}$ fam 1611^{2344} Andr f^{2073}; *tempus adhuc modicum*] it^{2} vg^{AFT}. (3) μικρὸν ἔτι χρόνον] Cyprian (*brevi adhuc tempore*).

(4) ἔτι μικρὸν χρόνον] Oecumenius^{2053} Andr h n^{2429} 2019 cop Beatus (*adhuc brevi tempore*). (5) ἔτι χρόνον] 046 Andr f^{2023} 94 Byzantine. (6) τίνα χρόνον] fam 1611^{2329} Andr l. (7) ἔτι μικρόν] it^{gig} (*adhuc modicum*). (8) μικρόν] 2351. (9) ἐπὶ χρόνον μικρόν] ℵ. Since ἐπί in (9) is an obvious error for ἔτι, ℵ actually supports reading (1).

11.f-f. A probable instance of epexegetical or explanatory καί (Bratcher-Hatton, *Revelation*, 5, 117).

11.g-g. Variants: (1) ἀποκτέννεσθαι] ℵ A C Oecumenius^{2053} Andr g 94; Tischendorf, *NT Graece;* von Soden, *Text;* Nestle-Aland^{27}; UBSGNT^{4}. (2) ἀποκτένεσθαι] fam 1006^{1006} fam 1611^{2329} Andr d e^{2026} f^{-2056} i^{2042} 2019 Byzantine. (3) ἀποκτείνεσθαι] 025 046 fam 1006^{1841} fam 1611$^{1854\ 2344}$ 2351 Andreas. (4) ἀποκταίνεσθαι] Andr b^{-2059} e^{2057} f^{2056} h l^{2080} (+ μετ᾽ αὐτούς).

11.h-h. Variants: (1) πληρωθῶσιν (aor. pass. subjunctive)] A C fam 1611^{2344} it$^{gig\ 61}$ vg syr$^{h\ ph}$; WHort; B. Weiss, *Johannes-Apokalypse,* 106; Merk, *NT;* Nestle-Aland^{27}; UBSGNT^{4}; *TCGNT*^{1}, 739. (2) πληρώσωσιν (aor. active subjunctive)] ℵ 025 046 fam 1006^{1006} fam 1611^{1854} Oecumenius^{2053text} 2351 Andreas Byzantine; Tischendorf, *NT Graece;* von Soden, *Text.* (3) πληρώσουσιν (fut. active ind.)] fam 1611$^{1611\ 2329}$ Oecumenius^{2053comm}. (4) πληρώσονται (fut. middle ind.)] TR. Reading (1), a typically intransitive use of πληροῦν, was apparently misunderstood because of the tendency to use πληροῦν as an abbreviated expression (for examples, see Stuhlmann, *Maß,* 9, 14, 21) and was therefore changed to readings (2) and (3), which are both transitive (a usage for which Bauer-Aland, ad loc., presents little evidence). Readings (2) and (3) must be understood to have some unstated obj. in view, e.g., τὸν δρόμον, "course"; cf. Acts 13:25, i.e., ἕως πληρώσωσιν τὸν δρόμον, "until they should complete their course," or τὸν ἀριθμόν, i.e., ἕως πληρώσωσιν τὸν ἀριθμόν, "until they have filled the [appointed] number" (Stuhlmann, *Maß,* 159–60).

12.a-a. Variant: (1) εἶδον] *lectio originalis;* spelled ἶδον: A C 046 fam 1611$^{1854\ 2329}$. (2) omit εἶδον] 94 Byzantine^{part}; Tyc^{2}. See similar omission in *Note* 6:1.a.

12.b. Variants: (1) ὅτε] *lectio originalis.* (2) καὶ ὅτε] 025 fam 1611^{2344} Andreas Primasius; vg^{mss}. (3) καί] fam 1611^{2329}.

12.c. Variant: ἔνυξεν] ℵ*.

12.d. καί introduces a coordinate clause that functions as the obj. of the verb εἶδον and should therefore be translated as "that." Variant: omit καί] Andr d; 2019. Omitted because it was thought unnecessary (*TCGNT*^{1}, 739).

12.e. Variant: insert ἰδού] A Byzantine. This is an attempt to conform this passage to the author's style elsewhere (6:2, 5, 8; cf. 4:1; 7:9; 14:1, 14).

12.f-f. Variant: ἐγένετο μέγας] A Andr i$^{1685\ 2042\ 2074}$.

12.g-g. Variants: (1) ἐγένετο μέλας] *lectio originalis.* (2) μέλας ἐγένετο] ℵ 046 fam 1611^{1854} 2351 Byzantine.

12.h. σάκκος, "sackcloth," is used here with the adj. τρίχινος, "made of hair" (making the translation "haircloth" appropriate), a combination attested in the papyri (MM, 567), referring to coarse cloth woven from the hair of goats and other domesticated animals, and usually very dark in color.

12.i-i. The phrase ἡ σελήνη ὅλη has been construed to mean either "the whole moon" (NIV; Charles, 2:403; Kraft, 121) or "the full moon" (RSV, NRSV). The translation of the NEB, "the moon all red as blood," and the REB, "the moon turned all red as blood" (cf. Lohse, 49: "und 'der Mond' wurde ganz wie 'Blut'"), are not literal translations but a paraphrastic rendering of the first alternation mentioned above, "the whole moon." Since the use of ὅλη in the postposition is frequently a means for emphasizing the substantive (BDR § 275.5), i.e., "the whole moon [rather than only part of the moon]," the construction emphasizes not that the full moon became blood but that the entire moon turned to blood. Variants: (1) ἡ σελήνη ὅλη] ℵ A C 046 Oecumenius^{2053} vg syr cop^{bo} Tischendorf, *NT Graece.* (2) ἡ σελήνη (omit ὅλη)] fam 1006$^{1006\ 1841}$ fam 1611$^{1611\ 2329\ 2344}$ Andreas Primasius it^{a} cop^{sa}.

13.a. Variants: (1) βάλλει] A C 046 fam 1006 Andreas. (2) βάλλουσα] ℵ fam 1611$^{1611\ 1854}$ Oecumenius^{2053} 2351. (3) βάλουσα] Byzantine.

13.b. The term τοὺς ὀλύνθους, lit. "late figs," refers to figs produced late in the summer, which often fall off the tree before ripening, and so can be translated "unripe figs" (Louw-Nida, § 3.37). LSJ, s.v. ὄλονθος, understand it to refer to "the sterile summer fruit of the cultivated fig."

14.a. The aor. pass. verb ἀπεχωρίσθη, from ἀποχωρίζεσθαι, can mean "to split" (BAGD, 102; cf. Louw-Nida, § 63.30), though this meaning does not fit the simile of a book rolling up. The verb is best understood in this context as meaning "to move away from a normal location, with the implication of disappearing" in the sense that the heaven could no longer be seen (Louw-Nida, § 15.14). Then the simile of a scroll rolled up makes sense, since it can be understood as lying open for reading and then snapping together quickly like a window shade.

15.a. The term χιλίαρχοι, "chiliarchs," refers to military officers in charge of 1,000 troops and so can be translated "commanding officers" or "generals."

16.a. While λίθος refers to separate pieces of stone or rock, or stone as a substance, πέτρα refers to bedrock (sometimes covered with a thin layer of soil) or to exposed outcroppings of rock such as precipices and cliffs (Louw-Nida, § 2.21). Here the pl. term πέτραι must refer to cliffs, rocky ridges, or precipices.

16.b. The phrase ἀπὸ προσώπου, lit "from the face," or "from the presence," is a *phraseological* Hebraism found three times in Revelation (6:16; 12:14; 20:11) and just four other times in the rest of the NT (Acts 3:20; 5:31; 7:45; 2 Thess 1:9). The force of the gen. noun προσώπου is frequently redundant so that the entire phrase constitutes a prep. meaning "from." The phrase is also found four times in the Apostolic Fathers (*Barn.* 6:9; 11:7 [since the accompanying gen. in both cases is τῆς γῆς, the idiom can mean "from the surface of the earth"]; *1 Clem.* 4:8, 10). For ἀπὸ τοῦ προσώπου, see *1 Clem.* 18:11; 28:3 [allusion to Ps 138:7 [MT 139:7]). In the LXX ἀπὸ προσώπου is used to translate several different Heb. "semiprepositions" (i.e., combinations of the simple preps. ב *bĕ*, ל *lĕ*, כ *kĕ*, על *ʿal*, and מן *min*, together with, in most cases, the name for a part of the body). The phrase ἀπὸ προσώπου is used to translate (1) מפני *mipnê*, 194 times (see Sollamo, *Semiprepositions*, 82–83), (2) מלפני *millipnê*, "from before, from," 34 times (Sollamo, *Semiprepositions*, 96), and (3) לפני *lipnê* 12 times (Sollamo, *Semiprepositions*, 33–34). According to Sollamo (*Semiprepositions*, 329), "The phrase ἀπὸ προσώπου is unknown in Classical Greek and is not attested in the Koine or Modern Greek, either. It is a peculiarity of translation Greek. For this reason it could be regarded as a phraseological Hebraism." Sollamo has missed the use of ἀπὸ προσώπου in Ctesias *Pers.* 2 (see BAGD, 721) and has not considered the six occurrences of ἀπὸ προσώπου in the NT, nor the four occurrences in the Apostolic Fathers; it is doubtful that all six instances should be regarded as translation Gk. The phrase ἀπὸ προσώπου in the LXX is *always* followed by a gen., as are the Gk. translations for other Heb. semipreps. (e.g., ἔμπροσθεν, ἀνὰ μέσον, ἐν μέσῳ; Sollamo, *Semiprepositions*, 298).

17.a. Variant readings: (1) αὐτοῦ] A P 046 1 fam 1006^{1006} 2351 Andreas Byzantine cop arm eth Primasius (*irae eius*); Arethas; B. Weiss, *Johannes-Apocalypse*, 175; Bousset (1906) 275 n. 5; Charles, 2:278. (2) αὐτῶν] ℵ C Oecumenius^{2053} fam 1611$^{1611\ 1854\ 2329\ 2344}$ 1828 2020 Andreas l 94 it$^{ar\ gig}$ (*ipsorum*); Tyc^{3} (*irae eorum*); Beatus (*irae eorum*); De promissionibus (*irae illorum*); Fulgentius (*irae illorum*); vg syr$^{ph\ h}$; Tischendorf, *NT Graece;* WHort; Merk, *NT;* Nestle-Aland^{27}; UBSGNT^{4}; *TCGNT*^{1}, 739–40; *TCGNT*^{2}, 668. Reading (1) is preferable on exegetical grounds, since only the wrath of the *Lamb* is in view in v 16 (ἀπὸ τῆς ὀργῆς τοῦ ἀρνίου), and it is therefore "*his* wrath [τῆς ὀργῆς αὐτοῦ]" that is referred to in v 17 (Schmid, *Studien* 2:100). Further, if the αὐτῶν of reading (2) were original, it would be difficult to account for the origin of αὐτοῦ, while if the αὐτοῦ of reading (1) were original, αὐτῶν could be understood as a correction. *TCGNT*^{1}, 739–40, and *TCGNT*^{2}, 668, improbably maintain that αὐτοῦ is the *easier* reading (since it continues the reference to τῆς ὀργῆς τοῦ ἀρνίου of v 16), introduced to avoid the ambiguity of αὐτῶν. Yet αὐτῶν is not ambiguous, since it is clearly intended to refer to the One seated on the throne and to the Lamb, both mentioned in v 16.

Form/Structure/Setting

I. OUTLINE

3. The Lamb breaks the first six seals (6:1–17)
    a. The first four seal visions (vv 1–8)
        (1) The first seal (vv 1–2)
            (a) Vision: the Lamb breaks the first seal (v 1a)
            (b) Audition: one of the four cherubim summons the first cavalier (v 1b)
            (c) Vision of the first cavalier (v 2)
                [1] Description of the cavalier (v 2a)
                    [a] Mounted on a white horse
                    [b] Wielding a bow
                [2] Action of the cavalier (v 2b)
                    [a] He is given a crown

[b] He rides out to conquer
(2) The second seal (vv 3–4)
(a) The Lamb breaks the second seal (v 3a)
(b) Audition: the second cherub summons the second cavalier (v 3b)
(c) Vision of the second cavalier (v 4)
[1] Description: mounted on a fiery red horse (v 4a)
[2] Action (v 4bc)
[a] The cavalier is given power
{1} Purpose: to remove peace from the earth
{2} Result: that people might slaughter each other
[b] The cavalier is given a large sword (v 4c)
(3) The third seal (vv 5–6)
(a) The Lamb breaks the third seal (v 5a)
(b) Audition: the third cherub dispatches the third cavalier (v 5a)
(c) Vision of the third cavalier (v 5b–6)
[1] Description (v 5bc)
[a] Mounted on a black horse
[b] Holding a balance scale
[2] A divine commission given to the cavalier (v 6)
[a] Source of commission: a voice from the midst of the four cherubim (v 6a)
[b] Content of the commission (v 6bc)
{1} A liter of wheat for a denarius
{2} Three liters of barley for one denarius
{3} Do not harm the oil and the wine
(4) The fourth seal (vv 7–8)
(a) The Lamb breaks the fourth seal (v 7a)
(b) Audition: the fourth cherub summons the fourth cavalier (v 7b)
(c) Vision of the fourth cavalier and his companion (v 8)
[1] Description of the cavalier (v 8ab)
[a] Mounted on a pale-colored horse
[b] His name is Death
[c] Hades followed him
[2] Death and Hades given authority over one-fourth of the earth (8c)
[a] To kill with the sword
[b] To kill with famine
[c] To kill with plague
[d] To kill with the wild animals of the earth
b. The fifth seal (vv 9–11)
(1) The Lamb breaks the fifth seal (v 9a)
(2) Vision of the souls of the martyrs (v 9b)
(a) Location: under the [heavenly] altar
(b) Cause of martyrdom (v 9c)
[1] Because of the word of God

[2] Because of the witness they bore
(3) The martyrs pray for vengeance (v 10)
(a) They cry out loudly (v 10a)
(b) Their collective prayer (v 10b)
[1] Invocation: O Master, holy and true
[2] Petition: How long till you avenge our deaths caused by those who dwell on the earth?
(c) God's response (v 11)
[1] Each martyr given a white robe (v 11a)
[2] Exhortation to the martyrs: Rest (11bc)
[a] A while longer (v 11b)
[b] Until the number of martyrs is complete (v 11c)
{1} Their fellow servants
{2} Their brothers who would be slain as they were
c. Vision of the sixth seal (vv 12–17)
(1) The Lamb breaks the sixth seal (v 12a)
(2) Cosmic upheavals (vv 12–14)
(a) A great earthquake occurs (v 12a)
(b) The sun disturbed (v 12b)
[1] The event: becomes dark
[2] The simile: as haircloth
(c) The moon disturbed (v 12c)
[1] The event: becomes red
[2] The simile: as blood
(d) Stars disturbed (v 13)
[1] The event: the stars of heaven fall to earth (v 13a)
[2] The simile: As a tree loses unripe figs when shaken by a strong wind (v 13b)
(e) The destruction of heaven (v 14a)
[1] The event: heaven disappears from sight
[2] The simile: like a scroll rolled up
(f) Every mountain and island shaken from its place
(3) Human reactions (vv 15–17)
(a) Everyone affected (v 15a)
[1] Important people
[2] Generals
[3] The wealthy
[4] The powerful
[5] Every slave
[6] Every free person
(b) Everyone tries to hide (v 15b)
[1] In caves
[2] In the mountain rocks
(c) Their collective cry of despair (vv 16–17)
[1] Address (v 16a)
[a] To the mountains
[b] To the cliffs

[2] Entreaty (v 16bc)
  [a] Fall on us (v 16b)
  [b] Hide us (v 16bc)
    {1} From the one who sits on the throne
    {2} From the wrath of the Lamb (v 16c)
[3] Motivation (v 17)
  [a] The day of his wrath has come (v 17a)
  [b] Who is able to withstand [his wrath]? (v 17b)

II. Literary Analysis

Rev 6:1–17 is part of the larger formal structure that began with the two-part throne scene in 4:2b–11; 5:1–14 and includes the breaking open of all seven seals (6:1–8:1). However, despite the fact that the seventh seal is broken open in 8:1, the results appear anticlimactic (the result is a half hour of silence in heaven), so that the act of breaking the seventh seal serves primarily as an introduction to the series of seven trumpet plagues that follows (8:2–11:18). Rev 7:1–17, which is placed between the breaking of the sixth and seventh seals and often designated as an "interlude," "intermission," or "intercalation" because of its apparently intrusive character, functions to separate the seventh seal from those that precede it.

A. *The Four Cavaliers (6:1–8)*

Within the literary framework of the breaking of the seven seals, the first four seals constitute a coherent literary unit. This is obvious in view of the stereotypical structure with variations that characterizes the brief narrative describing the breaking of the first four seals. Further, the cumulative effect of the four cavaliers on the inhabitants of the earth is described in v 8b, even though those effects (death by the sword, famine, plague, and wild animals) appear to be the work of the fourth cavalier and his companion (Death and Hades). Rev 6:1–8 contains five occurrences of the author's typical audition word, ἤκουσα, "I heard," in vv 1b, 3b, 5a, 6a, 7 and three occurrences of one of his typical vision phrases, καὶ εἶδον, καὶ ἰδού, "I saw, and behold," in vv 2a, 5b, 8a. Both of these stereotypical expressions do not serve to introduce either a new audition or vision; rather they function to call attention to a new or significant feature or action within a continuing vision narrative audition or vision (5:2, 6, 11; 6:2, 5, 8, 12; 7:2; 9:1; 16:13; 17:3, 6; cf. Acts 11:6; Dan 12:5; Ezek 37:8; 44:4; see *Comment* on 5:1). Despite the stereotypical structure of vv 1–8, variation is introduced in a number of ways. First, the phrase καὶ εἶδον, καὶ ἰδού, "I saw, and behold," is unexpectedly missing from v 4a, and in its place is the single verb ἐξῆλθεν, "he rode out." Second, only the first cavalier is said to ἐξῆλθεν, "ride away," to execute his task (v 2b), whereas the text is silent about whether the following three cavaliers actually executed their tasks. Third, the aorist passive verb ἐδόθη, "it was given," a circumlocution for divine activity or authorization, is used of the first, second, and fourth cavaliers (vv 2b, 4b, 4c, 8c) but not of the third. Fourth, the pericope dealing with the third cavalier is further distinguished by the insertion of a divine commission (v 6), which can only be attributed to God himself since it originates from the midst of the four cherubim.

The four cavaliers described in Rev 6:1–8 are in part allusions to Zech 1:7–11; 6:1–8. The four chariots drawn by horses in Zech 6:1–8 are identified with the four winds (v 5), though nothing is said about the four directions. The four cavaliers of Zech 1:8 ride red, dappled gray, sorrel, and white horses, while the horses that draw the four chariots in Zech 6:1–3 are red, black, white, and dappled gray, and the four horses of Rev 6:1–8 are white, red, black, and pale (gray or yellowish green). Rev 9:7 alludes to the comparison of a plague of locusts with horses riding to battle. In this connection, according to S. R. Driver (*Joel and Amos* [Cambridge: Cambridge UP, 1934] 88 n. 1), the Arabs claim that there are four different kinds of locusts: yellow, white, red, and black. Feuillet (*ZNW* 57 [1966] 229–59) regards the first cavalier as an agent of divine judgment bearing a bow, while the next three cavaliers are "arrows," which inflict the specific judgments of war, famine, and pestilence; this explains why the summary of the plagues in v 8 alludes only to the last three cavaliers and not to the first. Malina (*Revelation*, 121–28) proposes an astrological interpretation of the four cavaliers, construing the horses as comets and the riders as constellations that control the year and have particular attributes: Leo (Regulus, the "ruler of the stars," associated with damage through wild animals), Virgo (the vine-tender's knife), Libra (scales), and Scorpio (Death and Hades). The colors of the horses, he believes, indicate the planet and the cardinal directions: white (Jupiter, east), red (Mars, south), pale white (Venus, west), and black (Mercury, north).

An interesting parallel is found in Dio Chrysostom *Or.* 36.42–53 (LCL tr.), who wants to validate the Stoic view of the conflagration of the cosmos by showing how it is compatible with a myth of the magi, who speak of the perfect charioteer Zeus, whose chariot is pulled by *four* heavenly horses: (1) The first is sacred to Zeus, a "winged creature, brilliant in colour with the brilliance of the purest flame." This horse once caused a fiery blast to scorch the earth. This first horse also deserved victory and a crown (τὴν νίκην καὶ τὸν στέφανον; see Rev 6:2, where the rider of the first horse is given a crown [στέφανος] and rides out "conquering and to conquer [νικῶν καὶ ἵνα νικήσῃ]"). (2) The second is Hera's horse, which is a bit slower and is black. This horse once caused a flood on earth. (3) The third, still slower, is sacred to Poseidon and once caused a fountain to spring forth by pawing the earth with its hoof. (4) The fourth, named after Hestia, is firm and immovable. This entire scheme is clearly astrological (Boll, *Offenbarung*, 78–97; Betz, *Lukian von Samosata*, 97–98 n. 6).

B. Rev 6:9–11: The Martyrs' Cry for Vengeance

While the first four seals form a unit by the device of four successive cavaliers with mounts of different colors—each cavalier is summoned by one of the four cherubim, and each cavalier either brings or is commissioned to bring various destructive judgments upon the people of the earth (death by sword, famine, pestilence, and wild animals)—the fifth seal in vv 9–11 is set apart by its particular subject matter, the seer's vision of the souls of the martyrs under the heavenly altar. It seems somewhat out of place that the martyrs demand vengeance on the inhabitants of the earth when that appears to be precisely what has been dispensed by the four horsemen in vv 2–8. This section consists of three subunits: (1) The seer's attention is called to the souls of the martyrs under the altar (v 9). (2) The focus then turns to the martyrs, who appeal to God for vengeance on those who have killed them (v 10). (3) The divine response is twofold: (a) they are invested with a white robe (v 11a), and (b) they are told to rest until the *numerus martyrum*, "number of martyrs," is complete.

The entire scene in vv 9–11 has close parallels in both form and content with *1 Enoch* 47:4 and 4 Ezra 4:35–37. According to *1 Enoch* 47:4 (tr. Black, *1 Enoch*, 49),

> And the hearts of the holy were filled with joy;
> Because the number of righteous had been reached,
> And the prayer of the righteous had been heard,
> And the blood of the righteous ones had been avenged before the Lord of spirits.

Despite some difficulties with the text (Knibb, *Enoch* 2:133, note on 47.4), the reference is probably to the predetermined number of the elect (Black, *1 Enoch*, 209–10). Here we find the juxtaposition of two motifs, *the complete number of the righteous* and *the prayer for vengeance by righteous martyrs*. Similarly, in 4 Ezra 4:35–37, we find a comparable sequence of motifs consisting of a brief question put by the righteous dead (beginning with the phrase "How long . . . ?" as in Rev 6:11; see Westermann, *ZAW* 66 [1954] 53) and the comforting answer by a supernatural being, which contains the motif of the *numerus iustorum*, i.e., *the complete number of the righteous* (RSV):

> Did not the souls of the righteous in their chambers ask about these matters, saying, "How long are we to remain here? And when will come the harvest of our reward?" And Jeremiel the archangel answered them and said, "When the number of those like yourselves is completed; for he has weighed the age in the balance, and measured the times by measure, and numbered the times by number; and he will not move or arouse them until that measure is fulfilled."

This same passage is also quoted in an Amharic commentary on Revelation (R. W. Cowley, *Apocalypse*, 238).

C. Rev 6:12–17: The Day of Wrath

The breaking of the sixth seal introduces a brief narrative consisting of two subunits: (1) cosmic upheavals (vv 12–14) and (2) human reactions (vv 15–17). The description of the upheavals of the cosmos in vv 12–14 is a pastiche of traditional motifs arranged in a quasi-poetic manner (as the arrangement of the translation above in stichoi suggests). The first and last lines describe without the use of figurative language the great earthquake and the shaking of every mountain and island, while each of the four lines they frame makes use of a simile. All the inhabitants of the earth react to these cosmic disturbances with terror and try in vain to hide themselves from these events. The speech in 6:15–17 is a rhetorical device in which the reaction of everyone who has reason to fear the great day of wrath is expressed as a collective cry of despair. The speech itself is based on an allusion to Hos 10:8, where the unidentified speakers address the mountains with the entreaty "Cover us" and the hills with "Fall upon us." The continued existence of the caves, rocks, and mountains indicates that cosmic destruction is not in view. It is striking that the significance of the cosmic upheavals is not made explicit until the very end of the pericope when the upheaval is given a theophanic interpretation as a prelude to the great day of wrath (v 17).

Comment

1a καὶ εἶδον ὅτε ἤνοιξεν τὸ ἀρνίον μίαν ἐκ τῶν ἑπτὰ σφραγίδων, "Then I saw when the Lamb opened one of the seven seals." The Lamb is explicitly mentioned only here as the subject of the verb ἤνοιξεν, which occurs six more times with the subject τὸ ἀρνίον assumed (6:3, 5, 7, 9, 12; 8:1). Since it is obviously very difficult to imagine a lamb opening a sealed scroll, it is possible that the figure of the Lamb has subsequently been superimposed on an originally anthropomorphic figure. The act of the sequential opening of each of the seven seals (6:1, 3, 5, 7, 9, 12; 8:1) symbolizes the gradual unfolding of the contents of the scroll in the visions accompanying each opening. The visions introduced by the opened seals form two subgroups of four (6:1–8) and three (6:9–17; 8:1). The group of four visions in 6:1–8 is structured by using the four cherubim, each of whom summons one of the four horsemen, which afflict the world with a variety of plagues. A similar 4 + 3 structure is found in the trumpet visions (8:2–9:21; 11:15–18). On καὶ εἶδον, see *Comment* on 5:1.

"Seven" is frequently used as a structuring device in Revelation. The heptad (i.e., a series of seven) of the seven seals (6:1–8:1) is the first of two more heptads, the seven trumpets (8:2–9:21; 11:15–18) and the seven bowls (15:1–16:21). While the metaphor of the breaking open of a series of seven seals is unique to Revelation, there is some late evidence for a series of seven used to narrate the events that will occur just before the inauguration of the eschaton. The first text is *b. Sanh.* 97a (tr. Epstein, *Babylonian Talmud*):

> Our Rabbis taught: In the seven year cycle at the end of which the son of David will come—in the first year, this verse will be fulfilled: *And I will cause it to rain upon one city and cause it not to rain upon another city* [Amos 4:7]; in the second, the arrows of hunger will be sent forth; in the third, a great famine, in the course of which men, women, and children, pious men and saints will die, and the Torah will be forgotten by its students; in the fourth, partial plenty; in the fifth, great plenty, when men will eat, drink and rejoice, and the Torah will return to its disciples; in the sixth, [Heavenly] sounds; in the seventh, wars; and at the conclusion of the septennate the son of David will come.

The last three of these years are also mentioned in *b. Meg.* 17b (tr. Epstein, *Babylonian Talmud*):

> What was their reason for mentioning redemption in the seventh blessing? Raba replied: Because they [Israel] are destined to be redeemed in the seventh year [of the coming of the Messiah], therefore the mention of redemption was placed in the seventh blessing. But a Master has said, "in the sixth year will be thunderings, in the seventh wars, at the end of the seventh the son of David will come"? War is also the beginning of redemption.

1b καὶ ἤκουσα ἑνὸς ἐκ τῶν τεσσάρων ζῴων λέγοντος ὡς φωνὴ βροντῆς· ἔρχου, "and I heard one of the four cherubim saying, as though with a voice of thunder, 'Come!'" This is the first instance of a phenomenon in Revelation in which some angelic beings give orders to other angels or supernatural beings, thus implying a hierarchical structure that is never made explicit (see 7:2–3; 14:15, 18; cf. Zech 2:3–

5). The magical use of the command "Come!" (ἔρχεσθαι can mean either "go" or "come" depending on the context) occurs in *T. Sol.* 1:9, 11; 3:1, where it is addressed to demons: "Come! Solomon summons you!" The phrase "like the sound of thunder" occurs only here in connection with the summoning of the first cavalier. Thunder is used elsewhere in Revelation as a metaphor to characterize an extremely loud voice in 14:2; 19:6 (cf. *2 Apoc. Bar.* 11:3; 14:1–2). God's voice is frequently compared with the sound of thunder (2 Sam 22:14; Job 37:2–5; Pss 18:13; 29:3–9; Isa 29:6; 30:30–31; Jer 25:30; Amos 1:2), a simile perhaps derived from the theophanic imagery of the Sinai tradition.

2a καὶ εἶδον, καὶ ἰδού, ἵππος λευκός, καὶ ὁ καθήμενος ἐπ' αὐτὸν ἔχων τόξον, "And I looked, and behold, there was a white horse, and the cavalier had a bow." On καὶ εἶδον, see *Comment* on 5:1. The motif of four cavaliers is loosely based on Zech 1:11–17, while the motif of four horses of different colors (white, red, black, and pale) is just as loosely based on the variously colored horses drawing chariots in Zech 6:1–8. In *Metam.* 8.25–36, Ovid depicts the legendary Minos as mounted on a white horse and as carrying a bow as well as a spear (*Neuer Wettstein,* ad loc.). The stereotypical phrase καὶ εἶδον, καὶ ἰδού occurs seven times in Revelation (6:2, 5, 8; 7:9; 14:1, 14; 19:11; the phrase is also found as a *var. lect.* in 6:4 [א]; on the function of ἰδού in such contexts, see *Comment* on 4:1). This has influenced the textual transmission of Revelation, since scribes occasionally added καὶ ἰδού to καὶ εἶδον (see *Note* 5:6.a.), or added καὶ εἶδον to καὶ ἰδού, or deleted one or the other phrase (see *Note* 6:2.a-a.). The phrase [καὶ] εἶδον [= ἴδον] καὶ ἰδού does occur in the LXX (where it translates the Hebrew phrases וארא והנה *wāʾēreʾ wĕhinnēh* or ראיתי והנה *rāʾîtî wĕhinnēh,* particularly in Ezekiel (1:4, 15; 2:9; 8:7, 10; 10:1, 9; 37:8; 44:4; cf. Gen 33:1; Jer 4:2; 2 Chr 23:13), though it is relatively rare in Jewish-Greek literature (see *Jos. As.* 10:16; 14:9). It is possible that the author is imitating the LXX style of Ezekiel.

The phrase καὶ ἰδοὺ ἵππος λευκὸς καὶ ὁ καθήμενος ἐπ' αὐτόν, literally "and behold, a white horse and the one seated on it," is repeated verbatim in 19:11, a fact that suggests some kind of literary correlation between the two passages, perhaps even the identity of the two cavaliers. The white horse is an allusion based on the team of white horses in the vision of Zech 6:3. It is possible to interpret the figure of the cavalier in either a positive or a negative manner, though the fact that the second, third, and fourth seals are negative makes it difficult to maintain that the first seal is positive. (1) *Positive interpretations.* (a) Christ, the Messiah, or the Divine Warrior. Since the cavalier on the white horse in 19:11–16 is called "the Word of God" and represents the Messiah, interpreters beginning with Irenaeus (*Adv. haer.* 4.21.3) have understood the cavalier in 6:2 as Christ (Methodius *Symp.* 8.7, quoted by Andreas *Comm. in Apoc.* 6:2; Schmid, *Studien* 1/1:60; Vos, *Synoptic Traditions,* 181–92; Bachmann, *Bib* 67 [1986] 240–75; Hodges, *BSac* 119 [1962] 324–34; Heil, *Bib* 74 [1993] 223). The appearance of the white horse in 19:11–16 might suggest that the cavalier here in 6:2, like the cavalier there, is the Messiah. Despite the verbal similarity between 6:2 and 19:12, however, the two cavaliers have actually very little in common: though both have white mounts, the cavalier in 6:2 carries a bow and wears a wreath (στέφανος) of victory, while the cavalier in 19:11–16 has a sharp two-edged sword in his mouth and wears many diadems (διαδήματα), symbols of sovereignty (Swete, 86). The first cavalier should not be identified with the Messiah of 19:11–16 since it is obviously the Lamb himself who is opening the seals, and it is therefore unlikely that the Lamb is also the cavalier summoned by the breaking of the first seal (see Zahn, 2:352–53). Further, the Messiah is not expected to appear before the Messianic woes are complete (Charles, 1:164). (b) The victorious progress of the Gospel. Since there appear to be insuperable obstacles in identifying Christ as the first cavalier, a number of interpreters have suggested that the conquering activity of the cavalier can represent the triumph of the Gospel (Zahn, 2:352–53; J. Weiss, *Offenbarung,* 60–62; Allo, 87–88). In the Christian adaptation of Jewish apocalyptic, the proclamation of the gospel occupies a position of some importance in the events of the last days; according to Mark 13:10 (Matt 24:14; Luke 21:12), "the gospel must first be preached to all nations." Oecumenius combines the two preceding views by claiming that the white horse represents the gospel and Christ is the cavalier (*Comm. in Apoc.* 6:2; Hoskier, *Oecumenius,* 84). (c) A general argument for interpreting the four horsemen in a *positive* way is the fact that the image of the celestial cavalier is widely understood in the Greco-Roman world as a savior who delivers people from various types of trouble, e.g., the Dioscuri, Heron the Thracian cavalier god, Horus, or Mithras (see Johnston, *CP* 87 [1992] 307–16). (2) *Negative interpretations.* (a) Military conquest (Swete, 86; Mounce, 154; Roloff, 80–81) or, more specifically, a Parthian invasion (Wettstein, *NT Graecum;* Bousset [1906] 265–66; Ramsay, *Letters,* 58; Swete, 86; Charles, 1:164 [a secondary meaning overlayed on the text by the author]; Lohse, 47; Boring, 122; Metzger, *Code,* 58). (b) The Antichrist or false Messiahs. This view is usually based on the supposition that the sequence of eschatological events in the eschatological discourse (Mark 13 and par.) is somehow being replicated in Rev 6:1–17. Since the first theme in Mark 13:5–6 is the warning that many will attempt to lead Christians astray, the first cavalier must be understood in that light (R. W. Cowley, *Apocalypse,* 229; Rissi, *Zeit,* 89–94; id., *Int* 18 [1964] 407–18; Vos, *Synoptic Traditions,* 191). However, there are no convincing arguments for accepting this identification. (c) Gunkel suggested that the first cavalier represents the sun god Mithras (*Verständnis,* 53–54 n. 6), but this is extremely speculative since it is only one of several uses of the divine cavalier image (see Johnston, *CP* 87 [1992] 307–16).

The cavalier carries a bow (arrows are not mentioned, though certainly implied). For bow and arrows as proverbial instruments of death along with the sword and asps, see *T. Abr.* [Rec. B] 14:4. Archers were an important offensive force in ancient armies (Isa 21:17; Jer 50:29; 51:3). The bow was not, however, a Roman weapon but one widely used in Greece, Anatolia, and the Near East, especially Parthia (Ramsay, *Letters,* 58). The bow (together with arrows) is used in the OT as a symbol for divine chastisement (Deut 32:42; Isa 34:6; Hab 3:9; Lam 3:12–13; Ps 7:13–14). According to Deut 32:23–25 (perhaps reworked in Ezek 5:16–17), the arrows of the Lord cause the plagues of famine, plague, wild animals, and the sword. That these four plagues are mentioned specifically in v 8 suggests that they are the "arrows" unleashed by the first cavalier. However, that the bow alone is mentioned here militates against the full relevance of these parallels. The close association of the bow with Apollo has led some interpreters to regard the bow either as a symbol of the majesty of Apollo, used here to symbolize the majesty of Christ (Bachmann, *Bib* 67 [1986] 263–64), or as a symbol for Apollo himself (Kerkeslager, *JBL* 112 [1993] 118–21), whose arrows can bring death.

2b καὶ ἐδόθη αὐτῷ στέφανος καὶ ἐξῆλθεν νικῶν καὶ ἵνα νικήσῃ, "A crown was given to him, and the conqueror went out that he might conquer even more." This is the first occurrence of the aorist passive ἐδόθη, a *passivum divinum,* "passive of divine activity," used twenty-two times in Revelation (the third plural ἐδόθησαν occurs twice in 8:2; 12:14; on the *passivum divinum,* see *Comment* on 9:3). The use of the divine passive does not of itself appear to indicate the positive or negative aspects of divine enablement envisaged (Bachmann, *Bib* 67 [1986] 245). The verb ἐδόθη is used five times in vv 1–8, referring to a divine commission or divine enablement bestowed on all the cavaliers with the exception of the third (vv 5–6). Both the white horse (Vergil *Aeneid* 3.537–47; cf. Servius *In Aeneidem* III.538, where the scholiast interprets the phrase *candore nivali,* "snow white," as an omen presaging victory) and the crown can be construed to represent victory (Tertullian *De corona* 15). That the cavalier is awarded a crown *before* he rides out may be construed as a promise of victory. The phrase νικῶν καὶ ἵνα νικήσῃ, literally "conquering that he might conquer," is very obscure Greek and syntactically problematic. S. Thompson has proposed that this construction reflects the use of the Hebrew verb + cognate infinitive absolute, which he suggests should be emended to ἐξῆλθεν ἵνα νικῶν καὶ νικήσῃ, "he departed, in order that he might thoroughly conquer," the usual way in which the LXX translates the Hebrew verb + cognate infinitive absolute, i.e., with a Greek verb + cognate participle (*Apocalypse,* 80–81). Krause ("Participle," 202–4) has suggested that νικῶν is a nominative and should be linked with the subject of the verb (see *Note* 2.d.), while the connecting καί can be construed as introducing a heightened insertion (BAGD, s.v. καί, II.2), resulting in the translation "the conquering one left to conquer even more." The first cavalier primarily represents warfare, and each of the three following cavaliers represents one of the stereotypical evils of war: sword, famine, and plague.

3–4a Καὶ ὅτε ἤνοιξεν τὴν σφραγῖδα τὴν δευτέραν, ἤκουσα τοῦ δευτέρου ζῴου λέγοντες· ἔρχου, καὶ ἐξῆλθεν ἄλλος ἵππος πυρρός, "When he opened the second seal, I heard the second cherub saying, 'Come!' Then another horse, a fiery red one, rode out." On the first phrase, see *Comment* on 6:1b. The adjective ἄλλος has been construed as indicating that the first cavalier is separate from the following three, which would then form a distinct and unified group (Bachmann, *Bib* 67 [1986] 247–48). The color red may symbolize blood, representing the death and destruction caused by the second cavalier (Lohmeyer, 60). The author has omitted the characteristic phrase καὶ εἶδον, καὶ ἰδού, "I saw, and behold," used in connection with all the other cavaliers, and substituted the verb ἐξῆλθεν, "he rode out," though it is not clear whence the cavalier comes.

4b καὶ τῷ καθημένῳ ἐπ' αὐτὸν ἐδόθη αὐτῷ λαβεῖν τὴν εἰρήνην ἐκ τῆς γῆς καὶ ἵνα ἀλλήλους σφάξουσιν, "and the cavalier was given the power to remove peace from the earth so that people might slaughter each other." When the verb σφάζειν is used with reference to people, the connotations of violence and savagery are clearly present (Louw-Nida, § 20.72). The function of the cavalier in taking peace from the earth is portrayed as a universal phenomenon, perhaps as a conscious reversal of the Roman achievement of *pax Romana,* "Roman peace," by Augustus. Augustus closed the doors of the Temple of Janus three times, in January 29 B.C., at the end of the civil war inaugurating a new era of the *pax Romana* again in 25 B.C., and a third time, though the specific date of that closing is unknown (*Res Gestae Divi Augusti* 13). In Rome, the *templum Iani*, "Temple of Janus" (actually a gateway rather than a temple), was opened as a means of officially declaring war (Vergil *Aeneid* 1.294; Servius on *Aeneid* 1.294; Macrobius *Saturnalia* 1.9.17–18; Livy 1.19.2–4; Varro *De lingua Latina* 5.165; Horace *Ep.* 2.1.255; Ovid *Fasti* 1.121–24).

4c καὶ ἐδόθη αὐτῷ μάχαιρα μεγάλη, "He was given a large sword." In this phrase the sword is the symbol of the authority given to the cavalier expressed elliptically in v 4a: ἐδόθη αὐτῷ λαβεῖν τὴν εἰρήνην ἐκ τῆς γῆς, "he was given [the power] to remove peace from the earth"; i.e., the interpretation precedes the symbol. τὴν μάχαιραν φορεῖν, "to bear the sword" (Rom 13:4), is a metaphor for the power over life and death possessed by governing authorities (see Philostratus *Vitae Soph.* 1.532, δικαστοῦ γὰρ δεῖσθαι αὐτὰς ξίφος ἔχοντος, "they needed a judge with a sword"). Roman emperors carried a dagger or sword as an emblem of office (Tacitus *Hist.* 3.68 [*pugio*]; Suetonius *Galba* 11; Dio Cassius 42.27 [ξίφος]; Ulpian *Digest* 1.18.6.8). The *ius gladii,* "right of the sword," in cases of capital punishment was a symbol of imperium exclusively exercised by the emperor in Rome but delegated to provincial officials (A. Berger, *Roman Law,* 529). Wearing a sword was also the right of only the highest military officials during the Roman Republic (Dio Cassius 42.27.2), and during the Empire a sword was worn exclusively by the emperor (Mommsen, *Römisches Saatsrecht* 1:433–35; 2:806). That this cavalier was given a sword, therefore, indicates the authority and power with which he was temporarily entrusted by God (ἐδόθη is a divine passive; see *Comments* on 6:2b and 9:3). The sword was a typical weapon used by ancient cavalry in warfare. One would have expected that the sword would be mentioned *before* the anticipated slaughter of v 4b is described. This is another instance of the author's use of *hysteron-proteron,* "last-first," i.e., the reversal of the logical order of events, a literary device used frequently in Revelation (3:3, 17; 5:5; 10:4, 9; 20:4–5, 12–13; 22:14). Unlike the description of the first cavalier, who is said to have "ridden away" (ἐξῆλθεν), nothing in this text suggests that the cavalier executed his task.

5a καὶ ὅτε ἤνοιξεν τὴν σφραγῖδα τὴν τρίτην, ἤκουσα τοῦ τρίτου ζῴου λέγοντος· ἔρχου, "When he opened the third seal, I heard the third cherub saying, 'Come!'" This is part of the author's use of the four cherubim to provide a literary framework for the opening of the first four seals. See 6:1, 3, 5, 7, with *Comment* on 6:1b.

5b καὶ εἶδον, καὶ ἰδοὺ ἵππος μέλας, "Then I looked, and behold, there was a black horse." On καὶ εἶδον, see *Comment* on 5:1. The color black had strong negative connotations in antiquity because of its association with darkness and its consequent use as a symbol for death, the underworld, and (in the medieval Church) the Devil. The mention of a black horse is an allusion to one of the four teams of horses pulling chariots in the vision in Zech 6:2, 6. Here the color black apparently symbolizes famine, which is frequently associated with death.

5c καὶ ὁ καθήμενος ἐπ' αὐτὸν ἔχων ζυγὸν ἐν τῇ χειρὶ αὐτοῦ, "and the cavalier had a balance scale in his hand." A balance scale consisted of a crossbeam suspended by a hook or cord with a pan suspended from each end of the crossbeam. Weights placed in one pan were used to determine the weight of commodities placed in the other pan. Balance scales are mentioned several times in the OT, often with the protest that they were rigged to cheat customers (Prov 11:1; 16:11; 20:23; Isa 40:12; 46:6; Hos 12:7; Amos 8:5; Mic 6:11). The presence of the balance scales means that in a context of famine bread must be severely rationed and therefore sold by weight, a measure only necessary when bread is an extremely scarce commodity (Lev 26:26; Ezek 4:16). However, since balance scales are useful only for determining *weight,* and the focus in v 6 is the exorbitant cost of grain by *volume,* there appears to be a basic inconsistency present. Against Bousset ([1906] 267), then, the presence of the scales is not illuminated by what follows.

6a καὶ ἤκουσα ὡς φωνὴν ἐν μέσῳ τῶν τεσσάρων ζῴων λέγουσαν, "Then I heard a voice in the midst of the cherubim." Unidentified heavenly voices were relatively rare in Greek tradition according to E. Bevan, *Sibyls and Seers* (London, 1928) 99–100, but they are common in Revelation (9:13; 10:4, 8; 11:12, 15; 12:10; 16:1, 17; 18:4; 19:5; 21:3). A voice from heaven is heard in *Mart. Pol.* 9:1 encouraging Polycarp to be strong. According to Josephus *J.W.* 6.300, those in the temple heard a voice of a host say, "We are departing hence" (see Tacitus *Hist.* 5.13). On heavenly voices in early Judaism, see Kuhn, *Offenbarungsstimmen.* Since the unidentified voice comes from the midst of the cherubim, it is likely that both author and readers would have assumed that it was God who was speaking.

6b χοῖνιξ σίτου δηναρίου καὶ τρεῖς χοίνικες κριθῶν δηναρίου, "A liter of wheat for a denarius, and three liters of barley for a denarius." This statement suggests an exorbitant price for basic commodities during a period of famine caused either by drought or by war (about eight times the normal price for wheat and five-and-one-third times the normal price for barley) and indicates the relative value of wheat and barley. According to *b. Soṭa* 49b, produce will soar in price with the advent of the Messiah. One liter of wheat and three liters of barley are mentioned together here because it is the appropriate ration for a cavalryman and his mount, or for an individual and his domestic animals. Here the term "liter" is used as an equivalent to the Greek dry measure called a χοῖνιξ *(choinix,* pl. *choinikes),* roughly equal to a day's ration of wheat for one person (Herodotus 7.187; Xenophon *Anabasis* 7.3.23; Athenaeus *Deipn.* 3.98e; Diogenes Laertius 8.18; Livy 4.15.6). Three *choinikes* of barley was the approximate amount of daily fodder necessary to feed a horse (Polybius 6.39.13; see Stolle, *Der römische Legionar,* 59), while the ration of wheat for a Roman soldier was thirty-two *choinikes* per month (Polybius 6.39.13–15; two-thirds of a *medimnos,* which was forty-eight *choinikes*). 8 χοίνικες = 1 ἑκτεύς; 6 ἑκτεῖς = 1 μέδιμνος, i.e., a χοῖνιξ is 1/48 of a μέδιμνος. A *choinix* of barley or a half *choinix* of wheat per day was regarded as the normal ration for a slave (Thucydides 4.16.1; Athenaeus *Deipn.* 6.272c). Wheat (*Triticum durum;* Hebrew חִטָּה *ḥiṭṭâ*) was the grain of preference for making bread (Deut 32:14; 1 Kgs 5:21; Isa 28:28; Pss 81:16; 141:14; Ezek 27:17; Sir 39:26; Matt 13:33; Luke 13:21; for a discussion of the varieties of wheat found in the ancient Mediterranean world, see Pliny *Hist. nat.* 18.63–70). Barley (*Hordeum vulgare;* Hebrew שְׂעֹרָה *śĕʿorâ*) survives heat and drought better than other cereal grains and has a shorter growing season than wheat. It was used for a beverage called in Latin *tisana* or "barley-water," for beer (in Egypt), and for porridge, and the stalk was used for fodder (1 Kgs 4:28; Pliny *Hist. nat.* 18.74) but was not usually used for bread (Pliny *Hist. nat.* 18.71–75), except among the poorer people and slaves (Judg 7:13 [cf. 6:15–16]; 2 Kgs 4:42; Jos. *Ant.* 5.220–21; John 6:9, 13). According to the Romans, a shortage in the grain supply could be considered a *prodigium,* i.e., a divinely sent sign foreshadowing coming disasters (Tacitus *Annals* 12.43; see *Excursus 6A: Ancient Prodigies and the Plagues of Revelation*).

The author's emphasis on a *denarius* as the cost of a liter of wheat and three liters of barley presupposes that this amount represents a daily wage for an average worker (Matt 20:1–16; Tob 5:14). The normal cost for a *choinix* of wheat was about one-eighth of a Greek denarius or two Roman asses, while barley was about half the cost of wheat, i.e., one-sixteenth of a Greek denarius or one Roman ass (2 Kgs 7:1, 16; Polybius 2.15.1; Cicero *Verrine Orations* 3.81.188). During times of famine, grain prices could rise steeply. The prices mentioned in Xenophon *Anabasis* 1.5.5–6, for example, are fifty times the normal rates.

6c καὶ τὸ ἔλαιον καὶ τὸν οἶνον μὴ ἀδικήσῃς, "but do not harm the oil and the wine." This command is directed to the third cavalier as the second-person singular aorist subjunctive verb ἀδικήσῃς indicates. Further, μὴ ἀδικήσῃς, "do not harm," is an aorist of prohibition suggesting that no harm has yet been done. A close parallel occurs in 7:3, where four angels are commanded not to harm (μὴ ἀδικήσητε) the earth, sea, or trees. Here the terms τὸ ἔλαιον, "oil," and ὁ οἶνος, "wine," probably refer, by metonymy, i.e., the effect for the cause (cf. LXX Joel 1:10), to olive trees and vines (cf. the REB translation: "But do not damage the olive and the vine"), for the devastation of olive trees and vines would impede production of oil and wine for several years (Swete, 88; Bratcher-Hatton, *Revelation,* 113; BAGD, 248). This phrase can be construed to refer to either an alleviation or an aggravation of the famine. Most commentators have argued that the intent of the prohibition is to lessen the severity of the famine (i.e., an olive tree must be cultivated five years before fruiting, and fifteen to twenty years to mature; vineyards also take several years to establish); i.e., the scarcity of wheat and barley is a partial judgment (Schlier, *TDNT* 2:471; Kraft, 117; I. Broer, *EDNT* 1:426). However, if oil and wine are regarded as luxuries (Lohse, 47), the famine could be said to be aggravated by the fact that necessities of life are scarce while the luxuries are unaffected (Moffatt, *The Expositor* 6 [1908] 362–64). Following this line of interpretation, the phrase "do not harm the olives and the vines" can be construed as irony (Moffatt, *The Expositor* 6 [1908] 368–69). However, while oil and wine must be considered of lesser importance than wheat and barley, they cannot be considered luxury products. The sparing of the vineyards has been linked to the vine edict of Domitian (see below), though this is far from certain. During the first Jewish revolt (A.D. 66–70), Titus had the "gardens" (presumably consisting of olive trees and vineyards) on the outskirts of Jerusalem destroyed (Jos. *J.W.* 6.7; these gardens are also mentioned by Timocrates quoted in Eusebius *Praep.* 9.35 [452b–c]), though normally conquering armies avoided cutting down olive trees and burning vineyards (Pausanias 4.7.1; Ramsay, *Cities,* 431–32). Vines and olive trees are generally less affected in the short term by drought, and dry years can in fact be excellent years for the production of wine. In a late rabbinic tradition in *b. Soṭa* 49b, it is said that when the Messiah comes the vine will yield its fruit but the wine will be costly, and according to *Jub.* 23:18, there will be no grapes or oil during the last wicked generation. The meaning of the verb ἀδικεῖν is particularly problematic here. Charles proposes that nine of the eleven occurrences of ἀδικεῖν in Revelation mean "to hurt, damage" (2:11; 6:6; 7:2, 3; 9:4, 10, 19; 11:5[2x]), while the remaining two occurrences mean "to act unjustly, to sin" (Charles, 1:59; 2:222). Black observes that in the LXX ἀδικεῖν is often used to translate עשק *ʿāšaq,* "to oppress, wrong, extort, defraud" (e.g., Hos 12:8), and suggests that in Rev 6:6 it means "do not (fraudulently) withhold the oil and the wine (with the intention of obtaining an exorbitant price)" (Black, "Some Greek Words," 144).

The phrase καὶ τὸν οἶνον ... μὴ ἀδικήσῃς, "do not harm the wine," has been read by Reinach ("l'Apocalypse," 356–80), followed by many others (Gsell, *Essai,* 152; Robinson, *TAPA* 55 [1924] 18; Rostovtzeff, *History* 1:201; 2:599–600; Magie, *Roman Rule* 1:581; Levick, *Latomus* 41 [1982] 68), against the background of an edict that Domitian issued between A.D. 90 and 93 (the edict is dated to A.D. 91–92 by Eusebius-Jerome *Chron.* 3.160 and to A.D. 90 by the Byzantine *Chronicon Paschale* 1.466, but is mentioned only in literary sources) to restrict the growing of vines in the provinces by cutting down half the existing vineyards and prohibiting the planting of new ones (the decree is referred to by several ancient authors: Suetonius *Dom.* 7.2; 14.2; Philostratus *Vita Apoll.* 6.42; *Vit. Soph.* 1.21; Statius *Silvae* 4.3.11–12). Reinach argued that the motivation for this edict was the economic protection of Italian vintners from the overproduction of wine ("l'Apocalypse," 367–77), while Magie proposed that the edict was intended to reduce the dependence of Italy on imported grain (*Roman Rule* 1:580). However, Sherwin-White argued convincingly that the edict was motivated by the fear of famine and was intended to encourage grain production (*Letters,* 258) since, according to Suetonius, this occurred "on the occasion of a plentiful wine crop coinciding with a scarcity of grain" (*Dom.* 7.2; see P. Garnsey, *Famine and Food Supply in the Graeco-Roman World: Responses to Risk and Crisis* [Cambridge: Cambridge UP, 1988] 225). As Millar phrased it, "too much wine and too little corn was being produced" (*Emperor,* 391–92). This view has now been widely accepted (Levick, *Latomus* 41 [1982] 67; Hemer, *Letters,* 158; Mitchell, *Anatolia* 1:146). The edict was exceedingly unpopular in Asia Minor. According to Philostratus, the Ionians reportedly sent a delegation to Rome to try to persuade Domitian to change his mind (Philostratus *Vita Apoll.* 6.42). In *Vita. Soph.* 1.21, Philostratus is more specific, describing how Scopelian of Clazomenae was part of a delegation from Asia to Domitian that successfully persuaded the emperor to rescind his edict (see Reinach, "Apocalypse," 361–63). There is some skepticism among modern scholars on this point, however, for there are indications that, apart from Asia Minor, the edict was actually put into effect in various times and places (Levick, *Latomus* 41 [1982] 69–71).

Famines in Anatolia occurred with relative frequency in antiquity (Magie, *Roman Rule* 1:481; Garnsey, *Famine,* 218–27, highlights twenty-three food crises experienced in the Roman empire, with emphasis on the city of Rome; Mitchell, *Anatolia,* 145–46, discusses the famines in Asia Minor during the first century A.D.), in part because the region was urbanized, had an unreliable climate, and was largely dependent on grain imported from the Black Sea. According to Rostovtzeff, "the spectre of famine now hovered continually before the Greek cities" (*History* 1:201). Acts 11:28 reports a supposedly worldwide famine under Claudius in A.D. 44; there were famines during his reign (Suetonius *Claud.* 19; Tacitus *Annals* 12.43), but this one was almost certainly limited to Palestine. Another famine occurred in Palestine during the rule of Tiberius Alexander (A.D. 46–48) according to Josephus (*Ant.* 20.101), though this may be identical to that reported in Acts 11:28. At Aspendius in Pamphylia, during the reign of Tiberius (A.D. 14–37), there was a famine that was exacerbated by grain merchants who hoarded their stores (Philostratus *Vita Apoll.* 1.15). Toward the end of Vespasian's reign, there was a famine in Prusa and a consequent riot against the rich, who were thought to have hoarded grain (Dio Chrysostom *Orat.* 46). However, if the dating of the vine edict of Domitian to A.D. 91–92 discussed above is correct, it is possible to correlate this edict with the widespread famine in Asia Minor addressed by the edict of L. Antitius Rusticus the legate of Galatia-Cappadocia, published at Pisidian Antioch in A.D. 91–94 (Rostovtzeff, *History* 1:201; 2:599–600; Magie, *Roman Rule* 1:581). Following a severe winter, there was a serious famine in Asia Minor causing the price of grain to soar, and the inhabitants of Pisidian Antioch had responded to the crisis by hoarding. The legate ordered all colonists (*coloni*) and residents (*incolae*) of Antioch to report within thirty days the quantity of grain they possessed and the amount needed to support each household for that year and the next planting. Excess grain had to be sold to the grain merchants at not more than one denarius per *modius,* i.e., double the pre-famine price, which was eight asses per *modius.*

Does the vine edict of Domitian, when coordinated with the emergency famine edict of L. Antitius Rusticus, suggest that Revelation was written ca. A.D. 93, late in the reign of Domitian? While several scholars have argued for this position (Bousset [1906] 135; Robinson, *TAPA* 55 [1924] 18; Hemer, *Letters,* 158; Roloff [ET] 87), others have rejected it (Wellhausen, *Analyse,* 10 n. 1; Beckwith, 522; S. Krauss, *ZNW* 10 [1909] 81–89; Charles, 1:168; H. Schlier, "ἔλαιον," *TDNT* 2:471). Several important points can be made: (1) The prohibition against harming oil and wine in Rev 6:6 can be correlated with the fact that, at least in Asia Minor, the vine edict of Domitian was apparently rescinded, perhaps suggesting divine intervention (the voice prohibiting the harming of olive trees and vines comes from the midst of the four cherubim and is evidently the voice of God). (2) There is little evidence that the vine edict of Domitian was promulgated because of a famine (Beckwith, 522). Indeed, such a measure can only be construed in terms of its long-term effects, i.e., to encourage the planting of grains rather than vineyards, though the vine edict may have been provoked by the famine in Asia (Mitchell, *Anatolia* 1:146). (3) The frequency of famines in various parts of the empire means that it is difficult to correlate the famine anticipated in Rev 6:6 with any particular historical event (see Torrey, *Apocalypse,* 79; J. A. T. Robinson, *Redating,* 238). (4) The motif of famine occurs frequently in Jewish apocalyptic expectation (Isa 14:30; Ezek 6:11–12; Mark 13:8 = Matt 24:7 = Luke 21:11; 4 Ezra 15:5, 49; 16:18–22, 34, 46). (5) While vineyards are explicitly mentioned in the vine edict of Domitian, oil or olive trees are not mentioned, an omission requiring explanation (Beckwith, 522; J. A. T. Robinson, *Redating,* 238 n. 94; Prigent, 111). (6) Famines occurred with some frequency in the ancient world and were often understood as prodigies, i.e., as signs warning of divine anger (Dionysius Hal. *Ant. Rom.* 6.17.3; Wülker, *Prodigienwesens,* 21–22; see *Excursus 6A: Ancient Prodigies and the Plagues of Revelation*). It may be concluded that the reference to prohibiting the harming of oil and wine (olive trees and vineyards) cannot be certainly correlated with the vine edict of Domitian.

7 καὶ ὅτε ἤνοιξεν τὴν σφραγῖδα τὴν τετάρτην ἤκουσα φωνὴν τοῦ τετάρτου ζῴου λέγοντος· ἔρχου, "When he opened the fourth seal, I heard the voice of the fourth cherub saying, 'Come!'" On this fourth repetition of the introductory formula, see *Comment* on 1b.

8a καὶ εἶδον, καὶ ἰδοὺ ἵππος χλωρός, "I saw, and behold, a pale-colored horse." On καὶ εἶδον, see *Comment* on 6:1. The adjective χλωρός means "green, pale green," often used to describe the color of grass and other vegetation (Gen 1:30; 4 Kgdms 19:26; Ezek 17:24; Mark 6:39; MM, 639). In Gen 2:5 and Rev 9:4, πᾶν χλωρόν, literally "every green thing," means "every plant." χλωρός also means "pale greenish gray" (Louw-Nida, § 79.34–35), the color associated with the faces of the sick (Hippocrates *Progn.* 2) and the pallor of corpses. χλωρός is also used to describe fear (*Iliad* 7.479; *Odyssey* 11.43, 633, ἐμὲ δὲ χλωρὸν δέος ᾕρει, "pale fear seized me"). Sappho describes the anticipated symptoms of lovesickness: "I am greener [χλωροτέρα] than the grass; I feel very near to death" (Longinus *De sublimate* 10.2). The author continues the allusion to the fourth team of horses drawing a chariot in Zech 6:3, 7, where the horses are referred to as אֲמֻצִּים *'ămuṣṣîm* (rendered "fleshcolored, piebald" in KB³, 63, and "dappled gray" in the NRSV), which usually means "strong" but here apparently is used as the fourth of four colors, translated by the LXX as ποικίλος ψαρός, a peculiar combination because both adjectives mean "spotted, dappled" and have no particular connection with a specific color. By translating אֲמֻצִּים *'ămuṣṣîm* with χλωρός, the author of Revelation presumably wished to emphasize the associations of the Greek term with sickness, fear, and death.

8b καὶ ὁ καθήμενος ἐπάνω αὐτοῦ ὄνομα αὐτῷ ὁ θάνατος καὶ ὁ ᾅδης ἠκολούθει μετ' αὐτοῦ, "and the name of the cavalier was Death, and Hades was following after him." Death is personified four times in Revelation (1:18; 6:8; 20:13, 14), and each time it is linked to a personified Hades (though in 1:18 τοῦ θανάτου καὶ τοῦ ᾅδου are probably objective genitives and therefore, using hendiadys, refer to a *place;* see *Comment* on 1:18). Since "Death" always comes before "Hades" in those four references, it is probable that "Death" is considered the one who reigns over "Hades"; i.e., "Death" is a person while "Hades" is his kingdom. In Greek literature, the expression "to go to the house of Hades" means "to die," indicating that these two notions are closely associated. While Death is occasionally personified alone (Isa 25:8; Jer 9:21; Job 18:13; Prov 13:14; in *T. Abr.* Death is personified as an angel: *T. Abr.* [Rec. A] 16–20; [Rec. B] 13–14; see the Greek conception of Hades with wings in Kaibel, *Epigrammata Graeca,* 89.4), when Sheol or Hades is personified, it is equated with Death, and so both Death and Hades (מות *māwet* and שׁאול *šĕ'ôl*), or Mot and Sheol, are occasionally personified together in the OT (Isa 28:15, 18; Hos 13:14; Hab 2:5; Pss 18:5–6; 49:14[MT 15]; 116:3), always in poetic contexts. Death and Hades are also paired in some early Jewish texts, usually in poetic contexts (Sir 14:12; *Pss. Sol.* 16:2; 4 Ezra 8:53 [*mors* and *infernum*]). Mot was a Canaanite god (N. J. Tromp, *Death;* M. S. Smith, *God,* 52–53). Death or Thanatos is also personified in Greek and Latin texts (Hesiod *Theog.* 211; *Orphic Hymns* 87; Aristophanes *Frogs* 1392; Euripides *Alcestis,* passim; Cicero *De natura deorum* 3.17.44; Vergil *Aeneid* 11.197) but is never worshiped (*Kleine Pauly* 5:648–49). Hades was almost never worshiped, though in Elis there was a temple to Hades (Strabo 8.3.14; Pausanias 6.25.2). In early Christian literature, Hades is occasionally personified in order to identify it with Death (*Acts of Pilate* 20–24; Melito *Pass.* 22, 55, 102; see Lampe, *PGL,* 32). In Greek tradition Hades is both an underworld deity and a name for the underworld itself (see *Comment* on 1:18). Hades is occasionally personified in early Jewish literature (*3 Apoc. Bar.* 4:6; *Sib. Or.* 3.393, 480). The clause "and Hades was following after him" is regarded as an interpolation by Charles (1:274). Charles is probably correct, for the phrase is awkward at this point since either *two* figures are understood as mounted on the third horse (in which case ὁ καθήμενος should be οἱ καθήμενοι), or Hades follows on *another* mount, which seems improbable since only one horse is mentioned.

In Greek mythology the underworld is personified by the god Hades (*Iliad* 15.188; Hesiod *Theog.* 455), who figures prominently in many myths. Though in classical Greek Hades is referred to always as a person and never a place (*Iliad* 23.244), in Hellenistic Greek Hades can be referred to either as a person or as a place (Jos. *Ant.* 6.332; *J.W.* 1.596; 2.156; 3.375; *PGM* I.179; IV.2317; XVI.8, 17, 25). Hades can be represented as a malevolent being who causes a person's death (Lattimore, *Epitaphs,* 147–48). Death and Sleep (Thanatos and Hypnos) are personified as a famous pair of brothers (Hesiod *Theog.* 211–12, 756–57; *Iliad* 14.231; 16.672, 682); Pausanias reports that there were statues of them at Sparta

(3.18.1). They represent the cessation of life but are not depicted as killers (E. Vermeule, *Death,* 37–41, 145–46; J. Hjertén, *Hypnos och Thanatos i Dict och Konst* [Stockholm: Almqvist & Wiksel, 1951]).

8c καὶ ἐδόθη αὐτοῖς ἐξουσία ἐπὶ τὸ τέταρτον τῆς γῆς ἀποκτεῖναι ἐν ῥομφαίᾳ καὶ ἐν λιμῷ καὶ ἐν θανάτῳ καὶ ὑπὸ τῶν θηρίων τῆς γῆς, "They were given authority over a fourth of the earth to kill with the sword and with famine and with plague and by the wild animals of the earth." The plural pronoun αὐτοῖς, "to them," either refers to Death and Hades and this sentence forms a conclusion to the fourth seal, or the pronoun refers to all four cavaliers and this sentence forms a conclusion to the entire textual unit in 6:1–8 (Lohmeyer, 62; Rissi, *Zeit,* 89). Although four plagues are included in this summary of the activity of the four cavaliers, it is not possible to correlate each plague with a particular cavalier. The term for "sword" in v 3 (μάχαιρα) is different from the term for "sword" here in v 8 (ῥομφαία). The reason for this is simply that the list of plagues is a traditional list of disasters that ensue from divine judgment or chastisement. That several early Jewish texts place ῥομφαία, λιμός, and θάνατος (the latter meaning "pestilence") in close association, and one even includes the mention of wild animals, indicates the traditional and formulaic character of this list of types of misfortune. A triad of afflictions occurs frequently in certain portions of the OT, namely, the Deuteronomic portions of Jeremiah, Ezekiel, and Chronicles: (1) חרב *ḥereb,* "sword," (2) רעב *rāʿāb,* "famine," and (3) דבר *deber,* "plague, pestilence" (Jer 14:12; 21:9; 24:10; 27:8, 13; 29:17–18; 32:24, 36; 38:2; 42:17, 22; 44:13; Ezek 6:11; 12:16; 4QpPs[a] 1–10 ii 1); see O. Kaiser, *TDOT* 5:164–65. Rev 6:8 may allude to Ezek 14:21 (see Ezek 5:16–17; Deut 32:23–25), where the triad is supplemented by the addition of "evil beasts" (וחיה רעה *wĕḥayyâ rāʿâ*): "For thus says the Lord God: How much more when I send upon Jerusalem my four sore acts of judgment, sword, famine, evil beasts, and pestilence, to cut off from it man and beast!" (cf. the "four kinds of destroyers" in Jer 15:3). Yet the closest verbal parallel with all four types of destruction that includes the four plagues in the very same order in which they occur in Rev 6:8 is *Pss. Sol.* 13:2–3 (my tr.), "The arm of the Lord saved us from the sword [ῥομφαία], which passes through, from the famine [λιμός] and pestilence [θάνατος] belonging to sinners. Wild animals [θηρία] rushed upon them; with their teeth they tore their flesh"). Other parallels include Jer 14:12 (sword, famine, plague); Jer 15:3 (plague, sword, famine, captivity); Jer 43:11 (pestilence, captivity, sword); *Pss. Sol.* 15:7 (famine, sword, and pestilence are far from the righteous); *Sib. Or.* 3.335 (sword, famine, plague); *Sib. Or.* 3.316–17 (sword, famine, plague). Also of some interest is the report of the casualties suffered by the Jews in the second revolt of A.D. 132–35 preserved in the epitome of Dio Cassius 69.1–2 (LCL tr.):

> Five hundred and eighty thousand men were slain in the various raids and battles [i.e., the *sword*], and the number of those that perished by *famine, disease* and fire was past finding out. Thus nearly the whole of Judaea was made desolate, a result of which the people had had forewarning before the war. For the tomb of Solomon, which the Jews regard as an object of veneration, fell to pieces of itself and collapsed, and many *wolves and hyenas* rushed howling into their cities.

Here we find battle, famine, disease, fire, and wild animals, with the entire description following the stereotyped conception of such a destruction.

According to Dio Chrysostom *Or.* 38.20 (see Mussies, *Dio,* 248), a plague (λοιμός) or an earthquake can be attributed to the gods, who are thought to use such apparently natural disasters to punish people for their sins, though no one attributes war to the gods. Similarly, Hierocles the Stoic (second century A.D.) has a stereotypical list of natural disasters that he thinks are sometimes caused by the gods (*On Duties* 1.3.54; tr. Malherbe, *Moral Exhortation,* 87):

> For just as pestilence and drought, and also deluges of rain, earthquakes, and everything of this kind are for the most part produced by certain other physical causes, but at times are caused by the gods when it is critical that the sins of the masses be punished publicly and generally . . . .

The Romans regarded both plagues (F. B. Krauss, *Interpretation,* 80–87) and earthquakes (Krauss, *Interpretation,* 49–53) as prodigies, i.e., warnings of a breach in the relationship between people and the gods, a breach requiring expiation (see *Excursus 6A: Ancient Prodigies and the Plagues of Revelation*). The terms λιμός, "famine," and λοιμός, "plague"—the latter closely related to θάνατος, "pestilence"—are often linked (Hesiod *Works and Days* 243; Herodotus 7.171; 8.115; Thucydides 1.23.3 [a list of disasters that affected the Athenians during the Peloponnesian war: earthquakes, eclipses, droughts, famines, and pestilence]; Oenomaus of Gadara in Eusebius *Praep. evang.* 5.19.1; *Sib. Or.* 2.23; 3.332; Luke 21:11; Eusebius *Hist. eccl.* 9.8.11; Andreas *Comm. in Apoc.* 6:8). The mention of people killed by wild animals occurs as a separate motif in *T. Abr.* (Rec. A) 10:6–7; (Rec. B) 12:10–11.

"To kill with the sword" sounds like a parody of the Roman *ius gladii,* "law of the sword," i.e., the power to punish individual criminals (*Digest* 2.1.3; A. Berger, *Roman Law,* 529). Several OT prophetic oracles of doom predict that wild animals will devour both domesticated animals and people as a punishment (Lev 26:22; Deut 28:38, 39, 42; 32:24; Jer 5:6; 8:17; Ezek 5:17; Hos 13:7–8; Lam 3:10–11; see Hillers, *Treaty-Curses,* 54–56). Blessings are sometimes couched in terms of the *absence* of such ferocious wild animals (Isa 35:9; Hos 2:20). A number of ancient Near Eastern treaty curses state that wild animals will come upon a land as a punishment for violating the terms of the treaty, e.g., "May Bethel and Anath Bethel put you at the mercy of a devouring lion" (Hillers, *Treaty-Curses,* 54–55).

9 καὶ ὅτε ἤνοιξεν τὴν πέμπτην σφραγῖδα εἶδον ὑποκάτω τοῦ θυσιαστηρίου τὰς ψυχὰς τῶν ἐσφαγμένων διὰ τὸν λόγον τοῦ θεοῦ καὶ διὰ τὴν μαρτυρίαν ἣν εἶχον, "When he opened the fifth seal, I saw under the altar the souls of those who had been slain for the word of God and because of the witness which they bore." It is theologically significant that here the dead are in some way present in heaven; from the perspective of the OT it is not possible for mortals to go to heaven after their death (Houtman, *Himmel,* 3–5). Nevertheless, there are several passages in the Pauline letters, and perhaps two in the Fourth Gospel, that suggest that immediately following death believers are ushered into the heavenly presence of God (2 Cor 5:1, 8; Phil 1:23; 1 Thess 3:13 [however, here ἅγιοι may refer to angels rather than to "saints" = deceased Christians]; 4:14; 5:9; cf. John 14:2–3; 17:24). The widespread ancient conception (found in both the OT and Homer) that the dead go to the underworld (Sheol or Hades) presupposes a three-tiered cosmology consisting of heaven, earth, and underworld (this is precisely the cosmology of Revelation; see *Excursus 4C: The Cosmology of Ancient Ascent Narratives*). The view that the postmortem destination of the righteous is heaven is largely based on the implications of the so-called new cosmology, which became prevalent in the Hellenistic period. The Hellenistic version of this cosmology imagined the earth as stationary at the lowest or innermost part of the cosmos and surrounded by seven planetary spheres enclosed by an eighth sphere consisting of the fixed stars; the gods were thought to dwell in the highest sphere. During the late Hellenistic period, Judaism, too, adopted an analogous geocentric view of the universe in which the earth was surmounted by three or seven heavens, with God enthroned in the highest heaven (A. Yarbro Collins, "The Seven Heavens in Jewish and Christian Apocalypses," in *Cosmology and Eschatology in Jewish and Christian Apocalypticism* [Leiden: Brill, 1996] 21–54). Paul's cosmology consisted of at least three heavens, if not the full seven (2 Cor 12:2–3). In *Asc. Isa.* 9:7, "Isaiah" reports that in the seventh heaven he "saw all the righteous ones from the time of Adam." Since according to this cosmology the throne of God is located in the seventh heaven, the conception here is very similar to that expressed in *ʾAbot R. Nat.* 12 and *b. Šabb.* 152b (quoted above). Similarly, in *Sepher ha-Razim* 7.1–3 (tr. Morgan, 81):

> The seventh firmament, all of it is sevenfold light, and from its light all the (seven) heavens shine. Within it is the throne of glory, set on the four glorious *Hayot*. Also within it are the storehouses of lives, and the storehouse of souls.

The new cosmology was prevalent in Greco-Roman paganism, providing the basis for the belief that upon death, the soul, the true self, ascends to a heavenly region, to the realm of the gods. Seneca, a Roman Stoic reflecting a strong Platonic influence, states this belief (*Ep. mor.* 102.22; LCL tr.):

> When the day comes to separate the heavenly from the earthly blend, I shall leave the body here where I found it and shall of my own volution betake myself to the gods. I am not apart from them now, but am merely detained in a heavy and earthly prison. These delays of mortal existence are a prelude to the larger and better life.

This is very close to the Pauline view that "whether we wake or sleep, we might live with him" (1 Thess 5:9).

The term ψυχή here (and in 20:4) refers to "an essence which differs from the body and is not dissolved by death" (Thayer, *Lexicon*, 677) or to the "seat and center of life that transcends the earthly" (BAGD, 893); n.b. that the three meanings for ψυχή suggested by Louw-Nida, 2:266 ("inner self," "life," "person"), do not provide for such a possible conception (see *Diogn.* 6:1–9; Wis 3:1). The problem of how it is possible for John to *see* a (presumably) disembodied ψυχή immediately suggests itself, though this never appears to be a problem for visionaries in either Jewish or Hellenistic texts. For Tertullian, of course, the Stoic view of the corporeality of the soul was the answer (*De anima* 8). However, even in Plato *Phaedo* 81C–D (Tertullian argues against the Platonic views of the incorporeality of the soul in *De anima* 6) unpurified souls are conceived of not as immaterial substances but as phantoms or insubstantial wraiths (Gallop, *Plato*, 143–44). The location under the *altar* symbolizes the nearness of these martyrs to God; the same motif is apparently at work in early Jewish traditions, which conceive of souls under the throne of God (*b. Šabb.* 152b). It is interesting that the Greek term βωμός and the Latin term *ara*, both meaning "altar," were used in antiquity by pagans and Jews to mean "tomb" (van der Horst, *Epitaphs*, 42–43). According to Tacitus *Hist.* 5.5 (LCL tr.), Jews "believe that the souls [*animos*] of those who are killed in battle or by the executioner are immortal [*aeternos putant*]; hence comes their passion for begetting children and their scorn of death." According to *'Abot R. Nat.* 12 (see *b. Šabb.* 152b), "Nor is the soul of Moses alone in safekeeping under the throne of glory; rather the souls of all the righteous are in safekeeping under the throne of glory" (tr. Goldin, *Fathers,* 65). There is an interesting tradition in the *'Abot R. Nat.* 26: "He who is buried in the land of Israel is as though he were buried under the altar; for the whole land of Israel is fit to be the site of the altar. And he who is buried under the altar is as though he were buried under the throne of glory" (tr. Goldin, *Fathers,* 111). The problem, of course, is that a body buried under the altar would render it unclean. Lieberman, however, provides an explanation for this problem by referring to the rabbinic view that the "ashes of Isaac," which formed the foundations of the inner altar, are identified with the "ashes of the ram" sacrificed by Abraham (Lieberman, *Hellenism,* 161–63). Porphyry (*De abst.* 2.56.6) reports that the Doumatenoi of Arabia sacrificed a young boy whom they then buried beneath an altar; they thereafter treated the altar as a cult statue (Millar, *Near East,* 12–13).

The noun θυσιαστήριον, "altar," found eight times in Revelation (here; 8:3[2x]; 8:5; 9:13; 11:1; 14:8; 16:7), is derived from the verb θυσιάζειν, "to sacrifice," and is linked to the compound suffix -τηριον (the agentive -τηρ with the addition of -ιο-, a morpheme with diminutive significance), which is added to verbal stems to provide names for establishments, instruments, and utensils (an extension of the agentive significance); in this case the noun indicates the *place* where the sacrifice is made, i.e., the altar. The term appears for the first time in the LXX where it occurs over four hundred times (primarily as a translation of the Hebrew מזבח *mizbēaḥ,* "altar"), where it is used of the altar of burnt offering (2 Kgs 16:10–15), of the incense altar (1 Chr 6:49), and of altars generally (Gen 8:20). Until the third century A.D. the term is limited to Jewish and Christian authors (Klauck, *ZNW* 71 [1980] 277). In the NT it is primarily used of the altar for burnt offerings in the Jerusalem temple (Matt 5:23–24; 23:28–20, 35; Luke 11:51; 1 Cor 9:13; 10:18; Heb 7:13; cf. *1 Clem.* 41:2), four times for the altar of incense (Rev 8:3[2x], 5; 9:13), or for altars generally (Rom 11:3; Jas 2:21). In Revelation θυσιαστήριον is used four times of the altar of incense (8:3[2x], 5; 9:13), three times of the altar of burn offerings (6:9; 11:1; 16:7), and twice by figurative extension with the meaning "sanctuary" (11:1; 14:18; see *Comment* on 11:1). In the NT θυσιαστήριον refers to the heavenly altar only in Revelation (with the possible exception of Heb 13:10; see J. W. Thompson, "Outside the Camp: A Study of Heb 13:9–14," *CBQ* 40 [1978] 58–59). In Hermas *Mand.* 10.3.2–3, the term occurs twice of the heavenly altar, which is the goal of prayers, and the same conception is found in Irenaeus *Adv. haer.* 4.18.6 (Harvey 4.31.5) and Gregory Nazianzus (*Or.* 42). In Hermas *Sim.* 8.2.5 the heavenly altar is again mentioned as the place for testing or judgment. The conception of an altar in the heavenly temple is apparently of Jewish origin. The view of some that the presence of an altar in the heavenly temple is modeled after the presence of an altar in earthly churches is anachronistic. Minucius Felix (*Octavius* 32.1) observed *aras non habemus,* "we have no altars" (see Origen *Contra Cels.* 8.17).

Since in Jewish thought the earthly temple was modeled after the heavenly temple, it is appropriate to ask to what the eight occurrences of the term "altar" in Revelation refer (discussed in some detail in Charles, 1:226–230). The tabernacle (in part an idealization of the Solomonic temple; see Haran, *Temples,* 189–204), the

Solomonic temple, and the Herodian temple had two distinct altars, the "outer" altar or the "altar of burnt offering," located (along with the bronze laver) in the court before the entrance to the holy place, i.e., in the "Court of Priests" (Jos. *J.W.* 5.225), and the "inner" altar or the golden altar of incense, situated just in front of the *pāroket* or curtain separating the holy place or nave from the *dĕbîr* or most holy place (Lev 4:18). The holy place also housed the menorah (or menorahs) and the table for the bread of the presence (Jos. *J.W.* 5.216).

Boll (*Offenbarung*, 32–35; followed by Sattler, *ZNW* 20 [1921] 234, and Malina, *Revelation*, 128–32) reminds us that there was a constellation called Altar located in the southern sky in the Milky Way (Greek βωμός, θυτήριον, or θυμιατήριον; Latin *ara* or *turibulum;* see Aratus *Phaenomena* 403; Quintus Smyrnaeus 4.554; Ptolemy *Tetrabiblos* 28; Hipparchus 1.8.14–15; Eudoxus according to Hipparchus 1.11.6; Cicero *De natura deorum* 2.44; 3.40; *Arat.* 428 [184]; Ovid *Metamorphoses* 2.139; Manilius *Astron.* 1.421, 431; 5.18; Vitruvius 9.5.1 [*turibulum*]). Boll considered the souls clothed in white under the altar to be the stars in the Milky Way, over which the Altar constellation is situated. This interpretation seems forced, however, since the altar mentioned here in v 9 is one of the furnishings of the heavenly temple referred to elsewhere in Revelation (8:3[2x], 5; 9:13; 14:18; 16:7; cf. 11:1), and astral deification is not so much as hinted at in the rest of Revelation, though it is certainly known in Jewish apocalyptic (e.g., Dan 12:3). It is perhaps worth noting that the seven planets are represented by a row of (seven) altars in the fresco from the Barberini Mithraeum (*CIMRM,* 390) and the Mithraic monument of Ottaviano Zeno (*CIMRM,* 335; see Beck, *Planetary Gods,* plates III, IV). The symbolism of seven altars representing the seven planets occurs frequently in Mithraic iconography (index s.v. "altar—seven," *CIMRM* 1:333; 2:403).

While it is obvious that "those who had been slain for the word of God and because of the testimony which they bore" are martyrs, their specific identity is unclear. There are several variations of this phrase found throughout Revelation. The focal motifs are "the word of God" and "the testimony (of Jesus)" (1:2, 9; 20:4) or "the word of God" and "their testimony" (12:11). The closest parallel is 20:4, which speaks of those who had been beheaded διὰ τὴν μαρτυρίαν Ἰησοῦ καὶ διὰ τὸν λόγον τοῦ θεοῦ, "because of the testimony borne by Jesus and because of the word of God." Feuillet (*NTR* 99 [1977] 189–207) argues that the motif of "their testimony" rather than "the testimony of Jesus" indicates that here their number includes all pre-Christian martyrs who gave their lives for the cause of moral and religious truth (see Matt 23:31–35; Heb 11:4; 12:24). It is more probable that Christian martyrs are particularly in view, including those who died in the Neronian persecution in A.D. 64. The phrase ἣν εἶχον, "which they maintained," refers not to the testimony they bore to Jesus Christ but rather to the testimony they had received and preserved (for ἔχειν μαρτυρίαν, see 12:17; Beckwith, 526; Charles, 1:174).

10 καὶ ἔκραξαν φωνῇ μεγάλῃ λέγοντες, ἕως πότε, ὁ δεσπότης ὁ ἅγιος καὶ ἀληθινός, οὐ κρίνεις καὶ ἐκδικεῖς τὸ αἷμα ἡμῶν ἐκ τῶν κατοικούντων ἐπὶ τῆς γῆς; "They cried loudly saying, 'O Master, holy and true, how long will it be until you judge and avenge our deaths caused by those who dwell on the earth?'" The term κράζειν here has juridical overtones since the martyrs are crying out to God for justice (see POxy IV.717; PLond I.113,11b; Daniel-Maltomini, *Supplementum Magicum* 2:5–6). Using the קל וחומר *qal wāḥômer,* "lesser to greater," argument, it is argued in rabbinic Judaism that if God hears an individual cry to him, how much more will he hear when many cry (*Mek. de-Rabbi Ishmael, Nezikin* 18; Lauterbach, *Mekilta De-Rabbi Ishmael* 3:143)? In this instance the appeal for vengeance is uttered by many martyrs. The term δεσπότης, "lord, master," used only here in Revelation, is a general designation for people in authority (slaveowners: 1 Tim 6:1; Titus 2:9; 1 Pet 2:18; *T. Job* 7:9; householders: 2 Tim 2:20; *T. Jos.* 3:2), which is also used occasionally of Christ (2 Pet 2:1; Jude 4), but used seventeen times of God in the LXX (e.g., Gen 15:2, 8; Josh 5:14; Job 5:8; Prov 6:7; Isa 1:24; Jer 1:6; Jonah 4:3), and frequently in early Jewish literature (*Adam and Eve* 8:1; 19:2; *T. Abr.* [Rec. A] 1:4, 7; 4:5; 8:2–3; *T. Job* 38:1), as well as in early Christian literature (Luke 2:29; Acts 4:24; *Gk. Apoc. Ezra* 2:23; 4:5; 5:1, 6, 16). That δεσπότης refers to Christ, not God, is argued unconvincingly by Heil, *Bib* 74 [1993] 227 n. 22. The term δεσπότης, "master," is a regular Greek translation of two Latin terms for the Roman emperor, *dominus* and *princeps* (Philo *Flacc.* 4.23; see Mason, *Greek Terms*, 34). Dio Chrysostom *Or.* 45.1 (see Mussies, *Dio*, 248) states that though both Greeks and barbarians addressed Domitian as δεσπότης, "master," and θεός, "god," he was in reality an evil daimon (δαίμονα πονηρόν). This identification of a Roman emperor as an evil supernatural being comes close to John's perception of the real powers at work behind the emperor and the Roman empire.

The divine titles "holy and true" are used in the asyndetic form "the holy, the true" in 3:14 as titles of Christ (for the christological use of those titles, see *Comment* on 3:14). Neither the phrase "the holy, the true" nor the phrase "holy and true" is used elsewhere in early Jewish or early Christian literature of God or Christ. However, the title "the holy one" (ὁ ἅγιος) is used frequently of God in the LXX, often in the expression "the Holy One of Israel," which occurs twenty-nine times in Isaiah alone (see 2 Kgs 19:22; Pss 71:22; 78:41; 89:18; Isa 1:4; 5:19, 24; 10:20; 12:6; 17:7; 29:19; 41:14; Jer 2:3; 3:16; 50:29; 51:5). Less frequently, the title "true" is applied to God, often in the sense that other gods are false (Exod 34:6; 2 Chr 15:3; Neh 9:6; Isa 65:19; Jer 10:10; John 7:13; 17:3; 1 John 5:20; *1 Clem.* 43:14; *Diogn.* 8:9; Jos. *Ant.* 8.335, 337, 338, 343, 402; 9.256; 10.263), or it is stated that he does not lie (Jer 42:5; Rom 3:3), as in the titles ἀληθινὸς καὶ δίκαιος, "true and righteous" (Jos. *Ant.* 11.55).

Rev 6:10 reads like a dramatization of the rhetorical questions attributed to Jesus in Luke 18:7: "Will not God vindicate [ποιήσῃ τὴν ἐκδίκησιν] his elect who cry to him day and night? Will he long delay over them?" The phrase "how long?" in the context of impatient prayer (i.e., the perception that too long a period has intervened between the commission of an outrage and its just recompense) occurs several times in the OT (Pss 6:3–4; 13:1–2; 35:17; 74:9–10; 79:5; 80:4; 89:6; 1 Macc 6:22; 4 Ezra 4:35; cf. Luke 18:7; see Westermann, *ZAW* 66 [1954] 53). Rev 6:10 is essentially a prayer for vengeance, with precedents in the OT in the so-called imprecatory psalms (Pss 7, 35, 55, 58, 59, 69, 79, 83, 109, 137, 139), which are inappropriately labeled "imprecatory" since wishes or prayers for retribution are found in various types of psalms, though no single psalm has a completely imprecatory character. Wishes or prayers for divine vengeance also occur with some frequency in other contexts in the OT (2 Sam 3:28–29; 2 Kgs 1:10, 12; 2 Chr 22:22; Neh 4:4–5; Jer 11:20; 15:15; 17:18; 18:21–23; 20:12; Amos 7:17). The verb ἐκδικεῖν, "to avenge," occurs only here and in 19:2, where the vengeance prayed for is clearly fulfilled. In the OT, the shedding of human blood is a crime that requires compensation, often the death of the murderer (Gen 9:5–6; Num 35:33; cf. the formula "his blood is on his head" in Josh 2:19; 2 Sam 1:16; 1 Kgs 2:33, 37; Ezek 33:4; Matt 27:25). Once human blood has been shed, it is frequently said that such blood "cries out," i.e., to God who hears it, for vengeance (Gen 4:10; 2 Macc 8:3; 2 Esdr 15:8; *Sib. Or.* 3.313; cf. Ezek 3:18, 20; 35:6; see *TDOT* 3:249–50). Yahweh is depicted as the דֹּרֵשׁ דָּמִים *dōrēš dāmîm,* "avenger of blood" (Pss 9:13; 72:14), i.e., the one who sees that justice is done to those who murder his people (Deut 32:43; 2 Kgs 9:7; Pss 9:12; 79:10). This brief episode in Rev 6:10 is based on a type scene in which, as it were, the clients of a patron petition him or her for justice or vindication. One instance of this type scene is found in 1 Macc 6:22, where subjects appeal to their king for satisfaction (n.b. the use of the two terms κρίσις, "judgment," and ἐκδικεῖν, "to avenge"): "They went to the king and said, 'How long [ἕως πότε] will you fail to do justice and to avenge [οὐ ποιήσῃ κρίσιν καὶ ἐκδικήσεις] our brethren?'" In two nearly identical inscriptions containing Jewish prayers for vengeance inscribed on two tombstones from Delos and dating to the second or first century B.C. (Deissmann, *Light,* 413–24), we have a close parallel to Rev 6:9:

> I call upon and pray the Most High God, the Lord of the spirits and of all flesh, against those who with guile murdered or poisoned the wretched, untimely lost Heraclea, shedding her innocent blood wickedly: that it may be so with them that murdered or poisoned her, and with their children; O Lord that seeth all things, and ye angels of God, Thou before whom every soul is afflicted this same day with supplication: that Thou mayst avenge [ἐγδικήσῃς] the innocent blood and require it again right speedily!

The prayer for vengeance by the martyrs in Rev 6:10 also has a close parallel in *1 Enoch* 47:4 and 4 Ezra 4:35–37, texts composed during the late first century A.D. A partial parallel is found in *1 Enoch* 8:4–11:2 (a continuation of 7:1–6, since 8:1–3 is probably an interpolation; see Black, *1 Enoch,* 128): The destruction of humanity by the giants motivates the survivors to cry to heaven for help (8:4). The four archangels convey their prayer to God (9:1–11), specifically stating (9:10; tr. Knibb, *Enoch*):

> And now behold the souls which have died cry out and complain unto the gate of heaven, and their lament has ascended, and they cannot go out in the face of the iniquity which is being committed on the earth.

God responds by revealing that the wicked will be punished in several stages (10:1–15), and ultimately the righteous will flourish on the earth (10:16–11:2). Threats of vengeance on those who have tormented and murdered the righteous are found in Ps 79:10; 2 Macc 7:36; 8:2–4; *T. Mos.* 9:6–7 (see Charles, 1:176). A close parallel is found in *Sib. Or.* 3.307–13 (Charlesworth, *OTP* 1:369), where the future judgment of Babylon (based on the principle of the *lex talionis*) is partly the result of the crying out of the blood of those whose deaths have gone unavenged:

> For a heavenly eternal destruction will come upon you, Babylon,
> one day, from above, and on the children of wrath,
> (but it will come down upon you from heaven from the holy ones).
> Then you will be as you were before, as if you had not been.
> Then you will be filled with blood, as you yourself formerly
> poured out the blood of good men and righteous men,
> whose blood even now cries out [αἷμα βοᾷ] to high heaven.

In the *Testament of Moses,* the Jewish martyr Taxo, speaking to his seven sons, says, "Let us die rather than transgress the commandments of the Lord of Lords, the God of our fathers. For if we do this, and do die, our blood will be avenged before the Lord" (*T. Mos.* 9:6b–7). Taxo has recently been interpreted as the one who provokes divine vengeance, thereby inaugurating the eschaton (Licht, *JJS* 12 [1961] 95–103), though this view has been contested by J. Priest (in Charlesworth, *OTP* 1:923). Similarly, in *Mart. Marian* 12.7 (tr. Musurillo, *Acts,* 211),

> [Marian] foretold that the blood of the just would soon be avenged, and as though he were speaking already from heaven's heights he threatened various temporal scourges, such as epidemics, enslavement, famine, earthquakes, and the torment of poisonous flies.

Here divine retribution for the slaughter of God's people is understood in terms of plagues upon the people of the world.

The martyrs' prayer for vengeance on their enemies has many similarities to the so-called *defixiones tabellae,* i.e., curses preserved on lead and papyrus requesting the gods to do justice (Versnel, "Prayer," 33). In fact, such "prayers of revenge" constitute a particular literary type of ancient magical adjuration in Greco-Roman as well as early Christian magic; see Watson, *Arae,* 6–7, and Björck, *Fluch.* In ancient fiction, such prayers for revenge can be attributed to the dead, as was this prayer, which is placed in the mouth of the unjustly murdered Deiphobus (Vergil *Aeneid* 6.529–30; LCL tr.): "Ye gods, with like penalties requite the Greeks, if with pious lips I pray for vengeance." A Greek epitaph reads οἱ μὲν ἐμὲ κτείναντες ὁμοίως ἀντιτύχοισαν, Ζεῦ ξένιε, "May those who killed me meet a like fate, O Zeus, god of guests" (W. Peek, *Griechische Versinschriften* [Berlin: Akademie, 1955] 1362), a curse that suggests that the Greek tradition of hospitality has been violated (a theme of many Greek myths, including several about the house of Atreus and the story about Procrustes in the Theseus cycle of legends).

The imprecatory prayers and prayers for vengeance in the OT are often discussed in terms of the apparent antithesis that exists between them and the NT commands to love rather than curse one's enemies (Matt 5:39, 44; Luke 23:34; Rom 12:14; 1 Cor 4:12; 1 Thess 5:15); this theological problem is particularly striking when the curses of the NT are brought into the picture (Matt 21:18–21; 25:41; Acts 8:20; 13:10–11; Gal 1:8–9; 1 Cor 16:22; Rev 6:10; 22:18–19). There are several aspects of the problem that need consideration (see the discussion of Peels, *Vengeance,* 234–46): (1) The psalmists and others who utter prayers for vengeance are not cursing others but pray that God will act justly, though it is clear that the negative features of such prayers are derived from ancient curse traditions. (2) The curse played an important role in ancient social life and was used in a variety of contexts: to force obedience to treaties, to frighten off thieves and grave robbers, to guarantee honesty in transactions. (3) Curses were widely used as a legal device that posited justice against injustice, and a distinction was often made between legitimate and illegitimate curses (illegitimate curses were attributed to enemies; cf. Pss 10:7; 59:13; 62:5; 109:17, 28). (4) In the OT, curses were an integral part of the covenant relationship (derived from Near Eastern treaties, commonly sanctioned by curses) and were not simply unrestrained examples of human wickedness but originated from the conception of a holy and just God who curses those who do not turn from evil (Maiberger, *TTK* 97 [1988] 183–216). The commandments stipulated in the covenant between God and Israel required obedience rather than disobedience, which resulted in salvation, grace, and blessing on the one hand and destruction, judgment, and curse on the other. "The enemy is a covenant breaker and stands already, ipso facto, under the curse of God" (Peels, *Vengeance,* 240; cf. Maiberger, *TTK* 97 [1988] 210). (5) In the OT, imprecatory prayers typically arise in situations in which the wicked appear to prosper while the righteous are victimized; in this apparent discrepancy between injustice and justice, the honor, majesty, and truth of God are in question, so that "the imprecatory prayer is a call for the breakthrough of God's kingdom in liberation and vengeance" (Peels, *Vengeance,* 243). (6) Imprecatory prayers occur less frequently in the NT than in the OT and are associated not with the blessing-curse alternatives of covenant theology but with the proclamation of the gospel and the eschatological judgment.

The phrase τῶν κατοικούντων ἐπὶ τῆς γῆς, "the inhabitants of the earth," is used nine times in Revelation (3:10; 6:10; 8:13; 11:10[2x]; 13:8, 14[2x]; 17:8), *always* of the enemies of Christianity; see *Comment* on 3:10.

11a καὶ ἐδόθη αὐτοῖς ἑκάστῳ στολὴ λευκή, "Then each of them was given a white robe." The timing of this investiture is puzzling, for garments are given to the souls of the martyrs (separated from their earthly bodies) only when they complain that they have not been avenged. This seems to presuppose an "intermediate state" of indeterminate duration between death and the assumption of the heavenly mode of existence symbolized by the white robe (Roloff [ET] 89). Elsewhere in the NT the notion of an intermediate state has often been read into 2 Cor 5:1–5 (e.g., C. K. Barrett, *The Second Epistle to the Corinthians,* HNTC [New York: Harper & Row, 1973] 154–55; R. P. Martin, *2 Corinthians,* WBC 40 [Waco, TX: Word, 1986] 106), though this view is doubtful. The conception of such an intermediate state is reflected in 4 Ezra 7:100–101, where it is said that after the souls of the righteous have been separated from their bodies they will have seven days before "they shall be gathered in their habitations [*congregabuntur in habitaculis suis*]," a view closely parallel to the Jewish notion that the souls of the righteous dead are protected near the heavenly presence of God, dwelling in the "treasury of souls" (*1 Enoch* 39:4–5; 41:2; 61:12; 70:2–4; Urbach, *Sages,* 238–42), and close to the view of Philo, who conceived of heaven as the paternal οἶκος (*Som.* 1.256), the place to which souls return (*Conf.* 78; *Quis Her.* 274; *Mos.* 2.228). Some scholars understand the white robe as a reference to a heavenly body that the martyrs alone possess (Bousset [1906] 271; Charles, 1:176, 184–88; Lohmeyer, 64; cf. Caird, 86), but this is doubtful, particularly in view of the resurrection of the martyrs in 20:4. White robes, the characteristic garb of heavenly beings (see *Comment* on 3:5a), are also used as a polyvalent metaphor for salvation, immortality, victory, and purity (see στολή in Rev 7:9, 13, 14; 22:14; ἱμάτιον in 3:5, 18; *Comment* on 3:5a; Roloff [ET] 90; Mounce, 160). The passive verbs in this verse are passives of divine activity used as circumlocutions for the name of God (see *Comment* on 9:3), so these phrases could be translated "Then God gave each of them a white robe and told them to rest a while longer."

11b καὶ ἐρρέθη αὐτοῖς ἵνα ἀναπαύσονται ἔτι χρόνον μικρόν, "and they were told that they should rest a while longer." The rhetoric of this verse is peculiar, for the divine response to the martyrs is in *oratio obliqua,* i.e., indirect discourse, which occurs only here in Revelation. Strikingly, *oratio obliqua* is also used in *1 Enoch* 47:2, in a context closely parallel to Rev 6:9–11, where the holy ones in heaven pray to God giving thanks that he has forgotten neither the blood nor the prayers of the righteous. The speaker in Rev 6:11b is certainly God, who is indirectly referred to by ἐρρέθη, the passive of divine activity (similar passives occur in vv 2b and 11a; 8:3b; 13:5–7, 10b); on this use of the passive, see the detailed discussion in the *Comment* on 9:3. The implication of the divine response to the petition from the martyrs indicates the necessity of suffering in the plan of God, for more Christians must yet die before the eschaton can be inaugurated. Christian suffering does not hinder the fulfillment of the eschaton but rather inevitably leads to its inauguration. It is also evident that the prayer of the martyrs cannot alter the predetermined plan of God (see Luke 18:6–8, which is quite different). The terms ἀνάπαυσις and ἀναπαύειν (and cognates, particularly κατάπαυσις and καταπαύειν) are used as metaphors for death in early Judaism (as are κοίμησις, "sleep," and κοιμᾶσθαι, "to sleep"; see Louw-Nida, § 23.104; van der Horst, *Epitaphs,* 115–18); a few references are found in *TDNT* 1:350. In early Judaism, the situation of the dead, particularly the righteous dead, is sometimes described as one of rest and repose; see *Comment* on Rev 14:13 (which is similar in form to an epitaph). Sometimes the metaphor of rest is used of burial (Prov 21:16, the ignorant man "will rest [MT ינוח *yānûaḥ;* LXX ἀναπαύσεται] in the assembly of the dead"; Sir 30:17, "eternal rest [ἀνάπαυσις αἰῶνος]"; 38:23, "when the dead are at rest [ἐν ἀναπαύσει νεκροῦ]"; 47:23, "Solomon rested [ἀνεπαύσατο] with his fathers"; see also Wis 4:7). The rest or repose of the *soul* in heaven is sometimes mentioned (*Jos. As.* 8:11; 15:7, "a place of rest [τὸν τόπον τῆς καταπαύσεως] in the heavens"; 22:13; *1 Enoch* 39:4–9; *T. Abr.* [Rec. B] 7:9; *T. Isaac* 2:13, 15), sometimes referred to as Paradise (4 Ezra 7:36 [*locus requietionis*], 38, 75, 91, 95; 8:52; *Gk. Apoc. Ezra* 1:12), or Eden (*T. Dan.* 5:12), or the lap of Abraham (Luke 16:22). The *place* of rest for the righteous dead is often left unspecified (4 Ezra 2:34; *Par. Jer.* 5:32). The phrase εἰρήνη καὶ ἀνάπαυσις occurs on a Jewish grave inscription (*CIJ,* 688; fourth century A.D.; see Delling, *Lehre,* 30–31). The notion of the מנוח *mānôaḥ,* "rest," of the righteous dead also occurs in rabbinic literature (*b. Šabb.* 152b; see Str-B, 3:817). In Rev 6:11, the rest of the dead martyrs is clearly temporary, a notion presupposed in the question of "Ezra" in 4 Ezra 7:75: "after death, as soon as every one of us yields up his soul, shall we be kept in rest [A: *in requie;* L: *in requiem*] until those times come when you will renew the creation?" (the question is answered positively in 4 Ezra 7:88–99, which describes the seven orders of rest that the righteous will enjoy).

11c ἕως πληρωθῶσιν καὶ οἱ σύνδουλοι αὐτῶν καὶ οἱ ἀδελφοὶ αὐτῶν οἱ μέλλοντες ἀποκτέννεσθαι ὡς καὶ αὐτοί, lit. "until the number of their fellow servants and brothers who were to be killed as they were was complete." In the phrase "their fellow servants and brothers," that both plural nouns are articular and both are preceded by the conjunction καί, "and," suggests the possibility that two separate groups are in view (Zahn, 2:362; Ulfgard, *Feast,* 56). However, the connecting καί may well be epexegetical so that the phrase should probably be construed as meaning "their fellow servants, that is, their brothers," thus describing a single group from two perspectives (Beckwith, 527; Charles, 1:177; Mounce, 160). The term σύνδουλοι, "fellow servants," is a title found three times in Revelation (6:11; 19:10; 22:9). Elsewhere, it occurs in the NT in Col 1:7; 4:7 and in the Apostolic Fathers (Ign. *Eph.* 2:1; *Magn.* 2; *Phld.* 4; *Smyrn.* 12:2; *Rom.* 4:3). In these contexts it is *always* a title of honor (H. Gülzow, *Christentum und Sklaverei in den ersten drei Jahrhunderten* [Bonn: Habelt, 1969] 32). A parallel from the religious institutions of Asia Minor is found in the title συνιερόδουλος, "sacred slave," "colleague," in an inscription from Lydia; see G. Petzl, "Vier Inschriften aus Lydien," in *Studien zur*

Religion und Kultur Kleinasiens, FS F. K. Dörner, ed. S. Sahin, E. Schwertheim, and J. Wagner (Leiden: Brill, 1978) 745.61, 746.50.

This verse indicates that a *numerus praedestinatorum,* i.e., a "predetermined number," of martyrs must die before God will avenge them. πληροῦν can mean "to make something total or complete, to complete the number of" (Louw–Nida, § 59.33), so the entire clause can be translated "until the number of their fellow servants and brothers would be complete" (this verb is extremely problematic; see *Note* 6:11.h-h.). In the *Mart. Pol.* 14 (tr. Musurillo, *Acts,* 13), Polycarp gives thanks that he is able "to have a share among the number [ἐν ἀριθμῷ] of the martyrs." Since Polycarp died ca. A.D. 156 (the date is disputed; see Musurillo, *Acts,* xiii–xiv), this notion *could* have been drawn from Revelation, though it seems unlikely. A similar statement is made in the *Ep. Lugd.* 13 (Eusebius *Hist. eccl.* 5.1.13; Musurillo, *Acts,* 64–65), "every day the worthy were arrested to fill up the number of the martyrs [τὸν ἐκείνων ἀναπληροῦντες ἀριθμόν]." This martyrdom occurred ca. A.D. 177, and the work was written shortly thereafter. Since it alludes to Revelation twice (Rev 14:4 in chap. 10, and Rev 22:11 in chap. 57), the conception of a predetermined number of martyrs may very well be drawn from Revelation.

In early Judaism, the view that the *numerus iustorum,* "number of the righteous," has been predetermined by God is first expressed clearly in apocalypses nearly contemporary with Revelation (*1 Enoch* 37–71; 4 Ezra; *2 Apocalypse of Baruch;* see Räisänen, *Divine Hardening,* 67–78). In *1 Enoch* 47:4 it is said that the hearts of the holy ones rejoiced that the number of the righteous had been reached, that their prayer had been heard, and that their blood had been required before the Lord of Spirits. 4 Ezra 4:36 contains the phrase "when the number of those like yourselves is completed," referring to a predetermined number of the elect, though martyrdom is not in view. A similar view is reflected in *2 Apoc. Bar.* 23:5 (tr. Klijn in Charlesworth, *OTP* 1:629), "No creature will live again unless the number that has been appointed is completed" (see 30:2; 75:6). The notion also occurs in early Christianity. Paul claims that Israel will be unresponsive to the gospel until "the full number of the Gentiles come in" (Rom 11:25). The author of *1 Clement* uses the phrases ὁ ἀριθμὸς τῶν ἐκλεκτῶν, "the number of the elect" (2:4; 59:2), and ὁ ἀριθμὸς τῶν σῳζομένων, "the number of the saved" (58:2), in such a way as to suggest that it is already a well-known concept (van Unnik, *RHPR* 42 [1962] 237–46). Similarly, Justin says that Christ will not return in judgment "until the number is completed of those whom he foreknows [συντελεσθῇ ὁ ἀριθμὸς τῶν προεγνωσμένων]" (*1 Apol.* 45.1). *Apost. Const.* 15.3 (perhaps dependent on *1 Clement*) speaks of "the fullness of the number of the saved."

While Rev 6:11 speaks of the number of martyrs that must be completed, in the *Pistis Sophia* the phrase "the number of perfect souls is completed [*afjôk ebol n i parithmos nnepsuchooue nntelios*]" (or its equivalent) occurs frequently (1.23, 26, 27, 45, 50; 2.86, 96, 98; 3.125[4x]) and obviously refers to Gnostics. The phrase is apparently a *terminus technicus,* which the author incorporated within the framework of his Gnostic eschatology (van Unnik, "Pistis Sophia," 473). The "completion of the number of perfect souls" will occur at the "end of the aeon" (Coptic: *tsunteleia mpaion* = συντέλεια τοῦ αἰῶνος; 2.86), at the decisive point in the eschatological drama (van Unnik, "Pistis Sophia," 473). According to *Pistis Sophia* 1.50 (tr. MacDermot, 89–90), "Now at this time truly I say to you, when the perfect number is completed and the All is raised up, I will sit in the Treasury of the Light and you yourselves will sit on twelve light-powers, until we have set up again all the ranks of the twelve saviours at the place of the inheritance of each of them."

12a καὶ εἶδον ὅτε ἤνοιξεν τὴν σφραγῖδα τὴν ἕκτην, καὶ σεισμὸς μέγας ἐγένετο, "Then I saw, when he opened the fifth seal, that a great earthquake occurred." On καὶ εἶδον, see *Comment* on 5:1. The term σεισμός, "shaking," probably refers to an earthquake, but in the context it could refer to a "shaking" of "the heavens and earth" (Hag 2:6–7, 21–22), which caused the disruption of the heavenly bodies. In biblical tradition, earthquakes are often expected to occur in the end time as one effect of the presence or coming of God (Joel 2:10; 3:16[MT 4:16]; Isa 24:18–23; 29:6; Mic 1:4; Nah 1:5; see *Comment* on the theophany form in Rev 20:11); see Bauckham, "Earthquake," 199–209. Earthquakes are often perceived as prodigies (Plutarch *Cicero* 14; Appian *Bell. civ.* 1.83; Aulus Gelius *Noctes Atticae* 2.28.1–3; Wülker, *Prodigienwesens,* 18).

12bc καὶ ὁ ἥλιος ἐγένετο μέλας ὡς σάκκος τρίχινος, καὶ ἡ σελήνη ὅλη ἐγένετο ὡς αἷμα, "and the sun became dark as haircloth, and the entire moon became red as blood." This is an allusion to Joel 2:31 (MT 3:4):

> The sun shall be turned to darkness,
> and the moon to blood,
> before the great and terrible day of the Lord comes.

The addition of ὅλη as a modifier of σελήνη in such lists of portents is found only in *T. Moses* 10:5, *Sol non dabit lumen et in tenebris convertent se cornua lunae et confringentur, et [luna] tota convertit se in sanguine,* "The sun will not give its light, and the horns of the moon will turn into darkness, and [the moon] will entirely be turned into blood" (tr. J. Tromp, *Assumption of Moses,* 18–19). Charles (1:180) thought that the presence of *tota* in *T. Moses* 10:5 and ὅλη in Rev 6:12 suggested that the author of Revelation had some form of the *Testament of Moses* before him when he wrote, though direct literary dependence is not the only possible explanation. The darkening of the sun and moon is a motif that occurs elsewhere (Isa 13:10), while the haircloth or sackcloth motif was perhaps derived from Isa 50:3, "I clothe the heavens with blackness and I make sackcloth their covering" (on "sackcloth," see *Comment* on 11:3). From a Roman perspective, such a phenomenon would be considered *auspicia oblativa,* i.e., "unsought signs" (see Vergil *Georg.* 1.438–65). The darkenings and eclipses of the sun and the moon are frequently mentioned as prodigies (Apollonius Rhod. 4.1286; Cicero *Rep.* 1.16.25; Vergil *Georg.* 1.463–68; Dionysius Hal. *Ant. Rom.* 1.77.2; Ovid *Metam.* 15.785; Philo *Mos.* 1.123; Plutarch *Pelopidas* 31; Cassius Dio 47.40.2; Aulus Gelius *Noctes Atticae* 2.28.4–7; Diogenes Laertius 4.64; Lactantius *Div. Inst.* 7.169; Luterbacher, *Prodigienglaube,* 11–12; Wülker, *Prodigienwesens,* 7–8; F. B. Krauss, *Interpretation,* 70–71; see also F. Boll, "Finsternisse," *RE* [1909] 6:2329ff.). In Greco-Roman dream interpretation, a sun "dim or suffused with blood, or hideous to behold, it is inauspicious and evil for all men" (Artemidorus *Oneirocritica* 2.36; tr. White, *Interpretation,* 115). The motif of the darkening or destruction of the sun when God judges the world occurs frequently (Isa 13:10b; 24:23; Amos 8:9; Joel 2:31 [MT 3:4]; Zeph 1:15 (the Day of the Lord is a day of darkness and gloom); *T. Moses* 10:5; Mark 13:24–25 = Matt 24:29; Luke 21:25; Acts 2:20; 2 Pet 3:10 [the coming of the Day of the Lord will be accompanied by the destruction of the heavens and the earth]; *Barn.* 15:5). The three stichs in vv 12b, 12c, and 13 all have a similar pattern: a declarative statement of what occurred in the aorist, followed by a simile introduced with ὡς, "as, like." The motif of darkness on the Day of Yahweh found in the prophets (Amos 8:9) is developed into the motif of the darkening or destruction of the sun, moon, and stars on the day of judgment (Isa 13:9–10; Ezek 32:7–8; Joel 2:10; 3:15[MT 4:15]; *T. Levi* 4:1; *Sib. Or.* 5.477–82; 7.125; 4 Ezra 7:39; Oracle of Hystaspes frag. 14; Lactantius *Div. Inst.* 7.16.8 [Bidez-Cumont, *Mages* 2:368–69]; *Barn.* 15:5). *Barn.* 15:5 is interesting because the sequence of motifs it contains is as follows: (1) the coming of the Son, (2) the destruction of the time of the wicked one, (3) the judgment of the godless, and (4) the changing of the sun, moon, and stars. In view of this widespread association, it is obvious that the author of Revelation intends the readers to think that the Day of the Lord is ushered in with the sixth trumpet. An example is found in *Sib. Or.* 5.346–51 (tr. J. Collins in Charlesworth, *OTP* 1:401):

> The imperishable flames of the sun itself will no longer be
> nor will the shining light of the moon be anymore
> in the last time [ὑστατίῳ καιρῷ], when God assumes command.
> Everything will be blackened, there will be darkness throughout the earth,
> and blind men, evil wild beasts, and woe.
> That day [ἦμαρ ἐκεῖνο] will last a long time . . . .

A similar prediction is found in Ps.-Philo *Bib. Ant.* 19.13 (tr. Harrington in Charlesworth, *OTP* 2:328):

> And when the time draws near to visit the world, I will command the years and order the times and they will be shortened, and the stars will hasten and the light of the sun will hurry to fall and the light of the moon will not remain; for I will hurry to raise up you who are sleeping in order that all who can live may dwell in the place of sanctification I showed you.

The consequences attendant upon the coming of God are described in *T. Moses* 10:5–6 (tr. Priest in Charlesworth, *OTP* 2:932):

> The sun will not give light.
> And in darkness the horns of the moon will flee.
> Yea, they will be broken in pieces.
> It will be turned wholly into blood.
> Yea, even the circles of the stars will be thrown into disarray.

Finally, from the *Oracle of Hystaspes* frag. 14 (Lactantius *Div. Inst.* 7.16.8; see Bidez-Cumont, *Mages* 2:368–69):

> Then, too, strange prodigies [*prodigia*] in the sky will confound the minds of men with the greatest terror: the tails of comets, the eclipses of the sun, the color of the moon, and the fallings of stars.

A similar description is contained in Lactantius *Epitome* 71 (tr. Blakeney, *Epitome,* 121):

> To these plagues will be added also miraculous signs [*prodigia*] from heaven, that everything may combine to increase human alarm. Comets will frequently be seen. The sun will be darkened with perpetual gloom; the moon will be dyed in blood, nor will it

renew its lost light; all the stars will fall, nor will the seasons observe their proper course, for winter and summer will be confounded.

13 καὶ οἱ ἀστέρες τοῦ οὐρανοῦ ἔπεσαν εἰς τὴν γῆν, ὡς συκῆ βάλλει τοὺς ὀλύνθους αὐτῆς ὑπὸ ἀνέμου μεγάλου σειομένη, "and the stars of heaven fell to earth, as a fig tree drops its unripe figs when shaken by a strong wind." This is an allusion to Isa 34:4, where the leaves rather than the fruit of the fig tree are described: "All their host shall fall, as leaves fall from the vine, like leaves falling from the fig tree" (n.b. that the author has inverted the allusion to Isa 34:4 by first alluding to v 4b [in Rev 6:13a] and then to v 4a [alluded to in Rev 6:14a]). Isa 34:4 is also alluded to in the Synoptic apocalypse (Mark 13:25 = Matt 24:29 = Luke 21:26). However, the combination of the two motifs, the darkening of the sun and moon and the falling of the stars, occurs in Rev 6:12–13 and in a few other places (Mark 13:24–25; *T. Moses* 10:5–6; Lactantius *Epitome* 71). Falling stars are mentioned several times in Revelation (8:10; 9:1; 12:4). Falling stars, or meteors, do not necessarily involve the destruction of the heavens but may be considered a prodigy or an omen needing interpretation (4 Ezra 5:5; Jos. *J.W.* 6.289; Manilius *Astron.* 1.814–875), or they may be an anticipation of the judgment of God (Ezek 32:7; Joel 2:10 [MT 3:4]; 3:15 [MT 4:15]; Mark 13:25 = Matt 24:29; *Sib. Or.* 8.190, 341). The fallen-star motif is frequently used as a metaphor for the fall of Satan and/or his angels (*1 Enoch* 86:1; 88:1–3; 90:24; Jude 13; *T. Sol.* 20:16; *Apoc. Elijah* 4:11; cf. Luke 10:18). In ancient dream interpretation, seeing stars falling down to the earth meant that many people would die (Artemidorus *Oneirocritica* 2.37; cf. 5.23). In the apocalyptic scenario of the Hermetic tractate *Asclepius* 3.25, Trismegistus says "heaven will not support the stars in their orbits, nor will the stars pursue their constant course in heaven" (tr. W. Scott, *Hermetica* 1:345). Such cosmic disturbances are a commonplace in apocalyptic literature; see Nock-Festugière, *Corp. Herm.* 2:381 n. 218. Meteors are also considered prodigies (Cassius Dio 40.47.2; Wülker, *Prodigienwesens,* 11). In some versions of the Gigantomachy (the battle between the Olympians and the giants depicted on the Great Altar of Zeus from Pergamon and the Temple of Apollo at Delphi [Euripides *Ion* 206–18]), the stars were shaken from their places by the tumultuous battle (Manilius *Astron.* 1.427).

14a καὶ ὁ οὐρανὸς ἀπεχωρίσθη ὡς βιβλίον ἑλισσόμενον, "Heaven disappeared from sight like a scroll rolled up." This is an allusion to Isa 34:4, "All the host of heaven shall rot away, and the skies roll up like a scroll." The same allusion occurs several times in the *Sibylline Oracles,* e.g., 3.82–83 (tr. Collins in Charlesworth, *OTP* 1:364), "when God who dwells in the sky rolls up the heaven as a scroll is rolled [οὐρανὸν εἱλίξῃ, καθ' ἅπερ βιβλίον εἱλεῖται]." Similarly, in *Sib. Or.* 8.233, 413, the phrases "He will roll up the heavens [οὐρανὸν εἱλίξε]" and "I will roll up the heavens [οὐρανὸν εἱλίξω]" occur. Other allusions to this metaphor from Isa 34:4 are found in Heb 1:12, where the rolling up of the heavens and the earth is compared to the rolling up of a garment, in *Gos. Thom.* 111 (see Stroker, *Extracanonical,* 112–13), in Tertullian *Ad Hermog.* 34, and in *Apocalypse of Peter* (Macarius Magnes *Apocrit.* 4.7). Similarly, in *Pistis Sophia* 1.10 (ed. Schmidt-Till, p. 4, lines 15–16; ed. Schmidt-MacDermot, p. 6), the disciples speculate, "Perhaps the world will be rolled up."

14b καὶ πᾶν ὄρος καὶ νῆσος ἐκ τῶν τόπων αὐτῶν ἐκινήθησαν, "Every mountain and island was shaken from its place." The verb κινεῖν, "to move, remove, shake," can refer to the effects of an earthquake (Herodotus 6.98; Thucydides 2.8), and a great earthquake has just been mentioned in v 12a. The metaphor of the most stable features of the world, such as mountains, islands, and coastlands, "shaken" and "moved" occurs in contexts of a divine theophany or divine judgment (Judg 5:5; Pss 18:7[LXX 17:7]; 46:2–3; Isa 5:25; 54:10; 64:1; Jer 4:24; Ezek 26:18; 38:20; Mic 1:4; Nah 1:5; Hab 1:6; Zech 14:4). In sapiential contexts, the movement of mountains is often regarded as impossible (Ps 125:1–2; Matt 17:20; 1 Cor 13:2; cf. Job 14:18, which recognizes the reality of erosion). This motif also occurs in Rev 20:11 in a theophanic context.

Excursus 6A: Ancient Prodigies and the Plagues of Revelation

Bibliography

Berger, K. "Hellenistisch-heidnische Prodigien und die Verzeichen in der jüdisch und christlichen Apokalyptik." *ANRW* II, 23/2:1428–69. **Binder, G.** *Aeneas und Augustus.* Meisenheim, 1971. **Bloch, R.** *Les prodiges dans l'antiquité classique (Grèce, Étrurie et Rome).* Paris: Presses Universitaires de France, 1963. ———. "Portents and Prodigies." *EncRel* 11:454–57. **Brenk, F. E.** *In Mist Apparelled: Religious Themes in Plutarch's Moralia and Lives.* Leiden: Brill, 1977. **Fowler, W. W.** *The Religious Experience of the Roman People from the Earliest Times to the Age of Augustus.* London: Macmillan, 1911. **Grassmann-Fischer, B.** *Die Prodigien in Vergils Aeneis.* Munich: Fink, 1966. **Günther, R.** "Der politisch-ideologische Kampf in der römischen Religion in den letzten zwei Jahrhunderten v. u. Z." *Klio* 42 (1964) 209–97. **Handel, P.** "Prodigia." *RE* 46 (Stuttgart, 1959), cols. 2283–96. *Kleine Pauly* 4:1151–53. **Krauss, F. B.** *An Interpretation of Omens, Portents, and Prodigies Recorded by Livy, Tacitus, and Suetonius.* Philadelphia: University of Pennsylvania, 1930. **Liebeschuetz, J. H. W. G.** *Continuity and Change in Roman Religion.* Oxford: Clarendon, 1979. **Luterbacher, F.** *Der Prodigienglaube und Prodigienstil der Römer.* Burgdorf: Langlois, 1880. **McBain, B.** *Prodigy and Expiation: A Study in Religion and Politics in Republican Rome.* Brussels: Latomus, 1982. **Momigliano, A.** "Prodigia." *EncRel* 12:3. **Riess, E.** "Omen." PW 28/1:350–78. **Wülker, L.** *Die geschichtliche Entwicklung des Prodigienwesens bei den Römern: Studien zur Geschichte und Überlieferung der Staatsprodigien.* Leipzig: Glausch, 1903.

The term *prodigium,* "prodigy" (the plural form is *prodigia*), often called a *portentum,* is a term in ancient Roman religion for an unnatural or extraordinary occurrence or phenomenon understood as a sign warning of divine anger (Wülker, *Prodigienwesens,* 1). In early Roman tradition the occurrence of a prodigy was thought to reveal the *ira deum,* "anger of a god," and ostensibly indicated the disruption of the *pax deorum,* "peace with the gods." Therefore, it required rites of expiation to repair the breach between the Roman people and their gods (*Kleine Pauly* 4:1151–53). Greeks used such terms as τέρας, σημεῖον, οἰωνός (the latter etymologically limited to birds), and φάσμα for *prodigium* (Appian *Bell. civ.* 4.1.4; Plutarch *Sept. sap. conv.* 149C; Bloch, *Les prodiges,* 15). Cicero defines many of the terms used for prodigies in *De div.* 1.42.93 (LCL tr.):

> Because they "make manifest" [*ostendunt*], "portend" [*portendunt*], "intimate" [*monstrant*], "predict" [*praedicunt*], they are called "manifestions," "portents," "intimations," and "prodigies" [*prodigia*].

These terms are essentially synonymous (Servius *Comm. in Aen.* 3.366; see F. B. Krauss, *Interpretation,* 31–34), though Joannes Lydus (*De ostentis* praef.) argued that σημεῖα occurred in the heavens, while τέρατα occurred upon earth.

The *prodigia* had first to be observed, then acknowledged and accepted by the Roman senate (e.g., Livy 43.13.6), then explicated (through the science of *divinatio*), and finally expiated (often by following the *disciplina Etrusca*). The procedure for expiating *prodigia* was called *procuratio prodigiorum*, "prodigy management," and involved the purification of the city of Rome through such means as sacrifices, banquets for the gods (*lectisternia*), games, and the introduction of new cults and special prayers. Phenomena considered to be prodigies included eclipses of the sun and moon (Plutarch *Alex.* 31), the raining of blood and stones, unusual hail, lightning, thunderclaps in a clear sky (Cassius Dio 37.25.2), comets, meteors, earthquakes, and the behavior of birds, the sight and sound of armies in the sky, the sound of clashing arms and horses (Appian *Bell. civ.* 4.1.4), and the sweating, weeping, or moving of statues (Appian *Bell. civ.* 4.1.4). Livy (died A.D. 12 or 17) observed that people no longer believed in signs of the future and consequently no longer reported prodigies to the senate (43.13.1–2). Plutarch, who certainly believed in divination through portents, used prodigy lists from his sources in composing the *Parallel Lives* but was often very selective in the particular prodigies that he included in his narrative, and he also tended to subordinate them to the dramatic requirements of the narrative (*Sulla* 7; *Marcellus* 28; cf. Livy 27.11; see Brenk, *In Mist Apparelled*, 184–213). Tacitus commented briefly on the role of prodigies in the history of the Roman people during the period following A.D. 69, in *Hist.* 1.3.3 (LCL tr.):

> Besides the manifold misfortunes that befell mankind, there were prodigies in the sky and on the earth, warnings given by thunderbolts, and prophecies of the future, both joyful and gloomy, uncertain and clear. For never was it more fully proved by awful disasters of the Roman people or by indubitable signs that the gods care not for our safety, but for our punishment.

Roman annalists and historians often included lists of prodigies that were sighted each year or in association with critical events in the history of Rome. Some, like Livy and Tacitus, thought them superstitious but recorded them anyway (F. B. Krauss, *Interpretation*, 29). Prodigies and prodigy lists occur with such frequency in Roman histories and biographies that they should be regarded as a literary form that plays a specific function in the larger literary genres within which they are embedded (references to prodigy lists in classical literature are found in K. Berger, *ANRW* II, 23/2:1443 n. 55). In times of great social and political stress and anxiety, the number of such prodigies sighted and reported increased enormously (Günther, *Klio* 42 [1964] 209–97). Lucan compiled a list of prodigies that reportedly occurred when Caesar crossed the Rubicon in 49 B.C. (1.522–83). Vergil assembled a list of prodigies that were sighted in 44 B.C., the year of Caesar's death (*Georg.* 1.466–97); many are similar to those reported by Josephus (*J.W.* 4.289–300). Livy complained that in his day *prodigia* were lacking in official records and in histories (43.13.1), yet Julius Obsequens compiled *Prodigiorum liber*, a collection of prodigies, probably from Livy *Annals* 137. Livy gives lists of prodigies for the years 194 B.C. (34.45.6–8), 193 B.C. (35.9.2–5), 192 B.C. (35.21.2–6), 191 B.C. (36.37), 190 B.C. (37.3.1–6), etc. Many prodigies were reported during the conflict between Otho and Vitellius in A.D. 68, concerning which Tacitus observed (*Hist.* 1.86; LCL tr.), "many other things had happened which in barbarous ages used to be noticed even during peace, but which now are only heard of in seasons of terror" (see Plutarch *Otho* 4.5; Suetonius *Vesp.* 5.7; on the problem of placing the overflowing of the Tiber during the reign of Otho, see Chilver, *Tacitus*, 154). Tacitus, who narrated the reigns of Tiberius, Claudius, and Nero, reports very few prodigies during the reigns of Tiberius and Claudius. During the reign of Nero, however, in *Annals* 11–16, the number of such prodigies increased noticeably (Liebeschuetz, *Roman Religion*, 155–66), though the reasons for this are disputed (Syme, *Tacitus* 1:312; R. H. Martin, *Tacitus*, 257 n. 29). The first list occurs in A.D. 51 (*Annals* 12.43), a second in A.D. 54 (12.64), a third in A.D. 59 (*Annals* 14.12), and a fourth at the close of A.D. 64 (15.47).

Biographers often inserted lists of prodigies that anticipated the births and deaths of great public figures such as Julius Caesar (Suetonius *Jul.* 81.1–3), Augustus (birth: Suetonius *Aug.* 94.1–4; death: Cassius Dio 56.29.2–6; 56.45.2), Caligula (Suetonius *Cal.* 57.1–4), Vespasian (Suetonius *Vesp.* 23.4), and Otho (Tacitus *Hist.* 2.50). Prodigies were also part of imperial propaganda signifying divine approval for a new ruler, e.g., Vespasian (Tacitus *Hist.* 2.78; Suetonius *Vesp.* 5; Cassius Dio 66.1; see Chilver, *Tacitus,* 237).

While the sighting, interpretation, and expiation of prodigies were prominent features of ancient Etruscan and Roman religion, phenomena analogous to prodigies were not unknown in ancient Judaism, though there was no formal attempt made to expiate them (this according to Tacitus *Hist.* 5.13). Early Jewish literature reflects the formal adaptation of some of the more common Roman prodigies into literary contexts. These include the sight of a sword or swords in the sky (*Sib. Or.* 3.798; Jos. *J.W.* 6.288; Lactantius *Div. Inst.* 7.19 [Oracle of Hystaspes]) and armies clashing in the sky (*Sib. Or.* 3.805; 2 Macc 5:2; Jos. *J.W.* 6.288; Tacitus *Hist.* 5.13; Pliny *Hist. nat.* 2.58.148).

Prodigies, then, tend to be presented as lists of unnatural events that require a diagnosis and a cure. Philo suggests that the sun and moon were created not only to give light but also to serve as σημεῖα μελλόντων, "signs of future events" (*Op.* 58–58; *Spec. Leg.* 1.92). Occasionally, apocalyptic literature presents lists of unnatural occurrences in connection with such events as the eschatological day of judgment (*2 Apoc. Bar.* 27:1–13; 4 Ezra 4:52–5:13; 6:20–24; see K. Berger, *ANRW* II, 23/2:1455–59), though often single signs are mentioned (*Sib. Or.* 2.35; 3.334, 457; 4.61; 10.55). 4 Ezra 5:4–13, for example, contains a list of signs that combines the features of cosmic upheaval with the unnatural phenomena characteristic of prodigy lists. The Jewish historian Flavius Josephus described, in the manner of Roman historians of his day (he was, after all, addressing a primarily Roman audience), a number of unusual signs that he understood as divine warnings of the imminent destruction of the Jewish temple in Jerusalem, including a comet that lasted a year, a light that shown around the altar at midnight, a cow intended for sacrifice that gave birth to a lamb, a very heavy gate of the temple court that opened of its own accord, an appearance of chariots and armed soldiers in the sky, and a voice that was heard to say "We are departing from here" (*J.W.* 6.289–300). Tacitus also described many of these events, which he considered "prodigies" (*prodigia*), and observed that the Jews were opposed to averting these warnings by sacrifices or vows, understanding them to be positive rather than negative signs (*Hist.* 5.13).

Christian authors like Lactantius could also describe the signs of the end using the language of prodigies (*Epitome* 71; tr. Blakeney, *Epitome*):

> To these plagues will be added also miraculous signs from heaven [*prodigia de coelo*], that everything may combine to increase human alarm [*hominibus ad timorem*]. Comets will frequently be seen. The sun will be darkened with perpetual gloom; the moon will be dyed in blood, nor will it renew its lost light; all the stars will fall, nor will the seasons observe their proper course, for winter and summer will be confounded [cf. *1 Enoch* 80:2–8]. Year and month and day will be shortened. That this is the old age of the world, and its declension, has been foretold by Trismegistus.

While the plagues of Exodus were afflicted on the Egyptians by God through Moses, the plagues of Revelation are like prodigies in that they do not occur through human agency but are seen as signs of divine anger.

The plagues of Revelation are restricted to certain categories of phenoma: (1) heavenly phenomena: (a) thunder and lightning (8:5; 16:18), (b) hail and fire mixed with blood (8:7), (c) comets falling to the earth (6:13; 8:8, 10), (d) darkening of the sun, moon, and stars (6:12–13; 8:12), (e) the moon turning to blood (6:12), and (f) gigantic hailstones (16:20); (2) terrestrial phenomena: (a) earthquakes (8:5; 16:18), (b) the sea turning to blood (8:9; 16:3), (d) rivers and springs turn to blood (16:4), (e) famines (6:6, 8), and (d) wild animals attacking people (6:8).

In contrast to Greco-Roman prodigies, the plagues of Revelation are never called σημεῖα, "signs," a term used of the miraculous deeds performed by the beast from the sea = false prophet (13:13, 14; 19:20) or the lying spirits (16:14). The plagues, however, are not meant to be ends in themselves but are meant to be stern messages of warning from God intended to produce repentance (9:20–21; 16:9), although this is never the result.

15a καὶ οἱ βασιλεῖς τῆς γῆς καὶ οἱ μεγιστᾶνες καὶ οἱ χιλίαρχοι καὶ οἱ πλούσιοι καὶ οἱ ἰσχυροὶ καὶ πᾶς δοῦλος καὶ ἐλεύθερος, "The kings of the earth and the important people and the generals and the wealthy and the powerful and every slave and free person." A very similar sequence of substantives occurs in 19:18:

Rev 6:15	*Rev 19:18*
The *kings* of the earth	The carrion of *kings*
and the important people	
and the *generals*	and the carrion of *generals*
	and the carrion of horses
	and their riders
and the wealthy	
and the *powerful*	and the carrion of the *powerful*
and *every slave*	and the carrion of *all*
and *free* person	*free* and *slave*

On the term χιλίαρχοι, see *Comment* on 19:15. Again in the Similitudes of Enoch (*1 Enoch* 37–71), the stereotypical phrase "the kings and the mighty and the exalted, and those who dwell on the earth" (with minor variations), the counterpart to Rev 6:15a, occurs with relative frequency as a collective way of characterizing the enemies of God (62:1, 9; 67.8). This phrase, when taken together with that found in v 15b, is a complex way of saying "everyone." In *T. Abr.* [Rec. A] 19:7, Death claims that he leads everyone down to Hades, "kings and rulers, rich and poor, slaves and free men." The phrase "the kings of the earth" is a phrase that was taken up into the eschatological vocabulary of early Judaism and early Christianity (Ps 2:1–2 quoted in Acts 4:25–26; Isa 24:21; *Sib. Or.* 3.663; 4 Ezra 15:20). The phrases "mighty kings," "powerful kings," and "the kings and the mighty" occur frequently in the so-called Similitudes of Enoch (*1 Enoch* 38:5; 55:4; 62:1, 3, 6, 9; 63:1, 2, 12; 67:8, 12), and though their historical identification is a matter of dispute, they clearly function as the enemies of God and his people. The same phrase is found in 13:16 and 19:18. This looks like a gloss inserted to democratize those who will be terrified by the imminent day of the wrath of God.

15b ἔκρυψαν ἑαυτοὺς εἰς τὰ σπήλαια καὶ εἰς τὰς πέτρας τῶν ὀρέων, "hid themselves in the caves and in the mountain rocks." This is an allusion to Isa 2:19–21 (cf. Isa 2:10; Ezek 7:16; *Sib. Or.* 3.607). During times of invasion or seige, residents of cities and towns would often flee to the mountainous regions to hide from their enemies (Judg 6:2; 1 Sam 13:16; 14:11; Job 30:6; Ezek 33:27; Jer 13:14; 16:16; 49:30; Jos. *Ant.* 6.99, 116; 12.272–75, 421; 14.429; *J.W.* 1.307; 6.370). This is precisely the advice given to those living in Jerusalem during the time of eschatological stress (Mark 13:14; Matt 24:16; Luke 21:21). In the OT, the major reason for fleeing from the presence of God is to avoid judgment (Gen 19:17; Ps 67:1; Hos 5:3; Zech 14:5).

16ab καὶ λέγουσιν τοῖς ὄρεσιν καὶ ταῖς πέτραις· πέσετε ἐφ' ἡμᾶς καὶ κρύψατε ἡμᾶς ἀπὸ προσώπου τοῦ καθημένου ἐπὶ τοῦ θρόνου, "They said to the mountains and the cliffs, 'Fall on us and hide us from the One who sits on the throne.'" This is an allusion to Hos 10:8b, in which an original couplet (καὶ ἐροῦσιν τοῖς ὄρεσιν Καλύψατε ἡμᾶς, καὶ τοῖς βουνοῖς Πέσατε ἐφ' ἡμᾶς, "and they will say to the mountains, 'Hide us,' and to the hills, 'Fall on us'") is transformed into a single line with the verbs reversed, with "stones" substituted for "hills." Hos 10:6 is also alluded to in the saying of Jesus preserved in Luke 23:30, and there too the order of the verbs is similarly reversed; i.e., the mountains are implored to "fall" (πέσατε) while the hills are implored to "hide" (καλύψατε). While Hosea refers to the judgment that will fall on Samaria when foreign nations capture her, Rev 6:16 refers to the terror felt by pagans when they realize that divine judgment is imminent (cf. Ezek 38:20). The phrase "the One who sits on the throne" is a typical circumlocution for the mention of God used in Revelation. Fekkes *(Isaiah,* 162–63) argues that there is an allusion here to Isa 2:19 (clearly alluded to in 2 Thess 1:9), which, like Rev 6:16, consists of a parallel couplet:

Rev 6:16	*LXX Isaiah 2:19*
ἀπὸ προσώπου from the presence of	ἀπὸ προσώπου from the presence of
τοῦ καθημένου ἐπὶ τοῦ θρόνου the One seated on the throne	τοῦ φόβου κυρίου the fear of the Lord
καὶ ἀπὸ τῆς ὀργῆς and from the wrath	καὶ ἀπὸ τῆς δόξης and from the glory
τοῦ ἀρνίου. of the Lamb.	τῆς ἰσχύος αὐτοῦ. of his might.

The supposed parallelism, however, is not at all striking, particularly since only the phrase ἀπὸ προσώπου, "from the presence of," links the two passages.

16c καὶ ἀπὸ τῆς ὀργῆς τοῦ ἀρνίου, "and from the wrath of the Lamb." This phrase is probably a redactional addition to the text, since the role of the Lamb as judge is rare in Revelation, the pronoun αὐτοῦ in v 7a clearly refers to God (see references to the wrath of God in 11:18; 14:10; 16:19; 19:15), and the entire phrase in v 17a can be read as a continuation of v 16c (see Müller, *Messias,* 166). The role of the Messiah in Judaism sometimes includes the execution of eschatological judgment as the agent of God *(Pss. Sol.* 17:21–25, 35 [cf. Rev 19:15, 21]; 4 Ezra 13:8–11, 37–38; 12:32–33), particularly in the Similitudes of Enoch, where he is called "the Chosen One," "the Messiah," and "the Son of man" (*1 Enoch* 46:4–6; 49:4; 52:9; 55:4). This judicial role is clearly depicted in *1 Enoch* 69:27 (trs. Knibb, *Enoch* 2:164):

> And he sat on the throne of his glory
> and the whole judgment was given to the Son of man.
> And he will cause the sinners to pass away
> and be destroyed from the face of the earth.

In early Christianity, Christ is frequently assigned the role of eschatological judge (John 5:22, 27; Acts 10:42; 17:31; Rom 2:16; 2 Cor 5:10; 2 Thess 2:9; 2 Tim 4:1; *Barn.* 15:5).

17a ὅτι ἦλθεν ἡ ἡμέρα ἡ μεγάλη τῆς ὀργῆς αὐτοῦ, "because the great day of his wrath has come." The article used with ἡμέρα, "day," and with the restrictive attributive adjective μεγάλη, "great," indicates that the author is referring to a very specific day, one that is well known to the readers, namely, the Day of the Lord, i.e., a climactic eschatological event set in the indefinite future when God will judge the world. A parallel phrase occurs in Rev 16:14, τῆς ἡμέρας τῆς μεγάλης τοῦ θεοῦ τοῦ παντοκράτορος, "the great day of God the Almighty." The pronoun αὐτοῦ, "his," in its present context (see *Note* 6:17.a.), refers to the Lamb, indicating the Christian tendency to place Christ in a central role in the inauguration of the eschaton. In *Barn.* 15:5, after interpreting the six creative days as a period of 6,000 years, the seventh day of rest is interpreted to mean "when his Son comes he will destroy the time of the wicked one, and will judge the godless, and will change the sun and the moon and the stars, and then he will truly rest on the seventh day." This is a time of judgment presided over by the Son (as in Rev 6:17), and it also refers to changes in the heavenly bodies, reflected in Rev 6:12–13. Both the author of Barnabas and the author of Revelation are dependent here upon an earlier Christian tradition. This phrase therefore corresponds to such phrases as "the day of the Lord [=Jesus]" (1 Cor 5:5; 1 Thess 5:2; 2 Thess 2:2; 2 Pet 3:10); "the day of [our] Lord Jesus" (1 Cor 1:8; 2 Cor 1:14; Phil 1:6), or "the day of Christ" (Phil 1:10; 2:16). In Rev 6:14, this eschatological event is referred to as ἡ ἡμέρα, "*the* day," in the phrase "the great Day of God" (see 2 Pet 3:12). Similar ambivalence regarding the role of God or Christ in the last judgment is found in Paul, who can speak of "the judgment seat of God" in Rom 14:10 but "the judgment seat of Christ" in 2 Cor 5:10 (see Kreitzer, *Eschatology,* 112–28). Occasionally, the phrase "day of judgment" occurs in the NT (2 Pet 3:7; 1 John 4:17), while "the day of God" occurs only in 2 Pet 3:12.

The specific phrase "*the great day* [Hebrew יוֹם־יְהוָה הַגָּדוֹל *yôm YHWH haggādôl;* Greek ἡ ἡμέρα κυρίου ἡ μεγάλη] of the Lord" is found only in Zeph 1:14, though similar phrases occur in Joel 2:11, 31; Mal 4:5. In *Apoc. Adam* 13:3; 37:5, the phrase "that great day" (ἡ ἡμέρα ἐκείνη ἡ μεγάλη) refers to the day of resurrection and judgment. In *1 Enoch* 10:6 the phrase "the great day of judgment" occurs (see 104:5, "on the day of great judgment"); see the corresponding phrase in Aramaic on an incantation bowl: ליומא רבה דדינא *lywm' rbh ddyn',* "for the great day of judgment" (Naveh-Shaked, *Amulets,* bowl 13, line 14). This is one of the ways in which the prophetic conception of the Day of the Lord was expressed (see Cerny, *Day of Yahweh;* Rowley, *Faith,* 177–201; M. Weiss, *HUCA* 37 [1966] 29–60). Hebrew idiom used the term "day" for particularly important historical events (Isa 9:4[MT 9:3]; Ezek 34:12; Hos 1:11[MT 2:2]; Obad 12–14; see E. Jenni, *IDB* 4:643–44). The OT prophets used the phrase "Day of the Lord" (and parallel phrases) in a pejorative way for the impending judgment of Israel (Isa 13:6, 9; Ezek 13:5; Joel 1:15; 2:1, 11; 3:4; 4:14; Amos 5:18–20; 6:3; 9:10; Obad 15; Zeph 1:14–18; Mal 3:23), as well as the judgment of other nations (Ezek 30:1–9; Obad 15). While the term occasionally refers to events of the past (Lam 1–2; Isa 22:1–14; Jer 46:2–12; Ezek 13:1–9; Everson, *JBL* 93 [1974] 331–37), more frequently it refers to a future event (Isa 2:12–17; 34:1–17; 61:1–3; Ezek 30:1–9; Amos 5:18–20; Obad 15:15–21; Zech 14:1–21; Mal 3:13–24; see Everson, *JBL* 93 [1974] 331). Even though the concept of the Day of the Lord was drawn into Israelite and early Jewish eschatology when the *final* activity of God was in view, the phrase often refers to expected *historical* events and can be defined as a prophetic interpretation of momentous events in the past, present, or future (Everson, *JBL* 93 [1974] 93). According to Lam 1:21, the overthrow of Jerusalem was a Day of Yahweh (*TDNT* 2:944). Using a phrase very similar to "the great day of their wrath" in Rev 6:17, Ezek 7:19 speaks of "the day of the wrath of the Lord" (cf. Zeph 2:2–3; *Jub.* 24:30 ["the day of the wrath of judgment"]; cf. 36:10). Jer 46:10 states that "That day is the day of the Lord God of hosts, a day of vengeance to avenge himself on his foes [i.e., Egypt]." Jeremiah speaks of "that time" or "those days" rather than of the "Day of Yahweh" (Jer 3:16–18; 4:11; 5:18; 8:1; 31:1, 29). After the fall of Jerusalem in 586 B.C., prophecies of the Day of the Lord emphasize restoration, deliverance, and ultimate salvation (Ezek 33:21–22; Zech 12:1–9; see *TDNT* 2:945).

The phrase "the Day of the Lord" occurs rarely in early Jewish apocrypha and pseudepigrapha: (1) "the great day of the Lord" (*2 Enoch* 18:6 [Rec. J]); (2) "the day of the judgment of the Lord [ἡμέρα κρίσεως κυρίου]" (*Pss. Sol.* 15:12); (3) "the Day of the Wrath of Yahweh" ([יום א]ף יהוה [*ywm ʾ*]*p YHWH;* 1QpZeph 4; the lemma quotes Zeph 2:2b); (4) "the Day of the Lord" (*Apoc. Zeph.* 12:7). However, many other equivalent phrases occur: In *2 Apoc. Bar.* 48:47, in addressing the Lord, Baruch says "your Law which they transgressed will repay them on *your day,*" and in 49:2 he asks the Mighty One, "In which shape will the living live in *your day*" (tr. Klijn in Charlesworth, *OTP* 1:637). *2 Apoc. Bar.* 55:6 speaks of "the day of the Mighty One" (tr. Klijn in Charlesworth, *OTP* 1:640). A number of nearly synonymous terms are found: (1) ἡ ἡμέρα τῆς κρίσεως, "day of judgment," which refers to the final eschatological judgment and occurs more frequently than any other term (in the Dead Sea Scrolls, the phrase יום המשפט *ywm hmšpṭ* occasionally occurs [1QpHab 12:14; 13:2; 1QpMic 10:6–7]; Jdt 16:17; *Frag. Jub.* 3:9; 10:7 [Denis, *Fragmenta,* 77, 86]; *Jub.* 24:30; *Apoc. Adam* 12:2; 26:4; *T. Levi* 1:1; *1 Enoch* 10:12; 16:1; 19:1; 22:4, 13; 27:3, 4; 100:4; 104:5; cf. 97:3; 98:8; 4 Ezra 7:38 [*die iudicii*], 102, 104, 113; 12:34; *Gk. Apoc. Ezra* 2:27, 29; *3 Apoc. Bar.* 1:7; cf. "day of great judgment" or "the great day of judgment" in *1 Enoch* 10:6; 19:1; 22:11; 84:4; 94:9; 98:10; 99:15; Matt 10:15; 11:22, 24; 12:36; 2 Pet 2:9; 3:7; 1 John 4:17; "the day of his judgment," *Gk. Apoc. Ezra* 7:11); (2) ἡ ἡμέρα τῆς ἀναστάσεως, "the day of resurrection" (*Apoc. Adam* 10.2; 43.2); (3) αἱ ἡμέραι τῆς θλίψεως, "the days of tribulation" (*1 Enoch* 103:9; 4 Ezra 16:74; *T. Levi* 3:5); (4) ἡ ἡμέρα ἐκείνη, "that day" (*1 Enoch* 106:1; *T. Zeb.* 4:7; *Sib. Or.* 3.55 [ἦμαρ ἐκεῖνο], 206; 5.243, 248, 351); (5) ἡ ἡμέρα ἐκείνη ἡ μεγάλη, "that great day" (*Gk. Apoc. Ezra* 3:3); and (6) "those days" (ἤμασι κείνοις: *Sib. Or.* 3.186, 380, 675, 714, 779). The view that "the day of judgment" represents a different eschatological concept from "the Day of the Lord" (G. S. Holland, *The Tradition That You Received from Us: 2 Thessalonians in the Pauline Tradition,* HUT 24 [Tübingen: Mohr, 1988] 97) is a view that assumes greater precision in the use of these and other terms in early Judaism than the extremely varied terminological evidence allows (n.b. how the two phrases are combined in *Pss. Sol.* 15:12, "the day of the Lord's judgment"). The phrase ἡμέρα ἀναγκῆς, "day of distress," occurs in *Gk. 1 Enoch* 1:1. The expectation of the Day of the Lord is also a central feature of Pauline eschatology (Kreitzer, *Eschatology,* 112–28). Paul speaks of a "day of wrath" (Rom 2:5) and "on a day when God will judge" (Rom 2:16). In John, where future eschatology is only of marginal concern to the author, the phrase "the last day" occurs several times as the time of resurrection and judgment (6:39–40, 44, 54; 11:24; 12:48). In the Apostolic Fathers, there are scarcely any references to the last "day," though the phrase "the day of judgment" occurs in *2 Clem.* 16:3; 17:6. The phrase ἡ ἡμέρα is used for *the* day on which Christ will appear (*Barn.* 7:9). The phrase "the last days" is used as a term for the inauguration of eschatological events in *Did.* 16:3 (this expression is also widespread in early Judaism; see *1 Enoch* 89:55, 66, 67; *Pss. Sol.* 17:44; 18:6; 4 Ezra 10:59; 14:22) but is also used more generally for the period in which the author lives, which is near the end (*Barn.* 4:9). In *Barn.* 12:9 the phrase "in the last days" is used for the time when the Son of God will destroy Amalek.

This verse makes it clear that the plagues unleashed by the opening of the first six seals are only preliminary in nature, indicating that the terrible events of the great day of wrath are about to begin.

17b καὶ τίς δύναται σταθῆναι, "and who is able to withstand it?" The implied answer to this desperate question is obvious: no one can withstand the day of divine wrath. Variations on the rhetorical question "Who is able to stand before the Lord?" uttered in a context of anticipated judgment occur occasionally in the OT (1 Sam 6:20; 2 Chr 20:6; Job 41:10; Ps 76:7; Prov 27:4; Jer 49:19; 50:44; Nah 1:6; Mal 3:2). It is likely that this rhetorical question provides the main link between the narrative of the opening of the first six seals and the following section on the sealing of the 144,000 in 7:1–17. The scenario of people cowering before the wrath of God has a parallel in *Sib. Or.* 3.556–61 (tr. J. Collins in Charlesworth, *OTP* 1:374):

> But when the wrath of the great God comes upon you,
> then indeed you will recognize the face of the great God.
> All the souls of men will groan mightily and
> stretch out their hands straight to broad heaven
> and begin to call on the great king as protector
> and seek who will be a deliverer from great wrath.

Explanation

The breaking of each of the seven seals of the scroll by the Lamb becomes the framework for narrating a series of eschatological plagues from 6:1 to 8:1. The constituent visions introduced by the breaking of the seals are arranged in a 4 + 3 pattern, with the first four seals constituting a group, in which each of the four cherubim serves to introduce yet another plague (vv 1–8), and the last three also constituting a group (vv 9–17; 8:1). A similar 4 + 3 structure also characterizes the trumpet visions (8:2–9:21; 11:15–18). Although the breaking of each of the first six seals does not open the entire scroll, the events accompanying the breaking of each seal (with the exception of the fifth) belong to traditional Jewish and early Christian conceptions of the tribulations that will introduce the end (see Mark 13:3–8, 24–27 and par.), though the scenario stops just short of the great day of wrath itself (vv 16–17). The opening of the first four seals sends out four horsemen (imagery adapted from Zech 1:8–11; 6:1–8), each inflicting a particular kind of judgment on humanity: irresistible conquest, war and bloodshed, famine, disease, and death. With the opening of the fifth seal, John sees the souls of martyrs beneath the altar (symbolizing nearness to God), crying out for vengeance, who are told to wait until their number is completed. They are given white robes, symbolizing salvation and immortality (vv 9–11). The notion that a predestined number of martyrs must die before God will avenge their deaths is found in both early Judaism and early Christianity. Their question "How long?" reflects the common perception that too long a period often intervenes between the commission of an outrage and its just recompense. While some regard all these martyrs as pre-Christian, it is more likely that they should be identified with Christian martyrs such as those killed under Nero in A.D. 64.

The opening of the sixth seal is followed by a series of cosmic disturbances. First there is a great earthquake (the entire province of Asia was prone to earthquakes; in the great earthquake of A.D. 17 alone, twelve cities were destroyed). This is followed by a solar eclipse, the moon becomes the color of blood, stars fall to earth (these aspects of cosmic upheaval have parallels in Mark 13:24; Matt. 24:29), the sky vanishes, and every mountain and island is moved. These terrible catastrophes, many of which were part of the lore of ancient prodigies, i.e., unusual occurrences in the world of nature that signal either the displeasure or approval of the gods, move the powerful people of the world to fear the judgment of God and the Lamb. For, they say, "Who can stand before the day of his wrath?" (v 17). This question is answered in Rev 7.

3. The Protective Sealing of the 144,000 (7:1–17)

Bibliography

Augrain, C. "La vision de la foule innombrable, Ap 7,9.14b–17." *AsSeign* 25 (1969) 39–44. **Bauckham, R.** "The Book of Revelation as a Christian War Scroll." *Neot* 22 (1988) 17–40 (= "The Apocalypse as a Christian War Scroll," in R. Bauckham, *Climax*, 210–37). ———. "The List of the Tribes in Revelation 7 Again." *JSNT* 42 (1991) 99–115. **Beagley, A. J.** *The "Sitz im Leben" of the Apocalypse with Particular Reference to the Role of the Church's Enemies.* BZNW 50. Berlin; New York: de Gruyter, 1987. **Bousset, W.** *The Antichrist Legend.* Trans. A. H. Keane. London: Hutchinson, 1896. **Brox, N.** *Der Hirt des Hermas.* KAV 7. Göttingen: Vandenhoeck & Ruprecht, 1991. **Comblin, J.** "La liturgie de la nouvelle Jérusalem." *ETL* 29 (1953) 5–40. ———. "Le reasemblement du peuple de Dieu: Ap 7, 2–4. 9–14." *AsSeign* 66 (1973) 42–49. **Corsini, E.** *The Apocalypse: The Perennial Revelation of Jesus Christ.* GNS 5. Wilmington, DE: Glazier, 1983. **Dölger, F. J.** *Sphragis: Eine altchristliche Taufbezeichnung in ihrer Beziehungen zur profanen und religiösen Kultur des Altertums.* Paderborn: Schöning, 1911. **Draper, J. A.** "The

Heavenly Feast of Tabernacles: Revelation 7:1–17." *JSNT* 19 (1985) 133–47. **Feuillet, A.** "Les 144,000 Israélites marqués d'un sceau." *NovT* 9 (1967) 191–224. **Finegan, J.** *The Archaeology of the New Testament.* Princeton: Princeton UP, 1969. **Geyser, A.** "The Twelve Tribes in Revelation: Judean and Judeo-Christian Apocalypticism." *NTS* 28 (1982) 388–99. **Goranson, S.** "The Exclusion of Ephraim in Rev. 7:4–8 and Essene Polemic against Pharisees." *DSD* 2 (1995) 80–85. **Greenup, A. W.** *Sukkah, Mishna and Tosefta.* London: SPCK, 1925. **Heinemann, J.** "The Messiah of Ephraim and the Premature Exodus of the Tribe of Ephraim." *HTR* 68 (1975) 1–15. **Heitmüller, W.** "ΣΦΡΑΓΙΣ." In *Neutestamentliche Studien.* FS G. Heinrici, ed. A. Deissmann and H. Windisch. Leipzig: Hinrichs, 1914. 40–59. **Hill, C. E.** "Antichrist from the Tribe of Dan." *JTS* 46 (1995) 99–117. **Klauser, T.** "Taufet in lebendigem Wasser! Zum religions- und kulturgeschichtlichen Verständnis von Didache 7:1–3." In *Pisciculi: Studien zur Religion und Kultur des Altertums Franz Joseph Dölger dargeboten.* Münster: Aschendorff, 1939. 157–64. **Koester, C. R.** *The Dwelling of God: The Tabernacle in the Old Testament, Intertestamental Jewish Literature, and the New Testament.* CBQMS 22. Washington, DC: Catholic Biblical Association, 1989. **Lampe G. W. H.** *The Seal of the Spirit: A Study in the Doctrine of Baptism and Confirmation in the New Testament and the Fathers.* 2nd ed. London: SPCK, 1967. **McCarthy, D. J.** "The Symbolism of Blood and Sacrifice." *JBL* 88 (1969) 166–76. **McKelvey, R. J.** *The New Temple: The Church in the New Testament.* Oxford: Clarendon, 1969. **MacKenzie, R. K.** *The Author of the Apocalypse: A Review of the Prevailing Hypothesis of Jewish-Christian Authorship.* Lewiston, NY: Mellen Biblical, 1997. **Norelli, E.** "La sabbia e le stelle: Gen 13,16; 15,5; 22,17 nell' esegesi cristiana dei prima tre secoli." *Aug* 22 (1982) 285–312. **O'Hagen, A. P.** "The Great Tribulation to Come in the Pastor of Hermas." *StudP* 6 [= TU 79] (1961) 305–11. **Page, D.** *Folktales in Homer's Odyssey.* Cambridge: Harvard UP, 1973. **Pietrantonio, R.** "El Mesías Asesinado: El Mesías ben Efraim en el Evangelio de Juan." *RevistB* 44 (1982) 1–64. **Pines, S.** "Notes on the Twelve Tribes in Qumran, Early Christianity and Jewish Tradition." In *Messiah and Christos: Studies in the Jewish Origins of Christianity,* ed. I. Gruenwald, S. Shaked, and G. G. Stroumsa. Tübingen: Mohr-Siebeck, 1992. 151–54. **Sanderson, G. V.** "In Defence of Dan." *Scripture* 3/4 (1948) 114–15. **Schwartz, D. R.** "To Join Oneself to the House of Judah (Damascus Document IV, 11)." *RevQ* 10 (1981) 435–46. **Smith, C. R.** "The Portrayal of the Church as the New Israel in the Names and Order of the Tribes in Revelation 7.5–8." *JSNT* 39 (1990) 111–18. ———. "The Tribes of Revelation 7 and the Literary Competence of John the Seer." *JETS* 38 (1995) 213–18. **Taeger, J.-W.** *Johannesapokalypse und johanneischer Kreis: Versuch einer traditionsgeschichtlichen Ortsbestimmung am Paradigma der Lebenswasser-Thematik.* BZNW 51. Berlin; New York: de Gruyter, 1989. **Trudinger, P.** "The Apocalypse and the Palestinian Targum." *BTB* 16 (1986) 78–79. **Ulfgard, H.** *Feast and Future: Revelation 7:9–17 and the Feast of Tabernacles.* Lund: Almqvist & Wiksell, 1989. **Vitringa, C.** *Anakrisis Apokalypsios Joannis apostoli.* Amsterdam: Strickii, 1719. **Wallert, I.** *Die Palmen im alten Ägypten: Eine Untersuchung ihrer praktischen, symbolischen und religiösen Bedeutung.* Berlin: Hessling, 1962. **Westermann, C.** *Die Verheißung an die Väter: Studien zur Vätergeschichte.* FRLANT 116. Göttingen: Vandenhoeck & Ruprecht, 1976. **Winkle, R. E.** "Another Look at the List of Tribes in Revelation 7." *AUSS* 27 (1989) 53–67. **Ysebaert, J.** *Greek Baptismal Terminology: Its Origins and Early Development.* Nijmegen: Dekker & Van de Vegt, 1962.

Translation

1 [a]*After this I saw* [b]*four* [c] *angels standing at the four* [d] *quarters of the earth, restraining*
the four [e] [f]*winds of the earth* [f] *so that no* [g]*wind* [h]*might blow* [h] *on* [i] *the earth, nor on the sea,*
[j]*nor on any tree.*[j] 2 *Then I saw another angel ascending from the east* [a] *with the* [b] *signet of*
the living God. [c]*He* [d]*cried out* [d] *with a booming voice to* [e]*the four angels* [e] *who were*
empowered [f] [g]*to harm* [g] *the earth and the sea:* 3 [a] *"Do* [b]*not harm the earth or the sea or* [b] *the*
trees [c]*until* [d] *we* [e] *mark with the signet* [c] *the servants of our God on their foreheads."* 4 [a]*I*

then heard the number of those who were [b]marked;[a] 144,000[c] were marked[d] from every tribe of the sons of Israel.

5 *From the tribe of Judah, 12,000 were marked.*
From the tribe of Reuben, 12,000.
From the tribe of Gad,[a] 12,000.
6 *[a]From the tribe of Asher, 12,000.[a]*
From the tribe of Naphtali, 12,000.
From the tribe of Manasseh, 12,000.
7 *[a]From the tribe of Simeon, 12,000.[a]*
From the tribe of Levi, 12,000.
From the tribe of Issachar, 12,000.
8 *From the tribe of Zebulon, 12,000.*
From the tribe of Joseph, 12,000.
From the tribe of Benjamin, 12,000 [a]were marked.[a]

9 *After this I looked, [a]and behold,[a] a huge[b] crowd[c] which[d] no one could even begin to*
number,[e] from [f]every nation[f] and tribe and people and language group, standing[g] before
the throne and before the Lamb, dressed[h] in [i]white robes.[i] They had [j]palm fronds[j] in their
hands. 10 *They[a] cried[b] with a loud voice, [c]"Victory belongs to our God[c] who sits upon [d]the*
throne[d] and to the Lamb."[e] 11 *All[a] the angels, who had been standing[b] around the throne,*
and the elders and the four cherubim fell prostrate before the throne and worshiped[c] God,
12 *saying, "Amen, praise[a] and glory and wisdom and thanksgiving and honor and power*
and might to our God for ever and ever; amen."[b] 13 *[a]One[b] of[c] the elders said[d] to me, "Who*
are these people dressed in white robes and where did they come from?" 14 *I[a] replied[b] to him,*
"Sir,[c] you know." He then responded to me, "These are those [d]who came[d] from the[e] great
tribulation. They[f] washed[g] their robes and made them[h] white by the blood of the Lamb.
15 *For this reason they are before the throne of God and serve him day and night in his temple.*
The one who sits on [a]the throne[a] will shelter[b] them. 16 *They will neither hunger any longer*
nor thirst any longer, neither[a] will the sun fall on them nor any[b] scorching heat, 17 *because*
the Lamb [a]in the midst of[a] the throne will shepherd[b] them and guide them to [c]the springs
of life.[c] And God will wipe away every tear from[d] their eyes."

Notes

1.a. Variants: (1) omit καί before μετὰ τοῦτο] A C fam 1006[1006 1841] fam 1611[1854] Oecumenius[2053] 2351; WHort; B. Weiss (*Johannes-Apokalypse,* 175); Charles (2:278); Merk, *NT;* Nestle-Aland[27]; UBSGNT[4]. (2) καί before μετὰ τοῦτο] ℵ 025 046 Andr f[2023] i[2042] 1 94 Byzantine syr arm eth. (3) καὶ μετὰ ταῦτα] Andreas.

1.b. The phrase τέσσαρας ἀγγέλους is anarthrous because this particular team of angels is first mentioned here and is apparently unknown to the readers. The second mention of these angels in v 2 is expectedly arthrous, with the anaphoric use of the definite article.

1.c. Variants: (1) τέσσαρες] A 025 fam 1611[2329] Byz 17[93]. (2) τέσσαρας] C Oecumenius[2053] Andreas Byzantine. The acc. ending -ες (a common ending in Doric dialects) appears to be considerably older than -ας in τέσσαρες, which is the only early cardinal number that ever had a separate acc. form (Moulton, *Grammar,* 243–44), and so it is likely that the autograph of Revelation exhibited the form τέσσαρες (Moulton, *Grammar,* 36). The problem in MSS is that since numerals are frequently written out from numerical letters, the original form of the numerals cannot always be determined with certainty.

1.d. Variant: τέσσαρας] A C Oecumenius[2053] Andreas Byzantine. The inconsistency of A, which reads τέσσαρες in 7:1.c. and 7:1.e. is striking, suggesting the inconsistent transposition of numerical letters to cardinal numbers.

1.e. Variant: τέσσαρας] C Oecumenius[2053] Andreas Byzantine. (2) τέσσαρες] A Byz 17[93].

1.f-f. Variant: ἀνέμους τῆς γῆς] A; B. Weiss (*Johannes-Apokalypse,* 175; follows A without comment).

1.g. Variant: ὁ before ἄνεμος] C fam 1611$^{1611\ 2329\ 1854}$ Oecumenius^{2053} 2351 Andr f$^{2056\ 2073}$ h^{2302} l 2019.

1.h-h. Variants: (1) πνέῃ] *lectio originalis.* (2) πνεύσῃ] ℵ fam 1006^{1841} fam 1611$^{1854\ 2344}$ Andr g 1773. (3) γένηται] fam 1611^{2329}.

1.i. Variant: omit ἐπὶ τῆς γῆς] A.

1.j-j. Variants: (1) μήτε ἐπὶ πᾶν δένδρον] ℵ fam 1611$^{1854\ 2344}$ Andreas syr^{ph}; Tischendorf, *NT Graece;* WHort; Nestle-Aland^{27}; UBSGNT^{4}. (2) μήτε ἐπί τι δένδρον] C 046 fam 1006$^{1006\ 1841}$ Oecumenius^{2053} 2351 Byzantine cop^{sa} vg Primasius; B. Weiss (*Johannes-Apokalypse,* 125). (3) μήτε ἐπὶ δένδρου] A fam 1611^{2329}. Reading (2) is unlikely (and is probably a correction) since the author of Revelation avoids using the adjectival τις; it is used only substantively and is always preceded by εἰ or ἐάν (Mussies, *Morphology,* 183). The phrase μήτε ἐπὶ πᾶν δένδρον, "nor on any tree," is a negative idiom meaning "no tree" (i.e., μήτε πᾶς is used in place of μηδέν) and is frequently judged to be a Semitism derived from the Heb. idiom כל ... לא *lo*ʾ... *col,* "no/not... all/any" (BDR § 302; Moulton-Howard, *Accidence,* 433–34); see Rev 7:16; 9:4; 21:27. A similar Heb. idiom, לא ... כל *col*... *lo*ʾ = πᾶς ... οὐ/μή, occurs in Rev 18:22; 22:3. However, Ljungvik (*Syntax,* 18–23) provides many examples that show that this idiom was at home in late Hellenistic popular Gk.

2.a. The prep. phrase ἀπὸ ἀνατολῆς ἡλίου, lit. "from the rising of the sun," simply means "east," with ἡλίου as a subjective gen. Variants: (1) ἀνατολῆς] ℵ C 025 046. (2) ἀνατολῶν] A 1773 Andr l^{1778corr} Byz 2$^{18\ 2039\ 2076\ 2258}$ Byz 17^{2436} cop$^{sa\ bo}$ syr^{ph}; B. Weiss (*Johannes-Apokalypse,* 109); WHort^{marg}. Torrey (*Apocalypse,* 92) argues that the Aram. exemplar certainly had the pl.; he cites *Tg. Ezek.* 1:1 and G. H. Dalman, *Grammatik* (1905) 215–16. Weiss argues that variant (1) is an improvement of variant (2), which is derived from the LXX. Certainly the phrases ἀπὸ ἀνατολῶν [ἡλίου] and ἀπὸ ἡλίου ἀνατολῶν occur many times in the LXX, where they are used to translate such Heb. phrases as ממזרח־שמש *mimmizraḥ šameš* or simply ממזרח *mimmizrāḥ* or מקדם *miqqedem* (Gen 11:2; 13:11; Deut 4:41; Josh 1:15; 12:1; 13:5; 19:27, 34; Ps 50:1; Isa 9:12; 11:11; 43:5; 45:6; 46:11; 59:19; Ezek 48:4; Dan 11:44; 3 Macc 4:15; Bar 4:37 [here A reads ἀνατολῆς]). In fact, there is only a single instance in which ἀπό is used with the gen. sing. form ἀνατολῆς (Num 3:38). Yet this passage is very revealing, for while B and others read ἀπὸ ἀνατολῆς, A has corrected it to ἀπὸ ἀνατολῶν. Weiss places an overly high value on A, for in this instance it appears probable that A has corrected ἀπὸ ἀνατολῆς in conformity with Septuagintal usage.

2.b. σφραγῖδα θεοῦ ζῶντος, "the signet of the living God," is anarthrous because it is mentioned here for the first time; the second and only further mention of this noun has the anaphoric article in 9:4.

2.c. The καί that begins this sentence has been left untranslated since it functions as a discourse marker indicating the beginning of a new sentence or clause and has no independent semantic value.

2.d-d. Variants: (1) ἔκραξεν] *lectio originalis.* (2) ἔκραζεν] A 025 Oecumenius^{2053}.

2.e-e. The phrase τοῖς τέσσαρσιν ἀγγέλοις, "to the four angels," is articular because they have already been mentioned in v 1.

2.f. In the phrase οἷς ἐδόθη αὐτοῖς, lit. "to whom was given them," the pronoun αὐτοῖς is resumptive or pleonastic and is considered by many to be a Hebraism, אשר נתן להם *ʾăšer nittan lāhem* (BDR § 297; Turner, *Syntax,* 325; Mussies, *Morphology,* 177), but is also an idiom used occasionally by native Gk. writers (at least twenty-six times in Koine Gk., aside from the LXX and NT). In v 2 this construction is a Semitism since it is *essential* (i.e., it occurs in a dependent relative clause). This construction, called the *pronomen abundans,* occurs nine times in Revelation (3:8; 7:2, 9; 12:6, 14; 13:8, 12; 17:9; 20:8). For a more extensive discussion, see *Note* 3:8.c. and *Introduction,* Section 7: Syntax, III. Pronouns. The text was therefore corrected by some copyists by omitting the "redundant" αὐτοῖς (fam 1611$^{1854\ 2329}$ Andr f i m$^{2037\ 2046}$ n^{2429} Byz 1^{2256} Byz 8$^{177\ 180}$ Andr/Byz 2$^{336\ 337}$ Andr/Byz 3$^{35\ 1732}$ Andr/Byz 4^{2034} it^{gig} Tyc^{2} Beatus).

2.g-g. The aor. inf. ἀδικῆσαι functions as the subject of the verb ἐδόθη (Votaw, *Infinitive,* 12).

3.a. The present masc. sing. ptcp. λέγων, "saying," has been left untranslated because it is a redundant Hebraism that functions to introduce direct discourse.

3.b-b. Variants: (1) μὴ ... μήτε ... μήτε] Andreas. (2) μὴ ... μηδὲ ... μηδέ] ℵ fam 1611^{1854} Andr e^{2057} h 94; Andr/Byz 2b Andr/Byz 3. (3) μὴ ... καὶ ... μήτε] A Andr l 2351; B. Weiss, *Johannes-Apokalypse,* 175 (without comment); WHort^{mg}. In 5:4; 7:1; 9:21; 21:4, οὔτε or μήτε is textually certain, while the same is true of οὔδε in 7:16; 9:14; 12:8; 21:23. The encroachment of οὐτέ on οὐδέ in the early MS history of Revelation makes it difficult to determine the original reading (Schmid, *Studien* 2:225).

3.c-c. The phrase ἄχρι σφραγίσωμεν, "until we seal," is here translated "until we mark with the signet."

3.d. Variants: (1) ἄχρι] *lectio originalis.* (2) ἄχρις οὗ] fam 1611$^{-2050\ -2344}$ 2351 Byzantine. ἄχρι + aor. subjunctive constituted an adverbial temporal clause meaning "until" (see 15:8; 17:17 [*var. lect.*]; 20:3, 5; BAGD, 129).

3.e. The angel is presented as referring to himself in the first-person *pl.* in the verb σφραγίσωμεν with an unexpressed subject; occasionally, pl. verb forms are used to refer to a single person, particularly in the so-called allusive plural (Smyth, *Greek Grammar,* § 1007; BDF § 141) and the pl. of modesty (Smyth, *Greek Grammar,* § 1008). The first-person sing. is attested in arm^{1} and arm^{3}, but in no Gk. or Latin MSS.

4.a-a. Variant: omit] A.

4.b. The pf. substantival ptcp. τῶν ἐσφραγισμένων emphasizes the resulting state of the action of sealing and only implies the anterior occurrence of sealing (see Fanning, *Verbal Aspect,* 416–18).

4.c. Variants: (1) ἑκατὸν τεσσεράκοντα τέσσαρες χιλιάδες, frequently written as ρμδ χιλιάδες] Andreas; WHort; Nestle-Aland^{27}; UBSGNT^{4}. (2) ἑκατὸν καὶ τεσσεράκοντα τέσσαρες χιλιάδες] C fam 1006$^{1006\ 1841}$ Andr f^{2073} h^{2302} l^{-1678} Byzantine. (3) ἑκατὸν τεσσαράκοντα δ' χιλιάδες] A (the δ was added as a correction, so the original number written by the scribe of A was 140,000). (4) ἑκατὸν τεσσαρακοντέσσαρας χιλιάδες] Oecumenius^{2053}. (5) ρκδ χιλιάδες (= 124,000] fam 1611^{2329}. These variants provide a sample of the numerical variations found in some of the more important MSS. Variant (4) represents a contraction in which the -τα of τεσσεράκοντα is elided when combined with τέσσαρας. In the phrase ἑκατὸν τεσσεράκοντα τέσσαρες χιλιάδες, χιλιάδες is a pl. fem. nom. noun, while τέσσαρες, a pl. form that can be masc., fem., or neut., must be fem. ἑκατόν and τεσσεράκοντα, on the other hand, are indeclinable pl. forms, which here modify the fem. pl. form χιλιάδες.

4.d. Variants: (1) ἐσφραγισμένοι] *lectio originalis.* (2) ἐσφραγισμένων] 2351 Andr i Byzantine. (3) ἐσφραγισμένοις] Andr f$^{2031\ 2056}$. (4) omit] 94. The original reading, ἐσφραγισμένοι, "those sealed, marked," a pf. pass. ptcp. (indicating that they were marked in the past and continue to bear that imprint), is both redundant in this context and a solecism, i.e., a nom. of apposition, which should have been an acc. modifying τὸν ἀριθμόν, "the number," but in fact has been attracted to the nom. pl. of χιλιάδες, "thousands," though the latter is a *fem.* noun. For a similar solecism, see 11:4, which links a fem. nom. pl. article with a masc. nom. pl. ptcp.: αἱ . . . ἑστῶτες.

5.a. Variants: (1) Δάν] fam 1611^{1854} Byz 14$^{324\ 456}$ Byz 15$^{42\ 367}$ Andr/Byz 2b^{-582}. (2) *gath*] Beatus Primasius.

6.a-a. Variant: omit ἐκ φυλῆς Ἀσὴρ δώδεκα χιλιάδες] 2351 Andr/Byz 3^{1957} Andr/Byz 4b$^{172\ 2018}$.

7.a-a. Variant: omit] ℵ.

8.a-a. Variants: (1) ἐσφραγισμένοι] *lectio originalis.* (2) ἐσφραγισμένων] fam 1611^{1854} Andr i$^{1685\ 2074}$. (3) ἐσφραγισμέναι] Andr d i^{2042} 94 Byzantine. (4) omit] fam 1611^{2329} Andr c e^{2057} n 2019.

9.a-a. Variants: (1) καὶ ἰδού] *lectio originalis.* (2) omit καὶ ἰδού] A Methodius syr^{ph} cop; B. Weiss, *Johannes-Apokalypse,* 110–11. (3) omit ἰδού] C fam 1611^{1611}. B. Weiss (*Johannes-Apokalypse,* 110–11) argues that καὶ ἰδού cannot simply have been omitted since A reads ὄχλον πολύν. Schmid argues that readings (2) and (3) are either errors or corrections (*Studien* 2:89).

9.b. Variant: omit πολύς] 2351.

9.c. In the phrase εἶδον, καὶ ἰδοὺ ὄχλος πολύς, "I saw, and behold, a huge crowd," ὄχλος πολύς is in the nom., but as the sight that John saw, it should be in the acc. However, John frequently uses the nom. immediately following the particle ἰδού (4:1, 2; 6:2, 5; 14:4; see Mussies, *Morphology,* 326).

9.d. Variant: καί instead of ὅν] A; B. Weiss (*Johannes-Apokalypse,* 176; follows A without comment).

9.e. The pronoun αὐτόν is an example of a resumptive or pleonastic pronoun that redundantly modifies the relative pronoun ὅν, "which," and is often considered a Semitism, i.e., אשר לא יוכל למנתו *ʾăšer loʾ yûkal limnotô.* This particular instance of the *pronomen abundans* is *essential* (i.e., it constitutes a dependent relative clause) and therefore must be considered a Semitism; i.e., it constitutes an elaboration of πολύς and helps to define the antecedent (Bakker, *Pronomen Abundans,* 41). This construction occurs several times in Revelation (see *Note* 7:2.f.). For a more extensive discussion, see *Note* 3:8.c. and *Introduction,* Section 7: Syntax, III. Pronouns. αὐτόν was consequently omitted as redundant by many copyists (046 2020 2058 2329 Andr c d f^{2023} i 94 598 Byzantine).

9.f-f. In the phrase παντὸς ἔθνους, "every nation," ἔθνους is a neut. gen. sing. noun appropriately modified by παντός, which lacks the article and so is distributive (meaning "every") rather than collective (meaning "all"). The three nouns that follow are gen. pls., φυλῶν, λαῶν, and γλωσσῶν, and it is clear that the author intends the reader to extend the distributive sense of παντός to each of these nouns.

9.g. Variants: (1) ἑστῶτες] ℵ A fam 1611^{2344} Andreas. (2) ἑστῶτας (masc. pl. acc. ptcp.)] fam 1006 fam 1611$^{1611\ 1854\ 2329}$ Oecumenius^{2053} 2351 Andr i^{-2074} n^{2429} Byzantine; B. Weiss (*Johannes-Apokalypse,* 176). (3) ἑστώτων] C Andr c l. The adj. ptcp. ἑστῶτες, "standing" (masc. nom. pl. ptcp.), modifies the nom. sing. noun phrase ὄχλος πολύς, "huge crowd," undoubtedly because the author considers ὄχλος a *collective* noun that can be modified by pl. ptcps. and finite verbs. There are several instances in Revelation of the *constructio ad sensum* in which a collective noun is used with a pl. verb form (8:9; 9:18;

13:3–4; 18:4; 19:1 [where ὄχλου πολλοῦ is the antecedent of λεγόντων]); see John 12:12, ὁ ὄχλος πολύς . . . ἀκούσαντες. Further, ἑστῶτες is nom. because the author understands it as congruent in gender and case with ὄχλος πολύς, which is in the nom. case because it follows εἶδον καὶ ἰδού; i.e., εἶδον would normally take an acc., but καὶ ἰδού, which is usually followed by the nom., overrides εἶδον (for other examples of this construction, see 4:1, 2; 6:2, 5, 8; 12:3; 14:1, 14; 19:11). A number of cursives reflect scribal attempts to solve some of the grammatical problems by correcting the text to reading (2). Reading (3) is also a correction that shows obvious assimilation to the preceding string of pl. gens.

9.h. Variants: (1) περιβεβλημένους] ℵ A C Andr c i$^{1685\ 2074}$ l n^{2429} Byzantine. (2) περιβεβλημένοι] ℵ^{1} fam 1611^{1854} Oecumenius^{2053} fam 1611$^{2329\ 2344}$ 2351 Andreas. Variant (1), περιβεβλημένους, "clothed," a pf. pass. acc. pl. ptcp., is in the acc. because the author construes it as the obj. of εἶδον, even though the phrase ἰδοὺ ὄχλος πολύς, "behold, a huge crowd," intervenes, a construction that requires the nom. pl., as the correction in reading (2) attests (see Mussies, *Morphology*, 100; BDF § 136.2; Schmid, *Studien* 2:246).

9.i-i. στολὰς λευκάς, "white robes," is the acc. of the thing used with the pass., with the person in the nom. (Robertson, *Grammar*, 485, 816); cf. 7:13, περιβεβλημένοι τὰς στολὰς τὰς λευκάς, "clothed in white robes"; see 10:1; 11:3; 12:1; 17:4; 18:16; 19:13, but cf. 4:4, περιβεβλημένους ἱματίοις, "clothed with garments."

9.j-j. Variants: (1) φοίνικες] A C Andreas. (2) φοίνικας] ℵ* 2351 Andr f^{2023} i$^{1685\ 2074}$ n Byzantine; Tischendorf, *NT Graece*. Since the preceding ptcp. phrase περιβεβλημένους στολὰς λευκάς is in the acc. because it is apparently dependent on the verb εἶδον in v 9a, reading (2), an acc. pl., is a correction intended to agree with the case of that phrase. Since reading (1) is a *nom.* pl., it is either dependent on καὶ ἰδού, or it begins a new clause (Schmid, *Studien* 2:246). It is important to see the connections between some of the variants discussed above in v 9 (with simply a summary attestation):

(a) ἑστῶτες . . . περιβεβλημένους . . . φοίνικες] A
(b) ἑστώτων . . . περιβεβλημένους . . . φοίνικες] C
(c) ἑστῶτας . . . περιβεβλημένους . . . φοίνικας] Byzantine
(d) ἑστῶτες . . . περιβεβλημένοι . . . φοίνικες] Andreas
(e) ἑστῶτες . . . περιβεβλημένους . . . φοίνικας] ℵ*

10.a. See *Note* 2.c.

10.b. Variants: (1) κράζουσι] A 025 046 Oecumenius^{2053} Andreas Byzantine; WHort. (2) κράζουσιν] ℵ C fam 1611^{1611}; Tischendorf, *NT Graece;* B. Weiss, *Johannes-Apokalypse*, 176; Charles, 2:281; von Soden, *Text;* Nestle-Aland^{27}; UBSGNT^{4}. (3) κράζοντες] 1 cop$^{samss\ bo}$ Andr a^{-2186} d Byzantine TR. (4) ἔκραζον] it^{gig} vg cop^{sa} Cyprian Primasius. (5) ἔκραξαν] fam 1611^{2329} cop^{samss}. The impf. and aor. verbs in readings (4) and (5) represent attempts to eliminate the problematic present tense. Reading (3) is an attempt to improve the syntax. Reading (1) has superior attestation, but reading (2) often appears in modern texts because of the presence of the final moveable ν, which is used very irregularly (cf. Gignac, *Grammar* 1:114–16; BDF § 20). Moveable ν is missing in A in only seven places where it might be found (7:10; 9:4; 10:5; 17:16; 19:17; 21:8[2x]; see Mussies, *Morphology*, 28–29). κράζουσι is in the present tense, probably to make the scene more vivid to the reader, though it is translated as a past tense, "cried," in conformity with normal Eng. usage. The subject of κράζουσι is the sing. noun cluster ὄχλος πολύς in v 9a, making this a *constructio ad sensum;* see εἴρηκαν in 19:3 for an exactly similar grammatical parallel, and for parallels see Matt 20:29; Mark 5:21, 24; 9:14; Luke 8:4; John 6:2.

10.c-c. Bousset ([1906] 285) claims that the phrase ἡ σωτηρία τῷ θεῷ is a Hebraism with a parallel in Ps 3:9 (ליהוה הישועה *lYHWH hayšûʿâ;* cf. LXX Ps 3:9, τοῦ κυρίου ἡ σωτηρία); he also finds the same Hebraism in Rev 12:10; 19:1 (though both passages have τοῦ θεοῦ ἡμῶν rather than τῷ θεῷ ἡμῶν). BAGD, 801, also labels these three passages as Hebraisms; the same claim is made in Bauer-Aland, 1598, with the citation of an additional passage, *Pss. Sol.* 10:8, τοῦ κυρίου ἡ σωτηρία, "the Lord's salvation" or "the salvation of the Lord." The same phrase also occurs in *Pss. Sol.* 12:6. This construction need not be taken as a Hebraism, however, for it can be construed simply as a dat. of possession, which can best be translated "deliverance belongs to God" (the gen. of possession is used in the same way in 12:10; 19:1). The same construction occurs in doxologies when various attributes are ascribed to God or Christ in the dat. (e.g., Rev 1:5b–6; 4:9; 5:13; 7:12; cf. 19:1). The term σωτηρία, usually translated "salvation," must refer here to salvation in the sense of "deliverance" or "victory" over persecution rather than exclusively in a religious sense (Caird, 100–101; Turner, *Style*, 153).

10.d–d. Variant: τοῦ θρόνου] 2351.

10.e. Variant: a concluding doxology is a scribal interpolation based on 7:12b and found in ℵ* alone: εἰς τοὺς αἰῶνας τῶν αἰώνων· ἀμήν, "to the ages of ages, amen."

11.a. See *Note* 2.c.

11.b. The plupf. εἱστήκεισαν, lit. "they had stood," the only occurrence of the plupf. in Revelation, does not function as an impf. (contra Mussies, *Morphology,* 347), nor is there any reason to suppose that the perfect and plupf. forms of ἵστημι are influenced by Heb. (contra S. Thompson, *Apocalypse,* 73). Rather, εἱστήκεισαν refers to the position the angels had before they fell down to worship God; i.e., the plupf. is used to indicate the state resulting from the completion of the verbal action existing in the past (Rijksbaron, *Syntax,* 36–37). Porter (*Verbal Aspect,* 221–22) views the plupf. from an exclusively aspectual standpoint and defines it as stative, like the pf., but with the added aspectual feature of remoteness. According to K. L. McKay, *NovT* 23 (1981) 322, the plupf. "always signals a state (usually based on a previous action) which is either past or in some other way remote (e.g. unreal), irrespective of time. In narrative its use is parallel to that of the imperfect in filling in descriptive background to the events, and of course most perfect participles in narrative are replacements for clauses which would have had pluperfect verbs." In translating the εἱστήκεισαν as "who had been standing" (a substantival pf. ptcp. in Eng.), the appropriate verbal aspect is conveyed in Eng., even though the sentence has been turned into a relative clause.

11.c. The verb προσκυνεῖν, "to prostrate oneself, to worship," is very complex semantically since it refers to the physical position of the body as well as to the attitude of honor and reverence; both aspects can be present but one or the other emphasized depending on the context (Louw-Nida, §§ 17.21; 53.56). On the use of προσκυνεῖν + dat. or acc., see *Note* 4:10.b.

12.a. See *Note* 5:12.c.

12.b. Variants: (1) ἀμήν] ℵ A 025 046 fam 1006^{1006} fam 1611$^{1611\ 1854\ 2344}$ Oecumenius^{2053} 2351; Andreas it$^{ar\ c\ dem\ div\ gig\ haf\ z}$ vg syr$^{h\ ph}$ cop$^{sa\ bo}$ arm eth; Nestle-Aland^{27}; UBSGNT^{4}; *TCGNT*^{1}, 740 (variant omitted in *TCGNT*^{2}). (2) omit ἀμήν] C Andr d 2019 it^{t} Primasius.

13.a. See *Note* 2.c.

13.b. Here εἷς, "a, a certain," is used as an indefinite pronoun referring to a single indefinite person or thing, with a meaning similar to the indefinite pronoun τίς and often used where τίς would be appropriate (Zerwick, *Greek,* § 155; BDR § 247.2; MM, 187). Mussies (*Morphology,* 183) maintains, I think correctly, that it is a different word from the εἷς ordinal number that means "one" in contrast to more than one (e.g., Rev 17:12, 13, 17; 6 18:8, 10, 17, 19; 21:21). εἷς is used here and elsewhere in Revelation as an indefinite pronoun followed by the partitive gen. (5:5; 8:13; 9:13; 17:1; 21:9; cf. Matt 18:6; Luke 5:12, 17; 17:2; *1 Clem.* 46:8). This construction cannot be construed as a Hebraism since it has many parallels in pagan Gk. (MM, 187), or as a pronominal adj., i.e., as an indefinite article (8:13; 18:21; 19:17; cf. Mark 11:29); see Bauer-Aland, 466, 3b; BAGD, 231, 3b. In spite of the arguments that this is a Hebraism (Black, *Aramaic,* 104ff.; BDR § 247; Turner, *Syntax.* 195–96), it is not a Hebraism when followed by the partitive gen.

13.c. Variant: omit ἐκ] ℵ fam 1611$^{1611\ 1854}$ Andr f^{2254} Andr/Byz 3^{1957} Byz 17$^{2078\ 2436}$.

13.d. ἀπεκρίθη, "said," is a deponent aor. pass. verb used frequently in dialogue in the narrative sections of the LXX and in the NT Gospels and Acts. In Revelation, however, the term occurs here only, doubtless because of the lack of dialogue in the visions. The phrase ἀπεκρίθη . . . λέγων reflects the Heb. idiom ענה לאמר *ʿānâ lēʾmor.* See *Comment* on v 13.

14.a. See *Note* 2.c.

14.b. Variants: (1) εἴρηκα] *lectio originalis.* (2) εἶπον] fam 1611$^{1854\ 2329}$ Andr f^{2023} i^{2042} 1 94 Byzantine. The verb in reading (1), which is certainly original, is the 1st person sing. pf. εἴρηκα, which appears to function as an aor. (see 5:7; 8:5; 19:3; Zerwick, *Greek,* § 289; Turner, *Syntax,* 69–70; Mussies, *Morphology,* 264–65).

14.c. Variant: omit μου] A fam 1611^{1611} Andr a c g it$^{a\ gig}$ vg cop$^{bo\ samss}$ Cyprian Primatius Beatus.

14.d-d. The present substantival ptcp. οἱ ἐρχόμενοι is usually and correctly understood to refer to the past in modern translations (RSV, NRSV, "who have come"; NIV, "who have come"; NEB, "who have passed through"). The tenses of ptcps. generally indicate aspect (in the case of present ptcps., continuous, repeated, habitual, or characteristic action) rather than time, which is inferred from the context. Most often the present ptcp. denotes action simultaneous with the action of the main verb or verbs (Burton, *Syntax,* 53–59; Turner, *Syntax,* 79–81; Dougherty, *Syntax,* 395–97), in this case ἔπλυναν and ἐλεύκαναν. It is therefore correct to translate οἱ ἐρχόμενοι as a past tense.

14.e. The definite article used with θλῖψις indicates that the word refers to *the* great tribulation of Jewish eschatological expectation.

14.f. See *Note* 2.c.

14.g. Variants: (1) ἔπλυναν] *lectio originalis;* Oecumenius^{2053comm}. (2) ἐπλάτυναν] fam 1611$^{1854\ 2329}$ Oecumenius^{2053txt} Byzantine.

14.h. Variant: omit αὐτάς after ἐλεύκαναν] 2351 Andr i^{2042} 94 Byzantine.

15.a-a. Variants: (1) τοῦ θρόνου] ℵ A (lacuna in C) Andreas. (2) τῷ θρόνῳ] 025 fam 1611^{1854} Oecumenius^{2053} 2351 Andr e^{2026} f h i^{2042} n^{-2429} Byzantine. Reading (1) violates the stylistic "rule" that the case of ὁ θρόνος after ἐπί is acc. when ὁ καθήμενος is nom. or acc., but gen. if ὁ καθήμενος is gen. and dat. if ὁ καθήμενος is dat. See *Comment* on 4:2c.

15.b. The underlying Gk. phrase σκηνώσει ἐπ' αὐτούς, lit., "he will dwell over them," means "he will shelter, protect them" (BAGD, 755).

16.a. Variants: (1) οὐδὲ μή] *lectio originalis;* Andreas. (2) οὐδ' οὐ μή] 2351. (3) οὐδ' οὐ] 052 fam 1611^{2329} 2351 Andr c d e f^{2023} g^{-2045} $i^{1685\ 2042}$ l 598 Byzantine.

16.b. οὐδὲ πᾶν καῦμα, "any scorching heat," is an idiom used in place of the more proper οὐδὲν καῦμα, which is found in late popular Gk. and Gk. translated from Heb.

17.a-a. The phrase ἀνὰ μέσον is problematic as a compound prep. describing the location of the Lamb on the throne, since it means "among, in the midst of," or "between" (BAGD, 49; Dougherty, *Syntax,* 270).

17.b. Variant: (1) ποιμανεῖ] *lectio originalis.* (2) ποιμαίνει] 2351 Byzantine.

17.c-c. The phrase ζωῆς πηγὰς ὑδάτων, lit. "springs of waters of life," exhibits peculiar word order (Winer, *Grammar,* 689), since two gens. are dependent on the same noun (for examples of this phenomenon in the NT, see Acts 5:32; 2 Cor 5:1; Phil 2:30; 2 Pet 3:2; cf. Turner, *Syntax,* 218; BDR § 168.1). Scribes attempted to resolve the awkwardness by changing ζωῆς to ζώσας, a fem. pl. acc. ptcp. modifying πηγάς (052 fam $1611^{2329\ 2344}$ Andr a b c d l 598 Byzantine). This phrase occurs only here in Revelation, though the phrase πηγὰς ὑδάτων occurs four times, three times in the pl. (8:10; 14:7; 16:4) and once in the sing. (21:6), either with both nouns anarthrous (7:17; 14:7) or both nouns arthrous (8:10; 16:4). ὑδάτων is a gen. of apposition, so it can be translated "springs, that is, waters," i.e., "springs." Both forms of the phrase (the anarthrous and arthrous) occur in the LXX as a translation of the Heb. phrase עינת מים *ʿênot mayim* or עין מים *ʿên mayim* (Gen 16:7; 24:13; Exod 15:27; Lev 11:36; Num 33:9; Josh 15:9; Isa 35:7; 49:10). מים *mayim* is a *plurale tantum* (GKC § 124f), and עין *ʿayin* may be either in the construct state followed by מים *mayim* in the gen., i.e., "spring of water," or מים *mayim* may be in apposition to עין *ʿayin,* i.e., "a spring, that is, water" (Mussies, *Morphology,* 82 n. 1). Cf. 16:4, where the nouns are both pl. and arthrous, τὰς πηγὰς τῶν ὑδάτων, and 14:7, where they are both pl. and anarthrous, πηγὰς ὑδάτων. Several modern versions translate the phrase lit.: REB, "springs of the water of life," and RSV, NIV, "springs of living water."

17.d. Variant: ἀπό] ℵ fam 1611^{1854} Oecumenius^{2053} 2351 Andr e i^{-2042} $l^{1678\ 2080}$ 2019. See 21:4, where Isa 25:8 is also quoted but in a slightly different form. The substitution of ἀπό for ἐκ may in fact be an assimilation to Isa 25:8 (see Ps.-Epiphanius *Testimonia* 34).

Form/Structure/Setting

I. Outline

3. The protective sealing of the 144,000 (7:1–17)
   a. The sealing of the 144,000 (vv 1–8)
      (1) Vision of the four angels (v 1)
         (a) Location: standing at the four corners of the earth (v 1a)
         (b) Task: restraining the four winds of the earth (v 1b)
         (c) Purpose: so that no wind might blow (v 1c)
            [1] On the earth
            [2] On the sea
            [3] On any tree
      (2) An angelic speech (vv 2–3)
         (a) Vision of another angel (v 2)
            [1] Description (v 2)
               [a] Ascends from the east (v 2a)
               [b] Bears the signet of the living God (v 2a)
               [c] Speaks with loud voice (v 2b)

[2] Intended audience: the four angels who have power to harm (v 2b)
[a] The earth
[b] The sea
(b) The speech (v 3)
[1] Command: Do not harm natural elements (v 3a)
[a] The earth
[b] The sea
[c] The trees
[2] Time limit: until the servants of God are sealed on their foreheads (v 3b)
(3) Audition of the sealing of 144,000 Israelites (vv 4–8)
(a) Introductory summary: the number sealed: 144,000 from all the tribes of the sons of Israel (v 4)
(b) Enumeration of those sealed (vv 5–8)
[1] From the tribe of Judah: 12,000 (v 5a)
[2] From the tribe of Reuben: 12,000 (v 5b)
[3] From the tribe of Gad: 12,000 (v 5c)
[4] From the tribe of Asher: 12,000 (v 6a)
[5] From the tribe of Naphtali: 12,000 (v 6b)
[6] From the tribe of Manasseh: 12,000 (v 6c)
[7] From the tribe of Simeon: 12,000 (v 7a)
[8] From the tribe of Levi: 12,000 (v 7b)
[9] From the tribe of Issachar: 12,000 (v 7c)
[10] From the tribe of Zebulun: 12,000 (v 8a)
[11] From the tribe of Joseph: 12,000 (v 8b)
[12] From the tribe of Benjamin: 12,000 (v 8c)
b. Vision of a triumphant throng in the heavenly throne room (vv 9–17)
(1) Introductory vision formulas (v 9a)
(a) "After this"
(b) "I looked, and behold"
(2) The innumerable heavenly multitude (vv 9a–12)
(a) No person can count them (v 9a)
(b) Their universal origin (v 9b)
[1] From every nation
[2] From every tribe
[3] From every people
[4] From every language
(c) Their appearance (v 9c)
[1] They are standing
[a] Before the throne
[b] Before the Lamb
[2] They are dressed in white robes (v 9d)
[3] They hold palm fronds (v 9d)
(d) Their victory cry (v 10)
[1] Introductory formula: "They cried with a loud voice" (v 10a)

[2] Announcement of victory (v 10b)
[3] Addressees (v 10c)
[a] To our God who sits on the throne
[b] To the Lamb
(e) Response of the heavenly court (vv 11–12)
[1] Those who surround the throne (v 11a)
[a] The angels
[b] The elders
[c] The four cherubim
[2] Their worship (v 11b)
[a] They fall prostrate
{1} Before the throne
{2} On their faces
[b] They worship God
[3] Their antiphonal response
[a] Introductory response: amen (v 12a)
[b] Seven divine attributes (v 12b)
{1} Praise
{2} Glory
{3} Wisdom
{4} Thanksgiving
{5} Honor
{6} Power
{7} Might
[c] Addressee: to our God (v 12c)
[d] Eternity formula: "for ever and ever" (v 12d)
[e] Concluding amen (v 12e)
(3) The scene explained (vv 13–17)
(a) Introductory questions to the seer by one of the elders (v 13)
[1] Who are these people dressed in white robes? (v 13b)
[2] Where did they come from? (v 13b)
(b) John's response: "Sir, you know" (v 14a)
(c) The elder's explanation (vv 14b–17)
[1] Where they came from: the great tribulation (v 14b)
[2] The robes they wear (v 14c)
[a] They washed them
[b] They made them white by the blood of the Lamb
[3] Their location (v 15a)
[a] Before the throne of God
[b] They serve him day and night in his temple
[4] The One who sits on the throne will shelter them (vv 15b–16)
[a] They will not hunger (v 16a)
[b] They will not thirst (v 16b)
[c] The sun will not fall on them (v 16c)
[d] Scorching heat will not affect them (v 16d)
[5] Reasons (v 17)

[a] The Lamb in the midst of the throne will shepherd them (v 17a)
[b] The Lamb will guide them to the springs of life (v 17b)
[c] God will wipe away every tear from their eyes (v 17c)

II. Literary Analysis

Rev 7:1–17 consists of two main scenes, arranged in a "before" and "after" pattern: (1) 7:1–8 is introduced with the stereotyped phrase "After this I saw" (v 1), and it apparently takes place on earth. (2) 7:9–17 is introduced with a similar phrase, "After this I looked, and behold" (v 9), but the vantage point of the seer is apparently heaven (where the throne of God is located, vv 9–12, and where the heavenly temple is found, v 15).

(1) The three textual units in the first scene in 7:1–8 are: (a) a vision of the four angels restraining the winds (7:1); (b) a vision of another angel with the seal of God, who tells the first four angels not to harm the earth, the sea, or the trees until the servants of God have been sealed (7:2–3); and (c) a census list of the number and tribal affiliation of those sealed, which is overheard (not seen) by John (vv 4–8). Noteworthy by its absence is a scene in which the actual sealing takes place. There seems to be a lacuna between 7:3 and 7:4, at least in terms of narrative logic. However, in Ezek 9:4–8 also, to which this passage probably alludes and after which it is modeled, the actual marking of Jews who are to be protected from slaughter is not narrated but simply mentioned.

(2) The second scene in 7:9–17 consists of two units: (a) John sees a vision of a great multitude and hears their hymn of salvation to God and the liturgy of the angels, elders, and four cherubim surrounding the throne (7:9–12). (b) An elder voluntarily interprets the scene for John (7:13–17). Just as there is a disjuncture between v 3 and v 4, so there is also a major disjuncture between 7:1–8 and 7:9–17; i.e., there is no narrative of the great tribulation and the wrath of the ungodly inflicted on Christians from which those in 7:1–8 have been protectively sealed and out of which those in 7:9–17 have been delivered.

Two observations can be made about 7:1–17 as a whole. First, it is likely that 7:1–8 has been placed here because of the formal occurrence of the catchword σφραγίς, "signet, seal," found twelve times in Rev 5:1–8:1. Second, the author is interpreting 7:1–8 (which exhibits no distinctively Christian features, as many commentators have noted) by juxtaposing it with 7:9–17.

III. Literary Forms

A. *The Angelophanies in Rev 7:1–3*

This brief section contains two literary forms that have few parallels in Jewish or Christian apocalyptic literature outside of Revelation. For this reason they can reasonably be regarded as literary forms created by the author, and they provide an important index for distinguishing between the author's redaction of traditional material and sources and his own contributions to the composition of the text.

The first form, the *angelic action,* occurs four times and exhibits the following structural features (7:1; 8:2; 15:1; 20:1–3): (1) introductory phrase: καὶ εἶδον or μετὰ τοῦτο εἶδον (7:1; 8:2; 15:1), (2) object of vision: ἄγγελον or ἀγγέλους (7:1; 8:2; 15:1; 20:1), (3) brief description of the action performed by or to the angel or angels (7:1; 8:2; 15:1; 20:1–3), and (4) an abrupt change of subject (7:2; 8:3; 15:2; 20:4). In addition, the author presents these brief angelophanies strictly as an observer; the angel or angels he sees and whose action he describes do not interact with him, and he does not interact with them.

The second form, the *angelic speech,* occurs nine times in Revelation (7:2–3; 10:1–7; 14:6–7, 8, 9–11, 14–16, 18–20; 18:1–3; 19:17–18) and is once inserted immediately following an *angelic action* (7:2–3). The *angelic speech* in Revelation exhibits the following structural features: (1) introductory phrase: καὶ εἶδον (7:2; 10:1; 14:6; 18:1; 19:17), (2) object of vision: ἄλλον ἄγγελον (7:2; 10:1; 14:6, 8, 9; 18:1; 19:17), (3) movement of the angel (ascend, descend, fly, emerge, follow) to the center of the action (7:2; 10:1; 14:6, 8, 9, 15, 18; 18:1; 19:17), (4) a statement that the angel "cries with a loud voice" (7:2; 10:3; 14:7, 9, 15, 18; 18:2a; 19:17), and (5) a brief statement uttered by the angel (7:3; 10:3 [what he says is not mentioned; only "he cried with a loud voice as a lion roars"]; 14:7, 8, 9b–11, 15b, 18b; 18:2b–3; 19:17b–18). This brief statement is the focus of this literary form.

A mixed form, the *angelic speech and action,* occurs twice (14:14–16, 17–20), though both occurrences constitute two episodes within the larger literary form 14:14–20. It consists of several elements: (1) introductory phrase: καὶ εἶδον (14:14), (2) object of vision: an angelic figure (14:14 ["one like a son of man"], 17), (3) description of the figure (14:14, 17), (4) introduction of a second angel (14:15a, 18a), (5) a command given by the second angel to the first (14:15b, 18b), and (6) the fulfillment of the command by the first angel (14:16, 19–20).

This form has a striking parallel in *2 Apoc. Bar.* 6:4–6 (tr. A. F. J. Klijn in Charlesworth, *OTP* 1:622–23):

(1) Introductory phrase:	And I saw, and behold
(2) Object of vision:	there were standing four angels at the four corners of the city,
(3) Description:	each of them with a burning torch in his hands.
(4) Introduction of second angel	And another angel came down from heaven and said to them,
(5) Command of second angel	"Hold your torches and do not light them before I say it to you. Because I was sent first to speak a word to the earth and then to deposit in it what the Lord, the Most High, has commanded me."
(6) Fulfillment of command	[missing]

B. The Census List in 7:4–8

The census is a specific form of list that occurs with some frequency in the OT, where it is used for purposes of taxation (Exod 30:11–16; 2 Kgs 15:19–20), for labor conscription (2 Chr 2:17–18; cf. 1 Kgs 5:13–18), for determining the cultic duties and social structure of members of the tribe of Levi (Num 3:14–4:49), for determining Israelite descent (Ezra 2 and par. in Neh 7 and 1 Esdr 5), but most commonly as a means for determining military strength (Num 1:2–46, esp. vv 2–3; 26:1–56, esp. vv 1–2; 2 Sam 24:1–9 [and par. 1 Chr 21:1–6]; 1 Chr 27:1–24). This suggests that the census in Rev 7:4–8 is for *military purposes,* a possibility that is partially confirmed by the present literary context of this pericope since, according to Rev 14:3–4, the group of 144,000 consists exclusively of adult males who practice sexual abstinence, an ancient Israelite requirement for holy warriors (Bauckham, *JSNT* 42 [1991] 104; id., *Neot* 22 [1988] 217). However, the absence of all military and holy war imagery from Rev 7:4–8 makes this suggestion doubtful. The author's insistence on an equal number (12,000) from each of *twelve* tribes indicates his interest in the eschatological restoration of the the twelve-tribe nation of Israel (Luke 22:30; 24:21; Acts 1:6; see Geyser, *NTS* 28 [1982] 389). The eschatology of the late OT and early Jewish periods emphasized the hope of the restoration of Israel (Deut 30:3–5; Isa 11:11–16; 27:12–13; 49:5–6; 54:7–10; Jer 31:7–14; Ezek 37:15–23; Hos 11:10–11; Pss 106:47; 147:2; Bar 5:5–9; 2 Macc 2:7; Sir 36:11; Tob 13:13; *1 Enoch* 57; 90:33; 4 Ezra 13:12–13, 39–47; *2 Apoc. Bar.* 78:5–7; *T. Jos.* 19:4; *Pss. Sol.* 11:2–7; 17:26; *Shemoneh Esreh* 10; *m. Sanh.* 10:3; Matt 19:28). In *m. Sanh.* 10:3 the opinions that the ten tribes will not return and that they will return are juxtaposed. This motif of the restoration of Israel was transmuted in early Christianity into the gathering of the elect from the four winds at the Parousia (Mark 13:27 = Matt 24:31; 1 Thess 4:16–17; 2 Thess 2:1).

C. The Eschatological Heavenly Worship of God as an Apocalyptic Type Scene in 7:9–17

The throne vision, a literary form that occurs quite frequently in Jewish apocalyptic literature (e.g., *1 Enoch* 14:8–25; 4 Ezra 2:42–48; Ezekiel Trag. *Exagoge* 68–82), consists of several subtypes, including the eschatological heavenly worship of God, the eschatological reward scene, and the eschatological judgment scene. There are enough striking structural and thematic similarities between Rev 7:9–17 (particularly vv 9–12) and other passages in early Jewish and early Christian literature to suggest the presence of a "type scene," i.e., a brief recurring narrative episode (primarily limited to apocalyptic contexts) that is constituted by a restricted constellation of motifs (see R. Alter, *The Art of Biblical Narrative* [New York: Basic Books, 1981] 47–62). Perhaps the closest and most complete example of this type scene is found in Heb 12:22–24, though examples are also found in Rev 14:1–5, 5 Ezra 2:42–45, 4 Ezra 13:5–50, and *Odes Sol.* 36.

The motifs of this scene can clearly be seen in Heb 12:22–24 (RSV):

22But you have come to Mount Zion
and to the city of the living God, the heavenly Jerusalem,
and to innumerable angels in festal gathering,
23and to the assembly of the first-born who are enrolled in heaven,

and to a judge who is God of all,
and to the spirits of just men made perfect,
[24]and to Jesus, the mediator of a new covenant,
and to the sprinkled blood that speaks more graciously than the blood of Abel.

The introductory verb προσεληλύθατε, "you have come," suggests that this type scene is being used in a metaphorical sense (see v 18, "for you have not come to what may be touched"), which indicates the widespread familiarity of this particular scene with its constituent elements. The main motifs in this type scene include a concentric arrangement beginning with the setting and then proceeding from the outside to the inside: (1) Mount Zion, the heavenly Jerusalem (the setting), (2) an innumerable angelic host in festal gathering, (3) the assembly of the firstborn, (4) God the judge of all, (5) the assembly of righteous people, (6) Jesus, and (7) the sprinkled blood (implying the figurative presence of the ark).

Another variant of this type scene is found in 4 Ezra 2:42–45 (a late Christian addition to 4 Ezra often called 5 Ezra):

[42]I, Ezra, saw on Mount Zion a great multitude,
which I could not number,
and they all were praising the Lord with songs.
[43]In their midst was a young man of great stature,
taller than any of the others,
and on the head of each of them he placed a crown,
but he was more exalted than they.
And I was held spellbound.
[44]Then I asked an angel, "Who are these, my Lord?"
[45]He answered and said to me,
"These are they who have put off mortal clothing
and have put on the immortal,
and they have confessed the name of God;
now they are being crowned, and receive palms."

The primary motifs of this type scene are the following: (1) Mount Zion (the setting), (2) an innumerable multitude who praised God with song (2:42), (3) the young man of great stature, i.e., Christ (2:43), (4) the coronation of each member of the innumerable multitude (2:45), (5) the presentation of palms to each member of the innumerable multitude (2:45), and (6) the seer who asks an angel about the meaning of this scene, followed by (7) an explanation. The unknown author of this passage (and those that precede and follow it) has based much of it on Rev 7:4–17, including (1) reference to God as shepherd (v 34), (2) reference to the number of those sealed (v 38), (3) the multitude clothed in white (v 40), (4) their praise of God with songs (v 42), and (5) the palms they carry (v 45–46).

There are also a number of striking thematic similarities between 7:9–17 and 21:1–22:5. These include: (1) the seal on the forehead, (2) mention of the twelve tribes, (3) the nations of the world, (4) the throne of God, (5) worship, (6) the temple (present in 7:15; explicitly absent in 21:22), (7) God's dwelling with the faithful (7:15; 21:3), (8) the end to thirst (7:16; 21:6), (9) the absence of the sun (7:16; 21:23), (10) the springs of living water (7:17; 21:6), and (11) the wiping away of tears (7:17; 21:4); see Comblin, *ETL* 29 [1953] 38 n. 87. J. Comblin, who argues that Rev 21:1–22:5

reflects the celebration of the Feast of Tabernacles, suggests that the multitude in Rev 7:9–17 is presented as celebrating the Feast of Tabernacles, a conclusion suggested by the palm fronds (v 9) and their σωτηρία exclamation (*ETL* 29 [1953] 38–39).

IV. Tense Sequences

The tense sequences of Rev 7:1–17 obviously play an important role in the narrative. 7:1–8 contains a sequence of nine aorist verbs, interrupted only by the present subjunctive πνέῃ, "might blow," in the ἵνα clause in v 1. More irregularity is evident in 7:9–17, where the overall pattern is a sequence of past-tense verbs, then a sequence of present-tense verbs, followed by a sequence of future-tense verbs. Even though this vision sequence begins with the aorist verb εἶδον, "I saw," the author immediately switches to the imperfect in v 9 (ἐδύνατο, "could even begin"), in a parenthetical relative clause. This is followed by a present tense in 7:10, where κράζουσιν, "they cry," introduces the hymn sung by the innumerable multitude. This is followed by a series of four aorists in 7:11–13, interrupted by one of the few pluperfect verbs in Revelation, εἱστήκεισαν, "had been standing" (v 11). The explanatory speech of the elder (7:13–17) is introduced with an aorist verb (ἀπεκρίθη, "said"), and his question to John contains a present and an aorist verb: "Who are [εἰσίν] these dressed in white robes, and where did they come from [ἦλθον]" (v 13). The explanatory speech of the elder in vv 14b–17 contains thirteen verbs, beginning with a present tense (εἰσίν, "are"), followed by two aorists that explain that they washed (ἔπλυναν) their robes and made them white (ἐλεύκαναν). Two present tenses follow in v 15, εἰσίν, "they are," and λατρεύουσιν, "they worship," followed unexpectedly by a sequence of eight verbs, all futures with the exception of the aorist subjunctive πέσῃ in v 16: (1) σκηνώσει, "he will dwell," (2) πεινάσουσιν, "they will [not] sorrow," (3) διψήσουσιν, "they will [not] thirst," (4) πέσῃ, "it might [not] fall," an aorist subjunctive (n.b. that the future and the subjunctive are closely related), (5) ποιμανεῖ, "he will shepherd," (6) ὁδηγήσει, "he will guide," and (7) ἐξαλείψει, "he will wipe away." While the aorist subjunctive (e.g., πέσῃ) has the semantic features of projection with no expectation of fulfillment, the future semantically designates the speaker's expectation that an event is occurring (Porter, *Verbal Aspect,* 129, 134). Thus the problem in interpreting 7:13–17 is that vv 14b–15a describe what is already occurring, i.e., the present, while vv 15b–17 describe what is expected to occur, i.e., the future. This is a sequence-of-tense pattern that occurs frequently in the visions of Revelation, namely, the movement from past tenses to present tenses to future tenses (Mussies, *Morphology,* 334–36; see 4:8–10; 9:4–6; 18:4–15; 19:14–16; 20:4–7; 21:22–26). The author uses this sequence of tenses to convey visions (purportedly) seen in the past and described vividly in the present, which at the same time predict future events. The future tenses describe the final state of the innumerable host, but John does not actually claim to *see* them enjoying that state. Further, the presence of this innumerable host before God in the heavenly temple is *not* a final state of salvation, since the destruction of the old heaven and earth and the creation of a new heaven and earth provide the necessary setting for the earthly presence of the New Jerusalem.

V. Source Criticism of Rev 7:1–17

Some have attempted to solve the problem of the strange juxtaposition of Rev 7:1–8 and 7:9–17 by the hypothesis that two different sources lie behind 7:1–17

(Beckwith, 535; Kraft, 126; Beasley-Murray, 141; cf. Charles, 1:191–93, 199–203), though this is denied by Lohmeyer (70), who argues that there are no linguistic or stylistic criteria present that would validate such a hypothesis. Wellhausen (*Analyse,* 12) and Bousset ([1906] 288–89) think that while 7:1–8 is based on a pre-existing source, 7:9–17 certainly reflects the style of the author. The redaction of earlier literary material has resulted in the imposition of a later understanding of the significance of the passage over an earlier one. The mention of the 144,000 in 7:4–8 and 14:1–5 indicates that, in their present contexts, both passages refer to the Christian community of the end time, made up of both Jews and Gentiles. However, that 12,000 are sealed from each of the twelve tribes of Israel suggests (1) that this text derives from a Jewish provenance (argued by Charles, 1:188–91; Beckwith, 535), (2) that a Christian author is referring to Christian Jews who are but a part of the entire Jewish people and therefore need this "sealing" to be identifiable, or (3) that a Christian author is affirming the indissoluble connection between Israel and the Church (Karrer, *Brief,* 283; Rissi, *Babylon,* 17).

One of the problematic features of 7:9–17 in the present text of Revelation is that it appears to take place in heaven. The members of the innumerable multitude are gathered before the throne and the Lamb singing praises to God and to the Lamb and are accompanied by the elders and the four cherubim. The innumerable multitude consists of those who have died (v 14) and who now act as priests before the throne of God, serving him in his temple (v 15). Since the New Jerusalem contains no temple (21:22), the setting appears to be heaven. Yet it would be most unusual in Jewish apocalyptic to place the final consummation in heaven rather than on earth. Just two Jewish apocalypses, *2 Apoc. Bar.* 51:7–16 and *2 Enoch,* reject the notion of a messianic kingdom on earth and situate the final eschatological state in the heavenly paradise (see Joachim Jeremias, *TDNT* 5:767 n. 18). Further, in the present text, Rev 7:9–17 probably refers not only to Christians who have died but more specifically to Christian *martyrs.* Earlier, however, this text referred not exclusively to martyrs but rather to the whole Christian community (J. Weiss, *Offenbarung,* 67–68).

VI. Central Interpretive Issues

A. *Introduction*

The literary context of Rev 7 is provided by the narrative framework of the opening of the sixth seal in Rev 6:12–17, the effects of which are not actual judgments but rather a series of cosmic signs of impending disaster that throw fear and consternation into the hearts of people everywhere. These all speak with one voice in v 17 (a literary device that occurs frequently in the OT and Jewish literature; cf. Ruth 1:19; Matt 2:3), "The great day of their [i.e., God's and the Lamb's] wrath has come, and who can stand before it?" The answer to this rhetorical question is implied in 7:1–8, i.e., "No one except those protected by God."

Rev 7:1–17 is a literary diptych in which both scenes present similar interpretive problems: Who are the 144,000 sealed in 7:4–8? Who constitute the innumerable multitude described in 7:9–17? What is the temporal setting of each of these scenes, the present or the future? Does the Feast of Tabernacles provide the salient imagery for interpreting 7:9–17? This passage has proven to be one of the most difficult to interpret in Revelation, and each of the questions posed above has been answered in a variety of ways, often with few, if any, supporting arguments. After reviewing each major position, I will argue for the interpretation that I consider most likely.

B. Identifying the 144,000 (Rev 7:1–8)

1. *Interpretive Constraints.* While the 144,000 have been identified in a variety of ways, there are several interpretive constraints that limit the range of acceptable solutions: (a) According to Rev 7:4b, "144,000 were marked from every tribe of the sons of Israel [ἐκ πάσης φυλῆς υἱῶν Ἰσραήλ]"; i.e., those who are sealed are part of a larger group, for ἐκ + genitive here is a partitive genitive, indicating that a limited number are separated from a larger group. Whatever "the tribes of the sons of Israel" represents, 12,000 from each tribe can only mean a portion of those who make up the whole "tribe" (Caird, 96). This view is confirmed by the allusion to Ezek 9:4 in Rev 7:4–8, for in Ezekiel's vision only *some* of the inhabitants of Jerusalem were marked with a taw so that they would be saved by the angelic destroyers (in turn an allusion to the protective marking during Passover in Exod 12:23). (b) There are striking differences between the two groups described in Rev 7:4–8 and 7:9–17 that must be borne in mind: (i) There is a clear contrast between the specific enumeration of the 144,000 (7:4–8) and the vast size of the great multitude, which "no one was able to number" (7:9); the latter is obviously a much larger group than the former and therefore very probably a different group (Allo, 92). (ii) The 144,000 are composed of 12,000 drawn from each of the twelve tribes of the sons of Israel, while the members of the great multitude in explicit contrast, according to 7:9, are drawn from "every nation and tribe and people and language group" (Zahn, 368). (iii) The 144,000 are apparently located on earth while the innumerable multitude is in heaven before the throne of God (7:11). (iv) In 7:4–8, the 144,000 are in a situation of imminent peril that requires protective sealing (see Rev 9:4), while the innumerable multitude in 7:9–17 has passed victoriously through the great tribulation and has received a heavenly reward. (c) The 144,000 appear once again in 14:1–5, and the determination of their identity must be based on this passage as well, at least so far as the final edition of Revelation is concerned (J. Weiss, *Offenbarung,* 65), though some deny the identity of these groups (Allo, 92). (d) Whether or not 7:4–8 is based on a Jewish source, the passage must be interpreted in terms of how it functions in its present literary context (Taeger, *Johannesapokalypse,* 30). (e) The seal of God explicitly provides special protection for the wrath of God that is coming upon the world (9:4); there is no explicit indication that the sealed are not protected from the wrath of the ungodly (even though this is the claim of many commentators). In many early Christian texts, the eschatological tribulation was thought to be a present feature of Christian experience in the world, and no distinction was made between plagues and punishments sent by God upon humankind and the hostility and persecution inflicted on Christians by Jews and pagans (Mark 13:9–20 = Matt 24:9–22 = Luke 21:12–24; *Did.* 16:5).

2. *The 144,000 as Jews or Jewish Christians,* i.e., the faithful remnant of Israel (Eichhorn, 1:228; Bousset [1906] 287; Zahn, 368; Allo, 93; Comblin, *AsSeign* 66 [1973] 42–49; Corsini, *Apocalypse,* 158–60; Draper, *JSNT* 19 [1985] 136; Glasson, 52; W. J. Harrington, *Apocalypse,* 129; Kraft, 126; Rowland, 91). Many who think that Rev 7:4–8 is based on a Jewish source hold that while the 144,000 may have *originally* referred to Jews or the real Israel, that source has been reinterpreted by the author

to refer to a different group, such as the Christian church or Christian martyrs (J. Weiss, *Offenbarung,* 67; Beckwith, 535; Beasley-Murray, 141). There are others, however, who think that whether or not 7:4–8 is based on a Jewish source, the text in its present context refers to Jews (Draper, *JSNT* 19 [1985] 133–47; Comblin, *AsSeign* 66 [1973] 42–49; Buchanan, 189–91).

There are several arguments that proponents of this view put forward: (a) The detailed enumeration of 12,000 sealed from each of the twelve tribes of Israel suggests that Jews or Jewish Christians are in view, for while "the twelve tribes in dispersion" (Jas 1:1; cf. Herm. *Sim.* 9.17.1) can be used in a Christian context to represent the Christian church, a detailed enumeration of 12,000 from each of the twelve tribes does not lend itself easily to allegorization (Bousset [1906] 283, 287). (b) Since the author is undoubtedly a Jewish Christian (contra MacKenzie, *Author of the Apocalypse*), it is not particularly surprising that he would have envisioned a special role in the eschaton for Christians of Jewish origin (Bousset [1906] 288–89; Allo, 93). Paul struggled with the problem of the rejection of the gospel by most Jews in Rom 9–11, recognizing that not everyone descended from Israel belongs to the true Israel (Rom 9:6), yet nevertheless held out the eschatological hope that Israel would eventually be converted (Rom 11:25–27). The eschatological tradition of the future gathering of Israel and the Gentiles at the New Jerusalem at the coming of Christ is found elsewhere in early Christian literature, e.g., *T. Benj.* 9:2, "and there [at the temple of God] the twelve tribes and all the Gentiles will be gathered together" (see also Justin *Dial.* 24.3; 80.1). (c) Those who argue that the 144,000 are Jewish Christians frequently cite Rom 11:7, where Paul refers to the "elect" (ἐκλογή) or "remnant" (λεῖμμα) of Israel (i.e., Jewish Christians; see v 5) who believed that Jesus was the Messiah of Israel while the rest of Israel had rejected the messianic status of Jesus. The idea of a remnant of Israel that remains faithful to the covenant, as found in the OT (*TDNT* 4:196–209; *NIDNTT* 3:247–51), has certainly informed Paul in Rom 11:1–10 (*TDNT* 4:209–14; *NIDNTT* 3:251–53), and may well provide the background against which Rev 7:4–8 should be read. (d) The 144,000 as Jewish Christians are the "first fruits" of those first chosen to receive the gospel (Allo, 93). (e) Zahn suggests that the number 144,000 approximated the real number of Christians of Jewish origin at the time Revelation was written (371–72). Acts 21:20 speaks of the many ten thousands of Jews who have believed the gospel. (f) For those who assume that "sealing" symbolizes baptism or salvation, it is more likely that those who remained "unsealed" are Jews rather than Christians, for it is easier to conceive of "unsealed" Jews than "unsealed" Christians. (g) The distinction between Jewish and gentile Christians (sometimes called the "circumcised" and "uncircumcised," or "Jews" and "Greeks," respectively) pervades early Christian literature even though there is a complementary recognition that the latter as well as the former are part of the new people of God (Acts 10:45; 11:1, 19–20; 13:16–17, 26; 19:10; Rom 1:16; 3:29–30; 9:6–8; 10:12–13; 1 Cor 1:24; 12:13; Gal 2:7–8; 3:28; Eph 2:11–19). It would therefore not be surprising to find ethnic Jews distinguished from Christians of gentile origin. (h) The term σφραγίς, "seal," is sometimes used of the rite of circumcision (Rom 4:11; *Barn.* 9:6–8).

Opponents of this view have proposed a number of arguments against interpreting the 144,000 as Jews or Jewish Christians: (a) The twelve tribes did not literally exist in the first century A.D., and the hope of their eventual restoration belonged not to the real but to the ideal world (Behm, 45; Caird, 95; Mounce, 168; Boring,

129; E. Schüssler Fiorenza, *Revelation: Vision of a Just World* [Minneapolis: Fortress, 1991] 67). Against this objection it can be countered that Josephus, writing at the end of the first century A.D., reckoned with the existence of twelve tribes in his day (*Ant.* 11.133) and that the widespread Jewish eschatological hope of the regathering of the twelve tribes of Israel was certainly based on the assumption of their actual existence in the world (see *Comment* on Rev 7:4b). (b) The distinction between Jewish Christianity and gentile Christianity, common in the early decades of the apostolic age, was no longer current at the end of the first century (Behm, 45). Against this position it may be argued that the debate between Christianity and Judaism continued well into the second century, as evident in *Barnabas* and the *Dialogue* of Justin (Hvalvik, *Struggle,* 213–321). (c) So many ways of describing the real Israel have been applied to the Church in Revelation that it would be perverse to treat Rev 7:4–8 as an exception to the rule (Caird, 95). To this it may be replied that, while certain OT language used of Israel is applied to Christians, e.g., that Christians are a "kingdom" and "priests" (an allusion to Exod 19:6 found in Rev 1:6; 5:10; 20:6; probably traditional since it also occurs in 1 Pet 2:9), the use of other traditional language in Revelation suggests that the Church is constituted of both Jews and Gentiles; e.g., the twelve gates of the New Jerusalem bear the names of the twelve tribes of the sons of Israel (20:12–13; an eschatological tradition found in Ezek 48:30–35; 1QTemple 39:13–13; 40:11–14; description of the New Jerusalem: *4Q554* 2:12–3:9), while the twelve foundations of the city bear the names of the twelve apostles. (d) The author equates the 144,000 in Rev 7:4–8 with the 144,000 in 14:1–5, and the latter cannot be considered Jews or Jewish Christians (Boring, 129). To this it may be countered that since the author *contrasts* the two groups it cannot be assumed without detailed argumentation that they are identical.

3. *The 144,000 as the Christian church inclusive of both Jewish and gentile Christians* (Wellhausen, *Analyse,* 12; Charles, 1:200; Ladd, 114–17; Beasley-Murray, 140; Beagley, *Apocalypse,* 47; Boring, 129–32; W. J. Harrington, 98, 101; Giblin, 91–92; Rissi, *Babylon,* 17–19; Giesen, 193; Taeger, *Johannesapokalypse,* 30–31). According to this view, which has come to be held by a majority of scholars since the early part of the twentieth century, the references to the 12,000 sealed from each tribe of the sons of Israel must be understood metaphorically of all Christians. Arguments for this position include the following: (a) The Church was widely understood in early Christianity as the true Israel. The term "Jew" could be understood in a spiritual sense (Rom 2:28–29), and the "Israel of God" could be used as a metaphor for the Christian Church (Gal 6:16; cf. Rom 9:6). Similarly, "the twelve tribes in dispersion" could be understood as Christians (Jas 1:1; Herm. *Sim.* 9.17.1 [see Brox, *Der Hirt des Hermas,* 441–41]; close parallels to Rev 7:4–8 for those who construe the twelve tribes as a metaphor for Christians). Similarly, in terms from Jewish tradition, 1 Pet 1:1 refers to Christians in Asia Minor metaphorically as "elect exiles of the diaspora [ἐκλεκτοῖς παρεπιδήμοις διασπορᾶς]" (see P. J. Achtemeier, *1 Peter,* Hermeneia [Minneapolis: Fortress, 1996] 81–82), while throughout the entire letter the author applies to the Church language normally used of Israel and apparently no longer regards Israel as an independent entity (Achtemeier, *1 Peter,* 69–72). Paul argued that people of faith were sons of Abraham (Gal 3:7; Rom 4:11–17). (b) In Rev 9:4, the demonic scorpions are told only to harm those who do not have the seal of God upon their foreheads, suggesting that all Christians have such a seal

(Beasley-Murray, 140). (c) The irregular list of twelve tribes in Rev 7:5–8 is a subtle clue from the author indicating that empirical Israel is not in view (Ladd, 114–15).

4. *The 144,000 as Christian martyrs,* whose complete number must be fulfilled before the end; see Rev 6:9–11 (Kiddle-Ross, 133–37; Lohmeyer, 70; Caird, 94–98, 178–81). In a variation of this view, the 144,000 represent a holy army (Caird, 178) or "the Israelite army of the military Messiah of David" (Bauckham, "War Scroll," 216). According to Bauckham ("War Scroll," 210–37), the author has reworked Jewish military traditions and language to show that the decisive battle against evil has already been won through non-military means by the faithful witness and death of Jesus. Disciples are therefore urged to participate in this war by witnessing faithfully as Jesus did even to the point of death.

There are a number of arguments in support of this view (Bauckham, "War Scroll," 217–20): (a) Rev 7:4–8 has the literary form of a census of the tribes of Israel, and every OT census is a *military* census. (b) An Israelite army composed of twelve equal tribal contingents conforms to OT practice (e.g., according to Num 31:4–6, one thousand troops from each of the twelve tribes were dispatched against Midian; in 1QM 6:11, a contingent of six thousand horsemen is described, five hundred drawn from each tribe). (c) The notion of a messianic army composed of *all* twelve tribes fits the Jewish eschatological expectation of the regathering of the tribes to fight in the eschatological war. The eschatological army in the War Scroll (1QM), for example, is made up of continents from each of the twelve tribes. (d) This eschatological war tradition, however, is used both metaphorically and non-militaristically in Revelation. In Rev 5:5–6, an elder announces that the lion of the tribe of Judah, the root of David, has conquered, but when the seer turns to look, he rather sees a Lamb standing as though slaughtered. John rejects nationalistic militarism in Rev 7 just as he does in 5:5–6. According to 14:4, the 144,000 are all adult *male* Israelites, while the martyrs they symbolize in both 7:4–8 and 14:1–5 certainly include women and children (Bauckham, "War Scroll," 230–31). (e) While the 144,000 represent Christian martyrs, they are only a portion of the whole Church, represented by the twelve tribes of the sons of Israel (Kiddle-Ross, 136).

5. *When does this scene take place?* The imagined future just preceding the onset of the great tribulation (Sweet, 150), or the present (Giesen, 196).

6. *Solving the Problem.* Ultimately, none of the three ways of interpreting the 144,000 surveyed above (i.e., the 144,000 as the remnant of Jews or Jewish Christians, as all Christians, or as Christian martyrs) proves to be entirely convincing. Scholars have often failed to recognize or take seriously the interpretive constraints mentioned at the outset of this discussion (under B.1. *Interpretive Constraints*). Further, few scholars have drawn appropriate conclusions in considering which Jewish eschatological traditions provided a model for the author of Rev 7:4–8 and 14:1–5. In my view, *the 144,000 of Rev 7:4-8 represent that particular group of Christians (including all ages and both genders) who have been specially protected by God from both divine plagues and human persecution just before the final eschatological tribulation begins and who consequently survive that tribulation and the great eschatological battle that is the culmination of that tribulation.* The preservation of this group of "survivors" ensures that the number of the elect will not be cut off (Mark 13:20; *Barn.* 4:3) and guarantees the continued witness to Jesus during the unfolding end-time events. According to Jewish eschatological tradition contemporaneous with

the final edition of Revelation in 4 Ezra and *2 Apocalypse of Baruch,* those who are in the land of Israel (i.e., the last generation of Jews) will be protected by the presence of God from the messianic woes and the great eschatological battle waged by God, and they are therefore particularly fortunate (Dan 12:12; 4 Ezra 5:41; 6:25; 7:27; 9:7–8; 12:34; 13:48; *2 Apoc. Bar.* 29:1–2; 32:1; 40:2; 71:1; Mark 13:13; 1 Thess 4:15–17 [emphasizes the salvation of those who remain at the Parousia]; see Stone, *4 Ezra,* 148–49, 296–97, 369–70). This type of eschatological scenario is replayed, with variations, with particular frequency in 4 Ezra. Many of these brief scenarios emphasize that the deliverance of the survivors is linked to their presence in the land of Israel and presuppose the regathering of the twelve tribes of Israel (W. D. Davies, *The Gospel and the Land* [Berkeley; Los Angeles: University of California, 1974] 49–52). One such text is 4 Ezra 9:7–8:

> And it shall be that every one who will be saved and will be able to escape on account of his works, or on account of the faith by which he has believed, will survive the dangers that have been predicted, and will see my salvation in my land and within my borders, which I have sanctified for myself from the beginning.

Another similar text is found in 4 Ezra 12:34:

> But he will deliver in mercy the remnant of my people, those who have been saved throughout my borders, and he will make them joyful until the end comes, the day of judgment.

Again, the focus on the land is clear from 4 Ezra 13:48–49 (earlier in this chapter, in 13:15, it is said that the Messiah will appear and will stand on Mount Zion):

> But those who are left of your people, who are found within my holy borders, shall be saved. Therefore when he destroys the multitude of the nations that are gathered together, he will defend the people who remain.

The role of the Messiah in leading this remnant is mentioned in 4 Ezra 13:26:

> This is he [the man from the sea = the Son of man] whom the Most High has been keeping for many ages, who will himself deliver his creation; and he will direct those who are left.

A close parallel is also found two centuries earlier in CD 1:4: "But recalling the covenant with the first ones, he left a remnant of Israel and did not give them up to destruction" (here the remnant is apparently the Qumran sectarians).

The number 144,000 (12 [tribes] x 12 [apostles] x 1000) is a Christian symbol for the fullness of the new people of God, composed of both Jews and Gentiles, constituting the remnant of Christians who survive the eschatological woes. They form, as it were, an eschatological army of those who keep the commandments of God and follow the Lamb. They are not martyrs, for they have received divine immunity from all forms of suffering and death. There is no allusion to martyrdom in Rev 7:4–8, and only one phrase in 14:3 ("redeemed from the earth") has been wrongly construed to mean martyrdom in 14:1–5 (see *Comment* on 14:3). Further, the 144,000 are not identical with the innumerable multitude of 7:9–17, who must be identified as the greater number of Christians from whom the 144,000 have been drawn and who have borne witness to their faith and laid down their lives achieving victory through death just as Jesus did (see below).

The 144,000 are mentioned in Rev 14:1–5, and probably also in 17:14. The first passage, Rev 14:1–5, contains a brief narrative vignette of the Lamb and the 144,000 on Mount Zion (see *Form/Structure/Setting* in Rev 14). This is the only place where the 144,000 are localized in terms of known geography, and this localization (even though used symbolically by the author) coheres with the texts cited above relating to the preservation of the remnant of Israel in the land of Israel. The virginity of the 144,000, an allusion to the celibacy requirement for participants in holy wars, should be understood as symbolizing obedience to the commands of God and to the witness of Jesus.

The second passage, Rev 17:14, appears to be a brief fragment of an eschatological scenario (described differently in 16:12–16 and 19:11–21), in which it is said that the Lamb was victorious over the ten kings who have given their power and authority over to the beast, and *those who accompany the Lamb are called and elect and faithful* (see *Comment* on 17:14). In 17:14, the victory of the Lamb and his followers cannot be construed as a metaphor for death; rather it stands in the Jewish eschatological tradition of eschatological war in which the Messiah as leader of an army of Israel conquers the hostile nations who have gathered to oppose his rule.

C. The Identity of the Innumerable Host (Rev 7:9–17)

1. *Interpretive Constraints.* In identifying the innumerable host, there are features of this textual unit that constrain the interpretive possibilities for this passage. (a) The group must be identified as Christians since, according to v 14, "they have washed their robes and made them white in the blood of the Lamb." (b) The phrase "a great multitude which no one could number" (on the number of early Christians, see *Comment* on 7:9a) must be understood as an ancient hyperbole for a large number of people (Aeschylus describes the Lydian contingents of the ancient Persian army as a πλῆθος ἀνάριθμοι, an "innumerable multitude" [*Persians* 40]; Justin speaks of the Christians of his day as τὸ ἀναρίθμητον πλῆθος, "the innumerable multitude" [*Apol.* 15.7]; Origen in the early third century spoke of "innumerable souls" converted to Christianity [*Contra Celsum* 1.27]) and as the fulfillment of the promise to Abraham that his descendents would be like the stars of the sky and the sand of the sea for multitude.

2. *The innumerable multitude as Christian martyrs* (J. Weiss, *Offenbarung,* 66–67; Bousset [1906] 288; Behm, 46; Kiddle-Ross, 138–43; Caird, 95; W. J. Harrington, *Apocalpyse,* 131; Bauckham, "War Scroll," 210–37). There are several reasons that this group could be identified as martyrs. (a) There is evidence in both pagan and Christian writers that the number of Christian martyrs was extremely large. In Tacitus' account of the Neronian persecution, he claimed that "vast numbers" (*multitudo ingens*) were convicted and executed under Nero (*Annals* 15.44; for occurrences of the phrase *ingens multitudo* or *multitudo ingens,* "huge crowd," in Livy, see 2.39.9; 4.33.2; 5.7.2; 9.23.16; 34.29.5). *1 Clem.* 6:1 refers to unnamed martyrs as πολὺ πλῆθος ἐκλεκτῶν, "a great multitude of the elect." (b) In Rev 7:14, they are described as "coming out of the great tribulation," which implies their death (Boring, 131). (c) If one assumes that the 144,000 and the innumerable

multitude are identical, and if the 144,000 of 7:4–8 are identified as martyrs, then the innumerable multitude of 7:9–17 must also consist of martyrs. (d) If 7:14c is an allusion to Dan 11:35 (see *Comment* on 7:14c), then it is possible that John understands Dan 12:1 as the time when the people of God triumph, not through waging war but through martyrdom (Bauckham, "War Scroll," 227–28). (e) Their presence before the throne of God implies that they have died, perhaps as martyrs.

3. *The innumerable multitude as Christian Gentiles* (Bousset [1906] 287; Kraft, 126; Allo, 93). Major arguments for this view include the following: (a) This view is primarily held by those who regard the 144,000 as the remnant of Jews or Jewish Christians. The innumerable multitude is then thought to represent the rest of humankind, the Gentiles. (b) Also supporting this position is the statement that the innumerable multitude is composed of people from "every nation and tribe and people and language group" (v 9b), though this text cannot be construed to exclude Jews. The chief weakness of this interpretation is that while 7:14 makes it clear that the innumerable multitude must consist of Christians (against E. Schüssler Fiorenza, *Revelation: Vision of a Just World* [Edinburgh: T. & T. Clark, 1993] 68), there is no clear indication in the text itself that the group is limited to Gentiles. It has also been argued against this position that it makes no sense that gentile Christians have not been sealed to protect them from the wrath of God referred to in 9:4 (Giesen, 194).

4. *The innumerable multitude as all Christians,* Jews and Gentiles, martyrs and non-martyrs (Beckwith, 535–39; Lohse, 53; Lohmeyer, 70–71; Ulfgard, *Feast,* 70–79; Taeger, *Johannesapokalypse,* 30–31; Beagley, *Apocalypse,* 47; Boring, 129–32; Prigent, 121–23; W. J. Harrington, 98, 101; Giblin, 91–92; Rissi, *Babylon,* 17–19; Giesen, 193). The arguments for this view, which is held by the majority of scholars, include the following: (a) The innumerable multitude is explicitly interpreted as those "who have washed their robes and made them white in the blood of the Lamb" (v 14c), a vivid metaphor for belief in the atoning death of Christ, indicating that the multitude consists of Christians. (b) While those in the innumerable multitude have "come out of the great tribulation" (v 14b), i.e., have died and are now standing before the heavenly throne of God, there is no clear indication that all of them have suffered martyrdom. (c) Since they are drawn from "every nation and tribe and people and language group" (v 9c), there is no reason to exclude Jews from this inclusive list.

5. *The innumerable multitude as Jews from the Diaspora* (Buchanan, 189–92). There are at least two arguments for this minority view. (a) If Rev 7 is based on a Jewish source with some light Christian redaction (vv 10, 14), it would be possible to regard the innumerable multitude "from every nation [ἐκ παντὸς ἔθνους] and tribe and people and language group" (v 9) as diaspora Jews gathered from the places of their dispersion throughout the world. (b) Josephus can speak of the ten Jewish tribes east of the Euphrates as "countless myriads whose number cannot be ascertained [μυριάδες ἄπειροι καὶ ἀριθμῷ γνωσθῆναι μὴ δυνάμεναι]" (*Ant.* 11.133), a hyperbolic conception that could have been adopted by the author of Revelation.

There are also two obvious arguments against this view. (a) Rev 7:9–17 shows clear signs of having been composed by the primary author of Revelation (Wellhausen, *Analyse,* 12; Bousset [1906] 288–89; Lohmeyer, 70). (b) Even if 7:9–17 were based on an earlier Jewish source, the present shape of the text (with the obviously Christian references in vv 10, 14) indicates that at the very least the author has provided a Christian reading of the "source."

6. *When does this scene take place?* Several views regarding the temporal orientation of this scene have been proposed by scholars. Most interpreters view this scene as a proleptic vision of the future eschatological consummation (Beckwith, 530, 539; Zahn, 377; Mounce, 171; Prigent, 123; Giesen, 196). A second view is that the vision focuses on the reward of Christians who die before the Parousia of Christ and during the period when heaven and earth are still separate (Rissi, *Babylon*, 18). A third and more nuanced view recognizes that the vision links the perspectives of the present in vv 9–15b and the eschatological consummation in vv 15c–17 (Taeger, *Johannesapokalypse*, 31–33). A fourth view is articulated by Swete (100), who regards the scene as an allegory for the Christian life dominated by the joyful consciousness of the divine presence and glory.

7. *Solving the Problem.* In my view the innumerable multitude represents all Christians who have died, whether naturally or by martyrdom, before the completion of eschatological events, which conclude with the victory of the Lamb and his faithful followers (Rev 17:14). However, this group cannot represent *all* Christians for the simple reason that the 144,000 are still living on the earth under divine protection. The temporal setting of this vision is the future, emphasizing the heavenly reward enjoyed by those who were faithful to the point of death.

D. Two Groups or One Group in Rev 7:1–17?

Even though I have discussed separately the problems of identifying the 144,000 of Rev 7:4–8 and identifying the innumerable multitude of Rev 7:9–17, it is nevertheless important to keep in mind that the two parts of the chapter are closely related. Some have argued that *two different* groups are in view, the prevailing opinion when Bousset wrote the second edition of his commentary in 1906 (287): (1) martyrs and all Christians including the martyrs (Lohmeyer, 70–71); (2) the remnant of believing Jews and the gentile Christians (Kraft, 126–28); (3) Jews or Jewish Christians and martyrs (Bousset, [1906] 283–84, 287; Comblin, *AsSeign* 66 [1973] 42–49); or (4) Jews or Jewish Christians, representing the fullness of Israel, and the "survivors" of the Gentiles (Draper, *JSNT* 19 [1985] 136–37), or Israel and the gentile remnant (Bousset [1906] 287; Corsini, *Apocalypse*, 158–60; Rowland, 91). These views have all been surveyed above. (5) One scholar suggests that the two groups are the Palestinian Jews and the diaspora Jews (Buchanan, 189–92).

Most scholars now contend, however, that a single group is described from two different perspectives: (1) the Christian church, consisting of both Jews and Gentiles (Beckwith, 535–39; Lohse, 53; Ladd, 114–17; Ulfgard, *Feast*, 70–79; Taeger, *Johannesapokalypse*, 30–31; Beagley, *Apocalypse*, 47; Boring, 129–32; Prigent, 121–23; W. J. Harrington, 98, 101; Giblin, 91–92; Rissi, *Babylon*, 17–19; Giesen, 193), symbolically presented as the *ecclesia militans*, "church militant," and the *ecclesia triumphans*, "church triumphant" (Swete, 99; Hadorn, 92–94; Schrenk, *Weissagung*, 199–202; Roloff [ET] 97–98; Ulfgard, *Feast*, 72–73; Metzger, *Code*, 61), or (2) the Christian martyrs (Kiddle-Ross, 133, 138–40; Caird, 94–98).

E. The Relationship between Rev 7:1–8 and Rev 14:1–5

Since the group of 144,000 is mentioned only three times in Revelation, in 7:4 and 14:1, 3, it is important to determine whether 7:4–8 and 14:1–5 refer to the *same group* (Schrenk, *Weissagung,* 73–74 n. 91) or to *two different groups* (Bousset [1906] 122–23, 380, 383; Sickenberger, *Erklärung,* 137). A comparison and contrast between the two passages is in order: (1) In both passages groups of 144,000 are mentioned (7:4; 14:1, 3). (2) In both passages the members of the group of 144,000 are marked on their foreheads; in 7:3, the term σφραγίζειν, "to seal," is used, but what this seal looks like is not mentioned; in 14:1 the term "seal" is not used, but the 144,000 are said to bear the name of the Lamb and his Father's name on their foreheads. (3) The 144,000 sealed in 7:1–8 are drawn from a larger group, i.e., from Israelite tribes (ἐκ φυλῆς), and those in 14:1–5 have been redeemed from humankind as first fruits. (4) The scene in 7:1–8 is placed before the 144,000 are subjected to any opposition while that in 14:1–5 is a proleptic eschatological scene that depicts the 144,000 as either already victorious in the eschatological battle mentioned in 17:14, or else preparing for the gathering of nations that precedes the final battle. (5) In 7:1–8, nothing is mentioned that is distinctively Christian while in 14:1–5 the 144,000 are described as followers of the Lamb (14:4), bearing the name of the Lamb and of his Father on their foreheads (14:1), and so are clearly Christians. (6) In 14:1–5, in contrast to 7:1–8, there is no mention of Israelite tribes. (7) In 14:1–5, the 144,000 have several characteristics that are not mentioned in 7:1–8: (a) they are virgins (i.e., celibate), (b) they follow (ἀκολουθοῦντες) the Lamb wherever he goes (discipleship language), (c) they have been redeemed from humankind (ἀπὸ τῶν ἀνθρώπων) as first fruits for God and the Lamb, implying that others will be redeemed later (i.e., while 14:1–5 is a proleptic scene, it does not present the eschaton as fully present), and (d) the moral character of the 144,000 is stressed: they do not lie for they are blameless.

Despite the differences between the two passages, and despite the fact that the mention of the 144,000 does not have the anaphoric definite article referring back to 7:4, it appears that the author intends to equate the 144,000 in 7:4–8 and 14:1–5.

F. Rev 7:9–17 and the Feast of Booths

One particularly debated problem in the interpretation of Rev 7:9–17 deals with the issue of whether the author incorporated imagery from the Jewish Feast of Booths or Tabernacles (Succoth), the most important of all ancient Jewish festivals. In the early eighteenth century, C. Vitringa (*Anakrisis,* 295–319), followed by Eichhorn (217–33), argued that the presentation of heavenly worship in Rev 7:9–17 was based in part on imagery derived from the Jewish Feast of Booths (for the Jewish literary sources for this feast, see Greenup, *Sukkah,* 5–26). More recently, scholars such as J. Comblin (*AsSeign* 66 [1973] 42–49), H. Kraft (129); J. Sweet (151-52), and J. Draper (*JSNT* 19 [1985] 133–47) have repeated this proposal, sometimes developing it further. McKelvey, impressed with Comblin's argument ("La liturgie de la nouvelle Jérusalem [Apoc. xxi. 1–xxii. 5]," *ETL* 29 [1953] 5–40) that Rev 21:1–22:5 is based on the Feast of Booths, suggests that *all* of the liturgical scenes in the heavenly temple in Revelation, including Rev 7:9–17, are based on imagery drawn from this feast (*Temple,* 161–66). More recently, the most detailed exegetical argument for this position is that of H. Ulfgard (*Feast,* 108–58). Draper wants to show how Rev 7:1–17 has been influenced by the Jewish interpretation of Zech 14, and especially the focus on the eschatological celebration of the Feast of

Booths in vv 16–19, which he thinks is fulfilled in the universal celebration of the Feast of Booths depicted in Rev 7.

A brief summary of Zech 14 may be helpful at this point. This chapter centers on an apocalyptic vision of the New Jerusalem and consists of several pericopes: (1) the announcement of the future battle over Jerusalem between Yahweh and the nations (Zech 14:1–5); (2) utopian conditions in the land and the New Jerusalem (Zech 14:6–11); (3) description of the plague that will afflict all who fight against Jerusalem (Zech 14:12–15); and (4) the pilgrimage of all nations to Jerusalem for the Feast of Booths and the sanctification of all things in the eschaton (Zech 14:16-21).

Based on his view that Rev 7 contains structurally significant allusions to Zech 14, Draper understands Rev 7:1–8 to refer to the remnant of Israel (Draper, *JSNT* 19 [1985] 136) although there is no mention in this text of the regathering of the tribes. Draper understands Rev 7:9–17 to refer to the Gentiles who come to Jerusalem annually to celebrate the Feast of Booths, according to Zech 14:16–19 (*JSNT* 19 [1985] 137). Crucial to Draper's thesis is the unity of Rev 7:1–17, which reflects two aspects of Zech 14. His arguments for imagery from the Feast of Booths are strongest, however, for Rev 7:9–17, where several features found in Rev 7:9–17 may have parallels in this feast: (1) the festal gathering (v 9); (2) focus on the temple (vv 9b, 15) (3) the participants' palm fronds (v 9c); (4) the salvation exclamation (v 10); and (5) the allusion to (living) water (v 17). These parallels, however, are not sufficient to demonstrate that the author's conscious intention was to use imagery from the traditional features associated with the Feast of Booths to portray the final gathering of believers before the throne of God (Charles, 1:211; Greenup, *Sukkah,* 19).

The most detailed attempt to link Rev 7:9–17 with the Feast of Booths is that of Ulfgard, though the methodological approach of the study is flawed and leads to unconvincing and disappointing results. He provides a synchronic reconstruction of the popular features of the Feast of Booths and their interpretation in the first century A.D., using a variety of biblical and early Jewish literary and numismatic sources (*Feast,* 108–47). For Ulfgard, the "Exodus pattern" is of central importance, not only in Rev 7:9–17 but throughout Revelation, for the depiction of Christian existence as the redeemed people of God under the biblical type of Israel, liberated from "Egypt" and on the way to the "promised land" (*Feast,* 150–51). However, if we restrict ourselves to Rev 7:9–17, allusions to the Exodus event and its interpretation in the OT and later Jewish literature of the kind proposed by Ulfgard are so general and vague that to approach a difficult passage like Rev 7:9–17 with such an abstract key to its meaning is a case of trying to interpret *obscurum per obscurius.* The Feast of Booths, then, according to Ulfgard, is of secondary importance in understanding Rev 7:9–17. More important is what it represents, i.e., the joyful celebration of the past salvation of God, pointing back to the saving act of God in the Exodus event. While Ulfgard suggests, following several other scholars, that the liturgical activity before the throne of God, waving palm branches and uttering praise to God, can be understood as a kind of Booths celebration, his main interest is not in the liturgical imagery of the Feast of Booths itself but its theological significance. He is therefore not particularly interested in mining Rev 7:9–17 for possible allusions to the ritual of the Feast of Booths, nor is he concerned with arguing that the constellation of images reflects features associated with the ritual of this feast. Ulfgard argues that Draper is wrong in restricting his analysis of Rev 7 to Zech 14, for he misses the Exodus theme that is even more basic to that chapter. In emphasizing salvation as a past event, Ulfgard must argue against both Daniélou ("Le symbolisme eschatologique de la Fête des Tabernacles," *Irénikon* 31 [1958] 19–40) and Comblin (*AsSeign* 66 [1973] 42–49), who emphasize the eschatological character of the Feast of Booths. Ulfgard essentially discounts the clear eschatological setting given to the feast in Zech 14 (a passage that Ulfgard hardly discusses). What Ulfgard has done is to construct a theology of Revelation based on the "Exodus pattern" (*Feast,* 20–68), which he proceeds to read into Rev 7:9–17 by linking together themes and motifs from elsewhere in the book (*Feast,* 69–107). While Ulfgard's thesis is problematic, it does contain many fine exegetical insights, some of which are referred to in the *Comment* on Rev 7.

Comment

1a Μετὰ τοῦτο εἶδον τέσσαρας ἀγγέλους ἑστῶτας ἐπὶ τὰς τέσσαρας γωνίας τῆς γῆς, "After this I saw four angels standing at the four quarters of the earth." The formulaic phrase μετὰ τοῦτο εἶδον, "after this I saw," is used here to signal a change in subject and to introduce a new unit of text (the same formula is used in 4:1; 7:9; 15:5; 18:1). Since the author normally uses ταῦτα, "these things," however, this slight change in style may indicate an intrusive element in the composition. The phrase αἱ τέσσαρες γωνίαι as "the four quarters" of the compass is a widespread cosmological conception in the ancient world and is also found in Rev 20:8 (see Job 37:3; Isa 11:12 [literally "the four wings, MT כַּנְפוֹת *kanpôt;* LXX πτερύγων] of the earth"; Jer 49:36 uses the phrase "from the four ends [MT קְצוֹת *qĕṣôt;* LXX Jer 25:16, ἄκρων] of the earth"; Ptolemy *Tetrabiblos* 29; *T. Asher* 7:2; Pliny *Hist. nat.* 2.46.119). *PGM* VIII.8 speaks of αἱ δ' γωνίαι οὐρανοῦ, "the four quarters of heaven," while *PGM* 15a.8–11 refers to "the light from the four corners of the cosmos [κόσμου]" (see Kropp, *Koptische Zaubertexte* 2:103). The perspective of the author is determined by his presence in a prophetic trance in the heavenly court from 4:1 to 6:17. That heavenly perspective continues to be presupposed since the author claims to see the four angels standing at the four corners of the earth (conceived of as a flat, square shape).

1b κρατοῦντας τοὺς τέσσαρας ἀνέμους τῆς γῆς, "restraining the four winds of the earth." In ancient Israel, as in the rest of the ancient world, the four winds represented the four cardinal points of the compass and included all winds (see Ezek 37:9; Jer 49:36; Dan 7:2; 8:8; 11:4; Zech 2:6; 6:5; 4 Ezra 13:5; *1 Enoch* 18:2; Mark 13:27 = Matt 24:31; Jos. *J.W.* 6.300; *Adam and Eve* 38.3 [Denis, *Concordance,* 817]; *PGM* IV.3066; Kropp, *Koptische Zaubertexte* 2:103). Greco-Roman texts also refer to the four winds (Pliny *Hist. nat.* 2.46.119 [who insists that there are really two winds from each direction]; Vettius Valens 140.6; *P. Flor.* 20.19; 50.104; *PGM* III.273, 496; IV.1606). The storehouses of the winds are mentioned in *1 Enoch* 18:1; *2 Enoch* (J) 40:10. God controls the winds, bringing them from their storehouses (Ps 135:7; Jer 10:13; 51:16), a view also expressed in the Jewish magical papyrus entitled the "Recipe of Pibeches" (*PGM* IV.3007–86; see J. van Haelst, *Catalogue,* no. 1074), referring to God as "the one who stirs up the four winds" (line 3066). *1 Enoch* 76:1–14 describes the twelve gates through which come the winds from the four directions; through four of those gates come good winds, and through eight come winds of punishment. 4 Ezra 8:22 indicates that angels are changed to wind and fire at the command of God (probably based on Ps 104:4, quoted in Heb 1:7), and 1QH 1:10–11 speaks of the winds as "angels of holiness." In *Jub.* 2:2, the "angels of the spirit of the winds" are mentioned, and in 3 Enoch 14:4, the angel Ruhiel is said to be in charge of the wind. The four winds are also described as supports for the earth and the firmament of heaven (*1 Enoch* 18:2). The four winds can also be agents of divine judgment in scattering a people (Jer 49:36). In *Gos. Bartholomew* 31–36, which originated in the third century (Hennecke-Schneemelcher, *NTA* 1:498), the four angels who are in charge of the winds are named and described: (1) Chairum rules over Boreas and prevents the earth from drying up. (2) Oertha rules over Aparktias and prevents the earth from freezing. (3) Kerkutha rules over the south wind and prevents the earth from shaking. (4) Naoutha rules over the southwest wind and prevents the earth from burning up. Jerome (*Comm. in Dan.* 7:2–3) suggests that the four winds mentioned in Daniel are angelic powers. In line with this there is also a tradition in early Judaism that angels were identical with the winds, a notion based on Ps 104:4 (1QH 1:10–11; *Jub.* 2:2; 4 Ezra 8:22; *Pirqe R. El.* 4; Str-B, 3:678–79). Ptolemy *Tetrabiblos* 29 reflects the view that the winds originate at the four quarters of the horizon. In the Greek and Roman worlds, the four winds were often personified. In several Mithraic monuments, two or four great winds (Favonius, Auster, Eurus, Aquilo) are depicted with wings on their heads and blowing from the four points of the compass (Vermaseren, *CIMRM*, 1083, 1283, 1292, 1300, 1331, 1388, 1685); on the representation of the winds on Mithraic monuments, see L. A. Campbell, *Mithraic Iconography and Ideology* (Leiden: Brill, 1968) 162–80. According to the Coptic-Gnostic tractate *Paraph. Shem* 27.26–27 (tr. J. M. Robinson, *Nag Hammadi*, 353), "For without wind and star nothing happens upon the earth."

Many folktales deal with the problem of controlling the winds (see S. Thompson, *Motif-Index*, D2142). Many of these stories have been collected by J. G. Frazer, *The Golden Bough*, 2nd ed. (New York: Macmillan, 1911) 1:319–20; see Page, *Folktales*, 74–78. The earliest Greek story of an attempt to control the winds (and thus the weather) is found in *Odyssey* 10.1–76, where Odysseus narrates the story of Aeolus, whom Zeus had made steward of the winds. To provide safe passage home to Ithaca for Odysseus and his crew, Aeolus presented him with an ox-hide bag of storm winds tied with a silver cord so that he could reach home without experiencing contrary winds. While Odysseus slept, and when they were in sight of Ithaca, the crew opened the bag thinking it was treasure. The released storm winds drove them back to the island of Aeolus, where they received a chilly reception.

1c ἵνα μὴ πνέῃ ἄνεμος ἐπὶ τῆς γῆς μήτε ἐπὶ τῆς θαλάσσης μήτε ἐπὶ πᾶν δένδρον, "so that no wind might blow on the earth, nor on the sea, nor on any tree." Each of the four angels is presumably restraining one of the four winds, but it is not immediately evident *why* the winds should be restrained from blowing, though the assumption is that they will cause some type of terrible damage. In a fragment of Empedocles (Diels-Kranz, *FVS* 1:353, frag. B111), he appears to refer to the powers of a divine man: "You stop the power of tireless winds which move upon the earth, and by their blowing destroy the farmland; and again, if you have the will, you can summon the winds to return." In v 2 these angels are further characterized as those with the power to harm the earth and the sea. Presumably, this harm will come from the winds they are restraining. The trees are not mentioned here as they are in v 1. However, the potentially dangerous winds are not referred to again elsewhere in Revelation. Some have regarded this scene as a doublet of the opening of the first four seals, each of which unleashes a different plague on the world. A close parallel occurs in *2 Apoc. Bar.* 6:4–5 (tr. A. F. J. Klijn in Charlesworth, *OTP* 1:622–23), "And I saw, and behold, there were standing four angels at the four corners of the city [i.e., 'Jerusalem'], each of them with a burning torch in his hands. And another angel came down from heaven and said to them, 'Hold your torches and do not light them before I say it to you.'" J. Weiss understands the restraining of the four plague-bringing winds as a flashback introducing the protection of the 144,000 by sealing *before* the first six seals are opened (*Offenbarung,* 72); there is no indication in the text, however, that the author or the final redactor understood Rev 7 in this way.

2a καὶ εἶδον ἄλλον ἄγγελον ἀναβαίνοντα ἀπὸ ἀνατολῆς ἡλίου ἔχοντα σφραγῖδα θεοῦ ζῶντος, "Then I saw another angel ascending from the east with the signet of the living God." On καὶ εἶδον, see *Comment* on 5:1. The signet or seal is not further described (though it is assumed that it is an object, like a signet ring or a cylinder seal, that can make an impression on something), nor is that which is sealed on the foreheads of the servants of God explained (v 3). Not until 14:1 is it made clear that the name of the Lamb and the name of his Father are written (the term σφραγίζειν, "to seal," is not used) on the foreheads of the faithful. The seal is understood, at least in the final revision of Revelation, as the name of the Lamb and of his Father, mentioned explicitly in 14:1 (see 3:12; 22:4); see Dölger, *Sphragis,* 57. The terms σφραγίς, "seal, signet" (7:2; 9:4), and σφραγίζειν, "to seal" (7:3, 4[2x], 5, 8), are used in this chapter (and in 9:4) in an eschatological sense, as in Ezek 9:4–6 [cited in CD 19:12]; *Pss. Sol.* 15:6 (σημεῖον τοῦ θεοῦ, "mark of God"), 9 (σημεῖον τῆς ἀπωλείας, "mark of destruction"); 4 Ezra 6:5; 8:53. Further, sealing is used here as a symbol of *divine protection,* as Rev 9:4 makes clear: the demonic locusts are told to harm "only those people who do not have the seal of God on their foreheads" (this is the only other use of σφραγ- terms in Revelation). Further, both Ezek 9:4–6 and *Pss. Sol.* 15:6 use the metaphor of sealing in the context of the concept of the remnant. The currency of the sealing notion in apocalyptic circles is supported by 4 Ezra 6:5, which refers to eschatological sealing as if it were a well-known concept: "the schemes of its sinners had not yet been outlawed, nor had God's seal yet been set on those who have stored up a treasure of fidelity." The notion of sealing is combined with the motif of the *numerus iustorum* in 5 Ezra 2:38, 40:

> Rise, stand up, and see the whole company of those who bear the Lord's mark and sit at his table. . . . Receive, O Zion, your full number, and close the roll of those arrayed in white who have faithfully kept the law of the Lord.

Gen 4:15 offers a further parallel for a protective mark (the nature of which cannot be known) within the context of a curse: "And the Lord put a mark on Cain, lest any who came upon him should kill him" (see Westermann, "Excursus: The Mark of Cain," in *Genesis* 1:312–14). The protective function of sealing is made explicit in the Coptic-Gnostic tractate *Ap. John* 31.22–25 (tr. J. M. Robinson, *Nag Hammadi,* 122), "And I raised him up and sealed him in the light of the water with five seals, in order that death might not have power over him from this time on." The protective or apotropaic function of magical sealing is a motif frequently encountered in ancient texts and in inscriptions on amulets and other *materia magica.* An inscription on an Aramaic incantation bowl reads "that seal with which the First Adam sealed his son Seth to protect him from demons" (Isbell, *Incantation,* text 16.3, p. 54). Similarly, in *Acts Andrew* 27 (ed. MacDonald, *Acts*), seven demons will not attack Andrew because of the seal on his forehead. On an apotropaic copper amulet from Smyrna, which contains Jewish motifs and a magical formula with a few Christian additions, is the inscription on the obverse, "Seal of the living God, guard him who wears this," and on the reverse, "Get out hated one. Araaph the angel and Solomon drive you away from him who wears this" (Goodenough, *Jewish Symbols* 2:231; vol. 3, fig. 1054). For other amulets containing depictions of Solomon and the inscription σφραγὶς θεοῦ, "seal of God," see G. Schlumberger, "Amulettes Byzantines anciens destinés à combattre les maléfices & maladies," *REG* 5 (1892) 84; P. Perdrizet, "Σφραγὶς Σολομῶντος," *REG* 16 (1903) 42–61.

In the OT and early Judaism, there was the anthropomorphic notion that Yahweh, like all kings, had a seal (Job 9:7; Sir 17:22; *T. Moses* 12:9; *Apoc. Moses* 42:1; see Ysebaert, *Greek Baptismal Terminology,* 246). The signet ring (חותם *ḥôtām*) of God (conceived of either as a cylinder seal worn on a cord around the neck or a seal mounted on a ring) can be a metaphor for the king of Israel (Jer 22:24; Hag 2:23). According to *Pr. Man.* 3, God has "confined the deep [τὴν ἄβυσσον] and sealed [σφραγισάμενος] it with thy terrible and glorious name." On the basis of the evidence presented below, the idea of sealing people with the seal or signet ring of God is a metaphor drawn from the world of ancient magic, where sealing functions either to protect the person sealed or to control the evil spirit that is sealed.

The language of sealing and signet rings frequently occurs in ancient magic, where it is often difficult to distinguish between Jewish magic and Greco-Roman magic because of the enormous influence that the former had on the latter. *PGM* VII.583 speaks of an amulet that "is the powerful name and seal of the great god [ὄνομα τοῦ μεγάλου θεοῦ καὶ σφραγίς]." Here καί is probably epexegetical so that the phrase could be translated "the powerful name or seal of the great god." Similarly, in *PGM* I.306 and III.226 the phrase ὁρκίζω [σε] σφραγῖδα θεοῦ, "I adjure [you] by the seal of God," very likely refers to the *name* of the god (perhaps as inscribed or otherwise depicted on *materia magica,* e.g., amulets, papyri, etc.). This is suggested by the hexameter lines parallel to I.306 and III.226 in I.309, "I adjure you by Aion the eternal god of all," and III.229, "I adjure you by the great god Apollo." Thus σφραγίς = ὄνομα = θεός. T. Kraabel published the Wilshere jasper ringstone (ca. third century A.D.), with the divine names ΙΑΩ ΣΑΩ ΑΔΩΝΙ (i.e., Iao, Sabaoth, Adonai) written in reverse in three lines ΩΑΙ ΩΑΣ ΙΝΩΔΑ ("Jews in Imperial Rome: More Archaeological Evidence from an Oxford Collection," *JJS* 30 [1979] 50–55). Though magical formulas are frequently written backwards for magical effect (see J. Naveh, "Lamp Inscriptions and Inverted Writing," *IEJ* 38 [1988] 36–43), this particular ringstone is probably incised backwards so that it will imprint the divine names correctly when used as a stamp. Though these three divine names occur together frequently in the magical papyri (*PGM* III.266–67; IV.1485–86, 1534–35, 1561, 1621, 2315, 2326, 3053; VII.220, 311, 595–96), they are ultimately derived from three Hebrew names for God, which magical practitioners regarded as three separate deities. The name "Iao" is particularly important, for it represents a Greek transliteration of a shortened form of the covenant name for God, יהוה *YHWH,* usually vocalized as "Yahweh" (see Aune, "Iao," *RAC* 17:1–12).

In the *Testament of Solomon,* in magical gems that show a strong Jewish influence, and in the Jewish Aramaic incantation bowls, the use of seals and sealing in Jewish magical practice is very prominent. According to *T. Sol.* 1:6–7, Solomon received a magic ring from God through Michael, which he used to control evil spirits (Aramaic incantation bowl texts refer to "the sealing of Solomon the king [ובחותמא דישלומו מלכא *wbḥwtmʾ dyšlwmw mlkʾ*]" [Isbell, *Incantation,* 31–33], and "the signet-ring [עיזקתא *ʿyzqtʾ*] of King Solomon" [Isbell, *Incantation,* 108]); the ring is referred to as the σφραγὶς τοῦ θεοῦ, "the seal of God" (1:7; 10:6; 15:7), and ὁ δακτύλιος τοῦ θεοῦ, "the ring of God" (7:3; 8:12; 10:7). The ring of Solomon referred to in Josephus *Ant.* 8.47 is mentioned in *b. Giṭ.* 68a as "a ring on which was graven the Name." One type of magical gem or amulet depicts Solomon as a mounted warrior about to pierce a supine female figure with his lance. The rider is often labeled "Solomon," frequently with the inscription Σφραγὶς Θεοῦ, "seal of God," on the reverse (Bonner, *Magical Amulets,* 208–11; Delatte-Derchain, *Les intailles magiques,* nos. 369–73, 376–77 [pp. 261–64]). The Jewish Aramaic incantation bowls contain a number of relevant parallels. In text 3.4 (Isbell, *Incantation,* 21–22) we find this formula: "in the name of the great God and with the great seal of Shadda El [בישמיה דאלהא רבא ובחתמא רבא דשדא אל *byšmyh dʾlhʾ rbʾ ubḥtmʾ rbʾ dšdʾ ʾl*]"; here the term "seal" is parallel to the term "name," indicating their identity (a parallel text occurs in Isbell, *Incantation,* 4.1–2 [p. 24]). Similarly, text 48.4 speaks of being "sealed with the signet ring of El Shaddai [חתיהין בעיזקתא דאל שדי *ḥtyhyn bʿyzqtʾ dʾl šdy*]" (see 12.11; Isbell, *Incantation,* 48–49); a variation is to be "sealed with the great seal of the Holy One" (19.9; Isbell, *Incantation,* 62). Thus "seal" (חתמא *ḥatmāʾ*) and "signet-ring" (עזקא *ʿizqāʾ*) are used as equivalents. Another inscription reads "By the seal on which has been carved and engraved the Ineffable Name [שׁם מפורשׁ *šēm mĕpôrāš*]" (Isbell, *Incantation,* 17.9 [pp. 56–57]). The effectiveness of such sealing is emphasized in text 51.6–7 (Isbell, *Incantation,* 116), which speaks of "the great seal of the Lord of the Universe [whose] knot cannot be untied and whose seal cannot be broken." The protective function of the seal from plagues (פגעין *pĕgāʾîn*) with supernatural origins is expressed in text 31.2–4 (Isbell, *Incantation,* 83):

> . . . so that you may not come near the house and threshold of ʾAdaq the son of Maḥlapta who is sealed with the three [signet]-rings and doubly-sealed with the seven seals from all evil plagues [פגעין בישין *pĕgāʾîn bîšîn*], from all bad spirits, from monsters, from liliths, and from all blast-demons and harmers.

God is often called "the living God" (Heb. אלהים חיים *ʾĕlohîm ḥayyîm;* Gk. θεὸς ζῶν) in Jewish and early Christian tradition (the term κύριος, "Lord," is never used in this way), though in Revelation the phrase occurs only here in 7:2 (Deut 5:26; Josh 3:10; 1 Sam 7:26; 2 Kgs 19:4; Pss 42:2[LXX 41:2]; 84:2[LXX 83:2]; Isa 37:4, 17; Jer 10:10; 23:36; Dan 6:20, 26; Hos 1:10; LXX Deut 4:33; LXX Esth 6:13; 8:13; *Gk. 1 Enoch* 5:1; *T. Abra.* [Rec. A] 17:11; *Jos. As.* 8:5, 6; 11:10; *T. Job* 37.2; Matt 16:16; 26:63; John 6:69 [*var. lect.*]; Acts 14:15; Rom 9:26; 2 Cor 3:3; 6:16; 1 Thess 1:9; 1 Tim 3:15; 4:10; Heb 3:12; 9:14; 10:31; 12:22; *2 Clem.* 20:2; Hermas *Vis.* 2.3.2; 3.7.2; *Sim.* 6.2.2).

2b καὶ ἔκραξεν φωνῇ μεγάλῃ τοῖς τέσσαρσιν ἀγγέλοις οἷς ἐδόθη αὐτοῖς ἀδικῆσαι τὴν γῆν καὶ τὴν θάλασσαν, "He cried out with a booming voice to the four angels who were empowered to harm the earth and the sea." There are just two certain instances in Revelation in which particular angelic beings issue commands to others (7:2; 14:18; cf. 16:1), perhaps reflecting an implicit assumption of an angelic hierarchy. The aorist passive verb ἐδόθη is another example of the *passivum divinum,* indicating that God has given these angels the task in question (see *Comment* on 9:3).

3 λέγων· μὴ ἀδικήσητε τὴν γῆν μήτε τὴν θάλασσαν μήτε τὰ δένδρα ἄχρι σφραγίσωμεν τοὺς δούλους τοῦ θεοῦ ἡμῶν ἐπὶ τῶν μετώπων αὐτῶν, "Do not harm the earth or the sea or the trees until we seal the servants of our God upon their foreheads." The first-person plural form of the verb σφραγίσωμεν, "we seal," is enigmatic since it is not clear who in addition to the angel bearing the signet of God could be part of the subject of this verb. This sealing is a sign of divine protection, which is explicitly said to protect those sealed from the fifth trumpet plague in 9:4: "But they were instructed not to harm the grass of the earth nor any plant nor any tree, with the exception of people who do not have the seal of God upon their foreheads." See also *T. Job* 5.1, where after promising Job that he will not die, an angel seals Job before Satan begins to torment him (parallels in B. Schaller, *Das Testament Hiobs,* JSHRZ 3.3 [Gütersloh: Mohn, 1979] 330). The combination of the notions of sealing or tattooing with the term δοῦλοι, "slaves, servants," indicates that this metaphor is derived from the Eastern practice of tattooing secular and religious slaves (Dölger, *Sphragis,* 58). One important issue in this verse is the problem of determining whether the verb σφραγίζειν, "seal," has any connection with Christian baptism or the complex of rituals associated with baptism (see *Excursus 7A: Marking, Branding, and Tattooing in the Ancient World*). While the notion of "sealing" in 7:2–8 certainly is a metaphor for ownership, it is unlikely that it is a metaphor for either Christian baptism or the reception of the Holy Spirit (against Prigent, 120; Roloff [ET] 97; Giesen, 194). While Prigent, Roloff, and Giesen understand "sealing" as baptism, and the 144,000 as Christians, the fact that some but not all the "twelve tribes of the sons of Israel" were sealed means that the group from which the sealed were selected was obviously not sealed and hence cannot be Christians. To understand "sealing" as baptism, these scholars must ignore the basic character of the metaphor that presents the 144,000 as sealed from a presumably larger "unsealed" group.

This verse alludes to LXX Ezek 9:4, where those who mourned the pollution of the temple are marked on the forehead to protect them from the angels about to destroy Jerusalem: δὸς τὸ σημεῖον ἐπὶ τὰ μέτωπα τῶν ἀνδρῶν, "Place a sign on the foreheads of the men." The significance of this marking is that it indicates both divine protection and divine ownership (Lampe, *Seal,* 16). In CD (MS B) 19:10–12, Ezek 9:4 is referred to in connection with the protection of the faithful members of the covenant community, called the "little ones" and "the poor of the flock" (tr. P. R. Davies, *Covenant,* 257):

> These shall escape at the time of the visitation, and those who are left shall be delivered to the sword when the Messiah of Israel and Aaron comes. (It will be) as it was in the time of the first visitation, as He said by the hand of Ezekiel: "to make a mark upon the foreheads of those who sigh and groan."

Isa 44:5 is an appropriate parallel (RSV): "This one will say, 'I am the Lord's,' another will call himself by the name of Jacob, and another will write on his hand, 'The Lord's' [LXX καὶ ἕτερος ἐπιγράψει Τοῦ θεοῦ εἰμι], and surname himself by the name of Israel." J. Finegan (*Archaeology*, 224–25) argues that the use of the definite article with תו *tāw*, as in CD (MS B) 19:12 quoted above, which reads התיו *hattāyw*, or in Origen *Selecta in Ezech.* 9, where τοῦ Θαῦ is said to stand in the Greek versions of Aquila and Theodotion, refers to an alphabetic character, taw, a letter represented in archaic Hebrew script with *X* (see the "Table of Scripts" in Gibson, *Inscriptions* 1:117–18). Brownlee (*Ezekiel*, 140) translates the relevant phrase in Ezek 9:4 "mark with an *X* the foreheads of people." Ezek 9:4 has also influenced *Pss. Sol.* 15:8, 10, where we read "The mark of God is upon the righteous that they may be saved, whereas it is said of sinners that 'the mark of destruction is upon their forehead.'" In *b. Šabb.* 55a (tr. Epstein, *Talmud*), "a *taw* of ink upon the foreheads of the righteous" and "a *taw* of blood upon the foreheads of the wicked" are mentioned. In *b. Šabb.* 120b, bathing is forbidden to one who has the divine name written (כתב *kĕtāb*) on his skin (see *b. Yoma* 8a); see Ysebaert, *Greek Baptismal Terminology*, 244. An allusion to Rev 22:4 may be reflected in what appears to be a Christian interpolation into *T. Sol.* 17:4 (tr. Charlesworth, *OTP* 1:977):

> So I said to him, "Fear the God of heaven and earth and tell me by what angel you are thwarted." He replied, "He who is about to return (as) Savior thwarts me. If his mark [στοιχεῖον] is written on (one's) forehead, it thwarts me, and because I am afraid of it, I quickly turn and flee from him. This is the sign of the cross."

Divine protection was provided for Israelites who marked the doorposts of their homes with the blood of a sacrificial lamb (Exod 12:7), and many have seen Exodus imagery in this chapter. That this sealing is for the purpose of protecting the 144,000 is clear from 9:4, which explicitly states that only people who do not have the seal of God on their foreheads are to be harmed by the plague unleashed by the fifth trumpet.

Excursus 7A: Marking, Branding, and Tattooing in the Ancient World

Bibliography

Beskow, P. "Branding in the Mysteries of Mithras?" In *Mysteria Mithrae*, ed. U. Bianchi. Leiden: Brill, 1979. 487–501. **Dinkler, E.** *Signum Crucis.* Tübingen: Mohr-Siebeck, 1967. **Dix, G.** "'The Seal' in the Second Century." *Theology* 51 (1948) 7–12. **Dölger, F. J.** "Profane und religiöse Brandmark und der Tiere in der heidnischen und christlichen Antike." *AC* 3 (1932) 25–61. ———. "Die Sphragis der Mithrasmysterien." *AC* 1 (1929) 88–91. ———. *Sphragis: Eine altchristliche Taufbezeichnung in ihrer Beziehungen zur profanen und religiösen Kultur des Altertums.* Paderborn: Schöning, 1911. ———. "Die religiöse Brandmarkung in den Kybele-Attis-Mysterien nach einem Texte des christlichen Dichters Prudentius." *AC* 1 (1929) 88–91. ———. "Zum zweiten salomonischen Psalm." *AC* 1 (1929) 291ff. **Donfried, K.** *The Setting of Second Clement in Early Christianity.* NovTSup 38. Leiden: Brill, 1974. **Gustafson, W. M.** "*Inscripta in fronte:* Penal Tattooing in Late Antiquity." *CA* 16 (1997) 79–105. **Heintze, H. von.** "Studien zu den Porträts des 3. Jahrhunderts nach Chr." *MDAIRA* 64 (1957) 69–91. **Heitmüller, W.** "Σφραγίς." In *Neutestamentliche Studien.* FS G. Heinrici. Leipzig: Hinrichs, 1914. 40–59. **Jones, C. P.** "*Stigma:* Tattooing and Branding in Graeco-Roman Antiquity." *JRS* 77 (1987) 139–55.

Lampe, G. W. H. *The Seal of the Spirit: A Study in the Doctrine of Baptism and Confirmation in the New Testament and the Fathers.* 2nd ed. London: SPCK, 1967. **Lilliebjörn, H.** *Über religiöse Signierung in der Antike, mit besonderer Berüchsichtigung der Kreuzsignierung, nebst einem Exkurs über die Apokalypse und die Mithras-Monumente.* Uppsala: Almquist & Wiksell, 1933. **Michaelis, W.** "Zeichen, Siegel, Kreuz: Ein Ausschnitt aus der Bedeutungsgeschichte biblischer Begriffe." *TZ* 12 (1956) 505–25. **Ysebaert, J.** *Greek Baptismal Terminology: Its Origins and Early Development.* Nijmegen: Dekker & Van de Vegt, 1962.

The terms σφραγίς and σφραγίζειν refer to the impression of a seal in clay or wax; since seals could be attached to people, they can be confused with tattoos or brands. The term σφραγίς refers both to the seal and to the impression made by it; the term also represents the power and authority of its owner. The instruments used in sealing (e.g., cylinders, rings), often made of precious stones, were important as symbols of power. Individuals, temples, and cities frequently had seals. This is even more true of the gods, for Orphica *Hymni* 34.26 says of Apollo, "you have the master seal [σφραγῖδα] of the cosmos." Seals in wax or clay were attached to many types of objects to guarantee their authenticity (e.g., weights and measures). The mode of sealing is of interest particularly when it is used in connection with people. Seals could be worn suspended from a chain or cord worn around the neck (Xenophon *Vect.* 4.21). A play on the word *signaculum* is found in the *Acts of Maximilian* 2 (tr. Musurillo, *Acts*):

> Dion said to Maximilian: "Agree to serve and receive the military seal." "I will not accept the seal," he replied. "I already have the seal of Christ who is my God."

Here the *signaculum* (= σφραγίς) of soldiers is a military seal impressed on a lead *tessera* or *bulla,* though some argue that it was a tattoo or brand on the hand, forehead, or neck that functioned as a sign of service, a mark of recognition, and a precaution against desertion (Lampe, *Seal of the Spirit,* 11).

Branding or tattooing was used in several different ways in the ancient world: (1) as a barbarian custom, (2) as a punishment or mark of disgrace among the Greeks and later the Romans, (3) as a mark of ownership in the Roman empire, (4) as a sacral rite in some cults, and (5) as a term for Christian baptism or for the rite following baptism that conveyed the gift of the Holy Spirit. In the OT tattooing (the technical term for which was קעקע *qaʿăqaʿ*) was forbidden in Lev 19:28, translated in the LXX as γράμματα στικτά, "tattooed writing." Yet an emancipated slave could receive a tattooed inscription (כתובת קעקע *kĕtôbet qaʿăqaʿ*) according to *b. Giṭ.* 20b. Permissible and impermissible marks on the skin are discussed in *m. Mak.* 3:6 (tr. Danby, *Mishnah*):

> If a man wrote [on his skin] pricked-in writing [he is culpable]. If he wrote but did not prick it in, or pricked it in but did not write it, he is not culpable, but only if he writes it and pricks it in with ink or eye-paint or aught that leaves a lasting mark. R. Simeon b. Judah says in the name of R. Simeon: He is not culpable unless he writes there the name [of a god], for it is written, "Nor print any marks upon you: I am the Lord."

(1) Barbarian tribes in antiquity practiced tattooing often for reasons of tribal identity or as marks of ownership with religious significance (Strabo 7.5.4; Xenophon *Anab.* 5.4.32; Sextus Empiricus *Pyrhh.* 1.148; 3.202). The Greeks, who looked down on the custom, particularly associated the practice with the Thracians (Herodotus 5.6; Cicero *De offic.* 2.7.25).

(2) The Greeks used tattoos primarily as a punishment for slaves and criminals, a custom they apparently learned from the Persians, and hence it was a mark of disgrace (Ysebaert, *Greek Baptismal Terminology,* 190–91). Disobedient or runaway slaves were

sometimes branded or tattooed on their foreheads (Gustafson, *CA* 16 [1977] 81–85). In Petronius *Satyricon* 103, Eumolpus thinks that the head and eyebrows of Encolpius should be shaved: "Then I will come and mark your foreheads [*frontes*] with some neat inscription so that you look like slaves punished by branding" (LCL tr.). Then in *Satyricon* 105, "Tryphaena, thinking that the marks on our foreheads were real prisoners' brands [*vera enim stigmata credebat captivorum frontibus* (n.b. that *frons* can mean either face or forehead) *impressa*], cried bitterly over our supposed punishment." Herodas 5.65–67, 77–79 also refers to having a slave tattooed on the forehead: "when he has this inscription on his forehead [ἐν τῷ μετώπῳ τὸ ἐπίγραμμ' ἔχων τοῦτο]." C. P. Jones argues that *stigma* almost always refers to tattooing and not branding (*JRS* 77 [1987] 140). Lucian *Nigrinus* 27, at his satirical best, refers to philosophers who train students to endure cold baths and whipping, "while the more humane mark their skins with iron" (tr. Jones, *JRS* 77 [1987] 142). Among the ancients, tattooing was nearly always a sign of punishment and degradation (i.e., a lowering of status since it was normally reserved for slaves), so ancient medical literature frequently deals with the problem of removing tattoos (Jones, *JRS* 77 [1987] 143). Delinquent slaves were often tattooed (Aristophanes *Birds* 760–61; *Frogs* 1508–14; Menander *Samia* 321–24; Petronius *Sat.* 103.2; Suetonius *Caligula* 27.3; Diogenes Laertius 4.46). Slaves were tattooed on their foreheads, on the entire face, and sometimes on parts of the body such as the arm, hand, or leg. The tattoos could consist of texts, perhaps mentioning the crime committed; see Plato *Leges* 9.854D (LCL tr.), "Whosoever is caught robbing a temple, if he be a foreigner or a slave, his curse shall be branded on his forehead and on his hands."

(3) Tattooing could also be a mark of ownership (Ysebaert, *Greek Baptismal Terminology,* 191–94). The practice of branding cattle or sheep with the name of the owner was as common in antiquity as it is in modern times. Documentary evidence from the Egyptian Jewish colony at Elephantine indicates that slaves were marked on the arm with Aramaic letters (A. Cowley, *Aramaic Papyri,* 28,2). *Pss. Sol.* 2:6 speaks of the Jewish experience during the exile: "The sons and daughters (were) in harsh captivity, their neck in a seal, a spectacle among the Gentiles."

(4) Further, in a number of Levantine religions, tattooing had a religious significance involving dedication to a deity, a custom that also implies ownership (Ysebaert, *Greek Baptismal Terminology,* 194–96). Isa 44:5 predicts that at the end of days some Jews will write on their hands ליהוה אני *lYHWH ʾānî,* "I am the Lord's" (LXX Τοῦ θεοῦ εἰμι). Herodotus 2.113.1 refers to the fact that a slave could flee for refuge to a particular temple and be marked with στίγματα, "stigmata," thus ἑωυτὸν διδοὺς τῷ θεῷ, "giving himself to the god." In Lucian *De dea Syria* 59 (tr. Attridge-Oden, *Goddess*), the author observes, in connection with the cult of Atargatis at Hierapolis, that "All people are marked, some on their wrists and some on their necks. For this reason all Assyrians carry a mark." Prudentius, the Christian poet, provides evidence that branding was practiced in the mysteries of Cybele–Attis in the fourth century A.D. (Dölger, *AC* 1 [1929] 88–91). Tertullian (*De praescr. haer.* 40) claimed that Mithras "sets his marks on the foreheads of his soldiers [*signat illic in frontibus milites suos*]," and Cumont (*Mithra,* 157) concluded that initiates into Mithraism received a brand on their forehead (see Vermaseren, *Mithras,* 145); n.b. that in Mithraism the *miles,* "soldier," grade is one of seven levels of initiation. There is no archaeological evidence, however, to confirm Tertullian's claim. Lilliebjörn (*Signierung,* 62–78) lists twenty-six sculptures, all of which have a cross or an *X* on their foreheads, and concludes that they are Isiac or Mithraic religious stigmata directly relevant for understanding Rev 13:16–18. However, Beskow ("Branding," 487–501) has argued that this view is incorrect, though the crosses or *X* marks on the foreheads of the marble busts have yet to receive a satisfactory explanation.

(5) The rite of baptism and the reception of the Holy Spirit are not necessarily identical in earliest Christianity. The ritual that accomplished the postbaptismal bestowal of the

Spirit on those who had received baptism was designated in several ways: (a) "laying on of hands" (Acts 8:17ff.; 19:6; see Heb 6:2), (b) "anointing" (2 Cor 1:21–22; 1 John 2:20, 27), and (c) "sealing" (2 Cor 1:21–22; Eph 1:13; 4:30; *Testim. Truth* 69.10–11); see Ysebaert, *Greek Baptismal Terminology,* 259–65. In this metaphorical use of sealing in 2 Cor 1:21–22, it is *God* who does the sealing (θεός, ὁ καὶ σφραγισάμενος ἡμᾶς, "God, who also seals us"). There are at least two ways of understanding the metaphor of sealing in this passage: (a) as a mark of ownership or (b) as confirmation of something with a seal (Ysebaert, *Greek Baptismal Terminology,* 265–66). Paul also referred to circumcision as a sealing (Rom 4:11), a metaphor that was probably already in use in Judaism (see *Aramaic Levi* 2; J. C. Greenfield and M. E. Stone, "Remarks on the Aramaic Testament of Levi," *RB* 86 [1979] 218). Dunn (*Romans* 1:209) thinks it may have been current in Judaism, but he can point to no text earlier than Paul. Believers are therefore sealed by God and are his property (Ysebaert, *Greek Baptismal Terminology,* 265). Beginning in the second century, the "sealing" (σφραγίς and σφραγίζειν) that Christians receive at baptism becomes a term for baptism. According to Heitmüller, the earliest clear designations of baptism with the term σφραγίς are Hermas *Sim.* 8.6.3; 9.16.2ff.; 9.17.4; *2 Clem.* 7:6; 8:6 ("Σφραγίς," 40). The texts are probably more ambiguous, however, for while σφραγίς in *2 Clem.* 7:6; 8:6 can be understood as referring to the seal of baptism (Dinkler, *Signum Crucis,* 109; Donfried, *Clement,* 125), it can also be used primarily to refer to a mark of ownership (as in Rev 7:2–8), closely linked to baptism as the means whereby the seal is conferred (Ysebaert, *Greek Baptismal Terminology,* 390). The possibility of breaking the seal and receiving the seal anew is broached in Hermas *Sim.* 8.6.3. The seal is clearly identified with baptism in Hermas *Sim.* 9.16.4: ἡ σφραγὶς τὸ ὕδωρ ἐστίν, "the seal is the water." This sealing is also explained as "bearing the name of the Son of God" (Hermas *Sim.* 9.16.3). While Hermas readers apparently understood "water" as "baptism," the fact that he must explain that "the seal is the water" means that this use of the term "seal" is novel (Ysebaert, *Greek Baptismal Terminology,* 391). He proposes that "sealing" in the sense of ownership (from Rev 7:2–8) and "sealing" in the Pauline sense of a sealing with the Holy Spirit combined to become the "sealing" at baptism. Heitmüller, to be sure, was convinced that σφραγίς in Rev 7 was used of baptism and finds confirmation for this view particularly in the fact that the 144,000 when mentioned in Rev 14:1 bear the name of the Lamb and the Father on their foreheads ("Σφραγίς," 59). At any rate, this new meaning of seal = baptism first appears in Asia Minor and Syria (*Acts Thom.* 26–27, 49–50, 87, 120, 131; Clement of Alexandria *Exc. ex Theod.* 80.3, 83; *Odes Sol.* 39.6–7; *Acts Pet.* 5; *Acts Paul* 25 [*Pap. Heid.*, p. 28]; *Mart. Paul* 5; Irenaeus *Dem.* 3; see Ysebaert, *Greek Baptismal Terminology,* 391–95). Baptism can be construed as a "sealing" since it involves an appeal to the *name* of Christ (2 Cor 1:22; Eph 1:13; 4:30; Hermas *Sim.* 8.6; *2 Clem.* 7:6; 8:6). In Marcion, baptismal ritual included a bath, anointing, and sealing (Tertullian *Adv. Marc.* 1.14.3; 1.28.3).

Apart from the use of σφραγίς in a baptismal context, the term is also used as a metaphor for the name of the Son of God (Hermas *Sim.* 9.16.3–5; *Odes Sol.* 8:16ff.; 39.6–7; see Ysebaert, *Greek Baptismal Terminology,* 408–9). It is possible that during the course of the second century, the postbaptismal ritual of anointing was performed using the sign of the cross (Ysebaert, *Greek Baptismal Terminology,* 412), and in this way the term σφραγίς became a term used for the sign of the cross.

4a καὶ ἤκουσα τὸν ἀριθμὸν τῶν ἐσφραγισμένων, "I then heard the number of those who were sealed." This statement is a literary device used to explain how John knew that which was not part of this audition (cf. 9:16), namely, the actual number of those who were sealed. John does not *see* the 144,000 until 14:1–5. It is also clear that vv 4–8 constitute an *audition* rather than a vision (the visionary section is limited to vv 1–3), for this section does not narrate the sealing of the 144,000; rather it consists of a list that John claims to have heard.

4b ἑκατὸν τεσσεράκοντα τέσσαρες χιλιάδες ἐσφραγισμένοι ἐκ πάσης φυλῆς υἱῶν Ἰσραήλ, "144,000 were marked from every tribe of the sons of Israel." In Revelation, the term "Israel" occurs only here and in 21:12 in the phrase φυλή/φυλαὶ υἱῶν Ἰσραήλ and is unusual since "Israel" was normally the self-designation of Jews in postbiblical Jewish literature (oddly, the term "Israel" occurs fourteen times in *Barnabas,* but "Jews" never; see Hvalvik, *Struggle,* 140). The term Ἰουδαῖοι, "Jews," normally used in the non-Jewish world occurs only two times, in 2:9; 3:9, in a polemical context. The redundant phrase "the tribes of the sons of" is a characteristic redactional expansion found in *Targum Neofiti (Tg. Neof.* Num 1:5–15, 21, 29, 31, 35, and passim; cf. McNamara, *Tg. Neof. Num.,* 7), and it also occurs in the LXX (e.g., Gen 10:32; Num 10:15, 16, 19, 20, 23, 24, 26, 27; 34:23, 24, 26, 27; 36:3; Josh 19:8, 9, 16, 23) as a translation of the Hebrew phrase מַטֵּה בְּנֵי *maṭṭēh bĕnê,* "tribe of the sons of." It is important to note that those who are sealed are only part of a larger group, a factor that has an important bearing on identifying the 144,000. If the twelve tribes of Israel are interpreted literally, then some Jews are specially designated over others through sealing. If the twelve tribes of Israel are interpreted figuratively, then some Christians are specially designated over others through sealing. The literal interpretation reflects the notion of the remnant, which can be construed as either a Jewish remnant or Jews who become Christians and thereby become separated from their fellow Jews (Rom 11:7).

The 144,000 are also mentioned in 14:1–5, and since the number does not occur elsewhere in early Jewish or early Christian literature, it is widely assumed that in both places the number refers to the same group. However, there is wide disagreement over whom the 144,000 represent: (1) the faithful remnant of Israel, (2) Jewish Christians, (3) Christian martyrs, (4) Christians generally, the Israel of God, consisting of both Jews and Gentiles (Eph 2:11–19), or (5) primarily gentile Christians, since the Jews have rejected their place. Several texts in the NT refer to Christians as the "true Israel" (Gal 6:16; 1 Pet 2:9; Justin *Dial.* 11.5; 82.1), and Jas 1:1 refers to Christians as the "twelve tribes in dispersion." Ignatius goes so far as to suggest that the Jewish patriarchs were really Christians (*Phil.* 9:1). The number 144,000, explicitly based on 12 x 12,000 (enumerated in vv 5–8), likely arrived at by calculating 12 x 12 x 1,000, is probably to be understood as predicated on a Christian eschatology that understood the people of God to be built upon both the twelve tribes of Israel and the twelve apostles (cf. 21:12–14). The enumeration of twelve tribes (despite the peculiarities of this particular list; see *Excursus 7B*), reflects the great importance placed on the *restoration* of Israel found in the OT and early Judaism (Isa 49:6; 63:17 [all the tribes are God's possession]; Ezek 47:13, 21–23 [a new allotment of land]; 48:30–35 [gates of the New Jerusalem named after the twelve tribes]; Zech 9:1 [Yahweh sees all the tribes]; 4 Ezra 13:12–13, 39–49 [ten tribes]; Sir 36:10 [Sirach prays for their restoration]; *Pss. Sol.* 17:26–28, 43–44; 1QM 2:2–3; 3:12–13 [banners for the twelve tribes borne in the eschatological war]; 3.14–15; 1QSa 1:15, 29; a prayer for the regathering of Israel is found in the tenth benediction of the *Shemoneh Esreh* [Eighteen Benedictions]; Jos. *Ant.* 11.133 [knows of many survivors of the ten tribes in Mesopotamia]). See also Maurer, "φυλή," *TDNT* 9:248–50; Rengstorf, "δώδεκα," *TDNT* 2:321–28; Volz, *Eschatologie,* 344–48, 398; Russell, *Apocalyptic,* 297–98. That a particular number are selected from each of the twelve tribes presupposes that the eschatological restoration of the people of Israel as constituted by the twelve tribes has already taken place. Understood literally, then, 7:4–8 is a proleptic audition of a future eschatological event.

The twelve tribes referred to here as "every tribe of the sons of Israel," followed by the mention of a very irregular list of twelve tribes in vv 5–8 (see *Excursus 7B*), are often understood metaphorically of the Christian Church as the true Israel. Some commentators support this view by claiming that twelve Israelite tribes did not exist in the first century A.D. (Caird, 95; Boring, 129). The question, however, is not whether the twelve tribes actually existed in the first century A.D. but rather whether they were thought to exist. A number of early writers clearly assume the existence of the twelve tribes. Ezek 48:1–29 (written 150 years after the exile of the ten northern tribes) describes the allotments of each of the twelve tribes, and Ezek 48:30–35 describes the twelve gates of the eschatological Jerusalem, each named for one of the twelve tribes. The precedent of Ezekiel in naming the twelve gates of the eschatological Jerusalem after the twelve tribes was picked up in 11QTemple 39:12–13; 40:11–14 and 4Q*554* 2:12–3:9 (one of the "Description of the New Jerusalem" texts), as well as in Rev 21:12–13, suggesting the central character of the ideology of a regathered and reunified Israel in the eschaton. In the legend of the origins of the LXX found in the *Letter of Aristeas,* it is claimed that the seventy-two translators were composed of six men from each of the twelve tribes (*Ep. Arist.* 32, 39, 46; see Jos. *Ant.* 12.39, 49, 56; Augustine *City of God* 18.42). The tradition of the continued existence east of the Euphrates of ten or nine and one-half tribes (Manasseh was frequently considered a half-tribe), based in part on 2 Kgs 17:23 and 1 Chr 5:26, is preserved in a variety of contexts in early Jewish literature. Josephus mentions the existence of two tribes in Asia and claims that "until now there have been ten tribes beyond the Euphrates—countless myriads whose number cannot be ascertained [μυριάδες ἄπειροι καὶ ἀριθμῷ γνωσθῆναι μὴ δυνάμεναι]" (*Ant.* 11.133). The eschatological expectation of the return of the ten tribes from the east is preserved in several Jewish texts (*Sib. Or.* 2.171; 4 Ezra 13:39–50; *T. Moses* 4:9 [on the ways of construing this garbled Latin text, see Tromp, *Assumption,* 183–84]; *2 Apoc. Bar.* 77:17–26).

According to a widespread Jewish tradition, the Gentiles will be judged in the eschaton by the twelve tribes of Israel (*T. Abr.* 13.6; Dan 7:12; *Jub.* 32:19; Wis 3:8; 1QpHab 5:4). The Synoptic tradition that the twelve disciples will judge the twelve tribes of Israel, found in the Q saying in Matt 19:28 (= Luke 22:30), is related to this tradition: "Truly, I say to you, in the new world, when the Son of man shall sit on his glorious throne, you who have followed me will also sit on twelve thrones, judging the twelve tribes of Israel" (RSV). The existence of the twelve tribes of Israel is referred to in other early Christian texts as well. In Acts 26:6–7, Paul speaks of "the promise made by God to our ancestors, a promise that our twelve tribes [τὸ δωδεκάφυλον ἡμῶν] hope to attain." Justin, referring to a prophetic proof text in Zech 12:10–12, predicted that twelve tribes would mourn at the return of Christ (*Dial.* 126.2). Irenaeus claimed that Jesus sent forth disciples to the twelve tribes (*Adv. haer.* 1.20.2), and Hippolytus thought that Jesus chose twelve disciples from the twelve tribes of Israel (*Ref.* 5.3). An earlier form of the tradition found in Irenaeus and Hippolytus occurs in *Barn.* 8:3, "and there are twelve as a testimony to the tribes, because there are twelve tribes of Israel." Several references to the twelve tribes occur in the *Protevangelium Jacobi,* written ca. A.D. 150 (1.1, 3; 6.2).

5 ἐκ φυλῆς Ἰούδα δώδεκα χιλιάδες ἐσφραγισμένοι, "From the tribe of Judah, 12,000 were marked." This formula appears to be based on the phrase ἐκ τῆς φυλῆς, "of the tribe," found repeated twelve times in Num 1 (vv 21, 23, 25, etc.) in the context of a census of the tribes of Israel (cf. the second census in Num 26:1–56). The difference is that here 12,000 are marked from what is presumably a greater number of the members of each tribe (ἐκ + genitive is a partitive genitive), whereas in Num 1 the various census figures ostensibly reflect the actual number of adult males twenty years old and older, the appropriate age for military service. Though the list that follows conforms to no list of tribes found in the OT or early Jewish literature (on this basis Ladd, 114–15, argues improbably that these tribes do not literally represent Israel), the tribe of Judah is listed first in lists of tribes that are geographically arranged, starting from the south and moving north (Num 34:19–28; Josh 21:4–7; 1 Chr 12:23–37). There is general agreement that Judah is placed first here because it is the tribe from which the Messiah came (Swete, 98; Charles, 1:194, 208; Mounce, 169; Beasley-Murray, 43). However, this does not guarantee the Christian character of the list, for the tribe of Judah is also listed first in the military order of the tribes in the camp (Num 2:3; 7:12; 10:14), perhaps because of the later importance of Judah as the tribe of the Davidic dynasty. Judah also appears first in tribal lists in early Judaism, perhaps because Judah was the tribe of the Davidic Messiah (Ps.-Philo *Bib. Ant.* 25:4, 9–13). The Qumran community used the designation "Judah" as a positive way of referring to themselves (see Schwartz, *RevQ* 10 [1981] 435–46). Smith has argued that the tribal list has been Christianized and that the author replaced the tribe of Levi, which probably headed the list, with Judah, since the author has already referred to the Lamb as the messianic lion of the tribe of Judah in 5:5 (C. R. Smith, *JSNT* 39 [1990] 115–16; id., *JETS* 38 [1995] 215–16). However, Smith's insistence that Levi headed the traditional list, which John modified, has little to commend it.

6 The tribe of Dan is conspicuous by its absence in this list and has apparently been replaced here by Manasseh (n.b. that the tribe of Levi, often absent from tribal lists in the OT, is included in the tribal roster in v 7b). Dan and Naphtali are absent from the tribal list in Ps.-Philo *Bib. Ant.* 25:4 (certainly on the basis of corrupt transmission), though they are present in 25:9. Several possible reasons have been suggested for this substitution: (1) The tribe of Dan had a negative reputation in the OT (Gen 49:17; Judg 18:30; Jer 8:16) and early Judaism (in *Vitae Proph.* 3.17–20, the prophet Ezekiel pronounces judgment on the tribes of Dan and Gad for persecuting those who kept the law). However, Dan was not blacklisted in early Judaism, for none of the many lists of the twelve tribes in early Jewish literature omits Dan (with the exception of Ps.-Philo *Bib. Ant.* 25:4, an accidental omission). Not only that, but there is a tradition that the mother of the Messiah would be a Danite (*Gen. Rab.* 97.9; ed. Theodor-Albeck): "This is the Messiah ben David who will arise from two tribes: his father from Judah and his mother from Dan." (2) Dan was thought to be an apostate tribe (Str-B, 3:804–5), a postbiblical development of the tradition mentioned in the biblical passages listed under (1). *T. Dan* 5:4–8 predicts the apostasy of the tribe of Dan, though the restoration of Dan is predicted in 5:9–13. (3) Antichrist was expected to come from the tribe of Dan (Bousset, *Antichrist,* 26, 171–74; K. Berger, *Daniel-Diegese,* 101 [with additional references to the connection of Antichrist with Dan in Christian apocalypses]; C. R. Smith, *JETS* 38 [1995] 217). However, the earliest references to this tradition are found in Irenaeus 5.30.2, commenting on Jer 8:16, understood as a prophecy of the coming of Antichrist from the tribe of Dan in the east ("This too is the reason that this tribe is not reckoned in the Apocalypse along with those which are saved"), and in Hippolytus *de Ant.* 14.5–6 ("Just as Christ is born of the tribe of Judah, so Antichrist shall be born from the tribe of Dan"). Hill suggests that the tradition may be quite old even though it first appears in Irenaeus (*JTS* 46 [1995] 99–117). The tradition is not found in any Jewish sources and cannot therefore be confidently thought to be pre-Christian, despite Bousset's arguments (*Antichrist,* 171–74). The views of Irenaeus and Hippolytus influenced the Christian understanding of Rev 7:8; Andreas *Comm. in Apoc. ad* 7:8, and 16:12: "It is likely that the Antichrist will come from the eastern section of the land of Persia, where the tribe of Dan of Hebrew extraction is." (4) This list of twelve tribes has been partially assimilated to the list of twelve apostles in which, just as Matthias replaced the apostate Judas, so Dan has been replaced by Manasseh (C. R. Smith, *JSNT* 39 [1990] 115–16). (5) Sanderson (*Scripture* 3/4 [1948] 114–15) speculated that "Δάν" was omitted through a scribal error in which the abbreviation "Μαν [ασσῆ]" replaced "Δάν." (6) The simplest and most likely solution, however, is that Dan was dropped to keep the total number of tribes to twelve (Bauckham, *JSNT* 42 [1991] 113).

The mention of the tribe of Manasseh along with the tribe of Joseph in v 8 (see below) is unique and requires explanation, for Manasseh is always paired with Ephraim in lists of tribes in the OT, since both are sons of Joseph (and the omission of Levi required an adjustment to maintain the significant number twelve). A peculiar interpretation is found in *Barn.* 13:4–6, in which Ephraim and Manasseh, the elder and the younger, represent Christianity and Judaism, respectively, and thus Manasseh is given a pejorative interpretation in this connection. Bauckham points to Ezek 37:16, 19 (in the context of a prophecy of the reunion of the Northern and Southern Kingdoms in vv 15–28), in which the name "Joseph" is linked to "Ephraim," perhaps suggesting that "Joseph" is an appropriate designation for "Ephraim" in a list of the reunited tribes of eschatological Israel (*Neot* 11 [1988] 221–22). There is a negative symbolic use of the name Ephraim, who is identified with the "seekers after smooth things," i.e., the Pharisees in 4QpNah 3–4 ii 2,8 (Horgan, *Pesharim,* 181). On the slim basis of this single text, Goranson argues unconvincingly that the omission of the name Ephraim means that the author polemically excluded the Pharisees from among the sealed, predestined elect (*DSD* 2 [1995] 80–85). There is, on the other hand, a very positive evaluation of Ephraim in some rabbinic traditions (which may be pre-Hadrianic) in which the victorious Messiah of Ephraim (or Joseph) is expected to precede the Messiah of Judah; eventually Bar Kokhba was regarded by some as the Messiah of Ephraim (see Heinemann, *HTR* 68 [1975] 1–15; Pietrantonio, *RevistB* 44 [1982] 1–64).

7 The tribe of Levi is often omitted in OT lists of Israelite tribes for the simple reason that Levi had no traditional allotment of land. His place in the twelve tribes was taken by dropping Joseph and substituting the sons of Joseph, Ephraim, and Manasseh. It seems peculiar here that the name "Levi" occurs in the context of what may be a military roster when Levi is explicitly omitted from military censuses in the OT (Num 1:49; 2:33; 26:1–51; cf. 1 Chr 21:6) but included in nonmilitary censuses (Num 3:14–39; 26:57–62); see Bauckham, *Neot* 22 [1988] 222. However, Levi, like the other tribes, is organized for participation in the eschatological war depicted in 1QM 1:2; 2:2.

8 The tribe of Joseph is mentioned, while that of Manasseh has already been mentioned in v 6. Usually the tribe of Joseph is omitted and Ephraim and Manasseh put in its place, along with other modifications to ensure that the total number of tribes is always twelve. This may have some similarity to Num 13:4–16, where the tribe of Ephraim is mentioned in v 8, and in a gloss in v 11 it says, "from the tribe of Joseph (that is from the tribe of Manasseh)." In Rev 7:8 it is possible that by the tribe of Joseph, the author may have actually meant Ephraim.

Excursus 7B: The Order of the Tribes in Rev 7:4–8

Bibliography

Bauckham, R. "The List of the Tribes in Revelation 7 Again." *JSNT* 42 (1991) 99–115. **Geyser, A.** "The Twelve Tribes in Revelation: Judean and Judeo-Christian Apocalypticism." *NTS* 28 (1982) 388–99. **Gray, G. B.** "The Lists of the Twelve Tribes." *Expositor* ser. 6, 5 (1902) 225–40. **Smith, C. R.** "The Portrayal of the Church as the New Israel in the Names and Order of the Tribes in Revelation 7.5–8." *JSNT* 39 (1990) 111–18. **Winkle, R. E.** "Another Look at the List of Tribes in Revelation 7." *AUSS* 27 (1989) 53–67.

What determines the order of the tribes of Israel listed in 7:4–8? There is no list of the sons of Israel or of the tribes of Israel in the OT that corresponds exactly to the list in Rev 7:4–8, with regard to either order or content. It must also be observed, however, that few lists of the tribes of Israel within the OT itself are exactly identical with regard to order or number. This means that even though agreement in order or content cannot be expected, it might be possible to account for the particular order of the list in Revelation. There are several lists of the sons or tribes of Israel in the OT (Gen 35:22b–26; 46:8–27; Exod 1:2–4 [Joseph omitted for narrative purposes]; Num 1:4–15; 13:4–16). The first list is found in Gen 35:22b–26 (reproduced in *Jub.* 33:22 and Ps.-Philo *Bib. Ant.* 8:6):

A. Sons of Leah
 1. Reuben
 2. Simeon
 3. Levi
 4. Judah
 5. Issachar
 6. Zebulun
B. Sons of Rachel
 7. Joseph
 8. Benjamin
C. Sons of Bilhah (Rachel's maid)
 9. Dan
 10. Naphtali
D. Sons of Zilpah (Leah's maid)
 11. Gad
 12. Asher

In such lists the six Leah tribes remain relatively constant except for the eventual omission of Levi and the inclusion of Ephraim and Manasseh in place of Joseph, as in Num 1:5–15 and 13:2–14:

Num 1:5–15	*Num 13:4–14*
1. Reuben	1. Reuben
2. Simeon	2. Simeon
3. Judah	3. Judah
4. Issachar	4. Issachar
5. Zebulon	5. Ephraim
6. Ephraim	6. Benjamin
7. Manasseh	7. Zebulun
8. Benjamin	8. Joseph (i.e., Manasseh)
9. Dan	9. Dan
10. Asher	10. Asher
11. Gad	11. Naphtali
12. Naphtali	12. Gad

This order is not determined by the traditional order of birth, which is narrated in Gen 29–30 (reproduced in *Jub.* 28:17–24; 32:3):

A. Sons of Leah
  1. Reuben
  2. Simeon
  3. Levi
  4. Judah
B. Sons of Bilhah (Rachel's maid)
  5. Dan
  6. Naphtali
C. Sons of Zilpah (Leah's maid)
  7. Gad
  8. Asher
D. Sons of Leah
  9. Issachar
  10. Zebulun
E. Sons of Rachel
  11. Joseph
  12. Benjamin

A different order is preserved in the blessing of Jacob (Gen 49): (1) Reuben, (2) Simeon, (3) Levi, (4) Judah, (5) Zebulun, (6) Issachar, (7) Dan, (8) Gad, (9) Asher, (10) Naphtali, (11) Joseph, and (12) Benjamin. Yet another list is preserved in the blessing of Moses (Deut 33): (1) Reuben, (2) Judah, (3) Levi, (4) Benjamin, (5) Joseph, (6) Zebulun, (7) Issachar, (8) Gad, (9) Dan, (10) Naphtali, and (11) Asher (Simeon is omitted, possibly because it was absorbed into the tribe of Judah and ceased to have independent existence; see Gen 49:5–7; Ps.-Philo *Bib. Ant.* 25:9–13). Two other lists of the twelve tribes are found in Ezek 48 in the context of a list of thirteen tribal land allotments (48:1–29) and a list of twelve gates named after the twelve tribes (48:30–35). Joseph is listed rather than Ephraim and Manasseh.

Lists of the names and order of the twelve tribes are found in early Jewish literature in *Jubilees,* in 11QTemple (24; 39–41, 44–45), in Ps.-Philo *Biblical Antiquities* (six lists: 8:6; 8:11–14; 10:3; 25:4; 25:9–13; 26:10–11), and in Demetrius the Chronographer (two identical lists in frag. 2; Eusebius *Praep. evang.* 9.21.3–10, 17).

According to Gray, Rev 7:5c–6 has been displaced, and if restored to a position after v 8, the whole list makes sense: (1) Judah, (2) Reuben, (3) Simeon, (4) Levi, (5) Issachar, (6) Zebulun, (7) Joseph, (8) Benjamin, (9) Gad, (10) Asher, (11) Naphtali, and (12) Manasseh.

9a Μετὰ ταῦτα εἶδον, καὶ ἰδοὺ ὄχλος πολὺς ὃν ἀριθμῆσαι αὐτὸν οὐδεὶς ἐδύνατο, "After this I looked, and behold, a huge crowd which no one could even begin to number." This represents an intentional contrast with 7:4, where the author hears that the number of those sealed from the tribes of the sons of Israel is 144,000. In seeking to equate the 144,000 of 7:4–8 with the innumerable host of 7:9–17, some have argued unpersuasively that 144,000 would have appeared innumerable had the seer not been told their number (Giesen, 193). However, 7:4–8 is not a vision but an *audition;* that is, the seer does not claim to see those who were sealed but simply reports that he heard their number. This crowd is identified in 7:14 as those who have come through the great tribulation. That they have washed their robes in the blood of the Lamb suggests that they are certainly Christians and possibly martyrs (Bousset [1906] 280; Lohmeyer, 70–72), though some commentators have denied the latter (Wellhausen, *Analyse,* 12; Holtz, *Christologie,* 73–74). Comblin (*AsSeign* 66 [1973] 42–49) and Buchanan (193–95) are among the very few commentators who regard this group as diaspora Jews. In Tacitus' account of the Neronian persecution, he claimed that "vast numbers" (*multitudo ingens*) were convicted and executed under Nero (*Annals* 15.44). This phrase in Tacitus has an obviously indeterminate meaning. For the phrase *ingens multitudo,* "huge crowd," in Livy, see 4.33.2; 5.7.2; 9.23.16; 34.29.5; for *multitudo ingens,* see 2.39.9. *1 Clem.* 6:1 refers to unnamed martyrs as πολὺ πλῆθος ἐκλεκτῶν, "a great multitude of the elect," while Justin speaks of Christians generally as τὸ ἀναρίθμητον πλῆθος, "the innumerable multitude" (*1 Apol.* 15.7). The emphasis on the *innumerable* multitude intentionally sets up a contrast with the specific number 144,000 mentioned above in v 4, suggesting that the two groups are not identical, though the larger group in v 10 probably contains the smaller group enumerated in vv 4–8.

This innumerable multitude suggests the fulfillment of the promise to Abraham, which had two distinct traditional aspects: (1) *The promise of innumerable descendants,* "as the dust of the earth," "as the stars of the sky," or "as the sand of the sea" (Gen 13:16; 15:5; 16:10 ["I will so greatly multiply your descendants that they cannot be numbered for multitude"]; 22:17–18), a promise repeated to Isaac (Gen 26:4) and to Jacob (Gen 28:14; 32:12). This promise or its fulfillment is frequently repeated in later contexts (Exod 32:13; Deut 1:10; 10:22; 28:62; 2 Sam 17:11; 1 Kgs 3:8; 4:20; Neh 9:23; Isa 10:22; 48:19; 51:2; Hos 1:10[MT 2:1]; Sir 44:21; *Jub.* 13:20; 18:15; 25:16; 27:23; *Ladder of Jacob* 1:10; Pr Azar 1:13; *T. Abr.* [Rec. A] 1:5; *Gk. Apoc. Ezra* 3:10; 1Q*20* = 1QGenesis Apocryphon 21:13; Rom 9:27 [quoting Isa 10:22]; Heb 11:12). (2) *The promise that Abraham would be the father of many nations* (Gen 17:4–6, 16), a promise repeated to Isaac and to Jacob (Gen 28:14; 32:12; 35:11; 48:19) and found occasionally in later contexts (Sir 44:19), and one that is particularly emphasized in Christian authors (Rom 4:16–18; Justin *Dial.* 11.5; 119.4; Tertullian *De monogamia* 6; *Adv. Marcionem* 4.34; 5.3[2x]). See Norelli, *Aug* 22 (1982) 285–312; Westermann, *Verheißung,* 138–43. Occasionally, the notion of a census was seen to conflict with the promise of innumerable progeny made by God to Abraham (1 Chr 27:23; Ps.-Philo *Bib. Ant.* 14:2; cf. 1 Chr 21:1–6). This passage implies that the promise to Abraham has been fulfilled, though not through physical descent from Abraham. The spiritualization of the promise to Abraham is found in Rom 9:6–13. In Gal 3:16, Paul interprets the "offspring" of Abraham to mean Christ.

The enormous size of this group, which must be in the millions, is striking since the number of Christians, both Jews and Gentiles, living toward the end of the first century A.D. cannot have been very large. Attempts to estimate the Christian population of the Roman empire during the first three centuries, however, vary greatly because of the paucity of evidence. Zahn estimated (in part on the basis of Acts 21:20) that there were between 70,000 and 75,000 Jewish Christians in Palestine about A.D. 58 (372). B. Reicke estimated that there were about 40,000 Christians in A.D. 67, with a total of ca. 320,000 about the turn of the century, 80,000 of whom lived in Asia Minor (Reicke, *New Testament Era,* 302–4; cf. Elliott, *I Peter,* 63–64). In contrast to these bloated figures, R. L. Wilken estimated that by the end of the first century there were fewer than 50,000 Christians living in forty to fifty different cities of the Roman empire (*The Christians as the Romans Saw Them* [New Haven: Yale UP, 1984] 31; this view is shared by W. H. C. Frend, *The Rise of Christianity* [Philadelphia: Westminster, 1984] 968). L. von Hartling estimated that there were about two million Christians in the Roman empire by the end of the third century ("Die Zahl der Christen zu Beginn des 4. Jahrhunderts," *ZKT* 68 [1934] 234–52), and R. L. Fox estimated that by A.D. 250 the Christian population of the empire was perhaps 2 percent of the population of the Roman empire (*Pagans and Christians* [New York: Knopf, 1989] 317). R. MacMullen, on the other hand, estimates the Christian population by A.D. 300 to have been approximately five million (*Christianizing the Roman Empire* [New Haven: Yale UP, 1984] 32–33, 135–36 n. 26). Ancient evidence for the size of the Christian population in the first centuries of the Christian era is assembled and discussed by A. von Harnack, but without any specific numerical estimates (*Die Mission und Ausbreitung des Christentums in den ersten drei Jahrhunderten,* 4th ed. [Leipzig: Hinrichs, 1924] 2:529–52, 948), and more recently by R. M. Grant in a very careful way (*Early Christianity and Society* [New York: Harper and Row, 1977] 1–12, with bibliography on 193–94).

9b ἐκ παντὸς ἔθνους καὶ φυλῶν καὶ λαῶν καὶ γλωσσῶν, "from every nation and tribe and people and language group." This statement is intended to contrast with the 144,000 mentioned in vv 4–8, who are taken only from the constituent tribes of a single nation, Israel. The promise to Abraham took two forms, the promise of innumerable descendants and the promise that Abraham would be the father of many nations (see *Comment* on 7:9a); v 9a alludes to the former, while v 9b refers to the latter (Gen 17:4–6; 35:11; 48:19; Rom 4:16–18; Justin *Dial.* 119–20; cf. Jos. *Ant.* 4.115–16). A similar comprehensive enumeration of social and national groups emphasizing the international character of the Christian church occurs several other times in Revelation, though in varying order (5:9; 10:11; 11:9; 13:7; 14:6; 17:15; see *Comment* on 5:9), an emphasis that is atypical for Jewish apocalyptic literature, which usually defines the righteous as a restricted group within Israel. This expression has several parallels in Daniel, which is its origin (3:4, 7, 29[LXX 96]; 5:19; 6:25[LXX 26]; 7:14). Zeno, the founder of Stoicism, reportedly held that people should not live separated in different cities and groups but should share a common life (Plutarch *De fort. Alex.* 6).

9c ἑστῶτες ἐνώπιον τοῦ θρόνου καὶ ἐνώπιον τοῦ ἀρνίου, "standing before the throne and before the Lamb." Here ὁ θρόνος, "the throne," functions as a circumlocution for the name of God (see also 4:10; 8:3). It is likely that the phrase "and before the Lamb" was added by the author during one of the final stages of the composition of Revelation (for other interpolations that add "and the Lamb" after a mention of God, see 7:10; 22:1, 3).

9d περιβεβλημένους στολὰς λευκὰς καὶ φοίνικες ἐν ταῖς χερσὶν αὐτῶν, "dressed in white robes and with palm fronds in their hands." White robes are mentioned in 6:11; 7:13; in 3:4 the phrase ἐν λευκοῖς, "in white [garments]," is a reward for those in Sardis who have not soiled their garments, a reward reiterated in 3:5. In Revelation, white robes appear to symbolize heavenly existence or worthiness of heaven (Ulfgard, *Feast,* 85). White was worn during festive occasions (Eccl 9:8) and was also the typical color of garments thought to be worn by supernatural revealers or other heavenly figures, including God himself (Dan 7:9; 2 Macc 11:8; *1 Enoch* 14:20; *T. Levi* 8:2; Matt 17:2 = Mark 9:3 = Luke 9:29; Matt 28:3; Mark 16:5; John 20:12; Acts 1:10). While palm fronds were symbols of victory throughout the ancient Mediterranean world, in Egypt they symbolized length of life and life after death, and in Judaism they could suggest the Feast of Tabernacles (Meshorer, *Jewish Coins,* no. 161). They also appear to have symbolized blessing (see Zazoff, *Gemmen,* 301). The palm frond was used by metonymy to mean "victory." A mosaic in the Museum of Sousse (Tunisia) depicts Dionysus/Bacchus in a triumphal procession in a chariot drawn by four tigers; beside him stands winged Victory, carrying a palm frond, not (as one would expect) a thyrsus (M. Simon, *La Civilisation de l'Antiquité et le Christianisme* [Paris: Arthaud, 1972] plate 33). The association of the palm with victory is so close that statues of the goddess Nike or Victory can be described by metonymy as *palmaris deae facies,* "with the appearance of the goddess of the palm." In Apuleius *Metamorphoses* 9.4, Isis is described as wearing sandals woven with "leaves of victorious palm" (*palmae victricis*). *Venus Victrix,* "Victorious Aphrodite," is depicted holding a palm frond (Zazoff, *Gemmen,* 334; plate 104, 5). Olympic victors were given a frond of palm to symbolize victory (Pausanias 8.48.1–2), and in Hermas *Sim.* 8.2.1 the righteous are rewarded with wreaths and palm fronds. The true palm, *phoenix dactylifera,* was not native to the northern shores of the Mediterranean, and when grown there it did not produce fruit. Dioscorides, a first-century A.D. physician and pharmacologist, discusses the medicinal value of the date palm (*phoenix dactylifera*), which grows in Egypt (*Materia medica* 1.109.1–2; ed. Wellmann, *Pedanii* 1:102), as well as the φοῖνιξ θηβαικαί (*hyphaene coriacea*) or doum palm found in Greece and Turkey (1.109.2–3; ed. Wellmann, *Pedanii* 1:102). In *Quaest. conv.* 8.4 (723A–724F), Plutarch and his friends puzzle over the fact that the palm frond (ὁ φοῖνιξ) is awarded to victors at *all* athletic festivals. This practice was borrowed by the Romans, ca. 292 B.C., to reward victors in the Roman games (Livy 10.47.3); Vergil refers to *palmae, pretium victoribus,* "palms, the prize of the victor" (*Aeneid* 6.111). After 293 B.C., victorious Roman generals wore the *toga palmata* when celebrating a triumph (Livy 10.7.9). Tertullian identified the palms as signs of victory (*Scorpiace* 20). According to 1 Macc 13:51, palms were carried in Simon the Hasmonean's victorious entry into Jerusalem:

> The Jews entered it [the citadel in Jerusalem] with praise and palm fronds [βαΐων], and with harps and cymbals and stringed instruments, and with hymns and songs, because a great enemy had been crushed and removed from Israel.

In 2 Macc 14:4, an ex-priest named Alcimus presented the Syrian king Demetrius I Soter (187–150 B.C.) with a gold crown and a palm, probably symbols of a victorious ruler, and similar gifts were given to Demetrius II Nicator (161–125 B.C.)

by Simon the Hasmonean (1 Macc 13:36–37). The frequency with which palm fronds occur on Jewish coins together with the name of the current ruler suggests that they symbolize, like the wreath, an ascendant ruler (Meshorer, *Jewish Coins,* nos. 6, 21, 24, 40, 46, 48, 49, 66–74, 160). In John 12:13, the crowds welcomed Jesus to Jerusalem by waving palm fronds (not by cutting branches of trees and strewing them in his path, as in Mark 11:8 = Matt 21:8) and shouting, "Hosanna! Blessed is he who comes in the name of the Lord, even the King of Israel." Here also, palms apparently symbolize victory (see Schnackenburg, *John* 2:374–75). According to *Lev. Rab.* 30 (Str-B, 2:789), "We do not know who the victor is, but whoever carries the palm frond in his hand, by this we know that he is the victor." These references demonstrate that palm fronds could be used in various contexts in early Judaism to symbolize victory, and they suggest that those who understand the palms in Rev 7:9 as symbolic of victory are essentially correct (Charles, 1:211; Prigent, 124). Deissmann (*Bible Studies,* 370; cf. K. Berger et al., *Hellenistic Commentary,* no. 942) cites as an instructive parallel to Rev 7:9–10 an inscription from Stratonicea in Caria (*CIG* 2:2715, lines 8–10), which refers to thirty noble youths who are obligated to sing a hymn in the *bouleuterion* "clothed in white and crowned with olive branches, and bearing olive branches in their hands. These boys shall be accompanied by a zither player and a herald and shall sing a hymn composed by Sosandros the secretary, the son of Diomedes." Since the festal use of both white garments and palm fronds connotes victory in the Near East as well as in the Greco-Roman world, Bousset suggests that it is not necessary for Deissmann to emphasize parallels found in the practices of Greek religious cults ([1906] 284–85). The major objection to understanding the palms as symbols of victory is that this significance was primarily pagan (Kraft, 128; Ulfgard, *Feast,* 90). Yet the texts discussed above make it problematic to regard palms as symbolic of victory only in Greco-Roman culture.

In Egypt the palm frond symbolized length of life and in a funerary context was a symbol for life after death (Wallert, *Die Palmen*). Thoth, the "Lord of time," is depicted as holding a palm frond symbolizing length of life (Wallert, *Die Palmen,* 101ff.). Palm fronds were also placed on the breast of a mummy when it was carried in a funeral procession. In a procession honoring Isis, described in Apuleius *Metamorphoses* 11.9, set in Cenchreae near Corinth, five priests are described as dressed in white linen, and one of them carried a palm frond with leaves of gold and a caduceus; the god Anubis (the Egyptian mortuary god and the god of embalming and of cemeteries) is often represented holding these two objects (see Griffiths, *Isis-Book,* 198–200; Witt, *Isis,* 199). The palm as a symbol of victory appears to have originated in the Greek world, possibly on Delos in the seventh century B.C., and only in Roman times is it to be found with this significance in Egypt (Wallert, *Die Palmen,* 103–4).

Since Jews carried palm fronds around and into the temple in Jerusalem in connection with the celebrations of the Feast of Tabernacles, it is possible to understand the palms in Rev 7:9 in that connection (Ulfgard, *Feast,* 89–92). The sheaf carried in the celebration during the Feast of Tabernacles was called the לולב, *lûlāb* (literally "palm frond," but it actually consisted of palm, myrtle, and willow branches tied together into a bundle in accordance with Lev 23:40; see *m. Sukk.* 3:1–8; Draper, *JSNT* 19 [1985] 137). According to Neh 8:15, branches of olive, wild olive, myrtle, and palm are used to construct booths to celebrate the Feast of

Tabernacles. Josephus (*Ant.* 3.245; LCL tr.) speaks of those who celebrate Tabernacles as "bearing in their hands a bouquet composed of myrtle and willow with a frond of palm [κράδη φοίνικος], along with fruit of the persea" (see 13.372). In Plutarch's discussion of the Feast of Tabernacles (*Quaest. conv.* 4.6.2, 671E), he describes the festival as a "procession of branches" (κραδηφορία), in which each Jew entered the temple carrying a thyrsus (θύρσος is a Greek term for the combined palm, myrtle, and willow branches Jews carried during the festival). *Jub.* 16:31 retrojects a later ritual of Tabernacles to the practice of Abraham (Charlesworth, *OTP* 2:89):

> And Abraham took branches of palm trees and fruit of good trees and each of the days he used to go around the altar with branches. Seven times per day, in the morning, he was praising and giving thanks to his God for all things.

10 καὶ κράζουσιν φωνῇ μεγάλῃ λέγοντες ἡ σωτηρία τῷ θεῷ ἡμῶν τῷ καθημένῳ ἐπὶ τῷ θρόνῳ καὶ τῷ ἀρνίῳ, "They cried with a loud voice, 'Victory belongs to our God who sits upon the throne and to the Lamb.'" This short cry of victory or *Siegesruf* (Deichgräber, *Gotteshymnus,* 53–54; see Westermann, *Praise,* 90–93) in the *er-Stil,* or "he style," is a proleptic celebration of the eschatological triumph of God. A close parallel to ἡ σωτηρία τῷ θεῷ occurs in the phrase ליהוה הישועה *lYHWH hayĕšûʿâ,* "victory belongs to Yahweh" (Ps 3:9; Jonah 2:9; cf. *TDOT* 6:458). The term σωτηρία, usually translated "salvation," is not exclusively a religious term but is closely associated with eschatological victory in Revelation and refers here to salvation in the sense of "deliverance" or "victory" over persecution. Bousset has argued that ἡ σωτηρία τῷ θεῷ is a Hebraism parallel to Ps 3:9 and Jonah 2:9 (ליהוה הישועה *lYHWH hayĕšûʿâ;* cf. LXX Ps 3:9, τοῦ κυρίου ἡ σωτηρία; cf. Rev 12:10 and 19:1), though both passages have τοῦ θεοῦ ἡμῶν rather than τῷ θεῷ ἡμῶν (Bousset [1906] 285). Further parallels occur in the phrase τοῦ κυρίου ἡ σωτηρία, "the Lord's salvation" or "the salvation of the Lord," found in *Pss. Sol.* 10:8; 12:6. This construction need not be taken as a Hebraism, however, for it can be construed simply as a dative of possession, which can best be translated "deliverance belongs to God" or "victory belongs to God" (the genitive of possession is used in the same way in 12:10; 19:1). The same construction occurs in doxologies when various attributes are ascribed to God or Christ in the dative (e.g., Rev 1:5b–6; 4:9; 5:13; 7:12; cf. 19:1). On the other hand, σωτηρία can be construed as a semantic Hebraism based on the frequent meaning of יְשׁוּעָה *yĕšûʿâ* as "victory" (Exod 14:13, 30; 15:2; BDB, 447; *TDNT* 7:976; *TDOT* 6:450–51), a view held by many commentators (Eichhorn, 2:96; Bousset [1906] 342; Charles, 1:326; Beasley-Murray, 202; *TDNT* 7:998; BAGD, 801; Bauer-Aland, 1598; Caird, 100–101; Turner, *Style,* 153). This phrase may be an allusion to the *hosanna* of Ps 118:25, used at the Feast of Tabernacles according to *m. Sukk.* 4:5 (McKelvey, *New Temple,* 163). Here "salvation" refers to deliverance from tribulation, which belongs to God, who has sealed his servants on their foreheads and thus protected them.

11a καὶ πάντες οἱ ἄγγελοι εἱστήκεισαν κύκλῳ τοῦ θρόνου καὶ τῶν πρεσβυτέρων καὶ τῶν τεσσάρων ζῴων, "All the angels, who had been standing around the throne, and the elders and the four cherubim." Three categories of heavenly beings are listed, beginning with the angels, the outermost group encircling the throne, then the elders, and finally the four cherubim. The verb εἱστήκεισαν, "they stood," applies only to the angels who surround God's throne (no angel in Revelation is ever described as seated) but not to the elders, who are elsewhere described as seated (4:4), nor to the four cherubim, whose posture is never described. The description of angels *standing* before God suggests an awareness of the Jewish tradition that angels had no knees and therefore were unable to sit (*y. Ber.* 2c; *Gen. Rab.* 65.21 [ed. Theodor-Albeck, *Midrash,* 738]; see Gruenwald, *Apocalyptic,* 66–67). This tradition was apparently based on the phrase ורגליהם רגל ישרה *wĕraglêhem regel yĕšārâ,* "and their legs were straight," in Ezek 1:7. In Jewish tradition there was a widespread view that no one is permitted to sit in the presence of God (4Q*405* 20 ii 2 [see Newsom, *Songs,* 303–9]; *b. Ḥag.* 15a; *3 Enoch* 16), though in Revelation the twenty-four elders constitute an exception (see *Comment* on 4:4). While the innumerable multitude is described as standing before the throne (v 9), it appears to be presupposed that they encircle the angels. The closest parallel is found in Rev 5:11, where myriads of angels along with the cherubim and the elders are described as encircling the throne of God.

11b καὶ ἔπεσαν ἐνώπιον τοῦ θρόνου ἐπὶ τὰ πρόσωπα αὐτῶν καὶ προσεκύνησαν τῷ θεῷ, "fell prostrate before the throne and worshiped God." The motif of the adoration of heavenly beings who fall prostrate before the throne of God is normally limited to the twenty-four elders (4:10; 5:14; 11:16; 19:4). Here they are joined by the angels encircling the throne and the four living creatures, while in 5:8 the twenty-four elders are joined by the four living creatures (though in 5:8 the object of worship is the Lamb rather than God).

12 λέγοντες· ἀμήν, ἡ εὐλογία καὶ ἡ δόξα καὶ ἡ σοφία καὶ ἡ εὐχαριστία καὶ ἡ τιμὴ καὶ ἡ δύναμις καὶ ἡ ἰσχὺς τῷ θεῷ ἡμῶν εἰς τοὺς αἰῶνας τῶν αἰώνων· ἀμήν, "saying, 'Amen, praise and glory and wisdom and thanksgiving and honor and power and might to our God for ever and ever; amen.'" This verse constitutes a doxology with seven doxological predicates. The introductory "amen" actually functions as a response to the song of victory in v 10 (Bousset [1906] 285; Lohmeyer, 71; Deichgräber, *Gotteshymnus,* 45; Boring, *Sayings,* 132–33). Seven attributes are ascribed to God here, while a similar list of seven attributes ascribed to the Lamb appears in 5:12 (see *Comment*). Four of the attributes used in this doxology (εὐλογία, σοφία, εὐχαριστία, ἰσχύς) occur in doxologies only in Rev 4:9; 5:12 (Deichgräber, *Gotteshymnus,* 59). The attribution of wisdom to God, found only here in Revelation, occurs elsewhere in the NT (Luke 11:49; 1 Cor 1:24; 2:7), while it is ascribed to the Lamb in Rev 5:12. The phrase ὁ θεὸς ἡμῶν, "our God," occurs nine times in Revelation (4:11; 5:10; 7:10, 12; 12:10[2x]; 19:1, 5, 6).

13a καὶ ἀπεκρίθη εἷς ἐκ τῶν πρεσβυτέρων λέγων μοι, "One of the elders said to me." The phrase καὶ ἀπεκρίθη is not a response to an unspoken question (Bousset [1906] 285; Beckwith, 544; Charles, 1:212) but reflects the Hebrew use of the verb ענה *ʿānâ,* meaning "begin to speak," referring to something that has already occurred to which the remarks refer (LXX Isa 14:10; LXX Zech 1:10; 3:4; Matt 11:25; 12:38; 15:15; 17:4; 22:1; 28:5; Mark 9:5; 10:24; 11:14; 12:35; 15:12; Luke 14:3; John 2:18; 5:7; Acts 3:12; see BDB, 773; Thayer, *Lexicon,* 63; BAGD, 93). Here the phrase καὶ ἀπεκρίθη . . . λέγων, "and he answered . . . saying" (an idiom found only here in Revelation, but common in various forms in the Gospels and Acts), is a Semitism reflecting the Hebrew phrase וַיַּעַן לֵאמֹר *wayyaʿan lēʾmor,* "and he answered, saying," translated in the Greek phrase καὶ ἀποκριθεὶς εἶπεν with a participle followed by a finite verb (e.g., Luke 1:19, 35; 4:12; 5:5) or with a finite verb followed by a redundant participle, as in ἀπεκρίθη λέγων (LXX Ezek 9:11; Theod Dan 3:16; *Gk. 1 Enoch* 22:7, 9; 25:3; 106:9, 13; *T. Job* 23:5; John 1:26) and ἀπεκρίνατο λέγων (Luke 3:16). Asyndeton is characteristic of the introductory biblical Aramaic phrase עָנֵה וְאָמַר *ʿānēh wĕʾāmar,* "he answered and said" (Turner, *Style,* 150; Black, *Aramaic,* 56–57), rendered in the LXX as ἀποκριθεὶς εἶπεν, "answering he said," a locution frequently found in the Gospels. One of the distinctive features of Revelation is that the author never asks the meaning of any of the symbols in his visions. Nevertheless, the elder volunteers to interpret the scene for the seer, and this constitutes a variation on the motif of the *angelus interpres,* or "interpreting angel" (see *Comment* on 1:1), typical of many Jewish apocalypses (see H. Reichelt, *Angelus,* 175–76). Reichelt draws attention to an analogous setting in Dan 7:9–18, where there is a vision of a great judgment scene in which an enormous number of angelic beings attended God and one like a son of man appeared to the Ancient of Days and received dominion. Unlike the seer in Rev 7:13, who is approached by one of the elders, the narrator in Dan 7:16 approached "one of those who stood there" to ask the meaning of the vision.

13b οὗτοι οἱ περιβεβλημένοι τὰς στολὰς τὰς λευκὰς τίνες εἰσὶν καὶ πόθεν ἦλθον; "'Who are these dressed in white robes and where did they come from?'" The use of the interrogative pronoun and interrogative adverb τίς, "who," and πόθεν, "from where," together is a standard formula used for the interrogation of visitors in epic dialogue (*Odyssey* 1.170; 14.188; 16.57–58) and as a literary device to identify the deceased in funerary epigrams (see L. Robert, *Hellenica* 4:47ff., and Roueché, *Aphrodisias,* 63–64). When Aeneas is touring the underworld, he asks his deceased father Anchises about some of the sights he sees (Vergil *Aeneid* 6.711–12; tr. LCL): "What is [*quae sint*] that river yonder, and who are the men [*quive viri*] thronging the banks in such a host?" These questions serve to focus the interest in the preceding scene on the identity, the clothing, and the origin of the innumerable host. The elder answers these questions in reverse order in v 14, while in vv 15–17 he deals with the present and future of this throng.

14a καὶ εἴρηκα αὐτῷ· κύριέ μου, σὺ οἶδας, "I replied to him, 'Sir, you know.'" The juxtaposition of the perfect εἴρηκα, "replied," with the aorist εἶπεν, "said" (v 14b), suggests that the perfect functions as an aorist; see *Comment* on 5:7 (Fanning, *Verbal Aspect,* 302–3). A similar response is made by Ezekiel (Ezek 37:3) when God asks him (NRSV), "Mortal, can these bones live?" and Ezekiel replies "O Lord God, you know." While angelic beings are never considered omniscient, knowledge is one of most prominent qualities associated with them in 4QShirShabb (Newsom, *Songs,* 30), where they are called אלי דעת *ʾēlê daʿat,* "angels of knowledge" (4Q*400* 2:1; 4Q*403* 1 i 31; 4Q*405* 23 i 8), or ידעים *yodʿîm,* "those who know" (4Q*400* 3 ii 5; 4Q*401* 35:1).

14b καὶ εἶπέν μοι· οὗτοί εἰσιν οἱ ἐρχόμενοι ἐκ τῆς θλίψεως τῆς μεγάλης, "Then he said to me, 'These are those who have emerged from the great tribulation.'" The phrase οὗτοί εἰσιν, "these are," introduces a "demonstrative explanation" (i.e., a demonstrative pronoun with the verb "to be" expressed or understood) and is a stylistic feature of Jewish apocalypses that has been investigated in some detail by Himmelfarb (*Tours,* 41–67). Demonstrative explanations (often in response to a demonstrative question, e.g., "who (or 'what') is this?") are usually introduced by a demonstrative pronoun or adjective, primarily the Greek demonstrative pronoun οὗτος, "this," the Latin pronouns *hic* or *iste,* or the Hebrew terms אלה *ʾēlleh* or

זה *zeh.* Himmelfarb (*Tours,* 48–50) argues that the supposed Greco–Roman antecedents to Jewish and Christian apocalyptic tours of hell lack such demonstrative questions and explanations, while such demonstrative pronouns as "this" and "these" are characteristic of Jewish and Christian apocalypses. The only exceptions she cites are found in Aeneas' tour of Hades narrated in Vergil's *Aeneid* (6.621, 623; Himmelfarb, *Tours,* 49–50). Himmelfarb has overlooked the satirical work of Lucian *Dial. mort.* 6(20), in which Aeacus, the gatekeeper of Hades, conducts Menippus on a tour of the underworld. "This is Cerberus" (οὗτος μὲν ὅτι Κέρβερός ἐστιν), he begins, but Menippus wants to be shown the really famous men of antiquity. Aeacus then proceeds: "This is Agamemnon, this is Achilles, this is Idomeneus next, and this is Odysseus." Shortly, Menippus asks, "But who is this, Aeacus?" (οὗτος δέ, ὦ Αἰακέ, τίς ἐστιν;), to which Aeacus replies, "Cyrus, and this is Croesus" (Κῦρός ἐστιν· οὗτος δὲ Κροῖσος). The presence of this dialogical form in a second-century A.D. satirist (the style itself is probably an adaptation from that used by ancient tour guides) suggests that Himmelfarb has exaggerated its exclusively Jewish character.

Demonstrative questions and answers are also found in other literary genres, such as the lengthy *ekphrasis* (detailed description of a work of art) in Cebes *Tabula* (4.3; 5.3; 6.2; 7.2; 8.2–3; 12.3; 15.3). While the earliest revelatory tour is Ezekiel's guided tour of the eschatological temple in Ezek 40–48 (Himmelfarb, *Tours,* 56–60), Zech 1–8 provides the closest biblical model for the early second-century B.C. "Book of the Watchers" in *1 Enoch* 1–36 (Himmelfarb, *Tours,* 50–56), the earliest extrabiblical tour apocalypse to make elaborate use of demonstrative questions and answers (Himmelfarb, *Tours,* 58). Examples of demonstrative explanations are found in the Greek fragments of *1 Enoch* 18:14, 15; 21:6, 10; 22:3, 7, 9; 23:4; 25:3, 4; 32:6, and 4 Ezra 10:44–48. One of the distinctive characteristics of Revelation is that the question-and-answer form typical of many Jewish and Christian apocalypses is almost completely missing. Demonstrative explanations introduced by demonstrative pronouns, however, occur five times (7:14; 11:4; 14:4; 20:5, 14). Only here in 7:14 is the explanation a response to a question (v 13), but the question is asked not by John but by one of the heavenly elders.

In the phrase οἱ ἐρχόμενοι ἐκ τῆς θλίψεως τῆς μεγάλης, "those who have emerged from the great tribulation," οἱ ἐρχόμενοι is translated in a past tense because it represents action simultaneous with the two main verbs ἔπλυναν, "washed," and ἐλεύκαναν, "made white," both of which are aorists (see *Note* 7:14.d-d.; Beckwith, 545). It is therefore grammatically improbable to translate the present substantival participle οἱ ἐρχόμενοι as "those who are coming," as if the scene in 7:9–17 were occurring precisely when it was narrated by the author, and to regard the martyrdom of Christians as a process that will not be completed as long as the eschatological consummation remains in the future (against Charles, 1:212–13; Rissi, *Babylon,* 18; cf. Ulfgard, *Feast,* 100–104). The articular phrase τῆς θλίψεως τῆς μεγάλης, "the great tribulation," is anaphoric and assumes that the readers know the final tribulation or period of woes that will introduce the eschaton, first mentioned in Dan 12:1 (עת צרה *ʿēt ṣārâ,* "time of distress"; see Jer 30:7) and thereafter part of a series of events associated with the arrival of the eschaton in early Judaism and early Christianity (*T. Moses* 8:1; *Jub.* 23:11–21; 4 Ezra 13:16–19; *2 Apoc. Bar.* 27.1–15; Mark 13:7–19; Matt 24:6–28 [esp. v 21]; 1 Cor 7:26; Rev 3:21; *Did.* 16:4–5; Hermas *Vis.* 2.2.7; see Volz, *Eschatologie,* 147–63; Str-B, 4:977–

86). The phrase θλῖψις μεγάλη also occurs in Matt 24:21, while in Hermas *Vis.* 2.2.7 the concept has already become a formal part of traditional eschatological expectation with the expression τὴν θλῖψιν τὴν ἐρχομένην τὴν μεγάλην, "the impending great tribulation" (see *Vis.* 4.1.1; 4.2.4; 4.2.5; 4.3.6; O'Hagen, *StudP* 6 [1961] 305–11). Since the Danielic phrase "time of distress" was interpreted as the time of the battle against the Kittim in 1QM 1:11–12; 15:1, Bauckham suggests that the phrase "those who emerged from the great tribulation" here means "those who emerge victorious from the eschatological war" ("War Scroll," 226). To argue, as Ulfgard does (*Feast,* 101–2), that the deaths of those making up the innumerable multitude are not implied, even though not explicitly mentioned, is to deny the obvious. Since the innumerable multitude has come out of the great tribulation, it is a reasonable inference that they, or at least some of them, are martyrs. It appears that while "the great tribulation" belonged to a discrete series of events in Jewish eschatological expectation, early Christians regarded their frequent experience of persecution and opposition (see Rev 1:9; 2:9–10; Matt 10:16–23; Acts 8:1) as part of this eschatological period of tribulation presaging the end (Mark 13:9–20 = Matt 24:9–22 = Luke 21:12–24; *Did.* 16:5). If the 144,000 of 7:4–8 are protected from this tribulation, then they cannot be identical with the innumerable multitude of 7:9–17, whose members have come out of the great tribulation.

14c καὶ ἔπλυναν τὰς στολὰς αὐτῶν καὶ ἐλεύκαναν αὐτὰς [i.e., στολάς] ἐν τῷ αἵματι τοῦ ἀρνίου, "They washed their robes and made them [i.e., 'robes'] white by the blood of the Lamb." The first phrase has an extremely close parallel in 22:14, where in the context of a beatitude a blessing is pronounced on "those who wash their robes" (perhaps an allusion to Exod 19:10, 14; argued by Fekkes, *Isaiah,* 167), though no explicit mention of atonement is present there. More probably this is an allusion to Dan 11:35, understood by the author as a testing and purifying process (Bauckham, "War Scroll," 227; J. J. Collins, *Comm. Daniel,* 386): "and some of those who are wise shall fall, to refine and to cleanse them and to make them white, until the time of the end, for it is yet for the time appointed" (RSV). It is possible that the washing of clothes referred to here is part of the ritual purification required after the shedding of blood (Num 31:19–20, 24; cf. 19:19), applied to the aftermath of the eschatological war in 1QM 14:2–3 (cf. Bauckham, "War Scroll," 226): "In the morning they shall clean their garments and wash themselves of the blood of the guilty corpses" (tr. J. Duhaime, in J. H. Charlesworth, ed., *Damascus Document, War Scroll, and Related Documents,* vol. 2 of *The Dead Sea Scrolls: Hebrew, Aramaic, and Greek Texts with English Translation* [Tübingen: Mohr-Siebeck; Louisville: Westminster John Knox, 1995] 125). In the sphere of Greek religious practices, there is a paradoxical Greek ritual of purification by blood, often in cases in which the defiled person has killed another person (Burkert, *Greek Religion,* 80–82). In the context of the "time of distress" mentioned in Dan 12:1, the "wise" who fall victims to sword and fire, captivity and pillage (Dan 11:35), are said to have been "tested, refined, and made shining white" (Dan 11:35; cf. 12:10); John interprets the purification mentioned in Dan 11:35; 12:10 to be that of the martyrs who purify themselves through martyrdom (Bauckham, "War Scroll," 228). The phrase "made them white by the blood of the Lamb" is a paradoxical metaphor (see other such paradoxical metaphors in 5:5–6; 7:17; see *Comment* on these passages). The phrase "the blood of the Lamb" occurs elsewhere in Revelation only in 12:11, where the notion of atonement is absent, though the idea of martyrdom is very much present as it is here. The phrase "the blood of the Lamb" or "the blood of Christ" (1 Cor 10:16; Eph 1:7; 2:13; 1 Pet 1:19; Heb 9:14) or "the blood of Jesus" (1 Pet 1:2; Heb 10:19; 1 John 1:7) is metonymy for the death of Christ or more particularly the atoning death of Christ. This language is drawn from the practice of expiatory sacrifice in Israelite-Jewish cultic tradition. Unlike Greek, Roman, and Near Eastern sacrificial protocol generally, the Israelite sacrificial ritual placed great emphasis on the significance of blood and its use in various purifying and atoning rituals (McCarthy, *JBL* 88 [1969] 166–76). One Israelite theory of the meaning of blood ritual is expressed in Lev 17:11, "For the life of the flesh is in the blood; and I have given it for you upon the altar to make atonement for your souls; for it is the blood that makes atonement, by reason of the life" (see also Heb 9:22). Lev 14:52 speaks of "cleansing [LXX ἀφαγνιεῖ] the house with blood." In the OT, blood derived from sacrificial animals both removes sin and consecrates only the persons or objects to which it is *physically* applied for purposes of purification (Exod 29:12, 16, 20–21). This is a striking metaphor for atonement. In Heb 9:14 the blood of Christ is said to καθαριεῖ, "purify," the conscience, and 9:22 says that "under the law almost everything is purified [καθαρίζεται] with blood, and without the shedding of blood there is no forgiveness of sins." In 1 John 1:7, the blood of Jesus is said to καθαρίζει, "cleanse," from all sin (the metaphor of "cleansing" from sin, which is analogous to dirt, occurs with some frequency: Sir 23:13; 38:10; Acts 15:9; 2 Cor 7:1; Heb 9:13; 2 Pet 1:9; 1 John 1:9). This suggests that the innumerable multitude is made up largely of martyrs who are in heaven (see 12:11; 15:2).

According to Gen 49:11, garments are washed in wine and vesture in the blood of grapes, i.e., red wine. The Jerusalem Targum on Gen 49:11, however, reads "his garments will be dipped in blood" (Trudinger, *BTB* 16 [1986] 79). This phrase has been interpreted to refer to (1) martyrdom, (2) baptism (Prigent, 123, 126), or (3) more generally victory, purity, holiness, or festal participation. The metaphorical character of the white robes is evident in this passage, where they are washed white by the blood of the Lamb; i.e., the sin of those who wear them has been atoned for by the sacrificial death of Christ. The term ἐλεύκαναν, "made white," suggests a possible allusion to Isa 1:18 (quoted in *1 Clem.* 8:4), where scarlet sins are to be made "white as snow [ὡς χιόνα λευκανῶ]."

15a διὰ τοῦτό εἰσιν ἐνώπιον τοῦ θρόνου τοῦ θεοῦ καὶ λατρεύουσιν αὐτῷ ἡμέρας καὶ νυκτὸς ἐν τῷ ναῷ αὐτοῦ, "For this reason they are before the throne of God, and they serve him day and night in his temple." The martyrs are able to stand before God only because of their purity, based on the atoning death of Christ. The worship of God in the heavenly temple by heavenly beings continues unendingly (4:8), and the righteous will eventually become full participants in this unceasing worship (3:12). Normal worship at the temple in Jerusalem involved the closing of the gates following the evening sacrifice and the opening of the gates at the morning sacrifice (Ezek 46:1–3; *m. Tamid;* Schürer, *History* 2:286–87). Using a metaphor for continual worship, Acts 26:7 states that "the twelve tribes worship day and night." On the hendiadys "day and night" (or "night and day"), which means "unceasingly," see *Comment* on 4:8. Occasionally this metaphor is used, usually hyperbolically, in connection with prayer and other forms of religious observance (Jer 16:13 [used negatively]; Pss 1:2; 88:1; Neh 1:6; Jdt 11:17; Luke 18:7; 1 Thess 3:10; 1 Tim 5:5; 2 Tim 1:3). The presence of a temple in heaven is frequently mentioned in Revelation (11:19; 14:15, 17; 15:5, 6, 8; 16:1, 17; cf. 22:3, "and his servants will serve [λατρεύσουσιν] him"). The heavenly temple is mentioned in early Jewish literature as the location of the throne of God (*T. Levi* 5:1; 18:6). God dwells in the heavenly holy of holies (*T. Levi* 3:4), where bloodless sacrifices are made (*T. Levi* 3:5–6). According to *b. Pesaḥ.* 54a, the temple was one of the seven things created before the creation of the world, and according to *2 Apoc. Bar.* 4:3, it was made when God created Paradise. The heavenly tabernacle, the pattern for the earthly tabernacle (Exod 25:9, 40; 26:30; 27:8; *2 Apoc. Bar.* 4:5), is referred to in Wis 9:8; Heb 8:2; 9:11–12.

15b καὶ ὁ καθήμενος ἐπὶ τοῦ θρόνου σκηνώσει ἐπ' αὐτούς, "The one who sits on the throne will shelter them." This passage alludes to Ezek 37:27 (RSV), "My dwelling place [MT מִשְׁכָּנִי *miškanî;* LXX κατασκήνωσίς μου] shall be with them; and I will be their God, and they shall be my people." See also Lev 26:11 (RSV), "And I will make my abode [MT מִשְׁכָּנִי *miškanî*] among you." The verb σκηνοῦν means "to live, dwell" and suggests nothing about the *mode* of dwelling (i.e., whether in tents or houses, though τὸ σκῆνος means "tent," implying that the *extent* of time involved in such a dwelling is temporary). Lohmeyer contrasts the phrase σκηνώσει ἐπ' αὐτούς, "he will dwell with them," with the similar phrase σκηνώσει μετ' αὐτῶν, "will shelter them," in 21:3, and Rissi (*Babylon,* 18) argues that the former refers to the dwelling of the dead saints in heaven until the time of eschatological fulfillment. However, the notion that σκηνοῦν refers to God's "tabernacling presence" (Koester, *Dwelling,* 118) is linguistically untenable. If Exodus imagery is involved in this verse, it is possible to find a contrast between God's presence with Israel, represented by a cloud by day and a pillar of fire by night, and his unmediated presence with his people here. The term "Shekinah" means the presence of God in cloud and fire. The biblical instructions for the Feast of Tabernacles (חג הסכות *ḥag hassukkôt*) prescribed that the people of Israel live in booths (סכות *sukkôt*) during the seven-day feast because "I [Yahweh] made the people of Israel dwell in booths when I brought them out of the land of Egypt" (Lev 23:42–43). This use of booths (not tents) was probably taken over from Canaanite religious practice and projected back into the wilderness experience of Israel. Later rabbinic interpretation understood סכות *sukkôt* to mean the "clouds of glory" (here "glory" is a circumlocution for "God") with which God covered and protected his people during their wandering in the wilderness (see Ulfgard, *Feast,* 121–27, for references). According to *Tg. Onq.* Lev 23:42–43 (tr. Grossfeld):

> You should dwell in *booths* [Hebrew סכות *sukkôt,* from סכך *sākak,* meaning "to cover," rendered here in Aramaic as מיטללייה *myṭllyh,* from טלל *ṭělal,* meaning both "to cover" and "to protect"] for seven days; every native born among Israel should dwell in *booths,* in order that your future generations should recognize that I made the Israelites dwell *under the protection of My cloud* [Hebrew "in booths"] when I brought them out of the land of Egypt; I am the Lord your God.

The interpretation of the phrase "in booths" to mean "under the protection of My cloud" is attributed to R. Akiba in *Sipra Lev.* 103a and *Mek. de-Rabbi Ishmael* 35.10 (references in Grossfeld, *Targum Onqelos,* 53–55 n. 12; Ulfgard, *Feast,* 124 n. 522). Ulfgard (*Feast,* 125–26) thinks that since the various targumic versions of Lev 23:43 agree with the interpretation attributed to R. Akiba and R. Eliezer, this tradition goes back to the end of the NT period. According to this tradition, "God's protective presence during the wilderness wandering is conceptualized in the theological term 'cloud(s) of glory,' in which the desert generation is said to have dwelt" (Ulfgard, *Feast*, 126). Ulfgard, however, sees the reference to booths in Lev 23:43 as an example of the early theologization of the festival in which they are associated with God's presence in the desert (*Feast*, 146). There is absolutely no evidence supporting this interpretation, which is not demonstrably earlier than the late second century A.D.

16 οὐ πεινάσουσιν ἔτι οὐδὲ διψήσουσιν ἔτι, οὐδὲ μὴ πέσῃ ἐπ' αὐτοὺς ὁ ἥλιος οὐδὲ πᾶν καῦμα, "They will neither hunger any longer nor thirst any longer, neither will the sun fall on them nor any scorching heat." This is the longest allusion to an OT passage found in Revelation, and it is clearly drawn from Isa 9:10, "They shall not hunger [οὐ πεινάσουσιν] or thirst [οὐδὲ διψήσουσιν]; neither scorching wind nor sun shall smite them, for he who has pity on them will lead them, and by springs of water [πηγῶν ὑδάτων] will lead [ἄξει] them" (cf. Rev 7:17b). The very opposite is said to happen to those afflicted by the fourth bowl in 16:7, for there it is said that the sun was allowed to burn people with fire.

17a ὅτι τὸ ἀρνίον τὸ ἀνὰ μέσον τοῦ θρόνου ποιμανεῖ αὐτούς, "because the Lamb in the midst of the throne will shepherd them." The author has interrupted his allusion to Isa 49:10 to insert this statement regarding the role of the Lamb, which may be an allusion to Ezek 34:23. There is a close relationship between this passage and Rev 14:1–5, where the Lamb is described as standing on Mount Zion (v 1), but the throne is also mentioned (v 3), and the 144,000 are said to "follow the Lamb wherever he leads" (v 4), which appears to conflate both discipleship and shepherd/sheep imagery (see John 10:4). Rev 7:17 reflects the use of a common ancient pastoral metaphor in which the relationship between leader and those under him (usually a king and his people) is compared to a shepherd and his flock, and the term "shepherd" was a stock term for "king" (Zimmerli, *Ezekiel* 2:213–14). This imagery occurs frequently in the OT (2 Sam 7:7; Isa 44:28; Jer 3:15; 10:21; 25:34–36; Nah 3:18) and is very common in Greek literature (*Iliad* 2.243 and passim [where Agamemnon is called "shepherd of the people"]; Plato *Republic* 4.440d; *Politicus* 271e; Xenophon *Cyropaedia* 1.1.2; Dio Chrysostom *Or.* 1.13; 4.41; 4.44–45; Plutarch *De Alex. virt.* 329A–B; in pseudo-Pythagorean literature [Stobaeus 4.5.61 = 36.4–5; 7.64 = 82.5–6]; see J. B. Skemp, *Plato's Statesman* [London: Routledge & Kegan Paul, 1952] 52–66]). The verb ποιμαίνειν is used four times in Revelation (2:27; 7:17; 12:5; 19:15); in 7:17 it means "to shepherd" (Louw-Nida, § 44.3) or "to guide or help" (Louw-Nida, § 36.2), while in 2:27; 12:5; 19:15 it means "to rule" (Louw-Nida, § 37.57). The metaphor of shepherd is applied to Paul in *Acts of Paul* 21, "But Thecla sought for Paul, as a lamb [ὡς ἀμνός] in the wilderness looks about for the shepherd." It appears at first peculiar that it is a *lamb* who plays the role of a shepherd, yet it must be noted that the Lamb in Revelation is the Davidic Messiah (a figure described as a shepherd), as is Jesus, who is called a shepherd several times in the NT and early Christian literature (Matt 15:24; 25:32; Mark 14:27–28 = Matt 26:31–32 [an allusion to Zech 13:7, which is also found in *Barn.* 5:12]; Luke 19:10; John 10:2, 11, 12, 14; Heb 13:20; 1 Pet 2:25; 5:4; *1 Clem.* 16:1; Clement *Paed.* 3.101.3).

In early Christian art, Jesus is frequently depicted as the Good Shepherd, typically carrying a sheep on his shoulders; see Tertullian *On Modesty* 7.1–4; J. Quasten, "Der gute Hirte in hellenistische und frühchristliche Theologie," *Heilige Überlieferung* (Münster: Aschendorff, 1938) 51–58; W. Schumacher, *Hirt und Guter Hirt*, RQSup 34 (Freiburg: Herder, 1977); B. Ramsay, "A Note on the Disappearance of the Good Shepherd from

Early Christian Art," *HTR* 76 (1983) 375–78; A. Pollastri and A. M. Giuntella, "Shepherd, the Good," and "Iconography," *Encyclopedia of the Early Church,* ed. A. Di Berardino (New York: Oxford UP, 1992) 2:776–78.

In the Abercius epitaph (ca. A.D. 200), lines 3–6, Jesus is called the "pure shepherd who feeds his flocks of sheep on mountains and plains" (text in J. B. Lightfoot, *Apostolic Fathers,* 2/1:496; see W. M. Calder, "The Epitaph of Avircius Marcellus," *JRS* 29 [1939] 1–4). This metaphor occupies a significant place in John 10:1–16 (esp. in vv 2, 11, 12, 14, 16), a fact that has been used to argue for a close relationship between John and Revelation (Böcher, *NTS* 27 [1981] 312). Yet since the Fourth Gospel uses only the noun ποιμήν of Jesus, and Revelation uses only the verb ποιμαίνειν, the Johannine metaphor is in fact closer to the use of the metaphor in other NT passages such as Heb 13:20, where the exalted Jesus is called "the great shepherd of the sheep," and 1 Pet 2:25, where he is called "the shepherd and overseer of your souls." In the OT, God as the shepherd of Israel is an ancient metaphor (Gen 49:24 [Jahwist writer]; 48:15 [Elohist writer]), which continued to be used with some frequency (Pss 23:1, 3; 68:7–10; 80:1; Isa 40:11; 49:10; Jer 50:19). In the NT, God is referred to as a shepherd only in a single parable of Jesus found in Q (Luke 15:4–7 = Matt 18:12–14), and in the Apostolic Fathers only in Ignatius *Rom.* 9:1 (this metaphor, however, is based on the fact that Ignatius regards the bishop as the shepherd of the local flock of Christians; see *Phld.* 2:1; Ps.-Clement *Hom.* 3.72.1). The conception of Christians as the flock of God who are shepherded by church leaders occurs with some frequency in early Christian literature (Mark 14:27 = Matt 26:31; Acts 20:28; 1 Pet 5:2; *1 Clem.* 16:1; 44:3; 54:2; 57:2; see Joachim Jeremias, *TDNT* 6:500–502). This metaphor is based on the common application of the shepherd/flock imagery applied to the king and his people. Mic 5:4 (interpreted messianically in Matt 2:6) prophesies the coming of a ruler who will shepherd the people of Israel (see Mic 5:4). The role of David *redivivus* is described in Ezek 34:23, NRSV (see 37:24), "I will set up over them one shepherd, my servant David, and he shall feed them: he shall feed them and be their shepherd." This same metaphor is explicitly used of the Davidic Messiah in *Pss. Sol.* 17:40, where the flock is carefully described as the Lord's (tr. Charlesworth, *OTP* 2:668): "Faithfully and righteously shepherding the Lord's flock [ποιμαίνων τὸ ποίμνιον κυρίου].... He will lead [ἄξει] them in all holiness." It seems clear, then, that the imagery of Rev 7:17 is based on traditional conceptions associated with the Davidic Messiah.

17b καὶ ὁδηγήσει αὐτοὺς ἐπὶ ζωῆς πηγὰς ὑδάτων, "and guide them to the springs of life." The author, who in v 16 began to allude to Isa 49:10, now continues the allusion (cf. LXX Isa 49:10d, καὶ διὰ πηγῶν ὑδάτων ἄξει αὐτούς, "he will lead them through springs of water"). The phrase ζωῆς πηγὰς ὑδάτων, literally "springs of the waters of life," is very close to the Hebrew phrase מבוע מים חיים *mabbûaʿ mayim ḥayyim,* found in 1QH 8:16 (where it is a metaphor for the elect who will, like the Teacher of Righteousness, be a "fountain of living water"). The phrase מקור מים חיים *māqôr mayim ḥayyim,* "fountain of living water," also occurs in 4Q*416, 418,* frag. 2, line 5 (Eisenman-Wise, *Scrolls,* 245, 250), though the context is not clear. The image of "living water" also occurs in Rev 21:6; 22:1, 17 and is perhaps the most striking common metaphor that Revelation shares with John (4:14; 6:35; 7:17–18; see Taeger, *Johannesapokalypse,* 29–66). The phrase ὕδωρ ζῶν, literally "living water," means "flowing water," i.e., a spring or river rather than water standing in a cistern

(LXX Gen 26:19; Lev 14:5; Jer 2:13; Zech 14:8; *Did.* 7:1–2; Klauser, "Taufet," 157–64, esp. 157–59; see Ps.-Clement *Diamart.* 1, cited in Rordorf-Tulier, *Doctrine,* 170–71 n. 5). The Hebrew phrase מים חיים *mayim ḥayyim,* "waters of life," occurs in 1QH 8:7, and in 1QH 8:16 the author says that "Thou, O my God, have put in my mouth . . . a spring of living waters [מבוע מים חיים *mabbûaʿ mayim ḥayyim*] which shall not run dry." The phrase in Rev 21:6 is δώσω ἐκ τῆς πηγῆς τοῦ ὕδατος τῆς ζωῆς δωρεάν, "I will freely give from the well of living water," while 22:1 has ποταμὸν ὕδατος ζωῆς, "river of living water," and 22:17 has λαβέτω ὕδωρ ζωῆς δωρεάν, "let him receive as a gift the water of life." A relatively close parallel is found in LXX Jer 2:13, πηγὴ ὕδατος ζωῆς, "spring of living water," a metaphor for Yahweh (in the *Tg. Neb.* Jer 2:13, this is changed to a metaphor for goodness). In the early church, ὕδωρ ζῶν, "living water," or ὕδωρ τῆς ζωῆς, "water of life," is used as a metaphor for prophetic inspiration (Ignatius *Rom.* 7:2), baptism (Justin *Dial.* 14.1), Christ (Justin *Dial.* 69.6), the teaching of Christ (Clement of Alex. *Strom.* 7.16), and the Holy Spirit (Didymus *Trin.* 2.22; *PGL,* 1425). The phrase "spring [of the] water of life" also occurs in the Coptic-Gnostic treatise *Ap. John* 4.21–24.

17c καὶ ἐξαλείψει ὁ θεὸς πᾶν δάκρυον ἐκ τῶν ὀφθαλμῶν αὐτῶν, "And God will wipe away every tear from their eyes." This is a clear allusion to Isa 25:8, "Then the Lord God will wipe away the tears from all faces," probably based on the Hebrew text (cf. Jer 31:16[LXX 38:16]). The same allusion is also used in Rev 21:4, καὶ ἐξαλείψει πᾶν δάκρυον ἐκ τῶν ὀφθαλμῶν αὐτῶν, "he will wipe away every tear from their eyes," differing only in the omission of ὁ θεός, "God." See *Comment* on 21:4 for a discussion of the eschatological elimination of sorrow and pain.

Explanation

The question that concludes Rev 6 provides an introduction to 7:1–17, for it deals with the problem of how the "servants of God" (7:3) will fare during the catastrophes unleashed by the sixth seal. To answer this question, John inserts 7:1–17, which accomplishes two things. First, in vv 1–8 the effect of the plagues on Christians is temporarily held in abeyance while 144,000 "servants of God," 12,000 from each of the twelve tribes of Israel, are sealed on their foreheads by the signet ring of the living God, an act symbolizing both ownership and protection. While the number of those sealed is mentioned, the sealing itself is not narrated. Although the reference to the twelve tribes of Israel may have been understood literally in the source or tradition underlying this text, it now refers to a particular group of Christians who have been specially protected by God from both divine plagues and human persecution just prior to the beginning of the eschatological tribulation and who will consequently survive that tribulation and the great eschatological conflict with which it culminates. The particular list of tribes used in vv 4–8 has no exact parallel in other early Jewish or early Christian sources (see *Excursus 7B: The Order of the Tribes in Rev 7:4–8*), and its form probably reflects the author's inclinations. The unusual placement of the tribe of Judah at the head of the list occurs because the Messiah belongs to that tribe. The omission of Dan has no particular theological significance, and both Joseph and Manasseh are probably included because of an early error. ("Joseph" may have been occasionally substituted for "Ephraim.") The sealing, which cannot refer to Christian baptism, protects them against the plagues unleashed upon the unbelieving world as well as against those Romans and Anatolians who would kill them. This conception of immunity from the plagues is ultimately derived from the tradition that the plagues harmed Egyptians only, not Israelites (Exod 8:22; 9:4–7, 26; 10:23; Philo *Mos.* 1.143–46). Although the Last Judgment appears to be inaugurated by the opening of the sixth seal, the eschatological scenario of Revelation yet requires the plagues unleashed by the seven trumpets and the seven bowls. This suggests either that the seven seals were derived from a source that John prefixed to his narratives of the seven trumpets and seven bowls or (more likely) that the seven trumpets and seven bowls are derived from two Jewish sources that consolidated the ten plagues of Exod 7–12 into seven eschatological plagues.

Vv 9–17 consist of two related units of text, both of which focus on the eschatological heavenly worship of God. The first section (vv 9–12) consists of a great hymn of salvation sung to God by the innumerable multitude (vv 9–10) and is matched by an antiphonal response sung by the angels surrounding the throne, the twenty-four elders, and the four cherubim (vv 11–12). The second section (vv 13–17) consists of an explanation volunteered by one of the elders in which he interprets the foregoing scenes. It is clear that the "innumerable multitude" (v 9), which suggests the fulfillment of the promise to Abraham, consists of the large number Christians who have died or suffered martyrdom during the period of eschatological tribulation, during the same period that the 144,000 have been divinely protected from defeat and death. The deliberate contrast of the innumerable multitude with the 144,000 (the former is drawn from every nation) indicates that the groups are not identical.

C. *The Seventh Seal and the First Six Trumpets (8:1–11:14)*

1. *The Seventh Seal (8:1)*

2. *Vision of the First Six Trumpets (8:2–9:21)*

Bibliography

Allison, D. C. "The Silence of the Angels: Reflections on the Songs of the Sabbath Sacrifice." *RevQ* 13 (1988) 189–97. **Andiñach, P. R.** "The Locusts in the Message of Joel." *VT* 42 (1992) 433–41. **Arnold, W. N.** "Absinthe." *Scientific American* 260 (1989) 112–17. **Barton, B. H.** *The British Flora Medica: A History of the Medical Plants of Great Britain.* London: Chatto & Windis, 1877. **Bauckham, R.** "The Eschatological Earthquake." In Bauckham, *Climax.* 199–209. **Böcher, O.** "Lasterkataloge in der Apokalypse des Johannes." In *Leben lernen im Horizont des Glaubens.* FS S. Wibbing, ed. B. Buschbeck and F. Lemke. Landau: Pfalz, 1986. 75–84. **Delling, G.** "Josephus und die heidnischen Religionen." *Klio* 43–45 (1965) 263–69. **DeVries, L. F.** "Cult Stands: A Bewildering Variety of Shapes and Sizes." *BARev* 13 (1987) 27–37. **Eitrem, S.** "Der Skorpion in Mythologie und Religionsgeschichte." *SO* 7 (1928) 53–82. **Goodman, M.** *Mission and Conversion: Proselytizing in the Religious History of the Roman Empire.*

Oxford: Clarendon, 1994. **Gordon, R. P.** "Loricate Locusts in the Targum to Nahum 3:17 and Revelation 9:9." *VT* 33 (1983) 338–39. **Haran, M.** "The Use of Incense in the Ancient Israelite Ritual." *VT* 10 (1960) 113ff. **Holm-Nielsen, S.** "The Exodus Traditions in Psalm 105." *ASTI* 11 (1978) 22–30. **Keel, O.** *Vögel als Boten.* OBO 14. Freiburg: Universitätsverlag; Göttingen: Vandenhoeck & Ruprecht, 1977. **Kehnscherper, G.** "*. . . und die Sonne verfinsterte sich": Die Santorinkatastrophe und die archäologischen Forschungen um das letzte Buch der Bibel.* Aalen: Scientia, 1980. **Kittel, G.** "Die Fünfzahl als geläufige Zahl und als stilistisches Motiv." In *Arbeiten zur Religionsgeschichte des Urchristentums,* ed. J. Leipoldt. Vol. 1/3. Leipzig: Hinrichs, 1920. 39ff. **Knohl, I.** "Between Voice and Silence: The Relationship between Prayer and the Temple Cult." *JBL* 115 (1991) 17–30. ———. *The Sanctuary of Silence.* Minneapolis: Fortress, 1995. **Kobelski, P. J.** *Melchizedek and Melchiresa.* Washington, DC: Catholic Biblical Association of America, 1991. **Loehr, M.** *Das Räucheropfer im Alten Testament.* Halle: Niemeyer, 1927. **Loewenstamm, S. E.** "The Number of Plagues in Psalm 105." *Bib* 52 (1971) 34–38. ———. *The Tradition of the Exodus in Its Development.* Jerusalem: Magnes, 1965. **Macholz, C.** "Das 'Passivum divinum,' seine Anfänge im Alten Testament under der 'Hofstil.'" *ZNW* 81 (1990) 247–53. **Margulis, B.** "The Plagues Tradition in Psalm 105." *Bib* 50 (1969) 491–96. **McCarter, K.** "Exodus." In *Harper's Bible Commentary,* ed. J. L. Mays. San Francisco: Harper & Row, 1988. 129–56. **Mensching, G.** *Das heilige Schweigen: Eine religionsgeschichtliche Untersuchung.* RVV 20.2. Giessen: Töpelmann, 1926. **Morton, J. F.** *Atlas of Medicinal Plants of Middle America.* Springfield, IL: Thomas, 1981. **Müller, H.-P.** "Die Plagen der Apokalypse." *ZNW* 51 (1960) 268–78. **Mussies, G.** "*DYO* in Apocalypse ix 12 and 16." *NovT* 9 (1967) 151–54. **Nielsen, K.** *Incense in Ancient Israel.* Leiden: Brill, 1986. **Oppenheim, A. L.** *The Interpretation of Dreams in the Ancient Near East.* Transactions of the American Philosophical Society n.s. 46/3. Philadelphia: American Philosophical Association, 1956. **Paulien, J.** *Decoding Revelation's Trumpets: Literary Allusions and the Interpretation of Revelation 8:7–12.* Berrien Springs, MI: Andrews UP, 1987. **Petuchowsky, J. J.** "Jewish Prayer Texts of the Rabbinic Period." In *The Lord's Prayer and Jewish Liturgy,* ed. J. J. Petuchowsky and M. Brocke. New York: Seabury, 1978. 29. **Reeves, J. C.** "An Enochic Citation in *Barnabas* 4.3 and the *Oracles of Hystaspes.*" In *Pursuing the Text.* FS B. Z. Wacholder, ed. J. C. Reeves and J. Kampen. Sheffield: Sheffield Academic, 1994. 260–77. **Schäfer, P.** *Rivalität zwischen Engeln und Menschen: Untersuchungen zur rabbinischen Engelvorstellung.* SJ 8. Berlin; New York: de Gruyter, 1975. **Taylor, N.** *Plant Drugs That Changed the World.* New York: Dodd, Mead, 1965. **Thompson, J. A.** "Joel's Locusts in the Light of Near Eastern Parallels." *JNES* 14 (1955) 52–55. **Whiting, J.** "Jerusalem's Locust Plague." *NGM* 38 (1915) 511–50. **Wolff, H. W.** *Joel and Amos.* Tr. W. Janzen, S. D. McBride, Jr., and C. A. Muenchow. Philadelphia: Fortress, 1979. **Zahn, T.** "Der Ausbruch des Vesuvs vom J. 79 n. Chr. nach seinem Eindruck auf Heiden, Juden und Christen." In *Festschrift zu A. Schlatters 70. Geburtstag.* Stuttgart: Calwer, 1922. 151–69. **Zwickel, W.** *Räucherkult und Räuchergeräte: Exegetische und archäologische Studien zum Räuchopfer im Alten Testament.* OBO 97. Freiburg: Universitätsverlag; Göttingen: Vandenhoeck & Ruprecht, 1990.

Translation

1 *When* [ab] *he opened the seventh seal, there was silence in heaven for a half hour.* 2 *Then I saw the* [a] *seven angels (the ones who stand* [b] *before God), and seven trumpets* [c]*were given* [c] *to them.* 3 *Another angel came and stood* [a]*before the altar* [a] *of incense with a golden censer. A large quantity of incense was given to him* [b]*to offer* [b] *as a complement to the prayers of all* [c]*God's people* [c] *upon the golden altar before* [d] *the throne.* 4 *The smoke of the incense* [a]*with the prayers* [a] *of* [b]*God's people* [b] *went up from the hand of the angel before God.* 5 *The* [a] *angel received the censer and filled it with some glowing embers from the altar of incense and threw them upon the earth, and there were* [b]*thunder and rumbling and lightning* [b] *and an*

earthquake.[c] 6 *The*[a] *seven angels*[b] *with the seven trumpets got ready*[c] *to sound*[c] [d] *them.* 7 *The*[a]
first angel[b] *sounded his trumpet, and there was hail and fire mixed with blood, and it was*
thrown down to the earth[c] *with the result that*[c] *a third part of the earth was burned up, and*
a third part of the trees were burned up, and all the green grass was burned up. 8 *The second*
angel sounded his trumpet, and something like a great[a] *mountain burning*[b] *with fire*[b] *was*
cast into the sea[c] *with the result that*[c] *a third part of the sea became blood,* 9 *and a third part*
of the living[a] *creatures in the sea died, and a third part of the boats were destroyed.*[b] 10 *The*[a]
third angel sounded his trumpet, and a huge star fell from heaven burning like[b] *a torch and*
fell on a third part of the rivers and on the springs of water. 11 *Now the name of the star is*
[a]*Apsinth,*[b] *and a third part*[c] *of the water became bitter like*[d] *wormwood*[e] *so that*[f] *many people*
died as a result of[g] *the water because*[h] *it had turned bitter.*[h] 12 *Then*[a] *the fourth angel sounded*
his trumpet, and a third of the sun was struck and a third of the moon and a third of the stars
with the result that a third part of them was darkened and[b] *a third*[c] *part of the day did not*
[d]*appear*[b] *and the night similarly.*

13 *I looked and heard an*[a] *eagle*[b] *flying in*[c] *midheaven crying with a loud voice: "Woe, woe,*
[d]*woe*[e] *to the inhabitants*[e] *of the earth*[f] *because of*[f] *the remaining blasts of the trumpet which*
the three angels are about to sound!" 9:1 *Then the fifth angel sounded his trumpet, and then*
I saw a star which had fallen from heaven to earth. He was given the key to the shaft of the
abyss. 2 [a]*He opened the shaft of the abyss,*[a] *and smoke arose from the shaft as smoke from a great*[b]
furnace,[c] *so that*[c] *the sun and the air*[d] *were darkened*[d] *by*[e] *the smoke*[f] *from the shaft.* 3 *Out of*
the smoke[a] *emerged locusts upon the earth, and they*[b] *were given authority as scorpions have*
authority over the earth. 4 *But*[a] [b]*they were instructed*[b] *not to harm*[c] *the grass of the earth*[d] *nor*
any plant nor any tree,[d] *with the exception of people*[e] *who do not have*[f] *the*[g] *seal of God upon*
[h]*their foreheads.*[h] 5 *But*[a] *they were ordered*[b] *not to kill them but to torment*[c] *them for five months*
(their torment was like the torment of a scorpion when it stings a person).

6 *In*[a] *those*[b] *days people will seek death*
but[c] [d]*not*[e] *be able to find*[d] *it;*
they will desire to die,
but[f] *death*[g] *will elude*[g] *them.*[h]

7 *The*[a] *appearance of the locusts was like*[b] *horses prepared for battle. On their heads were*
[c]*something*[d] *like gold*[d] *crowns, and their faces were like human faces* 8 *with hair like that*[a] *of*
women, and their teeth were like those of lions. 9 *They had thoraxes like iron breastplates, and*
the sound of their wings was like the sound of many chariots with teams of warhorses[a] *rushing*
into battle. 10 *They have*[a] *tails*[b] *with stingers like*[c] *scorpions,*[d] *so that*[d] *with their tails they have*
power to harm[b] *people for five months.* 11 [a]*As*[b] *king they have over them*[b] *the angel of the abyss,*
whose name[c] *in Hebrew*[d] *is*[e] *Abaddon,*[f] *and in Greek*[g] [h]*he has the name*[h] *Apollyon.* 12 *The*
first[a] *disaster*[b] *has occurred; behold twice*[c] *more a disaster*[b] [d]*will come*[d] [e]*after these things.*

13 [a]*Then*[b] *the sixth angel sounded his trumpet, and I heard a*[c] *voice*[d] *from the*[e] *corners*[df] *of the*
golden altar of incense before God, 14 *announcing*[a] *to the sixth angel with the trumpet,*[b] *"Release*
the four[c] *angels bound*[d] *at the great river Euphrates."*[d] 15 *Then the four angels*[a] *who were prepared*[a]
for the hour[b] *and the day*[b] *and the month and the year were released to*[c] *kill a third of humanity.*
16 *The number of soldiers, or cavalry,*[a] *was twice ten thousand times ten thousand*[b] *(I heard their*
number). 17 *The horses*[a] *and their riders*[b] *I saw in my vision looked like this: they had breastplates*
which were fiery red and blue like hyacinth[c] *and yellow like sulfur. The heads of the horses were like*
the heads of lions, and from their mouths proceeded fire and smoke and sulfur. 18 *A third of humanity*
was killed[a] *by*[b] *these*[c] *three*[d] *plagues,*[e] *by the fire and*[f] *the smoke and*[g] *the sulfur which proceeded*
from their[h] *mouths.* 19 *For*[a] *the power of the horses is in their mouths and in their tails, for their tails,*
which resemble snakes, have[b] *heads, and they inflict injury with them.*

20 *The rest of humanity, those not killed by these plagues,*[a] *did not* [b] [c]*repent of*[c] *the products of their own manufacture; that is, they did not cease to worship* [d] [e]*the demons,*[e] [f]*or idols,*[f] *made of gold* [g] *and silver* [h] [i]*and bronze*[i] *and stone and* [j]*wood, which can* [k] *neither see nor hear nor walk,* 21 *and they did not* [a]*repent of*[a] *their murders, nor of their sorcery,*[b] [c]*nor of their immorality,*[d] [e]*nor of their thefts.*[ce]

Notes

1.a. The conjunction καί, "and," is left untranslated because it lacks semantic value here and functions as a discourse marker indicating the beginning of a new sentence or clause (Louw-Nida, 1:vi).

1.b. Variant: (1) ὅταν] A C fam 1006$^{1006\ 1841}$ fam 1611^{1611}; Tischendorf, *NT Graece;* WHort; von Soden, *Text;* UBSGNT^{4}; Nestle-Aland^{27}; *TCGNT*^{1}; *TCGNT*^{2}. (2) ὅτε] ℵ 025 052 Andreas Byzantine. According to the plausible argument in *TCGNT*^{1}, 740, and *TCGNT*^{2}, ὅτε resulted from the assimilation of the frequent occurrence of ὅτε ἤνοιξεν in Rev 6. The term ὅταν, which usually means "whenever" (and implies repetition), here clearly is used to mean "when" (referring to a unique event) and is used as an equivalent for ὅτε, "when," which occupies a similar position in the six preceding instances in which John has narrated the opening of a seal by the Lamb (6:1, 3, 5, 7, 9, 12; see Mussies, *Morphology,* 345; Lohmeyer, 49); see 4:9; 11:7; 12:4.

2.a. Variant: omit τούς before ἀγγέλους] fam 1611^{2329}.

2.b. The pf. verb ἑστήκασιν, lit. "they have stood," is used statively (appropriate for a stative or durative verb), here with no reference to the result of prior action (McKay, *Grammar,* 139). Further, ἑστήκασιν is the only 3rd pl. pf. in Revelation that retains the older pf. -ασι(ν) ending: see πέπωκαν (18:3); εἴρηκαν (19:3); γέγοναν (21:6); see Mussies, *Morphology,* 265.

2.c-c. Variants: (1) ἐδώθησαν] fam 1611^{2329}. (2) ἐδόθη] A Andr h l$^{052\ 2080}$. Variant (1) is a scribal error reflecting the ο = ω interchange (see Gignac, *Grammar* 1:275–77). Variant (2) is simply an error (Mussies, *Morphology,* 231 n. 1). The use of a finite verb in the beginning of this coordinate clause, καὶ ἐδόθησαν, is an example of the author's avoidance of hypotaxis in favor of parataxis, since in ordinary Gk. a ptcp. would be expected here (see Ljungvik, *Syntax,* 80; BDR § 471).

3.a-a. Variants: (1) ἐπὶ τοῦ θυσιαστηρίου] ℵ Byzantine; Tischendorf, *NT Graece;* WHort; Bousset (1906) 292; von Soden, *Text;* Merk, *NT;* Nestle-Aland^{27}; UBSGNT^{4}. (2) ἐπὶ τὸ θυσιαστήριον] A fam 1006 fam 1611$^{1611\ 1854\ 2329}$ Oecumenius^{2053} Andreas; Charles, 2:284.

3.b-b. Variants: (1) δώσει (fut. ind.)] ℵ A C Andr a f$^{2031\ 2056}$ g^{2045} h i^{-2074} l$^{1778\ 2080}$ 598 1773. (2) δώσῃ (aor. subjunctive)] 052 2351 Andreas Byzantine; Bousset (1906) 293; von Soden, *Text;* (3) δῷ (aor. subjunctive)] fam 1006 Oecumenius^{2053}. See Rev 3:9.

3.c-c. The pl. substantive οἱ ἅγιοι, lit. "holy ones," is used here, as frequently elsewhere in early Christian literature, with the meaning "God's people," with the emphasis on their relationship with God, not their sanctity (Louw-Nida, § 11.27); see *Comment* on 5:8.

3.d. Variant: omit τό before ἐνώπιον] ℵ fam 1611^{2329} Andr/Byz 4c^{-2022} TR eth arm.

4.a-a. See v 8:3c, where the phrase ταῖς προσευχαῖς also occurs. Moulton (*Prolegomena,* 75; followed by Robertson, *Grammar,* 529) understands it as a "sociative instrumental" (i.e., a dat. of association) meaning "with the prayers," while Swete (109), Bousset ([1906] 294), Beckwith (553), Charles (1:231), and Turner (*Syntax,* 238) construe the phrase as a *dativus commodi,* "in favour of," "in behalf of," "to help" their prayers. Moule (*Idiom-Book,* 43) suggests that this is a temporal dat., which should be translated "simultaneously with the prayers."

4.b-b. See *Note* on 8:3.c-c.

5.a. See *Note* 1.a.

5.b-b. Variants: (1) βρονταὶ καὶ φωναὶ καὶ ἀστραπαί] ℵ 025 046 fam 1006^{-1006} fam 1611^{1611} 2351 Andr g^{-2045} Byzantine latt syr^{ph} cop; Tischendorf, *NT Graece;* WHort; Bousset (1906) 295; von Soden, *Text;* Merk, *NT;* Nestle-Aland^{27}; UBSGNT^{4}. (2) βρονταὶ καὶ ἀστραπαί] fam 1006^{1006}. (3) βρονταὶ καὶ ἀστραπαὶ καὶ φωναί] A (lacuna in C) 052 fam 1611$^{2329\ 2344}$ Andr i^{2042} l syr^{h}; WHort^{mg}; B. Weiss, *Johannes-Apokalypse,* 108; Charles, 2:285. (4) φωναὶ καὶ βρονταὶ καὶ ἀστραπαί] fam 1611^{1854} Oecumenius^{2053} Andreas Tyc^{1} Beatus TR. There are three close parallels in Rev: 4:5; 11:19; 16:18, all of which read ἀστραπαὶ καὶ φωναὶ καὶ βρονταί. Rev 4:5 and 11:19 are textually secure, supported by A and Andr^{mss}, and suggest that the same order was used in 16:18. The rationale for this is in part because one logically expects lightning before thunder (but cf. LXX Exod 19:16, ἐγίνοντο φωναὶ καὶ ἀστραπαί; but quoted by Oecumenius [Hoskier, *Oecumenius,* 105]: καὶ ἐγένοντο βρονταὶ καὶ φωναὶ καὶ σάλπιγγες καὶ ἀστραπαί). Since the word order found in 4:5, 11:19, and 16:18 is not found in any textual witness for 8:5, it is almost certain that this could not have been the original reading (Schmid, *Studien* 2:228). Charles thinks that this was the original order here but that the interpolator botched the original order and placed them in the order found in reading (3); reading (1) is an attempt at correction (Charles 2:285). Readings (1) and (4) place ἀστραπαί in the third position, which is probably original, considering the weight of the textual evidence. Reading (1) is probably original (Schmid, *Studien* 2:228).

5.c. Variant: σεισμοί] 2351 Andr c g h 1773.

6.a. See *Note* 1.a.

6.b. Variant: omit οἱ before ἔχοντες] ℵ 052 Oecumenius^{2053} 2351.

6.c-c. Variants: (1) σαλπίσωσιν] ℵ A (lacuna in C) 025 046 fam 1006^{1006} fam 1611^{1854}. (2) σαλπίσουσιν] fam 1611^{2329} Andr/Byz 4a^{2084}. Reading (2) is a correction based on the phonetic similarity of ω and ου, coupled with the increasing use of the fut. ind. in ἵνα clauses.

6.d. Variants: (1) αὐτούς] *lectio originalis; TCGNT*^{1}, 740. (2) ἑαυτούς] ℵ^{1} 052 2351 Andreas Byzantine.

7.a. See *Note* 1.a.

7.b. Variant: ἄγγελος after πρῶτος] fam 1611^{2329} TR.

7.c-c. Here καί introduces a clause that describes the consequences of the action described in the preceding clause and is therefore an instance of καί *consecutivum.*

8.a. Variant: omit μέγα] Andr l^{-052}.

8.b-b. Variants: (1) πυρί] ℵ A 025 052 fam 1006^{1006} fam 1611$^{1611\ 1854\ 2344}$ Oecumenius^{2053} Andreas it^{ar,c,dem,div,gig,haf,z} vg syr^{h} cop$^{sa\ bo}$ arm Primasius *(ignis)* Tyc^{3} Beatus; Nestle-Aland^{27}; UBSGNT^{4}. (2) omit πυρί] 046 Andr c f^{2023} i^{2042} Byzantine syr^{h} Tyc^{1} Cassiodorus. Reading (1) is broadly supported by the major witnesses and was perhaps omitted because it appeared redundant next to καιόμενον (*TCGNT*^{1}, 740; *TCGNT*^{2}, 669). πύρ is missing with καιόμενος in 8:10, but καιόμενος [ἐν] πυρί occurs in 21:8 and elsewhere in Greco-Jewish literature (*Gk. 1 Enoch* 14:12; 21:3; *Vit. Proph.* 4.21B).

8.c-c. καί introduces a clause that describes the consequences of the action of the previous clause and is therefore an example of καί *consecutivum.*

9.a. The substantival ptcp. τὰ ἔχοντα, "those with" or "those having," is a solecism since it should modify τῶν κτισμάτων, "the creatures," but instead is a nom. in apposition to τῶν κτισμάτων (BDR § 136.1)

9.b. Variants: (1) διεφθάρησαν] A (lacuna in C) ℵ 046 Oecumenius^{2053} fam 1611$^{1611\ 1854\ 2329}$ Andreas. (2) διεφθάρη] Andr c d e^{2057} i^{2042} l n 94 598 1773 2019 2351 Byzantine TR. Variant (1) has the strongest external support and, because of the *constructio ad sensum,* is the *lectio difficilior* and therefore the original reading on internal grounds as well. Variant (2) is obviously a correction. The 3rd pl. aor. pass. verb διεφθάρησαν has the sing. substantive τὸ τρίτον as subject. The author understands this as a collective noun, however, which is congruent with a pl. verb form; this is therefore an instance of the *constructio ad sensum* found several times in Revelation (7:9; 9:18; 13:3–4; 18:4; 19:1, 6); see *Introduction,* Section 7, Syntax, XI. Agreement.

10.a. See *Note* 1.a.

10.b. Variant: ὥσπερ] fam 1611^{2329} Andr l; (it^{gig} vg: *tanquam*); Tyc^{2} (*velut).*

11.a. Variants: (1) ὁ before Ἄψινθος] A 025 Andr e^{2026} f$^{2031\ 2073}$ g i n^{-2429} 94 1773 Byzantine. (2) omit ὁ before Ἄψινθος] ℵ 052 Oecumenius^{2053} fam 1611$^{2329\ 2344}$ Andreas TR. Reading (2) is a correction; for similar corrections in the MS tradition, which omits the article from proper names in Revelation, see 6:8; 9:11; 12:9; 19:13, 16. These are all nouns whose transposition to the class of proper names is incomplete (Mussies, *Morphology,* 142). Yet, since they are unfamiliar to the readers, they should be anarthrous.

11.b. Variant spelling: Ἀψίνθιον] ℵ* fam 1611^{2344} Andr h i^{-2042} it^{h} vg^{cl} Tyconius Beatus.

11.c. Variant: insert μέρος before τῶν ὑδάτων] 2351. The meaning of the partitive gen. is made explicit by this scribal addition.

11.d. Variant: ὡς for εἰς] fam 1611^{2329} 2322 2351 Andr l$^{052\ 1678\ 1778\ 2080}$ Byz 1^{2256} it^{h} syr^{ph} Primasius. The two words have a similar appearance, and both make good sense, though εἰς is certainly original. The author says not that the water became *like* wormwood but that the water *became* wormwood.

11.e. The Gk. text reads καὶ ἐγένετο τὸ τρίτον τῶν ὑδάτων εἰς ἄψινθον, "and a third of the waters became *wormwood,*" yet the point is not that the waters became an herb (which is what wormwood is) but that they became *bitter* like the herb itself is. See Charles, 1:235–36. Variant spelling: ἀψίνθιον] ℵ* 052 fam 1611$^{1611\ 2329}$.

11.f. See *Note* 7.c-c.

11.g. Here ἐκ + the gen. functions as a marker of instrument implying the result (Louw-Nida, § 90.12).

11.h-h. The subject of the aor. pass. 3rd pl. verb ἐπικράνθησαν is unexpressed in the subordinate clause within which the verb occurs; the subject is the pl. noun "waters," which occurs in an oblique case in the preceding clause within a prep. phrase: ἐκ τῶν ὑδάτων. Third-person pl. verbs with an unexpressed subject occur 108 times in Revelation; see E. C. A. Dougherty, "The Syntax of the Apocalypse," Diss., The Catholic University of America, 1990, 39–47.

12.a. See *Note* 5:1.a.

12.b-b. Variant: (1) ἡ ἡμέρα μὴ φάνῃ τὸ τρίτον αὐτῆς] א A fam $1006^{1006\ 1841}$ fam $1611^{1611\ 1854\ 2329}$ Oecumenius^{2053} it^{gig} (*et dies non luceat terciam partem*); $\text{syr}^{ph\ h}$. (2) ἡ ἡμέρα μὴ φαίνῃ τὸ τρίτον αὐτῆς] Andreas. (3) τὸ τρίτον αὐτῆς μὴ φάνῃ ἡ ἡμέρα] 046 2351 Byzantine. (4) καὶ τὸ τρίτον αὐτῶν μὴ φάνῃ ἡμέρας καὶ ὁμοίως νύκτος] cop^{bo}; Charles, 1:237.

12.c. Variant: τέταρτον] A.

12.d. Variants: (1) φάνῃ] א A 052 fam $1006^{1006\ 1841}$ fam 1611^{1611} (φάνηι) ^{1854}; Oecumenius^{2053}. (2) φανεῖ] fam 1611^{2329}. (3) φαίνηται] Andr e^{2057}.

13.a. Variant: omit ἑνός] א. In the phrase ἑνὸς ἀετοῦ, "an eagle," ἑνός (masc. gen. sing. from εἷς, "one") functions as an indefinite article, a usage that occurs three times elsewhere in Revelation (9:13; 18:21; 19:17) and several times in the Gospels (Matt 8:19; 26:69; Mark 11:29), and also in early Jewish literature (*T. Abr.* [Rec. A] 4:9; 9:15); see Bauer-Aland, 466, 3b; BAGD, 231, 3b; Moulton, *Prolegomena,* 96–97). אחד *ʾeḥād* sometimes functions as an indefinite article in Heb. (see Dan 8:3). In spite of the arguments that this may be a Hebraism (Conybeare-Stock, *Septuagint,* 25–26; Black, *Aramaic,* 104ff.; BDR § 247; Turner, *Syntax,* 195–96), parallels in pagan Gk. papyri indicate that this is not the case (MM, 187; Horsley, *New Docs* 4:252, commenting on PKöln 2.109, lines 13, 18).

13.b. Variants: (1) ἀετοῦ] א A 046 fam 1006 fam 1611 $\text{Oecumenius}^{2053\ 2062}$ Andr f^{2073} i^{2042} l n 94 $\text{it}^{gig\ h}$ vg $\text{syr}^{h\ ph}$ $\text{cop}^{sa\ bo}$ eth Cassiodorus Beatus $\text{Tyc}^{1\ 2}$. (2) ἀγγέλου] 025 Andreas arm. (3) ἑνὸς ἀγγέλου ὡς ἀετοῦ] Byz 15^{42}; Primasius. Reading (2) is a substitution based on 14:6 (*TCGNT*[1], 741; *TCGNT*[2], 669), while the rare reading (3) is a combination of readings (1) and (2).

13.c. Variant: omit ἐν] א $\text{Oecumenius}^{2053txt}$.

13.d. Variant: omit οὐαί] fam 1611^{2329} Tyc^{1}.

13.e-e. Variants: (1) τοὺς κατοικοῦντας] א fam $1611^{1611\ 1854}$ Oecumenius^{2053} 2351 Andr i^{2042} Byzantine. (2) τοῖς κατοικοῦσιν] A (lacuna in C) fam $1006^{1006\ 1841}$ fam 1611^{2329} Andreas; WHort^{mg}; Charles, 1:237; 2:286. Because of the rarity of οὐαί + acc. (found elsewhere only in Rev 12:12; *Gk. Apoc. Ezra* 1:9, 24; 4:12), reading (2) arose as a correction, since οὐαί is frequently followed by the dat. of the person or thing concerned (Schmid, *Studien* 2:132, 204).

13.f-f. Here ἐκ + gen. is a marker of cause or reason (Louw-Nida, § 89.25).

9:2.a-a. Variants: (1) include καὶ ἤνοιξεν τὸ φρέαρ τῆς ἀβύσσου] A 025 fam 1006 fam 1611^{2329} syr^{h}. (2) omit καὶ ἤνοιξεν τὸ φρέαρ τῆς ἀβύσσου] א 046 fam $1611^{1611\ 1854}$ Oecumenius^{2053} Byzantine it^{a} vg^{mss} syr^{ph} $\text{cop}^{bo\ samss}$ arm^{1}.

2.b. Variant: καιομένης instead of μεγάλης] 2351 Andr f^{2023} i^{2042} n 94 Byzantine syr^{h}. The conflated reading μεγάλης καιομένης is found in Andr $\text{f}^{2073marg}$ 2019.

2.c-c. καί is used here to introduce the result of the previous clause.

2.d-d. Variants: (1) ἐσκοτώθη] A 0207 fam 1006 Andreas Byzantine. (2) ἐσκοτίσθη] א 2351 Andreas Byzantine; Bousset (1906) 298. The same choice between the aor. pass. forms of σκοτοῦν and σκοτίζειν occurs at 19:10, where the Attic form is certainly original. Though the choice here is more difficult (n.b. that σκοτισθῇ is found in 8:12), it appears that the Attic form in reading (1) was corrected to a more current Hellenistic form in reading (2); see Schmid, *Studien* 2:179–80. The verb is sing. because when a compound subject follows the verb, the latter normally agrees in number with the first subject (Smyth, *Greek Grammar,* § 966; BDF § 135; BDR § 135).

2.e. Variant: omit ἐκ] 0207.

2.f-3.a. Variant: omit τοῦ φρέατος καὶ ἐκ τοῦ καπνοῦ] א* $\text{Oecumenius}^{2053text}$ Byz 16^{69}.

3.a. See *Note* 9:2.f-3.a.

3.b. Variants: (1) αὐταῖς] *lectio originalis.* (2) αὐτοῖς] א 046 fam 1611^{2329}. Since αὐτοῖς (dat. masc. pl.) does not agree in gender with ἀκρίδες, which it modifies, αὐταῖς could be construed as a correction were it not so widely and strongly attested. αὐτοῖς probably originated as an attempt to construe the locust-demons as male warriors.

4.a. The καί that introduces this sentence functions syntactically as καί *adversativum* and so must be translated "but."

4.b-b. Variants: (1) ἐρρέθη] *lectio originalis.* (2) ἐρρήθη] 046 fam 1611^{1854} 1862 Andr $c^{2028\ 2029\ 2044\ 2054\ 2083}$ Byz 4^{141} Byz 7^{2024} Byz 17^{93} Andr/Byz 3^{1746} Andr/Byz 4a Andr/Byz 4b. The short ε in reading (1), which is certainly original, is a Hellenistic form (and the one regularly found in the LXX; see Thackeray, *Grammar,* 219) in contrast to reading (2), which is an Attic form. In this instance, copyists have replaced a Hellenistic form with an Attic one. Note that Andreas' comments in *Comm. in Apoc.* on 22:18 imply the scribal preference for Attic forms (Schmid, *Studien* 1/1:262).

4.c. Variants: (1) ἀδικήσουσιν (fut. ind.)] A 025 fam 1611^{2329} 2351. (2) ἀδικήσωσιν (aor. subjunctive)] ℵ 0207 Andreas Byzantine. ἀδικήσουσιν is a fut. ind. used in a ἵνα clause; ἵνα + fut. ind. occurs twelve times in Revelation (though there are often textual variants): 2:10; 3:9(2x); 6:4, 11; 8:3; 9:4, 5, 20; 13:12; 14:13; 22:14 (see *Note* 2:10.f.). This reading is supported by A fam 1611^{2329} 2351, though the confusion among ω = ου = ο (Gignac, *Grammar* 1:275–77, 211–14) has resulted in a variety of variants, including ἀδικήσοσιν (2256), ἀδικήσωυσι (1828), and ἀδικήσωσοι (680 2258). There is a tendency in the MS tradition to waver between present ind. (which should be considered the more difficult reading because it occurs just a few times in ἵνα clauses in the rest of the NT) and aor. subjunctive, although the latter occurs more frequently in Revelation (forty times in Nestle-Aland^{27}). It is worth noting that MS A, the best extant witness to the text of Revelation, uses the fut. ind. sixteen times in ἵνα clauses (2:22, 25; 3:9[2x]; 6:4, 11; 8:3; 9:4, 5, 20; 13:12; 14:13; 15:4; 17:17; 18:14; 22:14) and twice in ὅταν clauses (4:9, 10); see Mussies, *Morphology,* 322.

4.d-d. The two noun phrases οὐδὲ πᾶν χλωρόν, "nor any plant," and οὐδὲ πᾶν δένδρον, "nor any tree," both use οὐδὲ πᾶν in place of the more proper οὐδέν. On this idiom, which has parallels in popular Hellenistic Gk. as well as in Gk. translated from Heb., see Mussies, *Morphology,* 183, and see *Note* 7:1.j-j.

4.e. The word μόνους follows εἰ μὴ τοὺς ἀνθρώπους in the TR (Andr/Byz $3^{1957\ 2023}$) but is omitted in ℵ A 025 046.

4.f. Variant: (1) ἔχουσι] A Andreas Byzantine. (2) ἔχουσιν] ℵ 025. Though the moveable ν is used irregularly, there is a tendency to omit it when a consonant follows, a practice widely followed in the Andreas and Byzantine MS traditions. Moveable ν is only missing in seven places where it might have been included in A (see *Note* 7:10.b.).

4.g. τὴν σφραγῖδα τοῦ θεοῦ is articular because the first anarthrous mention of the σφραγίς in 7:2 is here referred to through the anaphoric use of the definite article.

4.h-h. Variants: (1) τῶν μετώπων] A ℵ 025 fam $1611^{1854\ 2050}$ $\text{Oecumenius}^{2053\text{comm}\ 2062}$ $\text{it}^{\text{a gig}}$; von Soden, *Text;* Nestle-Aland^{27}; UBSGNT^{4}. (2) τῶν μετώπων αὐτῶν] fam 1006 fam $1611^{1611\ 2329}$ $\text{Oecumenius}^{2053\text{txt}}$ Tyc^{1} Primasius Beatus. (3) τῶν μετώπων αὐτοῦ] 2351. (4) τοῦ μετώπου αὐτοῦ] 0207.

5.a. See *Note* 9:4.a.

5.b. For this translation of ἐδόθη (3rd sing. aor. pass.), see LSJ, 422–23, II.5; cf. LXX Mic 3:5.

5.c. Variants: (1) βασανισθήσονται] A ℵ 025 fam 1611^{2329} $\text{Oecumenius}^{2053\text{txt}}$ Andreas. (2) βασανισθῶσι] fam 1006 fam 1611^{1611} 2351 Andr d f^{2023} g i^{2074} 94 Byzantine. (3) βασανισθήσωνται] Andr a^{2186} b^{2081} e^{2057} f^{2056} h^{2302} l^{2080} n^{2429}.

6.a. See *Note* 8:1.a.

6.b. ἐκεῖνος differs from οὗτος in that the latter points to persons or things present in or contemporaneous with the communication situation (regardless of the distinction between the author and the addressee), while the ἐκεῖνος refers to things separated by some time or distance from the communication situation; here the phrase ἐν ταῖς ἡμέραις ἐκείναις, "in those days," refers to the future and should be understood as "in those [future] days" (Mussies, *Morphology,* 179–80). In Revelation, ἐκεῖνος occurs just twice (here and 11:13), or 2 times per 10,000 words, while it occurs 70 times in John, or 44 times per 10,000 words, while οὗτος occurs 51 times (in Nestle-Aland^{27}).

6.c. See *Note* 9:4.a.

6.d-d. Variants: (1) εὕρωσιν] A C 025 fam $1006^{1006\ 1841}$ fam $1611^{1854\ 2344}$ Oecumenius^{2053} Andreas; B. Weiss, *Johannes-Apokalypse,* 116; Bousset (1906) 299; Charles, 2:290. (2) εὑρήσωσιν] Andr a. (3) εὑρήσουσιν] ℵ 046 (εὑρίσουσιν); 0207 94 fam $1611^{1611\ 2329}$ (εὑρίσουσιν) 2019; Andr c d Byzantine; Tischendorf, *NT Graece;* WHort; von Soden, *Text;* Merk, *NT.* (4) εὑροῦσιν] 598. While οὐ μή + fut. ind. is the *lectio difficilior,* because of its rarity in the NT (it occurs in Revelation only in 3:5 and 18:14; see *Note* 3:5.b-b.), the external evidence strongly supports reading (1). The characteristic usage of Revelation suggests that reading (2) is the *lectio originalis* (Schmid, *Studien* 2:133), perhaps altered under the influence of the two fut. verbs that bracket this verb, ζητήσουσιν and ἐπιθυμήσουσιν (B. Weiss, *Johannes-Apokalypse,* 116); cf. the analogous alteration in 3:3 (Schmid, *Studien* 2:223). In favor of reading (2), however, is the tendency in the MS tradition to alter fut. inds. into aor. subjunctives (Mussies, *Morphology,* 322).

6.e. Variants: (1) οὐ μή] *lectio originalis.* (2) οὐχ] 2351.

6.f. See *Note* 9:4.a.

6.g-g. Variant: φεύξεται] fam 1611$^{1854\ 2329}$ 2351 Byzantine lat cop^{bo}. The original reading, φεύγει, is a futuristic present, as the preceding three fut. verbs make clear (Fanning, *Verbal Aspect,* 225), and for that reason was corrected to the fut. φεύξεται.

6.h. Variants: ἀπ' αὐτῶν ὁ θάνατος] 2351.

7.a. The καί with which this paragraph begins is not reflected in the translation since it functions here as a marker indicating the beginning of a new sentence or paragraph and lacks semantic content.

7.b. Variants: (1) ὅμοια] 0207 Oecumenius^{2053} Andreas Byzantine lat; WHort; Bousset (1906) 299; Merk, *NT;* Charles, 1:244; 2:290; von Soden, *Text;* Nestle-Aland^{27}; UBSGNT^{4}. (2) ὅμοιοι] ℵ 792 fam 1611^{2344} Andr e$^{2026\ 2057}$; Primasius (*similes*); it^{gig} (*similis*); Tyc^{3} (*similes*); Beatus (*similes*); it^{h}; Tischendorf, *NT Graece;* WHort^{mg}; B. Weiss, *Johannes-Apocalypse,* 181 (who suggests unconvincingly that ὅμοιοι matches the masc. gender of the pl. dat. pronoun αὐτοῖς in vv 3, 4, 5); Charles, 2:290^{margin}. (3) ὁμοίωμα] Andr i^{2047} 2351 Tyc^{1} (*similitudo*). (4) ὁμοιώματα] A (lacuna in C). Reading (1) is grammatically correct (neut. nom. pl.) and modifies the preceding τὰ ὁμοιώματα. It is not impossible that reading (2), the masc. nom. pl., certainly the *lectio difficilior,* may represent the primitive text that has been corrected by the MS tradition represented by reading (1), though it is more easily explained as an error by the scribe of ℵ (Schmid, *Studien* 2:75–76, 245–46). Reading (3) can be more easily explained as presupposing ὅμοια rather than ὅμοιοι.

7.c. Variant: ὁμοίωμα before ὡς] 2351.

7.d-d. Variants: (1) ὅμοιοι χρυσῷ] ℵ A 025 fam 1006^{1006} fam 1611$^{1611\ 2344}$ Oecumenius^{2053}. (2) χρυσοί] 0207 cop^{sa} Byzantine. (3) χρυσοί ὅμοιοι χρυσῷ] 2351. The phrase of which this variant is part, ὡς στέφανοι ὅμοιοι χρυσῷ, "like wreaths, like gold," is awkward because of the juxtaposition of the comparative particle ὡς and the comparative adj. ὅμοιος, introducing similes for the appearance of the heads of the locusts.

8.a. Variant: omit ὡς τρίχας] 2351.

9.a. The phrase ἁρμάτων ἵππων πολλῶν is a difficult expression, consisting of two juxtaposed nouns in the gen. pl. ἵππων may perhaps be construed as a gen. of association (usually with μετά), so that the expression means "many chariots with horses." Another possibility is that both pl. gens. are dependent on the preceding noun φωνή and should be translated "the sound of chariots, of many warhorses." In spite of the awkwardness of this expression, it has overwhelming MS support. Some copyists dealt with the problem by deleting the term ἁρμάτων (1 82 arm arab), while others deleted ἵππων (Andr f$^{2023–2056}$ 94). Bousset considered ἵππων an awkward gloss ([1906] 300), but very few copyists apparently shared that perception.

10.a. Variants: (1) ἔχουσιν] *lectio originalis.* (2) εἶχον] fam 1611^{2329} (ἦχαν); Andr d l; *habebant*] vg it^{gig} Tyc$^{1\ 2\ 3}$ Primasius Beatus eth arm. (3) ἔχοντες] cop.

10.b-b. Variants: (1) καὶ κέντρα, καὶ ἐν ταῖς οὐραῖς αὐτῶν ἡ ἐξουσία αὐτῶν ἀδικῆσαι] 𝔓^{47} ℵ A 025 fam 1006$^{1006\ 1841}$ fam 1611^{1611} Oecumenius^{2053}; WHort; von Soden, *Text;* Nestle-Aland^{27}; UBSGNT^{4}. (2) καὶ κέντρα ἐν ταῖς οὐραῖς αὐτῶν, καὶ ἡ ἐξουσία αὐτῶν ἀδικῆσαι] fam 1611^{1854} (καὶ αἱ ἐξουσίαι αὐτῶν ἀδικῆσαι); Andreas it^{a} vg^{cl} syr^{ph} (= καὶ κέντρα †δὲ ἐν, with the Syriac equivalent of δέ obelized; Gwynn, *Apocalypse,* 18). (3) καὶ κέντρα, καὶ ἐν ταῖς οὐραῖς αὐτῶν ἐξουσίαν ἔχουσιν τοῦ ἀδικῆσαι] fam 1611^{2329} (ἔχουσαι); Byzantine syr^{h} (-τοῦ). (4) καὶ κέντρα ἦν ἐν ταῖς οὐραῖς αὐτῶν ἡ ἐξουσία αὐτῶν ἀδικῆσαι] TR.

10.c. Variants: (1) ὁμοίας] 025 046 Oecumenius$^{2053\ 2062}$ fam 1006^{1841} fam 1611 Andreas Byzantine Compl. (2) ὁμοίοις] ℵ A (lacuna in C) 94 792 fam 1006^{1006} Andr f^{2031} Andr h^{2302} Andr/Byz 3^{35} Andr/Byz 4b^{1828} Byz 5^{808} Byz 15^{367} Byz 16^{69} Byz19$^{2075\ 2077}$ WHort^{marg}. (3) ὁμοίως] Andr e f$^{2073\ 2254}$ Byz 2^{2200} Byz 8^{180}. (4) ὅμοια] conjecture; WHort, 588, suggest that ὁμοίας is probably a primitive error for ὅμοια. Even though reading (2) is the *lectio difficilior,* this is probably an inferior reading. Schmid has proposed that it is a solecism resulting from mechanical assimilation of an original ὁμοίας to the dat. σκορπίοις (Schmid, *Studien* 2:75–76; see B. Weiss, *Johannes-Apokalypse,* 101). For contemporary examples of ὅμοιος with the dat., see Rev 13:11 and Rydbeck, *Fachprosa,* 78–79, 180 (BDF § 194.1 gives only *Iliad* 17.51). A related solecism is the phrase ὅμοιον υἱὸν ἀνθρώπου, "like a son of man," in 1:13; 14:14 (see *Notes* and *Comments* on both passages), though in this case υἱόν (an acc. that should be a dat.) has incorrectly been attracted to the case of ὅμοιον. Mussies speculates that since the Heb. and Aram. prefix -כְּ *kĕ-,* "as, like," is part of the following word, the author may have assumed that ὅμοιος and its complement should exhibit grammatical agreement (*Morphology,* 139); see 𝔓^{47} on Rev 13:11: ὁμοίῳ ἀρνίῳ.

10.d-d. Here καί *consecutivum* introduces a coordinate clause containing the result of the situation described in the main clause.

11.a. Variants: (1) καὶ ἔχουσιν] 025 fam 1611^{1854} 2351. (2) ἔχουσι δέ] fam 1611$^{1611\ 2329}$.

11.b-b. Variation in word order: βασιλέα ἐπ' αὐτῶν] 2351.

11.c. In the phrase ὄνομα αὐτῷ, ὄνομα is a parenthetical nom. (BDR § 144), while αὐτῷ is a dat. of possession, a construction also found in 6:8; see *Note* 6:8.f-f. Here 𝔓^{47} has ᾧ ὄνομα (with 94 and fam 1611^{2344}), while ℵ* reads ᾧ ὄνομα αὐτῷ, using a redundant resumptive pronoun that is a conflation of an original ὄνομα αὐτῷ with the altered form ᾧ ὄνομα. ὄνομα αὐτῷ is supported by the TR and nearly all other major and minor MSS.

11.d. The noun διαλέκτῳ is understood.

11.e. Variant: τόν before Ἀβαδδών] ℵ 0207.

11.f. Variant: βάττων] 𝔓^{47}, a singular reading, but similar to βάδδον in Oecumenius^{2053}.

11.g. The noun διαλέκτῳ is understood.

11.h-h. Variants: (1) ἔχει ὄνομα] 𝔓^{47} ℵ fam 1611^{2344} 2019 Andr/Byz 2b^{582}. (2) αὐτῷ ὄνομα] Andr e^{2026}. (3) ἔχων ὄνομα] 1773. Reading (2) is based on the same phrase that occurs earlier in v 11. On the idiom ὄνομα αὐτῷ, see *Note* 6:8.f-f.

12.a. The phrase ἡ οὐαὶ ἡ μία, lit. "the disaster the one," i.e., "the first disaster," has often been regarded as a Hebraism since the Heb. cardinal number אחד *ʾeḥād,* "one," could also be used as an ordinal meaning "first" (BDF § 247; Mussies, *Morphology,* 216). However, the Semitic influence on this expression is doubtful in view of the many parallels in ordinary Gk. usage (see *Note* 6:1.d.). Variants: (1) ἡ οὐαὶ ἡ μία] Andreas Byzantine and the other major MSS. (2) οὐαὶ ἡ μία] 𝔓^{47} ℵ^{1} Oecumenius^{2053text} Andr l Andr/Byz 4a^{-2022} Byz 1^{2256}. (3) οὐαὶ μία] ℵ* cop^{sa}. The omission of the article in variant (2) perhaps occurs because in the rest of the NT and in the LXX, οὐαί is *never* articular; in Revelation, however, it takes the fem. article both here in 9:12 and twice in 11:14 (where the article with the first οὐαί is also omitted by ℵ* and a number of minuscules; see *Note* 11:14.b-b.). See Rev 11:14, where the author uses Gk. ordinals: ἡ οὐαὶ ἡ δευτέρα, "the second disaster," and ἡ οὐαὶ ἡ τρίτη, "the third disaster."

12.b. οὐαί refers to a state of great hardship or distress and can here be translated "disaster" or "horror" (Louw-Nida, § 22.9).

12.c. The word δύο is used here with a multiplicative meaning, "twice" (Mussies, *Morphology,* 216–17, who cites as an example LXX Ps 61:12[MT 62:12], ἅπαξ [MT אחת *ʾaḥat*] ἐλάλησεν ὁ θεός, δύο [שתים *šĕtayim*] ταῦτα ἤκουσα, "Once God spoke, twice I heard these things"). Though this reflects Heb. influence (Mussies, *Morphology,* 217), there are examples from pagan Gk.: PRoss III.4, 9.

12.d-d. The verb ἔρχεται, "comes," is a sing., which appears to be incongruent with the subject, δύο οὐαί, "two woes" (Schmid, *Studien* 2:246). ἔρχεται has the support of A (lacuna in C) 𝔓^{47} ℵ Andreas Byzantine. B. Weiss (*Johannes-Apocalypse,* 181) suggested that the author perhaps considered οὐαί a neut. pl. noun that could take a 3rd pl. verb, but the author's use of the fem. gender in this same verse, ἡ οὐαὶ ἡ μία, invalidates that proposal. This difficulty was corrected by scribes who used the 3rd pl. form ἔρχονται (ℵ^{1} 046^{cor} 0207 Oecumenius^{2053} fam 1611$^{2329\ 2344}$ lat cop^{sa}). Since δύο is used here in a *multiplicative* sense (see *Note* 9:12.c.), οὐαί must be considered a sing. requiring a 3rd sing. verb.

12.e-13.b. Variants: (1) μετὰ ταῦτα. Καί] A 025 fam 1006^{1841} fam 1611^{1611} Oecumenius^{2053com} lat vg syr^{h} Cyprian Tyc$^{1\ 3}$ Beatus Andreas. (2) Μετὰ δὲ ταῦτα] 0207. (3) Μετὰ ταῦτα καί] fam 1006^{1006} fam 1611$^{1854\ 2329}$ 2351 Byzantine. (4) καὶ μετὰ ταῦτα] 046 Tyc^{2} (*et post haec*). (5) Καί (omit μετὰ ταῦτα)] Oecumenius^{2053txt} Primasius. Since the phrase μετὰ ταῦτα normally begins sentences in Revelation (two exceptions in addition to 9:12 are 1:19 and 4:1), there were various scribal attempts to link μετὰ ταῦτα to v 13, including the omission of the καί at the beginning of v 13 (see *Note* 9:13.a.); see *TCGNT*^{1}, 741.

13.a. Variant: (1) καί] A 025 Andreas it vg syr^{h}. (2) omit καί] 𝔓^{47} ℵ* fam 1611^{2344} Byz 13^{2058} Byz 14^{456} Byz 16$^{61\ 69}$ Byz 17^{469} Byz 19^{664} arab cop$^{sa\ bo}$ syr^{ph}. If the omission of καί were the *lectio originalis* (which is doubtful), this would mean that μετὰ ταῦτα would begin the sentence in v 13, rather than conclude the sentence in v 12. Aside from 9:12, μετὰ ταῦτα concludes sentences in Revelation only in 1:19 and 4:1. Variant (1) conforms to the way in which angels are introduced in 8:1, 8, 10, 12; 9:1 (*TCGNT*^{1}; 741, *TCGNT*^{2}, 669–70).

13.b. See *Note* 9:12.e-13.b.

13.c. The cardinal number εἷς is occasionally used in Revelation as a substitute for the adj. τις and functions like the indefinite article "a, an" in Eng., so that here φωνὴν μίαν means "a [certain] voice"; see Rev 8:13; 18:21; 19:17 (Mussies, *Morphology,* 183). See *Note* 8:13.a.

13.d-d. Variant: ℵ* omits the following phrase: μίαν ἐκ τῶν τεσσάρων κεράτων, "one of the four horns," but the phrase was inserted by a corrector, ℵ^{1}. Since ℵ averages twelve letters per line, it might appear that *two* lines have been omitted, since the omitted letters total twenty-four, and ΦΩΝΗΝ ends one line and ΤΟΥΘΥΣΙΑΣΤΗΡΙΟΥ constitutes the next line, though it must be admitted that the length of the lines or *stichoi* in the exemplar of ℵ is unknown. Nevertheless, it is likely that τεσσάρων stood in the exemplar of ℵ. Since a MS of Revelation like 𝔓^{47} contained twenty-five to thirty letters per line, it is possible that the omitted portion constituted a single line.

13.e. Variants: (1) omit τεσσάρων] 𝔓^{47} ℵ^{1} A (lacuna in C) 0207 fam 1611$^{1611\ 2344}$ Oecumenius^{2053} it^{ar,c,div,gig,haf,z} syr^{h} cop$^{sa\ bo}$ Andr i^{-2042} Andr l 94; WHort; Charles (2:293); Merk, *NT;* [Nestle-Aland^{27}]; [UBSGNT^{4}]. (2) τεσσάρων] 025 046 fam 1006^{1006} fam 1611^{1854} it^{dem} vg syr^{ph} Cyprian Primasius Andreas Arethas Byzantine; Tischendorf, *NT Graece;* von Soden, *Text;* NRSV. Though no obvious motivation can be discerned for *adding* τεσσάρων, the evidence that it was interpolated into the text is compelling (Schmid, *Studien* 2:76). Accidental omission of τεσσάρων is suggested by *TCGNT*^{1}, 742; *TCGNT*^{2}, 670.

13.f. The term κεράτων, lit. "horns," refers to the upward projections found at the corners of ancient altars (Exod 27:2; 29:12; Lev 4:7, 18, 25, 30, 34; Jer 17:1; Ezek 43:15, 20; Ps 118:27).

14.a. Variants: (1) λέγοντα] ℵ* A 149 fam 1611^{2344} it^{gig} Cyprian Tyconius Primasius Beatus. (2) λέγοντος] 046 fam 1006$^{1006\ 1841}$ fam 1611$^{1854\ 2329}$ 2351 Byzantine. (3) λέγουσαν] 𝔓^{47} 0207 fam 1611^{1611} Oecumenius^{2053} Andreas. (4) λέγουσα] Andr e f^{2031} 1773. λέγοντα, "announcing," is a masc. sing. acc. ptcp., which modifies φωνὴν μίαν, "a voice" (fem. sing. acc.), and so should have the form λέγουσαν, a correction found in reading (3). This is not the only place in Revelation where a fem. noun is modified by a masc. adj. or ptcp. (see 4:1; 11:4, 15; 17:3). Occasionally in Heb. the masc. gender is used to refer back to females or to fem. nouns in instances where no stress is placed on gender (Laughlin, *Solecisms,* 13–14; GKC § 144*a;* cf. 110*k*). For examples in the MT of masc. pronouns referring to females, see Exod 1:21; 2:17; Num 36:6; Judg 11:34; 21:12; 19:24; 1 Sam 6:7; 2 Sam 6:22; Ezek 23:49; Ruth 1:8; for examples of masc. pronouns referring to fem. nouns, see Exod 11:6; 22:25; Lev 6:8; 27:9; Num 3:27, 33; Deut 27:5; 1 Sam 10:18; Isa 34:17.

14.b. Variant: σάλπιγγαν] 𝔓^{47}. For slight variations in spelling, but all ending with -αν, see 42 792 2061.

14.c. Variant: omit τέσσαρας] 𝔓^{47} 2029 (also omits τούς before δεδεμένους). It is interesting that 𝔓^{47} also omits τεσσάρων from v 13.

14.d-d. Variant: ἐπὶ τοῦ ποταμοῦ τοῦ μεγάλου Εὐφράτου] 𝔓^{47} Andr l (the three minuscules in this group insert τῇ ψάμμῳ, "at the beach," after ἐπί).

15.a-a. The pf. substantival ptcp. οἱ ἡτοιμασμένοι emphasizes the resulting state of the verbal action (Fanning, *Verbal Aspect,* 416–18).

15.b-b. Variants: (1) εἰς τήν before ἡμέραν] 2351 Andr i^{2042} Byzantine. (2) τήν before ἡμέραν] Andr f^{2023} i l Compl. (3) omit καὶ ἡμέραν] ℵ Andr a^{-2428}.

15.c. Variant: ℵ inserts μή between ἵνα and ἀποκτείνωσιν, a singular reading, certainly the result of scribal error.

16.a. In the phrase τῶν στρατευμάτων τοῦ ἱππικοῦ, the first articular gen. is a gen. of measure or quantity, while τοῦ ἱππικοῦ is a gen. of apposition since it is identical with τῶν στρατευμάτων but is more specific.

16.b. Variants: (1) δισμυριάδες μυριάδων] A 025 (which reads δεὶς μυριάδες μυριάδων); fam 1611^{2344} 2351 Andreas Origen it^{gig} (*milies dena milia*); vg Cyprian (*dismyriades myriadon;* Vogels, *Untersuchungen,* 226). (2) δύο μυριάδων μυριάδας] ℵ. (3) δύο μυριάδες μυριάδων] 𝔓^{47} Andr i^{-2042} cop^{bo}. (4) μυριάδες μυριάδων] 046 Oecumenius^{2053txt} fam 1006$^{1006\ 1841}$ fam 1611$^{1611\ 2329}$ Andr a^{1} c d f^{2023} i^{2042} 1773 Byzantine cop^{samss}; Tyc^{1} Tyc^{2} Beatus (all *myriades miriadum*). (5) δισμυριάδας μυριάδων] Andr l n^{-2432}. (6) *octoginta milia*] Primasius. Reading (1) is the *lectio difficilior* because it is unusual and therefore probably the original reading. In reading (2) the acc. is probably dependent on the ἤκουσα of v 16b.

17.a. Variant: ἱππικούς] 2351.

17.b. The phrase τοὺς καθημένους ἐπ' αὐτῶν means "those sitting on them," i.e., "their riders." The author has a tendency to use an acc. following καθήμενος (nom.) or καθήμενον (acc.) sing. and pl., though here he uses a gen.; see Mussies, *Morphology,* 101. Variant: ἐπάνω] 𝔓^{47} ℵ.

17.c. ὑακινθίνους means being the color of the hyacinth, probably blue; see Louw-Nida, § 79.37.

18.a. Variants: (1) ἀπεκτάνθησαν] A C ℵ Andreas Byzantine. (2) ἀπεκτάνθη] 𝔓^{47} (but n.b. that 𝔓^{47} uses the 3rd pl. in the verb ἀποκτείνωσιν in v 15); 2019 2078 2436 Andr l 94 254 2019 Byz 13 Byz 15^{-42} Andr m$^{2037\ 2046}$. Variant (1) has overwhelmingly strong support and is an instance of the *constructio ad sensum,* corrected in variant (2). The subject of the 3rd pl. aor. pass. verb ἀπεκτάνθησαν is τὸ τρίτον τῶν ἀνθρώπων; τὸ τρίτον is construed by the author as a collective noun requiring a pl. verb form (see *Note* 8:9.b.). This is an example of the *constructio ad sensum* found several times in Revelation (7:9; 8:9; 13:3–4; 18:4; 19:1, 6).

18.b. ἀπό is supported by ℵ A C P 046 Andreas cop$^{sa\ bo}$ arm eth arab lat syr; ὑπό is supported by Andr a; Byzantine.

18.c. Variant: omit τούτων] 𝔓^{47}.
18.d. Variant: omit τριῶν before πληγῶν] 2351.
18.e. Variant: add καί before ἐκ] 2351.
18.f. Variant: ἐκ before τοῦ καπνοῦ] 𝔓^{47}.
18.g. Variant: ἐκ before τοῦ θείου] 𝔓^{47}.
18.h. Variant: omit αὐτῶν] 𝔓^{47}.
19.a. Variant: ἦν γὰρ ἡ] 𝔓^{47}.

19.b. The nom. pl. fem. ptcp. ἔχουσαι functions as a finite verb in this clause (Mussies, *Morphology*, 325); for further examples of ptcps. used as finite verbs in Revelation, see 1:16; 4:2, 4; 10:8; 14:1, 4; 21:14; ptcps. formed from ἔχω are frequently used in this way (1:16; 4:7, 8; 6:2, 5; 9:17, 19; 10:2; 12:2; 19:12; 21:12). Several Andreas MSS reflect a scribal correction of ἔχουσαι to the finite verb ἔχουσι (Andr a^{2428} d i^{2074} l^{1778}). The reading ἐχούσαις (which would modify ταῖς οὐραῖς, thus making a parenthesis of αἱ γὰρ ... ὄφεσιν) occurs in א* (in what appears to be a correction by the original scribe, who wrote ΕΧΟΥΣΑΣ and then inserted a small superlinear iota between the alpha and the sigma), 025 Oecumenius^{2053} 181 598 2019 (equal to A & C); 2059 2060 2065 2081 2286 2302 Andr a^{-2428} c e f$^{2023–2073}$ g i^{-2074} l^{-1778} 94 1773 (Schmid, *Studien* 1/1:103, brackets the final ς in ἐχούσαι[ς] in his Andreas text).

20.a. Variants: (1) omit αὐτῶν after πληγαῖς] (𝔓^{85}; though there are many lacunae in this MS, there is no room for αὐτῶν); Andr a b e f$^{2031–2056}$ h 598 1773 (πληγαῖς bracketed in Schmid's edition of Andreas) Byzantine. (2) αὐτῶν after πληγαῖς] 𝔓^{47} (πληγὲς αὐτῶν); א.

20.b. Variants: (1) οὐδέ] 𝔓^{47} א 046 Oecumenius^{2053txt} fam 1611^{2344} Andr l; Bousset (1906) 306; Tischendorf, *NT Graece;* Nestle-Aland^{27}; UBSGNT^{4}. (2) οὔτε] A fam 1611^{1611} Oecumenius^{2053com} Andreas; B. Weiss, *Johannes-Apokalypse,* 134; (Bousset [1906] 306); von Soden, *Text.* (3) οὐ instead of οὔτε] C fam 1006 fam 1611^{1854} 2351 Andr d e f$^{2023\ 2073}$ i 94 2019 Byzantine; WHort; Merk, *NT.* (3) καὶ οὐ] fam 1611^{2329}. Reading (1) probably preserves the *lectio originalis* (Schmid, *Studien* 2:225). Scribes may have changed οὐδέ to οὔτε to fit the οὔτε . . . οὔτε sequence later in v 20 (*TCGNT*^{1}, 742).

20.c-c. On μετανοεῖν ἐκ, see *Note* 2:21.c-c.

20.d. Variants: (1) προσκυνήσουσιν (fut. ind.)] 𝔓^{47} א A C Andr i^{2082} Andr/Byz 2a$^{104\ 459\ 922}$ Andr/Byz 4b^{1828} Byz 9$^{452\ 467\ 2021}$ 2019. (2) προσκυνήσωσι (aor. subjunctive)] 025 Oecumenius^{2053} 2351 Andreas Byzantine TR. For a discussion of ἵνα + fut. ind. in Revelation, see *Note* 2:10.f.

20.e-e. On the use of προσκυνεῖν + dat. or acc., see *Note* 4:10.b.

20.f-f. Variant: omit καὶ τὰ εἴδωλα] 𝔓^{47} cop^{sa} eth; this very weakly attested reading originated through accidental omission.

20.g. Variants: (1) χρύσεα] 2351^{com}. (2) χρυσαῖα] א 2351^{txt}.
20.h. Variant: ἀργύρεα] 2351.
20.i-i. Variant: omit καὶ τὰ χαλκᾶ] Byzantine vg^{mss} Tyconius.

20.j. Variant: omit τά before ξύλινα] 𝔓^{47} 𝔓^{85} ([κ]αι ξ[υλινα], restored by J. Schwartz, "Papyrus et tradition manuscrite," *ZPE* 4 [1969] 181); 2019 fam 1611$^{1854\ 2329}$ Byz 2^{2200}.

20.k. Variants: (1) δύνανται] 𝔓^{85} א A C 025 Oecumenius^{2053} fam 1006 fam 1611$^{1854\ 2050\ 2329}$ 2351 Andreas. (2) δύναται] 𝔓^{47} 598 fam 1611^{1611} Andr a Byzantine TR.

21.a-a. On μετανοεῖν ἐκ, see *Note* 2:21.c-c.

21.b. Variants: (1) φαρμάκων] 𝔓^{47} א C fam 1006 fam 1611$^{1611\ 1854}$ Andr i^{2042} Byzantine; WHort; von Soden, *Text;* Nestle-Aland^{27}; UBSGNT^{4}. (2) φαρμακειῶν] A 046 Oecumenius^{2053} fam 1611$^{2329\ 2344}$ 2351 (φαρμακιῶν); Andreas. The external support for reading (2) is strong, and copyists would have been more inclined to change φαρμάκων to the more specific φαρμακ(ε)ιῶν, rather than the reverse (*TCGNT*^{1}, 742; *TCGNT*^{2}, 670).

21.c-c. Variant: 𝔓^{85} (very fragmentary here) omits the end of v 21, probably including οὔτε ἐκ τῆς πορνείας αὐτῶν οὔτε ἐκ τῶν κλεμμάτων αὐτῶν, i.e., an error of omission through haplography.

21.d. Variants: (1) πορνείας] 𝔓^{47} C Andreas Byzantine. (2) πονηρίας] א* A Andr l. Even though reading (2) is the result of scribal error, the agreement of א* and A is striking (Schmid, *Studien* 2:101).

21.e-e. Variant: (1) omit οὔτε ἐκ τῶν κλεμμάτων αὐτῶν] 𝔓^{47} syr^{s} cop^{sa} Primasius. The similar phraseology of the last three clauses in v 21 (οὔτε ἐκ . . . αὐτῶν) is probably the result of accidental omission. Other accidental omissions in this verse include (2) οὔτε ἐκ τῶν φαρμάκων αὐτῶν] Andr c^{2033} Andr/Byz 4b22^{1828} Byz 3^{522} Byz 9$^{203\ 506}$ Byz 12$^{110\ 627\ 2048}$. (3) οὔτε ἐκ τῆς πορνείας αὐτῶν] Oecumenius^{2053} Andr g^{2071} Byz 18^{256}.

Form/Structure/Setting

I. Outline

C. The seventh seal and the first six trumpets (8:1–11:14)
  1. The seventh seal (8:1)
    a. Lamb opens seventh seal (v 1a)
    b. Result: silence in heaven for one-half hour (v 1b)
  2. Vision of the first six trumpets (8:2–9:21)
    a. Prologue: the third throne-room scene (8:2–6)
      (1) Commission of the seven angels (v 2)
        (a) Description: they stand before God (v 2a)
        (b) Investiture: they are given seven trumpets (v 2b)
      (2) Metaphor of the incense offering: the prayers of the saints for revenge are heard by God (vv 3–5)
        (a) An angel acts as priest (v 3)
          [1] Stands at the altar (v 3ab)
            [a] Has golden censer (v 3a)
            [b] Receives much incense (v 3b)
          [2] Offers incense with prayers of saints (v 3c)
            [a] On the golden altar
            [b] Before the throne
        (b) The offerings rise to God (v 4)
          [1] The smoke of the incense
          [2] The prayers of the saints
        (c) The prayers answered: the embers, symbolizing the trumpet plagues, are thrown down to the earth (v 5)
          [1] Angel fills censer with embers from the altar (v 5a)
          [2] Angel throws embers to the earth (v 5a)
          [3] Theophanic manifestations (v 5b)
            [a] Thunder
            [b] Rumbling
            [c] Lightning
            [d] Earthquake
      (3) The seven trumpet angels prepare to sound their trumpets (v 6)
    b. The first four trumpets (8:7–12)
      (1) The first trumpet plague (v 7)
        (a) The first angel sounds his trumpet (v 7a)
        (b) Plague: hail and fire mixed with blood are thrown down to the earth (v 7b)
        (c) Destructive effect (v 7c)
          [1] One-third of the earth burned
          [2] One-third of the trees burned
          [3] All the green grass burned
      (2) The second trumpet plague (vv 8–9)
        (a) The second angel sounds his trumpet (v 8a)
        (b) Plague: great burning mountainlike mass thrown into the

sea (v 8a)
(c) Destructive effects (vv 8b–9)
[1] One-third of the sea becomes blood (v 8b)
[2] One-third of the sea life dies (v 9)
[3] One-third of the ships destroyed (v 9)
(3) The third trumpet plague (vv 10–11)
(a) The third angel sounds his trumpet (v 10a)
(b) Plague: a great fiery star falls from heaven (vv 10a–11a)
[1] Falls on one-third of the rivers (v 10b)
[2] Falls on one-third of the springs (v 10b)
[3] Name of star: Wormwood (v 11a)
(c) Destructive effects (v 11bc)
[1] One-third of the waters become wormwood (v 11b)
[2] Many people die of the bitter water (v 11c)
(4) The fourth trumpet plague (v 12)
(a) The fourth angel sounds his trumpet (v 12a)
(b) Plague: the heavenly bodies are struck (v 12b)
[1] One-third of the sun
[2] One-third of the moon
[3] One-third of the stars
(c) Destructive effects (v 12c)
[1] One-third of their light darkened
[2] They do not appear one-third of the day
[3] They do not appear one-third of the night
c. The last three trumpets or the three woes (8:13–9:21; see 11:15–18 for seventh trumpet)
(1) Introduction to the last three trumpets as the three woes (8:13)
(a) Vision: an eagle flying in midheaven (v 13a)
(b) Audition: the eagle's announcement (v 13b)
[1] Pronouncement of triple woes for the people of the earth
[2] Cause of woes: the final three trumpet blasts
(2) The fifth trumpet, or first woe: demonic locusts (9:1–12)
(a) Introduction: the fifth angel sounds his trumpet (v 1a)
(b) Vision of the demonic locust army (vv 1a–11)
[1] Their emergence from the abyss (vv 1a–2)
[a] A star falls from heaven (v 1a)
[b] Star given key to abyss (v 1b)
[c] Star opens abyss (v 2a)
[d] The smoke arises from the abyss (v 2b)
{1} Like smoke from a great furnace
{2} Sun and air darkened
[2] Horde of demonic locusts released from the abyss (vv 3–11)
[a] Given scorpion-like authority on the earth (v 3b)
[b] Their instructions (v 4)
{1} Do not harm plant life (v 4a)
{2} Harm those lacking the seal of God (v 4b)

{3} Do not kill them, but torment them for five months (v 5ab)
{4} Parenthetical remark: their torment was like that of a scorpion (v 5c)
[c] The result of their torment (v 6)
{1} People will seek death but not find it (v 6a)
{2} People will desire death, but it will elude them (v 6b)
[d] Description of the demonic locusts (vv 7–10a)
{1} General appearance: like horses ready for battle (v 7a)
{2} Detailed description (vv 7b–10)
{a} Wearing gold crowns (v 7b)
{b} Human faces (v 7b)
{c} Long hair (v 8a)
{d} Teeth like lions (v 8b)
{e} Thoraxes like iron breastplates (v 9a)
{f} Wings sound like chariots in battle (v 9b)
{g} Tails with stingers like scorpions (v 10a)
[e] They have power to hurt people with their tails for five months (v 10b)
[f] Identity of their king (v 11)
{1} Angel of abyss (v 11a)
{2} Hebrew name: Abaddon (v 11a)
{3} Greek name: Apollyon (v 11b)
(c) Concluding enumeration of woes (v 12)
[1] First woe has passed
[2] Two more woes remain
(3) The sixth trumpet, or second woe: a demonic cavalry (9:13–21)
(a) Introduction: sixth angel sounds his trumpet (v 13a)
(b) Release of the four bound angels (13b–15)
[1] Heavenly command to release the four angels
[a] Source of command: voice from altar
[b] Addressee: sixth angel with trumpet
[c] Command: release four angels bound at the Euphrates
[2] The command executed (v 15)
[a] Four angels released (v 15a)
[b] Prepared for a specific time (v 15a)
[c] Prepared for a special task: kill one-third of humanity (15b)
(c) Onslaught of the demonic cavalry (vv 16–21)
[1] Number of cavalry: 200 million (v 16)
[2] Description of horses and riders (v 17)
[a] Colors of riders' breastplates (v 17a)
{1} Fiery red
{2} Blue like hyacinth
{3} Yellow like sulfur

[b] The horses' heads (v 17bc)
{1} Like lions' heads (v 17b)
{2} Plagues from their mouths (v 17c)
{a} Fire
{b} Smoke
{c} Sulfur
[3] Result: one-third of humanity killed (vv 18–19)
[a] Cause: the three plagues from the horses' mouths (v 18)
{1} Fire
{2} Smoke
{3} Sulfur
[b] Cause: authority of horses in their tails as well as their mouths (v 19)
{1} Tails have heads like serpents (v 19a)
{2} Tails inflict injury (v 19b)
[4] The response of the survivors of these three plagues (vv 20–21)
[a] They do not repent of worshiping demons-idols (v 20)
{1} Idols are manmade of natural material (v 20b)
{a} Gold
{b} Silver
{c} Bronze
{d} Stone
{e} Wood
{2} Idols are powerless (20c)
{a} Cannot see
{b} Cannot hear
{c} Cannot walk
[b] They do not repent of their wickedness (v 21)
{1} Murders
{2} Sorceries
{3} Fornication
{4} Thefts

II. LITERARY ANALYSIS

A. *The Structure of 8:2–9:21 and 11:15–18*

The series of seven trumpet plagues narrated in 8:7–9:21 and 11:15–18 is introduced with a scene in the heavenly temple in 8:2–6. This prelude (the fitting term *Vorspiel* is used by Rissi, *Babylon,* 15), like the prelude to the seven seals in 4:1–5:14 and the prelude to the seven bowls in 15:1–8, is set in the heavenly temple. It is framed by the mention of the seven trumpet angels in vv 2 and 6 and centers on two focal actions: the offering of incense to God, accompanied by the prayers of the saints, and the throwing of fiery embers down to the earth. If the coals of fire from the heavenly altar symbolize the series of judgments that are about to be inflicted on the people of the earth, then the prayers of the saints must be construed as prayers for divine vengeance upon those who have persecuted them, such as the prayer for vengeance uttered by the souls of the martyrs under the heavenly altar in 6:9–10.

The series of plagues introduced by the seven trumpets in Rev 8:7–9:21 and 11:15–19 begins with a series of four plagues, which are narrated only very briefly (similar to the rapid narrative of the results of the opening of the first four seals in 6:1–8): (1) Hail, fire, and blood fall, burning up one-third of the earth (v 7; resembles the seventh plague in Exod 9:22–26 and the fourth and seventh bowls in Rev 16:8–9, 19–21). (2) A great mountain is thrown into the sea, which becomes blood; one-third of sea creatures and ships are destroyed (vv 8–9; resembles the first plague of Exod 7:20–21 and the second bowl in Rev 16:3). (3) A star named Wormwood (Greek Ἄψινθος, *Apsinthos*; named for its effect, since no actual star had that name) falls on a third of the rivers and springs, poisoning them (vv 10–11; no model in Exod 7–12 or counterpart in Rev 15–16). (4) One-third of the sun, moon, and stars become darkened (v 12; similar to the ninth plague of Exod 10:21 and the fifth bowl plague in Rev 16:10).

The final three trumpets form a group of three woes announced in 8:13 by an eagle, who cries "Woe, woe, woe to those who dwell on the earth." The author subsequently inserts notices that the first and second woe have occurred (9:12; 11:14), but he does not explicitly mention when the third woe takes place (though it should certainly be identified with the woe of 12:12; cf. Vanni, *La struttura letteraria,* 131–32). This would then be the Satanic woe (11:14b–13:18; cf. Charles, 1:xxvii). Though the third woe may coincide with the sounding of the seventh trumpet (11:15–18), it is more likely that it encompasses all the plagues unleashed by the seven bowls (15:1–16:21). (5) The fifth trumpet causes a star to fall from heaven to earth (possibly Satan; cf. 12:9; probably an angelic messenger; cf. *Comment* on 9:1a); this star releases from the bottomless pit a plague of locusts who harm only those lacking God's seal (9:1–12; cf. the eighth plague of locusts in Exod 10:4–20; no counterpart in Rev 15–16). This locust plague, one of several terrible ordeals that people in the eastern Mediterranean could experience, is clearly modeled after Joel 2:1–14 (note the common motifs of the trumpet call, the comparison to an enormous army, the destruction of everything in their path). Since the angel of the abyss is their king (9:11), this must be an army of demons. (6) The sixth trumpet involves the release of the four angels bound at the Euphrates river (perhaps symbolizing four nations), who kill one-third of humankind (vv 13–19). This plague has no counterpart among the Exodus plagues. The effects are similar to the drying up of the Euphrates, the result of the sixth bowl plague, described in Rev 16:12. (7) The seventh trumpet is not narrated until 11:15–18.

The author concludes the lengthy section narrating the sixth trumpet plague in 9:13–19 with a description of the reaction of those people who were not killed by the demonic army: they did not repent of their idolatry and immorality (9:20–21). Does this mean that these punishments were intended to serve as a deterrent or to provoke repentance? Since John's narrative of the plagues connected with the trumpets and bowls does not have repentance as its purpose, references to the fact that people did not repent (9:20–21; 16:9, 11) have been regarded as indications that these two heptads were Jewish sources used by John though with a different purpose. Yet this proposal is unnecessary, since Exodus indicates that God judicially hardened Pharoah's heart, making repentance impossible (Exod 7:3–4a;

10:1). In the Exodus plague narrative, at the conclusion of each of the ten plagues, Pharaoh is depicted as reacting negatively, i.e., as hardening his heart (Exod 7:22–23; 8:15, 19, 32; 9:7, 12, 34–35; 10:20, 27; 14:6). Since eschatological tribulations and plagues in Jewish apocalypses are *never* intended to elicit the repentance of pagans, it is unlikely that they would have functioned that way in John's hypothetical source. The failure to repent is simply John's utilization of a recurring motif from Exod 7–14. The negative reaction of Pharaoh in the revision of the Exodus plague tradition is also found in Josephus (*Ant.* 2.295, 299, 304, 305, 309 [οὐ μετανόει], 320) though not with the formal regularity found in Exod 7–14.

The plagues unleashed by the seven trumpets consist of a group of four that have a homogeneous character and are described very succinctly (8:7–12). The last three trumpets also have a homogeneous framework in that they presumably consist of a series of three woes (8:13–9:21; 11:14–18). The first four seals also form a group that has a strikingly homogeneous formulation and structure and is also (like the first four trumpets) described only briefly (6:1–8). Only the seven bowls have a homogeneous character and do not exhibit the subgrouping of four + three.

The composition of the seven trumpet plagues appears to have been an expansion of the series of three woes (8:13–21; 11:14–18) created by prefixing the first four trumpets (8:7–12; cf. J. Weiss, *Offenbarung,* 75–76). The reason for this expansion was simply to achieve a heptad of trumpet plagues to complement the heptad of bowl plagues and the heptad of seals. There are several indications that an original series of three woes has been expanded to seven trumpet plagues: (1) Since one-third of humanity is killed after the blowing of the sixth trumpet (9:15, 18), the author suppresses the pattern of thirds in 8:11 and observes only that "many people died of the water." (2) The first four trumpet plagues are introduced like objective events, whereas the last three are introduced with vision formulas such as "I saw" (9:1) and "I heard" (9:13), though the last (11:15) is not so introduced.

Rev 9:7–11, which is appended to the section narrating the blowing of the fifth trumpet and its consequences (9:1–11), constitutes an unusually descriptive passage in which the author makes frequent use of the comparative particle ὡς, "as, like," and the comparative adjective ὅμοιος, "like, similar." This section is essentially an *ekphrasis* (description of a work of art). Since this passage could be omitted without interrupting the movement from 9:6 to 9:12, it is possible that this descriptive passage was added by the author when revising the entire work. The reason for the detailed description of demons in the form of locusts is to underline their evil origin. The author follows a particular pattern in this description: (1) overall appearance (like warhorses), (2) heads (wearing crowns), (3) faces (human), (4) hair (like women), (5) teeth (like lions), (6) scales (like iron breastplates), (7) sound of wings (like horses and chariots rushing to battle), and (8) tails (like scorpions). A similar description is found in *Apoc. Zeph.* 4:1–4 of ugly angels whose task it is to carry off the souls of the unrighteous and cast them into their eternal punishment (tr. Wintermute in Charlesworth, *OTP* 1:511):

> Then I walked with the angel of the Lord. I looked before me and I saw a place there. [Thousands] of thousands and myriads of myriads of an[gels] entered through [it]. Their faces were like a leopar[d], their tusks being outside their mouth [like] the wild boars. Their eyes were mixed with blood. Their hair was loose like the hair of women, and fiery scourges were in their hands.

This description is less detailed and focuses on: (1) faces (like leopards), (2) mouths (tusks outside), (3) eyes (mixed with blood), (4) hair (like women), and (5) hands (held scourges).

B. Trumpets as a Structuring Device

Rev 8:1–9:21 (with 11:14–18) constitutes a clearly defined textual unit that focuses on a series of seven tribulations unleashed upon the sounding of seven trumpets. The structure and content of this section are dependent on the framework provided by seven trumpets blown in succession by seven angels and on the sequence of seven plagues, which owes something to the Egyptian plague tradition in the OT and early Judaism. The use of the metaphor of the sounding of a trumpet for introducing a series of eschatological divine punishments has an inherent logic, if only because of the use of the trumpet in ancient warfare to deploy successive units of troops and cavalry in attacking the enemy forces at a variety of points. The only apocalyptic text that uses the blowing of trumpets as a structural device is *Apoc. Zeph.* 9–12 (first century B.C. to first century A.D.). The same "great angel" blows a golden trumpet to introduce three different scenes. Although the MS lacks the concluding four pages, which cannot be examined, it is not impossible that the same formal device was used to introduce subsequent scenes. The first scene is introduced with three blasts on a golden trumpet by a great angel proclaiming the triumph of Zephaniah over the accuser and his access to the place where famous righteous Israelites reside (*Apoc. Zeph.* 9:1–5). The second scene is introduced with a blast toward heaven of the golden trumpet, resulting in the opening of heaven and Zephaniah's vision of the place where souls were being punished; a daily trumpet call summons the righteous to intercede for those in torment (10:1–11:6). The third blast of the golden trumpet by the great angel is directed toward earth and then again toward heaven as a prelude to the destruction of earth and heaven and the judgment of all people before God (12:1–8). Despite the many differences between this text and that of the heptad of trumpets in Rev 8:1–11:19, the use of an angelic figure blowing a trumpet as a formal structuring device is significant.

C. Parallels between the Fifth and Sixth Trumpet Plagues

There are a number of similarities between the narratives associated with the fifth and sixth trumpets, which suggest that the two passages are doublets.

Rev 9:1–11 (Fifth Trumpet)	*Rev 9:13–19 (Sixth Trumpet)*
1. Nature of the plague (vv 1–6)	1. Nature of the plague (vv 13–16)
a. Abyss opened (v 2)	a. Four angels released (vv 14–15a)
b. Purpose of plague (vv 4–5)	b. Purpose of plague (vv 15b–16)
2. Description of locust army (vv 7–10)	2. Description of cavalry of 200 million (v 17)
a. Lethal nature of their tails (v 10)	a. Lethal nature of mouths and tails of horses (v 19)

D. Parallels between Seven Trumpets and Seven Bowls

Seven Trumpets of Rev 8:1–11:19	*Seven Bowls of Rev 15:1–16:21*
1. Hail and fire mixed with blood One-third of earth, trees, and grass burned up (8:7)	1. Foul and evil sores (16:2)
2. Burning mountain falls into the sea (8:8) One-third of sea becomes blood One-third of sea life dies One-third of ships destroyed (8:9)	2. Sea becomes blood (16:3) All sea animals die
3. Blazing star falls on one-third of rivers and fountains (8:10) One-third of waters poisoned and many people die (8:11)	3. Rivers and fountains become blood (16:4)
4. One-third of sun, moon, and stars darkened One-third of day and one-third of night kept from shining (8:12)	4. Sun allowed to scorch people People curse God and do not repent (16:8)
5. Star falls from heaven to earth; opens bottomless pit and locusts emerge (9:1–11)	5. Kingdom of beast in darkness People curse God and did not repent (16:10–11)
6. Four angels bound at Euphrates released; large cavalry kills one-third of humankind (9:13–19) Rest of humankind do not repent of evil (9:20–21)	6. Euphrates dries up, opening way for kings of east; kings of whole world assemble at Armageddon (16:12–16)
7. Kingdom of this world becomes the kingdom of Christ (11:15–18)	7. Earthquake splits Babylon in three parts; cities destroyed (16:17–21)

III. Tradition Criticism

A. *The Exodus Plague Tradition*

The narrative of the punishments unleashed with the blowing of each successive trumpet (8:1–9:21 and 11:15–18), similar to that of the pouring out of the seven bowls or cups of God's wrath (15:1–16:21), is an *eschatological* application of the ten plagues inflicted on Egypt by God (Exod 7–12). One of the major interpretive problems of Revelation has been the matter of determining whether the plagues unleashed by the seven bowls are recapitulations of the plagues unleashed by the seven trumpets. Another problem has been the relationship between the seven trumpets and seven bowls and the ten plagues of Exod 7:8–12:36, a problem complicated by the fact that two other OT versions of the Egyptian plagues are preserved in Pss 78:43–51 and 105:27–36, where *seven* rather than ten plagues are enumerated (see also Amos 4:6–11, in which seven plagues are mentioned, though apparently not directly related to the Egyptian plague tradition of Exodus; the passage from Amos will be considered below). There is also the further, though perhaps related, compositional problem of the intercalation of Rev 10:1–11:13 between the sixth and seventh trumpets, which may be structurally related to the parenthetical discussion of the Passover festival in Exod 12:1–28, inserted between the ninth and tenth plagues. Though the Egyptian plagues were a recurring theme in early Jewish literature, they are rarely interpreted *eschatologically*. An important major exception is found in *Apoc. Abr.* 30.14–16 (Charlesworth, *OTP* 1:704):

> Before the age of justice starts to grow, my judgment will come upon the heathen who have acted wickedly through the people of your seed who have been set apart for me. In those days I will bring upon all earthly creation ten plagues through evil and disease and the groaning of the bitterness of souls. Such will I bring upon the generations of those who are on it, out of anger and corruption of their creation with which they provoke me.

There are several features of this brief narrative that require some discussion. (1) Though there is no explicit mention of the plague narrative of Exodus, the fact that *ten* plagues are mentioned strongly suggests an allusion to the ten canonical plagues of Exod 7:8–12:36. (2) The ten plagues of the biblical tradition are considered a typological anticipation of the eschatological plagues, which God will unleash on the world and which constitute the eschatological judgment of God. (3) The ten eschatological plagues are primarily *punitive;* i.e., they appear to have no remedial function, and the possibility of repentance is not mentioned. (4) These ten eschatological plagues will be inflicted upon "all earthly creation"; i.e., they will affect the entire cosmos and its inhabitants. (5) This text contains all the necessary features of the seal plagues, the trumpet plagues, and the bowl plagues, which have been incorporated into Revelation.

In another Jewish text, the *Testament of Dan* (5:8), there is a prediction that the sons of Dan, together with the sons of Levi and Judah, because of their apostasy, will be led off to captivity and there experience "all the plagues of Egypt" (πάσας τὰς πληγὰς Αἰγύπτου). The purpose of these plagues, however, is remedial; i.e., they function to insure the eschatological restoration of both tribes (*T. Dan* 5:9). Further, the number seven can be used as a way of structuring history (*1 Enoch* 93:3–10, part of the Apocalypse of Weeks).

The notion of eschatological plagues in general as part of the period of great tribulation that precedes the end of the world, however, was a widespread notion in Jewish eschatological expectation. In *1 Enoch* 91:7–9 (tr. Knibb, *Enoch*), we read:

> And when iniquity and sin and blasphemy and wrong and all kinds of (evil) deeds increase, and (when) apostasy and wickedness and uncleanness increase, a great punishment will come from heaven upon all these, and the holy Lord will come in anger and in wrath to execute judgment on the earth. In those days wrongdoing will be cut off at its roots, and the roots of iniquity together with deceit will be destroyed from under heaven. And all the idols of the nations will be given up; (their) towers will be burnt in fire, and they will remove them from the whole earth; and they will be thrown down into the judgment of fire and will be destroyed in anger and in the severe judgment which (is) for ever.

Another list of eschatological plagues that have no explicit connection with the Exodus plague tradition, though there are a number of shared motifs, is found in *3 Apoc. Bar.* 16:3 (tr. Charlesworth, *OTP* 1:677; the archangel Michael is speaking): "Moreover, send forth caterpillars and locusts, rust and grasshoppers, hail with lightning and fury. Punish them with the sword and death, and their children with demons."

The preliminary character of the divine punishments unleashed by the blowing of the seven trumpets is indicated by the fact that only *one-third* of the specific parts of the world are affected (8:7–12). Two-thirds of the cosmos and its inhabitants thus survive for the final round of tribulations effected by the seven bowls. This pattern is not found in any other Jewish apocalypse and is the author's way of accommodating a doubling of the final punishments. The tribulations unleashed by the seven trumpets, in a synoptic table with the plagues of the seven bowls (Rev 15–16) and the ten plagues of Exodus (Exod 7–13), are as follows:

Seven Trumpets of Rev 8:1–11:19	*Seven Bowls of Rev 15:1–16:21*	*Ten Plagues of Exod 7:8–13:16*
1. Hail and fire mixed with blood	1. Foul and evil sores (16:2)	1. Nile turned to blood (דם *dām*) (7:17–21)
One-third of earth, trees, and grass burned up (8:7).		
2. Burning mountain falls into the sea (8:8)	2. Sea becomes blood (16:3)	2. Frogs (צפרדע *sĕpardēaʿ*) (8:1–7)
One-third of sea becomes blood	All sea animals die	
One-third of sea life dies One-third of ships destroyed (8:9)		

3. Blazing star falls on one-third of rivers and fountains (8:10) One-third of waters poisoned and many people die (8:11)	3. Rivers and fountains become blood (16:4)	3. Gnats (כנים *kinnim*) (8:16–19)
4. One-third of sun, moon, and stars darkened One-third of day and one-third of night kept from shining (8:12)	4. Sun allowed to scorch people People curse God and do not repent (16:8)	4. Flies (ערב *ʿārob*) (8:20–24)
5. Star falls from heaven to earth; opens bottomless pit and locusts emerge (9:1–11)	5. Kingdom of beast in darkness People curse God and do not repent (16:10–11)	5. Cattle disease (דבר *deber*) (9:1–7)
6. Four angels bound at Euphrates released; large cavalry kills one-third of humankind (9:13–19) Rest of humankind does not repent of evil (9:20–21)	6. Euphrates dries up, opening way for kings of east; kings of whole world assemble at Armageddon (16:12–16)	6. Sores and boils on people and animals (שחין *šĕḥîn*) (9:8–12)
7. Kingdom of this world becomes the kingdom of Christ (11:15–18)	7. Earthquake splits Babylon in three parts; cities destroyed (16:17–21)	7. Hail and thunderstorm (ברד *bārād*) (9:22–26)
		8. Locusts (ארבה *ʾarbeh*) (10:12–20)
		9. Darkness (חשך *ḥošek*) (10:21–29)
		10. Death of firstborn people and animals (מכה כל־בכור *makkēh kol-bĕkôr*) (12:29–32)

These comparisons are incomplete, however, since there is evidence in the OT for a widespread ancient tradition of *seven plagues* in addition to the narrative of ten plagues inflicted on the Egyptians according to Exod 7–13. In his 1965 book on the Exodus tradition, S. Loewenstamm argued persuasively that the seven-plague tradition is reflected in both Ps 78:43–52 and Ps 105:27–36 (*Exodus,* 32–34; cf. McCarter, "Exodus," 139). The Exodus account of ten plagues is a combination of the Yahwistic (J) account of *seven* plagues with the Priestly (P) account, which had *ten* plagues (Mihelic and Wright, *IDB* 3:822–24; McCarter, "Exodus," 139). The number *seven* is important, according to Loewenstamm, since it is the number of a *climactic series.* Scholars in general regard Ps 78:43–52 as a strand of tradition nearly identical with J(E), though antecedent to and independent of P (cf. C. A. Briggs, *A Critical and Exegetical Commentary on the Book of Exodus* [Edinburgh: T. & T. Clark, 1906] 2:181). B. Margulis, on the other hand, has argued that the narration in Exod 7–13 is the source of Ps 105 (the Exilic dating of Ps 105 by S. Holm-Nielsen, *ASTI* 11 [1978] 22–30, is based on supposed dependency on Pentateuchal traditions). He argues that in order to get a seven-plague tradition in Ps 105, Loewenstamm must combine the third and fourth traditional plagues, ערב *ʿārob,* "gnats," and כנים *kinnim,* "flies." Loewenstamm (*Bib* 52 [1971] 34–38), however, responds that the crucial issue is whether the Psalmist counted ערב and כנים as two plagues or one. Since all the plagues in Ps 105 are dealt with in two or more stichoi, a structural analysis of v 31 proves that the poet considered ערב and כנים to be one plague only (Loewenstamm, *Bib* 52 [1971] 35).

Another plague tradition, one not mentioned by Loewenstamm, is that found in Amos 4:6–11, which, like Ezekiel *Exagoge* 132–51, is presented as a first-person speech of God. The speech focuses on the prior judgments meted out to Israel by God and their failure to move the people to repentance. With each plague, God expected Israel to repent. H. W. Wolff (*Joel and Amos,* 213; cf. Andersen-Freedman, *Amos,* 440), though he does not enumerate the plagues of Amos 4:6–11 or suggest any relationship with the plague traditions of Pss 78 and 105, nevertheless provides seven unnumbered rubrics: (1) hunger (v 6), (2) drought (vv 7–8), (3) crop failure (v 9), (4) locusts (v 9), (5) pestilence (v 10), (6) sword (v 10), and (7) "overthrow" (v 11). Here it is relatively obvious that these seven plagues are arranged in a climactic order with "overthrow" as the most intense form of punishment. There is here, however, as Andersen and Freedman insist, "no canonical schedule of plagues, curses, destructions" (*Amos,* 440). While Wolff does refer to similarities between Amos 4:6–11 and Exodus 7–12, he finds significant verbal similarities with the announcements of reward and punishment at the end of the Holiness Code (Lev 26) and with the curses of Deut 28 and the royal intercessory prayer of Solomon in 1 Kgs 8:33–37. Included in Amos 4:6–11 is the classical triad of plagues: hunger, sword, pestilence (Jer 14:12; 21:7, 9; Ezek 6:11–12; 12:6).

Seven Plagues of Ps 78:43–52	*Seven Plagues of Ps 105:27–36*	*Seven Plagues of Amos 4:6–13*
1. Rivers turn to blood (v 44)	1. Darkness (v 28)	1. Famine
		Yet people do not return to God (v 6)

2. Flies (v 45a)	2. Waters become blood; fish die (v 29a)	2. Drought Yet people do not return to God (vv 7–8)
3. Frogs (v 45b)	3. Frogs (v 30)	3. Blight and mildew destroy crops (v 9a)
4. Caterpillars and locusts (v 46)	4. Flies and gnats (v 31)	4. Locusts devour trees Yet people do not return to God (v 9b)
5. Hail and frost destroy vegetation (v 47)	5. Hail and lightning destroy vines and trees (vv 32–33)	5. Pestilence (v 10a)
6. Hail and lightning destroy livestock (v 48)	6. Locusts destroy crops (vv 34–35)	6. Conquest in war Yet people do not return to God (v 10bc)
7. Death of firstborn (vv 49–51)	7. Destruction of firstborn (v 36)	7. Some overthrown as were Sodom and Gomorrah (v 11) Yet people do not repent (v 11)

The tradition of the Egyptian plagues also vacillates in early Jewish literature with regard to their number, order, and character. It is true, of course, that the plagues are not enumerated in Exodus, thus leaving open the possibility for a certain degree of imprecision and vagueness. The influence of Pentateuchal tradition in Exod 7–13 is traceable to a certain extent in these later narratives, but other traditions of various origins have also been incorporated. Josephus (*Ant.* 2.293–314), obviously dependent on the Pentateuchal account, leaves out the fifth plague, cattle disease.

(1) In the *Exagoge* of Ezekiel the Tragedian, the ten plagues of the Exodus are presented not as a narrative but by means of a prophetic speech attributed to God (132–51; for an extensive discussion of this text, cf. Jacobson, *Exagoge,* 112–21). However, certain features are at variance with the Pentateuchal account: (a) The plague of boils strikes *people* only in Ezekiel while in Exodus both people and animals are affected. (b) In Ezekiel the plague of boils is fourth (between gnats and

flies) rather than sixth (after pestilence) as in Exodus. (c) In Ezekiel darkness comes before locusts; in Exodus locusts come before darkness. (d) In Ezekiel the plague of pestilence kills people while in Exodus only animals are killed (cf. Ps 78:50). Jacobson points out that some rabbinic accounts reconcile these two traditions by having the pestilence indirectly affect people (*Exagoge,* 117; cf. *Midr. Exod.* 9:1–3; *Pesiq. R.* 197a)

(2) An extensive fragment of a work by Artapanus (Eusebius *Praep. evang.* 9.27.1–37; cf. Holladay, *FHJA* 1:209–25) retells the story of the plagues, which occur in the following order: (a) The Nile floods, with the result that the water becomes stagnant and both people and animals die of thirst (28–29). (b) Winged creatures torment the Egyptians producing incurable body sores (31), possibly a reference to flies, the fourth biblical plague, while the sores may refer to the sixth biblical plague. (c) Artapanus then combines into a single plague frogs, locusts, and fleas or lice (32), the second, eighth, and third plagues of Exodus. (d) Artapanus combines hail and earthquakes, both of which destroy people, into a single plague (33); hail is the seventh plague of Exodus; earthquakes are not mentioned in Exodus. The king of Egypt then releases the Jews (34). It appears, then, that Artapanus preserves a list of *seven* plagues: (a) flooding, (b) winged creatures who inflict sores, (c) frogs, (d) locusts, (e) fleas or lice, (f) hail, and (g) earthquakes. The ninth plague of Exodus, darkness, is conspicuous by its absence.

(3) In *Jub.* 48:5–8, the plagues inflicted on the Egyptians are enumerated as (a) blood, (b) frogs, (c) lice, (d) dog flies, (e) boils (the sixth plague of Exodus), (f) death of cattle (the fifth plague of Exodus), (g) hailstones that destroyed crops, (h) locusts that ate everything else, (i) darkness, and (j) the death of firstborn men and cattle. This list is faithful to the narrative in Exod 7–13 with the exception of the interchange of the fifth and sixth plagues.

(4) In *Bib. Ant.* 10:1 of Ps.-Philo, the canonical number of ten plagues is mentioned (Philo *Congr.* 118 also specifies *ten* plagues), though the list that follows contains only *nine,* perhaps an oversight: (a) blood, (b) frogs, (c) all manner of beasts, (d) hail, (e) death of cattle, (f) locusts, (g) gnats, (h) darkness, and (i) death of the firstborn. It is possible that by "all manner of beasts" the gnats and flies of the third and fourth plagues of Exodus are meant. In Exodus, hail is the seventh plague, following cattle disease (fifth) and boils (sixth); the latter is not mentioned here. Gnats are placed between locusts and darkness in Ps.-Philo, while in Exodus they are part of the third plague. *Bib. Ant.* 10:1 is also distinctive because it is in the form of a list rather than a narrative.

(5) The Egyptian plague tradition is also narrated in the Wisdom of Solomon in the framework of seven antitheses in which punishments meted out against the Egyptians are contrasted with blessings experienced by Israel (following D. Winston, *The Wisdom of Solomon* [Garden City: Doubleday, 1979] 224–325): (a) blood (11:1–14); (b) "a multitude of irrational creatures" (11:15) or "a multitude of animals" (16:1–4), i.e., possibly the frogs and/or gnats and/or flies and/or locusts of Exodus; (c) people slain by the bites of locusts and flies (16:9); (d) thunderstorms and fire (16:15–19); (e) darkness (17:1–20); (f) destruction of firstborn (18:5–25); and (g) the drowning of Egyptians in the sea (19:1–9). While the author does not follow the ten-plague schema of Exod 7–13 but uses a seven-plague schema, it is noteworthy that he exhibits no direct dependence on any of the earlier

seven-plague schemas found in Ps 78:43–52; Ps 105:27–36; Amos 4:6–13; and Artapanus. The author includes the drowning of the Egyptian army in his sevenfold schema and omits cattle disease (the fifth plague) and boils (the sixth plague).

(6) Philo's retelling of the Egyptian plagues is found in *Mos.* 1.90–146. Philo specifically mentions ten plagues (*Congr.* 118; *Mos.* 1.96), arguing that ten is the number of perfection; i.e., sin is brought to "perfection" (*Mos.* 1.96). Philo assigns the plagues to the basic elements of the cosmos—earth, fire, air, and water—though the schema is only very imperfectly superimposed on the rewritten narrative. Three plagues are assigned to the denser elements of earth and water, three are assigned to air and fire, the seventh plague is assigned to both air and fire, and the last three are reserved for God himself. The schema leads Philo to depart from the canonical order beginning with the fourth plague. The order of the plagues as presented by Philo is (with the particular element of the cosmos involved in italics): (a) In the plagues of *water,* the Nile and all lakes, springs, canals, wells, and fountains are turned to blood; fish and people die (98–101). (b) Frogs leave *water* for the land (103–5). (c) Gnats emerge from the *earth* (107–12). (The first three plagues are all in the canonical order.) (d) The *air* produces hail and lightning, which destroy trees and fruit; some animals are killed by hail and others by lightning (118–19). (This was the seventh plague in the canonical order [Exod 9:13–35].) (e) The *air* produces a scorching south wind (from a region where the intense heat of the sun burns up everything), which brings locusts, which destroy what was unharmed by the previous plague (120–22). (Locusts were the eighth plague in Exod 10:3–20.) (f) The *air* then produces darkness (123–25). (Darkness was the ninth plague in Exod 10:21–29.) (g) Moses scatters ashes into the *air,* which produces sores on both animals and people when the ashes fall to *earth* (126–29). (This was the sixth plague in Exod 9:8–12.) (h) Dogflies appear (130–32). (This was the fourth plague in Exod 8:20–32.) (i) A disease kills sheep, goats, and cattle (133). (This was the fifth plague in Exod 9:1–7.) (j) Death comes to the firstborn (134–39). According to Philo, the main reason that Moses performed wonders for Pharaoh was to convert him to belief in his word (*Mos.* 1.90). Further, Philo frequently mentions the negative reactions of Pharaoh and his courtiers.

(7) In *T. Ben.* 7:1–4, Cain was handed over by God for seven punishments, one plague (πληγή) for each century of his life, enumerated as: (a) envy (φθόνος), (b) destruction (ἀπώλεια), (c) oppression (θλῖψις), (d) captivity (αἰχμαλωσία), (e) poverty (ἔνδεια), (f) trouble (ταραχή), and (g) desolation (ἐρήμωσις). Cain's suffering began in his two hundredth year, and in his nine hundredth year he was destroyed in the flood (ἐρημοῦται ἐπὶ τοῦ κατακλυσμοῦ); since this verb corresponds with the seventh plague inflicted on Cain, his death must be seen as the climax in this series of seven punishments, just as the death of the firstborn climaxed the series of ten or seven plagues in the various Exodus plague traditions in the OT. Though there is no clear link to the plagues of Exod 7–12, the serialization of seven plagues climaxing with death makes this connection highly likely. A schema of seven punishments is explicitly mentioned in Lev 26:14–33; Sir 40:8–11; and *m. ʾAbot* 5:8 (Hollander-de Jonge, *Testaments,* 433).

(8) *M. ʾAbot* 5:8 specifically mentions *seven* kinds of retribution, which come upon the world for seven types of transgression: (a) famine from drought, (b) famine from tumult and drought, (c) all-consuming famine, (d) pestilence, (e)

sword, (f) noisome beasts, and (g) exile. This list is also arranged in terms of increasing severity but climaxes in exile rather than death, probably because exile is a punishment that affects an entire group of people.

(9) One of the few early Jewish compositions to enumerate a series of eschatological plagues is *Apoc. Abr.* 30:3–8 (tr. Rubinkiewicz in Charlesworth, *OTP* 1:704):

> And he said to me, "I will explain to you the things you desired in your heart, for you have sought to know the ten plagues which I prepared against the heathen, and I prepared them beforehand in the passing of the twelve hours on earth. Hear what I tell you, it will be thus. The first: sorrow from much need. The second: fiery conflagrations for the cities. The third: destruction by pestilence among the cattle. The fourth: famine of the world, of their generation. The fifth: among the rulers, destruction by earthquake and the sword. The sixth: increase of hail and snow. The seventh: wild beasts will be their grave. The eighth: pestilence and hunger will change their destruction. The ninth: execution by the sword and flight in distress. The tenth: thunder, voices, and destroying earthquakes.

These plagues are linked to the Exodus plague tradition only by their total number (*ten*) and by the thematic links between the third plague (cattle disease) and the fifth plague of Exodus 9:1–7 (cattle disease) and between the sixth plague (hail and snow) and the seventh plague of Exod 8:22–26 (hail and thunderstorms). In the eschatological scheme of the *Apocalypse of Abraham*, these plagues are followed by the sounding of the trumpet by God to summon his people and to begin the judgment of the wicked. The periodization of history into ten epochs is also reflected in *Sib. Or.* 4.47 and *1 Enoch* 91:1–19 (esp. 91:15).

The results of this extended discussion of the Egyptian plague tradition in the OT and early Judaism suggest that there was a strong tendency to reduce the ten-plague tradition of Exodus (itself the result of an expansion of an earlier seven-plague tradition) to a *seven*-plague schema. The following texts examined above appear to favor a seven-plague Exodus schema: (1) Ps 78:43–51; (2) Ps 105:27–36; (3) Amos 4:6–11; (4) Artapanus; (5) Wis 11:1–19:9; (6) *T. Benj.* 7:1–4; and (7) *m. ʾAbot* 5:8. While the last two schemas have no direct bearing on the Exodus plague tradition, they do exhibit the tendency to adopt seven as a number appropriate for a climactic series of punishments. Thus the tradition of a seven-plague divine scourge appears to have been well known in early Judaism.

B. Apocalyptic Lists of Cosmic Catastrophes

The list of cosmic catastrophes that will accompany the day of judgment is such a common phenomenon in Jewish and early Christian apocalyptic that it should be considered a literary form within the larger and more encompassing literary genres in which it is set. Within Judaism, such lists probably originated with theophany imagery, i.e., the atmospheric and seismic phenomena (e.g., earthquake, thunder, lightning, smoke, and darkness) associated with the revelation of God at Sinai. The phenomenon of darkness (Amos 8:9), for example, may have been elaborated as the darkening or destruction of the sun, moon, and stars (Joel 2:30–31; Isa 13:9–10; 34:4; Ezek 32:7–8). More general lists of cosmic catastrophes are also a commonplace (*Sib. Or.* 2.196–213; 3.81–92, 669–701; 4.171–78; 7.118–29; 8.225–

43, 336–58). Some of these lists are very similar to Roman prodigy lists (*Sib. Or.* 3.796–808; cf. Jos. *J.W.* 6.289–300).

A second early Jewish apocalypse that enumerates a series of eschatological plagues is *2 Apocalypse Baruch.* According to *2 Apoc. Bar.* 27:1–15, history will be divided into twelve periods (cf. 4 Ezra 14:11–12; *Apoc. Abr.* 29.2), and during each period a particular type of tribulation will afflict humanity before the appearance of the Messiah (*2 Apoc. Bar.* 30:1): (1) the beginning of commotions, (2) the slaughtering of the great, (3) the fall of many into death, (4) the drawing of the sword, (5) famine and drought, (6) earthquakes and terrors, [(7) missing,] (8) the appearance of ghosts and demons, (9) the fall of fire, (10) rape and violence, (11) injustice and unchastity, and (12) disorder and a mixture of all the preceding calamities.

Apocalyptic literature, in addition to transmitting lists detailing the destruction of the cosmos, also transmits lists of a quite different character, which focus not on the destruction of the cosmos but on the chaotic character of the cosmos (*1 Enoch* 80:2–8; *Sib. Or.* 2.6–26; 2.154–64; 5.447–83; 8.178–93; 4 Ezra 5:4–13). The individual catastrophes associated with the arrival of the eschatological day of judgment could easily be associated with the tradition of the plagues of Egypt as the author of Revelation has done.

Comment

1a καὶ ὅταν ἤνοιξεν τὴν σφραγῖδα τὴν ἑβδόμην, "When he opened the seventh seal." Bornkamm (*ZNW* 36 [1937] 133, 146) observes that since the scroll cannot be opened until all seven seals have been broken, 6:1–7:17 cannot be part of the contents of the scroll; rather it should be regarded as a short enigmatical outline of the contents of the scroll. The contents of the scroll can only be the remainder of Revelation, i.e., 8:2–22:5.

1b ἐγένετο σιγὴ ἐν τῷ οὐρανῷ ὡς ἡμιώριον, "there was silence in heaven for half an hour." In contrast to the eschatological events inaugurated by the opening of each of the first six seals, the silence following the opening of the seventh seal is anticlimactic and functions to retard the narrative action. The significance of this brief period of silence is problematic, and several explanations have been proposed: (1) Silence makes it possible for the prayers of the holy ones (8:3–5) to be heard before the throne (Charles, 1:223–24), a view Charles bolsters by referring to *b. Ḥag.* 12b, where the angels of the fifth heaven are said to sing during the day but be silent at night "because of the glory of Israel," i.e., so that the praises of Israel might be heard in heaven. This view is problematic, however, for nothing in Rev 8:1 suggests that noise would prevent God from hearing prayer. (2) Silence signals the eschatological return to primordial silence (4 Ezra 6:39; 7:30 ["the world shall be turned back to primeval silence for seven days, as it was at the first beginnings," i.e., a reversion to the chaos that preceded the first creation]; *2 Apoc. Bar.* 3:7; Ps.-Philo *Bib. Ant.* 60:2 ["there were darkness and silence before the world was"]; see Rissi, *Time,* 10–11). The weakness of this view lies in the fact that the text says nothing about a reversion to the silence that preceded creation. (3) Silence is sometimes a prelude to divine manifestations (Job 4:16; Zeph 1:7 ["Be silent before the Lord God for the day of the Lord is at hand"]; Zech 2:13; see Prigent, 130). (4)

Silence must be maintained in the presence of God, particularly during certain phases of the liturgy (Ps 62:1; Hab 2:20; according to *Ep. Arist.* 95, seven hundred priests in the temple in Jerusalem labor in complete silence [πᾶσα σιγή]; *T. Adam* 1.12 [fifth to sixth century A.D.]; see Mensching, *Das heilige Schweigen,* 80–89; Malina, *Revelation,* 136). In Greek tradition, silence was sometimes a ritual prelude to prayer (*Iliad* 9.171; Aristophanes *Thesmophoriazusai* 295–97; Thucydides 6.32.1; see Mensching, *Das heilige Schweigen,* 13–21). This view is the most convincing, for silence was very probably maintained during the incense offering in the Jerusalem temple cult (see *m. Tamid* 5:1–6; *T. Adam* 1.12), just as it is here during the heavenly incense offering narrated in vv 3–5. (5) The magnificence of God can be proclaimed not through speech but also, and perhaps even more profoundly, through silence (*Corpus Herm.* 1.31). Silence is an important motif in Ignatius, who says that it characterizes the bishop (*Eph.* 6:1; 15:1–2; *Phld.* 1:1), and silence appears to function as a metaphor for the role of bishop as a representative of God; i.e., God is silence, the bishop represents God, and therefore the silence of the bishop reflects divine silence (H. Chadwick, "The Silence of the Bishops in Ignatius," *HTR* 43 [1950] 169–72; but see Schoedel, *Ignatius,* 56–57, who disagrees with this view). According to one ancient view (*Corp. Herm.* 1.30; 10.5), the essence of God is σιγή or ἡσυχία, "silence" or "quietness," and he can only be approached in silence (Kroll, *Hermes,* 335–38). On Ignatius *Magn.* 8:2, which refers to Christ as the "Word which proceeded from silence," see Schoedel (*Ignatius,* 120–22), who understands this as a strategy of Ignatius in attempting to explain the inability of Jews and Judaizers to understand Scripture; the appearance of Christ is from silence in the sense that the previously hidden purpose of God is revealed. Plutarch refers to silence as something profound, mysterious (μυστηριώδης), and awesome (*De garrul.* 504a). Here he is probably alluding to the role of silence in initiations into the mysteries, for he then observes "in speaking we have men as teachers, but in keeping silent we have gods, and we receive from them this lesson of silence at initiations into the Mysteries" (*De garrul.* 505–6; LCL tr.); on silence in the mystery cults, see Hippolytus *Ref.* 5.8.39 and Grese, *Corp. Herm.,* 116–17.

There are few specialized studies on the ritual role and function of silence; see G. Mensching, *Das heilige Schweigen* (Giessen: Töpelmann, 1926); M. Picard, *The World of Silence* (Chicago: University of Chicago, 1952); E. McCumsey, "Silence," *EncRel* 13:321–24. For discussions of the phenomenon of silence in the ancient world, see R. Mortley, "The Theme of Silence in Clement of Alexandria," *JTS* 24 (1973) 197–202; O. Casel, *De philosophorum Graecorum silentio mystico* (Giessen: Töpelmann, 1919); L.-M. Dewailly, "Mystère et silence dans Rom. xvi.25," *NTS* 14 (1967) 111–18; id., "Den 'förtegade' hemligheten: Rom. 16.25," *SEÅ* 31 (1966) 114–21.

2a καὶ εἶδον τοὺς ἑπτὰ ἀγγέλους οἳ ἐνώπιον τοῦ θεοῦ ἑστήκασιν, "Then I saw the seven angels who stand before God." On καὶ εἶδον, see *Comment* on 5:1. The phrase ἱστάναι ἐνώπιον, literally "to stand before," can mean "to attend upon," "to be the servant of," so that the translation of v 2 could be "I saw the seven angels who serve God" (Charles, 1:225; R. Sollamo, "Some 'Improper Prepositions' such as ἐνώπιον, ἐνάντιον, ἐνάντι, etc. in the Septuagint and Early Koine Greek," *VT* 25 [1975] 778; K. G. C. Newport, "Semitic Influence on Revelation," *BT* 37 [1986] 332–33). Examples from the LXX include Judg 20:28; 1 Kgdms 16:22; 3 Kgdms

17:1; 18:18; 4 Kgdms 5:16; Jer 15:16; cf. Luke 1:19. However, to translate this verse as "the seven angels who serve God" is to say nothing more about them than about any other angel of God. These seven angels, however, are probably to be understood as the seven archangels who occupy a very particular role in the angelic hierarchy. The phrase ἱστάναι ἐνώπιον also occurs in 11:4 (see *Comment* there), where the translation "to be the servant of" is, however, appropriate. The phrase "who stand before God" has a close parallel in Luke 1:19, which refers to Gabriel, ὁ παρεστηκὼς ἐνώπιον τοῦ θεοῦ, "who stands before God."

Since the phrase τοὺς ἑπτὰ ἀγγέλους οἳ ἐνώπιον τοῦ θεοῦ ἑστήκασιν, "the seven angels who stand before God," is *articular,* this means either that they are being introduced here for the first time but are familiar to the readers, or that the anaphoric article refers back to the group of angels introduced anarthrously in 1:20 who are referred to individually thereafter with the definite article (2:1, 8, 12, 18; 3:1, 5, 7, 14). The first possibility is preferable because of the relative clause that defines their ordinary role in the heavenly court. Note that the definite article also occurs in Tob 12:15 (א) in the phrase εἷς τῶν ἑπτὰ ἀγγέλων, οἳ παρεστήκασιν καὶ εἰσπορεύονται ἐνώπιον τῆς δόξης κυρίου, "one of the seven angels who are present and go before the glory of the Lord," a reference to the seven archangels or the seven angels of the presence (Michl, *Engelvorstellung,* 184; Michel, "Engel II," *RAC* 5:77–78). It is possible that they are identical with the seven spirits of God referred to elsewhere in Revelation (1:4; 4:5; Michl, *Engelvorstellung,* 147–48, argues that they are not identical) and possibly identical with the "angels of the seven churches" (1:20); see *Comment* on 1:4d.

The tradition of the seven archangels appears for perhaps the first time in Tob 12:15, where Raphael identifies himself as "one of the seven angels who are present and go before the glory of the Lord." A group of four archangels is also occasionally mentioned (see *Comment* on 9:14; O. Böcher, "Engel IV," *TRE* 9:597; *EncJud* 2:958–59; Mach, *Engelglaubens,* 263–64 n. 425). Part of the Greek MS tradition of *1 Enoch* 20:1 (G^2 = Codex Panopolitanus) lists the following seven angels: Uriel, Raphael, Raguel, Michael, Sariel, Gabriel, Remeiel, though the Ethiopic MS tradition lists just six (Black, *Apocalypsis,* 32). In the Qumran document 4Q *Songs of the Sabbath Sacrifice,* the "seven chief princes [נשׂאי רושׁ *nĕśîʾê rôš* or ראשׁי נשׂיאים *rāʾšê nĕśîʾîm*]," referred to repeatedly (though they are never named), should be identified with the seven archangels (4Q*403* = 4QShirShabb[d] 1:23; 2:10–27; 4Q*404* = 4QShirShabb[e] frag. 1:1; frag. 2:4–5; 4Q*405* = 4QShirShabb[f] 3 ii 15; Newsom, *Songs,* 34). The tradition of seven archangels is referred to frequently in subsequent Jewish literature: *T. Levi* 8:2; *1 Enoch* 90:21; *3 Enoch* 17:1 (Pétrement, *Separate God,* 64–72). The phrase "angels of the presence," specifying no specific number, is used several times (*Jub.* 2:2, 18; 15:27; 1QSb 4:26; 1QH 6:13 [= 14:13]).

The emphasis on *standing* before God may be related to the Jewish tradition that angels had no knees and therefore were unable to sit (*y. Ber.* 2c; *Gen. Rab.* 65.21 [ed. Theodor-Albeck, 738]; see Gruenwald, *Apocalyptic,* 66–67). This tradition was apparently based on the phrase ורגליהם רגל ישׁרה *wĕraglêhem regel yĕšārâ,* "and their legs were straight," in Ezek 1:7. In Jewish tradition there was a widespread view that no one is permitted to sit in the presence of God (4Q*405* 20 ii 2 [see Newsom, *Songs,* 303–9]; *b. Ḥag.* 15a; *3 Enoch* 16).

The two phrases ἐνώπιον τοῦ θεοῦ, "before God" (3:2; 8:2, 4; 9:13; 11:16; 12:10;

15:4; 16:19), and ἐνώπιον τοῦ θρόνου, "before the throne" (1:4; 4:5, 6, 10; 7:11; 8:3; 14:3; 20:10), along with the two composite variant phrases ἐνώπιον τοῦ θρόνου τοῦ θεοῦ, "before the throne of God" (7:11), and ἐνώπιον τοῦ καθημένου ἐπὶ τοῦ θρόνου, "before the one sitting upon the throne" (4:10), constitute a major way of conceptualizing the divine presence. In the OT, the phrase "before God" was frequently used as an equivalent to "before the ark" (Lev 16:1–2; 1 Sam 10:25; 2 Sam 6:4–5, 14, 16, 17, 21; 1 Kgs 8:59; 2 Kgs 16:14).

2b καὶ ἐδόθησαν αὐτοῖς ἑπτὰ σάλπιγγες, "and seven trumpets were given to them." The sounding of the trumpet is occasionally part of the imagery used in early Christian apocalyptic to designate the point at which final events begin to unfold, particularly the Parousia (Matt 24:31; 1 Thess 4:16; 1 Cor 15:52; *Did.* 16:6; *Quaest. Esdr.* [Rec. B] 11, "until the coming of Christ when the trumpet of Gabriel sounds"; see the Gnostic appropriation of this metaphor in *Tri. Trac.* 138.8–12). According to *Ap. Jas.* 15.11–13, the ascension of Christ was accompanied by the sound of war, a trumpet blast, and a great uproar. This use of the trumpet in eschatological scenarios is usually assumed to have been derived from Judaism. The trumpet is used in Revelation as a metaphor for a loud voice (1:10; 4:1) and as a structuring device for the plagues unleashed upon the sounding of each of the seven trumpets in 8:2–9:21 and 11:15–18. In Revelation the trumpet is *never* used to signal the return of Christ as it is in other Christian texts. The seventh trumpet in 11:15–18 does, in some sense of course, mark the arrival of the end.

Series of trumpet blasts were used in various connections in the OT and early Jewish literature, however. Seven trumpets were used in the ritual that resulted in the destruction of Jericho (Josh 6), and in the Qumran War Scroll seven Levites carry seven rams' horns into the eschatological conflict (1QM 7:14). The trumpet (whether the שופר *šôpār,* "ram's horn," the יובל *yôbēl,* or the חצצרה *ḥăṣoṣrâ,* both "trumpet") was used in ancient Israel and in early Judaism for a number of purposes (see Str-B, 1:959–60; G. Friedrich, *TDNT* 7:71–88): (1) as a means of warning (Num 10:1–8; Ezek 33:3–6; Hos 8:1; Joel 2:1 [for the day of the Lord]); (2) to signal an attack by military forces (Num 31:6; Judg 7:8–22; 2 Chr 13:12; Zeph 1:16; 2 Macc 13:25; *Pss. Sol.* 8:1; *Sib. Or.* 8.253); (3) to give an alarm within a city to indicate an imminent attack (Jer 20:16; Hos 5:8; Amos 3:6; Zeph 1:16); (4) to signal a retreat (2 Sam 2:28; 18:16; 20:22; 2 Kgs 9:13); (5) as a cry to God for help (Num 10:9; 1 Macc 4:40); (6) to indicate that a victory has been won (Ps 47:5); (7) to signal the announcement of good news (*Pss. Sol.* 11:1); (8) as an accompaniment to religious ritual (Lev 25:9; Joel 2:15; 1 Macc 3:54; *m. Sukk.* 5:4; *m. Roš. Haš.* 3:3–4; *m. Tamid* 7:3); (9) as part of a theophany scene (Exod 19:13, 16, 19; 20:18; Aristobulus frag. 3 [10.13, 16–17; Denis, *Fragmenta,* 220]; Heb 12:19; Rev 1:10); and (10) in various eschatological contexts; the War Scroll exhibits an elaborate interest in describing various trumpets of the congregation, which have a variety of specific uses in the final eschatological war (1QM 2:16–3:11; 7:12–9:3; see P.R. Davies, *1QM,* 29–32, 63). The sound of the trumpet can therefore strike terror or joy or reverent expectation into the hearts of the hearers, depending on the context and their expectations.

The trumpet was absorbed into Jewish apocalyptic imagery, where it occasionally suggests eschatological salvation (Isa 27:13; Zech 9:14–15), though more commonly eschatological judgment (Isa 58:1; Joel 2:2–3; Zeph 1:14–16; 4 Ezra 6:23;

Sib. Or. 4.174–75; *Apoc. Mos.* 22:3; *Par. Jer.* 3:2; 4:1; *Apoc. Zeph.* 12:1; *Gk. Apoc. Ezra* 4:36). Michael is explicitly associated with the trumpet only rarely (*Apoc. Mos.* 22:1–3). The trumpet has an eschatological significance in the tenth of the Eighteen Benedictions in an ancient Palestinian version, which may allude to Isa 27:3 (tr. Petuchowsky, "Jewish Prayer Texts," 29):

> Sound the great horn for our freedom,
> and lift up a banner to gather in our exiles.
> You are praised, O Lord, who gathers in
> the outcasts of His people Israel.

Finally, it should be mentioned that comets could be referred to as having a trumpet shape (Ptolemy *Tetrabiblos* 2.90–91; see Malina, *Revelation,* 113).

3–5 This section appears to be inserted between vv 2 and 6 (n.b. that v 6 is little more than a repetition of v 2), since it has no obvious connections with the context in which it is presently found. Yet this brief episode does function as a kind of throne-room scene (more accurately a heavenly temple scene), which is artificially inserted into its present setting as is the scene in 15:2–4 that introduces the seven bowl plagues. When the angel is described as casting fiery coals on the earth, followed by thunder, voices, lightning, and an earthquake (v 5), he simply anticipates in a very general way the divine judgments that are unleashed upon the earth in 8:7–9:21 and 11:15–18.

3a καὶ ἄλλος ἄγγελος ἦλθεν καὶ ἐστάθη ἐπὶ τοῦ θυσιαστηρίου ἔχων λιβανωτὸν χρυσοῦν, "Another angel came and stood at the altar of incense with a golden censer." τὸ θυσιαστήριον, understood as the heavenly counterpart to the Israelite "altar of incense," is mentioned in Revelation four times (8:3[2x], 5; 9:13); the other five occurrences of θυσιαστήριον apparently refer to the altar of sacrifice of burnt offerings (6:9; 9:13; 11:1; 14:18; 16:7); see *Comment* on 6:9. Though the conception of a heavenly temple is an ancient one in Judaism, there is never any hint in the OT or in early Jewish literature that a counterpart to conventional sacrificial practice was carried out in the heavenly world. Rev 8:3–5 and 9:13 are the only passages in Jewish apocalyptic literature known to me in which either the incense offering or the golden altar of incense is mentioned. In the *Apoc. Paul* 44, however, which is clearly dependent on Revelation, the twenty-four elders, the four beasts, the altar, the veil, the throne, and the smoke of incense are mentioned in the throne vision. *T. Levi* 3:5–6 (reflecting a cosmology of seven heavens) describes the activities in the sixth heaven where "the angels of the presence of the Lord, who minister and make propitiation to the Lord for all the sins of ignorance of the righteous, . . . offer to the Lord a pleasant odor [ὀσμὴ εὐωδίας], a reasonable and bloodless offering [λογικὴν καὶ ἀναίμακτον προσφοράν]" (tr. Hollander-de Jonge, *Testaments,* 136). This is one of the few passages in which the incense offering is said to have an atoning function (the atoning function of the incense offering occurs in the OT only in Num 16:46–47; see also Sir 45:16; Wis 18:21; Zwickel, *Räucherkult,* 298). (On the phrase λογικὴ θυσία, "rational sacrifice," as a designation for a hymn of praise, see *Corp. Herm.* 1.31; 13.18–19.) In the heavenly mythology reflected in Rev 8:3–5, however, the seven angels of the presence do not officiate at the heavenly incense offering (as in *T. Levi* 3:5–6), but this task is assigned to a different angel. Since according to a common early Jewish cosmology, God is enthroned in the seventh heaven (symbolized by the *dĕbîr* or Most Holy Place), the sixth heaven (symbolized by the Holy Place) is where bloodless sacrifice is made, i.e., at the unmentioned "inner altar," the golden altar of incense.

λιβανωτός, here translated "censer," usually means "incense." It occurs in the LXX only in 1 Chr 9:29 (translating the Hebrew term לבונה *lĕbônâ*) and 3 Macc 5:3, where in both instances it means "incense." Greeks sometimes distinguished between λίβανος, the frankincense *tree,* and λιβανωτός, the *resin* from the tree, though in later Greek the words are used interchangeably.

The phrase "before the throne" is parallel to the phrase "before God" in v 4 (see Num 16:40, where incense is burned "before the Lord"), and "throne" is a circumlocution for the direct mention of God (see *Comment* on 4:10). Further, since the ark of the covenant was located in the *dĕbîr* or Holy of Holies separated by a curtain from the altar of incense, the term "throne" may also be a way of referring to the ark, since the ark originally appears to have functioned as a throne of Yahweh. In three passages in the Babylonian Talmud it is claimed that Michael ministers before the heavenly altar (*b. Menaḥ.* 110a; *b. Zebaḥ.* 62a; *b. Ḥag.* 12b; see Gruenwald, *Apocalyptic,* 65).

3b καὶ ἐδόθη αὐτῷ θυμιάματα πολλά, "and he was given a large quantity of incense." The use of the passive here (which may be the passive of divine activity, i.e., a circumlocution for the name of God) obscures the identification of the one who gives the angel the incense, though it is clear that the incense is placed in the λιβανωτὸς χρυσοῦς, the "golden censer." In *T. Levi* 8:10, as part of the priestly investiture of Levi by seven angels, the seventh angel "filled my [i.e., 'Levi's'] hands with incense [ἐπλήρωσεν τὰς χεῖράς μου θυμιάματος], that I might serve as priest for the Lord." It is interesting to note that many ancient censers are ladles shaped like a hand holding a shallow bowl (Nielsen, *Incense,* 5 [nos. 24–26], 38–40).

3c ἵνα δώσει ταῖς προσευχαῖς τῶν ἁγίων πάντων ἐπὶ τὸ θυσιαστήριον τὸ χρυσοῦν τὸ ἐνώπιον τοῦ θρόνου, "to offer (the incense) as a complement to the prayers of all God's people upon the golden incense altar before the throne." The dative phrase ταῖς προσευχαῖς, which occurs both here and in v 4, is problematic, and while the identical phrase occurs in 8:4, the two are not always construed similarly (see *Note* 8:4.a-a.). Bousset ([1906] 293) and Caird (107) consider it a dative of respect or reference, while Moule (*Idiom-Book,* 43–44) understands both phrases as examples of the temporal dative, which he translates "simultaneous with the prayers." The phrase ταῖς προσευχαῖς is sometimes considered a *dativus commodi,* or dative of advantage, in both vv 3 and 4; in v 3 the phrase ἵνα δώσει ταῖς προσευχαῖς could then be translated "to offer it in behalf of the prayers" (Mussies, *Morphology,* 99), or "as a complement to the prayers" (as I have rendered it above); then the incense functions as a supplement to the prayers to make them more acceptable or pleasing to God (Beckwith, 553; Charles, 1:230; Loisy, 172; Zahn, 2:383 n. 84; BDR § 188.1). If it is construed as a dative of association (as it is in the NRSV and REB), it can be translated "with the prayers," meaning that the smoke from the burning incense and the prayers of all God's people ascend to the throne together but have no intrinsic connection.

The prayers of the holy ones must be the prayers of Christians living on the earth (on "holy ones" = God's people or Christians, see *Comment* on 5:8). It is assumed that these prayers are prayers for divine vengeance on their opponents since the officiating angel mixes the prayers with incense on the heavenly altar and then throws fire down upon the earth with catastrophic effects (v 5). These prayers for vengeance are appeals to God from the living, analogous to the prayers for vengeance from the martyrs mentioned in 6:10 (Sattler, *ZNW* 20 [1921] 235).

As in v 4, the incense is not metaphorically understood as the prayers of Christians, but rather the incense and the smoke that result from its burning are understood to be closely associated with prayer (see *Comment* on 5:8, where incense is equated with prayer). The intimate connection between incense and prayer is reflected in Ps 141:2 (RSV):

> Let my prayer be counted as incense before thee,
> and the lifting up of my hands as an evening sacrifice.

The connection between prayer and incense is also found in *Par. Jer.* 9:1–4 (tr. R. A. Kraft and A.-E.Purintun, *Paraleipomena Jeremiou*, SBLTT 1 [Missoula, MT: SBL, 1972]):

> Now those who were with Jeremiah were rejoicing and offering sacrifices on behalf of the people for nine days. But on the tenth, Jeremiah alone offered sacrifice. And he prayed a prayer, saying: "Holy, holy, holy, fragrant aroma [τὸ θυμίαμα] of the living trees, true light that enlightens me until I ascend to you; for your mercy, I beg you—for the sweet voice of the two seraphim, I beg—for another fragrant aroma [εὐωδίας θυμιάματος]."

There is evidence to suggest that prayer was both appropriate and customary during the daily evening offerings (Ezra 9:5–15; Dan 9:21) when the regular incense offering occurred (Exod 30:8). In a Palestinian magical amulet in Jewish Aramaic, we find this prayer: "In your name, God of Israel, may the words rise up to heaven at the side of the throne of the great, powerful, aweful, sacred, magnified, praised and exalted God" (Naveh-Shaked, *Amulets*, amulet 7, lines 13–16); note the presence of no less than *seven* attributes of God. According to Plato (*Symp.* 202e), followed by Plutarch (*De Iside* 361c), it is *daimones*, a class of beings midway between gods and people, who convey the prayers and petitions of humans to the gods.

In ancient Israel there were three major ways in which incense was offered (Haran, *Temples*, 230–45): (1) Incense, or spice, could be burned with the grain offering (Lev 2:1, 15; 6:8, 14–15). There is no clear evidence that incense was sprinkled upon animal sacrifices (a characteristic feature of Greek sacrificial practice), yet the phrase, ריח־ניחח *rêaḥ-nî ḥoaḥ*, "pleasant odor," may indicate that spices were added to the burning victims, since burning flesh and fat produces unpleasant odors, and the addition of spices may have circumvented that eventuality. (2) The "outer" incense (simply designated קטרת *qĕṭōret*) was offered in a long-handled censer, מחתה *maḥtâ* (Lev 10:1; Num 16:6), or a מקטרת *miqṭeret*, "(upright) censer," and was not put on an altar. Evidence that this was a separate incense offering is found both in the Priestly writer and in Ezekiel (Lev 10:1–3; Ezek 8:10–11; 16:18; 23:41). This incense was usually burned within the temple precincts (Lev 10:1–2; Num 16:6–7), as the expression "burn incense before the Lord" (Num 16:40) suggests, though on rare occasions it would be burned outside (Num 17:11–12). The fire for this incense offering was gotten in the form of live coals from the brazen altar (Num 17:11; Lev 16:12), to which the incense was then added. (3) The "inner" incense (which was prepared in accordance with a special recipe, Exod 30:34–38) was offered on the golden incense altar twice each day, in the morning and evening in coordination with the *Tamid* offering, i.e., the "perpetual" daily offering of a lamb every morning and every afternoon (Exod 30:7–9; cf. Exod 29:38–42; Num 28:2–8), and is therefore called the קטרת תמיד *qĕṭōret tāmîd,* "regular incense offering." According to *m. Tamid* 5:1–6:3, coals from the great altar were spread out upon the inner altar, i.e., the golden altar of incense, and the incense then spread on top of them. In Luke 1:8–10, Zechariah is about to offer one of these twice-daily incense offerings when he receives an angelic revelation. This incense offering is made "before the Lord" because the golden altar of incense was positioned just in front of the curtain separating the Holy of Holies from the Holy Place. In surviving Aramaic letters, the Egyptian Jews at Elephantine refer several times to the meal offering, incense offering, and sacrifices (Cowley, *Aramaic Papyri,* no. 27, lines 14–15; no. 30, lines 21, 25; no. 33, line 11), but the use of this incense offering is left unspecified. In Rev 9:13–14, when John hears "a voice from the four horns of the golden altar before God," this can be explained because the throne of God in the heavenly temple would be located just behind the golden altar of incense; i.e., here God could well be the speaker. The reference to the "horns" of the altar conforms to the prescription found in the Priestly writer, Exod 30:1–8, and may be seen in the famous horned altar from Megiddo (drawing in Haran, *Temples,* 236, and a photograph in DeVries, *BARev* 13 [1987] 31); it is now virtually certain, however, that such altars were not actually *incense* altars. (4) In addition, there is the special incense offering made within the Holy of Holies on the Day of Atonement (Lev 16:11–14). This is described in *m. Yoma* 5:1: The high priest on the Day of Atonement took a ladle with two handfuls of incense and a fire pan (with coals from the altar) and entered through the curtain into the Holy of Holies; "when he reached the Ark he put the fire-pan between the two bars. He heaped up the incense on the coals and the whole place became filled with smoke" (tr. Danby, *Mishnah*).

Incense played a particularly important role in Greek religion (Burkert, *Greek Religion,* 62; M. Detienne, *The Gardens of Adonis: Spices in Greek Mythology* [Atlantic Highlands, NJ: Humanities, 1977] 37–58). In the Greek magical papyri, incense is often prescribed as part of the magical procedure (PGM III.665; IV.210, 1310, 1830, 2640, 2870, 2891; V.220, 395; VII.535, 925; VIII.55; XIII.1, 15, 25, 225; XIV.415). In the Jewish magical handbook *Sepher ha-Razim,* incense composed of myrrh and frankincense is placed on burning coals (tr. M. Morgan, *Sepher ha-Razim,* 24, 41, 51).

θυμιάματα, "incense," is a term used forty times in the LXX to translate the term קטרת *qĕṭōret,* which can mean (1) incense material, (2) incense offering, (3) the smoke or smell of any offering, or (4) sacrifice in general (Nielsen, *Incense,* 54).

4a καὶ ἀνέβη ὁ καπνὸς τῶν θυμιαμάτων ταῖς προσευχαῖς τῶν ἁγίων, "The smoke of the incense went up with the prayers of God's people." During the incense offering, coals from the altar are heaped in the fire pan and the incense is sprinkled on top of the coals (*m. Yoma* 5). Here again (cf. v 3) the smoke from the burning incense is not spiritualized or interpreted figuratively as the prayers of Christians (on "holy ones" = God's people or Christians, see *Comment* on 5:8), but rather the analogy between smoke and prayer is emphasized. This is unlike Rev 5:8 (see *Comment* on 5:8), where the incense is explicitly identified with the prayers of the holy ones. *3 Apoc. Bar.* 11:3 mentions Michael descending to receive the prayers of people, though precisely what he does with them is left unstated. Philo (*Quis Her.* 205), apparently using traditions about Michael as a model, says that the Logos, the archangel of the Father, "pleads with the immortal as suppliant for afflicted mortality." The scene in Rev 8:3–4 is similar in several ways to that in *Apoc. Adam* 33:4 (Charlesworth, *OTP* 2:289), "I myself saw golden censers [θυμιατήρια χρυσᾶ] and three bowls [τρεῖς φιάλας], and behold, all the angels with frankincense and the censers and the bowls came to the altar [θυσιαστήριον; the same term as in Rev 8:3] and breathed on them, and the fumes of the incense hid the sky." The location of this scene is on the earth, though the particular altar used is left unspecified.

4b ἐκ χειρὸς τοῦ ἀγγέλου ἐνώπιον τοῦ θεοῦ, "from the hand of the angel before God." The definite article before ἀγγέλου, "angel," here is anaphoric, referring to the ἄλλος ἄγγελος, "other angel," just mentioned in v 3a. There is every likelihood that this angel would be identified as Michael by readers acquainted with early Jewish angelology; see *Apoc. Paul* 43 (tr. Hennecke-Schneemelcher, *NTA* 2:787):

> And Michael answered and said: Listen when Michael speaks: It is I who stand in the presence of God every hour. As the Lord lives, in whose presence I stand, for one day or one night I do not cease from praying continually for the human race, and I pray for those who are (still) on earth.

While this apocryphal apocalypse is quite late, and is itself heavily influenced by Revelation, it nevertheless is part of the traditional conception of Michael as one of the angels of the presence, and as an intercessor; both of these features are present in vv 3–4.

5a καὶ εἴληφεν ὁ ἄγγελος τὸν λιβανωτὸν καὶ ἐγέμισεν αὐτὸν ἐκ τοῦ πυρὸς τοῦ θυσιαστηρίου καὶ ἔβαλεν εἰς τὴν γῆν, "The angel received the censer and filled it with some glowing embers from the altar of incense and threw them upon the earth." Rev 8:5 alludes to Ezek 10:2 (cf. Isa 6:6), where a voice commands a man (= angel) clothed in linen: "fill your hands with burning coals [πλῆσον τὰς δράκας σου ἀνθράκων πυρός] from between the cherubim, and scatter them over the city," i.e., in judgment (see Zimmerli, *Ezekiel* 1:250–51). There is a discussion of this passage in *b. Yoma* 77a (tr. I. Epstein):

> Were it not for the fact that the coals in the hand of the cherub became cold [in the process of coming] in to the hands of Gabriel, there would not have been left over from the "enemies of Israel" [i.e., Israel] one to remain or one to escape.

John, however, applies this imagery to the punishment of pagans rather than to the punishment of the disobedient people of God. While the incense offering is directed toward God, only the hot coals are directed toward the earth. This brief scene involving the casting of fire upon the earth is clearly a metaphor anticipating the judgments that attend the blowing of each of the seven trumpets. This divine punishment is implicity linked with the prayers of the saints offered with the incense to God in v 4, while the prayers themselves should be read in light of the prayer for revenge uttered by the souls under the altar in 6:9–10. See *Tg. Ezek.* 1:8 (Levey, *Tg. Ezekiel,* 20):

> Hands like the hands of a man were fashioned for them [the four living creatures] from beneath their wings on their four sides, with which to take out burning coals of fire from

> among the cherubim underneath the expanse which was over their heads, placing them into the hands of the seraphim to sprinkle on the place of the wicked, to destroy the sinners who transgress His word.

Fire that falls from heaven to earth is frequently a symbol of judgment (Gen 19:24; 2 Kgs 1:10, 12, 14; Job 1:6; Ps 11:6; 2 Thess 1:8). There is a reference to taking fire from the altar in Isa 6:6. On the term θυσιαστήριον, see *Comment* on 6:9.

The phrase ἐγέμισεν αὐτὸν ἐκ τοῦ πυρὸς τοῦ θυσιαστηρίου, literally "he filled it from the fire of the altar," presents some difficulty. The prepositional phrase can be construed in two ways: (1) as a genitive of content in which the preposition is redundant or (2) as a partitive genitive that functions as a dative. Though I prefer the second alternative, each possibility must be considered separately.

(1) ἐκ τοῦ πυρός *as a genitive of content.* If the ἐκ were omitted, the noun phrase in the genitive could be construed as a genitive of material or content, i.e. to fill something (τί, accusative) with something (τινός, genitive); see Mark 15:36; John 2:7; *Par. Jer.* 2:5, γεμίσωμεν αὐτὰς [sc. τὰς ποτίσατρας] δακρύων, "let us fill them [i.e., 'the watering troughs'] with tears." There are a few rare examples of the expression γεμίζειν τί ἐκ/ἀπὸ τινός: (a) Luke 15:16 (TR) reads καὶ ἐπεθύμει γεμίσαι τὴν κοιλίαν αὐτοῦ ἀπὸ τῶν κερατίων, "and he desired to fill his stomach with the carob pods" (for a full textual apparatus, see *The Gospel according to St. Luke* [Oxford: Clarendon, 1984–87] 2:43). (b) PEnteux 24, 14, γεμίσαι τὸ πλοῖον ἐκ τῶν τόπων, "to fill the boat [with goods] from the regions" (cited in Bauer-Aland, 307; BAGD, 153), is not an appropriate parallel since τῶν τόπων does not designate that with which the boat is filled. (c) 4 Macc 3:14 (cited by Bauer-Aland, 307; BAGD, 153) reads (MS A) καὶ ἀνευράμενοι τὴν πηγὴν θαρραλέως ἐξ αὐτῆς ἐγέμισαν τῷ βασιλεῖ τὸ ποτόν, "And when they found the spring, they boldly filled a drink from it for the king." The reading ἐγέμισαν is almost certainly incorrect (it should rather read ἐκόμισαν, "they brought"), for one cannot "fill" a ποτός, which is always a beverage, never a container.

(2) ἐκ τοῦ πυρός *as a partitive genitive functioning as a dative.* γεμίζειν is occasionally used with an accusative (of that which is filled) and a dative (of that which is used to fill), e.g., PGM IV.3191, γέμισον λύχνον ἐλαίῳ, "fill the lamp with oil." For other uses of the partitive genitive in Revelation as subject and object of a verb, see Rev 2:7, 10, 17; 5:7, 9; 11:9; 21:6; 22:19. In my view, an indefinite relative pronoun in the dative case, such as τινί, "some," should be supplied immediately before the prepositional phrase ἐκ τοῦ πυρός, resulting in the following translation: "The angel took the censer and filled it with some glowing embers from the incense altar." While rare, this use of the partitive genitive is not without parallel. One clear example is found in John 3:25, ἐγένετο οὖν ζήτησίς [τινι] ἐκ τῶν μαθητῶν Ἰωάννου μετὰ Ἰουδαίου περὶ καθαρισμοῦ, "Now a dispute arose between some of the disciples of John and the Jews concerning purification." Here, despite the demurrer of BDR § 164.2, ἐκ τῶν μαθητῶν functions as a dative (Nachmanson, *Partitives,* 27–28). Luke 15:16 (TR) can also be read as a partitive genitive functioning as a dative: καὶ ἐπεθύμει γεμίσαι τὴν κοιλίαν αὐτοῦ [τισι] ἀπὸ τῶν κερατίων ὧν ἤσθιον οἱ χοῖροι, "And he desired to fill his stomach [with some] of the carob pods which the swine ate."

Further, the term πῦρ cannot simply be understood as "fire" since something combustible must be added to a censer; therefore πῦρ should be translated "hot coals" or "glowing embers." This meaning is found in LXX Lev 10:1, where Nadab and Abihu ἐπέθηκαν ἐπ᾽ αὐτὸ [i.e, τὸ πυρεῖον] πῦρ, "they placed fire [i.e., 'coals'] in it [i.e., 'their censer(s)']." The resultant translation is "he filled it with some fiery coals from the altar."

5b καὶ ἐγένοντο βρονταὶ καὶ φωναὶ καὶ ἀστραπαὶ καὶ σεισμός, "and there were thunder and rumbling and lightning and an earthquake." In this series of atmospheric phenomena (cf. similar series in 4:5; 11:19; 16:18; see *Comment* on 4:5), βρονταί, "thunder," comes before ἀστραπαί, "lightning," though this order occurs in none of the other parallel passages in Revelation. The Phoenician cosmology of Philo of Byblos (Eusebius *Praep. evang.* 1.10.4) states that βρονταί τε ἀπετελέσθησαν καὶ ἀστραπαί, "thunder and lightning were produced." In American English it is more natural to refer to "thunder and lightning" than to "lightning and thunder," though flashes of lightning often precede the sound of thunder. The hearing of voices (φωναί) with no obvious origin is frequently regarded as a prodigy in Roman religion (Dionysius Halicarnassus *Ant. Rom.* 10.2.3; Krauss, *Interpretation,* 161–64).

In three of the four references to atmospheric disturbances, an *earthquake* is mentioned; here is a synopsis of those passages:

Rev 8:5b: καὶ ἐγένοντο βρονταὶ καὶ φωναὶ καὶ ἀστραπαὶ καὶ σεισμός
"and there were thunder and rumbling and lightning *and an earthquake.*"

Rev 11:19c: καὶ ἐγένοντο ἀστραπαὶ καὶ φωναὶ καὶ βρονταὶ καὶ σεισμὸς καὶ χάλαζα μεγάλη
"and there were lightning and rumbling and thunder *and an earthquake* and great hail."

Rev 16:18–21: καὶ ἐγένοντο ἀστραπαὶ καὶ φωναὶ καὶ βρονταὶ καὶ σεισμὸς ἐγένετο μέγας . . . καὶ χάλαζα μεγάλη
"Then there were lightning and rumbling and thunder and *there was a great earthquake* . . . and great hail."

The comparison of these passages requires some comment: (1) Each passage has a narrative function different from the others: (a) 8:5b anticipates the divine judgments that follow the sounding of the seven trumpets (Bauckham, "Earthquake," 203). (b) 11:19c is analogous to 4:5 (where lightning, rumblings, and thunder come from the throne of God) in that the atmospheric and seismic disturbances proceed from the heavenly ark as part of a manifestation of the power of God. Further, this theophanic manifestation functions as a conclusion to 11:15–18 but primarily as an introduction to 12:1–17. (c) In 16:18–21, the storm phenomena, but particularly the earthquake and the hail, constitute the destructive punishment of the seventh bowl.

(2) An earthquake associated with the Sinai theophany (Exod 19:18) is frequently referred to in allusions to the Sinai tradition (Ps 68:8; Isa 64:3) and is often part of the physical manifestations that accompany theophanies in subsequent tradition. Exod 19:16–18 mentions five natural phenomena that are associated with theophanies: thunder, lightning, a thick cloud, a loud trumpet blast, and an

earthquake. These five phenomena are essentially repeated in several subsequent revisions and expansions of Exodus in early Judaism, including *Tg. Onq.* Exod 19:16, *Tg. Ps.-Jon.* Exod 19:16, and Ps.-Philo *Bib. Ant.* 11:4. However, this list is enormously expanded, primarily through the use of seismic disturbances in *Bib. Ant.* 11:5 (tr. Charlesworth, *OTP* 2:318):

> And behold the mountains burned with fire, and the earth quaked, and the hills were disturbed, and the mountains were rolled about, and the abysses boiled, and every habitable place was shaken, and the heavens were folded up, and the clouds drew up water, and flames of fire burned, and thunderings and lightnings were many, and winds and storms roared, the stars gathered together. . . .

(3) Earthquakes can be assigned several different kinds of religious significance (see *TDNT* 7:196–200; *EDNT* 3:236–37): (a) An earthquake can either *anticipate* divine judgment (8:5) or be an *instrument* of divine judgment (Rev 16:18–21; 2 Sam 22:8; Isa 24:18–20; Hag 2:6–7, 21; Heb 12:26). In *Exod. Rab.* 29.9, the sages express the view that the occurrence of an earthquake when God punishes the wicked matches the function of the earthquake at Sinai. (b) An earthquake, in concert with other atmospheric phenomena, can symbolize the presence or imminent arrival of God or of an agent of God (Judg 5:4; Pss 68:8; 114:6–7; 1 Kgs 19:11; Matt 28:2). (c) An earthquake can function like a prodigy and accompany an event of particular significance (Matt 27:51; Vergil *Georgics* 1.475) or be a sign of impending events (Mark 13:8 = Matt 24:7 = Luke 21:11).

(4) Though Bauckham proposes that the earthquake language in particular is a conscious allusion to the Sinai theophany, it appears that such language has become so conventional that no direct allusion to the Sinai tradition should automatically be assumed. An earthquake is also linked to the Exodus tradition (Pss 77:18; 114:4–7). A similar list of four atmospheric and seismic disturbances, including the earthquake, for example, is found in LXX Esth 1:1de, where they are part of a dream in which violence against the Jews is anticipated:

> And this was his dream: Behold, there were sounds and tumult, thunderings and an earthquake [φωναὶ καὶ θόρυβος, βρονταὶ καὶ σεισμός], confusion on earth. And behold two great dragons [δράκοντες] came forth, both ready for battle, and their cry was great.

Further, the earthquake as a theophanic manifestation is also part of Greek tradition. In Callimachus *Hymn to Apollo* 1–8 (ca. 305–240 B.C.), several signs outside Apollo's temple reveal the imminent epiphany of the god: the quivering laurel, the shaking of the temple, a palm tree nodding, a swan singing, and the temple doors opening by themselves (for other occurrences of the theophanic earthquake, see *Homeric Hymn* 3.403; Apollonius Rhodius *Argonautica* 2.679–80; *PGM* I.305; III.255).

6 καὶ οἱ ἑπτὰ ἄγγελοι οἱ ἔχοντες τὰς ἑπτὰ σάλπιγγας ἡτοίμασαν αὐτοὺς ἵνα σαλπίσωσιν, "The seven angels with the seven trumpets got ready to sound them." This verse appears to be a redactional addition that functions as a repetitive resumption (this passage repeats v 2), added after vv 3–5 were inserted into the narrative.

7a καὶ ὁ πρῶτος ἐσάλπισεν, "The first angel sounded his trumpet." The mysterious sounding of a trumpet was sometimes considered a prodigy, i.e., a sign warning people of divine anger (Caesar *Civ.* 3.105; Lucan 1.578; Cassius Dio 47.40.2; Plutarch *Sulla* 7.3; *Sib. Or.* 8.239; Lactantius *Div. Inst.* 7.16; see *Excursus 6A: Ancient Prodigies and the Plagues of Revelation*). Plutarch mentions that the Etruscan diviners considered the prodigy of the sounding of a trumpet to be the harbinger of a new age, one of eight ages in all (*Sulla* 7.3–4). The sounding of the trumpet is called a σημεῖον in *Did.* 16:6 and *Sib. Or.* 4.124 and a *signum* in Commodian *Instr.* 43.1. The sounding of the trumpet is also found in some of the later OT prophets and in early Judaism as a signal for the arrival of the day of the Lord (Zech 9:14; Zeph 1:14–16; *Apoc. Abr.* 31:1; 4 Ezra 6:23; *Sib. Or.* 4.124; *Gk. Apoc. Ezra* 4:36). It was taken over into early Christian eschatology as a way of announcing the return of Christ (1 Thess 4:16; Matt 24:31; 1 Cor 15:52; *Did.* 16:6; Clement of Alex. *Quis dives salv.* 3; *Questions of Ezra* [Rec. B] 11; Commodian *Instr.* 43.1; *Apost. Const.* 7.32.3).

7b καὶ ἐγένετο χάλαζα καὶ πῦρ μιμιγμένα ἐν αἵματι καὶ ἐβλήθη εἰς τὴν γῆν, "and there was hail and fire mixed with blood, and it was thrown down to the earth." The phenomenon of blood raining from the sky (the recurring technical phrase is *sanguinem pluit*) occurs frequently in Roman prodigy lists (Cicero *De div.* 1.43.98; 2.27.58; Pliny *Hist. nat.* 2.57.147; Luterbacher, *Prodigienglaube,* 14; Wülker, *Prodigienswesens,* 11; see *Excursus 6A*). A parallel occurs in *Sib. Or.* 5.377–80 (tr. Collins in Charlesworth, *OTP* 1:402), "For fire will rain on men from the floors of heaven, fire and blood, water, lightning bolt, darkness, heavenly night." According to *Mek. de-Rabbi Ishmael, Beshallah* 7 (Lauterbach, *Ishmael* 1:245), after the Israelites had passed through the sea on dry ground, the ministering angels hurled arrows, great hailstones, fire, and brimstone down on the pursuing Egyptians.

7c καὶ τὸ τρίτον τῆς γῆς κατεκάη καὶ τὸ τρίτον τῶν δένδρων κατεκάη καὶ πᾶς χόρτος χλωρὸς κατεκάη, "with the result that a third part of the earth was burned up, and a third part of the trees were burned up, and all the green grass was burned up." The eschatological destructions of one-third of various aspects of the cosmos (a consistent theme throughout 8:2–9:21: 8:7[2x], 9[3x], 10, 11, 12[5x]; 9:15, 18) is loosely based on Ezek 5:2(3x), 12(3x), where three different fates befall each third of the population of Jerusalem, represented by what Ezekiel does to each third of the hairs of his head and beard. The motif of one-third destruction also appears later in *b. B. Meṣ.* 59b, where an anecdote is told of R. Eliezer, whose declarations had been rejected by his peers and cursed. In order to keep R. Eliezer from destroying the world with a curse, R. Akiba personally informed him. R. Eliezer then tore his garments, took off his shoes, and sat on the ground, whereupon only one-third of the olives, wheat, and barley of the world were blighted.

8a καὶ ὁ δεύτερος ἄγγελος ἐσάλπισεν καὶ ὡς ὄρος μέγα πυρὶ καιόμενον ἐβλήθη εἰς τὴν θάλασσαν, "The second angel sounded his trumpet, and something like a great mountain burning with fire was cast into the sea." In 8:10 it is said that a huge star burning like a torch fell on the rivers and springs. This is virtually a doublet of 8:8b. This sounds like extraordinary volcanic activity such as the tragic eruption of Vesuvius on 24 August A.D. 79, which radically affected the Bay of Naples from Capri to Cumae. Debris from Vesuvius fell into the bay making it impossible to land boats (Pliny *Ep.* 6.16.11), though no streams of lava were emitted from the crater. Zahn has argued that the details of the vision in 8:7–12 reflect aspects of the eruption of Vesuvius (2:390–94; id., "Der Ausbruch des Vesuvs," 151–69; cf. Kehnscherper, *Sonne,* 26–29; Metzger, *Code,* 64). While there are several brief notices of the eruption (Tacitus *Annals* 4.67; Jos. *Ant.* 20.144; Suetonius *Titus* 8.3–4), an eyewitness account of the eruption is provided by Pliny the Younger (*Ep.* 6.16, 20), and an epitomized account is preserved in Dio 66.21–23. Dio, including a stereotypical theme from Roman prodigy lore, claims that the sound of trumpets was heard before the disaster (66.23.1). The eruption of Vesuvius is described in *Sib. Or.* 4.130–34 (written ca. A.D. 80) in the context of divine judgment (tr. J. J. Collins in Charlesworth, *OTP* 1:387):

> But when a firebrand, turned away from a cleft in the earth
> in the land of Italy, reaches to broad heaven,
> it will burn many cities and destroy men.
> Much smoking ashes will fill the great sky,
> and showers will fall from heaven like red earth.

Seven stars like great burning mountains are mentioned in *1 Enoch* 18:13; 21:3, and it would make sense to speak of stars like burning mountains cast into the sea though that motif is not found in *1 Enoch*. *Sib. Or.* 5.158–59 speaks of a star from heaven that burns the sea and Babylon.

8b καὶ ἐγένετο τὸ τρίτον τῆς θαλάσσης αἷμα, "with the result that a third part of the sea became blood." As part of the extensive prodigy list linked to Caesar's crossing of the Rubicon (1.522–83), Lucan reports that "Black Charybdis churned up waves of blood from the bottom of the sea" (1.547–48). In an oracle against the Gauls in *Sib. Or.* 5.201, the prediction is made that "the ocean will be resounding, filled with much blood [πληρούμενος αἵματι πολλῷ]," though here the reference is probably to the blood that will flow from the slaughtered Gauls.

9 καὶ ἀπέθανεν τὸ τρίτον τῶν κτισμάτων τῶν ἐν τῇ θαλάσσῃ τὰ ἔχοντα ψυχὰς καὶ τὸ τρίτον τῶν πλοίων διεφθάρησαν, "and a third part of the living creatures in the sea died and a third part of the boats were destroyed." Speaking of the eruption of Vesuvius (see *Comment* on 8:8a), Dio (66.23.2; LCL tr.) claims that "it wrought much injury of various kinds, as chance befell, to men and farms and cattle, and in particular it destroyed all fish and birds." Pliny the Younger, an eyewitness of the eruption of Vesuvius, observed that the sea level went down and many sea creatures were left stranded on the dry sand (*Ep.* 6.20.9). It has been estimated that from 12,000 to 15,000 people lost their lives.

10a καὶ ὁ τρίτος ἄγγελος ἐσάλπισεν· καὶ ἔπεσεν ἐκ τοῦ οὐρανοῦ ἀστὴρ μέγας καιόμενος ὡς λαμπάς, "The third angel sounded his trumpet, and a huge star fell from heaven burning like a torch." This appears to be a doublet of 8:8. On falling stars, see *Comment* on 6:13. In the ancient world, comets were considered prodigies that signaled the imminence of death and disaster (Manilius *Astron.* 1.892–926). Pliny describes one type of comet as "torches" (*Hist. nat.* 2.22.90; 2.25.96). On the motif of the star falling from heaven to earth, i.e., a meteor or a comet, see *Comment* on 9:1. According to Artemidorus (*Oneirocritica* 2.36; 5.23), a falling star means the death of a person, and that certainly happens in Rev 8:10–11. Boll proposed that the poisonous influence of the star Apsinth or Wormwood on the rivers and fountains of the earth was through the Hellenistic conception of ἀπόρροια, "emanations," from stars, which gave off πνεύματα, "emissions, emanations," which came to earth (*Offenbarung*, 41–42). A closer parallel is found in *Sib. Or.* 5.155–61 (see Collins, *Sibylline Oracles*, 89–92), which predicts that a star will shine that will destroy the entire earth. Apparently the same "great star will come from heaven [ἥξει δ' οὐρανόθεν ἀστὴρ μέγας] to the wondrous sea and will burn the deep sea and Babylon itself and the land of Italy" (*Sib. Or.* 5.158–59; tr. Charlesworth, *OTP* 1:397). Here the sea and Babylon (= Rome) are negative symbols, and their destruction implies the deliverance of the just. There are two major differences between these passages (Collins, *Sibylline Oracles*, 90): (1) In Rev 8:10–11, the star *poisons* the waters, while the star in *Sib. Or.* 5.158–59 *destroys* the waters. (2) In Rev 8:10–11 the star is a physical element instrumental in causing a plague on earth, while in *Sib. Or.* 5.158–59 the star is a savior figure.

10b καὶ ἔπεσεν ἐπὶ τὸ τρίτον τῶν ποταμῶν καὶ ἐπὶ τὰς πηγὰς τῶν ὑδάτων, "and fell on a third part of the rivers and on the springs of water." Since a single star cannot fall on a third of the rivers and springs, this description cannot be construed literally; rather it means that the burning star *affected* a third part of the rivers and springs.

11a καὶ τὸ ὄνομα τοῦ ἀστέρος λέγεται ὁ Ἄψινθος, "Now the name of the star is Apsinth." There is no evidence that any star was called by this name in antiquity; rather, the star is given an *ad hoc* name in conformity with its effect upon the world. This phrase is very probably an explanatory gloss added by the author since it interrupts the thought (Charles, 1:235). Several forms of nouns formed on the stem Ἄψινθ- are attested: (1) the neuter τὸ ἀψίνθιον, (2) the feminine ἡ ἄψινθος, (3) the feminine ἡ ἀψινθία, and (4) the masculine ὁ ἄψινθος (see LSJ, 299; Bauer-Aland, 260; BAGD, 129). ἄψινθος is either a back formation from ἀψίνθιον or a survival of a pre-Greek word (-νθ-) accidentally unattested in earlier literature (Mussies, *Morphology*, 113–14). Ἄψινθος is probably masculine because it is the name of a star, ὁ ἀστήρ, which is also masculine in gender. Normally, proper names are anarthrous, while here ὁ Ἄψινθος is articular. Perhaps the explanation is that the author uses the article with words first used as proper names (Schmid, *Studien* 2:199). It is possible that Ἄψινθος is articular because it is a notion known in ancient apocalyptic tradition but unknown to us (Mussies, *Morphology*, 199).

11b καὶ ἐγένετο τὸ τρίτον τῶν ὑδάτων εἰς ἄψινθον, "and a third part of the water became bitter like wormwood." The transformation of fresh water to salt water at the eschaton is found in 4 Ezra 5:9, which is also found in a verbatim formulation in *Par. Jer.* 9:18. The plant genus *Artemisia*, to which absinthe or wormwood belongs (*Artemisia absinthium l.*), is the type associated with the constellation of Scorpio (an arachnid of the order Scorpionida), which has a stinging, poisonous tail (Boll, *Offenbarung*, 42). Wormwood belongs to the daisy family (Compositae) and is native to central and southern Europe, North Africa, Siberia, and northwestern India (Morton, *Atlas*, 908). It is also found in North America, Central America, and South America. The spice tarragon and the plant sagebrush belong to the same genus. The medicinal properties of three types of *absinthium* are discussed in some detail by Dioscorides Pedanius, an army physician and pharmacologist who lived in the first century A.D. during the reigns of Claudius and Nero (A.D. 41–68). The first type of absinthe is called ἀψίνθιον βαθύπρικον, "extremely bitter absinthe," i.e., wormwood (*Materia medica* 3.23.1–4; ed. Wellmann, 2:30–33), the best of which grows in Pontus and Cappadocia and is used primarily for external use since it is bad for the stomach and causes headache, though it is used to flavor wine. The second type, ἀψίνθιον θαλάσσιον, *absinthium marinum* (3.23.5–6), found in Cappadocia and Egypt, is an effective vermifuge. The third variety, ἀψίνθιον σαντονικόν (3.23.6), grows in alpine Galatia and gets its name from Santonicum, where it is found. The bitterness of wormwood was proverbial throughout the ancient world (Prov 5:4; Theophrastus *Hist. plant.* 1.12.1). A single ounce diluted in 524 gallons of water can still be tasted! The term "wormwood," apparently an alteration of "wormwort," is based on the medicinal use of the herb as a vermifuge, i.e., a specific use to expel worms from the intestines, an "intestinal insecticide" (N. Taylor, *Plant Drugs,* 44–45). It is still widely used for this purpose in Central and South America (Morton, *Atlas,* 908). The German term for wormwood, *Wermut,* is related to "vermouth," a wine containing an extract from wormwood. One ingredient in wormwood is the toxic agent thujone, a chemical that can cause intoxication, hallucinations, convulsions, and permanent damage to the nervous system. Oil of wormwood was extracted from the herb's stem, flowers, and leaves. The Hebrew term לענה *laʿănâ,* "wormwood," occurs several times in the OT (e.g., Prov 5:4; Lam 3:15, 19; Amos 5:7; 6:12), though in these cases a different species, *Artemisia judaica,* is probably in view.

11c καὶ πολλοὶ τῶν ἀνθρώπων ἀπέθανον ἐκ τῶν ὑδάτων ὅτι ἐπικράνθησαν, "so that many people died as a result of the water because it had turned bitter." The poisonous effects of absinthe or wormwood are problematic since the plant is bitter but not lethal. The connection between wormwood and poison is probably based on the parallelism in Jer 9:15, "Behold, I will feed this people with wormwood, and give them poisonous water to drink" (repeated verbatim in Jer 23:15). The phrase "and has given us poisoned water to drink" occurs also in Jer 8:14, though its parallel, "I will feed this people with wormwood," occurs only in Jer 9:15; 23:15. Here one would expect the pattern of thirds to continue and that the poisoning of one-third of the waters would result in the deaths of one-third of humanity. It is possible that the number one-third is missing here because one-third of humanity is killed in the plague unleashed by the sixth trumpet (9:15). This in turn suggests that the group of three woes (9:12; 11:14) was transformed into a group of seven trumpets by prefixing the first four trumpet plagues (8:7–12) in order to form a series of seven (J. Weiss, *Offenbarung,* 75).

12 καὶ ὁ τέταρτος ἄγγελος ἐσάλπισεν· καὶ ἐπλήγη τὸ τρίτον τοῦ ἡλίου καὶ τὸ τρίτον τῆς σελήνης καὶ τὸ τρίτον τῶν ἀστέρων, ἵνα σκοτισθῇ τὸ τρίτον αὐτῶν καὶ ἡ ἡμέρα μὴ φάνῃ τὸ τρίτον αὐτῆς καὶ ἡ νὺξ ὁμοίως, "Then the fourth angel sounded his trumpet, and a third of the sun was struck and a third of the moon and a third of the stars with the result that a third part of them were darkened and a third part of the day did not appear and the night similarly." If one-third of the lighted heavenly bodies are darkened, the result would necessarily involve the diminishing of their light by one-third, *not* their failure to appear during one-third of the day and one-third of the night. The author apparently thinks of the lighted heavenly bodies like torches, which burn out after a certain length of time, or an eclipse, in which the light of the sun or the moon is suddenly, if temporarily, obscured. Cf. Amos 8:9, "On that day, says the Lord God, I will make the sun go down at noon, and darken the earth in broad daylight," and Herodotus 7.37.2, "the sun, leaving his place in the heavens, disappeared, though there were no clouds and the sky was absolutely clear; and there was night instead of day" (see Bousset [1906] 296; Charles, 1:236–37). A similar prodigy is reported by Lucan (1.536–43; LCL tr.):

> [The moon] suddenly was smitten by earth's shadow and grew dim. The sun himself, while rearing his head in the zenith, hid his burning chariot in black darkness and veiled his sphere in gloom, forcing mankind to despair of daylight.

The effects of the fourth trumpet are in some tension with effects of the opening of the sixth seal (6:12–14), where the sun is blackened, the moon turns red, and the stars fall to earth—a scenario that involves virtually complete cosmic destruction. It is perhaps not mere coincidence that on the *fourth* creative day, God is reported to have created the sun, moon, and stars (Gen 1:14–19), so that the cosmic destruction that occurs here can be understood against the background of the creation account. In Zonara's epitomized account of Dio in which he described the eruption of Vesuvius (see *Comment* on 8:8a), he notes that the airborne volcanic ash darkened the sun for several days running (66.22.4; 66.23.4–5); this darkness during daylight hours agrees with the eyewitness report of Pliny the Younger (*Ep.* 6.16.17; 6.20.15).

13a καὶ εἶδον, καὶ ἤκουσα ἑνὸς ἀετοῦ πετομένου ἐν μεσουρανήματι, "I looked and heard an eagle flying in midheaven." On καὶ εἶδον, see *Comment* on 5:1a. Here the verbs appear problematic, for while John may have *seen* an eagle flying in midheaven, he obviously could not have *heard* the eagle flying. What he purportedly *heard* was, of course, the human speech of the eagle. The eagle was regarded as the messenger (διάκτωρ or ἄγγελος) of Zeus, and, in an epigram of Antipater of Sidon, the eagle of Zeus begins his proclamation with the term ἀγγέλλω, "I announce," and has already been identified as ὄρνι, Διὸς Κρονίδαο διάκτορε, "eagle, messenger of Zeus son of Kronos" (*Anth. Pal.* 7.161); cf. Sophocles *Elec.* 149 and *Anth. Graec.* 9.223.1–2, where the eagle is specifically designated a Διὸς ἄγγελος, or ἀγγελίην πὰρ Ζηνός, a "messenger of Zeus." For the bird as messenger in the ancient Near East, see Keel, *Vögel als Boten.*

The noun τὸ μεσουράνημα, "midheaven," occurs three times in Revelation (8:13; 14:6; 19:17). The term also occurs on a magical amulet, probably of Jewish origin, with a sun, moon, and two stars on the obverse and this inscription on the reverse: "One God in the heavens, who exists and who preexists [ὁ ὢν καὶ προών], who is greater than all, who dominates all the beings in midheaven [μεσουρανῶν]" (Delatte-Derchain, *Les intailles magiques,* 266, no. 381; extensive commentary in Peterson, *Εἷς Θεός,* 260–64). Midheaven is the location of the sun, moon, stars, and planets; one constellation is named Aquila, "Eagle," the bird of Zeus/Jupiter (Varro *Res rusticae* 2.2.13; Cicero *Arat.* 328; Manilius *Astron.* 1.343–45; Vitruvius 9.4.3; Pliny *Hist. nat.* 8.187). The eagle is a bird who has strong solar associations (Boll, *Offenbarung,* 38–39), and these associations are suggested by the fact that the angel in Rev 19:17 who "stands in the sun" calls to the birds who fly in midheaven (Peterson, *Εἷς Θεός,* 263). Cf. PGM XII.45, which contains an invocation to "Beetle [Scarabaeus], winged ruler of midheaven [μεσουρανῶν]."

13b λέγοντος φωνῇ μεγάλῃ· οὐαὶ οὐαὶ οὐαὶ τοὺς κατοικοῦντας ἐπὶ τῆς γῆς ἐκ τῶν λοιπῶν φωνῶν τῆς σάλπιγγος τῶν τριῶν ἀγγέλων τῶν μελλόντων σαλπίζειν, "crying with a loud voice: 'Woe, woe, woe to the inhabitants of the earth because of the remaining blasts of the trumpet which the three angels are about to sound!'" Here the eagle speaks on behalf of God (see *Comment* on Rev 4:7). A speaking eagle is part of the fifth vision in 4 Ezra 11:7–8. Baruch reportedly used an eagle as a messenger to bring a prophetic letter to the Israelites in captivity (*2 Apoc. Bar.* 77:19–26), and, in his commission to the eagle, Baruch reminded the eagle of earlier birds in the Bible who had served as messengers of God (in a recital that A. P. Wikgren labeled "kerygmatic ornithology," in "Aspects of Kerygmatic History," *MQ* 20 [1967] 292–300). In the *Par. Jer.* 7:15–16, which recounts a similiar episode of an eagle sent to Jeremiah by Baruch, it is said that "the eagle cried out in a loud voice," with which he delivered his message. In *Par. Jer.* 6:15–7:36, an eagle, who has the ability to speak, is miraculously provided to carry Baruch's letter to Jeremiah in exile. When the eagle resuscitates a dead man, the people think that God is appearing to them in the form of the eagle (*Par. Jer.* 7:20). For angels with the appearance of eagles, see *3 Enoch* 2:1; 24:11; 26:3; 44:5. In an interesting parallel in *PGM* XIII.146–47 (repeated in 454–55), "the first angel calls out in the language of bird-hieroglyphs [ὀρνεογλυφιστί], 'Arai ['Αραί],' which means 'Woe [οὐαί] to my enemy'" (the term ἀραί is the nominative plural form of ἀρά, meaning "curse").

The threefold repetition of the term "woe" is correlated with the sounding of next three trumpets. The first woe is specifically enumerated at the conclusion of the fifth trumpet (9:12), and the second woe is similarly enumerated at the conclusion of the sixth trumpet (11:14). The third woe, however, is not specifically enumerated at the conclusion of the seventh trumpet. There are several possible reasons for this omission. The author may have redesigned the textual unit dealing with the effects of the sounding of the seventh trumpet and, since it no longer contained any elements of punishment, omitted the phrase as inappropriate. It is also possible to argue that, since no plague is unleashed by the seventh trumpet (but rather a scene of victory in the heavenly court is presented), the author understands the third "woe" to consist of the judgment of Babylon in 17:1–19:8, where the phrase "Woe, woe, you great city" is repeated three times (18:10, 16, 19).

Here the threefold repetition of οὐαί is followed by the accusative τοὺς κατοικοῦντας, "those who dwell," without a preposition. On the negative designation τοὺς κατοικοῦντας ἐπὶ τῆς γῆς, "the inhabitants of the earth," which occurs nine times in Revelation, see *Comment* on 3:10c. οὐαί with the accusative also occurs in 12:12, and rarely elsewhere in Greek literature (no other examples are cited in BAGD, 561, or BDR § 190.2). The phrase οὐαὶ τοὺς ἁμαρτωλούς, "woe to the sinners," occurs in *Gk. Apoc. Ezra* 1:9, 24, and the phrase οὐαὶ τὴν ψυχὴν αὐτοῦ, "woe to his soul," in *Gk. Apoc. Ezra* 4:12. The Greek interjection οἴ, however, is occasionally used with the accusative (see *Anth. Pal.* 9.408, οἴ ἐμὲ δειλήν, "woe to poor me!"), and it is also possible that οὐαί + accusative is a Latinism since *uae* is used with both the dative (*uae mihi*) and the accusative case (*uae me*) in Latin (OLD, 2003); see *Note* 12:12.e. οὐαί + nominative (functioning as vocative) does occur in Rev 18:10, 16, 19 (see *Note* 18:10.a-a.). In the LXX, οὐαί is often used with the dative of the person or thing to whom the woe is directed (Num 21:29; 1 Sam 4:8; Jdt 16:17; Prov 23:29; Isa 3:9, 11; 10:1, 5; 33:1; Jer 4:3; Hos 7:13; 9:12; see MM, 464) and with articular nominatives used as vocatives (Zech 2:5; Isa 1:24; 5:8, 11, 18, 20, 21, 22; 31:1; *1 Enoch* 99:13, 14). Occasionally, οὐαί is used with ἐπί + the accusative in the LXX (Jer 10:19; 28:2[MT 51:2]; 31:1[MT 48:1]; Ezek 7:26). οὐαί appears for the first time in the LXX, where it occurs seventy-three times, with particular frequency in Isaiah and Jeremiah. The two Hebrew interjections אוי *ʾôy* and הוי *hôy* (cf. the similar Aramaic וי *way,* found in rabbinic literature) lie behind most of these occurrences. הוי *hôy,* though not אוי *ʾôy,* is peculiar to the prophets, for the single occurrence outside the prophetic writings of the OT is in 1 Kgs 13:30, where it is uttered by a prophet (Berlin, *Zephaniah,* 104). In prophetic discourse, however, it is likely that הוי *hôy* functions as a particle to get the attention of the hearer, like "hey," and it is usually followed by direct address (J. J. M. Roberts, *Nahum, Habakkuk, and Zephaniah: A Commentary,* OTL [Louisville: Westminster/John Knox, 1991] 114, 118). Though it was once assumed that οὐαί was derived from these words, it is more likely that the word first appeared in Greek in the fourth century B.C. and was selected by the LXX translators because of its phonetic similarity to the equivalent Hebrew terms (see A. D. Lowe, "The Origin of οὐαί," *Hermathena* 105 [1967] 34–39).

9:1a καὶ ὁ πέμπτος ἄγγελος ἐσάλπισεν καὶ εἶδον ἀστέρα ἐκ τοῦ οὐρανοῦ πεπτωκότα εἰς τὴν γῆν, "Then the fifth angel sounded his trumpet, and then I saw a star which had fallen from heaven to earth." On καὶ εἶδον, see *Comment* on 5:1a. πεπτωκότα, "had fallen," is a perfect active participle modifying ἀστέρα, "star." John does not say that he actually *saw* the star fall; he says only that he saw the star *after* it had fallen. In 9:1b–2a it becomes obvious that the "star" is a supernatural being, i.e., an angel. In early Jewish literature, stars can represent angelic beings (Judg 5:20; Job 38:7; Dan 8:10); in *PGM* I.74–75 a star is called an angel, and Platonists (among others) regarded stars as divine beings (Plato *Leges* 898D–899D; *Timaeus* 37B; 40A–B; Philo *Plant.* 12); see A. Scott, *Origen and the Life of the Stars* (Oxford: Clarendon, 1991). Falling stars often represent evil angelic beings or demons (*1 Enoch* 86:3; 88:1; 90:24; *T. Sol.* 20.14–17; Jude 13), or even Satan (*1 Enoch* 86:1; *Apoc. Elijah* 4:11; Luke 10:18; Rev 12:9; see *Comment* on 6:13). Here the fallen star should be understood as an angelic messenger (see 20:1) and not be identified with the angel of the abyss named Abaddon or Apollyon in 9:11 or Satan in 12:9. In *1 Enoch* 86:1, Enoch sees a star falling from heaven, followed (v 3) by many stars, all obviously fallen angelic beings. For a discussion of the significance of falling stars in dreams in the ancient Near East (where the "falling" of stars is generally considered a bad omen), see Oppenheim, *Interpretation,* 283–84; Artemidorus *Oneirocritica* 2.36; 5.23. In Ezekiel *Exagoge* 85, the stars represent the host of angelic beings: "A multitude of stars fell before my knees and I counted them all. They paraded past me like a battalion of men" (Jacobson, *Exagoge,* 55). The falling star in *Sib. Or.* 5.155–61 has some parallels with Rev 9:1–2 (tr. Charlesworth, *OTP* 2:397):

> A great star will come from heaven to the wondrous sea
> and will burn the deep sea and Babylon itself
> and the land of Italy, because of which many
> holy faithful Hebrews and a true people perished.

In both Rev 9:1–2 and *Sib. Or.* 5.158–61 the star is a messenger of God sent to earth, though God is only indirectly responsible for the destruction caused by the release of the locusts in vv 3–11. There was a view in the Hellenistic world that "none of the gods of heaven will ever quit heaven, and pass its boundary, and come down to earth" (*Corp. Herm.* 10.25). Manilius (*Astron.* 1.384–86; see 1.799) compares Augustus to a star that has fallen into the world.

1b καὶ ἐδόθη αὐτῷ ἡ κλεὶς τοῦ φρέατος τῆς ἀβύσσου, "He was given the key to the shaft of the abyss." The "star" is obviously some kind of supernatural being, as this verse and the following make clear. The two definite articles in the phrase "*the* shaft of *the* abyss" indicate that the notion of a shaft to the abyss, as well as the concept of the abyss itself, was well known to the readers (Mussies, *Morphology,* 188). The term ἀ-βύσσος (= βυθός), with the prefixed alpha privative, means "without depth," i.e., "fathomless, boundless," and was used to refer to the infinite void or a subterranean region beneath the earth (in accordance with a three-level view of the universe). The term ἄβυσσος occurs seven times in Revelation (9:1, 2, 11; 11:7;

17:8; 20:1, 3). Five of these occur in two passages in which the three-level cosmology of Revelation is implied (9:1–11; 20:1–3). Here, in 9:1, a star (= angelic being) descends from *heaven* to *earth* and is given a key to the *abyss,* while in 20:1 an angel descends from *heaven* (to *earth* is implied) with a key to the *abyss;* both passages imply a three-level cosmos. This coheres with the cosmology, consisting of heaven, earth, and sea, found elsewhere in Revelation (10:6; 12:12; 14:7; 21:1; see *Comment* on 10:6), though the three realms of heaven, earth, and below the earth are mentioned in 15:3 (see *Comment*), and the four realms of heaven, earth, below the earth, and the sea are referred to in 15:13 (see *Comment*). In 9:1–11 the abyss is the dwelling place of locust-demons who can be released only when the shaft (φρέαρ) to the abyss is opened by someone entrusted with the key (the φρέαρ, "shaft," to the abyss is mentioned just four times in Revelation, all occurrences in 9:1–2). While the key to the abyss is mentioned again in 20:1, the notion of a shaft that could be locked and unlocked is implied rather than explicitly stated. In the other two references, in Rev 11:7 and 17:8, the abyss is the place from which the beast is said to ascend. *PGM* XIII.169–70, 481–83 indicates a belief in a supernatural being who rules over the abyss: "a god appeared, he was put in charge of the abyss" (though here "abyss" probably refers to the primeval or celestial ocean as a source of moisture for the cosmos). The term ἄβυσσος is used in the LXX as the usual translation for Hebrew תְּהוֹם *tĕhôm,* "deep, primeval ocean, sea" (KB, 1557–59), and in Greco-Jewish literature for the *sea* (Gen 1:2; 7:11; Job 28:14; 36:16; 41:22, 23; Eccl 1:3; 16:18) and for the *depths of the earth* (Ps 71:20; Deut 8:7; *1 Enoch* 17:7, 8; *T. Levi* 3:9; *Jos. As.* 12:2; *Pss. Sol.* 17:19; *Jub.* 2:2, 16). It is sometimes synonymous with the underworld, which is the abode of the dead (*Jos. As.* 15:12; Ps 71:20; Rom 10:7; Diogenes Laertes 4.27 mentions "the abyss of Pluto" = Hades) and the place where demons are imprisoned (Luke 8:31; *1 Enoch* 18–21 [the term ἄβυσσος is used in the Greek version of 21:7]; *Jub.* 10:7 [the Greek fragment reads "to cast them into the abyss until the day of judgment"; see Denis, *Fragmenta,* 86], 9 [the Greek fragment reads "and the remaining nine parts were cast into the abyss"; Denis, *Fragmenta,* 87]). In Revelation the beast ascends from the abyss (11:7; 17:8), and it is also the abode of Satan (20:1–3), of the angel of the abyss, Abaddon or Apollyon (9:11), and of demons (9:1–10). In *Tri. Trac.* 89.25–28, the "pit of ignorance" is a metaphorical interpretation of "the Outer Darkness," "Chaos," "Hades," and "the abyss," revealing that these four designations are regarded as synonymous. In his astrological reading of Revelation, Malina argues that the abyss referred to here is the "celestial Abyss," which was thought to be the counterpart of the "terrestrial Abyss" (*Revelation,* 142–43), a conception found nowhere in ancient literature. Apart from the fact that he ignores the archaic three-tiered cosmology of Revelation (evident in *Revelation,* 2–5), he also combines several ancient opinions that are mutually contradictory. Malina cites Plutarch (*De genio Socr.* 590B–592E) as evidence for the view that the entrance to Hades (which he assumes is equivalent to the abyss) was located between Scorpio and Sagittarius, while Plutarch appears rather to have held that the region between the earth and the moon was "Hades" (*De genio Socr.* 591A–C; *De facie* 942F).

2a καὶ ἤνοιξεν τὸ φρέαρ τῆς ἀβύσσου, "He opened the shaft of the abyss." On the shaft to the abyss, see *Comment* on 9:1b. The shaft to the underworld, here specifically the region where demons dwell and the place from which the beast ascends (11:7; 17:8), is presented as if it were blocked by a door to which God alone holds the key. While this door can be locked (20:3) as well as unlocked (9:2a) by the one possessing the key (representing divine authority), the people of the world are protected as long as the door seals the realm of the earth from the subterranean abyss.

2b καὶ ἀνέβη καπνὸς ἐκ τοῦ φρέατος ὡς καπνὸς καμίνου μεγάλης, καὶ ἐσκοτώθη ὁ ἥλιος καὶ ὁ ἀὴρ ἐκ τοῦ καπνοῦ τοῦ φρέατος, "and smoke arose from the shaft as smoke from a great furnace so that the sun and the air were darkened by the smoke from the shaft." Locust plagues reportedly could darken the sky and obliterate the sun (Philo *Mos.* 1.123). The eruption of Vesuvius in A.D. 79 (see *Comment* on 8:8a) resulted in the obliteration of the sun for several days (see *Comment* on 8:12; see Pliny *Ep.* 6.16.17; 6.20.15; Cassius Dio 66.22.4; 66.23.4–5).

3a καὶ ἐκ τοῦ καπνοῦ ἐξῆλθον ἀκρίδες εἰς τὴν γῆν, "Out of the smoke emerged locusts upon the earth." These are demons in the guise of locusts, for their king is Abaddon, the angel of the abyss (v 11). This stands in tension with 12:7–12, which narrates the fall of the dragon (alias the devil and Satan) and his angels to the earth, and with 20:1–3, which describes the temporary imprisonment of Satan in the abyss; yet it is curiously concordant with the statements in 11:7 and 17:8 that the beast ascends from the abyss. An infestation of locusts constitutes the eighth plague of Exod 10:12–20 (cf. the other plague traditions in Pss 78:46; 105:34–35; Amos 4:9b; Ezekiel *Exogoge* 132–51; Artapanus [Eusebius *Praep. evang.* 9.27.32]; *Jub.* 48:5; *Bib. Ant.* 10:1; Wis 16:9 [though here the *bites* of the flies and locusts cause death]; Jos. *Ant.* 2.306; Philo *Mos.* 1.120–22). Locusts are also mentioned in lists of eschatological plagues that have no direct connection with the plagues of Exodus (*3 Apoc. Bar.* 16:3; *Sib. Or.* 5.454). Hermas refers to fiery locusts that came out of the mouth of the great beast he saw in a vision (*Vis.* 4.1.6).

In connection with the motifs that link 8:1–9:21 with the eruption of Vesuvius in A.D. 79 (see *Comments* on 8:8–12; 9:2), it is perhaps worth noting that in the fanciful account found in Zonara's epitome of Cassius Dio, giants were reportedly seen in the area, some of them flying through the air (66.22.2), and some people thought that the giants, who had been conquered in the Gigantomachy by Zeus and the Olympians and had been imprisoned in Tartarus by Zeus under several volcanoes in Italy and Greece (Apollodorus 1.6.1), were again rising in revolt, "for at that time many of their forms could be discerned in the smoke [πολλὰ γὰρ καὶ τότε εἴδωλα αὐτῶν ἐν τῷ καπνῷ διεφαίνετο]" (66.23.1).

3b καὶ ἐδόθη αὐταῖς ἐξουσία ὡς ἔχουσιν ἐξουσίαν οἱ σκορπίοι τῆς γῆς, "and they were given authority as scorpions have authority over the earth." There is a repeated effort to compare these demonic locusts with scorpions (see 9:5, 10). The phrase ἔχουσιν ἐξουσίαν οἱ σκορπίοι, "the *authority* scorpions have" (NRSV), is problematic, for it hardly conveys what it obviously means, namely, the "respect" and the leeway people and animals give to scorpions because they fear their venomous sting, which is extremely painful and sometimes lethal. The "authority" scorpions have, then, is the inherent ability to *intimidate* and *tyrannize* and, in the case of the demonic locusts, to *terrorize.* According to 2 Chr 7:13, it is God who has the power to command locusts to devour the land.

In vv 3–5, a series of statements is made using passive verbs (v 3, ἐδόθη, "was given"; v 4, ἐρρέθη, "were instructed"; v 5, ἐδόθη, "was given"). These verbs are in the *passive of divine activity,* which is a circumlocution used for avoiding the direct mention of the activity of God (Dalman, *Die Worte Jesu,* 183; BDR § 130; Joachim

Jeremias, *Theology,* 9–14; N. Perrin, *Jesus,* 189). The agent of passive verbs is often specified with a noun clause introduced by ἐκ or ἀπό, even when a divine agent is in view (e.g., John 3:27, ᾖ δεδομένον αὐτῷ ἐκ τοῦ οὐρανοῦ, "it was given to him by heaven [i.e., 'God']"; see John 6:65; *T. Levi* 2:2); διδόναι in the passive voice is sometimes accompanied by the adverb ἄνωθεν, "from above," as an alternate way of indicating divine agency (John 19:11; *Gk. 1 Enoch* 98:5[2x]). For other examples of διδόναι in the passive of divine activity, see *Gk. 1 Enoch* 25:4; 98:5 (ἐδόθη occurs three times in the Greek text, which is longer than the Ethiopic text); *T. Levi* 4:4; *T. Sim.* 6:6; *T. Iss.* 5:5, 8; *Vit. Proph.* 1:5(8). Ordinarily, Hebrew and Aramaic do not make frequent use of the passive voice; the impersonal plural is often preferred. While the *passivum divinum,* the passive of divine activity (a term coined by Joachim Jeremias), occurs frequently in the canonical Gospels (see Matt 5:4, παρακληθήσονται, "they will be comforted," i.e., "God will comfort them"; cf. Matt 5:6, 7, 9; Mark 2:5; Luke 22:16), according to Jeremias (*Eucharistic Words,* 202), it occurs only rarely in rabbinic literature. Jeremias thought that the primary setting of the *passivum divinum* was *apocalyptic* (Joachim Jeremias, *Theology,* 9–14), which might explain why it occurs frequently in Revelation. However, Macholz (*ZNW* 81 [1990] 247–53) has shown that the use of the passive as a way of avoiding the mention of God as the subject of various actions is widely found in later strata of the OT (Gen 42:22, 28; Num 4:20, 26, 31, 35; 5:6, 10, 13, 16, 18, 26; 2 Kgs 18:30 = Isa 36:15; Ps 18:4 = 2 Sam 22:4; Ps 130:4; Dan 9:9; Neh 9:17) and in early Jewish literature as well (Sir 44:16, 18; 45:24; 46:8; 49:7). The so-called *passivum divinum* is also used in nonreligious contexts when referring to rulers and may well have its origin as a *passivum regium.*

4a καὶ ἐρρέθη αὐταῖς ἵνα μὴ ἀδικήσουσιν τὸν χόρτον τῆς γῆς οὐδὲ πᾶν χλωρὸν οὐδὲ πᾶν δένδρον, "But they were instructed not to damage the grass of the earth nor any plant nor any tree." The speaker is not identified, but the ancient reader would assume that it is God (or an angelic agent of God), using the *passivum divinum,* the passive of divine activity, indicating that the scope of divine punishment is limited. The protection of the grass of the earth, however, is inconsistent with 8:7, where *all* the grass was burned up (Charles, 1:220). This passage (taken with 9:4b) is closely parallel to that in 7:3, where the angels who restrain the four winds (7:1), and are also said to have been empowered to destroy the earth and the sea (7:3), are told not to harm the earth, sea, or trees. The verbal similarities are evident in this synoptic comparison (with verbal equivalencies italicized):

Rev 7:2b	*Rev 7:3b*	*Rev 9:4a*
ἐδόθη αὐτοῖς they were empowered	μὴ ἀδικήσητε Do not *harm*	μὴ ἀδικήσουσιν not to *harm*
ἀδικῆσαι to *harm*		
τὴν γῆν *the earth*	τὴν γῆν *the earth*	τὸν χόρτον τῆς γῆς the grass of *the earth*
καὶ τὴν θάλασσαν and the sea	μήτε τὴν θάλασσαν or the sea	οὐδὲ πᾶν χλωρὸν nor any plant

μήτε τὰ δένδρα or the trees	οὐδὲ πᾶν δένδρον nor any tree
ἄχρι σφραγίσωμεν until we *seal*	
τοὺς δούλους τοῦ the servants of	εἰ μὴ τοὺς ἀνθρώπους except those people
θεοῦ ἡμῶν our God	οἵτινες οὐκ ἔχουσι who do not have
	τὴν σφραγῖδα the *seal*
	τοῦ θεοῦ of God
ἐπὶ τῶν μετώπων αὐτῶν *on their foreheads*	ἐπὶ τῶν μετώπων *on their foreheads*

The similarities between these two passages, which are essentially doublets, is striking: (1) In the first part of the saying, supernatural beings (angels or locust-demons) are commanded not to harm the trees (7:3, and the earth and sea; 9:4, and the grass of the earth and plants). (2) The second part focuses on the exemption for those sealed. Rev 7:3 has a *positive* formulation: the harming of earth, sea, and trees is delayed until the sealing of the servants of God is completed. Rev 9:4 has a *negative* formulation: only those people who do not have the seal of God on their foreheads are to be harmed. As it stands, 9:4 is an analeptic reference linking this textual unit to 7:1–8 (see *Introduction*, Section 5: Source Criticism, p. cxxix). If this literary tradition had an original context in the material available to the author, 9:4 is the obvious choice, for it is part of a complete narrative in 9:1–6, in a context where it makes good sense: locust-demons, paradoxically, harm not vegetation but only people, i.e., those who lack the seal of God. Rev 7:1–3, on the other hand, is truncated, for the four angels never do release the winds to harm the people of the world.

This prohibition prevents precisely the kind of activity for which locust plagues were justly infamous (Deut 28:38, 42; 1 Kgs 8:37; 2 Chr 6:28; 7:13; Pss 78:46; 105:34–35; Joel 1:4; 2:25; Amos 4:9; 7:2; Nah 3:15; Philo *Mos.* 1.123; *Praem.* 128). An eyewitness account of such a famine from A.D. 499–500 is found in W. Wright, *The Chronicle of Ps.-Joshua the Stylite* (Cambridge: Cambridge UP, 1882) chap. 38:

> In the month of Adar of this year the locusts came upon us out of the ground, so that, because of their number, we imagined that not only had the eggs that were in the ground been hatched to our harm, but that the very air was vomiting them against us, and that they were descending from the sky upon us. When they were only able to crawl, they devoured and consumed all the Arab territory and all that of Rasain and Tella and Edessa. But after they were able to fly, the stretch of their radii was from the border of Assyria to the Western sea [the Mediterranean] and they went northwards as far as the boundary of the Ortaye. They ate up and desolated these districts and utterly consumed everything that was in them.

The last locust plague in Jerusalem occurred in June 1915, when millions of locusts obscured the sun and ate every green thing in the vicinity (Whiting, *NGM* 38 [1915] 511–50).

4b εἰ μὴ τοὺς ἀνθρώπους οἵτινες οὐκ ἔχουσι τὴν σφραγῖδα τοῦ θεοῦ ἐπὶ τῶν μετώπων, "except those people who do not have the seal of God upon their foreheads." This refers the reader back to 7:2–8 and makes it explicit that the purpose of sealing is that of protection. The motif of protection is central in the sealing episode in Ezek 9:3–8, as it is in *Pss. Sol.* 15:4–9 (tr. Sparks, *AOT*), a passage that expands on Ezek 9 and contrasts the mark of God with the mark of destruction:

> He who performs these things shall never be shaken by evil:
> The flame of fire and the wrath against the unrighteous shall not touch him,
> When it goes forth from before the Lord against sinners,
> To destroy all the substance of sinners;
> For the *mark of God* [τὸ σημεῖον τοῦ θεοῦ] is upon the righteous for salvation.
> *Famine* and *sword* and *death* [λιμὸς καὶ ῥομφαία καὶ θάνατος;
> cf. Rev 6:8] shall be far from the righteous,
> For they shall flee from the holy as men pursued in war;
> But they shall pursue sinners and overtake them,
> And those who act lawlessly shall not escape the judgment of the Lord:
> As by enemies skilled in war shall they be overtaken,
> For the *mark of destruction* [τὸ γὰρ σημεῖον τῆς ἀπωλείας] is
> *upon their forehead* [ἐπὶ τοῦ μετώπου αὐτῶν].

On τὴν σφραγῖδα τοῦ θεοῦ, "the seal of God," see *Comment* on 7:2. This passage may be an interpolation.

5a καὶ ἐδόθη αὐτοῖς ἵνα μὴ ἀποκτείνωσιν αὐτούς, "But they were ordered not to kill them." In Job 2:6, God allows Satan to afflict Job, but not to the extent of actually killing him (the same motif is also picked up in *T. Job* 4.4; 20.3). This restriction leads to the intensified punishment connected with the sixth trumpet, namely, the slaughter of one-third of the people of the earth (9:15, 18).

5b ἀλλ' ἵνα βασανισθήσονται μῆνας πέντε, "but to torment them for five months." The number "five" here is apparently symbolic. The number five is frequently used in contexts in which it obviously functions as a round number meaning "a few" (1 Cor 14:19, "five words"; Matt 17:17–19 = Mark 6:38–41 = Luke 19:13–16, "five loaves"; Luke 12:6, "five sparrows"; Luke 12:52, "five in one family"; Jdt 7:30; 8:9, 15; Acts 20:6; 24:1, "five days later"; Lev 26:8 [cf. Isa 30:17], "five of you shall chase a hundred"; cf. Judg 18:2, 7, 14, 17; 1 Sam 17:40; see Kittel, "Fünfzahl," 39ff.; Str-B, 3:461–62; Hemer, *NIDNTT* 2:689–90). The five-month period may reflect the life cycle of the locust; i.e., they are hatched in the spring and die at the end of summer (Charles, 1:243). The specific limitation of the plague to *five* months, however, suggests the possible symbolic significance of that number; i.e., it is a round number meaning "a few" and indicates a limited period of tribulation.

5c καὶ ὁ βασανισμὸς αὐτῶν ὡς βασανισμὸς σκορίου ὅταν παίσῃ ἄνθρωπον, "(their torment was like the torment of a scorpion when it stings a person)." Scorpions belong to the Arachnida class (with spiders, ticks, and mites), and the sting they use to kill the insects on which they feed is very painful, though rarely fatal, to humans. Scorpions were common in the southern and eastern theaters of the Mediterranean world (particularly in the regions of the Nile and

Mesopotamia), but they were also found in Greek areas (particularly Crete). In these regions scorpion amulets were popular apotropaic devices to ward off scorpions and other poisonous and painful insects, spiders, and snakes (Eitrem, *SO* 7 [1928] 70–73). Scorpions are one of nine instruments of destruction that God created to punish the wicked, according to Sir 39:30. Scorpions are a metaphor for punishment in 1 Kgs 12:11, 14 (cf. 2 Chr 10:11, 14). A boundary stone of Nebuchadrezzar I (twelfth century B.C.) depicts a scorpion-man with a bow and arrow (*ISBE,* rev. ed., 4:358).

6a καὶ ἐν ταῖς ἡμέραις ἐκείναις ζητήσουσιν οἱ ἄνθρωποι τὸν θάνατον καὶ οὐ μὴ εὑρήσουσιν αὐτόν, "In those days people will seek death / but will not find it." The effects of the demonic locusts on the humans they terrorize is given in poetic form. V 6 (here divided into 6a and 6b) consists of two parallel couplets, and each couplet is an instance of antithetical parallelism. The entire verse is either a short digression or an interpolation made by the author for the second edition of Revelation. V 6 is also distinguished from the context by the presence of three verbs in the future tense (the only other verbs in the future tense in 8:1–9:21 are the two future subjunctives in vv 4 and 5). A similar description of despair appears in *Apoc. Elijah* [P. Chester Beatty 2018] 9.1–7 (tr. Pietersma): "They will desire death but death will flee from them. They will climb onto rocks and jump down on them, and say, 'Fall on us!' And they will not die but death runs away from them" (the last sentence is closely parallel to Rev 6:16). In his eyewitness report of the eruption of Vesuvius in A.D. 79, Pliny the Younger reports that in the ensuing panic "People bewailed their own fate or that of their relatives, and there were some who prayed for death in their terror of dying" (*Ep.* 6.20.14; LCL tr.; see *Comments* on 8:8–12).

6b καὶ ἐπιθυμήσουσιν ἀποθανεῖν καὶ φεύγει ὁ θάνατος ἀπ' αὐτῶν, "they will desire to die, / but death will elude them." This is an ancient commonplace that occurs in Judaism (Job 3:21; *Sib. Or.* 2.307–8; 8.353; 13.118; *Apoc. Elijah* 2:5, 32) as well as in Greco-Roman literature, e.g., Ovid *Ibis* 123–24, "May you have cause enough for death but no means of dying; may your life be forced to avoid the death it longs for" (cf. Seneca *Troad.* 954; Cornelius Gallus *Eleg.* 1; Sophocles *Electra* 1007–8). The preference of death over life, in the apocalyptic context of a variety of reversals that will characterize the end, occurs in *Asclepius* 25 of the *Corpus Hermeticum* (Nock-Festugière, *Hermès Trismégiste,* 329): "Darkness will be preferred to light and death will be preferred to life [*et mors vita utilior iudicabitur*]" (cf. the Coptic version in *Asclepius* 72.18 in J. M. Robinson, *Nag Hammadi,* 304). The desirability of death is discussed in Plato *Apol.* 40c, and some Greek writers (using a theme from consolation literature) refer to death as preferable to the troubles and suffering of life (Aeschylus *Prom.* 747–51; Sophocles *Antig.* 463–64; see Moran, *Consolations,* 31–39, and *Comment* on 22:4).

7a καὶ τὰ ὁμοιώματα τῶν ἀκρίδων ὅμοια ἵπποις ἡτοιμασμένοις εἰς πόλεμον, "The appearance of the locusts was like horses prepared for battle." On the image of horses arrayed for battle, see v 9a. Horses are specifically compared to "bristling locusts" in Jer 51:27; implicit is the comparison of a large cavalry and a locust plague. An invading enemy could devastate the crops and livestock and could therefore readily be compared to a plague of locusts (Judg 6:5; 7:12; Jer 15:27). Using locust imagery, an author can describe such an enemy cavalry as "covering the land" (*T. Mos.* 3:1) and as "devouring the land and all that fills it" (Jer 8:16), or a vast enemy army is compared in number to locusts (Judg 6:5; 7:12; Jer 46:23;

51:14; Joel 1–2; Amos 4:9; Nah 3:15–17; Jdt 2:20; Jos. *J.W.* 4.536; J. A. Thompson, *JNES* 14 [1955] 52–55; Andiñach, *VT* 42 [1992] 438–39).

7b καὶ ἐπὶ τὰς κεφαλὰς αὐτῶν ὡς στέφανοι ὅμοιοι χρυσῷ, καὶ τὰ πρόσωπα αὐτῶν ὡς πρόσωπα ἀνθρώπων, "On their heads were something like gold wreaths, and their faces were like human faces." Though the author has begun by describing the demonic beings that emerge from the shaft of the abyss as locusts (9:3a), in vv 7–9 they are described first in theriomorphic terms (i.e., they look like warhorses, v 7a), then in anthropomorphic terms (i.e., they wear something like gold wreaths on their heads, v 7b; their faces look human, v 7b; and they have disheveled hair, v 8a), after which the author resorts again to theriomorphic imagery in that they are described as having teeth like lions (v 8b). The mention of gold wreaths is a simile that may imply that the demon-locust horde is invincible.

8a καὶ εἶχον τρίχας ὡς τρίχας γυναικῶν, "they had hair like the hair of women." This probably means that their hair was long and possibly disheveled. Disheveled hair had several meanings in the OT: (1) as a sign of uncleanness for people with leprosy (Lev 13:45), (2) as a sign of mourning (Lev 10:6; 21:10), and (3) as part of the sacrificial protocol for a woman accused of adultery (Num 5:18). One of the demons who reportedly appeared before Solomon had disheveled hair (*T. Sol.* 13:1). Occasionally, the Jewish demon *lilith* is depicted with loose, disheveled hair in crude pictures on Aramaic incantation bowls (see Montgomery, *Aramaic,* 190). *Apoc. Zeph.* 4:4 describes the loose hair of the ugly angels who carry off the souls of the wicked and cast them into eternal punishment as similar to the hair of women. Similarly, in *Apoc. Zeph.* 6:8, the hair of the Accuser (i.e., Satan) is described: "His hair was spread out like women's." While both men and women could have long hair in the ancient world, in the Greek world both sexes could elaborately braid and bind their hair attractively (Blümner, *Greeks,* 64–77). Paul mentions that women normally have *long* hair (1 Cor 11:15; cf. Plutarch *Quaest. Rom.* 267B), which is perfectly appropriate, for in the first century A.D., women wore long hair and men had theirs cut (Plutarch *Quaest. Rom.* 267B). Paul also claims that it is degrading for men to wear their hair long (1 Cor 11:14; Ps.-Phocylides 212). Jewish men could wear their hair long in fulfillment of the Nazirite vow (Num 6:1–12; Judg 13:5; 16:17; 1 Sam 1:11; Acts 18:18). Long hair was often regarded by the Greeks as a sign of effeminacy in a male (H. Herter, "Effeminatus," *RAC* 4:629) or moral laxity in a female (Ps.-Phocylides 212). Fashions change, however, for Greek men once favored long hair (Herodotus 1.82; Plutarch *Lysander* 1; cf. Plato *Phaedo* 89B–C) though by the fifth century B.C., only Spartan men wore their hair long (Aristophanes *Aves* 1281–82; Philostratus *Vita Apoll.* 8.7). The Romans wore their hair long until the third century B.C., after which they considered long hair either barbaric or old fashioned (Juvenal 5.30). The Gauls wore their hair long, and as a result northern Gaul was called *Gallia Comata,* "long-haired Gaul." Apollonius of Tyana, following the practice of philosophers, wore his hair disheveled (Philostratus *Vita Apoll.* 8.7). Parthian warriors wore their hair long (Plutarch *Crassus* 24.2), and many interpreters have understood the demonic locust army as mytho-poetic imagery for the Parthian threat (see *Excursus 16A: Rome and Parthia*).

8b καὶ οἱ ὀδόντες αὐτῶν ὡς λεόντων ἦσαν, "and their teeth were like those of lions." "Like the teeth of a lion" is a proverbial expression for something irresistibly and fatally destructive (Sir 21:2–3; cf. Job 4:10). This is an allusion to Joel 1:6, in which it is said that the nation invading Israel "has the teeth of a lion." In Ps 57:4

the psalmist compares his enemies with man-eating lions with teeth like spears and arrows (see Ps 58:6). The mention of teeth like lions apparently has nothing to do with how the demonic locusts harm people, which they explicitly are said to do with the scorpion-like tails (v 10).

9a καὶ εἶχον θώρακας ὡς θώρακας σιδηροῦς, "They had thoraxes like iron breastplates." The *Tg. Nah.* 3:17 expands the Hebrew phrase מנזריך כארבה *minnĕzārayik kā'arbeh,* "Your princes [?] are like grasshoppers," from Nah 3:17, to the Aramaic phrase הא טסך מצלהבין כגובא *hā' ṭassak mĕṣalhĕbîn kĕgôbā',* "Behold, your plates [?] gleam like the locust," comparing the "scaled armour of the Assyrian warriors and the scaled thoraces of the locusts" (Gordon, *VT* 33 [1983] 338–39). Since Rev 9:7 compares locusts with horses, "the protective armour [προστερνίδιον] of the warhorse" could be the meaning of the phrase in Rev 9:9, "breastplates like breastplates of iron." In ancient warfare, the *kataphracts* (ἡ κατάφρακτος ἵππος, ἵπποι κατάφρακτοι or simply οἱ κατάφρακτοι [Plutarch *Crassus* 21.6; 24.1–2; 25.4; Polybius 30.25.9; Athenaeus *Deipn.* 5.194–95) were heavily armored cavalry (both horse and rider) particularly favored by the Parthians, whose archers and armored cavalry caused the disastrous defeat of the Romans under Crassus at Carrhae in Mesopotamia in 54 B.C. (Ziegler, *Parth.,* 32–34). For a discussion of possible allusions to the Parthians in Revelation, see *Excursus 16A: Rome and Parthia.*

9b καὶ ἡ φωνὴ τῶν πτερύγων αὐτῶν ὡς φωνὴ ἁρμάτων ἵππων πολλῶν τρεχόντων εἰς πόλεμον, "and the sound of their wings was like the sound of many chariots with teams of warhorses rushing into battle." Joel 2:4–9 compares a swarm of locusts with a marauding army, and it is clear that John modeled 9:7–10 on this passage. According to Joel 2:4–5a, "Their appearance is like the appearance of horses, / and like warhorses they run. / As with the rumbling of chariots [LXX φωνὴ ἁρμάτων], / they leap on the tops of the mountains" (RSV). 4 Kgdms 7:6, referring to the divine intervention that frustrates the Syrian king Ben-hadad's siege of Samaria, mentions the φωνὴν ἅρματος καὶ φωνὴν ἵππου καὶ φωνὴν δυνάμεως μεγάλης, "the sound of chariot and the sound of a cavalry and the sound of a great force." Swete (119) cites a parallel to ἁρμάτων ἵππων in 3 Kgdms 12:24b (part of an extensive Greek interpolation), ἦσαν αὐτῷ ἅρματα τριακόσια ἵππων, "he had three hundred chariots with teams."

10a καὶ ἔχουσιν οὐρὰς ὁμοίας σκορπίοις καὶ κέντρα, "They have tails with stingers like scorpions." It is not clear whether the author means "tails like [the tails of] scorpions" (see 13:11, "horns like [the horns of] a lamb") or that the tails of the locust-horses are being compared with scorpions (see Charles, 1:245); the former is more probable.

10b καὶ ἐν ταῖς οὐραῖς αὐτῶν ἡ ἐξουσία αὐτῶν ἀδικῆσαι τοὺς ἀνθρώπους μῆνας πέντε, "so that with their tails they have power to harm people for five months." Most versions of the locust plague of Exod 10:12–20 mention only the power of the locusts to destroy vegetation (see *Comment* on 9:3), though according to Wis 16:9 people were slain by the *bites* of the locusts and flies. On the significance of "five" as a round number indicating a limited period of time, see *Comment* on 9:5b.

11a ἔχουσιν ἐπ' αὐτῶν βασιλέα τὸν ἄγγελον τῆς ἀβύσσου, ὄνομα αὐτῷ Ἑβραϊστὶ Ἀβαδδών, "As king they have over them the angel of the abyss, whose name in Hebrew is Abaddon." The adverb Ἑβραϊστί, "in Hebrew," first occurs in the Greek translation of Sirach (praef.); in Revelation it occurs only here and in 16:16, and elsewhere in the NT only in the Fourth Gospel (John 5:2; 19:13, 17, 20; 20:6). The term occurs five times in other literary contexts in the first century A.D. (Jos. *Ant.* 10.8[2x]; 11.159; Heron Mech. *De mens.* 60.4; 61.4), and thereafter with increasing frequency (Herodian *Partitiones* 7.3; 31.5; *Acts of Paul* 5.13; Theophilus *Ad Autolycum* 2.24; 3.19; Origen *Contra Celsum* 6.32; *Comm. in Joan.* 13.26.161; *Ep. ad Afric.* 11.61, 80). In a Greek letter from the Bar Kosiba period found in the "Cave of Letters" in Naḥal Ḥever, the author says that he has written in Greek (Ἑλληνεστί) rather than in Hebrew (Ἑβραϊστί) for a reason that remains unclear because of a gap in the text (see B. Lifshitz, "Papyrus grecs du désert de Juda," *Aegyptus* 42 [1962] 240, no. 1; *SB* 8 [1967] no. 9843; G. Howard and J. C. Shelton, "The Bar-Kochba Letters and Palestinian Greek," *IEJ* 23 [1973] 101). Here the term means "in Hebrew," though it is also used for "in Aramaic" (Jos. *Ant.* 10.8). In Greek texts, terms such as Αἰγυπτιστί, Ἑλληνιστί, Ἀβραϊστί, and Ἑβραϊστί are used particularly for distinguishing among Egyptian, Greek, and Hebrew names for the gods (Herodotus 2.46, 79, 156; Plato *Tim.* 21E; Plutarch *De Iside* 375F), and in magical texts there is a concern to write or chant the spell or the divine name in the proper language (*PGM* V.475; XIII.82, 84, 594, 596, 975–96; Daniel-Maltomini, *Supplementum Magicum* II.70, 1–2 [comments]).

Though the star that had fallen from heaven mentioned in v 1 must be understood as an angel (cf. 20:1), it should not be identified with this particular angel. This angel is named only here in Revelation, and elsewhere in the OT and early Jewish literature is mentioned only in 4Q*280* 10 ii 7: [ארור אתה מלא]ך השחה ורו[ח האב]דון [*ʾrwr ʾth mlʾ*] *k hšḥh wrw*[*ḥ hʾb*] *dwn,* "[Cursed be you Ange]l of the Pit, and Spir[it of Aba]ddon" (Kobelski, *Melchizedek,* 43–44). While in 4Q*280* and related texts these two titles are alternate ways of describing Belial, in Revelation it is not at all clear that the angel of the abyss is a designation for Satan, for he is carefully named elsewhere with a selection of aliases in two different contexts (12:9; 20:2), and neither Abaddon nor the angel of the abyss is mentioned again. The fact that ἄγγελον is articular here, however, suggests that the author expected the readers to be familiar with this figure, i.e., that the angel of the abyss is none other than Satan-Belial. *Mart. Isa.* 10:9 (tr. Charlesworth, *OTP* 2:173) refers to the descent of Christ "as far as the angel who (is) in Sheol, but you shall not go as far as Perdition [i.e., the final place of punishment]." Abaddon (אֲבַדּוֹן *ʾăbaddôn*) is a Hebrew term for the kingdom of the dead (Prov 15:11; Job 26:6; 28:22; 31:12; Ps 88:12), used as a poetic parallel to Sheol (Job 26:6; Prov 15:11; 27:20; 1QH 3:16–19), death (Job 28:22), the grave (Ps 88:11 [MT 88:12]), and the abyss (4Q*504* = 4QDibHam[a] 7:8). Abaddon is personified as the place of destruction in Job 26:6; 28:22, and the conception of Abaddon as an angel appears to have originated as such a personification of the place of the dead (Olyan, *Thousands,* 74–75). Thus far Abaddon is known to occur in just one Aramaic text, *Tg. Job* (4Q*157* or 11QtgJob) 31:12 (van der Ploeg and van der Woude, *Le Targum de Job,* 46–47; Beyer, *Texte,* 290, 504). In the LXX the Hebrew word אֲבַדּוֹן *ʾăbaddôn* is often translated ἀπώλεια, "destruction" (Prov 15:11; Ps 87:12; Theod Job 26:6; 28:22). Similarly, the eschatological antagonist is called ὁ υἱὸς τῆς ἀπωλείας, "the son of destruction" (2 Thess 2:3), while the term "son of destruction" is also used of those destined for destruction (John 17:12; *Acts of Paul* 1:1).

The designation βασιλεύς, "king," is somewhat unexpected (n.b. that in Prov 30:27 it is said that "locusts have no king"), though the peculiar tradition reflected in LXX Amos 7:1 (which differs considerably from the MT) does link the concept of kingship to the locust swarm, which then becomes a transparent metaphor for Gog and Magog coming from the ends of the earth: οὕτως ἔδειξέν μοι κύριος καὶ ἰδοὺ ἐπιγονὴ ἀκρίδων ἐρχομένη ἑωθινή, καὶ ἰδοὺ βροῦχος εἷς Γωγ ὁ βασιλεύς, "Thus the Lord showed me, and behold, the offspring of locusts were coming in the morning, and behold, one locust was the king of Gog." Terms such as στρατηγός, "commander," ἡγεμών, "leader," or ἄρχων, "ruler, prince," would appear a more appropriate designation for a demonic leader. Satan is often called the "prince" or "ruler" (ἄρχων) of demons (Matt 9:24; 12:24; Mark 3:22; Luke 11:15; *Asc. Isa.* 2:4; *T. Sol.* 2:9; 3:5–6; 6:1), though ἄρχων is sometimes used to mean "king" (Rev 1:5). In *Maʿaseh Merkavah* § 587, the figure Zeʿufiel, the שר גיהנם *śar gêhinnām,* "prince of Gehinnom," is mentioned; the same figure (called Zaʿafiʾel) is mentioned in *3 Enoch* 44:3, as one whose task it is to escort the souls of the wicked from the presence of God to Gehinnom. Beliar is explicitly called "the king of this world" in *Asc. Isa.* 4:2 (Latin MSS *rex huius mundi*; Greek ὁ κοσμοκράτωρ τοῦ αἰῶνος τούτου), and some Qumran texts attest a demonic figure named Melchiresha (מלכי רשע *malkî rešaʿ*), meaning "my king is evil," clearly an alternate designation for Belial opposed by Melchizedek (11QMelch; 4QʿAmram frag. 2, line 3 [= 4Q*543, 545–48;* Eisenman-Wise, *Scrolls,* 151–56]; 4Q*280;* 4Q*286;* see Kobelski, *Melchizedek,* 75–83). Related appellations occur in the *Ascension of Isaiah,* where the name Sammael Malkira (the latter, derived from מלכי רע *malkî raʿ,* means "my king is evil") occurs in 1:8 (Sammael is identified elsewhere as the Angel of Death; see *Tg. Yer. I* Gen 3:6), and the leader of the false prophets, Belchira or Melchira (there are several variant spellings in the MS tradition), is the chief accuser of Isaiah (5:2–15). In medieval Jewish texts the figure of מלך השדים *melek haššēdî m,* "king of demons," appears. The "prince of darkness" (שר החשך *śar hāḥošek*) is mentioned twice in *Pesiq. R.* (95, 203), in the latter passage as identical with Satan and the leader of the angels who rebelled against God (see Schäfer, *Rivalität,* 56). The demon named Ashmedai, widely mentioned in Jewish literature (Tob 3:8 [name apparently missing from Aramaic fragments; see Beyer, *Ergänzungsband,* 137]; 8:3; *T. Sol.* 5:1–13; *JE* 2:217–20; Ginzberg, *Legends* 4:165–69), is called "king of the demons" in *b. Pesaḥ.* 110a, a designation that also occurs in the Cairo Genizah text TS K1.30, line 17, where demons are exorcised "in the name of Ashmedai your king [בשם אשמדי מלככון *bšm ʾšmdy mlkkwn*]," who is earlier given the specific title "Ashmedai, king of demons [אשמדי מלכא דשידין *ʾšmdy mlkʾ dšydyn*]" (Schiffman-Swartz, *Incantation,* 34, 71, 74–75).

11b καὶ ἐν τῇ Ἑλληνικῇ ὄνομα ἔχει Ἀπολλύων, "and in Greek he has the name Apollyon." The name "Apollyon" is a formation from the Greek verb ἀπολλύναι, "to destroy," and means "destroyer." In Aeschylus *Agamemnon* 1080–82, the name of the god Apollo is etymologically linked to the verb ἀπολλύναι, which appears to reflect a widespread ancient view (see Euripides *Phaethon* [frag. 781, lines 11–12]; Archilochus frag. 30D; Plato *Cratylus* 404D–E, 405E; Menander *Peric.* 440; Macrobius 1.17.9; see Fraenkel, *Aeschylus* 3:492). It is possible that an allusion to Nero is intended, for Nero, identified with Belial in some early Jewish literature, claimed a special relationship to Apollo (see Bell, *NTS* 25 [1978] 98–99). Commodian, a late third-century Christian poet, used the name Apollyon for the king of the Goths who had crossed the Danube and whose invasion had stopped the persecution of Christians by the emperor Decius (*Carmen apologeticum* 810–11; Martin, *Commodiani Carmina,* 102–3).

12 ἡ οὐαὶ ἡ μία ἀπῆλθεν· ἰδοὺ ἔρχεται ἔτι δύο οὐαὶ μετὰ ταῦτα, "The first disaster has occurred; behold, two more disasters will follow." This passage reminds the reader of the three "woes" or "disasters" announced earlier by the eagle in 8:13 and anticipates the parallel announcement of the accomplishment of the second woe and the imminent anticipation of the third woe in 11:14 (the accomplishment of the third woe is never mentioned in Revelation). There is, however, a striking difference between this passage (and 11:14) and 8:13. In 8:13 there is no indication that the interjection of mourning, οὐαί, is synonymous with a noun such as πληγή, "plague, misfortune." It appears likely that the author used the threefold repetition of the term οὐαί, "woe," secondarily as a structuring device to describe the plagues attendant on the sounding of the fifth (9:12) and sixth trumpets (11:14). This statement is abrupt in its function to conclude the vision segment that began in 9:1 with the blowing of the fifth trumpet. However, that the author resumes in v 17 the description of another aspect of the vision described in vv 1–11 suggests the presence of an editorial intrusion. οὐαί usually functions as an interjection; there are just two examples known to me of its use as a substantive outside Revelation: LXX Ezek 2:10, καὶ ἐγέγραπτο εἰς αὐτὴν θρῆνος καὶ μέλος καὶ οὐαί, "lamentation and mourning and woe are written in it" (where οὐαί translates the Hebrew masculine substantive הִי *hî*, a *hapax legomenon* in the OT; see BDB, 222), and LXX Ezek 7:26, οὐαὶ ἐπὶ οὐαὶ ἔσται, "there will be disaster upon disaster" (where οὐαί renders the Hebrew הוה *hôwâ*, an interjection without gender; BDB, 217). There is no obvious reason for the author to nominalize οὐαί in the feminine gender, which he treats as a neuter in view of the use of the third-person singular verb ἔρχεται (plural neuter nouns are regularly used as subjects of third-person singular verbs).

13 καὶ ὁ ἕκτος ἄγγελος ἐσάλπισεν, καὶ ἤκουσα φωνὴν μίαν ἐκ τῶν κεράτων τοῦ θυσιαστηρίου τοῦ χρυσοῦ τοῦ ἐνώπιον τοῦ θεοῦ, "Then the sixth angel sounded his trumpet, and I heard a voice from the corners of the golden altar of incense before God." The term θυσιαστήριον occurs eight times in Revelation, four of which refer to the heavenly counterpart of the Israelite *incense altar* (8:3[2x], 5; 9:13), and four to the heavenly counterpart of the *altar of burnt offerings* (6:9; 11:1; 14:18; 16:7). Since it is explicitly said that the golden altar is "before God," the voice from the four horns of the altar cannot be the voice of God. In 8:3–5 an angel functioning as a heavenly priest was depicted as standing by the golden altar, and it is possible that this unidentified voice could be his. However, it is probably best to read the text "literally" and assume that the altar "horn" or "corner" was endowed with speech that conveyed the divine will.

14 λέγοντα τῷ ἕκτῳ ἀγγέλῳ, ὁ ἔχων τὴν σάλπιγγα, λῦσον τοὺς τέσσαρας ἀγγέλους τοὺς δεδεμένους ἐπὶ τῷ ποταμῷ τῷ μεγάλῳ Εὐφράτῃ, "announcing to the sixth angel with the trumpet, 'Release the four angels bound at the great river Euphrates.'" This is the only instance in which one of the trumpet angels actively participates in the events that follow the blowing of the trumpet. The occurrence here of the antithetical verbs λύειν, "loose," and δεῖν, "bind," suggests that these are evil angels who have been restrained until an appointed day (Rev 20:2; Tob 3:17; 8:3), though how they have been bound is not specified. That the phrase "the four angels" is articular suggests either that it refers back to the four angels standing at the four corners of the earth in 7:1 (where the phrase is anarthrous) or that it refers to a group of four angels that the author assumes are familiar to his readers. Charles argues that they cannot be identified with the four angels of 7:1 since the only common element is their number (1:223, 250). There are two arguments for linking this group of four angels with that mentioned in 7:1: (1) The articular phrase τοὺς τέσσαρας ἀγγέλους in v 14b can be taken as anaphoric, referring back to the four angels introduced for the first time in 7:1. (2) While the four angels in 7:1 are described as restraining the four winds, they are never said to have released those winds, unless they are referred to in 9:14–15, where one could assume that they now fulfill their destructive task. (3) The two passages, 7:1–3 and 9:14–15, are functionally parallel in that the potential activity of each group of four angels is described but never accomplished. On the other hand, their location "standing at the four corners of the earth" (7:1) has no apparent connection with this group of four angels who are bound by the Euphrates, and these four angels are "bound" while the four in 7:1–3 are not.

Apart from Rev 7:1–3 and 9:14–15, no groups of four angels of *punishment* are known in Jewish apocalyptic literature (see *Comment* on 9:15b). Other groups of four angels that function quite differently are mentioned, however. There are occasional references to a group of four archangels: *1 Enoch* 9:1 (Syncellus) mentions οἱ τέσσαρες μεγάλοι ἀρχάγγελλοι, "the four great archangels," Michael, Ourael, Raphael, and Gabriel, while in the Ethiopic MS tradition of *1 Enoch* 20:1 they are simply named: Michael, Gabriel, Suriel, and Uriel. In *1 Enoch* 40:1–10 and 71:9–13, a group of four angels (differing somewhat in content and order from 20:1) is simply listed: Michael, Raphael, Gabriel, and Phanuel. A similar group of four is mentioned in 1QM 9:15–16—Michael, Gabriel, Sariel, and Raphael—and in *Apoc. Moses* 40:4—Michael, Gabriel, Uriel, and Raphael (the same list of four in this order occurs on a Jewish amulet; see Goodenough, *Jewish Symbols* 2:229; vol. 3, plate 1052). In an unrelated tradition, *3 Apoc. Bar.* 8:4 mentions four angels who daily take the crown of the sun to heaven for renewal. Ezekiel reports a vision of a group of six "men" (presumably angels; *b. Šabb.* 55a understands the "man" who marks people with the taw as Gabriel, and the group of six "men" are called "destroying angels") who kill all those not marked with a taw on their foreheads (Ezek 9:1–7), a passage alluded to in both Rev 7:3 and 9:4.

15a καὶ ἐλύθησαν οἱ τέσσαρες ἄγγελοι οἱ ἡτοιμασμένοι εἰς τὴν ὥραν καὶ ἡμέραν καὶ μῆνα καὶ ἐνιαυτόν, "Then the four angels who were prepared for the hour and the day and the month and the year were released." The phrase "the hour and the day and the month and the year" emphasizes the role God has predetermined for these angelic beings in the eschatological drama. While the sixth trumpet angel is directly commanded to release the four bound angels, their actual release is expressed through the passive verb ἐλύθησαν rather than an active form of λύειν, with the sixth angel as subject of the action, perhaps to emphasize their role as agents of the divine will.

15b ἵνα ἀποκτείνωσιν τὸ τρίτον τῶν ἀνθρώπων, "to kill a third of humanity." The role of these angels is clearly described through the purpose clause introduced with ἵνα, "in order that," as that of killing one-third of humanity. The phrase "the third part of humanity" is repeated in v 18. Because the author depicts the destruction of one-third of humanity here, it appears that he was forced to depart from his one-third destruction pattern in 8:11b, where it simply says that while one-third of the waters were poisoned, "many people" die. These are angels of punishment whose task it is to lead a demonic army to punish the people of the world. *1 Enoch* 66:1 mentioned "the angels of punishment who are prepared to come" and destroy humanity by the flood. Angels of punishment who act as agents of divine judgment on the earth are mentioned with some frequency in Jewish apocalyptic and in rabbinic literature (*1 Enoch* 53:3; 56:1; 62:11; 63:1; 66:1; *3 Enoch* 31:2; 32:1; 33:1; *b. Šabb.* 55a; 88a; cf. P. S. Alexander in Charlesworth, *OTP* 1:285 n. 31f; K. E. Grözinger, "Engel III," *TRE* 9:591; Michl, "Engel II," *RAC* 5:75–76). Though the reader is led to expect that the angels will directly carry out their mission of destruction, there is an abrupt transition to v 16, and the four angels are not mentioned again. It is possible, however, that the four angels represent four nations, for Dan 10:13, 20–21 mention angelic beings designated as the "prince of Persia" and the "prince of Greece," who are opposed only by Michael, the prince of Israel.

16a καὶ ὁ ἀριθμὸς τῶν στρατευμάτων τοῦ ἱππικοῦ δισμυριάδες μυριάδων, "The number of soldiers, or cavalry, was twice ten thousand times ten thousand." There is an apparent gap in the narrative (or the narrative logic) between v 15 and v 16, for there is no obvious connection between the four angels whose task it is to kill one-third of all humanity and the ravages of the enormous demonic cavalry described in vv 16–19 (Wellhausen, *Analyse,* 13), except the repetition of the phrase ἀποκτείνειν τὸ τρίτον τῶν ἀνθρώπων, "to kill one-third of humanity," in vv 15 and 18. It would perhaps make greater sense if the demonic army, rather than the four angels, were "bound at the Euphrates" (cf. 16:12–14), for the Euphrates marked the carefully guarded frontier between the Roman and the Parthian empires. Commentators often assume that the four angels act as instigators and leaders of the demonic cavalry, but this is not made at all explicit in the text in its present form. It is therefore quite possible that 9:14b–15 is a redactional modification of an earlier schema in which the angels explicitly functioned to incite the kings of the east to gather their armies and attack Israel. Just such a schema is reflected in *1 Enoch* 56:5–6 (Bousset [1906] 304; tr. Knibb, *Enoch*):

> And in those days the angels will gather together, and will throw themselves towards the east upon the Parthians and Medes; they will stir up the kings, so that a disturbing spirit will come upon them, and they will drive them from their thrones; and they will come out like lions from their lairs, and like hungry wolves in the middle of their flocks. And they will go up and trample upon the land of my chosen ones, and the land of my chosen ones will become before them a tramping-ground and a beaten track.

Just as the articular phrase "the four angels" in v 15a assumes that these angels are known to the readers (note the definite article in "the angels" in *1 Enoch* 56:5, quoted above), so the phrase τῶν στρατευμάτων, "the soldiers," is articular and therefore an entity the author assumes his readers recognize. Obviously, the author intends us to understand that these angels have been restraining the armies of various nations from devastating the civilized world. In 5:11 the author was apparently dependent on Dan 7:10 (μύριαι μυριάδες παρειστήκεισαν αὐτῷ, "ten thousand [times] ten thousands stood before him," though he avoids the numbers χίλιαι and μύριαι: μυριάδες μυριάδων καὶ χιλιάδες χιλιάδων, "ten thousands of ten thousands and thousands of thousands." Numbers compounded with χιλιάδες or μυριάδες can mean either (1) "*x* thousand" or "*x*-ty thousand," or (2) "thousands of," or "ten thousands of," while χίλιοι and μύριοι carry the meaning "one thousand" and "ten thousand," respectively (Mussies, *Morphology,* 223). The number διςχίλιας, "two thousand," occurs just once in the LXX in 1 Macc 9:4 (*var. lect.* MS A). Mussies (*Morphology*, 224–25) proposes that Rev 9:16 alludes to Ps 68:17 (MT 18), "With mighty chariotry, twice ten thousand [רבתים *ribbotayim*, a dual numeral], thousands upon thousands [אלפי שנאן *ʾalpê šinʾan*], the Lord came from Sinai into the holy place," suggesting that δισμυριάδες is a literal way of rendering the Hebrew dual form רבותים *ribbôtayim*. If this suggestion is correct, it means that the phrase δισμυριάδες μυριάδων should be translated not "twice ten thousands of ten thousands" but "ten thousand times tens of thousands." Further, the phrase should not be translated "two hundred million" or "one hundred million" (if the δίς is regarded as a mistranslation of the Hebrew dual), since the round number ten thousand implies a complete army.

This cavalry of two hundred million riders appears to be a demonic rather than a human army. Huge armies of destroying angels (though not this large) are twice mentioned in the Babylonian Talmud. In *b. Šabb.* 88a, it is said that 1.2 million angels of destruction punished the Israelites who sinned in the golden calf incident, and according to *b. Pesaḥ.* 112b, Igrath, the daughter of Mahalath, and 180 thousand angels of destruction go out every night (and previously they went out both day and night).

16b ἤκουσα τὸν ἀριθμὸν αὐτῶν, "(I heard their number)." This reads like an afterthought and is therefore placed in parentheses. A similar phrase is found in 7:4, where the author claims to have "heard the number" of those sealed, i.e., 144 thousand. The author knows the size of this gigantic army and must account for this knowledge by claiming in a gloss that this number was revealed to him (see *Comment* on 21:15).

17a καὶ οὕτως εἶδον τοὺς ἵππους ἐν τῇ ὁράσει καὶ τοὺς καθημένους ἐπ' αὐτῶν, ἔχοντας θώρακας πυρίνους καὶ ὑακινθίνους καὶ θειώδεις, "The horses and their riders I saw in my vision looked like this: they had breastplates which were fiery red and blue like hyacinth and yellow like sulfur." This reference to what the author saw in his vision is unique in Revelation, though relatively common in Daniel (7:1, 7, 13; 8:2, 15; 9:21), and appears to be an editorial comment intended to pick up the threads of the vision described in vv 7–11, which he has interrupted for some reason with the insertions found in v 12 and vv 13–16. He uses the term ὅρασις twice elsewhere (both times in 4:3) with the meaning "appearance." The colors of the breastplates of the cavalry soldiers (red, blue, and yellow) are correlated with the fire, smoke, and sulfur that proceed from the mouths of their mounts.

17b καὶ αἱ κεφαλαὶ τῶν ἵππων ὡς κεφαλαὶ λεόντων, "The heads of the horses were like the heads of lions." The description of these monsters is segmented in vv 17b–19, but they are a combination of three creatures, with the body of a horse, the head of a lion, and the tail of snake heads. The closest approximation to such a creature in antiquity is probably the Chimaera slain by the hero Bellerophon with the aid of Pegasus as described in Greek and Roman mythology. The Chimaera is consistently described as having the head of a lion, the tail of a dragon or serpent, and the body of a goat and belching fire (*Iliad* 6.181–82; Hesiod *Theog.* 319–24; Euripides *Ion* 203–4; *Electra* 474–75; Apollodorus 2.3.1; Lucretius *De rerum natura* 2.705; 5.905–7; Hyginus *Fabulae* 57.2). The extensive iconographic tradition is extremely consistent, depicting the Chimaera as a lion with the head of a goat coming from the top middle of its body, with a long snake's body and head for a tail (*LIMC* 3/1:249–69; 3/2:197–217). The similarity to the monster horses of 9:17–

19 is sufficiently close to suggest that the widely distributed depictions of the Chimaera may have served as a model for these trimorphic monsters.

17c καὶ ἐκ τῶν στομάτων αὐτῶν ἐκπορεύεται πῦρ καὶ καπνὸς καὶ θεῖον, "and from their mouths proceeded fire and smoke and sulfur." In a context that deals with an interpretation of the plagues of Egypt, Wis 11:18 mentions that God did *not* send bears or lions or unknown monsters to plague the Egyptians, "such as breathe out fiery breath, or belch forth a thick pall of smoke, or flash terrible sparks from their eyes." This may be connected with an isolated tradition concerning a fire-breathing Leviathan found in Job 41:19–21 (LXX 41:11–13):

> From its mouth go flaming torches; sparks of fire leap out. Out of its nostrils comes smoke, as from a boiling pot and burning rushes. Its breath kindles coals, and a flame comes out of its mouth.

Fire-breathing monsters are comparatively rare in Greco-Roman mythology, but far more common than in the Israelite-Jewish tradition. There are three main mythical monsters with this characteristic in Greco-Roman mythology: (1) The brazen-hooved bulls conquered by Jason in Colchis reportedly breathed fire from their nostrils (Pindar *Pyth.* 4.225; Apollodorus 1.9.23; Apollonius Rhodius 3.1302–5; Ovid *Metam.* 7.104–5; Vergil *Georgics* 2.140; however, in the iconographic tradition the bulls are never shown breathing fire; cf. *LIMC* 5/1:631–32; 5/2:427, plates 17–30). (2) Other mythological creatures occasionally described as breathing fire are the cannibalistic horses of Diomedes, conquered by Hercules (Euripides *Alcestis* 493; Lucretius *De rerum natura* 5.29), though this detail is more frequently omitted (Apollodorus 2.5.8; Diodorus Siculus 4.15.3), as it is in the iconographic tradition (*LIMC* 5/1:67–71; 5/2:81–82, plates 2414–54). (3) The Chimaera is described as belching fire (see above under *Comment* on v 17b). In addition, there is a giant boar depicted as having lightning flashing from its mouth and breath hot enough to scorch vegetation (Ovid *Metam.* 8.289), and there are occasional descriptions of horses that snort fire (Vergil *Georgics* 3.85; Silius Italicus 6.228; Nonnus *Dion.* 29.19).

Note the use of *inclusio* that characterizes vv 17b–18b and gives this passage a poetic flavor: v 17b, "from their mouths proceeded fire and smoke and sulfur"; v 18b, "from the fire and smoke and sulfur which proceeded from their mouths." This *inclusio* gives the passage a chiastic arrangement:

A [17b]from their mouths
B proceeded
C fire and smoke and sulfur
D [18a]From these three plagues a third of humanity was killed,
C´ [18b]from the fire and smoke and sulfur
B´ which proceeded
A´ from their mouths

18 ἀπὸ τῶν τριῶν πληγῶν τούτων ἀπεκτάνθησαν τὸ τρίτον τῶν ἀνθρώπων ἐκ τοῦ πυρὸς καὶ τοῦ καπνοῦ καὶ τοῦ θείου τοῦ ἐκπορευομένου ἐκ τῶν στομάτων αὐτῶν, "A third of humanity was killed by these three plagues, by the fire and the smoke and the sulfur which proceeded from their mouths." Fire, smoke, and sulfur are all mentioned in Philo's highly stylized account of God's destruction of Sodom and

Gomorrah (*Mos.* 2.55–58). The number "one-third" is used in *Sib. Or.* 3.544 of the survivors rather than the victims: "one-third of all mankind will survive" a plague of fire (see v 15). The motif of judgment of a city or a land by fire and brimstone is a fixed notion in the OT and early Judaism for which the destruction of Sodom and Gomorrah by fire and brimstone narrated in Gen 19:24 is prototypical (Deut 29:23; Ps 11:6; Ezek 38:22; Isa 30:33; 34:9; *Sib. Or.* 3.53–61, 689–92; Luke 17:29; *1 Clem.* 11:1). Fire and sulfur are frequently mentioned in Revelation as vehicles of divine judgment (9:17–18; 14:10; 19:20; 20:10; 21:8).

19a ἡ γὰρ ἐξουσία τῶν ἵππων ἐν τῷ στόματι αὐτῶν ἐστιν καὶ ἐν ταῖς οὐραῖς αὐτῶν, "For the power of the horses is in their mouths and in their tails." Since the lethal character of the mouths of the lion-headed horses has already been described in vv 17b–18, this phrase is meant to emphasize the lethal character of their tails as well and should probably be understood as "For the power of the horses is in their tails as well as in their mouths."

19b αἱ γὰρ οὐραὶ αὐτῶν ὅμοιαι ὄφεσιν, ἔχουσαι κεφαλὰς καὶ ἐν αὐταῖς ἀδικοῦσιν, "for their tails, which resemble snakes, have heads, and they inflict injury with them." On the mythical Greek monster the Chimaera, which was thought to have a snake's body and head for a tail, see *Comment* on v 17b.

20a καὶ οἱ λοιποὶ τῶν ἀνθρώπων, οἳ οὐκ ἀπεκτάνθησαν ἐν ταῖς πληγαῖς ταύταις, οὐδὲ μετενόησαν ἐκ τῶν ἔργων τῶν χειρῶν αὐτῶν, "The rest of humanity, those not killed by these plagues, did not repent of the products of their own manufacture." While it is possible that vv 20–21 are intended to form a conclusion to the entire series of six trumpet plagues in 8:7–9:19, the fact that the term "killed" is used here suggests that it is primarily a conclusion to the slaughter inflicted by the demonic army that composes the sixth trumpet plague. The motif of repentance appears here quite unexpectedly. Nowhere in the narrative of the seven trumpets (8:2–9:20; 15:15–18) is there any mention of the *purpose* of the trumpet plagues, whether as divine punishment for earlier transgressions or as attempts to "encourage" general repentance on the part of the people of the world. In fact, the motif of repentance occurs only rarely in Rev 4:1–22:5, and only in the context of a *negative* reaction to the eschatological punishments sent by God (9:20, 21; 16:9, 11). This repentance motif is a formal motif that has been derived by the author from the plague story in Exodus (Exod 7:13, 22; 8:15, 19, 32; 9:7, 12, 34–35; 10:1, 20; 11:9–10; 14:4), where it is couched in such a way that there is no doubt that a change of mind on the part of the pharaoh of Egypt was never considered a real possibility. In the parenesis of Rev 2–3, however, μετανοεῖν occurs eight times in contexts in which the Christian community is called upon to repent (2:5[2x], 16, 21[2x], 22; 3:3, 19; see *Comment* on 2:5).

The phrase τὰ ἔργα τῶν χειρῶν αὐτῶν, "the works of their hands" or "the products of their own manufacture," is a stereotypical Semitic phrase that often refers to idols as lifeless, impotent, manufactured objects (Deut 31:29; 1 Kgs 16:7; 2 Kgs 22:17; 2 Chr 34:25; Isa 2:8; 17:8; Jer 1:16; 25:6–7; 32:30; Mic 5:13; Acts 7:41; Justin *1 Apol.* 20.5; *Dial.* 35.6). This meaning is clear in Ps 115:4 (LXX 113:2; with a doublet in Ps 135:15[LXX 134:15]): "Their idols are silver and gold, the work of human hands." The equivalent Greek term χειροποίητος, "handmade, artificial," is occasionally used for idols also (*Sib. Or.* 3.606, 722; 4.28a; Justin *1 Apol.* 58.3; *Dial.* 35.6; Athenagoras *Leg.* 17.3). The phrase "the works of their hands" can also be used of people's deeds (Pss 28:4; 90:17; Isa 65:22; *1 Enoch* 100:9; *Pss. Sol.* 4:16; 6:2;

9:4; 16:9) or of the creative work of God (Pss 8:6; 19:1; 138:8; 142:5; Isa 45:11; 60:21; *Adam and Eve* 33:5; *Pss. Sol.* 18:1; *Gk. Apoc. Ezra* 1:10).

20b ἵνα μὴ προσκυνήσουσιν τὰ δαιμόνια καὶ τὰ εἴδωλα τὰ χρυσᾶ καὶ τὰ ἀργυρᾶ καὶ τὰ χαλκᾶ καὶ τὰ λίθινα καὶ τὰ ξύλινα, "that is, they did not cease to worship the demons, or idols, made of gold and silver and bronze and stone and wood." Vv 20–21 constitute a kind of vice catalog (there are three other such catalogs in 21:8, 27; 22:15). The ἵνα clause here functions as a result clause; i.e., they did not repent *with the result that* they might no longer worship idols.

The term δαιμόνιον, a faded diminutive form of δαίμων (the latter occurs only once in the NT in Matt 8:31), occurs three times in Revelation (9:20; 16:14; 18:2). Charles (1:254) observes that this text "carefully distinguishes demons and idols." But is that so? It is probable that καί here is epexegetical or explanatory and that the phrase should be translated "that they might not worship demons, *that is,* idols" (see Theophilus *Ad Autolycum* 1.10, where he says of the Olympians, "For they are not gods, but idols [εἴδωλα] . . . and [that is,] unclean demons [καὶ δαιμόνια ἀκάθαρτα]"). How are demons worshiped? In 1 Cor 10:19–20, Paul says that idols are nothing (cf. 1 Cor 8:4, 11), but that pagans actually offer sacrifices to *demons* and not to gods (a notion probably derived from Deut 32:17). There was a conviction expressed several places in the OT that pagan gods are really demons (Deut 32:17, ἔθυσαν δαιμονίοις καὶ οὐ θεῷ, "they sacrifice to demons and not to God"; see Ps 95:5, πάντες οἱ θεοὶ τῶν ἐθνῶν δαιμόνια, "all the gods of the nations are demons" [a passage quoted by Trypho in Justin *Dial.* 55.2]; Ps 105:37 [LXX 106:37]), a view that persisted in early Judaism (*Jub.* 1:11; 11:4–6; 22:17; *1 Enoch* 19:1; 99:7; *T. Judah* 23:1). The early Christian apologists were similarly convinced that the "gods" were really evil demons (Justin *1 Apol.* 5.2; 9.1; Tatian *Oratio* 8.1–4; 12.4; Tertullian *De spect.* 9; *Apol.* 23.4; *De idol.* 4; 15.5; *De test. an.* 2; *Ad Scap.* 2; Clement of Alex. *Protrepticus* 2; *Strom.* 6.3). Celsus thought that people should pray and sacrifice to idols even if they are daimons (Origen *Contra Celsum* 8.24). Of course for Celsus, as well as for the Greeks generally, the term "demon" or "daimon" was simply a term for a minor type of deity. Some Greeks identified some of the gods of Greek mythology with daimons, a term used nonpejoratively (Plutarch *De def. orac.* 421C–E; see Brenk, *In Mist Apparelled,* 85–112). Origen thought that some cult statues were inhabited by daimons (*Contra Celsum* 8.41). The notion of worshiping demons is mentioned in Tatian *Oratio* 16.2. In *Acts of Bartholomew* 6 (Lipsius-Bonnet, *AAA* 2/1:142), a demon conveniently confesses, "We are worshiped [προσκυνούμεθα] by them [i.e., 'pagans'] as gods, but we are actually demons" (on this motif, see Pohlenz, *Zorne,* 140ff.). In the late Greco-Roman period, there was a widespread belief that demons fed on sacrifices (1 Cor 10:20; Philo *Decal.* 74; Porphyry *De abst.* 11, 42; Oenomaus in Eusebius *Praep. evang.* 5.21.5 [213b]; Origen *Contra Celsum* 3.28; 7.6; see *Iliad* 4.49; 9.500; 24.70), in continuity with the ancient belief that the gods were nourished by sacrifices.

Jewish and Christian denunciations of idolatry frequently include a list of the materials out of which pagan deities were constructed (e.g., gold, silver, bronze, iron, wood, stone, clay), with the implication that this is incompatible with the belief that they are living beings (Hab 2:18–19; Dan 5:23; Ps 115:4–6; 3 Macc 4:16; 2 Macc 2:3; Wis 15:8–9; Ep Jer 8–9, 30, 50, 57, 70; Acts 17:29; 4QPrNab; 4Q*267* = 4QD[b] 17 ii 8–9; 4Q*268* = 4QD[c] 1 ii 8–9; 4Q*270* = 4QD[e] frag. 7, lines 20–21).

Surprisingly, in Revelation the general denunciation of pagan idolatry occurs only here and as part of a vice list in 22:15, though *specific* forms of idolatry are mentioned, such as eating meat sacrificed to idols, a problem within the Christian communities (2:14, 20), and the worship of the dragon, the beast, or his image, an issue involving people generally (13:4, 14–15; 14:9, 11; 16:2; 19:20; 20:4). Denunciations of idolatry occur frequently in the OT, where the influences of pagan worship within the land or people of Israel are regarded as a threat to the worship of Yahweh. In Hellenistic Jewish literature, particularly in apologetic contexts in which Jewish monotheism is being defended, idolatry was frequently derided as foolish and ridiculous (Philo *Spec. Leg.* 1.28; *Leg.* 139, 290; *Decal.* 72–79; Ps.-Aristeas *Ep.* 134–39; Jos. *Ant.* 19.290). The LXX translation of Exod 22:28 was very influential in the toleration of pagan worship advocated by some Hellenistic Jews. While the translation of Exod 22:28[MT and LXX 27] reads "You shall not revile God [אֱלֹהִים *ʾĕlōhîm*]," the LXX reads θεοὺς οὐ κακολογήσεις, "You shall not revile the *gods.*" This reading is cited several times in Philo and Josephus, where it was interpreted to mean that it was all right for Gentiles to worship pagan gods (Philo *Spec. Leg.* 1.53; *Mos.* 2.203–5; *Quaest. in Exod.* 2.5; Jos. *Ant.* 4.207; *Ag. Ap.* 2.236–37; see Le Boulluec-Sandevoir, *L'Exode,* 230–31; Delling, *Klio* 43–45 [1965] 263–69). However, only occasionally were Jewish writers concerned that Gentiles give up their own forms of worship in contexts in which Jews were unaffected (M. Goodman, *Proselytizing,* 40–59). Those few sources that sharply denounce pagan forms of worship generally (Wis 13–15; *Sib. Or.* 3.545–72, 601–7; Rom 1:18–23), often linking such worship with divine punishment, presuppose a universal eschatology in which all people will abandon their traditional forms of worship and turn to the worship of the true God (Tob 4:6; Philo *Mos.* 2.44; see *Comments* on 21:24–26). Therefore, the general denunciation of idolatry in Rev 9:20 and 22:15 is one aspect of the author's Christian universalism (for other aspects, see *Comments* on 14:6–7).

There was clear Jewish antagonism to idolatry in Palestine (1 Macc 2:23–28; Jos. *Ant.* 12.344; *Ag. Ap.* 1.193), and there is some evidence that when a Jewish community was relatively strong they might attack pagan shrines (1 Macc 5:68; 10:84; Jos. *Ag. Ap.* 1.248–50; cf. Bel 1:1–22). One basis for a Jewish denunciation of pagan idolatry was presumably the tradition of the "Noachic laws," which Jews believed were incumbent on all Gentiles, who, like the Jews, were descendants of Noah (they may be reflected in Acts 15:19–21, 28–29). The earliest form of these laws occurs in a section of the Tosepta called *ʿAboda Zara,* "alien worship," where seven Noachic requirements are discussed: (1) setting up courts of justice, (2) idolatry, (3) blasphemy, (4) fornication, (5) bloodshed, (6) thievery, and (7) limbs cut from living animals (*t. ʿAbod. Zar.* 8.4–6). However, there are other strands of Hellenistic Judaism that, though they might denounce gentile homosexuality, are soft on idolatry (*Testament of Abraham;* Ps.-Phocylides *Sententiae;* see Goodman, *Proselytizing,* 54). Prophetic critiques of idolatry are particularly frequent in Deutero-Isaiah, reflecting internal conflicts in the post-exilic Jewish community (Isa 40:18–20; 42:17; 44:9–20; 45:16, 20; cf. Jer 10:1–16; Ps 115:3–8).

Antagonism to idolatry is also expressed in the NT (1 Cor 14:15), and critiques of idolatry (often borrowing from Hellenistic Jewish apologetic) are also found among the early Christian apologists (Tatian *Oratio* 4.2; Theophilus *Ad Autolycum* 1.9–10; 2.2). Celsus charged that Christians cannot bear to see temples, altars, and images (Origen *Contra Cels.* 7.62). It is important to recognize that there was also a critique of "idolatry" expressed by Hellenistic intellectuals (Ps.-Heraclitus *Ep.* 4.; see H. W. Attridge, *First-Century Cynicism in the Epistles of Heraclitus,* HTS 29 [Missoula, MT: Scholars, 1976] 13–23, where there are a number of references to ancient sources). Plutarch (*De Iside* 379C–D) observes that some Greeks speak of the bronze, painted, and stone effigies as *gods,* rather than as *statues* (ἀγάλματα) of the gods, which is what they really are (see Acts 19:26; cf. v 23). Zeno, the founder of Stoicism, reportedly thought that the making of temples and images was unnecessary, for such human products are not worthy of the gods (von Arnim, *SVF* vol. 1, frag. 264 [quoted in Clement Alex. *Strom.* 5.12.76]).

20c ἃ οὔτε βλέπειν δύνανται οὔτε ἀκούειν οὔτε περιπατεῖν, "which can neither see nor hear nor walk." Probably an allusion to Ps 115:4–7:

> Their idols are silver and gold,
> the work of men's hands.
> They have mouths, but do not speak;
> eyes, but do not see.
> They have ears, but do not hear;
> noses, but do not smell.
> They have hands, but do not feel;
> feet, but do not walk;
> And they do not make a sound in their throat. (RSV)

Ps 115:4–6 may also be alluded to in this statement from an Aramaic incantation bowl (Naveh-Shaked, *Amulet,* bowl 6, line 4): "In the same way as you have eyes but do not see, as you have ears but do not hear, so shall you give me a stone from you to silence from me." Jewish and Christian critiques of idolatry often mention that pagan images lack the sense perceptions of living beings (Dan 5:23; 3 Macc 4:16; Wis 15:15; Ep Jer 8–9; Sir 30:19; 1 Cor 12:1).

21 καὶ οὐ μετενόησαν ἐκ τῶν φόνων αὐτῶν οὔτε ἐκ τῶν φαρμάκων αὐτῶν οὔτε ἐκ τῆς πορνείας αὐτῶν οὔτε ἐκ τῶν κλεμμάτων αὐτῶν, "and they did not repent of their murders nor of their sorcery nor of their immorality nor of their thefts." On the theme of repentance, see *Comment* on v 20. The mention of murder, immorality, and theft reflects concerns of the fifth, sixth, and seventh commandments of the Decalogue (Exod 20:13–15; Deut 5:17–19); the same three vices are mentioned in Rom 13:9 (together with covetousness) and also occur in the longer vice list in Mark 7:21–22. The term φάρμακον occurs only here in 9:21, while φαρμακεία, "sorcery," occurs in 18:23, and the cognate noun φάρμακος, "sorcerer," occurs twice in the plural in the other two vice lists in Revelation (21:8; 22:15). These φαρμακ- cognates all occur in lists, with the exception of 18:23. While φάρμακον can mean medicine, in pejorative contexts such as this it means either "poison" (Jos. *Ant.* 15.89; *J.W.* 1.581–83; cf. *PGM* VIII.33; note the close proximity of the terms φόνος, "murder," here in 9:21, and φονεύς, "murderer," in 21:8; 22:15) or "magical spell" (Jos. *J.W.* 1.571; POxy III.472; *PGM* IV.2176; VIII.33; XIII.253). The practice of magic was widespread in the ancient world and was particularly prevalent in Asia Minor and Egypt. Modern anthropologists, following E. E. Evans-Pritchard, have distinguished between *sorcery,* which manipulates magical techniques and substances, and *witchcraft,* which is an inborn quality in which adepts use hereditary psychophysical skills to attain their objectives *(Witchcraft, Oracles and Magic among the*

Azande [Oxford: Clarendon, 1976] 63–64, 176; see L. Mair, *Witchcraft* [New York; Toronto: McGraw-Hill, 1969] 7–32). The term βασκαίνειν, "to bewitch," connected with the evil eye in the LXX and Greek literature and used by Paul in Gal 3:1, fits this definition of witchcraft (see J. Neyrey, "Bewitched in Galatia: Paul and Cultural Anthropology," *CBQ* 50 [1988] 72–75).

The term πορνεία is a generic term for various forms of "sexual immorality," including homosexuality (Balsdon, *Romans,* 225–27).

A synoptic comparison of the three vice lists in Revelation is instructive:

Rev 9:20–21	*Rev 21:8*	*Rev 22:15*
[εἰδωλολατρία] [idolatry]	δειλοί cowards	
	ἄπιστοι unfaithful	
	ἐβδελυγμένοι abominable	κύνες dogs
φόνοι murders	φονεῖς murderers	φάρμακοι magicians
φάρμακα sorcery	πόρνοι immoral	πόρνοι fornicators
πορνεία immorality	φάρμακοι sorcerers	φονεῖς murderers
κλέμματα thefts	εἰδωλολάτραι idolaters	εἰδωλολάτραι idolaters
	πάντες οἱ ψευδεῖς all liars	πᾶς φιλῶν καὶ ποιῶν ψεῦδος everyone who both loves and practices lying

Explanation

The series of seven trumpet plagues narrated in 8:7–9:21 and 11:15–18 is introduced with a scene in the heavenly temple in 8:2–5, like the prelude to the seven seals in 4:1–5:14 and the prelude to the seven bowls in 15:1–8. The seven trumpet plagues, like the seven seals, exhibit a 4 + 3 structure, with the first four characterized by a succinct, tight structure (8:7–12) and the last three unified through identification with the structure of the three woes announced by the eagle in 8:13 (cf. 9:14; 11:12). Although the people of the earth afflicted by the seven trumpet plagues reportedly do not repent (9:20–21), the purpose of the plagues is not to elicit repentance but to exact punishment. The report of failure to repent is derived from a recurring motif found in Exod 7–14.

In the opening scene in the heavenly temple (8:2–5), an angel stands at the heavenly altar before the throne of God, where the prayers of Christians (probably offered for deliverance and justice) are like smoke mingled with incense, which rises up before God. The substitution or equation of prayer with sacrifice is a very ancient one and emphasized in Judaism since the cessation of animal sacrifices accompanying the destruction of the last two Jewish temples, the main one in Jerusalem in A.D. 70 and the schismatic temple of Onias in Leontopolis, Egypt, in A.D. 73. The censer filled with fire from the altar, which the angel casts down to the earth, symbolizes the punishment of humanity that will follow the blowing of each of the trumpets.

Like the seal plagues, the trumpet plagues exhibit a preliminary character in that the divine punishments narrated affect only *one-third* of the specified parts of the world (8:7–12), while two-thirds of the cosmos and its inhabitants survive until a final round of tribulations effected by the seven bowls. The parallels between Exod 7:8–13:16 (the ten Exodus plagues) and Rev 8:1–11:19 and 15:1–16:21 indicate that Exodus provided the model for the author's vision of the eschatological punishments inflicted by God on the unbelieving inhabitants of the world. There is also evidence in the OT for a seven-plague Exodus tradition in Ps 78:43–52, Ps 105:27–36, and Amos 4:6–13, and it appears that the Exodus account of *ten* plagues is a combination of the Yahwistic (J) account of *seven* plagues with the Priestly (P) account, which had *ten* plagues, thus providing a precedent for John's preference for the climactic symbolism of *seven* plagues. The use of seven *trumpets* had significance in both Greco-Roman and Israelite-Jewish tradition, for in the Greco-Roman world the mysterious sound of the trumpet could be a prodigy signaling a disruption in divine-human relations, while in Judaism trumpets were used to signal the beginning of battle.

In the *first* trumpet plague, hail, fire, and blood fall, burning up one-third of the earth (8:7, similar to the seventh plague of Exod 9:22–26 and the fourth and seventh bowl plagues in Rev 16:8–9, 19–21). A rain of blood would be considered a prodigy in the Greco-Roman world, indicating the anger of the gods. In the *second* trumpet plague, a great mountain is thrown into the sea, which becomes blood, resulting in the destruction of one-third of sea creatures and ships (8:8–9, similar to the first plague of Exod 7:20–21 and the second bowl plague of Rev 16:3). In the *third* trumpet plague, a star named Wormwood or Apsinthos (named for its poisonous effects since no actual star had that name) falls on a third of the rivers and springs, poisoning them (8:10–11, a plague with no model in Exod 7–12 or parallel in Rev 15–16). In the *fourth* trumpet plague, one-third of the sun, moon, and stars become darkened (8:12, like the ninth plague of Exod 10:21 and the fifth bowl plague of Rev 16:10).

The last three trumpet plagues form a group of three "woes" announced by an eagle in 8:13. It is likely that the author began with an apocalyptic tradition of three woes, which he expanded into a heptad of trumpets. The *fifth* trumpet plague produces the vision of a star that falls to earth (certainly an angelic messenger, less probably Satan; cf. 12:9), which releases from the bottomless pit a plague of locusts who harm only those lacking God's seal (9:1–12, modeled after the eighth plague of locusts in Exod 10:4–20 and the locust metaphor of Joel 2:1–14). This is a demonic army with the angel of the abyss, named Abaddon or Apollyon, as its king (9:11). While the demonic locusts are not permitted by God to kill people, they torment them with their painful sting for a limited period of five months. The *sixth* trumpet plague releases the four angels bound at the Euphrates River (perhaps symbolizing four nations), who in turn lead a huge demonic cavalry of two hundred million riders who kill one-third of humankind (9:13–19, a plague with no counterpart in the Exodus tradition). The *seventh* trumpet is delayed until 11:15–18.

3. The Angel and the Little Scroll (10:1–11)

Bibliography

Barr, J. *Biblical Words for Time.* London: SCM, 1962. **Bauckham, R.** "The Conversion of the Nations." In Bauckham, *Climax.* 238–337. **Bergmeier, R.** "Die Buchrolle und das Lamm (Apk 5 und 10)." *ZNW* 76 (1985) 225–42. **Birt, T.** *Die Buchrolle in der Kunst: Archäologisch-antiquarische Untersuchungen zum antiken Buchwesen.* Leipzig: Teubner, 1907. **Cullmann, O.** *Christ and Time.* Tr. F. V. Filson. Philadelphia: Westminster, 1950. **Day, J.** "Echoes of Baal's Seven Thunders and Lightnings in Psalm XXIX and Habakkuk III 9 and the Identity of the Seraphim in Isaiah VI." *VT* 29 (1979) 143–51. **Delcor, M.** "Les attaches littéraires, l'origine et la signification de l'expression biblique 'Prendre à témoin le ciel et la terre.'" *VT* 16 (1966) 8–25. **Elliott, K.** "Nouns with Diminutive Endings in the New Testament." *NovT* 12 (1970) 391–98. **Feuillet, A.** "Le chapitre X de l'Apocalypse, son apport dans la solution du probleme eschatologique." In *Sacra Pagina,* ed. J. Coppens, A. Descamps, and E. Massaux. BETL 12–13. Gembloux: Duculot, 1959. 414–29. **Fontenrose, J.** *Didyma: Apollo's Oracle, Cult, and Companions.* Berkeley: University of California, 1988. **Giblin, C. H.** "Revelation 11.1–13: Its Form, Function and Contextual Integration." *NTS* 30 (1984) 433–59. **Hirzel, R.** *Der Eid.* Leipzig: Hirzel, 1902. **Horn, F. W.** "Die sieben Donner: Erwägungen zu Offb 10." *SNTU* 17 (1992) 215–29. **Jeremias, Joachim.** *Jesu Verheissung für die Völker.* 2nd ed. Stuttgart, 1956 (ET: *Jesus' Promise to the Nations.* SBT 24. Rev. ed. London: SCM, 1967). **Koep, L.** *Das himmlische Buch in Antike und Christentum: Eine religionsgeschichtliche Untersuchung zur altchristlichen Bildersprache.* Bonn: Hanstein, 1952. **Koester, H.** *Ancient Christian Gospels: Their History and Development.* Philadelphia: Trinity, 1990. **Kreuzer, S.** *Der lebendige Gott: Bedeutung, Herkunft und Entwicklung einer alttestamentlichen Gottesbezeichnung.* Stuttgart: Kohlhammer, 1983. **Lührmann, D.** *Die Offenbarungsverständnis des Paulus und in paulinischen Gemeinden.* Neukirchen: Neukirchener, 1965. **Lust, J.** "For I lift up my hand to heaven and swear: Deut 32:40." In *Studies in Deuteronomy.* FS C. J. Labuschagne, ed. F. García Martínez, A. Hilhorst, J. T. A. G. M. van Reuiten, and A. S. van der Woude. VTSup 53. Leiden: Brill, 1994. 155–64. **Michael, J. H.** "The Unrecorded Thunder-Voices (Apoc 10:3)." *ExpTim* 36 (1924–25) 424–27. **Mussies, G.** "Identification and Self-Identification of the Gods." In *Knowledge of God in the Graeco-Roman World,* ed. R. van den Broek, T. Baara, and J. Mansfeld. EPRO 112. Leiden: Brill, 1988. 1–18. **Newport, K. G. C.** "Semitic Influence on Revelation." *BT* 37 (1986) 328–34. **Rowland, C.** "A Man Clothed in Linen: Daniel 10.6ff. and Jewish Angelology." *JSNT* 24 (1985) 99–110. **Schaik, A. P. Van.** "Ἄλλος ἄγγελος in Apk 14." In *L'Apocalypse,* ed. J. Lambrecht. 217–28. **Stadelmann, L. I.** *The Hebrew Conception of the World.* AnBib 39. Rome: Biblical Institute, 1970. **Stuhlmacher, P.** *Das paulinische Evangelium.* Vol. 1: *Vorgeschichte.* FRLANT 95. Göttingen: Vandenhoeck & Ruprecht, 1968. **Swanson, D. C.** "Diminutives in the Greek New Testament." *JBL* 77 (1958) 134–51. **Wilcox, M. F.** *The Semitisms of Acts.* Oxford: Clarendon, 1965.

Translation

[1]Then I saw another[a] mighty angel descending from heaven, wrapped in a cloud with a[b] halo[c] on his head,[d] and his face was like the sun and his legs[e] like fiery columns. [2]He[a] held[b] a small open[c] scroll[d] in his hand. He placed his right[e] foot on the sea but his left on the land. [3]Then he cried with a loud voice like a roaring[a] lion. And when he cried out, the[b] seven[c] thunders[d] uttered[e] their own sounds.[e] [4][a]When[b] the seven[c] thunders[d] spoke, [e]I was about to[e] write it down when I heard a voice[f] from heaven saying:[g] "Conceal[h] the message[i] of the seven[j] thunders; [k]don't even think about writing[l] it[m] down!"[k] [5]Then the angel, whom I saw standing on the sea and on the land, raised[a] his [b]right [c]hand[b] to heaven [6]and swore[a] an oath by[b] the One who lives for ever, who created heaven [c]and what is in it,[c] [d]the earth and what is in it,[d] [e]and the sea and what is in it:[e] [f]"There will be no more interval of time, [7]but in the days of the sound of [a]the seventh angel,[a] when he will sound the trumpet, then[b] the [c]secret plan[c] of God will have been fulfilled,[d] as he announced[e] [f]to his servants,[g] the prophets."[f] [8][ab]The[c] voice,[d] which I heard from heaven, again spoke[e] to me[f] and said,[ga] "Go, take the little scroll[h] [i]which lies open[i] in the hand of the angel standing on the sea and on the land." [9]I then went[a] to the angel and asked him [b]to give[b] me the scroll.[c] He said to me, "Take it [d]and eat it,[d] and though it will irritate[e] your[f] stomach,[g] it will be sweet as honey in your mouth." [10]Then I took the scroll[a] from the hand[b] of the angel and tasted[c] it, and it was sweet as honey in my mouth, and when [d]I swallowed it, my stomach[e] became irritated.[d] [11]Then [a]I was told,[a] "You[b] must again prophesy against[c] peoples and [d]nations and languages and many kings."[e]

Notes

1.a. Variants: (1) ἄλλον] A C Andreas Tyc$^{1\ 2}$ [*alium angelum*]; Tyc^{3} [*alterum angelum*]; Primasius [*alterum angelum; var. lect.: alium angelum*]; Beatus [*alium angelum*]; Cassiodorus [*alium angelum*]; it^{gig} [*alium angelum*]. (2) omit ἄλλον] 025 046 Oecumenius^{2053} fam 1006^{911} Andr a c f i 94; Byzantine Victorinus. Reading (2) is a correction of the text, since there is no obvious previous angel to which the adj. ἄλλος could refer (a similar textual problem occurs in 14:6).

1.b. Though not translated, ἡ ἶρις, "*the* halo," is articular, perhaps because an ἶρις was previously mentioned in 4:3; the article is therefore anaphoric. Yet since no two rainbows are really the same, the presence of the article is the *lectio difficilior* and the preferred reading (Schmid, *Studien* 2:194–95). Variants: (1) ἡ before ἶρις] A C fam 1006 fam 1611$^{1611\ 1854\ 2329}$. (2) omit ἡ] ℵ^{1} Oecumenius^{2053} Andreas. (3) ἡ θρίξ for ἡ ἶρις] ℵ*.

1.c. ἡ ἶρις is a nom. sing. introduced abruptly after a series of accs. governed by εἶδον. The term ἡ ἶρις, "halo," is found only here and in Rev 4:3 in the NT. It can mean a "circle of light," whether colored or not, and so can be translated "rainbow" (as in 4:3) or "halo" (Louw-Nida, § 1.38).

1.d. Variants: (1) ἐπὶ τὴν κεφαλήν] A C Byz 19^{2075} WHort; B. Weiss, *Johannes-Apokalypse,* 183. (2) ἐπὶ τῆς κεφαλῆς] 𝔓^{47} ℵ Andreas Byzantine; von Soden, *Text;* Merk, *NT;* Nestle-Aland^{27}; UBSGNT^{4}. While B. Weiss claims that reading (1) conforms to the style of Revelation (*Johannes-Apokalypse,* 106), the phrase ἐπὶ τῆς κεφαλῆς in a textually secure passage occurs only in 12:1; 14:14, while ἐπὶ τὰς κεφαλάς occurs in 4:4; 9:7; 13:1; 18:19; ἐπὶ τὴν κεφαλήν occurs in 19:12. The evidence is therefore mixed, and it appears that the author used ἐπί with the gen. and the acc. indiscriminately.

1.e. The term "legs" is used here to translate οἱ πόδες, lit. "the feet" (with RSV, NRSV, REB, NIV; cf. Bratcher-Hatton, *Revelation,* 156; Kraft, 147), since it makes little sense to describe "feet" rather than "legs" as fiery *columns.* Charles made the attractive suggestion that πόδες is a Hebraism, since the Heb. term רֶגֶל *regel* can mean "leg" (cf. 1 Sam 17:6 [רַגְלָיו *raglāyw* = "his legs" is translated τῶν σκελῶν αὐτοῦ = "his legs"]; Ezek 1:7 [וְרַגְלֵיהֶם *wĕraglêhem* = "and their legs" is translated καὶ τὰ σκέλη αὐτῶν = "and their legs"]), as well as "foot" (cf. Ezek 16:25); see Charles, 1:cxlvii, 259–60; Lohmeyer, 84; Turner, *Syntax,* 154; KB^{3}, 1105–7. MacKenzie's attempt to refute this proposal by claiming that flames from the foot would travel upward giving the legs the appearance of pillars is ludicrous (R. K. MacKenzie, *The Author of the Apocalypse* [Lewiston: Mellen Biblical Press, 1997] 144–45). There are occurrences of πούς, "foot," in Gk. texts written by native speakers in which the meaning must be "leg" (Lucian *Zeuxis* 4; Achilles Tatius 1.1.10; see BAGD, 696; MM, 531–32).

2.a. The καί, "and," with which this sentence begins has not been translated since it lacks semantic value and functions as a discourse marker indicating the beginning of a new clause or sentence (Louw-Nida, 1:vi).

2.b. The present masc. nom. ptcp. ἔχων, "held" (here the ptcp. functions as a finite verb, which is translated as a past tense in conformity with Eng. usage), is a solecism since it should modify the noun phrase ἄλλον ἄγγελον ἰσχυρόν, "another mighty angel" (and therefore be the masc. sing. *acc.* ptcp. ἔχοντα). Here ἔχων is a nom. of apposition. Variants: (1) εἶχεν] Andreas latt (Victorinus Tyc^{1} Tyc^{3} Beatus it^{gig} (*habebat*). (2) omit καὶ ἔχων . . . ἠνεῳγμένον] Tyc^{2}.

2.c. Variants: (1) ἠνεῳγμένον] *lectio originalis.* (2) ἀνεῳγμένον] 2351 Andr e f^{2023} h^{-2060} i 194 1773 2019 Byzantine. (3) omit] A cop^{bo}.

2.d. Variants: (1) βιβλαρίδιον] ℵ* A C^{2} 025 1 2351 Andr a b c d e f^{-2023} 94 2351. (2) βίβλιον] 𝔓^{47} Byzantine it^{gig} vg^{mss} Victorinus Tyconius Primasius. (3) βιβλιδάριον] C* fam 1006 fam 1611$^{1611\ 2344}$ Oecumenius^{2053} Andreas. (4) βιβλάριον] fam 1611^{2329}. The reading that is probably original, βιβλαρίδιον, "small scroll," is a true diminutive (which occurs three times, here and in vv 9, 10), and for each occurrence the variant βιβλιδάριον occurs. A morphological study of diminutive suffixes shows that -ιον = -ίδιον = -άριον = -ίσκος; i.e., these suffixes are semantically identical. Swete (127) and Charles (1:260) are, therefore, incorrect in proposing that βιβλαρίδιον is a diminutive of βιβλάριον. These two variants show that a sequence of three morphemes is involved: -αρ-ιδ-ιον, and -ιδ-αρ-ιον. Swanson has demonstrated that the suffix -ιδαριον is almost entirely classical in attestation, while -αριδιον is almost entirely post-classical (βιβλαρίδιον is attested in two second-century A.D. authors, Hermas *Vis.* 2.1.3 [MS A reads βιβλιδάριον]; 2.4.3, where MS A reads βιβλιδάρια for βιβλαρίδια [for the textual evidence, see the critical edition by M. Whittaker, ed., *Der Hirt des Hermas* (Berlin: Akademie, 1967)], and Galen 16.5). Using this linguistic criterion, then, βιβλαρίδιον must be the original reading with βιβλιδάριον as a scholarly alternative that would have been archaic in the Christian era (Swanson, *JBL* 77 [1958] 144–45).

2.e. Variant: omit τὸν δεξιόν] C.

3.a. Variants: (1) μοίκαται] C. (2) μοικώμενος] fam 1611^{2329} Primasius (*rugiens*); eth. (3) μυκόμενος] Byz 17^{93}; Beatus^{mss} (*fremens;* Lo Bue, *Tyconius,* 129n.). (4) μύκατε] ℵ*.

3.b. Variants: (1) αἱ ἑπτά] ℵ^{1} Andreas. (2) omit αἱ] ℵ* Andr a b d 94. (3) omit αἱ ἑπτά] Andr i$^{1876\ 2043\ 2082}$.

3.c. Variant: omit ἑπτά] 𝔓^{47}.

3.d. Variant: φωναί for βρονταί] ℵ*.

3.e-e. Variants: (1) ταῖς ἑαυτῶν φωναῖς] ℵ fam 1611^{2329} Andr/Byz 2a$^{104\ 459\ 922}$ Andr/Byz 3^{2196} it^{gig} arm. (2) omit ταῖς ἑαυτῶν φωναῖς] Primasius.

4.a. See *Note* 2.a.

4.b. Variant: (1) ὅτε] A C 025 046 fam 1006^{1006} fam 1611$^{1611\ 1854\ 2344}$ Oecumenius^{2053}. (2) ὅσα] 𝔓^{47} ℵ it^{gig} cop$^{sa\ bo}$ Andr i^{-2042} Tyc^{1} Primasius Beatus. Possibly an "exegetical modification" (*TCGNT*^{1}, 742–43; *TCGNT*^{2}, 670).

4.c. Variant: omit ἑπτά] 𝔓^{47}, a singular reading; see *Note* 4.j.

4.d. Variant: after βρονταί, 𝔓^{47} adds τὰς ἑαυτῶν φωνὰς καὶ ἤκουσα ὅσα ἐλάλησαν αἱ βρονταὶ καί, "their voices and I heard what the thunders said and." Singular reading.

4.e-e. Variant: after ἤμελλον add αὐτά] 𝔓^{47} fam 1611^{1854} cop.

4.f. Variant: φωνῆς] 𝔓^{47} Andr d.

4.g. Variant: λεγούσης] 𝔓^{47} 469 Andr d.

4.h. The aor. imper. verb σφράγισον, lit. "seal," does not refer to the action of rolling up and sealing a partially written message; rather it is a figurative extension of the term meaning "to keep secret, conceal" (Bauer-Aland, 1587; BAGD, 796). However, the prohibition μὴ σφραγίσῃς, "do not seal up," in 22:10 is the literal (it is a *topos* connected with apocalyptic writings; see *Comment* on 22:10), not the figurative, use of this verb, contra Bauer-Aland, 1587; BAGD, 796.

4.i. Variant: ὅσα] 𝔓^{47} ℵ fam 1611^{2344} 94.

4.j. Variant: omit ἑπτά] 𝔓^{47}; then corrected by another hand with the insertion of a superlinear ζ (= 7); singular reading.

4.k-k. Variant: μετὰ ταῦτα γράφεις for μὴ αὐτὰ γράψῃς] Andreas. Scribal correction intended to solve the problem that the sealing is mentioned before the command not to write; the command to seal appears to presuppose that something was written down (see *Comment* on 10:4).

4.l. The prohibition μὴ γράψῃς, "do not begin to write," uses the aor. subjunctive in an ingressive manner, emphasizing the necessity of not beginning the proscribed action, expressing a strong desire that something should not occur (J. P. Louw, "On Greek Prohibitions," *AcCl* 2 [1959] 52). As a specific command (as opposed to a general command), it fits the rule that a prohibition with the present prohibits an action in progress (i.e., "stop doing"), while the prohibition with the aor. forbids an action that has not yet begun (i.e., "do not begin to do"); Moulton, *Prolegomena,* 122–26.

4.m. Variant: αὐτάς (fem. acc. pl.)] 𝔓^{47}.

5.a. Variants: (1) ἦρεν] ℵ C 025 046 fam 1006^{1841} fam 1611^{2329} Andreas Byzantine. (2) ἦρε] A fam 1006^{1006} fam 1611$^{1611\ 1854\ 2050}$ Oecumenius$^{2053\ 2062}$. On the problem of moveable ν in the textual criticism of Revelation, see *Note* 7:10.b.

5.b-b. Variants: (1) τὴν δεξιάν] ℵ C 025 Andr c d f$^{2023\ 2073}$ g i l 94 Byzantine it^{gig} Tyc^{1} Primasius Beatus. (2) omit τὴν δεξιάν] A Andreas Tyc^{3} vg syr^{ph} cop$^{bo\ mss}$. While there is no obvious mechanical reason that τὴν δεξιάν should have been omitted, one material reason is that the uplifted right hand is associated with taking an oath only in LXX Deut 32:40 (see *Comment* on 10:5).

5.c. Variant: χεῖρας (acc. pl.)] 𝔓^{47}; singular reading.

6.a. Variant: ὤμωσεν] 𝔓^{85} with a scattering of minuscules; Andr b$^{2059\ 2081}$ Andr i$^{2015\ 2074}$; Byz 7^{2024} Byz 12^{2048} Andr/Byz 2b^{628} Andr/Byz 4a^{616} Andr/Byz 4b$^{172\ 1828}$.

6.b. Variant: omit ἐν] 𝔓^{47} ℵ* ℵ^{1} (added by ℵ^{3}) 046 fam 1611$^{2329\ 2344}$ 2351 Andr i^{2042} l 94 Byzantine. The absence of ἐν is the *lectio difficilior,* and the strong MS support for its omission suggests that it was an early insertion into Rev 10:6. ὀμνύω or ὄμνυμι can be used with several different constructions to mean "swear [an oath] by," including (1) the acc. (LXX Isa 65:16; Hos 4:15; LXX Dan 12:7), (2) κατά + gen. (LXX Gen 31:53; Exod 32:13; Deut 9:27; 1 Kgdms 30:5), (3) κατά + acc. (LXX Josh 9:18, 19), (4) dat. (LXX Isa 19:18; 48:1; Zech 5:4; Mal 3:5; Jer 12:16; 51:26[MT 44:26]), and (5) ἐν + dat. (Judg 21:7, 18; 1 Kgdms 24:22; 2 Kgdms 19:8[MT 7]). The use of the simple dat., however, is open to misunderstanding since it is often used of the one to whom one swears (2 Kgdms 19:24, καὶ ὤμοσεν αὐτῷ ὁ βασιλεύς, "and the king swore to him"; 3 Kgdms 1:17; 2:8; Isa 54:9). Rev 10:6 clearly alludes to Theod Dan 12:7, καὶ ὕψωσεν τὴν δεξιὰν αὐτοῦ καὶ . . . ὤμοσεν ἐν τῷ ζῶντι τὸν αἰῶνα, "and he raised his right hand and . . . swore by the one who lives for ever." The central problem with Rev 10:6, however, is to account for the presence or absence of ἐν before τῷ ζῶντι. While it is easy to account for its insertion if originally absent (it would remove the ambiguity of the expression, which without ἐν *could* mean "he swore to the one who lives . . ."), it is difficult to account for its omission except by error. I conclude that the strength of the MS evidence for the omission of ἐν, together with the fact that this reading is the *lectio difficilior,* suggests that ἐν was not found in the original text of Rev 10:6, although it is accepted by modern editions of the Gk. NT (Tischendorf, *NT Graece;* WHort; von Soden, *Text;* Merk, *NT;* Nestle-Aland^{27}; UBSGNT^{4}). It is possible that ἐν was inserted to conform more closely to Theod Dan 12:7.

6.c-c. Variant: omit καὶ τὰ ἐν αὐτῷ] fam 1611^{1611} and several minuscules.

6.d-d. Variant: omit καὶ τὴν γῆν καὶ τὰ ἐν αὐτῇ] A Andr a b e^{2057} f$^{2031\ 2056}$ h^{-2302} 598. Accidental omission.

6.e-e. Variant: (1) καὶ τὴν θάλασσαν καὶ τὰ ἐν αὐτῇ] 𝔓^{47} C 025 fam 1006^{1006} fam 1611^{1854} Oecumenius^{2053} vg cop^{bo}. (2) omit καὶ τὴν θάλασσαν καὶ τὰ ἐν αὐτῇ] ℵ* A fam 1611$^{1611\ 2344}$ Andr f^{2023} g i^{2042} l^{-2080} it^{gig} syr^{ph} cop^{sa} [WHort]. This was probably an accidental omission (*TCGNT*^{1}, 743; *TCGNT*^{2}, 671).

6.f. καὶ ὤμοσεν . . . ὅτι, "he swore an oath . . . that. . . ." The obj. of the verb ὤμοσεν is introduced with ὅτι, which introduces direct discourse and therefore cannot be translated.

7.a-a. Variants: (1) τοῦ ἑβδόμου ἀγγέλου] *lectio originalis.* (2) τοῦ ἀγγέλου τοῦ ζ] 𝔓^{47} ℵ (τοῦ ἀγγέλου τοῦ ἑβδόμου); syr.

7.b. καί is translated "then" because it follows a dependent clause (protasis) and introduces an independent clause (apodosis); the same phenomenon occurs in Rev 3:3 (the καί before εἰσελεύσομαι is probably original); 6:12; 14:9–10; cf. Luke 1:59; 2:21; Acts 13:19; Phil 1:22; 2 Cor 2:2; Jas 4:15. There are many instances of this construction in Gk. (*Iliad* 1.494; 5.897; 8.69; *Odyssey* 14.112; Thucydides 2.93.4; Hermetica 13.1 [Nock-Festugière, *Hermès Trismégiste* 2:219]; LSJ, 857, s.v. "καί," B.3). The construction can also be the result of Semitic influence (LXX Gen 24:30; BDR § 442.5; Beyer, *Semitische Syntax,* 66–72, esp. 69).

7.c-c. Here μυστήριον, lit. "mystery," refers to the "secret counsel" of God (Hatch, *Essays,* 59); see *Comment* on 10:7.

7.d. Variants: (1) ἐτελέσθη (aor. ind.)] ℵ A C 025 fam 1006^{1006} (lacuna in Oecumenius^{2053}) fam 1611^{2329} Andr f^{2073cor} i^{2042} l 94 598 2019. (2) τελεσθῇ (aor. subjunctive)] fam 1611^{1854} 2351 Andreas syr^{h}. Reading (1) is original, since it is the main clause in the sentence and not governed by ὅταν as many scribes apparently assumed. Here the context seems to require that the aor. pass. ἐτελέσθη be understood in a fut. sense since it follows the temporal clause consisting of ὅταν, "when, whenever," with the periphrastic fut. subjunctive μέλλῃ σαλπίζειν, "he will sound the trumpet." There are several other instances in Revelation in which the aor. ind. has a fut. meaning (11:10; 15:1; 21:4; see 11:2). There are three possible explanations: (1) The aor. can be used in a future sense (Radermacher, *Grammatik,* 152; Robertson, *Grammar,* 847; Burton, *Syntax,* § 50, speaks of a "proleptic" use of the aor.). (2) The aor. can be used like the Heb. prophetic pf., which presented fut. events as though they had already occurred (Fanning, *Verbal Aspect,* 274). (3) The phrase καὶ ἐτελέσθη, "and it was completed," could reflect the Heb. waw consecutive, which provides a fut. meaning when used with a pf. tense and should therefore be translated as if it read τελεσθήσεται (Allo, 141; Bousset [1906] 310; Beyer, *Semitische Syntax,* 69; S. Thompson, *Apocalypse,* 56; Lohmeyer, 86). (4) ἐτελέσθη could also be understood as reflecting the sense of a Heb. or Aram. pf. (S. Thompson, *Apocalypse,* 40; Mussies, *Morphology,* 337; Lancellotti, *Sintassi Ebraica,* 56). The verb ἐτελέσθη is also used with a fut. meaning in 15:1 (Lancellotti, *Sintassi Ebraica,* 56).

7.e. Only here and in Rev 14:6 is εὐαγγελίζειν found in the active voice in the NT; the only attestation of εὐαγγελίζειν in the active voice in non-Christian sources is PGiss 27 = *CPJ* 2:439, line 6 (see *New Docs,* 3:12).

7.f-f. Variants: (1) τοὺς ἑαυτοῦ δούλους τοὺς προφήτας] A C fam 1611$^{1611\ 1854\ 2329}$ Oecumenius^{2053} 2351 Andreas. (2) τοὺς δούλους αὐτοῦ τοὺς προφήτας] 046 fam 1006 Byzantine. (3) τοῖς ἑαυτους δούλοις τοῖς προφήταις] Andr a d. (4) τοῖς αὐτοῦ δούλοις τοῖς προφήταις] Andr i^{2036}. (5) τοῖς δούλοις αὐτους τοῖς προφήταις] 94 792 Byz 13$^{498\ 1704}$ Andr/Byz 2a$^{680\ 922}$ it^{gig} (*servis suis prophetis*). The acc. following εὐηγγέλισεν is problematic, since normally the one to whom something is proclaimed is in the dat. and that which is proclaimed in the acc. (e.g., Luke 1:19; 8:35). The obj. of εὐηγγέλισεν is corrected to the dat. in readings (3), (4), and (5); see *TCGNT*^{1}, 743. Kraft (149), therefore, understands the acc. phrase τους ἑαυτοῦ δούλους τοὺς προφήτας as an acc. of relation, arguing that the prophets are the content, not the recipients, of the revelation. Yet there are a number of instances in Luke-Acts in which the one to whom the proclamation is made is in the acc. (Luke 3:18 [εὐηγγελίζετο τὸν λαόν, "he proclaimed the good news to the people" (NRSV)]; cf. Acts 8:25, 40; 13:32; 14:21; 16:10).

7.g. Variant: insert καί after δούλους] 𝔓^{47} 𝔓^{85} א fam 1611$^{2329\ 2344}$ Byzantine cop^{sa} eth. Despite the relatively weak attestation, this reading conforms to the style of Revelation, since the καί is probably epexegetical, so that the entire phrase could be translated "his servants, that is, the prophets." The insertion of καί, however, destroys the stereotyped phrase "his servants the prophets" (*TCGNT*^{1}, 743).

8.a-a. Variant: καὶ φωνὴν ἤκουσα πάλιν ἐκ τοῦ οὐρανοῦ λαλοῦσαν] fam 1611^{2329}.

8.b. See *Note* 2.a.

8.c. Variant: omit ἡ] 𝔓^{47}; singular reading.

8.d. The syntax of this sentence is extremely clumsy. ἡ φωνή, "the voice," is in the nom. case but functions as a pendent nom. or nom. abs. since it is left dangling with no syntactical relationship to the clauses that follow. The author then introduces a relative clause ἣν ἤκουσα ἐκ τοῦ οὐρανοῦ πάλιν λαλοῦσαν μετ' ἐμοῦ καὶ λέγουσαν, "which I heard from heaven again speaking with me and saying." The Byzantine tradition corrected the two ptcps. to read λαλοῦσα and λέγουσα (fem. nom. sing. ptcps.) to modify ἡ φωνή, thus reducing the relative clause to ἣν ἤκουσα ἐκ τοῦ οὐρανοῦ. The syntactical problems caused by the phrase ἡ φωνὴ ἣν were solved by copyists by various strategies that focused on replacing the nom. φωνή (certainly the *lectio difficilior* and therefore the original reading, supported by 𝔓^{47} [- ἡ]; א A C Andreas Byzantine) with the acc. φωνήν: (1) καὶ ἤκουσα φωνήν is supported by 104 459 680 922 (all four MSS have a common archetype); 2091 Primasius Vulgate. (2) καὶ φωνὴν ἤκουσα has much stronger support: fam 1006$^{1006\ 1841}$ fam 1611^{2329} Oecumenius^{2053} 2057 Tyconius Beatus. (3) καὶ τὴν φωνὴν ἤκουσα] 1854.

8.e. Variants: (1) λαλοῦσαν] *lectio originalis.* (2) λαλοῦσα] 2351 Byzantine. λαλοῦσαν is a present fem. acc. ptcp. (modifying the relative pronoun ἥν, which refers to the preceding noun ἡ φωνή, "the voice"), an example of the Aram. or Mishnaic Heb. use of a ptcp. following a finite verb and functioning itself as a finite verb (Torrey, *Apocalypse,* 119–20; Mussies, *Morphology,* 324–26). In Aram. the ptcp. was widely used to indicate action simultaneous with that of the main verb, with the result that such present ptcps. should be translated as past tenses (Rosenthal, *Aramaic,* 55), and for that reason λαλοῦσαν is translated above with a past tense in Eng. since it should be understood as simultaneous in time with the aor. verb ἤκουσα, "I heard." Ptcps. used as finite verbs also occur in 1:16; 4:2, 4, 5, 7, 8; 5:6; 6:2, 5; 9:17, 19; 10:2, 8; 12:2; 14:1, 14; 19:11, 12, 13; 21:12(2x), 14, 19; these ptcps. are scattered throughout Revelation and are not limited to any hypothetical source document (Mussies, *Morphology,* 350).

8.f. On λαλεῖν μετ' ἐμοῦ, see *Note* 1:12.b-b.

8.g. Variants: (1) λέγουσαν] *lectio originalis.* (2) λέγουσα] 2351 Byzantine. λέγουσαν is a present fem. acc. ptcp. that has been attracted to the fem. gender and acc. case of λαλοῦσαν (whereas it should have modified ἡ φωνή and taken the form of the present fem. *nom.* ptcp. λέγουσα); the result is an anacoluthon (Mussies, *Morphology,* 100). Further, like λαλοῦσαν (see *Note* 8.e. above with bibliography), it is a Semitism reflecting an Aram. or Mishnaic Heb. ptcp. functioning as a finite verb. For the use of the past tense in the above translation, see *Note* 8.e.

8.h. Variants: (1) βιβλίον] A C fam 1006 fam 1611$^{1611\ 1854}$ Oecumenius^{2053} latt. (2) βιβλαρίδιον] ℵ 025 1 fam 1611^{2344} 2351 Andr a b c d e f^{-2023} 94 598. (3) βιβλιδάριον] Andreas Byzantine. The reading that is probably original here, βιβλίον, is a word usually regarded in the Hellenistic period as a faded diminutive of βίβλος. Yet if βιβλίον is the original reading here, it is clearly a synonym of the true diminutive βιβλαρίδιον, "short scroll," used three times in the immediate context (10:2, 9, 10). βιβλίον is used twenty-three times in Revelation, always (with the possible exception of 10:8) as a *faded* diminutive. Yet βιβλίον has the strongest attestation since it is found in A C and a number of important minuscules, including fam 1006 fam 1611$^{1611\ 1854}$ Oecumenius^{2053} (for a discussion of the textual evidence, see Schmid, *Studien* 2:228–30), while βιβλαρίδιον is attested in ℵ and the Byzantine group, and βιβλιδάριον is read by Andreas and a few other witnesses. Since A and C agree on βιβλίον, it is the strongest reading. Yet a number of scholars have preferred βιβλαρίδιον (e.g., Bousset [1906] 312). Elliott (*NovT* 12 [1970] 396) suggests that βιβλαρίδιον is the original reading in all four passages in which it occurs as a variant in this chapter (10:2, 8, 9, 10), arguing that while diminutive forms became increasingly common in the Hellenistic period, some classicists (e.g., Phrynicus, second century A.D.) sought to eliminate such forms. Variant readings in the NT show the same tendency to replace diminutive forms with classical ones. βιβλίον is probably the original reading and, if so, must be understood (semantically as well as morphologically) as a true diminutive. It was always possible to use semantically as true diminutives words with diminutive suffixes that function as faded diminutives, even though the word usually functions as a faded diminutive in general usage. βιβλίον is also used in Hermas *Vis.* 2.4.2 as a synonym for βιβλαρίδιον (2.1.3; 2.4.3) and βιβλίδιον (2.1.3, 4 [*bis*]; 2.4.1). This is corroborative evidence for the originality of βιβλίον in 10:8.

8.i. Variants: (1) ἠνεῳγμένον] Andreas. (2) ἀνεῳγμένον] 𝔓^{47} (ἀνεω[γμ]ένον); 046 fam 1006^{1841} Andr c e^{2026} f^{2023} i l 94 2351. These are simply alternate forms of the pf. pass. ptcp.

9.a. Variants: (1) ἀπῆλθα] A 𝔓^{47} fam 1611^{2329} 2351 Byz 6 Byz 7 Byz 9$^{452\ 467\ 2021}$ Byz 10$^{935\ 1728}$ Byz 12^{-110} Byz 13 Byz 14$^{325\ 517}$ Byz 17^{1852} Andr/Byz 2b$^{336\ 620\ 628\ 1918}$. (2) ἀπῆλθον] ℵ C Andreas.

9.b-b. Variants: (1) δοῦναι] 𝔓^{47} ℵ A C 046 fam 1006 fam 1611$^{1611\ 1854}$ Andr i^{2042} n^{-2429} 94. (2) δός (2nd sing. aor. active imper.)] Oecumenius^{2053} fam 1611^{2329} (δώς); Andreas. (3) τὸ δοῦναι] Byz 17^{2017} (latt: *ut daret*). The present ptcp. λέγων in this verse is a verb of asking (λέγειν should not be understood as a verb of command here [contra BDR § 392.5b]), with δοῦναι as a complementary inf., i.e., an inf. introducing indirect discourse.

9.c. Variants: (1) βιβλαρίδιον] (𝔓^{85}; [. . .]βιβλαρ[. . .] is visible); A^{c} C P 1 2351 Andr a b c d e^{2026} f^{-2023}. (2) βιβλίον] 𝔓^{47} ℵ fam 1006 fam 1611^{1854} Oecumenius^{2053} Andr l$^{1678\ 1778\ 2080}$ latt. (3) βιβλιδάριον] 046 fam 1611^{1611} Andreas Byzantine. (4) βιβλάριον] (𝔓^{85}; [. . .]βιβλαρ[. . .] is visible); A* fam 1611^{2329} (βυβλάριον).

9.d-d. καὶ κατάφαγε αὐτό] αὐτὸ καὶ κατάφαγε 𝔓^{47} 𝔓^{85} ([λαβ]ε αυτο κα[ι] visible; see J. Schwartz, "Papyrus et tradition manuscrite," *ZPE* 4 [1969] 181); ℵ* (ℵ^{1}: αὐτὸ καὶ κατάφαγε αὐτό).

9.e. The verb πικραίνειν here and in v 10 is usually translated "to make bitter," though bitterness is normally perceived through the sense of taste. What is really meant is that the scroll upset, or irritated, the author's stomach.

9.f. The personal pronoun σου *precedes* the articular noun it modifies, τὴν κοιλίαν, whereas usually it *follows* its substantive. Revelation has 302 instances of a poss. pronoun in the gen. following an articular noun, but just 11 instances in which it precedes the noun. Seven of the 11 instances are clustered in Rev 2–3 (see *Notes* on 2:9.a.), while just four occurrences are found in Rev 4–22 (10:9; 14:18; 18:5, 14).

9.g. Variant: καρδίαν] A 2351 Andr l.

10.a. Variants: (1) βιβλαρίδιον] A C 025 fam 1611^{2344} 2351 Andr a b c d e f^{-2023} 94 598 TR; Tischendorf, *NT Graece;* von Soden, *Text;* Nestle-Aland^{27}; UBSGNT^{4}; cf. *TCGNT*^{1}, 743–44; *TCGNT*^{2}, 671. (2) βιβλίδιον] 𝔓^{47} Andreas n^{-2429}. (3) βιβλιδάριον] fam 1006 fam 1611^{1611} Oecumenius^{2053} Andreas. (4) βιβλίον] ℵ fam 1611^{1854} Andr i^{2042} l Byzantine lat. (5) βυβλάριον] fam 1611^{2329}. See discussion in *Note* 2.d.

10.b. Variant: αὐτοῦ after χειρός] fam 1611^{2329}.

10.c. Variant: κατέφαγα] fam 1611^{2329} 2351.

10.d-d. Variant: ἔφαγα ἀυτὸ ἐγεμίσθη ἡ κοιλία μου πικρίας] fam 1611^{2329}.

10.e. Variant: καρδία] 2351 (κοιλία written over καρδία); cop^{sa}.

11.a-a. Variants: (1) λέγουσιν] ℵ A (lacuna in C) fam 1006 fam 1611^{2329} Andr f^{2073corr} i^{2042}; B. Weiss, *Johannes-Apokalypse,* 184. (2) λέγει] fam 1611$^{1611\ 1854}$ Oecumenius^{2053} Andreas it syr cop$^{sa\ bo}$ Tyconius Primasius. The pl. verb in variant (1) is the *lectio difficilior* and was obviously subject to correction. Since the impersonal pl. was used as a substitute for the pass. in both Heb. and Aram. (GKC § 144g; Rosenthal,

Aramaic, § 181), the presence of the impersonal (3rd) pl. has been frequently but incorrectly regarded as a Semitism when it occurs in Gk. texts of Jewish or early Christian origin (Moulton-Howard, *Accidence,* 447–48; Doudna, *Greek,* 66–70; Black, *Aramaic,* 126–28; Wilcox, *Semitisms,* 127–28). Rydbeck has provided a wealth of examples of the impersonal pl. from both classical and Hellenistic Gk. authors, demonstrating how common this idiom actually was in the writings of native speakers of ancient Gk. (*Fachprosa,* 27–45). There are several more occurrences of the impersonal (3rd) pl. in Revelation (2:24; 12:6; 16:15; 18:14; 20:4). For similar impersonal pls. in Acts 2:3; 19:19, see Wilcox, *Semitisms,* 127. The phrase here in 10:11, καὶ λέγουσίν μοι, lit. "and they say to me," has therefore been translated as a pass. construction: "Then I was told." S. Thompson regards this impersonal pl. as a circumlocution for the mention of God and translates this phrase "and God said to me" (*Apocalypse,* 22).

11.b. Variant: σαι for σε] 𝔓47; singular reading (unusual spelling variation).

11.c. On the two possible meanings of ἐπί + dat. in this context, "against" and "about, concerning," see *Comment* on 10:11.

11.d. Variant: ἐπί before ἔθνεσιν] 046 2351 (according to Hoskier, *Text* 1:280; 2:658, 2351 supports this reading, whereas it is not found in the *editio princeps* of 2351 in Diobouniotis-Harnack, *Apokalypse-Johannis,* 17); Byzantine.

11.e. Variants: (1) βασιλεῦσιν] ℵ A 025 Andr i2082 Byz 72024 Byz 1661 Andr/Byz 2a104 459. (2) βασιλεῦσις] 𝔓47; singular reading.

Form/Structure/Setting

I. Outline

3. Vision of the mighty angel and the little scroll (10:1–11)
   a. The introduction of "another mighty angel" (vv 1–3a)
      (1) Description of the mighty angel (vv 1–2)
         (a) Descends from heaven (v 1a)
         (b) Wrapped in a cloud (v 1b)
         (c) Halo on his head (v 1b)
         (d) Face like the sun (v 1c)
         (e) Legs like fiery columns (v 1c)
         (f) Small open scroll in his hand (v 2a)
      (2) The actions of the mighty angel (vv 2b–3a)
         (a) He placed right foot on the sea (v 2b)
         (b) He placed left foot on the land (v 2b)
         (c) He cried out (v 3a)
            [1] With a loud voice
            [2] Like a roaring lion
   b. The episode of the seven thunders (vv 3b–4)
      (1) When the mighty angel cried out, the seven thunders spoke (v 3b)
      (2) When the seven thunders spoke, John began to write (v 4a)
      (3) The prohibition of the heavenly voice (v 4b)
         (a) Seal what the seven thunders said
         (b) Do not write it down
   c. The stance and oath of the mighty angel (vv 5–7)
      (1) Reiteration of his stance (v 5a)
         (a) Standing on the sea
         (b) Standing on the land
      (2) The sanctions for the oath (vv 5b–7)

(a) Raised his right hand to heaven (v 5b)
(b) Appealed to God as witness (v 6a)
[1] The One who lives for ever
[2] He created heaven and what is in it
[3] He created the earth and what is in it
[4] He created the sea and what is in it
(c) The angel's oath (vv 6b–7)
[1] Time will no longer continue (v 6b)
[2] The secret plan of God will shortly be fulfilled (v 7)
[a] In the days when the seventh angel sounds his trumpet
[b] As God earlier announced to his servants the prophets

d. The eating of the scroll: a symbolic commission to prophesy (vv 8–11)
(1) The heavenly voice commands the seer (v 8)
(a) The identification of the voice (v 8a)
[1] The one I had heard from heaven
[2] That voice spoke to me again
(b) The commands to the seer (v 8b)
[1] Go (to the angel)
[2] Take the open scroll
[a] Location of scroll: in the hand of the angel
[b] Identification of angel: the one standing
{1} On the sea
{2} On the land
(2) The seer obeys the heavenly voice (v 9a)
(a) The seer went to the angel
(b) The seer told the angel to give him the little scroll
(3) The speech of the angel (v 9b)
(a) The commands of the angel
[1] Take (the little scroll)
[2] Eat (the little scroll)
(b) The predictions of the angel
[1] It will irritate your stomach
[2] It will be sweet as honey in your mouth
(4) The seer obeys the angel (v 10)
(a) The taking and eating of the little scroll (v 10ab)
[1] He took the little scroll from the hand of the angel (v 10a)
[2] He ate (the little scroll) (v 10b)
(b) The result (v 10bc)
[1] It was sweet as honey in his mouth (v 10b)
[2] It irritated his stomach after he ate it (v 10c)
(5) The meaning of the consumed scroll as a commission to prophesy (v 11)

(a) The commissioning agent: "I was told" (v 11a)
(b) You must prophesy against many (v 11b)
   [1] Peoples
   [2] Nations
   [3] Languages
   [4] Kings

II. Literary Analysis

After the sixth angel has sounded his trumpet (9:13–21), the author abruptly inserts two episodes (10:1–11; 11:1–13) that function to delay the sounding of the seventh trumpet in 11:15–18 (just as he delayed the opening of the seventh seal by inserting 7:1–17). The function of these two episodes within their larger literary context has been a source of controversy among commentators (Bousset [1906] 313–15). Further, though Rev 10:1–11 and 11:1–13 are juxtaposed, they are linked only superficially, though it is true that the author-editor does not indicate the beginning of a new unit of text in 11:1, where he simply says "I was given a reed, like a staff, with these instructions." Those to whom John is to prophesy in 10:11 (peoples and nations and languages and kings) are verbally linked with those who gaze at the corpses of the two witnesses in 11:9 (peoples and tribes and languages and nations; there is no reference to kings). Giblin (*NTS* 30 [1984] 435–36) tries to link 10:1–11 with 11:1–13 but is not completely successful in doing so. One link he suggests is that in both 10:8–10 and 11:1–2 the seer performs a prophetic action. This connection is part of the *prophecy* motif that occurs in both sections: the verb προφητεύειν occurs in 10:11; 11:3; the noun προφήτης occurs in 10:7; 11:10; and the noun προφητεία occurs in 11:6. This is significant in view of the fact that the five προφητ- cognates found in these sections occur only sporadically elsewhere in Revelation (1:3; 11:18; 16:6; 18:20, 24; 19:10; 22:6, 9). Rev 10:7 specifically mentions the sounding of the seventh trumpet, serving to link this section to 11:15–18, where the seventh trumpet is sounded, and the specific phrase "his/your servants, the prophets," occurs in 10:7; 11:18.

Rev 10:1–11, part of an apparently parenthetical intrusion in the narrative of the seven trumpet plagues in 8:1–9:21; 11:15–18, is introduced in a disjunctive manner with the phrase "Then I saw another mighty angel." Taken literally, the adjective ἄλλον, "other," can only refer back to the ἄγγελος ἰσχυρός, "mighty angel," mentioned in 5:2 (the angel in 18:21 is later referred to as an ἄγγελος ἰσχυρός). Since both narratives deal with mysterious scrolls, it is apparently the intention of the author-editor to remind the reader of this previous narrative. The narrative consists of four subunits: the introduction of the mighty angel (vv 1–3a), the episode of the seven thunders (vv 3b–4), the oath of the mighty angel (vv 5–7), and the eating of the little scroll as a symbolic commission to prophesy (vv 8–11).

The focal narrative segments, however, are the oath of the mighty angel, in which the imminence of the end is predicted to coincide with the sounding of the seventh trumpet, and the symbolic commission to prophesy. Both are implicit in v 2, where the two central features of each of these two textual units are mentioned in reverse order: the angel had a little open scroll in his hand (anticipating the symbolic commission), and he stood with his right foot on the sea and his left foot on the land (anticipating the oath). These two units are closely related because the imminence of the end makes the task of prophesying all the more urgent.

III. Rev 10 and the Colossos of Rhodes

John's conception of the angel is based in part on allusions to Dan 12:5–7, where a man clothed in linen (an angelic figure in priestly garb) raises his right and left hands toward heaven and swears an oath "by him who lives forever, that it would be for a time, two times, and half a time; and that when the shattering of the power of the holy people comes to an end all these things should be accomplished." John's conception of this angelic figure also appears to have been modeled after ancient conceptions of the famous Colossos of Rhodes. The Colossos of Rhodes (mentioned along with the Colossos of Rome as the two largest in the world by Pausanias 1.18.6) was a famous bronze statue erected ca. 280 B.C. by Chares of Lindos, a pupil of Lysippos who had himself made colossi at Tarentum. The Colossos was a bronze (see Rev 10:1, "his legs [were like] pillars of fire") representation of Helios (see Rev 10:1, "a halo was on his head" and "his face was like the sun"), which was destroyed in an earthquake in 224 B.C., after which it lay in ruins for centuries. According to John Malalas, Hadrian restored the Colossos, which had lain on the ground since an earthquake 312 years earlier (*Chron.* 11.18). Since the statue broke at the knees, the lower legs remained standing for many years until they were pulled down and the bronze salvaged. The Colossos was about 70 cubits high (ca. 105 feet; see Rev 10:5, "the angel . . . lifted up his right hand to heaven"). According to a popular but erroneous view, the Colossos stood astride the harbor of Rhodes permitting ships to pass through its legs; actually it stood on a promontory overlooking the harbor (see 10:5, "the angel whom I saw standing on sea and land"). The most prominent cult on Rhodes (an island of ca. 420 square miles) was that of Helios, whose three children, Lindos, Ialysos, and Camiros, were eponyms for the three city-states on Rhodes. The main ancient sources for information concerning the Colossos include Pliny *Hist. nat.* 34.18.41; Strabo 14.2.5; Sextus Empiricus *Adv. math.* 7.107; and Philo of Byzantium *De septem orbis spec.* 4.1–6 (the first ancient author to list the Colossos among the seven wonders of the ancient world; for a collection of testimonia, see J. Overbeck, *Die antiken Schriftquellen zur Geschichte der bildenen Künste bei den Griechen* [Leipzig: Teubner, 1868] 1539–54). The information in Pliny (and Strabo earlier) indicates that the broken pieces of this gigantic statue could still be seen and admired in the first century A.D. See also H. Maryon, "The Colossus of Rhodes," *JHS* 76 (1956) 68–86; A. Gabriel, "La construction, l'attitude et l'emplacement du colosse de Rhodes," *BCH* 56 (1932) 331–59. Gabriel (*BCH* 56 [1932] 345–46; p. 337 has a drawing) suggests that the right arm of the Colossos was upright holding a torch (the Statue of Liberty follows the same convention), a possibility suggested by the phrase φέγγος ἐλευθερίας, "torch of freedom," in *Pal. Anth.* 6.171, which also refers to the statue as raised "to Olympus" (see Rev 10:5, where it says that "he lifted his *right* hand to heaven"). Yet in what appears to be a bas relief depicting the Colossos, his right hand is raised to his forehead, apparently to shade his eyes from the sun; see G. Jacopi, *Monumenti de scultura del Museo Archeologico di Rodi,* II, Vol. 5 of *Clara Rhodos* (Bergamo: Istituto Storico-Archeologico-Rodi, 1932–40) fig. 15, pp. 24–26. The many similarities between the description of the angel in 10:1–6 and that which is known of the Colossos of Rhodes suggest that the imagery involved was widely known and generally connected with the magnificent Colossos.

Comment

1a καὶ εἶδον ἄλλον ἄγγελον ἰσχυρὸν καταβαίνοντα ἐκ τοῦ οὐρανοῦ, "Then I saw another mighty angel descending from heaven." On καὶ εἶδον, see *Comment* on 5:1. The ἄλλος, "another," apparently refers to the only ἄγγελος ἰσχυρός, "mighty angel," mentioned earlier, i.e., in 5:2 (on the phrase "mighty angel," see *Comment* on 5:2). Van Schaik argues that while this angel is modeled after the angel in Dan 12:5–7, his words and message are changed enough so that the author refers to him as ἄλλος ἄγγελος ("Ἄλλος ἄγγελος," 221). Charles (1:258–59) has speculated that Gabriel could be identified as the mighty angel, since the Hebrew term גִּבּוֹר *gibbôr,* "mighty one," can refer to "Gabriel" (which means "mighty one of God"). There is, however, no reason to suppose that the author had any particular angel in view. This is a formal link between two text units that deal with scrolls. Bauckham argues that the unique role of this angel and the majestic way in which he is described suggest that he should be identified with the centrally significant revelatory angel of Rev 1:1; 22:16 because it is the scroll in Rev 10 that contains the primary content of John's prophetic revelation ("Conversion," 254–55): (1) God gave the revelation to Jesus Christ (Rev 1:1) = the Lamb received the scroll from the hand of the one seated on the throne (Rev 5:7). (2) The revelation of Jesus Christ (1:1) = the Lamb opened the scroll and revealed its contents (Rev 6:1–8:1). (3) He made it known by sending his angel to his servant John (1:1) = the angel brings the opened scroll from heaven and gives it to John (10:2, 8).

1b περιβεβλημένον νεφέλην, καὶ ἡ ἶρις ἐπὶ τῆς κεφαλῆς αὐτοῦ, "wrapped in a cloud with a halo on his head." The presence of the cloud, rainbow or halo, sun, and fire (v 1c) are all optional features of theophanies. It is perhaps appropriate that ἶρις can refer not only to a rainbow but also to Iris, the personification of the rainbow (which Zeus has set in the clouds, *Iliad* 11.27–28), who is the messenger (ἄγγελος, *Iliad* 3.121; 18.182; μετάγγελος, *Iliad* 15.144) of the Olympian gods (*Iliad* 2.786–87; 8.398, 409; 11.185; 15.158–59; *Hymni Hom.* 2.314–15). On the cloud as a means of transport for supernatural beings, see *Comment* on 14:14. A text in Dionysius Hal. *Ant. Rom.* 1.77.2 narrates the story of a god who mated with a human woman and then was "wrapped in a cloud" (νέφει περικαλυφθῆναι) and was lifted from the earth. On the use of ἶρις for rainbow rather than the LXX term τόξον, see *Comment* on 4:3.

1c καὶ τὸ πρόσωπον αὐτοῦ ὡς ὁ ἥλιος καὶ οἱ πόδες αὐτοῦ ὡς στῦλοι πυρός, "and his face was like the sun and his legs like fiery columns." Comparing the face to the sun is a metaphor used in theophanies (Rev 1:16; Matt 17:2; *Apoc. Zeph.* 6:11; *Apoc. Peter* 1), of angels (*2 Enoch* [Rec. A] 1:5; *2 Enoch* [Rec. J] 19:1; *T. Abr.* [Rec. A] 7:3–4; 12:5; 16:6; *Apoc. Paul* 12; see Dan 10:6), and to describe the transformed appearance of the righteous in the eschaton (4 Ezra 7:97; Matt 13:43; *b. Ber.* 17a; see Dan 12:3; 4 Ezra 7:125) or as a result of their experience of the presence of God. Moses, whose face shone when he descended from Mount Sinai, is a paradigmatic figure for such imagery (Philo *Mos.* 2.70; see Exod 34:30; *Tg. Onq.* Exod 34:30; Jos.

Ant. 3.83; 2 Cor 3:7). The reference to the mighty angel's legs (lit. "feet"; see *Note* 1.e.) as "pillars of fire" is often considered an allusion to Exod 13:21 (Wis 18:3; *Sib. Or.* 3.250; Ezekiel Trag. *Exagoge* 247 [in the latter the στῦλος πυρός is understood as a σημεῖον or "sign"]), where the guiding presence of God is described as a עַמּוּד אֵשׁ *ʿammûd ʾēš* (LXX στῦλος πυρός), "a pillar of fire," though it is not clear that this is anything but a formal allusion without material significance. In 1 Enoch 18:11 and 21:7, Enoch sees "pillars of fire" (στύλοι [τοῦ] πυρός) falling from heaven, both in contexts of divine punishment.

2a καὶ ἔχων ἐν τῇ χειρὶ αὐτοῦ βιβλαρίδιον ἠνεῳγμένον, "He had a small scroll open in his hand." This is a clear allusion to Ezek 2:9–10, where "a hand" holding an open scroll is extended to the prophet (see *Comment* on 5:1, where the same OT passage is used in a strikingly different way). This clause appears to be either part of a summary introduction to 10:2b–11 or an interpolation since the small scroll plays no role in the scene that follows in vv 1–7 and is not mentioned again until v 8, where it dominates the narrative in vv 8–11. The "open," i.e., unrolled, scroll is a common motif in Greco-Roman art (see Birt, *Buchrolle,* 124–96). Though partially open scrolls are normally held in both hands, the normal way to read them (Birt, *Buchrolle,* 130–71), there are numerous iconographical parallels to figures holding an open book in either the right or the left hand, which usually indicates that reading has been interrupted (Birt, *Buchrolle,* 181–96). It is assumed here that the open scroll is in the left hand of the mighty angel since in v 5 he is said to raise his right hand to heaven. This book (mentioned repeatedly in vv 8–10) is a book that originated in heaven but is intended for use by people on earth, just like the book in Hermas *Vis.* 2.1.3; 2.4.1–3 (see Koep, *Buch,* 1–2). The adjectival participle ἠνεῳγμένον, "open," should not be construed as meaning "unrolled" (i.e., somehow draped over the hand of the mighty angel); rather it means "unsealed," i.e., in contrast to the sealed scroll first mentioned in 5:1.

βιβλαρίδιον, "little (papyrus) roll," is a diminutive of βίβλος, "book, roll." In Hermas *Vis.* 2.1.3; 2.4.1–3, βιβλαρίδιον and βιβλίδιον are used as synonyms (βιβλάριον is only attested in early Christian literature as a variant of βιβλίον in Rev 10:8 in minuscule 2329). βιβλαρίδιον used here and in vv 9, 10 and βιβλίον in v 8 are the only true diminutives found in Revelation. On the morphological and semantic analysis of diminutive forms, see Moulton-Howard, *Accidence,* 344–46, 375, 380; D. C. Swanson, "Diminutives in the Greek New Testament," *JBL* 77 (1958) 134–51; Elliott, "Nouns," 391–98; and Mussies, *Morphology,* 108–11 (where the morphological discussion fails to deal with diminutives in Revelation). ἀρνίον, originally a diminutive of ἀρήν, "lamb" (see Luke 10:3), which occurs twenty-four times in Revelation, is a faded diminutive because it has replaced ἀρήν or ἀρνός in general usage (Mussies, *Morphology,* 108; incorrectly classified as a true diminutive by Swanson, *JBL* 77 [1958] 137). βιβλαρίδιον, on the other hand, a conglutinative of -ιον (-άριον, -ίδιον, etc.), is a true diminutive. The word from which it is formed, βίβλος, occurs twice in Revelation (3:5; 20:15, though both in traditional formulations), while the faded diminutive βιβλίον occurs twenty-two times in Revelation, not including one occurrence of the term in 10:8, where (if it is the correct reading; see *Note* 8.h.) it is a synonym of βιβλαρίδιον (vv 2, 9, 10). Yet must βιβλίον *always* be regarded as a faded diminutive? The textual variants in 10:2, 8, 9, 10 indicate that βιβλίον *can* on occasion be used as a true diminutive (for the textual evidence and a brief discussion, see Schmid, *Studien* 2:228–30). Recognition of this fact is important for evaluating the textual evidence for 10:8.

2b καὶ ἔθηκεν τὸν πόδα αὐτοῦ τὸν δεξιὸν ἐπὶ τῆς θαλάσσης, τὸν δὲ εὐώνυμον ἐπὶ τῆς γῆς, "He placed his right foot on the sea but his left on the land." The stance of the angel symbolically corresponds to the oath that he takes in v 6, in which he appeals to heaven (toward which he extends his right hand in v 5), earth, and sea. The reference to the stance of the angel on earth and sea becomes a descriptive participial phrase used twice to identify the mighty angel in vv 5 and 6a. In a magical amulet from Palestine, there is an instance of three divine beings, perhaps angels, who are standing in the ocean and therefore apparently have power over both the ocean and the world (Naveh-Shaked, *Amulets,* no. 6, lines 3–7): "These three are standing in the great ford of the ocean and directing the water and the world in the ford of the world."

3a καὶ ἔκραξεν φωνῇ μεγάλῃ ὥσπερ λέων μυκᾶται, "Then he cried with a loud voice like a roaring lion." The description of the angel crying with a loud voice (supernatural beings in Revelation are regularly described as speaking loudly: Rev 1:10; 6:1; 7:10; 11:15; 12:10; 14:2, 7, 9, 15, 18; 16:1; 18:2; 19:1, 6, 17; 21:3) is a literary technique that emphasizes both the importance of what is said and the supernatural origin of the speaker (Mussies, "Gods," 7; see *Iliad* 20.375–80; *Odyssey* 24.529–53; Apollonius Rhodius 4.640–42; Sophocles *Aias* 14–18). The verb μυκᾶται, "roars," is a general or gnomic present, used to express customary actions and general truths (Burton, *Syntax,* 8–9). The voice of God is compared to a roaring, sometimes the roaring of a lion, in the OT (Hos 11:10; Joel 3:16; Amos 1:2; 3:8; Jer 25:30).

3b καὶ ὅτε ἔκραξεν, ἐλάλησαν αἱ ἑπτὰ βρονταὶ τὰς ἑαυτῶν φωνάς, "And when he cried out, the seven thunders uttered their own sounds." This is the only place in Revelation where a speech by an angelic being is introduced but not reproduced, though some have suggested that what he said was incomprehensible (and therefore could not be reproduced), and then interpreted by the seven thunders. Vv 3–5 exhibit some dramatic features, for it appears that the seven thunders are somehow responding to the powerful angel, perhaps even interrupting him. It is also possible, of course, that the seven thunders are interpreting the incomprehensible sounds made by the mighty angel.

It is tempting to regard vv 3–4 as a later interpretive expansion of the narrative, for the passage is neatly framed in v 2b by a reference to the angel standing on the sea and the land, a reference that is repeated in v 5a (a so-called framing repetition, often used to insert a source or a digression). The presence of the definite article with the phrase "*the* seven thunders" appears to function in an anaphoric manner, "referring back" to something familiar to the audience; i.e., it implies that "the seven thunders" are an entity already known to them (Swete, 127; Zahn, 414–15; Bousset [1906] 308; Hadorn, 114–15; Mussies, *Morphology,* 188).

Though Horn (*SNTU* 17 [1992] 215–29) attempts to disprove that a well-known apocalyptic conception is referred to, his attempt is abortive, for there were undoubtedly many more apocalyptic themes and motifs used in the ancient world than have survived in documentary form. For similar anaphoric uses of the article with a noun or noun phrase occurring for the first time in Revelation, see 6:4; 9:1; 11:3, 19; 16:14. Ps 29 contains a sevenfold manifestation of God in thunder (vv 3a, 4a, 4b, 5, 7, 8, 9). The voice of God is often compared with the sound of thunder (2 Sam 22:14; Job 37:2–5; Ps 18:13; Isa 29:6; 30:30–31; Jer 25:30; Amos 1:2) though only in Ps 29:3–9 with *seven* thunders. However, in LXX Hab 3:11, where the MT is possibly corrupt, the LXX has been reconstructed by J. Ziegler (*Duodecim prophetae,* 270) to read ἑπτὰ σκῆπτρα, "seven scepters," i.e., seven thunders (Day, *VT* 29 [1979] 146–47). Since this psalm is widely regarded as either of Canaanite origin or strongly influenced by Canaanite mythology (Day, *Conflict,* 57–61), it is interesting to note that Baal is associated with *seven thunders,* which suggests an ancient mythological tradition behind the phrase αἱ ἑπτὰ βρονταί (Day, *Conflict,* 59; id., *VT* 29 [1979] 143–51). There is a relatively late rabbinic tradition that the voice of Yahweh on Sinai was heard as seven thunders; *Exod. Rab.* 28:6 interprets Job 37:5 ("God thunders with his voice") in light of Exod 20:18, where the text has הַקּוֹלֹת *haqqôlōt,* "voices, sounds, thunders": "It was one voice that divided itself into seven voices and these into seventy languages" (see also *Exod. Rab.* 5:9). For further references, see Ginzberg, *Legends* 6:39. O. Betz (*TDNT* 9:296) speculates that this reflects rabbinic exegesis of Ps 29:3–9, but he provides no supporting evidence.

A no less distant parallel is found in the Greco-Roman magical tradition of a group of seven gods, the Pole Lords of Heaven (πολοκράτορες τοῦ οὐρανοῦ [*PGM* IV.676–77]), who use lightning, thunder, and earthquakes to punish the impious (*PGM* IV.679–84; part of the so-called Mithras Liturgy). This is related to Boll's view that the seven thunders represent the sounds made by the seven heavens, i.e., the seven planetary spheres (*Offenbarung,* 22). The phrase αἱ ἑπτὰ βρονταί, "the seven thunders," is a more specific way of rendering αἱ ἑπτὰ φωναί, "the seven voices (sounds, or thunders)." Magical texts and Gnostic texts contain a tradition of "the seven voices," which appears to be a relatively old tradition, perhaps originally based on an exegesis of Ps 29. The phrase "the seven voices" occurs in Coptic-Gnostic treatises as *ntz mphônai* or *ntz mphônê,* in which the Greek loanword φωναί or φωνή is preserved (*Pistis Sophia* [ed. Schmidt-Till] 1.1 [p. 2, line 21]; 1.10 [p. 11, lines 26–27]; 2.86 [3x: p. 123, lines 19, 25; pp. 123, line 25 to p. 124, line 16; p. 127, lines 2–3, 24]; 4.143 [p. 245, line 37]; *The Books of Jeu* [ed. Schmidt-MacDermot] 2.42 [p. 303, lines 27–28]; 2.44 [p. 306, lines 18–19, 25–26; p. 307, lines 17–18]; 2.45 [p. 308, lines 21–22]; 2.47 [p. 312, lines 3–4]; *Gos. Eg.* III, 42; IV, 52 [Böhlig-Wisse-Labib, *Gos. Eg.,* 62–63]). The "seven voices" usually refer to the seven Greek vowels αεηιουω, which often function as a mysterious divine name (Dieterich, *Abraxas,* 22–24), sometimes in the form AΩ as an abbreviated way of referring to all seven vowels (Aune, *NTS* 33 [1987] 489–91). In *PGM* XIII.39 there is a command to "write the great name with the seven vowels [ταῖς ἑπτὰ φωναῖς]," and *PGM* XXI.11–14 refers to "your name which is seven-lettered in harmony with the seven sounds [φωνάς]." Occasionally, the seven-vowel divine name is used in self-predications, as in *PGM* III.661, "I am AEHIOΥ[Ω AEHIOΥΩ]," and sometimes the ineffable name of God, the Tetragrammaton, was transliterated using all seven of the Greek vowels (Aune, *NTS* 33 [1987] 491). The command not to write down what the seven thunders said (v 4b) may reflect the view that the ineffable name of God should not be written down.

4a καὶ ὅτε ἐλάλησαν αἱ ἑπτὰ βρονταί, ἤμελλον γράφειν, καὶ ἤκουσα φωνὴν ἐκ τοῦ οὐρανοῦ λέγουσαν, "When the seven thunders spoke, I was about to write it down when I heard a voice from heaven saying." The phrase φωνὴ βροντῆς, "sound/voice of thunder," occurs in Rev 6:1; 14:2; 19:6, always as a metaphor for articulate speech by supernatural beings. Some strands of Jewish tradition mention an angel of thunder (*3 Enoch* 14:4; *Jub.* 2:2; *T. Adam* 4.3). There were various ways in the ancient world whereby thunder was interpreted as a communication from the divine world to the world of people: (1) In the OT and less commonly in early Judaism, the voice of God is often equated with thunder (Exod 19:19; 1 Sam 7:10; Job 37:2, 4, 5; 40:9;

Pss 18:13; 29:3; 68:33; 103:7; Isa 30:30; Jer 10:13; Amos 1:2; Sir 43:17; *Sib. Or.* 5.344–45 [tr. Charlesworth, *OTP* 1:401], "a heavenly crash of thunder, the voice of God"; see *TDNT* 9:282–83). In Phrygian inscriptions, βροντῶν θεός, "god of thunder," is a regular title for the sky god, similar to *Iuppiter Tonans* in Rome (MM, 118). (2) Less commonly, the voice of angels is associated with the sound of thunder (*3 Apoc. Bar.* 11:3; 14:1; *Sepher ha-Razim* 2.43–44, "their voice is like the voice of thunder" [tr. Morgan, 47]). (3) The *bat qol* (literally "daughter of a voice") is a heavenly voice or sound, which is sometimes compared to thunder (*Apoc. Abr.* 8.2, 6) or a voice accompanied by thunder (*y. Pe'a* 1.1). In John 12:28–29, a heavenly voice is interpreted by some bystanders as thunder while others understand it as an angelic revelation (Lindblom, *Gesichte,* 17). (4) In the Greek tradition, Zeus is sometimes thought to respond to prayer by thunder, which is understood as a good omen indicating the acceptance of the prayer (*Iliad* 2.353; 9.236; *Odyssey* 20.101–4; Pindar *Pyth.* 4.23). (5) Hellenistic divination included Greek *brontologia* or *brontiskopia* and the *brontomanteia* that was part of Roman divination based on the *Disciplina Etrusca.* This form of divination was practiced by Greeks and Romans (Bouché-Leclercq, *Histoire* 1:198–204), as well as the Jews (see *Sepher ha-Razim* praef. 15–16; ed. M. Morgan). The fragmentary Qumran text 4Q*318* is in part a *brontologion* (see Eisenman-Wise, *Scrolls,* 258–63; M. Wise, "Thunder in Gemini: An Aramaic Brontologion [4Q*318*]," in *Thunder in Gemini and Other Essays in the History, Language and Literature of Second Temple Judaism,* JSPSup 15 [Sheffield: Sheffield Academic Press, 1994] 13–50).

The identity of the heavenly voice is not specified, a phenomenon that frequently occurs in Revelation in audition reports (10:4, 8; 11:12; 12:10–12; 14:2, 13; 16:1, 7 [*var. lect.*], 17; 18:4–8; 19:5; 21:3). The unidentified revelatory voice is a motif that occurs only occasionally in the OT, though, when it does, the speaker is usually understood to be God (Num 7:89; Ezek 1:28; Dan 4:31–32; 8:16); in early Judaism the term "voice" is frequently used as a circumlocution for the name of God. Unidentified revelatory voices are mentioned with some frequency in the literature of early Judaism (*Gk. 1 Enoch* 13:8; *Apoc. Ezra* 6:3; 7:13; *Apoc. Abr.* 9.1; 10.1, 3; 19.1 [a voice from the midst of a fire]; *T. Job* 3.1; *Apoc. Sedr.* 2:1–4; *3 Apoc. Bar.* [Gk.] 8:14; [Syr.] 8:14; *Bib. Ant.* 28:8 [within a dream of Kenaz]; Philo *Decal.* 46–49 [fire from heaven became articulate speech]; Jos. *Ant.* 1.185). These unidentified voices come from the heavenly temple (16:1; see *2 Apoc. Bar.* 8:1–2; *T. Levi* 18:6 [perhaps a Christian interpolation; see Ulrichsen, *Grundschrift,* 204–5; Kuhn, *Offenbarungsstimmen,* 21–22]; see Jos. *J.W.* 6.300 and Tacitus *Hist.* 5.13), from *both* the temple and the throne (16:17), from the throne alone (19:5; 21:3), and perhaps from the altar (16:7 [*var. lect.*]). Most frequently, when the vantage point of the seer is earth, the unidentified voice comes "from heaven" (10:4, 8; 11:12; 14:2, 13; 18:4–8; 21:3 [*var. lect.*]; see Ezek 1:28; Dan 4:31–32; *T. Abr.* [Rec. A] 10:12; 14:13–15; *2 Apoc. Bar.* 13:1–2; 22:1; *Apoc. Abr.* 8.1 [identified as the voice of the Mighty One]; *Bib. Ant.* 53:3–5); when the vantage point is heaven itself, the voice is heard "in heaven" (12:10–12). See Kuhn, *Offenbarungsstimmen;* id., *Bat Qol: Die Offenbarungsstimme in der rabbinischen Literature* (Regensburg: Pustet, 1990). The unidentified voice is a motif that occurs in Gnostic literature (*Tri. Trac.* 119.3; *Ap. John* II/1 14.13; *Hyp. Arch.* 88.17–18; *Apoc. Adam* 84.4–24; *Paraph. Shem* 1.16–17; 40.6; *Ep. Pet. Phil.* 134.13 [identified as Jesus Christ in 134.17]; 135.3; 137.19; 138.21). The unidentified revelatory voice is also a phenomenon of the Greco-

Roman world (Plutarch *De def. orac.* 419b–c; Vergil *Aeneid* 3.93 [though the context indicates the voice is that of Apollo; see Servius *In Aeneidem Commentarii* 3.92–93]; 9.112). See Herodotus 1.159.3 (LCL tr.), "But while he so did, a voice [φωνήν] (they say) came out of the inner shrine [ἐκ τοῦ ἀδύτου] calling to Aristodicus, and saying . . . [an oracle follows]." The implication is clear that since this fictitious event is set in the temple of Apollo at Didyma, a famous oracle shrine, the voice must be that of Apollo (see Fontenrose, *Didyma,* 212–14). Strange voices were often regarded as prodigies in the Greco-Roman world (Tacitus *Hist.* 5.13 [see Jos. *J.W.* 6.300]; Cassius Dio 62.1.1–2).

4b σφράγισον ἃ ἐλάλησαν αἱ ἑπτὰ βρονταί, καὶ μὴ αὐτὰ γράψῃς, "Conceal the message of the seven thunders; don't even think about writing it down!" There is nothing in this text to suggest that John wrote anything down revealed by the seven thunders. To suggest, therefore, that what the seven thunders said was intended to be revealed only later (Horn, *SNTU* 17 [1992] 226) is simply wrong. The verb σφραγίζειν, "seal up," seems inappropriate here since nothing has yet been written that can be sealed, unless it is construed to mean something that should be kept secret by not writing it down. This is an example of *hysteron-proteron* ("last-first," i.e., placing two events in reverse order, a phenomenon that occurs frequently in Revelation: 3:3, 17; 5:5; 6:4; 10:9; 20:4–5, 12–13; 22:14), since one would normally expect the mention of "writing" to precede that of "sealing" (the scribal correction by the Andreas MSS in 10:3 solved this problem; see *Notes*). While O. Betz has suggested that the speech could not be written down because it could not be understood (*TDNT* 9:296), the text seems to make that suggestion improbable since John was on the point of writing down what he heard. Bousset suggested that John has intentionally omitted a "seven thunder" source (analogous to the seven trumpets and seven bowls), which contained a series of seven plagues introduced by the seven thunders, but mentions it here so his audience will know that he has omitted this source on divine authority ([1906] 309, followed by Müller, 201, and Metzger, *Code,* 67). In a late rabbinic tradition, the meaning of Job 26:14 ("But the thunder of his power who can understand?") is discussed in *Gen. Rab.* 12:1 (tr. Epstein, *Babylonian Talmud*):

> When thunder goes forth in its full force, no creature can understand it. It is not written, none understands, but "who can understand [מִי יִתְבּוֹנָן *mî yitbônān*]"? The intelligent ones they know [הַפִּקְחִים יוֹדְעִים *happiqḥîm yôdʿîm*] his hints and his thoughts.

Here thunder is regarded as a divine means of communication that only the wise will understand.

This prohibition to write reflects a curious convention in ancient revelatory literature in which *all but one thing is revealed.* The following passages are examples of the motif of oracular secrecy: (1) In *T. Sol.* 6:6, "I [Solomon] responded, 'Tell me why he is in the abyss of the Red Sea and what his name is.' He, however, said, 'Do not ask me; you are not able to learn that from me.'" (2) In *Apoc. Zeph.* 5:6, during Zephaniah's vision of the heavenly city, we read "Now my mouth was shut therein." This translation suggests that the author was presenting Zephaniah as seeing a vision that he could not or did not want to reveal. (3) The most famous example is 2 Cor 12:4, "And [in the third heaven] I heard things that cannot be told [ἄρρητα ῥήματα], which a person may not utter." Though some scholars have suggested that the Greek phrase ἄρρητα ῥήματα was originally derived from mystery religions (Lührmann, *Offenbarungsverständnis,* 57–58; Bietenhard, *Die himmlische Welt,* 166–67), its usage is actually much more widespread than that. (4) *Acts of Paul* 21 says "And the angel answered and said to me: Whatever I now show you here and whatever you will hear, do not make it known to anyone on earth." This is obviously based on 2 Cor 12:4, but in order to have anything at all to say, the author then has the angel observe "Follow me further and I shall show you what you ought to tell openly and report." (5) The same reveal/conceal pattern is reflected in 4 Ezra 14:5b–6 (God tells Ezra what he had told Moses), "Then I commanded him, saying, 'These words you shall publish openly, and these you shall keep secret.'" Similarly, Ezra is then commissioned to reconstitute the Law that has been destroyed (14:26): "And when you have finished [writing], some things you shall make public, and some you shall deliver in secret to the wise." This procedure is then narrated (14:37–48), with the result that twenty-four books were made public, but seventy reserved for the wise. (6) In Josephus *Ant.* 10.210, we read "And Daniel also revealed to the king the meaning of the stone, but I have not thought it proper to relate this, since I am expected to write of what is past and done and not of what is to be." (7) In Dan 12:4 are these instructions, "But you, Daniel, shut up the words, and seal the book, until the time of the end." Cf. Dan 8:26, "But seal up the vision, for it pertains to many days hence." (8) *3 Apoc. Bar.* 1:7 [Slavonic] relates "And I Baruch said, 'As the Lord lives, if you disclose a word to me and I hear it from you, I shall speak no further. May God add to me punishment on the Day of Judgment if I speak in the future'" (Charlesworth, *OTP* 1:663; the Greek version, which probably is closer to the original, contains not the oracular secrecy motif but the integrity formula; see *Comment* on 22:18–19). (9) In Virgil *Aeneid* 3.377–80, the prophet Helenus says, "I'll tell you a little, to help you cross strange waters more safely to Ausonia, and come there to harbor; all the rest the Fates forbid me to know, or Juno says I may not tell" (tr. Copely, *Vergil,* 59). (10) Josephus *Ant.* 3.90, in describing the giving of the Law on Sinai, states "And all heard a voice which came from on high to the ears of all, in such wise that not one of those ten words escaped them which Moses has left inscribed on the two tables. These words it is not permitted us to state explicitly, to the letter, but we will indicate their purport." This is the only evidence from early Judaism that the precise wording of the Ten Commandments was a ritual secret.

Though the contexts of these prohibitions vary, two general observations can be made. First, in a document filled with revelations, a refusal to reveal some possibly important detail lends credibility to the whole composition. Second, since the ostensible author is forbidden by supernatural intervention to reveal something to his audience, he is therefore more knowledgeable than they are about supernatural realities; i.e., he is in a superior position. There are other examples when various authors refuse to divulge information that they have taken an oath not to reveal, including these two instances from Pausanias: (1) Pausanias 1.14.3, "After I had intended to go further into this story . . . , I was stayed by a vision in a dream. I shall therefore turn to those things it is lawful to write of to all men." (2) Pausanias 1.38, "My dream forbade the description of the things within the wall of the sanctuary."

5 καὶ ὁ ἄγγελος, ὃν εἶδον ἑστῶτα ἐπὶ τῆς θαλάσσης καὶ ἐπὶ τῆς γῆς, ἦρεν τὴν χεῖρα αὐτοῦ τὴν δεξιὰν εἰς τὸν οὐρανόν, "Then the angel, whom I saw standing on the sea and on the land, raised his right hand to heaven." Since the phrase "standing on the sea and on the land" repeats what is said about the angel in v 2b, it is possible that vv 3–4 are a redactional insertion. Here it appears that raising the right hand to heaven when an oath is taken is a gesture that symbolically appeals to God, who dwells in heaven and therefore sees and knows everything, as a witness to the oath (Deut 32:40; Ps 106:26; Houtman, *Himmel,* 352–53). In Dan 12:7 (to which this passage alludes), the angel who swears an oath lifts *both* the right and the left hand to heaven. It has usually been assumed that the Hebrew phrase נשא יד *nāśāʾ yād,* which means "lift up the hand," is an idiom that means "to swear" (like the niphal form of the verb שבע *šābaʿ,* "swear"). This is reflected in the NRSV translation of Deut 32:40, "For I lift up my hand to heaven, / and swear: As I live forever . . ." (cf. Gen 14:22; Ezek 20:5–6, 15, 23, 28, 42; see *TDOT* 5:411). There is a danger, however, that the modern practice of raising the right hand when taking oaths has unduly influenced the exegesis of Deut 32:40 and similar passages. The phrase נשא יד *nāśāʾ yād* literally means "(the Lord) lifts up (his) hand" (Lust, "Deut 32:40," 155). In the OT, lifting up the hand or hands can have a variety of connotations: it can be a gesture accompanying prayer (Pss 28:2; 63:5; 134:2) or blessing (Lev 9:22), or a gesture for or against someone (Ezek 20:6, "I lifted up my hand to them to bring them out of the land of Egypt"; cf. Ezek 36:7; 44:12; 1QM 15:13; 18:1, 3). Nowhere in the OT, however, is it said that people lift up their hand or hands to swear (Lust, "Deut 32:40," 161), though swearing with the right hand is found in LXX Deut 32:40, for which there is no corresponding parallel in the MT (according to Dogniez-Harl, *Le Deutéronome,* 339, the line was added to create parallelism). LXX Deut 32:40 reads as follows (text of J.W. Wevers, *Deuteronomium,* Septuaginta: VTG 3.2 [Göttingen: Vandenhoeck & Ruprecht, 1977]):

> ὅτι ἀρῶ εἰς τὸν οὐρανὸν τὴν χεῖρά μου
> Because I lift up my hand to heaven
>
> καὶ ὀμοῦμαι τῇ δεξιᾷ μου.
> And I swear with my right hand.

Lust argues convincingly that נשא יד *nāśāʾ yād* with God as subject signifies the active intervention by the Lord (Ps 10:12; Isa 49:22); e.g., he can lift up his hand in punishment (Ezek 36:7; 44:12). Raising the hand is certainly not a typical gesture used to accompany an oath (e.g., Gen 24:9, where the servant of Abraham swears by putting his hand under Abraham's thigh). This gesture *is* used in Dan 12:7 (where, however, the phrase נשא יד *nāśāʾ yād* is not used, and where God is the witness rather than the subject of the oath; cf. Lust, "Deut 32:40," 163), and this is clearly the source of the gesture in Rev 10:5–6, even though in Dan 12:7 the angel lifts *both* hands. In LXX Deut 32:40 and Rev 10:5 *alone,* however, is the right hand raised as a gesture accompanying an oath. In the important passage in Deut 32:40, the first line of v 40 can be construed as the second part of the last line of v 39, i.e., "and no one can deliver from my hand, for I lift up my hand to heaven. I swear: As I live forever. . . ."

The stance of the mighty angel is paralleled in 1 Chr 21:16 (see 2 Sam 24:17), where David saw the gigantic figure of the angel of the Lord, who inflicted a plague on Israel, standing between the earth and the heaven.

In vv 5–6, the angel enacts an oath sworn by the one who lives forever, who created the heaven, earth, and sea by standing on the earth and in the sea and by lifting his hand up toward heaven. There are several instances in Israelite and Jewish literature where heaven and earth are summoned as witnesses (Deut 4:26; 30:19; 31:28; LXX Deut 8:19; *2 Apoc. Bar.* 19:1; *T. Moses* 3:12; *Tg. Ps.-J.* Deut 32:1; *Sipre Deut.* 32:1 [S. Horowitz and L. Finkelstein, eds., *Sifre on Deuteronomy,* Corpus Tannaiticum 3.3.2 [New York: Jewish Theological Seminary of America, 1969] 334]; see Delcor, *VT* 16 [1966] 8–25, who regards swearing by heaven and earth as a demythologization of the practice of swearing by the *gods* of heaven and earth). There are no instances in which the sea is included as it is here. According to *m. Šeb.* 4.13 (see *b. Šeb.* 35a), oaths taken "by heaven and earth" are invalid, while those taken by a name or circumlocution for God are valid. Normally heaven and earth are called upon as witnesses, not because they serve as guardians or protectors of the covenant but because they are stable and permanent aspects of reality (Delcor, *VT* 16 [1966] 11ff.). That is not done here because the heaven, the earth, and the sea will all pass away (Rev 21:1). The only truly stable reality is God himself.

6a καὶ ὤμοσεν [ἐν] τῷ ζῶντι εἰς τοὺς αἰῶνας τῶν αἰώνων, ὃς ἔκτισεν τὸν οὐρανὸν καὶ τὰ ἐν αὐτῷ καὶ τὴν γῆν καὶ τὰ ἐν αὐτῇ καὶ τὴν θάλασσαν καὶ τὰ ἐν αὐτῇ, "and swore an oath by the One who lives for ever, who created heaven and what is in it, the earth and what is in it, and the sea and what is in it." Two elaborate divine epithets form the sanction for the oath that follows. The first refers to God as "the one who lives for ever and ever," an epithet found elsewhere in Revelation in 4:9–10; 5:14 [*var. lect.*]; 7:2; 10:6; 15:7 (see *Comment* on 4:9). The substantival participle τῷ ζῶντι, "the One who lives," here is a circumlocution used to avoid the direct mention of the name of God, though his identity is, of course, not left in doubt but defined in the second epithet as the creator of heaven, earth, and sea. The second epithet reflects the ancient Israelite and Near Eastern conception of a two-level cosmos consisting of (1) heaven and (2) the earth and sea. The third level, the underworld, mentioned elsewhere in Revelation, is omitted (see *Comments* on 5:3 and 5:13).

This verse reproduces a variant of an ancient Israelite cult formula that occurs in several liturgical contexts and that emphasizes the denizens that populate each sector of the cosmos, as in Exod 20:11, "the Lord God made heaven, and earth and the sea, and all that is in them" (see also Neh 9:6 [LXX 2 Esdr 19:6]; Ps 146:6[MT 145:6]; Jdt 9:12; *T. Job* 2.4; *Sib. Or.* 3.20–23, 35; Acts 4:24; 14:15). Simpler versions of this formula refer to "the one who created heaven and earth," later taken up into the Nicene Creed (Gen 14:19, 22; Jdt 13:18 [an allusion to Gen 14:19, 22]; Bel 1:5; 1 Esdr 6:13), or "the one who created heaven and earth and sea" (Jdt 9:13; *Jub.* 2:2); see Houtman, *Himmel,* 96–97. The former was originally a Canaanite cult formula with parallels in both West Semitic and Mesopotamian sources (see C. H. Gordon, *Ugaritic Textbook* [Rome: Pontifical Biblical Institute, 1965] no. 2427; Cross, *Canaanite Myth,* 15–16 n. 20, 50–51 n. 25; Westermann, *Genesis* 2:205–6).

The cosmology referred to in this verse conceives of the universe as a two-level cosmos consisting of heaven, on the other hand, and the earth and sea, on the other, though in some texts the sea can be understood as the chaotic waters under the earth (the תְּהוֹם *tĕhôm,* "deep," of Gen 1:1), so that heaven, earth, and sea actually constitute a three-level cosmos (Deut 5:8 [refers to heaven above, earth beneath, and the water under the earth]; Jdt 9:12; *Jub.* 2:16; T. Abr. [Rec. B] 15:12; *Gk. Apoc. Ezra* 4:38; Rev 5:13 [here a fourth zone is added: "under the earth"]; 12:12; 14:7;

21:1; *PGM* V.459–63; VII.261; see Bietenhard, *Die himmlische Welt,* 14–17). An extremely close parallel to the divine title of Rev 10:6 is found in Acts 14:15 (though not in the context of an oath), "a living God who made the heaven and the earth and the sea and all that is in them," a description of God made in a polytheistic context, and perhaps derived from the apologetic theology developed in Hellenistic Judaism. *PGM* VII.270–71, a magical papyrus influenced by Judaism, contains the divine epithet "the one who made the heaven and the earth and everything in it." The divine epithet "maker of heaven and earth" occurs in Gen 14:19, 22. The epithet "creator of heaven and earth" also survives in magical texts reflecting Jewish influence (*PGM* V.99; XXXV.37–41; see V.459–63, "You who created earth and bones . . . who established the sea and suspended the heavens"). Greco-Roman literature also makes mention of the three divisions of the cosmos as sky, land, and sea (Manilius *Astron.* 2.61).

This is the only instance in Revelation where swearing an oath is mentioned, and there is a clear allusion to Dan 12:7, where the LXX reads καὶ ὤμοσε τὸν ζῶντα εἰς τὸν αἰῶνα θεόν, "and he swore by the God who lives forever," while Theodotion is even closer to the version found in Revelation: καὶ ὤμοσεν ἐν τῷ ζῶντι τὸν αἰῶνα, "and he swore by the one who lives for ever." The relative clause introduced by ὅς, "who," is the author's expansion of the allusion to Dan 12:7.

Deut 6:13 and 10:20 require that oaths be taken in the name of God (cf. 1Q*20* = 1QapGen 2 iv 6–7). The high priest in Matt 26:63 takes an oath κατὰ τοῦ θεοῦ τοῦ ζῶντος, "by the living God," reflecting the Hebrew oath formula חַי־יְהוָה *ḥay YHWH,* "as Yahweh lives," found forty-one times in the OT and thirty times in the Deuteronomist (e.g., Judg 8:19; Ruth 3:13; 1 Sam 14:39; 20:3; 2 Sam 4:9; 1 Kgs 1:29; Jer 4:2; 5:2; 16:14–15; 23:7–8; 38:16; 44:26; Hos 4:15; Amos 8:14; see *3 Apoc. Bar.* 1:7; cf. Kreuzer, *Der lebendige Gott,* 37–145, esp. 23). A Christian development of this formula into a trinitarian form is found in *1 Clem.* 58:2, ". . . for as God lives and as the Lord Jesus Christ lives and the Holy Spirit. . . ." According to *m. Šeb.* 4:13, oaths taken by one of the names of God or even abbreviations of the names of God are binding, as are such circumlocutions as "by the Merciful and Gracious" or "by him that is longsuffering and of great kindness."

It is perhaps not purely coincidental that in texts in which the early Jewish and Christian debate about the swearing of oaths is reflected mention is often made of swearing "by heaven" and "by earth" directly; see Matt 5:34–35 (where the "heaven"/"throne" and "earth"/"footstool" combination is an allusion to Isa 66:1; cf. Acts 7:49); Jas 5:12; Epiphanius *Pan.* 19.6.2; *2 Enoch* (Rec. J) 49:1 (probably a Christian interpolation; on this passage, see D. Duling, "'[Do not swear . . .] by Jerusalem because it is the city of the Great King' [Matthew 5:35]," *JBL* 110 [1991] 291–309); Deut 4:26; *T. Moses* 3:12. Swearing by heaven and earth is referred to in Philo in *Spec. Leg.* 2.5, where mention is also made of swearing by the sun, the stars, and the entire universe. In rabbinic literature (*m. Šeb.* 4:14; *b. Šeb.* 34a; see Str-B, 1:332–33) and in the Gnostic treatise *Disc. 8-9* 63.15–23, an oath by heaven and earth is mentioned (tr. J. M. Robinson, *Nag Hammadi*): "I make him who will read this holy book swear by heaven and earth [equal to the primal elements of air and earth] and fire and water and seven rulers of substance and the creating spirit in them and the unbegotten God and the self-begotten one and him who has been begotten. . . ." Agamemnon reportedly swore by Zeus, the sun, the rivers, the earth, and the underworld avengers (*Iliad* 3.276–80). Burkert (*Greek Religion,* 251) provides evidence to demonstrate that the tripartite oath formula of sun/sky, earth/rivers, and underworld, i.e., the entire cosmos, derives from Near Eastern tradition. In *Iliad* 15.36–40 Hera swears by Earth, Heaven, the Styx, the head of Zeus, and their marriage bed. The narrator in Achilles Tatius' *Leucippe and Clitophon* sees a picture of Eros and exclaims, "To think that a child can have such power over heaven and earth and sea" (1.2.1; tr. B. P. Reardon, *Collected Ancient Greek Novels* [Berkeley: University of California, 1989]). Though this has nothing to do with oaths, it does deal with universal sovereignty in terms of the three major regions of the cosmos.

When God is presented as swearing an oath in the OT, it is sometimes phrased ζῶ ἐγώ, "as I live" (LXX Num 14:21, 28; Deut 32:40; Jer 26:18; cf. Heb 6:13). The phrase ὀμνύειν κατά, "to swear by," is found in Hermas *Vis.* 2.2.5, 8 (in both instances God is the one who swears, first "by his glory" and then "by his Son"). The ancient Greeks invoked the names of specific deities (Burkert, *Greek Religion,* 253), as well as deities in general in their oaths (LSJ, 1223; *TDNT* 5:177). A typical example is found in Xenophon *Anab.* 6.6.17, "I, gentlemen, swear by the gods and goddesses" (cf. 6.1.31). Some Jewish texts strongly suggest that the name of God *not* be used in oaths (CD[a] 15:1). The third commandment in Exod 20:7 ("You shall not take the name of the Lord your God in vain") was widely interpreted in early Judaism as referring to the use of the divine name in oaths (Jos. *Ant.* 3.91; Philo *Spec. Leg.* 2.2; 4.40; Str-B, 1:326–27). The phrase ὀμνύειν ἐν, "to swear by," occurs three times in Matt 5:34–36, and God is referred to directly in LXX Judg 21:7, ὠμόσαμεν ἐν κυρίῳ, "we swore by the Lord." Some early Jewish and Hellenistic texts suggest that swearing be resorted to only rarely (Sir 23:9–11; Epictetus *Ench.* 33) or that it be entirely avoided (Matt 5:33–37; Jas 5:12; Justin *1 Apol.* 16.5; Irenaeus *Adv. haer.* 2.32.1; Epiphanius *Pan.* 19.6.2; Philo *Decal.* 82–95).

6b ὅτι χρόνος οὐκέτι ἔσται, "There will be no more interval of time." The introductory ὅτι, the object of the verb ὤμοσεν, "he swore," is a *hoti recitativum* introducing direct discourse, untranslated because it functions like quotation marks (BDR §§ 397.3; 470.1; Burton, *Syntax,* § 345). For similar constructions involving the verb ὀμνύειν followed by ὅτι introducing direct discourse, see Matt 26:74 = Mark 14:71; Mark 6:23; LXX 2 Kgdms 3:9–10; 19:8(MT 19:7); 3 Kgdms 1:13, 17, 30 (all three verses have λέγων ὅτι); Amos 4:2 (διότι); 6:8 (διότι); Jer 28:14(MT 51:14) (διότι); 30:7(MT 49:13). Direct discourse following ὀμνύειν can also be introduced by the conditional particle εἰ, "if," used to introduce oaths (but left untranslated because it introduces a condition assumed as real), though this is equivalent to simply beginning direct discourse after the verb of swearing (Heb 3:11; 4:3 [quotation of Ps 95:11(LXX 94:11)]; Judg 8:19; 1 Kgdms 3:14; 3 Kgdms 1:51; Ps 131:2–5[MT 132:2–5]; Amos 8:7; Isa 62:8), and by a participle of saying or speaking, always λέγων in the LXX (LXX Num 32:10–12; Deut 1:34–36; Judg 15:13; 21:1, 18; 1 Kgdms 19:6; 20:42; 28:10; 2 Kgdms 3:35; 21:17; 3 Kgdms 2:8 [λέγων εἰ], 23; Jer 22:5; 45:16[MT 38:16]; 47:9[MT 40:9]; 1 Macc 7:15, 35). ὀμνύειν followed by ὅτι can also introduce indirect discourse (LXX 1 Kgdms 24:22), though the infinitive normally functions in this way. The quotation includes the whole of v 7. This statement of the angel is modeled after Dan 12:7, in which an angel swears an oath (the verb ὤμοσε[ν] is similarly followed by a ὅτι clause introducing direct discourse): "It will be for a time, two times, and half a time; and when the shattering of the power of the holy people comes to an end all these things will be accomplished."

The term χρόνος here is not used in contrast to timeless eternity, which begins when χρόνος ceases (in this respect only, Cullmann, *Christ and Time,* 49, is correct). This was the view of Andreas of Caesarea, *Apoc.* 10.6 (Schmid, *Studien* 1/1:108) and other church fathers from the third century on. This view, however, contradicts the sense of v 7, for the prepositional phrase ἐν ταῖς ἡμεραῖς, "in the days," refers to the period of time inaugurated by the seventh trumpet; time can hardly be said to come to an end when the end itself is described as a period of days. The real question is whether the phrase χρόνος οὐκέτι ἔσται means "there will be no more delay" or "the time will be up" and the eschatological events will begin to unfold. Most commentators construe χρόνος, "time," in the sense of "delay," i.e., "There will be no more delay" (Swete, 129, translated the phrase as "interval of time" or "further delay"; Charles, 1:263; Allo, 140–41; Cullmann, *Christ and Time,* 49–50; Caird, 128; BAGD, 888; Goodspeed, *Problems,* 200–201). The argument is primarily based on the verb χρονίζειν, which certainly means "delay, linger." BAGD, 887, suggests the parallel usage ὁ ἐρχόμενος ἥξει καὶ οὐ χρονίσει, "the coming one will come and will not delay" (Hab 2:3, quoted in Heb 10:37; see Delling *TDNT* 9:592). Yet χρονίζειν is not χρόνος, and the latter rarely means "delay," and then only as the object of certain verbs (Barr, *Time,* 76 n. 2), such as ποιεῖν (Demosthenes *De fals. leg.* 163), ἐμποιεῖν (Demosthenes *Or.* 23.93; cf. Thucydides 3.38.1), or ἔχειν (Theocritus 21.25). "Delay" is an inappropriate translation of χρόνος in v 6, for it assumes that eschatological events have been postponed; there is no hint that this is the case in Revelation. In Rev 6:11 the phrase ἔτι χρόνον μικρόν means "for a little while longer," just as μικρὸν χρόνον in Rev 20:3 means "a little while" or "a short time."

7a ἀλλ' ἐν ταῖς ἡμέραις τῆς φωνῆς τοῦ ἑβδόμου ἀγγέλου, ὅταν μέλλῃ σαλπίζειν, "but in the days of the sound of the seventh angel, when he will sound the trumpet." According to J. Weiss (*Offenbarung,* 41; in agreement with Spitta, 110), this sentence is the redactional peg that links a previously existing source (which underlies 10:1–11:13) to the present text of Revelation. While Weiss is correct that v 7 is an interpolation, his view that 10:1–11:13 was based on an existing source is probably wrong. Though Weiss argued that this clause disturbs the parallelism of vv 6–7, Bousset countered that Rev 10 exhibits very little parallelism to begin with ([1906] 310 n. 3). Charles also regards this phrase as a possible interpolation but argues that the hand that inserted it misunderstood the *proleptic* character of 11:1–13 (1:264–65). It is probable that the author added this expansion when he inserted 10:1–11 into the seven-trumpet scheme in 8:2–9:21 and 11:15–18.

7b καὶ ἐτελέσθη τὸ μυστήριον τοῦ θεοῦ, ὡς εὐηγγέλισεν τοὺς ἑαυτοῦ δούλους τοὺς προφήτας, "then the secret plan of God will have been fulfilled, as he announced to his servants the prophets." This phrase perhaps alludes to Amos 3:7, כי אם־גלה סודו אל־עבדיו הנביאים *kî ʾim-gālâ sôdô ʾel-ʿăbādayw hannĕbîʾim,* "unless he reveals his counsel to his servants the prophets." The LXX text reads ἐὰν μὴ ἀποκαλύψῃ παιδείαν αὐτοῦ πρὸς τοὺς δούλους αὐτοῦ τοὺς προφήτας, "unless he reveal his *instruction* to his servants the prophets." Charles (1:266) argues that the author could not have relied on the LXX here, because the LXX reads παιδείαν, perhaps erroneously reflecting a form of the Hebrew stem יסר *yāsar,* "to chasten, admonish, instruct," such as מוסר *mûsār,* "warning, admonition" (Andersen-Freedman, *Amos,* 399). This is one of many clear instances in which the author follows the MT rather than the LXX. The term μυστήριον, "mystery," occurs just four times in Revelation

(1:20; 10:7; 17:5, 7) and is an important term in Jewish apocalyptic texts, though in Revelation only here does μυστήριον refer to the eschatological plan of God concealed in the prophetic books of the OT. In *3 Apoc. Bar.* 1:6, 8; 2:6, the angelic guide promises to reveal mysteries (plural) to the seer with the statement "I will show you (the greater) mysteries (of God)." The Aramaic term רז *rāz,* "mystery," a Persian loanword, occurs seven times in Aramaic portions of Daniel (2:17, 19, 27, 28, 29, 30, 47), and in each instance the various Greek versions (LXX, Aquila, Theodotion, Symmachus) translate it with the Greek term μυστήριον. In early Jewish literature, the term μυστήριον sometimes refers to "secrets of state" or "the plans of the king [which he kept to himself]" (Hatch, *Essays,* 57–58), as in the following texts: (1) Tob 12:7, 11 states "It is good to guard the secret of a king [μυστήριον βασιλέως], but glorious to reveal the works of God." (2) In Jdt 2:2, Nebuchadnezzar sets forth his secret plan (τὸ μυστήριον τῆς βουλῆς) to his officers and nobles. (3) 2 Macc 13:21 reports that Rhodocus, a Jew, provided "secret information" (τὰ μυστήρια) to the enemies of the Jews. Just as a king's counsel was a secret known only to himself, naturally the plans of God are secret. Thus Wis 2:22 claims that the wicked "did not know the secret purposes of God [μυστήρια θεοῦ]." The term רז *rāz,* "mystery," occurs frequently in the Dead Sea Scrolls (1QH 1:21; 2:13; 4:27–29). In the Habakkuk commentary from Qumran (1QpHab 7:5), רז *rāz,* "mystery," refers to that which is obscure and requires interpretation regarding what the OT prophets said about the last days. John's elaborate use of allusions to prophetic books, particularly Daniel and Ezekiel, reveals that he saw their prophecies as pointing to final fulfillment in his own day.

The view that God communicated to the prophets mysteries that are not fully understood until the time of their fulfillment is a view at home in some phases of early Judaism and early Christianity. This view is reflected in 1QpHab 2:8–10 (tr. Vermes, *Dead Sea Scrolls*), where the author refers to

> the Priest [in whose heart] God set [understanding] that he might interpret [לפשור *lipšôr*] all the words of His servants the prophets, through whom he foretold all that would happen to His people and [His land].

A similar statement is made in 1QpHab 7:1–5 (tr. Vermes, *Dead Sea Scrolls*):

> And God told Habakkuk to write down that which would happen to the final generation, but He did not make known to him when the time would come to an end. And as for that which He said, *That he who reads may read it speedily:* interpreted [פשרו *pišrô*] this concerns the Teacher of Righteousness, to whom God made known [הודיעו *hôdî'ô*] all the mysteries [רזי *rāzê*] of His servants the prophets.

These two texts reflect three presuppositions: (1) The events of the final generation have been predicted beforehand by God through the prophets. (2) The true meaning of the biblical text refers to historical events that have or will occur in the final generation. (3) The words of the prophets are mysteries (רזים *rāzîm*), the meaning of which God has revealed to the Teacher of Righteousness (probably identical with the Priest of 1QpHab 2:8; cf. 4QpPs[a] 3:15). A similar understanding of the OT is found in some phases of early Christianity. In 1 Cor 2:6–16, Paul claimed that the Spirit of God enabled Christians to understand the secret and hidden wisdom of God, which had been concealed for ages but was now revealed to those who had received the Spirit. The idea of a "mystery of God hidden for ages but now revealed" is a conception that some have labeled the "revelation schema" (Lührmann, *Offenbarungsverständnis,* 113–17). It occurs frequently in Pauline and particularly Deutero-Pauline literature (Rom 16:26–26; Col 1:26–27; Eph 3:5, 9–10; cf. 2 Tim 1:9–10; Titus 1:2–3; 1 Pet 1:20).

In early Christian literature, only here and in Rev 14:6 is the verb εὐαγγελίζειν, "to proclaim," found in the active voice, a relatively rare phenomenon (MM, 259), attested only twice in the LXX (1 Kgdms 13:9; 2 Kgdms 18:19), and thereafter in neither non-Jewish nor non-Christian Greek until the second century A.D. Further, the noun εὐαγγέλιον occurs only once in Revelation (14:6; see *Comment* on that complex passage), and these are the *only* occurrences of εὐαγγελ- words in the Johannine corpus. Further, the use of the verb εὐαγγελίζειν in 10:7 is so completely different from its use in 14:6 that the two usages reflect no common traditional usage. In 10:7 εὐαγγελίζειν is a verb of communication used in a semantically neutral sense; only the context indicates whether the message communicated is positive or negative. If this verse alludes to Amos 3:7 (which is possible), then εὐαγγελίζειν functions like the verb גלה *gālâ* or ἀποκαλύπτειν, i.e., "to reveal, make known." Further, in neither passage is εὐαγγελίζειν used in the technical sense of "to proclaim *the* gospel"; rather it is used in the more general sense of a message originating with God (Lohmeyer, 123–24). Here God is the subject of the verb εὐηγγέλισεν, and the object of the verb is τὸ μυστήριον, i.e., that which God communicated to the prophets, which is now "fulfilled." According to some scholars, the use of εὐαγγελίζειν in Rev 10:7; 14:6 reflects pre-Pauline usage (Jeremias, *Jesu Verheissung,* 19–20, 59; Stuhlmacher, *Evangelium,* 210–18). In Stuhlmacher's opinion, the use of εὐαγγελίζειν in Rev 10:7; 14:6 (as well as in Matt 11:2–6; Luke 7:18–23) reflects the usage of early Palestinian Jewish Christianity in which that which is proclaimed is the message of the coming of God to judge and to save. This usage is reflected in the phrase εὐαγγελίζεσθαι τὴν βασιλείαν τοῦ θεοῦ, "to proclaim the kingdom of God," in Luke 4:16–30; Mark 1:14–15. There is no relationship between this usage and the technical use found in Paul, i.e., to proclaim the message of the death and resurrection of Christ (Koester, *Gospels,* 9 n. 2). There is, however, no really convincing proof that Rev 10:7 and 14:6 reflect anything other than Jewish usage adopted by the author.

The phrase "his servants the prophets" is a designation for OT prophets that also occurs in 11:18. The conception of the prophets as servants of Yahweh (עבדיו הנבאים *ʿăbādāyw hannĕbîʾîm,* "his servants the prophets") is originally a Deuteronomistic conception (2 Kgs 9:7; 17:13, 23; 21:10; 24:2; Jer 7:25; 25:4; 26:5; 29:19; 35:15) that passed into general usage (Amos 3:7 [possibly a later interpolation; see the pro and con arguments in Andersen-Freedman, *Amos,* 391–92]; Ezra 9:11; Dan 9:6, 10; Zech 1:6; 1QS 1:3; 1QpHab 2:9; 7:5; 1QpHos[a] 2:5; 4Q*390* = 4QPseudo-Moses Apocalypse 2 i 5).

8a καὶ ἡ φωνὴ ἣν ἤκουσα ἐκ τοῦ οὐρανοῦ πάλιν λαλοῦσαν μετ᾽ ἐμοῦ καὶ λέγουσαν, "The voice, which I heard from heaven, again spoke to me and said." The articular noun ἡ φωνή, "the voice," refers back to the anarthrous noun φωνή in v 4 and is one of several devices used by the author to link vv 1–7 with vv 8–11. On the motif of the unidentified heavenly voice in Revelation, see *Comment* on 10:4.

8b ὕπαγε λάβε τὸ βιβλίον τὸ ἠνεῳγμένον ἐν τῇ χειρὶ τοῦ ἀγγέλου τοῦ ἑστῶτος ἐπὶ τῆς θαλάσσης καὶ ἐπὶ τῆς γῆς, "Go, take the little scroll which lies open in the hand of the angel standing on the sea and on the land." Vv 8–10 are modeled after Ezek 2:8–3:3, in which God serves Ezekiel an unpalatable scroll to eat, and, like an obedient child, Ezekiel does as he is told. Here in Revelation, the author amplifies the narrative in Ezekiel by introducing a second speaking part. It is God who addresses Ezekiel in Ezek 2:8–3:3 and tells him to "open your mouth and eat what I give you" (2:8), and it can then be inferred that the outstretched hand is none other than the hand of God. In Revelation it is an unidentified heavenly voice (the voice of God?) that commands the seer to approach the mighty angel and take the little scroll lying open in his hand, though the voice does not indicate what the seer is to do with it. The mighty angel is given a speaking part, and it is he who tells the seer to eat the scroll and predicts what it will taste like in his mouth and in his stomach.

Since the scroll with seven seals was the central focus of the throne scene in Rev 5 and the opening of each of the seals was the structuring device for the first series of seven plagues in 6:1–8:1, it is important to ask whether the author intends the audience to identify the two scrolls. Some have recently argued for this *identity* (Mazzaferri, *Genre,* 265–79; Bauckham, "Conversion," 243–57): (1) βιβλίον (used in Rev 5:1–9; 10:8) and βιβλαρίδιον and βιβλιδάριον (used in Rev 10:2, 9–10) are synonymous. (2) The phrase "I saw another mighty angel" (10:1) refers back to the phrase "I saw a mighty angel" in Rev 5:2, thereby linking the two passages. (3) The scroll in the hand of God in Rev 5:1 is modeled after Ezek 2:9–10, which is also the model for Rev 10:8–10; the allusions to Ezek 2:8–3:3 indicate that the seer intends to tell a single story in Rev 5 and 10 of the prophecy he received symbolized by the scroll. (4) Identifying the scrolls of Rev 5 and 10 solves the problem of the nature and content of the scroll introduced in Rev 5, for its contents cannot be identified with the narrative in 6:1–8:1 since the scroll cannot be opened until *all* seven seals are broken; the last seal of the scroll introduced in Rev 5 is broken at 8:1 and thereafter appears opened at 10:2. (5) The relationship between Rev 10 and Dan 12:6–9 indicates that John regarded the scroll of Rev 10 as one that had been sealed but had now been opened. (6) Since the revelation that John's prophecy is intended to communicate is contained in the scroll he received in Rev 10, the real content of the scroll is only revealed following Rev 10.

There are, however, weighty arguments *against* identifying the scrolls of Rev 5 and 10: (1) A strong grammatical argument against their identity is that while τὸ βιβλίον in 10:8 has an anaphoric article (referring back to the synonymous βιβλαρίδιον in 10:2), the term βιβλαρίδιον introduced in 10:2 is anarthrous and therefore cannot refer to the βιβλίον of Rev 5. (2) The scroll in Ezekiel is open, while the scroll in Rev 5 is sealed with seven seals, which are gradually opened (6:1–8:1), and is then brought down from heaven to the seer opened (10:2a). (3) The mission of John, as described in 10:11, is to "prophesy again *against* peoples and nations and languages and many kings," not *to* them.

Whether or not the scrolls of Rev 5 and 10 are the same, the question still remains, Does the scroll in Rev 10 contain any or all of the following visionary narrative beginning with Rev 11? Since the scroll with seven seals provides the structure, if not the content, of Rev 6:1–8:1, it is worth considering whether the same is true for the little open scroll of Rev 10. Since the author provides no clear literary indications that might aid in the solution of this problem, the answers to this question are necessarily speculative. The content of the scroll in Rev 10 has been identified with the following segments of Revelation: (1) Rev 10–11 (G. Bornkamm, "Komposition der apokalyptischen Visionen in der Offenbarung Johannis," in *Studien zu Antike und Urchristentum: Gesammelte Aufsätze* [Munich: Kaiser, 1959] 217), (2) Rev 11:1–13 (Charles, 1:260, 269; Schrenk, *TDNT* 1:618;

Lohmeyer, 87, 89; Lohse, 60–61), (3) Rev 11:1–15:4 (Schüssler Fiorenza, *CBQ* 30 [1968] 565–66; id., *CBQ* 39 [1977] 363), (4) Rev 12:1–22:5 (Bousset [1906] 312), (5) Rev 12 or 17 (Yarbro Collins, *Combat Myth,* 26), (6) Rev 15:1–22:9 (Giblin, *NTS* 30 [1984] 455 n. 10), and (7) Rev 20–22 (Beasley-Murray, 82).

9a καὶ ἀπῆλθα πρὸς τὸν ἄγγελον λέγων αὐτῷ δοῦναί μοι τὸ βιβλαρίδιον, "I then went to the angel and asked him to give me the scroll." The narrative at this point is extremely repetitive, following biblical (and hence ancient Near Eastern) literary traditions. Each action of the narrative tends to be first mentioned in speech and then descriptively narrated.

9b καὶ λέγει μοι· λάβε καὶ κατάφαγε αὐτό, καὶ πικρανεῖ σου τὴν κοιλίαν, ἀλλ' ἐν τῷ στόματί σου ἔσται γλυκὺ ὡς μέλι, "He said to me, 'Take it and eat it, and though it will irritate your stomach, it will be sweet as honey in your mouth.'" This is an example of *hysteron-proteron,* i.e., two events placed in reverse order, for one would first expect the mention of eating and only then the mention of the reaction of the stomach (see 3:3, 17; 5:5; 6:4; 10:4; 20:4–5, 12–13; 22:14 [Bratcher-Hatton, *Revelation,* 6]).

The phrase "take and eat" has a parallel in the eucharistic words of Jesus (Matt 26:26; Mark 14:22 [*var. lect.*], λάβετε φάγετε, "take, eat"), as well as in the story of Aseneth, who is given a heavenly honeycomb (with virtually sacramental connotations since its consumption bestows eternal life) by an angelic figure and told "'Eat!' And she ate [καὶ εἶπεν αὐτῇ φάγε. καὶ ἔφαγεν]" (*Jos. As.* 16:15). Here the sweetness of honey in her mouth is clearly symbolic of the supernatural origin and benefits of the honeycomb. The metaphor "sweet as honey" is occasionally used of the commands of God in the OT (Pss 19:10; 119:100–103) and is a metaphor used for agreeable speech (Prov 16:24). The phrase "sweet of speech" or "sweet words" was widely used for agreeable or pleasing speech in antiquity and was a metaphor particularly favored by Pindar (*Iliad* 1.247–49; Pindar *Nemean Odes* 3.78; *Olympian Odes* 1.19; Sir 12:16; 27:23).

The bitterness of the scroll after it is eaten is a detail not based on Ezek 2:8–3:3 though it may be the author's interpretation of the description of the scroll as filled with "dirges and laments and words of woe" (Ezek 2:10). γλυκύς, "sweet," and πικρός, "bitter," were frequently used as antonyms (Herodotus 4.52).

10a καὶ ἔλαβον τὸ βιβλαρίδιον ἐκ τῆς χειρὸς τοῦ ἀγγέλου, "Then I took the scroll from the hand of the angel." The one who handed the scroll to Ezekiel is not identified in Ezek 2:9 ("I saw a hand stretched out to me, holding a scroll") though it can be inferred that it is the hand of God, for in Ezek 2:8 the prophet is commanded "open your mouth, and eat what I give you."

10b καὶ κατέφαγον αὐτό, καὶ ἦν ἐν τῷ στόματί μου ὡς μέλι γλυκύ, "and ate it, and it was sweet as honey in my mouth." This phrase is a relatively close translation of the Hebrew text of Ezek 3:3, which is also very similar to the LXX version (Vanhoye, *Bib* 43 [1962] 437); for two other exact citations of Ezekiel, see Rev 1:15 (Ezek 43:2) and Rev 18:1 (Ezek 43:2). Ezekiel may have based this passage on the metaphor found in Jer 15:16, "Thy words were found, and I ate them, and thy words became to me a joy and the delight of my heart." The widespread use of this metaphor is suggested by its occurrence in Ps 119:103, "How sweet are thy words to my taste, sweeter than honey to my mouth!" (cf. Ps 19:10). It is clear that the metaphor of the sweet taste of honey refers to the emotions of joy and delight (see Sir 49:1). In 4Q*418* = 4QSapiential Work A[a] frag. 9, line 17, it is said that after a person investigates the paths of truth and the roots of evil (tr. García Martínez, *Dead*

Sea Scrolls, 389), "[Then you shall know what is bitter for man] and what is sweet for a man."

In *Oneirocritica* 2.45, Artemidorus discusses book symbolism in dreams; a book can represent the dreamer's life, as well as the remembrance of past events (which are recorded in books), while "eating books [βιβλία] signifies benefits for teachers, sophists, and for all those who earn a living for words or books. But for others, it portends sudden death" (tr. R. J. White, *Interpretation*). Bauer has therefore suggested that for gentile Christians in Asia Minor, the phrase ἐσθίειν βιβλία would suggest dream books in which the phrase was interpreted as an early death (BAGD, xxv). For Victorinus, "eating" a book meant memorizing it (*Comm. in Apoc.* X.3; ed. Haussleiter, *Victorinus,* 92).

10c καὶ ὅτε ἔφαγον αὐτό, ἐπικράνθη ἡ κοιλία μου, "and when I swallowed it, my stomach became irritated." On the effect of the scroll after it was eaten, see *Comment* on 10:9b.

11a καὶ λέγουσίν μοι, "And they said to me." The plural form of the verb is problematic. Several solutions are possible: (1) The mighty angel (vv 1, 9) and the heavenly voice (vv 4, 8) are speaking to John in tandem (B. Weiss, *Johannes-Apokalypse,* 184). (2) The angel of v 1 and the fictive *angelus interpres,* who mediates the entire vision of John and who is introduced by the editor in 1:1, are addressing John together (J. Weiss, *Offenbarung,* 42, attributes this verse, along with 10:8–11 to a redactor). (3) The indefinite plural is a substitute for the passive, an idiom that occurs in Hebrew and Aramaic (GKC § 144g; Rosenthal, *Aramaic,* § 181; Moulton-Howard, *Accidence,* 447–48; Doudna, *Greek,* 66–70; Black, *Aramaic,* 126–28; Wilcox, *Semitisms,* 127–28); see 13:16; 16:15 (see *Notes* on both passages); see Charles, 1:269. The third possibility is probably correct.

11b δεῖ σε πάλιν προφητεῦσαι ἐπὶ λαοῖς καὶ ἔθνεσιν καὶ γλώσσαις καὶ βασιλεῦσιν πολλοῖς, "You must again prophesy against peoples and nations and languages and many kings." The scroll that John just consumed is transparently metaphorical and provides the basis for his renewed prophetic commission. The verb δεῖ, "must," suggests the unavoidable necessity of prophesying (not considered in Grundmann's discussion of δεῖ in *TDNT* 2:21–25), while the adverb πάλιν, "again," suggests that this is a renewal of a mission that has already begun. The term δεῖ, "one must, it is necessary," is sometimes used in literary accounts of divine commissions (Acts 9:6; 27:24) and is perhaps related to the theme of divine compulsion to proclaim the message of God sometimes expressed by prophets or attributed to them (Amos 3:7–8; Jer 4:19; 6:11; 20:7–9; *Sib. Or.* 3.162–64; *Eccl. Rab.* 8:1; 1 Cor 9:16–17; see Sandnes, *Paul,* 122–29).

It is of critical importance to decide how the preposition ἐπί is used in this verse. There are at least two possible meanings of ἐπί + dative in this context: "against" (reflecting a more typically negative apocalyptic attitude toward the ungodly nations of the world) or "about, concerning" (reflecting a relatively neutral, perhaps prophetic, attitude toward the nations). The negative way of construing ἐπί is supported in part by the exclusively negative contents of the scroll mentioned in Ezek 2:9–10 (to which this passage alludes), which are described as "words of lamentation and mourning and woe" (Ezek 2:10).

(1) The translation "against" adopted here reflects the usage in which ἐπί + dative (or accusative) functions as "a marker of opposition in a judicial or quasi-judicial context" and means "against" with the *dativus incommodi* (Louw-Nida, § 90.34). Since John's

message to the nations is primarily one of judgment, the use of ἐπί with the dative in 10:11 is best understood in the sense of "to prophesy *against* the people." In LXX Jer 32:30[MT 25:30] we find καὶ σὺ προφητεύσεις ἐπ' αὐτοὺς τοὺς λόγους τούτους, "and you will prophesy these words *against* them." This reflects the Hebrew idiom נִבָּא עַל *nibbā' ʿal* (Jer 25:13, 14; Ezek 4:7; 11:4; 13:16; 25:2).

In LXX Ezek 25:2 the prophet is told προφήτευσον ἐπ' αὐτούς, "prophesy *against* them" (the same meaning of προφητεύειν ἐπί is found in Ezek 4:7; 6:2; 11:4; 13:2, 17; 21:2; 25:2; 28:21; 29:2; 34:2; 35:2; 38:2; 39:1); see Newport, *BT* 37 [1986] 330–31. According to *Sib. Or.* 3.162–64 (tr. Charlesworth, *OTP* 1:365–66), "Then the utterance of the great God rose in my breast and bade me prophesy concerning [i.e., 'against'; προφητεῦσαι κατά] every land and remind kings of the things that are to be" (doublet in 3.298; partial doublet in 3.491).

(2) ἐπί + genitive can mean "about, concerning" (Louw-Nida, § 90.23). Rev 10:11 is frequently appealed to as a parallel to ἐπί + dative in Rev 22:16 (Bousset [1906] 166; Charles, 1:cxxxiii; Allo, 360; Prigent, 357 n. 19; Kraft, 281; Bauer-Aland, col. 582 [II.1.b.δ]), so that this view construes the phrase to mean "to prophesy *about* the people."

Construing ἐπί as "against" is confirmed by the negative character of the Christian witness described in Matt 10:18, "And you will be brought to rulers and kings for my sake for a testimony against them and against the Gentiles [εἰς μαρτύριον αὐτοῖς καὶ τοῖς ἔθνεσιν]" (= Luke 12:11). Here αὐτοῖς and τοῖς ἔθνεσιν are probably datives of disadvantage (*dativus incommodi*). A close parallel is found in the Olivet Discourse in Mark 13:9, "and you will stand before governors and kings for my sake, to bear testimony against them [αὐτοῖς]" (= Luke 21:12). These sayings may be allusions to Ps 119:46 (LXX 118:46), "I will speak of your testimonies before kings." Predictions that Paul would bear witness to his faith before rulers is found in Acts 9:15 (Paul will carry the name of Jesus before Gentiles, kings, and Jews; cf. *1 Clem.* 5:7), fulfilled in Acts 25:13-26:32 and in Acts 27:24 (Paul is told that he must stand before Caesar). The "kings" referred to in Rev 10:11 are probably those referred to in 6:15; 16:12, 14; 17:2, 9, 12, 14; 18:3, 9.

On the fourfold list of ethnic units, which occurs seven times in Revelation, see *Comment* on 5:9. Here the first three nouns, "peoples, nations, languages," occur in the form regularly found in Daniel (3:4, 7, 29[LXX 96]; 5:19; 6:25[LXX 26]; 7:14). The universal character of John's prophetic witness is underscored by this list. This witness is in a sense fulfilled in 11:13 with the conversion of those in the city where the two witnesses were killed, who are earlier identified as representatives from the peoples, tribes, languages, and nations of the world (11:9).

Explanation

Following the sounding of the sixth trumpet (9:13–21), the author abruptly inserts two episodes (10:1–11 and 11:1–14) that function to delay the sounding of the seventh trumpet in 11:15–18, much as the opening of the seventh seal was delayed by the insertion of 7:1–17. The vision in Rev 10 consists of four subunits: the introduction of the mighty angel (vv 1–3a), the episode of the seven thunders (vv 3b–4), the oath of the mighty angel (vv 5–7), and the eating of the little scroll as a symbolic commission to prophesy (vv 8–11), though the focus is on the oath of the mighty angel (the imminence of the end is predicted to coincide with the sounding of the seventh trumpet) and the symbolic commission to prophesy.

The angel introduced as the vision narrative begins in v 1 is described magnificently as "wrapped in a cloud with a halo on his head, and his face was like the sun and his feet like fiery columns," using imagry perhaps associated with the Colossos of Rhodes. The status and importance of this angelic messenger is clearly being emphasized, for only the one like a son of man in 1:13–16 is described with more stiking imagery. The open scroll that the angel holds, apparently in his left hand, should not be identified with the sealed scroll in Rev 5, even though both passages contain allusions to Ezek 2–3. The oath of the angel (an allusion to Dan 12:7), in which mention is made of the eschatological significance of the sounding of the seventh and last trumpet, finds a mysterious response from the seven thunders, whose message John is forbidden to disclose. The substance of the oath is that the mystery or secret plan of God that was proclaimed (in veiled form) to the OT prophets will be fulfilled. This reflects the convention in revelatory literature that not everything can be disclosed to humans.

John is commanded to take the scroll from the angel (v 8), and when he asks for the scroll the angel tells him to eat it (v 9). This odd prophetic symbolic action is based on Ezek 2:8–3:3, where the episode is integral to the account of Ezekiel's prophetic call (Ezek 1:1–3:27). There the act of eating the scroll is a metaphor symbolizing the prophetic word that enters into Ezekiel (see Ezek 3:1). The meaning is similar in Rev 10:10–11, for as soon as John has eaten the scroll he is commissioned to prophesy against many nations and kings; that is, he is commanded to denounce the wickedness of those who have not responded to the Christian gospel.

4. The Temple and the Two Witnesses (11:1–14)

Bibliography

Allison, D. C., Jr. *The New Moses: A Matthean Typology.* Minneapolis: Fortress, 1993. **Andrews, D. K.** "Yahweh the God of the Heavens." In *The Seed of Wisdom.* Toronto: University of Toronto, 1964. 45–57. **Avigad, N.** *Discovering Jerusalem.* Nashville: Abingdon, 1983. ———. "Excavations in the Jewish Quarter of the Old City of Jerusalem (Third Preliminary Report)." *IEJ* 22 (1972) 198–99. **Bachmann, M.** "Himmlisch: Der 'Tempel Gottes' von Apk. 11.1." *NTS* 40 (1994) 474–80. **Bacon, B. W.** "The Elder John in Jerusalem." *ZNW* 26 (1927) 187–202. ———. *The Gospel of the Hellenists.* New York: Holt, 1932. **Bauckham, R.** "The Conversion of the Nations." In *The Climax of Prophecy: Studies in the Book of Revelation.* Edinburgh: T. & T. Clark, 1993. 238–337. ———. "Enoch and Elijah in the Coptic Apocalypse of Elijah." *StudP* 16 (1985) 69–76. ———. "The Martyrdom of Enoch and Elijah: Jewish or Christian?" *JBL* 95 (1976) 447–58. **Beagley, A. J.** *The 'Sitz im Leben' of the Apocalypse with Particular Reference to the Role of the Church's Enemies.* BZNW 50. Berlin; New York: de Gruyter, 1987. **Ben-Dov, M.** *In the Shadow of the Temple: The Discovery of Ancient Jerusalem.* New York: Harper & Row, 1982. **Berger, K.** *Die Auferstehung des Propheten und die Erhöhung des Menschensohnes: Traditionsgeschichtliche Untersuchungen zur Deutung des Geschicks Jesu in frühchristlichen Texten.* SUNT 13. Göttingen: Vandenhoeck & Ruprecht, 1976. **Black, M.** "The 'Two Witnesses' of Rev. 11:3f. in Jewish and Christian Apocalyptic Tradition." In *Donum Gentilicum.* FS D. Daube, ed. E. Bammel, C. K. Barrett, and W. D. Davies. Oxford: Clarendon, 1978. 227–37. **Böcher, O.** "Johannes der Täufer in der neutestamentlichen Überlieferung." In O. Böcher, *Kirche.* 70–89. **Boismard, M. E.** "'L'Apocalypse' ou 'les Apocalypses' de s. Jean." *RB* 56 (1949) 507–27. **Bornkamm, G.** "Die Komposition der apocalyptischen Visionen in der

Offenbarung Johannis." In *Studien zu Antike und Urchristentum.* BEvT 28. Munich: Kaiser, 1959. 2: . **Bousset, W.** *The Antichrist Legend: A Chapter in Christian and Jewish Folklore.* London: Hutchinson, 1896. **Broshi, M.** "Estimating the Population of Ancient Jerusalem." *BAR* 4 (1978) 10–15. ———. "La population de l'ancienne Jérusalem." *RB* 82 (1975) 5–14. ———. "Standards of Street Widths in the Roman-Byzantine Period." *IEJ* 24 (1977) 232–35. **Byatt, A.** "Josephus and Population Numbers in First Century Palestine." *PEQ* 105 (1973) 51–60. **Chaplin, T.** "Note on the Population of Jerusalem during the Siege of Titus." *Athenaeum* 23 (1878) 255–56. **Chyutin, M.** *The New Jerusalem Scroll from Qumran: A Comprehensive Reconstruction.* JSPSup 25. Sheffield: Sheffield Academic, 1997. **Collins, J. J.** *Apocalypticism in the Dead Sea Scrolls.* London; New York: Routledge, 1997. ———. *The Scepter and the Star: The Messiahs of the Dead Sea Scrolls and Other Ancient Literature.* New York: Doubleday, 1997. **Considine, J. S.** "The Two Witnesses: Apoc 11:3–13." *CBQ* 8 (1946) 377–92. **Cothenet, E.** "Le symbolisme du culte dans l'Apocalypse." In *Le symbolisme dans le culte des grandes religions,* ed. J. Ries. Louvain-la-Neuve: Centre d'Histoire des Religions, 1985. 223–38. **Derenbourg, J.** *Essai sur l'histoire et la geographie de la Palestine d'après les Thalmuds et les autres sources rabbiniques.* 1867. Repr. Hildesheim: Gerstenberg, 1975. **Ernst, J.** *Die eschatologischen Gegenspieler in den Schriften des Neuen Testaments.* Regensburg: Pustet, 1967. **Feuillet, A.** "Essai d'interpretation du chapitre XI del'Apocalypse." *NTS* 4 (1957–58) 183–200. **Flusser, D.** "Hystaspes and John of Patmos." In *Irano-Judaica: Studies Relating to Jewish Contacts with Persian Culture throughout the Ages,* ed. S. Shaked. Jerusalem: Makhon Ben-Tsevi, 1982. 12–75 (= *Judaism and the Origins of Christianity.* Jerusalem: Magnes, 1988. 390–453). **García Martínez, F.** "The 'New Jerusalem' and the Future Temple of the Manuscripts from Qumran." In *Qumran and Apocalyptic: Studies on the Aramaic Texts from Qumran.* Leiden: Brill, 1994. 180–213. **Giblin, C. H.** "Revelation 11:1–13: Its Form, Function and Contextual Integration." *NTS* 30 (1984) 433–59. **Greve, A.** "'Mine to vidner': Et forsøg på at identificere de to jerusalemitiske vidner (Apok. 11:3–13)." *DTT* 40 (1977) 128–38. **Gry, L.** "Les chapitres xi et xii de l'Apocalypse." *RB* 31 (1922) 203–14. **Gutman, J.** *The Jewish Sanctuary.* Iconography of Religions 23/1. Leiden: Brill, 1983. **Hahn, F.** "Zum Aufbau der Johannesoffenbarung." In *Kirche und Bibel.* FS B. E. Schick, ed. A. Winter et al. Paderborn: Schönigh, 1979. 145–54. **Haugg, D.** *Die Zwei Zeugen: Eine exegetische Studie über Apok 11:1–13.* NTAbh 17/1. Münster: Aschendorff, 1936. **Heitmüller, W.** "Zur Johannes-Tradition." *ZNW* 15 (1914) 189–209. **Hill, D. E.** "The Two Witnesses (Ap 11,3)." *Expositor* 22 (1921) 311–18. **Kellermann, U.** *Auferstanden in den Himmel: 2 Maccabäer 7 und die Auferstehung der Märtyrer.* SBS 95. Stuttgart: Katholisches Bibelwerk, 1979. **Ketter, P.** "Die apocalyptische Tempelmessung." *TTZ* 52 (1941) 93–99. **Kittel, G.** "Rundezahlen." In *Rabbinic.* Leipzig: Hinrichs, 1920. 31–47. **Lacy, T. A.** "The Two Witnesses." *JTS* 11 (1910) 55–60. **Levine, L. I.** "Josephus' Description of the Jerusalem Temple." In *Josephus and the History of the Greco-Roman Period.* FS M. Smith, ed. F. Parente and J. Sievers. Leiden: Brill, 1994. 233–46. **Lohfink, G.** *Die Himmelfahrt Jesu: Untersuchungen zu den Himmelfahrts- und Erhöhungstexten bei Lukas.* Munich: Kösel, 1971. **Luzarraga, J.** *Las tradiciones de la nube en la Biblia y en el Judaismo primitivo.* Rome: Biblical Institute, 1973. **Mazar, B.** "The Archaeological Excavations near the Temple Mount." In *Jerusalem Revealed: Archaeology in the Holy City 1968–1974,* ed. Y. Yadin. New Haven: Yale UP; London: The Israel Exploration Society, 1976. 25–40. **McNicol, A.** "Revelation 11:1–14 and the Structure of the Apocalypse." *ResQ* 22 (1979) 193–202. **Meeks, W. A.** *The Prophet-King: Moses Traditions and the Johannine Christology.* NovTSup 14. Leiden: Brill, 1967. **Milik, J. T.** *The Books of Enoch: Aramaic Fragments of Qumran Cave 4.* Oxford: Clarendon, 1976. **Min, P. B.-S.** *I Due Testimoni di Apocalisse 11,1–13: Storia—Interpretazione—Teologia.* Rome: Pontificia Universitate Gregoriana, 1991. **Minear, P. S.** "Ontology and Ecclesiology in the Apocalypse." *NTS* 12 (1965–66) 89–105. **Munck, J.** *Petrus und Paulus in der Offenbarung Johannes.* Copenhagen: Rosenskilde og Bagger, 1950. **Nützel, J. M.** "Zum Schicksal des eschatologischen Propheten." *BZ* 20 (1976) 59–94. **O'Brien, P. T.** *Introductory Thanksgivings in the Letters of Paul.* NovTSup 49. Leiden: Brill, 1977. **O'Connor, D. W.** *Peter in Rome: The Literary, Liturgical, and Archaeological Evidence.* New York;

London: Columbia UP, 1969. **Ogilvie, R. M.** *The Library of Lactantius.* Oxford: Clarendon, 1978. **Patai, R.** "The 'Control of Rain' in Ancient Palestine." *HUCA* 14 (1939) 251–86. **Pfleiderer, O.** *Das Urchristentum: Seine Schriften und Lehren in geschichtlichen Zusammengang.* 2nd ed. 2 vols. Berlin: Reimer, 1902. **Reader, W.** "The Riddle of the Identification of the Polis in Rev. 11:1–13." *SE* 7 [= TU 126] (1982) 407–14. **Reymond, P.** *L'eau, sa vie et sa signification dans l'Ancient Testament.* Leiden: Brill, 1958. **Richardson, L.** *A New Topographical Dictionary of Ancient Rome.* Baltimore: Johns Hopkins UP, 1992. **Royse, J. R.** "'Their Fifteen Enemies': The Text of Rev. xi 12 in $\mathfrak{P}^{47}$ and 1611." *JTS* 31 (1980) 78–80. **Sabourin, L.** "The Biblical Cloud: Terminology and Traditions." *BTB* 4 (1974) 290–311. **Safrai, Z.** *The Economy of Roman Palestine.* London; New York: Routledge, 1994. **Schubert, P.** *Form and Function of the Pauline Thanksgivings.* BZNW 20. Berlin: Töpelmann, 1939. **Schwier, H.** *Tempel und Tempelzerstörung: Untersuchungen zu den theologischen und ideologischen Faktoren im ersten jüdisch- römischen Krieg (66–74 n. Chr.).* NTOA 11. Freiburg: Universitätsverlag; Göttingen: Vandenhoeck & Ruprecht, 1989. **Segal, A. F.** "Heavenly Ascent in Hellenistic Judaism, Early Christianity, and Their Environment." *ANRW* II, 23/2:1333–94. **Spiro, A.** "The Ascension of Phinehas." *PAAJR* 22 (1953) 91–114. **Stahl, R.** "'Eine Zeit, Zeiten und die Hälfte einer Zeit': Die Versuche der Eingrenzung der bösen Macht im Danielbuch." In *The Book of Daniel in the Light of New Findings,* ed. A. S. van der Woude. BETL 106. Leuven: Peeters, 1993. 480–93. **Stambaugh, J. E.** *The Ancient Roman City.* Baltimore; London: Johns Hopkins UP, 1988. **Strand, K. A.** "An Overlooked Old Testament Background to Revelation 11:1." *AUSS* 22 (1984) 317–25. ———. "The Two Olive Trees of Zechariah 4 and Revelation 11." *AUSS* 20 (1982) 257–61. ———. "The Two Witnesses of Rev. 11:3–12." *AUSS* 19 (1981) 127–35. **Tabor, J. D.** "'Returning to the Divinity': Josephus's Portrayal of the Disappearances of Enoch, Elijah, and Moses." *JBL* 108 (1989) 225–38. **Talmon, S.** "The Concept of *Mashiach* and Messianism in Early Judaism." In *The Messiah: Developments in Earliest Judaism and Christianity,* ed. J. H. Charlesworth. Minneapolis: Fortress, 1992. 75–115. **Tilly, M.** *Johannes der Täufer und die Biographie der Propheten.* BWANT 17. Stuttgart: Kohlhammer, 1994. **Villiers, P. G. R. de.** "The Lord was Crucified in Sodom and Egypt: Symbols in the Apocalypse of John." *Neot* 22 (1988) 125–38. **Wilkinson, J.** *Jerusalem as Jesus Knew It.* London: Thames & Hudson, 1978. ———. "The Streets of Jerusalem." *Levant* 7 (1975) 118–36. **Yarden, L.** *Tree of Light: A Study of the Menorah, the Seven-Branched Lampstand.* Ithaca, NY: Cornell UP, 1971. **Zanker, P.** *Forum Romanum: Die Neugestaltung durch Augustus.* Tübingen: Mohr-Siebeck, 1972. **Zeron, A.** "The Martyrdom of Phineas-Elijah." *JBL* 98 (1979) 99–100. **Zwiep, A. W.** *The Ascension of the Messiah in Lukan Christology.* NovTSup 87. Leiden: Brill, 1997.

Translation

[1] *I was given a reed,*[a] *like a staff,* [b]*with these instructions:* [c] *"Go* [d] *and measure the temple of God, including the altar area, and count* [e] *those who worship within it.* [2]*But* [a] *exclude* [b] [c]*the courtyard* [c] *outside* [d] *the temple and do not measure it, for the Gentiles* [e]*will be permitted* [e] [fg]*to keep* [gh] *the holy city under subjection for forty-two months.*[i]

[3]*"I* [a] *will permit* [b] *my* [c]*two witnesses* [c] [d]*to prophesy* [d] *1,260 days clothed* [e] *in sackcloth."* [4]*These* [a] *are the* [b] *two olive trees and the* [c] *two menorahs which* [d] *stand* [e] [f]*before the Lord of the earth.* [5] [a]*If* [b] *anyone wants* [c] *to harm them, fire proceeds* [d] *from their mouths and utterly destroys their enemies, since* [e] *if anyone should wish* [f] *to harm* [g] *them, it is necessary that they should die* [h]*in such a way.*[h] [6]*They have* [a]*power* [b] [c]*to shut up* [c] *heaven that rain might not fall* [d]*during the period* [d] *when they prophesy. They also have power over the waters,* [e]*that is, to turn them to blood,*[e] *and to strike the earth with every type of plague* [f] *whenever* [g] [h]*they might wish.*[h] [7]*When* [a] *they finish* [b] *their* [c]*witness, the beast* [d]*who ascends* [d] *from the abyss will wage war on them, that* [e] *he might conquer them and kill them.* [8]*Their bodies* [a]

[b]will lie[b] in the[c] [d]public square[d] of the great city, which is called, prophetically,[e] "Sodom"
and "Egypt," where their[f] Lord was also[g] crucified. [9]And some[a] of the peoples and tribes
and tongues and nations will see[b] their bodies[c] for three and one-half days, but[d] people[e]
will not permit[f] their bodies[g] to be buried. [10]The inhabitants of the earth will rejoice[a] over
them, and they will be joyful[b] and will exchange[c] gifts with one another, for [d]these[e] two
prophets[e] tormented the inhabitants of the earth. [11]Now after [a]the three and one-half days
the breath of life from God entered [b]into them[b] so that[c] they stood on their feet, [d]with the
result that[d] great fear fell on those who saw them. [12a]They heard[a] [b]a loud voice from heaven,
saying[b] to them, [c]"Come up[c] here." They ascended to heaven on a [d]cloud while[e] their
[f]enemies [g]looked on.[g] [13]And in that hour there was a great earthquake, so that[a] a tenth of
the city was destroyed and[b] seven thousand people[c] were killed in the earthquake, with the
result that[d] the survivors were terrified[e] and gave glory to the God of heaven.
[14]The second disaster has occurred;[a] [b]behold, the third disaster will come[b] shortly!

Notes

1.a. Variant: καλάμονος for κάλαμος ὅμοιος] 𝔓[47]; singular error.

1.b. Variants: (1) καὶ εἱστήκει ὁ ἄγγελος, "and the angel stood," inserted before λέγων] ℵ[2] 046 fam 1611[1854 2329] 2351 Andr f[2023] Andr/Byz 3 Andr/Byz 4ab arm syr Tyc[1] Beatus (*et stabat angelus*); Victorinus. Cf. Tyc[3] (*et dixit mihi angelus*). (2) καὶ ἐλέχθη μοι, "it was told me," inserted before λέγων] Andr d[743 2051 2055 2064 2067]. This interpolation was made by copyists to make sense of a garbled sentence (λέγων has no grammatical antecedent; though κάλαμος is the correct gender and number, it obviously cannot be the antecedent of λέγων); see *TCGNT*[2], 671.

1.c. The present sing. masc. ptcp. λέγων, "saying," occurs here without an antecedent (since the agent of the aor. pass. ἐδόθη is not mentioned), so I have translated it with the ambiguous phrase "with these instructions." It is likely that the unidentified speaker was understood by the author to be the one who gave him the reed. The author probably intended to say Καὶ ἔδωκεν μοι κάλαμον ὅμοιον ῥάβδῳ λέγων, "He gave me a reed like a stick, saying," but his preference for the pass. ἐδόθη resulted in an impossibly rough construction. The syntactical problems in this verse were solved by the insertion, before λέγων, of the phrase καὶ εἱστήκει ὁ ἄγγελος, "and the angel stood" (see *Note* 1.b.).

1.d. Here the present imper. ἔγειρε, lit. "arise," is a formula that means to take action in contrast to one's present state of inaction and does not assume the person so addressed is either sitting or lying down.

1.e. The translation "count" is used here because μετρεῖν can mean both "measure" and "count."

2.a. καί is used here as an adversative particle for which the appropriate translation is "yet, but."

2.b. Variants: (1) ἔξωθεν] ℵ[1] A fam 1006[1006 1841] fam 1611[1611 1854] Oecumenius[2053] Andreas. (2) ἔξω] 𝔓[47] Andr c d e[2026] f[2023 2073mg] g i[2042] n Byzantine. (3) ἔσω] ℵ*. (4) ἔσωθεν] 025 ℵ fam 1611[2329] Victorinus; von Soden, *Text*.

2.c-c. Variant: omit τὴν αὐλήν] 𝔓[47].

2.d. Variants: (1) ἔξωθεν] 𝔓[47] ℵ[1] A 025 046 fam 1006[1006] fam 1611[1611 1854] Oecumenius[2053] Andreas vg syr[h] cop[sa bo]. (2) ἔσωθεν] ℵ* fam 1611[2329] Andr a b[2059] c syr[ph] Victorinus Byzantine. Reading (2) may have arisen as a correction for the puzzling expression "the outer court" (*TCGNT*[1], 744; *TCGNT*[2], 671).

2.e-e. ἐδόθη may be an instance of the so-called aor. of divine decree; i.e., a future event that is certain because it has been predetermined by God is spoken of in a past tense (Fanning, *Verbal Aspect*, 274).

2.f. Variant: insert καί] 𝔓[47] ℵ*.

2.g-g. Variant: μετρήσουσιν] A.

2.h. The verb πατεῖν is a figurative extension of its literal meaning, "to walk on," and can mean either (1) "to subdue by force," "to trample on" (Louw-Nida, § 20.22) or (2) "to conquer and keep under subjection" (Louw-Nida, § 39.54).

2.i. Variants: (1) καὶ δύο] A 046 fam 1611[1611] Andr d l[1678 2080] 2351. (2) δύο (omit καί)] ℵ Andreas Byzantine.

3.a. The καί that begins this sentence is left untranslated since it functions here as a discourse marker indicating the beginning of a new clause or sentence but without independent semantic value.

3.b. Here the fut. ind. verb δώσω, lit. "I will give," reflects the Hebraism נתן ל *nātan lĕ*, which can mean "to allow, permit." See Charles, 1:280; Allo, 149; Lancellotti, *Sintassi Ebraica*, 108.

3.c-c. That τοῖς δυσὶν μάρτυσιν is articular indicates that it refers to figures well known to the readers. In this case it is likely that the author assumes the readers' familiarity with Zech 4:2–14.

3.d-d. In the phrase καὶ προφητεύσουσιν, lit. "and they will prophesy," καί is used as a consecutive particle meaning "so that" (Zerwick, *Greek*, § 455; Aejmelaeus, *Parataxis*, 15–18; Ljungvik, *Syntax*, 82–83, provides examples of this use of paratactic καί as a substitute for a ἵνα clause or an inf.). Mussies thinks that the final-consecutive aspect has been taken over by the fut. ind. (*Morphology*, 342). It would be more accurate to say that καί + fut. ind. can have final-consecutive meaning; see 2:23; 3:10; 14:10; 20:10.

3.e. Variants: (1) περιβεβλημένοι] C Oecumenius^{2053} Andreas Byzantine Hippolytus; Tischendorf, *NT Graece;* von Soden, *Text;* Merk, *NT;* UBSGNT^{4}; Nestle-Aland^{27}. (2) περιβεβλημένους] ℵ* A (lacuna in 𝔓^{47}) 025 046 fam 1611^{2329} Andr d f^{-2023} h i^{-2042}; WHort; Charles (2:300). (3) περιβεβλημένοις] Andr f^{2076} g^{2071} Byz 2^{2039} Byz 5^{808} Byz 19$^{2075\ 2077}$. The circumstantial ptcp. περιβεβλημένοι, "clothed," in reading (1) should modify the noun group τοῖς δυσὶν μάρτυσίν μου, "my two witnesses," which, however, is in the dat. case. This ptcp. must therefore be construed *ad sensum* as congruent with the logical subject (masc. pl. nom.) of προφητεύσουσιν. Copyists attempted to correct this solecism by changing it to (2) περιβεβλημένους, a masc. pl. acc., which makes no better sense in the context and appears to be a mere mechanical assimilation to the form of σάκκους (Schmid, *Studien* 2:101; *TCGNT*^{1}, 744), or to (3) περιβεβλημένοις, a masc. pl. dat. Reading (1), however, is certainly the *lectio difficilior* (Min, *Apocalisse*, 227) and probably the original reading. Schmid points out that A and ℵ share common errors elsewhere, e.g., 9:10, ὁμοίοις σκορπίοις (*Studien* 2:246).

4.a. The demonstrative pronoun οὗτοι (masc. nom. pl.) is discordant with the articular predicate αἱ δύο ἐλαῖαι (fem. nom. pl.), "the two olive trees," because fem. and neut. terms are often used in apocalyptic as metaphors for male persons (Mussies, *Morphology*, 138).

4.b. Variants: (1) αἱ before δύο ἐλαῖαι] Oecumenius^{2053comm} Andreas. (2) οἱ before δύο ἐλαῖαι] ℵ. (3) omit αἱ δύο ἐλαῖαι] Oecumenius^{2053text}.

4.c. Variants: (1) αἱ before δύο λυχνίαι] Andreas. (2) omit αἱ before δύο λυχνίαι] ℵ Andr g.

4.d. Variants: (1) αἱ before ἐνώπιον] *lectio originalis* [WHort]. (2) omit αἱ before ἐνώπιον] ℵ fam 1611$^{1611\ 2329}$ 2351 Andr g$^{209\ 2045}$ h l^{1778} n^{-2429}. The peculiar text of ℵ should be quoted at this point, for it involves *Notes* 4.b., 4.c., and 4.d.: οἱ δύο ἐλαῖαι καὶ δύο λυχνίαι ἐνώπιον, "the two olive trees and two menorahs before." The omission of αἱ in reading (2) is understandable in view of the incongruence between it and the ptcp. ἑστῶτες, which follows (see *Note* 4.e.). The incongruence remains even with the omission because of the preceding arthrous nouns αἱ ἐλαῖαι and αἱ λυχνίαι, but it is softened (Schmid, *Studien* 2:238).

4.e. Variant: ἑστῶσαι] ℵ^{2} fam 1006 fam 1611^{1854} Oecumenius^{2053} Andreas Hippolytus (*de Ant.* 47). In a glaring grammatical blunder, the author matches the masc. nom. pl. pf. ptcp. ἑστῶτες, "standing," with the fem. nom. pl. definite article αἱ. Since he is using the symbol of "the two olive trees" (αἱ δύο ἐλαῖαι, fem. nom. pl.), he probably uses ἑστῶτες because he has in view the two men that the olive trees symbolize (οὗτοί εἰσιν); i.e., this is a construction *ad sensum*. The error is somewhat softened by the prep. phrase that separates αἱ from ἑστῶτες.

4.f. Variants: (1) αἱ before ἐνώπιον] *lectio originalis.* (2) omit αἱ] ℵ fam 1611$^{1611\ 2329}$ 2351 lat.

5.a. See *Note* 11:3.a.

5.b. Variant: ὅστις for εἴ τις] Andr l.

5.c. Variants: (1) αὐτοὺς θέλει] A Andreas. (2) θέλει αὐτούς] C Oecumenius^{2053} Byzantine. (3) θελήσει αὐτούς] 𝔓^{47} fam 1006^{1841} Andr l^{-1678}. (4) αὐτοὺς θελήσει] Hippolytus (*de Ant.* 47). Reading (3), a 3rd sing. fut. ind., arose as a correction conforming the *lectio originalis* θέλει to θελήσει, which follows in the next clause. Reading (2) is an attempt to impose the same word order in v 5a as is found in the parallel clause in v 5b. Many MSS therefore read:

> 11:5a: καὶ εἴ τις θέλει αὐτοὺς ἀδικῆσαι . . .
>
> 11:5b: καὶ εἴ τις θέλει αὐτοὺς ἀδικῆσαι . . . .

5.d. Variants: (1) ἐκπορεύεται (pres. ind.)] *lectio originalis.* (2) ἐκπορεύσεται (fut. ind.)] 2351 Byz 16$^{61\ 69}$ Andr/Byz 4c^{-2022} latt arm arab eth syr^{ph}.

5.e. καί is translated "since," because the clause it introduces provides the reason for the statement made in the previous clause (for a similar use of καί in the LXX, see Aejmelaeus, *Parataxis*, 23–24).

5.f. Variants: (1) θελήσῃ] ℵ A; WHort. (2) θέλει] C Oecumenius^{2053} Andreas Byzantine Hippolytus (*de Ant.* 47); Primasius; WHort^{marg}; von Soden, *Text.* (3) θελήσει] 𝔓^{47} fam 1006 fam 1611$^{1611\ 2329}$ 2351; WHort^{marg}; BDF § 372 (3). Reading (1) is 3rd sing. aor. subjunctive. Reading (2), a 3rd sing. present ind., has been corrected to fit the form of the previous θέλει. Reading (3), a 3rd sing. fut. ind., arose because of the confusion between η = ει (e.g., C has HTIΣ for EITIΣ twice in 11:5; see Gignac, *Grammar* 1:239–40). For evidence of the occasional use of εἰ + subjunctive, see BDR § 372.4 (to which add Ign. *Magn.* 8:1).

5.g. Variants: (1) ἀδικῆσαι] *lectio originalis.* (2) ἀποκτεῖναι] Andr i[2015].

5.h-h. Variants: (1) οὕτως] C ℵ 025 046 Oecumenius[2053] Andreas. (2) οὕτω] fam 1006 fam 1611 2351 Byzantine. (3) omit οὕτως] A. Since οὕτως is normally used before words with an initial vowel in Revelation (2:15; 3:16; 9:17; 18:21) and οὕτω before words with an initial consonant (16:18), reading (1) is the *lectio difficilior.*

6.a. Variants: (1) τήν before ἐξουσίαν] 𝔓[47] A C P fam 1611 Oecumenius[2053] 2351 Andr l. (2) omit τήν before ἐξουσίαν] ℵ Andreas Byzantine Hippolytus (*de Ant.* 47); Tischendorf, *NT Graece;* Bousset ([1906] 320). Bousset argues that an arthrous ἐξουσία is contrary to the style of the author, who always uses ἐχουσίαν ἔχειν or ἐχουσίαν δοθῆναι when followed by an inf. Yet ἐξουσία ἐδόθη + inf. occurs only twice (6:8; 13:5) and ἐξουσίαν ἔχουσιν + inf. only once (11:6)—hardly enough times to establish a rule. In this instance it is easier to explain the omission of the article than to justify its insertion (Schmid, *Studien* 2:118–19). This is one of a number of readings in which 𝔓[47] and ℵ disagree and the former preserves the *lectio originalis* (Schmid, *Studien* 2:118–19).

6.b. Variant: add καί before κλεῖσαι] 2351.

6.c-c. In the phrase τὴν ἐξουσίαν κλεῖσαι, the anarthrous inf. κλεῖσαι functions to supplement or complete the meaning of the noun. The other instance of this function of the inf. in Revelation is found in 11:18 (see *Note* 11:18.d.); Votaw, *Infinitive,* 15–16.

6.d-d. τὰς ἡμέρας, "the days," is an acc. of extent of time (see BDR § 161.4), which can be translated "during the period."

6.e-e. στρέφειν is an epexegetical or explanatory inf. introducing a clause that more closely defines the meaning of the preceding clause καὶ ἐξουσίαν ἔχουσιν ἐπὶ τῶν ὑδάτων, and so has been translated "that is, to turn . . . ." It can also be explained as an inf. that complements a noun (Votaw, *Infinitive,* 15–16).

6.f. πληγή here can mean a contagious disease (Louw-Nida, § 23.158), or it can be used more generically with the meaning "distress, great suffering" (Louw-Nida, § 22.13).

6.g. Variants: (1) ὁσάκις ἐάν] 𝔓[47] ℵ A Andreas Byzantine. (2) ὁσάκις ἄν] C fam 1611[1611 1854 2329] Oecumenius[2053] 2351 Andr l; Hippolytus (*de Ant.* 47). The problem reflected here is found throughout the MS tradition of the NT and the LXX (Conybeare-Stock, *Septuagint,* § 105) and involves the interchange ἄν/ἐάν (BDF § 107; BDR § 107). Variation between ἄν and ἐάν in which the more important MSS are divided occurs in Rev 2:25; 3:19; 11:6; 13:15; 14:4. Modern editions of the Gk. NT read ἄν in 2:25; 14:4, but ἐάν in 3:19; 11:6; 13:15, solely on the basis of external evidence.

6.h-h. Variants: (1) θελήσωσιν] ℵ A Andreas Byzantine Hippolytus (*de Ant.* 47); all modern editions. (2) θελήσουσιν] C. (3) θέλωσιν] 𝔓[47] fam 1611[2329] Byz 16 2351. Reading (2), a fut. ind., is unlikely on the basis of internal as well as external evidence, since ἐάν never occurs with the fut. ind. in Revelation; rather it always occurs with the present or aor. subjunctive.

7.a. ὅταν here describes a unique event and must be translated "when" rather than "whenever" (see 4:9; 8:1; 11:7; 12:4; Mussies, *Morphology,* 345). On καί, see *Note* 11:3.a.

7.b. Variants: (1) τελέσωσιν] *lectio originalis.* (2) τελῶσι] Hippolytus (*de Ant.* 47).

7.c. Variant: add τὸν δρόμον αὐτῶν before τὴν μαρτυρίαν] Hippolytus (*de Ant.* 47).

7.d-d. Variants: (1) τὸ ἀναβαῖνον] C Andreas Byzantine 2351. (2) τὸ ἀναβαίνων] A 2060 2286 Andr h[-2301] Andr/Byz 2a. Here the confusion between ο and ω is probably responsible for this variant (Schmid, *Studien* 2:234–35), though there is a tendency in Revelation to modify τὸ θηρίον with masc. ptcps. and pronouns (see 13:11, 14; 17:11).

7.e. See *Note* 11:3.d-d.

8.a. Variants: (1) τὸ πτῶμα] A C fam 1006 Oecumenius[2053] 2351 Byzantine Tyconius. (2) τὰ πτώματα] 𝔓[47] ℵ fam 1611[1611 1854 2329] Andreas lat syr. τὸ πτῶμα, though sing., is a distributive noun referring to something possessed by each member of a particular group and so must be rendered as a pl. in Eng.; see Mussies, *Morphology,* 84. On καί, see *Note* 11:3.a.

8.b-b. Since this sentence lacks a verb, "will lie" has been supplied. A few MSS have supplied the missing verb; e.g., ἔσται, "will be," is inserted after τὸ πτῶμα αὐτῶν in ℵ[2], and ἐάσει . . . ἀταφά, "will leave unburied," is inserted by Andr i[2036], with ἐάσει inserted following τὸ πτῶμα αὐτῶν and ἀταφά after μεγάλης.

8.c. Since τῆς πλατείας, "the street," is articular and the noun occurs here for the first time in Revelation, it is anaphoric in the sense that it must refer to a street well known (or at least that the author assumes to be well known) to the readers. See *Comment* on 11:8.

8.d-d. The fem. noun ἡ πλατεῖα can mean "street" or "public square" or "plaza" (MM, 517); here it appears to mean "public square." In the similar account found in the *Apoc. Elijah,* Elijah and Enoch are killed and lie dead for three and one-half days in "the market place [Coptic *tagora ntn mpolis*] of the great city."

8.e. πνευματικῶς, "prophetically," is translated in various ways in the versions: "allegorically" (RSV), "prophetically" (NRSV), "figuratively" (NIV), "in allegory" (NEB), and "in prophetic language" (REB). The literal translation "spiritually" is too vague in Eng. Schweizer correctly argues that the term should be understood to connote "in prophetic rather than in ordinary speech" (E. Schweizer, *TDNT* 6:449), so translations such as "allegorically," "figuratively," or "metaphorically" are not fully adequate. BAGD, 679, suggests this periphrastic translation: "if one follows the *spiritual* understanding of scripture."

8.f. Variants: (1) αὐτῶν] *lectio originalis.* (2) omit αὐτῶν] $\mathfrak{P}^{47}$ א*.

8.g. Variant: omit καί] $\mathfrak{P}^{47}$ א^{1} fam 1611^{1611} Andreas.

9.a. Here the partitive gen. phrase ἐκ τῶν λαῶν . . . , "some of the peoples . . . ," functions as the subject of the verb βλέπουσιν, "see" (see BDR § 164). See *Introduction,* Section 7, Syntax, under "partitive genitive," pp. clxxi–clxxiii.

9.b. Though βλέπουσιν is a present ind., it is translated as a fut.

9.c. See *Note* 8.a.

9.d. καί here functions in an adversative sense and so is translated "but."

9.e. οὐκ ἀφίουσιν, "they do not permit," is an indefinite pl., which can be translated "*people* do not permit" (identical with the subject of βλέπουσιν, which is the partitive gen. ἐκ τῶν λαῶν . . . , functioning as subject of the verb. Charles (1:288) suggests that ἀφίουσιν is either an Aramaism or the indefinite pl.

9.f. Variants: (1) ἀφίουσιν (present ind.)] *lectio originalis,* here translated as future (see *Note* 9.b.). (2) ἀφήσουσι (fut. ind.)] Oecumenius^{2053} Andr d f$^{2023\ 2073}$ h i^{2042} 94 Byzantine it^{gig} vg^{cl} cop^{bo}. (3) ἀφίησιν (present ind.)] 2351.

9.g. τὰ πτώματα, "bodies," occurs here in the pl., referring to the sum total of things possessed by each member of a particular group (Mussies, *Morphology,* 84); cf. the use of the distributive sing. τὸ πτῶμα in 11:8, 9.

10.a. Variant: χαρήσονται] Andr d l latt cop. On translation as fut., see *Note* 11:9.b.

10.b. Variant: εὐφρανθήσονται] fam 1611^{2329} Andr d f^{2023} l 94 Byzantine latt.

10.c. Variants: (1) πέμπουσιν] א* $\mathfrak{P}^{47}$ 025 Andr i n^{2429} 598 2019. (2) πέμψωσιν] Andr b. (3) δώσουσιν] Andr d 94 Byzantine.

10.d. Variant: omit οὗτοι] $\mathfrak{P}^{47}$ Andr g^{2045*} n^{-2429}.

10.e-e. Variants: (1) οἱ προφῆται οἱ δύο] $\mathfrak{P}^{47}$ א 2344. (2) omit οἱ προφῆται] Primasius (*hi duo*).

11.a. Variants: (1) τάς before τρεῖς] A C Oecumenius^{2053} Andr a^{-1} b^{-2059*} d^{2051} g i^{-1685} n^{-2429} Andr Ø$^{94\ 1773}$ 2019 Byzantine Andr/Byz 3 lat cop eth. (2) omit τάς before τρεῖς] א P fam 1611$^{1854\ 2344}$ Andreas; Tischendorf, *NT Graece;* [WHort]. Reading (1) is the *lectio originalis* because the anaphoric use of the article (which refers back to the anarthrous phrase ἡμέρας τρεῖς καὶ ἥμισυ in 11:9) conforms to the style of Revelation (B. Weiss, *Johannes-Apokalypse,* 125; Bousset [1906] 323; Schmid, *Studien* 2:195).

11.b-b. Variants: (1) ἐν αὐτοῖς] A fam 1006 fam 1611$^{1854\ 2329}$ 2351 Tyconius; Andreas (ἐν) (Andr e f^{2073} h i n 94 1773 2019); Tischendorf, *NT Graece;* WHort (ἐν); B. Weiss, *Johannes-Apokalypse;* Bousset (1906); Charles; Merk, *NT;* Nestle-Aland^{27}; UBSGNT^{4}. (2) αὐτοῖς] C 025 fam 1611^{1611} Oecumenius^{2053} Andr a b$^{-2059corr}$ c f$^{2031\ 2056}$ l 508. (3) εἰς αὐτούς] $\mathfrak{P}^{47}$ א Andr b^{2059corr} d g Byzantine. (4) ἐπ' αὐτούς] Andr f^{2023} Andr/Byz 3. Reading (2) probably arose through an error of haplography since the word immediately preceding it is εἰσῆλθεν (Schmid, *Studien 2*:106). Reading (3) doubtless arose as a correction of (1), which is the *lectio difficilior,* since in the vast majority of instances in the LXX and the NT the prep. used with εἰσέρχεσθαι is εἰς. Stylistically, ἐν is used as an equivalent to εἰς in Revelation only in 11:11 (Schmid, *Studien* 2:217). In Koine, ἐν is often used with verbs of motion where εἰς is expected (BAGD, 260 [I.6]; BDF § 218; BDR § 218.3). Parallels to εἰσέρχεσθαι εἰς + acc. in Rev 11:11 occur but are not common. For parallels to εἰσέρχεσθαι ἐν + dat., see Luke 9:46, εἰσῆλθεν δὲ διαλογισμὸς ἐν αὐτοῖς, "an argument entered into them"; *1 Clem.* 48:2, εἰσελθὼν ἐν αὐταῖς, "after entering into them [i.e., 'gates']" (allusion to Ps 118:19[LXX 117:19]); 48:3; *Apoc. Mos.* 5:3, ἐν ᾧ εἰσήρχετο, "in which he used to enter"; *T. Abr.* [Rec. A] 7:1; *T. Abr.* [Rec. B] 9:3, 4; *T. Jude* 9:4; *3 Apoc. Bar.* 13:4; *Gk. Apoc. Ezra* 1:6. Elsewhere the author uses εἰσέρχεσθαι εἰς + acc. in 15:8; 21:27; 22:14; εἰσέρχεσθαι πρός + acc. occurs only in 3:20 (see Mark 15:43; Luke 1:28). In the LXX εἰσέρχεσθαι is followed by εἰς + acc. (sometimes εἰς represents בְּ *bĕ,* e.g., Isa 26:20) and occasionally by the simple acc. (Helbing, *Kasussyntax,* 83; he has overlooked Ps 117:19). According to Winer, the use of ἐν with verbs of motion where εἰς is expected emphasizes the *result* of that motion, namely, *rest* (*Grammar,* 514–15).

11.c. καί functions here as a particle introducing a consecutive or purpose clause; see *Note* 11:3.d-d.

11.d-d. See *Note* 11:3.d-d.

12.a-a. Variants: (1) ἤκουσαν] ℵ* A C 025 Oecumenius^{2053} Tyc^{3} vg syr^{ph} TR Nestle-Aland^{27}; KJV; ASV; RSV; NRSV; NEB; REB ("a loud voice from heaven was heard"); Tischendorf, *NT Graece;* WHort; B. Weiss, *Johannes-Apokalypse,* 187; von Soden, *Text,* ἤκουσα[ν]; Charles, 2:304; UBSGNT^{4}. (2) ἤκουσα] 𝔓^{47} ℵ^{3} Andreas Byzantine it$^{a\ gig}$ syr^{h} cop 2351 Tyc^{1} Tyc^{2} Beatus; Bousset (1906) 323; NJB. (3) ἀκούσονται] 2329 Andr l. While reading (1) is certainly the *lectio originalis,* it is not completely clear whether the subject of ἤκουσαν is the two witnesses or the hostile bystanders. Reading (2) is obviously a correction made to include the typical εἶδον or ἤκουσα terminology, which is strikingly absent from 11:1–13 (*TCGNT*^{1}, 744; *TCGNT*^{2}, 672. On καί, see *Note* 11:3.a.

12.b-b. Variants: (1) φωνὴν μεγάλην . . . λέγουσαν] A fam 1611$^{1611\ 2329}$ Oecumenius^{2053} 2351 Byzantine; Charles (1:290; 2:304). (2) φωνῆς μεγάλης . . . λεγούσης] 𝔓^{47} C ℵ Andreas; Tischendorf, *NT Graece;* WHort^{marg}; B. Weiss, *Johannes-Apokalypse,* 187; Merk, *NT;* Nestle-Aland^{27}; UBSGNT^{4}. According to Schmid, *Studien* 2:102, "No certain decision is possible here." Normally ἀκούειν is used with the gen. of the person (6:1, 3, 5; 8:13; 16:5, 7) and the acc. of the thing (1:3; 7:4; 9:16; 22:8, 18). When φωνή is the obj. of ἀκούειν, however, it is sometimes in the gen. (3:20; 14:13; 16:1; 21:3) but more frequently in the acc. (1:10; 4:1; 5:11; 6:6, 7; 9:13; 10:4, 8; 12:10; 14:2; 18:4; 19:1, 6).

12.c-c. Variants: (1) ἀνάβατε (2nd pl. aor. imper.)] 𝔓^{47} A C ℵ 025 1773 2019; von Soden, *Text.* (2) ἀνάβητε] Andreas Byzantine. Reading (1) is an unusual form that was apparently avoided by Andreas Byzantine (Schmid, *Studien* 2:76; Gignac, *Grammar* 2:391; BDR § 95.7). Moulton-Howard (*Accidence,* 209–10) suggest that by analogy to τίμα, τιμᾶτε, the accent on ἀναβατε should be ἀναβᾶτε.

12.d. The definite article before νεφέλῃ suggests that the author assumed that this tradition was known to his audience (Charles, 1:291).

12.e. καί here introduces a temporal clause and can be translated "while."

12.f. Variant: ιε (= δεκαπέντε) before ἐχθροί] fam 1611^{1611} (𝔓^{47}). This variant, which specifies "fifteen enemies," is the result of an error of the eye in which the ιε (an abbreviation for fifteen) in the expression οιεχθροι, "the enemies," assumed separate existence (Royse, *JTS* 31 [1980] 78–80).

12.g-g. Variant: ἐμέτρησαν] 𝔓^{47}. A senseless variant, "they measured" (from μετρεῖν), based on the confusion of ἐμέτρησαν for ἐθεώρησαν, since both have the same beginning (ε) and ending (-ρησαν).

13.a. καί is used here in a consecutive sense to indicate the result of the verbal action in the preceding clause.

13.b. See *Note* 11:13.a.

13.c. In the redundant phrase ὀνόματα ἀνθρώπων, lit. "names of men," both ὄνομα and ἄνθρωπος belong to the semantic domain "people" (Louw-Nida, § 9.2, 19) and occur together here without any distinction in meaning. If ἀνθρώπων is a gen. of apposition, the phrase lit. means "names, that is, people." See *Note* 3:4.a. on ὀνόματα. Variant: ἀνδρῶν] fam 1611$^{1854\ 2329}$ Tyconius.

13.d. See *Note* 11:13.a.

13.e. Variant: ἐν φόβῳ] ℵ 2351 lat syr^{ph}.

14.a. Variants: (1) ἀπῆλθεν] majority. (2) παρῆλθεν] ℵ Andr i^{2042}. παρέρχεσθαι does not occur elsewhere in Revelation, while ἀπέρχεσθαι occurs seven times apart from 11:14 and in a similarly worded formula in 9:12.

14.b-b. Variants: (1) ἰδοὺ ἡ οὐαὶ ἡ τρίτη ἔρχεται] A C fam 1006$^{1006\ 1841}$ fam 1611$^{1611\ 2329}$ Oecumenius^{2053} 2351 Andreas. (2) ἰδοὺ ἔρχεται ἡ οὐαὶ ἡ τρίτη] 𝔓^{47} ℵ^{2} fam 1611^{2344} 2019 it^{gig}. (3) ἡ οὐαὶ ἡ τρίτη ἰδοὺ ἔρχεται] Byzantine.

Form/Structure/Setting

I. OUTLINE

4. The temple and the two witnesses (11:1–14)
   a. The command to measure the temple (vv 1–2)
      (1) John given a measure (v 1a)
      (2) The double command (vv 1b–2)
         (a) What should be measured (v 1b)
            [1] The temple of God
            [2] The sanctuary

[3] Those who worship there
(b) What should not be measured (v 2)
[1] Area: the outer court (v 2a)
[2] Location: outside the temple (v 2a)
[3] Reason (v 2b)
[a] It is given to the nations
[b] They will trample the holy city for forty-two months
b. The careers of the two witnesses (vv 3–13)
(1) Their mission and authority (vv 3–6)
(a) Their mission and status (vv 3–4)
[1] God authorizes his two witnesses to prophesy (v 3)
[a] For 1,260 days (v 3a)
[b] Clothed in sackcloth (v 3b)
[2] Their symbolic status (v 4)
[a] They are the two olive trees (that stand before the Lord of the earth) (v 4a)
[b] They are the two lampstands that stand before the Lord of the earth (v 4ab)
(b) Their inviolability (v 5)
[1] If anyone wants to harm them, fire issues from their mouths to destroy their enemies (v 5a)
[2] If anyone wants to harm them, they must die in such a way (v 5b)
(c) Their authority (v 6)
[1] They have power to shut the heavens (v 6a)
[a] Purpose: that no rain may fall
[b] Length of time: during the days of their prophesying
[2] They have power over the waters, to turn them into blood (v 6b)
[3] They have power to strike the earth (v 6c)
[a] With every plague
[b] As often as they wish
(2) The fate of the two witnesses (vv 7–10)
(a) The death of the two witnesses (v 7)
[1] The period of their inviolability ends: "when they complete their testimony" (v 7a)
[2] The role of the beast (v 7ab)
[a] His origin: he ascends from the abyss (v 7a)
[b] His hostility (v 7ab)
{1} He will wage war on them
{2} He will conquer them
{3} He will kill them
(b) The desecration of their corpses (vv 8–10)
[1] Mode of desecration: public exposure of their corpses (v 8a)
[2] Place of desecration: the square of the great city (v 8ab)

[a] First symbolic name: Sodom (v 8b)
[b] Second symbolic name: Egypt (v 8b)
[c] Description: where their Lord was crucified (v 8c)
[3] Their corpses are a public spectacle (vv 9–10)
[a] Length of time: three and one-half days (v 9a)
[b] Identity of the onlookers (v 9a)
{1} Some from the peoples
{2} Some from the tribes
{3} Some from the languages
{4} Some from the nations
[c] Activity of onlookers (v 9ab)
{1} They look at the corpses (v 9a)
{2} They will not permit burial in a tomb (v 9b)
[d] The reaction of the onlookers (v 10ab)
{1} They rejoice over the corpses (v 10a)
{2} They are joyful (v 10b)
{3} They exchange gifts (v 10b)
[e] Reasons for behavior: the two prophets had tormented the people of the earth (v 10c)
(3) The ultimate triumph of the two witnesses (vv 11–12)
(a) Their resurrection (v 11)
[1] Facts concerning the event (v 11a)
[a] Preceding time period: three and one-half days
[b] Means: the breath of life from God enters them
[2] The reaction: great fear falls on those who saw them (v 11b)
(b) Their ascension (v 12)
[1] Their summons to heaven (v 12a)
[a] They hear a loud voice from heaven
[b] The message: "Come up here!"
[2] Their ascension to heaven (v 12bc)
[a] Means: in a cloud (v 12b)
[b] Circumstances: in the sight of their enemies (v 12c)
(4) Concluding scene of judgment and repentance (v 13)
(a) The judgment (v 13a)
[1] Reference to time: at that hour
[2] There is a great earthquake
(b) Negative effects of the judgment (v 13bc)
[1] One-tenth of the city falls (v 13b)
[2] Seven thousand people are killed (v 13c)
(c) Positive effects of the judgment (v 13d)
[1] The rest are terrified
[2] The rest give glory to God
c. The second and third woes (v 14)
(1) The announcement that the second woe has passed (v 14a)
(2) The imminence of the third woe (v 14b)

II. Literary Analysis

Rev 11:1–13 is a coherent literary unit consisting of two major subunits, vv 1–2 and vv 3–13. Rev 11:14 functions both as a conclusion to 11:1–13 and as an introduction to 11:15–18. The view that 11:1–19 constitutes a single vision that begins with a focus on the earthly temple and concludes with an emphasis on the heavenly temple (Boismard, *RB* 56 [1949] 311) ignores other formal structural features. A number of interpreters regard 11:1–13 as the beginning of the content of the little scroll mentioned in 10:8–11 (Lohmeyer, 89; Bornkamm, "Komposition," 2:216–18; Court, *Myth and History,* 84; Bauckham, "Conversion," 266 [for whom the little scroll in 10:8–11 represents the scroll with seven seals of 5:1 *in nuce*]), though others argue convincingly that it is not (Yarbro Collins, *Combat Myth,* 27; A. J. P. Garrow, *Revelation* [London; New York: Routledge, 1997] 32).

The analysis of the composition of 11:1–13 presents several difficult compositional and interpretive problems. The author, addressed by an unidentified person (see *Comment* on v 1b), is given a series of instructions in direct discourse introduced by the present participle λέγων, "saying" (v 1). It is not clear where this speech ends. Many interpreters and translations simply assume (as indicated by quotation marks or paragraphing) that the speech concludes with v 3 (RSV; NRSV; NIV; REB; Allo, 149; Lohse, 63; Sweet, 180). The reference in v 8 to the city "where their Lord was crucified" suggests that the speech has already concluded. It is important to observe that the narrative about the two witnesses in vv 4–13 is *not* in the form of a vision report. Either the speech of the unidentified speaker found in vv 1–3 continues through to v 13 (unlikely), *or* the speech concludes with v 4, which contains brief allusions to Zech 4:1–14. In spite of the nonvisionary character of 11:1–13, John has couched this narrative in a style very similar to the visions found in the rest of the book. Vv 1–2 contain five main verbs in past tenses. The narrative that begins in v 3 continues through v 13 (on the tenses in Rev 11, see Min, *Apocalisse,* 71–76). This entire section is presented not as a vision that John saw and is now reporting but as a narrative prophecy focusing on the two witnesses.

A. *Rev 11:1–2*

In Rev 11:1–2, the seer is instructed to measure the temple and the altar (i.e., the inner portion of the temple), but he is expressly told not to measure the court outside the temple, "for the Gentiles will be permitted to keep the holy city under subjection for forty-two months." This short text is obviously fragmentary: (1) It does not cohere well with the preceding unit of text in 10:10–11, where the last speakers (λέγουσιν, "they say," v 11) are not identified, and the speaker in 11:1 is identified only with the participle λέγων, "saying," which has no obvious antecedent. (2) 11:1–2 consists largely of a command given to the author by an unspecified person, but it is a command that the author does not fulfill; i.e., he is told to measure the temple, but there is no accompanying narrative suggesting that he actually did so. This is surprising since the reader has been led to expect that angelic or divine commands to the seer will be immediately obeyed (e.g., in 10:8 the author is told to take the little scroll from the angel, which he does in v 9; in 10:9 he is told to eat the book, which he does in v 10). (3) The location or point of view of the author is problematic. In 10:1–2, 4, 5, 8, it is presupposed that the author is on earth, while

11:1–2 suggests that he is either in the vicinity of Jerusalem (where the temple was) or in heaven if the temple he is to measure is the heavenly temple. However, there is no indication of *how* he has access to the temple, whether in a vision or through physical transport (or both). (4) Though Revelation was finally edited toward the end of the first century A.D., a generation after the destruction of Jerusalem in A.D. 70, there is no indication in this brief pericope that the temple was actually described. The implicit point of view of the pericope is *before* A.D. 70.

Many commentators see two originally separate sources behind vv 1–2 and vv 3–13 (Yarbro Collins, *Combat Myth,* 195 n. 60). These sources are frequently thought to be two Jewish oracles that have been combined, with perhaps just one Christian interpolation in v 8 (Wellhausen, *Analyse,* 15; Pfleiderer, *Urchristentum* 2:283; Bousset [1906] 326–27; Charles, 1:270, 273; Loisy, 204; Beasley-Murray, 37–38; Giblin, *NTS* 30 [1984] 454 n. 4), while others regard 11:1–13 as a single oracle (Beckwith, 584–85; argued in detail by Min, *Apocalisse,* 84–90). With regard to vocabulary, it is quite remarkable that *none* of the 107 *hapax legomena* in Revelation (words used only in Revelation in the NT) occurs in 11:1–13.

B. Rev 11:3–13

Rev 11:3–13 is a prophetic narrative at first dominated by verbs in the future tense (vv 3–10) and then by verbs in the past tense. The narrative has an essentially parabolic or allegorical character (Bauckham, "Conversion," 373–74), for the two prophets seem to represent the Christian witness in the world while "the great city" in which the narrative is set represents Jerusalem, but in a wider sense the world of humankind. This section can be divided up into three text units: (1) the mission and authority of the two witnesses (vv 3–6); (2) the lynching of the two witnesses (vv 7–10); and (3) the victory of the two witnesses, followed by the punishment of their enemies (vv 11–13a) and the conversion of the survivors (v 13b).

(1) The first unit, vv 3–6, begins with a speech that could be attributed to either God or Christ because of the use of the first person: "*I* will grant *my* two witnesses authority to prophesy" (v 3a). It is clear that the speaker-narrator has changed by v 8, which speaks of the place where "*their* Lord was crucified." It is likely that the divine speech ends with v 3 and that vv 4–6 form the beginning of the narrative description of the ministry of the two witnesses. This is one of several formal ways of linking vv 1–2 with vv 3–13. The period of the ministry of the two witnesses is limited to 1,260 days (v 3), a symbolic number for a limited eschatological period, equivalent to the forty-two months of v 2 (another formal link between vv 1–2 and 3–13). The role and identity of the two witnesses are understood as identical with the two olive trees and two lampstands of Zech 4:3, 14, though Zech 4 is not mined further after Rev 11:4.

The ministry of the two witnesses is described succinctly in negative terms in two synonymous couplets in vv 5–6. Their ability to launch preemptive strikes against those who intend to harm them is emphasized, but nothing is said of their prophetic role in preaching repentance, which is briefly alluded to by mentioning that they were clothed in sackcloth (v 3). The absence of any positive emphasis on the nature of their prophetic ministry suggests that, for whatever reason, the source used by the author has been truncated.

(2) The lynching of the two witnesses is described in vv 7–10. When the

prophetic ministry of the two witnesses has concluded, presumably after the conclusion of the forty-two-month period mentioned in v 3, a new and unexpected character appears in the drama. The beast, identified by the participial phrase "who ascends from the abyss," is described as making war against the two witnesses, a war that concludes with his victory over them and their death (v 7). The term τὸ θηρίον, "*the* beast," has a definite article, which suggests that the author assumed that this figure was well known to the audience (the beast next appears in 13:1, this time *without* the definite article, as if he had not been mentioned previously). Nothing is said about the beast's motivation for attacking and killing the two witnesses, and after he has finished his grisly task he disappears from the narrative as abruptly as he appeared. The reader's many unanswered questions about this narrative suggest that the author has omitted a number of features from his source, which presumably existed in a more coherent form.

The unburied bodies of the two witnesses lie in the public square of the great city, which we learn is Jerusalem since it is "the great city where their Lord was crucified" (v 8). An implicit parallel is thus drawn between the death of Christ and the deaths of the two witnesses. "The great city," however, which the reader initially identifies with Jerusalem, is identified prophetically or spiritually with "Sodom" and "Egypt," ancient cities that symbolize depravity and bondage. Since representatives of "peoples and tribes and tongues and nations" are present to gloat over the deaths of the two witnesses (vv 9–10), "the great city" suddenly seems to symbolize the world.

(3) The next segment of the narrative (vv 11–13) centers on the unexpected event of the resurrection and ascension of the two witnesses as well as the punishment of their enemies. Somewhat surprisingly, this section is dominated by verbs in the past tense, as if it were a narrative of a past sequence of events. The statement that the two prophets were lying dead in the public square for *three and one-half* days suggests a partial parallel to the three-day period between the death and resurrection of Jesus, while three and one-half days is also reminiscent of the Danielic phrase "time, times, and half a time," or "year, two years, and half a year" (Dan 7:25; 12:7; cf. Rev 12:14), which are variants of the forty-two months of Rev 11:2 (and Rev 13:5) and the 1,260 days of Rev 11:3 (and Rev 12:6). Three striking events follow in quick succession. First, the resurrection of the two prophets results in great fear on the part of those who had rejoiced over their deaths (a stereotypical reaction). Second, the summons of the heavenly voice, followed by the ascension of the two prophets to heaven, produces astonishment in their enemies (another stereotypical reaction). Third, a great earthquake occurs immediately, destroying a tenth of the city and killing seven thousand people. The rest "gave glory to God," i.e., repented (v 13). This result is striking, for it is the only instance in Revelation in which punitive judgment produces repentance on the part of those who experience such judgment.

C. Revelation 11:14

This passage, which refers to the completion of the "second woe," both concludes the lengthy interruption to the series of seven trumpets from 10:1 to 11:13 and serves as an introduction to the "third woe," which is never referred to in the following narrative as having taken place. More specifically, the author uses this structural device to connect 10:1–11:13 to the sixth trumpet in 9:12–21, though the connection is strictly formal and hardly serves to unify such diverse material.

III. SOURCE CRITICISM OF REV 11:1–13

The geographical center of interest of Rev 11:1–13 is Palestine, as indicated by (1) the symbolic significance of the temple in Jerusalem (vv 1–2), (2) the mention of "the holy city" where the temple is located (v 2), (3) the identification of the city where the two witnesses were killed as the place where Jesus was crucified, i.e., Jerusalem (v 8), and (4) the threat of drought (v 6), a dominating concern in much of Palestine (Reymond, *L'eau,* 1ff., 31ff.; note that the threat of drought is not part of the seal plagues, the bowl plagues, or the trumpet plagues elsewhere in Revelation). It is also apparent that this unit of text reflects a Palestinian tradition dating from before the fall of Jerusalem in A.D. 70, a tradition that has been reworked by the author, and may be one the earliest partial texts out of which Revelation was fashioned. Some have argued that Rev 11:3–13 is a Christianized version of a Jewish Antichrist myth, though this is problematic in view of the singular and unexpected mention of the beast who ascends from the abyss in 11:7. The setting within which this tradition was reworked was very probably a situation of persecution. Apart from the obvious interpolation in 11:8, there is nothing in 11:1–13 that suggests a Christian origin (Bousset [1906] 326).

A. *Parallels with the* Apoc. Elijah *4:7–19*

Though the Coptic *Apocalypse of Elijah* is of uncertain date (A.D. 150 to 275; see Wintermute in Charlesworth, *OTP* 1:729–30), in its present form, it is a Christian document that is probably a revision of an earlier Jewish composition that perhaps originated during the first century B.C. (Rosenstiehl, *L'Apocalypse d'Elie,* 75–76). It exists in Greek in one fragmentary text and two quotations (Denis, *Fragmenta,* 103–4). It is clear that *Apoc. Elijah* 4:7–19 is either dependent on Rev 11:3–13, or that both passages are dependent on an earlier source. For reasons that will be discussed below, the latter hypothesis appears the most likely (see Joachim Jeremias, *TDNT* 2:939–41). The parallels and differences are indicated in the following synoptic summaries:

Rev 11:3–13	*Apoc. Elijah 4:7–19*
	Elijah and Enoch hear from heaven that the shameless one has revealed himself in the holy place and they descend.
God empowers his two witnesses to prophesy for 1,260 days (three and one-half years).	
	They give a speech denouncing the shameless one.
The beast from the abyss will make war on them, conquer and kill them.	The shameless one, angry, fights with them for seven days in the marketplace of the great city.

Their corpses will lie in the street of the great city.	Killed, they lie for three and one-half days in the marketplace.
After three and one-half days they will rise up; fear will fall on those who see them.	On the fourth day they rise up and again denounce the shameless one.
	Again angry, the shameless one fights with them, and the whole city will surround them.
A voice from heaven invites them to come, after which they ascend.	On that day they will shout up to heaven as they shine, and all the people of the world will see them.
At that hour a great quake destroys one-tenth of the city and kills seven thousand. The rest give glory to God.	

The narrative begins with the two Israelite worthies in heaven, where they had been raptured according to OT and Jewish tradition, and they only make their appearance through a descent from heaven after they learn that the eschatological adversary has revealed himself in Jerusalem, presumably in the temple. Thus this text provides an explanation for the presence of the two witnesses, which is mysteriously left unaccounted for in Rev 11:3–13. Unlike in Rev 11:3–13, they are said to address the adversary (see the Tabitha account below). The conflict between the adversary and Enoch and Elijah lasts seven days, and when they are killed, their bodies lie for three and one-half days in the marketplace. As in Rev 11:11, they are resurrected (though the mention of the *fourth* day seems to presuppose that they were dead for *three* days in an earlier version). They again denounce the adversary in a speech (as in the Tabitha account below), and this time the adversary and the population of the city surround them, doubtless intending to do away with them again. They shout *to* heaven (unlike in Rev 11:12, where the two witnesses are addressed by a heavenly voice), implicitly for divine assistance. This assistance is apparently provided, for they take on a glorified shining appearance, and since all the people in the world can see them, they apparently ascend to heaven (cf. Rev 1:7, "every eye will see him"). Though there is a basic similarity between these two texts, the only clear instance of the dependence of *Apoc. Elijah* 4:7–19 on Rev 11:3–13 is *Apoc. Elijah* 4:13–14 (the Shameless One fights and kills Elijah and Enoch in the marketplace of the great city, where they lie dead for three and one-half days) on Rev 11:7–9 (the beast fights and kills the two witnesses, and their corpses lie on the street of the great city for three and one-half days). It is probable, however, that this similarity is based on a later Christian revision of an earlier Jewish source.

The relationship between the two texts is more complex, however, because of a doublet involving a woman named Tabitha in *Apoc. Elijah* 14:9–15:7, with italicized portions containing parallels to the noted texts (P. Chester Beatty 2018; tr. Pietersma, *Apoc. Elijah*):

The young woman whose name is Tabitha
will hear that the shameless one
has made his appearance in the holy places. She will
dress in her linen clothes and hurry
to Judaea and reprove him
as far as Jerusalem, and say
to him, "O you shameless one, O you lawless
one, O you enemy of all
the saints!" *Then the shameless one will become*
angry with the young woman [Rev 12:17a].
He will pursue her to the region of the setting of the sun [Rev 12:6, 13–14].
He will suck her blood in the evening
and toss her onto the temple,
and she will become salvation for the people.
At dawn she will rise up alive and
rebuke him saying, "You shameless one,
You have no power over my soul, nor over my body,
because I live in the Lord always,
and even my blood which you spilled
on the temple became salvation for the people."

In this text, as in the following one from Lactantius, a single messenger from God is involved rather than two. In this case it is a woman named Tabitha. While the scenario is strikingly similar to Rev 11:3–13, the differences are such that there appears to be no literary relationship between the two texts. As in Rev 11:7, there is a single enemy, who is the eschatological adversary. This adversary appears in the "holy places," i.e., "Jerusalem," and Tabitha dons a special linen garment (suggesting purity and priesthood) and meets the adversary. Unlike Rev 11:3–13, but similar to *Apoc. Elijah* 4:8–12, Tabitha reproves the adversary with a brief speech, which angers him (note the parallel to Rev 12:17). He pursues her to the east (again cf. Rev 12:6, 13–14) and kills her and (using the vampire motif) sucks her blood. That he is suddenly back in Jerusalem with her body suggests that the italicized portions in the translation above have been interpolated into an earlier text. After she has been thrown onto the temple, she will rise from the dead the next morning (an interval of one day, not three or three and one-half days) and again reprove the adversary with a brief speech to the effect that throwing her on the temple has provided salvation for the people, a motif drawn from Jewish martyrological literature. Further, nothing is said about an ascension to heaven.

B. The Source Underlying Rev 11:1–13: Parallels with Lactantius Div. Inst. *7.17.1–3*

Lactantius *Div. Inst.* 7.17 exhibits close parallels with Rev 11:3–13 (see the discussion in K. Berger, *Auferstehung,* 66–74; Flusser, "Hystaspes," 12–75). After quoting the relevant text, it will be arranged in order to facilitate a synoptic comparison with Rev 11:3–13 (tr. M. F. McDonald, *Lactantius,* 517–18; italicized portions have no parallels in Rev 11:3–13):

> Now, when the end of these times is imminent, a great prophet [*magnus propheta*] will be sent from God to convert men to a recognition of God, and he will have the power of working miracles. Whenever men will not hear him, he will close heaven and will hold

back the rains; he will change water into blood, and will torture them with thirst and hunger; and fire will proceed from his mouth and burn whoever will attempt to hurt him. *By these prodigies and powers, he will convert many to the worship of God. When these works of his have been carried out, another king will rise from Syria, born of the evil spirit, the overthrower and destroyer of the human race, who will destroy the remains of that previous evil one together with itself.* This one will fight against the prophet of God; he will conquer and kill him and suffer him to lie unburied. But after the third day, he will rise again and will be taken into heaven while all look on and marvel.

The parallels can be seen more clearly in a synoptic presentation in which the only change in order is the placement of Rev 11:6 before 11:5 (adapted from Flusser, "Hystaspes," 68–69):

Rev 11:3–12	*Lactantius* Div. Inst. *7.17.1–8*
[3]I will permit my two witnesses to prophesy.	[1]Now, when the end of these times is imminent, a great prophet will be sent by God to convert men to a recognition of God,
	and he will have the power of working miracles.
[6a]They have power to shut up heaven that rain might not fall during the period when they prophesy.	[2]Wherever men will not hear him, he will close heaven and will hold back the rains.
[6b]They also have power over the waters, that is, to turn them to blood.	He will change water into blood, and will torture them with thirst and hunger.
[5]If anyone wants to harm them, fire proceeds from their mouths and utterly destroys their enemies.	And fire will proceed from his mouth and burn whoever will attempt to hurt him.
[7]When they finish their witness, the beast who ascends from the abyss will wage war on them that he might conquer them and kill them.	[3]This one will fight against the prophet of God; he will conquer and kill him
[9]But people would not permit their bodies to be buried.	and suffer him to lie unburied.
[11]Now after three and one-half days a spirit of life from God entered into them so that they stood on their feet with the result that great fear fell on	But after the third day, he will rise again

those who saw them.	
[12]They heard a loud voice	
from heaven saying to them,	
"Come up here." They ascended	and will be taken into heaven
to heaven on a cloud while their	while all look on and marvel.
enemies looked on.	

Since Lactantius lived from ca. A.D. 250 to 325, it is certainly possible that he may have been influenced by the text of Revelation. In *Epitome* 66.9, a later work in which the *Divine Institutes* are presented in abbreviated form, Lactantius writes, "By these miracles he will seduce many of them so that they will worship him and receive his sign on the hand and on the forehead" (*Quibus prodigiis inliciet multos ut adorent eum signumque eius in manu aut fronte suscipiant;* text in Perrin, *Épitomé,* 264). This reflects an alteration of what he had originally written in *Div. Inst.* 7.17.7 (tr. McDonald, *Lactantius,* 518), "Those who believe and come to him will be branded by him as though cattle," an alteration apparently made in the later text in light of Rev 13:16. Outside of *Div. Inst.* 7.17, Lactantius appears to reflect an awareness of Revelation when he speaks of the second resurrection after a thousand years (*Div. Inst.* 7.26.5–7; cf. Rev 20:11–13, though the term "second resurrection" does not occur in Revelation). Lactantius was thoroughly familiar with classical sources, the Sibylline Oracles and Hermetic writings (Ogilvie, *Lactantius,* 28–36), and even early Christian extracanonical literature (Ogilvie, *Lactantius,* 105–8), but less familiar with the Bible (see Ogilvie, *Lactantius,* 96–110, where he concludes that the seventy-three biblical quotations in *Div. Inst.* 4 are closely related to Cyprian's *Ad Quirinum,* though Lactantius cannot have drawn these quotations from the *Ad Quirinum* in its present state). Outside of *Div. Inst.* 7 (with its seventy-three quotations of the Bible), the rest of *Divine Institutes* contains just seven quotations (Ogilvie, *Lactantius,* 107–8), and the other works of Lactantius contain no biblical quotations at all (with the exception of the *Epitome*).

But there are, in fact, several reasons for supposing that Lactantius is dependent here on the *Oracles of Hystaspes* or some Jewish source and *not* on Rev 11:3–13, based on similarities and differences between these two texts. (1) A single prophet is found in Lactantius (who probably is dependent on an Elijah tradition); two prophets are found in Revelation. (2) The result of closing the heavens and turning the waters into blood in Lactantius is to torment people with hunger and thirst, while this effect is absent from Revelation. (3) The narrative in Revelation is consistently told with verbs in *past* tenses, while that in Lactantius is told using *future* tenses. (4) The text in Revelation contains a number of explanatory glosses (see *Comment*), none of which appear in the account of Lactantius. (5) The narrative in Lactantius continues on to describe events similar to those in Rev 13:1–10 (see *Form/Structure/Setting* under Rev 13:1–18), but with no apparent allusions to Rev 11:14–12:17. (6) The concluding earthquake that destroys one-tenth of the city, kills seven thousand people, and results in the mass conversion of survivors in Rev 11:13 is not mentioned in Lactantius, which suggests that this element has been added by John. (7) There is no mention in Lactantius of the variations on three and one-half found in Rev 11:3, 9, 11, namely 1,260 days (v 3) and three and one-half days (vv 9, 11), which also suggests that these have been added by John. (8) There is no mention in Lactantius of the city or its inhabitants, though these elements are essential for Rev 11:3–13 (K. Berger, *Auferstehung,* 71). (9) The identification of the enemies of the two witnesses as two separate entities, the beast and the representatives of all nations found in Rev 11:3–13, is missing in Lactantius. (10) The preliminary successes of the witness in converting his hearers has no parallel in Rev 11:3–13. (11) Lactantius places this event "when the end of these times is imminent," while there is no explicit link with the eschaton in Rev 11:3–13.

The determination of the source or sources used by Lactantius is problematic. It is perhaps a likely conjecture that a Christian compiler, writing in Greek and probably dependent to a certain extent on Porphyry, had placed the Oracles of Hystaspes together with certain Sibylline Oracles, the Oracles of Clarian Apollo, and the catalogue of Sibyls, which originated with Varro (Ogilvie, *Lactantius,* 54–55). It was this compilation upon which Lactantius was dependent.

C. *Editorial Expansions of Rev 11:1–13*

In the text of Rev 11:1–13 given below, the italicized portions are interpolations, revisions, or substitutions made in an earlier text by John, who adapted them to the larger apocalyptic narrative of his work (see *Comment* on each phrase for an explanation). The space between vv 1–2 and 3–14 indicates that they were in all probability separate traditions linked together by John.

1 I was given a reed, like a staff, with these instructions: "Go and measure the temple of God, including the sanctuary, and count those who worship within it. 2 But exclude the courtyard outside the temple and do not measure it, for the Gentiles will be permitted to keep the holy city under subjection for *forty-two months.*

3 "I will permit my *two* witness*es* to prophesy *1,260 days* clothed in sackcloth." 4 *These are the two olive trees and the two menorahs which stand before the Lord of the earth.* 5 If anyone wants to harm them, fire proceeds from their mouths and utterly destroys their enemies, since if anyone should wish to harm them, it is necessary that they should die in such a way. 6 They have power to shut up heaven that rain might not fall during the period when they prophesy. They also have power over the waters, that is, to turn them to blood, and to strike the earth with every type of plague whenever they might wish. 7 When they finish their witness, *the beast who ascends from the abyss will wage war on them,* that he might conquer them and kill them. 8 Their bodies will lie in the public square of the great city, *which is called, prophetically, "Sodom" and "Egypt," where their Lord was also crucified.* 9 And some of the *peoples and tribes and tongues and nations* will see their bodies for *three and one-half days,* but people will not permit their bodies to be buried. 10 The inhabitants of the earth will rejoice over them, and they will be joyful and will exchange gifts with one another, for these two prophets tormented the inhabitants of the earth. 11 Now after the *three and one-half days* the breath of life from God entered into them so that they stood on their feet, with the result that great fear fell on those who saw them. 12 They heard a loud voice from heaven saying to them, "Come up here." They ascended to heaven on a cloud while their enemies looked on. 13 And in that hour there was a great earthquake, so that a tenth of the city was destroyed and seven thousand people were killed in the earthquake, with the result that the survivors were terrified and gave glory to the God of heaven.

IV. Central Interpretive Issues

A. *The Symbolic Act of Measuring the Temple (Rev 11:1–2)*

1. The Main Issues. There are several clusters of interpretive problems presented by vv 1–2: (a) Is Rev 11:1–2 based on an earlier prophetic oracle formulated before the destruction of the temple in A.D. 70, perhaps by Zealots, or was the brief narrative of the symbolic measuring of the temple formulated by the author decades after the temple had been destroyed? (b) Is the temple referred to in vv 1–2 the physical temple in Jerusalem, or is it the heavenly temple? (c) How should the apparently symbolic references to the "temple," "altar," "worshipers," "outer court," and "holy city" be interpreted? The following discussion will attempt to show the range of possible answers to each of these problems.

2. The Origin of Rev 11:1–2. Rev 11:1–2 rests somewhat uneasily in its present context. It is tenuously linked with the immediately preceding unit of text in 10:8–11 (the commission to prophesy), in that it is a symbolic prophetic action enacting both salvation and judgment and can therefore be considered the first step in carrying out the prophetic commission of 10:11. It is more clearly linked to the text unit that follows in 11:3–13 (the story of the two witnesses) by the temporal reference to forty-two months specified for the subjugation of the outer court and the holy city to the Gentiles (v 2), which is equivalent to the 1,260 days of the ministry of the two witnesses (v 3), and by the reference to "the holy city" in v 2, which is matched by the reference to "the great city" in v 8 (both presumably referring to Jerusalem). Further, 10:8–11 is linked to 11:3–13 by the occurrence of the verb προφητεῦειν, "prophesy," in 10:11 and 11:3 (and the noun προφήτης, "prophet," in 11:10).

There are a series of difficulties within 11:1–2 as well: (a) The abrupt introduction of the passage (the subject of the participle λέγων, "saying," is unspecified; the usual visionary formulas such as "I saw" or "I heard" are absent). (b) The command to the visionary to measure the temple is never actually carried out. (c) Nothing is said about when or how the visionary could have access to the temple to carry out the task of measuring. (d) The Jerusalem temple is mentioned only here in Revelation and otherwise is apparently of little or no concern to the author. (e) Although the temple had been destroyed in A.D. 70, decades before the final composition of Revelation, nothing is said about that destruction, except that the outer court and the city will be overrun by the Gentiles. (f) The promise that the sanctuary of the temple complex will not be profaned by the Gentiles contradicts the expectation in Daniel, which predicts that the entire (second) temple will be desecrated but not destroyed (Dan 8:11–14; 9:26–27 [see Collins, *Daniel,* 357]), reflecting the conquest of Jerusalem and the temple mount by Antioches Epiphanes in 167 B.C., and the expectation that the temple will be completely destroyed, found in the eschatological discourse of Jesus (Mark 13:2 = Matt 24:2 = Luke 21:6) and alluded to in other sayings of Jesus (Mark 14:58 = Matt 26:61; Mark 15:29 = Matt 27:40; Acts 6:14; cf. John 2:19).

These are some of the factors that motivated Wellhausen to propose that 11:1–2 was a fragment of a Zealot prophecy from the weeks before the fall of Jerusalem in A.D. 70, expressing the belief that the Romans would take the city and the temple court but would be unable to penetrate the inner parts of the temple, which were held by the Zealots themselves (Wellhausen, *Skizzen* 6:221–23; id., *Analyse,* 15). This proposal has been accepted by many other scholars, including Bousset (1906) 324–30; J. Weiss, *Offenbarung,* 128–29 (who dates this prophecy to the few months between May and August A.D. 70); Beckwith, 586–87; Charles, 1:270–74; Behm, 58; Kraft, 152–54; Lohse, 64; Beasley-Murray, 176–77; Hengel, *Zealots,* 243; Müller, 206–7; Boring, 143. Toward the end of the war, the Zealots retreated into the sanctuary itself, the holy place and the holy of holies, as a place of last resort (Jos. *J.W.* 6.122 [tr. LCL]):

> Into those hallowed and inviolable precincts they rushed in arms, their hands yet hot with the blood of their countrymen; and to such lengths of crime did they proceed, that the indignation which the Jews might naturally have displayed had the Romans inflicted such wanton outrages upon them, was now manifested by the Romans against the Jews, for profaning their own sacred places.

Wellhausen's proposal is based in part on Josephus's attestation to intense prophetic activity during the last weeks and months of the war (*J.W.* 6.285–87; tr. LCL):

> They owed their destruction to a false prophet, who had on that day proclaimed to the people in the city that God commanded them to go up to the temple court [τὸ ἱερόν], to receive there the tokens of their deliverance. Numerous prophets, indeed, were at this period suborned by the tyrants to delude the people, by bidding them await help from God, in order that desertions might be checked and that those who were above fear and precaution might be encouraged by hope.

As a result of this prophecy and perhaps others like it, some six thousand Jews waited in the inner courts of the temple in expectation of divine intervention, but all were killed by the Romans or died in the fire (Jos. *J.W.* 6.283–84). Caird (131) dismisses Wellhausen's proposal cavalierly as "improbable, useless, and absurd," while Flusser ("Hystaspes," 13–14) disputes the idea that such a written prophecy might have survived the destruction of the temple and argues that even had it done so, it would quickly have been proven wrong by the fate of the temple. Others have similarly argued that a Zealot oracle that had been proven wrong would hardly have been accepted by Christians (Roloff [ET] 129; Giesen [1997] 240). Against this argument, it must be noted that oracles are rarely, if ever, "proven wrong" and are always capable of manipulation and reinterpretation, so that this objection has no great weight. Flusser rather suggests that 11:1–2 reflects a widespread apocalyptic conviction from the second temple period of the essential inviolability of Jerusalem and the temple (Zech 12:2–6; *1 Enoch* 56:5–8; *Sib. Or.* 5.101–10; Jos. *J.W.* 6.98). Dio Cassius, for example, reports the existence of a Jewish rumor that Jerusalem was impregnable (65.5.4; cf. Jos. *J.W.* 5.458–59). This view is also maintained by Feuillet (*NTS* 4 [1957–58] 188), who suggests that an echo of this view is found in *2 Apoc. Bar.* 6:3–9, where, just before the destruction of Jerusalem, an angel descended to the holy of holies and removed the veil, the holy ephod, the mercy seat, the two tables, the priestly vestments, the altar of incense, the forty-eight precious stones worn by the priests, and all the holy vessels, which were then buried in a secret place in the earth until the eschaton (cf. *2 Apoc. Bar.* 80:2–3; *Par. Jer.* 3:10–11, 18–19; other apocalyptic traditions recognize that the temple furniture and vessels were destroyed or carried off as booty: *Apoc. Abr.* 27; 4 Ezra 10:21–23). For the Jews, the temple was both the center and the stronghold against the siege of Titus (Hengel, *Zealots,* 221–24; cf. Dio Cassius 65.6.1–3). However, it is only the inviolability of the temple (ναός), altar, and those who worship there that is preserved according to Rev 11:1–2, for the outer court and the holy city are destined to be controlled by the nations for a restricted period of time (n.b. that the *destruction* of Jerusalem and the temple is not even suggested).

Lohmeyer (88–89) proposed that rather than regard vv 1–2 as a Zealot oracle from before A.D. 70, the reader should understand it as an early Christian oracle in which the "temple" and "those that worship in it" represent Christians and the act of measuring is equivalent to the sealing of 7:3–8. Similarly, vv 1–2, according to Roloff ([ET] 129), are based on an early Christian prophetic saying interpreting the events of A.D. 70 from a Christian perspective.

3. Earthly or Heavenly Temple? Another problem is whether the temple referred to in 11:1–2 is the literal temple in Jerusalem (presumably reflecting a period before A.D. 70), or whether the text was formulated with the transcendent, heavenly temple in view. If the author incorporated a prophetic oracle that originated *before* A.D. 70, as many interpreters propose, into his composition more than two decades after the destruction of Jerusalem and the temple in A.D. 70, he *must* have understood it symbolically.

(a) Most interpreters understand the primary reference in vv 1–2 to be to the literal temple in Jerusalem (Zahn, 421–22; Allo, 129; Lohmeyer, 87; Lohse, 64; Giesen [1997] 241). Some interpreters base this view on the proposal made by J. Wellhausen that a Jewish oracle, probably of Zealot origin, concerning the inviolability of the temple despite the capture of the city was made and circulated during the brief period A.D. 67–70 (Wellhausen, *Analyse,* 15; Bousset [1906] 324–30; Beckwith, 586–87; Charles, 1:270–73). Of course, those who think that the Revelation of John was written *before* A.D. 70 can simply regard 11:1–2 as a prophecy by the author that was not fulfilled. Arguments supporting the interpretation of the temple and the altar and those who worship there as references to the *historical temple* in Jerusalem are the following: (i) The notion that the heavenly worshipers of God need protection seems unnecessary. (ii) According to 10:1, the seer is on earth when he witnesses the descent of the mighty angel. There is nothing to suggest that the seer's position on the earth has changed when he is commanded to measure the temple of God in 11:1. (iii) The symbolic interpretation of vv 1–2, advocated by many interpreters who regard the primary reference to be the temple in Jerusalem (Roloff [ET] 128–29; Beasley-Murray, 176–77; Mounce, , 219–20), makes it unnecessary to suppose that a heavenly temple is in view. (iv) The local references in vv 1–2 (as well as in vv 7–9) suggest that the author is using a source that originated at least with Palestinian Christianity, perhaps interpreting the traumatic events of A.D. 70 (Roloff [ET] 129). (v) The temple in vv 1–2 cannot be the heavenly temple because part of the precinct cannot be measured since it will be taken over by the Gentiles for forty-two months (Kraft, 152). (vi) The temple at Jerusalem is never used elsewhere in early Christian literature to symbolize Christians or the Church.

(b) Recognizing the difficulties in interpreting vv 1–2 as a reference to the temple in Jerusalem that was destroyed by the Romans in A.D. 70, a number of scholars have argued that the heavenly temple is in view (Feuillet, *NTS* 4 [1957–58] 183–200). Recently Giblin (112; id., *NTS* 30 [1984] 438–40) has argued that it is only in the heavenly sphere where the temple, the altar (i.e., "altar" in Revelation is never connected with animal sacrifice), and those who worship there (the heavenly court) are protected from any assault; the excluded forecourt represents the profaned earth, the "forecourt" of heaven. The following are the arguments for a spiritual or allegorical understanding of the temple and altar: (i) The model for Rev 11:1–2 is Ezek 40:1–42:20, where Ezekiel is transported to a "high mountain" in the land of Israel where he watched a man carefully measure a visionary temple that would eventually be rebuilt but that was not yet actually in existence. (ii) If Revelation was written after A.D. 70, as most scholars agree, the temple would no longer have been in existence. (iii) The notion of a heavenly temple, based on the model of the tabernacle revealed to Moses (Exod 25:9, 40; 26:30; 1 Chr 28:11–19), was widespread during the late second temple period; the inviolability of the eschatological temple that God will build, identified as the community, is emphasized in 4QFlor 1:2–6 (Bachmann, *NTS* 40 [1994] 476–77). (iv) Rev 11:1–2 distinguishes the temple and altar from the outer court in a way analogous to the cosmic significance of the holy of holies, like heaven, accessible only to God, and the holy place, like the earth and the sea, accessible to mortals (Jos. *Ant.* 3.123, 181). (v) The phrase οἱ προσκυνοῦντοι, "those who worship," is formed from a verb used characteristically of the heavenly worship of God (e.g., Rev 4:10; 5:14; 7:11; 14:7; 19:14) or of the antithetical worship on earth of the dragon and the beast. (vi) In Revelation, heavenly realities are normally designated by the terms ναός, "temple" (3:12; 7:15; 11:19; 14:15, 17; 15:5, 6, 8; 16:1, 17), and θυσιαστήριον, "altar" (6:9; 8:3[2x], 5; 9:13; 14:18; 16:7). The specific phrase ὁ ναὸς τοῦ θεοῦ, "the temple of God," is used elsewhere in Revelation only in 11:19, where it is explicitly the heavenly temple.

4. *Symbolic Significance of Rev 11:1–2.* (a) The symbolic interpretation of vv 1–2 most widely held among modern interpreters is that the temple of God is not a literal building but, together with the altar and the worshipers, represents the Christian community who worship God, while the court outside the temple and the holy city refer to the outer life of the Church, the vulnerability of the people of God to suffering and death (Behm, 58; Allo, 130; Lohse, 64; Sweet, 182; Mounce, 220; Beagley, *Apocalypse,* 61; Boring, 143; Bauckham, "Conversion," 272; id., *Theology,* 127). This interpretation is based in part on the frequent use of the temple as a symbol for the Church in early Christian literature (1 Cor 3:16–17; 2 Cor 6:16; Eph 2:19–22; 1 Pet 2:5; Ign. *Eph.* 9:1; 15:3 [here the individual Christian is a temple of God]; *Magn.* 7:2; *Barn.* 4:11; 6:15; 16:10; cf. Ign. *Phld.* 7:2 and *2 Clem.* 9:3, where Christians are urged to keep their flesh as the temple of God). A corollary of this view frequently expressed by those who hold it is that the protection symbolized by measuring does not mean security against physical suffering and death; rather it assures support in and through suffering and death and protection from spiritual danger (Loisy, 205; Caird, 132; Mounce, 219; Sweet, 182; Harrington, 119; Boring, 143–44).

(b) A second symbolic interpretation is that the protective measuring of the temple, altar, and worshipers symbolizes the preservation of Christians, the true worshipers of God, while the conquest of the outer court and the holy city represents the rejection and punishment of unbelieving Judaism (Swete, 132–33; Feuillet, *NTS* 4 [1957–58] 187–88; McNicol, *ResQ* 22 [1979] 193–202; Beagley, *Apocalypse,* 62–63; close to the view of Andreas of Caesarea, who thought that the temple represented Christians who offered true sacrifice to God while the outer court represented the unbelieving synagogue of Gentiles and Jews [*Comm. in Apoc.* ad 11:2–3; J. Schmid, *Studien* 1/1:111–12]). Early Jewish sources understand the destruction of the temple as the punishment of Judaism for disobedience (*Apoc. Abr.* 27.5–7; *2 Apoc. Bar.* 1:3–4; *Par. Jer.* 1:8; 4:7–8; *Sib. Or.* 3.273–79; *T. Levi* 10:3; *T. Judah* 23:1–3).

(c) A third view is that the temple, altar, and worshipers refer to the Jewish remnant, while the outer court and the holy refer to Israel, which will be given up to the Gentiles for the punishment of the sins of the Jews (Beckwith, 588–90; M. Rissi, *Future,* 16, 64–65; id., "Das Judenproblem im Lichte der Johannesapokalypse," *TZ* 13 [1957] 241–59).

(d) Finally, a fourth view is that the temple, altar, and worshipers refer to that which was fundamental and essential in Judaism while the outer court and the holy city refer to all that was external and expendable in Judaism (Eichhorn, 2:51–53; Stuart, 2:214).

5. *Conclusion.* The many problems inherent in 11:1–2 suggest that the passage was based on a source consisting of a prophetic oracle predicting the inviolability of the sanctuary within the temple precincts in Jerusalem. In its present literary setting, however, it is clear that this originally Jewish oracle has been reinterpreted and must now be understood symbolically. However, the history of the symbolic or allegorical interpretation of this passage (reviewed above under 4), has shown little restraint, and I find such an interpretation to be generally unsatisfactory. It should first be emphasized that the deep theological structure of 11:1–2, in its present context, centers on the salvation and protection that lie at the center (the temple of God), while danger and destruction lie at the periphery (the outer court and the holy city). The worshipers, however, find salvation and protection in the temple and the altar area only insofar as they have been measured and so divinely protected by God. The author therefore regards the temple as a locus of salvation, much as the wilderness functions as a locus of salvation in Rev 12:6, 14, where the woman hides from the dragon at a place prepared by God in the wilderness. Here the wilderness, normally a place of danger and chaos, is transformed into a place of refuge and salvation. The Zealots, it will be remembered, regarded the wilderness and the temple, by turns, as places of refuge and salvation (Hengel, *Zealots,* 249–55). Second, while the temple and the altar area generally represent the place of salvation, those who worship there represent the remnant of God's people who will physically survive the tribulation and the eschatological war as well as the divine plagues sent to punish the wickedness of humankind. The divine protection that God provides for his people is not just spiritual (the view of most interpreters); it is also physical, for it entails the survival of God's chosen people at the end of days. The over-allegorization of the passage has essentially removed the clear apocalyptic orientation that the passage exhibits. How, one asks, can the temple, the altar, and the worshipers *all* stand for the people of God? What does divine protection symbolized by measuring and counting mean when that protection has nothing to do with the safety and security of the people of God? Thus the worshipers in the temple of God, in my view, are analogous to the 144,000 whom God has sealed (7:3–8; see *Form/Structure/Setting* on Rev 7:1–17), for they too are divinely protected against the divine punitive plagues as well as the murderous intent of the enemies of God.

B. The Two Witnesses (11:3–13)

1. *The Problem.* The origin of the idea of *two* eschatological witnesses or eschatological prophets is problematic. Bousset thought that this idea could not have been derived from a Jewish source since in Judaism the return of a single eschatological prophet, Elijah, was the normal expectation (*Antichrist,* 210). But the presence of *two* eschatological figures can be based formally on Zech 4, a

passage that suggests a possible relationship with the early Jewish expectation of *two* messianic figures, a priestly Messiah of Aaron and a Davidic lay Messiah of Israel, based on the two figures in Zech 3–4; 6:9–14, Zerubbabel the Davidic heir and Joshua the high priest (1QS 9:10–11; CD 12:22–23; 13:20–22; 19:34–20:1; 14:18–19; 19:9–11; 4QTestim 1–20; see Talmon, "Messianism," 79–115; J. J. Collins, *The Scepter and the Star,* 74–101; id., *Apocalypticism,* 71–90). O. Böcher parlays this double messianic expectation into his interpretation of the two witnesses as John the Baptist and Jesus (see below).

Various identifications for the two witnesses have been proposed, but the problem of identification has two levels: (a) First, which traditional figures (particularly prophetic figures) of Jewish eschatology, if any, served as models for the two witnesses? (b) The second level involves the question of whether (i) two *historical* figures figuratively embody characteristics of ancient prophetic figures (as, for example, John the Baptist was identified by some as Elijah; see Matt 11:11–13; Mark 9:11–13 = Matt 17:9–13; Luke 1:17), (ii) the two witnesses should be regarded as two ancient prophets returned to life, or (iii) the two witnesses are intended as *symbols.* Though the two witnesses are intentionally not named explicitly, the presence of an anaphoric definite article in the phrase τοῖς δυσὶν μάρτυσίν μου, "my two witnesses," suggests that they were well known to the author's intended audience.

2. The major options for traditional Jewish eschatological figures that could have served as models for the "two witnesses" are the following:

(a) *Enoch and Elijah* (see Min, *Apocalisse,* 113–23). Andreas (*Apoc.* 11:3–4) notes that most scholars identify the two witnesses as Enoch and Elijah, a view that was virtually unanimous in patristic exegesis after the time of Irenaeus and Tertullian (Tertullian *De anima* 50; Hippolytus *de Ant.* 46.3–4; *Comm. in Dan.* 4.35.3; 4.50.1–2; Augustine *Ep.* 193.3, 5; *De Gen. ad litt.* 9.5; Jerome *Comm. in Evang. Mt.* 3.57; Bousset, *Antichrist,* 27, 203–8; cf. *History of Joseph the Carpenter* 31). This view was based on the widespread belief that Enoch and Elijah were the only two human beings who had not died but had ascended to heaven and that one or the other (or both) would return at the end of the age to complete the mission interrupted by their removal from the world. Here is a summary of the primary textual evidence: (i) *Traditions of Enoch's ascension:* Gen 5:24; *1 Enoch* 70:1–4; 89:52; *2 Enoch* 36:1–2 [both recensions]; *3 Enoch* 6:1; Sir 44:16; 49:14; Wis 4:10–11; *Jub.* 4:23; Jos. *Ant.* 1.85; Heb 11:5; *1 Clem.* 9:4; *Vit. Proph.* 21.12; Epiphanius *Pan.* 1.5; 26.13.4; *Qoh. Rab.* 7.32; *Lev. Rab.* 32.4 (see Zwiep, *Ascension,* 41–58). (ii) *Traditions of Elijah's ascension:* 2 Kgs 2:1–11; Sir 48:9, 12; 1 Macc 2:58; *1 Enoch* 93:8; *Vit. Proph.* 21.15; Jos. *Ant.* 9.28; *Apoc. Ezra* 7:6; *Kerygmata Petrou* (Clementine Homilies 2.17.1); *Acts Pilate* 15.1 (see Zwiep, *Ascension,* 58–63); for iconography on the apotheosis of Elijah, see *EEC* 1:269. (iii) *Traditions of Elijah's eschatological return:* Mal 4:5; Sir 48:10; Matt 11:4; 16:4; 17:10–12 = Mark 9:11–13; Luke 1:17; 9:8, 19; *Sib. Or.* 2.187–89; Justin *Dial.* 49.2; Hippolytus *de Ant.* 46; *Quest. Barth.* 1.17 (*NTA* 1:542); see Joachim Jeremias, *TDNT* 2:928–41; Volz, *Eschatologie,* 195–97, 200–201; Str-B, 4/2:764–98. (iv) *Traditions that mention the ascension of both Enoch and Elijah:* Jos. *Ant.* 9.28; Philo *Quaest. in Gn.* 1.86 (see Meeks, *Prophet-King,* 122–25); *Mut.* 38; *1 Enoch* 90:31 (Enoch relates that a ram [= Elijah] seized him and together they descended into the midst of the angels and the seventy shepherds just before the judgment); 4 Ezra 6:26; Irenaeus *Adv. haer.* 5.5.1; Tertullian *De anima* 50; Ps.-Titus (*NTA* 2:61); *Apost. Const.* 8.41. (v) *Traditions that mention the return of both Enoch and*

Elijah: Apoc. Elijah 4:7; *Apoc. Dan.* 14:1–3; *Apoc. Paul* 20; *Apoc. Peter* (Ethiopic) 2; *Acts Pilate* 25; Augustine *Ep.* 193.3, 5; *De Gen. ad litt.* 9.5.

(b) *Moses and Elijah* (see Min, *Apocalisse,* 123–29). Most modern scholars, on the other hand, think that the author intended to use Moses and Elijah as prophetic models, since consuming enemies with fire from heaven and shutting up the heavens to cause drought (Rev 11:5–6a) are punitive miracles associated with Elijah in biblical tradition (n.b. that in Num 16:23–35 God through Moses rains fire from heaven, which incinerates those violating the sacrificial laws) and turning water to blood and afflicting the earth with every sort of plague are associated with Moses and the Exodus tradition (Bousset [1906] 318–20; id., *Antichrist,* 208; Charles, 1:281; Zahn, 2:427–31; Ernst, *Gegenspieler,* 129; Joachim Jeremias, *TDNT* 2:939). While there is abundant literary evidence to suggest that, according to widespread tradition in Judaism, Elijah was translated and expected to return as an eschatological prophet, the evidence for a belief in the ascension of Moses occurs only occasionally (Jos. *Ant.* 4.326 [here the phrase πρὸς τὸ θεῖον ἀναχωρῆσαι, "to return to the divinity," is used to mean bodily removed from the human realm; see Tabor, *JBL* 108 (1989) 227]; Philo *Sac.* 8 [where he claims that Moses was μετανίσταται, "translated"]; *Mos.* 2.288; *Acts Pilate* 16.7; Ambrose *De Cain et Abel* 1.2.8 [Migne, *PL* 14.337C]; for rabbinic references, see Joachim Jeremias, *TDNT* 4:855; Meeks, *Prophet-King,* 209–11; Lohfink, *Himmelfahrt,* 68–69; Zwiep, *Ascension,* 64–71). Deut 34:5–6 clearly speaks of the death of Moses, as does *T. Moses* 1:15; 10:14. It is sometimes supposed that the lost ending of the *Testament of Moses* (or the *Assumptio Mosis*) narrated the physical ascension of Moses to heaven. However, the terms ἀνάλημψις and *assumptio,* "taken away," often refer to the removal to heaven of a person's *soul* following death (Tromp, *Assumption,* 281–85; Lohfink, *Himmelfahrt,* 61–69). There was, however, a widespread belief that a prophet like Moses, or even Moses *redivivus,* would appear as an eschatological figure at the end of the age, based on Deut 18:15, 18 (see Aune, *Prophecy,* 125–26; Allison, *Moses,* passim). Deut 18:15, 18 is interpreted eschatologically in 4QTestim 1–20, where three OT passages (Deut 18:18–19; Num 24:15–17; Deut 33:8–11) are used to distinguish between an eschatological Mosaic prophet and the Messiah of Aaron and Israel. An important connection between Moses and Elijah in Christian tradition lies in their joint appearance at the Transfiguration of Jesus (Mark 9:4–5; Matt 17:3–4; Luke 9:30–30–33; *Treat. Res.* 48.6; Tertullian *Adv. Marc.* 4.22.1), perhaps representing the Law and the Prophets (Luke 16:29). The joint return of Elijah and Moses is mentioned in *Deut. Rab.* 3.17 (tr. Freedman and Simon, *Midrash Rabbah* 6:88):

> He [God] added: "Moses, I swear to you, as you devoted your life to their service in this world, so too in the time to come when I bring Elijah, the prophet, unto them, the two of you shall come together."

(c) *Elijah and Jeremiah* (see Min, *Apocalisse,* 129–32). Victorinus thought that since both Elisha and Moses had died, neither could be considered to be one of the two witnesses (*Comm. in Apoc.* XI.3; ed. Haussleiter, *Victorinus,* 98), though there was a tradition in early Judaism, presumably unknown to Victorinus, that Moses did not die (Jos *Ant.* 3.96; 4.326; see the discussion above). Victorinus himself thought that the two witnesses should be identified as Elijah and Jeremiah, for he held that Jeremiah (like Elijah) had not died but had been translated (*Comm. in Apoc.* XI.3;

ed. Haussleiter, *Victorinus,* 98). Only in Matthew's version of the confession of Peter is Jeremiah mentioned as a possible identification of Jesus (Matt 16:14; cf. 5 Ezra 2:18; 2 Macc 15:12–16 [where Jeremiah appears to Onias III and gives him a magical golden sword]).

(d) Eschatological prophets that should not be specifically identified with past Israelite prophets (Zahn, 424–28; Haugg, *Die zwei Zeugen,* 130–36; Wikenhauser, 126).

3. Historical figures that scholars have variously identified as the two witnesses include the following:

(a) *Peter and Paul* (see Min, *Apocalisse,* 133–38). J. Munck identified the two witnesses as Peter and Paul (both martyrs and both mentioned together as martyrs in Ign. *Rom.* 4:3; *1 Clem.* 5:4–7; Dionysius of Corinth [mid-second century] in Eusebius *Hist. eccl.* 2.25.8 [who claims that Peter and Paul ἐμαρτύρησαν κατὰ τὸν αὐτὸν καιρόν, "were martyred at the same time"; see Tajra, *Martyrdom,* 178–83]; Gaius in Eusebius *Hist. eccl.* 2.25.6–7; Tertullian *Scorp.* 15; *Ad Marc.* 4.5; *De praescr. haer.* 36; Peter's martyrdom is hinted at in John 21:18–19 and 2 Pet 1:14), since none of the traditional solutions mentioned above involved *martyrs* in the strict sense. Munck regards the clause that identifies the city as Jerusalem in v 8c ("where also their Lord was crucified") as a later interpolation (*Petrus und Paulus,* 33–34). However, there is the "Quo vadis?" tradition in the *Acts Pet.* 25, where, when Peter asks the Christ where he is going ("Quo vadis?), the answer is that he is going again to be crucified, though this time the city is Rome. John Malalas preserves a tradition involving the deaths of Peter and Paul in Rome (*Chron.* 10.37): "Nero ordered that the bodies of the holy apostles should not be handed over for burial, but should remain unburied [cf. Rev 11:9]." The earliest identification of Peter and Paul with the two witnesses of Rev 11 was by J. de Marianas (*Scholia in Vetus et Novum Testamentum* [Madrid: Ludovicus Santius, 1619] 1101), a view also held by Boismard (*RB* 56 [1949] 534, 540), and Giet (*L'Apocalypse,* 40). A critical but sympathetic critique of Munck's proposal is found in O'Connor, *Peter in Rome,* 65–68. There are two major obstacles to this proposal: (i) the death of the two witnesses in Jerusalem (11:8) and (ii) the resurrection and ascension of the two witnesses (11:10–11); see Greve, *DTT* 40 (1977) 128, and P. Benoit, Review of *Petrus und Paulus,* by J. Munck, *RB* 58 (1951) 627.

(b) *Stephen and James the Just.* Earlier martyrs such as Stephen (Acts 7:54–60; 22:20), James (Acts 12:1–2), and James the Just (Eusebius *Hist. eccl.* 2.23.21–24), however, were actually lynched in Jerusalem (a possibility listed by Kraft, 156).

(c) *James and John, the sons of Zebedee.* James the son of Zebedee was killed by Herod Agrippa I in A.D. 44 (Acts 12:2), and several scholars have argued that the two witnesses are modeled after the historical figures of James and John, who in turn are modeled after the eschatological prophets Elijah and Moses *redivivi* (Bacon, *ZNW* 26 [1927] 188–89; E. Hirsch, *Studien zum 4. Evangelium* [Tübingen: Mohr-Siebeck, 1936] 142; a possibility listed by Kraft, 156). This is partly argued on the assumption that Mark 10:35–40 and Matt 20:20–28 reflect the martyrdom of the *two* sons of Zebedee; since Mark was probably composed by A.D. 70, John (according to this theory) must have been martyred some time before that date (Heitmüller, *ZNW* 15 [1914] 189–90).

(d) *John the Baptist and Jesus* are regarded as the two witnesses chiefly by O. Böcher ("Johannes," 81–86; John the Baptist is suggested as a possibility by Kraft,

156). Based on the early Christian view that John the Baptist was Elijah *redivivus* (Matt 11:14) and that Jesus was understood as Moses *redivivus,* combined with the Jewish expectation of two messiahs, a Messiah of Aaron (a priestly Messiah) and a Messiah of Israel (a Davidic Messiah), Böcher argues that John the Baptist corresponds to the priestly Messiah, while Jesus corresponds to the Davidic Messiah; note the juxtaposition of the two figures in Luke 1–2. He must therefore regard the statement in 11:8 ("where their Lord was crucified") as a gloss ("Johannes," 83).

(e) *James the Just and James the son of Zebedee.* It has been suggested that the two witnesses might be the two figures named James, James the son of Zebedee (whose martyrdom ca. A.D. 44 is briefly mentioned in Acts 12:2) and James the brother of the Lord (martyred ca. A.D. 62 according to the account of Hegesippus in Eusebius *Hist. eccl.* 2.23.10–18), both of whom belonged to the apostolic generation and both of whom were killed in Jerusalem (Greve, *DTT* 40 [1977] 137–38; Bacon, *Gospel*).

(f) *The high priests Ananus and Joshua,* who were killed by the Idumaeans and whose corpses were cast out on the street without burial (Jos. *J.W.* 4.314–17). K. Berger (*Auferstehung,* 27) considers this the simplest solution to the problem of the historical identity of the two witnesses.

4. *Symbolic interpretations of the two witnesses* (see Min, *Apocalisse,* 143–52):

(a) The two witnesses can be construed as representing the OT and the NT (an ancient view held by Tyconius, Primasius, Beatus, and Bede) or the Law and the Prophets, represented by Moses and Elijah (Gry, *RB* 31 [1922] 205; Feuillet, *NTS* 4 [1957–58] 196).

(b) More recently it has been proposed that the two witnesses represent the prophetic witness of the Church (Swete, 134; Allo, 160–61; Brütsch, 2:19–20; Cothenet, "Le symbolisme," 228; Metzger, *Code,* 70–71; Talbert, 45–46). Lacy (*JTS* 11 [1910] 55) suggests that the two witnesses are the witness of men and the witness of the Spirit, while Considine (*CBQ* 8 [1946] 391) thinks that the two witnesses represent "the universality of Christian preachers and teachers." The function of *two* witnesses (using the term "witness" in its legal sense) in Jewish tradition is a guarantee of the truth of the testimony, following the legal aphorism *testis unus, testis nullus,* "a single testimony is no testimony" (Num 35:30; Deut 17:6; 19:15; 1 Kgs 21:10; *T. Abr.* [Rec. A] 13:8 [here the necessity of *three* witnesses is emphasized]; Matt 18:16; 26:59–60; John 8:17; 2 Cor 13:1; 1 Tim 5:19; Heb 10:28; 11QTemple 61:6–7; 64:8; *Mek. de-Rabbi Ishmael, Nezekin* 4 [Lauterbach, 3:33], *Kaspa* 3 [Lauterbach, 3:170–71]; *Pistis Sophia* 1.43 [ed. Schmidt-Till, p. 45, lines 17–19 = ed. Schmidt-MacDermot, p. 72]). These two witnesses may therefore be construed as symbolizing the *truth* of the Christian testimony.

(c) The two witnesses may represent the true spiritual value of the Israelite religion preserved intact in Christianity (Feuillet, *NTS* 4 [1957–58] 192, 199).

(d) The Word of God and the testimony of Jesus Christ are regarded as the two witnesses, i.e., "the OT prophetic message and the NT apostolic witness," by Strand (*AUSS* 19 [1981] 127–35 [quotation from p. 134]; *AUSS* 20 [1982] 257–61).

5. *Conclusions.* It is my view that the author based 11:3–13 on an existing source or tradition that narrated the story of a lone prophetic figure who opposed an evil tyrant and was ultimately delivered by miraculous resurrection from suffering and death at the tyrant's hands, though the ascension motif is probably missing from pre-Christian traditions (see Nützel, *BZ* 20 [1976] 59–94). The prophetic figure in

this traditional story was doubled by our author, who used the traditional eschatological figures of Moses and Elijah (as most modern interpreters believe) as models for shaping this narrative in ways he found useful. In my view, it is unnecessary to identify any specific historical figures who might have served as models for the two witnesses of Rev 11:3–13 for the simple reason that the powerful ancient tradition of the dramatic conflict of good and evil represented by the confrontation of a prophet of God and a godless, evil tyrant is a mythical pattern that could easily be historicized in countless situations of conflict. The present form of the narrative has a symbolic character and should not be taken as a sequence of events that the author expected would take place literally. With regard to the symbolic significance of the two witnesses, it is relatively clear that they represent the witness of the people of God in a godless world and that they, like their Lord, will ultimately triumph over suffering and death.

Comment

1a καὶ ἐδόθη μοι κάλαμος ὅμοιος ῥάβδῳ λέγων, "I was given a reed, like a staff, with these instructions." This section of text begins abruptly with none of the typical introductory vision formulas favored by the author. This suggests that structurally vv 1–2 may be a continuation of 10:8–11 (Kraft, 150). The image of the measuring reed is drawn from Ezek 40:3, where Ezekiel sees a person with a וקנה המדה *ûqnēh hammiddâ* (LXX κάλαμος μέτρου), "reed of measurement," who proceeds to measure the eschatological temple in great detail, providing what is essentially a description of the temple in Ezek 40:3–42:20. The term שבט *šēbeṭ*, usually translated ῥάβδος in the LXX, also means "rod, staff." In the Coptic "Prayer of Mary in Bartos," Michael is described as having a "golden staff" (ῥάβδος) in his hand (Kropp, *Koptische Zaubertexte* 2:131; no. XXXIX.9).

1b ἔγειρε καὶ μέτρησον τὸ ναὸν τοῦ θεοῦ καὶ τὸ θυσιαστήριον καὶ τοὺς προσκυνοῦντας ἐν αὐτῷ, "Go and measure the temple of God, including the altar area, and count those who worship within it." While the speaker is not identified (the verb ἐδόθη, "was given," of v 1a can be construed as a passive of divine activity referring to God or Christ), interpreters have variously speculated that the speaker is God, inseparable from Christ (Zahn, 419; Giesen [1997] 241–42), Christ (Loisy, 204; Allo, 129; see the phrase "*my* two witnesses" in v 3), the Spirit (Giblin, 112), or an angel (Bousset [1906] 315; Kraft, 152). The abrupt beginning of this text unit already noted in connection with v 1a is compounded here, for nothing is said about when or how the visionary has or will be transported to the temple to carry out the command of the heavenly voice. The OT text on which this section has been modeled, Ezek 40–48, is introduced with an explanation of how the visionary was transported to a high mountain in the land of Israel, where he saw a structure like a city opposite him (Ezek 40:1–4). Similarly, in Rev 21:9–10, John describes how an angel transported him to a high mountain where, after seeing the New Jerusalem, the angel proceeds to measure parts of it (21:15–17).

The act of measuring (which is never actually performed in the narrative) can be considered a symbolic prophetic action (similar to the symbolic actions of OT prophets; see 1 Kgs 22:11; Isa 8:1–4; 20:1–6; Jer 13:3–11; 27:1–28:16; Ezek 24:3; Acts 21:11; Aune, *Prophecy,* 100–101; G. Fohrer, *Die symbolische Handlungen der Propheten* (Zürich: Zwingli, 1953). This then constitutes a link with the prophetic commission in Rev 10:11 (Behm, 57; Roloff [ET] 128; Kraft, 152; Prigent, 160; Bauckham, "Conversion," 266; Giesen [1997] 240). This passage (along with Rev 21:10–27) alludes to Ezek 40:3–42:20 and Zech 2:1–5, though the latter passage is much closer to Rev 11:1 because of the absence of the actual act of measuring and the focus on the theme of divine protection (a common tradition of literary dependence links Zech 2:5 and Ezek 40:3, 5; cf. C. Jeremias, *Sacharja,* 164–65). Strand (*AUSS* 22[1984] 317–25) has proposed that Lev 16 (which describes the ritual order of the Day of Atonement) is alluded to in Rev 11:1, based on the mention of the same subjects, temple, altar, and worshipers (Lev 16:33), therefore implying a spiritual rather than a physical "measuring." Such an allusion, however, is impossibly subtle and not entirely correspondent since Lev 16:13 names not just the temple, the altar, and the worshipers but rather the sanctuary, the tent of meeting, the altar, the priests, and all the people of the assembly.

"Measuring" can be a metaphor for destruction (2 Sam 8:2a; 2 Kgs 21:13; Amos 7:7–9; Isa 34:11; Lam 2:8) as well as for preservation (2 Sam 8:2b; Ezek 40:1–6; 42:20; Zech 2:5), though the latter is obviously intended here. The theme of divine protection calls to mind Rev 7:3–8, where the 144,000 are sealed for their protection (9:4), as well as the flight of the woman to a place of safety in the wilderness in Rev 12:6, 14. The view that protection in Revelation means not security against physical suffering and death but rather support in and through suffering and death and protection from spiritual danger (Caird, 132; Mounce, 219; Sweet, 182; Harrington, 119) seems to me to subvert the meaning of the text. Further, the two witnesses in vv 3–13 experience just such divine protection from physical harm until their testimony is complete, i.e., when the period of 1,260 days is over (vv 3, 7). The measuring of the eschatological temple in Ezek 40–42 is a device for providing a detailed description of the future temple. Measuring is the common theme that links these prophetic and apocalyptic texts, and measuring can be a means of indicating the essential structure of a thing, which in this case involves the holiness of that which is measured (L. L. Thompson, *Revelation,* 88–89), or it can indicate the preservation or destruction of that which is measured (Isa 34:11; 2 Kgs 21:13; Amos 7:7–9). In Ezek 40:3, a man (probably an angel) uses the measuring rod (as in Rev 20:15), and it is also a man, but again presumably an angel, who does the measuring in the Qumran fragments of an apocalypse on the heavenly Jerusalem (see *Comment* on 21:15 for a brief discussion of the various groups of fragments making up this work). This "Description of the New Jerusalem" text is dependent to some extent on Ezekiel for the general structure of the town, though Ezekiel has a square city of modest dimensions, while the "New Jerusalem" texts envisage the city as an enormous rectangle (García Martínez, *Qumran,* 186). In Zech 2:1–2 it is a man (probably an angel) who is on his way to measure Jerusalem. Measurements of the Jerusalem temple are also found in 11QTemple 3–48 and in *m. Middot.* Here in Rev 11:1–2 it is John who is commanded to do the measuring. In a very difficult passage in *1 Enoch* 61:1–5, angels are given long cords either for measuring the righteous themselves for their preservation or for measuring the future heritage of the righteous on analogy to the tribal land allotments (Josh 13–19) and to reveal the secrets of the depths of the earth. The present imperative ἔγειρε, "come!" "get up!" is formulaic when followed by a second verb in the imperative and functions as a call to action to a person without assuming that he or she is actually sitting or lying down (Matt 9:5; Mark 2:9, 11; 3:3;

10:49; Luke 5:23–24; 6:8; John 5:8; Eph 5:14). Grammatically, John is told to measure three things, the temple, the holy place, and those who worship near it (ἐν αὐτῷ), i.e., near the temple or near the altar or holy place. Measuring worshipers is often thought to make little sense and therefore suggests symbolic interpretation (Feuillet, *NTS* 4 [1957–58] 185; W. J. Harrington, *Apocalypse,* 151). However, since the verb μετρεῖν can mean "count" as well as "measure," this is not really problematic. This could be an example of zeugma, in which one verb is used with two objects but suits only one (BDF § 479). The context suggests that this task of measuring connotes *preservation* since what John is expressly told not to measure is the outer court, which will be given over to the nations (v 2). This digression (between the sixth and seventh trumpets) with its emphasis on preservation thus corresponds to the digression following the opening of the sixth seal in which the sealing of the 144,000 in 7:1–17 symbolizes their preservation. In other Jewish apocalyptic scenarios, there is no mention of the protection of the Jerusalem temple from conquest by the nations.

The phrase τὸ ναὸν τοῦ θεοῦ, "temple of God," is used elsewhere in Revelation only in 11:19, where it is qualified with the phrase ὁ ἐν τῇ οὐρανῇ, "which is in heaven," to distinguish it from the earthly temple of God in Jerusalem referred to here. The term ναός has a number of meanings but is frequently used of the temple building itself, including the holy place or sanctuary and the holy of holies. The temple described here is certainly the earthly temple in Jerusalem, for the distinction between the temple proper (ναός) and the forecourt holds for both the temple of Solomon and the Herodian temple, though the real or imagined architecture is somewhat more complex. In addition to the holy of holies and the holy place, the temple of Solomon had two courts: the inner court surrounded by a wall (1 Kgs 6:36; 7:12) and the outer court, which surrounded the royal palace and the temple precincts (1 Kgs 7:9, 12); see *TDOT* 5:135. The temple described in Ezek 40–42, modeled after the temple of Solomon, also had two courts, an oblong inner court (Ezek 40:23) and a square outer court (Ezek 40:17–20). The Herodian temple, described both in Josephus and in *m. Middot,* consisted of four courts (following *TDOT* 5:137). The inner court of priests was separated from the court of Israelites by a barrier one cubit high. The court of Israelites was adjacent to the court of women. This whole inner precinct (the holy of holies, the holy place, and the three courts) was enclosed by a high wall with gates. The very large court of Gentiles, essentially a huge marketplace, lay without. The term τὸ ἱερόν tended to be used of the entire temple complex, including the three areas into which the inner court of Herod's temple was divided, the court of priests, the court of Israelites and the court of women (*m. Kelim* 1:8; *m. Mid.* 2:5; Jos. *J.W.* 5.198–99; *Ag. Ap.* 2.103–4; see Schürer, *History* 2:296–99); these three areas together with the temple itself constituted the ἱερόν. The ναός, with the temple and its three courts, was separated from the outer court (called החצר החיצנה *heḥāṣēr haḥîṣōnâ*; LXX ἡ αὐλὴ ἡ ἐξωτέρα), or ὁ πρῶτος περίβολος, "first court" (Jos. *Ant.* 15.417), by a low stone barrier that enclosed an area known as the rampart (חיל *ḥêl*) and upon which were posted warnings that Gentiles were forbidden to pass through on pain of death (Jos. *Ant.* 15.410–17; *J.W.* 5.193–94; 6.124–26; Philo *Leg.* 212; *m. Mid.* 2:3; see Eph 2:14; for a plan of the Herodian temple, see Finegan, *Archaeology,* 117). One of these inscriptions has survived complete, along with fragments of two others (*CIJ* 2:1400; *OGIS,* 598; see Schürer, *History* 2:285–86 n. 57); the complete transcription reads (Finegan, *Archaeology,* 119–20):

No foreigner is to enter within the balustrade and enclosure around the temple area. Whoever is caught will have himself to blame for his death which will follow.

The outer court, which could be included in the designation τὸ ἱερόν (Mark 11:15–16; Matt 21:12; Luke 19:45, 47; John 10:23; see Jos. *J.W.* 2.400) and was later called the court of the Gentiles, was bounded by covered porticoes, open toward the inside but closed toward the outside, along the perimeter of the temple mount (the portico on the east side was called Solomon's portico; see John 10:23). The entire *temenos* (sacred precincts) measured approximately 1,455 feet along the western wall (fully excavated by 1992), 1,035 feet along the northern wall, 1,536 feet along the eastern wall, and 912 feet along the southern wall (Jos. *Ant.* 15.396). The Royal Stoa, a triple portico, was located along the southern wall of the temple mount (Jos. *Ant.* 15.411–416; *J.W.* 5.190–9). This outer forecourt or temple esplanade eventually came to be called the court of the Gentiles and was used for commercial activities (Mark 11:15–17; Matt 21:12–13; Luke 19:45–46). The Temple Scroll (11QTemple) describes the second courtyard as a square area 480 cubits long on each side and off-limits for women (11QTemple 38–39), while the third courtyard is described as a square area 1,600 cubits long on each side (11QTemple 40).

Here the term τὸ θυσιαστήριον, which normally means "altar," can refer either to the altar of incense (8:3[2x], 5; 9:13) or to the altar of burnt offerings (6:9; 14:18; 16:7; see *Comment* on 6:9), though the presence of the definite article suggests that here it refers to the altar of burnt offering (Swete, 132; Zahn, 424; Beckwith, 590; Loisy, 205; Allo, 129; *TDNT* 4:887–88). A number of interpreters insist that the altar of incense is referred to here (Bauckham, "Conversion," 269; Giesen [1997] 242), though the fact that both the holy of holies and the holy place (where the altar of incense is located) constitute the ναός of the temple precinct makes the reference to measuring τὸ θυσιαστήριον redundant if the altar of incense is meant. The altar of incense was located in the holy place, separated by the *pārōket* or curtain from the most holy place, both rooms together constituting the ναός or temple. In the Herodian temple, the altar of burnt offerings was located in the court of the priests, separated from the court of Israelites and the court of women, though the sacrificial ritual could be observed from both courts. A more substantial barrier separated the fourth court, the court of Gentiles, from the other three courts. τὸ θυσιαστήριον here appears to refer to the room in which the altar was situated, i.e., the "altar room," "holy place," or (as translated here) "altar area." This meaning is required by the context, i.e., καὶ τοὺς προσκυνοῦντας ἐν αὐτῷ, "and those who worship *in* it," unless ἐν can be construed to mean "near, in the vicinity of" (BAGD, 258; I.1.c). In *Par. Jer.* 2:10; 9:7, the context requires that the phrase ἐν τῷ θυσιαστηρίῳ mean "in the sanctuary" or "in the altar area" (the latter is the translation in R. A. Kraft and A. E. Purintun, *Paraleipomena Jeremiou* [Missoula, MT: Scholars, 1972] 15, 45). The same meaning is required in *Apoc. Ezra* 6:14, "And the prophet said, 'My feet walked in the sanctuary [ἐν τῷ θυσιαστηρίῳ].'" A parallel usage occurs in Ignatius *Eph.* 5:2–3 (see *Trall.* 7:2), ἐὰν μή τις ᾖ ἐντὸς τοῦ θυσιαστηρίου, "unless a person be within the sanctuary" (Bauer-Paulsen, *Ignatius*, 32, suggest this meaning also for θυσιαστήριον in Rev 11:1 and 14:18). Schoedel (*Ignatius*, 55) understands θυσιαστήριον in Ignatius *Eph.* 5:2–3 to simply mean "altar," used in a figurative sense. In both Ignatius *Eph.* 5:2–3 and *Trall.* 7:2, the θυσιαστήριον is a metaphor for the Christian community in subordination to the bishop (Wehr, *Unsterblichkeit,* 69–70).

2a καὶ τὴν αὐλὴν τὴν ἔξωθεν τοῦ ναοῦ ἔκβαλε ἔξωθεν καὶ μὴ αὐτὴν μετρήσῃς, "But exclude the courtyard outside the temple and do not measure it." The phrase ἔκβαλε ἔξωθεν, literally "cast it outside," translated literally in the Vulgate as *eice foras,* is problematic if taken literally (Feuillet, *NTS* 4 [1957–58] 186, however, exaggerates the problem); instead it must be figuratively understood to mean "exclude" rather than "cast out," for here ἔκβαλε = μὴ μετρήσῃς. Feuillet is correct, however, in suggesting that the phrase ἐκβάλλειν ἔξω is normally applied to people who are expelled or excluded (Luke 4:29; Acts 7:58; John 9:34–35 12:31), which coheres with a metaphorical interpretation of this passage construed as referring to excluded people. Luke 13:28, part of the conclusion of the parable of the narrow door, is particularly appropriate, for it refers to Abraham, Isaac, and Jacob and all the prophets in the kingdom of God and the unfaithful cast out (ἐκβαλλομένους ἔξω; Feuillet, *NTS* 4 [1957–58] 186–87). Bauckham, convinced that vv 1–2 are dependent on John's reading of Dan 8:11–14, has argued that the problematic phrase καὶ τὴν αὐλὴν τὴν ἔξωθεν τοῦ ναοῦ ἔκβαλε ἔξωθεν is John's translation of the last three words of Dan 8:11, והשלך מכון מקדשו *wĕhušlak mĕkôn miqdāšô,* "and the place of his sanctuary was cast down" ("Conversion," 269–70). Since שלך *šālak* would mean "cast down, overthrow" if used of the temple itself, John understands the phrase to refer to the court of the temple. From this perspective, argues Bauckham, ἐκβάλλειν is an appropriate translation, for John assumes that the court of the temple has been "cast out" because the Gentiles have defiled it. In Bauckham's favor, it may be said that the phrase והשלך מכון מקדשו *wĕhušlak mĕkôn miqdāšô,* in Dan 8:11 cannot refer to the destruction of the temple, which was not torn down by Antioches Ephiphanes; rather the phrase probably refers to the desecration of the altar of burnt sacrifices (Collins, *Comm. Daniel,* 334). Both the LXX and Theod translate שלך *šālak* with ἐρημοῦν, "to make desolate, lay waste," indicating that they fully understood the context. On the other hand, his explanation has weaknesses. First, the Hebrew verb שלך *šālak* is never used in the OT in the sense that Bauckham argues; the passages to which he refers all use other Hebrew words. Second, ἔκβαλε, "exclude," is a second-person singular aorist imperative, describing an action that the heavenly voice commands John to take.

2b ὅτι ἐδόθη τοῖς ἔθνεσιν, καὶ τὴν πόλιν τὴν ἁγίαν πατήσουσιν μῆνας τεσσεράκοντα καὶ δύο, "for the Gentiles will be permitted to keep the holy city under subjection for forty-two months." The relationship between the ὅτι, "for," clause and the καί, "and," clause that immediately follows is problematic. One solution is to regard ἐδόθη, "will be permitted," as a passive of divine activity and the καί clause as equivalent to an indirect object, i.e., as an alternate way of expressing the idea "because God allowed the Gentiles to conquer the holy city." A second (and preferred) solution is to regard καί + future indicative as a coordinate clause, which forms the subject of the verb ἐδόθη (i.e., as equivalent to the simple infinitive [e.g., *T. Iss.* 5:8, τῷ Γὰδ ἐδόθη ἀπολέσαι, "to destroy was permitted to Gad"], or a ὅτι, "that," or ἵνα, "that," clause [Rev 9:5, καὶ ἐδόθη αὐτοῖς ἵνα μὴ ἀποκτείνωσιν αὐτούς, "not to kill them was permitted to them"]), i.e., literally, "to conquer the holy city was permitted to the Gentiles" (Beckwith, 599, gives this as a possibility; Bousset [1906] 317). The construction in v 3 is similar, though not identical: δώσω τοῖς δυσὶν μάρτυσίν μου καὶ προφητεύσουσιν, "I will permit my two witnesses to prophesy." A third solution is to regard the logical subject of ἐδόθη as ἡ αὐλή, "the temple court" (Charles, 1:278), i.e., "because the outer court has been given over to the Gentiles, and they will trample the holy city . . . ."

A close parallel is found in Luke 21:24, καὶ Ἰερουσαλὴμ ἔσται πατουμένη ὑπὸ ἐθνῶν, ἄχρι οὗ πληρωθῶσιν καιροὶ ἐθνῶν, "and Jerusalem will be trampled on by the Gentiles until the times of the Gentiles are fulfilled" (see Vos, *Synoptic Traditions,* 120–25). Both v 2 and Luke 21:24 are allusions to LXX Zech 12:3, "And it will come to pass on that day I will make Jerusalem a stone trampled by all the Gentiles [καταπατούμενον πᾶσιν τοῖς ἔθνεσιν]." Since אבן מעמסה *'eben ma'ămāsâ,* "a stone of burden," i.e., "a heavy stone," in Zech 12:3 is incorrectly translated by καταπατεῖσθαι in the LXX phrase λίθον καταπατούμενον, "a trampled stone," the author appears to be dependent on the LXX rather than the MT. Cf. *Pss. Sol.* 8:12, "They walked on the place of sacrifice [Syriac 'temple'] of the Lord [ἐπατοῦσαν τὸ θυσιαστήριον κυρίου]." The Greek verbs πατεῖν and καταπατεῖν are frequently used in Jewish sources for the conquest of Jerusalem and the profanation of the temple (Isa 63:18; Dan 8:13; *Pss. Sol.* 2:2, 19; 8:12; 17:22; 1 Macc 3:45, 51; 4:60; 3 Macc 2:18 [here trampling means destruction]; *2 Apoc. Bar.* 67:2; Jos. *J.W.* 4.171, 261; see *TDNT* 5:940–45). The same motif occurs in 4QpNah 3–4, 1:3–4 (tr. Horgan, *Pesharim,* 163), "[but God did not give Jerusalem] into the power of the kings of Greece from Antiochus until the rise of the Kittim; but afterwards [the city] will be trampled [and will be given into the hand of the rulers of the Kittim]" (see the commentary on these lines in Horgan, *Pesharim,* 173–74). *Barn.* 16:5 claims that "it was made manifest that the city and the temple and the people of Israel were to be delivered up" (freely citing sections of *1 Enoch* 89:56–58).

The phrase "holy city" is a clear reference to Jerusalem, also referred to in v 8 (Lohmeyer, 87), though the phrase τὴν πόλιν τὴν ἁγίαν Ἰερουσαλήμ occurs in Rev 21:2, 10, where it just as clearly refers to the heavenly Jerusalem since the phrase is qualified both times by the participial phrase καταβαίνουσαν ἐκ τοῦ οὐρανοῦ ἀπὸ τοῦ θεοῦ, "descended out of heaven from God." The view that the term "holy city" in Rev 11 is used here rather than "Jerusalem" because the latter is used only for the new, heavenly city (Vos, *Synoptic Traditions,* 120–25) is undermined by the phrase "the holy city Jerusalem" in 21:2. Jerusalem is occasionally called "the holy city Jerusalem" in early Jewish literature (LXX Isa 66:20; LXX Joel 4:17; Tob 13:10 [MSS A B]; Dan 3:28; Pr Azar 5; *Pss. Sol.* 8:4; *b. B. Qam.* 97b; *b. Sanh.* 107b). The earliest occurrence of the phrase "Jerusalem the holy city" is found in Isa 52:1, and the earliest occurrence of "holy city" is in Isa 48:2; thereafter, there is an increasing tendency to use the term "the holy city" to mean "Jerusalem." During the early second temple period, therefore, Jerusalem is increasingly referred to as "the holy city" (Neh 11:1, 18 = 2 Esdr 21:1, 18 [*var. lect.*]; Theod Dan 9:24; 1 Macc 2:7; 2 Macc 3:1; 15:14; 3 Macc 6:5; Sir 36:12; 49:6; *Par. Jer.* 1:6; *b. Sanh.* 107b; 11QTemple 47:13; Matt 4:5; 27:53; *Gos. Naz.* frag. 3). Philo favors the compound term ἱερόπολις (Philo *Som.* 2.246; *Mos.* 2.72; *Leg.* 225, 299; *Flacc.* 46), while Josephus tends to use the phrase ἱερὰ πόλις (Jos. *Ant.* 4.70, 200, 209, 218, 227; 20.118; *J.W.* 2.397; 4.214; *Ag. Ap.* 1.282). The phrase "Jerusalem the holy" (in paleo-Hebrew script: ירושלים הכדושה *yrwšlym hkdwšh*) occurs on silver shekels minted during the first Jewish revolt in A.D. 66–70; see Matthiae and Schönert-Geiss, *Münzen,* 84–85, plate 38. Some have argued that "the holy city" is not the historical Jerusalem (or any other actual city) but rather a symbol for the "World City" or the "civilized world" (Giblin, *NTS* 30 [1984] 439; Beasley-Murray, 185–86), a view supported by the universal audience in vv 9a and 10a.

The period of forty-two months (also mentioned in Rev 13:5, where it is the period during which the beast exercises authority; see *Comment* there) is a symbolic apocalyptic number for a divinely restricted period of time (often a limited period of eschatological tribulation), ultimately derived from Dan 7:25; 12:7. Forty-two months is equivalent to three and one-half years, a period of time that the author expresses differently elsewhere as 1,260 days (11:3; 12:6) and as "a time, times, and half a time" (12:14). He uses the number three and one-half for the number of days between the death and the ascension of the two witnesses (11:9, 11). Therefore, while John uses three different time designations to express three and one-half years, the reference to "a time, times, and half a time" in 12:14 makes it clear that he is alluding to Daniel (7:25; 12:7). In Dan 7:25, both the LXX and Theodotion read ἕως καιροῦ καὶ καιρῶν καὶ ἕως ἡμίσους καιροῦ, "for a time and times and a half time," while LXX Dan 12:7 (εἰς καιρὸν καὶ καιροὺς καὶ ἥμισυ καιροῦ, "for a time and times and a half time") differs somewhat from Theod Dan 12:7 (εἰς καιρὸν καιρῶν καὶ ἥμισυ καιροῦ, "for a time of times and a half time"). It is often claimed that the Aramaic phrase עד־עדן ועדנין ופלג עדן *ʿad ʿiddān wĕʿiddānîn ûplag ʿiddān* in Dan 7:25 is a cryptic way of saying three and one-half years (BDB, 1105), just as the equivalent Hebrew phrase למועד מועדים וחצי *lĕmôʿēd môʿădîm wāḥēṣî* in Dan 12:7 is said to mean "for a set time, times, and a half = 3 1/2 appointed times = half the prophetic week of years" (BDB, 417). However, עדן *ʿiddān*, "period," is not just a substitute for שׁנה *šānâ*, "year"; rather it envisages a long period (a period, two periods, four periods = seven periods, i.e., eternity), which is suddenly and unexpectedly cut in half (a period, two periods, one-half period); see Goldingay, *Daniel,* 181. According to Justin, Jewish biblical interpreters speculated that the term καιρός or מועד *môʿēd* in Dan 12:7 meant one hundred years (*Dial.* 32.3). It is likely that the phrase "a time, times, and half a time" is purposefully vague, for it is both specific and indeterminate at the same time (Stahl, "Zeit," 480–93). The real issue, of course, is what the phrase might have meant to the author of Revelation. The Aramaic phrase ושבעה עדנין *wĕšibʿâ ʿiddānîn* is literally translated ἑπτὰ καιροί, "seven periods," in Theod Dan 4:32(MT 4:22), while LXX Dan 4:32 (followed by Jos. *Ant.* 10.216) has ἔτη ἑπτά, "seven years." In a first-century A.D. composition, the *Vitae Prophetarum,* the author claims that ὁ Δανιὴλ τὰ ἑπτὰ ἔτη ἃ εἶπεν ἑπτὰ καιρούς ἐποίησε γενέσθαι ἑπτὰ μῆνας, "Daniel made the seven years (which he called seven periods) become seven months." There is then ample evidence to suggest that the strange formula in Dan 7:25; 12:7 was understood to mean three and one-half years in early Judaism. The number "three and one-half days" (an allusion to three and one-half years) is used in Rev 11:9, 11 as the period between the death and the resurrection of the two witnesses. In the present context it is relevant that almost exactly three and one-half years elapsed between the beginning of the first Jewish revolt (fall of A.D. 66) and the siege of Jerusalem (Wellhausen, *Skizzen,* 222; Schwier, *Tempel,* 172). Gunkel disputed the view that three and one-half (as half of seven) was an unlucky number (*Schöpfung und Chaos,* 266–68), and Kittel ("Rundezahlen," 31–47) cited a number of rabbinic passages in which three and one-half is not an apocalyptic symbol but simply a "round" number for an extended period of time (e.g., *Lev. Rab.* 19; *y. Šabb.*

7.2; *b. Sanh.* 97b). It is in this context that the three and one-half years of famine during the time of Elijah (mentioned only in Luke 4:25 and Jas 5:17) should be interpreted.

3 καὶ δώσω τοῖς δυσὶν μάρτυσίν μου καὶ προφητεύσουσιν ἡμέρας χιλίας διακοσίας ἑξήκοντα περιβεβλημένοι σάκκους, "and I will permit my two witnesses to prophesy 1,260 days clothed in sackcloth." The abrupt way in which this text unit begins (i.e., without any of the typical introductory devices favored by the author) is an argument against considering 11:3–13 as a major text unit following 10:1–11:2 (F. Hahn, "Aufbau," 145) or 10:8–11:2 (Kraft, 150–52). The verb δώσω, "I will give," and the possessive pronoun μου, "my," suggest that the speaker in 11:1b–3 is God or Christ (Haugg, *Zeugen,* 16); this suggests the fragmentary character of 11:1–2 since it is likely that the unidentified speaker is an angel who gives the author a measuring stick and orders him to measure parts of the temple. The speech probably continues only through v 3. This is the only feature that betrays the identity of the speaker since the rest of Rev 11 (beginning with v 4) is narrated in the third person. The short commentary in 11:8 ("where their Lord was crucified"), however, reveals that there has been a shift in narrative perspective (at least in the final edition). The presence of the definite article apparently indicates that the readers were already familiar with *the* two witnesses (Haugg, *Zeugen,* 13–14). Since parallel texts regularly name Enoch and Elijah as the two eschatological prophets who will return at the end of the age, it can perhaps be assumed that the author has omitted their names intentionally, possibly because he regarded them as *Christian* prophets whose ministry takes place after that of Jesus, who is designated as "their Lord" in v 8, in view of the widely held view that John the Baptist was the eschatological Elijah (Mark 1:2; 9:11–13 = Matt 17:10–13; Matt 11:14; Luke 1:17; Justin *Dial.* 49.3, 5), though the author of the Fourth Gospel rejects that identification (John 1:19–28). Furthermore (see below), the author modifies the expectation of Enoch and Elijah *redivivi* to Moses and Elijah *redivivi.* The term "witness" in this context has the connotation "prophet" since the phrase οἱ δύο μάρτυρες, "my two witnesses," in v 3 is exactly parallel to οἱ δύο προφῆται, "the two prophets," in v 10 (note that the verb προφητεύειν, "prophesy," and the noun προφητεία, "prophecy," are used of their ministry in vv 3, 6 and that μαρτυρία, "testimony," in v 7 is parallel to προφητεία in v 6). It seems probable that the source reworked by our author read προφῆται uniformly, a term that he supplemented with μάρτυρες, a critical term within the theology of the book as a whole. The tradition of the violent death of the prophets provides the conceptual background to 11:3–13 (2 Chr 24:19; 36:15–16; Neh 9:26; Matt 5:11–12 = Luke 6:22–23; Matt 23:34–36 = Luke 11:49–51; Matt 23:37–39 = Luke 13:34–35; Acts 7:52; 1 Thess 2:15; *Barn.* 5:11; *Vit. Proph.* 1.1; 2.1; 3.2; 6.1; 7.1; 21.3; Aune, *Prophecy,* 157–59; Urbach, *Sages,* 558–63). This motif occurs in succinct form in *Jub.* 1:12 (Charlesworth, *OTP* 2:53), "And I shall send to them witnesses so that I might witness to them, but they will not hear. And they will even kill the witnesses."

The length of the ministry of the two witnesses is fixed at 1,260 days, another way of calculating the 42-month period mentioned in v 2 as the length of time that the nations will trample over the holy city (see *Comment* on 11:2). The 42 months of 11:2 and the 1,260 days of 11:3 constitute one of the few formal links between 11:1–2 and 11:3–13. This symbolic period of 3 1/2 years suggests that the period during which the nations will control Jerusalem is precisely the period when the two witnesses will exercise their ministry and provides the reason that he has linked vv 1–2 (originally an independent tradition) to vv 3–13 (another independent tradition). The end of that period, described in vv 7–13, involves the murder, resurrection, and ascension of the two witnesses as well as the earthquake that destroys a tenth part of the city and the conversion of the survivors.

The origin of the idea of *two* eschatological witnesses or eschatological prophets is problematic. Bousset thought that this idea could not have been derived from a Jewish source since in Judaism the return of a *single* eschatological prophet, Elijah, was expected (*Antichrist,* 210). But there was an early Jewish expectation of *two* messianic figures, a priestly Messiah of Aaron and a Davidic lay Messiah of Israel, based on the two figures in Zech 3–4; 6:9–14, Zerubbabel the Davidic heir and Joshua the high priest (1QS 9:10–11; CD 12:22–23; 13:20–22; 19:34–20:1; 14:18–19; 19:9–11; 4QTestim 1–20; see Talmon, "Messianism," 79–115; Collins, *Scepter,* 74–101; id., *Apocalypticism,* 71–90).

The author is extremely fond of the number 3 1/2, which he expresses in a variety of ways. The period of 1,260 days (see *Comment* on Rev 12:6) is equivalent to 42 months (Rev 11:2 [see *Comment* there]; 13:5) or 3 1/2 years, the length of time of a period of eschatological distress (Dan 7:25; 12:7). This period of time appears to have been added to the traditional material reworked by the author.

Sackcloth (a dark-colored fabric made of goat hair or camel hair originally used for making grain sacks) was worn for several reasons: (1) as a sign of individual mourning or national distress (Gen 37:34; 2 Sam 3:31; Lam 2:10; Esth 4:1; Ps 30:11 [MT 30:12]; Isa 15:3; 22:12; Joel 1:13; Amos 8:10; *Barn.* 7:12; Jos. *Ant.* 7.40; 10.11; 19.349; Cowley, *Aramaic Papyri,* no. 31, line 19 [= Porten-Yardeni, *Textbook* 1:74–75]), (2) as an indication of submission when supplicating people or offering prayers to God (1 Kgs 20:31–32; Jer 4:8; 6:26; Dan 9:3; Jos. *Ant.* 7.154; 12.300; 20.123; *J. W.* 2.236–37; *Barn.* 7:5), (3) as a penitential practice (1 Kgs 22:27–29; 2 Kgs 19:1–2; 1 Chr 21:16; Neh 9:1; Ps 35:13; Jonah 3:5–8; Matt 11:21 = Luke 10:13; Jos. *Ant.* 8.362; Plutarch *De superst.* 168D), and (4) as the garb appropriate for prophets, who could dress in clothes appropriate for mourning in anticipation of the calamity of coming judgment. When made of goat hair, it could be extremely dark or even black in color (Isa 50:3; Rev 6:12; *1 Clem.* 8:3).

Occasionally, prophets are depicted wearing sackcloth or something similar, probably to exemplify the need for repentance and humility before God (Isa 20:2 [here the term translated "sackcloth" may refer to the basic male undergarment]; Zech 13:4; *Asc. Isa.* 2:10; Mark 1:6; the sheepskins and goatskins of Heb 11:37, which are natural, have nothing to do with sackcloth, which is manufactured), though it was by no means the typical uniform of prophets (as claimed by K. Berger, *Auferstehung,* 28, and Hengel, *Leader,* 36 n. 71); see the careful discussions in Guelich, *Mark 1:1–8:26,* 20–21, and Tilly, *Johannes,* 167–75. In fact, the garments of the two witnesses provide the only clue to the nature of their message, for nothing whatever is said about the *content* of their prophetic testimony. Though it is often claimed that their message was a call to *repentance* (Bauckham, "Conversion," 278), the text is strangely silent on that point (Satake, *Gemeindeordnung,* 120–21; Müller, 209). Satake has argued that the two witnesses are concerned not with securing the repentance of the world but rather with acting as God's agents in judging the world; killing and tormenting the opposition are not normal tactics of evangelists (*Gemeindeordnung,* 119–33). Despite the generally negative role of the two witnesses, however, it must be borne in mind that most of the inhabitants of the city were converted following the resurrection and ascension of the witnesses (v 13), though this too may belong to the revision of a traditional source. The focus, therefore, is not on the character or the content of their message but rather on the fact that, whatever it is, it will surely be rejected as they themselves will be.

4a οὗτοί εἰσιν αἱ δύο ἐλαῖαι καὶ αἱ δύο λυχνίαι, "These are the two olive trees and the two menorahs." On the introductory phrase οὗτοί εἰσιν, "these are," see *Comment* on 7:14. This demonstrative explanation is not in response to a demonstration question (i.e., "What is this?"); nor is it the explanation of a supernatural guide typical of many apocalypses. It is striking that the two witnesses are *both* the two olive trees and the two menorahs. In the phrase αἱ δύο ἐλαῖαι, "the two olive trees," the noun is articular because it is an allusion to the well-known olive trees in Zech 4:3, yet the author probably understands this metaphor more comprehensively, i.e., as a reference to the anointing and, therefore, the official commissioning of these prophets (Kraft, 157). In *ʾAbot R. Nat.* 34 (Goldin, *Fathers,* 137–38), the two anointed ones who stand before the Lord of the whole earth (Zech 4:14) are interpreted as Aaron and the Messiah.

Again in the phrase αἱ δύο λυχνίαι, "the two menorahs," the noun is articular, perhaps because it is an allusion to the well-known menorah of Zech 4:2–3, 11. The mention of *two* menorahs, however, when only *one* is found in Zech 4, may indicate the presence of an exegetical tradition upon which John is dependent. Though biblical tradition mentions but a single menorah in the wilderness tabernacle, and ten are mentioned in connection with the temple of Solomon (see *Comment* on 1:13), ancient representations of the menorah often show *two* menorahs flanking the Torah shrine (Yarden, *Tree of Light,* plates 93–95, 101, 109–10, 114, 119, 130, 193–94, 206). In the mosaic floor of the Beth Alpha synagogue, a depiction of the Torah shrine shows a *pārōket,* "curtain," flanked by two seven-branched menorahs, each surrounded by the sacral symbols of the shofar and the incense shovel (Gutmann, *Jewish Sanctuary,* plate XLVIII; see the *nine*-branched menorah flanked by an incense shovel and shofar [ram's horn] carved in relief on an arch stone from Yahudiyye, in *BAR* 14 [1988] 62). Two menorahs flank the ark in four drawings from Beth Sheʿarim, in mosaics from Hammath Tiberias, Naʿaran, Beth Sheʾan, and Susiya (Hachlili, *Jewish Art,* 247–48, plates 101–5), and on the ʾAssalieh lintel (Hachlili, *Jewish Art,* plate 29a). It should be borne in mind that the term λύχνος, "light," is also used as a metaphor for witness. Just as the two witnesses are λυχνίαι, "lights," so John the Baptist is also spoken of figuratively as ὁ λύχνος ὁ καιόμενος καὶ φαίνων, "the light which burns and shines" (John 5:35). Similarly, 2 Pet 1:19 compares the prophetic message of the OT to a lamp (λύχνος) shining in a dark place.

4b αἱ ἐνώπιον τοῦ κυρίου τῆς γῆς ἑστῶτες, "which stand before the Lord of the earth." This is an allusion to Zech 4:14, "These are the two anointed ones who stand by the Lord of the whole earth [παρεστήκασιν τῷ κυρίῳ πάσης τῆς γῆς]." The title "prince, lord of the earth" is frequently ascribed to Baʿal in Ugaritic sources (*Baʿal* II iv 47; vii 43ff.; III* A.32; III i 1ff.; iii.8–9; iv 5–6; IV iii 2, 9; V i 2–4; v 35). In 4Q*171* = 4QPss^a 3:15–16, the priest, i.e., the Teacher of Righteousness, is referred to as the one whom God chose *to stand before him.* Elijah, Enoch, and Moses (the three ancient figures with whom the two witnesses have been identified, paired as either Elijah and Enoch or as Elijah and Moses; see *Comment* on v 3) were traditionally thought to have ascended to heaven, thereby making their eschatological return possible. The two witnesses, however, simply appear on the scene suddenly and unexpectedly (as OT prophets often did) without any indication of their origin apart from the statement that they were empowered to prophesy for a restricted period of time (v 3). That they are described as *standing in the presence of the Lord,* however, may intimate their heavenly origin. The idiom "standing in the presence of God" (see *Comment* on 8:2, where the phrase is used of the seven archangels) suggests their priestly or levitical function (cf. *Jub.* 30:18 [tr. Charlesworth, *OTP* 2:113], "And the seed of Levi was chosen for the priesthood and levitical (orders) to minister before the Lord always just as we [i.e., the host of angels] do"; see Exod 18:19; Deut 10:18; 18:7; 1 Kgs 17:1 [Elijah swears by "the Lord the God of Israel before whom I stand"]; 18:15; 2 Kgs 3:14; 5:16; 2 Chr 29:11; Ezek 44:15; Zech 3:1). The phrase ἱστάναι ἐνώπιον, literally "to stand before," can in some cases mean "to attend upon, to be the servant of" (see *Note* 8:2.c-c.). While the two witnesses are undoubtedly "servants of God," this passage has a double-entendre that has complicated the syntax, for while the two witnesses "stand before" God in the sense that they serve him, the two lampstands (metaphors for the two witnesses) are understood to be actually "standing before" God in his heavenly temple. Angels are also sometimes described as "standing before God," an aspect of their priestly role (Rev 8:2; Job 1:6; 2:1; Zech 6:5). The "Lord of the earth" here is not the Roman emperor (contra J. Munck, *Petrus und Paulus*) but God. Victorinus, however, understood the "Lord of the earth" to be the Antichrist (*Comm. in Apoc.* XI.4; ed. Haussleiter, *Victorinus,* 100), perhaps because of the similarity of "Lord of earth" to the phrase "ruler/prince of this world" (John 12:31; 14:30; 16:11; Ign. *Eph.* 17:1; 19:1; *Magn.* 1:3; *Trall.* 4:2; *Rom.* 7:1; *Phld.* 6:2; *Asc. Isa.* 1:3; 10:29).

5a καὶ εἴ τις αὐτοὺς θέλει ἀδικῆσαι πῦρ ἐκπορεύεται ἐκ τοῦ στόματος αὐτῶν καὶ κατεσθίει τοὺς ἐχθροὺς αὐτῶν, "If anyone wants to harm them, fire proceeds from their mouths and utterly destroys their enemies." This is a typical first-class conditional sentence in which the conditional particle εἰ + indicative in the protasis (here the present indicative), with any tense of the indicative or imperative in the apodosis (BDF §§ 371–72), emphasizes the reality of the condition; i.e., it is taken to be a real instance. There is no tradition that associates either Elijah or Moses with fire that comes from the mouth and destroys enemies (Munck, *Petrus und Paulus,* 21). The closest parallel is found in Lactantius *Div. Inst.* 7.17.2 (tr. McDonald, *Lactantius,* 518), "and fire will proceed from his mouth and burn whoever will attempt to hurt him." The motif of fire coming from a person's mouth also occurs in *2 Enoch* (Rec. J and A) 1:5; *3 Enoch* 19:25; 22:4. In early Judaism and in early Christianity, the ancient prophets were regarded as men of power who could perform miracles (Jos. *J.W.* 2.261–63; *Ant.* 20.97–99, 168–72; Sir 48:1–14; Mark 6:15; Luke 7:16; John 6:14–15; P. W. Barnett, "The Jewish Sign Prophets—A.D. 40–70—Their Intentions and Origin," *NTS* 27 [1981] 679–97; Hengel, *Judaism and Hellenism* 1:136; Aune, *Prophecy,* 82, 126–29; Barton, *Oracles of God,* 99–102). The motif of fire emanating from a person's mouth was used as a metaphor for speaking forth the word of God, usually in a situation of rebuke and condemnation (see Jer 5:14b, "Behold, I am making my words in your mouth a fire, and this people wood, and the fire shall devour them"; *Tg.* Jer 5:14 [tr. Hayward, *Targum of Jeremiah,* 64] has "the words *of my prophecy* in your mouth"). Victorinus regarded the fire that proceeded from their mouths to mean "the power of the word" (*Comm. in Apoc.*

XI.2, *potestatem uerbi dicit* [ed. Haussleiter, *Victorinus,* 98]). An equivalent view is found in Philo *Quaest. in Ex.* 2.47 (tr. Marcus, LCL), "just as the flame consumes all the material that comes its way, so, too, when the thought of God clearly reaches the soul, it destroys all the heterodox thoughts of piety, bringing the whole mind into (a state of) holiness." In *PGM* IV.617 there is a similar equation between speech and fire: "Speak all these with fire and spirit"; cf. *PGM* CII.5 (POxy 2753), "you who are hurling lightning [and who are thundering]; you are the one whose mouth [constantly pours forth] fire" (tr. Betz, *Greek Magical Papyri,* 309). Also we find in *PDM* iv.125 (tr. Betz, *Greek Magical Papyri,* 202) "the first servant of the great god, he who gives light exceedingly, the companion of the flame, he is whose mouth is the flame which is never extinguished." According to 4 Ezra 13:10 (RSV), the man from the sea (later identified as God's son, the Messiah)

> sent forth from his mouth as it were a stream of fire,
> and from his lips a flaming breath,
> and from his tongue he shot forth a storm of sparks.

When this aspect of Ezra's vision is interpreted in vv 37–38, each of the three elements is explained in reverse order:

> And he, my Son, will reprove the assembled nations for their ungodliness (this was symbolized by the storm), and will reproach them to their face with their evil thoughts and the torments with which they are to be tortured (which were symbolized by the flames), and will destroy them without effort by the law (which was symbolized by the fire).

God himself is depicted as breathing fire in 2 Sam 22:9, perhaps in language drawn from the Leviathan tradition (cf. Job 41:18–21). In Ps 18:13 the voice of God consists of thunder, hail, and fire. In Rev 9:17–18 the plague of the sixth trumpet includes an enormous number of cavalry, from the mouths of whose mounts come fire and smoke and sulfur, which killed one-third of humanity. The motif of fire and sulfur has a long biblical tradition beginning with the judgment of Sodom and Gomorrah by fire and brimstone (i.e., sulfur); see *Comments* on 9:17–18. The power of the word of God is expressed in a variety of other ways also, such as the rain that causes seed to germinate (Isa 55:11) and other metaphors (Isa 9:8; 11:4).

5b καὶ εἴ τις θελήσῃ αὐτοὺς ἀδικῆσαι, οὕτως δεῖ αὐτὸν ἀποκτανθῆναι, "since if anyone should wish to harm them, it is necessary that they should die in such a way." This clause is obviously parallel to the previous one in v 5a. Here the οὕτως clause introduces the apodosis (as in 1 Thess 4:14) and repeats and intensifies the unusual and frightful type of death inflicted on the enemies of the two witnesses in v 5a, namely, incineration by fire proceeding from the witnesses' mouths. The protasis of this condition, however, consists of εἰ + subjunctive (see *Note* 11:5.f.). This is unusual, but not impossible, since εἰ began to be used in place of ἐάν increasingly in papyri from the second century A.D. (Turner, *Syntax,* 116; cf. BDF § 372.3). Here εἰ + subjunctive is a third-class condition, which indicates that the condition is assumed as possible of realization. Note that elsewhere in Revelation ἐάν + subjunctive is found in the protasis of six conditional sentences (2:5, 22; 3:3, 20; 22:18, 19), all in those portions that belong to the Second Edition. Though the two witnesses possess these punitive powers, the text does not explicitly say that they used them, though v 10 does say that they "tormented" the people dwelling on the earth.

6a οὗτοι ἔχουσιν τὴν ἐξουσίαν κλεῖσαι τὸν οὐρανόν, ἵνα μὴ ὑετὸς βρέχῃ τὰς ἡμέρας τῆς προφητείας αὐτῶν, "They have the power to shut up heaven, that rain might not fall during the period when they prophesy." Like v 5, v 6 consists of two parallel clauses, each introduced with a similar phrase: οὗτοι ἔχουσιν τὴν ἐχουσίαν, "these have power" (v 6a), and καὶ ἐξουσίαν ἔχουσιν, "they also have power" (v 6b). The miraculous powers wielded by the two witnesses are without exception punitive. Shutting up heaven so that it would not rain was a sign performed by Elijah, who caused a drought for three years (1 Kgs 17:1; 18:1; Sir 48:2; the time reference is omitted in Jos. *Ant.* 8.319, 328). Though 1 Kgs 17–18 does not specifically mention the *prayer* of Elijah or the *length* of the drought, tradition emphasizes his prayer (*Vit. Proph.* 21.4–5; Luke 4:25; Jas 5:17), and tradition also regards the drought as lasting for three years and six months (Luke 4:25; Jas 5.17) or three years (*Vit. Proph.* 21.4). Rev 11:6 and Luke 4:25 share the notion of the "shutting up" (κλείειν) of the heavens (regarded as the storehouse of the rains), a notion not attested elsewhere for the Elijah tradition, though the verb עצר *ʿāṣar* (in the sense of "to shut, restrain") is used in connection with shutting the heavens so that it will not rain in 1 Kgs 8:35 = 2 Chr 6:26 (see Houtman, *Himmel,* 185). In 1Q22 (Words of Moses) 2:10, Moses threatens the Israelites with the wrath of God, which "closes the skies above, which make rain fall upon you" (García Martínez, *Dead Sea Scrolls,* 277). The ability to shut the heavens was also ascribed to Phineas (who is really Elijah; see Zeron, *JBL* 98 [1979] 99–100) in *Bib. Ant.* 48:1. In Jewish tradition, Elijah was called "the key to rain" and was connected with magical rainmaking (*m. Taʿan.* 2:4; *b. Sanh.* 113a; *y. Sanh.* 10.28b; *y. Ber.* 5.9b; *y. Taʿan.* 1.63d; Patai, *HUCA* 14 [1939] 257). In the tradition of Elijah, Honi the Circle-Drawer (*m. Taʿan.* 3.8; see J. Derenbourg, *Essai,* 111–13), Onias (Jos. *Ant.* 14.22), and Hanina ben Dosa (*b. Taʿan.* 24b; *b. Yoma* 53b) were also credited with being able to control rain through prayer. This Elijah tradition is also reflected in Lactantius *Div. Inst.* 7.17.2, in a version probably independent of Revelation (tr. M. F. McDonald, *Lactantius,* 517): "Wherever men shall not hear him, he will close heaven and will hold back the rains." The dominating importance of rainfall in Palestine for the life of the people who lived there meant that the possibility of withholding rain was a perennially effective threat (Reymond, *L'eau,* 1ff., 31ff.). For that reason, supernatural attempts to control the rainfall were common (Patai, *HUCA* 14 [1939] 251–86).

6b καὶ ἐξουσίαν ἔχουσιν ἐπὶ τῶν ὑδάτων στρέφειν αὐτὰ εἰς αἷμα, "They also have power over the waters, that is, to turn them to blood." This alludes to the first plague of the Exodus, in which Moses transformed the Nile into blood (Exod 7:14–19). The plague of blood is also alluded to in the second trumpet plague (8:9) and the third bowl plague (16:4). The allusion to Exod 7:14–19 is particularly apt if one of the two witnesses is identified with Moses. The Moses tradition is also reflected in Lactantius *Div. Inst.* 7.17.2 (tr. McDonald, *Lactantius,* 517–18), "He will change water into blood and will torture them with thirst and hunger."

6c καὶ πατάξαι τὴν γῆν ἐν πάσῃ πληγῇ ὁσάκις ἐὰν θελήσωσιν, "and to strike the earth with every type of plague whenever they might wish." This apparently alludes to 1 Sam 4:8, where the Philistines, learning that the ark of the covenant had arrived in the camp of the Israelites, said, "These are the gods who struck the Egyptians with every type of plague [LXX οἱ πατάξαντες τὴν Αἴγυπτον ἐν πάσῃ πληγῇ] in the wilderness." This refers, of course, to all of the other plagues afflicted on people, such as those inflicted upon the Egyptians by Moses in Exod 7:14–11:10, and strongly suggests that the Egyptian plagues are indeed the model for those inflicted by the two witnesses.

7a καὶ ὅταν τελέσωσιν τὴν μαρτυρίαν αὐτῶν τὸ θηρίον τὸ ἀναβαῖνον ἐκ τῆς ἀβύσσου ποιήσει μετ' αὐτῶν πόλεμον, "When they finish their witness, the beast who ascends from the abyss will wage war on them." The phrase "when they finish" refers back to the predetermined length of the ministry of the two witnesses as specified in v 3, i.e., 1,260 days or 3 1/2 years, a symbolic eschatological period that the author-editor uses in a variety of ways. According to Hippolytus (who is dependent on both Revelation and Daniel), when the three-and-one-half-year ministry of the two witnesses is concluded, the beast will spend the remaining three and one-half years of the full week of seven years fighting the saints (*Dan.* 4.50.2). There is a verbal parallel between 11:7a and 20:7 (καὶ ὅταν τελεσθῇ τὰ χίλια ἔτη, λυθήσεται ὁ σατανᾶς ἐκ τῆς φυλακῆς αὐτοῦ, "and when the thousand years were completed, Satan was released from his prison," and gathered Gog and Magog to make war), which, according to Feuillet (*NTS* 4 [1957–58] 194), indicates that the two witnesses represent the Church. The noun "witness" is used here as an equivalent to the verb "to prophesy" in v 3 and the noun "prophecy" in v 6.

The figure of the beast is introduced here unexpectedly and for the first time in Revelation. Surprisingly, he plays no further role in this pericope. The definite article with θηρίον indicates that it (or he) is familiar to the readers even though it is introduced here for the first time (K. Berger, *Auferstehung*, 23). Though one might assume that this beast is identical with the one from the sea (13:1–10), θηρίον is anarthrous in 13:1, suggesting that John assumes that it is unknown to his readers. Since a beast is also described in 17:8 in a similarly phrased statement as originating from the abyss (καὶ μέλλει ἀναβαίνειν ἐκ τῆς ἀβύσσου, "he will ascend from the abyss"), it might be assumed that the beast in Rev 17 is identified by the author with the one mentioned in 11:7; 13:1–10. Yet the fact that θηρίον, "beast," in 17:3 is anarthrous suggests that a different beast is being referred to by the author (or he has inconsistently edited a source). This actor, however, is introduced a bit too abruptly; the motivation for his actions is not evident, so the phrase "the beast who ascends from the abyss" (perhaps an allusion to the four beasts in Dan 7:3, who ἀνέβαινον ἐκ τῆς θαλάσσης, "ascend from the sea") is very probably a later redactional addition designed to tie Rev 11:3–13 more closely to Rev 13 and 17 (Kraft, 157–58), and the abyss from which he ascends is intended to be identical with the sea from which the beast emerges in 13:1 (on the abyss in Revelation, see *Comment* on 9:1b). The adjectival phrase τὸ ἀναβαῖνον ἐκ τῆς ἀβύσσου, "who ascended from the abyss," functions as a description of the origin of the beast and does not suggest that the beast ascended during the ministry of the two witnesses to oppose them. The author frequently uses descriptive participial phrases to identify various characters (12:9, 17; 17:1; 18:9, 15; 19:20; 21:9, 15). His war against the two witnesses is narrated not as an event that has already occurred but rather as a prophecy of that which will occur in the future, as the three future indicatives ποιήσει μετ' αὐτῶν πόλεμον, "he will make war against them," νικήσει αὐτούς, "he will conquer them," and ἀποκτενεῖ αὐτούς, "he will kill them," indicate. There is a close parallel in 13:7, where it is said of the beast from the sea that ἐδόθη αὐτῷ ποιῆσαι πόλεμον μετὰ τῶν ἁγίων καὶ νικῆσαι αὐτοῦς, "he was permitted to wage war with the saints and conquer them." The beast is probably modeled after the fourth beast in Dan 7:21, "who made war with the saints and prevailed over them." The fourth beast of Daniel was believed by some early Christian writers to be Rome (Hippolytus *de Ant.* 25.1–3; 28.1), and for Victorinus, the beast from the abyss is the Romans (*Comm. in Apoc.* 11.4). Though only the two witnesses are attacked by the beast, the phrase ποιήσει μετ' αὐτῶν πόλεμον, "he will wage war on them," is language that is hardly appropriate for attacking and killing just two individuals. Normally this kind of language in Revelation is used of war waged against the righteous by Satan or one of his representatives (see Rev 12:17; 13:7 [the beast makes war on the righteous as the agent of the dragon]; *T. Job* 4.4; 18.5; 27.2). The Christian life is described with martial imagery in Eph 6:10–17 and Ignatius *Trall.* 4:2. Satanic opposition as warfare is not found as frequently in early Jewish or early Christian sources as one might expect.

7b καὶ νικήσει αὐτοὺς καὶ ἀποκτενεῖ αὐτούς, "that he might conquer them and kill them." In this phrase, literally "and he will conquer and kill them," καί + future indicative functions as a final or purpose clause (S. Thompson, *Apocalypse,* 99). For other examples of final and consecutive clauses consisting of καί + future indicative, see 4:1; 5:10; 9:19; 13:7–8; 15:4; 20:7–8, 10 (see Aune, *Revelation,* WBC 52A, cxciii–cxciv; Zerwick, *Greek,* § 455γ [with NT examples: Matt 5:15; Luke 5:1; 24:26; Mark 8:25]).

The narrative is extremely abbreviated and enigmatical (as are *all* the battle descriptions in Revelation; cf. 12:7–8; 17:14; 19:19–20; 20:9). Nothing is specifically said about *how* these two witnesses were killed, though stoning was a frequent fate of prophets in Jewish and early Christian tradition (Deut 13:10; 2 Chr 24:21; Heb 11:37; Matt 21:35; 23:37; Luke 13:34; Acts 7:58–60; *Par. Jer.* 9:21; *Vit. Proph.* 2.1). According to Augustine, Elijah and Enoch will be killed together at the end of the world by the Antichrist (*Ep.* 193.3, 5; *De Gen. ad litt.* 9.5), an old tradition also reflected in *Acts Pil.* 25, undoubtedly influenced by Rev 11 (tr. Hennecke-Schneemelcher, *NTA* 1:525):

> I am Enoch, who pleased God and was removed here by him. And this is Elijah the Tishbite. We shall live until the end of the world. But then we shall be sent by God to withstand Antichrist and to be killed by him. And after three days we shall rise again and be caught up in the clouds to meet the Lord.

Note the use of the phrase "after three days" in imitation of the traditional period of time between Christ's death and resurrection, rather than the "three and one-half days" of Revelation. Lactantius *Div. Inst.* 7.17.3 states (tr. McDonald, *Lactantius,* 518), "This one will fight against the prophet of God; he will conquer and kill him and suffer him to lie unburied." Perhaps the earliest tradition of the return and subsequent death of Elijah is in *Bib. Ant.* 48:1, where Phineas (who will return as Elijah) "will taste what is death."

8a καὶ τὸ πτῶμα αὐτῶν ἐπὶ τῆς πλατείας τῆς πόλεως τῆς μεγάλης, "Their bodies will lie in the public square of the great city." The bodies of the two witnesses lie unburied on the street, perhaps a deliberate literary contrast to Jesus' burial, which occurred soon after his death (Mark 15:42–47; Matt 27:57–61; Luke 23:50–56; John 19:38–42). According to John 19:31–37, Pilate was particularly anxious to have the bodies of those executed buried before the Sabbath began (cf. Jos. *J.W.* 4.317).

That ἡ πλατεῖα is articular probably means that it refers to a well-known street or square in either pre-A.D.-70 Jerusalem or in Rome (a reference to Rome in the source may have been redacted to refer to Jerusalem; see *Comments* on vv 8b and 8c; the chief public square at Rome was the *Forum Romanum*), though an original reference to Jerusalem appears most likely. If so, this is one of several indications that the author was of Palestinian origin. Jewish apocalyptic certainly regarded Palestine generally and Jerusalem in particular as the focus of God's eschatological program. One evident problem, if the author wrote ca. A.D. 90, is that Jerusalem had been destroyed in A.D. 70 (though portions of Revelation were almost certainly composed before A.D. 70). Very little is known about the streets of Jerusalem during the period *before* Hadrian's reconstruction (see Wilkinson, *Jerusalem*, 54–65; a map of the gridded street layout of Jerusalem as completed by Herod the Great is found on p. 62; a more detailed discussion with street maps is found in Wilkinson, *Levant* 7 [1975] 118–36). Although portions of a significant ancient street have been excavated in Jerusalem, it dates from the Roman resettlement of Jerusalem, renamed Aelia Capitolina, during the principate of Hadrian (see Avigad, *Discovering Jerusalem*, 213–29; H. Geva, *NEAEHL* 2:762). This street is called the *cardo maximus*, which was the general designation for the major north-south axis of a typical Roman city. This main artery of Roman-Byzantine Jerusalem was twenty-two meters or seventy-two feet wide, four times the width of other streets, and so could certainly be described as ἡ πλατεῖα (Broshi, *IEJ* 24 [1977] 232–35). The *cardo maximus* of Jerusalem, now called Khan ez Zeit Street, is depicted in the Madaba mosaic map of Jerusalem from the Byzantine period, ca. A.D. 600 (Avigad, *Discovering Jerusalem*, 211–12; Finegan, *Archaeology*, 169–70; Wilkinson, *Levant* 7 [1975] 118–23; M. Avi-Yonah, "Jerusalem," *NEAEHL* 2:775–76). However, the late date of this construction reveals little about the street system of Jerusalem in the Herodian period. The only large streets or plazas found in pre-A.D.-70 Jerusalem excavated thus far are the following: (1) The main north-south street, ten meters wide, dubbed "Tyropoeon Valley Street," ran along the western side of the temple mount and under the pier of "Robinson's Arch" and served as the central market of Jerusalem during the Herodian period (Mazar, "Temple Mount," 25–26; Ben-Dov, *Temple*, 113–15 [photographs]; H. Geva, "Jerusalem," *NEAEHL* 2:741 [photographs]). According to Ben-Dov, it was "the most impressive commercial center in Jerusalem" (*Temple*, 114). The Roman-Byzantine Secondary (Eastern) Cardo, in its northern section, follows the earlier Tyropoeon Valley Street (H. Geva, "Jerusalem," *NEAEHL* 2:763–64; M. Avi-Yonah, "Jerusalem," *NEAEHL* 2:779). (2) Intersecting this street is "Hulda Gates Street," a narrow east-west street (6.4 meters wide and ca. 280 meters long), which ran along the southern wall of the temple mount in front of the Hulda Gates (Mazar, "Temple Mount," 26–27; Ben-Dov, *Temple*, 108; H. Geva, "Jerusalem," *NEAEHL* 2:742). (3) South of the monumental stairs leading up to the narrow street that ran past the "Double Gate" in the southern wall of the temple mount the remains of a plaza have been found (Mazar, "Temple Mount," 27–30). (4) In the middle of the Upper City in the Jewish Quarter, fifty meters of a paved east-west street of the late Herodian period have been excavated, which at one point measured thirteen meters in width (Avigad, *IEJ* 22 [1972] 198–99; id., *Discovering Jerusalem*, 88, 94; Ben-Dov, *Temple*, 115). This street, called "Upper

Market," ἡ ἄνω ἀγορά (Jos. *J.W.* 2.305, 315, 339; 5.137), branched off from Tyropoeon Valley Street and ran to the Upper City to the residential and commercial areas. (5) In addition, Wilkinson proposes two major street grids, one oriented around the temple enclosure and the other oriented around Herod's palace (completed 23 B.C.), with a major street, which he calls "Temple Street," proceeding west from the temple mount and connecting the two building complexes (Wilkinson, *Jerusalem,* 62; id., *Levant* 7 [1975] figs. 6–8). According to Wilkinson (*Levant* 7 [1975] 126), "Temple Street was probably never straight, even though *it was the most impressive in the whole city of Herod the Great* [emphasis added]." Prof. L. Levine, however, informs me that Wilkinson's "Temple Street" has no basis in archeological evidence. At this point, then, it appears that Tyropoeon Valley Street is the best candidate for ἡ πλατεῖα at the present stage of our knowledge of the archeology of pre-A.D.-70 Jerusalem. Even though the tradition of the ministry of the two witnesses is located in pre-A.D.-70 Jerusalem, however, this does not contradict the fact that the author has transformed the historical Jerusalem into a symbol of an unbelieving world (Considine, *CBQ* 8 [1946] 388), which violently rejected the divine messengers sent to proclaim the word of God to it.

Though "the great city" has been understood to be either Jerusalem or Rome, in this context it should probably be identified with Jerusalem (Swete, 137–38; Bousset [1906] 312; Lohmeyer, 93; Kraft, 158; Giesen [1997] 255). Jerusalem is called "the great city" in various sources (*var. lect.* in Rev 21:20 [see *Notes;* Jer 22:8; Jos. *Ag. Ap.* 1.197; *Sib. Or.* 5.154, 226, 413; *Apoc. Elijah* 4:13 [3:31; ed. Rosenstiehl]). Pliny (*Hist. nat.* 5.14.70) observes *Hierosolyma long clarissima urbium orientis, non Iudaeae modo,* "Jerusalem is by far the most famous city of the east and not of Judaea only." Technically, Jerusalem did not fit the formal definition of a πόλις (Byatt, *PEQ* 105 [1973] 53; cf. Safrai, *Economy,* 30), though Hecataeus and Agatharchides (fourth and second centuries B.C.), both quoted by Josephus, call Jerusalem a πόλις (*Ag. Ap.* 1.197–98, 209). πόλις was used by Greek writers with two meanings: (1) a town or city and (2) a city-state on the Greek model. Greek authors called Carthage, Nineveh, Babylon, Opis, and Ecbatana πολεῖς even though they did not fit the Greek model of a πόλις (Herodotus 1.178–89; 2.15; Xenophon *Anab.* 2.4.25). Aristotle, however, wondered whether Babylon should be called a πόλις (*Pol.* 1276a), a fact that suggests that others called it a πόλις. Elsewhere in Revelation the phrase "the great city" refers to Rome, implicitly or explicitly designated "Babylon" (17:18; 18:10, 16, 18, 19, 21; cf. 16:19). The phrase "the great city" could be used pejoratively, based on Jonah's designation of Nineveh as "the great city" (Jonah 1:2; 3:2, 3; 4:11; Jdt 1:1; see *Vit. Proph.* 10.3 [10:6B in Denis, *Concordance,* 869; Rosenstiehl, *L'Apocalypse d'Élie,* 43), i.e., as the city of a hated enemy. The phrase is also variously used of *heaven* (*T. Abr.* [Rec. A] 2:6), the Sicilian city of *Croton (Sib. Or.* 4.82), *Antioch* (John Malalas *Chron.* 10.18, 23 and frequently), and *Alexandria* (John Malalas *Chron.* 10.32).

A number of scholars, however, have maintained that "the great city" refers to Rome (Munck, *Petrus und Paulus,* 30–35), a view that must then regard the phrase "where their Lord was crucified" (v 8c) as an interpolation. Wellhausen (*Analyse,* 16) claimed that "the μεγάλη πόλις (11,8) cannot mean ἅγια πόλις, but only, as usual, Babylon-Rome." Rome was called *princeps urbium,* "the greatest of cities" (Horace *Carm.* 4.3.13).

8b ἥτις καλεῖται πνευματικῶς Σόδομα καὶ Αἴγυπτος, "which is called, prophetically, 'Sodom' and 'Egypt.'" This phrase is probably an explanatory interpolation (J. Weiss, *Offenbarung,* 42), but one added by the author. The term πνευματικῶς here means not simply "allegorically" or "metaphorically" but "prophetically" (Schweizer, *TDNT* 6:449), for it refers to the charismatic exegesis of the OT under the guidance of the Spirit of God (Aune, "Charismatic Exegesis," 126–50). In Isa 1:9–10, the prophet denounced Jerusalem as "Sodom" (see Jer 23:14; Ezek 16:46, 49; *Asc. Isa.* 3:10; cf. Fekkes, *Isaiah,* 176). In the OT, Sodom is frequently cited as a paradigmatic "wicked city" (Gen 18:16–19:29; Deut 29:23; Isa 1:9; Jer 49:18; Amos 4:11; Zeph 2:9), a reputation that continues in early Judaism (4 Ezra 2:8; 3 Macc 2:5; *T. Levi* 14:6; *T. Naph.* 3:4; 4:1; *T. Asher* 7:1; *Apoc. Ezra* 2:19; 7:12) and early Christianity (Matt 10:15; 11:23, 24; Luke 10:12; Rom 9:29; 2 Pet 2:6; Jude 7). Egypt is a symbol of idolatry (Isa 19:1; Ezek 20:7) and slavery (Exod 2:23; 6:6; Deut 5:6; 6:12; Josh 24:17; Judg 6:8; Neh 9:17; Jer 34:13; Mic 6:4; 2 Esdr 14:3), though it is hardly appropriate to refer to Egypt as a "city." In the Hymn of the Pearl in the *Acts of Thomas* 108–13, "Egypt" is a symbol for the material world, a metaphor widely used in Gnosticism (Hippolytus *Ref.* 5.7.41; 5.16.5; H. Jonas, *The Gnostic Religion,* 2nd ed. [Boston: Beacon Press, 1963] 118). As the home of the cult of the dead, Egypt became known as the Kingdom of Death.

8c ὅπου καὶ ὁ κύριος αὐτῶν ἐσταυρώθη, "where their Lord was also crucified." This phrase clearly identifies "the great city" as Jerusalem, yet in all other references to "the great city" in Revelation, Rome is meant. Wellhausen (*Analyse,* ad loc.) identified "the great city" as Rome. Charles thinks that Jerusalem was the city meant by "the original writer and also by our author" (1:288). If Rome is the city in question, what street or square could the author mean? Among the more obvious possibilities are the *Forum Romanum* or *Magnum* (Richardson, *Rome,* 170–74; Zanker, *Forum Romanum*), the business center of Republican Rome and the heart of the city, and the *Sacra Via,* the oldest and most famous street in Rome (Richardson, *Rome,* 338–40). However, Rev 11:1–2 clearly sets the scene in *Jerusalem,* and nothing in 11:3–13 suggests a change in scene. Since this is the only explicitly Christian reference in 11:1–13, a number of scholars have argued that it is a gloss inserted by John into his source (J. Weiss, *Offenbarung,* 127; Beckwith, 591; Charles, 1:287; Munck, *Petrus und Paulus,* 33–34; K. Berger, *Auferstehung,* 30, regards vv 8–10 as a redactional addition), while others argue against the interpolation hypothesis (Satake, *Gemeindeordnung,* 120; Giesen [1997] 253–55).

The term κύριος, "Lord," is used of Jesus here for the first time in Revelation and in a unique way (κύριος occurs twenty-three times in Revelation, fifteen times of God and eight times of Jesus); elsewhere Jesus is identified as "Lord of lords" (in 17:14; 19:16, where his role as world ruler is emphasized) and as the "Lord Jesus" (22:20, 21). In Rev 14:13 it is not certain that the phrase ἐν κυρίῳ refers to Jesus. In view of the extent to which the title κύριος is applied to Jesus in the rest of the NT (see *TDNT* 3:1088–94), its relative absence in Revelation is remarkable. The absolute use of κύριος here as a designation for Jesus is another indication that this verse is an interpolation.

The murder of the two witnesses in Jerusalem reflects the traditional view that prophets must die in Jerusalem, a tradition made explicit in Luke 13:33, where Jesus links his own mission to Jerusalem: "it is impossible for a prophet to be killed outside of Jerusalem." Prophets traditionally thought to have been killed in Jerusalem include Isaiah (*Asc. Isa.* 51.1–5; cf. *Vit. Proph.* 1.1; Justin *Dial.* 120.5; *Par. Jer.* 9:21–22; see Schwemer, *Vitae Prophetarum,* 91 n. 40), Uriah (Jer 26:20–23),

Zechariah son of Jehoiada (2 Chr 24:20–22; Luke 11:50–51 = Matt 23:35; *Vit. Proph.* 23.1), and some unnamed prophets (Jos. *Ant.* 10.38). In addition, there was a foiled attempt to murder Jeremiah in Jerusalem (Jer 38:4–6).

9a καὶ βλέπουσιν ἐκ τῶν λαῶν καὶ φυλῶν καὶ γλωσσῶν καὶ ἐθνῶν τὸ πτῶμα αὐτῶν ἡμέρας τρεῖς καὶ ἥμισυ, "And some of the peoples and tribes and tongues and nations will see their bodies for three and one-half days." The bodies of the two witnesses are not actually on universal display (note that the partitive genitive ἐκ τῶν λαῶν . . . , "of the peoples . . . ," functions as the subject of the verb βλέπουσιν, "will see, " indicating that some but not all of the people of the world will see the bodies of the two witnesses); rather, "representatives" from all over the world are present in the city where the two witnesses are martyred (on their conversion, see *Comment* on v 13). This suggests that the "great city" has become a symbol for the world. An analogous situation is found in Acts 2:5, where it is claimed hyperbolically that pious Jews from every nation under heaven were present in Jerusalem. On the fourfold list of ethnic groups, see the *Comment* on 5:9. In *Vit. Proph.* 10.8, Jonah reportedly predicts the destruction of Jerusalem; the emphasis on the presence of *all the nations* in Jerusalem is particularly relevant:

> καὶ ὅτε ἴδωσιν ἐν Ἰερουσαλὴμ πάντα τὰ ἔθνη,
> ὅτι ἡ πόλις ἕως ἐδάφους ἠφάνισται ὅλη.
>
> When people see all the nations in Jerusalem,
> that means that the city will be completely razed.

While the "great city" (v 8a) is identified as Jerusalem (v 8c), the international origin of the people present would actually be more appropriate for Rome, one of the most cosmopolitan (and most densely populated) cities of the ancient Mediterranean world (Stambaugh, *City,* 89–100). This is a kind of ironic reversal of the Day of Pentecost, in which people from "all nations under heaven" are present in Jerusalem and hear Peter's sermon (Acts 2:5–11).

The reference to 3 1/2 days (repeated in v 11) corresponds numerically to the 1,260 days, or 3 1/2 years, during which the two witnesses were active (11:3). This number, which is used for the stereotypical period of distress in apocalyptic literature (Dan 7:25; 12:7; see *Comment* on 11:2), corresponds to the length of the famine during the time of Elijah according to a tradition found only in Luke 4:25, Jas 4:17, and a few rabbinic sources (J. Lightfoot, *Horae Hebraicae* 3:72–75; Str-B, 3:761); the biblical tradition mentions only three years (1 Kgs 18:1). In rabbinic sources the number "three and one-half" occurs frequently, with the apparent meaning of "an extended period of time."

9b καὶ τὰ πτώματα αὐτῶν οὐκ ἀφίουσιν τεθῆναι εἰς μνῆμα, "but people will not permit their bodies to be buried." The sudden appearance of τὰ πτώματα, "bodies," when the collective singular was just used in v 9a, requires explanation. According to Swete (138–39), since separate treatment is required of each body for burial, the plural form is appropriate. The composition of vv 7–10 appears to have been influenced by Ps 79:1–3 (NRSV):

> O God, the nations have come into your inheritance;
> they have defiled your holy temple;
> they have laid Jerusalem in ruins.

> [2]They have given the bodies of your servants
> to the birds of the air for food,
> the flesh of your faithful to the wild animals of the earth.
> [3]They have poured out their blood like water
> all around Jerusalem,
> and there was no one to bury them.

The following motifs are common to both passages: (1) the presence of "the nations" in Jerusalem, (2) the murder of the servants of God, and (3) the slain servants of God lying unburied. Ps 79:1–3 may actually have influenced the formulation of the narrative of the two witnesses or one witness used by the author. Another text, 4Q*176*=4QTanhumin 1–2 i 1–4 from Qumran, also appears to allude to Ps 79:1–3, indicating the influence of this narrative (tr. García Martínez, *Dead Sea Scrolls,* 208):

> Perform your marvel, do your people justice and . . . [. . .] [2]your temple. Argue with kingdoms over the blood of [. . .] [3]Jerusalem. See the corpses of your priests [. . .] [4]there is no-one to bury them.

In 1 Macc 7:16–18, the slaughter of sixty Hasideans is explicitly understood as the fulfillment of Ps 79:2–3, and the same passage has apparently influenced the formulation of the narrative about the Idumean slaughter of Ananus and Joshua the high priests, after which their corpses were cast out without burial (Jos. *J.W.* 4.314–17; Schürer, *History* 1:497; see Eckhardt, *Johannes,* 68–70). In a passage in *Jub.* 23 that predicts a final eschatological battle in which the righteous will be slain, it is explicitly stated that there will be no one to bury them (*Jub.* 23:23).

To leave a body unburied in the ancient world was understood as an outrage; it was done to express great anger against the deceased (*Iliad* 23.21–23, 183; 24.15–21; *Odyssey* 11.51–78; Sophocles *Antigone* [passim]; 1 Kgs 14:11; 16:4; 21:24; 2 Kgs 9:10, 33–37; Jer 8:1–2; 14:16; Tob 2:3–10; Mark 12:8; Philo *Jos.* 25; *Mos.* 1.39; Jos. *J.W.* 3.377; 4.381–84; *Sib. Or.* 3.643; *1 Enoch* 98:13; see K. Berger, *Auferstehung,* 278–79 n. 118). According to Josephus (*J.W.* 4.317), the Jews observed such stringent burial practices that even crucified criminals were buried before sunset. In the Greek world, the failure to bury (or cremate) a body meant both dishonor and exclusion from the underworld (*Iliad* 71; N. D. Fustel de Coulanges, *The Ancient City* [Baltimore: Johns Hopkins UP, 1980] 13–17; Parker, *Miasma,* 45–46, 70). In *T. Job* 53.5–6, the widows and orphans of the town prevented the family of Job from placing him in the tomb (presumably in order to mourn him, though the motive is unstated); after three days Job is finally buried.

10a καὶ οἱ κατοικοῦντες ἐπὶ τῆς γῆς χαίρουσιν ἐπ' αὐτοῖς, "The inhabitants of the earth will rejoice over them." For the negative significance of the phrase "inhabitants of the earth" (which occurs nine times in Revelation), see *Comment* on 3:10. This favorite expression of the author-editor is used here as a parallel to the phrase "some of the peoples and tribes and tongues and nations" in v 9a, where the phrase was a partitive genitive and therefore referred to "[some] of the inhabitants of the earth," i.e., "[representatives] of the inhabitants of the earth," which could refer to Jerusalem. This unqualified use of the phrase "the inhabitants of the earth" suggests that *everyone in the world* rejoiced over the deaths of the two witnesses; i.e., "the great city" of v 8 has become the world. Some commentators construe these as inhabitants of Palestine (Bousset [1906] 322–23; Charles, 1:289–90), though here the universal significance of the "great city" suggests otherwise. On the perverse rejoicing of the wicked, see LXX Prov 2:14; Jos. *Ant.* 8.197; *Gos. Pet.* 6.23 (Jews rejoice over the death of Jesus); *Asc. Isa.* 5.2 (all the false prophets laugh and rejoice when they see Isaiah being sawn in two).

10b καὶ εὐφραίνονται καὶ δῶρα πέμψουσιν ἀλλήλοις, "and they will be joyful and will exchange gifts with one another." The two motifs of joy and gift exchange are closely connected. In the Greco-Roman world the exchange of gifts was an expression of mutual obligation and occupied an important role in both public and private life (*Iliad* 6.119–236). Gifts were exchanged on the occasion of religious festivals, such as the Saturnalia (Burkert, *Greek Religion,* 101; Scullard, *Festivals,* 207; H. S. Versnel, *Inconsistencies in Greek and Roman Religion* [Leiden: Brill, 1992] 2:148; see Herodian 1.16.2; Macrobius *Saturnalia* 1.7.18ff.). In ancient Israel, as in ancient Greece, the presentation of gifts was connected with birth (Matt 2:11), betrothal (*Odyssey* 15.16–18), and marriage (*Odyssey* 20.341–44), and on various occasions gifts were presented by parents to children (Matt 7:11 = Luke 11:13), i.e., all occasions associated with joy and rejoicing. Gift giving on most of these occasions, however, did not actually involve gift *exchange* (the Saturnalia and the New Year festival of Kalends are exceptions; see M. Meslin, *La fête des kalendes de janvier dans l'empire romain* [Brussels: Latomus, 1970] 39). Some of the traditions associated with the Saturnalia, including gift exchange, may have been adopted by the Christian celebration of the nativity of Christ on December 25 (first celebrated on that date in A.D. 336), just following the festival of Saturnalia, which was celebrated for seven days, December 17–23 (Scullard, *Festivals,* 205–7). The Jewish festival of Purim was a time of joy and gladness and also an occasion when people gave "gifts of food to one another and presents to the poor" (Esth 9:22, NRSV), indicating that this Jewish festival truly involved gift exchange. The word "gift," however, requires some definition, for in the ancient world no one ever gave something of value without expecting recompense (Finley, *World,* 64–66; Hands, *Charities,* 26–48).

10c ὅτι οὗτοι οἱ δύο προφῆται ἐβασάνισαν τοὺς κατοικοῦντας ἐπὶ τῆς γῆς, "for these two prophets tormented the inhabitants of the earth." The designation "prophets" occurs here for the first time, though in their role as "witnesses" their ministry was described as "prophesying" in v 3 and "prophecy" in v 6. Here the term ἐβασάνισαν, "tormented, tortured," refers not to the effect of their prophesying (the content of which is left unspecified) but rather to the plagues and punishments that they dished out. The notion that the testimony of the two witnesses was "unbearable," i.e., using the term βασανίζειν in the figurative sense of emotional anguish, is suggested by Giblin (*NTS* 30 [1984] 444). On the phrase "inhabitants of the earth" (cf. v 10a), see *Comment* on 3:10.

11a καὶ μετὰ τὰς τρεῖς ἡμέρας καὶ ἥμισυ πνεῦμα ζωῆς ἐκ τοῦ θεοῦ εἰσῆλθεν ἐν αὐτοῖς καὶ ἔστησαν ἐπὶ τοὺς πόδας αὐτῶν, "Now after the three and one-half days the breath of life from God entered into them so that they stood on their feet." The second part of this clause alludes to Ezek 37:10, "I prophesied as he commanded me, and the breath [πνεῦμα] came into them [the dry bones], and they lived, and stood on their feet, a vast multitude" (cf. v 5, where the phrase πνεῦμα ζωῆς occurs in the LXX). Bousset argued that this incident of the resurrection of the two witnesses after three days was of Jewish-Christian origin (*Antichrist,* 210), but he later came to regard it as fully explicable from a Jewish perspective ([1906] 323–

24). K. Berger maintains that there are no valid grounds for regarding vv 11–12 as having a Christian origin (*Auferstehung*, 39), though this judgment is methodologically suspect (one could similarly atomize the Pauline letters and conclude that many sentences were not "Christian"). The phrase "after three and one-half days" is repeated from v 9a. Since the resurrection of the two witnesses occurs in three and one-half days, it is reminiscent of the three days associated with the resurrection of Jesus. This tradition takes two forms: (1) Jesus rose "*on* the third day" (Matt 16:21 = Luke 9:22; Matt 17:23; Matt 20:19 = Luke 18:34; Luke 24:7, 21, 46; Acts 10:43; 1 Cor 15:4), and (2) Jesus rose "*after* three days" (Matt 27:60; Mark 8:31; 9:31; 10:34). The attempt to equate "after three days" with the "three and one-half days" of Rev 11:11 is problematic, for the 3 1/2 days is an analogous, though much shorter, period of time than the 42 months of v 2 and the 1,260 days of v 3 (both variations of 3 1/2 years) as periods of oppression (v 2) and witness (v 3).

The phrase "breath of life" occurs several times in Genesis (Gen 1:30; 2:7; 6:17; 7:15, 22; cf. Job 32:8; 33:4; 4 Ezra 3:5). God breathed the breath of life into the first human being. Lactantius *Div. Inst.* 7.17.3 says (tr. McDonald, *Lactantius*, 518), "But *after the third day*, he will rise again and will be taken into heaven while all look on and marvel." In *Par. Jer.* 9:7–14, after praying near the altar of the temple, Jeremiah collapses as though dead. When the sorrowing people are about to bury him, a voice says, "Do not bury one who still lives, because his soul will again return to his body." After *three days* of waiting, Jeremiah revives and praises and glorifies God. In *T. Abr.* [Rec. A] 18:11, Abraham prays and "God sent a spirit of life [ἀπέστειλεν ὁ θεὸς πνεῦμα ζωῆς]" into the dead servants of Abraham, and they were made alive again. The notion that the soul of a deceased person lingered around the corpse for three days was widespread in the ancient Near East (Plutarch *De num. vind.* 22; K. Berger, *Auferstehung*, 370–71).

The phrase "to stand on one's feet" is an expression used occasionally to underscore the fact that a dead person has come back to life (2 Kgs 13:21; Ezek 37:10; *Pesiq. Rab Kah.* 23.1 [Neusner, *Pesiqta* 2:83]; cf. Ezek 3:24). The phrase אם יקום והתהלך *'im yāqûm wĕhithallēk*, "if he rise and walk" (cf. Exod 21:19), refers to the recovery of a person seriously injured (*Mek. de-Rabbi Ishmael, Nezikin* 9 [Lauterbach, 3:53]).

11b καὶ φόβος μέγας ἐπέπεσεν ἐπὶ τοὺς θεωροῦντας αὐτούς, "with the result that great fear fell on those who saw them." The phrase "great fear fell on them" is a Semitic expression for a collective response of awe, either because the Israelites or Jews seem invincible (Exod 15:16; Deut 11:25; Esth 8:17; 9:2; 1 Macc 3:25; 7:18; 2 Macc 12:22) or as a reaction to a display of supernatural power (2 Macc 3:24; Luke 1:12, 65; Acts 5:5; 19:17). The verb θεωροῦν occurs just twice in Revelation (11:11, 12), while βλέπειν occurs nineteen times (in contrast, θεωροῦν is a favorite term in the Fourth Gospel, where it is used twenty-four times).

12a καὶ ἤκουσαν φωνῆς μεγάλης ἐκ τοῦ οὐρανοῦ λεγούσης αὐτοῖς, ἀνάβατε ὧδε, "They heard a loud voice from heaven, saying to them, 'Come up here.'" For the motif of the unidentified voice in Revelation, see *Comment* on 10:4. Here the voice simply commands the two witnesses to "Come up here!" a phrase identical with that found in 4:1. Voices from heaven occasionally provide strength and encouragement for martyrs (*Mart. Pol.* 9.1). Witnesses to the apotheosis of Apollonius of Tyana reportedly heard a chorus singing within the closed temple from which he disappeared: "Hasten from earth, hasten to heaven, hasten," i.e., "Go upwards from earth" (Philostratus *Vita Apoll.* 8.30).

12b καὶ ἀνέβησαν εἰς τὸν οὐρανὸν ἐν τῇ νεφέλῃ, "They ascended to heaven on a cloud." This event is presented as a miraculous divine rescue, a view underlined by the fact that the enemies of the two witnesses observe their ascension. There are some Jewish and Christian martyr legends in which it is reported that martyrs ascend to heaven after their deaths, where they stand before God, though in every text with the exception of one (*T. Job* 39.12–13; 40.3), it appears to be a matter of the ascension of the *souls* of the martyrs (Dan 12:2–3; 4 Macc 17:5; Jos. *J.W.* 2.153–55; *Mart. Justin* [Rec. A and B] 5; *Acts Scill.* 15 [*Hodie martyrer in caelis sumus*]; *Mart. Perpetua* 11.7–8; *Mart. Fruct.* 5; 7.2; see Kellermann, *Auferstanden in den Himmel* [who, however, does not refer to Rev 11]). In some passages the *resurrection* of the martyr is in view, but with no reference to an ascent to heaven (2 Macc 7:9, 11, 14, 23, 29; *Jub.* 23:30; see Hengel, *Zealots,* 269–70). Other texts mention the immortality that awaits the martyrs but similarly do not mention heaven (Jos. *J.W.* 1.650; 7.344–60; *Ag. Ap.* 2.218–19; 4 Macc 7:19; 9:8; 16:25).

Clouds are used as transport in a number of ways in Israelite and early Jewish tradition (see Sabourin, *BTB* 4 [1974] 290–311; Lohfink, *Himmelfahrt,* 187–93; Luzarraga, *Nube,* 220–25; Vermes, *Jesus,* 186–88: "Excursus I: the cloud, a means of heavenly transport"): (1) as a means of transport for Yahweh (Deut 33:26; Ps 68:34; see Houtman, *Himmel,* 324–26), (2) as a means of transport from earth to heaven (Acts 1:9; 1 Thess 4:17; Rev 11:12; 2 Kgs 2:11; *1 Enoch* 14:8; 39:3; 52:1; 70:2; *2 Enoch* 3:1; *T. Abr.* [Rec. A] 10:1; [Rec. B] 8:3; 10:2; Jos. *Ant.* 4.326 [a cloud descended on Moses, and he disappeared in a ravine]; *b. Yoma* 4a ["Moses ascended in the cloud"]; *Pesiq. Rab. Kah.* 20.4 (96b), "the cloud covered Moses and carried him up" [A. Jellinek, *Bet Ha-Midrash* 1:59]), (3) as a means of transport from one area of heaven to another (Pss 68:4; 104:3; Isa 19:1; Dan 7:13; *T. Abr.* [Rec. B] 12:1, 9; 4 Ezra 13:3), (4) as a means of transport from heaven to earth, often associated in early Christian sources with the coming of the Son of man (Rev 1:7; 10:1; Mark 13:26 = Matt 24:30 = Luke 21:27; Mark 14:62 = Matt 26:64; *Barn.* 16:8; *T. Abr.* [Rec. A] 9:8; 15:2), (5) as a mode of enthronement (Rev 14:14–16; Sir 24:4; *Mek. de-Rabbi Ishmael, Shirata* 6 [Lauterbach, 2:46], "Nebuchadnezzar said: 'I will make me a little cloud and will dwell in it'"), and (6) as a symbol associated with theophanies or angelophanies (Rev 10:1; Exod 14:24; 16:10; 24:16; Lev 16:2; Num 12:5; Deut 1:33; Lam 3:44; 2 Macc 2:8; Mark 9:7 = Matt 17:5 = Luke 9:34–35).

The ascension of the two witnesses narrated in vv 11–12 is essentially a *rapture story,* as distinguished from stories of the heavenly journey of the soul; that is, the two witnesses are physically taken up alive into heaven as the final conclusion of their earthly lives (Zwiep, *Ascension,* 22, 36 n. 1). K. Berger has pointed out that Luke 24 exhibits the threefold pattern of *resurrection, manifestation,* and *ascent to heaven,* a pattern also found in Rev 11:3–13, *Gos. Pet.* 10, and *Barn.* 15:9 (*Auferstehung,* 170–74, 471–75). This pattern is found in its most succinct form in *Barn.* 15:9, "Therefore we celebrate joyfully the eighth day on which Jesus rose from the dead, and after being manifested, ascended into the heavens." A central motif that this verse shares with Acts 1:9 is the cloud as a vehicle for carrying those ascending into heaven. Nevertheless, this rapture story is different from other early Jewish rapture stories involving Enoch, Elijah, Moses, Ezra (4 Ezra 14:7–9, 50), Baruch (*2 Apoc.*

Bar. 76:1-5), and Phinehas (*Bib. Ant.* 48:1–2), for all these figures were taken up alive into heaven to await the eschaton, at which time they would return (Mal 3:23–24; Acts 1:11; 3:21; 4 Ezra 14:9; *2 Apoc. Bar.* 76:2; *Bib. Ant.* 48:2; see Zwiep, *Ascension,* 76–79). The appearance of the two witnesses, on the other hand, is an eschatological event that presumes the return of Moses and Elijah. Their physical assumption into heaven apparently represents a second rapture, which is accomplished for their protection, not for their preservation until the eschaton.

The theme of the apparently permanent (as opposed to the *temporary*) translation or transport of the righteous to heaven is somewhat problematic since in biblical tradition heaven is not normally considered the abode of the righteous, whether living or dead. Traditions of the translations of Enoch (Gen 5:22, 24; Sir 44:16; Jos. *Ant.* 1.85; *1 Enoch* 39:3; Heb 11:5; *1 Clem.* 9:3; *Ps.-Titus Epistle* [Hennecke-Schmeemelcher, *NTA* 2:153]) and Elijah (2 Kgs 2:1–12; Mal 4:5), however, are obvious precedents. These and other texts that mention the ascension of Moses, Ezra, Baruch, Phinehas, and others (Zwiep, *Ascension,* 36–79) suggest that heaven could be considered the abode of certain righteous individuals (*Apoc. Paul* 20, 51; *Asc. Isa.* 9:7–9), just as only exceptional Greek heroes were rewarded with life on the Islands of the Blessed. On this theme see *T. Job* 39.12 (Charlesworth, *OTP* 1:859), "For you will not find my children, since they were taken up [ἀνελήφθησαν] into heaven by the Creator their King." The text seems to imply that Job's children, killed when their house collapsed, were taken up into heaven body and soul (see the extended discussion by Spittler in Charlesworth, *OTP* 1:859 n. e). A different form of assumption with an obvious body-soul dichotomy is found in *T. Abr.* (Rec. B^1; F. Schmidt, 62) 7:16–17, "and he [Abraham] will be taken up [ἀναλαμβάνεται] into the heavens, but his body remains on the earth." A similar text is found in the *Testament of Abraham* (Rec. B^2; F. Schmidt, 89): "You shall be taken up [ἀναλαμβάνεσαι] to the heavens but your body will remain on earth." In *Asc. Isa.* 9:9, Isaiah reportedly saw the righteous in the seventh heaven "stripped of the garment of the flesh" (tr. Hennecke-Schneemelcher, *NTA* 2:657). Part of Munck's argument that Peter and Paul are the two witnesses in Rev 11:3–13 is the tradition that they were taken into heaven after their deaths (*Petrus und Paulus,* 72ff.). He uses this argument apparently unaware that this is a widespread martyrological motif. Peter's "ascension" is described in *1 Clem.* 5:4, οὕτω μαρτυρήσας ἐπορεύθη εἰς τὸν ὀφειλόμενον τόπον τῆς δόξης, "after thus bearing witness, he [Peter] went to the well-deserved place of glory." Similarly, *1 Clem.* 5:7 says of Paul καὶ εἰς τὸν ἅγιον τόπον ἀνελήμφθη, "he was also taken up to the holy place." Similarly, in *Mart. Paul* 4 (Lipsius-Bonnet, *AAA* 1:114, line 15 through 1:115, line 1), Paul says in his swan song that "I am going to the Lord" (perhaps based on Phil 1:23). *Acts Thom.* 169–70 (Lipsius-Bonnet, *AAA* 2/2:286, lines 10–11) reports that when the grave of the apostle Thomas was opened by a person seeking a relic, his body was not there (on the motif of disappearance = heavenly ascent, see *Comment* on v 12c).

12c καὶ ἐθεώρησαν αὐτοὺς οἱ ἐχθροὶ αὐτῶν, "while their enemies looked on." *Witnessing* an ascent to heaven is a motif that occasionally occurs in ascension narratives (Judg 13:20; 2 Kgs 2:11–12; Luke 24:51; Acts 1:9–10 [as in Rev 11:12, Jesus is carried to heaven by a cloud]; *Jub.* 32:20; Jos. *Ant.* 5.284; *2 Enoch* [Rec. J and A] 67; *T. Abr.* [Rec. B] 7:14–16; *T. Job* 52.8–10; John Malalas *Chron.* 10.33, "I [Peter] am his [Christ's] disciple and in my presence he ascended into heaven"; see Lohfink, *Himmelfahrt,* 73). The same motif occurs in the Greco-Roman accounts of apotheosis or divinization through ascension to heaven (in Dio *Ant. Rom.* 4.3 [Versio 1, Cassius Dio Coeceianus, ed. Boissevain], Aeneas vanished from sight and was thereafter honored as a god; Livy 1.16.1–2 [Romulus was covered by a cloud and was no longer seen on earth]; cf. Cicero *De repub.* 2.10.17; Dionysius Hal. *Ant. Rom.* 2.56.2; Ovid *Metam.* 14.805–51; *Fasti* 2.481–509; Plutarch *Rom.* 27.6–8). Justin (*1 Apol.* 21.3) speaks of the necessity of having a witness swear that the deceased Caesar was seen ascending into heaven. In developed versions of the myth of the apotheosis of Romulus, the role of an eyewitness takes on legal as well as legitimating significance. Julius Proculus reportedly claimed "I have myself beheld Romulus ascending to the sky" (Dio 1.5.12; Plutarch *Rom.* 28.1–3; *Numa* 2.3; Aurelius Victor *De viris illustr.* 2.13; Dio 56.46.2). Similarly, Numerius Atticus, a Roman senator, swore that he had seen Augustus ascending to heaven (Dio 56.46.2; Suetonius *Aug.* 100.4). Apollonius of Tyana, after being miraculously released from chains, summoned his jailers to witness his disappearance from within a temple, presumably a heavenly ascent (Philostratus *Vita Apoll.* 8.30). The notion that disappearance = heavenly ascent also occurs in John Malalas *Chron.* 10.52, which records that when Domitian disappeared in a temple while sacrificing to Zeus, the people assumed that he had ascended to heaven, though he had really been assassinated.

13a Καὶ ἐν ἐκείνῃ τῇ ὥρᾳ ἐγένετο σεισμὸς μέγας, "And in that hour there was a great earthquake." The phrase "in that hour" or "in the same hour" is used to emphasize the immediacy of divine retribution (Dan 3:15) or the immediacy with which miraculous events occur (Dan 5:5; Matt 8:13; 10:19 = Mark 3:11 = Luke 12:12; Luke 7:21; John 4:53; Acts 22:13; cf. K. Berger, *Auferstehung,* 24, who uses the phrase *mirabilis coincidentia temporis*). In Revelation the demonstrative pronoun ἐκεῖνος, "that," occurs just twice (9:6; 11:13). Here the author shifts from his use of present tenses to the use of a verb in the past tense (ἐγένετο, "was") because having seen this vision in the past, he describes it as a phenomenon that occurred in the past (Mussies, *Morphology,* 181).

In view of the analogy of the death and resurrection of the two witnesses with that of Jesus, the earthquake mentioned in Matt 27:51 accompanying the death of Jesus is a relevant parallel. In Revelation, earthquakes (along with other seismic and atmospheric phenomena) usually have a theophanic function (6:12; 8:5; 11:19), but here and in 16:18 they are instruments of divine punishment. According to *PGM* IV.679–84, a group of seven gods sends thunder, lightning, and earthquakes to punish the impious. In legendary narratives, the ascension of heroes is often accompanied by atmospheric and seismic phenomena; in the case of Romulus there was an eclipse, thunder, lightning, and rain (Dionysius Hal. *Ant. Rom.* 2.56.2; Plutarch *Rom.* 27.6; Ovid *Metam.* 14.816–17; Dio 1.5.12). These phenomena are not punitive; rather they function primarily as signs that an extraordinary event is taking place.

13b καὶ τὸ δέκατον τῆς πόλεως ἔπεσεν, "so that a tenth of the city was destroyed." The city, which according to v 8 must be interpreted as Jerusalem, is represented here as still in existence just prior to the great earthquake (as the temple in vv 1–2 is represented as still in existence). There are a few indications in the OT that the figure of one-tenth is usually used for the *survivors* of divine judgment (Isa 6:13; Amos 5:3; *Jub.* 10:9), in which case this would be a reversal of that conception.

13c καὶ ἀπεκτάνθησαν ἐν τῷ σεισμῷ ὀνόματα ἀνθρώπων χιλιάδες ἑπτά, "and seven thousand people were killed in the earthquake." One *topos* found in ancient battle accounts is the enumeration of the slain in thousands (1 Sam 18:7; 21:11; 29:5; *Scrip. Hist. Aug., Div. Aurelianus* 6.5; 7.2). The figure 7,000 is used in 1 Kgs 19:18 for a remnant of 7,000 Israelites who have not worshiped Baal (in Rom 11:7–8, Paul uses the term οἱ λοιποί, "remnant," for just these 7,000 Israelites). The biblical conception of "remnant" frequently refers to that portion of the community that escaped (or will escape) death or exile (Jer 24:8; Ezra 9:13–15; Isa 10:20–22; 11:11–16; 17:5–8; 28:5; 37:31–32; Amos 7:1–6; CD 1:4–5; 1QH 6:8; Rom 9:24–29; 11:5). Since one-tenth of the city is said to be destroyed in this earthquake, the figure of 7,000 may represent a tenth part of a total population of 70,000. Josephus (*Ag. Ap.* 1.197), on the authority of Hecataeus, claims that there were 120,000 inhabitants of Jerusalem, a figure that many have thought too high for the early first century A.D., though Chaplin estimated a population of ca. 250,000. The population of Jerusalem before A.D. 66 has been estimated at something between 55,000 and 95,000 (Joachim Jeremias, *Jerusalem,* 83 n. 24), perhaps something more than 70,000 (Hengel, *Zealots,* 67 n. 38). Broshi (*RB* 82 [1975] 5–14; id., *BAR* 4 [1978] 10–15) suggests that (with a population density of 160 to 200 persons per acre) as many as 40,000 people occupied the 230 acres of Jerusalem during Herod's reign, while just before the destruction of the second temple in A.D. 70, it doubled in size with a population of ca. 80,000 occupying about 450 acres. Another argument for identifying "the great city" of v 8 with Jerusalem and not Rome is the great disparity in population; the population of Rome during the mid-first century A.D. was ca. 500,000 (Allo, 155).

13d καὶ οἱ λοιποὶ ἔμφοβοι ἐγένοντο καὶ ἔδωκαν δόξαν τῷ θεῷ τοῦ οὐρανοῦ, "with the result that the survivors were terrified and gave glory to the God of heaven." This is a typical conclusion to a miracle story (K. Berger, *Auferstehung,* 24; cf. Theissen, *Miracle,* 69–72), consisting of two stock reactions, "fear and amazement" (fear: Matt 17:6; 27:54; Mark 4:41; Luke 2:9; 7:16; 8:35; amazement: Matt 8:27; Mark 1:27; 5:42; 6:51; Luke 4:36). The phrase "they glorified God" at the conclusion of a miracle is an "acclamation" and is frequently found in Luke-Acts (Luke 8:47; 9:43; 13:13, 17; 18:43; 23:47; Acts 3:9). Sometimes, as here, both kinds of reactions are combined (Mark 2:12; 16:8). The phrase διδόναι δόξαν τῷ θεῷ, "to give glory to God," is an idiom with several meanings: (1) it can mean "to tell the truth" (John 9:24; Louw-Nida, § 33.468), (2) it can mean "give praise and honor to God" (this is a Lukan formula: Luke 8:47; 17:18; Acts 3:9; 4:21; 11:18; 12:23; 13:48; 21:20), and (3) it can a be verbal indication of *conversion,* which is probably the meaning here (Trites, *Witness,* 169–70; Sweet, 106–9; Bauckham, "Conversion," 278; disputed by Giesen [1997] 259). This is somewhat surprising, however, since it is the only instance in Revelation of people turning to the true God as a result of a punitive miracle. Yet there is strong evidence that διδόναι δόξαν τῷ θεῷ is an idiom for *conversion* (Haas, "Testament of Job," 141). In Rev 16:9, people blasphemed the name of God, and "they did not repent so as to give glory to him," suggesting that had they repented they would have given glory to God. In the angelic proclamation of the "eternal gospel" in 14:6–7, people are exhorted to "fear God and give him glory," i.e., become converted. Here in 11:13, giving glory to God is clearly the consequence of repentance, i.e., conversion (Loisy, 216). The "conversion" of Nebuchadrezzar is described in LXX Dan 4:34, using the phrase δὸς δόξαν τῷ ὑψίστῳ, "give glory to the Most High." Similarly, the phrase διδόναι δόξαν τῷ θεῷ, "to give glory to God," occurs in other contexts in which it clearly indicates that conversion has taken place (1 Esdr 9:8; Acts 13:48; Hermas *Sim.* 6.3.6; 8.6.3). The phrase διδόναι δόξαν τῷ θεῷ is also used of Christians as a sign of their adherence to God (*Mart. Justin* 6.1; *Mart. Agape* 7.2). The conversion of the remnant of Judaism is predicted by Paul in Rom 11:25–26.

The title "the God of heaven" (found in Revelation only here and in 16:11) occurs with some frequency in the post-exilic portions of the OT that reflect contact between Persians and Jews (Gen 24:7 [J; the only text that may be pre-exilic]; 2 Chr 36:23 = Ezra 1:2; 5:11, 12; 6:9, 10; 7:12, 21, 23; Neh 1:4, 5; 2:4, 20; Ps 136:26; Dan 2:18, 19, 37, 44; 5:23 ["Lord of heaven"]; Jonah 1:9; see Porten, *Elephantine,* 108). For various views on the origins of this title, see Houtman, *Himmel,* 98–107. The title "God of heaven" emphasizes the universal sovereignty of God and appears to have been primarily used by Jews when communicating with non-Jews. It is also striking that the title was also used with non-Jews by other non-Jews and in official correspondence of the Persians as a designation of Yahweh (Andrews, "Yahweh"), while Jews among themselves used the divine name Yahweh (Houtman, *Himmel,* 104). This suggests that those who repent in Rev 11:13 are not Jews but, as v 9 indicates, representative of the "peoples and tribes and tongues and nations" of the world (a fulfillment of Rev 10:11). The title (occasionally used in Persian letters and decrees relating to the Jews, e.g., 2 Chr 36:23 = Ezra 1:2; 7:12, 21, 23) may have originated as a Persian epithet for Ahura Mazda, which was then adapted by Jews in petitions to the Persian king (e.g., Ezra 5:11, 12) so that their cult would be recognized by the Persians (Andrews, "Yahweh"). The Aramaic phrase אלה שמיא *ʾĕlāh šĕmayyāʾ,* "the God of Heaven," occurs several times in the Jewish Aramaic papyri (Cowley, *Aramaic Papyri,* no. 27, line 15; no. 30, lines 2, 28 [= Porten-Yardeni, *Textbook* 1:71; here the full title is יהו אלהי השמים *yhw ʾlhy hšmym,* "Yahu the God of heaven"]; no. 31, lines 2, 26–27 [= Porten-Yardeni, *Textbook* 1:75]; no. 32, lines 3–4 [= Porten-Yardeni, *Textbook* 1:76]; no. 38, lines 2, 3, 5 [= Porten-Yardeni, *Textbook* 1:58]; no. 40, line 1 [= Porten-Yardeni, *Textbook* 1:38]; cf. Porten, *Elephantine,* 107–9). The title "God of heaven" also occurs in the Apocrypha (Tob 10:11; Jdt 5:8; 6:19; 11:7; 3 Macc 6:28; 7:6), along with such synonyms as "Lord of heaven" (Tob 7:18; 10:12; Jdt 9:12; Cowley, *Aramaic Papyri,* no. 30, line 15, מרא שמיא *mārēʾ šĕmayyāʾ,* "Lord of Heaven") and "King of heaven" (Tob 13:7, 11; 1 Esdr 4:46, 58; 3 Macc 2:2). There are some examples of the phrase in the pseudepigrapha as well (*T. Moses* 2:4; *T. Reub.* 1:6; 6:9; *T. Iss.* 7:7; *T. Ben.* 3:1; cf. *Jos. As.* 11:9; 18:11; 21:15; *Par. Jer.* 5:32; *Jub.* 12:4; 20:7). There are a few parallels in the magical papyri, such as ἐν τῷ οὐρανῷ θεὸς ὁ μονογενής, "the only god in heaven" (*PGM* XV.15); the phrase [θεὸν τῶ]ν οὐρανῶν καὶ θεὸν τῆς γῆς, "God of the heavens and God of the earth," occurs in *PGM* 16.1, a Christian magical papyrus of the fourth or fifth century, and it also occurs frequently in the *Testament of Solomon,* written from the first to third century A.D. (*T. Sol.* 1:8; 2:9; 3:6; 17:4; 18:41; 20:21). The Aramaic phrase "the servant of the God of Heaven [עבדה דאלה שומיה *ʿbdh dʾlh šwmyh*]" occurs on a Palestinian Jewish magical amulet for protection while traveling (fifth or sixth century A.D.), made for the use of a certain Rabbi Eleazar (Naveh-Shaked, *Amulets,* amulet 3, line 6). The title also occurs in a magical recipe from the Cairo Genizah (Naveh-Shaked, *Amulets,* Geniza 5, p. 1, line 10, "I adjure you, spirit, in [the name of] YHWH, the God of heaven." In the NT the title "Lord of heaven and earth" occurs in one Q logion (Matt 11:25 = Luke 10:21) and once in Acts 17:34.

14 ἡ οὐαὶ ἡ δευτέρα ἀπῆλθεν· ἰδοὺ ἡ οὐαὶ ἡ τρίτη ἔρχεται ταχύ, "The second disaster has occurred; behold, the third disaster will come shortly." Of the pattern of "three woes" announced by the eagle in 8:13, and anticipated by the reader, only two woes are explicitly mentioned as having occurred (9:12; 11:14). The statements here and in 9:12 are the author's editorial comments, which he does not present as transmitted to him by a heavenly revealer; rather he simply inserts them into what he considers the appropriate juncture in his narrative. This in turn suggests that the statement of the eagle in 8:13 was inserted by the author at an advanced stage of composition. This sentence would appear more appropriate if it were placed after 9:21, and it is also difficult to reconcile with the result of the sounding of the seventh trumpet in 11:15–18, which can hardly be described as a "woe." Its displacement results from the insertion of 10:1–11:13 between the sixth and seventh trumpets (similar to the author's insertion of 7:1–17 between the sixth and seventh seals) and the author's attempt to pick of the threads of that narrative in 11:15–18.

Explanation

Rev 11:1–13 is a self-contained literary unit that consists of two subunits, vv 1–2 and vv 3–13, while v 14 serves as a conclusion to vv 1–13 and as an introduction to vv 15–18. Vv 1–13 are introduced abruptly without any of the author's usual introductory formulas, thus suggesting a close link with the previous unit of text in 10:1–11. This section contains a narrative that centers on the apparently unsuccessful mission of two mysterious eschatological prophetic witnesses whose ministry is a thematic continuation of John's renewed prophetic commission in 10:8–11 and symbolizes the kind of testimony borne by John and his prophetic colleagues. It is likely that John has fused two earlier prophetic oracles (probably Jewish in origin), one in 11:1–2 and the other in 11:3–13; they are connected only by the motifs of the 42 months (v 2), which is equivalent to the 1,260 days of v 3, and the holy city (vv 2, 8).

In vv 1–2, John is given a measuring stick and told to measure the temple of God, the altar or holy place, and the worshipers who worship near it, a task that is not described as actually having been carried out. Is John referring to the literal earthly temple in Jerusalem that was destroyed by the Romans in A.D. 70 or the transcendent heavenly temple, or is he using the earthly temple as a symbol? Since the Herodian temple was destroyed when Jerusalem fell to the Romans in A.D. 70, vv 1–2 may preserve a prophetic oracle uttered by a Jewish prophet in besieged Jerusalem just before A.D. 70, hoping that the temple would be preserved (Jos. *J.W.* 6.286). Whether John has reinterpreted an older oracle or formulated the passage himself, the meaning is the same. The act of measuring signifies *preservation.* Thus vv 1–2, part of the larger unit in vv 1–13 that is placed between the sixth and seventh trumpets, emphasizes preservation just as the first part of 7:1–17 (placed between the sixth and seventh seals) emphasizes the preservation of the 144,000 through their sealing. In this new context, the worshipers represent the divinely protected remnant of Christians who will survive until the arrival of the eschaton. The pagan domination over the holy city will be for 42 months (v 2), while the prophetic witness will be active for 1,260 days (v 3); both figures are derived from the 3 1/2 years of Dan 7:25, symbolizing a strictly limited period of time. The period of 42 months is also mentioned in Rev 13:5 as the time during which the beast exercises authority.

The second oracle (vv 3–13) focuses on the ministry of the two prophetic witnesses, a ministry abruptly ended by the appearance of an eschatological adversary. The passage begins with an allusion to the two olive trees and the two (instead of seven) lamps or menorahs of Zech 4:1–14. In Zechariah the olive trees represent Zerubbabel, the claimant to the Davidic throne, and Joshua, the high priest, on whom the prophet Zechariah and others based their hopes for the restoration of Judah. This passage (together with the messianic prophecy of Balaam in Num 24:17 concerning the coming of the "star" [= priest] and "scepter" [= king]), with its emphasis on the importance of both the royal and priestly offices, became influential in circles of Jewish eschatological expectation that emphasized the coming of *two* messiahs, a royal Messiah of David and a priestly Messiah of Aaron. The description of the two witnesses also owes features to biblical and traditional conceptions of Enoch, Elijah, and Moses. These were all taken up alive into heaven according to Jewish tradition, as are the two witnesses in v 12. The two witnesses have the power to perform punitive miracles; they can destroy with fire those who attempt to harm them (like Elijah; see 2 Kgs 1:9–16), cause drought (also like Elijah; 1 Kgs 17:1), and smite the earth with plagues (like Moses; see Exod 7–10). Strangely, the *content* of their message is not mentioned, though it may be presumed that they demand repentance of the nations (though initially in vain). They are often interpreted as Elijah and Moses (who were expected to return in the last days, though not minister in tandem) or Enoch and Elijah (many other suggestions are detailed in *Form/Structure/Content,* III. Central Interpretive Issues). Since the people of God are both kings and priests (1:6; 5:10), it is likely that the two witnesses represent the Christian Church in its prophetic witness. Since the witnesses are identical in every respect, the fact that there are *two* of them is based on the notion of the reliability of two witnesses (Num 35:30; Deut 19:15; John 8:13–18). When the brief period of their immunity is over, they will be killed by the beast from the bottomless pit (v 7; presumably identical with the beast of Rev 13 and 17), who is introduced here very briefly for the first time in Revelation but plays no further role in this narrative unit. The equation of the eschatological adversary in Jerusalem with the chaos monster is a redactional addition by John. The scene of their prophetic activity and the place where their unburied bodies lie is in "*the* street of *the* great city" (my emphasis). If the city is Jerusalem (where, according to v 8, their Lord was crucified), which is denounced under the names of "Sodom" and "Egypt," then the street in view could be Tyropoeon Valley Street (see *Comment* on 11:8). Yet the city also represents the world that has rejected the gospel and slain its prophetic messengers. In early Judaism there was a widespread view that suffering and martyrdom in Jerusalem were the all but inevitable experience of the true prophet (Luke 13:33); thus the fate of the two witnesses replicates the fate of Jesus and many earlier prophetic messengers. The fact that the two witnesses lie dead on the streets of the great city for three and one-half days is intended to remind the audience of the period between the crucifixion and the resurrection of Jesus. The summons of the dead witnesses to heaven by an unidentified heavenly voice both replicates John's revelatory experience in 4:1 and is reminiscent of the ascension motif in 2 Kgs 2:11–12 (Elijah) and Luke 24 and Acts 1 (Jesus). The ascension of the two witnesses on a cloud before onlookers represents a miraculous divine rescue. The destruction of a tenth of the city and death of seven thousand inhabitants by a great earthquake result in the survivors giving glory to the God of heaven, language that suggests their conversion.

D. The Seventh Trumpet and the Seven Bowls (11:15–16:21)

1. The Seventh Trumpet (11:15–18)

Bibliography

Cassem, N. H. "A Grammatical and Contextual Inventory of the Use of *kosmos* in the Johannine Corpus with Some Implications for a Johannine Cosmology." *NovT* 19 (1972) 81–91. **Feuillet, A.** "Essai d'interpretation du chapitre XI de l'Apocalypse." *NTS* 4 (1957–58) 183–200. **Gelston, A.** "A Note on יהוה מלך." *VT* 16 (1966) 507–12. **Gerstenberger, E.** "Psalms." In *Old Testament Form Criticism,* ed. J. H. Hayes. San Antonio: Trinity UP, 1974. 179–223. **Gunkel, H.** *The Psalms: A Form Critical Introduction.* Philadelphia: Fortress, 1967. ——— and **Begrich, J.** *Einleitung in die Psalmen: Die Gattungen der religiösen Lyrik Israels.* Göttingen: Vandenhoeck & Ruprecht, 1933. **Hartman, L.** *Prophecy Interpreted: The Formation of Some Jewish Apocalyptic Texts and of the Eschatological Discourse Mark 13 par.* ConBNT 1. Lund: Gleerup, 1966. **Kittel, B.** *The Hymns of Qumran.* SBLDS 50. Atlanta: Scholars, 1981. **Mowinckel, S.** *Offersang og Sangoffer.* Oslo: Universitetsforlaget, 1951. **O'Rourke, J. J.** "The Hymns of the Apocalypse." *CBQ* 30 (1968) 399–409. **Schille, G.** "Das Leiden des Herrn." *ZTK* 52 (1955) 161–205. **Ulrichsen, J. H.** "JHWH MALAK: Einige sprachliche Beobachtungen." *VT* 27 (1977) 361–74. **Westermann, C.** *The Praise of God in the Psalms.* Tr. K. R. Crim. Richmond: John Knox, 1965.

Translation

15 *Then the* [a] *seventh angel sounded his trumpet, and there were loud voices in heaven, saying:* [b]

The kingdom of the world
[c]*has become* [c] [d]*the kingdom*[d] *of our Lord and his Messiah,*
who[e] *will reign for ever and ever.*[f]

16 *The* [a] *twenty-four elders who*[b] *were* [c]*seated* [d] *before* [e]*God* [f]*on their thrones* [f] [g]*fell on their faces and worshiped* [h]*God,* 17 *saying:*

We thank you, [a]*Lord* [b] *God* [c]*Almighty, who was and who is,*[ad]
[e]*because you have received your great authority and* [f]*have begun to reign.*[f]
18 *The nations* [a]*are enraged,*[a]
but [b] *your wrath came*
and the time [c] *for the dead to be judged*
and to reward [d] *your servants, the prophets,*
and [e]*God's people* [f]*and those who revere* [e] *your name,*

[g]both the insignificant and the important,[g]
and [h] to ruin utterly [i]those who ruin the earth.[i]

Notes

15.a. Variant: omit ὁ before ἕβδομος] A.

15.b. Variants: (1) λέγοντες (present pl. nom. masc. ptcp.)] A Oecumenius^{2053} 2351 Byzantine. (2) λέγουσαι (present pl. nom. fem. ptcp.)] 𝔓^{47} ℵ C 051 fam 1006$^{1006\ 1841}$ fam 1611$^{1611\ 1854\ 2329\ 2344}$ Andreas; von Soden, *Text.* Despite the strong attestation of reading (2), it is obviously a grammatical correction to make the ptcp. agree with its antecedent, φωναὶ μεγάλαι (Schmid, *Studien* 2:102). For similar corrections, see 4:1; 9:13 (Schmid, *Studien* 2:236).

15.c-c. Variants: (1) ἐγένετο ἡ βασιλεία] Andreas 94 025. (2) ἐγένοντο αἱ βασιλεῖαι] Andr a b c g h n 598 1773 2019. (3) omit ἐγένετο] Andr e.

15.d-d. In this sentence the author has elided the predicate nom. ἡ βασιλεία, upon which τοῦ κυρίου, "the Lord," and τοῦ χριστοῦ αὐτοῦ, "his Messiah," are dependent (perhaps for stylistic reasons), though this noun must be supplied in the translation.

15.e. The καί that introduces this coordinate clause functions like a relative clause and so has been translated "who." The subject of the 3rd sing. fut. verb βασιλεύσει can be either "the Lord" or "his Messiah," but is probably the former.

15.f. Variant: insert ἀμήν] ℵ fam 1612^{344} Andr l 494 vg^{COT} it$^{c\ dem\ diu\ haf\ t}$ cop^{bo}; Beatus.

16.a. Variants: (1) οἱ before εἴκοσι] C fam 1006 fam 1611 Oecumenius^{2053comm} 2062 Andreas Byzantine; Tischendorf, *NT Graece;* B. Weiss, *Johannes-Apokalypse,* 101; von Soden, *Text;* Bousset (1906) 331; Charles, 1:295; 2:305. (2) omit οἱ before εἴκοσι] ℵ* A Oecumenius^{2053text} Andr c^{2033} n^{2429} 1773. Variant (2) must be the result of scribal error (Schmid, *Studien* 2:102, 195) since the first occurrence of εἴκοσι τέσσαρες πρεσβύτεροι in 4:4 is anarthrous but thereafter arthrous, in conformity with the author's style (see 4:10; 5:5, 6, 11, 14; 7:11, 13; 14:3; 19:4).

16.b. Variant: (1) οἱ before ἐνώπιον] 025 2351 Andr d f$^{051\ 2023\ 2073}$ i l 94 2019 Tischendorf, *NT Graece;* [WHort]; von Soden, *Text;* Bousset (1906) 331; Charles, 1:295; 2:305; [Nestle-Aland^{27}]; [UBSGNT^{4}]. (2) omit οἱ] 𝔓^{47} A 046 fam 1006 Andreas. Variant (2) is the consequence of scribal error (Schmid, *Studien* 2:102), for the definite article is repeated before an attributive following an arthrous noun, whether an adj., a pronoun, an ordinal number, or a ptcp. (e.g., 1:4; 2:24; 5:5; 8:3; 11:19; Schmid, *Studien* 2:196).

16.c. Variants: (1) οἱ before καθήμενοι] 2351 Andr g. (2) οἱ before κάθηνται] ℵ* 94 Byzantine; Tischendorf, *NT Graece;* von Soden, *Text.* (3) omit οἱ] WHort; Nestle-Aland^{27}; UBSGNT^{4}.

16.d. Variants: (1) καθήμενοι] A 051 fam 1611$^{1854\ 2329}$ Andreas. (2) κάθηνται] 𝔓^{47} ℵ^{2} C Oecumenius^{2053} fam 1006$^{1006\ 1841}$ fam 1611^{2344} WHort^{mg}.

16.e. Variant: insert τοῦ θρόνου] 94 Byzantine. The phrase ὁ θρόνος τοῦ θεοῦ, "throne of God," which has influenced the copyist, occurs just three times in Revelation (7:15; 22:1, 3).

16.f-f. Variant: omit ἐπὶ τούς θρόνους] 𝔓^{47}.

16.g. Variant: add καί] ℵ fam 1006.

16.h. On the use of προσκυνεῖν + dat. or acc., see *Note* 4:10.b.

17.a-a. The phrase κύριε ὁ θεὸς ὁ παντοκράτωρ, ὁ ὢν καὶ ὁ ἦν consists of a vocative (κύριε) followed by four nom. substantives in apposition to κύριε, each of which functions as a vocative.

17.b. Variant: κύριος] ℵ (abbreviated κσ instead of κε); 598.

17.c. Variants: (1) insert ὁ θεός] 𝔓^{47}. (2) omit ὁ before παντοκράτωρ] ℵ*.

17.d. Variant: insert καὶ ὁ ἐρχόμενος] 051 fam 1006$^{1006\ 1841}$ Tyc^{1} (*qui es et qui venisti et qui venturus es*); Tyc^{3} Beatus (*qui es et qui venisti*). This phrase follows ὁ ὢν καὶ ὁ ἦν in 1:8; 4:8, and its presence in these two passages has doubtlessly led to its secondary insertion here. Jörns (*Evangelium,* 99–100) is of the opinion that ὁ ἐρχόμενος is missing here (though present in 1:8; 4:8) because the "coming" of God has occurred (or is occurring) in terms of the beginning of judgment.

17.e. Variant: (1) omit καί before ὅτι] ℵ^{3} A 025 046 fam 1611$^{1611\ 1854}$ Oecumenius^{2053} it^{gig} vg syr$^{h\ ph}$ cop^{sa}. (2) καί before ὅτι] 𝔓^{47} ℵ* C fam 1611^{2344} it^{a} vg^{F} (*et quia*); vg^{DΘIΠUW} (*et qui*). (3) καὶ ὁ ἐρχόμενος before ὅτι] 051 fam 1006$^{1006\ 1841}$ Andr e^{2026} f i n 1773 2019 Tyconius. Elsewhere in Revelation, ὅτι is preceded by καί only in 2:2. Among modern editors, this reading is accepted only by Tischendorf (*NT Graece*). The insertion of καί at this point is a careless error, probably occurring because of the frequency with which καί is used in Revelation to begin new clauses and sentences (Schmid, *Studien* 2:102). The MS attestation of reading (1) is quite strong (*TCGNT*^{1}, 744–45; *TCGNT*^{2}, 672). Reading (3), not widely attested, is based on assimilation to the tripartite expression in Rev 1:4, 8; 4:8.

17.f-f. ἐβασίλευσας is translated as an ingressive aor.; see *Comment* on v 17.

18.a-a. Variant: ὠργίσθη] 𝔓[47] ℵ*. Correction made to provide a neut. pl. noun (τὰ ἔθνη) with a 3rd sing. verb.

18.b. The καί with which this clause is introduced is used in an adversative sense and so is translated "but," though this is disputed by Jörns, *Evangelium,* 104.

18.c. Variant: κλῆρος for καιρός] C Oecumenius[2053comm] Andr n. 2065 has a distinctive reading here: καὶ ἦλθεν ἡ ὀργή σου καὶ ὁ κλῆρος τῶν νεκρῶν, "and your wrath came and the fate of the dead." This variant originated as a visual error (Schmid, *Studien* 2:102).

18.d. δοῦναι, an aor. active inf., like κριθῆναι (see *Note* 11:6.c-c.), is complementary and provides a closer definition of ὁ καιρός.

18.e-e. Variants: (1) καὶ τοὺς ἁγίους καὶ τοὺς φοβουμένους] 𝔓[47] A 2351; Charles, 1:295; Mussies, *Morphology,* 100. (2) τοῖς ἁγίοις καὶ τοῖς φοβουμένοις] Oecumenius[2053] Andreas Byzantine; WHort; Charles, 2:306; Merk, *NT;* Nestle-Aland[27]; UBSGNT[4]. Since this phrase is grammatically parallel to τοῖς δούλοις σου τοῖς προφήταις, it should be a dat. rather than an acc. (as the indirect obj. of the verb δοῦναι). The accs. of reading (1) can therefore be understood as in apposition to τοῖς δουλοῖς σου τοῖς προφήταις. Mussies (*Morphology,* 100) suggests that in the irregular accs. read by A, in reading (1) here and in *Note* 18.g-g. reading (1), may have an emphatic or adversative value reflecting an overly mechanical rendering of the Heb. אֶת־ *ʾet,* which in a few instances in the MT is not used as a *nota accusativi* but has a certain emphasis (GKC, § 117m). In this case, Schmid (*Studien* 2:76–77) argues that reading (2) represents the original text, both here and in *Note* 18.g-g., and that when 𝔓[47] and A are alone in agreeing on a reading, that reading is usually an error (*Studien* 2:119–20). On translating τοῖς ἁγίους, lit. "saints," as "God's people," see *Comment* on 5:8.

18.f. Variant: omit καί] 051 fam 1611[1854]. The result of this omission would be that τοῖς φοβουμένοις must be read as an adj. ptcp. modifying τοῖς ἁγίοις, i.e., "the saints who revere."

18.g-g. Variants: (1) τοὺς μικροὺς καὶ τοὺς μεγάλους] 𝔓[47] ℵ* A (see *Note* 18.e-e.); C fam 1611[2329 2344] 2351; WHort; Charles, 2:306; Nestle-Aland[27]; UBSGNT[4]. (2) τοῖς μικροῖς καὶ τοῖς μεγάλοις] ℵ[2] 025 046 Oecumenius[2053] Andreas Byzantine; B. Weiss, *Johannes-Apokalypse,* 188; Bousset (1906) 332; Merk, *NT.* Reading (1) is the *lectio difficilior,* and in addition it has the support of a number of important MSS (*TCGNT*[1], 745; *TCGNT*[2], 672). The accs. of reading (1) can be considered to be in apposition to τοῖς δούλοις σου τοῖς προφήταις (Robertson, *Grammar,* 414).

18.h. Variant: omit καί] A Andr i[2014 2034].

18.i-i. Variants: (1) διαφθείροντας] 𝔓[47] ℵ A Byzantine. (2) διαφθείραντας] C fam 1611 Andr f[051 2023 2073] 94 2019 syr. (3) φθείροντας] Andreas. (4) φθείραντας] Oecumenius[2053com] Andr n[-2429] 598. All these variants are present active acc. masc. pl. ptcps., though there has been an ο > α shift that is the result either of the influence of the aor. endings on the present system (Gignac, *Grammar* 2:329) or of the ο > α shift that is characteristic of Egyptian Gk. (Gignac, *Grammar* 1:287–89).

Form/Setting/ Structure

I. OUTLINE

1. The seventh trumpet (11:15–18)
   a. The seventh angel sounds his trumpet (v 15a)
   b. The hymnic response from heaven (vv 15a–18)
      (1) The song of victory from heaven (v 15a–c)
         (a) The singers: loud voices in heaven (v 15a)
         (b) The song (v 15bc)
            [1] The transfer of the kingdom of the world (v 15b)
               [a] To our God
               [b] To his Messiah
            [2] God will reign for ever (v 15c)
      (2) The antiphonal song of thanksgiving of the twenty-four elders (vv 16–18)
         (a) The worship of the twenty-four elders (v 16)
            [1] Their location

[a] They are before God
[b] They are seated on their thrones
[2] Their action
[a] They fall on their faces
[b] They worship God
(b) Their song of thanksgiving (vv 17–18)
[1] Introductory thanksgiving formula: "we give thanks" (v 17a)
[2] Addressee (v 17a)
[a] To you
[b] Lord God Almighty
[c] Who is and who was
[3] Basic reason for thanksgiving (v 17b)
[a] You have received your great authority
[b] You have begun to reign
[4] Eschatological retrospective (v 18)
[a] The nations are enraged (v 18a)
[b] But your wrath came (v 18b)
[c] And the time to judge the dead (v 18b)
[d] And to reward your people (v 18c)
{1} Your servants the prophets
{2} And God's people
{3} And those who revere your name
{a} The unimportant
{b} The important
[e] And to destroy the destroyers of the earth (v 18d)

II. Literary Analysis

Rev 11:15–18 is a short isolated textual unit that forms an apparently anticlimactic continuation of 8:1–9:21, interrupted by 10:1–11:14, and is immediately followed by 11:19–12:17 and two other sections (12:18–13:18 and 14:1–20), none of which is very carefully integrated into an overarching compositional plan. By separating 11:3–14 from 11:19–12:17, the author has partially obscured the lack of connection that exists between those two units. The sounding of the seventh trumpet does not introduce an expected seventh set of plagues; instead it functions to introduce a brief throne vision. While the characteristic "I saw" and "I heard" formulas that are usually used to introduce visions and auditions in Revelation are lacking, the author apparently *hears* loud voices in heaven, which utter an initial song of victory, which is followed by a throne vision that John apparently *sees,* complete with a thanksgiving hymn sung by the twenty-four elders.

Rev 11:15–18 consists of a two-part responsory hymn that juxtaposes the celebration of the reign of God with the final judgment in which all the dead are judged; the righteous are rewarded and the wicked are punished. The first part is spoken by anonymous "loud voices in heaven" (v 15b), while the response is given by the twenty-four elders (vv 17–18). Since the responsory hymn in vv 17–18 is introduced with the first-person plural verb εὐχαριστοῦμεν, "we give thanks" (which only occurs here in Revelation; the noun εὐχαριστία, "thanksgiving," however, occurs twice in formulaic phrases in Rev 4:9; 7:12), it is reasonable to expect that the hymn will conform to the OT and early Jewish traditions of the song of thanksgiving.

The OT contains both communal and individual songs of thanksgiving (Eissfeldt, *Introduction,* 120–24). OT thanksgiving songs, originally intended for use by individuals and groups in the temple, consist of three parts (Gunkel, *Psalms,* 17–19): (1) the description of the author's distress, (2) the cry for help, and (3) the description of deliverance. Since both the individual song of thanksgiving and the thank offering are called תודה *tôdâ* (Jonah 2:10; Pss 50:14, 23; 107:22), the former probably originated as a verbal accompaniment to the latter and then became independent of it, particularly in the post-exilic period following the cessation of the temple cult.

Some of the problems of the form of this hymn are solved if it is regarded as a hymnic adaptation of an eschatological scenario such as that found in *1 Enoch* 27:3 (tr. Knibb, *Enoch*):

> And in the last days there will be the spectacle of the righteous judgment upon them before the righteous for ever, for evermore; here the merciful will bless [εὐλογήσουσιν] the Lord of Glory, the Eternal King. And in the days of the judgment on them they will bless [εὐλογήσουσιν] him on account of (his) mercy, according as he has assigned to them (their lot).

The scene is that of the final judgment, in which both the wicked and the righteous will be judged. When that judgment occurs, the righteous will praise or bless God, though the text has no suggestions regarding how such a song of praise might be phrased. In Rev 11:15–18, God is praised upon his assumption of full rule and his inauguration of the final judgment, not by the righteous but rather by the twenty-four elders. The motifs in this eschatological scenario are not in chronological order, for the beginning of the reign of God must be considered the closing act in this eschatological drama: (1) God has begun to reign (v 17). (2) The hostile nations of the world are enraged (v 18a), a motif paired with the kingly rule of God in Ps 99:1 (LXX 98:1), ὁ κύριος ἐβασίλευσεν, ὀργιζέσθωσαν λαοί, "The Lord reigns; let the peoples be enraged." (3) The time of judgment has arrived (v 18b). (4) The righteous are rewarded (v 18c). (5) The destroyers of the earth are destroyed (v 18d).

The structure and arrangement of the thanksgiving hymn is problematic, primarily because the sequence of motifs is not in chronological order. Jörns (*Evangelium,* 101–2) suggests the following structure, in which part A is hymnic while part B is prose:

A	I a	We thank you, Lord God Almighty,
	b	who was and who is,
	II a	because you have received your great authority
	b	and have begun to reign.
B	I	The nations are enraged,
	IIa	but your wrath came
	b1	and the time to judge the dead
	b2	and to reward your servants
	α	the prophets and God's people
	β	and those who revere your name

γ both the insignificant and the important.
b3 and to ruin utterly those who ruin the earth.

In agreement with Jörn's analysis, it is appropriate that lines Ia and Ib of part A constitute a unit consisting of the introductory thanksgiving formula and a list of the titles of God, who is the addressee. It is also appropriate in part A to regard line IIa as introducing a second subunit within the thanksgiving song. In the overall scheme of the hymn, however, it is problematic to distinguish between a "hymnic" and a "prose" portion, given the necessarily loose definitions of prose and poetry that have been applied to NT hymnody (there is a noteworthy emphasis on prose hymnody in the Greek world of the late Hellenistic and early Roman periods).

The real analytical problem is how the five lines introduced with καί function in the hymn taken as a whole, given the fact that each eschatological event, represented by the five cola, appears to be out of chronological order. First, it is important to recognize that while the ὅτι clause in v 17b provides the basic reason for the song of thanksgiving, the five cola in v 18 together represent an *eschatological retrospective* on which the basic reason in v 17b is grounded. While the phrase "eschatological retrospective" appears somewhat peculiar, it is nevertheless appropriate since the eschatological events are all described through aorist verbs and infinitives as though they were events of the *past,* and all of these events taken together make it clear that God has begun his reign. Two main verbs govern the five cola. The verb ὀργίζειν dominates the first colon, where it is reported that the nations who are enraged (ὠργίσθησαν), i.e., in rebellion against God, are stopped. In the second colon, it is said that God's ὀργή, "wrath," has arrived (ἦλθεν), functioning as a divine response to the wrath of the heathen nations. In the third colon, the verb ἦλθεν must be supplied with ὁ καιρός, "the time," as its subject. Three complementary infinitives in the third, fourth, and fifth cola are dependent on the supplied ἦλθεν, κριθῆναι (the time came *to judge*), δοῦναι τὸν μισθόν (the time came *to give a reward*), and διαφθεῖραι (the time came *to destroy*).

The thanksgiving hymn in 11:15–18 appears in part to be a pastiche of stereotypical expressions found elsewhere in Revelation and in part to be a composition with features unique in the book. This suggests that an earlier composition has been reworded to cohere with some of the characteristic emphases and locutions of the final version of Revelation. The following phrases in vv 17–18 have close parallels elsewhere in Revelation: (1) κύριε ὁ θεὸς ὁ παντοκράτωρ (4:8; 15:3; 16:7; 19:6; 21:22), (2) ὁ ὢν καὶ ὁ ἦν (1:4, 8; 4:8; 16:5; the first three references include ὁ ἐρχόμενος as a third element), (3) ὅτι εἴληφας τὴν δύναμιν (4:11, λαβεῖν . . . τὴν δύναμιν), and (4) τοὺς μικροὺς καὶ τοὺς μεγάλους (13:16; 19:5, 18; 20:12).

Comment

15a καὶ ὁ ἕβδομος ἄγγελος ἐσάλπισεν· καὶ ἐγένοντο φωναὶ μεγάλαι ἐν τῷ οὐρανῷ λέγοντες, "Then the seventh angel sounded his trumpet, and there were loud voices in heaven, saying." The first clause constitutes a formulaic introduction that closely corresponds with the introductions to the previous six trumpet plagues (8:7, 8, 10, 12; 9:1, 13; only in 8:7 is the term ἄγγελος missing). While the phrase φωνὴ μεγάλη, "great sound, loud voice," occurs frequently in Revelation in a number of connections, only here does the phrase occur in the plural of the sound of chanting or singing, though it is not at all clear why the plural is used. The closest parallel to 11:15a occurs in the hymnic introduction in 12:10, καὶ ἤκουσα φωνὴν μεγάλην ἐν τῷ οὐρανῷ λέγουσαν, "and I heard a loud voice in heaven, saying" (cf. 19:1). The phrase ἐν τῷ οὐρανῷ, "in heaven," is given as the location where the seer hears the voices, and the same prepositional phrase occurs in 12:10 and 19:1, indicating the heavenly perspective of the seer and suggesting that these hymns could only be heard in the vicinity of the heavenly court (Jörns, *Evangelium,* 91). Elsewhere the earthly perspective of the seer is implied by the use of the phrase ἐκ τοῦ οὐρανοῦ, "from heaven" (10:4, 8; 11:12; 14:2, 13; 18:4). The climactic character of the seventh trumpet is anticipated in the angelic speech in 10:7, in which it is proclaimed that the secret plan of God, which he announced to his servants the prophets, will be revealed in the days when the seventh trumpet is sounded. The identity of the loud voices is left unspecified, and there is no reason to speculate with Swete (141) and Charles (1:293–94) that the voices are those of the cherubim or with Lohmeyer (95) that the voices are those of the twenty-four elders (see Beckwith, 608). The introductory λέγοντες (masculine nominative plural participle) is a solecism since it modifies φωναὶ μεγάλαι, and therefore should be λέγουσαι (feminine nominative plural participle; see *Note* 11:15.b).

15b ἐγένετο ἡ βασιλεία τοῦ κόσμου τοῦ κυρίου ἡμῶν καὶ τοῦ χριστοῦ αὐτοῦ, "The kingdom of the world / has become the kingdom of our Lord and his Messiah." V 15bc constitutes a song of victory (*Siegesruf*) comparable to those found in 7:10 and 12:10–12 (Deichgräber, *Gotteshymnus,* 54). The theme of this song of victory is the kingship or rule of God, and the song consists of two lines connected by καί. The verb ἐγένετο is used to introduce a hymnic section only here and in 12:10 (where the kingship of God is also emphasized). Although ἐγένετο is an aorist and therefore refers to God's assumption of kingship as a fact of the *past,* the context makes it clear that ἐγένετο is used proleptically, like the *perfectum propheticum,* "prophetic perfect," of a future event that prophetic certainty speaks of as an event of the past (GKC § 106n; Justin *1 Apol.* 42.1). The initial position of ἐγένετο emphasizes the certainty of the final and complete eschatological rule of God.

The term κόσμος, "world," which occurs 186 times in the NT, occurs only 3 times in Revelation (here and in a formula found in Rev 13:8 and 17:8). Most occurrences of the term κόσμος occur in the Gospel (78 times) and Letters (24 times) of John (i.e., 55 percent of the occurrences in the NT; see Cassem, *NovT* 19 [1972] 81–91), which suggests a major difference in cosmological emphases between the Gospel and Letters of John on the one hand and Revelation on the other. In the phrase ἡ βασιλεία τοῦ κόσμου, "the kingdom of the world," κόσμος could refer to the totality of creation, but more probably it refers to the human world that had been in opposition to God and in conflict with his purposes (*TDNT* 3:889–95). There is a verbal parallel elsewhere in the NT only in Matt 4:8 (in the context of the temptation of Jesus), where the plural phrase αἱ βασιλεῖαι τοῦ κόσμου, "the kingdoms of the world," occurs and refers to the many individual kingdoms, each with its particular ruler, which make up the world. Yet the implication is that all these kingdoms belong to Satan and that he is able to deliver them to whomever he pleases.

The phrase τὰ ἔθνη τοῦ κόσμου, "the nations of the world" (Luke 12:30), is reminiscent of the common rabbinic expression אֻמּוֹת הָעוֹלָם *ʾummôt hāʿôlām,* "nations of the world," for the human race apart from Israel (Str-B, 2:191; *TDNT*

3:888). The apocalyptic perspective recognized that Satan was "the god of this world" (2 Cor 4:4), "the prince of the power of the air" (Eph 2:2), the κοσμοκράτωρ, "world ruler" (Eph 6:12; Irenaeus *Adv. haer.* 1.5.4), "the ruler of this world" (John 12:31; 14:30; 16:11; *T. Sol.* 2:9; 3:5–6; 6:1; *Asc. Isa.* 1:3; 2:4; 10:29), and "the ruler of this age" (Ignatius *Eph.* 17:1; 19:1; *Magn.* 1:2; *Trall.* 4:2; *Rom.* 7:1; *Phld.* 6:2); see H. Kruse, "Das Reich Satans," *Bib* 58 (1977) 29–61, and D. E. Aune, "Archon," *DDD*, 156–57. According to 1 John 5:19, "the whole world lies in the power of the evil one."

The phrase καὶ τοῦ χριστοῦ αὐτοῦ, "and his Messiah," looks like an interpolation since the verb that follows, βασιλεύσει, "he will reign," is *singular* even though the subject should be plural, i.e., "our Lord and his Messiah" (Vischer, *Offenbarung*, 18–19). Since "his Messiah" immediately precedes the verb βασιλεύσει, however, it is possible that it is the implied subject of the verb. In Revelation the phrase "his Messiah" occurs only in 12:10 in the context of a song of victory with several parallels to the song of victory in 11:15. The phrase "his Messiah" certainly underscores the subordinate relationship of the Messiah to God, just as the subordinate relationship between the Israelite kings and God is presupposed in analogous statements in the OT (Jörns, *Evangelium*, 94). This way of referring to God and his anointed (i.e., the king or the Messiah) has parallels in 1 Sam 12:3 (cf. v 5), where the phrase "before the Lord and before his anointed" occurs, and in Ps 2:2 (quoted in Acts 4:26), where the phrase "against the Lord and his anointed" is found. The phrase "his anointed," referring to the king of Israel or Judah, occurs occasionally in the OT (1 Sam 2:10; 12:5; 2 Sam 22:51; Pss 18:50[LXX 17:50]; 20:6; 28:8[LXX 27:8]), while in Greco-Jewish literature ὁ χριστὸς αὐτοῦ, "his anointed," can be used of the Messiah (*Pss. Sol.* 18:5) or in Christian texts of Jesus as "his Messiah" (Acts 3:18; 4:26 [quotation of Ps 2:2]; *Par. Jer.* 9:17; *Odes Sol.* 9:3; 41:3 [Syriac *mšyḥh*]). "His Messiah" in Rev 11:15 and 12:10 is therefore a natural christological adaptation of the equivalent phrase in the OT and early Jewish literature (O'Rourke, *CBQ* 30 [1968] 405; Jörns, *Evangelium*, 95–97). The related phrases "the Lord's anointed" (1 Sam 24:6; 26:9, 11, 16, 23; Luke 2:26; 9:20; *Odes Sol.* 29:6 [Syriac *bmšyḥh dmry*ʾ], referring to Christ) and "my [God's] anointed" (1 Sam 2:35) also occur.

15c καὶ βασιλεύσει εἰς τοὺς αἰῶνας τῶν αἰώνων, "who will reign for ever and ever." While the grammatical subject of βασιλεύσει, "will reign," is ἡ βασιλεία, "the kingdom" (v 15b), this is clearly impossible, for the logical subject is certainly God, to be supplied from τοῦ κυρίου ἡμῶν, "our Lord," in v 15b. There are several parallel phrases from the OT that appear in the LXX, e.g., LXX Ps 9:37(MT: 10:16), βασιλεύσει κύριος εἰς τὸν αἰῶνα καὶ εἰς τὸν αἰῶνα τοῦ αἰῶνος, "the Lord will reign for ever and ever" (see other LXX passages: Exod 15:18; Zach 14:9; Dan 2:44; 7:14, 27; Ps 145:10; Wis 3:8). The eternal reign of God is also found in an eschatological context in *Jos. As.* 19:8, καὶ κύριος ὁ θεὸς βασιλεύσει αὐτῶν [i.e., τῶν υἱῶν τοῦ ζῶντος θεοῦ] εἰς τοὺς αἰῶνας τῶν αἰώνων, "and the Lord God will reign over them [i.e., 'the sons of the living God'] for ever." A parallel phrase is found in Rev 22:5, καὶ βασιλεύσουσιν εἰς τοὺς αἰῶνας τῶν αἰώνων, "and they will reign for ever and ever," but the subjects are the servants of God in the New Jerusalem. The verb βασιλευεῖν, "reign," is used three times in Revelation with God as the subject, all in hymnic contexts (here; 11:17; 19:6), with a strikingly close similarity between the usage in 11:17 and that in 19:6 (see *Comments* on those passages). The hymnic phrase here in 11:15 emphasizes the eternal nature of God's reign and has a number of close parallels in the OT and early Jewish literature, primarily in hymnic contexts. The oldest such text is Exod 15:18, the concluding line from the Song of Moses, arguably antedating the beginning of the Israelite monarchy (cf. Albright, *Archaeology,* 117, 132; Albright, *Yahweh,* 13; Brettler, *King,* 14): "The Lord will reign for ever and ever" (LXX κύριος βασιλεύων τὸν αἰῶνα καὶ ἐπ' αἰῶνα καὶ ἔτι). This phrase is alluded to in a number of later texts, including Ps 10:16(LXX 9:37), "The Lord will reign for ever and ever" (see also Pss 145:13[LXX 144:13]; 146:10[LXX 145:10]; Lam 5:19; Ezek 43:7; Dan 4:3, 34; 6:26; Mic 4:7; Wis 3:8; *Jos. As.* 19:5, 8). The metaphor "forever" is also used of the reign of the house of David (2 Sam 7:13–16; 22:51; 1 Kgs 2:45; 1 Chr 22:10; 28:4; 2 Chr 6:16; 7:18; 13:5; Pss 45:6; 61:7; 89:3–4, 35–37; Isa 9:7; Jer 33:17; Ezek 37:25; cf. 1 Sam 13:13 [of the house of Saul]), and by extension it refers to the Messiah (Luke 1:33; Heb 1:8).

16 καὶ οἱ εἴκοσι τέσσαρες πρεσβύτεροι οἱ ἐνώπιον τοῦ θεοῦ καθήμενοι ἐπὶ τοὺς θρόνους αὐτῶν ἔπεσαν ἐπὶ τὰ πρόσωπα αὐτῶν καὶ προσεκύνησαν τῷ θεῷ, "The twenty-four elders who were seated before God on their thrones fell on their faces and worshiped God." See *Comments* on 4:4 and 4:10 (the latter is a particularly close parallel, for there the elders also leave their thrones to prostrate themselves before God). The function of v 16 is to link the two parts of the antiphonal hymnic structure in v 15 and vv 17–18, which is similar to the role played by 4:10 in linking 4:9 to 4:11 and by 7:11 in linking 7:10b to 7:12 (Jörns, *Evangelium,* 98). The fact that the elders are *seated* before God is emphasized here. In biblical tradition, royal officials typically *stand* before the king or queen when attending him or her (1 Sam 16:21–22; Jer 36:21; Dan 1:19; 2:2), and such officials can therefore be called "the elders who stood before Solomon" (1 Kgs 12:6) or "those servants who stand before you" (1 Kgs 10:8; Gen 41:46; see Brettler, *King,* 101). In depictions of the heavenly court in Israelite literature, God is always *seated* (1 Kgs 22:19; Isa 6:1; Dan 7:9) and is surrounded by members of the heavenly court who are always *standing* (1 Kgs 22:19; Isa 6:2; Dan 7:10).

17a λέγοντες· εὐχαριστοῦμέν σοι, κύριε ὁ θεὸς ὁ παντοκράτωρ, ὁ ὢν καὶ ὁ ἦν, "saying: 'We thank you, Lord God Almighty, who was and who is.'" Vv 17–18 constitute a collective song of thanksgiving, *das kollektive Danklied* (K. Berger, *Formgeschichte,* 242), or a prayer of thanksgiving, *Dankgebet* (Deichgräber, *Gotteshymnus,* 54). The main basis for thanksgiving is that God has assumed kingly rule (v 17b), and this is followed by an "eschatological retrospective" in v 18, providing the specific eschatological acts of God upon which his assumption of kingship is based. This verse contains several features that are combined in a single line in 19:6b, ὅτι ἐβασίλευσεν κύριος ὁ θεὸς ἡμῶν ὁ παντοκράτωρ, "for the Lord our God the Almighty has begun to reign."

εὐχαριστοῦμέν σοι, "we thank you," is the only certain liturgical formula found in the hymns of Revelation (Deichgräber, *Gotteshymnus,* 54; Jörns, *Evangelium,* 99). The term does occur in the NT in the general context of giving thanks to God in prayer (John 11:41; Acts 28:15; cf. *TDNT* 9:411), particularly in the context of meals (Mark 8:6; Matt 15:36; John 6:11, 23; Acts 27:35). In the specific context of eucharistic prayers, the formula occurs in *Did.* 9:3, "We give thanks to you, our Father [εὐχαριστοῦμέν σοι, πάτερ ἡμῶν], for the life and knowledge which you made known to us through Jesus your servant. To you be the glory for ever" (similar eucharistic prayers of thanksgiving are found in *Did.* 9:3; 10:2–5; see Audet, *Didachè,*

377–98; *TDNT* 9:414–15). See also *Apost. Const.* 7.38.4, περὶ πάντων σοι διὰ Χριστοῦ εὐχαριστοῦμεν, "We give thanks to you for everything through Christ" (see also *Apost. Const.* 7.26.2). Yet these do not explicitly state the reason that God is thanked, which is introduced with the ὅτι clause in Rev 11:18. εὐχαριστοῦμέν σοι corresponds to the Hebrew formula מודים אנחנו לך *môdîm ʾănaḥnû lāk* found in rabbinic sources (*m. Ber.* 5:3; *b. Taʿan.* 6b; Deichgräber, *Gotteshymnus,* 54). Attestation of this formula raises the question of whether the author has preserved liturgical traditions derived from the celebration of the Eucharist (the view of Schille, *ZTK* 52 [1955] 174). The phrase does occur in other early Jewish writings in Greek (though the verb εὐλογεῖν is much more frequent), including Jdt 8:25, παρὰ ταῦτα πάντα εὐχαριστήσωμεν κυρίῳ τῷ θεῷ ἡμῶν, "for all these things let us give thanks to the Lord our God"; 2 Macc 1:11, μεγάλως εὐχαριστοῦμεν αὐτῷ, "we thank him [i.e., 'God'] greatly"; *T. Abr.* (Rec. A) 15:4, εὐχαριστῶ σοι κύριέ μου, "I give thanks to you, my Lord" (Sarah addressing Michael). Cf. 3 Macc 7:16:

> They departed from the city crowned with all manner of fragrant flowers, with gladness and with shouting, giving thanks to the God of their fathers [εὐχαριστοῦντες τῷ θεῷ τῶν πατέρων], the Eternal Savior of Israel, with praises and melodious hymns.

The phrase אודכה אדני כי *ʾôdkâ ʾădōnāy kî,* "I thank you, Lord, because," is a standard introductory formula that occurs several times in the Qumran Thanksgiving Psalms or Hodayoth (1QH 2:20, 31; 3:19, 37; 4:5; 5:5; 7:6, 26, 34; 9:37; 14:8 [כי *kî* not used]; 17:7 [כי *kî* not used]; cf. 11:3 [אודכה אלי כי *ʾôdkâ ʾēlî kî,* "I thank you, my God, because"). In these hymns, the כי *kî* is often followed by a general description of salvation from distress (e.g., 1QH 2:20–22; 3:19–21; 5:5–6). It is also found in early Jewish literature transmitted in Greek (Jdt 8:25; 2 Macc 1:11; Jos. *Ant.* 1.193). The song or prayer of thanksgiving was also adapted to epistolary contexts (2 Macc 1:11). Perhaps the best-known form of adaptation is found in the introductory prayer of thanksgiving with which many Pauline letters begin. These prayers of thanksgiving are introduced with either the first-person singular form of εὐχαριστῶ, "I give thanks" (Rom 1:8–17; 1 Cor 1:4–9; Phil 1:3–11; Philem 4), or the first-person plural form (as in 1 Thess 1:2; Col 1:3–8). In these prayers, God is referred to in the third person (the *er-Stil,* "he style"). In addition to the epistolary context for prayers of thanksgiving, the early Church also used the verb εὐχαριστεῖν, "give thanks," in a liturgical context in connection with the celebration of the Lord's Supper. Some examples of this type of prayer of thanksgiving are fairly close in form to the prayer of Rev 11:17–18.

The form εὐχαριστῶ with a ὅτι clause that introduces the reasons for gratitude is one of two main types of Pauline epistolary prayers of thanksgiving described and analyzed by P. Schubert (*Form and Function of the Pauline Thanksgivings,* BZNW 20 [Berlin: Töpelmann, 1939] 10–39; cf. P. T. O'Brien, *Introductory Thanksgivings in the Letters of Paul,* NovTSup 49 [Leiden: Brill, 1977] 6–15). There are several examples of this form in early Christian non-epistolary contexts (Luke 18:11; John 11:41; cf. Ignatius *Smyrn.* 10:1). A prayer of thanksgiving similar to the Pauline epistolary thanksgivings is found in 2 Macc 1:11 (part of a quoted letter).

In Hellenistic religions, prayers of gratitude are relatively rare (this issue is discussed in Versnel, "Prayer," 42–62). εὐχαριστεῖν, "to give thanks," is a term frequently used to express thankfulness both to people and to the gods, but the short formula εὐχαριστῶ, "I give thanks," occurs only in inscriptions of the imperial period and are then located primarily in Asia Minor (Versnel, "Prayer," 45).

The phrase κύριε ὁ θεὸς ὁ παντοκράτωρ, "Lord God Almighty," is a formula found 5 times in Revelation (4:8; 11:17; 15:3; 16:7; 21:22; see *Comment* on 4:8) that reflects a literal translation of the Hebrew phrase יהוה (אלהי) (ה)צבאות *YHWH* (*ʾĕlō hê*) (*haṣ*)*ṣĕbāʾôt,* "Yahweh (the God) of (the) Hosts," found 9 times in Amos (3:13; 4:13; 5:14, 15, 16, 27; 6:8, 14; 9:5) and only10 times in the rest of the OT (2 Sam 5:10; 1 Kgs 19:10, 14; Hos 12:6[5]; Jer 5:14; 15:16; 35:17; 38:17; 44:7; Ps 89:9[8]). The shorter form "Yahweh of Hosts" occurs 267 times in the OT. Both titles have *military* overtones. צבאות *ṣĕbāʾôt* understood as an abstract plural, however, could connote "mightiness" (cf. O. Eissfeldt, "Jahweh Zebaoth," in *Kleine Schriften,* ed. R. Sellheim and F. Maass [Tübingen: Mohr-Siebeck, 1962–73] 3:120). For this reason, the LXX often translates צבאות *ṣĕbāʾôt* with παντοκράτωρ. See the excursus in Wolff, *Joel and Amos,* 287–88. In the LXX the longer form is often translated κύριε παντοκράτωρ θεέ/θεός (2 Kgdms 7:25 [MS B], 26 [MS A], 27; 1 Chr 17:24). In LXX Amos this is consistently rendered κύριος ὁ θεὸς ὁ παντοκράτωρ (Amos 3:13; 4:13; 5:16; 9:5, 15); the same form also occurs in Nah 3:5; Zech 10:3; Mal 2:16 (MS A). In the NT, apart from the OT allusion to LXX 2 Sam 7:8 in 2 Cor 6:18 (λέγει κύριος παντοκράτωρ, "says the Lord Almighty"), the form κύριος ὁ θεὸς ὁ παντοκράτωρ occurs only in Revelation, where it occurs *seven* times (1:8; 4:8; 11:17; 15:3; 16:7; 19:6; 21:22) and twice more in the form ὁ θεὸς ὁ παντοκράτωρ (16:14; 19:15). On this title, cf. Bousset-Gressmann, *Religion des Judentums,* 312 n. 2, though the discussion is somewhat garbled and contains several errors. κύριε παντοκράτωρ occurs in *T. Abr.* (Rec. A) 15:12; *Par. Jer.* 1:5; 9:6, while the whole formula, though not in the vocative, appears in *3 Apoc. Bar.* 1.3, and it occurs in the form κύριε ὁ παντοκράτορ ὁ θεός in the *Prayer of Manassis* (Denis, *Fragmenta,* 115). It is particularly significant that the full title occurs in Revelation several times in close association with the title ὁ ὢν καὶ ὁ ἦν (καὶ ὁ ἐρχόμενος), "who was and is (and is to come)": 1:8; 4:8; 11:17. On the phrase ὁ ὢν καὶ ὁ ἦν, see *Comment* on 1:4.

17b ὅτι εἴληφας τὴν δύναμίν σου τὴν μεγάλην καὶ ἐβασίλευσας, "because you have received your great authority and have begun to reign." Vv 17b and 18a allude to Ps 99:1 (LXX 98:1), ὁ κύριος ἐβασίλευσεν, ὀργιζέσθωσαν λαοί, "The Lord reigns; let the peoples be enraged." The ὅτι clause, which introduces the reason for thanksgiving, is also used in hymns elsewhere in Revelation (4:11; 5:9; 12:10). The verb βασιλεύειν, "reign," with God as subject occurs three times in Revelation, all in hymnic contexts (here; 11:15; 19:6; see *Comments* on these passages). There is a particularly close similarity between 11:17 and 19:6, though in 11:17 ἐβασίλευσας, "you have begun to reign," is in the second person, while in 19:6 ἐβασίλευσεν, "he has begun to reign," is put in the third person, reflecting two hymnic styles (the *du-Stil,* "thou style," and the *er-Stil,* "he style"; see *Excursus 4B: Hymns in Revelation*). In 11:17 the subject of ἐβασίλευσας is κύριε ὁ θεὸς ὁ παντοκράτωρ, "Lord God Almighty," while in 19:6 the subject of ἐβασίλευσεν is κύριος ὁ θεὸς ἡμῶν ὁ παντοκράτωρ, "the Lord, our God, the Almighty." Both ἐβασίλευσας (here) and ἐβασίλευσεν (in 19:6) may be construed as ingressive aorists emphasizing the beginning of a state, i.e., "have/has begun to reign as king" (Delebecque, 206; Ford, 168; *EDNT* 1:207). Since ἐβασίλευσας is parallel to εἴληφας, "you have received," it has perfective value (Mussies, *Morphology,* 338; cf. Porter, *Verbal Aspect,* 251). The parallelism could run the other way, of course, and εἴληφας could be considered an *aoristic* perfect (Turner, *Syntax,* 69). The fact that εἴληφας and ἐβασίλευσας are in the second person does suggest a similarity with investiture formulas that confer royal authority on a new king (cf. 2 Kgs 9:6), though such formulas are never used of Yahweh in the OT, for who can confer royal authority on him? Yet construing ἐβασίλευσας as an ingressive aorist need not mean that God did not reign as king previously; rather it could mean that his kingship has only now become effective over the world. In the LXX several of the declarations of Yahweh's kingship in OT coronation hymns, expressed in Hebrew with the perfect verb מלך *mālak* in the phrase יהוה מלך *YHWH mālak,* "Yahweh reigns," are translated using the aorist of βασιλεύειν in the phrase ὁ κύριος ἐβασίλευσεν (Pss 92:1 [MT 93:1]; 95:10 [MT 96:10]; 96:1 [MT 97:1]; 98:1 [MT 99:1]). Closely related to this phrase in coronation psalms are the phrases מלך אלהים *mālak ʾĕlōhîm,* "God reigns" (in Ps 47:8 [MT 47:9]; LXX Ps 46:9 [not found in MT], ἐβασίλευσεν ὁ θεός), and מלך אלהיך *mālak ʾĕlōhāyik,* "your God reigns" (in Isa 52:7 [LXX βασιλεύσει σου ὁ θεός]). While the precise meaning of יהוה מלך *YHWH mālak,* which Mowinckel called an enthronement formula, has generated a great deal of debate in OT scholarship, the meaning of ὁ κύριος ἐβασίλευσεν is hardly less problematic. Some have regarded יהוה מלך *YHWH mālak* as a nominal sentence that describes not an event but rather the quality of the subject; therefore, it could be translated "Yahweh is the one who exercises kingship" (Gelston, *VT* 16 [1966] 507). Based on parallel declarations reportedly made on the occasion of the enthronement of Israelite kings (Absalom in 2 Sam 5:10 and Jehu in 2 Kgs 9:13), however, יהוה מלך *YHWH mālak* may mean "Yahweh has become king" or "it is Yahweh who is king." Mowinckel argued that such declarations were made of God during the cultic ritual of the annual New Year enthronement ceremony and that the translation "God has become king" is therefore appropriate and does not contradict the view that Yahweh has *always* been king (*Offersang,* 126–28). The OT emphasis on the eternality of the reign of God (see *Comment* on 11:15), however, does not appear to cohere well with the emphasis here on a time in the indeterminate past when God *received* his great power and began to reign (received from whom?), an event that seems to reflect the kind of investiture narrated of the Lamb (see 5:7, 9, 12).

18a καὶ τὰ ἔθνη ὠργίσθησαν, "The nations are enraged." Taken with the preceding phrase, καὶ ἐβασίλευσας, "and you have begun to reign," in v 17c, the unusual combination of the two motifs of the Lord reigning and the anger of the nations makes it certain that this is an allusion to LXX Ps 98:1, ὁ κύριος ἐβασίλευσεν, ὀργιζέσθωσαν λαοί (MT 99:1, יְהוָה מָלָךְ יִרְגְּזוּ עַמִּים *YHWH mālāk yirgĕzû ʿammîm*), "The Lord has begun to reign; the people are enraged." An allusion to the MT is also possible, however, since the Hebrew verb רגז *rāgaz,* "to excite, tremble, be agitated," is translated with ὀργίζειν, "enrage," eight times in the LXX (Gen 45:24; Exod 15:14; 4 Kgdms 19:28; Job 12:6; Pss 4:4; 98:1; Prov 28:9; Zech 1:2). Charles (1:296) favors the allusion to the LXX here since ὀργιζέσθωσαν, "they are enraged," is a possible, though not a correct, translation of ירגזו *yirgĕzû.* Another possible source for this allusion is Exod 15:14, ἤκουσαν ἔθνη καὶ ὠργίσθησαν, "the nations heard and were enraged" (here יִרְגָּזוּן *yirgāzûn* can be translated "tremble"). The juxtaposition of the two motifs of the rule or reign of God and the tumult of the heathen became traditional in Jewish eschatological scenarios. To be sure, the rule of God was originally conceptualized as a rule exercised through an Israelite king, a notion that was transferred to the Messiah in some strands of eschatological expectation. Thus, while the reign of God followed by the rage of the nations as found in Rev 11:17–18 makes little sense if the reign of God is involved, it fits perfectly if the reign of the Messiah is in view (see *Comments* on 20:7–10). The motif of the tumult and assault of the nations occurs frequently in eschatological scenarios (Pss 2:1–2; 46:6; 65:7; *1 Enoch* 55:5–6; 99:4; 4 Ezra 13:30–31; *Jub.* 23:23; *Sib. Or.* 3.660–68; Hartman, *Prophecy Interpreted,* 77–101), and the anger of the nations is concretely expressed by their gathering to wage war against God and his people in several eschatological scenarios in Revelation (16:14; 17:14; 19:19; 20:9).

18b καὶ ἦλθεν ἡ ὀργή σου καὶ ὁ καιρὸς τῶν νεκρῶν κριθῆναι, "but your wrath came / and the time for the dead to be judged." The day of God's wrath, יום עברת יהוה *yôm ʿebrat YHWH* or יום אף יהוה *yôm ʾap YHWH,* is tradition rooted in the OT (Ezek 7:19; Zeph 1:18; 2:2–3; Lam 2:2). Within the framework of Revelation, the coming of God's wrath may anticipate the seven angels with seven plagues mentioned in Rev 15:1, for with these plagues "the wrath of God is ended." This reference to the judgment of the dead (which has a parallel in Revelation only in 20:11–15) is peculiar at this juncture because it by no means follows the normal scenario expected, i.e., the judgment of the nations. κριθῆναι, "to be judged," an anarthrous aorist passive infinitive, is complementary, functioning to limit or further define the noun ὁ καιρός, "the time" (Votaw, *Infinitive,* 15; Robertson, *Grammar,* 1075–76); this type of infinitive is used to modify nouns (or adjectives) signifying ability, fitness, authority, need, or time. A close parallel using καιρός with an articular infinitive occurs in *3 Apoc. Bar.* 8:1, ὅταν ἦλθεν ὁ καιρὸς τοῦ δῦσαι, "when the time for sunset came" (for other parallels using καιρός with a complementary infinitive, see *T. Zeb.* 7:3; *Par. Jer.* 5:24 [or 21]; *Ep. Arist.* 12, 256). In the phrase τὴν ἐξουσίαν κλεῖσαι, "power to shut up," in 11:6, the infinitive functions similarly. Several MSS insert τοῦ before κριθῆναι in order to make this complementary relationship more explicit (Byz $12^{110\ 627\ 2048}$). The entire clause is perceived as problematic: ἦλθεν ὁ καιρὸς τῶν νεκρῶν κριθῆναι is equivalent to ἵνα κριθῶσιν οἱ νεκροί, "that the dead be judged," according to BDF § 393.3.

The reference to the judgment of the dead has a parallel in the frequent saying referring to Jesus Christ as κριτὴς ζώντων καὶ νεκρῶν, "the judge of the living and the dead" (Acts 10:42; 2 Tim 4:1; *Barn.* 7:2; *2 Clem.* 1:1; Polycarp *Phil.* 2:1; cf. Rom 14:9). In 1 Pet 4:5 and *Acts Thom.* 30, it is God, not Jesus Christ, who is regarded as the judge of the living and the dead (Michaels, *1 Peter,* 235), and in *2 Clem.* 1:1, the author urges that "we must think of Jesus Christ as of God, as 'the judge of the living and the dead.'" This phrase became part of the *Symbolum Romanum.* In a comprehensive sense, God is designated the "judge of all" in Heb 12:23. Apart from this widely used formula, the phrase "judge of the dead" is scarcely found except for the close parallel in Rev 20:12, where it is said that ἐκρίθησαν οἱ νεκροί, "the dead were judged."

18c καὶ δοῦναι τὸν μισθὸν τοῖς δούλοις σου τοῖς προφήταις καὶ τοῖς ἁγίοις καὶ τοῖς φοβουμένοις τὸ ὄνομά σου, τοὺς μικροὺς καὶ τοὺς μεγάλους, "and to reward your servants the prophets / and God's people and those who revere your name, / both the insignificant and the important." The term μισθός refers to the reward or recompense that is based upon what a person has earned or deserves; it can be either positive or negative (Louw-Nida, § 38.14). Elsewhere in Revelation, μισθός occurs only in a saying of the exalted Jesus in 22:12, "Behold, I am coming quickly, and my reward is with me" (here μισθός can be construed both positively and negatively). In Rev 11:18 μισθός is an umbrella term referring to the salvific benefits that God will bestow on the faithful in the eschaton (see M. Smith, *Tannaitic Parallels,* 49–70). The use of the metaphor of μισθός for spiritual recompense is evident in *Gk. Apoc. Ezra* 1:14, "a slave serves his masters to receive his wage [μισθός];

thus the righteous man receives his reward [μισθός] in the heavens." This reward is described elsewhere in Revelation using a variety of metaphors, including eating of the tree of life (2:7; 22:14), immunity from the second death (2:11), hidden manna and a white stone (2:17), authority over the nations (2:26–27), white garments (3:5; 7:14), the believer becoming a pillar in the temple of God and having written upon him or her the name of God and the New Jerusalem (3:12), sitting beside Christ on his heavenly throne (3:21), being present before God on his heavenly throne (7:15–17; 22:3–4), and having access to the New Jerusalem through its gates (22:14). While this list is scarcely exhaustive, it does convey some of the dimensions of the eschatological reward bestowed on believers by God.

The notion of reward or recompense is clearly expressed in Rev 2:23 (see *Comment* there), "I will give to each of you according to your works." Variants of this same proverbial expression are found in 22:12 ("to recompense [ἀποδοῦναι] each according to his work") and 20:13 ("each will be judged according to their works"). The tendency among NT scholars to denigrate the notion of reward for meritorious achievement is a theological overlay that distorts the NT views of reward and punishment (see Preisker's statements in *TDNT* 4:714–28). In the LXX a μισθός can be something that God grants those who do his will in heaven or in the eschaton (Matt 5:12 = Luke 6:23; 1 Cor 3:8, 14; 2 John 8; *TDNT* 4:699–701).

A syntactical problem in this verse is whether τοῖς δούλοις σου should be taken with τοῖς προφήταις, i.e., "your servants the prophets," or with τοῖς προφήταις καὶ τοῖς ἁγίοις, i.e., "your servants, namely, the prophets and the saints" (the latter view is argued by Beckwith, 609–10). The first interpretation is supported by the frequent use of the phrase "your servants the prophets," while the latter is supported by the fact that in Revelation the prophets and the saints are considered two groups in Rev 16:6 and 18:24. See LXX Ps 113:21 (MT 115:13), εὐλόγησεν τοὺς φοβουμένους τὸν κύριον, τοὺς μικροὺς μετὰ τῶν μεγάλων, "He blessed those who fear the Lord, both small and great." A doublet occurs in Rev 19:5, "Praise our God all you his servants and you who fear him, both small and great." On the phrase "insignificant and important" or "small and great," see *Comment* on 13:16. On "holy ones" = Christians, see *Comment* on 5:8.

The reference to "one who reveres God" (ὁ φοβούμενος τὸν θεόν) is found in a similar hymnic context in 19:5 and occurs several times in Acts (10:2, 22, 35; 13:16, 26; cf. Justin *Dial.* 10.4). The equivalent expression "one who worships (God)" (ὁ σεβόμενος [τὸν θεόν]) occurs six times in Acts (13:43, 50; 16:14; 17:4, 17; 18:7) and has often been taken as virtually a technical term for Gentiles who have been attracted to Judaism but have not actually become converts. Here and in 19:5, it is clear that this phrase is used in a nontechnical sense of a Jew or Gentile who reveres God, so that "those who revere your name" should be understood to refer to Christians of gentile origin, while "God's people" represent Christians of Jewish origin (Feuillet, *NTS* 4 [1957–58] 197–98).

18d καὶ διαφθεῖραι τοὺς διαφθείροντας τὴν γῆν, "and to ruin utterly those who ruin the earth." Here "earth" is metonymy for the "people of the earth." Judgment is justice based on the principle of *lex talionis,* the "law of retaliation" in kind. The statement here in Rev 11:18, like that in *Sib. Or.* 3.311–12 (quoted above under v 6a), expresses a form of limited liability; i.e., one could not inflict a punishment on an offender greater than the crime that he or she had perpetrated (cf. a similar emphasis in Rev 18:6–7). On the *lex talionis,* see R. Hirzel, *Die Talion,* Philologus

Supplementband 11 (Leipzig: Weicher, 1910) 407–82; A. Dihle, *Die goldene Regel* (Göttingen: Vandenhoeck & Ruprecht, 1962). A close parallel occurs in *Apoc. Abr.* 29.19 (tr. Charlesworth, *OTP* 1:704), where the righteous "will destroy those who have destroyed them, and they will rebuke those who have rebuked them through their mockery." Exod 21:24 expresses this in the famous principle "an eye for an eye, and a tooth for a tooth." The Twelve Tables, the first codified body of Roman law, which dates to ca. 450 B.C., expresses the same principle (8.2; tr. LCL): "If a person has maimed another's limb, let there be retaliation in kind [*talio esto*]." Similarly, Ovid *Artis amatoriae* 1.655–56 states (tr. LCL; with modifications), "for there is no law more just than that contrivers of death should perish by their own contrivances." In extralegal contexts the notion of "poetic justice" holds that "those who live by the sword die by the sword." A biblical example is that of Haman who, according to Esth 7:10, died on the gallows he had erected for Mordecai. Adoni-bezek, who had cut off the thumbs and big toes of seventy kings, suffered the same fate (Judg 1:7). The words of Samson in Judg 15:11 also reflect this principle: "As they did to me, so have I done to them." Other examples include Judg 9:56–57; Longus 1.20; Xenophon of Ephesus 4.4; 3 Macc 5:1–5, 21, 38; 6:21. The phrase "they are deserving" (Rev 3:4; 16:6) is used ironically, since ἄξιος, "worthy," is usually an attribute of God or the Lamb in Revelation. On the *lex talionis* in the prophets, see *Comment* on 18:6.

The phrase καὶ διαφθεῖραι τοὺς διαφθείροντες, "and to destroy utterly those who deprave," is an instance of paronomasia, in which both literal and figurative meanings of a word are used in the same context (for other examples in Revelation, see 2:2[2x], 22; 3:10; 14:8; 18:6[3x], 20, 21; 22:18, 19; cf. BDF § 488.1; Turner, *Syntax,* 148). The literal meaning of διαφθείρειν is "to destroy utterly" (Louw-Nida, § 22.40), while a figurative extension of the word means "to morally ruin, to deprave" (Louw-Nida, § 88.266).

Explanation

Rev 11:15–18 is a relatively isolated unit of text that completes the narrative of the trumpet plagues that began in 8:1–9:21 and then was unexpectedly broken off by two units of text (10:1–11 and 11:1–14), both of which emphasize the prophetic character of the seer's own mission as well as the prophetic career and martyrdom of the two witnesses (11:1–14). Following the sounding of the seventh trumpet by the angel in v 15a, the anticipated seventh trumpet plague does not materialize (somewhat surprising since the third woe has just been announced in 11:14), and in its place is a relatively brief vision of the heavenly throne room.

This unit begins with an unexpected focus on loud but unidentified voices from heaven, which chant the first part of an antiphonal hymn. This two-part hymn juxtaposes the celebration of the reign of God with the final judgment of all the dead; the righteous are rewarded, and the wicked are punished. The first hymn is a *song of victory* (v 15), while the second hymn, chanted in response to the first, is a *prayer of thanksgiving* (vv 17–18).

The first hymn consists of a proclamation that the kingdom of the world, i.e., the created world of mortal and immortal beings, which had hitherto been under the rule of Satan, has been transferred to the eternal rule of God. This means not that

God did not previously reign as king but rather that his kingship has now become effective over the world. While Jews and Christians had usually assumed that God was ultimately the sovereign ruler of his creation, his rule had not yet been recognized or accepted universally. The heavenly announcement that God has begun to reign must be understood as a proleptic or anticipatory announcement of a state of affairs that would shortly come to pass with the arrival of the eschaton.

The theme of the kingly rule of God is continued and expanded in the second hymn, which is attributed to the twenty-four elders who have prostrated themselves before the heavenly throne of God in worship. As a prayer of thanksgiving, the primary reason for the giving of thanks is the reception of power and the inauguration of kingly rule by God (v 17). Just as prayers of thanksgiving frequently provide a retrospective narrative of that for which the worshiper is thankful, so in the second major part of this hymn (v 18) the anticipated eschatological activity of God is celebrated in past tenses, as if the events had already taken place. These events consist of both judgment and salvation. The angry rebellion of the nations of the world has been checked by the coming of God's wrath in the form of divine punishments (see 15:1–16:21). The judgment of the dead (perhaps both the righteous and wicked dead are in view) and the destruction of those who destroy the earth (perhaps Rome and her allies) constitute the primary negative aspects of God's visitation, while the recompense of eschatological salvation is given to the righteous of all nations.

2. *The Woman, the Child, and the Dragon (11:19–12:17)*

Bibliography

Aarne, A., and **Thompson, S.** *The Types of the Folktale: A Classification and Biography.* 2nd ed. Helsinki: Suomalainen Tiedeakatemia, 1961. **Anderson, B. H.** *Creation versus Chaos: The Reinterpretation of Mythical Symbolism in the Bible.* New York: Association, 1967. **Anderson, R. T.** "The Role of the Desert in Israelite Thought." *JBR* 27 (1959) 41–44. **Aptowitzer, V.** "La chute de Satan et des anges." *REJ* 54 (1907) 59–63. **Aulén, G.** *Christus Victor: An Historical Study of the Three Main Types of the Idea of the Atonement.* Tr. A. G. Hebert. New York: Macmillan, 1969. **Aus, R. D.** "The Relevance of Isaiah 66:7 to Revelation 12 and 2 Thessalonians 1." *ZNW* 67 (1976) 252–68. **Barton, G. A.** "The Origin of Names of Angels and Demons in the Extra-Canonical Apocalyptic Literature to 100 A.D." *JBL* 31 (1912) 156–67. **Benson, I. M.** "Revelation 12 and the Dragon of Antiquity." *RevQ* 29 (1987) 97–102. **Bergman, J.** *Ich bin Isis: Studien zum memphitischen Hintergrund der griechischen Isisaretalogien.* Uppsala: Acta Universitatis Upsaliensis, 1968. **Bergmeier, R.** "Altes und Neues zur 'Sonnenfrau am Himmel' (Apk 12): Religionsgeschichtliche und quellenkritische Beobachtungen zu Apk 12:1–17." *ZNW* 73 (1982) 97–109. **Betz, O.** "Die Geburt der Gemeinde durch den Lehrer." *NTS* 3 (1956–57) 314–26. **Boll, F.** *Aus der Offenbarung Johannis.* Berlin: Teubner, 1914. **Braun, F.-M.** "La Femme et le dragon." *BVC* 7 (1954) 63–72. ———. "La Femme vetue de soleil (Apoc. XII): État du probleme." *RevThom*

55 (1955) 639–69. **Brommer, F.** *Herakles: The Twelve Labors of the Hero in Ancient Art and Literature.* New Rochelle: Caratzas, 1986. **Brunner, H.** *Die Geburt des Gottkönigs: Studien zur Überlieferung eines altägyptischen Mythos.* Ägyptologische Abhandlungen 10. Wiesbaden: Harrasowitz, 1964. **Bruns, J. E.** "The Contrasted Women of Apocalypse 12 and 17." *CBQ* 26 (1964) 459–63. **Brunvand, J. H.** *Folklore: A Study and Research Guide.* New York: St. Martin's, 1976. **Budge, E. A. W.** *The Gods of the Egyptians.* 2 vols. 1904. Repr. New York: Dover, 1969. ———. *Osiris and the Egyptian Resurrection.* 2 vols. 1911. Repr. New York: Dover, 1973. **Caird, G. B.** *Principalities and Powers: A Study in Pauline Theology.* Oxford: Clarendon, 1956. **Carr, W.** *Angels and Principalities.* SNTSMS 42. Cambridge: Cambridge UP, 1981. **Cerfaux, L.** "La vision de la femme et du dragon de l'Apocalypse en relation avec le protevangile." *ETL* 31 (1955) 21–33. **Childs, B. S.** "The Enemy from the North and the Chaos Tradition." *JBL* 78 (1959) 187–98. **Collins, J. J.** "The Mythology of the Holy War in Daniel and the Qumran War Scroll." *VT* 25 (1975) 496–512. **Cothenet, E.** "Le Signe de la Femme (Ap 12)." In *Exégèse et Liturgie.* Paris: Cerf, 1988. 305–23. **Cross, F. M.** *Canaanite Myth and Hebrew Epic.* Cambridge: Harvard UP, 1973. **Darr, K. P.** "Two Unifying Female Images in the Book of Isaiah." In *Uncovering Ancient Stones.* FS H. N. Richardson, ed. L. M. Hopfe. Winona Lake, IN: Eisenbrauns, 1994. 17–30. **Davenport, G. L.** *The Eschatology of the Book of Jubilees.* Leiden: Brill, 1971. **Day, J.** "Dragon and Sea, God's Conflict with." *ABD* 2:228–31. ———. *God's Conflict with the Dragon and the Sea.* Cambridge: Cambridge UP, 1985. **Delahaye, K.** *Ecclesia Mater chez les Pères des trois premiers siècles.* Paris: Cerf, 1964. **Dieterich, A.** *Abraxas: Studien zur Religionsgeschichte des späteren Altertums.* Leipzig: Teubner, 1891. **Dix, G. H.** "The Heavenly Wisdom and the Divine Logos in Jewish Apocalyptic: A Study of the Vision of the Woman and the Man-Child in Revelation 12:1–5, 13–17." *JTS* 26 (1924–25) 1–12. **Driver, G. R.** *Canaanite Myths and Legends.* Edinburgh: T. & T. Clark, 1956. ———. "Mythical Monsters in the Old Testament." In *Studi Orientalistici in onore di Giorgio Levi della Vida.* Rome: Instituto per l'Oriente, 1956. 1:234–49. **Emerton, J. A.** "Leviathan and *ltn:* The Vocalization of the Ugaritic Word for the Dragon." *VT* 32 (1982) 327–33. **Ernst, J.** "Die 'himmlische' Frau im 12. Kapitel der Apokalypse." *TGl* 58 (1968) 39–59. **Feuillet, A.** "Le chapitre XII de l'Apocalypse: Son caractère synthétique et sa richesse doctrinale." *Esprit et Vie* 49 (1978) 674–83. ———. "Le Messie et sa Mère d'apres l'chapitre XII de l'Apocalypse." *RB* 66 (1959) 55–86. **Foerster, W.** "Die Bilder in Offenbarung 12f. und 17f." *TSK* 104 (1932) 279–310. **Fonck, L.** "Das sonnenumglänzte und sternenbekränzte Weib in der Apokalypse." *ZTK* 28 (1904) 672–81. **Fontenrose, J.** *Python: A Study in Delphic Myth.* Berkeley: University of California, 1959. **Forbes Irving, P. M. C.** *Metamorphosis in Greek Myths.* Oxford: Clarendon, 1990. **Forsyth, N.** *The Old Enemy: Satan and the Combat Myth.* Princeton: Princeton UP, 1987. **Freundorfer, J.** *Die Apokalypse des Apostels Johannis und die hellenistische Kosmologie und Astrologie.* Freiburg: Herder, 1929. **Gokey, F. X.** *The Terminology for the Devil and Evil Spirits in the Apostolic Fathers.* Washington, DC: The Catholic University of America, 1961. **Gollinger, H.** "Das 'grosse Zeichen' Offb. 12—das zentrale Kapitel der Offenbarung des Johannes." *BK* 39 (1967) 401–16. ———. *Das "grosse Zeichen" von Apokalypse 12.* SBM 11. Würzburg: Echter, 1971. **Gollwitzer, H.** "Predigt über Offenbarung Johannes 12:7–12." *Festschrift für Ernst Fuchs,* ed. G. Ebeling et al. Tübingen: Mohr, 1973. **Grant, M.** *The Myths of Hyginus.* Lawrence: University of Kansas, 1960. **Griffiths, J. G.** *The Conflict of Horus and Seth from Egyptian and Classical Sources.* Liverpool: Liverpool UP, 1960. ———. *Plutarch's "De Iside et Osiride."* Cardiff: University of Wales, 1970. **Gunkel, H.** *Schöpfung und Chaos in Urzeit und Endzeit: Eine religionsgeschichtliche Untersuchung über Gen 1 und Ap. Joh. 12.* Göttingen: Vandenhoeck & Ruprecht, 1895. **Hani, J.** *La religion Égyptienne dans la pensée de Plutarque.* Paris: Société d'edition "Les belles lettres," 1976. **Hanson, P. D.** *The Dawn of Apocalyptic.* Philadelphia: Fortress, 1975. ———. "Rebellion in Heaven: Azazel and Euhemeristic Heroes in 1 Enoch 6–11." *JBL* 96 (1977) 195–233. **Hauret, C.** "Eve transfigurée: De la Genèse à l'Apocalypse." *RHPR* 59 (1979) 327–39. **Hedrick, W. K.** "The Sources and Use of Imagery in Apocalypse 12." Diss., Graduate Theological Union, Berkeley, 1970. **Henten, J. W. van.** "Egyptische goden in Openbaring 12–13." In *Tussen Nijl en Herengracht.* FS M. S. H. G. Heerma van Voss, ed. M. G. D. Harbers, G. M. Naarden, and J. E.

Vermeulen. Amsterdam: University of Amsterdam, Faculty of Theology, 1988. 71–83. ———. "'En de draak werd toornig op de vrouw' (Openb 12:17)." In *Kleine Encyclopedie van de Toorn,* ed. A. and A. de Jong. Den Haag: Koninklijke Bibliotheek, 1993. 57–76. **Hommel, P.** "Giebel und Himmel." *IM* 5 (1955) 11–55. **Jonge, M. de,** and **Woude, A. S. van der.** "11Q Melchizedek and the New Testament." *NTS* 12 (1966) 301–26. **Jossua, J. P.** "'Die alte Schlange wurde gestürzt' (Offenbarung 12:9)." *Concilium* 11 (1975) 207–14. **Joüon, P.** "Le grand dragon et l'ancient serpent (Apoc 12:9 et Gen 3:14)." *RSR* 17 (1927) 444–46. **Kalimi, I.,** and **Purvis, J. D.** "The Hiding of the Temple Vessels in Jewish and Samaritan Literature." *CBQ* 56 (1994) 679–85. **Kassing, A. T.** *Die Kirche und Maria: Ihr Verhältnis im 12. Kapital der Apocalypse.* Düsseldorf: Patmos, 1958. ———. "Das Weib, das den Mann gebar (Apk 12:13)." *Benediktinische Monatsschrift* 34 (1958) 427–33. ———. "Das Weib und der Drache (Apk. 12:1–6, 13–17)." *BK* 15 (1960) 114–16. **Kellermann, U.** "Das Danielbuch und die Märtyrertheologie." In *Die Entstehung der jüdischen Martyrologie,* ed. J. W. van Henten. Leiden: Brill, 1989. 51–75. **Kloos, C.** *Yahweh's Combat with the Sea.* Leiden: Brill, 1986. **Kobelski, P. J.** *Melchizedek and Melchiresa.* CBQMS 10. Washington, DC: Catholic Biblical Association, 1991. **Koch, J. E.** "'Das grosse Zeichen' Offb. Joh. 12: Der Versuch einer Israellogie nach dem prophetischen Wort." *Judaica* 13 (1957) 29–60. **Korpel, M. C. A.** *A Rift in the Clouds: Ugaritic and Hebrew Descriptions of the Divine.* Münster: Ugarit, 1990. **Kosnetter, J.** "Die Sonnenfrau in der neueren Exegese." In *Theologische Fragen der Gegenwart.* FS T. Innitzer. Vienna: Domverlag, 1952. **Le Déaut, R.** *Liturgie juive en Nouveau Testament.* Rome: Biblical Institute, 1965. **LeFrois, B. J.** *The Woman Clothed with the Sun (Ap. 12), Individual or Collective?* Rome: Orbis Catholicus, 1954. **Lehmann-Nitsche, R.** "Der apokalyptische Drache: Eine astralmythologische Untersuchung über Ap Joh 12." *Zeitschrift für Ethnologie* 65 (1934) 193–230. ———. "Die magische Verfolgung in der Offenbarung des Johannes." *Zeitschrift für Ethnologie* 67 (1935) 75–78. **Leivestad, R.** *Christ the Conqueror: Ideas of Conflict and Victory in the New Testament.* London: SPCK, 1954. **Lods, A.** "La chute des anges, origine et portée de cette speculation." *RHPR* 7 (1927) 295–315. **Lohmeyer, E.** "Das zwölfte Kapitel der Offenbarung Johannis." *TBl* 4 (1925) 285–91. **Lortzing, J.** "Die inneren Beziehungen zwischen Joh 2:1–11 und Offb 12: Eine Auseinandersetzung mit der religionsgeschichtlichen Schule." *TGl* 29 (1937) 498–529. **Lueken, W.** *Michael: Eine Darstellung und Vergleichung der jüdischen und der morgenländisch-christlichen Tradition vom Erzengel Michael.* Göttingen: Vandenhoeck & Ruprecht, 1898. **Marshall, P. K.,** ed. *Hyginus Fabulae.* Stuttgart; Leipzig: Teubner, 1993. **Mauser, U. W.** *Christ in the Wilderness.* SBT 39. Naperville, IL: Allenson, 1963. **Michl, J.** "Die Deutung der apokalyptischen Frau in der Gegenwart." *BZ* n.s. 3 (1959) 301–10. ———. "Der Weibessame (Gen 3:15) in spätjüdischer und frühchristlicher Auffassung." *Bib* 33 (1952) 396–401. **Miller, P. D.** *The Divine Warrior in Early Israel.* Cambridge: Harvard UP, 1973. **Milne, P. J.** *Vladimir Propp and the Study of Structure in Hebrew Biblical Narrative.* Sheffield: Sheffield Academic, 1988. **Minear, P. S.** "'Far as the Curse is Found': The Point of Revelation 12:15–16." *NovT* 33 (1991) 71–77. **Mitropoulou, E.** *Deities and Heroes in the Form of Snakes.* Athens: Pyli, 1977. **Montagnini, F.** "Le 'signe' d'Apocalypse 12 à la lumèrre de la christologie du Nouveau Testament." *NRT* 89 (1967) 401–16. **Morgen, M.** "Apocalypse 12, un targum de l'Ancient Testament." *Foi et Vie* 80 (1981) 63–74. **Müller, D.** *Ägypten und die Isis-Aretalogien.* Berlin: Akademie, 1961. **Müller, U. B.** "Vision und Botschaft: Erwägungen zur prophetischen Struktur der Verkündigung Jesu." *ZTK* 74 (1977) 416–48. **Newsom, C. A.** "The Development of 1 Enoch 6–19: Cosmology and Judgement." *CBQ* 42 (1980) 310–29. **Nickelsburg, G. W. E.** "Apocalyptic and Myth in 1 Enoch 6–11." *JBL* 96 (1977) 383–405. **Noack, B.** *Satanas und Soteria: Untersuchungen zur neutestamentlichen Dämonologie.* Copenhagen: Munksgaard, 1948. **Norden, E.** *Die Geburt des Kindes: Geschichte einer religiösen Idee.* Leipzig; Berlin: Teubner, 1924. **Osten-Sacken, P. von der.** *Gott und Belial.* Göttingen: Vandenhoeck & Ruprecht, 1969. **Parrott, D. M.** "The 13 Kingdoms of the Apocalypse of Adam: Origin, Meaning and Significance." *NovT* 31 (1989) 67–87. **Petrement, S.** "Une suggestion de Simone Weil à propos d'Apocalypse XII." *NTS* 11 (1964–65) 291–96. **Plumpe, J.** *Mater Ecclesia: An Inquiry into the Concept of the Church as Mother in Early Christianity.* Washington, DC: The Catholic University of America, 1943.

Prigent, P. *Apocalypse 12: Histoire de l'exégèse.* Tübingen: Mohr-Siebeck, 1959. **Propp, V.** *Morphology of the Folktale.* 2nd ed. Austin: University of Texas, 1968. ———. "Structure and History in the Study of the Fairy Tale." *Semeia* 10 (1978) 57–83. **Robinson, J. M.** "On the *Gattung* of Mark (and John)." In *Jesus and Man's Hope,* ed. D. G. Buttrick. 2 vols. Pittsburgh: Pittsburgh Theological Seminary, 1970. 99–129. **Roloff, D.** *Gottähnlichkeit, Vergöttlichung und Erhöhung zu seligem Leben: Untersuchungen zur Herkunft der platonischen Angleichung an Gott.* Berlin: de Gruyter, 1970. **Saffrey, H. D.** "Relire l'Apocalypse à Patmos." *RB* 82 (1975) 414–32. **Satake, A.** "Sieg Christi—Heil der Christen: Eine Betrachtung von Apc XII." *AJBI* 1 (1975) 105–25. **Schmidt, K. L.** "Lucifer als gefallene Engelmacht." *TZ* 7 (1951) 161–79. **Schreiber, T.** *Apollon Pythoktonos: Ein Beitrag zur griechischen Religions- und Kunstgeschichte.* Leipzig: Engelmann, 1879. **Shea, W. H.** "The Parallel Literary Structure of Revelation 12 and 20." *AUSS* 223 (1985) 37–54. **Sickenberger, J.** "Die Messiasmutter im 12. Kapitel der Apokalypse." *TQ* 126 (1946) 357–427. **Staalduine-Sulman, E. van.** "The Aramaic Song of the Lamb." In *Verse in Ancient Near Eastern Prose,* ed. J. C. de Moor and W. G. E. Watson. Neukirchen: Neukirchener, 1993. 265–92. **Talmon, S.** "The 'Desert Motif' in the Bible and in Qumran Literature." In *Biblical Motifs,* ed. A. Altmann. Cambridge: Harvard UP, 1966. 31–63. **Thorley, J.** "When Was Jesus Born?" *GR* 28 (1981) 81–89. **Vanni, U.** "Il 'grande segno': Ap 12:1–6." In *L'Apocalisse,* ed. J. Lambrecht. 227–51. **Voegtle, A.** "Mythos und Botschaft in Apokalypse 12." In *Tradition und Glaube.* FS K. G. Kuhn, ed. G. Jeremias, H.-W. Kuhn, and H. Stegemann. Göttingen: Vandenhoeck & Ruprecht, 1971. 395–415. **Vollenweider, S.** "Ich sah den Satan wie einen Blitz vom Himmel fallen (Lk 10,18)." *ZNW* 79 (1988) 187–203. **Wakeman, M. K.** *God's Battle with the Monster: A Study in Biblical Imagery.* Leiden: Brill, 1973. **Wallace, H.** "Leviathan and the Beast in Revelation." *BA* 11 (1948) 61–68. **Wikenhauser, A.** "Ποταμοφόρητος Apk 12,15, u.a." *BZ* 6 (1908) 171. **Wilhelmi, G.** "Der Hirt mit dem eisernen Szepter." *VT* 27 (1977) 196–204. **Yarbro Collins, A.** *The Combat Myth in the Book of Revelation.* Missoula, MT: Scholars, 1976. ———. "The Political Perspective of the Revelation to John." *JBL* 96 (1977) 241–56. **Zielinski, T.** "Die griechischen Quellen der Apokalypse." *FuF* 7 (1931) 155–56.

Translation

19 *Then the temple of God* [a]*in heaven*[b] *opened, and his*[c] *ark of the covenant appeared* [d]
in his temple, and there were lightning and rumbling and thunder [e]*and an earthquake*[e]
and great hail. 12:1 [a]*A great* [b] *sign then appeared* [c] *in heaven, a* [d]*woman*[e] [f]*clothed* [d] *with the*
sun; the[g] *moon was beneath her feet, and upon*[h] *her head was a crown of twelve stars.* 2 *She*
was pregnant and [a] *cried out* [b] *in labor, in*[c] *the throes of childbirth.*[d] 3 [a]*Then another sign*
appeared in heaven.[a] *And behold, a* [b]*great red* [b] *dragon with seven heads and ten horns*
and seven diadems upon his heads. 4 *His* [a] *tail swept down*[b] *a third of the stars* [c] *of heaven*
and cast them down to the earth.

Now the dragon stood [d] *before the woman who was about to give birth, so that when she*
gave birth he might swallow her child. 5 [a]*Then she bore a son, a* [b]*male child, who* [a] *will drive* [c]
all the nations [d]*with* [e] *an iron crook.*[d] *But her child* [f]*was caught*[f] *up to God and to* [g] *his*
throne. 6 *The woman then fled into the wilderness* [a]*where* [b] *she had* [c] *a place* [a] *prepared* [d]
there [e] *for her by*[f] *God, that she* [g] [h]*might be* [i]*taken care of*[h] *there for* [j]*1,260 days.*[j] [k]

7 *There was a battle in heaven.* [a]*Michael* [b] *and his angels* [c]*had to fight* [c] *with the dragon.*
The dragon and his angels fought back 8 *but were unable to* [a]*prevail,* [b]*nor*[c] *was* [d]*there a*
place[e] *for them*[d] *any longer in heaven.* 9 *Then was cast down* [a]*the great dragon,*[a] [b]*the*
ancient[b] *serpent,* [c]*who is called Devil* [c] *and* [d] *Satan, who leads the whole world astray; he*
was cast down to the earth, and his[e] *angels were cast down along* [f]*with him.*[f]

10 *Then I heard a loud voice in heaven saying:*

"The victory [a]*and the power and the kingship of our God*

and the[b] *authority*[c] *of his Messiah have now occurred,*
[d]*because the accuser*[e] *of our brothers and sisters*[f] [g]*was cast out*[g]
who accused[h] *them*[i] *before our God day and night.*
11 *And they*[a] *conquered him through the blood of the Lamb*
and [b]*through the word of their testimony,*[b]
for[c] *they did not love their life to the point of death.*
12 *Therefore rejoice,*[a] *O*[b] [c]*heaven,*[d]
and those who dwell therein.[c]
Woe[e] *to* [f]*the earth*[f] *and* [g]*the sea,*[g]
because the devil, who is very angry, was cast down to you,
because he knows that he has[h] *only a short time."*

13 *And when the dragon realized* [a]*that he had been cast down to the earth,*[a] *he pursued*[b]
the woman who had delivered[c]*the male child.*[c] 14 *Then the woman*[a]*was provided*[a] *with the*[b]
two wings of a[c] *large eagle that*[d]*she might fly*[d] [e]*to her place*[e] *in the wilderness*[fg]*where she*
will be taken care of[g] *for a time, times,* [h]*and half a time*[h] [i]*from the presence*[i] *of the serpent.*
15 *Then the serpent spewed water like a river from*[a] *his mouth behind*[b] *the woman that he*
might wash her[c] *away.* 16 *Yet the earth helped the woman, and*[a]*the earth*[a] *opened its mouth*
and swallowed[b]*the river which*[b] *the dragon spewed*[c] *out*[d] *of his mouth.* 17 *And the dragon*
was angry[a]*because of*[a] *the woman and left*[b]*to wage war*[b] *with the rest of her children who*
kept the commandments of God and maintained their witness [c]*to Jesus.*[c]

Notes

19.a. Variants: (1) ὁ before ἐν] A C fam 1006$^{1006\ 1841}$ fam 1611^{2329} 2351 Andr f^{2073} l; Victorinus (*quod est in caelo*); it$^{gig\ h}$ (*quod in caelo est*); eth cop^{bo} arm [von Soden, *Text*]. (2) omit ὁ] 𝔓^{47} ℵ 025 046 051 Andreas Byzantine cop$^{sams\ bomss}$. Since variant (1) corresponds to the style of Revelation, it is the original reading (see Schmid, *Studien* 2:89, 196). Reading (1) also has the strongest external attestation, and though it may have been a grammatical correction, it could also have been omitted by mistake (*TCGNT*^{1}, 745; *TCGNT*^{2}, 672).

19.b. Variant: add ἄνω] ℵ*.

19.c. Variants: (1) αὐτοῦ] *lectio originalis.* (2) τοῦ κυρίου] 𝔓^{47} Andr d^{-2051} f^{2023} Byzantine. (3) τοῦ θεοῦ] ℵ Andr d^{2051} e^{2026} l Byz 11$^{149\ 2025}$. Readings (2) and (3) are corrections based on the frequent OT phrase "the ark of the covenant of God/the Lord." The correction reflected in variant (3) presupposed variant (2); see Schmid, *Studien* 2:115.

19.d. Variant: ἐδόθη] C.

19.e-e. Variants: (1) καὶ σεισμός] ℵ (A C: σισμός) 025 051 Andreas vg (*terraemotus*). (2) καὶ σεισμοί] Oecumenius^{2053} Andr l^{1778} n^{2429}. (3) omit] Andr f^{2023text} 046 Byzantine syr^{ph}.

12:1.a. Variant: insert εἶδον before σημεῖον] Hippolytus (*de Ant.* 60).

1.b. Variant: insert καὶ θαυμαστόν after μέγα] Hippolytus (*de Ant.* 60).

1.c. Variant: omit ὤφθη] Hippolytus (*de Ant.* 60).

1.d-d. Variant: γυναῖκα περιβεβλημένην] Hippolytus (*de Ant.* 60). The omission of ὤφθη and insertion of εἶδον in Hippolytus necessitated the change from the nom. to the acc. case for this noun phrase.

1.e. The fem. nom. γυνή, "woman," is in apposition to σημεῖον, "sign," since it explains what the sign is.

1.f. Variant: περιβλεπομένη] A. Careless transcriptional error.

1.g. Variants: (1) ἡ] *lectio originalis.* (2) omit ἡ] Andr a b d f$^{2031\ 2056}$ l^{1678} n^{-2429}.

1.h. Here ἐπί, "on, upon," with the gen. noun cluster τῆς κεφαλῆς αὐτῆς, "her head," has a meaning semantically identical with ἐπί with the acc.; cf. v 3, ἐπὶ τὰς κεφαλὰς αὐτοῦ, "on his heads." Mussies, *Morphology*, 100–101, points out that ἐπί is used in Revelation with the gen., dat., or acc. without distinguishing location *in* a place or movement *to* a place.

2.a. Variants: (1) καί before κράζει] 𝔓^{47} ℵ C fam 1006 Oecumenius^{2053} Andr l$^{1778\ 2020}$ n^{2429}. (2) καί after κράζει] A. (3) omit καί before κράζει] fam 161$^{11611\ 1854\ 2329\ 2344}$ 2351 Andreas Byzantine Hippolytus (*de Ant.* 60); von Soden, *Text.*

2.b. Variants: (1) κράζει (present)] A 𝔓[47] ℵ Andreas Hippolytus (*de Ant.* 60). (2) ἔκραζεν (impf.)] C Byzantine 2351. (3) ἔκραξεν (aor.)] some Byzantine MSS. κράζει, "cries out," is a historical present, undoubtedly the original reading; cf. σύρει, another historical present in v 4. Schmid (*Studien* 2:208) has pointed out the marked tendency in Revelation MSS to change the tense of the verb κράζειν from impf. to aor. and from aor. to impf.

2.c. The καί, "and," is left untranslated since the two clauses that it ties together, καὶ κράζει ὠδίνουσα, "and cried out in labor," and καὶ βασανιζομένη τεκεῖν, "in the throes of childbirth," are synonymous, so that καί functions epexegetically; i.e., the second phrase explains or elaborates on the meaning of the first phrase.

2.d. In the phrase καὶ βασανιζομένη τεκεῖν, "in the throes of childbirth," the function of the aor. inf. τεκεῖν is problematic. Since it is probably dependent on the present pass. ptcp. βασανιζομένη, "tormented," it can be construed as epexegetical, explaining the reason for the torment. On the other hand, Burton (*Syntax*, § 389) construes τεκεῖν as the obj. of the verbal notion "desire," implicit though unexpressed in the preceding ptcps. This view may be reflected in the RSV translation "in anguish for delivery." τοῦ is inserted before τεκεῖν in Hippolytus (*de Ant.* 60) but omitted in the commentary (*de Ant.* 61).

3.a-a. καί here functions as a temporal particle like εἶτα or τότε.

3.b-b. Variants: (1) μέγας πυρ[ρ]ός] A 025 051 fam 1006[1841] Andreas lat cop[sa]; WHort; B. Weiss, *Johannes-Apokalypse,* 122; Nestle-Aland[27]; UBSGNT[4]. (2) πυρ[ρ]ὸς μέγας] 𝔓[47] ℵ C 046 Oecumenius[2053] fam 1611[-2050] 2351 Andr d l Byzantine Methodius Primasius cop syr eth; Tischendorf, *NT Graece;* Bousset (1906) 336 (in parentheses as second option). See Rev 20:11: θρόνον μέγαν λευκόν. The change from -ρρ- to -ρ- occurred relatively late. Here in Rev 12:3, C and 046 read πυρός (which can be confused with the gen. of πῦρ); see *Note* 6:4.b., and cf. Moulton-Howard, *Accidence* 2:101; MM, 560.

4.a. Here καί, "and," is a discourse marker indicating the beginning of a new sentence and is therefore left untranslated.

4.b. σύρει, "sweeps," is a historical present translated as a past tense.

4.c. Variant: ἀστρῶν] C Oecumenius[2053].

4.d. Note that εστηκεν can either be the impf. of the verb στήκω (i.e., ἕστηκεν) or the pf. of the intransitive verb ἵστημι (i.e., ἕστηκεν). There is no clear way to determine which form this is (BDF § 73; Mussies, *Morphology,* 265), though BAGD, 768, opts for the impf.

5.a-a. In the phrase καὶ ἔτεκεν υἱόν, ἄρσεν, ὅς, "then she bore a son, a male child, who," ἄρσεν is a sing. *neut.* acc. adj., which is used correctly in apposition to the sing. *masc.* acc. noun υἱόν, since the nom. sing. masc. relative pronoun ὅς, "who," modifies υἱόν (BDR § 136.3; Mussies, *Morphology,* 139–40). The phrase ἔτεκεν υἱόν is an allusion to LXX Isa 66:7, ἐξέφυγεν καὶ ἔτεκεν ἄρσεν, "she fled and bore a male" (cf. LXX Jer 20:15, ἐτέχθη σοι ἄρσεν, "a male was born to you").

5.b. Variants: (1) ἄρσεν (neut. acc.)] A C; Charles, 2:308; Tischendorf, *NT Graece;* WHort; Nestle-Aland[27]; UBSGNT[4]. (2) ἄρσενα (masc. acc.)] 051 fam 1006 fam 1611 Oecumenius[2053] Andreas (specifically Andr b e f[2023] h n 598); Byzantine Hippolytus (*de Ant.* 60); B. Weiss, *Johannes-Apokalypse,* 97–98 (regards ἄρσεν as a scribal error); Bousset (1906) 338 n. 1. (3) ἄρρενα] 𝔓[47] ℵ 2351 Andr l[1678 1778] Byzantine. Readings (2) and (3) could have been influenced by 12:13, where the phrase ἔτεκεν τὸν ἄρσενα occurs and ἄρσενα is a masc. acc. noun. In the LXX, Exod 2:2, Isa 66:7, and Jer 37:6 (MT 30:6) have the phrase ἔτεκεν ἄρσεν (the phrase also occurs in *T. Jos.* 3:7), and Jer 20:15 has the term ἄρσεν (B) or ἄρσην (A), used in an idiomatic translation of the Heb. phrase בן זכר *bēn zākār* (found only here in the OT), lit. "a son, a male," or more idiomatically "a male child" (KB[3], 260). These passages increase the likelihood that the original text is ἄρσεν, the *lectio difficilior,* attested to by A and C, and that readings (2) and (3) are corrections (Schmid, *Studien* 2:90). According to Schmid, ἄρσεν should be understood not in *apposition* to υἱόν but as an *attribute* of υἱόν. There was a fluctuation between -ρρ- (the Attic form) and -ρσ- (the Ionic form); the -ρρ- spelling is more frequent after the second century A.D. (Gignac, *Grammar* 1:143–44).

5.c. The periphrastic verb μέλλει ποιμαίνειν is the author's way of rendering the simple fut. ind. ποιμανεῖς found in the LXX Ps 2:9. Normally, ποιμαίνειν means "to pasture, herd or tend," but it is often used in ancient literature (both Near Eastern and Greco-Roman) as a metaphor for ruling. In the LXX version of Ps 2:9, where this phrase originated (see *Comment* on 2:27), the verb ποιμανεῖς represents an apparent departure from the Heb. text, where the corresponding verb is תרעם *tĕrōʿēm,* "you will break them," from רעע *rāʿaʿ,* "to break," so that the whole line reads "You shall break them with a rod of iron," paralleled by the second line of the couplet, "and dash them in pieces like a potter's vessel." However, the LXX translators apparently understood the verb behind תרעם *tĕrōʿēm* to be רעה *rāʿâ,* "pasture, tend," a verb that is also used figuratively for ruling; cf. KB[3], 1174–75). Though ποιμαίνειν can be used as a metaphor in a negative context, the view of Lohmeyer that it can mean "destroy" is not borne out by the lexical meaning of ποιμαίνειν in the LXX passages he cites (Mic 5:4; Jer 6:3; 22:22; Ps 48:14; *Pss. Sol.* 17:23; cf. Lohmeyer, 29). This view was expressed earlier by Charles, 1:75–76, who noted that ποιμαίνειν was used parallel to πατάσσειν, "to strike, strike down, slay," in Rev 19:15 and συντρίβειν, "to mistreat, beat, shatter," in Rev 2:27. The harsh treatment of a flock of sheep, however, can better be rendered with a term like "drive," "goad," rather than with the term "destroy," and it has the advantage in Eng. that it retains the flavor of the original pastoral metaphor.

5.d-d. Variant: omit ἐν ῥάβδῳ σιδηρᾷ] Hippolytus (*de Ant.* 60). The phrase ἐν ῥάβδῳ σιδηρᾷ, "with an iron rod," is still part of the pastoral image drawn from Ps 2:9. It is therefore appropriate to translate ῥάβδος as "(shepherd's) crook," with the adj. "iron" emphasizing the cruel and harsh use to which it will be put. See *Comment* on 2:27.

5.e. Variant: omit ἐν before ῥάβδῳ] C 051 fam $1006^{1006\ 1841}$ Oecumenius^{2053} Andreas.

5.f-f. Variants: (1) ἡρπάσθη] *lectio originalis.* (2) ἡρπάγη] ℵ Andr e^{2057} f^{2023} h^{2302} Andr/Byz 3. Reading (1), which is certainly original, is the Attic form of the aor. pass., while reading (2) is the Hellenistic form.

5.g. Variants: (1) πρός] Hippolytus (*de Ant.* 60). (2) omit πρός] Andreas.

6.a-a. In the phrase ὅπου ἔχει ἐκεῖ τόπον, lit. "where she has a place there," ἐκεῖ is a resumptive adverb, which appears to be a Semitism since it is redundant in Gk. (Mussies, *Morphology,* 177); the same idiom occurs in v 14. Here the clause is *essential;* i.e., it is a dependent clause, a characteristic of the Semitic resumptive pronoun (Bakker, *Pronomen Abundans,* 41–42); cf. 12:14, however, where the clause is *nonessential* and conforms to possible Gk. usage. The indeclinable personal pronoun אשׁר *ʾăšer,* "which," in Heb. is frequently elucidated by means of the adverb שׁם *šām,* "there." Though ὅπου occurs five times without a resumptive adverb in Revelation (2:13[2x]; 11:8; 14:4; 20:10) and once with a resumptive pronoun (17:9), this does not conflict with the author's style (as claimed by Charles, 1:clviii n. 1) since the same idiom occurs in LXX Judg 18:10 (B), ὅπου οὐκ ἔστιν ἐκεῖ, while in Judg 20:22 (B), ὅπου occurs *without* a resumptive adv. For two other examples of ὅπου and ἐκεῖ used resumptively, see Ruth 3:4; Eccl 9:10. The adverbs οὗ and ἐκεῖ are used resumptively in Gen 13:4, οὗ ἐποίησεν ἐκεῖ (אשׁר־עשׂה שׁם *ʾăšer-ʿāśâ šām,* "where he made there" (cf. Gen 20:13, 21; 31:13; 40:30; Exod 21:13; 24:10; Judg 18:10 [A]; 19:26; Ruth 1:7; 1 Sam 9:10; 14:11; 23:22; 26:5; 29:4, 10; 2 Sam 2:23; 15:32; 1 Kgs 7:7; 8:47; 2 Kgs 19:32; 2 Chr 1:3; 6:37; 8:11; 1 Esdr 6:33; 2 Esdr 1:4; Jdt 5:19; Joel 3:7; Jer 13:7; 23:3, 8; Bar 2:4, 13, 29; Ezek 12:16; 28:25; 29:13; 36:20, 21, 22; 37:21, 25; 46:20, 24; Theod Dan 9:7). For instances of resumptive pronouns, see *Note* 3:8.c.; *Introduction,* Section 7: Syntax, III. Pronouns.

6.b. Variants: (1) ἔχει ἐκεῖ] *lectio originalis.* (2) ἐκεῖ ἔχει] Hippolytus (*de Ant.* 60). (3) εἶχε ἐκεῖ] Andr l. (4) omit ἐκεῖ] C 051 fam $1006^{1006\ 1841}$ 1611^{2329} Oecumenius^{2053} Andr a b h l 598 2019 lat syr^{h} Tyconius Primasius. The visual similarity between these two words led to their transposition, or to the omission of ἐκεῖ as a redundant adverb. See *Note* 12:6.e.

6.c. ἔχει, lit. "has," is a historical present appropriately rendered in Eng. by the past tense "had."

6.d. The pf. ptcp. ἡτοιμασμένον, "prepared," is in apposition to τόπον, which in turn is the obj. of ἔχει; the pattern ἔχειν + obj. + pf. ptcp. (adj.) occurs several times in Revelation (14:1; 19:12, 16; 21:12). In all these cases ἔχειν + ptcp. is not a periphrastic construction (cf. W. J. Aerts, *Periphrastica* [Amsterdam: Hakkert, 1965] 161–62). Similar constructions also occur in Mark 3:1; 8:17; Luke 13:6; 14:18–19; 19:20; John 17:13; *Jos. As.* 2:6; 5:5; 27:9; *T. Job* 25.7.

6.e. Variant: omit ἐκεῖ] C fam 1611^{2329} Andr a b h l 598 2019 lat syr^{h} Tyc^{1} Primasius. Stylistic omission of a redundant adv.

6.f. Variants: (1) ὑπό] 046 fam 1611^{1611} 2351 Oecumenius^{2053comm} Andr d e i^{-2042} 2019 Byzantine. (2) παρά] Andr/Byz $4c^{2070}$. These variants are corrections because of the relatively uncommon use of ἀπό as a marker of agent; see also 9:18 (Louw-Nida, § 90.7); ὑπό + gen. as a marker of agent occurs in 6:8, 13.

6.g. Variant: αὐτόν for αὐτήν] ℵ*.

6.h-h. The 3rd pl. present subjunctive verb τρέφωσιν, lit. "they might nourish," has an indefinite character and "need not refer exclusively to speaker, addressee or a known non-participant, but may have a more general aspect of meaning which can best be rendered by the indefinite pronoun 'one'" (Mussies, *Morphology,* 231), or might also be the impersonal use of the third person as an equivalent to the pass.

6.i. Variants: (1) τρέφωσιν] A fam 1006 fam 1611^{-2329} Oecumenius^{2053} Andreas; Charles, 1:321; $2:309^{mg}$. (2) τρέφουσιν] ℵ C fam 1611^{2329} Andr f^{051} h $i^{1685\ 2074}$ 598 2019; Tischendorf, *NT Graece;* $WHort^{mg}$; Charles, 2:309. (3) ἐκτρέφωσιν] 94 Byzantine Hippolytus (*de Ant.* 60). (4) ἐκτρέφουσιν] Byz $3^{429\ 522}$ Byz 4^{1719} Byz 12^{2048} Byz 17^{469}. Because of the style of Revelation, the present ind. in variant (2) must be rejected; if original, it would be singular (B. Weiss, *Johannes-Apokalypse,* 100; Schmid, *Studien* 2:103, 221). A similar variant occurs in 16:15: ἵνα βλέπουσι ($\mathfrak{P}^{47}$ Andreas) for ἵνα βλέπωσι.

6.j-j. The number 1,260 (certainly original) was subject to confusion in the textual tradition, in part because of the alphabetical abbreviation of numbers, resulting in the following (selection of) variants:

(1) 3 1/2 years (Victorinus: *triennio et mensibus sex*), (2) 1,240 days (it[gig]: *diebus mille ducentis quadraginta),* (3) 1,265 days (ℵ[2] arm[1,2,3,4]), (4) 1,277 1/2 days, apparently 365 x 3 1/2 days (Byz 17[2078 2436]), and (5) 1,290 days (Beatus: *dies mille ducentos nonaginta;* cop[bo]).

6.k. Variant: insert πέντε] ℵ[2] arm[1,2,3,4].

7.a. Variant: insert τε after ὅ] A (= ὅτε).

7.b. "Michael" is articular because it is the name of a well-known figure in Jewish apocalyptic literature (cf. Jude 9).

7.c-c. Variants: (1) τοῦ πολεμῆσαι] A C P fam 1006 1611 Andr b[2059*] f n 2019 Andr/Byz 3. (2) πολεμῆσαι (omit τοῦ)] 𝔓[47] ℵ Andreas Byzantine; Tischendorf, *NT Graece.* (3) omit τοῦ πολεμῆσαι] 2351. Since the agreement of A and C constitutes strong evidence, and the presence of τοῦ is the more difficult reading, it is probably the original reading (Schmid, *Studien* 2:90). τοῦ πολεμῆσαι, "to fight," is the only secure instance of an articular inf. in Revelation (for the articular inf. in variant readings, see *Notes* on 10:9; 14:15) and functions as an inf. of purpose used as a predicate in a nominal clause. This can be compared with 27 occurrences of articular infs. in Matthew, 16 in Mark, 72 in Luke, 52 in Acts, and 111 in the seven genuine Pauline letters. In contrast to this relatively frequent usage, it is worthy of note that the articular inf. occurs just 4 times in John (1:48; 2:24; 13:19; 17:5), always as the obj. of a prep. Some have suggested that τοῦ was accidentally added by a copyist through dittography, since the word immediately preceding is αὐτοῦ (R. G. V. Tasker, "The Chester Beatty Papyrus of the Apocalypse of John," *JTS* 50 [1949] 62–63; Lancelotti, *Sintassi Ebraica,* 112). Charles has convincingly argued that Rev 12:7 has been formulated using Heb. idiom as a model (1:321–22; see also Howard-Moulton, *Accidence,* 448–49; Schmid, *Studien* 2:243; BDR § 400.7; Mussies, *Morphology,* 96; S. Thompson, *Apocalypse,* 62–63; Turner, *Insights,* 160–61). τοῦ πολεμῆσαι is a Hebraism reflecting the imperatival or jussive force of ל *lĕ* + inf. (cf. GKC § 114k): "they had to fight." "Michael and his angels" is in the nom. because in Heb. the subject before ל *lĕ* + inf. is in the nom. Parallel examples from the LXX are Hos 9:13; 1 Chr 9:25; Ps 24:14(MT 25:14); Eccl 3:15. Buttmann (*Grammar,* 268) and then Moulton (*Prolegomena,* 218; cf. Robertson, *Grammar,* 1066; Turner, *Syntax,* 141) suggested that τοῦ πολεμῆσαι was epexegetical, explaining πόλεμος, so that the problematic sentence could presumably be translated as follows: "There was a war in heaven, Michael and his angels fighting with the dragon." Some have suggested that a main verb, such as ἐγένετο, has been dropped out or should be supplied, so that τοῦ πολεμῆσαι would then express purpose: i.e., "Michael [arose] to fight" (Beckwith, 625; Turner, *Style,* 152). A. Lancelotti (*Sintassi Ebraica,* 112), apparently ignoring the explanation of Charles (that ל *lĕ* + inf. can have a jussive force), proposes that πολεμῆσαι (he rejects the article τοῦ as a scribal error) is an example of the Heb. inf. functioning as a finite verb (cf. GKC § 113y), indicated by the parallel aor. verb ἐπολέμησεν in v 7b. Among these varied explanations, the explanation given by Charles is the most persuasive.

8.a. Variants: (1) ἴσχυσεν] A fam 1611[1854] cop[bo] Oecumenius[2053comm] (ἴσχυσε); Andr f[2023] 94 Byzantine; WHort; B. Weiss, *Johannes-Apocalypse,* 109–10, 191; Charles, 2:309; Nestle-Aland[27]; UBSGNT[4]. (2) ἴσχυσαν] 𝔓[47] ℵ C 051 fam 1006[1006 1841] fam 1611[1611 2329] Oecumenius[2053] 2351 Andreas it vg syr; Tischendorf, *NT Graece;* WHort[mg]; von Soden, *Text;* [Bousset (1906) 341]; Charles, 2:309[mg]. (3) ἴσχυον] 046 Byz 16[61 69].

8.b. Variants: (1) insert πρὸς αὐτόν after ἴσχυσαν] ℵ. (2) insert πρὸς αὐτούς after ἴσχυσαν] cop[bo].

8.c. Variants: (1) οὐδέ] ℵ A C 046 fam 1006 fam 1611[1611 1854 2329] Oecumenius[2053] Andr d e[2026] f[2023] i l 94 it[gig h] vg Primasius Tyc[2] Beatus. (2) οὔτε] 051 2315 Andreas.

8.d-d. Variants: (1) τόπος εὑρέθη αὐτῶν] A Andreas. (2) τόπος εὑρέθη αὐτοῖς] ℵ[2] 051 Andr f[2023] 2019 syr[ph] cop[samss]. (3) τόπος εὑρέθη αὐτῷ] fam 1006[1006] fam 1611[1854] Oecumenius[2053] Andr e f[2023] g n[-2065] Byzantine cop[bo] Victorinus. (4) τόπος αὐτῶν εὑρέθη] fam 1006[1841] fam 1611[1611] Andr i[-2042] m[2046] it[h] Beatus Tyc[3]. (5) τόπος εὑρέθη] ℵ* 2042. The phrase within which reading (1) is found is very similar to a phrase in Rev 20:11; both are allusions to Theod Dan 2:35. Since reading (2), where αὐτοῖς is a dat. of possession, conforms more closely to the phrase in 20:11, which in turn is a verbatim allusion to Theod Dan 2:35, readings (2) and (3) are harmonizations. Reading (1) is the *lectio difficilior* since αὐτῶν is a gen. of possession but is separated from its governing noun by a verb; reading (4) is a correction intended to make its adnominal function clearer as a gen. of possession.

8.e. Variant: τότε for τόπος] ℵ*.

9.a-a. Variants: (1) ὁ μέγας, ὁ ὄφις] *lectio originalis.* (2) ὁ μέγας ὄφις] ℵ. (3) ὁ ὄφις ὁ μέγας] 𝔓[47] fam 1006[1006 1841] cop[bo].

9.b-b. Variant: omit ὁ ἀρχαῖος] 𝔓[47].

9.c-c. The term Διάβολος, "devil," is apparently anarthrous, though it *could* be considered articular since it is found in the phrase ὁ καλούμενος Διάβολος, "the one called Devil," and that article could also be connected with Διάβολος as well as the ptcp. If the article is connected to Διάβολος, the phrase could be translated "the so-called devil," but the fact that it is used anarthrously in 20:2 suggests that it is also anarthrous here in 12:9 (Mussies, *Morphology,* 196–97). However, Διάβολος does occur with the article in 2:10, where it is used as a title.

9.d. Variants: (1) καὶ ὁ] Andreas. (2) ὁ] ℵ fam 1611^{1854} cop^{bo}. (3) καί] $𝔓^{47}$ fam 1611^{2329} Byzantine. The omission of the article in variant (3) results from the preceding anarthrous Διάβολος (Schmid, *Studien* 2:199)

9.e. Variant: omit αὐτοῦ] $𝔓^{47}$ $Oecumenius^{2053}$ cop^{bo}.

9.f-f. Variant: omit μετ' αὐτοῦ] 051 fam 1611^{1854} Andreas.

10.a. Variants: (1) σωτηρία] fam 1611^{1854}. (2) ἐξουσία] 792.

10.b. Variant: omit ἡ] A Andr/Byz $2b^{628}$.

10.c. Variants: (1) σωτηρία] $𝔓^{47}$. (2) ἐξουσία] 792.

10.d. A rather free quotation of Rev 12:10 is found in Hippolytus *Frag. in Gen.* 34 (ed. H. Achelis, 64), ἐβλήθη εἰς τὴν γῆν ὁ διάβολος ὁ κατηγορῶν τοὺς ἀνθρώπους ἐνώπιον τοῦ θεοῦ, "The devil, who accuses people before God, was cast down to the earth."

10.e. Variants: (1) κατήγωρ] A; Tischendorf, *NT Graece;* B. Weiss, *Johannes-Apokalypse,* 109; WHort; Nestle-$Aland^{27}$; $UBSGNT^4$. (2) κατήγορος] $𝔓^{47}$ ℵ C 046 051 fam 1006 fam 1611 2351 Andreas Byzantine; von Soden, *Text.* Although κατήγωρ occurs only in A, that it occurs as a loanword in rabbinic literature makes it understandable why John wrote κατήγωρ and also makes it unlikely that a scribe would change κατήγορος to κατήγωρ, while a change from κατήγωρ to κατήγορος would not be difficult to imagine (see Schmid, *Studien* 2:103; *TCGNT* ¹, 745–46; *TCGNT* ², 673). R. V. G. Tasker argues, on the other hand, that the fifth-century copyist of A made the change based on the usage of his day ("The Chester Beatty Papyrus of the Apocalypse of John," *JTS* 50 [1949] 65). See *Comment* on 12:10.

10.f. "And sisters" added to indicate inclusive sense of τῶν ἀδελφῶν.

10.g-g. Variant: κατεβλήθη] 051 Andreas.

10.h. The present substantival ptcp. ὁ κατηγορῶν, lit. "the one who accuses," must be translated using a past tense because of the context; since the accuser has been expelled from heaven, he can no longer accuse Christians before God. Tenses of the ptcp. have no intrinsic temporal value in themselves (Burton, *Syntax,* § 118) but receive temporal value from the context. ὁ κατηγορῶν may simply identify the one who does the action defined by the verb, without reference to time.

10.i. Variants: (1) αὐτούς] $𝔓^{47}$ A 051 Andreas. (2) αὐτῶν] ℵ C fam 1006 fam 1611^{-2050} $Oecumenius^{2053}$ 2351 Andr c f^{2023} n 94 2351 Byzantine. Since the gen. following verbs of acc. is normal style in the NT (BDF § 178; BDR § 178), reading (1) is the *lectio difficilior,* for it is easier to understand how αὐτούς could be changed to αὐτῶν than the reverse (Schmid, *Studien* 2:103).

11.a. Variants: (1) αὐτοί] *lectio originalis.* (2) οὗτοι] ℵ. (3) αὐτοῦ] Andr $d^{2052\ 2067}$.

11.b-b. Variants: (1) omit τὸν λόγον] C. (2) omit διά] Andr $f^{2031\ 2056}$.

11.c. καί introduces a clause that provides the reason for the statement in the preceding clause and should therefore be translated in a causal sense, e.g., "for," "because." In the OT, causal clauses are occasionally introduced by waw (GKC § 158), and καί is similarly used in the LXX as a causal particle (Aejmelaeus, *Parataxis,* 23–24). However, this use of καί cannot be considered a strict Semitism since it is also found in pagan Gk. (Ljungvik, *Syntax,* 57–59). Charles (1:cxlviii) says that καί (= ו *wĕ*) "introduces a statement of the condition under which the action denoted by ἐνίκησαν took place." Two OT examples are Gen 8:18; 26:27. For the same syntactical phenomenon, cf. Rev 18:3; 19:3.

12.a. Variant: εὐφραίνεσθαι] A. Orthographical variation based on phonological interchange of αι > ε (Gignac, *Grammar* 1:192–93).

12.b. Variants: (1) οἱ before οὐρανοί] A Andreas fam 1006^{1006} fam $1611^{1611\ 2344}$ 2351; Bousset (1906) 343; Charles, 2:311. (2) omit οἱ] C ℵ 025 Byzantine fam $1611^{1854\ 2329}$ $Oecumenius^{2053}$; Tischendorf, *NT Graece;* B. Weiss, *Johannes-Apokalypse,* 192; WHort. It is bracketed in the text by $UBSGNT^4$ and Nestle-$Aland^{27}$. The article was probably in the original text since the nom. has almost completely replaced the vocative in Revelation and the articular nom. functioning as a vocative is characteristic of the author's style (Bousset [1906] 343 n. 1; Schmid, *Studien* 2:103; for this usage generally, cf. Robertson, *Grammar,* 769). There are twelve other occurrences of this construction in Revelation; cf. *Note* 4:11.a.

12.c-c. The articular substantives in the phrase οἱ οὐρανοὶ καὶ οἱ ἐν αὐτοῖς σκηνοῦντες are noms. functioning as vocatives; cf. *Note* 12.b.

12.d. The pl. form οἱ οὐρανοί is found only here in Revelation, while the sing. form occurs fifty-one times. In the NT there is apparently no semantic difference between the sing. and pl. forms (Louw-Nida, § 1.11). Since the Gk. pl. form, like the Heb. *plurale tantum* שׁמים *šāmayim,* "heavens," refers to a sing. "heaven," this usage has often been considered a Hebraism (BDF § 141.4; BDR § 141.1; Maloney, *Marcan Syntax,* 190–92). The pl. form of οὐρανός is found in the LXX, where it appears for the first time in Gk. literature. Although the pl. form שׁמים *šāmayim,* lit. "heavens" (the *plurale tantum,* explained by some as a "plural of extension"; cf. GKC § 124l; *TDNT* 5:502), frequently occurs in the MT, it is only translated with a pl. form of οὐρανός 51 times (*TDNT* 5:510), primarily in poetic contexts, while the sing. form is used more than 370 times (Mussies, *Morphology,* 85). The pl. form in Rev 12:12 cannot refer to a plurality of heavenly realms (as in other early Jewish apocalyptic and Merkavah literature, and even in the NT; cf. 2 Cor 12:2) since such a cosmology is nowhere else reflected in Revelation. Charles suggested that this usage indicates the presence of a source (1:clviii n. 1, 302, 329). The pl. form occurs only a very few times in Gk. literature (cf. *TDNT* 5:498 n. 2). Here οὐρανοί is very probably an allusion to the LXX (Isa 49:13, εὐφραίνεσθε, οὐρανοί, καὶ ἀγαλλιάσθω ἡ γῆ, "rejoice, O heavens, and let the earth be glad"; cf. Ps 95:11, εὐφραινέσθωσαν οἱ οὐρανοί, καὶ ἀγαλλιάσθω ἡ γῆ, "let the heavens rejoice and let the earth be glad"; Isa 44:23, εὐφράνθητε, οὐρανοί, "rejoice, O heavens"; *T. Levi* 18:5, οἱ οὐρανοὶ ἀγαλλιάσονται, "the heavens will rejoice"), i.e., a Septuagintism. Further, the term is found in a poetic context, and the poetic pl. characteristic of more elevated Hellenistic style may have influenced the author at this point (Mussies, *Morphology,* 84–85). The view that οὐρανοί referring to a single heaven is a Hebraism was contested by F. Torm ("Der pluralis οὐρανοί," *ZNW* 33 [1934] 48–50). He found instances of pl. forms of οὐρανός in pagan Gk. (though he failed to mention that most such instances refer to a *plurality* of heavens). Torm also proposed that since the pl. form was primarily found in poetic contexts in the LXX (cf. Doudna, *Greek,* 73–74), it functioned as a *pluralis majesticus,* "plural of majesty," or a *pluralis poeticus,* "poetic plural," i.e., a rhetorical plural rather than as the result of Semitic influence. P. Katz pointed out that the pl. forms of οὐρανός in the LXX tend to be used in contexts in which pl. forms (particularly pl. verbs) precede and follow שמים *šāmayim,* e.g., Gen 2:1; Pss 32:6; 68:35, 96:6, so that a lit. rendering required the Hebraistic Gk. pl. οὐρανοί (*Philo's Bible* [Cambridge: Cambridge UP, 1950] 141–46). Though there are exceptions, in general in the OT Apocrypha and pseudepigrapha, as well as in the NT and the NT Apocrypha, the pl. form is used of the place where God dwells, while the sing. form is used of the region above the earth (Torm, *ZNW* 33 [1934] 49–50). An example of their synonymity is the terminology found in the framework of a single vision; in Hermas *Vis.* 1.1.4, the heaven (sing.) is opened, and in *Vis.* 1.2.1, the heavens (pl.) are shut (cf. Hilhorst, *Sémitismes,* 126–29). In Mark, οὐρανός occurs seventeen times, four of which occur in the pl. (1:10, 11; 12:25; 13:25 [similar to LXX Isa 34:4 in MS B; not in MT]). These four pl. forms of οὐρανός in Mark are the result of Semitic interference or are Septuagintisms (Maloney, *Marcan Syntax,* 191–92). In the Gk. Jewish pseudepigrapha (Denis, *Fragmenta*), the term οὐρανός occurs 291 times, 46 times in the pl. Some of these refer to more than one heaven (*T. Levi* 2:9; 3:1; cf. 1 Enoch 1:4, ὁ οὐρανὸς τῶν οὐρανῶν, "the heaven of heavens," i.e., "the highest heaven").

12.e. The interjection οὐαί, "woe," is used here with the acc. without a prep., as it is in 8:13; apparently there are no other known examples of this unusual usage (cf. BAGD, 561; BDR § 190). οὐαί + nom. (functioning as vocative) does occur in Rev 18:10, 16, 19. Since the Latin interjection *uae* could be used with the acc. as well as the dat. (*OLD,* 2003), it is possible that οὐαί + acc. in Rev 8:13; 12:12 is a Latinism. In the LXX οὐαί is often used with the dat. of the person or thing to whom the woe is directed (Num 21:29; 1 Sam 4:8; Jdt 16:17; Prov 23:29; Isa 3:9, 11; 10:1, 5; 33:1; Jer 4:3; Hos 7:13; 9:12; cf. MM, 464) and with articular noms. used as vocatives (Zech 2:5; Isa 1:24; 5:8, 11, 18, 20, 21, 22; 31:1). Occasionally οὐαί is used with ἐπί + acc. in the LXX (Jer 10:19; 28:2 [MT 51:2]; 31:1 [MT 48:1]; Ezek 7:26). The unusual construction of οὐαί + the simple acc., which is certainly the *lectio difficilior,* encouraged scribal corrections. ℵ reads οὐαὶ εἰς τὴν γῆν, using a prep. to smooth over the ungrammatical construction. Other MSS transpose the phrase governed by οὐαί into the grammatically correct dat. case: οὐαὶ τῇ γῇ . . . , "woe to the earth . . ." (𝔓^{47} fam $1611^{1854\ 2329\ 2344}$ 2351 Byzantine). οὐαί appears for the first time in the LXX, where it occurs seventy-three times, particularly in Isaiah and Jeremiah. The two Heb. interjections אוי *ʾôy* and הוי *hôy* (cf. the similar Aramaic וי *way,* found in rabbinic literature) lie behind most of these occurrences. Though it was once assumed that οὐαί was derived from these words, it is more likely that the word first appeared in Gk. in the fourth century B.C. and was selected by the LXX translators because of its phonetic similarity to the equivalent Heb. terms (cf. A. D. Lowe, "The Origin of οὐαί," *Hermathena* 105 [1967] 34–39).

12.f-f. Variants: (1) τῇ γῇ] 𝔓^{47} fam $1611^{1854\ 2329\ 2344}$ 2351 Byzantine. (2) τὴν ἀγάπην] A. Nonsensical transcriptional error.

12.g-g. Variants: (1) τῇ θαλάσσῃ] 𝔓^{47} fam $1611^{1854\ 2329\ 2344}$ 2351 Byzantine. (2) τοῖς κατοικοῦσιν τὴν γῆν καὶ τὴν θάλασσαν] 1.

12.h. The present verb ἔχει, "has," is the only example in Revelation of the general present used in reported *thought;* it frequently occurs in reported speech (Mussies, *Morphology,* 333).

13.a-a. Variant: omit ὅτι ἐβλήθη εἰς τὴν γῆν] Hippolytus (*de Ant.* 60 [text and commentary]).

13.b. Variants: (1) ἐξεδίωξεν] ℵ^{2}. (2) ἔδωκεν] ℵ*. (3) ἀπῆλθεν ἐκδίωξαι] 𝔓^{47}. (4) ἐδίωκε] Oecumenius^{2053} (text and commentary) fam 1611^{1854} Andr $l^{1678\ 1778}$. Variant (2) is a scribal error in which a 3rd sing. aor. from διδόναι is mistakenly used (the difference is simply the presence or absence of an iota), while variant (4) is an error in which a 3rd sing. impf. form from διώκειν is used. Both (1) and (3) can be explained as derived from the 3rd sing. aor. ἐδίωξεν.

13.c-c. Variants: (1) ἄρσενα] ℵ C 025 051 fam $1006^{1006\ 1841}$ fam $1611^{1611\ 1854}$ Oecumenius^{2053} Andr e f n; WHort. (2) ἄρσεναν] A. (3) ἄρρενα] fam 1611^{2329} Andreas Byzantine. Variant (2) supports variant (1) since the addition of -ν to the acc. sing. of third-declension nouns in A (e.g., 13:14: εἰκόναν for εἰκόνα; 22:2: μῆναν for μῆνα) is based on the analogy of other acc. sings. of all first- and second-declension nouns (e.g., λόγον, πόλιν) and was a replacement that occurred gradually during the imperial period (Mussies, *Morphology*, 33, 104; Gignac, *Grammar* 1:45–46). On the fluctuation between the Attic form -ρρ- and the Ionic form -ρσ-, see Gignac, *Grammar* 1:143–44. τὸν ἄρσενα is a masc. acc., in contrast to ἄρσεν in v 5, which is a neut. acc.

14.a-a. Variant: ἐδόθη] 𝔓^{47} ℵ^{2} Andr g 209.

14.b. The article αἱ before δύο πτέρυγες, "two wings," is omitted by 𝔓^{47} ℵ fam 1611$^{1854\ 2329\ 2344}$ 2351 Byzantine Hippolytus (*de Ant.* 60; but present in the commentary in *de Ant.* 61). The article is present because parts of the human body (cf. 2:1) and parts of the bodies of animals, such as wings, are well known.

14.c. The articular phrase τοῦ ἀετοῦ τοῦ μεγάλου, lit. "the great eagle," is problematic. Since a substantive not previously mentioned is usually anarthrous, John may be referring here to "the great eagle" in a story well known to his audience but unfortunately unknown to us.

14.d-d. Variants: (1) πέτηται] *lectio originalis.* (2) πέτητε] A. (3) πέτεται] 046 051 fam 1611^{2329} Oecumenius^{2053} Andr f^{2023} g^{2045}. (4) πέταται] Andreas. (5) πετάσῃ] Andr Ø^{1773}. Apart from reading (5), all the variants represent phonological changes in transcription. Reading (2) reflects the frequent phonological diphthong interchange αι > ε (Gignac, *Grammar* 1:192), while reading (3) reflects the phonological vocalic change η > ε (Gignac, *Grammar* 1:242–43). The η > α change in (4) is more difficult to account for. πέτεσθαι occurs four times in Revelation (8:13; 12:14; 14:6; 19:17) and exhibits a variety of orthographical variations (BDF § 101; MM, 511).

14.e-e. Variant: omit εἰς τὸν τόπον αὐτῆς] Hippolytus (*de Ant.* 60; omitted also in commentary in *de Ant.* 61).

14.f. Variant: ἵνα before ὅπου] 2351.

14.g-g. The pronominal clause ὅπου τρέφεται ἐκεῖ, lit. "where she is nourished there," is an instance of the *pronomen abundans,* which has been considered a Semitism by many scholars. In this instance, however, ὅπου introduces a relative connection; i.e., it introduces an independent clause with a copulative sense and so must be considered within the parameters of Gk. usage (Bakker, *Pronomen Abundans,* 42). The *pronomen abundans* occurs nine times in Revelation (3:8; 7:2, 9; 12:6, 14; 13:8, 12; 17:9; 20:8). Of these occurrences, all are in essential or dependent clauses with the exception of 12:14 and 20:8. For a more extensive discussion, cf. *Note* 3:8.c. and *Introduction,* Section 7: Syntax, III. Pronouns.

14.h-h. Variant: omit καὶ ἥμισυ καιροῦ] C (Andr i^{2074} omits καὶ ἥμισυ in 11:11).

14.i-i. On the Semitism ἀπὸ προσώπου, see *Note* 6:16.b. Here the normal meaning "from the presence of" is possible, but ἀπὸ προσώπου is occasionally used with the meaning "because of, on account of" (LXX Isa 19:17; Hos 10:15; see Charles, 1:128; K. G. Newport, "Semitic Influence on Revelation," *BT* 37 [1986] 328–30).

15.a. Variant: ἀπό] 𝔓^{47} Andr l i^{2042}.

15.b. ὀπίσω + gen.; see *Note* 1:10.c.

15.c. Variant: ταύτην] 051 Andreas.

16.a-a. Variant: omit ἡ γῆ] 𝔓^{47} Byz 4^{-1424} 8 9$^{452\ 467\ 2021}$ Andr/Byz 2b^{628} 4a^{-250} 4b$^{172\ 1862\ 1888\ 2018}$ 2019 it^{gig} arm^{1} Primasius Victorinus Tyc^{1}.

16.b-b. Variant: τὸ ὕδωρ ὅ] A arm^{1}.

16.c. Variant: ἐνέβαλεν] 046 2351.

16.d. Variant: ἀπό] 𝔓^{47}.

17.a-a. Variants: (1) ἐπί] *lectio originalis.* (2) omit] 𝔓^{47} C. (3) ἐν] 2351. ἐπί + dat. following a verb of strong emotion (here ὀργίζεσθαι) can indicate the *cause* of the emotion (Helbing, *Kasussyntax,* 211; BDF § 196; BDR § 196.3); cf. LXX Gen 40:2; Num 31:14; 3 Kgdms 11:9; 4 Kgdms 19:28. The relatively rare use of ἐπί here resulted in the scribal corrections found in readings (2) and (3); see Schmid, *Studien* 2:104.

17.b-b. Variants: (1) ποιῆσαι πόλεμον] *lectio originalis.* (2) πόλεμον ποιῆσαι] ℵ fam 1611^{1854}; Tyc$^{2(MsV)}$: *bellum facere.*

17.c-c. The translation "to Jesus" indicates that the gen. Ἰησοῦ is construed as an obj. gen. (see *Comment* on 1:9).

Form/Structure/Setting

I. Outline

2. The woman, the dragon, and the child (11:19–12:17)
   a. Introductory divine manifestations (11:19)
      (1) The temple of God in heaven opens (v 19a)

(2) The ark of God's covenant appears in his temple (v 19b)
(3) Accompanying atmospheric and seismic manifestations (v 19c)
(a) Lightning
(b) Rumbling
(c) Thunder
(d) Earthquake
(e) Great hail

b. Introduction of the *dramatis personae:* the pregnant woman and the dragon (12:1–4a)
(1) The first great sign in heaven: a woman (12:1–2)
(a) Description (v 1)
[1] Clothed with the sun
[2] The moon beneath her feet
[3] Crown of twelve stars on her head
(b) Behavior (v 2)
[1] She is pregnant
[2] She cries out in labor
[3] She is in the throes of childbirth
(2) The second great sign in heaven: a great red dragon (vv 3–4a)
(a) Description (v 3)
[1] Seven heads
[2] Ten horns
[3] Seven diadems on his heads
(b) Behavior (v 4a)
[1] His tail sweeps down a third of the stars
[2] He casts the stars down to the earth

c. The first stage of conflict: the birth and escape of the child and the flight of the woman (vv 4b–6)
(1) The dragon's attack (v 4b)
(a) He stands before the woman
(b) She is about to give birth
(c) He waits to swallow her child
(2) The woman gives birth to a child (v 5ab)
(a) The description of the child (v 5a)
[1] The child is a son
[2] The child is a male
(b) The destiny of the child (v 5b)
[1] He will drive all nations
[2] He will use an iron crook
(3) The child escapes the dragon (v 5c)
(a) Caught up to God
(b) To the throne of God
(4) The woman flees from the dragon (v 6)
(a) To the wilderness (v 6a)
(b) To a place prepared by God (v 6b)

(c) Purpose: to be nourished there (v 6c)
(d) Period: for 1,260 days (v 6c)

d. The second stage of the conflict: the dragon's defeat and its positive and negative effects (vv 7–12)
 (1) The battle in heaven (vv 7–9)
  (a) Michael and his angels fight the dragon (v 7b)
  (b) The dragon and his angels fight (vv 7b–8)
   [1] They are unable to prevail (v 8)
   [2] No place found for them in heaven (v 8)
  (c) The dragon and his angels are cast down to earth (v 9)
   [1] The dragon is cast down (v 9a)
   [2] Parenthesis: the dragon's aliases (v 9a–c)
    [a] The great dragon
    [b] The ancient serpent
    [c] Devil
    [d] Satan
   [3] The dragon's role: he leads the whole world astray (v 9d)
   [4] The expulsion of the dragon (v 9e)
    [a] The dragon is cast down to the earth
    [b] His angels are cast down with him
 (2) A heavenly commentary: a song of victory (vv 10–12)
  (a) Introduction: John hears a loud sound in heaven (v 10a)
  (b) The song of victory (vv 10a–12)
   [1] The proclamation of God's victory (v 10a)
    [a] Aspects of God's sovereignty actualized
     {1} Victory
     {2} Power
     {3} Kingship
    [b] The authority of God's Messiah actualized
   [2] The basis for God's victory (v 10bc)
    [a] The Accuser is cast out
     {1} He accuses "our brothers and sisters"
     {2} He accuses them
      {a} Where: before God
      {b} When: day and night
    [b] "Our brothers and sisters" conquer the Accuser (v 11)
     {1} Means of conquest (v 11ab)
      {a} The blood of the Lamb
      {b} The word of their testimony
     {2} Reason: they did not love their lives to the point of death (v 11c)
   [3] Summons to rejoice (v 12a)
    [a] To the heavens
    [b] To those who dwell therein
   [4] Announcement of woe (v 12b–d)
    [a] Object of woe (v 12b)
     {1} The earth
     {2} The sea

[b] Reason for woe (v 12cd)
{1} The devil is cast down to you with great wrath
{2} He knows that he has only a short time
e. The third stage of the conflict: the dragon pursues the woman and her offspring (vv 13–17)
(1) Introduction (v 13)
(a) The dragon realizes that he has been cast down to the earth
(b) The dragon resumes pursuit of the woman who had delivered the male child
(2) The second escape of the woman (v 14)
(a) Divine provision: the two wings of a large eagle (v 14a)
(b) Purpose: to fly to her place in the wilderness (v 14b)
(c) There she finds temporary protection (v 14c)
[1] Period: a time, times, and half a time
[2] Purpose: protection from the presence of the serpent
(3) The serpent attacks the woman (vv 15–16)
(a) Means: he spews water from his mouth like a river (v 15a)
(b) Purpose: to wash the woman away (v 15b)
(c) The woman is rescued by the earth (v 16a)
(4) The dragon then turns his wrath on the offspring of the woman (v 17)
(a) Those who keep the commandments of God
(b) Those who maintain their witness to Jesus

II. Literary Analysis

A. The Relationship of Rev 11:19–12:17 to 11:19–14:20

Between the narrative describing the sounding of the seventh trumpet (11:15–18) and the narrative of the seven bowls (15:1–16:21) are three subtexts (11:19–12:17; 12:18–13:18; 14:1–20), which are framed by these narratives. The visions that make up this section form a roughly continuous narrative of eschatological events. Beginning with the birth of the child (= Messiah) who was "caught up" to heaven, the defeat and expulsion of the dragon (= Satan) from heaven by Michael are described and thereafter the persecution of the Church (chap. 12). The beast from the sea (= Rome) and the beast from the land (=imperial priesthood) then appear, and with the authority of the dragon kill those who will not worship the beast (chap. 13). John then sees the 144,000 members of the Christian remnant with the Lamb on Mount Zion (14:1–5). Angels then announce the gospel and the necessity of repentance, the fall of Babylon, and the terrible fate awaiting those who worship the beast (14:6–12). The eschatological harvest is then depicted with Christ gathering in the elect and an angel gathering in unbelievers for punishment (14:13–20).

B. The Analysis of Rev 11:19–12:17

The entire section can be broken down into five constituent textual subunits (see extended outline above): (1) introductory divine manifestations (11:19); (2)

introduction of the *dramatis personae:* the pregnant woman and the dragon (12:1–4a); (3) the first stage of conflict: the birth and escape of the child and the flight of the woman (12:4b–6); (4) the second stage of the conflict: the defeat and expulsion of the dragon from heaven (12:7–9); and (5) the third stage of the conflict: the dragon's pursuit of the woman and her offspring (12:13–17). Each of these requires more detailed discussion.

1. INTRODUCTORY DIVINE MANIFESTATIONS (11:19)

Most commentators have assumed that 11:19 concludes the previous textual unit (11:15–18) and that the unit of text in 12:1–17 is introduced with 12:1. A careful analysis of both internal structural features and analogous external literary forms, however, strongly suggests that 11:19 functions both as an introduction to 12:1–17 and as a conclusion to 11:15–18. Rev 12:1–17 consists of four episodes: (1) 12:1–4a, (2) 12:4b–6, (3) 12:7–12, and (4) 12:13–17, framed by 11:19 and 12:18. The three episodes in 12:4b–17 are interrelated and form a unit that is continued in 13:1, so that our analysis of 11:19–12:17 must form the first phase of what follows.

Three interpretations of the structural significance of 11:19 are possible: (a) that it forms a conclusion to 11:14–18 (consisting of "answering manifestations"; Beckwith, 274, 606, 610), (b) that it "interlocks" or acts as a transition between 11:14–18 and 12:1–17, or (c) that it introduces 12:1–17 (P. Minear, *New Testament Apocalyptic* [Nashville: Abingdon, 1981] 91–92). This is how it is understood in the lection from Rev 11:19; 12:1–6, 10 on the feast of the Assumption of the Blessed Virgin Mary, read on 15 August in Roman Catholic churches. It is my view that 11:19 introduces 12:1–17, a position supported by the two following lines of argument.

(i) The structural significance of the formulaic mention of thunderstorms and earthquakes in Revelation has been discussed by several scholars (e.g., Vanni, *La struttura letteraria,* 141–48; Bauckham, "Eschatological Earthquake," in *Climax,* 199–209; Lambrecht, "Structuration," in *L'Apocalypse,* ed. J. Lambrecht, 93–95). There are four such thunderstorm and earthquake passages in Revelation, each linked to the throne of God or the heavenly temple (4:5; 8:5; 11:19; 16:18–21). Lambrecht ("Structuration," 94–95) claims that the last three references climactically *follow* the seventh element of the heptads of seals (8:5), trumpets (11:19), and bowls (16:18–21). Yet this is true only of 16:18–21; the thunder and earthquake phenomena of 8:5 clearly *introduce* the seven trumpets (8:2–5); the function of the atmospheric and seismic phenomena in 11:19 is ambiguous.

Three motifs are found in 11:19: (1) the opening of the heavenly temple, (2) the sighting of the ark of the covenant within the temple, and (3) the occurrence of atmospheric and seismic phenomena (lightning, rumbling, thunder, earthquake, and heavy hail). The thunder and earthquake motif is clearly epiphanic in significance and further symbolizes the imminence of divine judgment (see *Comment* on 4:5). In 11:19 a further epiphanic motif is used, that of the opening of the heavenly temple. This is comparable to the opening of the heavenly temple in 15:5, which clearly serves to introduce the seven bowls. The opening of a temple door together with other epiphanic signs constitutes a ritual motif pointing to the imminence of a divine epiphany. The *Hymn to Apollo* of Callimachus (ca. 305–240 B.C.) begins outside Apollo's temple with several signs indicating the imminent epiphany of the god, including the quivering laurel, the shaking of the temple, a palm tree nodding, a swan singing, and the temple doors opening by themselves (lines 1–8). For these and other epiphanic signs anticipating the appearance of Apollo, see *Homeric Hymn* 3.403; Apollonius Rhodius *Argonautica* 2.680; *PGM* I.304; III.252–53. This Hellenistic literary motif is discussed by F. Williams, *Callimachus, Hymn to Apollo* (Oxford: Clarendon, 1978) 15–23; K. J. McKay, "Door Magic and the Epiphany Hymn," *CQ* 17 (1967) 184–94; and O. Weinreich, *Religionsgeschichtliche Studien* (Darmstadt: Wissenschaftliche Buchgesellschaft, 1968] 67–74. Within Revelation itself, the motifs of the opening of the heavenly door (see *Comment* on 4:1) and the opening of heaven (see *Comment* on 19:11) both serve to introduce revelatory visions. The Greek version of Esther begins with the narrative of a symbolic dream of Mordecai (LXX Esth 1:1de):

> And this was his dream: Behold, there were sounds and tumult, thunder and an earthquake [φωναὶ καὶ θόρυβος, βρονταὶ καὶ σεισμός], confusion on earth. And behold two great dragons [δράκοντες] came forth, both ready for battle, and their cry was great.

This dream is interpreted at the conclusion of the book (LXX Esth 10:3a–f).

(ii) A second line of argument for understanding 11:19 as the introduction to this pericope is the verbal and structural influences of Isa 66:6–7, which reflect a pattern similar to that in Rev 11:19–12:5a:

> Hark, an uproar from the city!
> A *voice from the temple* [φωνὴ ἐκ ναοῦ]!
> The *voice* of the Lord,
> rendering recompense to his enemies!
> Before she was in labor
> she gave birth;
> before her pain came upon her
> she was delivered of a son [ἔτεκεν ἄρσεν]. (RSV)

If this passage has influenced the composition of Rev 11:19–12:5, which is probable (the phrase ἔτεκεν ἄρσεν has arguably influenced the diction of 12:5; see Lindars, *Apologetic*, 143), the *introductory* function of the temple motif is assured. There is evidence that Isa 66:6–7 was interpreted messianically in Judaism (*Gen. Rab.* 38:1; *Lev. Rab.* 12:2; *Tg. Isa.* 66:7; see Aus, *ZNW* 67 [1976] 256–62) and the early Church (Justin *Dial.* 85.8–9; Ps.-Epiphanius *Test.* 11; Methodius *Sym. et Ann.* 3; *Symp.* 7). This passage can be compared with *Tg. Isa.* 66:6–8, which clearly seems to have a messianic character (tr. Chilton, *Isaiah Targum*, 127):

> A sound of tumult from the city of Jerusalem!
> A *voice from the temple!*
> The *voice* of the Memra of the Lord,
> rendering recompense to his enemies.
> Before distress comes to her
> she shall be delivered;
> and before shaking will come upon her,
> as pains upon a woman in travail,
> her king will be revealed.

First, the epiphanic phenomena are mentioned, followed by the metaphors of labor and birth. Second, the birth of the child is clearly interpreted as the birth of the Messiah.

2. INTRODUCTION OF THE *DRAMATIS PERSONAE:* THE PREGNANT WOMAN AND THE DRAGON (12:1–4A)

In this section the author skillfully introduces the protagonist and the antagonist of this mythological narrative in a parallel manner by presenting them as two astrological signs or constellations. The woman and the dragon are each introduced as a σημεῖον, "constellation," that "appeared in heaven"; each is described using a rich and complex set of traditional symbols. The activity or behavior of each character is then described. The vulnerability of the woman is emphasized by describing her as pregnant and in great pain since she is about to deliver. The aggressive character of the dragon is emphasized by describing him as sweeping stars down from heaven with his tail and casting them down to the earth. Even though the plot is interrupted by the switch in vv 7–9 to the great war in heaven between Michael and his army and the dragon and his army and then to the hymnic commentary on the outcome of this war in vv 10–12, the story is resumed in vv 13–17.

3. THE FIRST STAGE OF CONFLICT: THE BIRTH AND ESCAPE OF THE CHILD AND THE FLIGHT OF THE WOMAN (12:4B–6)

This section consists of three movements: (a) the dragon taking a hostile stance before the woman who is about to give birth to a child, with the express motive of devouring the child immediately upon its birth (v 4b); (b) the birth of the male child (clearly designated as the Messiah through an allusion to Ps 2:9) and its immediate rescue by being snatched up to heaven, to the throne of God (v 5); and (c) the flight of the woman to the wilderness to a place prepared for her by God for 1,260 days (v 6).

4. THE SECOND STAGE OF THE CONFLICT: THE DEFEAT AND EXPULSION OF THE DRAGON FROM HEAVEN (12:7–12)

This section consists of two subsections: (a) the narrative of the heavenly battle between Michael and his angels and the dragon and his angels, resulting in the defeat and expulsion of the dragon and his minions from heaven to the earth (vv 7–9), and (b) the hymnic commentary on the significance of the dragon's expulsion from heaven in the victory hymn in vv 10–12.

The hymnic section in Rev 12:10–12 was added by the author-editor both to supplement and to provide a commentary on the mythic narrative in vv 7–9 (Wellhausen, *Analyse,* 19; Charles, 1:326), which was sandwiched between vv 1–6 and vv 13–17. This section is framed by the mention of Satan's having been cast down to the earth in v 9 ("The great dragon . . . was cast down to the earth"), which is repeated in v 13 ("When the dragon saw that he was cast down to the earth"), thereby framing the insertion in vv 10–12. One of the distinctive features of this section is the abrupt use of the verb ἤκουσα, "I heard," in a text unit in which there are otherwise no first-person verbs, nor is the narrative in 11:19–12:17 presented as a vision in the author's usual vision-report style. Further, vv 10–12 largely consist of a pastiche of reworked phrases that occur with some frequency in other parts of Revelation.

The victory hymn functions in several ways: (i) it gives the significance for the history of salvation of the expulsion of Satan and his minions from heaven; (ii) it explains what Satan was doing in heaven in the first place (v 10); (iii) it mentions a favorite theme of the author's final redactional emphases, the faithfulness of the Christian martyrs (v 11); and (iv) it inserts a warning to the earth and the sea (v 12). See *Comments* on individual verses for elaboration.

The hymn is structured in three strophes. The first strophe (v 10) announces that the salvation, power, and kingship of God have now taken effect, and the reason (provided by the ὅτι clause) is because Satan, who had the role of accusing Christians before God, has been expelled from heaven. The second strophe (v 11) shifts to those who had been accused by Satan, namely Christians. They have been victorious in the sense that they, like the Lamb before them, have died for their testimony. The third strophe exhorts the heavens to rejoice, not because of the death of faithful Christians but because of the expulsion of Satan from heaven. This analysis suggests that the second strophe is a secondary insertion reflecting a very specific interest in the persecution and martyrdom of the faithful (Charles, 1:328).

5. THE THIRD STAGE OF THE CONFLICT: THE DRAGON PURSUES THE WOMAN AND HER OFFSPRING (12:13–17)

The section consists of four subsections. (a) In the first (v 13), the author-editor picks up the threads of the narrative that was interrupted with the insertion of vv 7–12. This is accomplished by causally linking the renewed pursuit of the woman with the dragon's realization that he has been cast down to the earth. (b) In the second subsection (v 14), the focus is on the miraculous rescue of the woman, who is provided by God with the two wings of the great eagle and flies to a special place in the wilderness where she is protected from the serpent (an alias of the dragon used twice in vv 14 and 15) and nourished for a definite but limited period of time. V 14 is essentially a doublet of v 6, though it contains more thoroughly mythological details. Further, v 14 seems out of place, at least chronologically, for in the third subsection (c), the serpent (= dragon) attacks the woman by trying to wash her away with a river of water, which he spews at her from his mouth, only to have the woman rescued by Earth, who swallows the water (vv 15–16). This brief episode would be appropriate *before* the woman reached her sanctuary in the wilderness mentioned in v 14. Otherwise (to keep a generally chronological order), one must suppose that the period of her protection ended in v 14 and that she was again vulnerable to the renewed attack of the serpent (= dragon). (d) The very fact that the dragon does not pursue his attack in the fourth and concluding subsection (v 17) but turns his anger on the offspring of the woman, however, suggests that she has indeed reached her sanctuary in the wilderness and is therefore not subject to further attack.

III. SOURCE-CRITICAL ANALYSIS

Rev 11:19–12:17 is a textual unit that appears to have been composed as an independent, largely self-contained narrative, which was only later adapted to the constraints of a more encompassing narrative structure (Bousset [1906] 356). The compositional history of this passage can be plausibly reconstructed by positing the following stages: (1) The author combined two mythological narratives that he thought complemented one another by inserting vv 7–9 into an existing narrative now found in vv 1–6, 13–17a. (2) The author inserted the hymnic commentary of vv 10 and 12 between v 9 and v 13. (3) The author then linked this composition to the larger narrative structure within which it is now located, connecting it with what precedes by inserting 11:19 and with what follows by inserting 12:18. (4) Perhaps at the same time the author added two further interpolations, those found in vv 11 and 17b. The justification for this analysis is found in the following paragraphs and in greater detail in the *Comment.*

There are a number of distinctive features of Rev 11:19–12:17 that suggest its original independence from its present narrative context: (1) The narrative does not, strictly speaking, exhibit the features characteristic of a vision report. The characteristic phrase "and I saw" is entirely absent, though the phrase "I heard" does occur in v 10, where it is very probably part of a later interpolation. (2) The introduction of the *dramatis personae* in v 1 is unique in Revelation, for the visual character of what follows is expressed by means of the aorist passive verb ὤφθη: "A great sign appeared [ὤφθη] in heaven." This phrase is repeated in v 3 and suggests that the narrative that follows may be a narrative interpretation of one or more constellations (Malina, *Revelation,* 153–62). (3) This unit of text interrupts the chronological progression of the narrative context and obviously involves the description of past events, namely, the birth of the Messiah who was subsequently taken up into heaven (as the language of v 5 makes clear). In fact, this text unit constitutes the kind of explicitly mythological material that some ancient authors thought appropriate for digressions in narratives (Plutarch *De Herodoti malignitate* 855D; Quintilian *Inst.* 4.3.12). There are persuasive arguments that the author has used both Hellenistic and Jewish traditions and sources in composing this chapter. This passage comprises a number of originally independent traditions that have been woven together by the author. (4) Of the two *dramatis personae* introduced in 12:1–4a (the child is a minor player), only the dragon is mentioned subsequently in Revelation, suggesting that the narrative was included primarily because of the prominence of the dragon. (5) The sequence of verb tenses in 11:19–12:17 exhibits some peculiarities. There are forty-seven finite verbs in this section (one perfect, nine presents, including five present indicatives, and thirty-seven aorists); as in most narratives the aorist is the basic tense used. The nine present-tense and the single perfect-tense verbs, however, are used in distinctive ways: (a) In the first subunit of text, 12:1–4a, two main verbs in the present tense are used to describe the two central *dramatis personae,* κράζει (the groaning of the woman in v 2) and σύρει (the sweeping down of the stars by the dragon in v 4a), both historical presents that function to highlight this part of the narrative by making it more vivid. (b) In the next subunit, 12:4b–6, the perfect verb ἕστηκεν, "he stood," is used to foreground the dramatic confrontation between the dragon and the woman. This is followed by a sequence of three present tenses: (i) μέλλει ποιμαίνειν, "who is to rule," describing the future victory of the male child, (ii) ἔχει, "has," used to describe the place of asylum available to the woman, and (iii) τρέφωσιν, "they might nourish," describing the sustenance of the woman in her place of asylum. (c) In the fourth subunit, 12:10–12, two present tenses are used: (i) εὐφραίνεσθε, "rejoice," a present imperative enjoining the heavens and its inhabitants to rejoice at the expulsion of Satan from heaven, and (ii) a corresponding verb ἔχει, "has," used of the recognition on the part of the devil that he has only a limited time to accomplish his evil intentions. (d) Finally, in the fifth subunit of text, 12:13–17, two present-tense verbs occur in v 14, which is a close parallel to v 6: (i) πέτηται, "flies," a present subjunctive verb used of the flight of the woman, and (ii) τρέφεται, "is nourished," used to describe the sustenance of the woman in her place of asylum.

The literary unity of Rev 12 has been a matter of considerable scholarly debate. Rev 12 is often thought to have been based on the combination of two or more sources with the possible addition of several redactional glosses. Two sources have frequently been identified behind Rev 12 (J. Weiss, *Offenbarung*, 87–91; Charles, 1:307): (1) a Jewish myth of the heavenly battle between Michael and the dragon (12:7–9), which appears to have been inserted into (2) a Jewish adaptation of a Greek myth of the woman who bears a child and is attacked by a great red dragon (12:1–6, 13–18). Wellhausen (*Analyse*, 18–19) considers vv 1–6 and vv 7–9, 13–14 as two parallel variants. It is interesting to note that when Hippolytus quotes Rev 12 in *de Ant.* 60, he quotes only vv 1–6 and 13–17, with no interruption between v 6 and v 13, almost as if he had a text of Revelation in which vv 7–12 were missing. It is, of course, possible that he simply omitted vv 7–12 because he recognized their extraneous character.

A. Yarbro Collins has shown how v 14 (in which the threads of the interrupted story are picked up again) has many verbal similarities with v 6 (*Combat Myth*, 102). The following similarities are evident: (1) general direction of flight: the woman flees "into the wilderness," εἰς τὴν ἔρημον (v 6); the woman is given wings and flies "into the wilderness," εἰς τὴν ἔρημον (v 14); (2) specific destination of flight: "where she has a place there [ὅπου ἔχει ἐκεῖ τόπον]" prepared for her by God (v 6); to "her place" (τόπον) in the wilderness (v 14); (3) purpose of flight: there "they will nourish her," ἐκεῖ τρέφωσιν αὐτήν (v 6); "where she will be nourished there," ὅπου τρέφεται ἐκεῖ (v 14); and (4) period of time: for 1,260 days, i.e., three and one-half years (v 6); for a time, times, and half a time, i.e., three and one-half years (v 14). Yarbro Collins describes this repetition as a common redactional device used when returning to the main source (*Combat Myth*, 102) and refers to J. M. Robinson, "The Johannine Trajectory," in *Trajectories through Early Christianity* (Philadelphia: Fortress, 1971) 244: "It would seem to be redactional policy, when splitting up a source in order to interpolate material, that one provide an overlapping or repetitious comment, as if one ought to resume the source with some reference to where one left off." U. C. von Wahlde uses the term "framing repetitions," which he describes as a technique used to resume the original text sequence after an editorial insertion ("A Redactional Technique in the Fourth Gospel," *CBQ* 38 [1976] 520–33). It is better to regard this literary phenomenon, however, as a *resumption* technique used in a variety of ways by Greek writers: (1) to link individual composition units in a paratactic style (cf. H. R. Immerwahr, *Form and Thought in Herodotus* [Cleveland: Western Reserve UP, 1966] 46–78; the origin of this technique in *oral* literature is emphasized by M. L. Lang, *Herodotean Narrative and Discourse* [Cambridge: Harvard UP, 1984] 1–17; R. E. Longacre refers to this narrative device rather awkwardly as "tail-head linkage via recapitulation," in T. A. Van Dijk, ed., *Discourse and Literature* [Amsterdam; Philadelphia: Benjamins, 1985] 171); (2) to link individual books of large compositions (compare Luke 24:36–54 with Acts 1:1–5; see Aune, *New Testament*, 117); (3) to resume the threads of a narrative after inserting a digression (compare Luke 3:21–22 with 4:1; see Aune, *New Testament*, 95); and (4) to interpolate sources.

IV. The Combat Myth and Rev 12

A. Ancient Versions of the Combat Myth

The legendary narrative pattern of a combat between a hero and his adversary or the mythic narrative pattern of a primordial cosmic struggle between two divine beings and their allies for sovereignty was widespread throughout the ancient world. In mythical combats the antagonist is often depicted as a monster, serpent, or dragon. The protagonist typically represents order and fertility, while the antagonist represents chaos and sterility. While the names of the combatants, as well as their roles, change from culture to culture, many of the constituent folklore motifs of the combat myth or legend either remain constant or are subject to a limited range of variation (Aarne-Thompson, *Types,* §§ 300–359, "The Ogre [Giant, Dragon, Devil, Cobold, etc.] is Defeated"). Some scholars have assumed that the common pattern exhibited by many combat myths suggests a unitary origin (Fontenrose, *Python,* 2–3). This "historical-geographical method," developed by the Finnish school of folklore, maintains that common patterns when correlated with geographical distribution provide clues in the quest for the archetypal version. More recently there has been a tendency in folklore studies to abandon the quest for the chimerical prototypical version (Brunvand, *Folklore,* 15–16; cf. C. Lévi-Strauss' view that a myth consists of all its versions: "The Structural Study of Myth," in *Myth: A Symposium,* ed. T. A. Sebeok [Bloomington: Indiana UP, 1958] 81–106). In Babylon the protagonist and antagonist were Marduk and Tiamat or Gilgamesh and Humbaba; in Canaan, Baal and Yamm (Sea) or Baal and Mot (Death); in Egypt Osiris and Set (or Typhon) or Rê (the Sun), to whom Pharaoh was assimilated, and Apophis (the serpent representing night). The Greek world knew many versions of the combat myth, often narrated as a succession myth: Ouranos and Kronos; Zeus and Kronos; Zeus and the Titans (the Titanomachy; Nonnos *Dionysiaca* 12.29–32); and Zeus and the Giants (the Gigantomachy; they reportedly had serpentine extremities; see Apollodorus 1.6.1–2). Otus and Ephialtes, giant sons of Zeus, tried to ascend to heaven (εἰς οὐρανὸν ἀναβήσεται) but were repulsed by Artemis (Apollodorus 1.7.4). Other Greek variants included Zeus and Typhoeus (Hesiod *Theog.* 820–68), Bellerophon and the Chimaera (Apollodorus 2.3.1–2), Helios and Phaethon (particularly important for Rev 12), and the Apollo and Python myth (cf. Fontenrose, *Python*). Satan becomes the chief adversary only in early Jewish apocalyptic literature and in the NT (1 Pet 5:8), though never in the OT (though in 1 Chr 21:1–17 he ceases to be a subordinate of Yahweh and becomes an independent instigator).

Various versions of the combat myth were adopted from other cultures and adapted to Israelite-Jewish traditions at various times and places throughout the history of Judaism. Canaanite myths of the struggle between Baal and Yamm or Mot (understood as a *Chaoskampf,* a struggle against chaos) were causally connected with creation (Pss 74:12–17; 89:9–14[MT 10–15]; Job 26; cf. Ps 104:6–9; Prov 8:29; Job 38:8–11; Day, *Conflict,* 1–61). In Israelite poetry these conflicts were transposed into stories of Yahweh's conquest of Rahab and Leviathan (Pss 74:13–14; 89:9–10; Job 7:12). While the name "Rahab" has not been found in any extrabiblical text, the Hebrew term לויתן *liwyātān,* "Leviathan," is related to the Ugaritic term for dragon, *ltn* (see Emerton, *VT* 32 [1982] 327–33). In Isaiah and Ezekiel, language from the cosmic rebellion aspect of the combat myth was used metaphorically to describe Israel's historical enemies (Isa 14:10b–15; Ezek 28:1–9; cf. Day, *Conflict,* 88–140; Eliade, *Sacred,* 47–50). Egypt or its pharaoh was designated as the primordial dragon Rahab (Isa 30:7; 51:9–10; Ps 87:4) or the dragon Tannin (Ezek 29:3–5; 32:2–8; probably also Isa 27:1). The application of language drawn from the primordial cosmic rebellion myths to the historical enemies of Israel is based on the perception of the paradigmatic character of the original conflict. Israel's memory of Egypt as an oppressor, coupled with the divine delivery through water that constituted the Exodus (cf. Isa 51:9–11; Exod 15:1–8), provided the link that made it possible to describe the historical conflict in mythical terms. The sea and rivers were used as metaphors for Assyria (Isa 17:12–14; 8:5–8) and Babylon (Hab 3:8–10, 15). Babylon was also designated as a *tannin* or sea monster (Jer 51:34). Further, the cosmic waters are probably a designation of hostile nations in general (Pss 18:5–18; 46:3–4; 144:5–7). God was expected to do to Israel's current historical enemies what he once did in the distant past to his mythological enemies. In some proto-apocalyptic texts such as Isa 27:1, God is expected to repeat in the *future* his primordial victories of the past: "In that day the Lord with his hard and great and strong sword will punish Leviathan the fleeing serpent, and he will slay the dragon that is in the sea." Such texts show the way in which *eschatological* combat myths were developed out of *protological* combat myths. In Dan 7, the four beasts from the sea represent Babylon, Media, Persia, and Greece; these beasts are conquered by divine intervention (v 12), with the introduction of an everlasting kingdom represented by the manlike figure in vv 13–14.

B. Jewish Versions of the Combat Myth

Jewish apocalyptic literature, which depicted the end time largely in terms of conflicts and judgments, reflects a renaissance of ancient mythic narratives, of which one of the more important was the combat myth. One of the primary functions of this myth was to ascribe the experience of suffering and evil in the world to an independent cosmic adversary, Satan. Satan is the primary adversary (variously conceived as a rebel, tempter, or tyrant) in early Judaism and early Christianity; his name suggests that his primary role is that of opposition (the Hebrew term *śāṭān* means "adversary," and the Greek term *diabolos* means "slanderer"). He also was known by many other aliases, including Beliar, Beelzebul, Abaddon, Apollyon, Lucifer, Sammael, Semihazeh, Asael, and the devil. The author of Revelation was particularly concerned to list several of Satan's aliases so there could be no doubt in the reader's mind that a *single* familiar cosmic adversary was involved. In Rev 12:9, for example, five aliases are listed: the great dragon, the ancient serpent, the devil, Satan, and the deceiver of the whole world.

In apocalyptic literature, imagery drawn from primordial combat stories is no longer limited to poetic metaphor but is used as a means of describing real events of the past or future. Gen 6:1–4 in particular was reinterpreted as a cosmic rebellion myth in the Enoch literature and thereafter became an essential part of early Jewish apocalyptic tradition. In *1 Enoch* 6–11 (perhaps dependent on the parallel myth in Hesiod's *Eoiae* frag. B.3–34), two hundred "Watchers" (angelic beings [cf. Dan 4:17], who function as a kind of cosmic security force), led by Semihazeh, rebel against God by lusting after mortal women, who conceive giants and bring evil to the earth. Azazel (the name of the fallen angelic chief in an originally independent version; cf. Nickelsburg, *JBL* 96 [1977] 384–99), who comes to the fore as a leader of the Watchers, is bound hand and foot and thrown into a fissure in the earth where he is to be confined in darkness until the great day of judgment when he will be cast into fire (*1 Enoch* 10:1–6; similarities with the Prometheus myth reflected in Hesiod *Theog.* 507–616, *Works and Days* 42–105, and Aeschylus *Prometheus Bound* suggest dependence on Greek sources; cf. Nickelsburg, *JBL* 96 [1977] 399–404). The initial binding of Azazel coincides with the judgment of the flood (*1 Enoch* 10:2). In the parallel story, Semihazeh and the rest of the Watchers are bound and confined under the hills of the earth until the day of judgment, when they will be cast into the abyss of fire (*1 Enoch* 10:11–14). After this, a period of perpetual righteousness and peace will dawn upon the earth (*1 Enoch* 10:16–11:2).

In *Jubilees* the chief of the fallen angels is called Mastema (formed from the Hebrew stem שׂטם *śṭm,* "animosity," etymologically related to שׂטן *śāṭān,* "adversary"). The author, explicitly dependent on the Enoch literature (*Jub.* 21:10) as well as on Genesis, narrates how God caused the sons of the Watchers to destroy each other, after which the rebellious angels themselves were bound and confined beneath the earth "forever," i.e., until the day of judgment (*Jub.* 5:6–11). The judgment of the Watchers apparently serves as a prototype of the coming judgment (Davenport, *Jubilees,* 73), though the phrase "until the day of judgment" (*Jub.* 4:19; 10:17, 22) is a stereotyped expression emphasizing temporal limits rather than eschatological expectation (Davenport, *Jubilees,* 83–87). The reference to the coming judgment with "fire and sword" (*Jub.* 9:15) suggests an eschatological combat but provides no details. After the flood the demonic offspring of the giants corrupt humanity (*Jub.* 10:1–3); nine-tenths are bound until the day of judgment with one-tenth active on the earth and subject to Satan, an alias of Mastema (*Jub.* 10:11), who is also called Beliar (in the phrase "sons of Beliar," *Jub.* 1:20; 16:33). In both *1 Enoch* 1–36 and *Jubilees,* the rebellion motif is an integral part of the combat myth. In both, the rebellious angels are conquered and confined by God until the last judgment. The primary function of these myths is to account for the origin of evil in the world. There is no hint that an eschatological conflict will take place between God and his rebellious angels; eschatology, indeed, plays very little role in *1 Enoch* 1–36; cf. *1 Enoch* 10:12–11:2; 16:1; 19:1; 25:4 (Newsom, *CBQ* 42 [1980] 311).

C. The Combat Myth in Rev 12

In the specifically Christian version of the combat myth, an exalted angelic being challenged the power of Yahweh and now has control of the earth. Christ functions as the divine warrior who, though Satan attempts to defeat him (cf. Luke 22:3, "Then Satan entered into Judas") through his crucifixion, has freed humanity from the tyranny of Satan, though his final banishment has yet to take place. According to Aulén (*Christus Victor,* 4), the classic idea of the atonement is based on divine conflict and victory. Christ fights against all the evil powers in the world under whom human beings were in bondage and suffering, and decisively triumphs over them, thereby reconciling the world to himself.

The presence of the combat myth in Revelation, particularly Rev 12, has been discussed by a number of scholars who have proposed that various myths from particular ancient cultures were somehow incorporated into Rev 12. H. Gunkel thought that Rev 12 reflected the Babylonian combat myth centering on the conflict between Damkina, with her son Marduk, and Tiamat (*Schöpfung und Chaos,* 171–398, esp. 379–98). A. Dieterich thought that a version of the Greek combat myth involving Apollo-Leto-Python was most persuasive (*Abraxas,* 117–22; cf. Prigent, *Apocalypse 12,* 120–21). W. Bousset was struck with the similarities among several variants of the Isis-Osiris-Horus-Typhon myth in Egyptian sources ([1906] 350–56). There are a number of important issues that need to be raised in this quest for the oral and literary traditions that have influenced Rev 12: (1) Is it reasonable to suppose that the author would have used pagan traditions in addition to OT-Jewish traditions in the composition of Rev 12, either directly or mediated through Hellenistic Judaism? (2) Are the parallels between Rev 12 and pagan myths phenomenological, or are there genetic, historical links indicating that the author has actually borrowed from pagan sources? (3) Did the author base his narrative in Rev 12 on a single coherent myth (the view of Yarbro Collins), or did he create a pastiche based on a variety of ancient mythical traditions?

1. POSSIBLE GREEK SOURCES

Recently this discussion has been advanced in important respects by J. Fontenrose, W. K. Hedrick, and A. Yarbro Collins. Fontenrose (*Python,* 210) observed that the combat myth in Rev 12 closely resembled his "version D" of the Python myth. According to that version, found in Lucan (*Bell.* 5.79–81), Lucian (*Dial. mar.* 9; cf. *Saltatio* 38), and Hyginus (*Fabulae* 140), Hera commanded Python to pursue the pregnant Leto and destroy her with her unborn children. With Poseidon's help, Leto found refuge on Delos, and after the twins Apollo and Artemis were delivered, Apollo killed Python at Delphi. The most complete form of this myth is found in Hyginus, who wrote before A.D. 207 and whose work was subsequently epitomized (tr. Grant, *Hyginus,* 115–16, with equivalent Greek names or Latin words inserted in brackets):

> Python, offspring of Terra, was a huge dragon [*draco*] who, before the time of Apollo, used to give oracular responses on Mount Parnassus. Death was fated to come to him from the offspring of Latona [Leto]. At that time Jove [Zeus] lay with Latona, daughter of Polus [Coeus]. When Juno [Hera] found this out, she decreed (?) that Latona should give birth at a place where the sun did not shine. When Python knew that Latona was pregnant by Jove, he followed her to kill her. But by order of Jove the wind Aquilo [Boreas] carried Latona away, and bore her to Neptune [Poseidon]. He protected her, but in order not to make void Juno's decree, he took her to the island Ortygia, and covered the island with waves. When Python did not find her, he returned to Parnassus. But Neptune brought the island of Ortygia up to a higher position; it was later called the island of Delos. There Latona, clinging to an olive tree, bore Apollo and Diana [Artemis], to whom Vulcan [Hephaestus] gave arrows as gifts. Four days after they were born, Apollo exacted vengeance for his mother. For he went to Parnassus and slew Python with his arrows. (Because of this deed he is called Pythian.) He put Python's bones in a caldron, deposited them in his temple, and instituted the funeral games for him which are called Pythian.

Yarbro Collins (*Combat Myth,* 58) argues that the combat myth in Rev 12 reflects combat traditions from both the Near East (12:7–9) and Hellenism (12:4b–6, 13–

17) and demonstrates that the Python-Leto-Apollo myth was well known in western Anatolia prior to the end of the first century A.D. (*Combat Myth,* 245–61). Saffrey even speculated (with no evidence) that there was a distinctive form of the myth of the birth of Apollo and Artemis on the Island of Patmos, where John may have become familiar with it (*RB* 82 [1975] 410–17). Yarbro Collins (*Combat Myth,* 61), closely following the Greek form of the myth proposed by Fontenrose (*Python,* 262–64), lists eight constituent motifs of the combat myth in Rev 12:

A. The dragon (v 3)
B. Chaos and disorder (v 4a)
C. The attack (v 4b)
D. The champion (v 5a)
E. The champion's "death" (v 5b)
G. Recovery of the champion (v 7a)
H. Battle renewed and victory (vv 7b–9)
I. Restoration and confirmation of order (vv 10–12a)
F. The dragon's reign (vv 12b–17)

She then summarizes the version of the Leto-Apollo myth found in Hyginus *Fabulae* 140 (*Combat Myth,* 66):

1. Reason for Python's attack: possession of oracle
2. Zeus impregnates Leto
3. Python pursues Leto to kill her
4.a. Zeus orders north wind to rescue Leto
4.b. Poseidon aids Leto
5. Birth of Apollo and Artemis
6. Apollo defeats Python
7. Apollo establishes Pythian games

Yarbro Collins then provides a brief analysis of similar motifs in Rev 12 that match (by number) the list above (*Combat Myth,* 66):

2. A woman on the point of giving birth (v 2)
3. A dragon intends to devour the child (v 4)
5. Birth of the child (v 5)
7. Kingship of the child (v 5)
4.a. Woman is aided by God (v 6)
4.b. Woman is aided by the great eagle (v 14)
4.c. Woman is aided by the earth (v 16)
6. Michael defeats the dragon (vv 7–9)

There are some flaws in Yarbro Collins' analysis of Rev 12, however, that need to be pointed out: (1) Rev 12 does not end with the defeat of the dragon (his final defeat is not mentioned until Rev 20:12). (2) The woman flees not to an island but to the wilderness. (3) In Rev 12, the woman gives birth *before* she flees, not after. (4) In the Apollo-Leto-Python myth, the motivation for Python to pursue Leto is to prevent the birth of her twins (Gollinger, "*Zeichen,*" 130); in Rev 12 there is no obvious motivation for the dragon to pursue the woman *after* she has given birth and *after* her child has been snatched away to heaven. In the Isis-Typhon myth, on the other hand, Typhon pursues Isis and her son Horus *after* she has given birth.

(5) The designation of the child as the "champion" is hardly appropriate in a narrative in which he plays merely a cameo role (the reference to Ps 2:9 is clearly a later christological interpolation). (6) Similarly, to speak of the "death" of the champion is also inappropriate, for the child was in fact "rescued" by God (*passivum divinum*) by being snatched up to heaven. Taken together, these criticisms suggest that the author has not used a coherent pagan myth; rather he has created a pastiche of mythological motifs.

2. POSSIBLE EGYPTIAN SOURCES

The Apollo-Leto-Python story, however, is not the only myth that scholars have thought might lie behind the myth in Rev 12. Bousset was equally impressed with the Isis-Osiris-Typhon myth ([1906] 353–55), which is particularly interesting because of the *interpretatio Graecae,* which made the following equations: Leto = Isis or Leto = Uto (Herodotus 2.59, 152, 155; A. B. Lloyd, *Herodotus, Book II* [Leiden: Brill, 1994] 270); Dionysus = Osiris; Typhon (in metathesized form, "Python") = Seth; Apollo = Horus.

The myth of Isis-Osiris-Horus-Typhon is preserved primarily in Plutarch *De Iside* 355D–358F (and passim), with a much shorter version containing a few variants in Diodorus 1.21–22; 1.88.4–7. Egyptian sources contain no connected account of this myth, though various episodes appear in Pyramid Texts and in the Memphite Theology from the third millennium B.C. (H. Frankfort, *Ancient Egyptian Religion* [New York: Columbia UP, 1948] 126–28). Myths and legends are rarely written down in anything like complete form since such stories were known by everyone and referred to in a variety of situations. "This means that stories were usually referred to or told only in an abbreviated form—everybody knew what they were all about" (R. Kvideland and H. K. Sehmsdorf, eds., *Scandinavian Folk Belief and Legend* [Minneapolis: University of Minnesota, 1988] 14). Like combat myths generally, and the myth in Rev 12 particularly, the conflict turns on the question of cosmic sovereignty. Through trickery, Typhon nailed Osiris the king of Egypt into a coffin, which was dumped into the Nile, thereby killing Osiris. Isis wandered everywhere in her grief trying to locate the coffin, which she eventually found at Byblos and transported to Buto (where the island of Chebt is found in a lake near the temple at Buto). At this point Plutarch omits mention of the sexual intercourse Isis had with the deceased Osiris, which produced Horus/Harpocrates (358E; cf. Hani, *La religion Égyptienne,* 80–83). Though Isis hid the coffin, Typhon discovered it and divided the body of Osiris into fourteen parts (or twenty-six parts; cf. Diodorus 1.21.2), scattering them in various places (which, according to Plutarch, accounts for the numerous tombs of Osiris). Isis found and assembled all of the body parts with the exception of the phallus, for which she substituted a prosthesis. Horus, Isis' son, who was raised by Leto at Buto (358F; 366A), conquered Typhon and turned him over to Isis bound in chains. Isis, however, released him rather than execute him (358D). Horus then snatched the crown from Isis and became king. Many motifs in this story have striking parallels in the myth of Demeter and Persephone preserved in *Homeric Hymn to Demeter,* and while many scholars have assumed Egyptian dependence on the Greek myth, the Greek version is probably dependent on the Egyptian (Burkert, *Ancient Mystery Cults,* 20–21).

The version of this myth found in Plutarch and Diodorus says nothing about Typhon pursuing Isis and her child, and therefore appears to be at best a distant parallel to Rev 12. While Yarbro Collins succinctly summarizes the possible Egyptian parallels to Rev 12 (*Combat Myth,* 62–63), she says very little about the version of the myth that impressed Bousset. Though the version of the Isis-Osiris-Typhon myth summarized by Bousset is derived from H. Brugsch, *Religion und Mythologie der alten Ägypter,* 2nd ed. (Leipzig: Hinrichs, 1891), Bousset actually drew his information from three sources: Herodotus, an Osiris hymn, and the Metternich Stele. Let us first consider the version of the myth preserved in Herodotus 2.156 (LCL tr.):

> The story told by the Egyptians who show why the island [Chemmis] moves is this: when Typhon [Seth] came seeking through the world for the son of Osiris, Leto [Isis], being one of the eight earliest gods, and dwelling in Buto where this oracle of hers is, received Apollo [Horus] in charge from Isis and hid him for safety in this island which was before immovable but is now said to float. Apollo and Artemis were (they say) children of Dionysus [Osiris] and Isis, and Leto was made their nurse and preserver; in Egyptian, Apollo is Horus, Demeter Isis, Artemis Bubastis.

In the Greek myth of Apollo-Leto-Python, Leto flees to the island of Delos, which, like Chemmis, was believed to be a floating island (Hecataeus *FrGrHist* 1.20, frag. 284, mentions the floating island Chemmis, which he spells Χέμβις, "Chembis," which is closer to the Egyptian "Chebt" than to Herodotus' spelling). According to some strands of Greek tradition, Delos was thought to be a floating island before the birth of Apollo (*Homeric Hymn to Demeter* 73–75; Pindar frag. 87–88 [LCL tr., 562]; Callimachus *Hymni* 4.35–38) and thereafter became fixed—just the reverse of Chemmis, which though once fixed was later thought to float, according to Herodotus. This mythic episode appears to fit into the account of Plutarch, where there is an obvious lacuna at the point where he passes over the impregnation of Isis by the deceased Osiris (Plutarch *De Iside* 357F, i.e., between chap. 17 and chap. 18). Bousset also quotes a relevant portion of an Osiris hymn from the Eighteenth Dynasty, ca. 1500 B.C., which supplies another episode, logically following the one just quoted, dealing with the impregnation of Isis and secret birth of Horus (cited here from the translation in Budge, *Osiris* 1:94):

> Isis the magician avenged her brother [i.e., Osiris]. She went about seeking him untiringly. She flew round and round over the earth uttering wailing cries of grief, and she did not alight on the ground until she had found him. She made light [to appear] from her feathers, she made air to come into being by means of her two wings, and she cried out the death cries for her brother. She made to rise up the helpless members of him whose heart was at rest, she drew from him his essence, and she made therefrom an heir. She suckled the child in solitariness, and none knew where his place was, and he grew in strength, and his arm increased in strength in the House of Keb (i.e., the earth).

(The entire hymn is found in both text and translation in Budge, *Gods* 2:148–52.) Egyptian wall paintings often depict Isis suckling Horus concealed by the papyrus plants of the island, analogous to later Christian paintings and sculptures of the Madonna and child. The Metternich Stele (inscribed ca. 350 B.C.) narrates how Isis escaped to the city of Buto (Pe-Tep) in the Delta after Seth had shut her up in a building (a translation of the relevant parts of this stele is found in Budge, *Gods* 2:205–12; the text with a literal translation is found in 2:222–40). There she gave birth to Horus and raised him secretly, unknown to anyone. While away one day, Horus was killed by a scorpion. As a result of the grief of Isis, her sister Nephthys appealed to Thoth, who provided Isis with the magic to restore Horus to life (Budge, *Osiris,* 95–96).

Perhaps the chief difficulty with Bousset's proposal is that the only version of this myth current in the Greek world (so far as we know) is the truncated version found in Herodotus 2.156. There is no evidence that this mythical episode was in circulation during the first century A.D. Nevertheless, there are parallels between these versions of the Isis-Typhon myth and Rev 12 not found in the Apollo-Leto-Python myth, such as the fact that Isis (like the woman in Rev 12:14) is depicted as having two wings.

3. A POSSIBLE GNOSTIC SOURCE

J. M. Robinson ("*Gattung,*" 119–24) called attention to the similarities that exist between part of the Coptic Gnostic *Apocalypse of Adam* and the myth in Rev 12 (critiqued by Hedrick, "Sources," 158–65, and Yarbro Collins, *Combat Myth,* 69–70). The relevant section describes fourteen statements about the gnostic redeemer; the first thirteen statements describe thirteen "kingdoms," and the last describes a kingless race (*Apoc. Adam* 77.26–83.4). These "kingdoms" are all apparently arranged in chronological succession. Each of these "kingdoms" involves the coming of the Illuminator (probably Seth), expressed through various mythological or folkloristic traditions (cf. Rudolf, *Gnosis,* 135–38). The only correct view, however, is that of the kingless race. A selected quotation from *Apoc. Adam* 78.6–26 will suggest the character of this scheme (J. M. Robinson, *Nag Hammadi,* 283):

> And the second kingdom says about him that he came from a great prophet. And a bird came, took the child who was born and brought him onto a high mountain. And he was nourished by the bird of heaven. An angel came forth there. He said to him, "Arise! God has given glory to you." He received glory and strength. And thus he came to the water.
>
> The third kingdom says of him that he came from a virgin womb. He was cast out of his city, he and his mother; he was brought to a desert place. He was nourished there. He came and received glory and power. And thus he came to the water.

While some of the thirteen mythic schemes have some similarities with Rev 12 (e.g., pregnancy, birth, removal to an isolated region, divinely arranged nourishment—but of the child, not the mother, as in Rev 12:14—see Yarbro Collins, *Combat Myth,* 69), there is no trace of the combat myth in any of them.

V. A FORMALIST ANALYSIS OF REV 11:19–12:17

Regardless of the sources that lie behind Rev 11:19–12:17, and irrespective of some of the awkward features of the final form of the text, it is nevertheless important that the *structure* of the passage be carefully analyzed. Rev 11:19–12:17 is one of the few textual units within Revelation that preserve a patently mythological narrative (comparable to the story of the two witnesses in 11:4–13). In view of the many folkloristic features of Rev 11:19–12:17, it seems appropriate to borrow the methodology of folklore studies to see if some further light might be shed on the structure of this passage. The following formal analysis of the surface structure of this unit of text has been guided by the programmatic work of the Russian formalist V. Propp, who analyzed one hundred Russian fairy tales (a subgenre of folk tales also called *Märchen*) by focusing on the identification of the *functions* of the *dramatis personae* in the surface structure of folk tales rather than on the identification of themes and motifs. Propp's method has been applied to some OT texts, such as Gen 32:23–33, Ruth, Tobit, and the "Court Tales" in Dan 1–6 (Milne, *Propp,* 125–75, 179–265). Propp has enumerated thirty-one such functions, *which always occur in the same temporal sequence* (Propp, *Semeia* 10 [1978] 74), though all of the functions are rarely present in every folk tale. He regarded these thirty-one functions as the morphological foundations of fairy tales in general (Propp, *Morphology,* 25; these are explained by Milne, *Propp,* 75–88). A. Dundes sought to replace the problematic term "function" with the term "motifeme" ("From Etic to Emic Units in the Structural Study of Folktales," *JAF* 75 [1962] 95–105; id., *Morphology of North American Indian Folktales* [Helsinki: Suomalainen Tiedeakatemia Academia Scientiarum Fennica, 1964]). Propp identified the basic compositional scheme common to the entire corpus of folk tales that he analyzed. From this scheme individual plots were constructed. Propp judged some functions more important than others, such as function 8 (A), *villainy,* or 8a (a), *lack,* with which the complication of the plot begins (Propp, *Morphology,* 62). The following analysis of Rev 12 attempts to identify the formal functions of the narrative by specifying the number and name of each function (discussed in Propp, *Morphology,* 25–65) together with Propp's abbreviations (listed in Propp, *Morphology,* 149–55).

In Propp's terms, 12:1–4a constitutes the *initial situation* (= α), in which the two major *dramatis personae,* the woman and the dragon, are introduced. The woman (vv 1–2) has three attributes (Propp, *Morphology,* 88): (1) she is located in heaven, (2) her description indicates that she is a female and suggests that she is a cosmic sovereign (she is clothed with the sun; she has the moon beneath her feet; she wears a wreath of twelve stars), and (3) she is vulnerable because she cries out in pain and is on the point of giving birth. The woman is clearly the *hero,* for her child makes only a very brief appearance and then leaves the story (v 5). Yet she is a *victim-hero* (rather than a seeker-hero) since she is entirely a passive figure; the actions of the story occur around her and happen to her. The dragon is then introduced (vv 3–4a), and he too has three attributes: (1) he is in heaven, (2) he is depicted as a sovereign, for he has seven heads and ten horns with a diadem on each head, and (3) he is a victorious cosmic warrior, for he has cast a third of the stars of heaven down to the earth. The dragon is clearly the *villain,* who characteristically makes two appearances in folk tales (Propp, *Morphology,* 84). The first is sudden and from outside (v 4a), while his second appearance is as one who is sought out when he is attacked in heaven by Michael and his angels (vv 7–9).

The dragon is alerted by the outcry of the woman (v 2), for her cries notify him of her condition (No. 5: *delivery* = ζ). He then confronts the woman (No. 8: *villainy* = A). Their conflict clearly centers on the child who is about to be born. Since the child is as yet unborn, this corresponds to No. 8a: *lack* of an individual (= a^1). The outcry of the woman (No. 9: *mediation* = B) is the means whereby the lack is made known. For the woman the child is the royal heir, and his ability to conquer is the basis upon which the hope of future sovereignty rests. This is made explicit by a direct allusion to Ps 2:9, "Who will drive all the nations with an iron crook." The dragon is motivated by the desire to swallow the child (No. 8: *villainy* = A), suggesting that he regards the child as a potential threat to his rule and feels the need to eliminate him (see Propp, *Morphology*, 76: "The actions of a Dragon and of very many other villains are not in any way motivated by the tale"). However, the child is caught up to God and to his throne, v 5 (No. 15: 11: *departure*), which indicates that the woman is in fact successful in her confrontation with the dragon. This implies that God is the father of the child, and the mention of the throne suggests that the coronation of the child has occurred (No. 19: *lack liquidated* = K).

The scene abruptly shifts to heaven, the new location of the child, where Michael and his angels are introduced as magical agents or helpers (No. 14: *magical agent* = F). They fight against the dragon, who has apparently pursued the child (No. 16: *struggle*, they fight in an open field = H^1). This fight must be understood as a struggle by proxy. The dragon is defeated (No. 18: *victory:* villain beaten in open combat = I^1) and cast down to Earth. The accompanying song of victory in 12:10–12 indicates that the dragon's downfall means that salvation, power, and kingship have been placed into the hands of God and authority into the hands of Christ (No. 19: *lack liquidated*, object of quest obtained as result of preceding actions = K^4). However, this has some mysterious connection with Christians on earth who have died for their faith (v 11).

When the dragon finds himself thrown down to Earth, he pursues the woman (No. 21: *pursuit*, pursuer attempts to kill hero = Pr^6). But the woman is magically provided with the two wings of an eagle (No. 22: *rescue*, is carried through the air = Rs^1). She flees to the wilderness to a place prepared (No. 22: *rescue*, fleeing with concealment of escapee = Rs^4). The dragon then attempts to inundate her with a flood of water he spews out of his mouth (No. 21: *pursuit*, pursuer attempts to kill hero = Pr^6). Thereupon the woman is rescued by Earth (No. 22: *rescue*, rescue or salvation from being destroyed = R^8), who opens her mouth to swallow the water. The dragon, angry at the woman, turns to pursue the rest of her offspring (No. 21: *pursuit*, pursuer attempts to kill surrogates of hero = Pr^6). Since Rev 12 ends before the story has been satisfactorily concluded, it must be regarded as the first "move," with other moves to follow. Several functions can serve to terminate a "move," such as a reward (F), liquidation of lack (K), or an escape (Rs) (Propp, *Morphology*, 92). In that respect, the first move ends with 12:16, in which Earth rescues the woman. Rev 13 narrates the appearance of two creatures, the beast from the sea (13:1–10) and the beast from the land (13:11–18) (No. 24: *claims of a false hero* = L).

Comment

19a καὶ ἠνοίγη ὁ ναὸς τοῦ θεοῦ ὁ ἐν τῷ οὐρανῷ, "Then the temple of God in heaven opened." Temple doors that opened by themselves were considered a prodigy in the ancient world (Xenophon *Hellenica* 6.4.7; Tacitus *Hist.* 5.13; Cassius Dio 66[64].8.2; see *Excursus 6A: Ancient Prodigies and the Plagues of Revelation*). There is a parallel to Rev 11:19 in Vergil *Aeneid* 3.90–96 (tr. Copeley, *Vergil*):

> Scarce had I spoken when suddenly all things shook, the temple, the sacred laurel; the whole hill moved around us. The shrine sprang open; the tripod clanged. As we fell prostrate, a voice came to our ears: "Oh Dardans! Hardy men! The land that first gave you and your fathers birth, with wealth and joy will take you back. Look for your ancient mother."

According to the tradition in *b. Yoma* 39b, forty years before the destruction of the temple the doors of the temple (הֵיכָל *hêkāl*) would open by themselves until they were rebuked by R. Johanan ben Zakkai. This kind of prodigy has been influenced by similar phenomena in the Greco-Roman world.

19b καὶ ὤφθη ἡ κιβωτὸς τῆς διαθήκης αὐτοῦ ἐν τῷ ναῷ αὐτοῦ, "and his ark of the covenant appeared in his temple." The presence of the ark of the covenant in the heavenly temple implies that it is the "true" ark, which served as an archetype for the construction of the ark housed in the earthly tabernacle and temple (cf. Exod 25:9, 40; 26:30; 27:8; 1 Chr 28:19; Wis 9:8; Acts 7:44; Heb 8:1–5; 9:24; *b. Hag.* 12b; *Gen. Rab.* 55.7; *Midr. Cant.* 4:4; Str-B, 3:702–4; Winston, *Wisdom,* 203–5). This is the only explicit reference in early Jewish and early Christian literature to a heavenly ark of the covenant, though "throne" can be used in a way corresponding to the earthly ark as in Jer 17:12, "A glorious throne set on high from the beginning is the place of our sanctuary." That the earthly temple corresponds to the heavenly throne is made explicit in *Tg. Ps.-J.* Exod 15:17 (tr. Maher, in McNamara et al., *Tg. Ps.-J.: Exodus*), "You have established, O Lord, a place that corresponds to the throne of your Glory, made ready opposite the dwelling place of your holy Shekinah."

The syntax is unclear here, for it is uncertain whether the possessive pronoun αὐτοῦ modifies the entire noun phrase ἡ κιβωτὸς τῆς διαθήκης, "the ark of the covenant," or just the preceding noun τῆς διαθήκης, "the covenant." Thus the phrase ἡ κιβωτὸς τῆς διαθήκης αὐτοῦ can be translated as "his ark of the covenant," as I have done here (see Seow, "Ark," *ABD* 1:393), or as "the ark of his covenant" (all major English versions: RSV; NRSV; NEB; REB; NIV; KJV, "ark of his testament"). In favor of the second translation is the frequency of the occurrence of the phrases "his [i.e., 'God's'] covenant" and "my [i.e., 'God's'] covenant" in the OT (e.g., Exod 2:24; Deut 4:13; 7:9, 12; 2 Kgs 13:23; 1 Chr 16:15; Ps 25:10, 14; Ezek 17:14; Dan 9:4), though they occur rarely in early Christian texts (Luke 1:72; *1 Clem.* 15:6; *Barn.* 9:41). Against this translation is the lack of emphasis on the διαθήκη or "covenant" here, the only place the word occurs in Revelation, making it more likely that it is the entire sacred object, "the ark of the covenant," that is modified by the personal pronoun "his." Supporting this translation is the occurrence of phrases such as "the ark of God" and "the ark of Yahweh" some eighty-two times in the OT indicating divine ownership and possession (Seow, *ABD* 1:387). The fuller expressions, such as "the ark of the covenant of Yahweh" and "the ark of the covenant of God," occur thirty times in the OT (e.g., Num 10:33; 14:44; Deut 10:8; 31:9; Josh 3:3; 4:7; 6:6; 1 Sam 4:3; 1 Kgs 3:15; 1 Chr 15:25–26; 2 Chr 5:7), and in all instances the term "covenant" seems to define "ark," meaning that possessive phrases such as "of Yahweh" and "of God" modify the entire phrase "the ark of the covenant" (Seow, *ABD* 1:387). In the NT, the ark of the covenant is mentioned only in Rev 11:19 and Heb 9:4.

In early Jewish literature, however, the ark is *never* mentioned as part of the sacred furnishings of the heavenly temple (though, as mentioned above, the throne could serve as a heavenly counterpart to the ark). In the list of the temple furnishings and vessels broken and carried to Babylon, the ark is conspicuous by its absence (2 Kgs 25:13–17; Jer 52:17–23). Yet in 4 Ezra 10:22 the plundering of the ark of the covenant is lamented by "Ezra," and *T. Moses* 3:2 explicitly mentions that the holy vessels were carried off (alluding to 2 Kgs 25:13–17 and Jer 52:17–23). There was some eschatological speculation in early Judaism that the temple vessels, including the ark, would be restored in the eschaton. Most of these speculations are part of the Jeremiah-Baruch tradition (see Wolff, *Jeremia,* 16–17, 20–26, 61–71), which maintains that the temple furnishings were *not* carried off by the Babylonians but were hidden locally until the end time by Jeremiah (2 Macc 2:4–8; *Par. Jer.* 3:8–11; *Vit. Proph.* 2.11–19) or angels (*2 Apoc. Bar.* 6:5–9); see Kalimi-Purvis, *CBQ* 56 [1994] 679–85. The Jeremiah legend was also preserved by Alexander Polyhistor, a first-century B.C. historian (preserved in Eusebius *Praep. evang.* 9.39; *FrGrHist* 723, F 5); he probably derived his version from the Jewish historian Eupolemus frag. 4, though according to this account Jeremiah retained only the ark and tablets of the Law (Holladay, *FHJA* 1:132–34). Josephus *Ant.* 18.85–87 preserves the Samaritan belief that Moses himself had concealed the sacred vessels on Mount Gerizim (see M. F. Collins, "The Hidden Vessels in Samaritan Traditions," *JSJ* 3 [1972] 97–116). In rabbinic tradition, on the basis of 2 Chr 35:3, the ark was thought to have been concealed by Josiah and would eventually be restored in the messianic age by Elijah (*b. Yoma* 52b; *b. Hor.* 12a; *y. Šeqal.* 6.1). For Talmudic traditions on the hiding of the temple vessels, see V. Aptowitzer, *Parteipolitik der Hasmonäerzeit in rabbinischen und pseudoepigraphischen Schriften* (Vienna: Kohut, 1927) 192–93 n. 2; for Jewish speculations about the lost ark, see M. Haran, "The Disappearance of the Ark," *IEJ* 13 (1963) 46–58. M. Haran argues that Jer 3:16 implies that the ark is no longer in existence (*IEJ* 13 [1963] 51) and notes that in the vision of the temple in Ezek 40–48 no mention is made of tables, lampstands, ark, or cherubim. Jewish coins minted during the Bar Kosiba rebellion (A.D. 132–35) depict the facade of the Jerusalem temple (at that time in ruins) with an object that looks like the ark between the pillars (Meshorer, *Jewish Coins,* 159 [no. 165], 161–62 [nos. 178–81], 165 [nos. 199–201]).

19c καὶ ἐγένοντο ἀστραπαὶ καὶ φωναὶ καὶ βρονταὶ καὶ σεισμὸς καὶ χάλαζα μεγάλη, "and there were lightning and rumbling and thunder and an earthquake and great hail." There are several lists of atmospheric and seismic phenomena in Revelation with a theophanic significance (4:5; 8:5; 11:19; 16:18; see *Comment* on 4:5). Parallel atmospheric and seismic phenomena introduce the dream of Mordecai in LXX Esth 1:1d, καὶ ἰδοὺ φωναὶ καὶ θόρυβος, βρονταὶ καὶ σεισμός, τάραχος ἐπὶ τῆς γῆς, "And behold there was rumbling and noise and thunder and earthquake, upheaval upon the earth." The Philistines were conquered when, according to 1 Sam 7:10, the Lord "thundered with a mighty voice" (for thunder as a weapon in holy wars, see 1 Sam 2:10; 2 Sam 22:14; Klein, *1 Samuel,* 68). The voice of the Lord is particularly emphasized in Ps 29, a hymn that is probably a Canaanite or Phoenician Baal hymn slightly modified (Cross, *Canaanite Myth,* 151–52; for an opposing view, see P. C. Craigie, *Psalms 1–50* [Waco, TX: Word, 1983] 241–49). In Ps 29:3–9 the various aspects of a thunderstorm are turned into metaphors for the voice of the Lord. Earthquakes are also frequently mentioned in descriptions of theophanies in Greco-Roman sources (Callimachus *Ap.* 1–2; Philostratus *Vita Apoll.* 4.16).

12:1a Καὶ σημεῖον μέγα ὤφθη ἐν τῷ οὐρανῷ, "A great sign then appeared in heaven." The term ὤφθη, "appeared," is an aorist passive verb that occurs in this form just three times in Revelation (11:19; 12:1, 3). The close proximity of these three occurrences of ὤφθη provides another formal indication that 11:19 is intended to introduce 12:1–17 (see *Form/Structure/Setting,* II. Literary Analysis). In early Jewish and early Christian literature, ὤφθη is often used to introduce theophanies (Gen 12:7; 26:2; Exod 6:3; 16:10; Judg 6:12; 13:3; Jer 38:3), angelophanies (Exod 3:2; Judg 13:3; Tob 12:22; Acts 7:2), and prophetic visions (Ezek 1:4; 2:1; 10:1; Dan 8:1). The term σημεῖον, "sign, portent," referring to a significant heavenly sight, occurs just three times in the singular in Revelation (12:1, 3; 15:1); each of these is connected, for 12:3 and 15:1 refer to ἄλλο σημεῖον, "another sign," referring respectively to 12:1 and 12:3. σημεῖον, regularly used to translate אוֹת *'ôt* in the LXX, means "sign" in a number of specific ways: (1) *a characteristic mark by which something is known or recognized* (Gen 1:14; Exod 12:13; Josh 2:12; Matt 16:3; 26:48); (2) *a monument that is a reminder of a past event* (Gen 9:12, 17; 17:11; Exod 13:9; Deut 6:8; 11:18); (3) *an omen or indication of something to come* (2 Kgs 19:29; Isa 7:14; Ezek 4:3; Matt 24:3; Luke 21:11, 25; Acts 2:19); (4) *a miracle,* which may be either genuine (Exod 7:3; Josh 24:17; Ps 77:43; Mark 16:20; John 2:11; 4:48; 6:30; 1 Cor 14:22) or a lie (Mark 13:22 = Matt 24:24; 2 Thess 2:9–10; Rev 13:13–14; 16:14); or (5) *a constellation,* for in Greco-Roman astrological lore the Greek term σημεῖον could mean "constellation" (Euripides *Rhesus* 528–33; *Ion* 1157 [in context of 1146–58]; Aratus *Phaen.* 10; LSJ, 1593). The corresponding Latin term *signum,* a translation equivalent of σημεῖον, was also used in the sense of "constellation" or "sign of the zodiac" (Manilius *Astron.* 1.34, 109, 215, 255, 295, 506; Cicero *De nat. deor.* 1.22; see *OLD,* 1760).

Mentioned in the eschatological scenario in *Did.* 16 are three heavenly τὰ σημεῖα τῆς ἀληθείας, "signs of truth," which include (1) "the sign spread out in heaven," (2) "the sign of the trumpet," and (3) "the resurrection of the dead." Similarly, Matt 24:30 refers enigmatically to "the sign of the Son of man in heaven" (RSV). The plural term σημεῖα occurs four times in Revelation, always of false miracles performed by the beast from the earth (13:13–14), by the three froglike demonic spirits (16:14), or by the false prophet (19:20). A celestial phenomenon can be referred to as a σημεῖον (Gen 1:14; 19:12–17; Matt 16:1; 24:23; Mark 8:11). The term can refer to an exceptional occurrence that serves as a forewarning of something that will happen in the future and can therefore be translated "portent" (see Luke 21:11, which speaks of ἀπ' οὐρανοῦ σημεῖα μεγάλα, "great signs from heaven"), or it can refer to a miracle that is a demonstration of supernatural power (John 20:30–31). The term σημεῖον is used of heavenly phenomena that presage impending events upon the earth (*Sib. Or.* 2.34–38; 3.796–803, 804–8; Luke 21:11; *Did.* 16:6, "a sign spread out in heaven"; see Josephus *J.W.* 6.289). The term σημεῖον also occurs in LXX Isa 7:14 (a passage with some connections to Isa 66:6–7), "Therefore, the Lord himself will give you a sign [σημεῖον]. Behold, a young woman shall conceive and bear a son, and shall call his name Immanuel." σημεῖον in Rev 12:1, 3 seems to have a different meaning, however, for here it means a symbol that has deeper significance. Although it is clear that John has incorporated an originally Greek myth (perhaps as mediated by Hellenistic Judaism) into his narrative in 12:4b–6, 13–18, he uses this earlier, older material *allegorically,* perhaps as an *interpretatio Iudaica* or *interpretatio Christiana.* John, however, is not concerned to interpret explicitly any of the figures or actions in the drama (unlike, for example, his procedure in Rev 17), with the single exception that he wants the reader to know who the dragon is and therefore lists his many aliases, which include Satan and Devil (v 9; cf. v 12). While it is not a close parallel to Rev 12:1–4a, there are some important similarities in the Star Hymn quoted by Ignatius *Eph.* 19:1–3 with its sidereal imagery; an incomparably bright star (= Christ) astonishes the other stars along with the sun and the moon (see the astral imagery in the Joseph story in Gen 37:9–11).

1b γυνὴ περιβεβλημένη τὸν ἥλιον, καὶ ἡ σελήνη ὑποκάτω τῶν ποδῶν αὐτῆς, "a woman clothed with the sun; and the moon was beneath her feet." The nominative singular noun γυνή, "woman," is in apposition to σημεῖον, "sign," in v 1a and provides a more detailed explanation of the sign or constellation. This female figure is portrayed as a "queen of the cosmos" through the powerful symbols of the sun, moon, and twelve stars (Boll, *Offenbarung,* 98–124; Yarbro Collins, *Combat Myth,* 71–76). A tessera from Palmyrene depicts an unidentified goddess standing on a crescent moon, with three stars, one over her head and the other two next to her right and left arms (Cumont, *Recherches,* 209).

It is perhaps significant that neither the woman nor the child (v 4) is named, though the author-editor is careful to emphasize the various names of the dragon (v 9). There are several opinions regarding the identity of this heavenly woman: (1) Throughout the history of Christian biblical interpretation, particularly in the patristic and medieval periods, the woman in Rev 12 has often, though not exclusively, been interpreted as Mary, the mother of Jesus (Oecumenius *Comm. in Apoc.* 12.1; LeFrois, *Woman,* 38–58). The modern Roman Catholic Marian interpretation still finds representatives (see LeFrois, *Woman,* 232–35). (2) Equally ancient is the view that the woman in Rev 12 represents the Church (LeFrois, *Woman,* 11–38; Hippolytus *de Ant.* 61; Methodius *Symp.* 8.5). (3) The woman is sometimes identified with the bride, the Heavenly Jerusalem of Rev 19:7–8; 21:9–10 (Harrington, 128). (4) From a Jewish perspective the woman can represent the persecuted people of God from whom the Messiah comes (Yarbro Collins, *Combat Myth,* 107). (5) The woman is sometimes considered an astrological figure, perhaps a particular constellation. Boll suggests that a specific astronomical reference to the constellation Virgo should be understood in Rev 12:1 (*Offenbarung,* 100–108). This constellation, whose Greek name was Παρθένος, "virgin," the second largest constellation, was well known in antiquity (Aratus *Phaen.* 96–146; Cicero *De nat. deor.* 2.42; Hyginus *Poetica Astronomica* 2.25; Nonnos *Dionysiaca* 2.655). Virgo was thought to have two wings (see Rev 12:14). Ps.-Eratosthenes *Catasterismi* 9 identified Virgo with various female divinities, such as Atargatis, Isis, Demeter, and Tyche. Several goddesses in the Greco-Roman world were similarly portrayed: Artemis of Ephesus, Atargatis of Syria, Isis, and Hekate. (6) The woman has been identified as Isis, the queen of heaven. Egyptian sources understand Isis as a cosmic queen connected with the sun and stars (Bergman, *Isis,* 162–63). Her usual headdress is a pair of horns, often stylized as an upturned crescent, and between the horns is a solar disk (Budge, *Gods* 2:202; *LIMC* 5/2:503 [plate 34], 508 [plate 124], 510 [plate 174], 511 [plate 195], 513 [plate 209]). Lucius refers to the moon-goddess as *regina caeli,* "queen of heaven" (cf. "lady of heaven," a title of Isis in Budge, *Gods* 2:213), along with various other names, and eventually identifies her with Isis (Apuleius *Metamorphoses* 11.2, 4; see Griffiths, *Isis-Book,* 114–15). The Isis aretalogy from

Memphis (line 13) suggests that she is a creator goddess: Ἐγὼ ἄστρων ὁδοὺς ἔδειξα, "I showed the paths of the stars" (Müller, *Isis-Aretalogien,* 39). Similarly, on the next line, her creative powers are associated with the sun and the moon, though Egyptian parallels to this predication are very rare: Ἐγὼ ἡλίου καὶ σελήνης πορείαν συνεταξάμην, "I commanded the course of the sun and the moon" (Müller, *Isis-Aretalogien,* 40). Sarapis and Isis are also identified as Helios (sun) and Selene (moon); see the Isis aretalogy from Maroneia, line 19 (Danker, *Benefactor,* 181). Female Egyptian deities, including Hathor, Satis, Sothis, and Isis, were given the title "mistress of the stars" (for references, see Müller, *Isis-Aretalogien,* 39). The moon beneath her feet has a parallel in *T. Naph.* 5:4b (tr. Hollander-de Jonge, *Testaments*), "and Judah was bright as the moon, and under his feet were twelve rays."

Ancient cities and peoples were frequently personified by female figures. Several *aurei* and *denarii* reverses from Rome with the legend *IVDAEA,* "Judea," depict a seated Jewess in mourning with the trophies of war displayed behind her (B. V. Head, *BMC, Empire* 2:5–6, nos. 31–42). *T. Moses* 10:9–10 (Charlesworth, *OTP* 1:932) depicts eschatological Israel as exalted to the heavens:

> And God will raise you to the heights.
> Yea, he will fix you firmly in the heaven of the stars,
> in the place of their habitations.
> And you will behold from on high.
> Yea, you will see your enemies on the earth.

The nimbus is reminiscent of Asian Artemis as she is portrayed in many ancient representations. Gems depict Artemis with a nimbus situated between stars and a halfmoon (Hommel, *IM* 5 [1955] 44).

1c καὶ ἐπὶ τῆς κεφαλῆς στέφανος ἀστέρων δώδεκα, "and upon her head was a crown of twelve stars." The twelve stars probably represent the zodiac, clearly mentioned in *2 Enoch* [long rec.] 21:6; 30:4–6 and in *Sib. Or.* 5.512–31 (Boll, *Offenbarung,* 100; Bousset [1906] 336, 355; Charles, 1:316; Hedrick, "Imagery," 44). The zodiac appears on a number of mosaic floors of Jewish synagogues in late antiquity. One important example is the Beth Alpha synagogue in Galilee, in which a depiction of Helios the sun god driving his quadriga or chariot is surrounded by the twelve signs of the zodiac, each accompanied by its Hebrew name (*NEAEHL* 1:190–92): (1) *Taleh* (Aries or Ram), (2) *Shor* (Taurus or Bull), (3) *Teomim* (Gemini or Twins), (4) *Sartan* (Cancer or Crab), (5) *Aryeh* (Leo or Lion), (6) *Betulah* (Virgo or Virgin), (7) *Meoznayim* (Libra or Scales), (8) *Aqrab* (Scorpio or Scorpion), (9) *Kashat* (Sagittarius or Archer), (10) *Gedi* (Capricorn or Goat), (11) *Deli* (Aquarius or Water Bearer), and (12) *Dagim* (Pisces or Fishes). The view that the crown of twelve stars represents the sum total of angels who support the woman and her child (LeFrois, *Woman,* 120) has no early evidential basis. A late Coptic magical text refers to a similar "crown of stars" on the head of Jesus (Kropp, *Koptische Zaubertexte* 2:22). Menedemus the Cynic, a very strange character who performed miracles and claimed to be on a mission from Hades, wore a similar crown. According to the report of Diogenes Laertius (6.102; LCL tr.), he wore

> a grey tunic reaching to the feet [ποδήρης], about it a crimson girdle [ζώνη φοινικῆ]; an Arcadian hat [πῖλος] on his head with the twelve signs of the zodiac [τὰ δώδεκα στοιχεῖα] inwrought in it.

2 καὶ ἐν γαστρὶ ἔχουσα, καὶ κράζει ὠδίνουσα καὶ βασανιζομένη τεκεῖν, "She was pregnant and cried out in labor, in the throes of childbirth." ἐν γαστρὶ ἔχουσα is a technical phrase for a pregnant woman (Matt 1:18, 23 [citing Isa 7:14]; Mark 713:17; 1 Thess 5:3). ἔχουσα, "has," the present active participle, is used as a finite verb (Mussies, *Morphology,* 325). Note that vv 1–2 begin with an aorist passive verb, ὤφθη, "appeared," but switch to the present with ἔχουσα, "has," and κράζει, "cries" (the same switch from a past to a present tense in a vision is found in vv 3–4). Israel in distress is frequently compared to a woman suffering birth pains (Isa 21:3; 26:17–18; 37:3; Jer 4:31; 6:24; 13:21; 22:23; 30:6; Mic 4:9; *1 Enoch* 62:4; 1QH 3:8–9), and various Hebrew phrases meaning "like a woman in labor" occur frequently in the OT and in ancient Near Eastern literature (Isa 13:8; 21:3; 42:14; Jer 4:31; 6:24; 13:21; 22:23; 30:6; 49:24; 50:43; Mic 4:9, 10; Ps 48:7; see Darr, "Female Images," 24–27). Isa 66:7 uses the metaphor of Israel bearing a male child to indicate the arrival of the period of salvation. Isa 26:17 also compares Israel's helplessness before her enemies to "a woman with child who writhes and cries out in her pangs, when she is near her time" (cf. Hedrick, "Imagery," 25–27, who doubts that John is alluding to this passage). Another similar passage appears in 1QH 3:7–12 (tr. Vermes, *Dead Sea Scrolls*):

> [and] like a woman in travail
> with her first-born child,
> upon whose belly pangs have come
> and grievous pains,
> filling with anguish her child-bearing crucible.
> For the children have come to the throes of Death
> and she labours in her pains who bears a man,
> For amid the throes of Death
> she shall bring forth a man-child,
> and amid the pains of Hell
> there shall spring from her child-bearing crucible
> a Marvellous Mighty Counsellor.
> And a man shall be delivered from out of the throes.
> When he is conceived
> all wombs shall quicken,
> and the time of their delivery
> shall be in grievous pains;
> they shall be appalled
> who are with child.
> And when he is brought forth
> every pang shall come upon the child-bearing crucible.

3a καὶ ὤφθη ἄλλο σημεῖον ἐν τῷ οὐρανῷ, "Then another sign appeared in heaven." The wording of this phrase corresponds closely to that phrase in v 1 and is intended as an introduction to the woman's antagonist. On the term σημεῖον, "sign," in Revelation, see *Comment* on 12:1. Both here and in v 1 the term very likely refers to a constellation.

3b καὶ ἰδοὺ δράκων μέγας πυρρός, "And behold, a great red dragon." Since the author has inserted καὶ ἰδού, "and behold," at this point, δράκων, "dragon," is a nominative singular since the nominative regularly follows (καὶ) ἰδού, and therefore δράκων is not grammatically in apposition to σημεῖον, "sign," as γυνή, "woman," is in v 1. The term δράκων occurs in the NT only in the second half of Revelation, where it is found thirteen times (12:3, 4, 7[2x], 9, 13, 16, 17; 13:2, 4, 11; 16:13; 20:2). "Dragon" is one of many designations of Satan in early Judaism (see 12:9); see *3 Apoc. Bar.* 4:3–5. δράκων is used four times in the LXX to translate the Hebrew term לויתן *liwyātān*, "Leviathan" (Job 40:25; Pss 73:14[MT 74:14]; 103:26[MT 104:26]; Isa 27:1), and fifteen times for תן *tan* or תנין *tannîn*, "serpent, sea-monster" (e.g., Exod 7:9–12; Job 7:12; Ps 73:13[MT 74:13]; Isa 27:1). An astronomical reference is possible here since Δράκων or Draco was the name of a constellation widely known in the Hellenistic period; Draco was understood to possess a long coiling tail and was seen in conjunction with the Kneeler, a constellation thought to depict Herakles (or Theseus, or Prometheus) with his foot on the head of the dragon (Aratus *Phaenomena* 45–70; Cicero *De nat. deor.* 2.42; Hyginus *Poetica Astronomica* 2.3; Nonnos *Dionysiaca* 2.672–73). In the elaborate retelling of the conflict between Zeus and Typhoeus in Nonnos *Dionysiaca* 154–218, the wild attack of Typhoeus is narrated in terms of the constellations with which Draco is associated.

The color red had generally positive associations for the Greeks, who considered it to have protective and apotropaic powers. Elsewhere in Revelation the adjective πυρρός is used only of the red horse in 6:5 (n.b. that the beast in 17:3 is described as κόκκινον, "scarlet"). The Egyptians believed that Typhon (the Greek name of the Egyptian god Seth), the mythical opponent of Isis and Osiris, was *red* (πυρρός; Plutarch *De Iside* 359E, 363B, 364B; Diodorus 1.88.4), and hence red had negative as well as positive associations (see Hopfner, *Offenbarungszauber*, vol. 1, § 615; A. Hermann, *RAC* 6:362–71, 405–8 [s.v. *Farben*]; J. G. Griffiths, "The Symbolism of Red in Egyptian Religion," in *Ex orbe religion: Studia G. Widengren oblata* [Leiden: Brill, 1972] 1:85–87). In Egyptian mythology, Seth-Typhon took many forms, including the snake, dragon, and crocodile (Apollodorus 1.6.3; see Fontenrose, *Python*, 185–87; Budge, *Gods* 2:245). According to *T. Abr.* 17:14; 19:6–7, Death sometimes appears as seven fiery red heads of dragons (κεφαλὰς δρακόντων πυρίνους ἑπτά), which symbolize the seven ages of the world (19:7). The color red as the color of the dragon has a partial parallel in Hermas *Vis.* 4.1.10, where the θηρίον, "beast," seen by Hermas has four colors on its head: black, flame and blood (πυροειδὲς καὶ αἱματῶδες, i.e., red), gold, and white. The flame and blood are later interpreted to mean that the world must be destroyed by blood and fire (Hermas *Vis.* 4.3.3).

3c ἔχων κεφαλὰς ἑπτὰ καὶ κέρατα δέκα καὶ ἐπὶ τὰς κεφαλὰς αὐτοῦ ἑπτὰ διαδήματα, "with seven heads and ten horns and seven diadems upon his heads." Since the dragon is described using imagery that is not further exploited or even referred to in the rest of this vision, it appears to be a redactional interpolation drawn from 17:3 (note that this clause can be omitted without disrupting the sequence of thought), for only in that context are the seven heads and the ten horns actually interpreted (17:9–14). Seven heads and ten horns are also attributed to the beast mentioned in 13:1 (here θήριον, "beast," is anarthrous even though he has already been mentioned in 11:7), but this figure is clearly differentiated from the dragon to whom he is subordinate (13:3). A beast with seven heads and ten horns is again mentioned in 17:3, but since the term θηρίον in 17:3 is anarthrous, it appears clear that either two *different* beasts are in view or the author did not successfully conceal his use of sources. Here the dragon has seven heads and ten horns, with seven diadems on his *heads* (i.e., the conclusion is inescapable that each of the diademed heads must, at least originally, have symbolized a ruler), while in

13:1 the beast has ten horns and seven heads with ten diadems on his *horns*. The reference to ten horns is an allusion to Dan 7:7, 20, 24, where they are interpreted to mean ten kings, by which is meant ten successive rulers of a single world power (cf. *Sib. Or.* 3.396–400, a Jewish interpolation based on Dan 7:7, 20). The reference to ten horns in *Sib. Or.* 3.397 (including an eleventh that sprouts from the side) clearly refers to ten kings and then an eleventh but has probably been added to the oracle by a Jewish Sibyllist (J. J. Collins in Charlesworth, *OTP* 1:359). Boll (*Offenbarung*, 102) notes that the constellations Corvus, "crow," and Crater, "goblet," are located next to Virgo and consist (according to ancient sidereal lore) of seven and ten stars, respectively (though how these are connected with heads and horns is problematic). In *T. Abr.* 17:12–19, Death reveals himself to Abraham in many terrifying forms, including appearances as seven fiery red heads of dragons (κεφαλὰς δρακόντων πυρίνους ἑπτά, 17:14; 19:6–7) and as a frightening three-headed dragon (δράκοντα τρικέφαλον φοβερόν, 17:16).

On the many diadems signifying rule over many kingdoms, see *Comment* on 19:12. In the allegory of kingship in Dio Chrysostom *Or.* 1.58–84 (see Mussies, *Dio,* 250), two allegorical female figures (one symbolizing "Kingship" and the other "Tyranny") are enthroned on two mountains. "Lady Tyranny" has many scepters and tiaras as well as diadems (1.79, πολλαὶ δὲ τιᾶραι καὶ διαδήματα ἐπὶ τῆς κεφαλῆς, "many tiaras and diadems on her head"), and the mountain upon which she is seated is called Typhon (1.67), obviously a name appropriate for wicked rule. Dio refers several times to people who, though they might have many scepters, tiaras, and diadems, are not thereby legitimate kings (Dio *Or.* 1.79; 3.41; 4.25; 14.22; Mussies, *Dio,* 250). The possession of these many outward symbols of kingship are regarded negatively by Dio.

The beasts of Rev 13:1 and 17:3 are also described as having *seven heads*. Ps 74:14 speaks of "the heads of Leviathan [ראשי לויתן *rā'šê liwyātān*]," but the number of heads is specified neither here nor elsewhere in the OT (M. S. Smith, *The Early History of God* [San Francisco: Harper & Row, 1990] 53, mistakenly speaks of Rahab as a seven-headed figure in Ps 89:10). *Odes Sol.* 22:5 refers to the overthrow of "the dragon with seven heads" (Syriac *ltnyn dšb' 'ryšwhy*). The same mythological imagery is reflected in *Pistis Sophia* 2.66 (ed. Schmidt-MacDermot, *Pistis Sophia,* 141), "For one of them [emanations] changed to the form of a great serpent; again another changed to the form of a basilisk, having seven heads; again another changed to the form of a dragon [Coptic *drakôn*]."

Other references to the seven-headed serpent or basilisk in *Pistis Sophia* occur in 2.66 (3x: ed. Schmidt-Till, p. 88, line 36; p. 91, lines 11, 14 = ed. Schmidt-MacDermot, pp. 137, 141, 142); 2.67 (ed. Schmidt-Till, p. 95, line 26 = ed. Schmidt-MacDermot, p. 149); 2.70 (ed. Schmidt-Till, p. 100, lines 5–6 = ed. Schmidt-MacDermot, p. 156); 2.71 (2x: ed. Schmidt-Till, p. 101, line 13; p. 102, lines 18–19 = Schmidt-MacDermot, pp. 157, 159).

This reptilian trinity is of interest because Isa 27:1 similarly mentions three separate monsters. Rabbinic tradition mentions the seven-headed dragon in *b. Qidd.* 29b. The seven-headed dragon appears much earlier in an ancient text from Ugarit (*CTA* 5.I.1–3; *ANET,* 138):

> If thou [Baal] smite Lotan [Leviathan],
> the serpent slant,

Destroy the serpent tortuous,
Shalyat of the seven heads.

Another Ugaritic text in the Baal epic indicates that Leviathan had seven heads (Driver, *Canaanite Myths,* 87; 3.IIID.39). The Lernaean Hydra of Greek myth was thought of as having *nine* heads (Apollodorus 2.5.2), or even as many as one hundred (Diodorus Siculus 4.11.5; Ovid *Metamorphoses* 9.69ff.), though Pausanias doubted that the monster had more than a single head (2.37.4). Yet other versions of the myth mention three, fifteen, or "many" heads (see *RAC* 16:905). Though nine snake heads were the norm in traditional mythical conceptions of Medusa, the number was apparently not very important since it varied even in the works of the same authors and artists (Brommer, *Herakles,* 13). Evidence for a seven-headed hydra is also discussed in Burkert, *Mythology and Ritual,* 80–83. Mesopotamian seal cylinders depict gods in combat with a seven-headed serpent; see Pritchard, *ANEP,* 221, no. 691; cf. no. 671. In the Coptic-Gnostic *Ap. John* II.11.29–31, one of the seven archons is of some relevance for the present discussion, for "the fourth is Iaô with the face of a dragon [*drakôn*] who has seven heads" (M. Krause and Labib, *Apokryphon des Johannes,* 141). The *Apocryphon of John* is preserved in four closely parallel Coptic versions, and the quoted passage occurs also in III.18.1–2; IV.18.18–20; BG.42.2. For the motif of the seven-headed dragon in folklore, see S. Thompson, *Motif-Index* 1:350: B11.2.3.1. In *T. Abr.* [Rec. A] 17:14; 19:6–7, a dragon with seven fiery heads symbolizes death, and at the same time the seven ages of the world (19:7), which are specified as seven thousand years in *T. Abr.* [Rec. B] 7:16.

The term διάδημα, "diadem-crown," occurs twice more in Revelation (13:1; 19:12). A diadem, regardless of its specific appearance, usually functioned as a *royal crown.* Diadems worn wrapped around upright tiaras by Persian kings are first mentioned in Greek literature in Xenophon *Cyr.* 8.3.13 (see also Plutarch *De fort. Alex.* 340B; *De frat. amore* 488D; LXX Esth 8:15; 1 Macc 13:32; Jos. *J.W.* 1.671) and could be called a διάδημα βασιλείας (Isa 62:3; *T. Sol.* D 7.4; *Apost. Const.* 20.3; *T. Judah* 12:4). A στέφανος, "garland, wreath," on the other hand, was made of real or stylized leaves (occasionally flowers and fruits) and functioned as an award or as ceremonial headgear for various occasions (see *Comment* on 2:10, and *Excursus 2C: Ancient Wreath and Crown Imagery*). The term diadem could also be used for a priestly crown, i.e., a διάδημα ἱερατείας, "diadem of priesthood" (see Philo *Mos.* 2.116, 131). Diadems in the Hellenistic period usually consisted of strips of gold embossed with various designs. Various pendants were often used to decorate diadems more elaborately. Josephus mentions that Aristobulus I was the first Jewish monarch to wear the diadem (*Ant.* 20.241), though coins minted under Alexander Yannai (103–76 B.C.) depict an anchor surrounded by a diadem with the inscription ΒΑΣΙΛΕΩΣ ΑΛΕΞΑΝΔΡΟΥ, "of King Alexander" (Meshorer, *Jewish Coins,* 118, no. 5A; 120, no. 17). Coins of Herod the Great also depict a diadem with the inscription ΗΡΩΔΟΥ ΒΑΣΙΛΕΩΣ, "of Herod the King" (Meshorer, *Jewish Coins,* 128, no. 41).

4a καὶ ἡ οὐρὰ αὐτοῦ σύρει τὸ τρίτον τῶν ἀστέρων τοῦ οὐρανοῦ καὶ ἔβαλεν αὐτοὺς εἰς τὴν γῆν, "His tail swept down a third of the stars of heaven and cast them down to the earth." This probably alludes to Dan 8:10, where it is said that a king, represented by the little horn, "grew great, even to the host of heaven; and some of the host of the stars it cast down to the ground, and trampled upon them" (metaphors emphasizing the excessive pride of this ruler). The destruction of one-third of the stars corresponds to the destruction of a third of various parts of the cosmos as the result of the plagues unleashed by the seven trumpets (8:7–9:19). It is possible that the description of the dragon sweeping a third of the stars and casting them down to the earth alludes to the story of the descent of Satan and his angels to earth in the traditional story of the Watchers (*1 Enoch* 6–11). In *1 Enoch*, stars can represent evil angels (18:14; 21:3–6; 86:1–3; 88:3); for the stars = angels metaphor, see *Comment* on 1:20. Isa 24:21–22 says, "On that day the Lord will punish the host of heaven in heaven, and the kings of the earth on the earth. They will be gathered together as prisoners in a pit; they will be shut up in a prison, and after many days they will be punished." In Apollodorus 1.6.3, the monster Typhon, with a hundred dragon heads (ἑκατὸν κεφαλαὶ δρακόντων), was so gigantic that his head touched the stars (ἡ δὲ κεφαλὴ πολλάκις καὶ τῶν ἄστρων ἔψαυε). In the late mythography of Nonnos, Typhoeus is depicted as attacking and pulling down the various constellations from the heavens (*Dionysiaca* 1.163–205). In the *Mart. Pionius* 12 (tr. Musurillo, *Acts,* 151), Pionius tells his visitors "I am tormented anew . . . when I see . . . the stars of heaven being swept down to earth by the dragon's tail." This is undoubtedly an allusion to Rev 12:4, allegorically interpreted as the physical harm inflicted on Christians by Satan. On falling stars, see *Comment* on 6:13.

4b Καὶ ὁ δράκων ἕστηκεν ἐνώπιον τῆς γυναικὸς τῆς μελλούσης τεκεῖν, ἵνα ὅταν τέκῃ τὸ τέκνον αὐτῆς καταφάγῃ, "Now the dragon stood before the woman who was about to give birth, so that when she gave birth he might swallow her child." This confrontation takes place in heaven since that is the location of the two great signs that appeared (Boll, *Offenbarung,* 101, argues that ἕστηκεν, "stood," is a *terminus technicus* for the location of a constellation in the sky, though the term is certainly used in other connections as well; see Freundorfer, *Apokalypse,* 132–34). Yet the statement that the child will be caught up to heaven (v 5) indicates that the confrontation between the dragon and the woman takes place on the earth. When the dragon is cast down to the earth (v 13), he pursues the woman, so her location on the earth in v 4b must be presumed. The term κατεσθίειν, "to devour, swallow," is a synonym of καταπίνειν, "to devour, swallow," used in 12:16 of Earth swallowing the floodwaters spewed out by the dragon. These terms frame the story in the sense that the attempt to "swallow" the child is the dragon's primary *offense* in 12:4b, while in 12:16 it is the primary *defense* of Earth, the champion of the woman. In LXX Jer 28:34 (MT 51:34), the Babylonian king Nebuchadrezzar is compared to a dragon: "Nebuchadrezzar king of Babylon has swallowed me like a dragon [κατέπιέν με ὡς δράκων]."

The myth in Ignatius *Eph.* 19:1 is quite different; there the virginity of Mary and her childbearing, together with the death of the Lord, were concealed from the prince of this world. Similarly, in Hippolytus *Theoph.* 4, Jesus appeared incognito at his baptism "that he might elude the wickedness of the dragon." Yet the motif of *concealment* is Rhea's first line of defense in the Kronos-Zeus succession myth discussed below. The antipathy between the dragon and the offspring of the woman can be seen in the version of the birth of Zeus found in *Sib. Or.* 3.132–41 (Charlesworth, *OTP* 1:365):

> Whenever Rhea gave birth, the Titans sat by her,
> and they tore apart all male children,
> but they allowed the females to live and be reared with their mother.

> But when Lady Rhea gave birth in the third child-bearing
> she brought forth Hera first. When they saw
> with their eyes the female species, the Titans, savage men,
> went home. Then Rhea bore a male child,
> whom she quickly sent away to be reared secretly in private,
> to Phrygia, having taken three Cretan men under oath.
> Therefore they named him Zeus, because he was sent away.

Rhea similarly conceals the births of Poseidon and Pluto; the story continues in lines 147–55:

> When the Titans heard that children existed
> in secret, whom Kronos had begotten with Rhea, his consort,
> Titan assembled sixty sons
> and held Kronos and Rhea, his consort, in fetters.
> He hid them in the earth and guarded them in bonds.
> Then indeed the sons of mighty Kronos heard it
> and they stirred up great war and din of battle against him.
> This is the beginning of war for all mortals
> for this is the first beginning of war for mortals.

This euhemeristic version of the Kronos-Zeus succession myth concludes with a list of kingdoms, beginning with the Titans and concluding with that of Rome (*Sib. Or.* 3.156–61), a tradition that views Rome as playing the same antagonistic role as the Titans. This mythological sequence is developed from Hesiod *Theog.* 453–91 (summarized in Apollodorus 1.1.5–7), in which Kronos, fearing the birth of a son who would overthrow him, swallowed [καταπίνειν] all his children shortly after Rhea gave birth to them. Upon Rhea's appeal to Earth and Ouranos, she was sent to Crete where Zeus was hidden in a cave after he was born, and Rhea presented Kronos with a rock wrapped in baby garments, which he promptly swallowed. The ancient world knew a number of terrifying baby-killing or baby-snatching demons (Mormo, Lamia, Gella, Empousa, Lilith, Lamashtu), all of which are traditionally understood to be female.

5a καὶ ἔτεκεν υἱόν, ἄρσεν, "Then she bore a son, a male child." This is probably an allusion to Isa 66:7, but a major grammatical incongruity is involved, for ἄρσεν, "male child," a *neuter* accusative adjective, is in apposition to υἱόν, "son," a *masculine* accusative noun. The phrase "a son, a male" can be construed as a Hebraism like that found in Jer 20:15, "A son, a male [בֵּן זָכָר *bēn zākār*] is born to you" (the LXX renders this ἐτέχθη σοι ἄρσεν, "a male is born to you"). More commonly, such idiomatic phrases as παῖς ἄρρην (Jos. *Ant.* 1.52, 304; 7.146; 20.92), παιδίον ἄρρεν (Jos. *Ant.* 3.271; 7.158; 9.65), and τέκνον ἄρρεν (Jos. *Ant.* 7.243) are used to mean "son." There is some evidence to suggest that υἱός in popular speech could mean "child," making it necessary to specify that the child was a male; see B. Olsson, "υἱὸς ἄρρην," *Glotta* 23 (1935) 112. Note that in the parallel noun cluster υἱὸς ἄρσην in Tob 6:12 (Codex א), ἄρσην is a masculine accusative adjective, so the phrase simply means "male son" and is redundant though not grammatically problematic like υἱόν, ἄρσεν in Rev 12:5 (see Isa 66:7; Jer 20:15). Vanni, who implies that this strange construction is intentional and conveys certain theological perspectives, suggests that ἄρσεν enlarges the conception of υἱός and, by virture of its neuter gender, universalizes the notion and suggests such ideas as strength, domination, and importance (Vanni, *L'Apocalisse*, 245–47, esp. 245). The messianic interpretation of Isa 66:7 in Judaism is suggested by *Gen. Rab.* 38:1; *Lev. Rab.* 12:2; *Tg. Isa.* 66:7 (Aus, *ZNW* 67 [1976] 256–62) and is also reflected in a few early Christian texts (Justin *Dial.* 85.8–9; Ps.-Epiphanius *Test.* 11; Methodius *Sym. et Ann.* 3; *Symp.* 7). The Hebrew term חבל *ḥēbel,* "birth pang," is associated with the conception of the חבלו של משיח *heblô šel māšîaḥ,* "birth pang(s) of the Messiah," a well-known eschatological motif for the trials and tribulations that are expected to precede the time of the end (Aus, *ZNW* 67 [1976] 260–62). LXX Isa 7:14 is another passage in which the child born is the Messiah (Swete, 148; Lohmeyer, 99; Hedrick, "Imagery," 31): "Therefore the Lord himself will give you a sign [σημεῖον; see 12:1]. Behold, a young woman shall conceive and bear a son [ἐν γαστρὶ ἕξει καὶ τέξεται υἱόν], and shall call his name Immanuel." If the woman of 12:1 represents Israel, the problem is that there is no OT passage that personifies Israel as a mother and also speaks of her bearing a child Messiah; according to Hedrick ("Imagery," 31), "there is no precedent for John's description of a personified Israel as giving birth to the Messiah."

5b ὃς μέλλει ποιμαίνειν πάντα τὰ ἔθνη ἐν ῥάβδῳ σιδηρᾷ, "who will drive all the nations with an iron crook." Here the masculine relative pronoun ὅς, "who," refers back to υἱόν, "son," rather than to ἄρσεν, "male child" (see *Comment* on v 5a and *Note* 5.a.). This is an allusion to Ps 2:9, a passage that was interpreted messianically in *Pss. Sol.* 17:23–24. Here the *judicial authority* of the Messiah is emphasized. This is one of three allusions to Ps 2:9 in the NT, all of which occur in Revelation; both 2:27 and 19:15 have ποιμανεῖ αὐτοὺς ἐν ῥάβδῳ σιδηρᾷ, "he will shepherd [or 'drive'] them with an iron crook." Only in 12:5 do μέλλει, "is about to," and πάντα τὰ ἔθνη, "all the nations," occur, which suggests that the author derived this allusion through different traditional channels. LXX Ps 2:9 reads ποιμανεῖς αὐτοὺς ἐν ῥάβδῳ σιδηρᾷ, "you will shephard [or 'drive'] them with an iron crook" (αὐτούς, "them" refers to the ἔθνη, "nations," in Ps 2:8). The author has just replaced the pronoun αὐτούς with the fuller expression πάντα τὰ ἔθνη and altered the phraseology from second person to the third person singular. This allusion is probably an explanatory gloss added by John to the Greek source he was revising (Charles, 1:clviii n. 2, 301). The gloss is intended to identify the male child as the Messiah of Jewish eschatological expectation and to place that rule in the *future.* The absence of any clear Christian features in this description of the woman and the child Messiah has led scholars since Vischer to propose that the author has incorporated a Jewish source into his composition, but one to which he assigns a Christian interpretation (J. Weiss, *Offenbarung,* 82–84). A. Yarbro Collins (*Combat Myth,* 105) thinks that this description of the Messiah and his role *cannot* be Christian but must be Jewish. Yet it must be admitted that there is no Jewish tradition that the Messiah would be persecuted by the dragon after his birth and then miraculously rescued by God (Bousset [1906] 349).

The phrase πάντα τὰ ἔθνη, "all the nations," is a fixed phrase that occurs five times in Revelation (12:5; 14:8; 15:4; 18:3, 23) and frequently elsewhere in the NT and early Christian literature (Matt 24:9, 14 [= Mark 13:10]; 25:32; 28:19; Mark 11:17 [Isa 56:7]; Luke 21:24; 24:47; Acts 14:16; 15:17; Rom 1:5; 15:11 [Ps 117:1]; Gal 3:8; 2 Tim 4:17; *Barn.* 9:5 [Jer 9:25–26]; *1 Clem.* 59:4; *2 Clem.* 13:2 [Isa 52:5]; 17:4; Hermas *Sim.* 9.17.4). The phrase occurs often in early Jewish literature (*T. Sim.* 7:2; *T. Levi* 4:4; 8:14; 14:1, 4; 15:1; *T. Jude* 22:2; *T. Zeb.* 9:8; *T. Asher* 7:3; *T. Jos.* 19:6; *T.*

Benj. 9:2; *Pss. Sol.* 9:9; 17:34; *Vit. Proph.* 2.10; 4.21B; 10.8; Jos. *Ant.* 11.215; *Ag. Ap.* 1.172). The phrase occurs about sixty times in the OT (e.g., Gen 22:18; Deut 17:14; Josh 23:3; 1 Sam 8:5, 20; 1 Chr 14:7; Isa 2:2; Jer 25:9; Joel 3:2; Amos 9:9).

5c καὶ ἡρπάσθη τὸ τέκνον αὐτῆς πρὸς τὸν θεὸν καὶ πρὸς τὸν θρόνον αὐτοῦ, "But her child was caught up to God and to his throne." The child is separated immediately from his mother, but he then joins his hitherto absent "father," i.e., God (in an enthronement context, the term "Father" is used of God in Revelation only in 3:21; on God as Father in Revelation, see *Comment* on 1:6). In its present context this statement probably refers to the ascension of Jesus, and that is clearly how Christian interpreters have traditionally understood the passage (Prigent, *Apocalypse 12,* 8, 136). There are convincing reasons, however, for maintaining that this is a secondary application: (1) Unlike the ascension narrative in Luke 24 and Acts 1, the snatching of the child here occurs *immediately* after birth (Yarbro Collins, *Combat Myth,* 105). (2) The ascension of Jesus is never presented as a supernatural "rescue" from Satan (Gollinger, *Apokalypse 12,* 151–57). (3) References to the cross and the resurrection are strikingly absent from the narrative. Joachim Jeremias suggests that in the ancient Near East there was a tendency to focus on both the beginning and the end of a story, while omitting what happens in between (*Parables,* 148). Rissi (*Zeit,* 44) applies this tendency specifically to Rev 12:5. Swete (151) notes that ἁρπάζειν, "snatch away," and ἀναλαμβάνειν, "take up," overlap in meaning and that the latter is used of the ascension of Jesus (Acts 1:2, 11, 23; 1 Tim 3:16). The ascension of Jesus is narrated only in Luke 24 and Acts 1 and also in the longer ending of Mark (16:9–20). It is alluded to in a credal context in 1 Tim 3:16. Otherwise, the ascension is presupposed by the use of Ps 110:1 to assert that Christ is seated at the right hand of God, the *sessio ad dextram dei* (Rom 8:34; 1 Cor 15:25; Eph 1:20; 2:6; Col 3:1–3; Heb 1:3, 13; 8:1; 10:12; 12:2; 1 Pet 3:20; *1 Clem.* 36:5; Pol. *Phil.* 2:1; *Barn.* 12:10; *Apoc. Peter* 6; *Sib. Or.* 2.243; *Ap. Jas.* 14.30; see Lindars, *Apologetic,* 45–51; Hay, *Psalm 110*). There is a possibility that the mention that the child was caught up "to God and to his throne" is an allusion to Ps 110:1 used to affirm the messianic status of Jesus *ad dextram dei,* "at the right hand of God," though nothing is explicitly said of the child's enthronement. Ps 110:1 is nowhere else alluded to in Revelation with the possible exception of 3:21, where the risen Christ says "as I also conquered and sat with my Father on his throne." The reference to God and his throne would have been sufficient to Christianize a Jewish source, for it is likely that the original Hellenistic tradition the author used simply read "her child was caught up to heaven" (ἡρπάσθη τὸ τέκνον αὐτῆς πρὸς τὸν οὐρανόν).

A central problematic issue, of course, is the identification of the child, particularly if the allusion to Ps 2:9 is regarded as a later addition. Since Isa 66:6–14 (alluded to twice in Rev 12:1–5) uses mother, birth, and child imagery to describe the emergence of a new city, with Zion as the "mother" and Jerusalem as the "child," it is possible that the woman in Rev 12:1–6 originally referred to Zion and the child to Jerusalem; the latter may have been only secondarily identified with the Messiah.

There are many Greek myths that deal with the popular theme of apotheosis or deification in which the *seizure motif* is central (verbs such as ἁρπάζειν and ἀνερείπεσθαι, both meaning "to seize," figure prominently; see Betz, *Lukian von Samosata,* 169 n. 3, for further references). In *Iliad* 20.234, it is said of Ganymede, τὸν καὶ ἀνηρείψαντο θεὸ Διὶ οἰνοχοεύειν, "him the gods snatched up to serve wine to Zeus" (see W. Dindorf, *Scholia Graeca in Homeri Iliadem* [Oxford: Clarendon, 1875] 2:202; Lucian *Dial. deorum* 8.1–2; Pausanias 5.24.5; Achilles Tatius 2.36.4; 2.37.2; Nonnos *Dionysiaca* 10.311). Pindar substitutes the story of how Pelops was seized (ἁρπάσαι) and carried up to Olympus by Poseidon in place of the traditional account of murder and cannibalism (*Olympian Odes* 1.40). *Odyssey* 15.250–51 mentions that Cleitus was seized (ἥρπασεν) by Dawn so that he might live with the gods. The motif of a *child* being carried off to heaven is found in Pausanias 73.18.11, where the child (παῖς) Dionysus is reported to have been carried off to heaven (ἐς οὐρανόν) by Hermes. One version of the legend of Europa speaks of her being seized (ἥρπασεν) by Zeus and transported to Crete (Lucian *De dea Syr.* 4; see Apollodorus 73.1.1), and Dawn seized (ἥρπασε) Orion and carried him off to Delos (Apollodorus 1.4.4). Artemis caught up Iphigeneia and made her immortal (Apollodorus *Epitome* 3.22), much as Philip was "seized" (ἥρπασεν) by the Spirit of the Lord from the side of the Ethiopian eunuch and transported to Caesarea (Acts 8:39), and Hermas is seized (here the term is αἴρει) by the Spirit and transported to a place of revelation (Hermas *Vis.* 2.1.1). This imagery is based on Greek abduction stories, which frequently pair the verbs ἁρπάζειν, "to snatch," and κομίζειν, "to carry away" (e.g., Theseus abducted Helen in Apollodorus 3.10.7; Dawn abducted Tithonius and carried him off to Ethiopia [Apollodorus 3.12.4]; Poseidon rescued his son Eumolpus by carrying him off to Ethiopia [Apollodorus 3.15.4]; Dionysus fell in love with Ariadne and carried her off to Lemnos [Apollodorus *Epitome* 1.9]). In another seizure story, Enoch was taken by angels and resettled in the Garden of Eden (*Jub.* 4:23). Other Greco-Roman seizure and removal stories include the following: Pluto seized Persephone and carried her off to Hades (Apollodorus 1.5.1); Phrixus and Helle were caught up (ἀνήρπασε) on a ram provided by their mother Nephele ("cloud") and transported across the Aegean (Apollodorus 1.9.1); a cloud was the vehicle that raised Herakles to heaven (εἰς οὐρανὸν ἀναπέμψει) and immortality (Apollodorus 2.7.7); Aphrodite carried off (ἁρπάσασα) Butes (Apollodorus 1.9.23); Dionysus, after liberating his mother Semele from Hades, ascended with her to heaven (Apollodorus 3.5.3); Zeus carried (εἰς οὐρανὸν ἀνάγει) Pollux up to heaven (Apollodorus 3.11.2); Zeus caught up (ἀναρπάσας) Ganymede to heaven on an eagle (Apollodorus 3.12.2; Lucian *Dial. deorum* 10.1). Paul uses the aorist passive verb ἡρπάγη, "caught up" (here the passive functions as a circumlocution for divine activity), to describe a visionary ascent (of himself or someone else) to the third heaven, to Paradise (2 Cor 12:2, 4), and he uses the same term in the future passive (ἁρπαγησόμεθα) to refer to the collective ascent of Christians at the Parousia of Jesus (1 Thess 4:17). In *Gk. Apoc. Ezra* 5:7, after a guided tour of Hades, Ezra says "While I was saying this a cloud came and seized me [ἥρπασέν με] and carried me [ἀπήνεγκέν με] to the heavens." Earlier in 1:7 the author refers to his original heavenly ascent: "Therefore I was taken up [ἀνελήφθην] to heaven" (for a revelatory experience). In *T. Job* 39.9–40.5, Job claims that the bodies of his children will not be found in the house that collapsed on them, for "they were taken up [ἀνελήφθησαν] into the heavens by the creator." When his hearers express doubt, they are permitted to see Job's children, wearing crowns, in heaven beside the Heavenly One.

6a καὶ ἡ γυνὴ ἔφυγεν εἰς τὴν ἔρημον, "The woman then fled into the wilderness." Since it appears that the mythological narrative described by the author in vv 1–3 occurs in heaven, the flight of the woman into the wilderness (presumably on earth) is problematic. If the signs in heaven are constellations that represent a narrative of conflict that the author then unfolds, however, the supposed contradiction is nonexistent. Here and in v 14 the woman appears to be understood as a personification of the Christian community, which began to experience persecution following the birth and ascension of the Messiah. The flight of the people of God for refuge into the wilderness (Mark 13:14–20 = Matt 24:15–22 = Luke 21:20–24) or "from desert to desert" (*Asc. Isa.* 4:13; Hippolytus *de Ant.* 61.9) occurs in a variety of apocalyptic contexts, though in 12:17 nothing is said of the people of God fleeing into the wilderness or anywhere else. The motif of the *wilderness* was extremely important in Israelite and early Jewish literature. For the Qumran community, the desert retreat was a prelude to the final eschatological battle; see 1QM 1:1–3 (P. von der Osten-Saken, *Gott und Belial,* 30–41). The desert was traditionally regarded as a place of refuge in times of trouble (1 Kgs 17:2–3; 19:3–4) and had a variety of theological associations in early Judaism (Yarbro Collins, *Combat Myth,* 120–22; Hengel, *Zealots,* 249–53). The flight of Mattathias and his sons into the desert is a historical application of these themes (1 Macc 2:28–29; 2 Macc 5:27; *Pss. Sol.* 17:16–17). The author does not mention that the scene has changed from heaven to earth; the desert is therefore not a geographical place but a symbol (Gollinger, *Apokalypse 12,* 100–101).

6b ὅπου ἔχει ἐκεῖ τόπον ἡτοιμασμένον ἀπὸ τοῦ θεοῦ, "where she had a place prepared there for her by God." The phrase ἑτοιμάζειν τόπον, "to prepare a place," occurs in John 14:2–3, but it can hardly be considered distinctive enough to indicate the common origin of John and Revelation in the Johannine circle (as suggested by Prigent, 369).

6c ἵνα ἐκεῖ τρέφωσιν αὐτὴν ἡμέρας χιλίας διακοσίας ἑξήκοντα, "that she might be taken care of there for 1,260 days." This symbolic apocalyptic number for a divinely restricted period of time consists of three and one-half years, variously expressed as "a time, times, and half a time" (Rev 12:14), "forty-two months" (Rev 11:2; 13:5), or "1,260 days" (Rev 11:3); see *Comment* on Rev 11:2.

7a καὶ ἐγένετο πόλεμος ἐν τῷ οὐρανῷ, "There was a battle in heaven." This verse introduces what many have considered to be an intrusive narrative fragment sandwiched between v 6 and v 9. There is no explicit connection between the interrupted narrative of the dragon's pursuit of the woman and her child in vv 1–6, continued in vv 10–17 with the dragon's pursuit of the woman and her offspring. This abrupt statement would probably have struck the original readers as somewhat shocking, for Israelite and early Jewish sources preserve few narratives of a heavenly battle such as that described here in vv 7–9. One such account narrates an eschatological battle among the stars involving Lucifer and the twelve constellations of the zodiac, at the conclusion of which the combatants are cast down to the earth (*Sib. Or.* 5.512–13; cf. Philo *Som.* 2.114–15). However, since v 5 discloses that the male child was snatched away and taken to God and his throne, i.e., in heaven, it is implicit that the heavenly battle was caused by the dragon's futile attempt to devour the male child. There was, however, a conception in the OT and early Judaism, widely adopted in early Christianity, that each nation on earth was represented in heaven by an angelic being. Deut 32:8 in the MT reads "he [God] fixed the boundaries of peoples according to the number of the sons of Israel [בני ישראל *bĕnê yiśrāʾēl*]." Yet the LXX (which has κατὰ ἀριθμὸν ἀγγέλων θεοῦ, "according to the number of the angels of God") and other MSS suggest that the original reading was probably בני אל *běnê ʾēl* or בני אלים *běnê ʾēlîm*, "sons of God," i.e., angels (*BHS*, 345). Isa 12:32 mentions "the messengers of the nations," referring to angelic representatives of the nations. In Dan 10:20, two of these angels are referred to as "the prince of Persia" and "the prince of Greece." In 1QM 17:6 the phrase משרת מיכאל *miśrat mîkāʾēl*, "kingdom of Michael," refers to Israel. Wars between earthly nations have a counterpart in wars between their heavenly representatives, each presumably accompanied by an angelic host (Collins, *Daniel*, 133–38). There is, however, an interesting passage in Ignatius (*Eph.* 13:2), where the unity of faith is the means "whereby every battle [πόλεμος] against heavenly beings and earthly beings [ἐπουρανίων καὶ ἐπιγείων] is abolished." In the context of Ignatius *Eph.* 13:1, however, it is clear that this is not a struggle *between* heavenly and earthly beings (though this may well be the original meaning of the formulation; see Wehr, *Unsterblichkeit*, 90); rather, the Christian community itself is opposed by heavenly beings (i.e., "invisible" beings; see *Trall.* 5.2), i.e., by evil supernatural beings, and by earthly beings (i.e., "visible" beings; see *Trall.* 5.2) or human opponents such as heretics (Wehr, *Unsterblichkeit*, 88–91). *Pistis Sophia* 1.27 (ed. Schmidt-Till, p. 23, lines 5–11; ed. Schmidt-MacDermot, pp. 37–38) describes how Adamas the tyrant and all the tyrants of the twelve eons began to wage war with the descending Jesus, whose radiance they wished to appropriate for themselves. While this is a heavenly war, it belongs to the constellation of myths associated with the secret descent of Jesus (see Ign. *Eph.* 19:1; *Asc. Isa.* 9:14–15; 11:16). There are several Hellenistic myths about heavenly wars. The mythical war between Athens and Atlantis was thought by some interpreters to refer to a primeval heavenly battle between the stars (the Athenians) and the planets (the people of Atlantis) because of their contrary revolutions: the stars appear to revolve from east to west, while the planets seem to revolve from west to east (Proclus *In Timaeus* 1.76.21–30; cf. Philo *Som.* 2.114–15).

7b ὁ Μιχαὴλ καὶ οἱ ἄγγελοι αὐτοῦ τοῦ πολεμῆσαι μετὰ τοῦ δράκοντος. καὶ ὁ δράκων ἐπολέμησεν καὶ οἱ ἄγγελοι αὐτοῦ, "Michael and his angels had to fight with the dragon. The dragon and his angels fought back." On a lead amulet of uncertain date discovered at Amorgos there is an adjuration for the purpose of curing a tumor, part of which reads "I adjure you, malign tumor, by the name of him who . . . killed the twelve-headed dragon [τὰ τὸν δωδεκακέφαλον δράκοντα] by the hand of Michael and Gabriel, his holy archangels" (T. Homolle, "Inscriptions d'Amorgos: Lames de plomb portant des imprécations," *Bulletin de Correspondance Hellénique* 25 [1910] 430–56; the text and translation are also included in H. Leclercq, "Amulettes," *DACL* 1:1796–99). In Revelation, of course, the dragon is depicted as having seven heads (v 3; cf. 13:1; 17:3). No other precisely similar primeval myth of the destruction of the dragon with seven heads by Michael and Gabriel is known to me, though the eschatological myth in vv 7–9 is clearly an adaptation of a variant of that myth. In 11QMelch 9–15, a text riddled with lacunae, an eschatological battle is described in which Melchizedek (apparently identical with Michael; see Vermes, *Dead Sea Scrolls*, 300), allied with God's holy ones (וקדושי אל *ûqdôšê ʾēl*), i.e., angels, will judge and vanquish Belial and the spirits of his lot (רוחי גורלו *rûḥê gôrālô*). Since this is presented as an interpretation of Ps 82:1 ("ELOHIM [a term used of Melchizedek/Michael] has taken his place in the divine council; in the midst of the ELOHIM [= angels] he holds judgment") and Ps 7:7b–8a ("Take your seat on high. EL [= Melchizedek/Michael] judges the peoples"), this appears to be an event that occurs in *heaven* and thus corresponds to the eschatological events narrated in Rev 12:7–9. There are Jewish texts in which Satan (also called Beliar and Mastema) is thought to accuse Israelites before God (Job 1:6–12; 2:1–6; *Jub.* 1:20; 17:15–16; 48:15–18; *1 Enoch* 40:7 [here the accusers are "satans"]) and so is present in heaven. There were also traditions that an angelic host would defeat Satan and his spirits on the day of judgment (*T. Levi* 3:3; 1QM 15–19, where the eschatological battle between the sons of light and the sons of darkness is joined by Michael [1QM 17:7] and his hosts and Belial and his hosts; see 4Q*491* frag. 11, the "Son of Michael"), or simply a general statement that Satan would be defeated without specifying precisely how (*1 Enoch* 10:6; *T. Jud.* 25:3; *Apoc. Ezra* 4:43), or that Christ would defeat Satan (the Christian interpolations in *T. Levi* 18:12; *T. Sim.* 6:6; *T. Dan* 5:10–11; *T. Zeb.* 9:8).

The conception of a heavenly army of angels (Mach, *Engelglaubens,* 241–55) occurs frequently in the OT, early Judaism, and early Christianity. According to an ancient Israelite conception, the army of Israel could be aided by a heavenly army (Josh 5:14; 2 Kgs 6:17; Dan 10:13, 21; 12:1; 2 Macc 2:21; 3:25–26; 5:2–4; 8:19–20; 11:6; 15:22–23; 3 Macc 6:18–21; 1QM 9:5–6; 11:11–13). In the Greek world there are stories about deities who miraculously protect their temples or cities (Herodotus 8.37–39; Diodorus 11:14.3–4; Pausanias 10.23.1–10; Doran, *Temple Propaganda,* 47–52). The conception of a heavenly host occurs in Luke 2:13 (see Acts 7:42), a variant of the LXX expression στρατιὰ τοῦ οὐρανοῦ, "army of heaven" (3 Kgdms 22:19; 2 Esdr 19:6[MT Neh 9:6]; Jer 19:13; Hos 13:4; 2 Chr 33:3, 5; Neh 9:6). In Matt 26:53, Jesus refers to "twelve legions of angels," a conception based on the analogy of the organization of the Roman army as the Latin loanword "legion" indicates (see 2 Kgs 6:17). This image of a "legion" of angels is unique to the NT but occurs occasionally in later rabbinic literature (Str-B, 1:997). The conception of Michael "and his angels" has a parallel in the coming of the Son of man "with his angels" (Matt 16:27; cf. 24:31; Mark 8:38).

Excursus 12A: Michael the Archangel

Bibliography

Bauckham, R. J. *Jude, 2 Peter.* WBC 50. Waco, TX: Word, 1983. **Betz, O.** *Der Paraklet: Fürsprecher im häretischen Spätjudentum, im Johannes-Evangelium und in neu gefundenen gnostischen Schriften.* Leiden: Brill, 1963. **Kobelski, P. J.** *Melchizedek and Melchiresa.* CBQMS 10. Washington, DC: Catholic Biblical Association, 1991. **Luecken, W.** *Michael: Eine Darstellung und Vergleichung der jüdischen und der morgenländisch-christlichen Tradition vom Erzengel Michael.* Göttingen: Vandenhoeck & Ruprecht, 1898. **Rohland, J. P.** *Der Erzengel Michael: Artzt und Feldherr: Zwei Aspekte des vor- und frühbyzantinischen Michaelskultes.* Leiden: Brill, 1977.

Michael, a major angelic figure in early Judaism, is mentioned just three times in the OT (Dan 10:13, 21; 12:1), twice in the NT (Jude 9; Rev 12:7), and once in the Apostolic Fathers (Hermas *Sim.* 8.3.3). In Dan 10:13–21, Gabriel (the only other angel specifically named in the OT, though here it is not absolutely certain that he is the angel referred to) claims that he and "the prince of the kingdom of Persia" (i.e., an angel representing Persia) were in conflict for twenty-one days when he was relieved by Michael. In Dan 10:20, the "prince of Persia" and the "prince of Greece" are mentioned, and again these are clearly national angels of Persia and Greece. Beginning with Daniel, Michael is considered "the great prince [Theod ἄρχων] who has charge of your people [i.e., 'Israel']" (Dan 12:1; see *1 Enoch* 20:5) or "the ruler [ἄρχοντα] of the Jewish people" (Ps.-Dionysius Areopagita *De caelesti hierarchia* 9.2). Though this appears to be a war fought by angels, nothing is mentioned about any angelic armies they might lead. Jude 9 alludes to the story of the archangel Michael disputing with Satan over the body of Moses from the lost ending of the *Testament of Moses* (Bauckham, *Jude, 2 Peter,* 65–76). This is related to Rev 12:7–9 in that Michael and Satan are presented as in conflict, though this cannot be described as a war, nor are they backed up by opposing armies. Michael is the only angel specifically named in Revelation (and only here in 12:7–9), and this passage is the earliest evidence that Christians held the view that Michael held the first position in an angelic hierarchy. Since he is depicted in Rev 12:7–9 as leading an angelic host, he is not simply an archangel but an ἀρχιστράτηγος, "field marshall," in function if not in title; see the evidence for this title in early Jewish texts below. In *Apoc. Paul* 14, evil angels fight with good angels to prevent a sinless soul from entering heaven; when the soul does enter heaven, "Michael and all the host of angels [*Michael et omnis exercitus angelorum*]" worship God. God then turns the soul that has not sinned over to Michael to lead it into the paradise of jubilation to await the resurrection. In *Apoc. Paul* 43, Michael is again depicted as descending from heaven "and with him the whole host of angels [*Michael cumomne exercitu angelorum*]." In the fourth-century *Gos. Bartholomew* 4.29 (Hennecke-Schneemelcher, *NTA* 1:497), Michael is called "the captain of the hosts above."

In early Jewish sources, Michael is called an ἀρχάγγελος or "archangel" (Sync *1 Enoch* 9:1 [Black, *Apocalypsis,* 23]; *T. Abr.* [Rec. A] 1:4, 6; 10:1; 20:10; this title is not linked to Michael in Rec. B, with the exception of the prescript [Denis, *Concordance,* 830]; *Adam and Eve* 22:1; 37:4; 38:1; 40:1; *Par. Jer.* 9:5; *3 Apoc. Bar.* [Gk.] 11:8; Jude 9; see *4 Bar.* 9:5; *Apoc. Sedr.* 14:1; *T. Moses* 9:1 [Denis, *Fragmenta,* 64, 67; lost source for Jude 9; *Jub.* 10:7 frag. [Denis, *Fragmenta,* 86]). Michael is also called an ἀρχιστράτηγος, "commander-in-chief" (*T. Abr.* [Rec. A] 1:4; 2:2; 3:9; 4:7; 5:1; 7:11; 9:8; 10:12; 14:5, 12; 15:1; 19:4 [this title is uniformly absent from Rec. B]; *3 Apoc. Bar.* [Gk.] 11:4, 7, 8; *Gk. Apoc. Ezra* 4:24), Greek equivalent for the title "the great prince" (MT השר הגדול *haśśar haggādôl;* LXX ὁ ἄρχων ὁ μέγας) in Dan 12:1 (and rabbinic literature, though Michael is not mentioned in the Mishna; see *b. Ḥag.* 12b; *b. Menaḥ.* 110a). In the LXX, the title ἀρχιστράτηγος is used twice of a heavenly being (Josh 5:14; Dan 8:11). Michael is usually associated in early Jewish tradition with a restricted group of heavenly beings called "angels of the presence," variously identified as a group of *four* archangels (*1 Enoch* 9:1; 40:9; 54:6; 71:8, 9, 13; *Apoc. Mos.* 40:3; *Sib. Or.* 2.215; *Num. Rab.* 2:10; *Pesiq. R.* 46; *Pirqe R. El.* 4; see Lueken, *Michael,* 34–35; Bousset-Gressmann, *Religion des Judentums,* 326–27; see *Epistula Apostolorum* 13) or *seven* archangels (Tob 12:15; *1 Enoch* 20:1–7; see Lueken, *Michael,* 36–37; Bousset-Gressmann, *Religion des Judentums,* 325–36), a number conforming to the seven planets. These angels are often thought to supervise certain activities: Raphael superintends healing, Gabriel supervises warfare, and Michael attends to the prayers and supplications of people (Origen *De principiis* 1.8.1). He is sometimes singled out as the foremost angel, as in *T. Abr.* [Rec. B] 4:5 (MS B), "The same Michael is the first of the angels." Michael is involved in the eschatological struggle of the sons of light against the sons of darkness. Though Michael is mentioned just three times in the War Scroll (1QM 9:15–16; 17:6–8), it is probable that he had a greater role in the angelology of the Qumran community than might first appear. The ethical dualism of Qumran saw people as ultimately influenced by two conflicting supernatural beings (1QS 3:18–19), the רוח האמת *rûaḥ ha'ĕmet,* "Spirit of Truth," and the רוח העול *rûaḥ hā'āwel,* "Spirit of Evil." The designation מלאך חושך *mal'ak ḥôšek,* "Angel of Darkness," undoubtedly refers to Belial, i.e., Satan (1QS 1:17–18; 3:20–21; CD 5:18–19), while the שר אורים *śar 'ôrîm,* "Prince of Lights" (1QS 3:20; CD 5:18), or שר מאור *śar mā'ôr,* "Prince of Light" (1QM 13:10), or "Angel of Truth" (1QS 3:24), refers to Michael; both have the same title שר *śar,* "prince," in 1QS 3:20 and Dan 12:1 (Betz, *Paraklet*, 66–69; Leaney, *Rule*, 43–44, 148). Michael and Melchizedek are probably identified in 4Q‘Amram 3:2 (Kobelski, *Melchizedek*, 71–74). Both the Angel of Light (Michael) and Belial have angelic armies at their disposal (1QM 13:10–12). Michael is presented in Dan 10:21 and Jude 9 as one who battles the forces of evil. He is "the holder of the keys of the kingdom" (Slavonic *3 Apoc. Bar.* 11:2) and is identified as the one who conveys the prayers of people to God (Slavonic *3 Apoc. Bar.* 11:4). He is designated as "the great prince" (Dan 12:1; *b. Ḥag.* 12b; *b. Menaḥ.* 1; *b. Zebaḥ.* 62a), the commander-in-chief of the angelic forces (Dan 10:13, 21; *2 Enoch* 22:6; 33:10 [Rec. A]; *T. Abr.* [Rec. A, Rec. B] 14; *3 Apoc. Bar.* [Gk.] 11:4, 6).

8 καὶ οὐκ ἴσχυσεν οὐδὲ τόπος εὑρέθη αὐτῶν ἔτι ἐν τῷ οὐρανῷ, "but were unable to prevail, nor was there a place for them any longer in heaven." A very similar phrase occurs in Rev 20:11, καὶ τόπος οὐχ εὑρέθη αὐτοῖς, "but there was no place for them," which is a verbatim allusion to Theod Dan 2:35; in both places the pronoun appears to indicate possession. A parallel to this verse occurs in *1 Clem.* 9:3, where it is said of Enoch καὶ οὐχ εὑρέθη αὐτοῦ θάνατος, literally "and his death was not found," i.e., "and his death did not occur" or "he did not die." Since the verb ἰσχύειν can be translated into Latin as *imperium habere*, "to have imperium" (Mason, *Greek Terms*, 58), this may well be a parody of what will happen to the Roman emperor.

9a καὶ ἐβλήθη ὁ δράκων ὁ μέγας, "Then was cast down the great dragon." V 9 has a clear chiastic arrangement caused by the parenthetical mention of the dragon's aliases and the resumption that follows:

a Then was cast down the great dragon,
b the ancient serpent, who is called Devil and Satan,
b′ who leads the whole world astray;
a′ he was cast down to the earth,
and his angels were cast down along with him.

Since the combat myths in which the hero fights a dragon regularly end with the destruction of the dragon, this variant has been adapted to the primeval Jewish myth of the fall of Satan. The passive voice of the two occurrences of the aorist verb ἐβλήθη, "he was cast out," functions as the passive of divine activity, i.e., a circumlocution that avoids the name "God" as the subject of the verb (see *Comment* on 9:3). Therefore, the dragon was cast out not by Michael and his angels but ultimately by God. The myth of the heavenly battle between Michael and Satan resulting in the defeat and expulsion of Satan and his angels from heaven (vv 7–9) is narrated as an *eschatological* event in 12:9 (as it is in Luke 10:18; cf. the language of John 12:31), but as an exclusively *primordial* or *protological* event in early Jewish and Islamic literature, a motif based on Isa 14:12–15. It is of course possible that the tradition of Satan's presence before the heavenly throne of God as an adversary of the righteous on earth (see *Comment* on 12:10) led to a reinterpretation of the tradition of his primordial expulsion from heaven, resulting in a tale of his eschatological expulsion (Bousset [1906] 351). In *Adam and Eve* 12–16 (esp. 13:1; 16:2), there is a dialogue between Satan and Adam in which the former blames the latter for his expulsion from heaven (see also *Gos. Bartholomew* 52–55; *Qu'ran* 7.11–17: Iblîs [= Satan] is expelled from heaven for not prostrating himself before Adam). This myth is frequently reiterated in the *Qu'ran* (see 2.34; 15.28–39; 17.61–64; 18.50;

20.116–17; 38.71–83). Related to these traditions of the protological expulsion of Satan from heaven is the soliloquy that God gives over Adam's corpse in *Apoc. Moses* 39 in which he says that Adam will be established on the throne of his seducer (Satan), who will be cast down to the earth so that Adam might be seated above him. This Greek redaction of *Adam and Eve* 47 may refer to the eschatological expulsion of Satan from heaven. The juxtaposition of the two motifs of pride and expulsion found in Isa 14:12–15 also occurs in the *Gos. Bartholomew* 52–55 (*NTA* 1:499–500) and in the longer text of the Jewish apocalypse of *2 Enoch* 29:4–5 (Bousset [1906] 350–51), perhaps from the late first century A.D. The image of the dragon thrown down to earth has a close parallel in the only vision of Jesus reported in the synoptic Gospels: "And he said to them [seventy disciples], 'I saw Satan fall like lightning from heaven'" (Luke 10:18). This tradition, in turn, has a verbal parallel in John 12:31, "Now the ruler of this world has been cast out [ἐκβληθήσεται ἔξω]" (see 16:11). Yet here Satan has been cast not out of heaven but out of the earth; i.e., he has been defeated by Jesus. The variant reading, βληθήσεται κάτω, "has been cast down" (Codex Θ and some versional evidence: it syr^{s} cop^{sa}), makes expulsion from heaven explicit but has no claim to originality and may well have been influenced by Rev 12:9–10, 13 (see Schnackenburg, *John* 2:392). As the text in John 12:31 stands, it may mean that Satan is now driven from the world, i.e., has finally been judged and conquered by the crucifixion of Jesus (John 12:32; 16:11). An analogous vision is reported by John in Rev 9:1, "I saw a star fallen from heaven to earth," though in this case the star cannot represent Satan since it apparently functions as a messenger of God in unleashing the plague of locusts upon the earth (see *Comment* on 9:1). The Jewish character of vv 7–9 is suggested by the fact that Michael (the guardian angel of Israel; see Dan 10:13, 21; 12:1; 1QM 17:4ff.; *3 Enoch* 44:10), rather than the Messiah, is the one who defeats Satan. John clearly wants to identify the dragon with Satan, for he piles up various names for Satan in v 9, including dragon, ancient serpent, Devil, and Satan. The expulsion of Satan is also mentioned in Irenaeus *Adv. haer.* 4.40.3. Apollodorus 1.6.3 preserves the myth of Typhon's attempted assault on heaven in which he was attacked by Zeus when he followed the gods to Egypt. In *Apoc. Abr.* 23, the dragon (with six pairs of wings and human hands and feet) is the instrument of Azazel, or Satan, in the temptation of Eve in the Garden of Eden.

9b ὁ ὄφις ὁ ἀρχαῖος, "the ancient serpent." This phrase begins a short excursus in which the aliases of the dragon are listed. While the woman and the child are neither named nor identified, the author-editor is careful to identify the dragon by listing his traditional names and designations in v 9. The phrase נחש הקדמוני *nāḥāš haqqaddĕmônî*, "the ancient serpent," as a designation of Satan occurs occasionally in rabbinic literature (*t. Soṭa* 4.17 [*var. lect.* in MSS W and A; see *Der Tosefta-Traktat Soṭa*, ed. H. Bietenhard, 289]; *Sipre Deut.* § 323 on 32:33 [S. Horovitz and L. Finkelstein, eds., *Sifre on Deuteronomy* (New York: Jewish Theological Seminary of America, 1969) p. 374,11]; *b. Ber.* 9b; *Gen. Rab.* 22:12 on Gen 4:15; Tanchuma מצורע *mĕṣôrāʿ* § 7 [S. Buber, ed., *Midrash Tanḥuma,* 2 vols. (Jerusalem: Eshkol, 1990) p. 24a,3]; see also Str-B, 3:814; *Der Tosefta-Traktat Soṭa*, ed. H. Bietenhard, 82 n. 151).

Rev 12:9 provides the only explicit biblical identification of Satan with the serpent who tempted Eve in Gen 3:1–7. However, such an identification *may* be presupposed in several other NT passages, such as in Rom 16:20, if the phrase "crush Satan under your feet" alludes to the "protevangelium" in Gen 3:15, and perhaps also in Luke 10:19, which links the fall of Satan (seen by Jesus in the vision reported in 10:18) with the ability to tread on serpents (and scorpions). In 2 Cor 11:3, Paul mentions that the serpent deceived Eve, and in 2 Cor 11:14 he observes that "Satan disguises himself as an angel of light" (these two statements may be connected in view of *Apoc. Moses* 17:1, where Satan came in the form of an angel to tempt Eve, apparently using the serpent as a kind of ventriloquist's dummy). Wis 2:24 presupposes the association or identity of the serpent with the devil, and the identity of Satan with the serpent is also presupposed in *Adam and Eve* 16:3. In *3 Apoc. Bar.* 9:7, it is Sammael (Syriac *Satanel*) who took the serpent as a garment. In the Latin version of Origen's *De principiis* 3.2.1, Michael the archangel reportedly says that the serpent was inspired by the devil and therefore caused Adam and Eve to sin. That John piles up synonyms for Satan suggests that he is consciously attempting to expose the real role of this antagonist of God throughout cosmic and human history. Isa 27:1 is an important OT passage in which imagery drawn from the primordial combat myth is given an *eschatological* application (Day, *Conflict,* 142–51). In this passage a single monster is described using three separate designations, Leviathan the twisting serpent, Leviathan the crooked serpent, and the dragon (a fact made evident by parallels in Ugaritic texts; see Day, *Conflict,* 142). Some have taken these three terms to refer to three constellations, Serpens, Draco, and Hydra (C. F. Burney, "The Three Serpents of Isaiah XXXVII 1," *JTS* 11 [1910] 443–47). Prior to Rev 12:9, an explicit identification of Satan with the serpent in Eden is hinted at in *Apoc. Moses* 16:4–5 (Charlesworth, *OTP* 2:277), where the serpent becomes the spokesperson for the devil. In *Adam and Eve* 9:1–11:3, Satan (later referred to as the devil) transforms himself into a luminous angel and deceives Eve a second time. At least in these related compositions, deriving from perhaps the first century A.D., it is clear that Satan is the real tempter of Eve. Wis 2:24 implies the connection by claiming that "by the envy of the devil death entered into the world." In *1 Enoch* 69:6, Gadreel, one of the lesser fallen angels, is credited with leading Eve astray, implying the identity of the serpent with a fallen angel. In *PGM* IV.1636, Helios is addressed as "the great Serpent, leader of all" (Betz, *Greek Magical Papyri,* 60).

9c ὁ καλούμενος Διάβολος καὶ ὁ Σατανᾶς, "the one called Devil and Satan." The phrase ὁ καλούμενος is a typical formula used for introducing an alternate name, perhaps more familiar to the hearer or reader. An alternative name or alias was frequently introduced by the phrase ὁ καί, or *qui et,* used after the first century B.C. (Acts 13:9; Jos. *Ant.* 1.240; 12.285; 13.320; *J.W.* 1.99; 2.530; Ign. *Eph. inscr.; Magn. inscr.*), or other expressions such as ὁ (ἐπι)καλούμενος, or ὁ λεγόμενος (Jos. *J.W.* 2.167; Acts 1:23; 4:36; 10:5, 18, 32; 11:13; 12:12, 25; 13:1; 15:22, 37); see M. Lambertz, "Zur Ausbreitung des Supernomen oder Signum im römischen Reiche," *Glotta* 4 (1912) 78–143; 5 (1914) 99–170. In the Coptic-Gnostic tractate *Testim. Truth* 47.5–6, a revisionist version of Gen 3, it is said that God "cursed the serpent and called him Devil." Satan is mentioned in just three OT books (1 Chr 21:1; Job 1:6, 9, 12; 2:3, 4, 6, 7; Zech 3:1, 2), meaning "accuser," "adversary." The name "Satan" also occurs in early Jewish literature (*T. Gad* 4:7; *T. Ash.* 6:4; *T. Dan* 3:6; 5:5–6; 6:1), but it never occurs in the literature from Qumran, where the name "Beliar" is preferred. Yet in the LXX, the Hebrew term שָׂטָן *śāṭān* is translated by (ὁ) διάβολος in 1 Chronicles, Job, and Zechariah, meaning "one who separates," "the seducer," "the enemy." The devil is called Sotona because his original name was Satanail, and he is the one who seduced Eve in the Garden (*2 Enoch* [Rec. J] 31:6). The designation "devil" occurs in some early Jewish texts (*T. Naph.* 3:1; 8:4, 6; *T. Gad* 5:2; *T. Ash.* 1:8–9; 3:2), thirty-six times in the NT ("Satan" occurs thirty-four times), and becomes the standard designation for Satan in the Apostolic Fathers, where the term "Satan" itself occurs just three times (*Barn.* 18:1; Ign. *Eph.* 13:1; Pol. *Phil.* 7:1, always with the article). The articular form of διάβολος occurs twenty-four times (Ign. *Eph.* 10:3; *Trall.* 8:1; *Rom.* 5:3; *Smyrn.* 9:1; Pol. *Phil.* 7:1; *2 Clem.* 5:3; *Mart. Pol.* 3:1; Hermas *Mand.* 4.3.4, 6; 5.1.3; 7.2, 3; 9.9, 11; 11.3, 17; 12.2.2; 12.4.6, 7; 12.5.1; 12.6.1, 2, 4; *Sim.* 8.3.6; see G. J. M. Bartelink, *Lexicologisch-semantische Studie over de Taal van de Apostolische Vaders* [Utrecht: Beyers, n.d.] 98–99).

The piling up of four aliases for Satan in this verse is reduplicated in 20:2 and has a general parallel in the reptilian trinity mentioned in Isa 27:1, "In that day the Lord with his hard and great and strong sword will punish Leviathan the fleeing serpent, Leviathan the twisting serpent, and he will slay the dragon that is in the sea." Justin speaks of "the prince of evil demons called serpent and Satan and Devil" in *1 Apol.* 28.1, and an extremely long list of aliases occurs in the longer recension of Ignatius *Phil.* 11:6–7 (fourth century A.D.), "Beliar, dragon, apostate, crooked serpent, rebel against God, outcast from Christ, alien from the Holy Spirit, exile from the chorus of angels, one who does violence to the laws of God, enemy of customs."

9d ὁ πλανῶν τὴν οἰκουμένην ὅλην, "who leads the whole world astray." The substantival participle ὁ πλανῶν, "the one who deceives," is used of Satan twice in Revelation, here and in 20:10. In both contexts ὁ πλανῶν does not, strictly speaking, function as a title (it has different objects), yet it is transformed into a title in the term ὁ κοσμοπλανής, "Deceiver of the World," in *Did.* 16:4. Yet in *Did.* 16:4 the title is used of the eschatological antagonist, not Satan, though it is widely assumed that the former is a tool of the latter. The motif of "leading someone astray" occurs frequently in Revelation and in early Jewish and early Christian literature generally. Subjects of the verb πλανᾶν in Revelation include "Jezebel" (2:20), the devil (12:9; 20:3, 8, 10), the beast from the land (13:14), also called the false prophet (19:20), and Rome (18:23). Satan is called the "Prince of Deceit" in *T. Sim.* 3:5; *T. Jud.* 19:4.

9e ἐβλήθη εἰς τὴν γῆν καὶ οἱ ἄγγελοι αὐτοῦ μετ' αὐτοῦ ἐβλήθησαν, "he was cast down to the earth, and his angels were cast down along with him." In ancient mythologies, expulsions from heaven are much rarer than (attempted) ascents to heaven (see *Comment* on v 5). In *1 Enoch* it is repeatedly stated that the Watchers *left* heaven (6:6; 12:4; 15:3; see *Jub.* 4:15; *2 Enoch* 18:3–4 [short version]). While they cannot ascend again to heaven (*1 Enoch* 14:5), nowhere does it say that they were actually *cast out* of heaven. This tradition is repeated in Jude 6, "And the angels that did not keep their own position but left their proper dwelling have been kept by him in eternal chains in the nether gloom until the judgment of the great day" (these angels are called "wandering stars" in v 13b). *2 Enoch* 29:4–5 does speak of the expulsion of an unnamed archangel from heaven on the second day of creation (tr. Andersen, in Charlesworth, *OTP* 1:148):

> He thought up the impossible idea, that he might place his throne higher than the clouds which are above the earth, and that he might become equal to my power. And I hurled him out from the height, together with his angels.

Yet this quotation with the motif of the fall of Satan through hubris is from the *longer* text of *2 Enoch* (an expansion of the shorter text rather than the source abridged to form the shorter text) and is relatively late (Milik, *Enoch,* 107–16; G. G. Scholem, *Major Trends in Jewish Mysticism* [New York: Schocken, 1960] 40–79; Forsyth, *The Old Enemy,* 242–47). *Sib. Or.* 5.512–31 narrates a battle among the stars of the zodiac, which concludes (lines 528–29; tr. Collins, in Charlesworth, *OTP* 1:405) "Heaven itself was roused until it shook the fighters. In anger it cast them headlong to earth." In the Coptic-Gnostic tractate *Orig. World* 121.30–35, Sophia Zoe is said to have expelled the seven "rulers of darkness" from their heavens and cast them down into the world, where they lived in the form of evil spirits. Later it is said that these seven rulers made demonic angels to serve them and these introduced humanity to a variety of errors (123.2–15).

According to a scholium on Apollonius Rhodius *Argonautica* 4.57, which alludes to a portion of Hesiod's lost work Μεγάλη Ἠοίαι, "Great Eoiae," Endymion was carried up (ἀνενεχθῆναι) to heaven by Zeus, but when he tried to make love to Hera, "he was thrown out, and descended into Hades [ἐκβληθέντα κατελθεῖν εἰς Ἀΐδου]" (C. Wendel, *Scholia in Apollonium Rhodium Vetera* [Berlin: Weidmann, 1935] 264–65). Similarly, Pindar claims that the raptured Pelops was later "released" (προῆκαν) from Olympus to live again in the human world (*Olympian Odes* 1.65). In *Iliad* 1.586–94, Hephaestus recounts to his mother Hera how Zeus had cast him down from Olympos to Lemnos, thereby accounting for his lameness (see Lucian *De sacrifiis* 6; the story of Hephaestus' [Mulciber's] fall is retold in Milton, *Paradise Lost* 1.740–516 in language drawn from the tradition of Satan's expulsion). Another variant is recorded in *Iliad* 18.394–99, in which Hera herself threw Hephaestus out of Olympus (see *Homeric Hymn to Apollo* 317–20). The two versions are harmonized in Apollodorus 1.3.5. Bellerophon, who tried to enter Olympus, was thrown from Pegasus (Pindar *Isthmian Odes* 7.43–47; Nonnos *Dionysiaca* 11.144–46; see P. Diel, *Symbolism in Greek Mythology* [Boulder, CO; London: Shambhala, 1980] 67). Other stories using the "cast out" motif include the tale of Side, whom Hera cast down into Hades (ἔρριψεν εἰς Ἀΐδου) because she was envious of her beauty (Apollodorus 1.4.3). A much closer parallel is found in Hesiod *Theog.* 820, where the author summarizes the results of the Titanomachy: "Then, after Zeus had expelled the Titans from heaven [ἀπ' οὐρανοῦ ἐξέλασεν]," for heaven was where Kronos reigned (Hesiod *Works and Days* 111), even though the Titans were said to have fought the Olympians from Mount Othrus (Hesiod *Theog.* 632; see West, *Theogony,* 340–41).

10a καὶ ἤκουσα φωνὴν μεγάλην ἐν τῷ οὐρανῷ λέγουσαν, ἄρτι ἐγένετο ἡ σωτηρία καὶ ἡ δύναμις καὶ ἡ βασιλεία τοῦ θεοῦ ἡμῶν καὶ ἡ ἐξουσία τοῦ χριστοῦ αὐτοῦ, "Then I heard a loud voice in heaven, saying, 'The victory and the power and the kingship of our God / and the authority of his Messiah have now occurred.'" On the motif of the unidentified sound or voice, see *Comment* on 10:4. In this instance an individual voice seems less likely or appropriate than the sound of a large group (cf. 11:15; 19:1; Jörns, *Evangelium,* 110). At this point the author inserts a hymnic passage consisting of vv 10–12, which comment on the significance of the expulsion of Satan from heaven. Satan's expulsion means nothing less than the victory of God and his Messiah. The temporal adverb ἄρτι, "now," together with the aorist verb ἐγένετο, which has perfective value ("has occurred, has happened"), indicates that the ascriptions of deliverance, power, and kingship to God are grounded in the specific temporal occurrence of Satan's expulsion from heaven narrated in v 9 and cited as the specific cause for this song of victory in v 10. Linking this occurrence of victory, power, and kingship with the salvation-historical period of Christ's lordship revealed by the cross and resurrection (Roloff, *Revelation,* 149), or even more specifically with the cross of Christ (Caird, 153–54; Sweet, 201; Beasley-Murray, 203), is based primarily on the interpretive overlay found in v 11, though it has a slim exegetical basis in the chapter taken as a whole. Some scholars have construed σωτηρία in 12:10 (and 7:10 and 19:1) to mean "victory" (Eichhorn, *Commentarius* 2:96; Bousset [1906] 342; Charles, 1:326; Beasley-Murray, 202; *TDNT* 7:998), a Hebraism based on a frequent meaning of יְשׁוּעָה *yĕšûʿâ* (Exod 14:13, 30; 15:2; BDB, 447; *TDNT* 7:976; *TDOT* 6:450–51). However, יָשָׁע *yāšāʿ* and יְשׁוּעָה *yĕšûʿâ* mean "bringing help to those in trouble" rather than rescuing them from trouble (*TDOT* 6:445). While σωτηρία certainly centers on the notion of "salvation" in the sense of the "deliverance, rescue" of the people of God (Bratcher-Hatton, *Revelation,* 187), the context of the heavenly battle between Michael and the dragon and the use of military imagery in v 11 suggest that "victory" is a particularly apt translation. This proclamation that deliverance *has occurred* is in some tension with 11:15, where it is said ἐγένετο ἡ βασιλεία τοῦ κόσμου τοῦ κυρίου, "the Lord's kingship over the world *has occurred.*" If God's kingship has already become a fact in 11:15, what can the duplicate statement in 12:10 mean? The answer must be that in the present text the coming or occurrence of the kingship of God is described proleptically.

This is the only place in Revelation where the ἐξουσία, "authority," of the Messiah or of Christ is mentioned, though in 2:26 the risen Christ promises ἐξουσία over the nations to the conquering Christian. Elsewhere in the NT and early Jewish literature, authority is said to be given by God to Jesus or to a Jewish redeemer figure (Matt 28:18; John 3:35; 5:27; 13:3; 17:2; Dan 7:13; *1 Enoch* 69:27; see *Corp. Herm.* 1.32). The delegation of authority by the dragon (Satan) to the beast from the sea (13:2, 4) is analogous. The term ἐξουσία is the Greek word most frequently used to translated *imperium,* a Latin term for supreme administrative power (in both war and in the interpretation of law), first exercised by Roman kings, then by magistrates, and finally by Roman emperors (Mason, *Greek Terms,* 132–34); other Greek terms for *imperium,* used less frequently, include ἰσχύς, "power, might," and more rarely δύναμις, "power, authority." In the early coinage issued by Augustus, the emperor prefers to emphasize his *auctoritas,* "prestige," rather than his *imperium,* "military force" (Hannestad, *Roman Art,* 47).

10b ὅτι ἐβλήθη ὁ κατήγωρ τῶν ἀδελφῶν ἡμῶν, "Because the accuser of our brothers and sisters was cast out." The *reason* Satan was cast out of heaven, i.e., the basis of the conflict between the dragon and his angels and Michael and his angels, is not specifically mentioned. The term κατήγωρ, "accuser," is a literal translation of the Hebrew שטן *śāṭān,* "Satan." In Job and Zechariah שטן *śāṭān* always occurs with the definite article, השטן *haśśāṭān,* as a way of indicating the title of the heavenly accuser. ὁ κατήγωρ is articular because it refers to this well-known figure in biblical and early Jewish tradition. Though the LXX regularly translates שָׂטָן *śāṭān* with διάβολος (e.g., Job 1:6, 7, 9, 12; Zach 3:1), the term κατήγωρ, "accuser," is equally appropriate, and it is perhaps for that reason that the term διάβολος is introduced in v 12. The term κατήγωρ is transliterated in rabbinic sources in the form קטיגור *qāṭêgôr* as one of the standard epithets of Satan (*m. ʾAbot* 4:11; *Tg. Exod.* 32:19; Str-B, 1:141–42). Some commentators have thus argued incorrectly that κατήγωρ is a Semitism (B. Weiss, *Johannes-Apokalypse,* 109; Bousset [1906] 342; Charles, 1:327;

TDNT 3:636). In support of this view it is sometimes argued that a Hebrew loanword with an analogous formation, סְנֵיגוֹר *sĕnêgôr,* is attested in Greek only in the form συνήγορος, "advocate," never συνήγωρ (*TDNT* 3:636). Rather, κατήγωρ is a colloquial back formation from the genitive plural κατηγόρων on the analogy of such forms as ῥήτωρ (genitive plural ῥητόρων) and διάκων (genitive plural διακονῶν); see Deissmann, *Light,* 90–91; BDF § 52; Moulton-Howard, *Accidence,* 127–28; *TDNT* 3:636; Mussies, *Morphology,* 114; Bauer-Aland, 861. The view that κατήγωρ is a colloquial Greek formation is confirmed by *PGM* X.25–26, where the term is used as part of an all-purpose charm: ποιεῖ γὰρ πρὸς ἐχθροὺς καὶ κατηγόρας, "for it works against enemies and accusers."

The phrase "our brothers" is problematic because the hymnic section in vv 10–12 was introduced as the utterance of "a loud voice," which seems to suggest that the speaker or singer is an unidentified *individual,* though it is, of course, possible for an individual to articulate the interests and concerns of the group to which he belongs. The expression "our brothers," however, seems to suggest that those in the heavenly group represented by the speaker are the peers of those who are yet on earth (i.e., the "we"/"they" dichotomy presupposed by this statement constitutes one single group). Though Bousset suggests that the singers must be angels rather than humans ([1906] 342), Charles is surely correct that Christian martyrs in heaven must be intended (1:327). Since it appears, however, that their earthly colleagues have been martyred (v 11), the dichotomy between "we" and "they" is problematic because at least some of the earthly Christians are part of the heavenly group.

10c ὁ κατηγορῶν αὐτοὺς ἐνώπιον τοῦ θεοῦ ἡμῶν ἡμέρας καὶ νυκτός, "who accused them before our God day and night." This part of the hymnic section in vv 10–12 serves as a partial commentary or explanation for Satan's role in heaven and hints at the reason for his expulsion. The conception of Satan as a member of the heavenly court (see 1 Kgs 22:19; Pss 82:1; 89:5–7; Jer 23:18, 22; the rabbis held that there was a heavenly law court presided over by God himself; see *b. Sanh.* 38b; *Exod. Rab.* 30:18; *Lev. Rab.* 24:2; P. Alexander in Charlesworth, *OTP* 1:244–45) indicates that Satan's traditional role was the accuser of the righteous before God. This tradition is found in the OT in Job 1:6–12; 2:1–7 (see *T. Job* 8:1–3; 16:2–4; 20:1–3) and Zech 3:1 (see 1 Chr 21:1). In Zech 3:1, the angel of the Lord and Satan play the roles of defender and prosecutor, respectively, of Joshua, and these opposing figures appear again in 4QʿAmramᵇ, where the opponents are Belial (also called the Prince of Darkness and Melchirešaʿ) and Michael (also called the Prince of Light and Melchizedek). A different form of the tradition is reflected in *1 Enoch* 40:7, part of a throne-room scene in 40:1–10, where שטנים *śĕṭānîm,* "satans," are mentioned as those "who come before the Lord of Spirits to accuse those who dwell on the dry ground" (tr. Knibb, *Enoch*) and are expelled from heaven. *Apoc. Zeph.* 3:8–9 describes "the angels of the accuser" who sit at the gate of heaven and write down the sins people commit and transmit that information to the accuser himself. Similarly, in *Apoc. Zeph.* 6:17, the great angel that "Zephaniah" saw in 6:8 is described by another angel as "the one who accuses men in the presence of the Lord." According to *3 Enoch* 26:12, each day Satan confers with Sammaʾel, prince of Rome, and Dubbiʾel, prince of Persia, and they record the sins of Israel and give them to the seraphim to transmit to God. Since there is no hint elsewhere in Revelation that Satan had a role to play in the heavenly court, it is likely that this tradition has been added here by way of explaining the presence of Satan in heaven in v 7. Hermas reportedly saw a vision of his mistress Rhoda in heaven in which she claimed that she had been taken up to heaven to accuse (ἐλέγχειν) him of his sins before the Lord (Hermas *Vis.* 1.1.4), much as a witness for the prosecution. On the hendiadys "day and night," meaning "continually," see *Comment* on 4:8.

11a καὶ αὐτοὶ ἐνίκησαν αὐτὸν διὰ τὸ αἷμα τοῦ ἀρνίου, "And they conquered him through the blood of the Lamb." The verb νικᾶν, "to conquer, be victorious," occurs seventeen times in Revelation; when Christ is the subject of this verb (5:5), it means that he conquered *through death,* and it means precisely the same thing when it is used eleven times of Christians, explicitly in 12:11 and implicitly in the other references (cf. 2:7, 11, 17, 26; 3:5, 12, 21[2x]; see A. T. Hanson, *The Wrath of the Lamb* [London: SPCK, 1957] 165). There is a close parallel to v 11a in 1 Cor 15:57, "Thanks to God who gave us victory [νῖκος] through our Lord Jesus Christ," where in the context of the entire chapter it is likely that the resurrection of Jesus is meant. Nevertheless, in both passages, one emphasizing Christ's death and the other his resurrection, victory is achieved by means of Christ (διά). *1 Enoch* 50:2 predicts that "the righteous will conquer in the name of the Lord of Spirits." The motif of Jewish martyrs "conquering" (νικᾶν) their besiegers and torturers by facing suffering and death nobly is emphasized in 4 Macc 6:10, "And like a noble athlete the old man, while being beaten, was victorious [ἐνίκα] over his torturers." See also 4 Macc 7:4b, "Although his sacred life was consumed by tortures and racks, he conquered [ἐνίκησεν] the besiegers with the shield of his devout reason" (see 4 Macc 9:6, 30; 11:20; 16:14; 17:15 [θεοσέβεια δὲ ἐνίκα]). The verb νικᾶν occurs fifteen times in 4 Maccabees, frequently of conquering through the ὑπομονή, "endurance," of torture (1:11b, "By their endurance [τῇ ὑπομονῇ] they conquered [νικήσαντες] the tyrant"). This endurance, however, is a Stoic virtue, since it is based on pure reason (4 Macc 3:17–18; 6:33; 8:1), which is able to conquer the emotions (13:7). In *T. Job* 27.3–9, Satan claims that Job conquered (ἐνίκησας) him through perseverance (καρτερία). The same motif occurs in Christian martyrological literature. In *Mart. Perpetua* 10.13–14, the martyr states (tr. Musurillo, *Acts,* 119), "Then I awoke. I realized that it was not with wild animals that I would fight [*pugnaturam*] but with the Devil, but I knew that I would win the victory [*uictoriam*]." Here, of course, *uictoria* means dying without renouncing faith in Christ.

This entire verse, as well as the entire section in vv 10–12, is probably a redactional interpolation by John (the view of many critics: E. Vischer, *Offenbarung,* 28; F. Spitta, 130; J. Weiss, *Offenbarung,* 80; Bousset [1906] 343, 356 [who considers vv 10–11 to be additions]; Charles, 1:328). There are several reasons for regarding vv 10–12 as later additions to the text: (1) These verses focus on the theme of Christian martyrdom, which is otherwise touched on only in 12:17. (2) The identity of the speaker or speakers is not mentioned, though they refer, in the third person, to the dragon as "the accuser of *our* brothers" (v 10), and it is they (αὐτοί, v 11) who have conquered him through martyrdom. However, what does the dragon's role as one who continually denounces them before God have to do with martyrdom? Is it that he receives temporary authority to test Christians as in *T. Job* 8.1–3; 16.2–4; 20.1–3? (3) The Lamb is mentioned here, though not in the rest of Rev 12 (the Lamb is frequently mentioned in interpolated passages). (4) The passage deals with the proleptic victory of Christian martyrs (Bousset [1906] 342) since in 12:17

the dragon is depicted as beginning to pursue the seed of the woman (i.e., Christians). Cf. Rev 2:10, "Be faithful to the point of death [ἄχρι θανάτου]." (5) The victory won over Satan reflected in this verse is not only a victory *in heaven* but also one that has been won on earth through martyrdom; it is not a victory that will be won in the future but one that is already a part of past experience.

11b καὶ διὰ τὸν λόγον τῆς μαρτυρίας αὐτῶν, "and through the word of their testimony." The genitive τῆς μαρτυρίας is a genitive of apposition, indicating that "their testimony" is a further specification of "the word." This phrase has several parallels in Revelation: (1) 1:9, "because of the word of God and my witness to Jesus"; (2) 6:9, "because of the word of God and because of the witness which they bore"; (3) 12:17, "who . . . maintained their witness to Jesus"; (4) 19:10, "who maintain the testimony concerning Jesus"; and (5) 20:4, "because of their witness to Jesus and because of the word of God."

11c καὶ οὐκ ἠγάπησαν τὴν ψυχὴν αὐτῶν ἄχρι θανάτου, "for they did not love their life to the point of death." The *topos* of "the love of life" standing in the way of a willingness to die for an important cause is typically Hellenistic (Euripides *Hecuba* 348; *Hercules* 518, 531–34; Philo *Leg.* 369; Jos. *Ant.* 6.344; 12.301; 13.198), e.g., Demosthenes *Or.* 60.28, "they preferred to be dead rather than through love of life [φιλοψυχήσαντες] to survive among the Greeks." The terms used in these texts, cognates of φιλοζω- and φιλοψυχ-, all meaning "love of life," are frequently considered equivalents of "cowardice." There is a saying of Jesus that occurs in three relatively independent versions in which the notion of "saving one's life" is found in paradoxical formulations (Crossan, *Fragments,* 89–94): (1) "loving life" and therefore losing it and "hating life" and therefore achieving it (John 12:25), (2) "saving one's life" and therefore losing it, and "losing it" and therefore finding it (Mark 8:35 = Matt 16:25 = Luke 9:24), and (3) "finding" or "seeking to gain one's life" and then losing it, versus "losing life" and then finding it (Matt 10:39 = Luke 17:33; see Stroker, *Extracanonical,* 131–32). There are a number of passages in the OT, early Judaism, and early Christianity in which the truism that people love their lives is used to motivate virtuous behavior (Jer 17:21; Prov 22:5; Luke 10:27; Eph 5:28; 1 Pet 3:10; Jos. *Ant.* 17.180). See also Ign. *Eph.* 9:3, "Love nothing according to human life, but God alone," in the context of the author's awareness of impending martyrdom.

12a διὰ τοῦτο εὐφραίνεσθε, οἱ οὐρανοὶ καὶ οἱ ἐν αὐτοῖς σκηνοῦντες, "Therefore rejoice, O heaven, / and those who dwell therein." The exultant call for the heavens to rejoice occurs several times in the OT, but it is usually paired with a parallel appeal to the earth to rejoice as well (Ps 96:11; Isa 44:23; 49:13; 4Q*176* = 4QTanhumin 1–2 ii 1–2; 4Q*88* = 4QPsalms[f] 10:5), though in this instance a woe is pronounced on the earth because of the devil's presence there (see v 12b). This passage probably alludes to LXX Deut 32:43, freely reformed, since the initial summons for the heavens to rejoice is paired with an appeal for heavenly beings to respond to God in worship:

εὐφράνθητε, οὐρανοί, ἅμα αὐτῷ,
Rejoice, heavens, together with him,

καὶ προσκυνησάτωσαν αὐτῷ πάντες υἱοὶ θεοῦ
and let all the sons of God worship him.

On the plural form of "heaven," see *Note* 12:12.d. On the three zones of the cosmos mentioned in v 12ab, heaven, earth, and sea, see *Comments* on 5:3 and 10:6.

12b οὐαὶ τὴν γῆν καὶ τὴν θάλασσαν, "Woe to the earth and the sea." The term οὐαί, "woe," in the NT occurs primarily in the synoptic Gospels (twelve times in Matthew; two in Mark; fifteen in Luke), *always* in sayings of Jesus. The term occurs fourteen times in Revelation. In both contexts it conveys a prophetic gravity that calls to mind the great prophetic speeches of denunciation in the OT, particularly in Isaiah and Jeremiah. While the term "earth" is a figure of speech for the people of the world (cf. 14:16), it is not immediately evident why the author includes the "sea" in his pronouncement of woe.

12c ὅτι κατέβη ὁ διάβολος πρὸς ὑμᾶς ἔχων θυμὸν μέγαν, "because the devil, who is very angry, was cast down to you." The term διάβολος, "devil," occurs just five times in Revelation (2:10; 12:9, 12; 20:2, 10), twice in nearly identical lists of aliases (12:9; 20:2). On the anger of the devil, see *Comment* on 12:17a.

12d εἰδὼς ὅτι ὀλίγον καιρὸν ἔχει, "because he knows that he has only a short time." The anger and hostility of Satan toward the people of God are here said to be based on his awareness of the temporal limitations God has placed on his activities. According to the eschatological schema of Rev 20:3, Satan is to be released for a short time (μικρὸς χρόνος) after his thousand-year confinement (in parallels in Jewish apocalypses, the evil angels are not released but are bound until the time of judgment; see *1 Enoch* 18:16; 21:6). In Rev 17:10, the period of activity of the seventh king is described as ὀλίγον (here used as an adverb of time), meaning a "short [time]," again reflecting the foreordained eschatological plan of God. Although the OT occasionally refers to the short time allotted to the wicked (Job 20:5; Prov 10:27), that limitation is based on the relatively short span of human life (Wis 2:1; 4 Ezra 8:5).

13 Καὶ ὅτε εἶδεν ὁ δράκων ὅτι ἐβλήθη εἰς τὴν γῆν ἐδίωξεν τὴν γυναῖκα ἥτις ἔτεκεν τὸν ἄρσενα, "And when the dragon realized that he had been cast down to the earth, he pursued the woman who had delivered the male child." The noun τὸν ἄρσενα, "male child," is a masculine accusative with an anaphoric article referring back to the anarthrous noun ἄρσεν in v 5, but there it is a neuter accusative. This discrepancy may reflect the editorial activity of the author-editor (Yarbro Collins, *Combat,* 147 n. 2). Charles conjectures that the original form of v 13 was καὶ ὁ δράκων ἐδίωξεν τὴν γυναῖκα, "and the dragon pursued the woman" (1:329–30). In Plutarch's retelling of the Isis-Osiris myth, he relates how many were transferring their allegiance from Seth/Typhon to Horus/Harpocrates (the son of Osiris), and when Thueris, the concubine of Typhon, came over to the side of Horus, "a serpent which was pursuing [ἐπιδιώκων] her was cut in pieces by the followers of Horus" (*De Iside* 358C–D). In a peculiar episode in *T. Sol.* 14:4, "Solomon" interviews a demon called the "Winged Dragon," who chases after only beautiful women with whom he has anal intercourse. He claims that one of the women he attacked bore a child named Eros. Only the motif of a dragon chasing a fleeing woman connects that passage to this.

14a καὶ ἐδόθησαν τῇ γυναικὶ αἱ δύο πτέρυγες τοῦ ἀετοῦ τοῦ μεγάλου, "Then the woman was provided with the two wings of a large eagle." The imagery suggests not that the woman is *rescued* by a large eagle, and is somehow borne into a wilderness fastness, but that she is outfitted with a pair of eagle's wings and is thereby enabled to fly into the wilderness herself. This suggests comparison with the many metamorphosis stories in Greek mythology in which people in danger are transformed into birds to enable them to escape (Forbes Irving, *Metamorphosis,* 96–127 [esp. 106–7], 235–36). Appearances of deities in the form of birds occur in the mythologies of the eastern Mediterranean world. Philo of Byblos reported that Canaanite deities took the form of birds (Attridge-Oden, *Philo,* 56–59), and the mythological Ugaritic texts provide numerous examples of this conception (Korpel, *Clouds,* 544–53). In an Osiris hymn from the Eighteenth Dynasty of Egypt (ca. 1500 B.C.), Isis is depicted as having two wings with which she searches for her brother Osiris (Budge, *Osiris* 1:94). In another Egyptian myth, the gods flee from Seth-Typhon and change themselves into various animals (Apollodorus 1.6.3; Ovid *Metam.* 5.321–31; J. G. Griffiths, "The Flight of the Gods before Typhon: An Unrecognized Myth?" *Hermes* 88 [1960] 374–76). After deities have appeared to people in disguise, they sometimes assume the form of birds when they leave (*Odyssey* 1.319–23, 420; 3.371–72). Since the word "eagle" has a definite article, the author appears to assume that this eagle is well known to his readers (Charles, 1:330). The argument that this could refer to the anarthrous ἀετός in 8:13 is specious (LeFrois, *Woman,* 183–84), as is the suggestion that the definite article indicates that the constellation Eagle is in view (Boll, 113). The notion of rescue by flying away like a bird is reflected in *1 Enoch* 96:2, where it is said that the young of the righteous will mount up and rise like eagles in the day of distress. The precedent for this is the well-known biblical association between the Exodus from Egypt and the wings of an eagle, expressed in Exod 19:4, "You have seen what I did to the Egyptians, and how I bore you on eagles' wings and brought you to myself" (cf. 4Q*504* = 4QDibHam[a] frag. 6, lines 6–7 [tr. García Martínez, *Dead Sea Scrolls,* 417], "You have lifted us wonderfully [upon the wings of] eagles and you have made us enter to you"). Deut 32:10–14, part of the Song of Moses, contains three motifs that also occur here: the wilderness, protection by an eagle, and nourishment. These themes are expanded in *Tg. Onq.* Deut 32:10–14 (Grossfeld, *Targum Onqelos,* 91–92) and in the Fragment-Targums on Deut 32:10–14 (Klein, *Fragment-Targums* 2:86, 183–84). In *T. Moses* 10:8, Israel will be rescued by mounting upon the neck and wings of an eagle (see *1 Enoch* 96:2). The Latin word for "eagle" is *aquila,* which could have been associated with *aquilo,* the Latin term for "north wind"; see Hyginus *Fabulae* 140 (tr. Grant, *Hyginus*), "by order of Jove the wind Aquilo [the Greek term is Βορέας] carried Latona [i.e., 'Leto'] away" (pointed out by Zielinski, *FuF* 7 [1931] 155–56). This motif brings the version of the Apollo-Leto-Typhon myth preserved by Hyginus closer to the version used by John in Rev 12.

14b ἵνα πέτηται εἰς τὴν ἔρημον εἰς τὸν τόπον αὐτῆς, "that she might fly to her place in the wilderness." This clause (see *Comment* on v 14c) is a revision of v 6ab, which serves to resume the narrative interrupted by the interpolations in vv 7–12: "The woman then fled into the wilderness where she had a place prepared there for her by God." The wilderness has both negative and positive associations in the OT and early Jewish literature (see Talmon, "'Desert Motif,'" 31–63). The connection of the Exodus theme with a flight into the wilderness for refuge is undoubtedly present. It is positively depicted as a place of refuge and salvation (Isa 40:3; Jer 31:2; 48:6; Ezek 34:25; Ps 55:7–8; see Talmon, '"Desert Motif,'" 42, 45–46). Hagar fled into the wilderness to escape the anger of Sarah (Gen 16:6–14). The Israelites escaped Egyptian bondage by fleeing into the wilderness, where they were guided by God (Deut 1:31; Ps 78:52; Jer 2:2, 6; Hos 2:16–17; Amos 2:10) and fed by him

(Exod 16:32). Individuals also fled to the wilderness for refuge, including Moses (Exod 2:15) and David, to escape Saul (1 Sam 22:1–2). Elijah fled to the brook Cherith, where ravens fed him (1 Kgs 17:1–7), and later to Horeb, where he was also miraculously fed (1 Kgs 19:4–8). The Qumran community, with its center in the wilderness of Judea northwest of the Dead Sea, understood their presence in the desert as an eschatological fulfillment of Isa 40:3 (1QS 8:12–14; 9:19–21). Isaiah and other prophets eluded Manasseh by hiding in the wilderness (*Mart. Isa.* 2:7–11; cf. Heb 11:37–38, which may allude to the Isaiah legend preserved in the *Martyrdom of Isaiah*). A quasi-historical event is the tradition of the flight to Pella (Mark 13:14–20 and par.; Eusebius *Hist. eccl.* 3.5.3; Epiphanius *Pan.* 29.7.7–8; 30.2.7; *De mens et pond.* 15; see C. Koester, "The Origin and Significance of the Flight to Pella Tradition," *CBQ* 51 [1989] 90–106). The flight of the woman into the desert in Rev 12:6, 14 should be understood in terms of the tradition of the wilderness as a place of refuge and security, and perhaps also in connection with the expectation that the Messiah will come from the desert (Matt 2:15; Hos 11:1).

There are several Greek myths in which women pursued by an antagonist become birds and thus escape (Procne, Philomela, and Tereus in Apollodorus 3.14.8; see Ovid *Metam.* 6.667–74). The constellation Virgo was depicted as having two wings (Aratus *Phaen.* 96–146). One nymph fleeing the wrath of Typhoeus expresses the desperate wish "O that I had wings to fly" (Nonnos *Dionysiaca* 2.126). Medea, after killing Pelias, is borne away by winged dragons (Ovid *Metam.* 7.350–51). This story suggests to Ovid many others that involve the escape from various dangers by figures of myth and legend who are miraculously provided with wings: (1) Ceramus of old was aided by the nymphs and escaped the flood by flying away with wings (Ovid *Metam.* 7.354–56). (2) Cygnus was transformed into a swan (Ovid *Metam.* 7.371–72). (3) Combe reportedly escaped on wings from her sons, who wanted to harm her (Ovid *Metam.* 7.382–83). (4) The king and queen of the island of Calaurea were both transformed into birds (Ovid *Metam.* 7.384–85).

14c ὅπου τρέφεται ἐκεῖ καιρὸν καὶ καιροὺς καὶ ἥμισυ καιροῦ ἀπὸ προσώπου τοῦ ὄφεως, "where she will be taken care of for a time, times, and half a time, from the presence of the serpent." Like v 14b, this clause is essentially a revised version of v 6c, which serves to resume the narrative broken off by the interpolations in vv 7–12: "that she might be taken care of there for 1,260 days." The phrase "a time, times, and half a time" is an allusion to Dan 7:25; 12:7; the author uses this cryptic apocalyptic period of time in two other forms: as 1,260 days in 11:3 and 12:6, and as 42 months in 11:2 and 13:5 (see *Comment* on 11:2).

Here the term ὄφις, "serpent," is used as the name for the enemy of the woman; the author has prepared us for this change in terminology by the redactional gloss in 12:9b. The phrase ἀπὸ προσώπου, a literal translation of the Hebrew מִפְּנֵי *mipnê,* means, literally, "from the presence of," but it may mean "because of," "for fear of" (Rev 6:16; 20:11; BDB, 818; KB, 889; Charles, 1:330; Thayer, *Lexicon,* 551).

15 καὶ ἔβαλεν ὁ ὄφις ἐκ τοῦ στόματος αὐτοῦ ὀπίσω τῆς γυναικὸς ὕδωρ ὡς ποταμόν ἵνα αὐτὴν ποταμοφόρητον ποιήσῃ, "Then the serpent spewed water like a river from his mouth behind the woman that he might wash her away." The term "serpent" is used here for a second time in the narrative (see v 14). In OT combat texts, the enemy of Yahweh is not only the sea but also the waters (Pss 29:3; 66:6; 74:15; 77:16[MT 17]; 93:4; Isa 50:26; 51:10) and rivers or floods, נהרות *nĕhārôt* or נהרים *nĕhārîm* (Ps 93:3; Nah 1:4; Hab 3:8–9). Baal's opponent in the Ugaritic texts in *CTA* 2 is not only Prince Yam but also Judge River (Day, *Conflict,* 7). *CTA* 3.IIID.35–36, "Surely I smote Yam, beloved of El, surely I made an end of River [*nhr*] the mighty god" (Day, *Conflict,* 13). In fact, they are synonymous terms used as a hendiadys for the same chaos monster (Wakeman, *God's Battle,* 92–97; see Hab 3:8; Pss 74:15b; 66:6; Isa 50:26). The author of the Qumran Ḥodayot used the metaphor "torrents of Belial [נחלי בליעל *naḥălê bĕliyyaʿal*]" (1QH 3:29, 32) for the onslaught of the enemies of God instigated by Satan. In some OT passages, the chaos waters can be identified as a generic term for the nations hostile to Israel (Pss 18:5–18; 46:3–4; 144:5–7; Hab 3:15[MT 13]; see Day, *Conflict,* 120–38). Aegina, daughter of the river Asopus, was carried off (ἥρπασε) by Zeus: "Asopus pursued him, but by throwing thunderbolts Zeus sent him back to his own channel" (Apollodorus 3.12.6). The river Scamander, outraged because of Trojan blood polluting its waters, attacked Achilles but was repulsed by the fire of Hephaestus (*Iliad* 20–21; Apollodorus *Epitome* 4.7; Lucian *Dial. mar.* 10). Typhoeus (who drank the rivers dry, Nonnos *Dionysiaca* 2.53–59) reportedly fought with Zeus by releasing the waters of the earth and causing great flooding (Nonnos *Dionysiaca* 2.68–76). Typhoeus claims that his brother Okeanos will bring his waters to Olympus and flood the stars (Nonnos *Dionysiaca* 2.277–80). In the so-called Aramaic Song of the Lamb (see *Comment* on 15:3), the giant Goliath (under the metaphor of a Bear) is pitted against the boy David (under the metaphor of a Lamb), and the former says (Staalduine-Sulman, "Aramaic Song," 270):

> Blessed be you, boy [*ṭly'* = lamb],
>   if you go away from before me,
> lest I spit on you,
>   and you would drown in my spittle.

The dragon's attempt to "wash her away" is, of course, an obvious metaphor for destruction.

16a καὶ ἐβοήθησεν ἡ γῆ τῇ γυναικί καὶ ἤνοιξεν ἡ γῆ τὸ στόμα αὐτῆς καὶ κατέπιεν τὸν ποταμόν, "Yet the earth helped the woman, and the earth opened its mouth and swallowed the river." Wakeman proposes that Eretz (Earth) is an alternate name for the earth-monster and a synonym for Mot (*God's Battle,* 108–12), but her arguments are weak (Day, *Conflict,* 84–86). Nevertheless, Earth is occasionally personified in the OT with verbs for "swallowing." Earth is said to have swallowed the pharaoh and his host (Exod 15:12) and later to have swallowed Korah, Dathan, and Abiram (Num 16:32–34). In these stories Earth acts to destroy the enemies of God just as she frustrates the serpent's attempt to inundate the woman in Rev 12:16. Similarly, in the *Acts of Andrew* 31 (ed. MacDonald, *Acts of Andrew,* 161), the earth opened in response to a prayer of Andrew and swallowed [κατέπιε] the water that had inundated the wicked people of the city. The "woman" at this point in the narrative is a collective symbol for the totality of the earthly Church, and as such she is essentially protected from the onslaught of Satan (Gollinger, *Apokalypse 12,* 179).

16b ὃν ἔβαλεν ὁ δράκων ἐκ τοῦ στόματος αὐτοῦ, "which the dragon spewed out of his mouth." This phrase repeats the statement made in v 15a, but it is probably inserted to make clear that the dragon is identical with the serpent in v 15a.

17a καὶ ὠργίσθη ὁ δράκων ἐπὶ τῇ γυναικί, "And the dragon was angry because of the woman." The motif of the anger or rage of a persecutor is a frequent *topos* in martyrdom stories in both early Judaism and early Christianity (Dan 3:13, 19; 11:30; 2 Macc 7:3, 39; 3 Macc 3:1; 5:1; 4:12–13; 4 Macc 8:2; 9:10; Acts 5:33; 7:54; *Mart. Pol.* 12:2; *Mart. Carpus* [Gk. rec.] 9; *Ep. Lugd.* 1.17; cf. *Pistis Sophia* [ed. Schmidt-Till] 1.55 [p. 66, lines 30, 36]; 2.80 [p. 113, line 30]; see Kellermann, "Märtyrertheologie," 74, where he lists the martyrological motif of the "outburst of anger by the tyrants"). The presence of this motif suggests that this part of the story is modeled after persecution and martyrological narratives.

17b καὶ ἀπῆλθεν ποιῆσαι πόλεμον μετὰ τῶν λοιπῶν τοῦ σπέρματος αὐτῆς, "and he left to wage war with the rest of her children." The term σπέρμα, "seed, offspring," occurs only here in Revelation and is unexpected since only the male child has been mentioned previously (vv 4–5, 13), with no hint that he has or will have any siblings (on the notion of Christians as siblings of Christ, see Heb 2:11–13). This abrupt mention of "the rest of her offspring," therefore, appears to be an interpolation intended to anticipate the mention of the war that the beast from the sea wages on the saints (13:7–10), i.e., to provide a transitional link from this textual unit to that found in Rev 13 (Bousset [1906] 356–57). However, since the phrase ἔτεκεν ἄρσεν, "she bore a male," in 12:5 is very probably an allusion to Isa 66:7, it is noteworthy that Isa 66:8 speaks of Zion delivering children. The phrase τὸ σπέρμα αὐτῆς, literally, "her seed," is a very unusual expression, for "seed" or "offspring" are normally associated with a male progenitor; but see P. W. van der Horst, "Sarah's Seminal Emission: Hebrews 11:11 in the Light of Ancient Embryology," in *Greeks, Romans, and Christians,* FS A. J. Malherbe, ed. D. L. Balch, E. Ferguson, and W. Meeks (Minneapolis: Fortress, 1990) 287–302. This expression, therefore, is probably an allusion to Gen 3:15 (J. Weiss, *Offenbarung,* 138), where God addresses the serpent in these words: "I will put enmity between you and the woman, and between your seed and her seed," a passage understood in some circles of early Judaism and by early Christians to refer to the birth of the Messiah (Prigent, *Apocalypse 12,* 143–44); in early Christianity the Hebrew term זרע *zeraʿ,* "seed," was understood (incorrectly) as having a singular rather than a collective sense (Westermann, *Genesis* 1:260–61; see Gal 3:16). This was facilitated by the fact that the masculine pronoun αὐτός, "he," occurs there, rather than the neuter pronoun αὐτό, "it," in the phrase "he will bruise your head, and you will bruise his heel." This messianic reading, however, was probably not the intention of the LXX translator (see Michl, *Bib* 33 [1952] 398, 401, 501). According to the tradition preserved in *Tg. Ps.-J.* Gen 3:15 (Bowker, *Targums,* 122) and in the fragmentary targums P and V on Gen 3:15 (Klein, *Fragment-Targums* 2:7, 91), when the offspring of the woman *keep* the Torah, they smite the offspring of the serpent on the heel, whereas in Rev 12:17, the offspring of the woman *keep* the commandments of God but are nevertheless attacked by the dragon (who is identified as the serpent in vv 9, 14, 15). The presence of the common motifs of the woman, her offspring, the serpent, and the importance of obeying the commandments strongly suggests that this aspect of the myth in Rev 12 appears to be a dramatization of the so-called *protevangelium* of Gen 3:15. The expression τὸ σπέρμα αὐτῆς symbolizes individual Christians, the spiritual children of the woman (Gollinger, *Apokalypse 12,* 179), perhaps specifically gentile Christians (Charles, 1:332).

A general parallel occurs in the Herakles cycle of legends: after the ascension of Herakles to Olympus, his sons (the Heraklidae) were forced to flee from his old nemesis Eurystheus (Apollodorus 2.8.1). In *Quʾran* 7.16–17, Iblīs (= Satan), who has been cast out of heaven, says (M. M. Pickthall, ed., *The Glorious Qurʾan: A Bi-*

Lingual Edition with English Translation, Introduction, and Notes [Albany, NY: SUNY, 1976]), "Now, because Thou hast sent me astray, verily I shall lurk in ambush for them on Thy Right Path. Then I shall come upon them from before them and from behind them and from their right hands and from their left hands, and Thou wilt not find most of them beholden (under Thee)." In *Qu'ran* 17.62, a sentiment very close to 12:17 is expressed (tr. Pickthall, *The Glorious Qur'an*): "He said: Seest Thou this (creature) whom Thou hast honoured above me, if Thou give me grace until the Day of Resurrection I verily will seize his [i.e., 'Adam's'] seed, save but a few."

17c τῶν τηρούντων τὰς ἐντολὰς τοῦ θεοῦ καὶ ἐχόντων τὴν μαρτυρίαν Ἰησοῦ, "who kept the commandments of God and maintained their witness to Jesus." This clause defines more closely the identity of "the rest of her offspring" mentioned in v 17b and conforms to the author's tendency to characterize the actors in the apocalyptic drama with descriptive participial phrases (cf. 11:7; 12:9; 17:1; 18:9, 15; 19:20; 21:9, 15). The phrase οἱ τηροῦντες τὰς ἐντολὰς τοῦ θεοῦ, "those who kept the commandments of God," occurs again verbatim in 14:12 (cf. the *lect. var.* οἱ ποιοῦντες τὰς ἐντολὰς αὐτοῦ, where the αὐτοῦ apparently refers to Christ, in 22:14). In 14:12, as in 12:17, the phrase is part of a couplet in which the first line refers to God and the second line to Jesus:

Rev 12:17	*Rev 14:12*
τῶν τηρούντων τὰς ἐντολὰς Those who keep the commandments	οἱ τηρούντες τὰς ἐντολὰς Those who keep the commands
τοῦ θεοῦ of God	τοῦ θεοῦ of God
καὶ ἐχόντων τὴν μαρτυρίαν and maintain the testimony	καὶ τὴν πίστιν and (maintain) faith
Ἰησοῦ of Jesus	Ἰησοῦ in Jesus

Though the second line is differently phrased than the first, it is apparent that the saying functions to link obedience to God (which here is very probably a reference to the ethical commands of the second table of the Decalogue and the love command [see *Excursus 12B: The Commandments of God and the Torah*]; cf. Rom 2:27–28; 1 Cor 7:19; Sir 32:23) to faith in or faithfulness to Jesus. This is in essence a definition of Christian faith, in which the traditional commands of God, understood from a Christian perspective, are seen as complementary rather than antithetical to the requirements of faith in (or faithfulness to) Jesus. The phrase τηρεῖν τὰς ἐντολάς, "keep the commandments," also occurs in the Matthaean version of the Synoptic pericope on the rich young ruler (Matt 19:17), where it refers to the Decalogue, three times in John (14:15, 21; 15:10), where it *always* refers to the commands of Jesus (ἐντολή, "commandments," whether in the singular or plural in John *never* refers to the Mosaic law), and five times in 1 John where it *always* (as here) refers to the commands of God (1 John 2:3, 4; 3:22, 24; 5:3; ποιεῖν τὰς ἐντολάς, "do the commandments," occurs once in 1 John 5:2; see Brown, *Epistles*, 251–52), which must at least include the Christian understanding of the Torah. The phrase ποιῆτε τὰς ἐντολάς μου, "do my commandments," occurs in an extracanonical saying of Jesus (*2 Clem.* 4:5; cf. Matt 7:24; see Stroker, *Extracanonical,* 71). This entire clause (like v 11) also appears to be an explanatory gloss inserted into an originally Jewish source to Christianize the story (Wellhausen, *Analyse,* 19; J. Weiss, *Offenbarung,* 136; Charles, 1:331), reflecting the final revision of Revelation (Bousset [1906] 345). Some have argued that only the phrase "and maintained their witness to Jesus" has been added since "who kept the commandments of God" is a descriptive phrase fully in line with Judaism (see Justin *Dial.* 10.3). Keeping the commands of God is one of the major reasons that martyrs give for their willingness to suffer and die rather than compromise their faith (1 Macc 1:60–63; 2 Macc 7:1–3; 3 Macc 1:23; 4 Macc 5:16–17, 29; 6:18; 7:8; 9:1–2; *Bib. Ant.* 38:2; see *Comment* on 14:12, and Kellermann, "Märtyrertheologie," 71–72, where the motif of obeying the Torah is listed as a frequent motif in martyrdom stories). Of course, "obeying the commandments of God" in such contexts refers primarily to circumcision, dietary laws, Sabbath observance, and avoidance of any participation in pagan sacrificial rituals (Dan 3:3–18; 1 Macc 1:60–63). In early Christianity, particularly in dialogue with Judaism, the phrase "keep the commandments of God" (e.g., *Barn.* 4:11, φυλάσσειν . . . τὰς ἐντολὰς αὐτοῦ) came to have a very particular meaning, i.e., the *ethical* as opposed to the ceremonial commands (see J. C. Paget, *The Epistle of Barnabas: Outlook and Background,* WUNT 2.64 [Tübingen: Mohr, 1994] 64–65).

Excursus 12B: The Commandments of God and the Torah

Bibliography

Bourgeault, G. *Décalogue et morale chrétienne: Enquête patristique sur l'utilisation et l'interpretation chrétiennes du décalogue de c. 60 à c. 220.* Paris: Desclée; Montreal: Belarmin, 1971. **Dunn, J. D. G.** "The New Perspective on Paul." *BJRL* 65 (1983) 95–122. ———. "Works of the Law and the Curse of the Law [Galatians 3:10–14]." *NTS* 31 (1985) 523–42. **Fuller, R. H.** "The Decalogue in the New Testament." *Int* 43 (1989) 243–55. **Grant. R. M.** "The Decalogue in Early Christianity." *HTR* 40 (1947) 1–17. **Harrelson, W.** *The Ten Commandments and Human Rights.* Philadelphia: Westminster, 1980. **Nissen, A.** *Gott und der Nächste im antiken Judentum: Untersuchungen zum Doppelgebot der Liebe.* WUNT 15. Tübingen: Mohr-Siebeck, 1974. **Reicke, B.** *Die zehn Worte in Geschichte und Gegenwart.* Tübingen: Mohr-Siebeck, 1973. **Rordorf, W.** "Beobachtungen zum Gebrauch des Dekalogs in der vorkonstantinischen Kirche." In *The New Testament Age.* FS B. Reicke, ed. W. C. Weinrich. Macon, GA: Mercer UP, 1984. 2:431–42. **Söding, T.** *Das Liebesgebot bei Paulus: Die Mahnung zur Agape im Rahmen der paulinischen Ethik.* NTAbh 26. Münster: Aschendorff, 1995. **Vokes, F. E.** "The Ten Commandments in the New Testament and in First Century Judaism." *TU* 103 (1968) 146–54.

For early Judaism, law included the entire Torah, while for early Christian authors, the central part of the law was the second table of the Decalogue (i.e., the ethical commands) and the love command. When such phrases as "the law" or "the commandments" are used in early Christian contexts, it is often difficult to decide exactly what is meant. Sometimes some or all of the Ten Commandments are in view (particularly those five dealing with human relations recorded on the second tablet), and at other times either the ritual aspects of Torah (e.g., primarily circumcision and *kašrût* or food laws; Sabbath observance was apparently not a central issue) or the ethical portions of the Torah (love of God and neighbor) are primarily in view.

While the Ten Commandments are first enumerated in the Torah (Exod 20:2–17; Deut 5:6–21), where they are called the "ten words" in both Hebrew and Greek (Exod 34:28; Deut 4:13; 10:4; cf. Jos. *Ant.* 3.90–92) and later the "decalogue" (Clement Alex. *Paed.* 3.12; Tertullian *De anima* 37.4), they are hardly mentioned elsewhere in the OT (1 Kgs 8:9 = 2 Chr 5:10; Jer 7:8–9; Hos 4:2) and virtually never in the apocrypha and pseudepigrapha. Josephus is the first to mention that five commandments were engraved on each of the two tablets of the law (*Ant.* 3.8), and much has been made of the fact that in the NT it is the laws on the *second* tablet of the Decalogue that are referred to almost exclusively. Perhaps reflecting the special interest in the Decalogue of Hellenistic Judaism, Philo devoted a treatise to the interpretation of the Ten Commandments (*De decalogo,* "On the Ten Commandments"), and he organized a subsequent treatise (*De specialibus legibus,* "On special laws") using the Ten Commandments as major headings. Philo characterizes the first five commandments as φιλόθεοι, "instructions concerning God," and the last five as φιλάνθρωποι, "instructions concerning humanity" (*Decal.* 110).

Paul can speak very positively about the necessity of τήρησις ἐντολῶν θεοῦ, "obeying the commandments of God" (1 Cor 7:19), though he excludes circumcision, which is certainly a part of the Torah unless "commandments" is understood to include ethical and exclude ceremonial elements. In the NT the Ten Commandments are not referred to with any specific designation, though the stone tablets received by Moses are mentioned in 2 Cor 3:7 and Heb 9:4 (cf. Exod 34:29; Deut 10:5; 1 Kgs 8:9 = 2 Chr 5:10), and the first and second commandments are mentioned (Mark 12:28–31 = Matt 22:36–40), implying the enumeration of the whole group. Short lists of commandments are also found (Mark 10:19 = Matt 19:17–19 = Luke 18:20; Rom 13:8–9; 1 Tim 1:8–11; *Did.* 2:1–3; Aristides *Apol.* 15.2–5; Athenagoras *De res.* 23; Tertullian *Adv. Marc.* 4.16–17; cf. Rev 9:20–21), and individual commandments are mentioned (honoring parents: Mark 7:9–10 = Matt 15:3–4; Eph 6:2; keeping the Sabbath: Luke 23:56; not coveting the possessions of others: Rom 7:8; 2 Macc 2:5). The importance of keeping the law is emphasized in some sources (Matt 19:17; 1 John 2:4–5), while the difficulty of obeying the whole law is stressed in others (John 5:45; Rom 3:19; Gal 5:3; Jas 2:10). The permanent validity of the law is sometimes stressed (Matt 5:17–20), while at other times the completion or even abolition of the law is in view (Rom 10:4; 2 Cor 3:14; Eph 2:15). There is also the tendency to see the whole law encapsulated in either the two commands to love God and love one's neighbor (Mark 12:28–31 = Matt 22:36–40; *Did.* 1:2; Justin *Dial.* 93.2; Theophilus *Ad Autol.* 2.34) or the command to love one's neighbor (Rom 13:8–10; Gal 5:14; Jas 2:8; cf. Söding, *Liebesgebot,* 200–203, 250–58).

This tendency to summarize the law under a single rubric was also found in Judaism (Vokes, *TU* 103 [1968] 150–51). The command to love one's neighbor, of course, is not part of the Decalogue but a quotation (in Mark 12:13) of LXX Lev 19:18 (cf. 19:33–34; Deut 10:19). This love command takes on a significant theological role in the NT (1 Thess 4:9; Rom 13:8–10).

Paul's negative perception of "the works of the law" is sometimes (though not entirely; cf. Rom 3:20; 7:7–25) restricted to the distinctive socio-religious markers of Judaism: circumcision, *kašrût,* and Sabbath observance (Dunn, *BJRL* 65 [1983] 95–122; id., *NTS* 31 [1985] 523–42). Even though the ethical requirements of the Torah may be used to play a negative theological role (Rom 7:7–11), in general they are regarded in an overwhelmingly positive light in early Christianity as reflecting the revealed will of God (Rom 7:12, "So the law is holy, and the commandment is holy and just and good" [RSV]). When Paul refers to the law of Christ (1 Cor 9:21; Gal 6:2), he is probably referring to the second table of the Decalogue plus the love command (Rom 13:8–9; cf. Fuller, *Int* 43 [1989] 253–54). While the phrase "to keep the commandments of God" obviously encompasses doing the will of God, the knowledge of God's will is mediated through the Torah, which is interpreted from a variety of early Christian perspectives. It is in this context that "keeping the commandments of God" in Rev 12:17 and 14:12 must be regarded as referring to the *ethical* requirements of the Torah.

Explanation

After beginning with the opening of the heavenly temple, the sighting of the ark within, and the listing of the attendant theophanic phenomena typical of divine manifestations consisting of lightning, thunder, rumblings, an earthquake, and hail (11:19), the two protagonists and the antagonist of the mythological narrative that follows are succinctly introduced: the vulnerable woman about to give birth to a son and the aggressive, proud, and violent dragon with seven heads and ten horns (12:1–4), not as part of a vision (the typical introductory phrases "I saw" and "I heard" are missing) but as if they were constellations telling a story. The ensuing narrative consists of three scenes of conflict: (1) the birth and escape of the child and the flight of the woman from the dragon (12:4b–6), (2) the defeat and expulsion of the dragon and his angels from heaven by Michael and his angelic host (12:7–9), and (3) the dragon's relentless pursuit of first the woman and then her offspring (12:13–17). Between vv 7–9 and vv 13–17, the author has sandwiched a victory hymn, which both supplements and provides a commentary on the mythic narrative in vv 7–9 by explaining the significance for the history of salvation of Satan's expulsion from heaven (a protological event in Jewish tradition presented here as an eschatological event), by sketching Satan's role in heaven before his expulsion and by emphasizing the faithfulness of the Christian martyrs.

Though both are combat myths (found in many versions throughout the ancient world), the narrative of the woman, the child, and the dragon (vv 4b–6, 13–17) has a completely different significance from the story of Michael's heavenly war with the dragon (vv 7–9), which has been inserted into it. The first myth must be understood allegorically but can be read in several ways. In a Christian context, it has seemed natural to construe the woman of vv 1–6 as Mary and her child as Jesus. Yet in vv 13–17, where "the rest of her offspring" (v 17) are mentioned, it seems more appropriate to understand the woman as the Church and her persecuted offspring as Christians. From a Jewish perspective, in an earlier version of this myth, the woman could be construed as Israel, the persecuted people of God. While in the present version the child is clearly the Messiah (=Jesus), described as "one who is to rule all the nations with a rod of iron" (v 5, alluding to Ps 2:9, a psalm interpreted messianically), this detail is probably a Jewish embellishment of the Hellenistic myth. That the child was "caught up" to God and to his throne (v 5) probably signifies the exaltation of the risen Jesus to the right hand of God, though its occurrence immediately following the child's birth and its depiction as a divine rescue indicate its earlier, pre-Christian character.

The presence of this ascension motif together with the fact that the messianic rule of the child has yet to be realized suggests that the ultimate origin of this myth, though it was probably refracted in Judaism, was a Hellenistic version of the combat myth. The version of the combat myth found in Rev 12 is closest to the Greek Leto-Apollo-Python myth, though there are numerous differences. The goddess, Leto, pregnant with Apollo, was pursued by the dragon Python. Leto fled to a distant island and eventually gave birth to Apollo, who, when just four days old, killed Python.

To his adaptation of the myth of Leto-Apollo-Python, John has prefixed a description of the two myth-images that served as a catalyst for his juxtaposition of two mythic traditions. The woman who appears as the queen of the cosmos and protagonist appears in heaven (v 1), followed by the appearance of the great red dragon, the antagonist (v 3), later drawn clearly into early Jewish and early Christian tradition by listing his aliases as a ancient serpent, Devil, Satan, and deceiver of the entire world. The woman is presented in astral imagery (clothed with the sun, the moon under her feet, and wearing the crown of the Zodiac) as the queen of the cosmos (v 1, probably based on popular conception of Artemis, Hekate, and Isis, who are often described with similar attributes). The dragon (equated with the devil, the ancient serpent, or Satan, v 12), the primary antagonist of God, first appears at this point in John's eschatological scenario (v 3). The ascension of the child in v 5 is described using the rapture motif commonly found in Greek myths involving deification through ascension to heaven. The use of motifs from Greek mythology in this way constitutes a kind of narrative apologetic in which traditional Greek stories are shown to validate important aspects of the Christian gospel.

3. The Two Beasts (12:18–13:18)

Bibliography

Aune, D. E. "Oral Tradition and the Aphorisms of Jesus." In *Jesus and the Oral Gospel Tradition,* ed. H. Wansbrough. JSNTSup 64. Sheffield: Sheffield Academic, 1991. 211–65. **Baines, W. G.** "The Number of the Beast in Revelation 13:18." *HeyJ* 16 (1975) 195–96. **Barclay, W.** "Great Themes of the New Testament: V. Revelation xiii." *ExpTim* 70 (1958–59) 260–64, 292–96. **Barrett, A. A.** *Caligula: The Corruption of Power.* London: Batsford, 1989. **Bauckham, R.** "The Conversion of the Nations." In R. Bauckham, *Climax.* 238–337. ———. "Nero and the Beast." In R. Bauckham, *Climax.* 384–452. **Beale, G. K.** "The Danielic Background for Revelation 13:18 and 17:9." *TynBul* 31 (1980) 163–70. **Bergh van Eysinga, G. A. van den.** "Die in der Apokalypse bekämpfte Gnosis." *ZNW* 13 (1912) 293–306. **Bergmeier, R.** "Die Erzhure und das Tier: Apk 12.18–13.18 und 17f.: Eine quellen- und redaktionskritische Analyse." *ANRW* II, 25/5:3899–3916. **Bilde, P.** "The Roman Emperor Gaius (Caligula)'s Attempt to Erect His Statue in the Temple of Jerusalem." *ST* 32 (1978) 67–93. **Birdsall, J. N.** "Rev XIII.6." *JTS* 14 (1963) 399–400. **Blidstein, G.** "Nullification of Idolatry in Rabbinic Law." *PAAJR* 42–43 (1973–74) 1–44. **Bousset, W.** *The Antichrist Legend: A Chapter in Christian and Jewish Folklore.* Tr. A. H. Keane. London: Hutchinson, 1896. **Bruins, E. M.** "The Number of the Beast." *NedTTs* 23 (1969) 401–7. **Brun, L.** "Die römischen Kaiser in der Apokalypse." *ZNW* 26 (1927) 128–51. **Burch, V.** "Reasons Why Nero Should Not Be Found in Revelation 13." *Expositor* 8 (1920) 18–28. **Burney, C. F.** "A Hebraic Construction in the Apocalypse." *JTS* 22 (1921) 371ff. **Caquot, A.** "Léviathan et Behémoth dans la troisième 'Parabole' d'Hénoch." *Semitica* 25 (1975) 111–22. **Clemen, C.** "Nochmals die Zahl des Tieres." *ZNW* 11 (1910) 204–23. ———. "Die Zahl des Tieres Apc 13:18." *ZNW* 2 (1901) 109–14. ———. "Die Zahl 666, ein Hinweis auf Trajan?" *Protestantische Monatshefte* 25 (1921) 144–48. **Corssen, P.** "Nocheinmal die Zahl des Tieres in der Apokalypse." *ZNW* 3 (1902) 238–46. ———. "Zur Verständigung über Apok 13:18." *ZNW* 4 (1903) 264–67. **Deininger, J.** *Die Provinziallandtage der römischen*

Kaiserzeit von Augustus bis zum Ende des dritten Jahrhunderts n. Chr. Munich; Berlin: Beck, 1965. **De Ste. Croix, G. E. M.** "Why Were Early Christians Persecuted?" In *Studies in Ancient Society,* ed. M. I. Finley. London: Routledge & Kegan Paul, 1974. 210–49. **Dornseiff, F.** "Die Rätsel-Zahl 666 in der Offenbarung des Johannes." *FuF* 12 (1936) 369 (= *Kleine Schriften.* II. *Sprach und Sprechender,* ed. J. Werner. Leipzig: Koehler & Amelung, 1964. 244–47). **Driver, G. R.** "Mythical Monsters in the Old Testament." In *Studi Orientalistici in onore di Giorgio Levi della Vida.* Rome: Instituto per l'Oriente, 1956. 1:234–49. ———. "The Number of the Beast." In *Bible und Qumran,* ed. S. Wagner. Berlin: Evangelische Haupt-Bibelgesellschaft, 1968. 75–81. **Ernst, J.** *Die eschatologischen Gegenspieler in den Schriften des Neuen Testaments.* Regensburg: Pustet, 1967. **Flusser, D.** "The Apocryphal Book of *Ascensio Isaiae* and the Dead Sea Sect." *IEJ* 3 (1953) 30–47. ———. "Hystaspes and John of Patmos." In *Judaism and the Origins of Christianity.* Jerusalem: Magnes, 1988. 390–453. **Gordon, C. H.** "Leviathan: A Symbol of Evil." In *Biblical Motifs,* ed. A. Altmann. Cambridge, MA: Harvard UP, 1966. **Grant, R. M.** "Sacrifices and Oaths as Required of Early Christians." In *KYRIAKON.* FS J. Quasten, ed. P. Granfield and J. A. Jungmann. 1973. Repr. London: Variorum Reprints, 1983. 1:12–17. **Gutman, J.** "Leviathan, Behemoth and Ziz: Jewish Messianic Symbols in Art." *HUCA* 39 (1968) 219–30. **Hadorn, W.** "Die Zahl 666, ein Hinweis auf Trajan." *ZNW* 19 (1919–20) 11–28. **Hanfmann, G. M. A.** *Letters from Sardis.* Cambridge, MA: Harvard UP, 1972. **Hanhart, K.** "The Four Beasts of Daniel's Vision in the Night in the Light of Rev. 13:2." *NTS* 27 (1981) 576–83. **Hartingsveld, L. van.** "Die Zahl des Tieres, die Zahl eines Menschen: Apokalypse XIII. 18." In *Miscellanea Neotestamentica,* ed. T. Baarda, A. F. J. Klijn, and W. C. van Unnik. Leiden: Brill, 1978. 2:191–201. **Hartman, L.** *Prophecy Interpreted: The Formation of Some Jewish Apocalyptic Texts and of the Eschatological Discourse Mark 13 par.* ConBNT 1. Lund: Gleerup, 1966. **Hillers, D. R.** "Revelation 13:18 and a Scroll from Murabbaʿat." *BASOR* 170 (1963) 65. **Inan, J.,** and **Alföldi-Rosenbaum, E.** *Römische und frühbyzantinische Porträtplastik aus der Türkei.* Mainz am Rhein: von Zabern, 1979. ——— and **Rosenbaum. E.** *Roman and Early Byzantine Portrait Sculpture in Asia Minor.* London: The British Academy, 1966. **Jacobs, I.** "Elements of Near-Eastern Mythology in Rabbinic Aggadah." *JJS* 28 (1977) 1–11. **Judge, E. A.** "The Mark of the Beast, Revelation 13:16." *TynBul* 42 (1991) 158–60. **Kautzsch, E.** "Zahlen." *RE* 21:598–607. **Kearsley, R.** "Asiarchs, *Archiereis,* and the *Archiereiai* of Asia." *GRBS* 27 (1986) 183–92. **Koonce, K.** "ΑΓΑΛΜΑ and ΕΙΚΩΝ." *AJP* 109 (1988) 108–10. **Kraybill, J. N.** *Imperial Cult and Commerce in John's Apocalypse.* JSNTSup 132. Sheffield: Sheffield Academic, 1996. **Labuschagne, C. J.** *The Incomparability of Yahweh in the Old Testament.* Leiden: Brill, 1966. **Majercik, R.** *The Chaldean Oracles: Text, Translation, and Commentary.* Leiden: Brill, 1989. **Minear, P. S.** "The Wounded Beast." *JBL* 72 (1953) 93–101. **Morgenthaler, R.** "Roma—Sedes Satanae: Röm 13,1ff. im Lichte von Luk 4,5–8." *TZ* 12 (1956) 289–304. **Murmellstein, B.** "Das zweite Tier in der Offenbarung Johannis (Kap 13B)." *TSK* 101 (1929) 447–57. **Oberweis, M.** "Die Bedeutung der neutestamentlichen 'Raetzelzahlen' 666 (Apk 13:18) und 153 (Joh 21:11)." *ZNW* 77 (1986) 226–41. **Prete, B.** "Il testo di Apocalisse 13,9–10: Una minaccia per i persecutori o un'esortazione al martirio?" *Studii biblici franciscani liber annuus* 27 (1977) 102–18. **Price, S. R. F.** "Between Man and God: Sacrifice in the Roman Imperial Cult." *JRS* 70 (1980) 28–43. ———. "Gods and Emperors: The Greek Language of the Roman Imperial Cult." *JHS* 104 (1984) 79–95. ———. *Rituals and Power: The Roman Imperial Cult in Asia Minor.* Cambridge: Cambridge UP, 1984. **Reicke, B.** "Die jüdische Apokalyptic und die johanneische Tiervision." *RSR* 60 (1972) 173–92. **Rigaux, B.** *L'Antéchrist et l'opposition du royaume messianique dans l'Ancien et le Nouveau Testament.* Gembloux: Duculot; Paris: Gabalda, 1932. **Ringgren, H.** *The Faith of Qumran: The Theology of the Dead Sea Scrolls.* Philadelphia: Fortress, 1963. **Robert, L.** "Inscription d'Athènes." *REA* (1964) 316–24 (= *Opera Minora Selecta* 2:832–40). **Rowland, C.** *The Open Heaven: A Study of Apocalyptic in Judaism and Early Christianity.* New York: Crossroad, 1982. **Sanders, H. A.** "The Number of the Beast in Revelation 13:18." *JBL* 37 (1918) 95–99. **Scherrer, S. J.** "Revelation 13 as an Historical Source for the Imperial Cult under Domitian." Th.D. Diss., Harvard, 1979. ———. "Signs and Wonders in the Imperial Cult: A New Look at a Roman Religious Institution in the Light of Rev 13:13–15." *JBL* 103 (1984) 599–610. **Schlier, H.** "Vom Antichrist: Zum 13. Kapitel der Offenbarung Johannis." In *Theologische Aufsätze.* FS K. Barth, ed. E. Wolf. Munich: Kaiser, 1936. **Schowalter, D. N.** *The Emperor and the Gods: Images from the Time of Trajan.* HDR 28. Minneapolis: Augsburg, 1993. **Scott, K.** *The Imperial Cult under the Flavians.* Stuttgart; Berlin: Kohlhammer, 1936. **Stauffer, E.** "666." In *In honorem Antonii Fridrichsen sexagenarii.* ConNT 11. Lund: Gleerup, 1947. 237–41. ———. *Christus und die Caesaren: Historische Skizzen.* 5th ed. Hamburg: Wittig, 1960. **Ulrichsen, J. H.** "Dyret i Åpenbaringen: En skisse til tidshistorisk forståelse av kapitlene 13 og 17." *NTT* 87 (1986) 167–77. **Urbach, E. E.** "The Rabbinical Laws of Idolatry in the Second and Third Centuries in the Light of Archaeological and Historical Facts." *IEJ* 9 (1959) 149ff., 229ff. **Venetz, H.-J.** "Zwischen Unterwerfung und Verweigerung: Widersprüchliches im Neuen Testament? Zu Röm 13 und Offb 13." *BK* 43 (1988) 153–63. **Vischer, E.** "Die Zahl 666: Apc 13:18." *ZNW* 13 (1912) 294–97. **Wallace, H.** "Leviathan and the Beast in Revelation." *BA* 11 (1948) 61–68 (repr. in *The Biblical Archaeologist Reader, 1,* ed. G. E. Wright and D. N. Freedman. Garden City: Doubleday, 1961. 290–98). **Wikenhauser, A.** "Ἐνώπιος—ἐνώπιον—κατενώπιον." *BZ* 8 (1910) 263–70. **Yarbro Collins, A.** "The Political Perspective of the Revelation to John." *JBL* 96 (1977) 241–56. **Ysebaert, J.** *Greek Baptismal Terminology: Its Origins and Early Development.* Nijmegen: Dekker and van de Vegt, 1962.

Translation

18 He stood [a] on the sand of the sea. 13:1 I [a] saw a beast rising up out of the sea, with ten
horns and seven heads, and on its horns were ten diadems and on its heads were
blasphemous [b] names.[c] 2 The [a] beast which I saw was [b] like a leopard, and its feet were like
those of a bear, and its mouth was like that of a lion.[c] The [d] dragon gave him his power
and his throne and great authority. 3 One [a] of [b] its heads [c] appeared to be fatally wounded,[c]
but [d] [e] its mortal wound [e] was healed. The whole [f] earth was astonished and followed [g] the
beast. 4 They worshiped [a] [b] the dragon [b] because [c] he gave authority [d] to the beast, [e] and they
also worshiped [f] the beast,[f] chanting, "Who is like the beast,[e] and who is able to fight against
it?" 5 It [a] [b] was given haughty and blasphemous things to say,[bc] and it was given the
authority [d] to be active [d] forty-two months.[e] 6 It [a] began to utter blasphemies [ab] against God,
that is, to blaspheme [c] his name [d] and his dwelling,[d] that is, [ef] those who dwell in heaven.[e]
7 [a] And it was permitted to make war against [b] God's people [b] and conquer them,[a] and it was
given authority over every tribe [c] and people [c] and language and nation. 8 All the
inhabitants of the earth will worship him,[a] everyone [b] whose [c] name was not written [b] since
the creation [d] of the world in [e] the book [e] of life of the Lamb [f] who was slaughtered.[f]

9 If anyone has an ear, let him hear:
10 If anyone is [a] for captivity,[a] [b] to captivity [b] he will go; [c]
If anyone with the sword [d] is to be slain,[d] he [e] [f] with the sword [f] will be slain.
[g] This indicates that [g] the endurance and faith of [h] God's people [h] are involved.

11 Then I saw another beast ascending [a] from the earth, and it had [b] two [c] horns like [d] a
ram,[e] but [f] it sounded [g] like a dragon. 12 It [a] exercised [b] the full authority of the first beast,
[c] on its behalf,[c] and compelled the earth, [d] that is,[d] those who dwell on it, to worship [e] [f] the first
beast,[f] whose [g] mortal wound was healed. 13 It performed [a] impressive miracles, [b] even
causing [c] fire [d] to fall from heaven [bd] to [e] earth before people. 14 It deceives those who dwell on
the earth through the miracles it was permitted to perform [a] on the authority of [a] the beast.
He told [b] those who dwell on the earth [c] to fashion [c] [d] a cult statue [d] in honor of [e] the beast
who [f] was wounded [g] with a sword but [h] lived.[ig] 15 It [a] was permitted [b] to give life [b] to the cult
statue [c] of the beast that the cult statue of the beast might speak and [c] [d] cause [e] whoever [d] did
not worship [f] [g] the cult statue [g] of the beast to be executed.[h] 16 It forced everyone, the

unimportant and the important, rich and poor, free and slave, [a]*to be given* [a] *a brand* [b] [cd]*on their right hand or on their forehead,*[c] 17 [a]*so that no one can*[b] *buy or sell unless he has,*[c]*as a brand,*[cd] [e]*the name of the beast* [e] *or the number of its name.* 18 *Here is wisdom. Let the one with understanding calculate the number of the beast, for it is also* [a]*a number referring to a person,*[a] [b]*and the number of that person* [b] *is six hundred sixty-six.*[c]

Notes

18.a. Variants: (1) ἐστάθη ("he stood," 3rd sing. aor. pass.)] 𝔓[47] A C ℵ fam 1611[1854 2344] 209 792 2351 Andr g n Byz 1[2256] Byz 16[61] Byz 17[469] Andr/Byz 2[582 628] Andr/Byz 3[1894] Andr/Byz 4[172 1828 1888] it[gig ar] Tyc[2] vg syr[h] eth arm; WHort; Nestle-Aland[27]; UBSGNT[4]. (2) ἐστάθην ("I stood," 1st sing. aor. pass.)] 025 Oecumenius[2053] Andreas Byzantine; Tischendorf, *NT Graece;* von Soden, *Text.* A number of scholars (B. Weiss, *Johannes-Apokalypse,* 5; Bousset [1906] 358 n. 1; Schmid, *Studien* 2:77; *TCGNT*[1], 746; *TCGNT*[2], 673) contend that reading (2) is a result of assimilation to καὶ εἶδον in 13:1. Von Soden (*Text* 1:2076), on the other hand, argued that ἐστάθη was a correction based on ὠργίσθη in 12:17a. This variant is important for the structure of Revelation, for reading (1) must refer to the dragon and so concludes 11:19–12:17 by providing a transition to 13:1–18, while reading (2) must refer to John and can also be understood as introducing a new text unit in 12:18–13:18.

13:1.a. The καί that begins this sentence is left untranslated since it is a discourse marker that functions to indicate the beginning of a new sentence or clause but has no independent semantic value.

1.b. βλασφημίας, "blasphemy," is a descriptive gen. that functions as an adj. modifying ὀνόματα, "names"; cf. 17:3 (G. Mussies, *Morphology,* 96).

1.c. Variants: (1) ὀνόματα] A 046 051 fam 1611[-2329] Oecumenius[2053 2058] Andr a[1] f g l n[2432] 94 1773 2019; Byzantine a it[gig] (*nomina blasphemiae;* erroneously listed by Nestle-Aland[27] as evidence for ὄνομα); vg syr[h] Tyc[3] (*nomina blasphemiae*); WHort; Charles, 2:313; Merk, *NT.* (2) ὄνομα] 𝔓[47] ℵ C 025 fam 1006 fam 1611[2329] Andreas vg[mss] syr[ph] cop arm Primasius (*nomen scriptum blasphemiae*); Beatus (*nomen blasphemiae;* Vogels, *Untersuchungen,* 201); WHort[marg]; von Soden, *Text.* An original ὄνομα could have been altered to ὀνόματα through the influence of the preceding pl. form κεφαλάς, or ὄνομα could be the result of the accidental omission of the τα after the μα (B. Weiss, *Johannes-Apokalypse,* 129–30; *TCGNT*[1], 746; *TCGNT*[2], 673). The pl. ending is bracketed in Nestle-Aland[27] and UBSGNT[4]. The originality of ὀνόματα is strongly suggested by the parallel in Rev 17:3.

2.a. See *Note* 1.a.

2.b. Variants: (1) ἦν] A C (Schmid, *Studien* 1/1:136, errs in having ἦν rather than ἦν as the variant for the following MSS: 025 Andr b[2081] d f[2023–2073] l n 94 1773); Irenaeus[Lat]; Priscillian (*erat similis*); Tischendorf, *NT Graece;* B. Weiss, *Johannes-Apokalypse,* 193; von Soden, *Text;* Nestle-Aland[27]; UBSGNT[4]. (2) omit ἦν] 𝔓[47] Andreas it[gig] arm. (3) ὅμοιος ἦν] Oecumenius[2053]; *similis erat:* Primasius Tyc[2] Beatus it[z].

2.c. Variant: λεόντων] ℵ fam 1611[1611] 2351 Victorinus.

2.d. See *Note* 1.a.

3.a. See *Note* 1.a. Here μίαν is unaccountably in the acc., unless it functions as the obj. of εἶδον, "I saw," in v 1.

3.b. Variants: (1) ἐκ] ℵ A C 025 046[corr] Andr f i l 94 Irenaeus[Lat] and Primasius (*ex capitibus*); it[gig] (*de capitibus*); Tyc[2] (*ex capitibus*); Beatus (*ex capitibus*); Irenaeus[Lat] (*ex capitibus;* Sanday-Turner, *Nouum Testamentum,* 197); cop[bo]; von Soden, *Text;* Nestle-Aland[27]; UBSGNT[4]. (2) omit ἐκ] 046* fam 1611[1854] Oecumenius[2053] Andreas TR.

3.c-c. In the phrase ὡς ἐσφαγμένην εἰς θάνατον, ἐσφαγμένην is a fem. acc. pf. pass. ptcp. from σφάζειν, "to slaughter" (modifying μίαν, "one"); with ὡς meaning "as if," the phrase means "appeared fatally wounded."

3.d. The καί introducing this clause functions as καί *adversativum* because this clause has a surprising element that contrasts with the previous clause.

3.e-e. ἡ πληγὴ τοῦ θανάτου αὐτοῦ, lit. "the wound of his death." τοῦ θανάτου, "death," is a descriptive gen. functioning as an adj. modifying the noun πληγή, "wound" (Mussies, *Morphology,* 96). The poss. pronoun αὐτοῦ, "his," reflects Semitic usage, for in both Heb. and Aram. noun clauses, the pronoun suffixed to the final word governs the entire group (for the Heb. idiom, see GKC § 440).

3.f. ὅλος, "whole," is used here *before* the noun it modifies, probably to emphasize the dazzling effect of the beast on the *entire* population of the world; elsewhere in Revelation ὅλος is only used in the postposition, normally to emphasize the substantive it modifies (3:10; 6:12; 12:9; 16:14; cf. BDR § 276.5).

3.g. ὀπίσω + gen.; for a different use, see *Note* 1:10.c.

4.a. προσεκύνησαν is a 3rd pl. verb, the subject of which is the noun phrase in v 3, ὅλη ἡ γῆ, "the entire earth," in which ἡ γῆ is grammatically sing. but regarded by the author as a collective noun (though ἡ γῆ is also the subject of the 3rd sing. verb ἐθαυμάσθη in v 3); this is an example of one type of *constructio ad sensum* (see *Introduction,* Section 7: Syntax, pp. cciv–ccvi).

4.b-b. On the use of προσκυνεῖν + dat. or acc., see *Note* 4:10.b.

4.c. Torrey *(Apocalypse,* 125) proposes that ὅτι, "because," makes no sense here and is a mistranslation of the Aram. די *dî,* which can also be translated "who"; i.e., "they worshiped the dragon *who* gave authority to the beast."

4.d. Variant: omit τήν before ἐξουσίαν] 2351.

4.e-e. 𝔓[47] omits καὶ προσεκύνησαν τῷ θηρίῳ λέγοντες τίς ὅμοιος τῷ θηρίῳ; undoubtedly an error of haplography in which the copyist's eye strayed from the first to the third occurrence of θηρίῳ.

4.f-f. Variant: τὸ θηρίον] A fam 1611[2344] Andr i[1876 2014 2043] Andr n[2066com]. Fee regards this reading as probably original since elsewhere in Revelation neut. nouns, especially τὸ θηρίον are in the acc. following προσκυνεῖν (see *Note* 4:10.b. and literature cited there), and he suggests that the dat. originated in conformity with the preceding τῷ δράκοντι.

5.a. See *Note* 1.a.

5.b-b. διδόναι στόμα is an idiom meaning "to help someone to say something" or "to give someone something to say" (Louw-Nida, § 33.105).

5.c. Variant: λαλοῦντα for λαλοῦν] 𝔓[47] Byz 1[2256].

5.d-d. Variants: (1) ποιῆσαι] *lectio originalis.* (2) πολεμῆσαι] 2351. (3) πόλεμον ποιῆσαι] 051 fam 1611[2329] Andr b[2081] c f[2023 2073] Byzantine. (4) ποιῆσαι ὃ θέλει] ℵ. Reading (3) is imported from v 7.

5.e. Variants: The number forty-two is found in three forms in the MSS: (1) μβ] 𝔓[47] 046 051 Oecumenius[1678 1778 2080]. (2) τεσσεράκοντα δύο] ℵ C Byzantine. (3) τεσσεράκοντα καὶ δύο] A fam 1006[1841] fam 1611[1854] Irenaeus[Lat] *(XL et duobus;* Sanday-Turner, *Nouum Testamentum,* 197); 2351. (4) σαρακονταδύο] Oecumenius[2053] (accidental omission of the initial τεσ in the text, not the commentary). The omission of the καί could have occurred as the result of converting the written cardinals to alphabetic symbols and then back to written cardinals again. In Revelation, καί is used to link cardinal numbers only in 11:2 (A 046 1611) and 13:5; these rare occurrences militate against regarding καί as part of the original text (cf. Luke 13:16; John 2:20; 5:5; Acts 13:20; Gal 3:17).

6.a-a. ἀνοίγειν στόμα is a Semitic idiom meaning "to begin to speak, to start to speak, to utter" (Louw-Nida, § 33.29); see *Comment* on 13:6.

6.b. Variants: (1) εἰς βλασφημίας (acc. pl.)] ℵ A C Andr a[1] f[2031] 94 598 1773; Andr/Byz 4a[-2084] 4b[-2018 -2032] 598 fam 1006 fam 1611[1854] Andr/Byz 4a[2084]; it[z] (*in blasphemias*); Nestle-Aland[27]; UBSGNT[4]. (2) βλασφημῆσαι (aor. inf.)] 𝔓[47] syr[ph] cop. (3) εἰς βλασφημίαν (acc. sing.)] 051 Andreas Oecumenius Byzantine it[gig] (*in blasphemiam*); Tyc[2] (*in blasphemiam*); Beatus (*in blasphemiam*); Irenaeus[Lat] (*ad blasphemium;* Sanday-Turner, *Nouum Testamentum,* 197); syr[h] TR; von Soden, *Text.*

6.c. The inf. βλασφημῆσαι, "to blaspheme," is used epexegetically in order to specify precisely how the beast blasphemed God: "that is, to blaspheme his name and dwelling."

6.d-d. Variant: omit καὶ τὴν σκηνὴν αὐτοῦ] C.

6.e-e. Variants: (1) τοὺς ἐν τῷ οὐρανῷ σκηνοῦντας] ℵ* A C fam 1611[1611 2344] Oecumenius[2053]. (2) omit τοὺς ἐν τῷ οὐρανῷ σκηνοῦντας] 𝔓[47] Primasius (Vogels, *Untersuchungen,* 216). (3) omit τούς] Andr/Byz 4b[2018] fam 1611[1854]. (4) omit σκηνοῦντας] 𝔓[47]. The insertion of a prep. phrase between the article and its substantive, as in τοὺς ἐν τῷ οὐρανῷ σκηνοῦντας, is rare in Revelation, occurring primarily in the introductions to each of the seven proclamations (2:1, 8, 12, 18; 3:1, 7, 14; 19:9). Reading (1) has superior external attestation (*TCGNT*[1], 746–47; *TCGNT*[2], 674).

6.f. Variant: add καί] ℵ[2] 025 046* 051 2023 Oecumenius[2053text] Andreas Irenaeus[Lat] (Sanday-Turner, *Nouum Testamentum,* 197) lat syr[ph] cop. Added to relieve strained syntax (*TCGNT*[1], 746; *TCGNT*[2], 674).

7.a-a. Variants: (1) καὶ ἐδόθη αὐτῷ ποιῆσαι πόλεμον μετὰ τῶν ἁγίων καὶ νικῆσαι αὐτούς] ℵ 046 051 94 fam 1006[1006] fam 1611[2344] Andr a[1*] i[-2042] f[2073] l n Byz 2[2138] 2019 syr[ph] it[gig] Tyc[2] Beatus cop[bo]; von Soden, *Text.* (2) καὶ ἐδόθη αὐτῷ πόλεμον ποιῆσαι μετὰ τῶν ἁγίων καὶ νικῆσαι αὐτούς] fam 1611[1611 1854] 2351; Andr/Byz 4b[1828] vg. (3) καὶ ἐδόθη αὐτῷ ἐξουσία ποιῆσαι πόλεμον μετὰ τῶν ἁγίων καὶ νικῆσαι αὐτούς] Byz 1[1859] Andr l[2020] Andr n[2065 2432]; Primasius (*et data est ei potestas* [ἐξουσία] *faciendi bellum cum sanctis et vicit eos*); Beatus. (4) omit καὶ ἐδόθη αὐτῷ ποιῆσαι πόλεμον μετὰ τῶν ἁγίων καὶ νικῆσαι αὐτούς] 𝔓[47] A C Oecumenius[2053] Andreas syr[h] cop[sa] arm Irenaeus[Lat]. In spite of the important witnesses that omit the clause in reading (2), it appears that the omission resulted from an early scribal error of the eye jumping from the first to the second occurrence of καὶ ἐδόθη αὐτῷ in v 7 (*TCGNT*[1], 747; *TCGNT*[2], 674). This is one of the rare instances in which ℵ and Byzantine preserve the original text (Schmid, *Studien* 2:120–21).

7.b-b. On translating οἱ ἅγιοι, lit. "saints, holy ones," as "God's people," see *Comment* on 5:8.

7.c-c. Variants: (1) καὶ λαόν] ℵ A 025 051 Andr f$^{2023\ 2073}$ g i^{-2042} l n 94 cop^{sa} it^{gig} it^{z} vg. (2) καὶ λαούς] C syr^{ph}. (3) omit καὶ λαόν] 𝔓^{47} 051 fam 1006^{1006} Andreas cop^{bo}.

8.a. αὐτόν is a masc. acc. pronoun used to refer to the neut. noun θηρίον because the latter is used to symbolize a male figure. The variant reading αὐτῷ, attested by ℵ 051 Oecumenius^{2053} fam 1006 fam 1611$^{1611\ 1854}$ 792 Andreas, is an attempt to correct the masc. acc. αὐτόν, by substituting the generically ambiguous pronoun αὐτῷ (which can be either masc. or neut.), and is also in a case that can function as the obj. of προσκυνεῖν, with which the acc. and the dat. can be used interchangeably (see *Note* 3:9.h.). On the use of προσκυνεῖν + dat. or acc., see *Note* 4:10.b.

8.b-b. Variants: (1) οὗ οὐ γέγραπται τὸ ὄνομα αὐτοῦ] C fam 1611$^{1854\ 2344}$ Oecumenius^{2053} Irenaeus^{Lat} Primasius; B. Weiss, *Johannes-Apokalypse,* 194; Charles, 2:315; Nestle-Aland^{27}; UBSGNT^{4}. (2) οὐ αἰγέγραπται τὸ ὄνομα αὐτοῦ] A. (3) οὐαὶ οὐαὶ οὗ οὐ γέγραπται τὸ ὄνομα αὐτοῦ] Andr l. (4) ὧν οὐ γέγραπται τὸ ὄνομα αὐτῶν] fam 1611^{1611} Andr h n Beatus. (5) ὧν οὐ γέγραπται τὰ ὀνόματα αὐτῶν] 𝔓^{47} (ℵ* omits οὐ) ℵ 025 051 fam 1006$^{1006\ 1841}$ fam 1611^{2329} Andr h n lat. (6) ὧν οὐ γέγραπται τὸ ὄνομα] 2351 Andreas Byzantine; von Soden, *Text.* (7) ὧν οὐ γέγραπται τὰ ὀνόματα] 025 Andr a c f^{2023} h i n 2019. (8) omit τὸ ὄνομα αὐτοῦ] Tertullian (*De coron.* 13). The original text is very probably found in reading (1) and is presupposed in readings (2) and (3), which reflect the mistaken reading of ουαι for ουου. In reading (2), οὐ αἰγέγραπται is perhaps an itacistic error for the plupf. form ἐγέγραπτο or more likely is based on the phrase οὐαὶ γέγραπται. Readings (4), (5), and (6) have corrected οὗ to ὧν to agree with the preceding masc. pl. noun cluster πάντες οἱ κατοικοῦντες, and the distributive sing. τὸ ὄνομα has similarly been corrected to the pl. form in reading (5). However, in reading (4) the use of ὄνομα where a plurality is referred to can be considered a Hebraism, which would explain a correction from ὧν . . . αὐτῶν to οὗ . . . αὐτοῦ on the one hand and from ὄνομα to ὀνόματα on the other (Charles, 1:354). For discussions of these variants, see B. Weiss, *Johannes-Apokalypse,* 105–6; Schmid, *Studien* 2:90; *TCGNT*^{1}, 747.

8.c. οὗ . . . αὐτοῦ is an example of a resumptive pronoun (cf. 3:12; 7:2, 9; 13:12; 17:2; 20:8), which has often been regarded as a Semitism but can be found also in pagan Gk. (Turner, *Syntax,* 325).

8.d. For καταβολή as "creation," see *Ep. Arist.* 129 and Louw-Nida, § 42.37.

8.e-e. Variants: (1) τῷ βιβλίῳ] A 2351 Andreas Byzantine; von Soden, *Text.* (2) βιβλίῳ] C. (3) τῇ βίβλῳ] 𝔓^{47} 250^{com} Andr a c i^{2042} l TR. (4) βίβλῳ] ℵ fam 1611$^{1611\ 1854\ 2344}$ 2019 Andr e$^{2026\ 2091}$ h$^{2060\ 2286\ 2302}$ Andr/Byz 4$^{2070\ 2305}$ 2084. (5) τῷ βίβλῳ] ℵ 181 256. Variant (1) represents a wide variety of MSS and, with the support of (2), which only lacks the definite article τῷ, is certainly the superior reading (Schmid, *Studien* 2:228). The author appears to have used ἡ βίβλος τῆς ζωῆς (3:5; 20:15) and τὸ βιβλίον τῆς ζωῆς (17:8; 20:12; 21:27) interchangeably.

8.f-f. Variant: τοῦ οὐρανοῦ τοῦ ἐσφραγισμένου] Oecumenius^{2053}. Here τοῦ οὐρανοῦ replaces τοῦ ἀρνίου by the accident of a copyist (cf. 21:27, where ℵ has the abbreviation ουνου for αρνιου). τοῦ ἐσφαγμένου is a pf. mid. ptcp. that, according to Mussies (*Morphology,* 348), has taken over the gerundive value of the *qatul* category of Semitic verbs, allowing the phrase to be translated "the Lamb *which was to be slaughtered* from the foundation of the world."

10.a-a. Variants: (1) εἰς αἰχμαλωσίαν] A C fam 1006 fam 1611 Oecumenius$^{2053\ 2062}$; W Hort; von Soden, *Text.* (2) εἰς αἰχμαλωσίαν ἀπάγει] 2351 Andr/Byz 4a^{616} Andr/Byz 4b$^{1828\ 1862\ 1888}$ it$^{(ar)\ e\ dem\ div\ gig\ haf\ z}$; vg^{A} (*qui in captivitatum ducit*); vg$^{I\ \Phi\ Clem}$ (*in captivitatum duxerit*); syr$^{ph\ h}$ Irenaeus^{Lat} Primasius; Bousset (1906) 364. (3) αἰχμαλωτίζει] Andr/Byz 2a$^{104\ 459}$ 2019 cop^{sa}. (4) ἔχει αἰχμαλωσίαν] Andr d f$^{051*\ 2023\ 2073}$ Byzantine. (5) αἰχμαλωσίαν] Andr a c. The lack of a verb in reading (1) has given rise to the scribal embellishments in readings (2) and (3). Reading (4) is an obvious scribal error in which ἔχει was mistakenly read for εἰς. See *TCGNT*^{1}, 747–48; *TCGNT*^{2}, 674–75.

10.b-b. Variants: (1) εἰς αἰχμαλωσίαν] A fam 1611^{2344} Primasius (*qui captivum duxerit et ipse capietur*); it^{gig} (*si quis in captivitatem duxerit in captivitatem vadit*); WHort; [von Soden, *Text*]; Nestle-Aland^{27}; UBSGNT^{4}; (*TCGNT*^{1}, 747). (2) omit εἰς αἰχμαλωσίαν] 𝔓^{47} ℵ C 051 Oecumenius^{2053} fam 1006 fam 1611$^{1611\ 1854}$ Andreas Byzantine Beatus (*si quis in captivatem vadit*); arm cop^{bo}. (3) omit εἰς] 1678 1778. For thorough discussions of the problems involved in this variant, see Schmid, *Studien* 2:139–41, and J. Delobel, "Le texte de l'Apocalypse," 162–65). Schmid regards the reading of A in 13:10 as proof of the general superiority of that MS (*Studien* 2:141). Though the double expression could be accounted for as an error of dittography (i.e., the repetition of a letter or letter group), it appears more likely that one of the two identical phrases was accidentally omitted through haplography (i.e., the omission of a letter or letter group that should be repeated). Yet the double expression does fit the pattern found in LXX Jer 15:2 (cf. LXX Jer 50:11[MT 43:11], καὶ ὅσοι εἰς αἰχμαλωσίαν εἰς αἰχμαλωσίαν [see *Comment* on v 10 below]). J. Delobel has collected the MS evidence for LXX Jer 15:2 showing that the four parallel phrases, including the one just quoted, suffered haplography in the MS tradition ("Le text de l'Apocalypse," 164 n. 55).

10.c. Variants: (1) ὑπάγει] A C 025 046 051 fam 1006 fam 1611 Oecumenius$^{2053\ 2062}$ Andreas Byzantine. (2) συνάγει] Andr a b c. (3) αἰχμαλωτισθήσεται] 94. The present ind. ὑπάγει, "he goes," according to Mussies (*Morphology*, 337), is "clearly jussive" and so could be translated "let him go." Yet it is probably more appropriate to regard this construction as a futuristic present ind.: "he will go" (cf. S. Thompson, *Apocalypse*, 120 n. 88). The proverbial style of the statement would also support interpreting ὑπάγει as a gnomic or general present (Burton, *Syntax*, § 12).

10.d-d. Variants: (1) ἀποκτανθῆναι] A; Charles, 1:355; Mussies, *Morphology*, 190; Nestle-Aland^{27}; UBSGNT^{4}. (2) ἀποκτενεῖ] 𝔓^{47} (only απ[οκτενει] is fully visible); C 025 051^{corr} fam 1611^{2329} Andreas lat syr^{h} Irenaeus^{Lat}; Tischendorf, *NT Graece;* B. Weiss, *Johannes-Apokalypse*, 194; WHort; Bousset (1906) 365; von Soden, *Text;* Nestle-Aland^{25}. (3) ἀποκτείνει] ℵ fam 1006^{1841} fam 1611$^{1611\ 1854}$ it^{gig} syr$^{\mathrm{ph\ h}}$ eth Irenaeus; WHort^{mg}. (4) ἀποκτέννει] fam 1006$^{911\ 1006\ 1841}$ fam 1611$^{1854\ 2344}$ 2351 Andr n^{2432} Andr/Byz 4a$^{250\ 424}$ Andr/Byz 4b$^{1862\ 2018}$. (5) ἀποκταινεῖ] Andr f^{051*} h. (6) ἀποκτενεῖν] Oecumenius^{2053}. (7) ἀποκτείνειν (present inf.) or ἀποκτεῖναι (aor. inf.)] conjecture by Westcott and Hort, *Introduction*, 138*. Reading (1) is supported only by A (for discussions arguing for the correctness of this reading, see Charles, 1:355–56; Schmid, *Studien* 2:138–41; *TCGNT* ^{1}, 748; *TCGNT* ^{2}, 675 (where it is called "the least unsatisfactory" of the available variant readings). Westcott and Hort (*Introduction*, 138*) observe that "the reading of A gives the right sense; for the former clause, as well as Jer xv 2, on which both clauses are founded, shows that not requital but fulfillment of a Divine appointment is intended." Critical of this use of a singular reading is J. Delobel, "Le text de l'Apocalypse," 162–65. Some of the variants originated in various Gk. dialects; doubling of the liquid ν in reading (5) is characteristic of the Aeolic dialect (cf. 6:11), while reading (6) is of Doric origin. Reading (1) can be construed as follows: εἴ τις ἐν μαχαίρῃ ἀποκτανθῆναι [aor. pass. inf.] αὐτὸν ἐν μαχαίρῃ ἀποκτανθῆναι, "If anyone *is slain* with a sword, he with a sword must be slain." Reading (2): εἴ τις ἐν μαχαίρῃ ἀποκτενεῖ [fut. ind. active] δεῖ αὐτὸν ἐν μαχαίρῃ, "If anyone *will kill* with a sword, he must be killed with a sword." Reading (3): εἴ τις ἐν μαχαίρῃ ἀποκτείνει [pres. ind. active] δεῖ αὐτὸν ἐν μαχαίρῃ ἀποκτανθῆναι, "If anyone *kills* with a sword, he must be killed with a sword."

10.e. Variants: (1) αὐτόν] A Byz 12^{2048} it^{gig} cop$^{\mathrm{sa\ bo}}$ Beatus; Nestle-Aland^{27}; UBSGNT^{4}. (2) δεῖ αὐτόν] 𝔓^{47} ℵ C 025 051* Oecumenius^{2053} fam 1006$^{911\ 1006\ 1841}$ fam 1611$^{1611\ 1854\ 2329\ 2344}$ 2351 Andreas Andr/Byz 4a$^{250\ 424}$ Andr/Byz 4b$^{1862\ 2018}$ latt eth syr$^{\mathrm{ph\ h}}$ Irenaeus^{Lat}; Tischendorf, *NT Graece;* B. Weiss, *Johannes-Apokalypse*, 194; WHort; Bousset (1906) 365; von Soden, *Text*. In favor of reading (1) is the fact that acc. pronouns functioning as the subject of infs. are placed *before* the inf. in 10:11; 11:5; 17:10; 20:3 (*var. lect.* ℵ); all these examples have the impersonal verb δεῖ with the inf.

10.f-f. Variant: omit ἐν μαχαίρῃ] Andr f$^{051\mathrm{cor}\ 2073\mathrm{cor}}$ Byzantine.

10.g-g. The adv. ὧδε, often used as an adv. of place indicating a position relatively near the speaker (Louw-Nida, § 83.1), is used here to refer to the relevance of the following statement to the altered allusion to Jer 15:2; i.e., it functions to introduce the *true significance* of the allusion. ὧδε is therefore paraphrased as the italicized portions indicate: "*This indicates that* the endurance and faith of the saints *is involved.*" Some modern versions render ὧδε in a problematic way. The RSV and NRSV translate it as "Here is a call for," and the NIV and REB have "This calls for." Both translations give the erroneous impression that an exhortation rather than an interpretation is involved. The more paraphrastic rendering of the NEB is appropriate: "Here the fortitude and faithfulness of God's people have their place."

10.h-h. See *Note* 13:7.b-b.

11.a. Variants: (1) ἀναβαῖνον] ℵ A C fam 1006 fam 1611 Oecumenius$^{2053\ 2062}$ 2351 Andreas Byzantine. (2) ἀναβαῖνων] 𝔓^{47} 792 Andr h$^{2060\ 2286}$ Byz 12^{2048} Andr/Byz 2$^{104\ 459\ 628\ 680\ 922}$ Andr/Byz 3$^{1894\ 2061}$. This variant results either from the confusion of ο = ω (Gignac, *Grammar* 1:275–77) or from the tendency in apocalyptic literature to regard symbols for people (e.g., the neut. θηρίον, "beast") as masc. (cf. the use of the masc. acc. pronoun αὐτόν in v 8). For a similar variant, see *Note* 11:7.d-d.

11.b. This verse contains a possible instance of two finite verbs coordinated with a preceding ptcp.: ἀναβαῖνον . . . εἶχεν . . . ἐλάλει; cf. Burney, *JTS* 22 (1921) 321ff. Mussies, however, thinks that, since this verse can be broken up into two sentences, the construction is probably not present (*Morphology*, 326–27).

11.c. Variant: omit δύο] Byzantine arm^{3}.

11.d. Variant: ὁμοίῳ] 𝔓^{47}. On the assimilation of ὅμοιος to the noun it governs, see *Notes* 1:13.c-c. and 9:10.c-c.

11.e. Though the term here is ἀρνίῳ (a dat. of association with ὅμοιος), usually translated "lamb," it must be translated "ram" since lambs do not have horns. ἀρνίον is clearly used here as a faded diminutive. It must therefore be translated "ram," referring to an adult male (cf. Louw-Nida, § 4.25).

11.f. Since the clauses joined by the conjunction καί are antithetical, this καί functions adversatively (καί *adversativum*) and should therefore be translated "but."

11.g. Variants: (1) λάλει] 𝔓^{47} it^{gig}. (2) ἐλάλησεν] Andr i^{2042}.

12.a. See *Note* 1.a.

12.b. The verb ποιεῖ, a historic present, is noteworthy because it occurs in the present ind. four times in vv 12–16, twice as an aor. inf. (v 14), once as a present subjunctive (v 13), and once as an aor. subjunctive (v 15).

12.c-c. Variant: omit ἐνώπιον αὐτοῦ] Hippolytus (*de Ant.* 49, from commentary, not text quoted in *de Ant.* 48). Error of omission by homoioteleuton; the copyist skipped from ποιεῖ to ποιεῖ. While ἐνώπιον + gen. can mean "in the presence of" or "before the eyes of," it makes little sense to understand it this way (as do Bratcher-Hatton, *Revelation,* 201–2). Here the expression means "by the authority of, on behalf of" (Thayer, *Lexicon,* 220; BAGD, 271).

12.d-d. καί functions in an epexegetical or explanatory way (BDF § 142.9).

12.e. Variants: (1) ἵνα προσκυνήσουσιν] 𝔓[47] A C Oecumenius[2053] 2351 Andr h[2060] 598 2019. (2) ἵνα προσκυνήσωσι] 051 2351 Andreas Byzantine Hippolytus (*de Ant.* 48); von Soden, *Text.* (3) προσκυνεῖν] ℵ a vg. In Revelation, ἵνα is used with either the fut. ind. or the subjunctive, and in passages in which there are variants (almost all), the fut. ind. appears to have the strongest MS support (see 3:9; 6:4, 11; 8:3; 9:4, 5, 20; 13:12; 14:13; 22:14); cf. Schmid, *Studien* 2:220.

12.f-f. On the use of προσκυνεῖν + dat. or acc., see *Note* 4:10.b.

12.g. The pronominal phrase οὗ . . . αὐτοῦ, ends with a resumptive pronoun, called a *pronomen abundans,* often thought to reflect a Semitism. This idiom occurs nine times in Revelation (3:8; 7:2, 9; 12:6, 14; 13:8, 12; 17:9; 20:8). In 13:12 the relative clause is *essential,* i.e., dependent, and therefore must be considered a Semitism. The relative clause defines the antecedent, τὸ θηρίον τὸ πρῶτον, "the first beast." For an extended discussion, see *Note* 3:8.c. and *Introduction,* Section 7: Syntax, pp. clxvi–clxvii.

13.a. Variants: (1) ποιεῖ] *lectio originalis.* (2) ἐποίει] 051 cop[bo]. (3) ποιήσει] 1006 Andr f[2032 2056] h Andr/Byz 4a Andr/Byz 4b cop[sa] Irrenaeus[Lat].

13.b-b. The clause ἵνα καὶ πῦρ ποιῇ ἐκ τοῦ οὐρανοῦ καταβαίνειν, "even making fire come down from heaven" (RSV), functions epexegetically, dependent on the phrase ποιεῖ σημεῖα μεγάλα, "he performs great signs" (Mussies, *Morphology,* 245: "and he does great signs, so that [namely that] he makes even fire to come down"). BDR § 391.5 construes this ἵνα clause as a *result* clause (cf. Matt 24:24).

13.c. Variants: (1) ποιῇ] *lectio originalis.* (2) ποιήσῃ (aor. subjunctive)] 𝔓[47] Andr b[2081] l[1678 2080] 1773. (3) ποιεῖ] 025 051 Oecumenius[2053]. (4) ποιήσει (fut. ind.)] fam 161 2329 Victorinus. (5) omit ποιῇ] Hippolytus (*de Ant.* 48).

13.d-d. Variants: (1) ἐκ τοῦ οὐρανοῦ καταβαίνειν] 𝔓[47] A C fam 1006 fam 1611 Oecumenius[2053]. (2) ἐκ τοῦ οὐρανοῦ καταβαίνῃ] 2351 2377 Byzantine. (3) καταβαίνειν ἐκ τοῦ οὐρανοῦ] 025 051 Andreas. (4) καταβῇ ἐκ τοῦ οὐρανοῦ] Hippolytus (*de Ant.* 48).

13.e. Variants: (1) εἰς] *lectio originalis.* (2) ἐπί] 𝔓[47].

14.a-a. See *Note* 12.c-c above..

14.b. The masc. sing. ptcp. λέγων functions as a predicate adj. modifying the neut. sing. noun θηρίον (v 11). This is clearly a solecism, but the construction reflects the narrator's practice of using adjs., pronouns, and ptcps. in the masc. gender to modify neut. nouns that symbolize men (Mussies, *Morphology,* 138).

14.c-c. ποιῆσαι is an inf. that complements the ptcp. λέγων and introduces indirect discourse.

14.d-d. Variant: εἰκόναν] A Andr Ø[598 2038]. On the addition of -ν to third-declension nouns in the imperial period, see *Note* 12:13.c-c.

14.e. The dat. τῷ θηρίῳ could be the dat. of indirect obj., "to make a cult statue *for* the beast," but the context makes it clear that it is a dat. of advantage and should be translated "to make a cult statue *in honor of* the beast."

14.f. Variants: (1) ὃς ἔχει] 𝔓[47] A C 025 046 051 fam 1611[1854] Andreas Primasius (*qui*); it[gig] (*qui*); B. Weiss, *Johannes-Apokalypse,* 195; Nestle-Aland[27]; UBSGNT[4]. (2) ὃ ἔχει] ℵ fam 1006[-911] fam 1611[2329] 2377 Byzantine Andr a c d f[2093] g l 94 TR; von Soden, *Text.* (3) ὡς ἔχει] Oecumenius[2053]. (4) ὡς εἶχεν] 2351. The masc. sing. relative pronoun ὅς modifies the neut. sing. τῷ θηρίῳ, because the latter is a symbol for a male individual (cf. Mussies, *Morphology,* 138); therefore readings (2), (3), and (4) must be regarded as corrections. However, note that the certain readings in 13:2 and 17:11 have τὸ θηρίον ὅ.

14.g-g. Variant: καὶ ἔζησεν ἀπὸ τῆς μαχαίρης] 2351 2377 Byzantine.

14.h. Since the clauses joined by the conjunction καί, "and," are antithetical, this is a contextual indication that this is an instance of καί *adversativum* and must be translated "but." It also has the idea of unexpectedness (Louw-Nida, § 91.12), and the entire phrase could be translated "who was wounded with the sword but (surprisingly) lived."

14.i. Variant: ζήσας] 𝔓[47].

15.a. Variants: (1) αὐτῷ] ℵ 025[corr] 046 Andreas Byzantine; Tischendorf, *NT Graece;* B. Weiss, *Johannes-*

Apokalypse, 136; von Soden, *Text;* Nestle-Aland^{27}; UBSGNT^{4}. (2) αὐτῇ] A C 025; WHort; Charles, 1:cxlvi; 2:318. Westcott and Hort, *Introduction,* 138*, suggest that either αὐτῷ and αὐτῇ are *both* interpolations or that τῇ γῇ was lost after αὐτῇ or substituted for it. It is difficult to account for the change from an original αὐτῷ to αὐτῇ since the latter is certainly the *lectio difficilior* (cf. Westcott, *Introduction,* 138*) and probably arose as a scribal error (Schmid, *Studien* 2:90–91; *TCGNT*^{1}, 748). Torrey (*Apocalypse,* 129) suggests that the author had the Aram. word חיתא *ḥayta'*, "beast" (a fem. noun), in mind when he wrote αὐτῇ.

15.b-b. Variants: (1) δοῦναι πνεῦμα] *lectio originalis.* (2) πνεῦμα δοῦναι] 2351 Andr c f^{2023} i^{2042} 94 Byzantine. πνεῦμα, lit. "spirit," is here rendered "life."

15.c-c. The textual history of this verse is exceedingly complicated and subject to a great deal of variation. Several groups of MSS attest to major omissions from Nestle-Aland^{27}: (1) omit θηρίου ἵνα καὶ λαλήσῃ ἡ εἰκὼν τοῦ θηρίου καί] 𝔓^{47}. (2) omit ἵνα καὶ λαλήσῃ ἡ εἰκὼν τοῦ θηρίου] Andr c^{2033} h^{2302} i$^{1876\ 2014\ 2034\ 2036\ 2043\ 2047\ 2082}$ n^{2429} Byz 14^{468*} Byz 15^{367} Byz 16$^{61\ 69}$ Byz 18^{617} Byz 19^{2016} Andr/Byz 2$^{336\ 620\ 628\ 1918}$ Andr/Byz 3^{2196} cop arm Beatus. (3) omit ἵνα καὶ λάλησῃ ἡ εἰκὼν τοῦ θηρίου καὶ ποιήσῃ [ἵνα] ὅσοι ἐὰν μὴ προσκυνήσωσιν τῇ εἰκόνι τοῦ θηρίου] Oecumenius^{2053}. These errors of haplography were caused by the two occurrences of τοῦ θηρίου.

15.d-d. Variants: (1) ποιήσῃ ἵνα ὅσοι] A 046 fam 1006^{1006} fam 1611$^{2329\ 2344}$ 2019 Andreas TR; [von Soden, *Text*]; [Nestle-Aland^{27}]; [UBSGNT^{4}]. (2) ποιήσῃ ὅσοι] 𝔓^{47} א 598 fam 1611^{1611} 2351 2377 Andreas Byzantine vgst Hippolytus (*de Ant.* 48); Tischendorf, *NT Graece.* (3) τοῦ ποιῆ(σαι) ὅσοι] 𝔓^{47}; a singular reading (the gen. of the definite article + inf. is rare in Revelation and occurs elsewhere only in 12:7; in a textually disputed passage, τοῦ + inf. occurs in Rev 14:15 [TR]). (4) ἵνα before ἀποκτανθῶσιν] 051 1 fam 1611^{1854} Andr f^{2073} TR. ἵνα, like ὥστε, is used with verbs meaning "to effect, to make, to persuade, to confer, to compel," etc. so that ποιῆσῃ ἵνα makes excellent sense. Textually, ἵνα is necessary because it goes with ἀποκτανθῶσιν, an aor. subjunctive, which has strong textual attestation (A C 025 046 051 fam 1611$^{1854\ 2329}$); cf. Schmid, *Studien* 2:91. Some Andreas MSS solved the problem of the aor. subjunctive ἀποκτανθῶσιν by placing a ἵνα immediately before it: Andr a c e^{2026*} f i^{2074}. Reading (1) is the *lectio difficilior,* and it is easier to account for its omission than its insertion. See *TCGNT*^{1}, 748–49; *TCGNT*^{2}, 675–76.

15.e. ἐάν = ἄν and frequently follows relative pronouns in the LXX and NT as here (BDF § 107; BDR § 107).

15.f. Variant: προσκυνήσουσιν] א 051 598 1006^{corr} 2019 2351 Andr c e^{2091} f$^{2023–2073}$ g^{2045} h^{2286} i^{2074} n^{2429} Byz 9$^{452\ 467\ 2021}$ Byz 12$^{2–48}$ Byz 16^{69} Byz 17^{459} Byz 19^{2016} Andr/Byz 2$^{104\ 459}$.

15.g-g. Variant: τὴν εἰκόνα] A. On the use of προσκυνεῖν + dat. or acc., see *Note* 4:10.b.

15.h. Variants: (1) ἀποκτανθῶσιν] *lectio originalis.* (2) ἀποκτανθῆναι] 1773 2351. (3) ἵνα ἀποκτανθῶσιν] Andr a c e^{2026} f i^{2074mg} Andr/Byz 3.

16.a-a. Variants: (1) ἵνα δῶσιν αὐτοῖς (aor. subjunctive)] 𝔓^{47} א* A C Andreas Hippolytus (*de Ant.* 48). (2) ἵνα δώσει αὐτοῖς (fut. ind.)] Oecumenius^{2053} Andr a^{-1} Andr f$^{2031–2056}$ Andr h^{2060} Hippolytus (*de Ant.* 48; MS E). (3) ἵνα δῶσιν αὐτῷ (aor. subjunctive)] Andr l$^{1678–1778}$. (4) ἵνα δώσωσιν αὐτοῖς (aor. subjunctive)] 2377 Andr g i^{-2042} Byzantine. (5) ἵνα δώσουσιν αὐτοῖς] 94 Andr d. (6) ἵνα δώσῃ αὐτοῖς (aor. subjunctive)] 051^{corr} fam 1611^{2329} Andr b^{2286} Hippolytus (*de Ant.* 48; MS R). (7) ἵνα λάβωσιν τὸ χάραγμα αὐτοῦ] fam 1006 Andr n; Victorinus. Reading (1) is certainly the original reading and is supported by extremely strong textual evidence. The verb δῶσιν is in the indefinite 3rd pl. (see also 2:24; 12:6; 16:15; 18:14; 20:4; cf. Charles, 1:362; Mussies, *Morphology,* 231–32) and is equivalent to a pass. (cf. ἐδόθη in v 15) and has therefore been translated "to be given."

16.b. Variant: χαράγματα] 2351. While χάραγμα is often translated with a general term like "mark," when applied to human or animal skin, it is always a *brand* (Ysebaert, *Greek Baptismal Terminology,* 285).

16.c-c. Note the peculiar use in this verse of ἐπί + gen. and ἐπί + acc. in synonymous ways in the two phrases "to place a mark" ἐπὶ τῆς χειρὸς αὐτῶν, "on their hand" (ἐπί + gen.), and ἐπὶ τὸ μέτωπον αὐτῶν, "on their forehead" (ἐπί + acc.). A peculiarity of the style of Revelation is that when God's people are sealed, the term "foreheads" is always the *pl.* form τῶν μετώπων (7:3; 9:4; 14:1; 22:4), while the *sing.* τὸν μέτωπον or τοῦ μετώπου is always used of allies of the beast (13:16; 14:9; 17:5; 20:4). Schmid (*Studien* 2:211) observes this phenomenon but attributes it to the author's stylistic variation.

16.d-17.d. The scribe of Oecumenius^{2053} accidentally omitted the phrases between χάραγμα in v 16 and χάραγμα in v 17.

17.a. Variants: (1) καί] 𝔓^{47} א A (lacuna); 025 046 051 fam 1006^{1006} fam 1611$^{1854\ 2344}$ it$^{gig\ ar}$ vg arm eth. (2) omit καί] א* C fam 1611^{1611} syr$^{h\ ph}$ cop$^{sa\ bo}$ Hippolytus Irenaeus Tyc^{2} Beatus. The καί was perhaps omitted when the following ἵνα clause was read as dependent on δῶσιν in v 16, whereas the ἵνα clause is dependent on ποιεῖ and coordinate with the ἵνα δῶσιν clause (*TCGNT*^{1}, 749; *TCGNT*^{2}, 676). The omission of the καί is based on a misunderstanding of the relationship between v 16 and v 17 (Schmid, *Studien* 2:104).

17.b. Variants: (1) δύνηται (pres. subjunctive)] 𝔓^{47} א A C (lacuna in Oecumenius^{2053}) fam 1006^{1841} 2351 Hippolytus Aretas; WHort. (2) δύναται (pres. ind.)] 051 Andreas Byzantine; WHort^{mg}; B. Weiss, *Johannes-Apokalypse,* 103. ἵνα + present subjunctive is rarely used in classical Gk. and occurs only once in the NT (1 John 5:20, ἵνα γινώσκομεν); in two other passages the verbs can be construed as either subjunctive or ind. (φυσιοῦσθε in 1 Cor 4:6 and ζηλοῦτε in Gal 4:17); cf. Robertson, *Grammar,* 984.

17.c-c. The neut. acc. τὸ χάραγμα is the direct obj. of the ptcp. ὁ ἔχων, while the neut. acc. τὸ ὄνομα and the masc. acc. τὸν ἀριθμόν, which follow, are in apposition to τὸ χάραγμα, so that the entire phrase could be translated "the one with the brand, that is, the name of the beast or the number of his name."

17.d. See *Note* 13:16.d-17.d.

17.e-e. Variant: (1) τὸ ὄνομα τοῦ θηρίου] A fam 1006 fam 1611$^{-1611\ -2329}$ 051 Andreas Byzantine. (2) τοῦ θηρίου] fam 1611^{1611} Andr e^{2026} i$^{1685\ 2074}$ n^{-2429}. (3) τοῦ ὀνόματος τοῦ θηρίου] C Andr c h^{2302} 598 1773 it^{a} vg syr arm^{3} eth. (4) ἢ τὸ ὄνομα τοῦ θηρίου] 𝔓^{47} it^{gig} Beatus. (5) τοῦ θηρίου ἢ τὸ ὄνομα αὐτοῦ] א Andr l 2019 cop. (6) ἐπὶ τοῦ μετώπου αὐτοῦ τὸ ὄνομα τοῦ θηρίου] fam 1611^{2329}. Variant (1) is in the acc. of apposition, which is expressed by some texts that place a comma after χάραγμα, though not Nestle-Aland^{27}.

18.a-a. On the translation "a number referring to a human being," see Peerbolte, *Antichrist,* 151.

18.b-b. Variants: omit καὶ ὁ ἀριθμὸς αὐτοῦ] 𝔓^{47} א Oecumenius^{2053com} syr^{ph} cop^{sa}.

18.c. Variants: (1) ἑξακόσιοι ἑξήκοντα ἕξ] A; the following have χξς = 666: 𝔓^{47} 051 fam 1611$^{1611\ 2329}$ Andreas Byzantine. (2) ἑξακόσιαι ἑξήκοντα ἕξ] א. (3) ἑξακόσιαι δέκα ἕξ] C arm^{4} Tyc^{2}. (4) ἑξακόσια ἑξήκοντα πέντε] fam 1611^{2344}. (5) ἑξακόσια ἑξήκοντα ἕξ] 025 fam 1611^{1854} Oecumenius^{2053} Andreas. (6) omit χξς] 2351. The number 666, despite the variation in grammatical forms of ἑξακόσιοι, is supported by readings (1), (2), and (5), where it is probably the original reading, based on the strong MS support of 𝔓^{47} א A 025 046 051, most minuscules, and many early versions: it^{gig} vg Beatus syr^{ph} cop arm. 𝔓^{47} 025 051 Hippolytus (*de Ant.* 48) Andr d e f^{2073} n 598 and the Byzantine text have three letters that function as numbers, χξς, the last of which is "digamma" (the first and last letters look the same as the first and last letters of the name Χριστός; cf. E. Zellweger, *Das neue Testament im Lichte der Papyrusfunde* [Frankfurt am Main: Lang, 1985] 151); the numerical value of this combination is 666: χ = 600; ξ = 60; ς or digamma = 6. Both ἑξήκοντα and ἕξ are indeclinable numerical adjs., while ἑξακόσιοι is declinable (-αι, -α). The pl. masc. nom. form ἑξακόσιοι, which is certainly the correct reading, fits the masc. gender of ἀνθρώπου (a human). The pl. neut. nom. form ἑξακόσια is attested by 025 and Andreas, and probably arose because τὸ θηρίον, "the beast," is a neut. noun. The fem. plur. nom. ἑξακόσιαι is a reading found in א and C (though C has the inferior reading: ἑξακόσιαι δέκα ἕξ, "six hundred sixteen"). The significance of the fem. form is difficult to explain. Most minuscules write the number 666 using the alphabetical signs χξς. Reading (3) has ἑξακόσιοι δέκα ἕξ, "six hundred sixteen," which is clearly inferior, though read by C, some MSS reported by Irenaeus (who thought it a scribal error, *Adv. haer.* 5.30.1), and Tyc^{2}. M. Oberweis has suggested that the origin of this variant is the result of the transliteration of the Gk. gen. noun θηρίου, "beast," from Rev 13:18 into Heb. characters as תריו *tryw,* which has the total numerical value of 616 (ת = 400; ר = 200; י = 10; ו = 6), and the name would make sense written on a person's forehead or hand, since it can mean "[belonging to the] beast." Yet the numerical value of the Gk. term θηρίον, "beast," is also 666! Since 616 is the numerical value of Gaius Caesar (usually called Caligula, A.D. 37–41), the possibilities for speculation seem limitless.

Form/Structure/Setting

I. OUTLINE

3. Vision of the two beasts (12:18–13:18)
    a. Introductory transition: the dragon stood on the sand of the sea (12:18)
    b. The emergence of the first beast from the sea (13:1–10)
        (1) Introductory vision formula: "Then I saw" (v 1a)
        (2) Subject of vision: a beast emerges from the sea (v 1a)
        (3) The description of the beast (vv 1b–2a)

(a) Initial description (v 1b)
[1] Has ten horns
[2] Has seven heads
(b) Closer description (v 1cd)
[1] Ten diadems on his horns
[2] Blasphemous names on his heads
(c) Detailed description of the beast (v 2a)
[1] Like a leopard
[2] Feet like a bear
[3] A mouth like a lion
(4) The dragon commissions the beast (v 2b)
(a) He gives him his power
(b) He gives him his throne
(c) He gives him great authority
(5) The healed wound of the beast (v 3a)
(a) One of his heads is fatally wounded
(b) The fatal wound is healed
(6) The reactions of the people of the world to the dragon and the beast (vv 3b–4)
(a) They are amazed at the beast (v 3b)
(b) They worship the dragon because he authorized the beast (v 4a)
(c) Hymnlike worship of the beast (v 4bc)
[1] Who is like the beast? (v 4b)
[2] Who can fight the beast? (v 4c)
(7) The program of the beast (vv 5–10)
(a) God's empowerment of the beast (v 5)
[1] Given ability to speak (v 5a)
[a] Haughty things
[b] Blasphemous things
[2] Given authority to be active forty-two months (v 5b)
(b) The activity of the beast (vv 6–8)
[1] He blasphemes God (v 6)
[a] He blasphemes God's name
[b] He blasphemes God's dwelling, i.e., those who dwell in heaven
[2] Actions against God's people (v 7a)
[a] He is permitted to fight against God's people
[b] He is permitted to conquer God's people
[3] Given worldwide authority (v 7b)
[a] Over every tribe
[b] Over every people
[c] Over every language
[d] Over every nation
[4] Those who worship the beast (v 8)
[a] Positive description: all inhabitants of the earth (v 8a)
[b] Negative description: those whose names were not

written in the book of life (v 8b)
{1} Book belongs to the slain Lamb
{2} When not written: at the foundation of the world
(c) Parenthetic call for endurance (vv 9–10)
[1] Proclamation formula: If any one has an ear, let him hear (v 9)
[2] Prophetic saying (v 10ab)
[3] Parenetic saying (v 10c)
c. Another beast emerges from the land (vv 11–18)
(1) Introductory vision formula: "Then I saw" (v 11a)
(2) Subject of vision: another beast ascending from the earth (v 11a)
(3) Description of the second beast (v 11b)
(a) Two horns like a ram
(b) It sounds like a dragon
(4) Relationship to the first beast (v 12a)
(a) It exercises the full authority of the first beast
(b) It acts on his behalf
(5) The second beast's program promoting the worship of the first beast (vv 12b–17)
(a) It compels the worship of the first beast (vv 12b–13)
[1] Those compelled (v 12b)
[a] The earth
[b] Those who dwell on the earth
[2] What they are compelled to do: worship (v 12b)
[3] Object of worship (v 12c)
[a] The first beast
[b] The one whose mortal wound was healed
[4] Means of compelling worship (v 13)
[a] Performance of impressive miracles (v 13a)
[b] Example: It causes fire to fall (v 13b)
{1} From heaven to earth
{2} Before people
(b) It deceives people (v 14)
[1] The deceived: those who dwell on the earth
[2] Means of deception: the miracles it is permitted to perform
[3] Nature of the deception: it tells them to make a cult statue
[a] In honor of the beast
[b] The beast who had a mortal wound but who lived
(c) The cult statue of the first beast (v 15)
[1] The second beast is permitted to give life to the cult statue (v 15)
[a] That it might speak (v 15b)
[b] That it might order the execution of those who did not worship his image (v 15c)

[2] The second beast compels everyone to be branded (v 16)
 [a] Everyone compelled (v 16a)
 {1} Unimportant and important
 {2} Rich and poor
 {3} Free and slave
 [b] Location of brand (v 16b)
 {1} On their right hand
 {2} Or on their forehead
 [c] What cannot be done without the brand (v 17a)
 {1} No one can buy
 {2} No one can sell
 [d] Content of the brand (v 17b)
 {1} The name of the beast
 {2} Or the number of its name
(6) Concluding numerical riddle (v 18)
 (a) Introduction: "Here is wisdom!" (v 18a)
 (b) Challenge to decode the number of the beast (v 18ab)
 [1] The number refers to a human being (v 18a)
 [2] The number is 666 (v 18b)

II. Literary Analysis

Rev 11:19–12:17 constitutes a coherent textual unit within Revelation (see *Form/Structure/Setting* on 11:19–12:17). Similarly, 12:18–13:18 also forms a coherent textual unit in the final revision of Revelation. These two blocks of material are connected by 12:18, "And he [i.e., 'the dragon'] stood [ἐστάθη] on the shore of the sea." This is a redactional attempt to link these two large units of text together (J. Weiss, *Offenbarung,* 85). The problematic character of this transitional editorial phrase is evident in the MS tradition in which the third-person singular ἐστάθη, "he stood," is altered or corrected to the first-person singular ἐστάθην, "I stood" (referring to John), which functions as an introduction to the vision narrated in 13:1–10. The dragon stands on the shore of the sea because (one must imagine) he has been frustrated in his pursuit of the woman of 12:1–17 and has turned his anger on her offspring. From the sea and from the land two beasts will emerge who will be empowered by the dragon to wage war against Christians. The problem, however, is that this explanation is not explicitly found in the text, though it appears to be the intention of the final redactor (Charles, 1:344). Since 12:18 is a redactional link joining 12:1–17 with 13:1–18, it is also likely that the dragon was not originally part of either of the two visions in 13:1–10 and 13:11–18 but was introduced into these visions in order to tie them more closely to 12:1–17 (where the term δράκων occurs eight times). Therefore, the sentence in 13:2d is redactional: "The dragon gave him his power and his throne and great authority." Similarly, v 4a also looks out of place: "They worshiped the dragon because he gave authority to the beast." The statement that the beast from the land spoke "like a dragon" (13:11) is probably redactional as well. Further, v 3a also looks redactional: "One of his heads appeared to be fatally wounded, but its mortal wound was healed." This insertion reflects the Nero *redivivus* legend. With these redactional glosses bracketed, vv 2–4 read as follows:

2a The beast which I saw was like a leopard,
and its feet were like those of a bear,
and its mouth was like that of a lion.
[2b] [The dragon gave him his power and his throne and great authority.]
[3a] [One of its heads appeared to be fatally wounded,]
[but its mortal wound was healed.]
3b The whole earth was astonished and followed the beast.
[4a] [They worshiped the dragon because he gave authority to the beast,]
4b and they also worshiped the beast, chanting,
"Who is like the beast,
4c and who is able to fight against it?"

Bousset was of the opinion that Rev 13 was, on the whole, composed by the final redactor of the book ([1906] 379).

The final version of the scene in Rev 12:18–13:10 is a perverse reflection of the investiture of the Lamb in Rev 5 (Roloff, 135). Just as the Lamb received the sealed scroll from the one seated upon the throne (5:7), and thereby received power and authority (5:12), so the beast from the sea receives authority from the dragon (13:2). Just as the Lamb is the ruler over people from all tribes, languages, and nations purchased through his blood (5:9), so the beast from the sea rules over tribes, peoples, languages, and nations (13:7). Just as the heavenly cherubim, representing the entire created order, offer their homage to the Lamb (5:12), so the inhabitants of the earth fall prostrate before the beast, pay him homage, and offer him a song of praise (13:4). Just as the sign of recognition of the Lamb is the marks of his slaughter (5:6), so the beast also bears a mortal wound that has been healed (13:3).

In the discussion of Rev 11:1–13 above under *Form/Structure/Setting*, I presented evidence for a source underlying Rev 11:1–13 based on a consideration of the striking similarities and differences between that passage and a source used by Lactantius in *Div. Inst.* 7.17.1–3. That argument receives further support from the number of sequential parallels between Rev 13:11–16 and *Div. Inst.* 7.17.4–8, which Lactantius seems to derive from the same source. The hypothesis of a common source underlying Rev 11:1–13 and 13:11–16 is strengthened by the fact that while the eschatological narrative in Revelation is interrupted by 11:14–12:18, Lactantius *Div. Inst.* 7.17.1–8 presents a continuous narrative, which is parallel to Rev 11:1–13 and 13:11–16. In the following translation of *Div. Inst.* 7.17.4–8, the italicized portions have no parallel in Rev 13:11–16 (tr. McDonald, *Lactantius,* 518):

> [4]*That king, indeed, will be most offensive and will himself, but as the prophet of liars, set himself up as and call himself a god. He will order himself to be worshiped as the son of God.* And there will be given to him power, so that he may do signs and wonders with the sight of which he may ensnare men to adore him. [5]He will order fire to descend from heaven, *and the sun to stand still in its course,* and a statue to speak; *and these things will be done at his word. By these miracles even many of the wise will be attracted to him.* [6]*Then, he will try to overturn the temple of God, and will persecute the just people, and there will be pressure and contrition such as there never has been from the beginning of the world.* [7]Those who believe and come to him will be branded by him as though cattle; those who reject his mark will either flee to the mountains, or

they will be seized and killed by well-contrived tortures. *He will pile the books of the prophets upon the just and thus he will burn them.* [8]And it will be given to him to make the earth desolate in forty-two months.

Flusser argues that the source behind Lactantius *Div. Inst.* 7.17.1–8 is the *Oracle of Hystaspes,* which he considers to be essentially of Jewish origin ("Hystaspes," 390–453). The parallels can be seen more clearly in a synoptic presentation of the two texts, in which two portions of the Revelation text, 13:15b and 13:5b, are not in their original sequence.

Rev 13:11–16	*Lactantius* Div. Inst. *7.17.4–8*
[13]It performed impressive miracles,	[4b]And there will be given to him power, so that he may do signs and wonders with the sight of which he may ensnare men to adore him.
even causing fire to fall from heaven to earth before people.	[5]He will order fire to descend from heaven,
[15a]It was permitted to give life to the cult statue of the beast that the cult statue of the beast might speak	and a statue to speak; . . .
[16]It forced everyone, small and great, rich and poor, free and slave, to be given a brand on their right hand or on their forehead,	[7]Those who believe and come to him will be branded by him as though cattle;
[17]so that no one can buy or sell unless he has a brand, that is, the name of the beast or the number of its name.	
[15b]and cause whoever did not worship the cult statue of the beast to be executed.	those who reject his mark will either flee into the mountains, or they will be seized and killed by well-contrived tortures.
[5b]and authority was given to it to be active for forty-two months.	And it will be given to him [*et dabitur ei*] to make the earth desolate in forty-two months.

There are a number of reasons for regarding Lactantius *Div. Inst.* 7.17.4–8 (as well as the earlier portion of the narrative in 7.17.1–3) as a source essentially *independent* of Revelation: (1) Most obviously, the eschatological narrative in Lactantius *Div. Inst.* 7.17.1–8 is *continuous* while that in Rev 11:1–13 and 13:11–16 is interrupted by two very different textual units, 11:14–18 (the conclusion of the seven-trumpet series with the sounding of the seventh trumpet, concluding the trumpet plagues, which was interrupted at Rev 9:21) and 11:19–12:18 (the narrative of the dragon, the woman, and the child). No one would have suspected that the narratives of Rev 11:1–13 and 13:11–16 were part of one continuous story were it not for the evidence of Lactantius (Flusser, "Hystaspes," 449). (2) Even though the sequence of motifs found in both Rev 13:11–16 and Lactantius *Div. Inst.* 7.17.4–8 is striking, there is not clear indication of the literary dependence of the latter on the former even though Lactantius (ca. A.D. 250–325) wrote two centuries after the composition of Revelation. The one possible exception is the reference to forty-two months used in combination with the divine passive in *Div. Inst.* 7.17.8. (3) Redactional features that clearly belong to the author of Revelation, such as the phrase "small and great, rich and poor, free and slave" (Rev 13:16), the economic motif (Rev 13:17a), and the reference to the "king" of Lactantius (usual in narratives dealing with the Antichrist) as the beast in Revelation (13:17b) do not occur in Lactantius, indicating that he did not derive his narrative from this source.

III. TRADITION HISTORY

Rev 12:18–13:18 consists of two main units of text: 12:18–13:10, on the beast from the sea, and 13:11–18, on the beast from the land. These two beasts clearly reflect the Jewish myth of Leviathan, the female monster from the sea, and Behemoth, the male monster from the desert. Though this allusion provides a visionary framework for 12:18–13:18, the unity thereby imposed on the text unit is only superficial since important features of the Leviathan-Behemoth myth are omitted and replaced with motifs derived from the myth of the eschatological antagonist. The Leviathan-Behemoth myth has both protological features (e.g., the two monsters were created on the fifth day of creation) and eschatological features (e.g., they will serve as food for the righteous in the eschaton). This myth is found in fragmentary form in short passages in three Jewish apocalypses that originated late in the first century A.D., i.e., at a time roughly contemporary with Revelation: (1) *1 Enoch* 60:7–11, 24 (vv 12–23 have been inserted, artificially separating vv 7–11 from v 24; cf. Caquot, *Semitica* 25 [1975] 115–16); (2) 4 Ezra 6:49–52; and (3) *2 Apoc. Bar.* 29:4. It is possible that 4 Ezra and *2 Apoc. Bar.* are dependent on *1 Enoch* for this myth (Black, *1 Enoch,* 227). More complete forms of the story are found in the Talmud and midrashim (*b. B. Bat.* 74b–75a) and have been synthesized by Ginzberg (*Legends* 1:27–28). Inspired by Gen 1:21, which describes God's creation of the great sea monsters on the fifth creative day, this legend claims that God then separated the pair (4 Ezra 6:47–52), appointing Leviathan to inhabit the sea (Job 41:1–34; Ps 104:25–26; 4 Ezra 6:52) and Behemoth the land (Job 40:15–24; 4 Ezra 6:51). Thus the *separation* of Leviathan from Behemoth, symbolizing the ordering of chaos by the separation of the sea from the land (a feature perhaps more appropriate to the *third* day of creation; cf. Caquot, *Semitica* 25 [1975] 120–21) was a *protological* act. Their emergence from the realms to which they were appointed, the sea (Rev 13:1) and the earth (Rev 13:11), however, is an *eschatological* action that signifies the emergence of chaos from order, i.e., the irruption of chaotic forces as the dying gasp of the old, worn-out creative order just before a period of restoration and renewal. Missing from Revelation, but present in the Jewish apocalyptic and rabbinic versions of the story, is the expectation that Leviathan and Behemoth will serve as food for the righteous in the eschaton (*1 Enoch* 60:24; 4 Ezra 6:52; *2 Apoc. Bar.* 29:4; *b. B. Bat.* 75a).

The superficiality of the Behemoth allusion in Rev 13:11–18 is evident by the fact that this beast is referred to elsewhere only as the false prophet (16:13; 19:20; 20:10). The identification of the beast from the land with the false prophet is assumed in 16:13 and 20:10 but made explicit only by the reference to 13:12–13 in 19:20, "the false prophet who perfomed miracles by his authority whereby he deceived those who received the mark of the beast and who worshiped his cultic image." Since the dragon, the beast, and the false prophet are referred to only very briefly in 16:13, 19:20, and 20:10, these references must all be regarded as redactional attempts to tie the various myths together into a relatively consistent pattern. Further, the beast and the false prophet are ultimately defeated and thrown into the lake of fire, not eaten (Rev 19:20).

Rev 12:18–13:18 reflects the systematization of the two main strands of the traditional Jewish myth of the eschatological antagonist (or the Antichrist), presented as two separate historical realities, each masked by superficial Leviathan-Behemoth imagery, the "godless tyrannical ruler" (modeled after Antiochus IV) and the "false seductive prophet" (Bousset-Gressmann, *Religion des Judentums,* 254); see *Excursus 13B: The Eschatological Antagonist Myth.* An eschatological tradition of *two* antagonists may be derived from the *Oracles of Hystaspes.* According to Lactantius, after ten kings have divided and ruled the world, a powerful enemy will conquer the three who possess Asia, and this conqueror will be regarded as the prince of the rest; a period of chaos will be inaugurated (*Div. Inst.* 7.16.1–14). However, after a prophet appears from God (*Div. Inst.* 7.17.1–2), another king will arise from Syria who will overthrow the previous king and will fight against and kill the prophet from God (*Div. Inst.* 7.17.2–11). Of course, while the two antagonists of Rev 13 are allies, the two in Lactantius *Div. Inst.* 7.16–17 succeed one another. Similarly, Commodian speaks of two kings who function as eschatological antagonists (one will be the king of the Goths, and the other a Syrian king). The Syrian king is described as Nero *redivivus,* who will be adored as God (*Carmen de duobis gentibus* 827–32). The Antichrist will kill the great prophet Elijah (*Carmen* 833–64); here both Lactantius (*Div. Inst.* 7.17.1–3) and Commodian (*Carmen* 833–64; *Instr.* 1.41) speak of the killing of a single great prophet.

The beast from the sea in 13:1–10 appears to represent the Roman Empire (not an individual), while the beast from the land in 13:11–18, the agent of the first beast, probably represents the *commune Asiae,* i.e., the Koinon of Asia. This presents a conceptual problem, for the antagonist myth that pervades this section is heavily dependent on identifying the antagonist with a diabolical *individual,* not a group or a nation. However, much of the antagonist imagery is concentrated in 13:11–18, where the figure of the false prophet appears wearing the mask of the second beast, i.e., Behemoth. The historical paradigm for the antagonist in early Judaism was Antiochus IV Epiphanes (Dan 11:36–39; 1 Macc 1:20–61; 2 Macc 5:11–6:11).

Many of these motifs are evident in *Asc. Isa.* 4:2–12, part of an extensive Christian addition (3:13–4:22), which probably dates to the end of the first century A.D. (Knibb in Charlesworth, *OTP* 2:147–49). The relevant motifs in *Asc. Isa.* 4:2–12, quoted here (tr. Knibb in Charlesworth, *OTP* 2:161–62), are in italics:

> [2]And after it has been brought to completion, *Beliar will descend* [Rev 12:9], the great angel, the king of this world, which he has ruled over since it existed. He will descend from

his firmament in the form of a man, a *king of iniquity* [2 Thess 2:8], a murderer of his mother—this is the king of the world—[3]and will *persecute the plant* [Rev 12:17] which the twelve apostles of the Beloved will have planted; some of the twelve will be given into his hand. [4]This angel, Beliar, will come in the form of that king [Rev 17:11], and with him will come all the powers of this world [Rev 12:9b] and they will obey him in every wish. [5]*By his word he will cause the sun to rise by night, and the moon also he will make to appear at the sixth hour* [Rev 13:13; 2 Thess 2:9; Mark 13:22 (= Matt 24:24)]. [6]And he will do everything he wishes in the world; he will act and speak like the Beloved [*Did.* 16:4], and will say, "I am the Lord, and before me there was no one" [Mark 13:6 (= Matt 24:5; Luke 21:8); 2 Thess 2:4–7]. [7]And all men in the world will believe in him [Rev 13:4, 8]. [8]*They will sacrifice to him* [Rev 13:14–15] and will serve him, saying, "*This is the Lord, and besides him there is no other* [Rev 13:4]." [9]And the majority of those who have associated together to receive the Beloved he will turn aside after him [Mark 13:22; *Did.* 16:3]. [10]And *the power of his miracles* [Rev 13:13; 2 Thess 2:9; Mark 13:22 (= Matt 24:24); *Did.* 16:4] will be in every city [11]and district, and *he will set up his image before him in every city* [Rev 13:15–16]. [12]And he will rule for three years and seven months and twenty-seven days [Rev 13:5].

The sequence of motifs in this apocalyptic discourse, as the references in brackets suggest, exhibits many parallels with the eschatological scenarios in Rev 13:1–18, Mark 13, Matt 24, 2 Thess 2, and *Did.* 16.

The Nero *redivivus* motif is apparent in *Asc. Isa.* 4:2, in which the incarnation of Beliar (= Satan) is described as a matricide and he is portrayed as one who persecutes the plant, i.e., Christians (during the infamous Neronic persecution of A.D. 64). The description of Beliar as a "king of iniquity" reflects the tradition that the Hebrew term בליעל *bĕliyyaʿal*, "Belial" (meaning "worthless"), stands behind the term ὁ ἄνομος, "the lawless one," in 2 Thess 2:8 (the Hebrew phrase אנשים בני בליעל *ʾănāšîm bĕnê bĕliyyaʿal* in Deut 13:14 is translated in the LXX as ἄνδρες παράνομοι, "lawless men"; cf. Hartman, *Prophecy,* 199; Bousset, *Antichrist,* 136–37; Flusser, *IEJ* 3 [1953] 32 n. 6). The Nero *redivivus* myth is also central to *Sib. Or.* 3.63–74 (see translation of this text in *Comment* on 13:13), in which the depiction of Beliar coming from the *Sebastenoi* indicates that he will be one of the Roman emperors.

IV. THE FORM OF REV 13:9–10

Rev 13:9–10 consists of three units: (1) the introductory proclamation formula (v 9), (2) a prophetic oracle in the form of a maxim (v 10ab), and (3) a concluding parenetic saying (v 10c).

(1) The proclamation formula in Rev 13:9 contains a variation of the proclamation formula found at the conclusion of each of the seven proclamations (2:7, 11, 17, 29; 3:6, 13, 22), though here it is used to introduce rather than conclude a unit of text. Because the proclamation formula is used in an oracular context in each of the seven proclamations, its association with this unit of text suggests that it too is oracular in character.

(2) The maxim in v 10ab is based in part on an allusion to Jer 15:2 (and perhaps also to Jer 43:11 [LXX 50:11]).

אֲשֶׁר לַמָּוֶת לַמָּוֶת וַאֲשֶׁר לַחֶרֶב לַחֶרֶב
ʾăšer lammāwet lammāwet waʾăšer laḥereb laḥereb
וַאֲשֶׁר לָרָעָב לָרָעָב וַאֲשֶׁר לַשְּׁבִי לַשֶּׁבִי
waʾăšer lārāʿāb lārāʿāb waʾăšer laššĕbî laššebî

ὅσοι εἰς θάνατον, εἰς θάνατον,
καὶ ὅσοι εἰς μάχαιραν, εἰς μάχαιραν,
καὶ ὅσοι εἰς λιμόν, εἰς λιμόν,
καὶ ὅσοι εἰς αἰχμαλωσίαν, εἰς αἰχμαλωσίαν.

Those who are destined for pestilence, to pestilence;
those who are destined for the sword, to the sword;
those who are destined for famine, to famine;
those who are destined for captivity, to captivity.

A similar formulation is found in LXX Jer 50:11 (MT 43:11):

οὓς εἰς θάνατον, εἰς θάνατον,
καὶ οὓς εἰς ἀποικισμόν, εἰς ἀποικισμόν,
καὶ οὓς εἰς ῥομφαίαν, εἰς ῥομφαίαν.

Those who are destined for pestilence, to pestilence,
and those who are destined for exile, to exile,
and those who are destined for the sword, to the sword.

The oracular character of v 10ab is supported by the fact that Jer 15:2 is in the form of a question-and-answer schema that concludes with an oracle introduced with the stereotypical phrase "thus says the Lord" (B. O. Long, "Two Question and Answer Schemata in the Prophets," *JBL* 90 [1971] 129–39). On the other hand, Jer 43:11 (MT 50:11), which is very similar in content and phraseology to Jer 15:2, is part of a larger prophetic oracle (Jer 43:8–13), which is unconnected to a question-and-answer schema.

Rev 13:10ab consists of a synonymous couplet comprising two conditional sayings introduced by the conditional particle εἰ, "if," which assumes that the condition is either real or possible (Aune, "Aphorisms," 229–31); each line contains a protasis and an apodosis closely similar in wording, i.e., in the form of an anadiplosis:

εἴ τις εἰς αἰχμαλωσίαν, εἰς αἰχμαλωσίαν ὑπάγει
εἴ τις ἐν μαχαίρῃ ἀποκτανθῆναι, αὐτὸν ἐν μαχαίρῃ ἀποκτανθῆναι.

If anyone is for captivity, to captivity he will go;
If anyone is to be slain with the sword, he will be slain with the sword.

This saying is obviously connected with the very real possibility of suffering or martyrdom. In that connection there is a similar saying attributed to Esther in the form of an anadiplosis in Esth 4:17, "If I perish, I perish." This is formally similar to the anadiplosis in Gen 43:14, "If I [Jacob] am bereaved of my children, I am bereaved" (cf. the translation of Westermann, *Genesis* 3:123, "But I—I am bereaved, bereaved!").

Comment

18 καὶ ἐστάθη ἐπὶ τὴν ἄμμον τῆς θαλάσσης, "He stood on the sand of the sea." This sentence is structurally problematic, for it is unclear whether it belongs with the previous text unit (11:19–12:17) or it introduces the next unit of text (13:1–18). In Oecumenius *Comm. in Apoc.*, the pericope he quotes for comment is 12:18–13:4, indicating that he understood 12:18 as the beginning of the unit in 13:1–4. However, ἐστάθη, "he stood," follows two other third-person singular verbs in v 17, ὠργίσθη, "was angry," and ἀπῆλθεν, "left." The subject of both is explicitly the dragon, and the sentence appears to mean that he has come to a standstill on the shore of the sea to await, or perhaps even to summon, the emergence of the beast from the sea described in 13:1–10 (B. Weiss, *Johannes-Apokalypse,* 193; Charles, 1:344; Lohse, 76). As an introduction to 13:1–18, however, the passage is awkward (reflected in the textual variants) since one would expect more details to be given regarding *how* the dragon summoned forth the beast (Bousset [1906] 358). This verse is therefore, in all probability, a redactional suture that links 12:1–17 with 13:1–18 (Bousset [1906] 357). On analogy with 17:1 and 21:9, Bergmeier (*ANRW* II, 25/5:3908) has reconstructed 12:18a to read "[And he carried me in the Spirit] to the beach of the sea." However, this reconstruction is unlikely since 17:1–3a and possibly 21:9–10a are themselves redactional introductions to 17:3b–19:10 and 21:10b–22:7, respectively (though it is probable that 17:1–3a was formulated on the basis of 21:9–10a; see *Comments* on both passages).

13:1a καὶ εἶδον ἐκ τῆς θαλάσσης θηρίον ἀναβαῖνον, "Then I saw a beast emerging from the sea." On καὶ εἶδον, see *Comment* on 5:1. The prepositional phrase ἐκ τῆς θαλάσσης, "from the sea," immediately following the verb and its object is unusual (cf. v 11 and LXX Theod Dan 7:3, which have a more normal word order), but this serves to emphasize the phrase "from the sea," thus showing that 13:1 is linked with 12:18, which mentions the sea as the place where the dragon took his stand (Kraft, 172). In LXX Dan 7:3, the passage to which this verse alludes, the Greek phrase is καὶ τέσσαρα θηρία ἀνέβαινον ἐκ τῆς θαλάσσης (cf. Theod Dan 7:3, καὶ τέσσαρα θηρία μεγάλα ἀνέβαινον ἐκ τῆς θαλάσσης), "and four beasts emerged from the sea." Further, that the term θηρίον, "beast," is anarthrous indicates that the author assumed it was unknown to his readers (this also suggests that the articular phrase τὸ θηρίον in 11:7 is a redactional gloss). It is also clear that the final redactor understood the sea as representing the abyss, as 11:7 indicates.

This beast from the sea is, at least in part, an allusion to the Jewish tradition of Leviathan, a female monster who was separated from Behemoth on the fifth day of creation and assigned to the sea (*1 Enoch* 60:7–11, 24; 4 Ezra 6:47–52; *2 Apoc. Bar.* 29:4; *b. B. Bat.* 74b–75a); for "Behemoth," see *Comment* on 13:12. The only previous mention of such a beast is in 11:7 in the phrase "the beast who ascends from the abyss." There τὸ θηρίον is articular, suggesting that the author assumed that his readers were already familiar with this creature. Here θηρίον is anarthrous, suggesting either that this is a different beast from the one mentioned in 11:7 or (more likely) that the clause in 11:7 quoted above is an interpolation.

According to Artemidorus (*Oneirocritica* 2.16), when a person dreams of any sea creature, no one will be benefited. In Judaism the sea monster could represent oppressive foreign nations (Dan 7:1–8). Occasionally, the chaos monster Rahab or Leviathan could be used to represent a particular foreign oppressor like Egypt (Pss 74:14; 87:4; Isa 30:7; Ezek 29:3; 32:2–3). In Jer 51:34, for example, Nebuchadrezzar is compared to a monster who will devour Israel. The figure of Leviathan as a symbol of evil was derived by Israel from Canaanite mythology (Gordon, "Leviathan," 1–9). In early Jewish literature the term δράκων, "dragon," is used as a symbol of chaos (*Sib. Or.* 8.85) and as a term for Satan (*Apoc. Abr.* 23:7). In CD 8:10 the תַּנִּינִים *tannînîm,* "dragons," of Deut 32:33 (the same word occurs in Gen 1:21; Job 7:12; Ps 74:13; Ezek 29:3; 32:2) are interpreted as "the kings of the peoples." The term תַּנִּינִים *tannînîm* is used of foreigners who invade Palestine and capture Jerusalem (G. R. Driver, "The Number of the Beast," 80). The first such invader is Nebuchadrezzar (described as a תַּנִּין *tannîn,* "monster," in MT Jer 51:34[LXX 28:34], translated δράκων, "dragon, monster," in the LXX). In *Pss. Sol.* 2:25, Pompey, who conquered Jerusalem in 63 B.C., is designated a δράκων, "dragon, monster."

The beast from the sea has frequently been understood in historical terms as the Roman governor; i.e., the proconsul representing the Roman emperor, who arrived each year in the Roman province of Asia, was bound to set foot first in Ephesus (*CAH* 11:581). Since he necessarily arrived by boat, it could be said that he came "from the sea" (Rowland, *Open Heaven,* 431–32). The proconsuls of the two most important Roman provinces, Asia and Africa, were always ex-consuls (Magie, *Roman Rule* 1:446). The fact that from the time of Augustus on there were also imperial procurators in the senatorial province of Asia suggests the presence of extensive property belonging to the emperor in this province (Magie, *Roman Rule,* 1:679). It is also possible that the beast from the sea represents the Roman state.

1b ἔχον κέρατα δέκα καὶ κεφαλὰς ἑπτά, "with ten horns and seven heads." This phrase (unaccountably omitted from early printings of the NRSV), in reverse order, occurs in 12:3 and 17:3, though in 12:3 it is the *dragon* who has seven heads and ten horns, while in 17:3 it is a *beast* who has these features (however, since θηρίον, "beast," is anarthrous in 17:3, it does not refer back to the θηρίον of Rev 13). The fact that the ten horns and seven heads are not interpreted here suggests that this phrase (like that in 12:3) is an interpolation based on 17:3, which occurs within a context in which the ten horns and seven heads are interpreted as rulers (17:9–14). The fourth beast of Daniel's vision in Dan 7:7 has ten horns, which are then interpreted as ten kings (7:24). Irenaeus understood the ten horns of Dan 7 to be ten kings who will subdivide the Roman empire (*Adv. haer.* 5.26.1; followed by Hippolytus *de Ant.* 25; *Comm. in Dan.* 4.5.3).

1c καὶ ἐπὶ τῶν κεράτων αὐτοῦ δέκα διαδήματα, "and on its horns were ten diadems." The red dragon in 12:3 has seven diadems, one on each of its seven heads (presumably meaning that the seven heads represent seven rulers). Here the diadem or crown is clearly a symbol of royal power and authority normally worn on the head (presumably, if interpreted, the ten crowns would refer to ten rulers). The wearing of several diadems in antiquity indicated sovereignty over as many nations (1 Macc 11:13; Jos. *J.W.* 13.113; see *Comment* on 19:12), certainly an appropriate image for the beast from the sea, if it represents the Roman empire. It should be noted, however, that Roman emperors themselves never wore diadems signifying royal status. The mention of diadems in addition to horns appears somewhat redundant since both can be construed as symbols of power. While Dan 7:7, 20 mention ten horns, there is no mention of crowns or diadems on the horns as a way of indicating that they represent kings.

1d καὶ ἐπὶ τὰς κεφαλὰς αὐτοῦ ὀνόματα βλασφημίας, "and on its heads were blasphemous names." The phrase "blasphemous names" also occurs in 17:3, where the great harlot is described as sitting on a red beast, which is covered with blasphemous names (ὀνόματα βλασφημίας) and which also has seven heads and ten horns, though it not specified whether the names are written only on the heads and horns. There are magical figures whose bodies are covered with magical inscriptions (Eitrem, *Papyri Osloenses,* 41). One of the magical figures in *PGM* XXXVI (see Betz, *Greek Magical Papyri,* 269) is divided into sections and inscribed with various magical names on the arms, legs, neck, chest, and stomach. The beast forces all people to be branded on their foreheads or hands (13:16, 17; cf. 14:9, 11; 16:2; 19:10; 20:4).

The beast and the whore and their followers are not the only ones who have distinguishing marks in Revelation. Christ bears a name no one knows but he himself (19:12), and the words "King of kings and Lord of Lords" are written on his robe and thigh (19:16). The 144,000 also have the name of the Lamb and his Father on their foreheads (14:1), just as the servants of the Lamb in the New Jerusalem have his name on their foreheads (22:4).

By "blasphemous names," the author could mean the titles and epithets used by Roman emperors, including κύριος, "lord," σωτήρ, "savior," and *divi filius,* "son of god"; cf. Cuss, *Imperial Cult,* 53–74. In various Hellenistic ruler cults, part of the characteristic paraphernalia for priestly colleges charged with overseeing various ruler cults was a crown bearing the image of particular divine rulers. Antiochus II, in 193 B.C., proclaimed the formation of a new group of priestesses for the purpose of superintending the worship of Laodice his wife. They were to bear "crowns of gold decorated with portraits of the queen" (C. B. Welles, *Royal Correspondence in the Hellenistic Age* [New Haven: Yale UP, 1934] nos. 36–37).

2a καὶ τὸ θηρίον ὃ εἶδον ἦν ὅμοιον παρδάλει καὶ οἱ πόδες αὐτοῦ ὡς ἄρκου καὶ τὸ στόμα αὐτοῦ ὡς στόμα λέοντος, "The beast which I saw was like a leopard, and its feet were like those of a bear, and its mouth was like that of a lion." This aspect of the vision is a pastiche based on Daniel's vision of the four beasts from the sea (Dan 7:1–8). The author of Revelation, who is concerned with a *single* kingdom rather than with a succession of four kingdoms, has created a single beast from characteristics of three of the four beasts in Daniel, one of which was like a lion (Dan 7:4), the second like a bear with three large teeth (7:5), and the third like a leopard with four wings and four heads (7:6). The fourth is an indescribably terrifying beast with ten horns (7:7, 20), similar to those that characterize this beast from the sea in v 1. The seven heads of the beast in 13:1 have no direct correspondence in the beasts described in Dan 7:1–8, though the third leopardlike beast is described as having four heads (Dan 7:6).

Dan 7:1–8 was interpreted in various ways in early Christian texts. *Barn.* 4:4–5 quotes Dan 7:24 and then 7:7–8, both of which deal with the ten horns and the small horn of the fourth beast, in an enigmatical passage referring to a series of Roman emperors. Similarly, in 4 Ezra 11:1–12:39, Ezra dreams of an eagle who emerged from the sea (*et ecce ascendebat de mari aquila*) with twelve wings and three heads (11:1). This eagle is the fourth beast, representing the fourth kingdom that was part of the vision of Daniel (4 Ezra 11:36–46; 12:11). Though nothing in the description of the fourth beast in Dan 7:7–8, 19–27 suggests identifying it with an eagle, the eagle was probably chosen because it clearly represents Rome (Myers, *Esdras,* 295–96). There are no demonstrable literary or exegetical traditions that link Rev 13:1–18 with 4 Ezra 11:1–12:39, though it is significant that *both* authors reinterpret the vision in Dan 7:1–9, *both* are concerned with a single beast, and *both* use the beast to symbolize Rome. *2 Apoc. Bar.* 39:5–7 and some early Christian authors express the view that the fourth beast of Dan 7 represents Rome (Hippolytus *de Ant.* 25.1–

3; 28.1; see Irenaeus *Adv. haer.* 5.25.3). The *os leoni,* "mouth of a lion," image may allude to Roman imperial power, since the lion was a symbol used for the Roman emperor (Jos. *Ant.* 18.228). The Paul of 2 Tim 4:17 was rescued ἐκ στόματος λέοντος, "from the mouth of the lion" (a phrase used in Ps 22:21 [cf. Heb 11:33] for rescue from great danger), referring to Roman imperial authority, which early Christian tradition equated with Nero (Eusebius *Hist. eccl.* 2.22.4).

A lengthy inscription in an Aramaic incantation bowl contains a description of the demon Bagdana, literally from head to toe (Naveh-Shaked, *Amulets,* bowl 13, lines 4–5), and has some analogies to the description of the beast from the sea:

> His head is the head of a lion, his molar teeth of a she-wolf, his teeth are the teeth of a tiger, the draughts of his mouth are furnaces of fire, his eyes are flowing lightnings, his shoulders are the spheres of a cloud, his temples are an anvil of iron, his arms are two hammers, his chest is the chest of an evil man . . . .

2b καὶ ἔδωκεν αὐτῷ ὁ δράκων τὴν δύναμιν αὐτοῦ καὶ τὸν θρόνον αὐτοῦ καὶ ἐξουσίαν μεγάλην, "The dragon gave him his power and throne and great authority." According to 2 Thess 2:9, the lawless one (a designation for the eschatological antagonist) comes as an agent of Satan, a view also found in later Christian writers (Irenaeus *Adv. haer.* 5.25.1). This statement is probably a redactional insertion into the narrative to link the activity of the dragon, who has been cast down to the earth (12:13–17), with the activity of the beast from the sea introduced in 13:1; see v 4a (J. Weiss, *Offenbarung,* 84–85; Bergmeier, *ANRW* II, 25/5:3909). This is supported by the fact that this statement is not part of John's vision but is revealed as something he, as an omniscient author, knows about the relationship between the beast and the dragon. The dragon, while he played a central role in 12:1–17, is essentially extraneous to the narratives in 13:1–18 and is mentioned only in redactional additions (12:18; 13:2d, 4a).

This transfer of power constitutes a brief "enthronization" scene (Roloff, 136–37), in which it is revealed that the beast is an agent or plenipotentiary of the dragon, i.e., Satan; the power of the Roman empire is therefore satanic in origin. In 1QM 15:2–3, a close connection is posited between the "king of the Kittim" and Satan (tr. Vermes, *Dead Sea Scrolls*):

> All [who are ready] for battle shall march out and shall pitch their camp before the king of the Kittim and before all the host of Satan [חיל בליעל *ḥêl bĕliyyaʿal*] gathered about him for the Day [of Revenge] by the Sword of God [בחרב אל *bĕḥerem ʾēl*].

The identification of the term "Kittim" is problematic; in the War Scroll the term designates nations who are the enemies of Israel, while in the Habbakuk Commentary and the Nahum Commentary the term probably refers to the Romans (Ringgren, *Qumran,* 26–31; J. Carmignac, "Les Kittim dans la Guerre des fils de lumière contre les fils de ténèbres," *NRT* 77 [1955] 737ff.; Horgan, *Pesharim,* 8, 26). Nevertheless, as in Rev 13:2, Belial or Satan is the ultimate authority behind the earthly world power. Similarly in *Asc. Isa.* 2.4, Manasseh, the Israelite king, is said to have become a servant of Beliar, the prince of unrighteousness who rules this world.

On Satan's ability to bestow power and glory on those who subordinate themselves to him, see the Lukan version of the temptation story found in Q (Luke

4:1–13 = Matt 4:1–11). After the devil showed Jesus all the kingdoms of the world (οἰκουμένη, a term Luke uses for the Roman empire in Luke 2:1 and Acts 17:6; Matt 4:8 has κόσμος), he then makes this promise in Luke 4:6: "And the devil said to him, 'To you I will give [δώσω] all this authority [ἐξουσίαν] and their glory; for it has been delivered to me [παραδέδοται], and I give [δίδωμι] it to whom I will.'" Satan is in possession of the Roman empire and can transfer this sovereignty to whomever he will; in Rev 13:2 this sovereignty is transferred to the Roman emperors, while in Luke 4:5–8 Satan offers the same sovereignty to Jesus (see Morgenthaler, *TZ* 12 [1956] 289–304). According to Theissen (*Gospels,* 212–15), the emperor Gaius (like Augustus before him) is the type of ruler with power over the kingdoms of the earth who could bestow these kingdoms to whomever he wished. A similar relationship exists between the lawless one and Satan in the eschatological scenario in 2 Thess 2:9, where it is claimed that "the coming of the lawless one by the activity of Satan [κατ' ἐνέργειαν τοῦ σατανᾶ], will be with all power and with pretended signs and wonders" (RSV). In the cosmic myth of the Gnostic Justin, Edem gives great authority (καὶ δίδωσιν ἐξουσίαν ἡ 'Εδὲμ μεγάλην) to her third angel Naas (Hippolytus *Ref.* 5.26.21; ed. Marcovich, *Hippolytus*).

The reference to the throne of the dragon calls to mind the throne of Satan mentioned in 2:13, metaphorically located in Pergamon. The throne of the beast is again mentioned in 16:10, where the fifth angel pours out his bowl on the throne of the beast, causing its kingdom to be in darkness. The throne of Satan is also mentioned in *2 Apoc. Enoch* [Rec. J] 29:4 (he sought to place his throne in a place equal to that of God and was thereafter expelled from heaven) and *Apoc. Mos.* 39:2 = *Adam and Eve* 47:3.

3a καὶ μίαν ἐκ τῶν κεφαλῶν αὐτοῦ ὡς ἐσφαγμένην εἰς θάνατον καὶ ἡ πληγὴ τοῦ θανάτου αὐτοῦ ἐθεραπεύθη, "One of its heads appeared to be fatally wounded, but its mortal wound was healed." Here the cardinal number μίαν, "one," can also be an ordinal number, "the first" (Sweet, 209; cf. Court, *Myth and History,* 128), referring either to Julius Caesar, who was assassinated on 15 March 44 B.C. (Plutarch *Caesar* 66.4–14; Suetonius Julius 82; Dio Cassius 44.19.1–5), or possibly to Nero, with whom the enumeration of emperors in 17:9–10 might begin (Court, *Myth and History,* 128). Further, the second occurrence of the pronoun αὐτοῦ, "its," refers not to the head but to the beast. This suggests that the seven heads mentioned in v 1 represent seven kings, one of which is presented as surviving an apparently mortal wound. In the narrative of the activities of the second beast in vv 11–18, the first beast is repeatedly mentioned. In v 12 he refers to τὸ θηρίον τὸ πρῶτον, οὗ ἐθεραπεύθη ἡ πληγὴ τοῦ θανάτου αὐτοῦ, "the first beast whose mortal wound was healed," while in v 14 he refers to τῷ θηρίῳ, ὃς ἔχει τὴν πληγὴν τῆς μαχαίρης καὶ ἔζησεν, "the beast who was wounded by the sword but lived." While in v 3a it is one of the seven heads of the first beast that is wounded, in vv 12 and 14 it is the beast itself that is mortally wounded. The seven heads of the scarlet beast of 17:3 are explicitly said to represent seven kings (17:9–10); heads of anomolous beasts are occasionally thought to represent kings (4 Ezra 12:22–26; Philostratus *Vita Apoll.* 5.13). Caligula had a dangerous illness and people wondered if he would recover (Suetonius *Caligula* 14.2; Dio Cassius 59.8.1–2; Philo *Leg.* 14–21; cf. A. A. Barrett, *Caligula,* 73–75). Yet it appears that Caligula must be excluded from consideration since 13:14 specifically mentions a wound inflicted by a *sword.* Nero, on the other hand, committed suicide by plunging a sword (*ferrum*) into his throat (Suetonius

Nero 49.3–4). Victorinus identified this head with Nero (*Comm. in Apoc.* XIII and XVII.3; ed. Haussleiter, *Victorinus,* 120). The healing of the mortal wound is probably an allusion to the legend of the return of Nero (see *Excursus 13A*).

3b καὶ ἐθαυμάσθη ὅλη ἡ γῆ ὀπίσω τοῦ θηρίου, "The whole earth was astonished and followed the beast." The phrase "the whole earth" is a metaphor for "all the people of the world," a figure made clear in the doublet in 17:8, "and those who dwell on the earth were astonished." A relatively close parallel is found in a nearly contemporary Jewish apocalypse, 4 Ezra 12:3, where the reaction to the burning of the body of the eagle (= Rome) is described: "And the earth was exceedingly terrified [*et expavescebat terra valde*]." Another close parallel is found in Jdt 11:16b, "and God has sent me [Judith] to accomplish with you things that will astonish the whole world [πράγματα ἐφ' οἷς ἐκστήσεται πᾶσα ἡ γῆ]." After her victory over Holofernes, this was the reaction (Jdt 13:17): "All the people were greatly astonished and bowed down and worshiped God."

The phrase καὶ ἐθαυμάσθη ὅλη ἡ γῆ ὀπίσω τοῦ θηρίου is a difficult, elliptical construction. BDR § 196.3 suggests that ἐθαύμασεν ὀπίσω τοῦ θηρίου, "it marvelled after the beast," is a pregnant construction for ἐθαύμασεν ἐπὶ τῷ θηρίῳ καὶ ἐπορεύθη ὀπίσω αὐτοῦ, "it marvelled at the beast and went after it" (θαυμάζειν, "marvel," is usually used with ἐπί + dative or περί + accusative). A verb, ἦλθε, "went," or ἠκολούθη, "followed," or ἐπορεύθη, "went," must certainly be supplied with ὀπίσω, "after." BDR § 196.3 also suggests a relatively close parallel in LXX Deut 31:16, ὁ λαὸς οὗτος ἐκπορνεύσει ὀπίσω [אחרי *ʾaḥărê*] θεῶν ἀλλοτρίων, "this people played the harlot [and followed] after strange gods." Torrey (*Apocalypse,* 124) understands ὀπίσω as an overly literal translation of the Aramaic אחרי *ʾaḥărê,* which, like על *ʿal,* can mean "concerning," so that this passage should be translated "the whole earth was in amazement *concerning* the beast." As an improper preposition with the genitive, ὀπίσω can mean "after" and is used with ἔρχεσθαι and ἀκολουθεῖν meaning "to go after" or "to follow after," i.e., "to become an adherent of" (BAGD, 575; Bauer-Aland, 1166).

Here the "earth" represents the people of the earth who are given a brief but significant speaking part in v 4. Since biblical writers in general tend to avoid indirect speech (see R. Alter, *The Art of Biblical Narrative* [New York: Basic Books, 1981] 63–87), this use of direct discourse is the author's way of revealing the attitude of all who worship the beast. The literary device of attributing a single statement to a large group of people is found often in the OT and early Jewish literature (Gen 11:3–4; Ruth 1:19; 1 Sam 4:6–9; 5:7; 7:6; 1 Macc 1:11; 2:37, 40–41; 3:43; 5:57; 7:6–7). It is also found in Greek literature. In *Pericles* 12.1–2, Plutarch quotes the kind of speech that critics of Pericles made publicly, though the speech is actually a literary device for articulating the opposition to Pericles' policies.

Excursus 13A: The Nero Redux or Redivivus Legend

Bibliography

Anderson, J. G. C. "Trajan on the Quinquennium Neronis." *JRS* 1 (1911) 173–79. **Bastomsky, S. J.** "The Emperor Nero in Talmudic Legend." *JQR* n.s. 59 (1969) 321–25. **Bishop, J.** *Nero: The Man and the Legend.* London, 1965. **Bodinger, M.** "Le mythe de Néron de l'Apocalypse de Saint Jean au Talmud de Babylone." *RHR* 206 (1989) 21–40. **Borleffs,**

J. W. P. "Institutum Neronianum." *VC* 6 (1952) 129–45. **Bradley, K. R.** *Suetonius' Life of Nero: An Historical Commentary.* Bruxelles: Revue d'Études Latines, 1978. **Charlesworth, M. P.** "Nero: Some Aspects." *JRS* 40 (1950) 69–76. **Chilver, G. E. F.** *A Historical Commentary on Tacitus' Histories I and II.* Oxford: Clarendon, 1979. **Collins, J. J.** *The Sibylline Oracles of Egyptian Judaism.* Missoula, MT: Scholars, 1974. **Gallivan, P. A.** "The False Neros: A Re-examination." *Historia* 22 (1973) 364–65. **Geffcken, J.** *Studien zur ältern Nerosage.* Göttingen: Nachrichten von der königl. Gesell. d. Wissen. zu Göttingen, 1899. **Griffin, M. T.** *Nero: The End of a Dynasty.* New Haven: Yale UP, 1984. **Henderson, B. W.** *The Life and Principate of the Emperor Nero.* London: Methuen, 1903. **Jakob-Sonnabend, W.** *Untersuchungen zum Nero-Bild der Spätantike.* Hildesheim; Zürich; New York: Olms-Weidmann, 1990. **Kreitzer, L.** "Hadrian and the Nero *Redivivus* Myth." *ZNW* 79 (1988) 92–115. **Lawrence, J.** "Nero Redivivus." *Fides et Historia* 11 (1978) 54–66. **Millar, F.** *A Study of Cassius Dio.* Oxford: Clarendon, 1964. **Momigliano, A.** "Nero." *CAH* 10:702–42. **Pappano, A. E.** "The False Neros." *CJ* 32 (1937) 385–92. **Scullard, H. H.** *From the Gracchi to Nero.* 4th ed. London: Methuen, 1976. **Syme, R.** "Flavian Wars and Frontiers." *CAH* 11:131–87. ———. *Some Arval Brethren.* Oxford: Clarendon, 1980. ———. *Tacitus.* 2 vols. Oxford: Clarendon, 1958. **Trudinger, P.** "The 'Nero Redivivus' Rumour and the Date of the Apocalypse of John." *St Mark's Review* 131 (1987) 43–44.

Nero Claudius Caesar was born on 15 December 37 and was the emperor of Rome A.D. 54–68. On 8 June 68 he was deposed by the Senate and declared a public enemy. He committed suicide on 9 June 68, but confusion surrounding his death together with the paucity of witnesses who actually saw his corpse and his burial (for details see Chilver, *Commentary,* 42) made it possible for rumors that he was still alive to circulate widely. Suetonius was the first to record the belief that Nero would shortly return and visit destruction on his enemies (*Nero* 57). The belief that Nero escaped to Parthia and would return with an army is reflected in the *Sibylline Oracles* (*Sib. Or.* 4.119–22, 137–39; 5.137–54, 214–27; 8.68–72; 12.78–94). This myth of Nero *redux,* i.e., "Nero returned," was based on a widespread refusal to accept the rumor of his death as true, while the related myth of Nero *redivivus,* i.e., "living again," was based on the notion that, though dead, he would return to life. During his lifetime, Nero had fostered good relations with the Parthians, and that contributed to the belief that he had sought asylum with them. Dio Chrysostom (A.D. 40–after 112) wrote "Even now everyone wishes that Nero were alive and most people actually believe it" (*Orat.* 21.10). After Nero's suicide, fictitious edicts were posted under his name threatening his enemies, revealing his high standing with many people.

Nero was as popular in the Greek east as he was despised in the west, and several false Neros appeared at various times. Lucian refers to ὁ ψευδονέρων in the singular (*Adv. ign.* 20), though a number of scholars think that *two* false Neros appeared (Bastomsky, *JQR* n.s. 59 [1969] 321–25; Henderson, *Life,* 420; Momigliano, *CAH* 10:741; Bishop, *Nero,* 167; Scullard, *Gracchi to Nero,* 332). Yet it is possible that there were as many as *three* false Neros (Syme, *Arval,* 87; id., *CAH* 11:144–45; id., *Tacitus,* 518; Gallivan, *Historia* 22 [1973] 364–65; Bradley, *Suetonius' Life,* 295; Pappano, *CJ* 32 [1937] 385–92; E. Hohl, *RE,* suppl. III, col. 393): (1) An unnamed impostor (Dio Cassius 63.9.3) who resembled Nero, either a slave from Pontus or a freedman from Italy (Tacitus *Hist.* 2.8), appeared in A.D. 69. Gathering an army of deserters, he sailed east from Greece and was forced by a storm to land on the island of Cynthus in the Cyclades. There he was executed by Calpurnius Asprenas, the new governor of Galatia and Pamphilia. The body was taken via Asia to Rome (Tacitus *Hist.* 2.8–9; Zonaras 11.15, p. 45, 11–16D). (2) The false Nero of A.D. 80 was Terentius Maximus, an Asiatic who looked and spoke like Nero (Dio Cassius 66.19.3) and who gathered an increasing number of followers from Asia to the Euphrates. (3) A third pretender, referred to in Suetonius *Nero* 57.2 (Gallivan, *Historia* 22 [1973] 365; against Bastomsky, *JQR* n.s. 59 [1969] 321–25), appeared in A.D. 88 (similarities to

Terentius Maximus can be accounted for by the tendency of pretenders to imitate the outward form of a royal march "in which the pretender assumes the outward appearance of the man whose identity he claims, and is given an escort and appropriate supplies and honors" [Millar, *Study,* 217]). Tacitus (*Hist.* 2.8.1) observes *ceterorum casus conatusque in contextu operis dicemus,* "the adventures and enterprises of the other pretenders we will relate in the course of the work," which indicates that Tacitus intended to discuss the brief careers of at least two other pretenders, though unfortunately those parts of Tacitus' work are lost. It is certainly significant in this context to note that Domitian was called "Nero" by Juvenal (*Satires* 4.38).

The oldest form of the Nero *redux* myth, which appears to have originated in Asia, is that Nero would return from the east as the champion of the east at the head of a Parthian army to retake the imperial throne in Rome. This basic version of the myth is reflected in *Sib. Or.* 4.138–39 (tr. Charlesworth, *OTP* 1:387), "the fugitive from Rome will also come, brandishing a great spear, having crossed the Euphrates with many myriads" (cf. *Sib. Or.* 5.28–34, 138–53, 215–24, 363–70; 3.63–74; 8.70–72, 140–47; cf. Jakob-Sonnabend, *Nero-Bild,* 138–44).

In Jewish and Christian tradition, however, this usually positive image of a triumphant messianic figure was transformed into a monstrous incarnation of evil and became part of the eschatological-antagonist myth. In Jewish tradition Nero is identified with Belial (*Sib. Or.* 3.63–74; *Asc. Isa.* 4:1–14), as revealed in *Asc. Isa.* 4:2 (tr. Hennecke-Schneemelcher, *NTA* 2:648):

> And after it [i.e., the world] has come to its consummation, Beliar, the great prince, the king of this world who has ruled it since it came into being, shall descend; he will come down from his firmament in the form of a man, a lawless king, a slayer of his mother, who himself (even) this king will persecute the plant which the Twelve Apostles of the beloved have planted; and one of the twelve [i.e., Peter] will be delivered into his hand.

In Christian tradition, Commodian (*Instr.* 41.7; Martin, *Commodiani,* 33) expected the resurrection of Nero from hell (*Cum fuerit autem Nero de inferno leuatus*), while at the same time Elijah would seal the beloved ones (*Instr.* 41.8; Martin, *Commodiani,* 34).

It is not difficult to understand how the Nero myth could be understood in a wholly negative manner and Nero himself could be considered a personification of evil by Jews and Christians. Both groups would be repelled by the imperial propaganda, spread throughout the eastern part of the Roman empire during the emperor's lifetime, retailing the notion of Nero's divinity (Griffin, *Nero,* 215–20). Nero, for example, authorized the minting of coins on which he was depicted wearing the radiate crown appropriate for the sun god (K. Scott, *Imperial Cult,* 32–33; Griffin, *Nero,* 217–18; Bodinger, *RHR* 206 [1989] 26–27). At the beginning of his reign Nero was more modest, for he vetoed the dedication of gold and silver statues of himself, metals that were normally reserved for statues of deities (Tacitus *Annals* 13.10). In *Sib. Or.* 5.28–34 (tr. J. J. Collins in Charlesworth, *OTP* 1:393), Nero *redux* is described metaphorically as a "terrible snake [δεινὸς ὄφις]," in a way comparable to Rev 17:8:

> One who has fifty as an initial [N = 50] will be commander,
> a terrible snake, breathing out grievous war, who one day
> will lay hands on his own family and slay them, and throw everything into confusion,
> athlete, charioteer, murderer, one who dares ten thousand things.
> He will also cut the mountain between two seas and defile it with gore.
> But even when he disappears he will be destructive. Then he will return
> declaring himself equal to God. But he will prove that he is not.

What factors encouraged the formation and circulation of the Nero *redux* or *redivivus* myth? Confusion surrounding the death of Nero certainly fueled the circulation of the myth. Further, it is possible that the Nero *redivivus* myth was encouraged by an atmosphere of "messianic" expectation that pervaded the Levant during the second half of the first century A.D. (Bodinger, *RHR* 206 [1989] 22).

There are other examples of rumors that great men of the past reappeared. A false Alexander the Great appeared in A.D. 221 (Dio Cassius 80.18.1–3; Lucian *Adv. indoctum* 20). Αψευδοφίλιππος, "false Philip" of Macedon, who was really Andriscus of Adramyttium, pretended to be Philip, the son of Perseus king of Macedon (d. 165 or 162 B.C.), though the real Philip had died in internment at Alba Fucens two years after the death of Perseus in 163 or 160 B.C. (Diodorus Siculus 32.17.1–7; Lucian *Adv. indoctum* 20; Strabo 13.4.2; Polybius 36.10.1–7; for a discussion of this figure, cf. Walbank, *Polybius* 3:668–69). Appian refers to a ψευδομάριος, a "false Marius," who pretended to be the grandson of Marius (*Bell. civ.* 3.1.2). Another false Alexander, this one pretending to be a son of the same name whom Herod the Great executed in 7 B.C., appeared in Crete shortly after the death of Herod in 4 B.C. (Jos. *J.W.* 2.101–10; *Ant.* 7.24–38). In A.D. 34 a false Drusus who arose in the Cyclades was eventually arrested and sent to Tiberius (Dio Cassius 58.25; Tacitus *Annals* 5.10). A ψευδοαντωνῖνος, a "false Antoninus," is mentioned several times in the fragments of Dio Cassius (80.17–19). Many years later impostors impersonated Frederick the Great and Louis XVI after their deaths. Even in late twentieth-century America, Elvis Presley has been sighted by hundreds of people.

4a καὶ προσεκύνησαν τῷ δράκοντι, ὅτι ἔδωκεν τὴν ἐχουσίαν τῷ θηρίῳ, "They worshiped the dragon because he gave authority to the beast." The worship of Satan is referred to in *Mart. Isa.* 2:7 in connection with Manasseh's heretical practices. In Jewish tradition God alone deserves worship (LXX Esth 4:17e [13:14], οὐ προσκυνήσω οὐδένα πλὴν σοῦ τοῦ κυρίου μου, "I will not worship anyone but you my Lord"). One of the striking features of the eschatological antagonist presented as the beast from the sea in 13:1–10 is that he is never explicitly made to claim that he is God and demand worship on that basis; nor does he take residence in the temple and broadcast his claim from there. The absence of these features, which figure prominently in many Jewish versions of the eschatological-antagonist myth, probably results from the author's reshaping of the myth in light of the historical realities that he wishes the myth to reflect. The author may fail to mention the temple because this narrative was formulated in the Diaspora or because it was formulated after the destruction of the Jerusalem temple in A.D. 70. In the eschatological-antagonist myth, the antagonist's claim to be God (2 Thess 2:4) in part reflects the remembered divine pretentions of Antioches IV Epiphanes (Dan 11:36–37; the epithet "epiphanes" means "[god] manifest," and he used the title θεός, "god," on coins), Gaius (Philo *Leg.* 197–337; Jos. *J.W.* 2.184–203; *Ant.* 18.256–309), and Nero (*Sib. Or.* 5.33–34), as well as the understanding that the cause of Satan's fall was his hubris in claiming to be the equal of God (said of the king of Babylon in Isa 14:13–14 and of the king of Tyre in Ezek 28:2). This motif became part of the myth of Satan's fall in early Judaism (*Asc. Isa.* 4:6; Lactantius *Div. Inst.* 7.17.4; *2 Apoc. Enoch* [Rec. J] 29:4).

Like v 2d (see *Comment*), this sentence is probably a redactional insertion for the purpose of connecting the beast with the dragon (the dragon is essentially extraneous to the visions in 13:1–10 and 11–18); see Bergmeier, *ANRW* II, 25/5:3909. This sentence can be omitted without interrupting the sense of the passage, and it should be noted that the following sentence begins in a way that is verbally identical to this sentence: καὶ προσεκύνησαν τῷ, "and they worshiped the." (On the use of προσκυνεῖν, "worship," in Revelation [here the object of worship is the dragon, an alias for Satan], see *Comment* on 3:9.)

4b καὶ προσεκύνησαν τῷ θηρίῳ λέγοντες· τίς ὅμοιος τῷ θηρίῳ, "and they also worshiped the beast, chanting, 'Who is like the beast?'" The worship of the beast from the sea (representing the Roman imperial cult), or its image, is mentioned here and several more times from this point on in Revelation (13:8, 12, 15; 14:9, 11; 16:2; 20:4), though nothing is explicitly stated about the mode of this worship. The verb προσκυνεῖν, "worship," is used of the Roman senators who were compelled to worship an empty chair representing the emperor Gaius in the Capitol (Dio 59.24.4; cf. Philo *Leg.* 116). Prayer and sacrifice are two important modes of worship of the imperial cult, and while personal prayers were made to both living and dead emperors (Price, *JHS* 104 [1984] 91), sacrifice in the imperial cult was normally made *on behalf of,* not *to,* the emperor, though the distinction between these two types of sacrifice was occasionally blurred in the provincial imperial cult (Price, *JRS* 70 [1980] 30).

This is a brief hymn of praise introduced with an *aporia,* i.e., the rhetorical question "Who is like?" (Labuschagne, *Incomparability,* 16–23; Weiser, *Psalms,* 54), and should be taken as an intentional parody of similar rhetorical questions used in OT hymns (Charles, 1:351; Deichgräber, *Gotteshymnus,* 55). Though there are a few examples of similar rhetorical questions set in the middle of several OT psalms (Exod 15:11; Pss 18:31; 35:10; 89:6, 8; 113:5; cf. 1 Sam 26:15; Isa 40:25; 46:5; Mic 7:18; *Mek. de-Rabbi Ishmael, Shirata* 8 [Lauterbach, 2:59–63]), such questions are not fundamental features of the structures of any OT psalm. In fact, this question appears to be an echo in reverse of Exod 15:11, "Who is like thee, O Lord, among the gods?" (cf. Pss 35:10; 71:19; 1QM 10:8–9; 13:13). It is of interest in this connection that the angelic name "Michael" (מיכאל *mîkāʾēl*) means "who is like God?" This same rhetorical question is found in hymnic portions of the Qumran literature: (1) 1QH 15:28 (= 7:28; cf. 1Q*35* = 1QHymns[b] frag. 1, line 2), מי כמוכה באלים אדוני *mî kamôkâ bāʾēlîm ʾădônāy,* "Who is like you among the gods, O Lord?" (2) 1QM 10:8–9, "Who (is) like you, God of Israel? . . . And who (is) like your people Israel?" (3) 4Q*381* = 4QNon-Canonical Psalms B frag. 15, line 6 (tr. García Martínez, *Dead Sea Scrolls,* 313), "Who in the heavens is like you, my God? And who among the sons of gods?" A similar question occurs in *Maʿaseh Merkavah* § 548.2 (tr. Swartz, *Prayer,* 226), "Blessed are you, God, great in power. Who is like you in heaven or on earth—Holy in heaven and holy on earth?" (see also §§ 548.4, 7). In Revelation the most extensive example of a hymn introduced with an *aporia* is Rev 5:2, 9–10, 12, 13, 14 (see *Form/Structure/Setting* on Rev 5). The star hymn in Ign. *Eph.* 19 is also introduced with an *aporia:* "How then was he revealed to the aeons?"

This is the first instance in Revelation in which the verb προσκυνεῖν, "to prostrate oneself in worship," is used of the beast, reflecting the protocol of the imperial cult. Prostration was part of the Persian court ceremonial, which Alexander introduced into his own court ceremonial even though Greeks generally found it objectionable. Since the Romans associated prostration (including kneeling) with the monarchy that they had abolished in the sixth century B.C., prostration or kneeling occurs only very rarely and in special circumstances during the late Republic and early Empire (see Cicero *Phil.* 2.86 [Alföldi, *Repräsentation,* 51, 54], where Mark Antony's kneeling before Julius Caesar to present him with a diadem was construed as indicating a claim to kingship and resulted in Caesar's assassination; Suetonius *Tiberius* 20). The emperor Gaius, however, apparently made *proskynesis* part of his court ceremonial (Seneca *De benef.* 2.12.1–2; Suetonius *Vitellius* 2; Dio Cassius 59.19.5; 59.24.4; 59.27.4–6; Philo *Leg.* 116–17; see Alföldi, *Repräsentation,* 50), a symbolic act that Gaius apparently insisted on as a public form for paying him divine honor but one that members of the senatorial aristocracy regarded as a perverted demand of an autocratic ruler. Claudius, in direct contrast to Gaius, prohibited prostration (Dio Cassius 60.5.4), though it was reintroduced into imperial court ceremonial by both Nero and Domitian.

4c καὶ τίς δύναται πολεμῆσαι μετ' αὐτοῦ; "and who is able to fight against it?" For a similar rhetorical question that is an expression of both impotence and despair, see 1 Sam 4:8, "Who can deliver us from the power of these mighty gods?" See also 1 Sam 10:27; Lam 5:8. "Sedrach" similarly expresses human impotence in opposition to the devil (*Apoc. Sedrach* 5:4; tr. Charlesworth, *OTP* 1:610): "Who can fight against an invisible spirit?"

5a καὶ ἐδόθη αὐτῷ στόμα λαλοῦν μεγάλα καὶ βλασφημίας, "It was given haughty and blasphemous things to say." In v 5, the beast is given permission to act as an antagonist of God, but he does not begin to exercise his authority until v 6. This phrase is a clear allusion to LXX Theod Dan 7:8, 20 where the little horn is said to have "a mouth speaking great things [στόμα λαλοῦν μεγάλα]." In Daniel, however, the ascription of a "mouth" to a little horn is a way of indicating that the horn symbolizes a person and a way of enabling it to speak; in Rev 13:5a, on the other hand, the beast presumably already has a mouth, and διδόναι στόμα, "give mouth," is a Semitic idiom meaning "to give someone something to say" (e.g., Luke 21:15; cf. Louw-Nida, § 33.105; see *Note* 13:5.b.).

The two motifs of hubris or vaunting pride and blasphemy against God are mentioned in this verse, as they are in Dan 11:36. These two motifs are sometimes combined in texts in which the eschatological antagonist is said to claim divine honors, i.e., to be God or the son of God, based on Ezek 28:2 and Dan 11:36 (2 Thess 2:5; *Did.* 16:4; *Asc. Isa.* 4:6, 12; Irenaeus *Adv. haer.* 5.25.1, 4; 5.28.2; Hippolytus *de Ant.* 18.1–4 [quoting Ezek 28:2–5]; 53 [quoting Ezek 28:2 and Isa 14:13]; Origen *Contra Celsum* 6.46 [quoting 2 Thess 2:4]). These two motifs are rarely combined in texts dealing with the eschatological antagonist. The *blasphemy motif,* based in part on Dan 7:25, is found in Justin *Dial.* 32.4, where he refers to the Man of Sin (probably an allusion to 2 Thess 2:3, though Peerbolte, *Antichrist,* 91–93, argues against dependence), who is about to appear and is prepared to speak bold and blasphemous things against the Most High (καὶ τοῦ βλάσφημα καὶ τολμηρὰ εἰς τὸν ὕψιστον μέλλοντος λαλεῖν); see also Justin *Dial.* 110. The emperor Gaius reportedly addressed the Jewish embassy from Alexandria with a blasphemous speech (Philo *Leg.* 352). The *hybris motif,* based on the descriptions of Antioches Epiphanes in Dan 8:10–11 and Lucifer in Isa 14:13–14, is found in *2 Apoc. Bar.* 67:7 (Charlesworth, *OTP* 1:644), "But the king of Babylon will arise, the one who now has destroyed Zion, and he will boast over the people and speak haughtily in his heart before the Most High" (see also 4 Ezra 11:43; *Apoc. Elijah* 4:8–12; Hippolytus *de Ant.* 16.2; 17.6–7 [quoting parts of Isa 14]; Cyprian *Ep.* 59.3 [quoting Isa 14:13]).

5b καὶ ἐδόθη αὐτῷ ἐξουσία ποιῆσαι μῆνας τεσσεράκοντα καὶ δύο, "and it was given authority to be active forty-two months." This statement reflects the view based on Dan 7:25; 8:14; 9:27 that the period of the Antichrist's dominion would last three and one-half years (in Dan 7:25, in the phrase "a time, times, and half a time," "time" means one year; see *Comment* on 11:2). According to Justin (*Dial.* 32.3–4), Jewish exegetical speculation that the eschatological tyrant mentioned in Dan 7:25 would reign for 350 years was based on their understanding that the term καιρός meant 100 years. The view that the eschatological antagonist would rule for "a time, times, and half a time" was widely held in early Christianity (Justin *Dial.* 32.3–4; Irenaeus *Adv. haer.* 5.25.3; 5.30.4; Hippolytus *de Ant.* 61.9; *Asc. Isa.* 4:12 [Beliar = Nero is said to have reigned *III annos et VII menses et dies XVIII,* "three years and seven months and eighteen days"]; *Apoc. Elijah* 2:52; Victorinus *Comm. in Apoc.* 11.2). In Rev 20:3 the phrase μικρὸν χρόνον, "short period," was interpreted by Victorinus to be three years and six months, based on this view. An identical period is given to the king from Syria to persecute the whole earth, according to Lactantius *Div. Inst.* 7.17.8 (tr. McDonald, *Lactantius,* 518), "And it will be given to him [*et dabitur ei*] to make the earth desolate in forty-two months."

This passage, which may have been part of the Greek *Oracle of Hystaspes* (Flusser, "Hystaspes," 390–453), also appears to be alluding to Dan 7:25 and 12:7; while this passage is probably independent of Revelation, it employs similar phrases with the passive of divine activity: *et dabitur* [future passive indicative] *ei* = καὶ ἐδόθη [aorist passive indicative] αὐτῷ (cf. the Vulgate translation of καὶ ἐδόθη αὐτῷ, *et datum est ei,* which uses the perfect passive participle *datum* with the present *est*). On the *passivum divinum,* see *Comment* on 9:3b.

A period of forty-two months was referred to earlier in Rev 11:2 as the period of time when the nations would hold the holy city under subjection. The two witnesses are also said to be granted 1,260 days to prophesy, i.e., 42 months of 30 days each (11:3). The woman in 12:6 was protected in the wilderness for 1,260 days, referred to in 12:14 as "a time, times, and half a time" (an allusion to Dan 7:25; 12:7). It is clear that the author intends the reader to understand that the period during which the first beast is active coincides with the period during which the holy city will be trampled on by the nations and the period during which the two witnesses will prophesy. Their death must therefore coincide with the end of this predestined period of time.

In vv 5–7, the singular aorist passive verb ἐδόθη, "was given," occurs four times in the identical phrase καὶ ἐδόθη αὐτῷ, "and it was given"; in each instance the passive voice of the verb can be construed as a passive of divine activity, i.e., as a circumlocution for the direct mention of God as subject of the action of the verb. This makes it clear that John does not see the conflict between God and Satan (historically manifested in the conflict between Christians and the state) in terms of a cosmic dualism; rather he emphasizes the ultimate sovereignty and control of God over events that occur in the world. Essentially the same view is expressed by Paul in Rom 13:1–2, when he asserts that all political authority has been instituted by God (Venetz, *BK* 43 [1988] 160). The phrase καὶ ἐδόθη αὐτῷ also occurs in v 15 as an introduction to vv 15–17 (cf. the closely related phrase τὰ σημεῖα ἃ ἐδόθη αὐτῷ ποιῆσαι, "the miracles which it was given to perform," in v 14 and the use of the active voice in v 2, καὶ ἔδωκεν αὐτῷ ὁ δράκων, "the dragon gave him").

6a καὶ ἤνοιξεν τὸ στόμα αὐτοῦ εἰς βλασφημίας πρὸς τὸν θεόν, "It began to utter blasphemies against God." This is an allusion to Dan 7:25a, "He shall speak words against the Most High" (cf. Dan 11:36c, "and [the king] shall speak astonishing things against the God of gods," and Dan 8:9–14). Though the term βλασφημεῖν, "blaspheme," occurs only a few times in the LXX, the object of the verb is usually God (2 Kgs 19:4, 6, 22; Isa 52:5; Dan 3:29[LXX 3:96]). The phrase "to open the mouth" is a Semitic idiom found with some frequency in Jewish and early Christian literature. The Hebrew phrase פָּתַח פֶּה *pātaḥ peh,* "to open the mouth," occurs some forty times in the MT (BDB, 835). By itself, the phrase "to open the mouth" can simply mean "to speak" (Job 35:16; Pss 38:13; 39:9; 78:2; Prov 24:7; 31:8; Isa 53:7; Ezek 16:63; Lam 2:16; LXX Exod 4:12, 15; Matt 13:35 quotation of Ps 78:2; Acts 18:14; *Adam and Eve* 10:3; 21:3; *Jos. As.* 11:15–18; *Sib. Or.* 3.497). However, in phrases like "he opened his mouth to speak" or "he opened his mouth and began to speak," the phrase "to open the mouth" functions as a preparation for speech reflecting Semitic redundancy and is often used as a solemn introduction to a speech or a prayer (Job 33:1–2; Ezek 3:27; Dan 10:16; LXX Theod Dan 3:25; *1 Enoch* 106:3; *T. Abr.* [Rec. B] 10:15; Matt 5:2; Acts 8:35; 10:34). The use of this phrase in Rev 13:6 suggests that the beast is speaking in an official, formal manner.

6b βλασφημῆσαι τὸ ὄνομα αὐτοῦ καὶ τὴν σκηνὴν αὐτοῦ, "that is, to blaspheme his name and his dwelling." The verb βλασφημεῖν, "blaspheme," is used four times in Revelation, twice with "God" as the object (16:11, 21) and twice with the "name" of God as the object (13:6; 16:9; cf. Rom 2:24; 1 Tim 6:1; Jas 2:7), while in the rest of the NT it is frequently used intransitively (Matt 9:3; 26:65; Mark 2:7; Acts 26:11; 1 Tim 1:20). A close parallel is found in Acts 6:11: the trumped-up charges against Stephen are that "he spoke blasphemous words against Moses and God [ῥήματα βλάσφημα εἰς Μωϋσῆν καὶ τὸν θεόν]," which is understood as "speaking words against this holy place [κατὰ τοῦ τόπου τοῦ ἁγίου τούτου] and against the law" (Acts 6:13), i.e., blasphemy against the temple = blasphemy against God (cf. Acts 21:28; 25:8). This text demonstrates that criticism of the temple could be generalized and understood as criticism of God. Blaspheming God or the name of God suggests a violation of the third commandment, i.e., the warning against wrongful use of the name of God (Exod 20:7 = Deut 5:11), a violation for which there was a capital penalty (Lev 24:16); cf. Reicke, *Die zehn Worte,* 54–56. In 1 Tim 6:1 "the name of God" is also the object the verb βλασφημεῖν. The motif of slandering the name of God apparently alludes to Isa 52:5, combined with Dan 7:25 and 11:36.

In early Christianity LXX Isa 52:5 is used in two primary ways (Schoedel, *Ignatius,* 150): (1) it is applied to the Jews who are blamed for causing the Gentiles to slander God's name (Rom 2:24; Justin *Dial.* 17.2; Tertullian *Adv. Marc.* 3.23.4; 4.14.16; 5.13.7), and (2) it is applied to Christians who through various types of sinful behavior provoke criticism from pagans (2 Pet 2:2; Ign. *Trall.* 8.2; Pol. *Phil.* 10.3; *2 Clem.* 13:2–4; Tertullian *De idol.* 14). These uses were encouraged by the peculiar form of the text of LXX Isa 52:5: δι' ὑμᾶς διὰ παντὸς τὸ ὄνομά μου βλασφημεῖται ἐν τοῖς ἔθνεσιν, "because of you my name is slandered continually among the Gentiles." The phrases δι' ὑμᾶς, "because of you," and ἐν τοῖς ἔθνεσιν, "among the Gentiles," are missing from the Hebrew text.

One interpretive issue here is the problem of whether σκηνή, "tent, dwelling," can refer to the temple in Jerusalem. The parallel in Acts 6:11, 13 mentioned above indicates that blasphemy against the temple could be understood as blasphemy against God. The following review of the evidence indicates that there is nothing to suggest that either the first or second temple was ever referred to with this term, for σκηνή *always* refers to a temporary structure, never a permanent building of brick or stone. The term ἡ σκηνή, "the tent, tabernacle," or ἡ σκηνὴ τοῦ μαρτυρίου, "the tent of witness," is used in the NT and early Christian literature of the entire ancient Israelite tabernacle (Acts 7:44; Heb 8:5; 9:2, 6, 8, 21; 13:11; *1 Clem.* 43:2–3, 5), but it can also refer to the most holy place within the tabernacle (Heb 9:3), usually called τὰ ἅγια, "the holy place," in Hebrews (Heb 8:2; 9:2, 3, 12, 24, 25). σκηνή can also refer to the heavenly tabernacle (Heb 8:2; 9:21; Rev 15:5), while (τὰ) ἅγια can be used of the most holy place in heaven (Heb 9:12; 10:19). The use of the term ἡ πρώτη σκηνή in Heb 9:6, 8, does not mean "the first tabernacle" in contrast with the heavenly tabernacle or even the temple of Solomon (as the phrase is used in Jos. *Ag. Ap.* 2.12); rather it means "the outer court" (היכל *hêkāl*) in contrast to the inner tent (דביר *dĕbîr*), i.e., the most holy place, which is called ἡ δευτέρα [σκηνή], "the second [tent]," in Heb 9:7 (Attridge, *Hebrews,* 218, 232). This is in continuity with the description of the tabernacle in the LXX as ἡ σκηνὴ τοῦ μαρτυρίου, "the tent of witness" (Exod 27:21; 29:4; Lev 1:1; Num 1:1), or simply ἡ σκηνή (משכן *miškān*), terms that continued to be used in early Judaism (*Vit. Proph.* 12.12; 18.1; Eupolemus frag. 2 [Eusebius *Praep. evang.* 9.30.1; 9.34.7; 9.34.14; C. R. Holladay, *FHJA* 1:114, 126, 130]). According to 4Q372 = Apocryphon of Joseph, frag. 1, line 13 (tr. García Martínez, *Dead Sea Scrolls,* 225), foreign people were guilty of "blaspheming against the tent of Zion."

The eschatological antagonist is occasionally depicted as assaulting the temple of God or of occupying the temple of God and as presenting himself as God (2 Thess 2:4; *Sib. Or.* 5.33–34). Hellenistic kings such as Philip of Macedon and Antiochus III are sometimes thought to have attacked and destroyed temples of the gods because of their excessive pride and later to have suffered divine retribution (Diodorus 28.3; 29.15; 31.18a; Jos. *Ant.* 12.358–59; Porphyry, *FrGrHist,* 260 F56). Antiochus IV Epiphanes is remembered as having violated, or attempted to violate, several temples (Polybius 31.9; 1 Macc 6:1–5; 2 Macc 1:14–17) as well as the temple in Jerusalem (1 Macc 1:20–24; Jos. *Ag. Ap.* 2.83–84). The Roman emperor Gaius (A.D. 12–41) intended to have his statue erected in the temple in Jerusalem (Jos. *Ant.* 18.261; *J.W.* 2.184–85; Philo *Leg.* 188, 207–8; Tacitus *Hist.* 5.9), but his death ended the imminent conflict with the Jews over this issue. There are several descriptions of the eschatological scenario in which the antagonist claims to be God (2 Thess 2:4; *Asc. Isa.* 4.6, 11; *Sib. Or.* 5.33–34; Hippolytus *de Ant.* 52; Lactantius *Div. Inst.* 7.17; *Epitome* 71), but the occupation of the temple (ὁ ναὸς τοῦ θεοῦ) is only mentioned in 2 Thess 2:4. This is the earliest mention of this motif, which is repeated in later Christian writers (Mark 13:14 = Matt 24:15 [cf. Dan 9:27; 11:31; 12:11; 1 Macc 1:54]; Irenaeus *Adv. haer.* 5.25.1; 5.30.4; Victorinus *Comm. in Apoc.* 13 and 17.4 [ed. Haussleiter, *Victorinus,* 128]; see Bousset, *Antichrist,* 160–64). It appears likely that 2 Thess 2:4 reflects the combined influence of Dan 11:36, Ezek 28:2, and perhaps Isa 14:13–14 (B. Rigaux, *L'Antéchrist,* 281; Ernst, *Gegenspieler,* 37) and that the abortive incident during the reign of Gaius has become incorporated as a new motif in the series of outrages committed by the antagonist, of which Antioches IV Epiphanes was the essential model (Ernst, *Gegenspieler,* 40, is rightly hesitant to interpret 2 Thess 2:4 in strictly historical terms).

6c [τοὺς ἐν τῷ οὐρανῷ σκηνοῦντας], "[that is, those who dwell in heaven]." This accusative phrase is used in apposition to τὴν σκηνήν, "the dwelling," and appears to be an interpretive gloss added at the final redaction of Revelation to remove the contradiction between ἡ σκηνὴ αὐτοῦ, "his [God's] dwelling," i.e., the temple, and 21:3, which states that "the dwelling [σκηνή] of God is with people," but there is no temple in the new Jerusalem (21:22). While it is perfectly possible and plausible to blaspheme God's sanctuary (cf. Acts 6:13), it makes little sense to blaspheme those who dwell in heaven. It appears then that blaspheming God's dwelling is metaphorically interpreted as referring to slandering the people of God. Ignatius *Trall.* 8:2 mentions Gentiles who, because of the foolish behavior of a few Christians, slander (βλασφημεῖν) the entire congregation of God.

7a καὶ ἐδόθη αὐτῷ ποιῆσαι πόλεμον μετὰ τῶν ἁγίων καὶ νικῆσαι αὐτούς, "And it was permitted to make war against God's people and conquer them." This phrase alludes to Dan 7:21, and perhaps also to LXX Dan 7:8. In Dan 7:21, it says that the little horn "made war with the holy ones and was prevailing over them" (cf. Theod Dan 7:21, ἐποίει πόλεμον μετὰ τῶν ἁγίων καὶ ἴσχυσεν πρὸς αὐτούς, "he made war against the saints and conquered them"). A similar phrase has been added to the text of Dan 7:8 in the LXX: καὶ ἐποίει πόλεμον πρὸς τοὺς ἁγίους, "and he waged war against the saints" (pointed out to me by J. W. van Henten). According to 11:7, the beast "waged war with them [the two witnesses] and conquered them and killed them," a proleptic interpolation referring to 13:7. Here the beast from the sea is allowed to persecute the people of God, just as the dragon who empowers him did (12:17). On the phrase "God's people" (literally "holy ones") as Christians, see *Comment* on 5:8.

7b καὶ ἐδόθη αὐτῷ ἐξουσία ἐπὶ πᾶσαν φυλὴν καὶ λαὸν καὶ γλῶσσαν καὶ ἔθνος, "and it was given authority over every tribe and people and language and nation." On the polysyndetic list of ethnic units, see *Comment* on 5:9. This list is meant to emphasize the universal authority exercised by the beast from the sea and reflects the extent of the Roman empire.

8a καὶ προσκυνήσουσιν αὐτὸν πάντες οἱ κατοικοῦντες ἐπὶ τῆς γῆς, "All the inhabitants of the earth will worship him." While that portion of the vision described in vv 1–7 probably refers not to the future but rather to a revelation of the significance of Rome, the sudden switch from the aorist in the previous verse (ἐδόθη, "was given") to the future indicative here suggests that this part of the vision, the adoration of the beast by all the inhabitants of the earth, lies in the future. The phrase "the inhabitants of the earth" occurs nine times in Revelation (see *Comment* on 3:10), but only here are *all* the inhabitants of the earth mentioned. This cannot then refer to any situation in the past or present but must refer to the eschatological future when the rule of the beast will include the entire known world.

8b οὗ οὐ γέγραπται τὸ ὄνομα αὐτοῦ ἐν τῷ βιβλίῳ τῆς ζωῆς [τοῦ ἀρνίου τοῦ ἐσφαγμένου] ἀπὸ καταβολῆς κόσμου, "everyone whose name was not written in the book of life [of the Lamb destined to be slaughtered] since the creation of the world." The syntax of this passage is ambiguous, and there are two quite different ways of understanding the meaning of this text. At first glance, it seems more natural, given the existing word order of the text, to connect the phrase ἀπὸ τῆς καταβολῆς κόσμου, "since the creation of the world," with ἐσφαγμένου, "slain," and to translate the passage so: "whose name has not been written in the book of life of the Lamb slaughtered from the foundation of the world" (AV; NIV; REB; Caird, 168; Mounce, 256; Sweet, 212; Harrington, 139). It is also grammatically possible to link the prepositional phrase ἀπὸ τῆς καταβολῆς κόσμου to γέγραπται, "written," as it must be understood in the parallel passage in 17:8 (Beckwith, 638), and therefore to translate the passage "whose name has not been written from the foundation of the world in the book of life of the Lamb that was slaughtered" (RSV; NRSV; B. Weiss,

Johannes-Apokalypse, 194). This interpretation is preferable since it is logically and theologically impossible to make sense of the statement that the Lamb "was slaughtered *before* the foundation of the world." According to Acts 2:23, Jesus was "delivered up according to the deliberate plan and foreknowledge [τῇ ὡρισμένῃ βουλῇ καὶ προγνώσει] of God," and there is even a closer parallel in 1 Pet 1:19–20, which refers to "the precious blood of Christ, like a blameless and spotless lamb, known already before the world was made [προεγνωσμένου μὲν πρὸ καταβολῆς κόσμου]." While it is possible to think of Christ as *destined* to die for the sins of the world, it is quite another thing to say that that he was *slain* before the creation of the world. This phrase has a doublet in 17:8, with the similarities and differences revealed by this comparison:

Rev 13:8	*Rev 17:8*
οὗ οὐ γέγραπται τὸ ὄνομα αὐτοῦ whose name was not written	ὧν οὐ γέγραπται τὸ ὄνομα whose name was not written
ἐν τῷ βιβλίῳ τῆς ζωῆς in the book of life	ἐπὶ τὸ βιβλίον τῆς ζωῆς in the book of life
τοῦ ἀρνίου τοῦ ἐσφαγμένου of the Lamb slaughtered	
ἀπὸ καταβολῆς κόσμου from the foundation of the world	ἀπὸ καταβολῆς κόσμου from the foundation of the world

This parallel suggests the possibility that the noun cluster τοῦ ἀρνίου τοῦ ἐσφαγμένου, "of the Lamb destined to be slaughtered" (bracketed in the translation above), is a redactional addition or gloss that has been inserted between ζωῆς, "life," and ἀπό, "since" (Bousset [1906] 364; Charles, 1:353). This proposal is supported by the syntactical awkwardness of the phrase as discussed above, for when the phrase τοῦ ἀρνίου τοῦ ἐσφαγμένου is removed, it is natural to take ἀπὸ καταβολῆς κόσμου with γέγραπται as in 17:8. This has the effect of suggesting that the slaying of the Lamb, i.e., the crucifixion of Jesus, was an event predetermined from the beginning of creation, whereas Rev 17:8 includes the curious statement that the names of the inhabitants of the earth who followed the beast were *not* written in the book of life from the beginning of creation. This unusual negative formulation appears to have encouraged redactional modification (see *Comment* on 17:8). It appears that the editor inserted the pronouncement from 17:8 here in 13:8 with two changes: (1) the problematic genitive plural relative pronoun ὧν was changed to οὗ, and (2) the phrase τοῦ ἀρνίου τοῦ ἐσφαγμένου was inserted. Apart from the interpolated phrase, the peculiar *negative* formulation of the pronouncement was probably a change introduced by the author from a *positive* version of the saying, i.e., "whose names were written in the book of life from the creation of the world." There is a striking parallel to Rev 13:8 in 1 Pet 1:18–20 in which several of the same motifs occur: "You were ransomed . . . with the precious blood of Christ, like that of a *lamb* [ἀμνοῦ] without defect or blemish. He was destined before the foundation of the world [πρὸ καταβολῆς κόσμου]."

An extremely close parallel to v 8b is found in the Coptic-Gnostic tractate *Gos.*

Phil. 53.8–9 (tr. J. M. Robinson, *Nag Hammadi,* 142), "he [Christ] voluntarily laid down his life from the very day the world came into being." Another version of this saying very close to Rev 13:8 is found in *Jos. As.* 15:4:

> For behold, your name was written in the book of the living [ἐν τῷ βίβλῳ τῶν ζώντων] in the beginning of the book, as the very first of all, your name was written by my finger, and it will not be erased [ἐξαλειφθήσεται] forever.

This is an antithetical formulation ("written"/"not erased"). (For a more extensive discussion of the motif of "the book of life," see *Comment* on 3:5.) The formula ἀπὸ καταβολῆς κόσμου, "from/before the beginning of the world," occurs four times (five including Matt 13:35) in the NT outside Revelation (Matt 13:35 [*var. lect.*]; 25:34; Luke 11:50; Heb 4:3; 9:26), twice in Revelation (here and 17:8), and once in the Apostolic Fathers, in *Barn.* 5:5, where God says to the Lord from the foundation of the world ἀπὸ καταβολῆς κόσμου, "Let us make man in our image and likeness." The very similar formula πρὸ καταβολῆς κόσμου, "before the creation of the world," occurs three times in the NT (John 17:24; Eph 1:4; 1 Pet 1:20). This formula, which uses the act of creation as a protological reference point in a variety of ways, was apparently widespread in early Judaism in view of its broad distribution and usage in the NT and early Christian literature; see H.-F. Weiss, *Kosmologie,* 139–45. A relatively close parallel formula is πρὸ τῶν αἰώνων, "before the ages" (1 Cor 2:7), or πρὸ παντὸς τοῦ αἰῶνος, "before all ages" (Jude 25); cf. τὸ ἀποκεκρυμμένον ἀπὸ τῶν αἰώνων, "hidden for ages" (= Eph 3:9). In the Coptic-Gnostic tractate *Treat. Seth* 65.33–37, the Assembly of Aeons in the Ogdoad is set "before the foundation of the world." A complementary formula with an *eschatological* reference point that occurs several times in Matthew is συντέλεια τοῦ αἰῶνος, "the consummation of the age/world" (Matt 13:39, 40, 49; 24:3; 28:20; cf. 1 Cor 10:11). The formula in either form is not really distinctively Judeo-Christian since the view was widespread in the Greco-Roman world that the *kosmos* had a beginning but would have no end (Hesiod, Pythagoras, Plato, the Stoics; cf. Arnim, *SVF* 2:574–78; Plato *Timaeus* 29d–30c). Aristotle (and a very few other ancient philosophers) held the unusual view that the *kosmos* was eternal, without beginning or end (Aristotle *De caelo* 1.10; Philo *Op.* 7). καταβολή can mean "beginning" or "foundation" (*1 Clem.* 57:1; cf. Polybius 1.36.8; 24.8.9; 13.6.2; Diodorus Siculus 12.32.2; Jos. *Ant.* 2.409, 417) and, more specifically, "creation" (*Ep. Arist.* 129). While neither phrase occurs in the LXX, the former occurs twice in *T. Mos.* 1:13, 14, though very rarely in rabbinic literature (Str-B, 1:982). In *Barn.* 5:5, Gen 1:26 is quoted as an utterance made ἀπὸ καταβολῆς κόσμου, "just after the beginning of the world," connecting the formula with the creative events narrated in Gen 1:3–25. In the NT, however, the formula is used (1) of the relationship between the Father and the Son before creation (John 17:24), (2) of the election of God's people from the outset of God's creative activity (Matt 25:34; Eph 1:4; Rev 17:8; cf. O. Hofius, "Erwählt vor Grundlegung der Welt [Eph 1:4]," *ZNW* 62 [1971] 123–28), (3) of events occurring since the beginning of history (Luke 11:50; Heb 9:26; cf. *T. Mos.* 1:13), (4) of the creation of the universe (Heb 4:3; *Barn.* 5:5), and (5) of the mission of Christ foreordained before the creation of the world (1 Pet 1:20; Rev 13:8; cf. *T. Mos.* 1:14 on the foreordained mission of Moses: καὶ προεθεάσατό με ὁ θεὸς πρὸ καταβολῆς κόσμου εἶναι με τῆς διαθήκης αὐτοῦ μεσίτην, "God foresaw before the foundation of the world that I would be a mediator of his covenant"; Greek text in Denis, *Fragmenta,* 63). In Judaism there is an emphasis on the selection of Israel at creation (*Jub.* 2:19–20); *Jos. As.* 8:9 refers to "your people that you have chosen before all (things) came into being."

9–10 These two verses have an altogether different literary character when compared with the vision narrated in 13:1–8, for they serve as commentary on the meaning of the vision. It is likely that this hermeneutical section is a redactional addition by the author (for a similar explanatory gloss, see *Comment* on 13:18). For a more detailed discussion of this proposal, see above under *Form/Structure/Setting.*

9 εἴ τις ἔχει οὖς ἀκουσάτω, "if anyone has an ear, let him hear." On this proclamation formula, which uses the third-person imperative, see *Comment* on 2:7 (Mussies, *Morphology,* 322–23). This formula calls attention to the allusion to Jer 15:2 that follows and suggests that 13:1–8 should be understood in the light of v 10a; i.e., it indicates how Christians should face the threat of the beast from the sea. Further, the allusion to Jer 15:2 in v 10a is followed in v 10b by an explanatory phrase that indicates how the allusion to Jer 15:2 must be understood. This address to the reader has functional parallels in 13:18, 14:12, and 17:9 (cf. Mark 13:14, and the discussion in J. Weiss, *Das älteste Evangelium* [Göttingen: Vandenhoeck & Ruprecht, 1903] 71–80), as well as at the conclusion of each of the proclamations to the seven churches (2:7, 11, 17, 29; 3:6, 13, 22).

10a εἴ τις εἰς αἰχμαλωσίαν, εἰς αἰχμαλωσίαν ὑπάγει, "If anyone is for captivity, to captivity he will go." The protasis introduced by εἰ, "if," lacks a verb, and appropriate verbs have subsequently been inserted in the textual tradition (see *Note* 13:10.a-a.). The formulation of the proverbial saying in vv 10a and 10b is based on an allusion to LXX Jer 15:2:

> ὅσοι εἰς θάνατον, εἰς θάνατον,
> καὶ ὅσοι εἰς μάχαιραν, εἰς μάχαιραν,
> καὶ ὅσοι εἰς λιμόν, εἰς λιμόν,
> καὶ ὅσοι εἰς αἰχμαλωσίαν, εἰς αἰχμαλωσίαν.
>
> Those who are destined for pestilence, to pestilence,
> those who are destined for the sword, to the sword;
> those who are destined for famine, to famine;
> those who are destined for captivity, to captivity.

A similar formulation is found in LXX Jer 50:11 (MT 43:11):

> ὃς εἰς θάνατον, εἰς θάνατον,
> καὶ οὓς εἰς ἀποικισμόν, εἰς ἀποικισμόν,
> καὶ οὓς εἰς ῥομφαίαν, εἰς ῥομφαίαν.
>
> Those who are destined for pestilence, to pestilence,
> and those who are destined for exile, to exile,
> and those who are destined for the sword, to the sword.

John alludes selectively to these texts since he does not want to include either pestilence or famine in the scenario of that which faithful Christians must face in the very near future. These texts in Jeremiah do not involve the principle of *lex talionis* (i.e., the law of retribution in kind); rather they indicate that those whose lot is death or the sword or famine or captivity will have to endure those fates. In Jeremiah, such punishments are the consequences of the sins of the people, whereas in Revelation the fates of captivity and the sword (i.e., death) are the fated consequences of those who practice the qualities of faith and endurance. That can be seen in 13:7, where the beast from the land is permitted to make war on God's people and conquer them. There is a close parallel in Esth 4:16, where Esther, before she goes unbidden into the presence of King Ahasuerus, fatefully says "If I perish, I perish" (MT וכאשר אבדתי אבדתי *wĕka'ăšer 'ābadtî 'ābādtî*). The difficulties in this text have spawned a large number of textual variants (see above under *Notes* 10.a-a., 10.b-b., and 10.c.).

10b εἴ τις ἐν μαχαίρῃ ἀποκτανθῆναι, αὐτὸν ἐν μαχαίρῃ ἀποκτανθῆναι, "If anyone with the sword is to be slain, he with the sword will be slain." This couplet is impossible Greek, and a variety of textual variants have arisen in scribal attempts to make sense of these clauses (the text above, adopted by Nestle-Aland[27] and UBSGNT[4], is attested to *only* by A). There are several possible ways of construing the infinitives. The first occurrence of ἀποκτανθῆναι, "to be slain" (aorist passive infinitive), can be understood as the object of a finite verb, which is understood and has been omitted, e.g., "If anyone *is destined* to be slain with the sword." Most MSS have solved the problem of construing this clause by replacing ἀποκτανθῆναι with a finite form of the same verb (e.g., ἀποκτενεῖ or ἀποκτεννεῖ [future active indicative], "he will kill," or ἀποκτείνει or ἀποκτέννει [present active indicative], "he kills" [see *Note* 13:10.d-d.]). In the second clause, ἀποκτανθῆναι can perhaps be construed as an imperatival infinitive (Turner, *Syntax,* 78; though according to BDF § 389 there are only two or three imperatival infinitives in the NT, both without a subject, Rom 12:15; Phil 3:16; Luke 9:3, where an imperative and an infinitive are interchanged) or as a future imperatival infinitive (Zerwick-Grosvenor, *Grammatical Analysis* 2:762). The variants, however, suggest that ἀποκτανθῆναι is elliptical and is the subject of an impersonal verb such as δεῖ (present in most MSS; cf. *Note* 13:10.d-d.).

It is also possible, at least in the first clause, that the protasis, ἀποκτανθῆναι, represents a Hebrew idiom literally translated into Greek, for which the only NT analogy is Rev 12:7 (Charles, 1:355; Schmid, *Studien* 2:140; Moulton-Howard, *Accidence,* 449–50). The Hebrew idiom would be אשר בחרב למות הוא בחרב למות *'ăšer bĕḥereb lāmût hû' bĕḥereb lāmût* (Charles, 1:355). The second clause, or apodosis, however, also presents a problem. Instead of the aorist passive infinitive ἀποκτανθῆναι, "to be slain," one would have expected a future passive such as ἀποκτανθήσεται, "he/she/it will be slain." Charles translates these two clauses in this way: "If any man is to be slain with the sword, he is to be slain with the sword" (1:356). In Hebrew the infinitive absolute can function as a substitute for a finite verb, such as the emphatic imperative, the jussive, and the cohortative (GKC § 113y), and in the LXX such infinitives are occasionally literally translated using Greek infinitives (1 Chr 9:25, ἀδελφοὶ αὐτῶν . . . τοῦ εἰσπορεύεσθαι, "their brothers . . . had to come in"; cf. Soisalon-Soininen, *Infinitive,* 31). The problem with Charles's proposal is that he must suppose that αὐτός, "he," has been corrupted to αὐτόν, "him." This adaptation of Jer 15:2 can be understood as an exhortation to perseverance in the face of the very real possibility of imprisonment and martyrdom (Prete, *Studii biblici franciscani liber annuus* 27 [1977] 102–18, followed by Prigent, in loc.).

10c Ὧδέ ἐστιν ἡ ὑπομονὴ καὶ ἡ πίστις τῶν ἁγίων, "This indicates that the endurance and faith of God's people are involved." This statement functions as an explanation for the difficult saying in v 10ab. It is important to observe that the allusion to Jer 15:2 in this verse is carefully framed by the proclamation formula in v 9 and by this interpretive formula, which provides a particular way of understanding the meaning of the statement in the first part of v 10. There are four instances in Revelation in which ὧδε introduces a comment by the implied author (13:10, 18; 14:12; 17:9). This first instance functions as an explanatory narrative aside (Lee, "Narrative Asides," 121). On the phrase "God's people," literally "holy ones," as Christians, see *Comment* on 5:8. In the phrase ἡ ὑπομονὴ καὶ ἡ πίστις τῶν ἁγίων, "the endurance and faith of God's people," the use of the article with both substantives may function to place the emphasis on each of them individually. Frequently, when two substantives of the same gender are connected with καί, the article is used with the first substantive and not repeated, though there are many exceptions to this practice in Revelation.

Excursus 13B: The Eschatological Antagonist

Bibliography

Bilde, P. "The Roman Emperor Gaius (Caligula)'s Attempt to Erect His Statue in the Temple of Jerusalem." *ST* 32 (1978) 67–93. **Bousset, W.** "Antichrist." *ERE* 1:578–81. ———. *The Antichrist Legend: A Chapter in Christian and Jewish Folklore.* Tr. A. H. Keane. London: Hutchinson, 1896. ——— and **Gressmann, H.** *Die Religion des Judentums.* Tübingen: Mohr-Siebeck, 1966. 254–59. **Buzy, D.** "Antéchrist." *DBSup* 1:297–306. **Charles, R. H.** *The Ascension of Isaiah.* London, 1900. li–lxxv. ———. *Revelation* 2:76–87. **Erbes, K.** "Der Antichrist in der Schriften des Neuen Testaments." *Theologische Arbeiten des rheinischen wissenschaftlichen Prediger-Vereins* n.s. 1 (1897) 1–59. **Ernst, J.** *Die eschatologischen Gegenspieler in den Schriften des Neuen Testaments.* Regensburg: Pustet, 1967. **Flusser, D.** "The Hubris of the Antichrist in a Fragment from Qumran." *Immanuel* 10 (1980) 31–37. **Förster, W.** "Βελιάρ," *TDNT* 1:607; "διάβολος," *TDNT* 2:72–81; "δράκων," *TDNT* 2:281–83; "θηρίον," *TDNT* 3:133–36; "ὄφις," *TDNT* 5:566–82. **Friedländer, M.** *Der Antichrist in den vorchristlichen jüdischen Quellen.* Göttingen: Vandenhoeck & Ruprecht, 1901. **Geffcken, J.** "Die Sage vom Antichrist." *Preussische Jahrbücher* 102 (1900) 385–99. **Grayston, K.** *The Johannine Epistles.* Grand Rapids, MI: Eerdmans, 1984. 76–82. **Hartman, S. S., Böcher, O.,** and **Benrath, G. A.** "Antichrist." *TRE* 3 (1978). **Henle, F. A.** *Der Evangelist Johannes und die Antichristen seiner Zeit.* Munich: Stahl, 1884. **Hilgenfeld, A.** "Nero der Antichrist." *ZWT* 12 (1869) 421–45. **Jenks, G. C.** *The Origins and Early Development of the Antichrist Myth.* BZNW 59. Berlin; New York: de Gruyter, 1991. **Keresztes, P.** "Nero, the Christians and the Jews in Tacitus and Clement of Rome." *Latomus* 43 (1984) 404–13. **Lebram, J. C. H.** "König Antiochus im Buch Daniel." *VT* 25 (1975) 737–72. **Lohmeyer, E.** "Antichrist." *RAC* 1:450–57. **McGinn, B.** "Antichrist." *EncRel* 1:321–23. **Osten-Saken, P. von der.** *Gott und Belial.* SUNT 6. Göttingen: Vandenhoeck & Ruprecht, 1969. **Peerbolte, L. J. L.** *The Antecedents of Antichrist: A Traditio-Historical Study of the Earliest Christian Views on Eschatological Opponents.* Leiden: Peerbolte, 1995. **Piper, O. A.** "1 John and the *Didache* of the Primitive Church." *JBL* 66 (1947) 437–51. **Preisker, H.** "Antichrist." *RGG*[2] 1:375–78. **Preuss, H.** *Der Antichrist.* Berlin, 1901. **Rigaux, B.** *L'Antéchrist et l'opposition du royaume messianique dans l'Ancien et le Nouveau Testament.* Gembloux: Duculot; Paris: Gabalda, 1932. **Renan, E.** *L'Antéchrist.* Paris, 1871. **Rosenstiel, J.-M.** "Le portrait de l'Antichrist." In *Pseudépigraphs de l'Ancien Testament et Manuscrits de la Mer Morte.* Paris: Presses Universitaires de France,

1967. 45–60. **Schlier, H.** "Vom Antichristen: Zum 13. Kapital der Offenbarung Johannes." In *Die Zeit der Kirche.* 2nd ed. Freiburg: Herder, 1958. 16–29. **Schmid, J.** "Der Antichrist und die hemmende Macht." *TQ* 129 (1949) 323–43. **Sirard, L.** "La Parousie de l'Antéchrist: 2 Thess. 2:3–9." In *Studiorum Paulinorum Congressus.* AnBib 18. Rome: Pontifical Biblical Institute, 1963. 2:89–100. **Stählin, W.** "Die Gestalt des Antichristen und das Katechon." In *Festgabe Joseph Lortz,* ed. E. Iserloh and P. Manns. Baden-Baden: Grimm, 1958. 2:1–12. **Stone, M. E.** "Antichrist." *EncJud* 3:59–62. **Strecker, G.** "Der Antichrist: Zum religionsgeschichtlichen Hintergrund von 1 Joh 2,18.22; 4,3 und 2 Joh 7." In *Text and Testimony: Essays on New Testament and Apocryphal Literature.* FS A. F. J. Klijn, ed. T. Baarda, A. Hilhorst, G. P. Luttikhuizen, and A. S. van der Woude. Kampen: Kok, 1988. 247–54. **Weinrich, W. C.** "Antichrist in the Early Church." *CTM* 49 (1985) 135–47. **Yate, R.** "The Antichrist." *EvQ* 46 (1974) 42–50.

The term ἀντίχριστος, "antichrist," occurs for the first time in early Christian literature in the Johannine letters; it is used four times in the singular (1 John 2:18, 22; 4:3; 2 John 7) and once in the plural (1 John 2:18). Though the term ἀντίχριστος is anarthrous in 1 John 2:18 (its first occurrence), the author assumes that the figure is known to the readers, for he claims that "you have heard that antichrist is coming." It is possible that they were familiar, therefore, with the eschatological role that this figure was expected to play and probably even with the term ἀντίχριστος. It is also possible that the author of 1 John coined this designation, for whenever the term occurs in later literature, it is used exclusively by Christians.

The author distinguishes this figure (or figures) from the devil, whom he mentions in 1 John 3:8, 10. The preposition ἀντί, when used as a prefix, can mean "against, in opposition to," or "instead of, in place of," i.e., "substitute, counterfeit" (LSJ, 153; Strecker, "Der Antichrist," 247 n. 2); i.e., the Antichrist figure can be understood primarily as an *opponent* of Christ or as a *counterfeit* Christ (the latter is emphasized by Weinrich, *CTM* 49 [1985] 142; see Origen *Comm. in Matt.* 27). It is not necessary to choose between etymologies, however, for Antichrist figures seem to function in *both* ways. 1 John 2:22 defines the role of the Antichrist as that of denying the Father and the Son (i.e., as an *opponent* of God and Christ). Polycarp, who uses the term "antichrist" in apparent dependence on 1 John 4:2–3 and 2 John 7 (Brown, *Epistles,* 8–9), says in *Phil.* 7:1, "For everyone who does not confess that Jesus Christ has come in the flesh is an antichrist [ἀντίχριστος] and whosoever does not confess the testimony of the cross is of the devil." In this couplet, "antichrist" is parallel to "of the devil," a phrase that both indicates the malevolent supernatural power behind the figure of the Antichrist and makes it clear that the Antichrist and the devil are distinct figures in Polycarp's view, as they are in the view of the author of 1 John. The term "antichrist," following the precedent of 1 John 2:18, 22; 4:3; 2 John 7; Polycarp *Phil.* 7:1, was also used of heretics in general by early Christian writers (Tertullian *Praescr.* 3.12–4.5; *Adv. Marc.* 3.8; *Ieiun.* 11; Cyprian *Ep.* 70.3).

The term ἀντίχριστος is a Christian term for an opponent of Christ and/or a counterfeit Christ, and as such it is too specific to describe other Jewish and Christian figures who play slightly different roles (Jenks, *Origins,* 23–24), for it is but one of many designations used for one or several human representatives of the devil or Satan who actively oppose the Messiah. For that reason the term "eschatological antagonist" is preferable, for it is sufficiently broad to include all such figures found in early Jewish and early Christian literature. Even in Christian texts there are a number of different designations for eschatological adversaries, including ψευδόχριστος, "false Christ" (a term very close in meaning to ἀντίχριστος), found in the plural in Mark 13:22 (= Matt 24:24) and occurring (along with designations for several other types of eschatological antagonists) in several other early Christian authors: Hegesippus in Eusebius *Hist. eccl.* 4.22.6 (who claims that false Christs and false prophets and false apostles emerge from the seven heresies); Justin *Dial.* 35.3 (false Christs and false apostles); 82.2 (false prophets and false Christs); Irenaeus *Hist. eccl.* 5.25.1–5; 5.28.1–4. Most of these passages in fact allude to Mark 13:22 and Matt 24:24. Other designations for human figures who represent Satan and therefore function as opponents of God, in addition to false Christs, include: (1) false apostles (Rev 2:2; Justin *Dial.* 35.3; Hegesippus in Eusebius *Hist. eccl.* 4.22.6; *Apost. Const.* 6.9.6); (2) false prophets (Mark 13:22 = Matt 24:24; Matt 7:15; 1 John 4:1–3; Rev 16:13; 19:20; 20:10; Hegesippus in Eusebius *Hist. eccl.* 4.22.6; *Didascalia* 11.5.6); (3) false teachers (2 Pet 2:1, compared with false prophets of the past), (4) the man of lawlessness (2 Thess 2:3, 8, 9; Justin *Dial.* 32.4; 110.2), (5) the son of perdition (2 Thess 2:3; this figure is an alternate designation for the man of lawlessness in 2 Thess 2:3, 8, 9), and (6) the son of lawlessness (*Apoc. Elijah* 1:10; 3:1, 5, 13, 18; 4:2, 15, 20, 28, 31; dependent on 2 Thessalonians). Occasionally, Satan and the Antichrist are identified, as in *Sib. Or.* 3.63–74 and *Asc. Isa.* 4:1–7, where Nero (= Antichrist) is regarded as Beliar (= Satan) incarnate.

From the time of Irenaeus on, the term ἀντίχριστος appears with some frequency in early Christian literature and is clearly a developed figure (Judas, a Christian commentator on Daniel quoted in Eusebius *Hist. eccl.* 6.7; Hippolytus *de Ant.*; Origen *Contra Celsum* 6.45). The major characteristics of the Antichrist in Christian literature from Irenaeus to the early fourth century A.D. are the following (Jenks, *Origins,* 49–76): (1) he is the agent of Satan, (2) he is a deceiver, (3) he performs false signs and wonders (Irenaeus *Adv. haer.* 5.28.2; Tertullian *De anima* 50.7; Origen *Contra Celsum* 2.50; 6.45; *Apoc. Elijah* 3:13), (4) he is extremely evil (Irenaeus *Adv. haer.* 5.25.3), (5) he persecutes the people of God (Irenaeus *Adv. haer.* 5.25.3; Hippolytus *de Ant.* 56.1; 58.4; 61.9; *Comm. in Dan.* 4.50.3; *Apoc. Elijah* 4:8–12), (6) he has excessive pride (Hippolytus *de Ant.* 16.2; 17.6–7; 18.1–4), and (7) he claims divine honors (Irenaeus *Adv. haer.* 5.25.1, 4; 5.28.2; Hippolytus *de Ant.* 53; Tertullian *Adv. Marc.* 5.16; Origen *Contra Celsum* 6.46).

The developed Antichrist figure found in Christian writers of the late second century appears to have been constructed out of two originally separate eschatological-antagonist traditions that are sometimes combined or juxtaposed in early Christian texts (Bousset-Gressmann, *Religion des Judentums,* 254; Strecker, "Der Antichrist," 247–54): (1) the tradition of the godless, tyrannical ruler (probably originating with the depiction of Antiochus IV in Daniel and augmented by traditions concerning the Roman emperors Caligula and Nero) and (2) the tradition of the false, seductive prophet (originally based on Deut 13:1–6). The two traditions are *combined* in 2 Thess 2:3–12 but juxtaposed in Rev 13:1–10, 11–18, and perhaps also in Mark 13 (compare v 14 with vv 6, 22; cf. Strecker, "Der Antichrist," 253). Charles (2:76–87) argued for *three* traditions, an Antichrist tradition, a Beliar tradition, and a Nero tradition; the first two were "fused" by A.D. 50, while all three were "fused" ca. A.D. 88. Ernst (*Gegenspieler,* 198–210) has proposed that the OT theme of the "enemy from the north" (Jer 1:15; 4:13; 5:15; 6:22; Isa 5:27–28; 8:8–9; 17:4–5; Ezek 1:4; Joel 2:20), particularly depicted as Gog and Magog (Ezek 38–39), was important for the Christian conception of the eschatological antagonist.

In a variety of early Jewish and early Christian texts, the eschatological antagonist is expected to perform signs and wonders (2 Thess 2:9–10; Rev 13:13; 16:14; 19:20; *Sib. Or.* 2.167; 3.63–67; *Asc. Isa.* 4.10–11; *Apoc. Elijah* 3:5–13; *Apoc. Dan.* 13:1–13; *Gk. Apoc. Ezra* 4:26–27; *Apoc. Pet.* 2). While early Jewish texts predating the Christian era do not mention a thaumaturgical eschatological antagonist, that notion was probably the result of an eschatological interpretation of Deut 13:2–6 (see *Comment* on 13:13). The Clementine literature, perhaps under the influence of Gnosticism, reflects the development of the doctrine of syzygies, i.e., a series of true and false prophets that are opposed to each other and that have appeared in various incarnations from the beginning of human history (G. Strecker, *Die Pseudoklementinen,* 3rd ed. [Berlin: Akademie, 1992] 145ff., 154ff.).

Apart from the Johannine literature in the NT, the apocalyptic conception of an eschatological antagonist is vested in the notion of a world ruler who becomes the adversary of God and/or his Messiah. This typically involves a historicization of the combat myth (discussed in detail in Rev 11:19–12:17 under *Form/Structure/Setting*). This very ancient and widespread myth normally involves two divine beings (one representing order and goodness, the other representing chaos and evil) and their supernatural allies in a struggle for control of the cosmos. The antithetical roles of these two supernatural combatants can be understood in terms of historical agents who are either inspired by such divine beings or are considered their incarnations. Thus Israel and the nations that were her traditional enemies could be understood as historical representatives of antagonistic spiritual powers. Early evidence for this tendency toward the historicization of the combat myth can be seen in the OT, where the chaos monsters Rahab and Leviathan are sometimes used as metaphors for foreign oppressors like Egypt (Pss 74:14; 87:4; Isa 30:7; Ezek 29:3; 32:2–4). In Jer 51:34 (LXX 28:32), Nebuchadrezzar is compared to a monster who will devour Israel. In *Pss. Sol.* 2:25–29, the arrogance of Pompey is compared to ἡ ὑπερηφανία τοῦ δράκοντος, "the arrogance of the dragon" (H. E. Ryle and M. R. James, *Ψαλμοὶ Σολομῶντος: Psalms of the Pharisees, Commonly Called the Psalms of Solomon* [Cambridge: Cambridge UP, 1891] 23). In early Judaism the sea monster continued to be used as a metaphor representing various oppressive foreign nations (Dan 7:1–8). The notion of an evil tyrant who would arise in the last generation, an important constituent theme in the antagonist myth, has antecedents in the OT (Ezek 28:2; Dan 7:24–25). However, even the depiction of Antioches Epiphanes in Dan 8:23–25; 11:29–39 appears to be based on a typology already in existence and not only or exclusively on the historical features of Antiochus (Lebram, *VT* 25 [1975] 737–72). Another important theme revolves around the leader of the forces of evil in the final battle (1QM 18:1; 1QS 4:18–19; *T. Dan* 5:10–11; *T. Mos.* 8). The Christian doctrine of the historical incarnation of Christ made it all but inevitable that a satanic counterpart to Christ (often labeled the Antichrist) be incorporated into early Christian eschatological expectation (for an extensive list of references to ἀντίχριστος in early Christian literature, see *PGL*, 160–62).

The antagonist myth was subject to continuous development through the combination of the historical features of various rulers hostile to Judaism with old themes and motifs drawn from various versions of the combat myth. The career of Antiochus IV Epiphanes was blended with mythical features and transformed into a figure representing incarnate evil (Lebram, *VT* 25 [1975] 737–72). The anti-Jewish actions of Antiochus are narrated in 1 Macc 1:20–61; 2 Macc 5:11–6:11 and presented in apocalyptic form in Dan 8:23–25; 11:29–39. The characterization of Antiochus in Dan 8:23–25, particularly the emphasis on his wisdom (see the parallel in Ezek 28:3), reveals the existence of an earlier typology (Lebram, *VT* 25 [1975] 738–43):

> At the end of their rule,
>   when the transgressions have reached their full measure,
> a king of bold countenance shall arise,
>   skilled in intrigue.
> He shall grow strong in power,
>   shall cause fearful destruction,
>   and shall succeed in what he does.
> He shall destroy the powerful
>   and the people of the holy ones.
> By his cunning
>   he shall make deceit prosper under his hand,
>   and in his own mind he shall be great.
> Without warning he shall destroy many

> and shall even rise up against the Prince of princes.
> But he shall be broken, and not by human hands. (NRSV)

One of the characteristic motifs that make up the image of the eschatological antagonist is the claim to be divine. The historical Antioches IV Epiphanes was remembered as claiming divinity (Dan 11:36–37), and that claim became integral to the Jewish myth of the eschatological antagonist (2 Thess 2:4; *Sib. Or.* 5.33–34; *Asc. Isa.* 4.6; *2 Enoch* [Rec. J] 29:4). This claim is reflected in Lactantius *Div. Inst.* 7.17.4 (tr. McDonald, *Lactantius,* 518), "That king, indeed, will be most offensive and will himself, as the prophet of liars, set himself up as and call himself a god. He will order himself to be worshiped as the son of God." The emperor Gaius reportedly claimed to be divine and intended to have erected in the temple in Jerusalem a statue of himself, which was to bear the name "Gaius the New Zeus Epiphanes" (Philo *Leg.* 188, 346; Jos. *J.W.* 2.184–85; *Ant.* 18.257–61; Tacitus *Hist.* 5.9), an act described as μανία, "madness," and ὕβρις, "insolence" (Jos. *Ant.* 18.277–78, 280).

The eschatological tyrant, considered the chief antagonist to the Messiah, is described in *2 Apoc. Bar.* 40:1–3 (Klijn in Charlesworth, *OTP* 1:633):

> The last ruler who is left alive at that time will be bound, whereas the entire host will be destroyed. And they will carry him on Mount Zion, and my Anointed One will convict him of all his wicked deeds and will assemble and set before him all the works of his hosts. And after these things he will kill him and protect the rest of my people who will be found in the place that I have chosen.

11a καὶ εἶδον ἄλλο θηρίον ἀναβαῖνον ἐκ τῆς γῆς, "Then I saw another beast ascending from the earth." (On καὶ εἶδον, see *Comment* on 5:1.) The adjective ἄλλος, "another," is used with some frequency by the author to signal a new scene (7:2; 8:3; 10:1; 18:1; 20:1).This second beast is referred to as a θηρίον, "beast," only here in Revelation, for throughout the remainder of this pericope (vv 11–18), it/he is referred to only by a series of eight third-person singular verbs (13:11 [2x], 12 [2x], 13 [2x], 14, 16) and two occurrences of the pronoun αὐτός (13:14, 15). This figure is elsewhere referred to as the "false prophet" (16:13; 19:20; 20:10), which clearly conveys the role the author assigns him. By referring to this figure as a beast (the result of a reworking of the Leviathan-Behemoth myth), the author-editor forestalls using the designation "false prophet."

The phrase "ascending from the earth" is expressly formulated as a complementary parallel to the description of the first beast "ascending from the sea." While it is clear what "emerging from the sea" means (i.e., emerging from the abyss), it is not at all clear what "ascending from the earth" means. Surely an opening of some kind in the surface of the earth, such as a cave or fissure, is imagined. In 11:7 "the beast who ascends from the abyss" is mentioned in a proleptic gloss, but it is not immediately clear whether this refers to the beast from the sea or the beast from the land, though it almost certainly refers to the former.

This mention of a second beast from the land is clearly an allusion to Behemoth, a mythical male monster who, according to Jewish tradition, was separated from Leviathan on the fifth day of creation and assigned to the land (*1 Enoch* 60:7–11, 24; 4 Ezra 6:47–54; *2 Apoc. Bar.* 29:4); on Leviathan, see *Comment* on 13:1. The version of the myth in *b. B. Bat.* 74b–75a mentions the castration of Behemoth by God. In several Greek myths of Near Eastern origin, the separation of Sky from Earth is achieved only by the castration of the former (Hesiod *Theog.* 178–87; see

H. Staudacher, *Die Trennung von Himmel und Erde* [Tübingen: Mohr-Siebeck, 1942]).

The identity of the beast from the earth is problematic. While it is clear that his behavior is sketched with the aid of that aspect of the eschatological-antagonist myth that anticipates the coming of a false prophet at the end, it is not clear whether the author thinks simply of the eschatological false prophet (whom Irenaeus calls the "armor bearer" of the Antichrist, *Adv. haer.* 5.28.2) or has in mind a specific contemporary individual or institution that promotes the imperial cult, e.g., the Roman emperor himself (Koester, *Introduction* 2:255), Roman provincial governors (Mommsen, *Römisches Staatsrecht*), the Greco-Roman priesthood, the provincial imperial priesthood (Bousset [1906] 365–66; J. Weiss, *Offenbarung;* Charles, 1:357; Müller, 253–54; Talbert, 55), the province of Asia in its double aspect of civil and religious administration, the proconsul and the *commune* (Ramsay, *Letters,* 97), a more general conception of propaganda for the imperial cult (Sweet, 214), the *koinon* of Asia as represented by priests of the imperial cult (Caird, 171), or all those individuals and institutions that actively promote the imperial cult (Roloff, [ET] 161).

Of these possibilities, the most likely solution is that the beast from the earth represents the imperial priesthood, which was centrally concerned with promoting the imperial cult (Cuss, *Imperial Cult,* 96; Beasley-Murray, 216). Very little is really known about priests in imperial cults, however. Between 29 B.C. and A.D. 26, there was just one priest in the imperial provincial cult in Asia (at Pergamon), who had the title ἀρχιερεὺς θεᾶς Ῥώμης καὶ Αὐτοκράτορος Καίσαρος θεοῦ υἱοῦ Σεβαστοῦ, "the high priest of the goddess Roma and the Emperor Caesar Augustus son of God." After the time of Augustus, the high priest of the first provincial imperial cult of Asia was also known as the ἀρχιερεὺς Ἀσίας, "high priest of Asia" (see Friesen, *Twice Neokoros,* 77–81). While scholars have generally accepted the notion that the high priestesses mentioned in inscriptions were wives of high priests (Magie, *Roman Rule* 1:149; Deininger, *Provinziallandtage,* 154), it appears that these high priestesses were legitimate cultic functionaries in their own right (Kearsley, *GRBS* 27 [1986] 183–92; Friesen, *Twice Neokoros,* 81–89) and functioned as high priests in the province of Asia by the middle of the first century A.D. Despite claims to the contrary (LSJ, 256), there does not appear to be any evidence suggesting that those who held the office of Asiarch functioned as priests in the imperial cult of Roman Asia (Acts 19:31; Strabo 14.1.42; *Digest* 27.1.6.14); see Friesen, *Twice Neokoros,* 92–112.

Priests of the imperial cult wore crowns that displayed the busts of the deified emperors and the gods whose cult they served. Suetonius reports how Domitian presided at athletic competitions wearing a golden crown depicting Jupiter, Juno, and Minerva, while the priest of Jupiter and the college of Flaviales (flamens or priests of deified Flavian emperors) had crowns depicting Jupiter, Juno, Minerva, and Domitian (*Dom.* 4.4). Priests of the imperial cult in the provinces were apparently persons of importance who wore their priestly crowns in public (see *Acts Paul* 26–39 and Price, *Rituals,* 170–71). Several sculptures have been preserved from the first to the third century A.D. depicting imperial priests wearing crowns on which were mounted miniature busts of deified Roman emperors (Inan and Rosenbaum, *Sculpture,* 109 [plate LXV], 124 [plate LXXXV, 1–2], 139–40 [plate CIII, 1–2]; Inan and Alföldi-Rosenbaum, *Porträtplastik,* no. 230, pp. 252–53, plate in vol. 2, no. 164; Hanfmann, *Sardis,* 65, figure 43), though some depict deities and not deified emperors (Inan and Rosenbaum, *Sculpture,* 31–32).

11b καὶ εἶχεν κέρατα δύο ὅμοια ἀρνίῳ καὶ ἐλάλει ὡς δράκων, "and it had two horns like a ram, but it sounded like a dragon." The two horns are not interpreted (normally only an abnormal number of horns is interpreted in apocalyptic texts), though the fact that they are only *two* in contrast to the *ten* of the first beast apparently indicates that the second is subordinate to the first. This may be an allusion to the ram with two horns of Dan 8:3, which symbolize the kings of Media and Persia, opponents of the people of God. Horns are used as symbols of power and authority in the OT (KB³, 1068–69), sometimes of powerful nations (Zech 1:18–21[MT 2:1–4]), of the power exercised by a particular nation (Jer 48:25), or of kings (the future Davidic king in Ezek 29:21 and Ps 132:17; Alexander the Great in Dan 8:8a; the Macedonian successors of Alexander, or Diadochi, in Dan 8:8b). This is in part an allusion to Dan 8:3, where a ram with two horns symbolizes the Persian empire, according to Dan 8:20 (in both the LXX and Theod of Dan 8:3, κριός, "ram," is used for the Hebrew term אַיִל *ʾayil,* "ram"). Though ἀρνίον is usually translated "lamb," that is problematic since lambs (in contrast to rams) do not have horns. The author is intentionally contrasting "ram" with "dragon," just as he contrasted the "lion" with the "lamb" in 5:5–6. A logion of Jesus preserved in Matt 7:15 (with no close parallels) warns against false prophets who appear to be sheep but within are rapacious wolves (allusions to this saying are found in Justin *Dial.* 35.3; *1 Apol.* 16.13; Irenaeus *Adv. haer.* 1, praef. 2; *Acts Thom.* 79; cf. *Did.* 16:3; Ign. *Phld.* 2:1–2; Ps.-Ign. *Eph.* 5; Ps.-Ign. *Hero* 2).

What does it mean to "speak like a dragon"? Aelian observes that a δράκων makes a hissing or whistling sound (he uses the verb συρίζειν in *De nat. anim.* 6.63; in 16.39 he uses the cognate nouns συριγμός and σῦριγξ). Aelian uses the terms συριγμός, "hiss," and φύσημα, "roar," together in *De nat. anim.* 15.21. In the *Acts of Andrew,* Gregory's Epitome 19 (ed. MacDonald, *The Acts of Andrew,* 262–63), an eighty-foot snake "gave a deep roar [*emittens gravem rugitum*]" and then retreated before Andrew. In a novella about Pinus and the dragon, Aelian implies that though Pinus could not see who was speaking, he heard a voice [φωνή], presumably the dragon's, which said "Touch not the fawns" (*De nat. anim.* 10.48). However, here "to speak like a dragon" undoubtedly means that the second beast acted as the agent or plenipotentiary of the first beast.

12a καὶ τὴν ἐξουσίαν τοῦ πρώτου θηρίου πᾶσαν ποιεῖ ἐνώπιον αὐτοῦ, "It exercised the full authority of the first beast, on its behalf." The author switches from past to present tenses in vv 12–18, though apart from producing a more vivid narrative, the reasons for this stylistic change are not immediately evident.

"The full authority" of the first beast was in turn based on the authority granted him by the dragon (13:2). The tertiary level of authority exercised by the second beast is thus somewhat problematic and perhaps reflects the author's attempt to connect the narrative in vv 11–18 to that in vv 1–10. The second beast clearly functions as his fully accredited representative or deputy. The phrase ἐνώπιον αὐτοῦ, literally "before him, in his presence," really means "by his authority, on his behalf" (Thayer, *Lexicon,* 220; BAGD, 271) or even "at his commissioning" (K. Krämer, *EDNT* 1:462). The view that ἐνώπιον + genitive should be taken literally as "in the presence of" the first beast (Beckwith, 640; Bratcher-Hatton, 201–2) or "in the presence of" the official representatives of the emperor (Charles,1:360) is doubtful, for the first beast is never referred to in vv 11–18 in an active way. ἐνώπιον αὐτοῦ is a Semitic idiom also used in13:14, where the second beast performs miracles ἐνώπιον τοῦ θηρίου, "by the authority of the beast" (13:14), a passage alluded to later in 19:20, where it is said that the false prophet performed miracles ἐνώπιον αὐτοῦ, "on his authority," i.e., the authority of the beast. This expression appears to have been formulated by the author in antithesis to the way in which this improper preposition is normally used in Revelation, that is, with reference to the presence of God.

ἐνώπιον + genitive is primarily used in Revelation in expressions such as ἐνώπιον τοῦ θεοῦ, "before God" (3:2; 8:2;9:13; 11:16; 12:10; 16:19; cf. 15:4), ἐνώπιον τοῦ θρόνου [τοῦ θεοῦ], "before the throne [of God]" (1:4; 4:5, 6, 10; 7:9, 11, 15; 8:3; 14:3; 20:12), ἐνώπιον τοῦ καθημένου ἐπὶ τοῦ θρόνου, "before the one seated on the throne" (4:10), ἐνώπιον τοῦ κυρίου, "before the Lord" (11:4), ἐνώπιον τοῦ πατρός μου, "before my Father" (3:5), and ἐνώπιον τοῦ ἀρνίου, "before the Lamb" (5:8; 7:9; 14:10). That the second beast or the false prophet is said to exercise authority and perform miracles *in the presence of* the beast hints at a priestly role for the false prophet.

12b καὶ ποιεῖ τὴν γῆν καὶ τοὺς ἐν αὐτῇ κατοικοῦντας ἵνα προσκυνήσουσιν τὸ θηρίον τὸ πρῶτον, "and made the earth, that is, those who dwell on it, to worship the first beast." The power over the people of the earth that the first beast has is such that the second beast, acting as his agent, has the ability to compel people to do his will. The phrase "the earth and those who inhabit it" is found only here in Revelation; more characteristic phrases are "the inhabitants of the earth," which occurs nine times (see *Comment* on 3:10), and "the whole earth" (3:10; 12:9; 13:3; 16:14). Charles regarded this phrase as betraying the hand of a different author (1:336), while Bauckham regards it as a deliberate and subtle parallel to "the heavens and those who dwell in them" in 12:12 ("Conversion," 240). There is, however, no reason to regard the parallelism as intentional.

12c οὗ ἐθεραπεύθη ἡ πληγὴ τοῦ θανάτου αὐτοῦ, "whose mortal wound was healed." This adjectival phrase refers back to v 3, where it is said that one of heads of the first beast ὡς ἐσφαγμένην εἰς θάνατον, καὶ ἡ πληγὴ τοῦ θανάτου αὐτοῦ ἐθεραπεύθη, "appeared to be fatally wounded, but its mortal wound was healed." However, there it was one of the *heads* (i.e., kings) that received a mortal wound, but here and in v 14 (where a similar relative clause is used) it is the beast itself that has sustained the wound. How could the beast itself have been mortally wounded if six heads were still living? This therefore appears to be an interpolation (J. Weiss, *Offenbarung*, 33–34), which has the analeptic function of linking the vision of the beast from the land (vv 11–18) with that of the beast from the sea (vv 1–10). V 14c, which is also a redactional addition, is more specific: ὅς ἔχει τὴν πληγὴν τῆς μαχαίρης καὶ ἔζησεν, "who was wounded by the sword but lived." The relative clause functions to identify the beast for the reader by referring to the event narrated in v 3a, though this narrative aside appears to be an explanatory interpolation included in the final revision of Revelation. For similar clauses used for identifying major players in the drama, cf. v 14.

13 καὶ ποιεῖ σημεῖα μεγάλα, ἵνα καὶ πῦρ ποιῇ ἐκ τοῦ οὐρανοῦ καταβαίνειν εἰς τὴν γῆν ἐνώπιον τῶν ἀνθρώπων, "It performed impressive miracles, even causing fire to fall from heaven to earth before people." The idiom ποιεῖν σημεῖα/σημεῖον, "perform miracles/miracle," occurs four times in Revelation (13:13, 14; 16:14; 19:20) but is a favorite expression in the Fourth Gospel, occurring thirteen times (John 2:23; 3:2; 4:54; 6:2, 14, 30; 7:31; 9:16; 10:41; 11:47; 12:18, 37; 20:30); see Ruckstuhl-Dschulnigg, *Stilkritik,* 153. The "impressive miracles" performed by the beast from the sea are reminiscent of Elijah's miracle of fire (1 Kgs 18:38; 2 Kgs 1:10; cf. Luke 9:54), on which they may have been intentionally modeled. So far as the Greco-Roman world is concerned, Artemidorus (*Oneirocritica* 2.9; tr. White, *Dreams*) observes that "worst of all is a dream in which fire is seen being carried down to earth." The miracles worked by this beast (= false prophet) are referred to again in 19:20, and the demonic spirits that came from the mouths of the dragon, the beast, and the false prophet are also said to perform miracles (16:14). The performance of miracles by the eschatological antagonist links this passage closely to 2 Thess 2:9–10:

> The coming of the lawless one by the activity of Satan [κατ' ἐνέργειαν τοῦ σατανᾶ] will be with all power and with pretended signs and wonders, and with all wicked deception for those who are to perish, because they refused to love the truth and so be saved.

In predictions of the coming of various evil eschatological figures (false Christs, false prophets, the eschatological antagonist), they are frequently expected to perform signs and wonders to lead people astray (Mark 13:21–23 = Matt 24:23–25; *Did.* 16:4; *Asc. Isa.* 4.10; *Sib. Or.* 2.167 [to Beliar]; 3.63–67; *Apoc. Elijah* 3:5–13; *Apoc. Dan.* 13:1–13; *Gk. Apoc. Ezra* 4:26–27 [the antagonist unsuccessfuly attempts to turn stones into bread]; *Apoc. Pet.* 2; Tertullian *De anima* 50.7; Hippolytus *Haer.* 528.2; Origen *Contra Celsum* 2.50; 6.45). The prediction that many will come saying "I am the Christ" is found in *Apoc. Pet.* 1–2, and the prediction that "many false messiahs and false apostles will arise and deceive many of the faithful" is found in Justin (*Dial.* 35.3). Simon Magus (never presented as the eschatological antagonist, though he is depicted as the adversary of Peter) purportedly performed miracles that persuaded people to follow him (*Acts Pet.* 12). According to Hartman (*Prophecy,* 199) and others (see Strecker, "Der Antichrist," 248–49, who suggests that Deut 13:2–6 may already have been eschatologized in early Judaism), it is likely that this sequence of motifs (false prophet/signs and wonders/deception) originated with Deut 13:1–3 (emphasis added):

> If a *prophet* arises among you, or a dreamer of dreams, and gives you a *sign or a wonder,* and the *sign or wonder* which he tells you comes to pass, and if he says, "*Let us go after other gods,*" which you have not known, "and let us serve them," you shall not listen to the words of that prophet or to that dreamer of dreams; for the Lord your God is testing you.

However, references in early Jewish and early Christian literature to false prophets or false Christs who perform miracles to deceive people do not clearly allude to Deut 13, apparently because these motifs were quickly transformed into apocalyptic traditions, thereby losing any direct reference to Deut 13. The second beast in Rev 13:11–18 is referred to subsequently only as the false prophet (Rev 16:13; 19:20; 20:10), thereby linking these two eschatological scenarios. For evidence that religious miracles were fabricated for political reasons in the Roman world, see G. W. Bowersock, "The Mechanics of Subversion in the Roman Provinces," in *Opposition et Résistances a l'Empire d'Auguste a Trajan,* Fondation Hardt, Entretiens 33 (Geneva: Fondation Hardt, 1987) 291–320.

The motif of fire falling from heaven to earth (often understood as lightning;

cf. 4 Ezra 4:16) as divine judgment is found in Rev 20:9, where fire falls from heaven and destroys the huge army that has surrounded Jerusalem. This motif occurs frequently in the OT and early Jewish literature (Gen 19:24 [cf. Wis 10:6; *Gk. Apoc. Ezra* 2:19]; 2 Kgs 1:10, 12, 14 [cf. Sir 48:3]; Job 1:16; Ps 11:6; Lam 1:13; Ezek 38:22; 39:6; *Sib. Or.* 2.196–200; 3.53–54, 84–85; 8.243; Aristeas *Hist.* frag. 1 [Holladay, *FHJA* 1:268–69; Denis, *Fragmenta,* 196]; Ep Jer 6:63; *T. Abr.* [A] 10:11). Several stories are told in the OT in which a man of God prays and fire comes down from heaven and consumes sacrifices (Lev 9:24; 1 Chr 21:26; 2 Chr 7:1 [cf. 2 Macc 2:10]; 1 Kgs 18:36–39 [cf. *Vit. Proph.* 21.10]). In some of these passages a person acting as an agent of God is able to call down fire from heaven (1 Kgs 18:38; 2 Kgs 1:10, 12, 14; *T. Abr.* [A] 10:11; *T. Abr.* [B] 12:3, 4; cf. Luke 9:54). There are several references to fire from heaven as divine judgment in early Christian literature (Luke 9:54; *1 Clem.* 11:1; Rev 20:9). *Sib. Or.* 3.63–74 (an addition to the text made after ca. A.D. 70) deals with Nero (= Beliar), his performance of "many signs for men" (σήματα πολλὰ ποιήσει ἀνθρώποις), and his fiery destruction (tr. Collins in Charlesworth, *OTP* 1:363):

> Then Beliar will come from the *Sebastenoi*
> and he will raise up the height of mountains,
> he will raise up the sea,
> the great fiery sun and shining moon,
> and he will raise up the dead, and perform many signs
> for men. But they will not be effective in him.
> But he will, indeed, also lead men astray,
> and he will lead astray many faithful, chosen Hebrews,
> and also other lawless men
> who have not yet listened to the word of God.
> But whenever the threats of the great God draw nigh
> and a burning power comes through the sea to land
> it will also burn Beliar and all overbearing men,
> as many as put faith in him.

14a καὶ πλανᾷ τοὺς κατοικοῦντας ἐπὶ τῆς γῆς διὰ τὰ σημεῖα ἃ ἐδόθη αὐτῷ ποιῆσαι ἐνώπιον τοῦ θηρίου, "It deceives the inhabitants of the earth through the miracles it was permitted to perform on the authority of the beast." The term "deceive" in this context is an alternate way of saying "he made the earth and those who dwell on it worship the first beast" (v 12). (On the negative designation "the inhabitants of the earth," see *Comment* on 3:10.) The phrase "deceiver of the whole world" (ὁ πλανῶν τὴν οἰκουμένην ὅλην) has already been used of Satan (12:9; see also 20:10), and an equivalent phrase is now used of the beast from the land, one type of eschatological antagonist in Revelation who is elsewhere in Revelation called the false prophet (16:13; 19:20). The motif of the eschatological antagonist as a deceiver occurs occasionally in early Christian tradition (2 Thess 2:9–10; 2 John 7; *Did.* 16:4; Hippolytus *Comm. in Dan.* 4.7.1; 4.16.1; 4.21.3; *de Ant.* 6). The phrase ἐδόθη αὐτῷ, literally "it was given to him," though more idiomatically translated "he was permitted," is another occurrence of the *passivum divinum* or "divine passive," used as a circumlocution for the name of God (see *Comment* on 9:3b). A close parallel to this performance of lying signs permitted by God is found in 2 Thess 2:9–11, where it is predicted that the eschatological antagonist will perform signs and wonders, which those doomed to destruction will believe because "God sends the power of deceit to them so that they might believe the falsehood" (v 11). On the idiom ποιεῖν σημεῖα, "to perform miracles," see *Comment* on 13:13.

14b λέγων τοῖς κατοικοῦσιν ἐπὶ τῆς γῆς ποιῆσαι εἰκόνα τῷ θηρίῳ, "He told those who dwell on the earth to make a cult image in honor of the beast." The author has clearly modeled vv 14–15 on Dan 3:4, where Nebuchadrezzar king of Babylon set up a golden image and ordered that all peoples, nations, and languages worship the image on pain of death. While nothing in Daniel suggests that the golden image represented the king, Hippolytus suggested that Nebuchadrezzar made this golden image of himself so that he might be worshiped by everyone as God (*Comm. in Dan.* 3.4). According to the version of the eschatological-antagonist myth found in *Asc. Isa.* 4:1–13 (part of the extensive Christian interpolation of 3:13–4:22 in an otherwise Jewish document), Beliar incarnate will set up images of himself in every city (4:11). Portraits were absolutely essential for the ruler cults of the Hellenistic and Roman periods, and thousands of portraits, busts, and statues were produced for ruler-cult shrines.

Two terms that can be translated "statue" were used by the Greeks, ἄγαλμα and εἰκών (Isocrates *Evagoras* 57). Some scholars still reflect the older view that an ἄγαλμα (like the Latin term *similacrum*) referred to a "(cult) statue," i.e., the main statue of the deity in a temple, while an εἰκών (like the Latin *imago*) referred to an "image," not used in connection with cultic worship (see Nock, *Essays* 1:204). F. W. Walbank (*CAH* 7/1:87–88), however, notes that the distinction between the two words was not always maintained. L. Robert proposed that an εἰκών was a representation of a human being, such as a living emperor or a local official, while an ἄγαλμα was a representation (normally a statue) of a god or a deified emperor. This distinction, borne out by the Latin equivalents *imago* (= εἰκών) and *simulacrum* (= ἄγαλμα) appears in Pliny *Ep.* 10.96.5–6: Pliny ordered Christians to make "offerings of wine and incense to your [i.e., 'Trajan's'] statue [*imagini tuae*] (which I had ordered to be brought into court for this purpose along with the images [*simulacris*] of the gods)." However, in Tacitus *Hist.* 5.5 and Suetonius *Div. Iul.* 88, the term *similacrum* is used of a statue of Julius Caesar (see Schowalter, *Emperor,* 5 n. 22). According to Price (*Rituals,* 178), the difference between an εἰκών and an ἄγαλμα was primarily one of *location.* Images placed in temples were generally called ἀγάλματα and were not limited to deities or deified emperors but could also be representations of private citizens who did not receive a public cult (a point confirmed by Koonce, *AJP* 109 [1988] 109). Price emphasizes that both ἀγάλματα and εἰκόνες could receive cultic worship (*Rituals,* 78). According to *Mart. Apollonius* 7, Perennis the proconsul ordered Apollonius to sacrifice "to the gods and to the image [εἰκόνι] of the emperor Commodus" (Commodus, A.D. 180–92, was the reigning emperor). In *Mart. Pionius* 5.2, the protagonist says, "we do not worship your gods, nor will we adore the golden statue [τῇ εἰκόνι τῇ χρυσῇ]" (the latter is an allusion to the golden statue of Nebuchadrezzar in Dan 3). In *Mart. Dasius* 7, Christians were asked to "venerate the statues [τοῖς εἰκόσι] of our lords the emperors." Koonce (*AJP* 109 [1988] 109–10) argues on the basis of a recently published inscription from the area of Thessaloniki, dated A.D. 1, that ἀγάλματα could be placed in conspicuous parts of an agora, i.e., in a nonsacral setting (a fact already known from Isocrates *Evagoras* 57). The mention of the εἰκών, "image," of the beast in Rev 13:14, therefore, refers to the fashioning of a cult image in honor of the emperor. On images in the imperial cult, see Cuss, *Imperial Cult,* 104–12.

The general aniconic stance of ancient Judaism is well known; see P. Prigent, *Le Judaïsme et l'image* (Tübingen: Mohr-Siebeck, 1990). In the OT Jews were encouraged to destroy idols (Exod 32:20; 34:13; Deut 7:5; 12:3; Judg 6:25–26; 2 Kgs 10:26–27; 23:6, 11–15, 20; see also 1 Macc 5:68; 13:47–48; Jos. *Ag. Ap.* 2.75), while the aniconic stance in rabbinic Judaism avoided violence but utilized the strategy of disregarding or nullifying the sacred status of pagan idols (Blidstein, *PAAJR* 42–43 [1973–74] 1–44). Proscriptions against imperial images were particularly important in Palestinian Judaism; see Urbach, *IEJ* 9 (1959) 149ff., 229ff.

14c ὃς ἔχει τὴν πληγὴν τῆς μαχαίρης καὶ ἔζησεν, "who was wounded with a sword but lived." This is a relative clause used to identify the θηρίον, "beast," with the event narrated cryptically in v 3a and repeated in v 12 with additional details: i.e., the wound was inflicted by a sword. The precise meaning of this detail is unknown, though historically it is true that Nero killed himself with a dagger (Suetonius *Nero* 49). For a similar relative clause, see v 12b. Like the relative clause in v 12, this one also appears to alter the event described in v 3, the mortal wounding of one of the seven heads of the beast (leaving six heads alive, whereas here the wound was suffered by the beast itself), and looks like an interpolation (J. Weiss, *Offenbarung,* 33–34), which functions analeptically; i.e., it refers back to the beast from the sea, linking this vision with that one.

15a καὶ ἐδόθη αὐτῷ δοῦναι πνεῦμα τῇ εἰκόνι τοῦ θηρίου, "It was permitted to give life to the cult image of the beast." This reflects the world of ancient magic in which the animation of images of the gods was an important means for securing oracles. The general Greek view was that images of the gods were not the actual gods themselves but only reminiscent of them (Cicero *De nat. deor.* 2.17; Dio Chrysostom *Or.* 12.60–61; Origen *Contra Celsum* 7.62). According to Heraclitus, people who approach lifeless things as gods act like a man who holds conversations with houses; they have no idea of the nature of gods or heroes (H. Diels and W. Kranz, *Die Fragmente der Vorsokratiker,* 6th ed. [Zürich; Hildesheim: Weidmann, 1951] 1:151–52 [Herakleitos, frag. B5]). Plato reflects this view: "we set up statues as images, and we believe that when we worship these, lifeless though they be [ἀψύχους], the living gods [τοὺς ἐμψύχους] beyond feel great good-will towards us and gratitude" (*Laws* 11.931A; LCL tr.). While ceremonies were used to consecrate cult images (Dionysius of Halicarnassus *Ant. Rom.* 8.56.2; Minucius Felix *Octavius* 23; the term for dedication is often ἱδρύειν; see Dio Chrysostom *Or.* 12.84), there is no evidence that the ancient Greeks used magical rituals for the purpose of giving life to such images (E. Bevan, *Holy Images: An Inquiry into Idolatry and Image-Worship in Ancient Paganism and in Christianity* [London: Allen & Unwin, 1940] 32; Burkert, *Greek Religion,* 91). The popular view in the Hellenistic and Roman world, however, was that the gods inhabited their statues (Plutarch *De Iside et Osiride* 379C–D; MacMullen, *Paganism,* 59–60).

There were many reports in the ancient world of statues turning (Dio Cassius 41.61; 54.7), sweating (Cicero, *De div.* 1.43.98; Plutarch *Cor.* 38.1; *Anton.* 60), weeping (Augustine *Civ. dei* 3.11), or speaking (Dionysius of Halicarnassus *Ant. Rom.* 8.56.2); several similar stories are collected in Plutarch *De pyth. orac.* 397E–398B; see C. Clarc, *Les théories relatives au Culte des Images chez les auteurs grecs du iime siècle aprés J.-C.* (Paris: Fontemoing, 1915) 45–49, and O. Weinreich, *Antike Heilungswunder* (Giessen: Töpelmann, 1909) 146. This popular view has links with the doctrine of ἔμψυχα ἀγάλματα, "animate images," which was held by some

Neoplatonists (such as Porphyry and Iambichus) and which is reflected in some of the Hermetic literature. Magical rituals for achieving animation are preserved in the magical papyri (see *PGM* XII.14–95; Hopfner, *Offenbarungszauber* 2:210–18). Christians such as Minucius Felix were convinced that unclean spirits concealed themselves inside cult images and were able to give oracles (*Octavius* 27). Much earlier, Babylonians had rituals intended to give life to statues of the gods (A. L. Oppenheim, *Ancient Mesopotamia* [Chicago: University of Chicago, 1964] 186). In ancient Egypt, beginning at an even earlier period, statues of the gods were vitalized through a ceremony of "opening the mouth" (Morenz, *Egyptian Religion,* 155–56; E. Otto, *Das altägyptische Mundöffnungsritual* [Wiesbaden, 1960]). Magical animation rituals were also performed on mummies (E. A. W. Budge, *Egyptian Magic* [New York: Dover, 1971] 201–3). The magical rituals for animating images of the gods in Egypt probably influenced that special branch of magic called theurgy, connected with Julian the Theurgist (the putative author of the *Chaldean Oracles;* see R. Majercik, *The Chaldean Oracles: Text, Translation, and Commentary* [Leiden: Brill, 1989] 1–5).

Theurgists developed a special complex of rituals called τελεστική (also called ἡ θεουργικὴ τέχνη by Iamblichus *De myst.* 5.23), which was primarily concerned with the consecration and animation of statues in order to receive oracles from them (Proclus *In Tim.* 3.6.13; *Asclepius* 3.37; see H. Lewy, *Chaldaean Oracles and Theurgy* [Paris: Études Augustiniennes, 1978] 495–96; E. R. Dodds, "Theurgy," Appendix II in *The Greeks and the Irrational* [Berkeley: University of California, 1951] 291–95). τελεστική apparently involved placing a selection of σύμβολα (various *materia magica* such as stones, herbs, animals, and scents) within the cavity of a statue for the purpose of establishing a sympathetic relationship with the god (Iamblichus *De myst.* 5.23; *Asclepius* 3.38; *Chaldaean Oracles* frag. 224). Images of the gods could thus be animated by placing those material elements that had a "sympathetic" connection with the deity inside the image, and with the prompting of a consecration ritual, the divinity could be persuaded to appear and answer oracular inquiries put to him or her by the theurgist (see Majercik, *Chaldean Oracles,* 27). This procedure is reflected in the Hermetic treatise *Asclepius* 3.38 (tr. W. Scott, *Hermetica* 1:361):

> And these gods who are called "terrestrial," Trismegistus, by what means are they induced to take up their abode among us? They are induced, Asclepius, by means of herbs and stones and scents which have in them something divine.

The doctrine of ἔμψυχα ἀγάλματα is also found in *Asclepius* 3.23B, "But the gods whose shapes are fashioned by mankind are made of both substances, that is, of the divine substance, which is purer and far nobler, and the substance which is lower than man, namely, the material of which they are wrought" (tr. W. Scott, *Hermetica* 1:339). When Asclepius doubts that Trismegistus is referring to statues, the god replies (3.24a; W. Scott, *Hermetica* 1:339–41):

> I mean statues, but statues living and conscious, filled with the breath of life [*statuas animatas sensu et spiritu plenas*], and doing many mighty works; statues which have foreknowledge, and predict future events by the drawing of lots, and by prophetic inspiration, and by dreams and in many other ways; statues which inflict diseases and heal them, dispensing sorrow and joy according to men's deserts.

The motif of statues coming to life occurs in Greek mythology; Ovid, for example, tells the story of Pygmalion, whose love turned an ivory statue named Galatea into a living woman (*Metamorphoses* 10.243–97).

15b ἵνα καὶ λαλήσῃ ἡ εἰκὼν τοῦ θηρίου, "that the cult image of the beast might speak." For the ancients, a statue that speaks is a statue that gives *oracles*. The Cynic philosopher Oenomaeus of Gadara (fl. A.D. 120), skeptical of oracles, wrote a lost work entitled Γοήτων φώρα, "On the Detection of Charlatans," preserved in fragmentary quotations in Eusebius, who summarizes his views (*Praep. evang.* 5.21.213c; Eusebius, *Preparation for the Gospel,* tr. E. H. Gifford [Oxford: Clarendon, 1903]):

> For he [Oenomaus] will not admit that the oracles which are admired among all the Greeks proceed from a daemon, much less from a god, but says that they are frauds and tricks of human imposters, cunningly contrived to deceive the multitude.

Alexander of Abonuteichos was presented by Lucian (hardly an objective reporter) as a charlatan who constructed a serpentine image representing Glaucon-Asklepios, complete with a movable mouth and concealed speaking tubes for giving oracles (*Alex.* 12–26). Similarly, Hippolytus describes a "talking skull" rigged up by combining a human skull with a windpipe of a crane to function as a speaking tube (*Ref.* 4.41). Other reports also mention talking statues (Suetonius *Gaius* 57.1; Ps.-Lucian *De Syria Dea* 10). According to Athenagoras (*Legatio* 26.3–4), statues of Nerullinus in Tralles and Peregrinus Proteus at Parium reportedly gave oracles (though whether such oracles were based on the interpretation of the "behavior" of the statues, such as movement, sweating, etc., or were thought to be communicated in human language is not mentioned; the former is more probable than the latter); see Nilsson, *GGR* 2:525. There is no evidence that imperial cult images were believed to actually give oracles, however. A close parallel to Rev 13:15 is found in the *Oracle of Hystaspes* (Lactantius *Div. Inst.* 7.17.5; tr. McDonald, *Lactantius,* 518): "He [a king from Syria] will order fire to descend from heaven, and the sun to stand still in its course and a statue to speak [*imaginem loqui*]." Plutarch reports that when a certain statue was set up in a temple, it spoke twice (*Coriolanus* 37.3). Plutarch, however, ever the rationalist, thought that articular speech from a lifeless object was impossible (*Coriolanus* 38.2). The third wonder, making a statue speak, was part of the repertoire of ancient magicians.

Religious fraud was not unknown in the ancient world. Scherrer (*JBL* 103 [1984] 601–10) has argued that "special effects equipment" were used to produce speaking and moving statues as well as simulated thunder and lightning in the imperial cult. Athenaeus reports a moving image (*Deipn.* 5.198F). Simon Magus reportedly tells Peter *statuas moveri feci, animavi exanima,* "I made statues move; I gave breath to inanimate objects" (Ps.-Clem. *Recog.* 3.47.2; cf. Ps.-Clem. *Hom.* 2.32). Theophilus *Ad Autolycum* 1.8, speaking to pagans, observes "you believe that statues [ἀγάλματα] made by men are gods and work miracles." According to Philostratus, *Vita Apoll.* 1.27, a satrap in charge of the gates of Babylon required that everyone who entered the city first worship a golden image (χρυσῆν εἰκόνα) of the king, though this requirement was not made of emissaries from the Roman emperor, and Apollonius himself also refused to perform this ritual (1.28).

15c καὶ ποιήσῃ ὅσοι ἐὰν μὴ προσκυνήσωσιν τῇ εἰκόνι τοῦ θηρίου ἀποκτανθῶσιν, "and cause whoever did not worship the cult image of the beast to be executed." The subject of the aorist subjunctive ποιήσῃ, "he might cause," is ambiguous. Since it is parallel to λαλήσῃ, "he might speak," in v 15b, the subject of which is ἡ εἰκών, "the cult statue," it is logical to understand ἡ εἰκών as the subject of ποιήσῃ so that it is the speaking statue who causes those who refuse it worship to be executed. It is possible, however, that the logical subject of ποιήσῃ is the second beast, acting on behalf of the first beast, who orders the executions. The execution of those who resist appears to be a doublet of v 7, in which it is said that the first beast made war on the saints and conquered them. Philo claims that the emperor Gaius organized "a great and truceless war" against the Jews for refusing to worship him (*Leg.* 119), though the historicity of this claim is doubtful (Bilde, *ST* 32 [1978] 72–73). Here the image of the beast is apparently given *exclusive* worship, though this is not characteristic of either Greek or Roman religious protocol.

According to some scholars, allegiance to Rome meant the worship of Caesar (Syme, *Tacitus* 2:469). Yet the primary issue reflected in the sources is not simply sacrificing to the emperor (strictly speaking the living emperor was not a *divus,* "god," until he was officially enrolled with the gods after his death by an act of the Senate, though two emperors, Gaius and Domitian, apparently claimed to be gods during their lifetime; see *Comment* on 4:11) but sacrificing to the gods (Pliny *Ep.* 10.97.1; *Acts Carpus* [Greek Rec.] 4; *Mart. Fruct.* 2.2; *Mart. Justin* 5.8). Yet toward the end of the second century A.D. Tertullian observed that the twin charges against Christians were that they did not worship the gods and they did not sacrifice on behalf of the emperors (*pro imperatoribus; Apol.* 10.1). The problem is understanding what is involved in the term προσκυνεῖν, "worship." Did this involve compulsory sacrificing to the emperor along with the other gods? In Pliny *Ep.* 10.96.5 (LCL tr.), the sincerity of *apostate* Christians was tested only by requiring that they sacrifice to the gods:

> Among these [i.e., those denounced as Christians] I considered that I should dismiss any who denied that they were or ever had been Christians when they had repeated after me a formula of invocation to the gods and had made offerings of wine and incense to your statue (which I had ordered to be brought into court for this purpose along with the images of the gods), and furthermore had reviled the name of Christ: none of which things, I understand, any genuine Christian can be induced to do.

The execution of Christians or Jews in connection with their rejection of the eschatological antagonist is reflected in *Apoc. Pet.* 2, where it is said that when the deceiver (who is not the Christ) is rejected, he will kill many with the sword.

16a καὶ ποιεῖ πάντας, τοὺς μικροὺς καὶ τοὺς μεγάλους, καὶ τοὺς πλουσίους καὶ τοὺς πτωχούς, καὶ τοὺς ἐλευθέρους καὶ τοὺς δούλους, "It forced everyone, unimportant and important, rich and poor, free and slave." The subject of ποιεῖ, "forced," is clearly the second beast. The first term, πάντας, "all," is comprehensive; then the following terms describe in various ways the social polarities that make up the "all." These antithetical terms (the rhetorical term is *divisio* or *merismus,* i.e., dividing a whole into its parts) constitute a figure of speech used to express the notion of totality (see P. Boccaccio, "I termini contrari come espressione della totalità in ebraico," *Bib* 33 [1952] 173–90; A. M. Honeyman, "Merismus in Biblical Hebrew," *JBL* 71 [1952] 11–18). The use of the stereotyped expression "insignificant and important," literally "small and great," occurs four times elsewhere in Revelation (11:18; 19:5, 18; 20:12) and often appears to be a redactional element used to unify the composition; in 19:18 it is accompanied by an analogous antithetical pair, "free and slave," as here in 13:16. A similar, but much larger, inclusive list occurs in Rev 19:18 (see *Comment* there). The phrase "the least and the greatest" as an idiom connoting social inclusivity occurs with some frequency in the OT and early Jewish literature (Gen 19:11; Deut 1:17; 1 Kgs 22:31; 2 Kgs 23:2; 25:26; 1 Chr 12:14; 25:8; 26:13; 2 Chr 18:30; 34:30; Job 3:19; Wis 6:7; Jdt 13:4, 13; Jer 6:13; 31:34[LXX 38:34]; 1 Macc 5:45) as well as in the NT (Acts 8:10; 26:22; Heb 8:11 [quoting Jer 38:34]). Used in this way the phrase "small and great" is an idiom meaning the totality of people of all ages or all stations in life, found in both Semitic and Greek literature.

A specifically Semitic idiom is מִקָּטֹן וְעַד־גָּדוֹל *miqqāṭōn wĕʿad gādôl,* "from small to great" (Gen 19:11), which occurs more than thirty times in the OT (*TDOT* 2:398–400), though there are also Greek parallels (e.g., Ign. [long rec.] *Ad Philippenses* 15.1, ἀπὸ μικροῦ ἕως μεγάλου; see also *Ad Antiochenos* 12.3; *Ad Hieronem* 8.2). The more typical Greek form of this idiom is μικρῷ τε καὶ μεγάλῳ, "to both small and great" (Acts 26:22). The phrase "small and great" is also applied to minor and major things (2 Chr 36:18; Amos 8:5; 2 Macc 5:20; 1 Esdr 1:54; Sir 5:15; 29:23; Plutarch *Pericles* 17.1; *Pompey* 57.1; *Quaest. conv.* 730A; Epictetus 2.19.29; 2.23.28; Ign. [long rec.] *Phld.* 6.9). It also occurs in the magical papyri in formulaic contexts in which the practitioner wishes to be inclusive: *PGM* 21.21, πρὸς πάντας ἀνθρώπους, μικροὺς καὶ μεγάλους, "for all people, small and great," an example of *merismus.* In *PGM* XXXV.17–19 the magician demands favor, influence, victory, and strength "before everyone, small men and great [ἔμπροσθεν πάντων, ἀνδρῶν μικρῶν καὶ μεγάλων], as well as gladiators, soldiers, civilians, women, girls, boys, and everybody [καὶ πάντων]." "Small and great" as groups or classes at the opposite end of the social pyramid are also referred to in Rev 11:18; 20:12 (see Wis 6:7; Jonah 3:5; Jer 6:13). *PGM* XII.49 refers to those whom the magical practitioner desires power over: "men or women, small or great." Similarly, *PGM* XV.18 refers to spirits the magician wants under his control: "whether male or female, small or great." In a magical procedure from the *Sepher ha-Razim* 1.135–40 (tr. Morgan, 34) we find the same inclusive language: "You angels who go around and circulate in the world, bring around (to me) all the citizens of this city, great and small, old and young, lowly and distinguished." In a famous inscription describing the foundation and regulations of a mystery cult published most recently by Sokolowski (*Lois,* 53–58, no. 20), the phrase "men and women, free persons and slaves" occurs three times (lines 5–6, 15–16, 53–54) of those who could have access to the cult (i.e., everyone). The term μικροί, literally "small ones," is a designation for people with little power or influence and is sometimes a term for disciples of Jesus (Matt 10:42; 18:6 = Mark 9:42 = Luke 17:2; Matt 18:10).

16b ἵνα δῶσιν αὐτοῖς χάραγμα ἐπὶ τῆς χειρὸς αὐτῶν τῆς δεξιᾶς ἢ ἐπὶ τὸ μέτωπον αὐτῶν, "to receive a brand on their right hand or on their forehead." The two motifs of the brand and the worship of the beast are connected not only here in vv 15–16 but also in 14:11; 15:2; 19:20; 20:4, though the prohibition of buying and selling occurs only here. The reception of the brand appears to be a *private* act of piety (or impiety), while the worship of the beast is a *public* action (J. Weiss, *Offenbarung,* 18). The only other place in Revelation where the possibility of having a brand on *both* the right hand and forehead occurs in 14:9. This same combination occurs in the Coptic *Apoc. Elijah* 2.7–8, which is probably dependent on Revelation (tr. Pietersma-Comstock, *Apocalypse of Elijah*): "I will write my name upon their foreheads and set a seal on their right hands."

There is a striking parallel to this verse in Lactantius *Div. Inst.* 7.17.7 (tr. McDonald, *Lactantius,* 518): "Those who believe and come to him will be branded by him as though cattle [*signabuntur ab eo tamquam pecudes*]; those who reject his mark will either flee into the mountains, or they will be seized and killed by well-contrived tortures." According to 3 Macc 2:28–29, Ptolemy IV Philopater (221–204 B.C.) inaugurated a program of persecution against Egyptian Jews in which he required them to enroll in a census and to be branded [χαράσσεσθαι] with the ivy leaf of Dionysus; those who did not cooperate were executed (it is likely that Ptolemy IV, who was particularly devoted to Dionysus, himself sported an ivy-leaf brand; see M. Hadas, *The Third and Fourth Book of Maccabees* [New York: Ktav, 1953] 45).

While the "mark of the beast" has a traditional basis in Ezek 9 and *Pss. Sol.* 15:9–10, and some scholars have preferred to understand it as a traditional eschatological motif (Bousset [1906] 132–33), others have suggested that a reference to one or another contemporary historical practice is also presupposed (Charles, 1:362–63; Judge, *TynBul* 42 [1991] 158–60). There are at least four possibilities: (1) as a reference to Jewish *tephillin* or phylacteries (Charles, 1:362–63; C. Schneider, *TDNT* 4:635–37); (2) as a reference to the tattooing of slaves, soldiers, or the devotees of a particular deity; (3) as a reference to Roman coins used to buy and sell commodities (Caird, 173; Stauffer, *Die Caesaren,* 126, 179; Kraft, 182–83; Yarbro Collins, *JBL* 96 [1977] 253–54); and (4) as a reference to imperial seals (Deissmann, *Light,* 341).

Each of these requires some comment. (1) Jewish *tefillin* (also called φυλακτήρια or "phylacteries") are leather boxes or amulets containing Scripture passages and are worn on the hand and forehead (*Ep. Arist.* 159; Matt 23:5; Jos. *Ant.* 4.213; *m. Šeb.* 3:8, 11). Though the hand phylactery is traditionally worn on the *left* arm (facing the heart), the χάραγμα of the beast is described as marking the *right* hand and forehead. Despite this slight discrepancy, the wearing of *tefillin* could be a model for the mark of the beast. (2) In connection with *tattoos on slaves or soldiers,* χάραγμα is a term that always means "brand" when applied to human or animal skin (Ysebaert, *Greek Baptismal Terminology,* 285). On the basis of no concrete evidence, Judge speculates that those entering the market of Ephesus, after first sacrificing, received a marking in ink on their wrist or forehead (as in Ezek 9:2–6), giving them the right to buy and sell (*TynBul* 42 [1991] 158–60). (3) The connection of buying and selling with the χάραγμα of the beast has been understood as a reference to the use of Roman coins, which bore the portraits and names of Roman emperors (Kraybill, *Imperial Cult,* 138–39). The inability to buy or sell would then be the result of refusing to use Roman coins. This has a parallel in the Jewish prohibition of images, which for some, such as the Zealots, included the image of the emperor on Roman coins (Hengel, *Zealots,* 190–95). However, the mark is said to be made on the right hand and forehead of people, which would exclude coins (Beckwith, 641; Charles, 1:363 n. 1). (4) Deissmann (*Bible Studies,* 240–47; id., *Light,* 345) found evidence in the papyri for a stamp printed on deeds of sale with the name and year of the reigning emperor and called a χάραγμα. Deissmann observed that the brand embodied the name or number of the beast (v 17), concerned buying and selling (v 16), and was technically known as a χάραγμα (*Bible Studies,* 241–42). An example of such an imperial seal is pictured in *Bible Studies,* 243, and *Light,* fig. 51. Some examples of these stamps found on papyri include one that reads [Αὐτ]οκρ[άτορος], "emperor," and Δομ[ιτιανοῦ], "Domitian," and another that reads on the outer circle [Αὐτ]οκράτορος Καίσαρος Ν[ερούα Τραϊανοῦ], "Emperor Caesar Nero Trajan"; see Deissmann, *Bible Studies,* 243–44. However, there is no evidence that *people* were stamped on their hands or foreheads (Swete, 173; Roloff [ET] 164).

The term χάραγμα occurs seven times in Revelation, always of the brand indicating loyalty to the beast (13:16, 17; 14:9, 11; 16:2; 19:20; 20:4). Three times this brand is referred to as located on either the forehead or the right hand (13:16; 14:9; 20:4). Christians, on the other hand, are spoken of as having the σφραγίς, "seal," of God on their foreheads (7:4; 9:4). This "seal" is spoken of in 7:2 as in the possession of an angel, who then proceeds to "seal" 12,000 from each of the twelve tribes of Israel (7:4[2x], 5, 8). There can be little doubt that this brand is a parody of the seal of God that is placed on the foreheads of his servants (7:3; 9:4).

17a καὶ ἵνα μή τις δύνηται ἀγοράσαι ἢ πωλῆσαι, "so that no one can buy or sell." The inability "to buy and sell" apparently refers to the interdiction of basic and essential economic activity. Whether this passage refers to a real or imagined situation has been the subject of debate. Ramsay understood this passage to refer to an otherwise unknown formal or informal economic boycott against Christians (Ramsay, *Letters,* 105–8). Hemer suggests that this passage refers to an existing problem and proposes that Thyatira was the most likely place where the imperial cult was connected to the "pagan system" so that Christians who did not participate could face commercial ruin (*Letters,* 126–27). Hemer is presumably referring to the presence of many trade guilds in Thyatira (*Letters,* 108–9; the epigraphical evidence for the presence of various guilds is listed on p. 246 n. 10). He rightly emphasizes the religious basis of such guilds, a feature that is analyzed in great detail by Kraybill (*Imperial Cult,* 113–41). Several prominent features of guilds emerge: (1) they were voluntary, private associations; (2) people from various strata of society could belong to the same guild (e.g., Roman citizens, resident foreigners, freedmen, slaves); (3) they were primarily social organizations not directly concerned with the business activities of their members; and (4) they generally had a cultic character, and many guilds in the imperial period gave some expression to the imperial cult. The guilds did not generally function as trade unions in the modern sense of the term, and they rarely if ever engaged in strikes or boycotts. Membership in the guilds, however, inevitably entailed participation in cultic ritual, which included eating the meat of sacrificial victims, a practice to which John was unalterably opposed (Charles, 1:69; Giesen [1997] 314–15). For the author, then, membership in the guilds was antithetical to faith in Christ (Yarbro Collins, *Crisis and Catharsis,* 124). It is possible that this economic function of the brand in v 17a was added, along with v 17b, by the author as a final redactional gloss (Flusser, "Hystaspes," 58). In general, Roman antipathy to the religious practices of various mystery cults, Judaism, and Christianity did not take the form of economic sanctions (Caird, 173).

17b εἰ μὴ ὁ ἔχων τὸ χάραγμα τὸ ὄνομα τοῦ θηρίου ἢ τὸν ἀριθμὸν τοῦ ὀνόματος αὐτοῦ, "unless he has, as a brand, the name of the beast or the number of its name." In Pindar *Olymp.* 3.29–30, the poet refers to a doe with golden horns that Taygete had inscribed with the name "Artemis," to whom she devoted the animal. This suggests that bearing the name of a divinity indicates divine ownership.

18a Ὧδε ἡ σοφία ἐστίν. ὁ ἔχων νοῦν ψηφισάτω τὸν ἀριθμὸν τοῦ θηρίου, ἀριθμὸς γὰρ ἀνθρώπου ἐστίν, "Here is wisdom. Let the one with understanding calculate the number of the beast, for it is also a number referring to a person." This verse is an explanatory redactional addition by the author-editor to the vision narrated in 13:11–17, much like 13:9–10 is an explanatory addition to 13:1–8. The introductory phrase Ὧδε ἡ σοφία ἐστίν. ὁ ἔχων νοῦν, "Here is wisdom. The one with understanding," has an extremely close parallel in 17:9: ὧδε ὁ νοῦς ὁ ἔχων σοφίαν, "This requires deep insight." The phrase ἔχειν νοῦς means "to have understanding" and is perhaps an allusion to Dan 12:10, "None of the wicked shall understand, but those who are wise shall understand [LXX οἱ διανοούμενοι προσέξουσιν; Theod οἱ νοήμονες συνήσουσιν]" (the same passage is also alluded to in Rev 22:11). Similar appeals to the understanding of the readers are found in other apocalyptic or prophetic contexts. In Mark 13:14, after the mention of "the desolating sacrilege set up where it ought not to be," the author inserts a parenthetic remark that calls attention to a new interpretation of Dan 11:31; 12:11: "let the reader understand [ὁ ἀναγινώσκων νοείτω]" (see H. A. Guy, "Mark 13:14: ὁ ἀναγινώσκων νοείτω," *ExpTim* 65 [1953–54] 30). Similarly, in *Barn.* 4:4–6, the author quotes from Dan 7:24 and 7:7–8 (the ten horns and the little horn of the fourth beast) and then says "You ought to understand [συνιέναι οὖν ὀφείλετε]." However, neither in Rev 13:18 nor in Rev 17:9 nor in the other parallels cited is there any *explicit* mention of the necessity for divinely aided insight into the meaning or meanings of the visions in question, as there is, for example, in the Joseph stories (Gen 40:8; 41:15–16) and the court tales of Daniel (1:17; 2:19, 30; 5:11–12; 8:15). In nonapocalyptic contexts, the saying "The one who is able to receive this, let him receive it" concludes a group of sayings on marriage in Matt 19:12, and a possible allusion to this saying is found in Ign. *Smyrn.* 6:1, "The one who receives, let him receive."

The phrase τὸν ἀριθμὸν τοῦ θηρίου, "the number of the beast," which we learn is also the number of a person, may refer to the fact that when the Greek word θηρίον, "beast," is transliterated into Hebrew, תריון *trywn,* the numerical value of these letters is 666: ת = 400; ר = 200; י = 10; ו = 6; נ = 50 (Hadorn, 146; *TDNT* 1:463; Bauckham, "Nero and the Beast," 389).

The phrase ἀριθμὸς γὰρ ἀνθρώπου ἐστίν, "for it is also a number referring to a person," is problematic, for ἀνθρώπου, "person," can be understood in at least two different ways: (1) ἀνθρώπου can be used in a generic sense (Mussies, *Morphology,* 81–82) so that the phrase ἀριθμὸς ἀνθρώπου can mean a number calculable according to human reckoning, not an unknowable divine number (cf. Rev 21:17), or the number only of a beast (Swete, 174–75). (2) ἀνθρώπου can be non-generic (Mussies, *Morphology,* 81–82) and refer to a specific individual, i.e., "for it is the number of a [certain] person" (Bousset [1906] 370–71; Charles, 2:365; Prigent, 214). The translation suggests that the second view is the correct one. This appeal to the reader (with parallels in 13:9–10; 14:12; 17:9) indicates that the beast is not a *future* but rather a *present* figure whose identity was probably well known to the readers of the book. ἀνθρώπου may lack an article because it is modeled after the Hebrew construct state, which is always anarthrous. An important parallel is Rev 21:17, where we find the phrase μέτρον ἀνθρώπου ὅ ἐστιν ἀγγέλου, "by human measurement, the same as angelic measurement," where ἀνθρώπου is clearly used generically. Rev 21:17, and possibly 13:18, reflects the ancient view that there are two languages or systems operative in the cosmos, the divine and the human (see *Comment* on 19:12).

18b καὶ ὁ ἀριθμὸς αὐτοῦ ἑξακόσιοι ἑξήκοντα ἕξ, "and the number of this person is six hundred sixty-six." That the number of the beast, "666," is in the masculine gender cannot be used as an argument supporting the identification of the beast as an individual man since it is probably in the masculine gender by virtue of having been attracted to the case of the preceding noun, ἀριθμός, "number" (see Mussies, *Morphology,* 225).

The symbolic meaning of the number 666 has been one of the most debated issues in the interpretation of Revelation. There are three major approaches to solving the meaning of this obviously symbolic number: (1) gematria, (2) triangular numbers, and (3) the general symbolic significance of numbers in apocalyptic literature (see *Excursus 13C* for a full discussion). One of the traditional Pythagorean *akousmata,* "oral teachings," is "What is the most wise? Number or that which gives names to things" (Aelian *Varia Historia* 4.17; cf. Iamblichus *Vita Pythagorica* 82; see W. Burkert, *Lore and Science in Ancient Pythagoreanism,* tr. E. L. Minar, Jr. [Cambridge: Harvard UP, 1972] 169 n. 22).

The ancient Christian commentators speculated on the name that might fit this numerical code. The earliest attempt to solve the riddle of 666 in Rev 13:18 was that of Irenaeus (*Adv. haer.* 5.30.3, followed by Hippolytus *De ant.* 50), who assumed that the name must be Greek and suggested three names for which the numerical values of the constituent letters total 666, Evanthas, Lateinos, and Teitan: ΕΥΑΝΘΑΣ (Ε = 5; Υ = 400; Α = 1; Ν = 50; Θ = 9; Α = 1; Σ = 200; total = 666), ΛΑΤΕΙΝΟΣ (Λ = 30; Α = 1; Τ = 300; Ε = 5; Ι = 10; Ν = 50; Ο = 70; Σ = 200; total = 666), and ΤΕΙΤΑΝ (Τ = 300; Ε = 5; Ι = 10; Τ = 300; Α = 1; Ν = 50; total = 666). In Ps.-Hippolytus *De consummatione mundi* 28 (ed. H. Achelis, *Schriften,* 301), the unknown author suggests the name ΑΡΝΟΥΜΕ (Α = 1; Ρ = 100; Ν = 50; Ο = 70; Υ = 40; Μ = 400; Ε = 5; total = 666), which means "deny me." Victorinus also used the name "Teitan" as an example of a name whose numerical values totaled 666 (*Comm. in Apoc.;* Haussleiter, *Victorinus,* 124), and he also suggests the names ΓΕΝΣΗΡΙΚΟΣ and ΑΝΤΕΜΟΣ, which similarly add up to 666 (Haussleiter, *Victorinus,* 125, 127).

This gematria riddle was probably formulated with the name of a specific individual in mind, and many commentators have thought that this person must be Nero. The Aramaic transliteration of "Nero Caesar" from Greek is קסרא נרון *qsrʾ nrwn,* the final aleph producing the numerical total 667, and therefore an invalid solution (unless the final quiescent aleph is not counted, in which case the total would be 666; see Driver, "The Number of the Beast," 79). However, the normal Hebrew transliteration of "Nero Caesar" is קיסר נרון *qysr nrwn,* but the numerical value of these letters is 676 (since the yod following the qoph has a numerical value of ten). If the name of "Nero Caesar" is transliterated into Hebrew from the Greek to form קסר נרון, the numerical value is 666: נרון *nrwn* = 306 plus קסר *qsr* = 360, making 666 (נ = 50; ר = 200; ו = 6; נ = 50; ק = 100; ס = 60; ר = 200). This possibility appears to have been confirmed by the discovery of an Aramaic document at Wadi Murabbaʿat that transliterates the name and title of Nero as קסר נרון *qsr nrwn,* "Neron Caesar," from the Greek form of the name, with the combined numerical value of 666 (Benoit et al., *Les grottes,* 100–104; Hillers, *BASOR* 170 [1963] 65), and most scholars agree that this is the most likely solution. One possible origin for 616 as a variant of 666 in the MS tradition is the fact that the Latin form "Nero Caesar" transliterated in Hebrew characters is spelled נרו קסר *nrw qsr,* the numerical equivalent of which is 616: נרו *nrw* = 256 plus קסר *qsr* = 360 (נ = 50; ר = 200; ו = 6; ק

= 100; ס = 60; ר = 200). On the association of Nero with the beast of Revelation, it is important to take account of the evidence from ancient writers that designate Nero as a θηρίον, "beast" (Philostratus *Vit. Apoll.* 4.38; *Sib. Or.* 5.343; 8.157).

A more complex solution has been proposed by Stauffer ("666," 237–41), who argues that the Greek name of Domitian, ΔΟΜΙΤΙΑΝΟΣ (= 755), complete with his official titles, was ΑΥΤΟΚΡΑΤΩΡ ΚΑΙΣΑΡ ΔΟΜΕΤΙΑΝΟΣ ΣΕΒΑΣΤΟΣ ΓΕΡΜΑΝΙΚΟΣ, occasionally found abbreviated on coins as Α ΚΑΙ ΔΟΜΕΤ ΣΕΒ ΓΕ (= 666):

Αυτοκρατωρ = 1	= 1
ΚΑΙσαρ = 20 + 1 + 10	= 31
ΔΟΜΕΤιανος = 4 + 70 + 40 + 5 + 300	= 419
ΣΕΒαστος = 200 + 5 + 2	= 207
ΓΕρμανικος = 3 + 5	= 8
Total	666

Excursus 13C: 666 and Gematria

Bibliography

Bauckham, R. "Nero and the Beast." In R. Bauckham, *Climax.* 384–452. **Bergh van Eysinga, G. A. van den.** "Die in der Apokalypse bekämpfte Gnosis." *ZNW* 13 (1912) 293–306. **Bohak, G.** "Greek-Hebrew Gematrias in *3 Baruch* and in Revelation." *JSP* 7 (1990) 119–21. **Bonner, C.** "The Numerical Value of a Magical Formula." *JES* 16 (1930) 6–9. **Dornseiff, F.** *Das Alphabet in Mystik und Magie.* 2nd ed. Leipzig; Berlin: Teubner, 1925. 91–118. **Forstner, D.** *Die Welt der Symbole.* 2nd ed. Innsbruck: Tyrolia, 1967. **Hvalvik, R.** "Barnabas 9.7–9 and the Author's Supposed Use of Gematria." *NTS* 33 (1987) 276–82. **Lieberman, S.** *Hellenism.* **Sambursky, S.** "On the Origin and Significance of the Term 'Gematria.'" *JJS* 29 (1978) 35–38. **Stauffer, E.** "666," *ConNT* 11 (1947) 237–44.

(1) Most interpreters have assumed that the number 666 in Rev 13:18 is a clear biblical example of *gematria* (a Hebrew loanword from the Greek term γεωμετρία, meaning "manipulation with numbers"), a form of coded wordplay in which the letters of the alphabet are assigned numerical values based on their position in the alphabet (Forstner, *Symbole,* 29–63). The appropriate Greek term is ἰσόψηφος, "equal in numerical value." Rule 29 of the 32 *Middot* (i.e., hermeneutical "rules" of the Haggadah) is *gematria* (for a translation of these *Middot,* see H. L. Strack, *Introduction to the Talmud and Midrash* [New York: Jewish Publication Society of America, 1931] 95–98). Possible examples of *gematria* are found both in the OT (G. R. Driver, "The Number of the Beast," 75–77) and in the NT (Driver, "The Number of the Beast," 77–78).

There are two types of gematria: (a) Gematria as an *exegetical method* was based on the mysterious significance accorded to numbers in sacred or traditional texts. All or parts of a given word in a traditional text are converted into a significant number, or a particular number found in a traditional text is converted into its significant alphabetical equivalent, which explains the hidden or encoded meaning of the number. Seneca reported that a grammarian named Apion claimed that by the first two letters of the Iliad, MH (M = 40; H = 8), Homer indicated the total number of books into which the Iliad and Odyssey were divided, i.e., twenty-four books each or forty-eight altogether (Seneca *Ep.* 88.40–41; unfortunately for this ancient theory, the book divisions in the Homeric epics were not made by the author-editors but were probably made during the Hellenistic period). In rabbinic tradition, the number 318 for the servants of Abraham mentioned in Gen 14:14 was understood as a gematria for Eliezer, a servant of Abraham, since the sum of the numerical value of the consonants in his name is 318 (*b. Ned.* 32a). A related (competing?) early Christian example of this type of gematria as an exegetical method occurs in *Barn.* 9:8; the number 318 for the men circumcised by Abraham (combining Gen 17:23 with 14:14) is understood as a reference to the first two letters of the name Ἰησοῦς, "Jesus" (I = 10; H = 8) and to the cross in the shape of the Greek letter tau (T = 300).

(b) In a second type of gematria, words or names independent of traditional texts are coded and transformed into *riddles* by converting them into numbers. Examples of such numerical riddles are found in Lucian *Alex.* 11 (a prophecy of Alexander of Abunoteichos); the *Palatine Anthology* 14.20, 105 (containing riddles based on the numerical values of letters); *Sib. Or.* 1.137–46 (a riddle on a name for God, which has not been solved); 1.324–30 (a Christian interpolation in which the number 888 stands for the Greek form of the name Ἰησοῦς: I = 10; H = 8; Σ = 200; O = 70; Υ = 400; Σ = 200). *Sib. Or.* 5.1–51 (the latest section of *Sib. Or.* 5, probably written before A.D. 132) is a prophecy of world leaders from Alexander to Hadrian, including eleven emperors referred to by gematria, i.e., numbers representing the first initials of their names. Deissmann cited two graffiti from Pompeii that fall into this category, both in Greek: "I love her whose number is 545 [ΦΜΕ]," and "The number of her honorable name is 45 (or 1035)" (*Light,* 276). In the later *Sibylline Oracles* (books 11 and 12 can be dated to about A.D. 235, book 13 to ca. A.D. 265, and book 14 was given final form by the seventh century A.D.), rulers, primarily Roman emperors, are referred to by numerals symbolizing their names (11.91) but more usually their initials (11.29–30, 92, 114, 189–90, 208, 256, 266; 12.39, 49–50, 68, 78, 96, 101, 121, 125, 144, 148, 189, 207, 246, 250, 258; 13.83–84; 14.21, 28, 44, 59–60, 79, 95, 106, 126, 137, 150, 163, 227, 248).

The major problem of decipherment lies in the fact that many different words or names can have the same numerical value. Yet it is important to observe that in all the riddles cited above, *a proper name is the answer to the riddle.*

A variation of this second type of gematria (proposed by M. Oberweis, *ZNW* 77 [1986] 226–41) consists in a number that is expressly formulated to be turned into its alphabetical equivalent. Since 666 cannot be written as a sensible Greek word because the alphabetic numeral for 6 is the archaic digamma (𝔓[47] and 051 write the number with the alphabetic numerals χ = 600, ξ = 60, digamma = 6), Oberweis prefers Hebrew, in which all letters stand for adjectival numerals. He proposes that the Greek verb ψηφισάτω in 13:18 be translated "write a number in numerals/letters," and therefore he suggests that the alphabetical Hebrew equivalent of 666 is תרסו (a second-person masculine plural qal imperfect meaning "you [masculine plural] should destroy"), a supposed allusion to Amos 6:11 also reflected in Rev 13:16. However, this Hebrew verb makes little sense in context since it is a second-person masculine plural.

(2) *666 as a triangular number.* Triangular numbers (known to Aristotle *Meteorologica* 1092b) are those that are the sum of a consecutive series of integers beginning with 1. Thus (according to Lohmeyer, 118–19), 666 is a triangular number of 36 (i.e., the sum of the integers 1 through 36 is 666), while 36 is itself the triangular number of 8 (i.e., the sum of the integers 1 through 8); in 17:11 the beast is specifically designated as "the eighth." A triangular number is understood to have the same symbolic significance as the last integer used to calculate it. However, the weakness of this view is that it is tautological: the number of the beast (666) is converted into another number (36) that represents the beast. Why should such a simplistic procedure require the wisdom and insight of the reader as 13:18a suggests (see Oberweis, *ZNW* 77 [1986] 227)? Bergh van Eysinga (*ZNW* 13 [1912] 293–306) has argued that the mention of the eighth king in Rev 17:11 underscores the importance of the number 8. The sum of the numbers from 1 through 8 is 36 (1 + 2 + 3 + 4 + 5 + 6 + 7 + 8 = 36). The significance of the number 36 becomes apparent since the sum of all the numbers from 1 through 36 is 666. However, this only reveals that the person whose number is 666 is identical with the eighth king of Rev 17:11, but it does not indicate the identity of that king (Peerbolte, *Antichrist,* 151).

(3) *666 as a symbolic or apocalyptic number.* Revelation contains many numbers that clearly have symbolic significance (e.g., 7, 12, 1,000, 12,000, 144,000) yet do not represent encoded words or names. Since 666 represents the only probable example of gematria in Revelation, it is possible that it should be interpreted more generally. A similar cryptogram for a divine name occurs in *PGM* II.128, "you have given me as a gift the knowledge of your great name, of which the number [ψῆφος] is 9999." Though this papyrus is written in Greek, the number 9999 is written not in numeral adjectives (as 666 is in Rev 13:18) but in alphabetic numbers and signs (theta = 9; sampi = 900; koppa = 90; theta prime = 9,000). Therefore, 9999 cannot be converted into a sensible Greek word since it must be written using two signs that are not part of the Greek alphabet. This reflects the so-called Chabrax formula found on magical papyri and gems (χαβραχ φνεσχηρ φιχρο γνυρω φωχω βωχ), which means "the greatest name, whose number is 9999"; i.e., the letters of the Chabrax formula have the numerical sum of 9999 (Bonner, *JES* 16 [1930] 6–9; id., *Magical Amulets,* 141–42; id., "A Miscellany of Engraved Stones," *Hesperia* 23 [1954] 145). The Pythagorean tradition associated numbers with the gods, though nine was associated with strength and constraint because it held back other numbers in the decad and was called Okeanos, the boundary of earth, and Prometheus, because of its strength (P. Gorman, *Pythagoras* [London: Routledge & Keegan Paul, 1979] 151).

Excursus 13D: The Provincial League (Koinon) of Asia

Bibliography

Buckler, W. H., and **Robinson, W. H.** *Greek and Latin Inscriptions.* Sardis: Publications of the American Society for the Excavation of Sardis 7/1. Leiden: Brill, 1932. **Deininger, J.** *Die Provinziallandtage der römischen Kaiserzeit von Augustus bis zum Ende des dritten Jahrhunderts n. Chr.* Munich; Berlin: Beck, 1965. **Duckworth, H. T. F.** "The Roman Provincial System." In *The Beginnings of Christianity.* Part 1: *The Acts of the Apostles,* ed. F. J. Foakes Jackson and K. Lake. London: Macmillan, 1920. 1:171–217. **Ehrenberg, V.** *Der Staat der Griechen.* 2nd ed. Leipzig: Teubner, 1957. ——— and **Jones, A. H. M.** *Documents Illustrating the Reigns of Augustus and Tiberius.* 2nd ed. Oxford: Clarendon, 1955. **Frank, T.** "Representive Government in the Ancient Polities." *CJ* 14 (1918–19) 549. **Guiraud, P.** *Les Assemblées provinciales dans l'Émpire romain.* Paris: Impremerie Nationale, 1887. **Horsley, G. H. R.** "The Inscriptions of Ephesos and the New Testament." *NovT* 34 (1992) 105–68. **Jones, A. H. M.** *The Cities of the Eastern Roman Provinces.* 2nd ed. Ed. M. Avi-Jonah. Amsterdam: Hakkert, 1983. **Kearsley, R. A.** "Asiarchs, *Archiereis,* and the *Archiereiai* of Asia." *GRBS* 27 (1986) 183–92. **Kornemann, E.** "Concilium." *RE* 4/1:803–20. ———. "Κοινόν." *RESup* 4:929–41. **Larsen, J. A. O.** *Representative Government in Greek and Roman History.* Berkeley; Los Angeles: University of California, 1955. ———. "The Position of Provincial Assemblies in the Government and Society of the Late Roman Empire." *CP* 29 (1934) 209–20. **Magie, D.** *Roman Rule in Asia Minor.* 2 vols. Princeton: Princeton UP, 1950. **Monceaux, P.** *De communi Asiae provinciae* (ΚΟΙΝΟΝ ΑΣΙΑΣ). Paris: Thorin, 1885. **Moretti, L.** "ΚΟΙΝΑ ΑΣΙΑΣ." *RF* n.s. 32 (1954) 276–89. **Oliver, J. H.** *The Sacred Gerousia.* Athens: American School of Classical Studies, 1941. **Rossner, M.** "Asiarchen und *Archiereis Asiae." Studii Clasice* 16 (1974) 101–42. **Taylor, L. R.** "The Asiarchs." In *The Beginnings of Christianity.* Part 1: *The Acts of the Apostles.* London: Macmillan, 1920. 5:256–62.

During the period when Revelation was written, the provincial league of the cities of Asia was called, as it had been for more than a century, τὸ κοινὸν τῶν ἀπὸ τῆς Ἀσίας Ἑλλήνων, "the league [or 'commonality'] of the Greeks in Asia," or οἱ ἀπὸ τῆς Ἀσίας Ἕλληνες, "the Greeks in Asia," i.e., like the Greeks of the Achaean peninsula but living apart from them (see Ehrenberg-Jones, *Documents,* no. 300.3–4; Deininger, *Provinziallandtage,* 36). It was also referred to as simply the κοινὸν Ἀσίας, "league of Asia," or, in Latin, *Commune Asiae.*

Unfortunately, little is known of the organization and character of provincial *concilia* or κοινά apart from inscriptional and numismatic evidence, notices in a few ancient authors (Tacitus, Pliny, and particularly Strabo 14.3.3), and preserved imperial *rescripta* in later compilations of Roman law.

In spite of the great size of the Roman empire, the provincial *concilia* or κοινά appear to have been remarkably uniform throughout the first three centuries A.D. (Deininger, *Provinziallandtage,* 6). This type of political organization was adapted by the Romans from Hellenistic models so that leagues of the eastern provinces of Rome remained fundamentally Hellenistic in character. The real political significance of the Greek κοινά ended in 146 B.C. with the Roman subjection of the Greek world. The basic structure of the provincial league was such that its connection to the Roman imperial cult was natural, for the ruler cults of the Hellenistic kingdoms had been closely connected with the municipal leagues linking Greek city-states. When a provincial imperial cult was combined with an existing provincial league, a feature that gave new importance to provincial κοινά, the basic pattern of the Roman imperial provincial league was created (Deininger, *Provinziallandtage,* 19).

The earliest evidence for the existence of the provincial league of Asia dates to the first century B.C. (*OGIS,* 438; Deininger, *Provinziallandtage,* 15). In the winter of 30/29 B.C., Octavian went to Asia, where he instituted a cult in honor of Roma and Augustus (i.e., himself) at Pergamon. His actions included the erection of a temple and the institution of sacred games called the κοινὰ Ἀσίας (Cassius Dio 51.20.7–9; Tacitus *Annals* 4.37; cf. Suetonius *Aug.* 52; Moretti, *RF* n.s. 32 [1954] 276–89; Deininger, *Provinziallandtage,* 54–55). In A.D. 26 a temple was erected in Smyrna in honor of Tiberius (Tacitus *Annals* 4.15, 55–56; Cassius Dio 59.28.1). Other temples were dedicated to the imperial cult in Cyzicus, Ephesus, Sardis, and possibly Miletus. The province of Asia had a single imperial temple in Pergamon with a chief priest. However, other temples were instituted, each with its own "high priest of Asia" (see the inscriptional evidence in Deininger, *Provinziallandtage,* 38–39), all equal in status, and all probably had seats in the provincial assembly of Asia. This assembly was headed by an official (called Ἀσιάρχης, "Asiarch," or ἀρχιερεύς, "chief priest"), the spokesman and president of the assembly (συνέδριον or *concilium*), who held office for one year. Though not religious specialists, they were drawn from prominent members of the local civic aristocracy and could hold office for shorter or longer periods (including lifetime tenure). The provincial assembly, which met once each year at one of the leading cities of the province, never possessed powers of legislation or taxation.

The office of Asiarch (Strabo 14.1.42; the plural form is found in Acts 19:31) has been a matter of great debate. Some scholars have argued that the terms Asiarch and ἀρχιερεύς, "chief priest," were essentially unconnected since the former is a municipal title of honor while the latter is a title for an elected official (Magie, *Roman Rule* 1:448–50, with notes 59, 61; 2:1279–1301), while others have contended that the two titles are synonymous (Taylor, "Asiarchs," 258–62; Deininger, *Provinziallandtage,* 44–50; Rossner, *Studii Clasice* 16 [1974] 101–7). Almost all the evidence for Asiarchs is epigraphical. Of the more than 200 Asiarchs now known from inscriptional evidence, 106 are connected with Ephesus (Horsley, *NovT* 34 [1992] 137). On the basis of this extensive evidence, Kearsley has concluded that the functions of the Asiarch and the Archiereus were quite distinct and that the usage of the title Asiarch was the same during the first and second centuries A.D.

One important feature of the provincial leagues was that they were completely separate from the Roman provincial administration, which consisted of the senatorial procurator, three legates (*legati pro praetore*), and a quaestor; whether the governor was a resident of Ephesus or Pergamon is a matter of dispute (*CAH* 11:581; *Kleine Pauly* 1:636). The *conventus civium Romanorum,* a permanent organization of Roman citizens in the provinces, existed side by side with the provincial assembly but had no relationship with it; nor was it very influential in its own right. The following are some of the major characteristics and functions of the League of Asia: (1) Like other provincial leagues, the League of Asia had an ἐκκλησία or συνέδριον, "assembly" (Latin *concilium*), which was a representative rather than a primary assembly. Representation was normally in proportion to population. Inscriptional evidence reveals that in 4 B.C. the assembly of the League of Asia numbered 150 members (Buckler-Robinson, *Inscriptions,* no. 8, doc. 7). During the reign of Antoninus Pius (A.D. 137–61), the cities of Asia were grouped into three classes, probably suggesting that the larger cities had three representatives, the medium-sized two, and the smaller one (*Digest* 27.1.6.2). (2) The League of Asia enjoyed administrative autonomy in choosing of its own officials, including the most important official, the provincial high priest or Asiarch. (3) The League of Asia also had the authority to mint a special series of silver coins, which appeared ca. 19/18 B.C. and which ended with the reign of Nerva (on the reverse side a provincial temple was depicted with the dedication ROM ET AUG and the inscription COM ASIAE [*Commune Asiae*]). (4) After 29 B.C. the central function of the League of Asia was the oversight of the imperial cult, including the building of temples and the institution of calendrical reforms, i.e., the introduction of the Julian calendar and the beginning of the year with 23 September, the birthday of Augustus. In contrast to the royal cults of the Hellenistic period, which were limited to cities, imperial cults were organized by provincial assemblies. There was intense competition among cities for the honor of having a provincial temple at which an imperial cult was celebrated. By the end of the first century A.D. the title νεωκόρος, "temple administrator," indicated that a city had been selected for that honor (see Friesen, *Twice Neokoros,* 50–75). (5) When the term of a Roman provincial governor was up, the provincial assembly reviewed his record and could vote him honors or prosecute him for extortion (Tacitus *Annals* 3.66–69; 4.15; 13.33, 43). (6) They also engaged in minor "political" activities (discussed in Deininger, *Provinziallandtage,* 55–60), including channeling appeals to the emperor on behalf of the province and making imperial decisions and intentions known to the Greeks of the province (Sherk, *Documents,* 328–37).

Excursus 13E: The Roman Imperial Cult in Asia Minor

Bibliography

Alföldi, A. "Die Ausgestaltung des monarchischen Zeremoniells am römischen Kaiserhofe." In *Mitteilungen des deutschen archaeologischen Instituts.* Römische Abteilung 49. Munich: Bruckmann, 1934. 3–118. (= "Die Ausgestaltung des monarchischen Zeremoniells am römischen Kaiserhofe." In *Die monarchische Repräsentation im römischen Kaiserreiche.* Darmstadt: Wissenschaftliche, 1970. 3–118). **Barrett, A. A.** *Caligula: The Corruption of Power.* London: Batsford, 1989. **Bickermann, E.** "*Consecratio.*" In *Le culte des souverains dans l'empire romain,* ed. W. den Boer. Geneva: Fondation Hardt, 1972. 1–37. ———. "Die römische Kaiserapotheose." *ARW* 27 (1929) 1–34. **Boer, W. den,** ed. *Le culte des souverains dans l'empire romain.* Entretiens sur l'Antiquité Classique 19. Geneva: Fondation Hardt, 1972. **Botha, P. J. J.** "God, Emperor Worship and Society: Contemporary Experiences and the Book of Revelation." *Neot* 22 (1988) 87–102. **Bowersock, G. W.** *Augustus and the Greek World.* Oxford: Clarendon, 1965. ———. "Greek Intellectuals and the Imperial Cult in the Second Century A.D." In *Le culte des souverains dans l'empire romain,* ed. W. den Boer. Geneva: Fondation Hardt, 1972. 177–212. ———. "The Imperial Cult: Perceptions and Persistence." In *Jewish and Christian Self-Definition,* ed. B. E. Meyer and E. P. Sanders. Philadelphia: Fortress, 1982. 3:171–82. **Cerfaux, L.,** and **Tondriau, J.** *Le culte des souverains dans la civilisation gréco-romaine.* Tournai: Desclee & Cie, 1957. **Charlesworth, M. P.** "Some Observations on Ruler Cult, Especially in Rome." *HTR* 28 (1935) 5–44. ———. "The Virtues of a Roman Emperor." *Proceedings of the British Academy* 23 (1937) 105–33. **Fayer, J. C.** *Il culto della dea Roma: Origine e diffusione nell'Impero.* Pescara: Trimestre, 1976. **Fishwick, D.** "AUGUSTUS DEUS and DEUS AUGUSTUS." In *Hommages à Martin*

Vermaseren. Leiden: Brill, 1978. 1:375–80. ———. "The Development of Provincial Ruler Worship in the Western Roman Empire." *ANRW* II, 16/2:1201–53. ———. *The Imperial Cult in the Latin West: Studies in the Ruler Cult of the Western Provinces of the Roman Empire.* Vol. 1/1. Leiden: Brill, 1987. **Fredricksmeyer, E.** "Three Notes on Alexander's Deification." *AJAH* 4 (1979) 1. **Friesen, S. J.** *Twice Neokoros: Ephesus, Asia and the Cult of the Flavian Imperial Family.* Leiden: Brill, 1993. **Geiger, F.** *De sacerdotibus Augustorum municipalibus.* Halle, 1913. **Habicht, C.** *Gottmenschtum und griechische Städte.* 2nd ed. Munich: Beck, 1970. ———. "New Evidence on the Province of Asia." *JRS* 65 (1975) 64–91. **Hänlein-Schäfer, H.** *Veneratio Augusti: Eine Studie zu den Tempeln des ersten römischen Kaisers.* Archaeologica 39. Rome: Bretschneider, 1985. **Herzog-Hauser, G.** "Kaiserkult." *RESup* 4:823ff. **Hopkins, K.** *Conquerors and Slaves: Sociological Studies in Roman History.* Vol. 1. Cambridge: Cambridge UP, 1978. **Jones, D. L.** "Christianity and the Roman Imperial Cult." *ANRW* II, 23/2:1023–54. **Keil, J.** "Die erste Kaiserneokorie von Ephesos." *Numismatische Zeitschrift* n.s. 12 (1919) 115–20. **Kornemann, E.** "Zur Geschichte der antiken Herrscherkulte." *Klio* 1 (1901) 51–146. **Langer, P.** "Alexander the Great at Siwah." *Ancient World* 4 (1981) 109–27. **Le Glay, M.** "Le culte de Rome et de Salus a Pergame, ou l'annonce du culte impérial." In *Studien zur Religion und Kultur Kleinasiens.* FS F. K. Dörner, ed. S. Sahin, E. Schwertheim, and J. Wagner. EPROER 66. Leiden: Brill, 1978. 2:546–64. **Liebeschuetz, J. H. W. G.** *Continuity and Change in Roman Religion.* Oxford: Clarendon, 1979. **MacCormack, S. G.** *Art and Ceremony in Late Antiquity.* Berkeley; Los Angeles: University of California, 1981. **Mellor, R.** "The Goddess Roma." *ANRW* II, 17/2:950–1030. ———. ΘΕΑ ΡΩΜΗ: *The Worship of the Goddess Roma in the Greek World.* Göttingen: Vandenhoeck & Ruprecht, 1975. **Millar, F.** "The Emperor, the Senate and the Provinces." *JRS* 56 (1966) 156–66. ———. "The Imperial Cult and the Persecutions." In *Le culte des souverains dans l'empire romain,* ed. W. den Boer. Geneva: Fondation Hardt, 1972. 145–65. ———. *The Roman Emperor in the Roman World (31 B.C.–A.D. 337).* Ithaca, NY: Cornell UP, 1977. **Momigliano, A.** "How Roman Emperors Became Gods." *American Scholar* 55 (1986) 181–93. **Nock, A. D.** "Religious Developments from the Close of the Republic to the Death of Nero." *CAH* 10:465–511. **Pick, B.** "Die Neokorien von Ephesos." In *Corolla Numismatica.* London: Oxford UP, 1906. 234–44. **Pleket, H. W.** "An Aspect of the Emperor Cult: Imperial Mysteries." *HTR* 58 (1965) 331. **Price, S. R. F.** "Between Man and God: Sacrifice in the Roman Imperial Cult." *JRS* 70 (1980) 28–43. ———. "Gods and Emperors: The Greek Language of the Roman Imperial Cult." *JHS* 104 (1984) 79–95. ———. "Noble Funeral to Divine Cult: The Consecration of Roman Emperors." In *Rituals of Royalty: Power and Ceremonial in Traditional Societies,* ed. D. Cannadine and S. Price. Cambridge: Cambridge UP, 1987. ———. *Rituals and Power: The Roman Imperial Cult in Asia Minor.* Cambridge: Cambridge UP, 1984. **Schowalter, D. N.** *The Emperor and the Gods: Images from the Time of Trajan.* HDR 28. Minneapolis: Augsburg, 1993. **Scott, K.** *The Imperial Cult under the Flavians.* Stuttgart; Berlin: Kohlhammer, 1936. **Taeger, F.** *Charisma: Studien zur Geschichte des antiken Herscherkultes.* 2 vols. Stuttgart: Kohlhammer, 1957–60. **Taylor, L. R.** *The Divinity of the Roman Emperor.* Middletown, CT: American Philological Association, 1931. **Wardman, A.** *Religion and Statecraft among the Romans.* Baltimore: Johns Hopkins UP, 1982. **Weinstock, J.** *Divus Julius.* Oxford: Clarendon, 1971. **Wlosok, A.,** ed. *Römischer Kaiserkult.* Darmstadt: Wissenschaftliche, 1978. **Wrede, H.** *Consecratio in Formam Deorum: Vergöttlichte Privatpersonen in der römischen Kaiserzeit.* Mainz am Rhein: von Zabern, 1981.

From Augustus to Constantine, thirty-six of the total of sixty emperors together with twenty-seven family members were apotheosized and given the title *divus,* "divine" (Price, "Divine Cult," 57). The antecedents of the Roman imperial cult lie primarily in the cults of the Hellenistic kings. While cults were founded in honor of various Greek rulers (Lysander of Sparta, Dion of Syracus, Philip of Macedon), the evidence that a divine cult was actually requested by Alexander the Great is problematic (see Fishwick, *Imperial Cult*

1/1:8–11). There is evidence to suggest that Alexander wanted to be deified, and it is also probable that it was on his famous trip to the oasis of Siwah in Libyah (see P. A. Brunt, ed. and tr., *Arrian,* LCL [Cambridge: Harvard UP, 1976] 1:467–80; extensive bibliography in Langer, *Ancient World* 4 [1981] 109–27) that he was recognized by the priest there as the son of Zeus-Ammon, which may have convinced Alexander of his own divine birth (Fredricksmeyer, *AJAH* 4 [1979] 1).

Greek cities that obtained various privileges and benefactions from Hellenistic rulers often established cults in their honor. These cults, modeled after the existing cults of the gods, were one of the major means whereby Hellenistic cities came to terms with a new form of unmanageable power, which was Greek and yet external to the structure of the city (Price, *Rituals,* 29–30). Price argues that by classifying rulers in divine terms, the novelty of the Hellenistic monarchies was disguised (*Rituals,* 52). Cities ordinarily took the initiative in founding ruler cults, and these cults were thereafter integral to the religious affairs of each city. It is possible that the connection of ruler cults with traditional cults played an important role in the revitalization of the latter. When rulers lost control of particular cities, the cities sometimes continued such cults, sometimes formally terminated them (as the Athenians did in the case of Philip V of Macedon; see Livy 31.44.4–8), or simply replaced them with cults dedicated to the new rulers and their dynasty.

Another important aspect of Hellenistic cults is the institution of public cults in honor of private citizens who had performed major services for their cities (Price, *Rituals,* 47–51). However, after 29 B.C., the institution of new cults to Roman officials or private citizens of Greek cities became increasingly rare. The last known cult honoring a Roman official was established after A.D. 27 for Capito in Miletus (Bowersock, *Augustus,* 120).

While the Hellenistic ruler cults focused on paying divine honors to the *living* ruler, the imperial cult in Rome tended to emphasize the posthumous divinity accorded to *deceased* emperors, who were thought to have ascended to the region of the stars after death in a ceremony of apotheosis (Cicero *Phil.* 1.13; 2.110; Pliny *Pan.* 10.4; 24.5; 89.2; Manilius 1.799–804; Herodian 4.2). Those who lived in the provinces, however, were free to worship a *living* emperor (Bickerman, "*Consecratio,*" 9–10). At this point, however, it is important to distinguish between *provincial* cults and *municipal* cults, which were local and subject to local customs. Provincial cults, which were established through the approval by the Senate and the emperor of requests made by provincial leagues, necessarily took cognizance of Roman traditions and therefore generally limited the title θεός, "god," to deceased emperors who had been officially deified by the Senate (Friesen, *Twice Neokoros,* 22–23; see *IGRom* 1:55–56; 4:1756). Yet in the case of Domitian, this line was crossed, and he appears to have demanded divine worship in Rome itself in the form of sacrifices (Pliny *Pan.* 52.1, 7).

Until very recently, the Roman imperial cult has been viewed in terms of its *political* rather than its *religious* significance for the ancients (Liebeschuetz, *Continuity,* 65–90). According to A. D. Nock (*Conversion: The Old and the New in Religion from Alexander the Great to Augustine of Hippo* [Oxford: Oxford UP, 1933] 229), "By the time of Claudius it [ruler worship] was an outward sign of loyalty which involved little sentiment." In his view the ruler cult involved homage rather than worship (Nock, *CAH* 10:481–82). However, the religious significance of the imperial cult has become increasingly clear in recent scholarship (Hopkins, *Conquerors,* 1:197–242; Price, *Rituals,* passim). Since divine kingship was absent from Greek and Roman history prior to the Hellenistic period, it is a problem to account for its prevalence during this period. According to Momigliano (*American Scholar* 55 [1986] 193), "The imperial cult was primarily a sign of indifference or doubt or anxiety about the gods; it was, furthermore, an expression of admiration for efficient, but alien, rule."

One of the religious antecedents of the ruler cults of the Hellenistic and Roman periods was the Greek conception of the "hero," a deceased person whose tomb was the focus of cultic observances and whose remains were thought imbued with power. Yet one disjunctive feature is that ruler cults focused on the divinity of the *living* monarch, an essentially Greek phenomenon. Since Hellenistic rulers could provide the blessings and protection earlier sought from the gods, the cult of the πολιοῦχος, "protector of the city," took its place beside the cults of the traditional gods.

The beginning of the Hellenistic period witnessed an increasing tendency to blur the traditional Greek distinction between mortal and immortal. Many cults of Roman magistrates existed in Greek cities from the end of the third century B.C. through the beginning of the first century A.D. (Bowersock, *Augustus*). There were limits to the ruler cult in Rome (Momigliano, *American Scholar* 55 [1986] 187): "Generally speaking, the emperor had to approve, to limit, and occasionally to refuse ruler-cult. He had to be worshipped, and yet he had to remain a man in order to live on social terms with the Roman aristocracy of which he was supposed to be the 'Princeps.'" Thus during the lifetime of a particular emperor "he was more of a god in his absence than in his presence" (Momigliano, *American Scholar* 55 [1986] 187). In the provinces, and particularly in the Province of Asia, the imperial cult mediated the presence of an absent emperor. Augustus, together with Roma, was the recipient of a provincial cult in A.D. 29 in Asia and Bithynia. In the catalogue of temples dedicated in whole or in part to the divine Augustus, Hänlein-Schäfer (*Veneratio Augusti*) has listed sixty-six such buildings. The number of cults dedicated to specific emperors fell off rapidly after Augustus with lesser numbers of cults instituted in honor of imperial successors such as Tiberius and Claudius. Cults honoring the emperors generically, however, were numerous and probably represent the successful institutionalization of the charisma of Augustus (Price, *Rituals*, 57–58). Thirteen inscriptions from A.D. 89–90 have been discovered relating to the first official provincial imperial cult in Ephesus, the Temple of Domitian (Price, *Rituals*, 255), or, more accurately, the ναὸς τῶν Σεβαστῶν, "Temple of the Sebastoi" (*I. Eph.* 2.233, lines 9–10); see *I. Eph.* 2.232, 232a, 233, 234, 235, 237, 238, 239, 240, 241, 242; 5.1498; 6.2048; collected and discussed in Friesen, *Twice Neokoros*, 29–49.

The term *neokorate*, derived from νεωκόρος, meaning "temple caretaker," was originally a term for an official who assisted priests and priestesses in the administration of a cult. The term was applied to cities in the first century A.D.; the three earliest examples of such usage are discussed by Friesen, *Twice Neokoros*, 53–56. Late in the first century A.D. the term was incorporated into the imperial cult and applied to cities who were permitted to establish an imperial cult by the Senate and emperor (an important discussion of this term is found in Friesen, *Twice Neokoros*, 50–75). In most instances the name of Domitian has been erased and that of Vespasian inserted. The Temple of Hadrian was the second imperial *neokorate* in Ephesus (Price, *Rituals*, 256).

Many of the acts of Christian martyrs reveal the seamy side of the imposition of the imperial cult, which sometimes took on brutal dimensions. The standard accusation raised against Christians was that they did not sacrifice to the emperor (Tertullian *Apol.* 10, *deus non colitis et pro imperatoribus sacrificia non penditis*). The test of loyalty involved the recognition of the imperial cult (Pliny *Ep.* 10.96; *Martyrdom of Polycarp; Acts of the Scillitan Martyrs; Martyrdom of Pionius*). Some Roman intellectuals, like Tacitus, spoke pejoratively about the imperial cult as *Graeca adjulatio*, "Greek adulation."

The Roman imperial cult also had a presence in Palestine. Herod the Great constructed a temple at Caesarea Maritima (built between 22 and 10 B.C.) in honor of the city's "ancestral" deities, Roma and Augustus (Jos. *J.W.* 1.414–15; *Ant.* 15.339; see *NEAEHL* 1:238). An inscription discovered at Caesarea in 1961 indicates that Pontius Pilate, the prefect Judea A.D. 26–36, had dedicated a Tiberieum, i.e., a small chapel in honor of Tiberius (A.D. 14–37), in Caesarea Maritima.

One interesting background aspect of the deification of Roman emperors is the tradition of the deification of private persons, a non-Greek tradition restricted to Rome and cities of the western part of the empire and expressed primarily in artistic representations (Wrede, *Consecratio,* 2–3). This deification tradition takes two major forms: (1) the depiction of the deceased through the use of mythological themes and exempla and (2) the depiction of the deification itself.

Explanation

From a narratological perspective, Rev 12:18–13:18 is loosely connected with 11:19–12:17, by the editorial transition in 12:18, "And he (i.e., the dragon) stood [ἐστάθη] on the shore of the sea." Rev 12:18–13:18 consists of two subunits, the first on the beast from the sea (12:18–13:11), who appeared earlier in a brief cameo as the one responsible for the deaths of the two witnesses (11:7), and the second on the beast from the land (vv 12–18). Since this second beast is completely subservient to the first beast, all of the activities of the former are performed in the service of the latter; therefore, the first beast also dominates vv 12–18. The investiture of the beast from the sea as viceregent of the dragon serves as a perverse antithesis of the narrative of the investiture of the Lamb in Rev 5. These two beasts are based on the Jewish myth of Leviathan, the female monster from the sea, and Behemoth, the male monster from the desert. Though this allusion provides a visionary framework for 12:18–13:18, the unity imposed on the text unit is relatively superficial since important features of the Leviathan-Behemoth myth are omitted and replaced with motifs derived from the myth of the eschatological antagonist or Antichrist (see *Excursus 13B*). The beast from the sea, probably representing the Roman empire rather than an individual ruler, is modeled after the "tyrannical ruler," while the beast from the land functions as the agent of the first beast and seems to represent the *commune Asiae,* i.e., the *Koinon* of Asia (the native political organization, which facilitated the policies of Rome), and is largely patterned after the "false seductive prophet."

Throughout the ancient world there were many versions of a primal myth of combat between the great gods and a sea dragon or similar monsters, representing the antithesis between order and chaos. The Greeks told stories about the conflict between Zeus and Typhon as well as Apollo and Python, the Babylonians about Marduk and Tiamat, and the Israelites about Yahweh and Rahab or Yahweh and Leviathan. According to Jewish primeval mythology, God created two sea monsters on the fifth day of creation, Leviathan and Behemoth. The male monster Leviathan was confined to the sea, while Behemoth, his female counterpart, was confined to the desert.

In a strand of Jewish eschatological expectation with which John shows familiarity in Rev 13, after the Messiah is revealed, Behemoth will appear from his place and Leviathan will ascend from the sea. John sees the first beast (the female Leviathan of Jewish legend) rise from the "sea" (representing the abyss or bottomless pit and symbolizing evil and chaos), with seven heads, upon which blasphemous names were written, and ten horns with a diadem on each (v 1). The appearance of the beast (v 2) indicates that it is a conflation of the four separate beasts from the sea described in Dan 7:2–7. Horns symbolize power, and the ten diadems suggest universal sovereignty, which parodies the rule of Christ (19:10).

In Judaism the sea monster came to represent oppressive foreign nations, and occasionally the chaos monsters Rahab or Leviathan could represent Egypt. Since this beast has the throne and power of the dragon (v 2b), it functions as Satan's earthly representative and also as a parody of Christ. The worship that is given to this beast (v 4) is that which occurred in the imperial cult. The "blasphemous names" referred to in v 1 may refer to the honorific titles (such as "lord" and "god") applied to living emperors in provincial imperial cults. One of the beast's seven heads, though fatally wounded, was miraculously healed (v 3), a parody of the death and resurrection of Christ.

Since the seven heads stand for seven kings (see *Comment* on 17:10), this obscure reference is usually thought to refer to the legend of Nero *redivivus*. Though Nero committed suicide on 9 June A.D. 68, few saw his corpse or witnessed his burial. He was as popular in the eastern provinces as he was despised in Italy. In the years following A.D. 68 at least three false Neros appeared, one in A.D. 69, a second in A.D. 80, and a third in A.D. 88. The statement that this beast warred against the saints and conquered them (v 7) may well refer to those who, like Antipas (2:13; cf. 6:9–11; 20:4), had been executed for refusing to sacrifice in connection with the imperial cult.

The second beast from the earth (the male Behemoth of Jewish legend) had two horns like a ram, and it spoke like a dragon—a wolf in sheep's clothing (v 11). Later referred to as the "false prophet" (16:13; 19:20; 20:10), the second beast performs deceptive miracles persuading people to fashion a cult statue of the beast, a statue that has the power of speech (vv 13–15). Christian eschatology anticipated the coming of such adversaries as "false Christs" and "false prophets" who would perform miracles. Religious fraud was not unknown in the ancient world, though there is no evidence that it occurred in connection with the imperial cult.

The second beast represents a local authority concerned with the worship of the first beast, probably the priesthood of the imperial cult, the most important cult in the province of Asia. It is likely that the foundation of the provincial cult of Domitian at Ephesus late in the first century (involving the participation of the entire province of Asia) provided a climate in which enormous pressure was placed on Christians to be loyal citizens and participate in the imperial cult. While sacrifices and prayers were not ordinarily directed toward the emperor himself, but to the gods on his behalf, this fine distinction was probably imperceptible to Christians. Emperors were not officially regarded as gods until they were posthumously pronounced *divus,* "divine," by the Roman senate (with the exceptions of Gaius and Domitian). In the provinces, however, and in Asia in particular, Roman emperors were often accorded cults during their reign.

The second beast compels everyone to be branded on the right hand and forehead with the name of the beast; unbelievers thus form an identifiable group in contrast to faithful Christians marked with God's seal (7:2–8). The coded name of the first beast is 666, a number that is the total of the numerical value of the letters spelling "Nero Caesar" in Aramaic (found in a document in Palestine at Wadi Muraba'at), though this is just one of many possible solutions to the riddle.

4. *Visions of Eschatological Salvation and Judgment (14:1–20)*

Bibliography

Altink, W. "Theological Motives for the Use of 1 Chronicles 16:8–36 as Background for Revelation 14:6–7." *AUSS* 24 (1986) 211–21. **Aune D. E.** "Following the Lamb: Discipleship in the Apocalypse." In *Patterns of Discipleship in the New Testament,* ed. R. N. Longenecker. Grand Rapids, MI: Eerdmans, 1996. 269–84. ———. "Luke 20:34–36: A 'Gnosticized' Logion of Jesus?" In *Geschichte—Tradition—Reflexion.* FS M. Hengel, ed. H. Cancik, H. Lichtenberger, and P. Schäfer. Tübingen: Mohr-Siebeck, 1996. 3:187–202. **Avemarie, F.** "Esaus Händer, Jakobs Stimme: Edom als Sinnbild Roms in der frühen rabbinischen Literatur." In *Die Heiden: Juden, Christen und das Problem des Fremden,* ed. R. Feldmeier and U. Heckel. WUNT 70. Tübingen: Mohr-Siebeck, 1994. 177–208. **Bauckham, R.** "The Apocalypse as a Christian War Scroll." In R. Bauckham, *Climax.* 210–37. ———. "The Conversion of the Nations." In R. Bauckham, *Climax.* 238–337. ———. "The Use of Apocalyptic Traditions." In R. Bauckham, *Climax.* 38–91. **Baus, K.** *Der Kranz in Antike und Christentum.* Theophaneia 2. Bonn: Hanstein, 1940. **Bentzen, A.** "Der Sichel." *VT* 1 (1951) 216–17. **Bergmeier, R.** "Die Erzhure und das Tier: Apk 12,18 und 17f. Eine quellen- und redaktionskritische Analyse." *ANRW* II, 25/5:3899–3916. **Betz, O.** "Jesu Heiliger Krieg." *NovT* 2 (1957) 116–37. **Borsch, F. H.** *The Son of Man in Myth and History.* London: SCM, 1967. **Brock, S. P.** "Early Syrian Asceticism." *Numen* 20 (1973) 1–19. **Brongers, H. A.** "Der Zornesbecher." *OTS* 15 (1969) 177–92. **Brown, S.** "Concerning the Origin of the *Nomina Sacra.*" *SPap* 9 (1970) 7–19. **Burrows, M.** "The Origin of the Term 'Gospel.'" *JBL* 44 (1925) 21–33. **Casey, P. M.** *Son of Man: The Interpretation and Influence of Daniel 7.* London: SPCK, 1979. **Cerfaux, L.** "L'Evangile Eternel (Apoc. XIV:6)." *ETL* 39 (1963) 672–81. **Coppens, J.** "La mention d'un Fils d'homme angélique en Ap 14,14." In *L'Apocalypse,* ed. J. Lambrecht. 229. **Culianu, I. P.** *Psychanodia:* Vol 1. *A Survey of the Evidence concerning the Ascension of the Soul and Its Relevance.* EPRO 99. Leiden: Brill, 1983. **Deer, D. S.** "Whose faith/loyalty in Revelation 2.13 and 14.12?" *BT* 38 (1987) 328–30. **Devine, R.** "The Virgin Followers of the Lamb." *Scripture* 16 (1964) 1–5. **Feuillet, A.** "Les 144.000 Israélites marqués d'un sceau." *NovT* 9 (1967) 191–224. ———. "La moisson et la vendange de l'Apocalypse (14,14–20): La signification chrétienne de la révélation johannique." *NRT* 94 (1972) 113–32, 225–50. **Ford, J. M.** "The Meaning of 'Virgin.'" *NTS* 12 (1966) 293–99. **Frankmölle, H.** *Evangelium: Begriff und Gattung.* Stuttgart: Katholisches Bibelwerk, 1994. **Galling, K.,** and **Altaner, B.** "Babylon." *RAC* 1:1118–34. **Grillmeier, A.** "'Ihre Werke folgen ihnen nach' (Offb 14:13)." *GL* 37 (1964) 321–24. **Huntzinger, C.-H.** "Babylon als Deckname für Rom und die Datierung des 1. Petrusbriefes." In *Gottes Wort und Gottes Land.* FS H.-W. Hertzberg, ed. H. G. Reventlow. Göttingen: Vandenhoeck & Ruprecht, 1965. 67–77. **Jeremias, Joachim.** *Jesu Verheissung für die Völker.* 2nd ed. Stuttgart: Kohlhammer, 1956 (ET: *Jesus' Promise to the Nations.* SBT 24. Rev. ed. London: SCM, 1967). **Kang, S.-M.** *Divine War in the Old Testament and in the Ancient Near East.* BZAW 177. Berlin: de Gruyter, 1989. **Lietzmann, H.** *Der Menschensohn: Ein Beitrag zur neutestamentlichen Theologie.* Freiburg i. B.; Leipzig: Mohr-Siebeck, 1896. **Lindijer, C. H.** "Die Jungfrauen in der Offenbarung des Johannes XIV 4." In *Studies in John,* FS J. N. Sevenster. NovTSup 24. Leiden: Brill, 1970. 124–42. **Lindsay, D. R.** *Josephus and Faith:* Πίστις *and* Πιστεύειν *as Faith Terminology in the Writings of Flavius Josephus and the New Testament.* AGJU 19. Leiden: Brill, 1993. **Lohse, E.** "Der Menschensohn in der Johannesapokalypse." In *Jesus und der Menschensohn,* ed. R. Pesch and R. Schnackenburg. Freiburg; Basel; Vienna: Herder, 1975. 415–20. **Masson, C.** "L'Évangile Eternel 14,6–7." In *Hommage de Reconnaissance à K.*

Barth, ed. J.-J. von Allmen. Neuchâtel; Paris: Delachaux & Niestlé, 1946. 63ff. **McArthur, H.** "Celibacy in Judaism at the Time of Christian Beginnings." *AUSS* 25 (1987) 163–81. **McCarthy, D. J.** "Vox bśr praeparat vocem 'evangelium.'" *VD* 42 (1964) 26–33. **McKane, W.** "Poison, Trial by Ordeal and the Cup of Wrath." *VT* 30 (1980) 474–92. **McNamara, M.** *Palestinian Targum.* 209–14 [14:1–5]. **Olson, D. C.** "'Those Who Have Not Defiled Themselves with Women': Revelation 14:4 and the *Book of Enoch.*" *CBQ* 59 (1997) 492–510. **Paap, A. H. R. E.** *Nomina Sacra in the Greek Papyri of the First Five Centuries.* Leiden: Brill, 1970. **Poucouta, P.** *La dynamique missionnaire de l'Apocalypse.* Paris: Cerf, 1991. **Power, E.** "A Pretended Interpolation in the Apocalypse (14:4e, 5ab)." *Bib* 4 (1923) 108–12. **Rad, G. von.** *Der heilige Krieg im alten Israel.* 3rd ed. Göttingen: Vandenhoeck & Ruprecht, 1958. **Ringgren, H.** "Vredens kalk." *SEÅ* 17 (1953) 19–30. **Roberts, C. H.** *Manuscript, Society and Belief in Early Christian Egypt.* London: Oxford UP, 1979. **Rückert, K.** "Die Begriffe παρθένος und ἀπαρχή in Apok. 14:4, 5." *TQ* 68 (1886) 391–448; 69 (1897) 105–32. **Schaik, A. P. van.** "'Ἄλλος ἄγγελος in Apk 14." In *L'Apocalypse,* ed. J. Lambrecht. 217–28. **Schüssler Fiorenza, E.** "The Followers of the Lamb: Visionary Rhetoric and Social-Political Situation." In *Discipleship in the New Testament,* ed. F. F. Segovia. Philadelphia: Fortress, 1985. 144–65. **Schwartz, J.** "Treading the Grapes of Wrath: The Wine Press in Ancient Jewish and Christian Tradition." *TZ* 49 (1993) 215–28, 311–24. **Seltman, C.** *Wine in the Ancient World.* London: Routledge & Kegan Paul, 1957. **Sissa, G.** *Greek Virginity.* Cambridge: Harvard UP, 1990. **Skrinjar, A.** "Virgines enim sunt." *VD* 15 (1935) 331–39. **Slater, T. B.** "*Homoion huion anthropou* in Rev 1.13 and 14.14." *BT* 44 (1993) 349–50. **Stadelmann, L. I. J.** *The Hebrew Conception of the World.* AnBib 39. Rome: Biblical Institute, 1970. **Steinberger, G.** *Der Weg dem Lamme nach (Apc. 14,4).* Munich, 1948. **Strecker, G.** "Das Evangelium Jesu Christi." In *Jesus Christus in Historie und Theologie.* FS H. Conzelmann, ed. G. Strecker. Tübingen: Mohr-Siebeck, 1975. 503–48. **Stuhlmacher, P.** *Das paulinische Evangelium:* Vol. 1. *Vorgeschichte.* Göttingen: Vandenhoeck & Ruprecht, 1968. **Tambyah, T. I.** "'Virgins' in Rev. XIV.4." *ExpTim* 32 (1920–21) 139. **Thiede, C. P.** "Babylon, der andere Ort: Anmerkungen zu Petr 5,13 und Apg 12,17." *Bib* 67 (1986) 532–38. **Tissot, Y.** "Encratisme et Actes Apocryphes." In *Les Actes Apocryphes des Apôtres,* ed. F. Bovon. Geneva: Labor et Fides, 1981. 109–19. **Traube, L.** *Nomina Sacra: Versuch einer Geschichte der christlichen Kürzung.* Munich: Beck, 1907. **Vööbus, A.** *Celibacy: A Requirement for Admission to Baptism in the Early Syrian Church.* Stockholm: Estonian Theological Society in Exile, 1951. **Weicht, W.** *Die dem Lamme folgen: Eine Untersuchung der Auslegung von Offb 14,1–5 in den letzten 80 Jahren.* Untermerzbach/Bamberg, 1976. **Wolff, C.** *Jeremia im Frühjudentum und Urchristentum.* Berlin: Akademie, 1976. **Yarbro Collins, A.** "The Political Perspective of the Revelation to John." *JBL* 96 (1977) 241–56. ———. "Women's History and the Book of Revelation." In *Society of Biblical Literature 1987 Seminar Papers,* ed. K. H. Richards. Atlanta: Scholars, 1987. **Zondervan, P.** "Het Woord 'Evangelium.'" *TT* 43 (1914) 178–213.

Translation

[1]*I*[a] *saw, and, behold, the*[b] *Lamb was standing*[c] *on*[d] *Mount Zion and with him a group of*[e] *144,000 with*[f] *his name and the name of his Father written*[g] *on their foreheads.*[h]
[2]*I*[a] *heard a sound*[b] [c]*from heaven like the roar of the sea*[d] *and like the sound of loud thunder.*
[e]*The*[f] *sound which*[g] *I heard was like*[h] *that*[i] *of kitharists*[e] *playing on their kitharas.* [3]*Then*
they sang,[a] *as it were,*[b] *a new song before the throne and before the four cherubim*[c] *and*[d] *the elders.*[c]

No one[e] *could learn the song except the 144,000 who had been redeemed*[f] *from the earth.*
[4]*These*[a] *are those who have not polluted themselves with women, for they are*[b] *chaste. These are those who follow the Lamb* [c]*where he would go.*[c] *These are those who have been redeemed*[d] *from humanity, servants devoted to*[e] *God and the Lamb,* [5]*and "in their mouths*[a] *guile was not found."*[b]*They are blameless.*

6 *Then I saw another*[a] *angel flying in midheaven, with an eternal message to proclaim*[b]
among[c] *those who dwell*[d] *on the earth and among*[e] *every nation and tribe and language*
and people, 7 *proclaiming*[a] *with a loud voice,*

"Fear God and give[b] *him glory, because the hour of his judgment has come, and*
[c]*worship the one who made*[c] *the heaven and the earth and the*[d] *sea and the springs."*

Then another[a] *angel, a second one,*[a] *followed,*[b] [c]*saying,*

"Fallen, fallen is Babylon the great who[d] *gave all nations*[e] *to drink*[e] *of*[f] *the wine which*
is her immoral [g]*passion."*

9 *Another angel, a third one, followed them,*[a] *proclaiming with a loud voice,*

"If anyone worships [b]*the beast*[b] *and his cultic image and receives a* [c]*brand*[d] [e]*on his*
forehead or upon his hand,[e] 10 *then*[a] *he too*[b] *will drink some*[c] *of the wine, which is*[d] *the*
fury[e] *of God poured unmixed*[f] *into the cup, which is*[g] *his anger,*[f] [h]*with the result that*[h]
he will be tormented[i] *in fire and sulfur before the holy angels and before the Lamb.*
11 *The*[a] *smoke of their*[b] *torment ascends forever. Those who worship* [c]*the beast*[c] *and its*
cultic image will have no rest day and night, and [d]*whoever*[d] *receives the brand*[e] *with*
its name.[f] 12 [a]*This*[b] *indicates that*[a] *the perseverance of*[c] *God's people*[c] *involves*[d] [e]*keeping*
the commands of God and [f]*maintaining* [g]*faithfulness to Jesus.*[g]

13 *Then I heard a voice from heaven saying,*[a] *"Write,*

[b]*'How fortunate*[b] *are the dead who die in*[c] *the Lord.*[c] [d]*Truly, says*[d] *the Spirit,* [e]*that*[f] *they*
might rest[e] *from their labors, for their works follow*[g] *after them.'"*

14 [a]*Then I looked,*[a] *and behold, a white cloud, and*[b] *upon the cloud was seated*[bc] *one like*
a [d]*human*[e] *being*[d] *with*[f] *a golden wreath upon his head and a sharp sickle in his hand.*
15 *Then another angel came out of the* [a]*temple,*[b] *exclaiming*[c] *with a loud voice to the one*
seated upon the cloud, [d]*"Use your* [e]*sickle*[d] *for*[f] *harvesting, for the hour to harvest has*
arrived,[g] *because the harvest of the earth is ripe."*[h] 16 *The one sitting upon* [a]*the cloud*[a]
[b]*began to swing his sickle*[b] *on the earth, and the earth was* [c]*harvested.*[c]

17 *Then another angel came*[a] *out of the temple* [b]*which is in* [c]*heaven,*[a] *and he also had a*
sharp sickle. 18 *Yet another angel emerged* [a]*from the sanctuary*[b] *(*[c]*the one*[c] *with authority*
over fire) and [d]*called with a loud voice to the one who had*[e] *the*[f] *sharp sickle, "Use your*[g]
[h]*sharp sickle and gather the grape clusters* [i]*from the vineyard which is the earth,*[i] *for its*
grapes are ripe. 19 *Then the*[a] *angel began to swing his sickle toward*[b] *the earth and gathered*
the vintage of the earth and cast it into the great winepress[c] *of the wrath of God.* 20 *The*
winepress was trodden[a] *outside of the city, and blood flowed from the winepress to*[b] *the height*
of the bridles of horses for [c]*one thousand six hundred stadia.*[c]

Notes

1.a. The καί with which this sentence begins has been left untranslated since it is a discourse marker that indicates the beginning of a new sentence but has no independent semantic value.

1.b. Variants: (1) τό before ἀρνίον] ℵ A C 046 fam 1006 fam 1611[1611 2329] Oecumenius[2053] Andr f[2073] i[-2042] 1 94; von Soden, *Text.* (2) omit τό] 𝔓[47] 051 fam 1611[1854] Andreas TR; Spitta, 146–47. The definite article is unquestionably original (despite the speculative suggestions of Spitta) and has an anaphoric function; i.e., it refers back to a concept or thing mentioned earlier that has occurred initially without the article (i.e., ἀρνίον first occurs without the article in 5:6, and when it is mentioned the next time in 5:8, it is articular). Of the twenty-eight other occurrences of ἀρνίον as a metaphor for Jesus in Revelation, only 5:6 is anarthrous. The omission of the article here is certainly the *lectio difficilior,* but the MS evidence favors reading (1). This variant is cryptically discussed in *TCGNT*[2], 677.

1.c. Variants: (1) ἑστός (neut. nom. or acc. sing. pf. ptcp.)] ℵ A C 025 fam 1611[2344] Andr h[-2286] i[-1685 -2074] 2019; Tischendorf, *NT Graece;* WHort; von Soden, *Text;* Bousset (1906) 379; Charles, 2:322; Merk, *NT;* Schmid, *Studien* 2:234; Nestle-Aland[27]; UBSGNT[4]. (2) ἑστώς (nom. sing. masc. pf. ptcp.)] 𝔓[47]

Oecumenius^{2053} Andreas. (3) ἑστηκός (nom. or acc. sing. neut. pf. ptcp.)] 2377 Andr d f^{2023} Byzantine. The original reading is probably ἑστός. The use of ἑστώς (which can either be the result of the phonetic equation ο = ω [Gignac, *Grammar* 1:275–77] or intentionally masc. [like the pronouns referring to τὸ θηρίον in Rev 13]), which can only be nom., indicates that the ambiguous neut. ἑστός is also nom. While the acc. normally follows εἶδον, here the author follows his tendency to use the nom. following ἰδού. In this context, ἑστός functions like a finite verb (cf. Mussies, *Morphology,* 325). For other instances in Revelation in which the ptcp. functions as a finite verb, cf. 1:16; 4:2, 4; 5:6; 10:8; 14:6, 14; 21:14.

1.d. ἐπί + acc. usually means resting at or on a place (which it means here), not motion toward a place. Yet ἐπί is not normally used with such consistency in Revelation.

1.e. The absence of the definite article αἱ before ἑκατὸν τεσσεράκοντα τέσσαρες χιλιάδες (cf. v 3, where the article is used with the second mention of this group) suggests that, despite the similarity in number, this is a different group than the one previously mentioned in 7:4 (Spitta, 145).

1.f. ἔχουσαι is a nom. *fem.* pl. pres. ptcp. because it modifies χιλιάδες, "thousands." Since this group is part of what John saw (εἶδον), it should be in the acc., yet he always reverts to the nom. after ἰδού.

1.g. The ptcp. γεγραμμένον is in apposition to τὸ ὄνομα, which is the obj. of the ptcp. ἔχουσαι. The pattern ἔχειν + obj. + pf. ptcp. occurs several times in Revelation (12:6; 19:12, 16; 21:12), and in each case the ptcp. is adj., modifying the obj. of ἔχειν. The suggestion that this is a periphrastic construction (ἔχειν + ptcp.) is unfounded (cf. W. J. Aerts, *Periphrastica* [Amsterdam: Hakkert, 1965] 161); cf. *Note* 12:6.d.

1.h. τῶν μετώπων αὐτῶν, "their foreheads," is a distributive noun usually found in the sing., e.g., 13:16, τὸ μέτωπον αὐτῶν, "their foreheads," referring to something possessed by everyone in a group. The occurrence of the pl. form μετώπων here refers to the sum total of things possessed by everyone in the group (Mussies, *Morphology,* 84).

2.a. See *Note* 1.a.

2.b. The term φωνή here must be translated "sound" since it cannot be a "voice" as the NRSV renders it, because "voice" must refer to the sound made by an individual, not a group.

2.c. Variant: ὡς inserted before ἐκ τοῦ οὐρανοῦ] 𝔓^{47}; singular reading.

2.d. ὡς φωνὴν ὑδάτων πολλῶν, lit. "like the sound of many waters," can be more idiomatically translated "like the roar of [the waves of] the sea" or "like the roar of water."

2.e-e. Variants: (1) καὶ ἡ φωνὴ ἣν ἤκουσα ὡς κιθαρῳδῶν] ℵ A C 046 051 fam 1611^{1611} fam 1006^{1841} 2020 2080; Andr f$^{2031\ -2056}$ g l n 94 2019 Andr/Byz 4b^{1862} ; Byzantine. (2) καὶ φωνὴν ἤκουσα κιθαρῳδῶν] 𝔓^{47} Oecumenius^{2053} Andreas; Kraft, 187–88. (3) καὶ φωνὴν ἤκουσα ὡς κιθαρῳδῶν] Andr i^{-2042}. Variant (1), which centers on ἡ φωνή *with* the definite article, means that what follows is another way of describing the same φωνή (anarthrous) mentioned in v 2a. In variants (2) and (3), on the other hand, since φωνή is *anarthrous,* it must refer to a second sound. All modern critical Gk. texts accept reading (1).

2.f. See *Note* 1.a.

2.g. Variant: omit ἥν (fem. sing. acc. relative pronoun) 𝔓^{47}.

2.h. Variants: (1) ὡς before κιθαρῳδῶν] ℵ A C 025 fam 1611^{2329} Oecumenius^{2053comm} Byz 7^{2024} Byz 17^{469} Andr/Byz 3$^{1248\ 1894\ 2196}$ Andr i$^{-1685\ -2042}$ Andr m$^{2037\ 2046}$; von Soden, *Text.* (2) omit ὡς] Andreas.

2.i. Variant: ὡς φωνήν before κιθαρῳδῶν] 𝔓^{47} Oecumenius^{2053}.

3.a. Though ᾄδουσιν is in the present tense, it has been translated here as a past tense in accordance with normal Eng. usage. Further, the identity of the *subject* of this 3rd pl. verb is not obvious (it is certainly not the 144,000), and so it can probably be construed as an impersonal 3rd pl., i.e., "people were singing" or perhaps in this case "heavenly beings were singing." This idiom is normally used with verbs of speaking or narrating, e.g., Dan 4:22, 28–29; Ezra 4:13; Luke 12:20; Matt 5:15; 9:2; 17:27; Mark 2:18; 3:21; 14:2 (cf. Turner, *Syntax,* 292–93; Black, *Aramaic,* 126–28; N. Turner, "Markan Usage," *JTS* 25 [1924] 377–86). The indefinite or impersonal pl. can also be used, like the pass., as a circumlocution for the name of God (Zerwick, *Greek,* §§ 1–6).

3.b. Variants: (1) ὡς] A C 051 fam 1006 Andreas it^{ar} syr^{ph}; WHort; Bousset; [von Soden, *Text*]; Charles; Merk, *NT;* [Nestle-Aland^{27}]; [UBSGNT^{4}]. (2) omit ὡς] 𝔓^{47} ℵ 025 046 Oecumenius^{2053} fam 1611^{-2050} 2377 Andr d e f$^{2023\text{-}2031}$ g^{-2045} l n^{2429} 94 2019 Byzantine it^{gig} syr^{h} Primasius; Tischendorf, *NT Graece.* This is a difficult decision. While ὡς is probably the *lectio difficilior,* it is nevertheless difficult to explain its omission from such different witnesses to the ancient text as 𝔓^{47} ℵ and Oecumenius^{2053}; see *TCGNT*^{1}, 750; *TCGNT*^{2}, 677. Schmid considers ὡς the original reading (*Studien,* 2:137; cf. 225–26, where he cites all the problematic texts containing a disputed ὡς). The use of ὡς in contexts in which the first term of comparison is omitted, as here, is in accord with the style of Revelation (see 4:6; 6:6; 9:7; 19:1, 6[3x]).

3.c-c. Variant: omit καὶ τῶν πρεσβυτέρων] C arm^{1}.

3.d. Variant: ἐνώπιον before τῶν πρεσβυτέρων] ℵ 2019 it^{gig} syr arm.

3.e. See *Note* 1.a.

3.f. The substantival ptcp. οἱ ἠγορασμένοι (masc. nom. pl. pf. pass.), "those who have been redeemed," is a solecism because it is a masc. nom. pl. in apposition to αἱ ἑκατὸν τεσσεράκοντα τέσσαρες χιλιάδες, "the 144,000," a fem. nom. pl. The same solecism occurs in 7:4, χιλιάδες ἐσφραγισμένοι. οἱ ἠγορασμένοι emphasizes the resulting state of the subjects rather than the action that produced the condition (Fanning, *Verbal Aspect,* 160).

4.a. οὗτοι is a nom. in apposition to οἱ ἠγορασμένοι.

4.b. The Gk. term παρθένοι, "[male] virgins," is here translated "chaste" (see *Comment* on 14:4).

4.c-c. Variants: (1) ὅπου ἂν ὑπάγῃ] ℵ Andreas Byzantine; B. Weiss, *Johannes-Apokalypse,* 98; Nestle-Aland^{27}; UBSGNT^{4}; Schmid, *Studien* 2:91. (2) ὅπου ἂν ὑπάγει] A C (lacuna in 𝔓^{47}) fam 1611^{2329} Andr i^{2015} e^{2091} f^{2031} g^{2071} Andr/Byz 2a$^{104\ 459\ 628\ 680}$ Andr/Byz 2b$^{336\ 620}$ Andr/Byz 3^{1745} Andr/Byz 4a^{2084} Andr/Byz 4b^{172} Byz 1^{2256} Byz 2^{2138} Byz 4^{1719} Byz 18^{256} 181 598 792 2019; WHort; Charles, 1:10, 323. On ἄν with the ind., see Porter, *Verbal Aspect,* 125–26. In view of the relative rarity of ἄν with the ind., reading (2) is the *lectio difficilior.* In the NT there are a few examples of ἄν with the *aor.* ind. (Mark 6:56; Luke 19:23 = Matt 25:27; Heb 10:2). Rev 8:1 has ὅταν with ἤνοιξεν, an aor. ind. There are also a few examples of ἄν with the impf. ind. (Mark 6:56; Acts 2:45; 4:35; 1 Cor 12:2) but no examples of ἄν with the present ind. in the NT apart from Rev 14:4. In addition to being the *lectio difficilior,* reading (2) is also attested by the strong combination of A and C and is arguably the superior reading. However, Schmid argues that an itacistic error (ῃ = ει; see Gignac, *Grammar* 1:239–42) is more likely than an original ind. (*Studien* 2:91, 218), and it appears that an original present ind. is highly unlikely here.

4.d. Variant: ὑπὸ Ἰησοῦ] Andr f$^{051\ 2023\ 2073}$ Byzantine.

4.e. ἀπαρχή, "devoted servants" (for this translation, see *Comment* on 14:4), is a nom. in apposition to the preceding οὗτοι. Variant: ἀπ' ἀρχῆς for ἀπαρχή] 𝔓^{47} ℵ Andr h^{-2302} Andr/Byz 2b; Primasius (*ab exordio*); Beatus (*ab initio*). A similar variant is found in 2 Thess 2:13, where ἀπαρχήν is read by B F G^{gr} P 33 81; Nestle-Aland^{27}; UBSGNT^{4}, and is certainly the *lectio difficilior,* while ἀπ' ἀρχῆς is strongly attested by ℵ D K L Ψ (evidence in *TCGNT*^{1}, 636–37).

5.a. τῷ στόματι, "mouth," is a distributive noun, which occurs here in the sing. but has been translated as pl.; cf. *Note* 1.h.

5.b. Variants: (1) omit γάρ] A C 025 fam 1611^{1854} Oecumenius^{2053}; Andr b e f^{2023} h i^{2042} 598 it$^{\text{c diu gig haf}}$ Augustine *(sine macula sunt)*; Beatus (*immaculati sunt*). (2) γάρ after ἄμωμοι] 𝔓^{47} ℵ* 046 fam 1006$^{1006\ 1841}$ fam 1611$^{1611\ 2329}$ 2351; [Andreas] (Schmid, *Studien* 1/1:148); Byzantine; it$^{\text{dem t}}$ vg^{ADDOΠTZ} (*sine macula enim sunt*); syr cop. (3) ὅτι before ἄμωμοι] Andr f^{2023}. One argument for the original presence of γάρ is that the line would then be parallel to παρθένοι γάρ εἰσιν in v 4a. Yet a similar asyndetic construction occurs in 16:6 (ἄξιοί εἰσιν). Reading (1) is supported by *TCGNT*^{1}, 750–51; *TCGNT*^{2}, 677.

6.a. Variants: (1) ἄλλον] ℵ A C 025 fam 1006 fam 1611$^{1611\ 2329\ 2344}$ Oecumenius^{2053} Andr f$^{2073\text{corr}}$ i^{-2042} l n^{-2429}. (2) omit ἄλλον] 𝔓^{47} ℵ* 046 Andreas Byzantine. The strength of the attestation of reading (1) indicates that the original text is preserved by A and C (Schmid, *Studien* 2:91), while the omission of ἄλλον is an attempt to correct the text since no angel is mentioned prior to this text. Reading (1) is also the *lectio difficilior,* which was probably deliberately excised since no angel has been mentioned since 11:15 (*TCGNT*^{1}, 751; *TCGNT*^{2}, 678). J. Weiss attempted to solve the problem by emending ἄλλον ἄγγελον to ἄλλον ἀετόν, "another eagle," referring back to the first eagle in 8:3 (*Offenbarung,* 96), an ingenious but unconvincing solution.

6.b. Variants: (1) εὐαγγελίσαι] *lectio originalis.* (2) εὐαγγελίσασθαι] 𝔓^{47} ℵ fam 1611$^{1854\ 2329}$ Andr e^{2026} f$^{051\ -2073}$ i^{-2042} l 2019. Reading (1), certainly original, is an aor. active inf.; the active form of the verb εὐαγγελίζειν occurs only here and in Rev 10:7 in the NT (in Acts 16:17, εὐαγγελίζοντες occurs as a *var. lect.* attested only in D*). The only other known occurrence of the active verb is in PGiss 27 = *CPJ,* vol. 3, no. 439; for a useful discussion of εὐαγγελ-words, see Horsley, *NewDocs* 3:12–15. εὐαγγελίζειν, though a *causative* verbal form, does not mean "*cause* the good news to be proclaimed" but is similar in meaning to the middle εὐαγγελίζεσθαι (BDR § 309.1).

6.c. Variants: (1) ἐπί] 𝔓^{47} ℵ A C P fam 1611$^{1611\ 1854\ 2329}$ Oecumenius^{2053} Andr l syr^{ph}. (2) omit ἐπί] 051 Andreas Byzantine syr^{h}; Bousset ([1906] 384) places ἐπί in brackets. Schmid correctly argues that only in the Andreas texts are ἐπί^{1} and ἐπί^{3} consistently absent; that only the first ἐπί is consistently missing in the Byzantine texts proves that the absence of the first is really a correction (*Studien* 2:78). The presence of *both* occurrences of ἐπί in the original text suggests that the author understood εὐαγγελίζειν ἐπί to mean "to proclaim among" (cf. Stuart, 2:294–95). φωτίζειν is used in precisely the same syntactical way as εὐαγγελίζειν in Revelation; in 21:23 it is used with the simple acc. (ἐφώτισεν αὐτήν), while in 22:5 it is used with ἐπί (φωτίσει ἐπ' αὐτούς).

6.d. Variants: (1) τοὺς καθημένους] 𝔓^{47} ℵ C 025 Andr d e^{2026} f$^{2023\ -2073\text{corr}}$ i^{1685} l 94 Byzantine. (2) τοὺς κατοικοῦντας] A 051 cop^{bo} eth^{comm} Beatus TR. Reading (1) is the more difficult reading (the verb is not similarly used elsewhere in Revelation) and probably the *lectio originalis.* The original reading in 𝔓^{47} ℵ C is conflated with the correction in A to produce the Andreas reading: τοὺς καθημένους τοὺς κατοικοῦντας (Schmid, *Studien* 2:137). καθῆσθαι can mean "live, dwell, reside" (BAGD, 389; Louw-Nida, § 85.63; cf. Luke 21:35, ἐπεισελεύσεται γὰρ ἐπὶ πάντας τοὺς καθημένους ἐπὶ πρόσωπον πάσης τῆς γῆς, "for it will come upon all those who inhabit the entire earth"); cf. Acts 2:2.

6.e. Variant: omit ἐπί] Andreas.

7.a. Variants: (1) λέγοντα] 𝔓^{47} 051 fam 1611^{1611} Oecumenius^{2053}. (2) omit λέγοντα] ℵ.

7.b. Variant: δοξάσατε] 𝔓^{47}.

7.c-c. Variants: (1) τῷ θεῷ τῷ ποιήσαντι] fam 1611^{2329} it^{gig}. (2) αὐτὸν τὸν ποιήσαντα] Byzantine. Reading (1) is a secondary expansion based on the frequent use of τῷ θεῷ as the obj. of προσκυνεῖν (see *Note* 4:10.b.). Reading (2) may be an Atticistic change; i.e., late grammarians condemned προσκυνεῖν + dat. and recommended the acc. (see *Note* 4:10.b.).

7.d. Variants: (1) omit τήν before θάλασσαν] A C 025 fam 1006 [Andreas] (Andr e h n^{2065} Andr Ø^{1773} 2019). (2) τήν before θάλασσαν] 𝔓^{47} ℵ 051 fam 1611^{1854} Oecumenius^{2053} 2329 Byzantine. (3) anarthrous θαλάσσας] Andr a b. Schmid argues that reading (2) is probably a later addition to the text, as the parallel but anarthrous noun phrase πηγὰς ὑδάτων strongly suggests (Schmid, *Studien* 2:91). The absence of the article is the *lectio difficilior,* though articles are frequently omitted from the second and following nouns in a series of nouns connected by καί (*Apoc. Mos.* 29:11; *T. Abr.* [Rec. A] 15:12), though that is not usually the practice of the author of Revelation. Nevertheless, θάλασσα is usually articular (BDR § 253.2); it occurs twenty-six times in Revelation and is anarthrous in only three instances (4:6; 14:7; 15:2), though two of those occurrences (4:6; 15:2) use the phrase ὡς θάλασσα (cf. *Note* 15:2.b.).

8.a-a. Variants: (1) ἄλλος ἄγγελος δεύτερος] ℵ* C (reads δεύτερον); 051 fam 1611$^{1611\ 2344}$ Oecumenius^{2053} Andreas it^{gig} syr^{h} Primasius; Tischendorf, *NT Graece;* B. Weiss, *Johannes-Apokalypse,* 132; Nestle-Aland^{27}; UBSGNT^{4}. (2) ἄλλος δεύτερος] 𝔓^{47} (has β instead of δεύτερος); ℵ* fam 1006$^{1006\ 1841}$ fam 1611^{1854} syr^{ph}. (3) ἄλλος δεύτερος ἄγγελος] A 1 fam 1611^{2329} Byzantine. Reading (2) probably reflects the accidental omission of ἄγγελος, which must have followed ἄλλος in the exemplar of ℵ*, for it would be easier to omit if it followed ἄλλος than if it followed δεύτερος (Schmid, *Studien* 2:104–5). Reading (1), according to some, best explains the origin of the other variants (*TCGNT*^{1}, 751–52; *TCGNT*^{2}, 678). A exhibits a tendency to place adjs. before the nouns they modify (cf. Rev 2:4; 4:4; 6:4; 19:14; B. Weiss, *Johannes-Apokalypse,* 87–88). The phrase ἄλλος ἄγγελος τρίτος in v 9 also suggests the originality of reading (1).

8.b. Variant: ἠκολούθει] 𝔓^{47}.

8.c-9.a. Variant: omitted by ℵ; the scribe's eye skipped from ἠκολούθησεν in v 8 to ἠκολούθησεν in v 9, omitting everything in between. A similar error of haplography (omission) occurs in ℵ at Luke 10:32 (cf. Metzger, *Text,* 109–10).

8.d. Variants: (1) ἥ] A C fam 1006 fam 1611^{2344} Oecumenius^{2053} Andr l Andr/Byz 4ab. (2) omit ἥ] 𝔓^{47} ℵ^{1} (lacuna in ℵ*) 051 Andreas Byzantine it^{gig}. Reading (1) is certainly the original reading because it has the strongest external support; since ἥ is preceded by μεγάλη, it could easily have been omitted by an error of haplography.

8.e-e. Variants: (1) πεπότικεν] A C 025 fam 1611^{2329} Byz 2$^{2004\ 2138}$ Byz 7^{2024} Byz 17$^{99\ 1852}$ Andr/Byz 3^{1894}. (2) πεπότικε (3rd sing. pf. ind. active from ποτίζειν, "to drink")] Oecumenius^{2053} Andreas Byzantine Tyc^{2} (*potavit*). (3) ἐπότισε] Andr i^{2074}. (4) πέπτωκαν (3rd pl. pf. ind. active from πίπτειν, "to fall")] ℵ^{2} (hiatus in ℵ*) Primasius (*ceciderunt*). (5) πέπτωκεν (3rd sing. pf. ind. active from πίπτειν)] fam 1611^{1854}; Beatus (*cecidit cecidit babylon illa magna cecidit babylon magna*). (6) πέπτω[. . .]ν] 𝔓^{47}. (7) πέπωκαν (pl. pf. ind. active from πίνειν)] attested by no Gk. MSS, but only by it^{gig} (*biberunt*). Since 14:8 and 18:3 (see *Comments*) both contain allusions to LXX Jer 28:7 (MT 51:7), where the verb is ἐπίοσαν (3rd pl. aor. ind. active from πίνειν, "to drink"), it is likely that πεπότικε (ν) is the original reading. It is also possible, however, that an original πέπτωκαν was corrected in light of the LXX text. The substitution of πέπτωκαν might have occurred through the influence of ἔπεσεν ἔπεσεν, which stands at the beginning of the verse (Schmid, *Studien* 2:143).

8.f. ἐκ τοῦ οἴνου is a partitive gen. functioning as the obj. of the pf. verb πεπότικεν, so that the entire sentence could be translated "She made all nations drink *some of the wine* of her passionate lust."

8.g. τοῦ θυμοῦ is a gen. of apposition providing, in effect, an allegorical interpretation of τοῦ οἴνου. In the noun clause τοῦ θυμοῦ τῆς πορνείας αὐτῆς, the second articular noun is a gen. of quality functioning like an adj.: "her immoral passion" (Zerwick, *Greek,* § 40; BDF § 165). θύμος has two distinct meanings; here it means "intense desire" (Louw-Nida, § 25.19), while in v 10 it means "fury, intense anger" (Louw-Nida, § 88.178), another instance of paronomasia (BDF § 488), though commentators generally have not recognized the author's play on words.

9.a. Variant: αὐτῷ] A cop^{bomss} Primasius.

9.b-b. Variant: τὸ θυσιαστήριον] A. A mistake in copying possibly resulting from misinterpreting an abbreviation. On the use of προσκυνεῖν + dat. or acc., see *Note* 4:10.b.

9.c. χάραγμα, "brand," should have the definite article τό (as in v 11) since the χάραγμα has already been mentioned in 13:16. However, the *lack* of a definite article suggests that this passage was not composed or inserted with an awareness of the previous reference in 13:16.

9.d. On this translation, see *Note* 13:16.b.

9.e-e. It is peculiar that in the same context the first ἐπί is used with the gen. τοῦ μετώπου, while the second is used with the acc. τὴν χεῖρα. τῆς χεῖρος, attested by $\mathfrak{P}^{47}$ fam $1611^{1611\ 2329}$ Andr d 94 1773, is an attempt to assimilate the acc. to the previous gen. (Schmid, *Studien* 2:212).

10.a. καί introduces the apodosis of the conditional sentence begun in v 9, which Charles (2:16, 423) labels a Hebraism but which Beyer (*Semitische Syntax,* 69–71) considers a Septuagintism.

10.b. The nom. αὐτός is probably emphatic and probably means "he *too* will drink," just like the nations in v 9, though a different drink (Mussies, *Morphology,* 169–70).

10.c. The prep. phrase ἐκ τοῦ οἴνου τοῦ θυμοῦ τοῦ θεοῦ, "of the wine which is the wrath of God," is a partitive gen. (intensified by the prep. ἐκ, "of/from"), functioning as the *obj.* of the verb πίεται, "will drink"; cf. BDR § 164. When a partitive gen. is used as the obj. of a verb, only *part* of the obj. is affected by the verb; therefore an indefinite pl., such as τινά, "some," is generally presupposed.

10.d. Here τοῦ θυμοῦ, "the wrath," is an epexegetical or appositive gen. that interprets the metaphor of the wine.

10.e. θυμός means "fury" here (Louw-Nida, § 88.178), while in v 8 it means "intense desire" (Louw-Nida, § 25.19), an instance of the figure of speech called paronomasia.

10.f-f. Variant: ἐκ τοῦ ποτηρίου] A Byz 17^{469} Andr/Byz 2a 2b.

10.g. Variants: (1) τῆς ὀργῆς] *lectio originalis.* (2) τὴν ὀργήν] A. (3) omit] Beatus. Here τῆς ὀργῆς is certainly original and is an epexegetical or appositive gen. that allegorically interprets the metaphor of the cup.

10.h-h. The καί introducing this phrase functions as a consecutive particle introducing a result clause (Zerwick, *Greek,* § 455; Ljungvik, *Syntax,* 62–63; Mussies, *Morphology,* 342; Aejmelaeus, *Parataxis,* 14–18). καί functions in a similar way in 3:7; 11:13; 20:10; cf. 2:23; 3:10 (see *Notes* on these passages).

10.i. Variants: (1) βασανισθήσεται (3rd sing. fut. pass. ind.)] C (lacuna in $\mathfrak{P}^{47}$) ℵ Oecumenius^{2053} Andreas Byzantine arm eth^{comm} it^{gig} Primasius Beatus; Charles, 2:326. (2) βασανισθήσονται (3rd pl. fut. pass. ind.)] A fam 1006 2019 Byz $16^{61\ 69}$ vg cop; B. Weiss, *Johannes-Apokalypse,* 109; Bousset (1906) 385. From v 10 to v 11, there is a transition from sing. (καὶ αὐτὸς πίεται) to pl. (ὁ κάπνος . . . αὐτῶν). In A and the rest of the witnesses in reading (2), this transition occurs earlier. Since the external attestation is stronger, reading (1) is preferred, though either could be original (Schmid, *Studien* 2:105).

11.a. See *Note* 10.d.

11.b. After a series of sing. pronouns, αὐτῶν (masc. pl.. gen.) occurs here.

11.c-c. On the use of προσκυνεῖν + dat. or acc., see *Note* 4:10.b.

11.d-d. Here εἴ τις, which was often regarded as one word (BDF § 475.2), was considered in Hellenistic Gk. to be the equivalent of ὅστις (BDF § 376; Ljungvik, *Syntax,* 11) and could introduce relative clauses (e.g., Matt 18:28). For a detailed discussion of εἴ τις, see Ljungvik, *Syntax,* 9–18. Charles suggests, for example, that εἴ τις λαμβάνει is equivalent to οἱ λαμβάνοντες (2:18); cf. Mark 4:23, εἴ τις ἔχει ὦτα, with Rev 2:7, ὁ ἔχων οὖς.

11.e. On this translation, see *Note* 13:16.b.

11.f. τοῦ ὀνόματος is an epexegetical or explanatory gen., so the phrase χάραγμα τοῦ ὀνόματος αὐτοῦ means "the brand consisting of its name."

12.a-a. ὧδε, used to refer to the relevance of that which immediately precedes for the present discourse; it can be translated "in this, in this case, in the case" (Louw-Nida, § 92.35). The major Eng. versions all translate this term appropriately, though in various ways: (1) "here is a call for" (RSV and NRSV), (2) "this is a call for" (NIV), (3) "this calls for" (REB).

12.b. Variant: ἐστίν is transposed by $\mathfrak{P}^{47}$ from after ἁγίων to after ὧδε; singular reading.

12.c-c. On translating οἱ ἅγιοι, lit. "saints," as "God's people," see *Comment* on 5:8.

12.d. Variant: insert ὧδε] 051 Andreas. This is a correction, which eliminates the problem of οἱ τηροῦντες (see *Note* 14:12.e).

12.e. Variants: (1) οἱ τηροῦντες] *lectio originalis.* (2) τῶν τηρούντων] ℵ fam $1006^{1006\ 1841}$ fam 1611^{1611} 2019 Andr l. οἱ τηροῦντες (nom. pl. masc. ptcp.) is the *lectio difficilior* because it is in apposition to τῶν ἁγίων (gen. pl. noun). It is therefore a solecism, which should read τῶν τηρούντων, and has been corrected in reading (2).

12.f. The term "maintaining" has been inserted even though a single ptcp. (οἱ τηροῦντες) has two objs., τὰς ἐντολάς and τὴν πίστιν, since in Eng. no single verb can be used with "the commandments" and "the faith" as objs.

12.g-g. In the phrase τὴν πίστιν Ἰησοῦ, "Jesus" is construed as an obj. gen. (see *Comments* on 1:9 and 14:12).

13.a. Variants: (1) omit μοι] ℵ A C 025 046 fam 1006 fam 1611. (2) insert μοι] 051 Oecumenius^{2053} ^{2062} Andreas it$^{dem\ diu\ gig}$ vg^{D} Primarsius Cassiodorus. The dat. pronoun μοι follows various forms of λέγειν thirteen times (7:13, 14; 10:9, 11; 17:7, 15; 19:9[2x], 10; 21:6; 22:6, 9, 10), suggesting that it was inserted here on analogy with these passages and in accordance with common Gk. usage.

13.b-b. On the translation "how fortunate," see *Note* 1:3.b.

13.c-c. Variants: (1) Χριστῷ] C 025 fam 1611^{1854} 792 Beatus. (2) θεῷ] fam 1611^{1611} eth syr^{h}. The *lectio originalis*, ἐν κυρίῳ, could refer to either God or Christ, while the two corrections, ἐν Χριστῷ and ἐν θεῷ, remove the ambiguity.

13.d-d. Variants: (1) ἀπαρτὶ λέγει] conjecture of A. Debrunner ("Über einige Lesarten der Chester Beatty Papyri des Neuen Testaments," ConNT 11 [1947] 45–59), based on the orthography of reading (2). (2) ἀπ' ἄρτι λέγει] 𝔓^{47} ℵ* Andr g^{205} Byz 3^{522} Byz 6^{218} Andr/Byz 2^{-336} cop^{bo} arm. (3) ἀπ' ἄρτι λέγει ναί] fam 1611^{2329} 94 Andr f^{2023} Andr/Byz 3 Byzantine. (4) ἀπ' ἄρτι ναὶ λέγει] ℵ^{c} A C 025 Andreas vg; Nestle-Aland^{27}; UBSGNT^{4}. (5) ἀπ' ἄρτι καὶ λέγει] Oecumenius^{2053}. (6) ἀπὸ ἄρτι ναὶ λέγει] Andr i^{-2042}. Reading (4) has the strongest external support, while reading (2) is the shortest (*TCGNT*^{1}, 752; *TCGNT*^{2}, 678–79). Reading (5) is probably the result of a simple copyist's error, confusing καί for ναί.

For all the readings other than (6), there is a problem of punctuation, i.e., whether ἀπ' ἄρτι, "from now on," belongs with the preceding or following sentence. Nestle-Aland^{27} places a period *after* ἀπ' ἄρτι, which suggests that the sentence be translated "Blessed are the dead who die in the Lord from now on." This punctuation is supported by Tischendorf, *NT Graece;* B. Weiss, *Johannes-Apokalypse,* 198; Bousset (1906) 386; Charles, 2:321; Merk, *NT;* UBSGNT^{4}. It is my opinion, however, that ἀπ' ἄρτι should be taken as ἀπαρτί, "certainly, exactly, truly," belonging to the same semantic domain as ἀμήν, "amen, truly," an Attic usage, and understood as the beginning of the following sentence (BDF § 12.3; BDR § 12.3), i.e., reading (1). The phrase οὐ μὴ πίω ἀπ' ἄρτι in Matt 26:29 reads οὐ μὴ πίω ἀπὸ τοῦ νῦν in the parallel in Luke 22:18, but a related formulation in John 13:19 has ἀπ' ἄρτι λέγω ὑμῖν, which makes little sense unless ἀπ' ἄρτι is construed as ἀπαρτί (a synonym of ἀμήν), so that ἀπ' ἄρτι λέγω ὑμῖν should perhaps be read ἀπαρτὶ λέγω ὑμῖν, "certainly I say to you" = ἀμὴν λέγω ὑμῖν, "truly I say to you." Another example of this confusion is found in Matt 26:64, "From now [ἀπ' ἄρτι] on you will see the Son of man seated at the right hand of Power and coming on the clouds of heaven." The parallel in Luke 22:69 reads "But from now on [ἀπὸ τοῦ νῦν] the Son of man will be seated at the right hand of the power of God." A closely related logion occurs in John 1:51, "He said to him 'Truly, truly, I say to you, you will see the heaven opened, and the angels of God ascending and descending on the Son of man." Here again the ἀμὴν ἀμὴν λέγω ὑμῖν of John 1:51 could be an equivalent to ἀπαρτὶ λέγω ὑμῖν.

13.e-e. Variants: (1) ἵνα ἀναπαήσονται (3rd pl. fut. pass. ind.] A ℵ; WHort. (2) ὅτι ἀναπαήσονται] 𝔓^{47}. (3) ἵνα ἀναπαύσωνται (3rd pl. aor. mid. subjunctive)] 051^{c} Oecumenius^{2053} Byzantine. (4) ἵνα ἀναπαύσονται (3rd pl. fut. mid. ind.)] C 046 fam 1611^{2329} 792 2019 2084 Andr a^{1} b^{2059} c e f$^{051*\ 2013\ 2056}$ g^{2071} h^{-2302} i^{2015} Ø$^{181\ 598}$ Byz 1^{2256} Byz 3^{429} Byz 4^{1719} Byz 7^{2024} Byz 12^{2048} Byz 13^{2058} Byz 17$^{1852\ 2017}$ Andr/Byz 1^{922} Andr/Byz 2a$^{104\ 459\ 620\ 680}$ Andr/Byz 2b^{336} Andr/Byz 3^{2061} Andr/Byz 4^{1828}. ἀναπαύσονται and ἀναπαύσωνται are both corrections of ἀναπαήσονται (Schmid, *Studien* 2:105, 220), the first changing it from a fut. pass. ind. to a fut. mid. ind., while the second (influenced by ἵνα) changes a fut. ind. to a more commonly used aor. subjunctive.

13.f. ἵνα is problematic here and can be construed in several ways (cf. also 16:15; 22:14): (1) It can be understood as causal (n.b. that 𝔓^{47} reads ὅτι ἀναπαήσονται here), i.e., as a virtual equivalent to ὅτι, and perhaps for that reason it is linked with the fut. ind. rather than with an aor. subjunctive (BDF § 369.2; the discussion of causal ἵνα is found in BDR § 456.2; cf. D. C. Hesseling and H. Pernot, "ἵνα = omdat," *Philologus* 12 [1927] 43–44). The three instances in which ἵνα may be understood as introducing a causal clause in Revelation (14:13; 16:15; 22:14) are formally similar in that all are μακάριοι sayings. Matt 5:3–10 has eight μακάριοι . . . ὅτι sayings (just three occur in Luke 6:20–21). On the causal use of ἵνα, see A. T. Robertson, "The Causal Use of ἵνα," in *Studies in Early Christianity,* ed. S. J. Case (New York: Century, 1928) 51–57. (2) It can be understood as imperatival or absolute, i.e., "let them rest from their labor" (Zerwick, *Greek,* § 414; A. R. George, "The Imperatival Use of ἵνα in the New Testament," *JTS* 45 [1944] 56–60). Cf. Eph 5:33. (3) It can be understood as introducing a final or purpose clause ("so that").

13.g. The sing. verb ἀκολουθεῖ has the neut. pl. subject τὰ ἔργα following Gk. syntactical usage (BDF § 133); other examples of this phenomenon are found in 18:14; 20:5; 19:14; 20:7.

14.a-a. Variant: omit καὶ εἶδον] ℵ fam 1611^{1854} 2324 syr^{ph}.

14.b-b. Variant: ὁ ἐπὶ τὴν νεφέλην καθημένος] 𝔓^{47}; a singular reading that violates a syntactical rule of the author that a prep. phrase cannot stand between the article and a substantive. This "rule," however, is violated in the *adscriptiones* of each of the seven proclamations in 2:1, 8, 12, 18; 3:1, 7, 14; for a discussion of this issue, see *Note* 2:1.a-a. This correction does, however, follow the author's tendency to place a nom. following the interjection ἰδού (see *Note* 14:14.c.). However, cf. Rev 19:9, where an extensive prep. phrase is inserted between the article and the substantivized ptcp.: οἱ εἰς τὸ δεῖπνον τοῦ γάμου τοῦ ἀρνίου κεκλημένοι.

14.c. Following the interjection ἰδού, "behold," the nom. regularly follows (Rev 4:1, 2; 5:5; 6:2, 5, 8; 7:9; 12:3; 14:1; 19:11; 21:3). Yet the author reverts to the acc. with the phrase καθήμενον ὅμοιον υἱὸν ἀνθρώπου, "one sitting like a son of man" (probably functioning as the obj. of the aor. εἶδον, "I saw"). Then after this acc. noun phrase, the author switches back to the masc. nom. sing. again with the adj. ptcp. ἔχων, "having" (see *Note* 14:14.b-b). Cf. *PGM* XII.367–9, ἐπικαλοῦμαί σε τὸν ἐπὶ κενῷ πνεύματι δεινόν, ἀόρατον, μέγαν θεόν, τὸν πατάξαντα γῆν καὶ σείοντα τὸν κόσμον, ὁ φιλῶν ταραχάς, "I call upon you powerful, invisible, great God in the empty wind, who smites the earth and shakes the cosmos, you who love disorder." Here ὁ φιλῶν should be τὸν φιλοῦντα, but apparently the author wants to use a vocative substantival ptcp. since τὸν θεόν functions like a vocative (cf. *PGM* XIII.618, where ἐπικαλοῦμαι σε is followed by a string of vocatives).

14.d-d. The phrase υἱὸς ἀνθρώπου is anarthrous, as it is in 1:13; both allusions appear to be based on Dan 7:13 (though this is denied by Casey, *Son of Man,* 144, 148). The phrase is anarthrous also in Heb 2:6, which is a quotation of Ps 8:4. In the canonical Gospels, ὁ υἱὸς τοῦ ἀνθρώπου is *always* articular, with the sole exception of John 5:27. On the implications of the articular use of the phrase as an anaphoric reference to *the* Son of man (of Dan 7:13), see C. F. D. Moule, *The Origin of Christology* (Cambridge: Cambridge UP, 1977) 11–22. Since the phrase υἱὸς ἀνθρώπου probably refers to an angelic being and not the exalted Jesus (see *Comment* on 14:14), the phrase has been translated "human being."

14.e. Variants: (1) υἱόν] A ℵ 046 fam 1611^{2329} Byzantine vg^{mss} Tyc^{2} Beatus. (2) υἱῷ] 𝔓^{47} C 051 fam 1006 fam 1611^{1611} Oecumenius^{2053} Andreas lat syr. (3) υἱός] fam 1611^{1854}. (4) υἱοῦ] 025 cop. Since the dat. follows ὅμοιος, despite the strong evidence for this reading, it is an attempt to correct the solecism υἱόν; see *Note* 1:13.c-c. ὅμοιος is found twenty-one times in Revelation, and in nineteen instances (one of which occurs in 1:15), it is properly used with the dat. of the person or thing to which something is compared, which suggests that in both 1:15 and 14:14 the author is following a fixed tradition. Reading (1) υἱόν as the *lectio difficilior* both here and in 1:13, where it is undoubtedly the original reading; see Schmidt, *Studien* 2:249).

14.f. Variants: (1) ἔχοντα] 𝔓^{47} ℵ* fam 1006 (2329) Oecumenius^{2053text} Andr g^{2071} i$^{-1685\ -2042}$ l$^{1678\ 1778\ 2080}$ Andr Ø^{254} Byz 1^{911} Byz 3^{385} Byz 5$^{808\ 1893}$ Byz 9$^{203\ 452\ 467\ 506}$ Byz 10$^{935\ 1728\ 2305}$ Byz 14$^{325\ 456\ 517}$ Byz 15$^{42\ 367}$ Byz 17^{469} Andr/Byz 3^{2196} Andr/Byz 4^{2305}. (2) ἔχον] ℵ^{1} C and a worthless scattering of late minuscules (Byz 4^{141} Byz 6$^{218\ 1352}$ Byz 7^{2024} Andr/Byz 4^{2018}); this variant probably originated in the phonetic similarity between ο and ω. The present masc. sing. ptcp. ἔχων (supported by Andr), "having," is a solecism since it modifies the antecedent noun phrase υἱὸν ἀνθρώπου, "son of man," and so should be ἔχοντα (though the possibility of the interchangeability in pronunciation of ο = ω should be considered [Gignac, *Grammar* 1:275–77; cf. BDR § 28]). Here ἔχων functions as a nom. of apposition, a relatively frequent use of the nom. in Revelation in modifying oblique cases. The same grammatical phenomenon occurs in 1:13–16, where υἱὸν ἀνθρώπου in v 13 is modified by ἔχων in v 16, and that is an argument in favor of the originality of ἔχων here.

15.a. Variants: (1) ναοῦ] *lectio originalis.* (2) οὐρανοῦ] 051 Oecumenius^{2053} Andreas. (3) ναοῦ αὐτοῦ] Andr l. Although the definite article before ναοῦ indicates that the *heavenly* temple is in view, reading (2) is an attempt to clarify the place from which the angel emerges, perhaps based on v 17, where a second angel is said to come ἐκ τοῦ ναοῦ τοῦ ἐν τῷ οὐρανῷ, "out of the temple which is in heaven."

15.b. Variant: insert αὐτοῦ] ℵ Andr l$^{1678\ 1778\ 2080}$ eth.

15.c. Variant: ἀνακράζων] 𝔓^{47}; a singular reading, except that κράζων is translated *proclamans* by Primasius, but *clamans* by it^{gig} Beatus.

15.d-d. The phrase πέμπειν τὸ δρέπανον, lit. "to send a sickle," is an idiom meaning "begin to harvest a crop by cutting ripe grain with a sickle" (Louw-Nida, § 43.17).

15.e. Variant: omit τό before δρέπανον] 𝔓^{47}; singular reading.

15.f. In the phrase καὶ θέρισον, lit. "and harvest," καί is used to introduce a purpose clause, "to harvest" (cf. Ljungvik, *Syntax,* 68–76, esp. 75).

15.g. Variant: ἐξῆλθεν ὁ θερισμός] 𝔓^{47}; singular reading, though ἐξῆλθεν is read by Andr/Byz 4a$^{172\ 2018}$. ἐξῆλθεν is an intensified form of ἦλθεν inserted here because of the occurrence of ἐξῆλθεν twice, in vv 15a and 17.

15.h. While ξηραίνειν normally means "dry," in the case of grains it means "ripe" (Louw-Nida, §

23.198). BAGD, 548, and Bauer-Aland, 1111, erroneously include Rev 14:15 among references under ξηραίνειν that refer to plants without good roots.

16.a-a. Variants: (1) τὴν νεφέλην] C 051 fam 1006$^{1006\ 1841}$ fam 1611$^{1854\ 2329\ 2344}$ Oecumenius^{2053} Andreas; WHort^{mg}; Bousset (1906) 389. (2) τῆς νεφέλης] ℵ A fam 1611^{1611} Andr i^{-2042}; Tischendorf, *NT Graece;* WHort; von Soden, *Text;* Charles, 2:327. (3) τῇ νεφέλῃ] 046 Byzantine. Reading (1) is probably original since it conforms to the author's customary usage (Schmid, *Studien* 2:105, 209–10); that is, after ὁ καθήμενος in the nom. or acc., the case following ἐπί is acc., while if ὁ καθήμενος is in the gen. or dat., the case following ἐπί is dat. B. Weiss has argued that reading (1) was emended under the influence of the phrase ἐπὶ τὴν νεφέλην in v 14 (*Johannes-Apokalypse,* 129).

16.b-b. The phrase βάλλειν τὸ δρέπανον is an idiom meaning "to begin to harvest" (Louw-Nida, § 43.17).

16.c-c. Variant: ἐκαθαρίσθη] fam 1611^{2329}; singular reading.

17.a-a. Variant: ἐκ τοῦ οὐρανοῦ instead of ἐκ τοῦ ναοῦ τοῦ ἐν τῷ οὐρανῷ] fam 1611^{1854} cop^{bo}.

17.b. Variant: αὐτοῦ for τοῦ] 𝔓^{47} eth; obvious transcriptional error.

17.c. Variant: omit τῷ] C; singular reading.

18.a. Variants: (1) omit ἐξῆλθεν] 𝔓^{47} A fam 1611^{1611} 2038 Oecumenius^{2053} Andr g^{2045} Andr h$^{2060\ 2286\ 2302}$ Andr i^{2042} Andr Ø^{598} it$^{ar\ c\ gig}$ (*et alius angelus de altare*); vg. (2) insert ἐξῆλθεν] ℵ C 025 fam 1006^{1006} it$^{dem\ div\ h\ haf}$ syr$^{h\ ph}$ cop$^{sa\ bo}$ arm Beatus (*et alius angelus exiit de ara*). Since the odds are greatly against the same error of omission occurring in 𝔓^{47}, A, and Oecumenius^{2053}, ἐξῆλθεν was probably missing from the ancient text of Revelation (Schmid, *Studien* 2:105). The omission of ἐξηλθεν in reading (1) may be accidental omission, while its presence reflects the kind of repetition characteristic of Revelation; cf. v 17 (*TCGNT*^{1}, 752; *TCGNT*^{2}, 679).

18.b Although θυσιαστήριον normally means "altar" (see *Comment* on 6:9), here (as in 11:1) the context requires that the reference be to the room within which the altar is found, i.e., the "sanctuary" or "holy place." See *Comment* on 11:1b and the references there to Ignatius *Eph.* 5:2–3 and *Trall.* 7:2, where θυσιαστήριον has the same meaning.

18.c-c. Variant: ὁ before ἔχων] A C fam 1611^{2329}; WHort^{mg}; B. Weiss, *Johannes-Apokalypse,* 199; Merk, *NT.* The articular substantival ptcp. ὁ ἔχων is original since the exegesis of the text indicates that this particular angel is identified as ὁ ἔχων ἐξουσίαν ἐπὶ τοῦ πυρός, "the one who has authority over fire" (Schmid, *Studien* 2:91). Charles, 2:328, omits ὁ ἔχων ἐξουσίαν ἐπὶ τοῦ πυρός as a gloss.

18.d. See *Note* 14:1.a.

18.e. Here the adj. ptcp. τῷ ἔχοντι (masc. sing. dat.), "who had," is a solecism since it should modify the noun phrase ἄλλος ἄγγελος, "another angel" (and thus have the form ὁ ἔχων), but instead it has been attracted to the case of φωνῇ μεγάλῃ, "loud voice."

18.f. The article in the ascriptive attributive phrase τὸ δρέπανον τὸ ὀξύ, "the sharp sickle," is anaphoric, referring to the first mention of δρέπανον ὀξύ in v 17.

18.g. The poss. pronoun σου precedes the articular noun it modifies, whereas in the great majority of instances (302) in Revelation it *follows* the noun; in only eleven instances does the pronoun precede the noun that governs it; seven of these occur in Rev 2–3 (cf. *Note* 2:9.k.), while the other four are scattered through Rev 4–22 (10:9; 14:18; 18:5, 14; cf. Mussies, *Morphology,* 120). Since personal categories in Heb. and Aram. are located in the final syllables of words, in the LXX gens. like μου and σου are placed immediately after the substantives they modify in the great majority of instances; cf. A. Wifstrand, "Die Stellung der enklitischen Personalpronomina bei den Septuaginta," *Bulletin Soc. Royale des Lettres de Lund* (1949–50) 44ff.

18.h. See *Note* 18.f.

18.i-i. τῆς ἀμπέλου τῆς γῆς, "from the ['grapevine' or] vineyard which is the earth." Here τῆς γῆς, "the earth," is a gen. of apposition since the vineyard or grapevine symbolizes the earth (M. Zerwick, *Greek,* § 33). Though ἄμπελος usually means "vine" or "grapevine," for the meaning "vineyard" (= ἀμπελών), see Aelian *De natura animalium* 11.32; MM, 27; Bauer-Aland, 91; BAGD, 46.

19.a. Variant: omit ὁ before ἄγγελος] 𝔓^{47}.

19.b. Variant: ἐπί for εἰς] 𝔓^{47}.

19.c. Variants: (1) τὸν μέγαν] C 025 046 051 Andreas Tyc^{2} (*magnum*); Primasius (*magnum*); Nestle-Aland^{27}; UBSGNT^{4}; *TCGNT*^{1}, 752–53. (2) τὸν μέγα] A fam 1611^{2329} Andr b^{-2081} 94. (3) τὴν μεγάλην] ℵ fam 1006$^{1006\ 1841}$ fam 1611^{1854} Oecumenius^{2053} Andr d f^{2023} g i l n^{-2429} cop$^{sa\ bo}$. (4) τοῦ μεγάλου] 𝔓^{47} fam 1611^{1611} Andr n^{2429} 2019. Though it might appear that τὸν μέγαν (masc. sing. acc.) is intended to modify τὴν ληνόν (fem. sing. acc.), it should then have the fem. sing. acc. form τὴν μεγάλην, indicating that reading (2) is probably a correction. The problem might lie in the ambiguous character of ἡ ληνός, a second declension fem. noun (Radermacher, *Grammatik,* 48), which apart from the article is declined like a second declension masc. noun. However, it is possible that the gender of τὸν μέγαν is in agreement with that of τοῦ θυμοῦ (second declension masc. noun), in which case the phrase should be translated "the winepress of the great wrath of God." The scribal correction τοῦ μεγάλου in reading (4), which can go with either θυμοῦ or θεοῦ, is intended to solve this problem. In that case, however, the gen. case of τοῦ θυμοῦ is not in accord with the acc. case of τὴν ληνόν. Torrey (*Apocalypse*, 133–34) thought that the problem of agreement could be solved by recourse to a mistranslated Aram. text. He proposed that this phrase was literally translated into Gk. from Aram.: רמא לדצרתא די לוטא די אלהא ההא רבא *rmʾ lmṣrtʾ dy lwṭʾ dy ʾlhʾ hhʾ rbʾ*, "the great winepress of the wrath of God," through a literal word-by-word translation. A more idiomatic translation would be "the winepress of the great wrath of God," since the Aram. adj. ההא רבא *hhʾ rbʾ* refers to the masc. word לוטא *lwṭʾ*, "curse, wrath." Weyland (*Omwerkings*, 136–37) suggested that the Heb. term behind ληνός was masc. and that the author had this word in mind when writing this sentence. Thayer (*Lexicon*, 377) mentions this construction and claims that "a variation in gender (though not rare in Heb. . . .) can hardly be matched in Grk." In Heb., masc. forms can be used to refer to fem. forms (GKC §§ 110k, 144a; for other irregularities in the use of gender in Heb., cf. GKC §§ 145p, 145t, 145u). Laughlin (*Solecisms*, 13) suggested the MT of Isa 63:3 as an example of double gender (פורה *purâ*, "winepress," is fem., while אדרכם *ʾedrĕkēm*, "I will trample them," is masc.). Laughlin misconstrues the text, however, for the pl. masc. suffix of אדרכם *ʾedrĕkēm* refers not to פורה *purâ* but to ומעמום *ûmēʿammîm*, "and from the people."

20.a. Variants: (1) ἔξωθεν] A C 025 046 fam 1006 fam 1611$^{1611\ 2329}$ Oecumenius^{2053text} Andr f^{2023} n^{-2429}. (2) ἔξω] ℵ 051 fam 1611^{1854} Oecumenius^{2053com} Andreas.

20.b. Variant: μέχρι for ἄχρι] $\mathfrak{P}^{47}$.

20.c-c. Variants: (1) χιλίων ἑξακοσίων, "1600 stadia"] ℵ^{c} A C 025 046 Andreas; *TCGNT*^{1}, 753; *TCGNT*^{2}, 679. (2) χιλίων διακοσίων, "1200 stadia"] ℵ* syr^{ph}. (3) χιλίων ἑξακοσίων ἕξ, "1606 stadia"] Andr i$^{1876\ 2014\ 2036\ 2042\ 2043\ 2047\ 2074\ 2082}$ m$^{2037\ 2046}$.

Form/Structure/Setting

I. Outline

- 4. Visions of eschatological salvation and judgment (14:1–20)
  - a. Eschatological salvation: the Lamb and the 144,000 (vv 1–5)
    - (1) Introductory formula: "Then I saw, and, behold" (v 1a)
    - (2) Vision of the Lamb and 144,000 (v 1)
      - (a) The Lamb stands on Mount Zion (v 1a)
      - (b) The 144,000 are with him (v 1b)
      - (c) Names written on their foreheads (v 1c)
        - [1] Name of the Lamb
        - [2] Name of his Father
    - (3) Audition of the new song (vv 2–3)
      - (a) Description of sound from heaven (v 2)
        - [1] Initial nature similes (v 2a)
          - [a] Like roaring water
          - [b] Like loud thunder
        - [2] Simile from human life: like the sound of kitharas being played (v 2b)
      - (b) The singing of the new song (v 3)
        - [1] Locationof the performance (v 3a)
          - [a] Before the throne
          - [b] Before the cherubim
          - [c] Before the elders
        - [2] The secrecy of the song (v 3bc)
          - [a] No one can learn the song

[b] Except the 144,000 who have been redeemed from the earth

(4) Description of the 144,000 (vv 4–5)

(a) Their sexual purity (v 4a)

[1] They are undefiled by women

[2] They are chaste

(b) They follow the Lamb wherever he goes (v 4b)

(c) They have been redeemed from humanity (vv 4c–5)

[1] They are devoted servants (v 4c)

[a] To God

[b] To the Lamb

[2] Moral character (v 5)

[a] They do not lie

[b] They are blameless

b. Vision of three angelic speeches (vv 6–12)

(1) The first angelic speech: invitation to worship the true God (vv 6–7)

(a) The revelatory angel (vv 6–7a)

[1] Another angel (the first) (v 6a)

[2] Location: flying in midheaven (v 6a)

[3] With an eternal message (v 6a)

[4] Intended audience (v 6b)

[a] Inhabitants of the earth

[b] All ethnic groups

{1} Every nation

{2} Every tribe

{3} Every tongue

{4} Every people

[5] Mode of communication: with a loud voice (v 7a)

(b) The angel's message (v 7)

[1] Necessary attitude toward God (v 7a)

[a] Fear him

[b] Give him glory

[2] Reason: the hour of his judgment has come (v 7b)

[3] Worship God (v 7c)

[a] Who created heaven

[b] Who created the earth

[c] Who created the sea

[d] Who created springs of water

(2) The second angelic speech: the fall of Babylon (v 8)

(a) The revelatory angel (v 8a)

[1] Another angel, a second

[2] Follows first angel

(b) The angel's message (v 8ab)

[1] Announcement of judgment: Babylon is fallen (v 8a)

[2] Reason: she corrupted all nations (v 8b)

(3) The third angelic speech: condemnation of those who worship the beast (vv 9–12)

(a) The revelatory angel (v 9a)
[1] Another angel, a third
[2] Follows second angel
[3] Proclaims with a loud voice
(b) The angel's message (vv 9a–11)
[1] Reasons for punishment (v 9a)
[a] Perverse worship
{1} The beast itself
{2} The beast's image
[b] Receiving brand (v 9b)
{1} On the forehead
{2} On the hand
[2] Description of judgment (vv 10a–11b)
[a] Metaphors of judgment (v 10a)
{1} Must drink the unmixed wine of God's wrath
{2} From the cup of God's anger
[b] Reality of judgment (vv 10b–11b)
{1} Kind of torment (v 10b)
{a} In fire
{b} In sulfur
{2} Place of torment (v 10b)
{a} Before the holy angels
{b} Before the Lamb
{3} Length of torment (v 11ab)
{a} Smoke of torment ascends forever (v 11a)
{b} No rest day or night (v 11b)
[3] Reiterated conditions for punishment (v 11bc)
[a] Perverse worship (v 11b)
{1} The beast itself
{2} The beast's image
[b] Receiving the brand of its name (v 11c)
(3) Parenetic call for the endurance of God's people (v 12)
(a) Those who keep the commands of God
(b) Those who maintain faithfulness to Jesus
c. Audition of antiphonal beatitude (v 13)
(1) Source of beatitude: command to write by heavenly voice (v 13a)
(2) Beatitude for martyrs (v 13b–d)
(a) Blessed are the dead who died in the Lord henceforth (v 13b)
(b) Confirmation by Spirit (v 13cd)
[1] They will rest from their labor (v 13c)
[2] Their works follow them (v 13d)
d. Vision of angelic reapers of the earth (vv 14–20)
(1) The grain harvest (vv 14–16)
(a) The two angelic actors (vv 14–15)
[1] One like a human being (v 14)
[a] Sits on a cloud
[b] Wears a golden wreath
[c] Holds a sharp sickle

[2] Another angel (v 15)
[a] Emerges from temple (v 15a)
[b] Issues command to the one seated on the cloud (v 15a–c)
{1} Use your sickle for harvesting (v 15b)
{2} Reason (v 15c)
{a} The harvest time has arrived
{b} The earth is ripe for harvesting
(b) The act of harvesting by the one sitting on the cloud (v 16)
[1] He swings his sickle on the earth
[2] The earth is harvested
(2) The grape harvest (vv 17–20)
(a) The two angelic actors (vv 17–18)
[1] Another angel (v 17)
[a] Emerges from the heavenly temple
[b] Holding a sharp sickle
[2] Another angel (v 18)
[a] Emerges from the sanctuary (v 18a)
[b] Identity: the one with authority over fire (v 18a)
[c] Issues command to first angel (v 18b)
{1} Use your sickle for gathering grapes from the earth
{2} Reason: the grapes are ripe
(b) The acts of gathering and pressing the grapes (vv 19–20)
[1] The gathering of the grapes (v 19)
[a] The angel swings his sickle toward the earth (v 19a)
[b] The angel gathers the grapes of the earth (v 19a)
[c] The angel puts the grapes into the great press of God's wrath (v 19b)
[2] The pressing of the grapes (v 20)
[a] The grapes are pressed (v 20a)
[b] Location: outside the city (v 20a)
[c] Metaphorical result: "blood" (v 20b)

II. Literary Analysis

The composition and structure of Rev 14 are extraordinarily complex. The text consists of four self-contained units of text framed at the beginning in 14:1 by one of the author's favorite introductory formulas, which is frequently used to introduce a new subject, "I saw, and behold," and at the end by the phrase that introduces a new unit of text in 15:1, "Then I saw another sign" (the term "another" in 15:1 in turn refers back to 12:1, 3), which also indicates a new subject. The chief structural problem is whether 14:14–20 should be considered part of the larger section 14:1–20 or a separate and equal unit. The phrase καὶ εἶδον, καὶ ἰδού, "then I saw, and behold" introduces 14:14, which would seem to suggest that a new unit of text is introduced parallel to 14:1–13. On the other hand, the phrase ἄλλον ἄγγελον, "another angel," which occurs three times in 14:6–13, also occurs three times in 14:14–20 and seems to function as a literary link between these units of text.

Several themes and motifs link 14:1–20 with what precedes and follows. First, the introduction in 13:11–18 of the worship of the beast and the possibility of being branded with the name or number of the beast on the right hand or the forehead is countered in 14:1–5 by the 144,000 who have the names of God and the Lamb written on their foreheads. Second, those who worship the beast and receive its brand in 13:11–18 are condemned in 14:9–11 to eternal torment, a consequence not mentioned in 13:11–18. Third, the call for endurance in 14:12 is similar in form to the call in 13:10 and is similar in content to 12:17, with the reference to keeping the commandments of God and maintaining the testimony of Jesus or faithfulness to Jesus. Fourth, the beatitude in 14:13 appears to be addressed to those who die for their faith, a possibility mentioned in 13:15. While these elements link 14:1–5, 14:9–11, 14:12, and 14:13 with 12:17–13:18, the other three units in Rev 14 (vv 6–7, 8, 14–20) exhibit no such evident connections.

There are four units of text in Rev 14: (1) 14:1–5; (2) 14:6–12; (3) 14:13; and (4) 14:14–20. Each presents a particular set of problems involving its internal structure and meaning and its structural relation to the other textual units. The phrase ἄλλος ἄγγελος, "another angel," is prominent in vv 6–18, where it occurs no less than six times (vv 6, 8, 9, 15, 17, 18). Since the same schema is present in these six verses, it is possible that vv 6–20 form an originally unified text, which the author has incorporated into the present context. However, it is more likely that the four units of text in vv 1–20 represent a pastiche of themes and motifs drawn from elsewhere in Revelation. Here is a synoptic list of parallels between Rev 14:1–20 and other parts of Revelation (the bracketed references are parallels of content though not verbally similar), and it is striking how few parallels there are between vv 14–20 and the rest of Revelation:

Rev 14:1–20		*Parallels in Revelation*
v 1	I saw, and behold,	4:1; 6:2, 5, 8; 7:9; 14:14; 19:11
	the Lamb was standing	5:6
	144,000	7:4
	his name and Father's name written on foreheads	7:3; 22:4b
v 2	I heard a voice from heaven	10:4
	like the roar of water	19:6a
	like the sound of loud thunder	19:6a
	like kitharists playing	[19:6a]
v 3	They sang a new song	5:9
v 4	They follow the Lamb	[7:17]
v 6	flying in midheaven	8:13
	those who dwell on the earth	6:10; 8:13; 11:10; 13:8, 14; 17:3, 8
	every nation, tribe, language, people	5:9; 7:9; 10:11; 13:7; 17:5
v 8	Fallen, fallen is Babylon the great	18:2
	who gave all nations to drink of the wine which is her immoral passion	17:2; 18:3a
v 9	If anyone worships the beast or his cultic image	13:15; 16:2b; 19:20b; 20:4b

	and receives a brand on his forehead or hand	13:16b; 16:2b; 19:20b; 20:4b
v 10	of the wine of the wrath of God	16:19b; 19:15
	fire and sulphur	19:20; 20:10; 21:9
v 11	Those who worship the beast and its cultic image	cf. v 9
	they have no rest day and night	4:8
	if anyone receives the brand with its name	cf. v 9
v 12	This indicates that the perseverance of God's people	13:10
	keeping the commands of God and maintain faithfulness to Jesus	12:17
v 13	Then I heard a voice from heaven	10:4, 8; 12:10; 4:2; 18:4
v 14	Then I saw, and behold,	4:1; 6:2, 5, 8; 7:9; 14:14; 19:11
	one like a son of man	1:13
v 15	Another angel came out of the temple	[15:6]
v 16	[No parallels]	
v 17	[No parallels]	
v 18	Angel and altar	[8:3, 5]
v 19	The great winepress of God's wrath	19:15
v 20	[No parallels]	

A. Rev 14:1–5: The Lamb and the 144,000

This section constitutes a clearly defined unit of text that provides an effective contrast to the terrifying developments narrated in Rev 13 (Bousset [1906] 146). At the literary level, the mention of the 144,000 must be connected with the earlier mention of the 144,000 who were sealed in Rev 7:4–8, whether or not the author has adapted both scenes from different sources. The entire pericope is introduced with the formula "I saw, and behold" (v 1), and is followed by three structural segments: (1) the vision of the 144,000 on earth (v 1); (2) the audition of the new song sung in heaven (vv 2–3); and (3) the interpretive explanation in vv 4–5, which elaborates on the identity of the 144,000 in three οὗτοι clauses. This explanatory section is compositionally problematic, for it is an elaboration of the author's characteristic use of participial phrases that more closely identify an individual or a group (cf. 11:7; 17:1; 18:9, 15; 19:20; 21:9, 15).

There are both thematic and structural similarities between 14:1–5 and 7:1–17. Like 14:1–5, 7:1–17 also exhibits a tripartite structure: (1) a vision of the sealing of the 144,000 on earth (7:1–8), (2) a vision of a great multitude praising God in his heavenly throne room (7:9–12), and (3) an interpretive explanation (7:13–17). In addition to an analogous structure, two motifs link the two passages: (1) the mention of 144,000 (7:4; 14:1) and (2) the mark of the seal of God (7:2–8; 14:1), though only in 14:1 is it made explicit that the seal consists of the *name* of the Lamb and his Father. The striking structural and thematic parallels between these two passages present an interpretive problem. What is the origin of this doublet?

B. Rev 14:6–12

This section introduces four subunits of text (vv 6–7, 8, 9–11, 12), which, despite the diversity of their content, form a literary unit. The first three subunits are presented as a single vision, beginning with the phrase καὶ εἶδον, "then I saw" (v 6); each of the three angelic speeches mentions yet another angelic revealer, referred to as "another angel" (v 6), "another angel, a second" (v 8), and "another angel, a third" (v 9); the second and third angels are described as "following" (ἠκολούθησεν) the previous one. There is yet a fourth formal link between these three units in that each conforms to the literary form that I have earlier designated the *angelic speech* (see Rev 7:1–17, *Form/Structure/Setting,* II. Literary Forms).

The first form, the *angelic action,* occurs four times (7:1; 8:2; 15:1; 20:1–3) and exhibits the following structural features: (1) introductory phrase: καὶ εἶδον, "then I saw" (μετὰ τοῦτο εἶδον, "after this I saw": 7:1; 8:2; 15:1); (2) object of vision: ἄγγελον, "angel," or ἀγγέλους, "angels" (7:1; 8:2; 15:1; 20:1); (3) brief description of the action performed by or to the angel or angels (7:1; 8:2; 15:1; 20:1–3); and (4) an abrupt change of subject (7:2; 8:3; 15:2; 20:4). In addition, the author presents these brief angelophanies strictly as an observer; the angel or angels he sees and whose action he describes neither interact with him nor he with them. The second form, the *angelic speech,* occurs nine times in Revelation (7:2–3; 10:1–7; 14:6–7, 8, 9–11, 14–16, 18–20; 18:1–3; 19:17–18) and is once inserted immediately following an *angelic action* (7:2–3). The *angelic speech* in Revelation exhibits the following structural features: (1) introductory phrase: καὶ εἶδον (7:2; 10:1; 14:6; 18:1; 19:17); (2) object of vision: ἄλλον ἄγγελον (7:2; 10:1; 14:6, 8, 9; 18:1; 19:17); (3) movement of the angel (ascension, descending, flight, emergence, following) to the center of the action (7:2; 10:1; 14:6, 8, 9, 15, 18; 18:1; 19:17); (4) a statement that the angel "cries with a loud voice" (7:2; 10:3; 14:7, 9, 15, 18; 18:2a; 19:17); and (5) a brief statement from the angel (7:3; 10:3 [what he says is not made explicit, only that "he cried with a loud voice as a lion roars"]; 14:7, 8, 9b–11, 15b, 18b; 18:2b–3; 19:17b–18). This brief statement is the focus of this literary form.

Rev 14:9–11 exhibits a chiastic pattern, for after the introduction in v 9a an angelic speech follows in vv 9b–11, in which vv 9b and 11b are closely parallel and serve to frame this brief unit:

Rev 14:9b	*Rev 14:11b*
εἴ τις προσκυνεῖ τὸ θηρίον If anyone worships the beast	οἱ προσκυνοῦντες τὸ θηρίον Those who worship the beast
καὶ τὴν εἰκόνα αὐτοῦ and its cultic image	καὶ τὴν εἰκόνα αὐτοῦ and its cultic image
καὶ λαμβάνει and receives	καὶ εἴ τις λαμβάνει and if anyone receives
χάραγμα a brand	τὸ χάραγμα τοῦ ὀνόματος αὐτοῦ the brand of its name
ἐπὶ τοῦ μετώπου αὐτοῦ on his forehead	
ἢ ἐπὶ τὴν χεῖρα αὐτοῦ or on his hand	

This section is striking in that it begins with *singular* pronouns and verb forms, switches to *plural* forms in vv 10–11a, and then in v 11b reverts again to the singular τὶς λαμβάνει, "anyone receives." This structure, however, indicates that v 12 is *not* part of vv 9–11 but constitutes an appended text unit, which nevertheless provides an exhortation based on vv 9–11. The third angelic vision (vv 9–11) appears to be an expansion constructed of statements drawn from other parts of Revelation.

Rev 14:12 is a parenetic saying introduced by ὦδε, which interrupts the narrative. The ὦδε introducing this statement calls attention to that which immediately precedes, and therefore this statement must be considered the concluding part of vv 9–11. There are three other such sayings in Revelation, each introduced by ὦδε (13:10, 18; 17:9). Each reads like a commentary on the preceding text made in view of the anticipated impact of the events narrated in that textual unit upon faithful Christians. The similarities between 14:12 and 13:10 are quite close:

Rev 13:10	*Rev 14:12*
ὦδέ ἐστιν This indicates that	ὦδε This indicates that
ἡ ὑπομονὴ the perseverance	ἡ ὑπομονὴ the perseverance
καὶ ἡ πίστις and faithfulness	
τῶν ἁγίων of God's people	τῶν ἁγίων ἐστίν of God's people

This verbal similarity suggests that 14:12 was drawn from 13:10.

C. *Rev 14:13*

The concluding beatitude in v 13 consists of two parts, (1) an unidentified voice from heaven commanding the seer to write and (2) the second of seven beatitudes in Revelation (1:3; 14:13; 16:15; 19:9; 20:6; 22:7, 14). This too appears to have originated as a compositional expansion by the author-editor (not a gloss).

D. *Rev 14:14–20*

Earlier critics tended to regard 14:14–20 as the conclusion of an independent apocalypse, or the conclusion of the *Grundschrift* underlying Revelation, though this view is problematic. This unit of text is introduced with one of the author's customary formulas for beginning a new subject, "I saw, and behold" (v 14), and concludes in v 20, which is followed by an introductory phrase indicating the beginning of a major new section of the composition: "I saw another sign" (15:1). Rev 14:14–20 consists of two units, the first in vv 14–16 and the second in vv 17–20, which are essentially doublets (Wellhausen, *Analyse,* 24). Since other doublets are also present in Revelation (e.g., 14:1–5 and 7:1–17), the problem to be solved is the relationship between these two versions. Were they taken from the author's apocalyptic sources and intentionally placed here as a pair? Should 14:15–17 be considered an interpolation (Charles, 2:20–21)?

Rev 14:14–16	*Rev 14:17–20*
figure with sickle seated on cloud	figure with sickle comes out of temple
another angel comes out of the temple	another angel comes out from the altar
calls with loud voice to first figure	calls with loud voice to first figure
"Put in your sickle" [πέμψον τὸ δρέπανόν σου]	"Put in your sickle" [πέμψον σου τὸ δρέπανον]
to harvest	to gather clusters
for harvest is ripe	for grapes are ripe
first figure used his sickle on the earth	first angel used his sickle on the earth
the earth was reaped	vintage of the earth gathered

The parallelism ceases with vv 19c–20, where the imagery of the grape harvest is continued by mentioning the "great winepress of the wrath of God," into which the grapes are placed. The winepress is then trodden outside the city, and the blood that flowed out of it is described in stereotypical apocalyptic language as being as high as a horse's bridle (see Bauckham, "Apocalyptic Traditions," 40–48).

The composition of Rev 14:14–20 is distinctive in Revelation and appears to combine the two literary forms that the author uses in various contexts in Revelation, the *angelic speech* and the *angelic action* (see *B. Rev 14:6–12* above), into a mixed form, the *angelic speech and action,* which occurs in vv 14–16 and 17–20 (Rev 7:1–17, *Form/Structure/Setting,* III. Literary Forms). This suggests that this section is not drawn from an existing source but is the composition of the author, though it contains many stereotypical apocalyptic motifs. It consists of several elements: (1) introductory phrase: καὶ εἶδον (14:14); (2) object of vision: an angelic figure (14:14 ["one like a son of man"], 17); (3) description of the figure (14:14, 17); (4) introduction of a second angel (14:15a, 18a); (5) a command given to the first angel by the second (14:15b, 18b); and (6) the fulfillment of the command by the first angel (14:16, 19–20).

The juxtaposition of the imagery of the grain harvest and the grape harvest as metaphors for divine judgment in vv 14–20 is based on Joel 3:13 (MT 4:13):

> Put in the sickle, for the harvest [קָצִיר *qāṣîr*] is ripe.
> Go in, tread, for the winepress is full.
> The vats overflow, for their wickedness is great.

While this passage originally centers on the metaphor of the vintage harvest alone, John understood it to refer *both* to the grain harvest and to the grape harvest (קציר *qāṣîr* is normally used of the grain harvest, while בציר *bāṣîr* is used of the vintage harvest). The tradition in Rev 14:14–16 is also reflected in Mark 4:29, which also alludes to Joel 3:13 as a grain harvest (see Bauckham, "Conversion," 290–96). Elsewhere the cutting of the grape clusters or the treading of the vintage is used alone as a metaphor for divine judgment (Lam 1:15; Isa 63:1–6; Jer 25:30–31), as is the metaphor of the grain harvest or the image of the threshing floor (Isa 17:4–5; Jer 51:33; Mic 4:13; Matt 3:12 [= Luke 3:17]; Matt 9:37–38 [= Luke 10:2; *Gos. Thom.* 73]; Mark 4:29; cf. Gal 6:7–9). Charles proposes that vv 15–17 contain an intrusive doublet whose removal makes sense of vv 14, 18–20. This is true, but it is also an unacceptable solution.

III. Interpreting Rev 14:14–20

The central interpretive problems in 14:14–20 are two: (1) Does the figure identified as "one like a son of man" in v 14 represent the Messiah or Christ, or should he be identified as an angel? (2) While all interpreters are agreed that the grape harvest in vv 17–20 is a metaphor for judgment, does the grain harvest narrated in vv 14–16 also represent judgment, or could it be a metaphor for the eschatological gathering of the elect by Christ?

A. *"One like a son of man" (Rev 14:14–16)*

Most interpretations of Rev 14:14–16 conclude that the "one like a son of man" is the Messiah, if this is a fragment of a Jewish apocalyptic composition (Bousset [1906] 388), or the exalted Christ (van Schaik, "Ἄλλος ἄγγελος," 222–25; Müller, 269–70). The strongest argument for identifying the "one like a son of man" figure with the exalted Christ is the fact that the identical phrase, "one like a son of man" (ὅμοιον υἱὸν ἀνθρώπου, distinctive because it is a solecism since υἱόν should be in the dative case), occurs in Rev 1:13, where it is also an allusion to Dan 7:13, and just as clearly describes a figure in 1:13–16 that most commentators agree is the exalted Christ (Prigent, 233; Roloff, 154). One obstacle to the identification of these two figures is the golden wreath mentioned in v 14, which has no counterpart in 1:13 (Kraft, 197). The exalted nature of the "one like a son of man" is sometimes emphasized by pointing out that this figure is preceded (14:6, 8, 9) and followed (14:15, 17, 18) by three angels and thus stands at the center as their head (Lohse, 86). While this is an imaginative reading of vv 6–20, it is not at all evident that the text was intentionally structured in this way. It must be recognized that the only common feature that 14:14–16 has with 1:12–16 is the phrase "one like a son of man" drawn from Dan 7:13. Only if the phrase "one like a son of man" (v 14b), and perhaps also the phrase "with a golden crown upon his head" (v 14c), is considered an *interpolation* in an earlier composition that the author revised at a later stage can it be effectively argued that the figure in v 14 represents an angel and not Christ. This also means that at the final stage of composition, the author-editor has equated the two figures and regards the "one like a son of man" in 14:14–16 as the exalted Christ.

Once this major hurdle is crossed, there are a number of weighty arguments in favor of construing the "one like a son of man" figure as representing an angelic being rather than the exalted Christ (Zahn, 2:524; Kiddle-Ross, 274–77; Kraft, 197–98; Coppens, "Fils d'homme angélique," 277; see the detailed remarks in *Comments* on vv 14–16): (1) The phrase "one like a son of man" is an allusion to Dan 7:13 but reflects no awareness of the Son of man traditions in the canonical Gospels. The phrase is used not as a title but rather as a simile and should be translated "one like a human being." Aside from a common allusion to Dan 7:13 in 1:13 and 14:14, nothing suggests the identity of the two figures (Coppens, "Fils d'homme angélique," 229). (2) The "one like a son of man" wears a gold στέφανος, "wreath, crown," which nowhere else in Revelation is part of the apparel of the Messiah or the exalted Christ (with the possible exception of 6:2, but see *Comment* there). (3) The "one like a son of man" is commanded by "another angel" to begin harvesting (v 15), though it seems inappropriate for the exalted Christ to be commanded by an angel (Zahn, 2:525). This difficulty is often met by claiming that the originator of the angel's command is God, since the angel emerges "from the [heavenly] temple" (Roloff, 154–55; Müller, *Messias,* 194; Harrington, *Apocalypse,* 192). Another way out of the difficulty is to claim that, since the Son of man does not know the day or the hour of the end (Mark 13:32; Acts 1:7), he must therefore be told by God (Wikenhauser, 102). (4) The phrase "another angel" (v 15a) suggests that the "one like a son of man" is in fact an angelic figure (Zahn, 2:524; Bousset [1906] 388; Coppens, "Fils d'homme angélique," 229). (5) If the grain harvest in vv 15–16 and the vintage harvest in vv 18–20 *both* symbolize judgment (see the discussion of this issue below), then the "one like a son of man" participates only in the first part, not the second. (6) The "one like a son of man" is described not as *coming* but rather as harvesting the earth while sitting on a cloud. (7) When the first figure is referred to twice in vv 15 and 16, it is by means of the epithet "the one sitting on the cloud," *not* as "one like a son of man," indicating that the latter epithet is not particularly important for the author. (8) The task of harvesting the earth is a task entrusted to angels: οἱ δὲ θερισταὶ ἄγγελοί εἰσιν, "the reapers are angels" (Matt 13:39; cf. Mark 13:26–27 = Matt 24:30–31, where the returning Son of man sends angels to gather the elect from all parts of the world).

B. The Grain Harvest (14:15–16)

The grain harvest in vv 14–16 has often been construed as a metaphor for the eschatological judgment, the position taken in this commentary. A variation on this view, suggested by Weiss-Heitmüller (4:298–99), is to interpret the grain harvest as the general judgment, while the grape harvest in vv 17–20 represents the judgment of Israel (since "vineyard" is a frequent metaphor for Israel). However, a number of scholars have argued that the grain harvest should be rather understood in the positive sense of the gathering of the elect by the Messiah or the exalted Christ (Hadorn, 156; Lohmeyer, 129; Prigent, 234) or, alternatively, as the conversion of people from the nations of the world (Bauckham, "Conversion," 283–96). A variation of this view is the suggestion that the grain harvest in vv 14–16 involves the gathering of both the good grain and the worthless weeds, with the burning of the latter (Zahn, 2:525), a view obviously influenced by such texts as Matt 3:12 = Luke 3:17 and Matt 13:36–43.

The most convincing arguments are those that understand the grain harvest in vv 14–16 as a *metaphor for the eschatological judgment* (essentially parallel to the metaphor of the gathering and treading of grapes in vv 17–20), a view held by most scholars (e.g., Wikenhauser, 102; Roloff, 154–55). The main arguments for this view are the following: (1) Rev 14:14–16, like 14:17–21, is a clear allusion to Joel 3:13(MT 4:13), a passage that deals only with divine judgment. (2) The harvest instrument in v 14 is called a δρέπανον ὀξύ, "*sharp* sickle" (the identical phrase describes the tool used for the grape harvest in v 17), indicating that *judgment* and *punishment* are in view, since the sickle is primarily a negative symbol (see *Comment* on 14:14). (3) The phrase ἦλθεν ἡ ὥρα θερίσαι, "the hour for harvest has come," uttered by the angel in v 15, can be construed as referring back to the phrase ἦλθεν ἡ ὥρα τῆς κρίσεως, "the hour of judgment has come," referred to in v 7 (Müller, *Messias,* 194). (4) For the harvest (grain, grape, or olive) as a metaphor for divine judgment, see Isa 17:5; 18:4–5; 24:13; Jer 51:33; Hos 6:11; Joel 3:13(MT 4:13); Mic 4:12–13; Matt 13:24–30, 36–43; Mark 4:29; 4 Ezra 4:28–32; *2 Apoc. Bar.* 70:20. In Matt 3:11–12 the threshing floor is the image used for the separation of the righteous from the wicked, resulting in the salvation of the former and the damnation of the latter. However, in some rabbinical texts, both harvests in Joel 3:13(MT 4:13) can be understood negatively. This is reflected in *Midr. Ps.* 8.1 (quoted in the *Comment* on v 16). (5) Interpreting the wheat harvest as either the gathering of the elect or the conversion of people from the nations of the world is problematic. On the one hand, the motif of the eschatological gathering of the elect occurs occasionally in early Christian eschatological narratives (Mark 13:26–27 = Matt 23:30–31; 1 Thess 4:16–17; 2 Thess 2:1), but it is strikingly absent from Revelation. The one text in Revelation generally thought to reflect the Parousia of the exalted Jesus is Rev 19:11–21, but it only deals with the conquest of the armies of the kings of the earth by the rider on the white horse and his heavenly army. The innumerable multitude of martyrs in heaven depicted in Rev 7:9–17 is there because the martyrs were killed, not because of an eschatological gathering. While the ideal of a reunited people of God may be symbolically represented by the New Jerusalem with twelve gates named for the twelve tribes of Israel and twelve foundations inscribed by the names of the twelve apostles (see *Comment* on 21:12), the eschatological event of gathering itself is nowhere depicted. The sealing of the 144,000 in Rev 7:4–8 could be construed as a gathering of God's people (cf. 14:1–5), but it shares no motifs with such texts as 1 Thess 4:16–17.

A number of arguments have been proposed in favor of interpreting vv 14–16 in a *positive* manner: (1) Just as the vintage image in 14:17–20 has an antecedent image earlier in the same chapter (vv 8, 10), so the grain harvest image in vv 15–16 has an antecedent image in the 144,000 who are the first-fruits (i.e., the first sheaf from the grain harvest; see Lev 23:9–14) for God and the Lamb; the martyrs of 14:4 are the first-fruits of all nations, while the reaping of the whole harvest is depicted in vv 15–16, i.e., as a metaphor for the gathering of the converted nations (Bauckham, "Conversion," 291–92). (2) While the metaphor of the grain harvest (and the threshing floor) can be used with the negative connotation of divine judgment, the grain harvest is also used in a *positive* sense as a metaphor for the gathering of the elect (Luke 10:2 = Matt 9:37–38 = *Gos. Thom.* 73; Matt 13:30, 43; John 4:35–38) or the reward of the righteous (4 Ezra 4:35). (3) Had the author wished to use the grain harvest as a metaphor for judgment he could have included the metaphors of threshing and winnowing, frequently used as metaphors for divine judgment (cf. Jer 51:33; Mic 4:12–13; Hab 3:12; Matt 3:2 = Luke 3:17). The metaphor of the grape harvest in vv 18–20 is clearly a metaphor for judgment since it concludes with the treading of the grapes in the winepress of God's wrath. (4) That the "one like a son of man" is seated on a *white* cloud is in itself a favorable sign (Allo, 243).

Comment

1a καὶ εἶδον, καὶ ἰδοὺ τὸ ἀρνίον ἑστὸς ἐπὶ τὸ ὄρος Σιών, "I saw, and behold, the Lamb was standing on Mount Zion." (On καὶ εἶδον, see *Comment* on 5:1.) The setting for this vision, which formally consists of vv 1–5, exhibits an oscillating ABA pattern between the *earth* (v 1) and *heaven* (vv 2–3) and then the *earth* again (vv 4–5). Note that a similar ABA oscillation is evident in Rev 12, where vv 1–6 and 13–17 presuppose a setting on the earth, while vv 7–12 switch to a vantage point in heaven.

That the Lamb is depicted as *standing* on Mount Zion, i.e., in Jerusalem, suggests that this pericope and 4 Ezra 13:29–50 are dependent on a common source or tradition, for 4 Ezra 13:35 expressly states, *Ipse autem stabit super cacumen montis Sion*, "But he will stand on the top of Mount Zion." The scene in v 1 is set on the earth (Swete, 177; Bousset [1906] 380; Beckwith, 657; Charles, 2:4–5; Allo, 195; Ladd, 189) since v 2 introduces an audition of a voice from heaven, clearly distinguishing between Mount Zion and heaven. In Jewish eschatological expectation, Mount Zion = Jerusalem served as the center of the eschatological kingdom (Joel 2:32; Isa 24:23; 31:4; Mic 4:7; Zech 14:4–5; *Jub.* 1:28; 4 Ezra 13:29–50; *2 Apoc. Bar.* 41:1–4; cf. *Sib. Or.* 5.414–33; Rev 17:14; see Volz, *Eschatologie*, 372). The Lamb, a thinly veiled metaphor for the Davidic Messiah, is depicted as *standing* in order to suggest that he functions as a warrior prepared to destroy his enemies (the Lamb is also depicted as "standing" when first seen by John in 5:6).

Why is the Lamb in Rev 14:1 depicted as *standing* and not as *enthroned?* At least one antecedent of that tradition is Ps 2:6, where God claims to have "set my king on Zion my holy hill," from whence he will conquer his enemies, vv 8–11, where there is no explicit mention of enthronement (this passage is interpreted messianically in *Pss. Sol.* 17:21–25). Further, while the imagery of Acts 7:56 is based on the conception of Christ seated at the right hand of the Father, the Son of man is nevertheless depicted as "standing" at the right hand of God.

Some commentators have understood Mount Zion in this pericope as a reference to heaven and suppose that the 144,000 have been exalted to heaven (Kiddle-Ross, 262–71; Lohmeyer; Mounce, 267; Giesen, 320), a view apparently reflected in 5 Ezra 2:42–48. There "Ezra" narrates a vision of the great and innumerable multitude on Mount Zion who were praising the Lord with songs. A young man of great stature placed victory crowns on their heads, and they were also given victory palms. The interpreting angel explained that these people are those that now put on immortality, and the young man is the Son of God whom they confessed in the world. The obvious similarities to Rev 7:9, 14:1, and Heb 12:22 are certainly the result of literary dependence of the Christian author of 5 Ezra 1–2 and 6 Ezra 15–16 upon the NT. Mount Zion in this case is the heavenly Jerusalem (Myers, *Esdras*,

153). However, the older, Jewish portion of 4 Ezra (chaps. 3–14) understands Mount Zion as an earthly mountain (13:33–36):

> And when all the nations hear his [God's Son's] voice, every man shall leave his own land and the warfare that they have against one another; and an innumerable multitude shall be gathered together, as you saw, desiring to come and conquer him. But he will stand on the top of Mount Zion. And Zion will come and be manifest to all people, prepared and built, as you saw the mountain carved out without hands. And he, my Son, will reprove the assembled nations for their ungodliness.

Here it appears that "the top of Mount Zion" refers to the temple mount in Jerusalem, while the phrase "Zion will come" refers to the descent or appearance of the heavenly Jerusalem. While the MT of Isa 24:23 expresses the eschatological hope that "the Lord of hosts will reign on Mount Zion," *Tg. Isa.* 24:23 (tr. Chilton, *Isaiah Targum*) substitutes the manifestation of God's *kingdom* for the visitation of God himself: "for the kingdom of the Lord of hosts will be revealed on the Mount of Zion." Similarly in *Tg. Isa.* 31:4 (tr. Chilton), "so the kingdom of the Lord of hosts will be revealed to settle upon the Mount of Zion and upon its hill."

The term "Zion" occurs only here in Revelation, elsewhere in the NT just six times (Matt 21:5; John 12:15; Rom 9:33; 11:26; Heb 12:22; 1 Pet 2:6), and once in the Apostolic Fathers (*Barn.* 6:2). Since "Zion" (= Jerusalem) occurs only here in Revelation, it is likely that this pericope is based on a particular source used by the author. The entire scene in 14:1–5 may have been modeled, at least in part, on Isa 40:9–11, where the people are told "Get you up to a high mountain, O Zion, herald of good tidings" (v 9), where they anticipate the coming of God who will "feed his flock like a shepherd" (v 11). In Jewish apocalyptic texts, Mount Zion is the place where the Messiah will defeat his foes and will judge them (*2 Apoc. Bar.* 40:1–3).

1b καὶ μετ' αὐτοῦ ἑκατὸν τεσσεράκοντα τέσσαρες χιλιάδες, "and with him a group of 144,000." The number 144,000 was used earlier in Rev 7:4, and it seems that it must be the author's intention that the reader correlate the two contexts within which this number is found. However, it is striking that though the 144,000 were previously mentioned in an anarthrous phrase in 7:4, here in 14:1 the phrase is also anarthrous (Spitta, 145), suggesting that a *different* group is in view (Bousset [1906] 380). There is, however, the problematic issue of whether the 144,000 represent a Christian elite, such as the martyrs or Jewish Christians, or the whole people of God. While the earlier mention of the 144,000 in 7:4 did not explicitly indicate that the group comprised Christians, it is probable that this group in 14:1–5 should be understood as the remnant of Christians who survive to the end. The mention of the 144,000 here and in v 3 forms an inclusio indicating that vv 1–3 form a small textual unit. It is not impossible that the number 144,000 could represent the approximate number of Christians in the Mediterranean world at the end of the first century B.C., but the author could not have known, even approximately, how many Christians there were (see *Comment* on 7:4).

1c ἔχουσαι τὸ ὄνομα αὐτοῦ καὶ τὸ ὄνομα τοῦ πατρὸς αὐτοῦ γεγραμμένον ἐπὶ τῶν μετώπων αὐτῶν, "with his name and the name of his Father written on their foreheads." This apparently refers to the sealing of the 144,000 in 7:3–8, and therefore it appears that both groups are identical in the final edition of Revelation. While the seal on the foreheads of the 144,000 is not further described in 7:3–8, here it becomes apparent that it consists of the name of the Lamb and of his Father (cf. 3:12; 22:4). This is one of just five references to God as Father in Revelation (1:6; 2:28; 3:5, 21; 14:1; see *Comment* on 1:6), and the only one that occurs in the First Edition (4:1–22:9), which might suggest that this section is a comparatively late addition to the text. A parallel to Rev 14:1 is found in *Odes Sol.* 42:20 (J. H. Charlesworth, tr. and ed., *The Odes of Solomon: The Syriac Texts* [Missoula, MT: Scholars, 1977]), "And I placed my name upon their head, / Because they are free and they are mine." Cf. *Odes Sol.* 39:7 (tr. Charlesworth, *Odes Sol.*), "Because the sign [Syriac *ʾtʾ*] on them is the Lord, / And the sign [Syriac *ʾtʾ*] is the Way for those who cross in the name of the Lord." Here *ʾtʾ* means "sign, mark, pledge, token" (R. P. Smith, *A Compendious Syriac Dictionary* [Oxford: Clarendon, 1903] 31). Another parallel from the Greco-Roman world contrasts physical signs with spiritual signs: "the 'Sown men,' as they were called, of Thebes had what seemed a spear mark on their bodies as a sign [σημεῖον] of their origin, and he who did not have this mark was not regarded as one of the 'Sown men.' And do you not think that in the souls of the offspring of Zeus also a sign [σημεῖον] is to be found by which those who have the power to judge will know whether they are of his seed or not?" (Dio Chrysostom *Or.* 4.23 [LCL tr.]; Mussies, *Dio,* 251).

It is difficult to make sense of the description in v 1 unless the names of Jesus and the Father are understood as written in an *abbreviated* form, though certainly the Israelite-Jewish name for God expressed in the tetragrammaton יהוה *YHWH* would not be inordinately lengthy. It is possible that the existence of Christian *nomina sacra,* i.e., the abbreviation of "sacred names" often found in NT MSS, is presupposed by this and other passages in Revelation (7:1–4; 19:16; see Roberts, *Manuscript,* 41–42).

In Christian papyri, the names contracted were primarily sacred names (with a supralinear horizontal stroke indicating the presence of an abbreviation), and the complete list of such contracted forms totals just fifteen words. The contracted forms were varied to indicate case. The most important *nomina sacra* were the four names κύριος and θεός (the nominative forms of which were contracted as κς and θς) and Ἰησοῦς and Χριστός (contracted as ιη or ιης and χς). Other abbreviated words include πνεῦμα, "Spirit," as πνα; ἄνθρωπος, "person," as ανος; σταυρός, "cross," great variation; πατήρ, "father," as πρ; σωτήρ, "savior," as σρ; μήτηρ, "mother," as μηρ; and οὐρανός, "heaven," as ουνς (Paap, *Nomina Sacra,* 76–99). Like names on coins, these *nomina sacra* were composed of the first two or three letters of a name.

Traube proposed that certain *nomina sacra,* i.e., κς and θς, arose in Judaism (*Nomina Sacra,* 30, followed by Paap, *Nomina Sacra,* 125–26), but this view has been proven wrong (Roberts, *Manuscript,* 34). Traube also proposed that the *nomina sacra* constituted a Greek equivalent to the Hebrew tetragrammaton, to prevent the full disclosure of the sacred name of God (*Nomina Sacra,* 30–32), a view that has been refuted by Brown (*SPap* 9 [1970] 7–12). Paap (*Nomina Sacra,* 124) argues that the *nomina sacra* originated with Jewish Christians with the abbreviation of θεός, since that word was the Greek equivalent to יהוה, *YHWH.* There is evidence that Alexandrian Jews occasionally wrote the tetragrammaton in gold letters (*Ep. Arist.* 176, followed by Jos. *Ant.* 12.89, who erroneously describes entire biblical rolls as written in gold; see Traube, *Nomina Sacra,* 21), which functioned to *emphasize* the divine name, a function achieved by leaving the tetragrammaton in Hebrew letters in Greek manuscripts of the LXX (Brown, *SPap* 7 [1970] 13–14). The uncial MS 022 of the Gospels (Codex Purpureus Petropolitanus), written in the sixth century A.D., has the names Lord, God, Jesus, Christ, Father, Spirit, and Son written in gold. In this respect the *function* of Christian *nomina sacra* was the same as some Jewish uses of the tetragrammaton, i.e., to emphasize the divine name by setting it apart from its context.

Evidence from Greek ostraca and inscriptions indicates that abbreviation by contraction was well known in the Greco-Roman world (Nachmanson and Rudberg, referred to in Paap, *Nomina Sacra,* 3). The earliest evidence for the abbreviation of the name Ἰησοῦς as ιη (this is suspension rather than contraction) is found in *Barn.* 9:8 (ca. A.D. 100; see Clement of Alex. *Strom.* 6.11); this is a form occasionally found in later papyri, probably because of its numerological significance (Paap, *Nomina Sacra,* 93). The date for the appearance of most of the important *nomina sacra* (God, Lord, Spirit, Father, Person, Israel, and Jesus) is from the first half of the second century A.D. (Paap, *Nomina Sacra,* 119). Though he goes well beyond the evidence, Roberts supposes that the *nomina sacra* were a Christian innovation and speculates that the guidelines for abbreviating sacred names were laid down by the church in Jerusalem prior to A.D. 70, and that they represent an "embryonic creed" expressed by the primitive Christian community (Roberts, *Manuscript,* 46; see 26–48: "*Nomina Sacra:* Origins and Significance").

2–3 This short section narrates an intercalated vision of the singing of a heavenly choir, which should not be identified with the 144,000. It cannot be determined, however, if this heavenly choir is composed of angels or of other Christians. This entire section appears to have been inserted by the author into a larger, perhaps truncated, version of a traditional unit that dealt with the Messiah's appearance on Mount Zion, followed by the decisive defeat of his enemies and the gathering in of his people.

2a καὶ ἤκουσα φωνὴν ἐκ τοῦ οὐρανοῦ ὡς φωνὴν ὑδάτων πολλῶν καὶ ὡς φωνὴν βροντῆς μεγάλης, "I heard a sound from heaven like the roar of the sea and like the sound of loud thunder." Here the seer hears the tremendously loud sound of heavenly singing but does not see the celestial throne room from which the singing emanates. For the motif of the unidentified voice in Revelation, see *Comment* on 10:4. The voice is not that of the 144,000 but rather the sound of the heavenly assembly (Swete, 177). The perspective of the seer is on the earth, and the setting of v 1 is, therefore, also on the earth. While the use of thunder as a metaphor for an extremely loud voice occurs elsewhere in Revelation only in 6:1 and 19:6, the phraseology in 14:2 and 19:6a is particularly similar, and in both passages there are three similes introduced with ὡς, "as, like," which the author uses to characterize the magnificent sound he hears.

Rev 14:2	*Rev 19:6a*
καὶ ἤκουσα Then I heard	καὶ ἤκουσα Then I heard
φωνὴν a sound	
ἐκ τοῦ οὐρανοῦ from heaven	
	ὡς φωνὴν like the sound

	ὄχλου πολλοῦ of a large multitude
ὡς φωνὴν like the sound	καὶ ὡς φωνὴν and like the sound
ὑδάτων πολλῶν of the roaring sea	ὑδάτων πολλῶν of the roaring sea
καὶ ὡς φωνὴν like the sound	καὶ ὡς φωνὴν and like the sound
βροντῆς μεγάλης of loud thunder	βροντῶν ἰσχυρῶν of loud thunder
καὶ ἡ φωνὴ ἣν ἤκουσα and the sound which I heard	
ὡς φωνὴν κιθαρῳδῶν like that of kitharists	
κιθαριζόντων playing	
ἐν ταῖς κιθάραις αὐτῶν on their kitharas	

The major difference between these two passages is that the two similes drawn from nature are placed first in 14:2 but last in 19:6. Correspondingly, the similes drawn from human life, a large crowd of people in 19:6 and a group of kithara players in 14:2, are both somewhat awkward since in both instances the groups named are not just similes but the groups who sing. Rev 14:2 is presented as an audition, and it is as if the author only gradually becomes aware of the sound he hears, for he first compares it to loud sounds found in nature, roaring water and loud thunder. In v 2b, on the other hand, his impression of the sound becomes much more specific.

2b καὶ ἡ φωνὴ ἣν ἤκουσα ὡς κιθαρῳδῶν κιθαριζόντων ἐν ταῖς κιθάραις αὐτῶν, "The sound which I heard was like that of kitharists playing their kitharas." The syntax of this verse is awkward since ἡ φωνή, "the sound," is a nominative that has no syntactical relationship to the rest of the sentence and must therefore be regarded as a nominative absolute or pendent nominative (the same construction occurs in 10:8; on the pendent nominative in Revelation, see 2:26; 3:12, 21). φωνή here has an anaphoric definite article referring to the previous anarthrous use of φωνή in v 2a, indicating that the metaphor of kitharists playing on their instruments refers to the *same* sound referred to in v 2a. Kraft, who is virtually alone in preferring the variant reading of the second φωνή as anarthrous (see *Note* 14:2.e-e.), thinks that two groups are referred to, one in heaven and the 144,000 on the earth, who he thinks should be identified with the kitharists (187–88).

This is the third of three similes that the author uses to describe the sound he hears (see *Comment* on v 2a), and the repetitive introductory phrase, "the sound which I heard" (v 2a), emphasizes that the author has a clearer impression of the sound he hears and uses a simile drawn from human life, namely, the sound of a group of kithara players, to characterize the sound. The phrase κιθαρῳδῶν κιθαριζόντων ἐν ταῖς κιθάραις αὐτῶν, literally "harpers harping on their harps," is as redundant and alliterative in Greek as it is in English.

3a καὶ ᾄδουσιν ὡς ᾠδὴν καινὴν ἐνώπιον τοῦ θρόνου καὶ ἐνώπιον τῶν τεσσάρων ζῴων καὶ τῶν πρεσβυτέρων, "Then they sang as it were a new song before the throne and before the four cherubim and the elders." The logical subject of the third-person plural verb ᾄδουσιν, "they sing," is the kitharists of v 2b, even though they are introduced with ὡς as the third simile for the sound from heaven mentioned in v 2a, and so grammatically are not necessarily the subjects of the verb. Who are the kitharists? The twenty-four elders are previously mentioned in heavenly court scenes as having kitharas (5:8), but they are excluded since the new song is sung before them. Those who have conquered the beast are described as using kitharas to accompany their singing in 15:2. There then are two possibilities: the heavenly angelic host (also mentioned in 4:11–12; 7:11–12; Bousset [1906] 380–81; Charles, 2:7; Beckwith, 651; Loymeyer, 119; Müller, 262), or the host of the redeemed (7:9–10; 15:3–4). If the innumerable angelic host is in view, that suggests that the 144,000 will eventually participate in angelic worship. If the host of the redeemed is meant, that suggests that the 144,000 will join them through martyrdom. There are other instances in which songs are sung by a great multitude that, like here, is not more closely identified (19:1–3, 6–8; cf. 12:10–12). Further, the appearance of ᾄδουσιν, "they sing," in the *present* tense is problematic since the audition is presented in the aorist tense as an occurrence of the past (see *Note* 3.a.).

On the phrase "new song," which occurs twice in Revelation, see the *Comment* on 5:9. Bauckham suggests that the phrase "new song" belongs to holy-war terminology ("War Scroll," 230), but while ancient military victories were celebrated with songs (2 Chr 20:27–28; 1 Macc 13:51; 1QM 4:4–5), the connection of the "new song" with such occasions occurs only rarely (Ps 144:9–10). The phrase ἐνώπιον τοῦ θρόνου, "before the throne," means "before God," for θρόνος here is a circumlocution for the name of God used just four times in Revelation (4:10; 7:9; 8:3; 14:3). Further, that the new song is sung before the throne (i.e., before God, the four cherubim, and the elders) suggests that *this is the only appropriate place for this new song to be sung,* and the recognition of this makes the statement in v 6b comprehensible. The motif of the Song of the Blessed Ones, i.e., gods, occurs frequently in Greco-Roman literature (Festugière, *Hermès Trismégiste* 2:133–37). In Diodorus 2.47.1–3 (in an account dependent on Hecataeus), the author describes an island in an ocean north of the land of the Celts, an island where Leto was reportedly born (2.47.2; LCL tr.):

> Furthermore, a city is there which is sacred to this god [Apollo], and the majority of its inhabitants are players on the cithara [κιθαριστάς]; and these continually play on this instrument in the temple and sing hymns [συνεχῶς ἐν τῷ ναῷ κιθαρίζοντας ὕμνους] of praise to the god, glorifying his deeds.

3b καὶ οὐδεὶς ἐδύνατο μαθεῖν τὴν ᾠδὴν εἰ μὴ αἱ ἑκατὸν τεσσεράκοντα τέσσαρες χιλιάδες, "No one could learn the song except the 144,000." The very fact that the author does not provide a transcript of the new song suggests that since he is not part of the 144,000, he himself cannot understand the song! This is the only place in Revelation where a song or hymn is mentioned but not quoted (a partial exception is the indirect way of referring to the hymn in 4:9). The emphasis on the fact that no one (on earth) can understand the new song except the 144,000 suggests that the song is only appropriate for singing before the throne of God.

Does this statement mean that, although the author himself claims to have "heard" the sound (v 2), the new song was heard by the 144,000 on Mount Zion as well? This is doubtful. The term μανθάνειν here could mean "to learn, to be instructed" in the ordinary sense, or it could also refer to the ability "to understand," a higher, more esoteric type of knowledge (Hadorn, 150; K. Rengstorf, *TDNT* 4:407). It is possible that the second kind of "understanding" is referred to here, and if so, there is an interesting parallel in 2 Cor 12:4 (Boll, *Offenbarung,* 19), where Paul claims that someone (probably referring to himself) was caught up to the third heaven and that "he heard things that cannot be told [ἄρρητα ῥήματα], which a person may not utter." Like the 144,000, Paul heard something in heaven that was impossible or inappropriate for others to hear or understand. One benefit of access to Noah's magical book, the *Sepher ha-Razim,* "Book of Mysteries," according to the compiler, is the ability "to comprehend the songs of heaven" (pref. 18; tr. M. Morgan, *Sepher ha-Razim*). Similarly, in *T. Abr.* 1:5 (an older, more obviously Jewish part of this work), "Adam" claims that he used to hear the praise of the seraphim (the trisagion), but after he sinned he was no longer able to hear it. A parallel from the Greco-Roman side (also suggested by Boll, *Offenbarung,* 19–20) is found in *Corp. Herm.* 13.15–16 (tr. Grese, *Corp. Herm.*):

> TAT: Father, I would like the hymn of praise [τὴν διὰ τοῦ ὕμνου εὐλογίαν] which you said that you heard from the powers [τῶν δυνάμεων] when you came to the Ogdoad, as Poimandres prophesied concerning the Ogdoad [probably referring to *Corp. Herm.* 1.26; see Nock-Festugière, *Hermès Trismégiste* 2:215–16 n. 65].
>
> HERMES: Child, you are right in your eagerness to dissolve the body, for now you are pure [κεκαθαρμένος]. Poimandres, the Mind of Absolute Authority, did not transmit to me more than is written, since he knew that by myself I would be able to understand all things, to hear what I wish, and to see all things, and he left it to me to do the beautiful things.
>
> TAT: Father, I want to hear these things, and I want to understand [νοῆσαι] them.
>
> HERMES: Be silent, child, and now hear a suitable blessing, the hymn of regeneration, which I had not decided to reveal so readily, except to you at the end of all [ἐπὶ τέλει τοῦ παντός]. Consequently, this is not taught [διδάσκεται], but is hidden in silence.

As in Rev 14:3, a hymn sung by heavenly powers is mentioned (in *Corp. Herm.* 13.17–20 the hymn is quoted). Knowledge of the heavenly hymns, however, is limited to those who are pure.

3c οἱ ἠγορασμένοι ἀπὸ τῆς γῆς, "who had been redeemed from the earth." The term γῆ, "earth," here can refer either to the earth in a geographical sense (emphasizing that the redeemed come from all parts of the world) or to the earth in the sense of that which is in opposition to God, as the "place of unbelief" (Lohmeyer, 122), similar to the Johannine understanding of κόσμος as the world hostile to God and his people (John 15:18–19; cf. 7:7; 17:14; 1 John 3:13; see Weicht, *Folge,* 89–90). While both views are possible, the first is more likely for two reasons: (1) In 5:9 the term ἀγοράζειν is applied to those redeemed "from every tribe and tongue and people and nation," emphasizing their universal origin. (2) The phrase οὗτοι ἠγοράσθησαν ἀπὸ τῶν ἀνθρώπων, "who are redeemed from humanity" (which occurs in 14:4), is clearly parallel to οἱ ἠγορασμένοι ἀπὸ τῆς γῆς, "redeemed from the earth" (v 3), so that "the earth" and "humanity" must be understood as interchangeable; i.e., both terms emphasize the *universality* of the people of God. On the other hand, it must be noted that "those who dwell on the earth," i.e., humanity, is a phrase used frequently in Revelation in the negative sense of those who are in opposition to God (3:10; 6:10; 8:13; 11:10; 13:8, 12, 14; 14:6; 17:2, 8). ἀγοράζειν occurs six times in Revelation, though only in 5:9 and 14:3, 4 does it have a religious meaning as a metaphor for salvation (and all three passages are closely related as we have seen above). Since vv 4–5 appear to have been a later addition to this narrative sequence (see *Comments* on vv 4–5), the clause in which ἀγοράζειν occurs in v 4 may have been included because of a catchword association with ἀγοράζειν in v 3. Charles considered the phrase to be an interpolation (2:7–8; id., *Lectures,* 27).

4a οὗτοί εἰσιν οἳ μετὰ γυναικῶν οὐκ ἐμολύνθησαν, παρθένοι γάρ εἰσιν, "These are those who have not polluted themselves with women, for they are chaste." This clause forms an inclusio with v 5, "and in their mouth guile was not found, for they are blameless." V 4a deals with *ritual purity,* while v 5 focuses on *moral purity.* This suggests that vv 4–5 constitute an explanatory interpolation whose purpose is the characterization of the 144,000. This clause was judged an interpolation by Charles (2:8–9; id., *Lectures,* 27, 43), whose views are disputed with weak arguments by Power (*Bib* 4 [1923] 108–12).

The phrase οὗτοί εἰσιν, "these are," introduces an explanatory passage that includes vv 4–5 (n.b. the threefold use of οὗτοι) and is therefore an interpretive expansion of the vision recounted in vv 1–3. The anaphoric character of such demonstrative pronouns means that when they are used at the beginning of sentences in Revelation, they are never preceded by καί, either as an interpretive explanation supplied by the author in his own person (11:4, 6, 10; 20:5, 14) or as the first word in a sentence introducing the direct discourse of a supernatural revealer (7:13, 14; 17:13, 14; 19:9; 21:5; 22:6).

The aorist passive form of the verb μολύνειν can be used literally with the meaning "to soil, to make dirty," as in Rev 3:4 (see Louw-Nida, § 79.56), or (as here in Rev 14:4) figuratively with the meaning "to defile, stain," i.e., "to cause something to be ceremonially impure," implying serious defilement (Louw-Nida, § 53.34). This is a *constative* aorist summing up the consistent behavior of these chaste males over an indefinite period of time (as in Rev 3:4). μολύνειν is used in a similar context in *Acts of Paul* 12: "Otherwise there will be no resurrection for you unless you remain pure and do not defile [μολύνητε] the flesh but keep it pure." This negative statement has its positive antithesis in the declaration that "they are virgins." μολύνειν can be understood to refer to ritual impurity that is the consequence of sexual intercourse, a view widely assumed in the OT world (Lev 15:18, 24; G. F. Moore, *Judaism* 2:76; C. M. Doughty, *Travels in Arabia Deserta* [Cambridge: Cambridge UP, 1888] 1:572). *Acts of Andrew* 14 (ed. D. R. MacDonald, *Acts of Andrew,* 98–99) refers to the requirement that priests, after having sexual intercourse with women, purify themselves for seven days before entering into the temple. The phrase "to defile themselves with women" is used of the behavior of the Watchers (in *1 Enoch* 7:1; 9:8; 10:11; 15:3; 69:5), who, as angels, are forbidden to marry (*1 Enoch* 15:2–7; cf. Luke 20:35; see Aune, "Luke 20:34–36," 187–202). The presence of an allusion here to *1 Enoch* 1–36 is recognized by Yarbro Collins ("Women's History," 89) and used by Olson to argue that the author of Revelation depicts the angelic status of the 144,000 of Rev 14:4, who stand in radical opposition to the fallen angels of *1 Enoch* 1–36 (*CBQ* 59 [1997] 496–500). The context of this emphasis on sexual purity or virginity is one of *discipleship* (cf. the "following" motif in v 4b), and there are discipleship sayings in the Gospels that emphasize asceticism, such as forsaking one's wife and children (Luke 14:26–27; 18:29; see Aune, "Following the Lamb," 272–74; Roloff [ET] 171–72; Yarbro Collins, "Women's History," 96).

An emphasis on sexual asceticism is particularly characteristic of Luke (Cadbury, *Luke-Acts,* 264–65, 272). In Mark 10:29, seven types of renunciation (home, brothers, sisters, mother, father, children, fields), all repeated in Matt 19:29, are reduced to five in Luke 18:29 with the addition of "wives" (house, wife, brothers, parents, children). In the Q passage in Luke 14:26–27 (= Matt 10:37–38), wives are also included in a list of that which followers of Jesus must "hate" (in the parallel in *Gos. Thom.* 53, only father, mother, brothers, and sisters are mentioned). According to Vermes (*Jesus,* 246 n. 79), however, the term "house" in Mark 10:29 and Matt 19:29 is synonymous with "wife," since in the vernacular Aramaic "one belonging to his house" is the wife of the owner. In the parable of the Great Supper (Luke 14:15–24; Matt 22:1–14), only Luke includes recent marriage as an excuse not to attend the banquet (v 20; marriage is not mentioned in the parallel in *Gos. Thom.* 64).

The term παρθένοι is unusual, for it is a term usually reserved for young women of marriageable age, though virginity is not always a connotation of the word (Horsley, *New Docs* 4:221–27). Here the term is clearly used of males (this conclusion is necessitated by v 4a, though the masculine gender of the substantival participles and pronouns in vv 1–5 could be construed as including both men and women). This masculine application of the term παρθένος is very rare and is certainly unknown before the first century A.D. Some have argued that παρθένος in 1 Cor 7:25–27 can be understood to refer to male as well as female παρθένοι (J. Weiss, *Korintherbrief,* 194–95; Black, *Scrolls,* 84–85), though the use of the term παρθένος of women in 1 Cor 7:28, 34, 36–38 makes this an unlikely possibility. Joseph is called a παρθένος in *Jos. As.* 4:9 (tr. Burchard in Charlesworth, *OTP* 2:206: "Joseph is a man who worships God, and self-controlled, and a virgin [παρθένος] like you [i.e., 'Aseneth'] today"; he is also called a παρθένος in 8:1). Along with Rev 14:4, this is one of the very first instances in which the term παρθένος is used of males (see C. Burchard, *Untersuchungen zu Joseph und Aseneth,* WUNT 8 [Tübingen: Mohr (Siebeck), 1965] 110 n. 1). In Achilles Tatius 5.20.5, Clitophon tells Leucippe by letter "you will find that I have imitated your virginity [παρθενίαν], if there be any virginity in men [ἐν ἀνδράσι παρθενία]." The term παρθένος is also used of males such as John the Apostle, referred to as "the holy virgin John" (Epiphanius *Pan.* 28.7.5) or "John the virgin," using the Greek loanword παρθένος (*Pistis Sophia* 1.41 [ed. Schmidt-Till, p. 42, line 27; ed. Schmidt-MacDermot, p. 68]; 2.96 [ed. Schmidt-Till, p. 148, line 25; ed. Schmidt-MacDermot, p. 233). It is also applied to such OT figures as Jeremiah (Olympiodorus *Frag. in Jer.* 52:1; Migne, *PG* XCIII.724), Abel (Adler, *Suidae Lexicon* 1:16), and Melchizedek (Adler, *Suidae Lexicon* 2:773); see references in Lindijer, "Die Jungfrauen," 128. The terms παρθένος and παρθενικός are sometimes used of men in Jewish epitaphs (*CIJ,* 81, 242), though here it means simply that the deceased were unmarried when they died. This might suggest that the 144,000 were executed as young men and are designated παρθένοι because they had died as yet unmarried. In two Jewish sepulchral inscriptions from Rome, the Greek adjective παρθενικός, "virginal," and the Latin adjective *virgineum* (= *virginio*) are used of husbands who had not been previously married (A. J. Leon, *The Jews of Ancient Rome* [New York: The Jewish Publication Society of America, 1960] 130, 231–32, 274–75 [no. 81], 299 [no. 242]). Against this background the reference to the 144,000 as παρθένοι in Rev 14:4 may plausibly be construed to mean that they have been married only once (Ford, *NTS* 12 [1966] 293–99).

The central interpretive problem here in v 4 is often reduced to a choice between understanding these statements to indicate literal asceticism, i.e., physical purity, and understanding them to imply figurative abstention from various forms of sin, i.e., moral purity. The term παρθένοι, "celibates," can be understood in several different ways. (1) The term παρθένοι is sometimes understood to refer to those who abstain from sexual immorality, whether or not they are married (Beckwith, Zahn, Hadorn). This view is generally unconvincing. (2) The term is also understood more literally to refer to those who remain celibate (Bousset, Lohmeyer, Lindijer, "Die Jungfrauen"), a view held earlier by Augustine (Migne, *PL* XL.410–11). It is also important to note that the author uses the metaphor of marriage for the relationship between Christ and his community, i.e., the New Jerusalem (Rev 19:7–10; 21:2, 9–14; 22:17). (3) Another traditional understanding of this term regards it as a figurative term for the purity of the faith of those who refuse to worship the beast. In the OT, unchastity is frequently used as a metaphor for turning away from the true worship of God to the idolatrous worship of false gods (Jer 3:2; 13:27; Ezek 16:15–58; 23:1–49; 43:7; Hos 5:4; 6:10; see *Comment* on 2:14). In 2 Cor 11:2, the metaphor of the "pure virgin" symbolizes the moral and spiritual purity of the Christian community, while in Hermas *Vis.* 4.2.1–2, Hermas sees a παρθένος who represents the Church. This view is reflected in the early Church in Ps.-Augustine (Migne, *PL* XXXV.2437), Ps.-Ambrose (Migne, *PL* XVII.891), and Ambrosiaster (Migne, *PL* XVII.319–20). (4) Finally, the chastity of the 144,000 males can be regarded as reflecting the purity regulations required of participants in a holy war (Lev 15:16; Deut 23:9–10; 1 Sam 21:5; 2 Sam 11:11; 1QM 7:3–7) or the abstinence requirements for priests under particular ritual circumstances (Lev 15:18); both soldiers and priests were exclusively male. Variations of this view are widely held by scholars (Lohmeyer, 120; Caird, 179; Beasley-Murray, 223; Sweet, 222; Yarbro Collins, *Combat Myth,* 129–30; id., *JBL* 96 [1977] 248).

4b οὗτοι οἱ ἀκολουθοῦντες τῷ ἀρνίῳ ὅπου ἂν ὑπάγῃ, "These are they who follow the Lamb where he would go." The peculiar metaphor of the *Lamb* as shepherd and guide is found here and in Rev 7:17, while the more conventional metaphor of the *Messiah* as shepherd (based on the ancient Near Eastern metaphor of the king as shepherd of his people) is found in *Frg. Tg.* Exod 12:42 (tr. Klein, *Fragment-Targums* 2:126), "and Moses will go forth from the midst of the wilderness and the King Messiah, from the midst of Rome: this one [Moses] will lead at the head of the flock, and that one [King Messiah] will lead at the head of the flock." The notion that the Messiah will shepherd the flock of the Lord (i.e., God's people) also occurs much earlier in *Pss. Sol.* 17:40–42 and has biblical antecedents in Isa 40:11 and Ezek 34:23.

One interpretation of the 144,000 suggests that their sexual abstinence is a result of their having forsaken everything, particularly normal marital relationships, to follow the Lamb. In the NT, ἀκολουθεῖν, "follow,"occurs primarily in the Gospels (seventy times), as well as six times in Revelation, three times in Acts, and once in Paul. ἀκολουθεῖν has two literal meanings, "to follow, go behind" (Louw-Nida, § 15.144) and "to follow" in the sense of "to accompany" (Louw-Nida, § 15.156). By figurative extension, the term means "to be a disciple of" in the sense of "adhering to the teachings or instructions of a leader and in promoting the cause of such a leader" (Louw-Nida, § 36.31; see Str-B, 1:187–88, 527–29). This meaning is found *only* in the four Gospels and Rev 14:4 (*TDNT* 1:213–15). The phrase "where he would go" in Rev 14:4 suggests that the 144,000 follow the Lamb regardless of the cost, i.e., even to the point of death (see Matt 10:38 = Luke 14:27; Mark 8:34–35 = Matt 16:24–25 = Luke 9:23–24; Luke 17:33; John 12:25–26; 1 Pet 2:21; Rev 12:11). In the interpretive explanation found in Rev 14:4, the term ἀκολουθεῖν is very probably modeled after Gospel traditions involving discipleship, such as the chreia in Q (Matt 8:19–20; Luke 9:57–58), introduced with the statement "As they were going along the road a man said to him, 'I will follow you wherever you go [ἀκολουθήσω σοι ὅπου ἐὰν ἀπέρχῃ].'" The saying so introduced ("Foxes have holes . . ."), like its close parallel in *Gos. Thom.* 86 (Kloppenborg, *Formation of Q,* 191), probably circulated as an independent saying and was turned into a chreia by introducing it with the brief narrative element in v 57 (Bultmann, *Geschichte,* 27). This narrative framework was in all probability formulated on the basis of a generic understanding of Christian discipleship, i.e., "following Jesus wherever he went." It is true, however, that the term ἀκολουθεῖν, "to follow after," occurs in connection with Jesus outside the Gospels only here in Rev 14:4 and in a figurative sense (Hengel, *Leader,* 62). And, of course, it is not the historical Jesus that is in view here but rather the exalted Christ (Hengel, *Leader,* 86 n. 9). A similar statement is found in *Acts of Paul* 25, "Thecla said to Paul, 'I will shave my head and follow you wherever you go [ἀκολουθήσω σοι ὅπου δἂν πορεύῃ].'" This possibility receives partial confirmation by the existence of several similarly worded statements in the Gospel of John. For example, in John 13:36, "Where I go [ὅπου ὑπάγω] you are unable to follow [ἀκολουθῆσαι] me now, but you will follow later." Here discipleship means following Jesus to death (see John 21:18–19; Mark 8:34–35 and par.). John 13:36 is thematically connected with John 12:26, "If any one serves me, he must follow me [ἐμοὶ ἀκολουθείτω]; and where I am [ὅπου εἰμὶ ἐγώ] there shall my servant be also."

Finally, in John 14:3, Jesus expresses the eventual reward for disciples who follow him to death: "where I am [ὅπου εἰμὶ ἐγώ] you may be also. And you know the way I am going [ὅπου ἐγὼ ὑπάγω οἴδατε τὴν ὁδόν]." These Johannine passages provide a form of the tradition found in Rev 14:1–5 but shorn of apocalyptic features; i.e., true discipleship means following Jesus to death with the promise of their "acceptance into Jesus' community with the Father" (Schnackenburg, *John* 3:55–56). Some of the consequences of discipleship are described in more traditionally eschatological terms in Matt 19:28, "Truly, I say to you, in the new world, when the Son of man shall sit on his glorious throne, you who have followed [οἱ ἀκολουθήσοντες] me will also sit on twelve thrones, judging the twelve tribes of Israel" (see Luke 22:28–30, which adds the motif of the messianic banquet). The term ἀκολουθεῖν is used metaphorically in Ign. *Phld.* 2:1, "Where the shepherd is, there follow as sheep [ὅπου δὲ ὁ ποιμήν ἐστιν, ἐκεῖ ὡς πρόβατα ἀκολουθεῖτε]"; cf. *Smyrn.* 8:17. In an early allusion to Rev 14:4 in *Ep. Lugd.* 10 (preserved in Eusebius *Hist. eccl.* 5.1.10; Musurillo, *Acts,* 64), it is said of a Christian martyr named Vettius

Epagathus that "he was and is a true disciple of Christ, *following the Lamb wherever he goes* [ἀκολουθῶν τῷ ἀρνίῳ ὅπου ἂν ὑπάγῃ]." In this allusion to Rev 14:4, following Christ is clearly a metaphor for martyrdom, conceived of as true discipleship.

4c οὗτοι ἠγοράσθησαν ἀπὸ τῶν ἀνθρώπων ἀπαρχὴ τῷ θεῷ καὶ τῷ ἀρνίῳ, "These are those who have been redeemed from humanity, servants devoted to God and the Lamb." This statement is parallel to a phrase used in a hymn of praise to the Lamb in Rev 5:9, "you were slain and you redeemed for God [ἠγόρασας τῷ θεῷ] by your death / People from every tribe [ἐκ πάσης φυλῆς] and tongue and people and nation." Since the 144,000 have already been redeemed from humanity and are depicted first with the Lamb on Mount Zion (v 1) and then as following the Lamb wherever he goes (v 4b), the Lamb they accompany has obviously already been slain. If the "Zion" referred to in v 1 is identical with the *earthly* Jerusalem, it appears that the 144,000 constitute a military force awaiting the final onslaught of the ungodly nations (cf. 16:12–16; 20:7–10). However, if "Zion" is construed as the *heavenly* Jerusalem, then 14:1–5 is closely parallel with 7:9–17 and 15:2–4 (where the song of Moses and the song of the Lamb may represent the new song of 14:3, which only the 144,000 could learn), and the 144,000 represent those who have been killed for their faithfulness. The scene in 14:1–5 should be understood as both highly symbolic and as set on the *earth.* The number 144,000 confirms this, for though it is a very large number, it is obviously a finite number (therefore representing earthly realities), which symbolizes the remnant of faithful Christians of the end time.

The term ἀπαρχή, "first-fruits," here translated "devoted servants," originated as a technical term drawn from the language of cultic offerings and sacrifice found throughout the ancient Mediterranean world. In the ancient Mediterranean world, there were three primary types of "sacrifice" or gifts to the gods (i.e., commodities withdrawn from regular human use): offerings of food, offerings of objects (votive offerings), and animal sacrifices. The offering of first-fruits (ἀπαρχή), which belongs to the first category, was regarded by the Greeks as "the simplest and most basic form of uncorrupted piety" (Burkert, *Mythology and Ritual,* 52). The means of offering first-fruits, however, exhibited a wide spectrum: they may be offered to any god; they may be left at a holy place until they decompose or are eaten by animals or scavengers; they may be thrown into ponds, rivers, or the sea; they may be burned.

The Hebrew word בְּכוֹר *bĕkôr* and its feminine plural form בְּכֹרוֹת *bekōrôt* refer to the "firstborn" of animals and humans beings, while the masculine plural form בִּכּוּרִים *bikkûrîm* refers to the "first-fruits" or "first portion" of cereal and fruit crops that are presented to God in a cultic context (Exod 23:19; 34:22; Lev 23:9–14; Num 28:26–27; Deut 16:9–12; Deut 26:1–11; 2 Kgs 4:42; Neh 10:35 [MT 36]; Prov 3:9–10; *Ep. Arist.* 158; *T. Levi* 9:7, 14; *T. Jud.* 21:5; *T. Iss.* 5:6; 1QS 6:5–6; 1QSa 2:18–19; Jos. *Ant.* 4.70; 9.273; *Apost. Const.* 8.40.2); see *TWAT* 1:644–45; 7:292–93; *EDNT* 1:116–17; J. Milgrom, "First Fruits, OT," *IDBSup,* 336–37; R. O. Rigsby, "First Fruits," *ADB* 2:796–97). Inexplicably, בִּכּוּרִים *bikkûrîm* is *never* translated ἀπαρχή in the LXX. רֵאשִׁית *rē'šît* is also used to refer to the "first-fruits" (of the field) in a cultic sense, but it is not at all clear what difference, if any, existed between רֵאשִׁית *rē'šît* and בִּכּוּרִים *bikkûrîm* in Israelite sacrificial protocol (Tsevat, *TDOT* 2:122). The semantic problem is compounded by the rare phrase רֵאשִׁית בִּכּוּרֵי *rē'šît bikkûrê,* τὰς ἀπαρχὰς τῶν πρωτογενημάτων, "first-fruits of first-fruits" (Exod 23:19 [cf. Philo *De sacr.* 72]; 34:26; Ezek 44:30). The term בְּכוֹר *bĕkôr,* "firstborn," a term often used synonymously with גָּדוֹל *gādôl,* "eldest," is based on the same root as בִּכּוּרִים *bikkûrîm,* "first-fruits," and the assumption is that the firstborn or firstlings of animals and people (i.e., the first and the best), as well as the first-fruits of the field, belong to God (Exod 13:2–16; Lev 27:26–27; Num 3:44–51; 18:13–17; Deut 14:23–26; Neh 10:36[MT 37]; Jos. *Ant.* 4.70; cf. Ezek 20:25–26). The presentation of the first-fruits of the harvest, which themselves cannot be consumed by the offerer (Jer 2:3b), sanctifies the entire harvest, which can then be consumed (Lev 23:14; cf. Prov 3:9–10). In the OT the offering of first-fruits was reserved for priests and Levites (Num 18:12–13; Deut 18:4; Ezek 44:30; Sir 45:20), a practice continued in some segments of early Christianity according to *Did.* 13:3–7. The term ἀπαρχή can also be used of booty presented to God (Jos. *Ant.* 5.26), and in *Pss. Sol.* 15:3, ἀπαρχή is used metaphorically of speech in praise of God. There is evidence in the OT that רֵאשִׁית *rēʾšît* takes on the meaning "the best" (Num 24:20; 1 Sam 15:21; Jer 49:35; Amos 6:6; see Weicht, *Folge,* 96–99; *TWNT* 1:644; 7:293; Rigsby, "First Fruits," *ADB* 2:796). It is important to observe that the term ἀπαρχή is *never* used of the firstborn of animals or people in the OT or early Jewish literature. Therefore the figurative use of the term ἀπαρχή when applied to people, whether individually or collectively, is a metaphor drawn from the first-fruits of the field (barley, wheat, bread, grapes, etc.).

The term ἀπαρχή occurs seventy-six times in the LXX, with the following meanings (Lust, *Lexicon,* 45): (1) "offering" (Exod 25:3), (2) "the first (offering)" (Deut 26:10), (3) "portion" (1 Sam 10:4), (4) "first-offerings" (Exod 23:19), and (5) "first-fruits" (Exod 22:28). The verb ἀπάρχομαι, "to offer first-fruits," occurs five times (2 Chr 30:24[2x]; 35:7, 8, 9). ἀπαρχή is used to translate several different Hebrew terms: תְּרוּמָה *tĕrûmâ,* "offering" (37x), רֵאשִׁית *rēʾšît,* "beginning, chief" (17x), תְּנוּפָה *tĕnûpâ,* "elevation offering" (1x: Exod 39:1[MT: 38:24]), חֵלֶב *ḥēleb,* "fat" (2x: Num 18:12), and מַעֲשֵׂר *maʿăśēr,* "tithe" (1x: Deut 12:16), though sometimes ἀπαρχή appears in the LXX without reflecting the Hebrew text (e.g., Exod 22:29; Num 18:1; 1 Kgs 10:4; Ezek 20:31). Though בִּכּוּרִים *bikkûrîm* can mean "first-fruits," it is inexplicably never translated with ἀπαρχή in the LXX, though rather frequently it is rendered by πρωτογενήματα, "first-fruits" (Exod 23:16, 19; 34:26; Lev 2:14; 23:17, 20; Num 18:13; 2 Kgs 4:42), once by ἀρχή, "beginning" (Exod 34.22), once by πρόδρομοι, "forerunners" (Num 13:20), and once by τὰ νέα "the new things" (Num 28:26).

There are just two passages in the LXX in which the term ἀπαρχή is used of human beings, Ps 77:51 (MT 78:51) and the closely parallel Ps 104:36 (MT 105:36). In both passages, ἀπαρχή is used in the second colon of a synonymous couplet as a term parallel to πρωτότοκος, both referring to the firstborn of Egypt who were destroyed in the plague narrated in Exod 12:29–36:

Ps 77:51	*Ps 104:367*
καὶ ἐπάταξεν πᾶν πρωτότοκον ἐν Αἰγύπτῳ,	καὶ ἐπάταξεν πᾶν πρωτότοκον ἐν τῇ γῇ αὐτῶν,
He struck all the firstborn in Egypt	He struck all the firstborn in their land,

ἀπαρχὴν τῶν πόνων αὐτῶν ἐν τοῖς σκηνώμασι Χαμ.	ἀπαρχὴν παντὸς πόνου αὐτῶν
first-fruits of their works in the tents of Ham.	first-fruits of all their work

In both passages (which are literal translations of the underlying Hebrew text), πρωτότοκος is used to translate בְּכוֹר *běkôr* and ἀπαρχή renders רֵאשִׁית *rēʾšît*. Even though ἀπαρχή is used in both Ps 77:51 and Ps 104:36 of human beings, ἀπαρχή does not have a cultic meaning and is therefore not used figuratively or metaphorically but simply means "the first (of a series)" (Louw-Nida, § 61.8), i.e., in this case the first or eldest son, closely associated in meaning with πρωτότοκος.

The cognate term ἀρχή is used figuratively in Jer 2:3, where it refers to *all Israel* and in this instance means "first-fruits".

ἅγιος Ἰσραὴλ τῷ κυρίῳ
Israel is holy to the Lord,

ἀρχὴ γενημάτων αὐτοῦ [רֵאשִׁית תְּבוּאָתֹה *rēʾšît tĕbûʾātōh*]
the first-fruits of his produce.

πάντες οἱ ἔσθοντες αὐτὸν πλημμελήσουσιν
All who eat it will transgress.

The phrase רֵאשִׁית תְּבוּאָתֹה *rēʾšît tĕbûʾātōh*, which underlies ἀρχὴ γενημάτων αὐτοῦ, can be translated "the first-fruits of his harvest." It is a metaphor that emphasizes the inviolability of Israel; just as consuming the first-fruits encurs the penalty of the law (though no specific penalty is mentioned in the Torah), so harming Israel will provoke punishment by Yahweh. This metaphor is paraphrastically translated in *Tg. Jer.* 2:3 (Hayward, *Tg. Jeremiah*, 48–49):

> The house of Israel are holy before the Lord—in respect of those who plunder them—like fruits of heave-offering of harvest, of which whoever eats is guilty of death; and like firstlings of harvest, the sheaf of the heave-offering, of which every one who eats, before the priests the sons of Aaron offer it as a sacrifice upon the altar, is guilty. Even so are all those who plunder the house of Israel guilty: evil shall come upon them, says the Lord.

The Mishnah has two tractates particularly relevant for the present discussion, *Bikkurim*, "first-fruits," and *Bekorot*, "firstlings," which contain most of the mishnaic discussion of various aspects of both cultic practices. All uses of בִּכּוּרִים *bikkûrîm* in the Mishnah are both literal and cultic. *M. Bik.* 1:3 refers to the seven types of agricultural products from which first-fruits can be brought, presumably the list of seven found in Deut 8:8: wheat, barley, grapes, figs, pomegranates, olive oil, and (date) honey (cf. *m. Ber.* 6:4). The first-fruits must be brought to the temple mount (*m. Bik.* 1:9; 2:10; 3:2; cf. Deut 26:2), and they are given to the priests (*m. Bik.* 2:1; *m. Maʿaś. Š.* 5:6). The rabbis were very conscious of the fact that no specific measure for the amount of first-fruits was prescribed in the Torah (*m. Peʾa* 1:1), and it was apparently possible for a person to designate an entire field of crops as first-fruits (*m. Bik.* 2:4). Philo refers to the practice of giving tithes of agricultural produce as first-fruits (*De virt.* 95).

Philo frequently mentions ἀπαρχή or ἀπαρχαί in his commentaries. When he refers to ἀπὸ τῶν πρωτοτόκων τὰς ἀπαρχάς (*De sacrificiis* 136), in all probability he means not "the *first-fruits* of the firstborn" but rather "the *offering* of the firstborn." Elsewhere he speaks of presenting firstborn males as a kind of ἀπαρχή, "offering," which he designates as a χαριστήριον, "thank-offering" (*Spec. leg.* 138).

ἀπαρχή or ἀπαρχαί (usually occurring in the plural form) exhibits a number of distinctive meanings in Greek literature. In Euripides *Orestes* 96, Helen refers to her κόμης ἀπαρχὰς καὶ χοάς, i.e., an "offering of hair and drink offering." However, a more appropriate gloss for ἀπαρχαί in this context might be "representative offering," and a working definition of this distinctive meaning of ἀπαρχαί might be "a category of sacrifice in which that which is offered to the deity, though only a small part of a whole, nevertheless carries with it the implication that the whole entity has been sacrificed, i.e., "made holy." The cultic meaning of ἀπαρχαί in Greek literature, as in the OT and early Jewish literature, refers most often to agricultural products (*Odyssey* 14.422 [verb ἀπάρχεσθαι]; Herodotus 4.71; Sophocles *Trach.* 183, 761; Euripides *Phoen.* 857, 1524; Thucydides 3.85; Isocrates *Archidamus* 96; Aristotle *Nic. Eth.* 8.11 [1160a]; *SIG,* 83.55; 200.10; 455.2; 502.40; 739.5; see Stephanus, *TGL* 1/2:1208–9; Delling, *TDNT* 1:484–85), in which case the gloss "first-fruits" is more appropriate than "representative offering." In the oldest occurrence of ἀπαρχή in Greek literature, it is a close synonym of ἀνάθεμα and refers to a "representative offering" by Croesus of the wealth he inherited from his father (Herodotus 1.92). In Greek cults there were three major forms of offerings to the gods—animal sacrifice, food offerings, and votive dedications—all of which could be designated ἀπαρχαί (Stengel, "Ἀπαρχαί," PW 1:2666–68; Burkert, *Mythology and Ritual,* 52–54). ἀπαρχαί, which tended to be regarded in a generally positive manner (in contrast to animal sacrifices, which were opposed by some Greek philosophical traditions such as Pythagoreanism and Neopythagoreanism), could consist of crops, wine, or booty (Sophocles *Trach.* 183; Euripides *Phoen.* 857), or in a metaphorical sense the speech that greets Apollo (Euripides *Ion* 401–2). The equivalent term in Latin is *primitiae,* which in Roman sacrificial ritual similarly refers to the offering of the first-fruits of a harvest (Pliny *Hist. nat.* 18.2.8; 18.30.119; Varro *De lingua latina* 6.16; Ovid *Fasti* 2.520; *Metam.* 8.274; Livy 26.11.9; Dionysius Hal. *Ant. Rom.* 7.72.15; Dio Cassius 73.16).

The key to understanding the meaning of ἀπαρχή in Rev 14:4 is the phrase ἀπαρχὴ ἀνθρώπων, "first-fruits consisting of people" or "first-fruits instead of people," which occurs occasionally in Greek literary and non-literary sources (Plutarch *Theseus* 16.2; *Quaest. Graec.* 298f; *De Pyth. orac.* 402a; Diodorus Siculus 4.66), where it is used to refer to offerings to the gods, which consisted of *people,* who may then have become temple servants or even released (Stengel, PW 1:2667; Bömer, *Sklaven* [2], 3:10–24). ἀπαρχαί can also refer to religious taxation, such as the grain tithe collected by officials of the cult of Demeter at Eleusis (Stengel, *Kultusaltertümer,* 174, 178, 235; Burkert, *Homo Necans,* 249–50 n. 7); it is also used of religious taxation in Judaism (Jos. *Ant.* 16.172).

In the NT, ἀπαρχή is never used in a literal sense, but it has several extended meanings: (1) the "first portion" of something that has been set aside and offered to God before the rest can be used (Rom 11:16; Louw-Nida, § 53.23), (2) the "first" of a group or class (1 Cor 15:20; Louw-Nida, § 61.8), and (3) "foretaste and pledge," similar in meaning to ἀρραβών (Rom 8:23; *Barn.* 1:7; Louw-Nida, § 57.171). Here in Rev 14:5 it is particularly important to notice that the term ἀπαρχή is used as a nominative in apposition to οὗτοι, the subject of the verb ἀγοράζειν, "to redeem," since the offerings of the first produce of agricultural commodities functions to redeem the rest of the crop. The term "first-fruits" is metaphorical in the OT only in Jer 2:3, where it refers to *all Israel:* "Israel was holy to the Lord, the first-fruits of his harvest" (RSV).

ἀπαρχή occurs nine times in the NT, seven of which occur in the Pauline corpus (Rom 8:23; 11:16; 16:5; 1 Cor 15:20, 23; 16:15; 2 Thess 2:13; Jas 1:18; Rev 14:4), and nine times in the Apostolic Fathers (*Did.* 13:3[2x], 5, 6, 7; *Barn.* 1:7; *1 Clem.* 24:1; 29:3; 42:4). ἀπαρχή is used five times in a figurative sense in the NT (various literal uses of the term occur in Rom 11:16, 1 Cor 15:20, 23; Rev 14:4). In the Apostolic Fathers there are just three uses of ἀπαρχή in a figurative sense (*Barn.* 1:7; *1 Clem.* 24:1; 42:4). In Judeo-Christian literature the term is usually in the collective singular, while in pagan Greek literature the term is usually found in the plural. However, plural forms occur in *Barn.* 1:7 and *1 Clem.* 42:4. Unlike the LXX, early Christian literature uses ἀπαρχή of human beings, both in a singular way of Christ (1 Cor 15:20, 23; *1 Clem.* 24:1) and to refer to initial converts to Christianity (Rom 16:5: 1 Cor 16:15; 2 Thess 2:13; Jas 1:18; *1 Clem.* 42:4).

One of the more problematic occurrences of ἀπαρχή in the NT occurs here in Rev 14:4, where the 144,000 are referred to as οὗτοι ἠγοράσθησαν ἀπὸ τῶν ἀνθρώπων ἀπαρχὴ τῷ θεῷ καὶ τῷ ἀρνίῳ, "these were ransomed from humanity as ἀπαρχή to God and the Lamb." Here ἀπαρχή is a collective singular functioning as a nominative of apposition modifying οὗτοι and gives the appearance of being a gloss on the text. This possibility is suggested by a parallel text in Rev 5:9 (part of a hymn addressed to the Lamb) where the term ἀπαρχή is missing: καὶ ἠγόρασας τῷ θεῷ ἐν τῷ αἵματί σου, ἐκ πάσης φυλῆς καὶ γλώσσης καὶ λαοῦ καὶ ἔθνους, "and you redeemed for God by your death / People from every tribe and tongue and people and nation." The parallelism between these two passages is even more clear when it is noted that ἀπὸ τῶν ἀνθρώπων, "from humanity," is a summary of the more typical ἐκ πάσης φυλῆς καὶ γλώσσης καὶ λαοῦ καὶ ἔθνους, "from every tribe and tongue and people and nation." The connection between οὗτοι ἠγοράσθησαν, "these were ransomed," and ἀπαρχή is far from clear. οὗτοι ἠγοράσθησαν is a metaphor drawn from the practice of manumission, i.e., the release of someone from slavery, while ἀπαργή may be a metaphorical reference to a type of ancient sacrifice; at any rate, this is a strange mixture of metaphors. In this context, ἀπαρχή represents 144,000 people who are part of a much larger group, all humanity. It makes little sense, however, to construe ἀπαρχή as the first of a set, the others of which will follow, i.e., all humanity. Rather, it seems appropriate to understand ἀπαρχή here in terms of a widespread Greek understanding of the term mentioned above, namely, as people who have been devoted to the deity as servants.

Excursus 14A: Celibacy in Antiquity

Bibliography

Anderson, G. "Celibacy or Consummation in the Garden? Reflection on Early Jewish and Christian Interpretations of the Garden of Eden." *HTR* 82 (1989) 121–48. **Baumgarten, J. M.** "The Qumran-Essene Restraints on Marriage." In *Archaeology and History in the Dead*

Sea Scrolls, ed. L. H. Schiffman. JSPSup 8. Sheffield: Sheffield Academic, 1990. 13–24. **Blinzler, J.** "Εἰσὶν εὐνοῦχοι." *ZNW* 48 (1957) 254–70. **Boring, M. E.** *The Continuing Voice of Jesus.* Louisville: Westminster/John Knox, 1991. **Brock, S. P.** "Early Syrian Asceticism." *Numen* 20 (1973) 1–19. **Burkitt, F. C.** *Early Eastern Christianity.* London: John Murray, 1904. **Cadbury, H. J.** *The Making of Luke-Acts.* London: SPCK, 1958. **Frank, S.** *Angelikos Bios.* Münster: Aschendorff, 1964. **Isaksson, A.** *Marriage and Ministry in the New Temple: A Study with Special Reference to Mt. 19:3–12 and 1 Cor. 11:3–16.* Lund: Gleerup, 1965. **Kretschmar, G.** "Ein Beitrag zur Frage nach dem Ursprung frühchristlicher Askese." *ZTK* 61 (1964) 27–67. **McArthur, H.** "Celibacy in Judaism at the Time of Christian Beginnings." *AUSS* 25 (1987) 163–81. **Michel, J.** "Engel IV (christlich)." *RAC* 5:156–58. **Pervo, R. I.** *Profit with Delight: The Literary Genre of the Acts of the Apostles.* Philadelphia: Fortress, 1987. **Qimron, E.** "Celibacy in the Dead Sea Scrolls and the Two Kinds of Sectarians." In *The Madrid Qumran Conference,* ed. J. L. Barrera and L. V. Montaner. STDJ 11. Leiden: Brill; Madrid: Editorial Complutense, 1992. 287–94. **Rad, G. von.** *Der heilige Krieg im alten Israel.* 4th ed. Göttingen: Vandenhoeck & Ruprecht, 1965. **Theissen, G.** "Wanderradikalismus." *ZTK* 70 (1973) 245ff. **Vermes, G.** *Jesus the Jew.* New York: Macmillan, 1974. **Vööbus, A.** *Celibacy: A Requirement for Admission to Baptism in the Early Syrian Church.* Stockholm: Estonian Theological Society in Exile, 1951.

Whether literally or figuratively understood, the language of Rev 14:4 reflects a *positive* estimation of sexual abstention. This extraordinary emphasis on the *sexual abstinence* of the followers of Jesus in Rev 14:5 requires explanation. It is important, however, to consider this text within the comparative framework of the various positive assessments of celibacy or sexual continence that existed in antiquity. The phenomenon of celibacy or sexual continence (which could be either temporary or permanent) in the ancient world was practiced for a number of very different reasons: (1) as a ritual requirement for male participants in holy wars, (2) as a ritual requirement for communion with the divine world, (3) as a prerequisite for becoming a disciple of Jesus or (in some phases of second- and third-century Christianity) a Christian, (4) as part of an ascetic program that sought a more spiritual form of existence through the denial of the needs and drives of the physical body, (5) as a prophetic characteristic according to some strands of early Jewish tradition, and (6) as a sign of participation in the Israelite cult (Exod 19:10–15; Jos. *J.W.* 5.227; CD[a] 12:1–2).

(1) The sexual abstention of these adult males is sometimes explained against the background of the requirement for *temporary* celibacy demanded of participants in a holy war as prescribed in the OT (1 Sam 21:4–5[MT 21:5–6]; 2 Sam 11:11–12; cf. Deut 23:9–14; von Rad, *Krieg,* 7; de Vaux, *Ancient Israel,* 258–59; J. Pedersen, *Israel,* 4 vols. in 2 [London: Cumberlege; Copenhagen: Branner og Korch, 1926] 3–4:10). The primary problem with understanding the sexual abstinence of the 144,000 in this ideological background is they are not described in vv 1–5 with other military metaphors or motifs based on Israelite holy war theology (unless they are linked to the 144,000 in Rev 7:4–8, and the latter passage is considered a military roster), though it is true that v 4a indicates that they are all males. It is also true, however, that in Rev 13:7 the beast makes war on the saints and conquers them. The conception of the holy war was not limited to Israel's distant past; it was also revitalized in connection with imaginative accounts of the impending eschatological conflict (see Giblin, 222–31). In the Qumran community, for example, there was a close connection between celibacy and holy-war theology (G. Anderson, *HTR* 82 [1989] 140). According to 1QM 7:3–6 (tr. Vermes, *Dead Sea Scrolls,* 132–33):

> No boy or woman shall enter their camps, from the time they leave Jerusalem and march out to war until they return. . . . And no man shall go down with them on the

day of battle who is impure because of his fount [i.e., a nocturnal emission] for the holy angels shall be with their hosts.

According to Philo (*Apol.* 11.14–17), Pliny (*Hist. nat.* 5.15), and Josephus (*J.W.* 2.120–21; *Ant.* 18.21), the Essenes rejected marriage, though Josephus does mention one branch of the sect that did marry (*J.W.* 2.160–61). While the practice of celibacy among the Essenes is not confirmed *directly* in the Dead Sea Scrolls (with the exception of the requirement of "temporary" abstention from sexual relations in 1QM 7:3–4 in anticipation of the eschatological holy war, which was expected to last forty years), that the Essenes did practice celibacy is confirmed by Philo (*Apol.* 11.14; Eusebius *Praep. evang.* 8.11), Josephus (*J.W.* 2.120–21; *Ant.* 18.21), and Pliny (*Hist. nat.* 5.17). Philo and Josephus attribute this practice of celibacy to misogyny (Philo *Apol.* 11.14–17; Jos. *J.W.* 2.121), but quite incorrectly (see Baumgartner, "Marriage," 13–14). Josephus, however, mentions another group of Essenes who did practice marriage (*J.W.* 2.160–61).

Pliny, Philo, and Josephus all agree on the reasons for the negative attitude of the Essenes toward marriage: ascetic renunciation of pleasure and the relatively low morals of women. These attitudes, however, are not confirmed in the Dead Sea Scrolls and appear to be based primarily on Hellenistic values. The evidence for celibacy among the residents of Qumran is ambiguous. Apparently only males were buried in the large central cemetery of Qumran (containing about 1,100 graves), while the remains of women and children have been found in adjacent (perhaps later) burial areas (F. M. Cross, *The Ancient Library of Qumran,* rev ed. [Garden City, NY: Doubleday, 1961] 96–99; J. C. VanderKam, *The Dead Sea Scrolls Today* [Grand Rapids, MI: Eerdmans, 1994] 14–15, 90–91). One female skeleton was found somewhat separated from the other graves in the main cemetery. However, only twenty-six graves have been excavated there. It is possible that members of the community over the age of twenty-five were required to abstain from sexual relations since they were considered soldiers mustered in readiness for the eschatological holy war; young men (נער זעטוט *naʿar zaʿăṭûṭ;* 1QM 7:3) between the ages of twenty and twenty-five were required to live celibately (Isaksson, *Marriage,* 55–56). This arrangement would have given some outsiders the impression that *all* members of the Qumran community were celibates. However, in view of the discussions by Baumgarten and Qimron, it appears that there were two kinds of members of the Qumran community: (a) those who lived at Khirbet Qumran and considered themselves a temporary substitute for Jerusalem and its temple and in consequence maintained a high degree of ritual purity appropriate for Jerusalem, i.e., permanent abstention from sexual relations (Qimron, "Celibacy," 291–92), and (b) those who lived in the "camps," i.e., the villages of Palestine, and did marry and have children (CD 7:6–7; Qimron, "Celibacy," 289–90). The asceticism of the Qumran community, then, is both *eschatologically* motivated, i.e., in order to be constantly prepared for the final conflict a strict regimen that included sexual abstinence in accord with OT prescriptions for the prosecution of a holy war was deemed necessary (1QM 7:3–6), and *cultically* motivated, i.e., the ritual demands of sexual abstinence within the temple were extended to Jerusalem (11QTemple 47:5–12; 46:16–18; CD 12:12), and since members of the community represented the temple, they practiced permanent sexual abstinence.

In his discussion of the Therapeutae (which some consider an Egyptian branch of the Essenes; see G. Vermes, "Essenes and Therapeutae," *RQ* 3 [1962] 495–502), Philo mentions that they had abandoned their possessions, brothers, children, wives, parents, and homeland (*Vit. Cont.* 18), and that the women among them were aged virgins (*Vit. Cont.* 68). However, the possibility of an eschatological motivation for celibacy is not mentioned. It must also be noted that a Roman in military service was not permitted to contract a legal marriage (*matrimonium iustum*) during service (this included soldiers in the legions, the praetorian guard, the urban guard, and the auxiliary units and sailors in the fleet); see Dio Cassius 60.24.3. This ancient regulation, which, however, did not prevent military personnel from keeping mistresses, was finally rescinded by Septimus Severus (Herodian 3.8.5).

(2) An entirely different role for celibacy is attested in some strands of early Jewish tradition linking celibacy to the reception of revelation, to the possession of the Spirit of God, or to prophecy. The Jewish tradition of the celibacy of the prophet and sage is reflected in rabbinic tradition (Vermes, *Jesus,* 99–102; A. Büchler, *Types of Jewish Palestinian Piety from 70 B.C.E. to 70 C.E.* [Oxford: Clarendon, 1926] 42–67; Boring, *Voice of Jesus,* 134–37). In a saying widely considered a later addition to the Mishnah, the second-century A.D. sage Phineas ben Jair proposes a graduated chain of virtues (tr. Danby, *Mishnah,* 306–7):

> Heedfulness leads to cleanliness, and cleanliness leads to purity, and purity leads to abstinence, and abstinence [פרישות *pĕrîšôt*] leads to holiness, and holiness leads to humility, and humility leads to the shunning of sin, and the shunning of sin leads to saintliness, and saintliness leads to [the gift of] the Holy Spirit, and the Holy Spirit leads to the resurrection of the dead.

Here, פרישות *pĕrîšôt,* "separation, abstinence," refers to *sexual* abstinence (Büchler, *Palestinian Piety,* 48–59). According to talmudic tradition, Moses had no sexual relations with his wife after his call, since if *temporary* communion with God required temporary continence, *uninterrupted* communion with God required permanent continence (*b. Šabb.* 87a; Vermes, *Jesus,* 100–101). A similar tradition is preserved earlier in Philo *Mos.* 2.68–69 (LCL tr.):

> But first he [Moses] had to be clean, as in soul so also in body, to have no dealings with any passion, purifying himself from all the calls of mortal nature, food and drink and intercourse with women. This last he had disdained for many a day, almost from the time when, possessed by the spirit, he entered on his work as a prophet, since he held it fitting to hold himself always in readiness to receive the oracular messages.

When Zipporah (the wife of Moses) heard that Eldad and Medad had begun to prophesy, she was overheard by Miriam to say "Woe to the wives of these men!" (*Sipre Num.* 12:1 [99]). Though these texts are relatively late, the tradition of the prophetic celibacy of Moses goes back to the first century A.D. since Philo also claims that Moses abstained from sexual intercourse after he began to function as a prophet (*Mos.* 2.68–69). Yet since from the rabbinic perspective prophecy was largely a phenomenon of the past, prophetic celibacy was not a current practice (Vermes, *Jesus,* 101–2).

The seven daughters of Philip are specifically designated as παρθένοι, perhaps because a connection was assumed between virginity and the gift of prophecy (Lindijer, "Die Jungfrauen," 129). A similar conception is expressed in the *Acts of Paul* 5, "Blessed are the continent [ἐγκρατεῖς] because God will speak to them."

(3) Sexual abstention was sometimes cited as a prerequisite for becoming a disciple of Jesus. The author of Luke-Acts does stress various aspects of asceticism, including celibacy (see below), but only in a relatively weak form. 1 Tim 4:3 (written ca. A.D. 100 or later) expresses opposition to Christians who forbid marriage and enjoin abstention from various types of food, though the identity of the author's opponents is unknown. A strong correlation between discipleship and sexual abstinence can be found in the Apocryphal Acts, widely regarded as originating in Asia Minor from ca. A.D. 175 to 225, though the Christian practice of sexual abstinence is certainly much earlier (see Tissot, "Encratisme," 109–19), and in the celibacy demanded as a prerequisite for baptism in Syrian Christianity (see Brock, *Numen* 20 [1973] 1–19; Vööbus, *Celibacy*).

Just as Philo (*Vit. Cont.* 18) emphasized how the Therapeutae had abandoned possessions, brothers, children, wives, parents, and homeland, so the Gospels emphasize the specific types of renunciation of those whom Jesus called to follow him. The seven types of renunciation enumerated in Mark 10:29 and repeated in Matt 19:29 (home, brothers, sisters, mother, father, children, fields) are reduced to five in Luke 18:29 with the addition of "wives" (an indication of Luke's concern with celibacy). In a passage possibly derived from Q (Luke 14:26; Matt 10:37–38), only Luke includes wives on a list of what followers of Jesus must "hate." Luke 20:34–36 (in contrast to Mark 12:24–25) indicates that sexual abstinence is a prerequisite for participation in the Resurrection. In the Parable of the Great Supper from Q (Luke 14:15–24; Matt 22:1–14), only Luke mentions recent marriage as an excuse not to attend the banquet. These passages all reflect a special Lukan emphasis on the abandonment of sexual relationships, an abstinence that is part of a larger emphasis on asceticism (Cadbury, *Luke–Acts,* 264–65, 272; Pervo, *Profit,* 127, 181–82 n. 79).

(4) Sexual abstinence was often considered part of an ascetic program that sought a more spiritual form of existence through the denial of the needs and drives of the physical body. Philo describes the ascetic practices of the Therapeutae, which included celibacy (*Vit. Cont.* 18, 32–33, 68–69, 83ff.). According to Matt 19:12, there are three types of eunuchs: (1) eunuchs by birth (i.e., born without normal sexual organs), (2) those made eunuchs by people (i.e., emasculated), and (3) those "who have made themselves eunuchs for the sake of the kingdom of heaven" (i.e., self-emasculation or more probably voluntary celibacy); see J. Blinzler, "'Εἰσὶν εὐνοῦχοι': Zur Auslegung von Mt. 19,12," *ZNW* 48 (1957) 254–70. Ben Azzai, an unmarried rabbi, reportedly claimed that he could not marry since his soul was joined to the Torah (Str-B, 1:807); perhaps Paul was also unmarried because he was "married" to his ministry (1 Cor 9:5; cf. 7:33–34). In Jesus' saying about forsaking homes and families (Mark 10:28–30 = Matt 19:27–29 = Luke 18:28–30; *Ap. James* 4:1), only Luke mentions leaving one's wife (v 29). In the negative version of that saying in Luke 14:26, hatred of wives is mentioned along with hatred of other family members as criteria for discipleship. Similarly, the Lukan version of the question about the resurrection (Mark 12:18–27 = Matt 22:23–33 = Luke 20:27–40) emphasizes celibacy for those who will be accounted worthy to attain to the age to come and the resurrection (20:34–36; see Aune, "Luke 20:34–36," 187–202). In 1 Cor 7:1, Paul recommends that a man not touch a woman, a suggestion made because of the nearness of the end (1 Cor 7:29–31); i.e., celibacy is eschatologically motivated. According to *1 Clem.* 35:1–2, one of the gifts of God is ἐγκράτεια ἐν ἁγιασμῷ, "continence in holiness" (cf. *1 Clem.* 38:2). ἐγκράτεια becomes increasingly emphasized in second-century Christianity (1 Tim 4:3; Ign. *Pol.* 5:2; *2 Clem.* 15:1; Hermas *Vis.* 1.2.4; 3.8.4; Justin *1 Apol.* 15.6; Athenagoras *Legatio* 33.1; Tatian, Marcion, and Saturninus emphasized celibacy; see Eusebius *Hist. eccl.* 4.29.3; Tertullian *Ad uxorem* 1.3–4; *De exhort. cast.* 9–10; Minucius Felix *Oct.* 31).

(5) The participation by priests in the Israelite cultus required temporary sexual abstinence (Exod 19:10–15; Jos. *J.W.* 5.227). In CD[a] 12:1–2 (cf. 4Q*268* = 4QD[c] 3 i 17) the rules for temporary priestly celibacy are extended from the temple itself to include the entire city of Jerusalem.

5 καὶ ἐν τῷ στόματι αὐτῶν οὐχ εὑρέθη ψεῦδος, ἄμωμοί εἰσιν, "and 'in their mouth guile was not found.' They are blameless." These sentences constitute the last part of an inclusio with v 4a, "These are those who have not polluted themselves with women, for they are chaste," indicating that vv 4–5 constitute a single short unit of text. V 5 indicates the moral purity of the 144,000, while v 4a emphasizes their ritual purity. It is likely that the term ἄμωμοι, "blameless, without defect," which like ἀπαρχή, "first-fruits," is a term associated with sacrificial offerings (Charles, 2:7), interprets the word παρθένοι of v 4a, giving it a metaphorical meaning (on ἄμωμος as a description of appropriate sacrificial victims, see Lev 22:21; 1 Pet 1:19; Heb 9:14, and note that the phrase ἀμνὸς ἄμωμος, "lamb without defect," or ἀμνοὶ ἄμωμοι, "lambs without defect," occurs some thirteen times in the LXX of acceptable sacrificial victims). The term "blameless" is also used of Christians (Phil 2:15; Col 1:22; Eph 1:4; 5:27).

"Guile is not found in their mouth" is a Semitic idiom for telling the truth, and there is a tendency within Judaism to favor the negative expression of this moral virtue. While this appears to be an ethical *topos,* it may be inspired by Zeph 3:13, where it is said of the remnant of Israel καὶ οὐ μὴ εὑρεθῇ ἐν τῷ στόματι αὐτῶν γλῶσσα δολία, "nor shall a deceitful tongue be found in their mouth." (This does not mean, however, that the author understands the 144,000 as the remnant of Israel.) Because this saying occurs in a variety of contexts in a stereotypical form, its dependence on Zeph 3:13 is somewhat weakened. A similar saying is found in Isa 53:9 (quoted in 1 Pet 2:23 and *1 Clem.* 16:10), where it is said of the Servant of the Lord: οὐδὲ εὑρέθη δόλος ἐν τῷ στόματι αὐτοῦ, "and there was no deceit in his mouth." Similar forms of this saying occur in LXX Ps 31:2 (MT 32:2) in the context of a beatitude: μακάριος ἀνήρ, οὗ οὐ μὴ λογίσηται κύριος ἁμαρτίαν, οὐδὲ ἔστιν ἐν τῷ στόματι αὐτοῦ [MT בְּרוּחוֹ *bĕrûḥô,* "in his spirit"] δόλος, "Blessed is the person to whom the Lord does not impute sin, nor is there guile in his mouth," and in Jdt 5:5, καὶ οὐκ ἐξελεύσεται ψεῦδος ἐκ τοῦ στόματος τοῦ δούλου σου, "and no lie will come forth from the mouth of your servant." The term ἄμωμος, "blameless," occurs only here in Revelation and can refer to a sacrificial offering that is without defect (Exod 29:1; Lev 1:3; 4:3; 5:15; Ezek 43:22–23; Philo *Leg. All.* 1.50; Christ in 1 Pet 1:19), to a priest who is in a state of ritual purity (1 Macc 4:43), and by extension to one who is morally blameless, i.e., faultless (Eph 1:4; 5:27; Col 1:22; Phil 2:15; Ign. *Trall.* 13:3).

In the OT and early Judaism there was an extremely large vocabulary devoted to the notions of deceit and treachery, suggesting that (along with idolatry, murder, and sexual immorality) lying was regarded as one of the major vices, though paradoxically there is not a single law in the OT that forbids lying generally, though there are injunctions against bearing false witness (Exod 20:16; Prov 21:28) and perjury (Lev 19:12). In the OT, God is associated with truth and idolatry with lying, and by the late second temple period this is transposed into the association of God with truth and Satan with lying (1QS 4:9; 10:22; Titus 1:22; John 8:41–47; Rom 3:4); see *NIDNTT* 2:470–74.

6a καὶ εἶδον ἄλλον ἄγγελον πετόμενον ἐν μεσουρανήματι, "Then I saw another angel flying in midheaven." (On καὶ εἶδον, see *Comment* on 5:1.) The phrase ἄλλος ἄγγελος, "another angel," which occurs five times in Rev 14 (vv 6, 8, 15, 17, 18), is a stylistic device that requires explanation, particularly since no previous angel has been mentioned to which the adjective ἄλλος can reasonably be thought to refer (see van Schaik, "Ἄλλος ἄγγελος," 217–28). Further, in v 8 the phrase ἄλλος ἄγγελος δεύτερος, "another angel, a second," indicates that the ἄλλος ἄγγελος here in v 6 is the first of the series. When "another angel" is mentioned elsewhere in Revelation (e.g., 7:2; 8:3), a previous angel has already been mentioned (e.g., 7:1; 8:2). J. Weiss suggested that the phrase be emended to ἄλλον ἀετόν, "another eagle," which could then be understood as referring back to the eagle mentioned in 8:13, similarly described as πετομένου ἐν μεσουρανήματι, "flying in midheaven" (*Offenbarung,* 96). Charles (2:12) deals with the problem unsatisfactorily by translating the phrase ἄλλον ἄγγελον, as "another, an angel."

It is of interest that this is the earliest reference in Jewish or Christian literature to an angel (apart from cherubim and seraphim) *flying*. While cherubim and seraphim are described as having wings and as flying, angels in general are not (1 Chr 21:16 merely states that the angel of the Lord was seen standing between heaven and earth, not that he had wings or was flying). Even in Rev 14:6, however, the flying angel is not necessarily described as winged. The first clear reference to angels (and demons) with wings is found in Tertullian *Apol.* 22.8. *1 Enoch* 61:1 mentions angels who "acquired wings for themselves, and flew" (Knibb, *Enoch* 2:148), though the Parables of Enoch (*1 Enoch* 37–71) should probably be dated after A.D. 70 (according to Milik, *Enoch,* 95–96, as late as A.D. 270).

The phrase πετόμενον ἐν μεσουρανήματι, "flying in midheaven" (*Comment* on 8:13), means that the angel appeared in the place where he could be seen and heard by everyone on earth (Masson, "L'Evangile," 63–64), since his message was directed to all human beings. This of course presupposes a world shaped like a flat disk rather than a sphere. While Aristotle thought the earth was spherical (*Cael.* 2.14; 298a), it was more commonly thought to be flat and circular with Delphi at the center and surrounded by Ocean (Herodotus 5.49) or flat and rectangular (Ephorus of Cyme according to Strabo 1.2.28). This conception of a flat, circular earth survived into Hellenistic and Roman times (*Anth. Graec.* 9.778 [Gow-Page, *Greek Anthology* 1:300–301]).

There is a doublet of this verse in 8:13, with the parallel phrases evident in this synoptic comparison:

Rev 8:13	*Rev 14:6*
καὶ εἶδον Then I saw	καὶ εἶδον Then I saw
καὶ ἤκουσα and heard	
ἑνὸς ἀετοῦ an eagle	ἄλλον ἄγγελον another angel
πετομένου ἐν μεσουρανήματι flying in midheaven	πετόμενον ἐν μεσουρανήματι flying in midheaven
	ἔχοντα εὐαγγέλιον αἰώνιον with an eternal message
	εὐαγγελίσαι to proclaim
λέγοντος φωνῇ μεγάλῃ saying with a loud voice,	
οὐαὶ οὐαὶ οὐαὶ Woe, woe, woe	

τοὺς κατοικοῦντας ἐπὶ τῆς γῆς
to the inhabitants on the earth.

ἐπὶ τοὺς καθημένους ἐπὶ τῆς γῆς
to the inhabitants on the earth.

6b ἔχοντα εὐαγγέλιον αἰώνιον εὐαγγελίσαι ἐπὶ τοὺς καθημένους ἐπὶ τῆς γῆς καὶ ἐπὶ πᾶν ἔθνος καὶ φυλὴν καὶ γλῶσσαν καὶ λαόν, "with an eternal message to proclaim among those who dwell on the earth and among every nation and tribe and language and people." The noun εὐαγγέλιον, "message," occurs only here in Revelation, though it occurs frequently in the NT. This usage is distinctive, however, for unlike the regular articular use of εὐαγγέλιον (to designate a well-known reality, the proclamation of the good news of the saving death and resurrection of Jesus the Messiah), this is the only occurrence in the NT where the definite article is not used. The active verb εὐαγγελίζειν, "proclaim," occurs just twice in Revelation, here and in 10:7. These are the only places where the active verb εὐαγγελίζειν occurs in the NT. The active verb is rare, occurring only twice in the LXX (1 Kgdms 13:9 and 2 Kgdms 18:19), in a *var. lect.* in Acts 16:17 (Codex Bezae), and in profane Greek, making its first appearance at the beginning of the second century A.D. The middle form εὐαγγελίζεσθαι, on the other hand, is used fifty-two times in the NT. No εὐαγγελ- words are found in the rest of the Johannine corpus. The content of this εὐαγγέλιον is given in v 7; it is an appeal for repentance and conversion to the God who created heaven and earth in the context of impending judgment (v 8). It is striking that this use of the phrase εὐαγγελίζειν εὐαγγέλιον, "to make a proclamation," has little in common with the technical Christian use of the term (found earliest in the Pauline letters), referring to the message of good news about the death and resurrection of Jesus.

An important lexicographical problem is whether εὐαγγελίζειν means "to tell the good news"(Louw-Nida, § 33.215) and its derivative εὐαγγέλιον means "good news" (Louw-Nida, § 33.17) or these two words (like the Hebrew words בשׂר *bāśar* and בשׂורה *bĕśôrâ*, consistently translated with εὐαγγελ- cognates in the LXX) are "neutral" (i.e., the verb means "to proclaim a [positive or negative] message," while the noun means "a [positive or negative] message" [KB, 1:165; *TDOT* 2:313–15]). Not surprisingly, recent lexical surveys of εὐαγγελ- words suggest that they tend to be positive, i.e., to refer to good news (Horsley, *New Docs* 3:11–15).

A. P. van Schaik ("'Ἄλλος ἄγγελος," 219–21) has suggested that the two scenes in Isa 40:9–10 and 52:7–9 served as models for Rev 14:1–5 and that the occurrence of the term εὐαγγελίζειν in 14:6 was derived from the occurrences of εὐαγγελίζεσθαι in LXX Isa 40:9(2x) and 52:7(2x), thereby linking 14:1–5 to 14:6–7. The noun εὐαγγέλιον is anarthrous and therefore refers to "a message" rather than to "*the* gospel" (Bousset [1906] 383; Lohse, 85). The same is true of the use of the verb εὐαγγελίζειν in 10:7 (see *Comment* on 10:7).

Stuhlmacher has argued for the pre-Pauline Christian usage of εὐαγγέλιον and εὐαγγελίζειν traceable to the early Palestinian Jewish Christian community. Examples of this usage occur in Rev 10:7; 14:6 (*Evangelium,* 1:210–18; Zondervan, *TT* 43 [1914] 200–201), as well as in several other passages in the NT, i.e., Matt 4:23; 9:35; 11:5 = Luke 7:22; Matt 16:13; 24:14; Mark 1:14 (*Evangelium,* 209–44). This is doubtful, however, for several reasons: (1) the meanings of εὐαγγελίζειν and εὐαγγέλιον in Rev 10:7; 14:6 are fully explicable from the perspective of Jewish apocalyptic; (2) the terms have no semantic connections to Pauline usage; and (3) the terms belong to the later strata of Revelation and do not constitute evidence for early Christian tradition (Strecker, "Evangelium," 515–17; id., "εὐαγγέλιον," *EDNT* 2:74; followed by Frankmölle, *Evangelium,* 122–23, 130).

The LXX exclusively used εὐαγγελ- words to translate terms based on the triliteral stem בשר *bśr.* The term בשורה *bĕśôrâ,* "message," occurs six times in the OT (2 Sam 4:10; 18:20, 22, 25, 27; 2 Kgs 7:9), always translated in the LXX as εὐαγγέλιον. The use of εὐαγγελίζειν with a cognate accusative in the phrase εὐαγγελίζειν εὐαγγέλιον, "to proclaim a message," would correspond to the Hebrew phrase בשר בשורה *bēśar bĕśôrâ* (unattested in the OT), which Stuhlmacher designated "translation Greek" (*Evangelium,* 213–14). In 14:6b, an *angel* is the proclaimer, and the εὐαγγέλιον is characterized as eternal; i.e., the message always has been and always will be valid.

In several passages in early Christian and early Jewish literature the verb εὐαγγελίσασθαι is used with angelic messengers as proclaimers (Jos. *Ant.* 5.282; Luke 1:19; 2:10; Gal 1:8–9; see Stuhlmacher, *Evangelium,* 212–13). With reference to the angelic proclamation in Rev 14:6–7, Jeremias has argued that an angelic messenger is also presupposed in the originally independent logia attributed to Jesus in Matt 24:14 = Mark 13:10 ("The gospel must first be proclaimed to all nations" [RSV]). Originally Matt 24:14 = Mark 13:10 envisaged not a gentile mission (as they do in their present context), he argues, but rather the angelic proclamation of the victory of God in the last days (Joachim Jeremias, *Jesus' Promise,* 22–23, 69). However, since the proclaimers in these texts are not explicitly identified, it is hardly credible to suggest that they are angels.

The phrase εὐαγγέλιον αἰώνιον, "eternal message," has been construed in several ways. The adjective αἰώνιος (which occurs only here in Revelation) emphasizes the extraordinary character of the εὐαγγέλιον and refers to the permanent validity of the proclamation, which is as enduring as the eternal God who authorizes its announcement (cf. *Sib. Or.* 3.47–48, which refers to "the very great kingdom of the immortal king [ἀθανάτου βασιλῆος]"). The context suggests that the message proclaimed is purely eschatological; i.e., it announces the necessity of repentance and conversion in view of the imminent end of the world and the judgment of God. Cerfaux suggests in passing that it is formulated in protest to the so-called good news of the imperial cult and therefore reveals that message to be of only temporary significance (*ETL* 39 [1963] 673).

A parallel phrase, ἀθάνατον κήρυγμα, "immortal proclamation," is used as a designation for the famous inscription of Antiochus I of Commogene (M. Guarducci, *Epigrafia Graeca* [Rome: Istituto Poligrafico dello Stato, 1969] 2:425–29, line 12), which Danker considers an instance of chancery style (*Benefactor,* 253). A similar phrase, τὸ ἱερὸν καὶ ἄφθαρτον κήρυγμα, "the sacred and imperishable proclamation," is used of the gospel in the so-called shorter ending of Mark. A possible origin of the phrase is Ps 96:2b, "proclaim his salvation from day to day" (MT בשרו מיום־ליום ישועתו *bĕśśĕrû miyyôm lĕyôm yĕšû'ātô*; LXX [95:2b] εὐαγγελίζεσθε ἡμέραν ἐξ ἡμέρας τὸ σωτήριον αὐτοῦ), which the author could conceivably have translated εὐαγγέλιον αἰώνιον (Bauckham, "Conversion," 286–89). This allusion is likely since Ps 96:3a (LXX 95:3a) continues "Declare his glory among the nations [ἔθνεσιν], his marvelous works among all peoples [λαοῖς]," and the "eternal gospel" is explicitly addressed to "every nation and tribe and language and people" (Rev 14:6).

The universal audience addressed by the angel is expressed in two parallel phrases. The first phrase, οἱ καθήμενοι ἐπὶ τῆς γῆς, "those who dwell on the earth," is found in LXX Jer 32:29, 30 [MT 25:29, 30]; cf. 51:13, 26 [MT 44:13, 26], alongside the expression οἱ κατοικοῦντες τὴν γῆν (LXX Jer 1:14; 4:7 [*var. lect.*]; 6:12; 10:18; 13:13; 29:2 [MT 47:2]), indicating that they are virtually equivalent. The second phrase, πᾶν ἔθνος καὶ φυλὴν καὶ γλῶσσαν καὶ λαόν, "every nation and tribe and language and people," occurs frequently with variations in Revelation (see *Comment* on 5:9). In view of this universal audience for the proclamation of the gospel, a frequently cited parallel to Rev 14:6–7 is Matt 24:14, "This good news of the kingdom will be proclaimed throughout the world as a testimony to all the nations; and then the end will come" (cf. Mark 13:10). The uncompromising universality of the proclamation of the message appealing to people to repent in view of the impending eschatological judgment of God is contrary to the normal parochialism inherent in Jewish apocalyptic literature, in which only a specific ethnic group, usually a Jewish remnant, is the object of God's saving activity in the world (*Pss. Sol.* 17–18; *2 Apoc. Bar.* 53–57; 4 Ezra 10–13; *Apoc. Abr.* 21–32). The author refuses to espouse religious nationalism, whether Jewish or pagan, and instead categorizes people only in terms of their faithfulness to the Lamb (Rev 7:9–10, 14, 17; 12:11; 13:16–17; 14:1, 4–5; 19:6–8) or their failure to repent and their adherence to the beast (9:20–21; 13:3–4, 8, 16–17; 14:9–11; 20:15).

7a λέγων ἐν φωνῇ μεγάλῃ, φοβήθητε τὸν θεὸν καὶ δότε αὐτῷ δόξαν, "proclaiming with a loud voice, 'Fear God and give him glory.'" This invitation to worship the true God because he created the heavens and the earth (v 7) is a theme found in Deut 10:12–15 and can be construed as a positive formulation of the third commandment (Exod 20:4–6). This describes the *content* of the message (εὐαγγέλιον) proclaimed by the angel; i.e., it is a call to repentance in view of God's judgment, which has arrived (v 7b). The conversion of the inhabitants of the city who escaped destruction in 11:13 is described with similar language: καὶ ἔδωκαν δόξαν τῷ θεῷ τοῦ οὐρανοῦ, "and they gave glory to the God of heaven" (see *Comment* on 11:13). This is not the gospel of early Christianity but the message proclaimed by Hellenistic Judaism and taken over by early Christianity, reflections of which are found in the NT (1 Thess 1:9–10; Acts 14:15–17; 17:22–31).

This verse contains four key words: φοβεῖν, "fear," δόξα, "glory," κρίσις, "judgment," and προσκυνεῖν, "worship." Their use in tandem suggests that the author is drawing on LXX 1 Chr 16:8–36, in addition to Ps 96 (Altink, *AUSS* 24 [1986] 187–96). The notion of the "fear of God" (φόβος τοῦ θεοῦ), more accurately rendered "reverence for God" or "respect for God," is a conception found frequently in the OT and refers to the awe and reverence that people should have toward God's authority and that enables them to obey his commands (Gen 22:12; Jer 32:40; Ps 111:10; Prov 8:13; *T. Reub.* 4:1; *T. Levi* 13:1; *T. Sim.* 3:4; Acts 9:31). The phrase "the fear of God" or "the fear of the Lord" is often used in a way synonymous with true faith (Ps 34:11). The phrase φοβούμενοι τὸν θεόν or σεβόμενοι τὸν θεόν, "God-fearers," is a technical term used in Luke-Acts of pagans who have become adherents to Judaism (Acts 10:2, 22; 13:16, 26).

7b ὅτι ἦλθεν ἡ ὥρα τῆς κρίσεως αὐτοῦ, "because the hour of his judgment has come." The urgency of the call for conversion in v 7a implies that the day of God's judgment of the world *has already arrived,* though an aorist verb ἦλθεν, "has come," is obviously used in a proleptic or anticipatory sense. The primary interpretive problem centers on how repentance or conversion remains a real possibility if the eschatological judgment of God has in fact arrived. No other exhortation to repent in the OT or NT suggests that the eschatological judgment has already arrived, though in Mark 1:15 Jesus demands repentance because the Kingdom of God ἤγγικεν, either "has arrived" or "has come near" (survey of interpretations in Guelich, *Mark,* 43–44). While the aorist verb ἦλθεν could be used here as a *perfectum confidentiae,* "perfect of assurance," i.e., a prophetic perfect (see *Comment* on 14:8a), that does not really solve the problem. The aorist verb ἦλθεν is probably used here with perfective value (Mussies, *Morphology,* 339; cf. Turner, *Syntax,* 72); i.e., the emphasis is on the continuing implications of the arrival of the eschatological judgment.

ἦλθεν is used in the context of eschatological judgment several times elsewhere in Revelation: (1) 6:17, "the great day of wrath has come [ἦλθεν]" (part of a collective cry of anguish uttered by those experiencing the plagues unleashed at the opening of the sixth seal); (2) 11:18, καὶ ἦλθεν ἡ ὀργή σου, "your wrath has come" (part of a hymn chanted by the twenty-four elders following the sounding of the seventh trumpet); (3) 18:10, μιᾷ ὥρᾳ ἦλθεν ἡ κρίσις σου, "in one hour your judgment came" (part of a collective speech of the kings of the earth who expressed shock at the sudden fall of Babylon); and (4) 14:15, ἦλθεν ἡ ὥρα θερίσαι, "the hour for harvesting has come" (part of an angelic speech providing the reason for harvesting the earth).

The noun κρίσις, "judgment," occurs here in the first of four occurrences in Revelation (see also 16:7; 18:10; 19:2). That it is articular means that it refers to the final day of judgment, which was a centrally important part of early Jewish and early Christian eschatological expectation (see the texts listed below). In Jewish and Christian eschatological traditions, the phrase "the hour of [his] judgment" is rare, though the synonymous phrase ἡ ἡμέρα τῆς κρίσεως, "day of judgment," which refers to the final eschatological judgment, occurs frequently (the Hebrew equivalent, יום המשפט *yôm hammišpāṭ,* occurs in the Dead Sea Scrolls): 1QpHab 12:14; 13:2; 1QpMic 10:6–7; Jdt 16:17; *Frag. Jub.* 3:9; 10:7 (Denis, *Fragmenta,* 77, 86); *Jub.* 24:30; *Apoc. Adam* 12:2; 26:4; *T. Levi* 1:1; *1 Enoch* 10:12; 16:1; 19:1; 22:4, 13; 27:3, 4; 100:4; 104:5; cf. 97:3; 98:8; 4 Ezra 7:38 (*die iudicii*), 102, 104, 113; 12:34; *Gk. Apoc. Ezra* 2:27, 29; *3 Apoc. Bar.* 1:7; cf. "day of great judgment" or "the great day of judgment" in *1 Enoch* 10:6; 19:1; 22:11; 84:4; 94:9; 98:10; 99:15; Matt 10:15; 11:22, 24; 12:36; 2 Pet 2:9; 3:7; 1 John 4:17; "the day of his judgment" in *Gk. Apoc. Ezra* 7:11 (see Volz, *Eschatologie,* 272–309).

7c καὶ προσκυνήσατε τῷ ποιήσαντι τὸν οὐρανὸν καὶ τὴν γῆν καὶ θάλασσαν καὶ πηγὰς ὑδάτων, "and worship the one who made the heaven and the earth and sea and the springs." The divine title "the one who made heaven and earth" occurs only here in Revelation, but it is a frequent designation for God in the OT (Gen 1:1; 14:18, 22; 2 Kgs 19:15; 2 Chr 2:12; Isa 37:16; Pss 115:15; 121:2; 124:8; 134:3; 146:6; see *Pr. Man.* 2; *Par. Jer.* 5:32) and is used occasionally in early Christianity (Acts 4:24; 14:15; cf. 17:24). Similarly, God's sovereignty over the universe is emphasized when he is addressed as "God of heaven and earth" (Gen 24:3; Ezra 5:11) or "Lord of heaven and earth" (Matt 11:25 = Luke 10:21; Acts 17:24). On the divine epithet describing a two-level cosmos in three sectors, "the one who created the heaven, the earth, and the sea," see *Comments* on 5:3, 13 and 10:6.

The "sea and the springs" constitute one sector of the cosmos, since the ancients thought that the sea, rivers, and springs were all fed by the subterranean ocean (Job 38:16; Stadelmann, *World,* 154–64). The phrase πηγὰς ὑδάτων, literally "springs of water" or "springs" (the same phrase occurs in 8:3), refers to sources of water flowing from below ground level into pools and should be distinguished from fountains and wells, which are constructed by people (see Louw-Nida, § 1.79). Reliable sources of water were important for any urban area, so much so that the travel guide Pausanias (second century A.D.) defined a πόλις (city-state) as consisting of government offices, a gymnasium, a theater, a market, and water descending to a fountain, as through an aqueduct (10.4.1).

8a καὶ ἄλλος ἄγγελος δεύτερος ἠκολούθησεν λέγων, ἔπεσεν ἔπεσεν Βαβυλὼν ἡ μεγάλη, "Then another angel, a second one, followed, saying, 'Fallen, fallen is Babylon the great!'" (On the phrase "another angel," see *Comment* on v 6.) The angel's declaration has an exact verbal parallel in 18:2b, whence it was probably derived (in many ways Rev 14 is a pastiche of other portions of Revelation; see *Form/Structure/Setting* on 14:1–20, II. Literary Analysis). Though this verse clearly alludes to Jer 51:7–8 (LXX 28:7–8), the doubling of the verb ἔπεσεν suggests the influence of LXX Isa 21:9, where MS B reads πέπτωκεν πέπτωκεν Βαβυλών (Wolff, *Jeremia,* 167); n.b. that this is a literal rendering of the Hebrew נָפְלָה נָפְלָה בָּבֶל *nāplâ nāplâ bābel,* "fallen, fallen, is Babylon." The aorist verbs ἔπεσεν ἔπεσεν, "fallen, fallen," emphasize the certainty of the fall of Babylon-Rome, which, from the standpoint of the speaker, is an event that has not yet occurred (this line also occurs in Rev 18:2). Lancellotti (*Sintassi Ebraica,* 42) refers to these aorists as "proleptic," i.e., to the use of the *perfectum confidentiae,* "perfect of assurance," or the *perfectum propheticum,* "prophetic perfect" (GKC § 106n; Mussies, *Morphology,* 338), in which an event of the future is described with a past tense as if it had already occurred. The use of the "prophetic perfect" in the OT was commented on by Justin *1 Apol.* 26:1, "Things he [the OT prophet] fully knows are to happen he speaks of in advance as if they had already occurred."

Babylon, a symbolic name for Rome, occurs here as the first of six occurrences in Revelation (see Rev 16:19; 17:6; 18:2, 10, 21). Babylon and Rome are comparable because both were centers for world empires and both captured Jerusalem and destroyed the temple. The fall of the *urbs aeterna,* the "eternal city," as Rome was designated, would have been virtually unthinkable for Romans (the sack of Rome by the Goths in A.D. 410 spurred Augustine to write *The City of God* in A.D. 413–26 to answer pagans who credited the disaster to the replacement of the old cult with the Christian religion). As a cipher for Rome, the term "Babylon" occurs occasionally in Jewish apocalyptic literature, though the fact that all the references occur in literature that postdates A.D. 70, the year when Jerusalem fell to Titus, has suggested to many scholars that the equation Babylon = Rome was not made until after that date and suggests that Revelation must have been written after that date (Yarbro Collins, *Crisis and Catharsis,* 57–58). 1 Pet 5:13, written ca. A.D. 80, may be the earliest application of the cover name "Babylon" for Rome, an equation made by Clement Alex. in Eusebius (*Hist. eccl.* 2.15.2) and also reflected in the substitution of Ῥώμη for Βαβυλών in the minuscule 2138 and the addition of ἐν Ῥώμῃ in two other minuscules. "Babylon" is the location of the author in 1 Pet 5:13 and corresponds to the location of the addressees in the "dispersion" (1 Pet 1:1). Since no opposition to "Babylon" is expressed in 1 Peter, "Babylon" primarily means "those in exile" and is not a pejorative code name for Rome (Souza Nogueira, "Widerstand," 154–55). The models for the use of "Babylon" in 1 Peter are the letters of Jeremiah purportedly sent to the exiles in Babylon in Jer 29:1–23 (LXX 36:1–23) and *2 Apoc.*

Bar. 78–87. The fictional setting of 4 Ezra and *2 Apocalypse of Baruch* is Babylon, which the authors equate with Rome, though writing in the late first and early second century A.D., respectively (4 Ezra 3:1–2, 28–31; 16:44, 46; *2 Apoc. Bar.* 10:2; 11:1; 67:7).

The comparison between Babylon and Rome is based implicitly on the parallels between the conquest of Jerusalem by Babylon in 587 B.C. and the conquest of Jerusalem by Rome in A.D. 70. The same fictional perspective with its implicit comparison of the two tragedies is found in *Paraleipomena Jeremiou* (*4 Baruch*), which was probably composed early in the second century A.D. (Nickelsburg, *Jewish Literature,* 315). The use of "Babylon" as a code name for Rome is also found in *Sib. Or.* 5.143, 159 (written ca. A.D. 90); while Babylon is also mentioned in *Sib. Or.* 5.434 and the Babylonians in 5.440, these citations appear to refer to the historical Babylon. Yet in the Jewish sources and 1 Pet 5:13, the term "Babylon" is not used with the hostility found in Revelation. John has read the OT prophets, has probably made the equation himself, and has transferred the prophetic hostility toward the historical Babylon to his own attitudes toward Rome (there are five oracles against Babylon in the OT; see Isa 13:1–22; 14:22–23; 21:1–10; Jer 25:12–14; 50:1–51:64). There were other symbolic names for Rome in use by early Judaism, including Edom, Kittim (Aramaic כתים *kittîm,* in Dan 11:30 is translated Ῥωμαῖοι in LXX Dan 11:30), and Egypt. The Kittim are frequently mentioned in 1QpHab and 1QM (see H. Ringgren, *The Faith of Qumran: Theology of the Dead Sea Scrolls* [Philadelphia: Fortress, 1963] 26–31).

Josephus claimed that Jeremiah predicted the recent (A.D. 70) destruction of Jerusalem (*Ant.* 10.79), as Daniel had (*Ant.* 10.276–77); Josephus therefore probably understood Babylon as a code word for the Romans who had destroyed Jerusalem most recently (Wolff, *Jeremia,* 11). In Aune, *Revelation,* WBC 52A, lxi, lxix, I accepted the view of A. Yarbro Collins that the use of the name "Babylon" as a code word for Rome pointed to a date after A.D. 70 for the composition of Revelation. However, that argument for dating is vulnerable, since the name "Babylon" is used to interpret "Assyria" in Isa 10:13–19 (part of an oracle against Assyria in Isa 10:5–19) in the pesher commentary 4QpIsa[c] 6–7 ii 4 (see Horgan, *Pesharim,* 97, though she does not comment on this feature of the text), which is certainly to be dated some years *before* A.D. 70. Although D. G. Meade has claimed that the name "Babylon" is used as an eschatological symbol of a world power in Dan 1:1–8; 3:8–12; 6:2–24, he is certainly not correct, for "Babylon" only occurs once with reference to the first regnal year of Belshazzar, king of Babylon (7:1), and not elsewhere in Dan 7–12, the apocalyptic section of Daniel (*Pseudonymity and Canon,* WUNT 39 [Tübingen: Mohr-Siebeck, 1986] 165).

This is the first of a series of predictions of the fall of Babylon-Rome (see also Rev 16:19; 17:16–17; 18:1–24). In the eastern Mediterranean, there was a great deal of political resistance to Roman domination, which found expression in various types of revelatory literature (in some instances earlier oracles against the Greeks were reapplied to the Romans). The *Oracles of Hystaspes* predicted the destruction of the Roman empire and the rise to power of the East (Bidez-Cumont, *Mages* 1:215–23; 2:359–77). After 6,000 years, Rome was expected to collapse, an event that would signal the beginning of natural disasters and wars. According to *Oracles of Hystaspes* frag. 13b (Bidez-Cumont, *Mages* 2:366–67; Lactantius *Div. Inst.* 7.15.11; tr. McDonald, *Lactantius*):

> This will be the cause of the destruction and confusion, that the Roman name, by which the world is now ruled . . . will be taken from the earth, and power will be returned to Asia, and again the Orient will dominate and the West will serve.

A period of one thousand years of peace was expected to follow. One Roman writer who envisaged the possibility of the fall of Rome was Ps.-Sallust, *Epistula ad Caesarem Secunda* 13.6 (LCL tr.), "For if this empire should succumb to decay or to fate, can anyone doubt but that all over the world devastation, wars, and bloodshed would ensue?"

The phrase "Babylon the Great" occurs four times in Revelation (14:8; 16:19; 17:7; 18:2; cf. 18:10, 21) and may have been drawn from Dan 4:27, Βαβυλὼν ἡ μεγάλη (Aramaic בבל רבתא *bābel rabtāʾ*). The phrase Βαβυλὼν μεγάλη, "great Babylon," also occurs in *Sib. Or.* 4.93. In the Greek poetic tradition, "the great city" was Troy. In an encomium on Smyrna, Aelius Aristides gives the title ἡ μεγάλη πόλις, "the great city," to the city of Smyrna (*Or.* 18.3), and in *Indica* 1.8, Arrian refers to Massaca with the anarthrous phrase "great city." Aside from its use in Rev 11:8 (where it refers to Jerusalem), the phrase "the great city" refers to Rome elsewhere in Revelation, implicitly or explicitly designated "Babylon" (16:19; 17:18; 18:10, 16, 18, 19, 21). It was widely known in the ancient world that Alexander had planned to make Babylon the capital of his empire (Strabo 15.2.10; Quintus Curtius 5.1.42; Arrian *Anab.* 3.16.4; 7.17.2). The phrase "the great city" could be used pejoratively, based on Jonah's designation of Nineveh as "the great city" (Jonah 1:2; 3:2, 3; 4:11; Jdt 1:1; see *Vit. Proph.* 10.3 [10:6B in Denis, *Concordance,* 869]; see Rosenstiehl, *L'Apocalypse d'Élie,* 43), i.e., as the city of a hated enemy. Jerusalem is called "the great city" in various writings (*var. lect.* in Rev 21:20 [see *Notes*]; Jer 22:8; Jos. *Ag. Ap.* 1.197; *Sib. Or.* 5.154, 226, 413; *Apoc. Elijah* 4:13 [3:31, ed. Rosenstiehl]). The phrase is used of heaven in *T. Abr.* [Rec. A] 2:6 and of the Sicilian city of Croton in *Sib. Or.* 4.82. Rome was called *princeps urbium,* "the greatest of cities," in Horace *Carmina* 4.3.13.

8b ἣ ἐκ τοῦ οἴνου τοῦ θυμοῦ τῆς πορνείας αὐτῆς πεπότικεν πάντα τὰ ἔθνη, "who gave all nations to drink of the wine which is her immoral passion." In this concatenation of four genitives, τοῦ οἴνου, "the wine," is a partitive genitive, τοῦ θυμοῦ, "passion," "appetite," is an appositive or epexegetical genitive, τῆς πορνείας, "fornication, immorality," is a descriptive genitive or genitive of quality (BDF § 165), to which some have given the unnecessary label "Hebraic" genitive (Zerwick, *Greek,* § 40; Turner, *Syntax* 3:212–14; see the brief criticism in Horsley, *New Docs* 4:58–59), and αὐτῆς is a genitive of possession. The term θυμός is used here meaning "intense desire" and in v 10 meaning "fury, intense anger." This play on words is one of the many instances of paronomasia in Revelation (see also 2:2[2x], 22; 3:10; 18:6[3x], 20, 21; 22:18, 19). The phrase πάντα τὰ ἔθνη, "all nations," is a fixed phrase that occurs five times in Revelation (12:5; 14:8; 15:4; 18:3, 23); see *Comment* on 12:5.

There are close verbal parallels between 14:8c and 18:3. When taken with the many other verbal similarities between Rev 14 and other portions of the book, this suggests that much of the chapter has been fashioned by borrowing from earlier sections of the composition.

Rev 14:8c	*Rev 18:3a*
ἣ ἐκ τοῦ οἴνου τοῦ θυμοῦ	ὅτι ἐκ τοῦ οἴνου τοῦ θυμοῦ
who from the wine which is	because from the wine which is

τῆς πορνείας αὐτῆς her immoral passion	τῆς πορνείας αὐτῆς her immoral passion
πεπότικεν πάντα τὰ ἔθνη. she gave all nations to drink.	πέπωκαν πάντα τὰ ἔθνη all nations collapsed.

A relatively close parallel phrase is found in Rev 17:2, ἐκ τοῦ οἴνου τῆς πορνείας αὐτῆς, "of the wine which is her fornication." These passages both allude to LXX Jer 28:7 (MT 51:7), ποτήριον χρυσοῦν Βαβυλὼν ἐν χειρὶ κυρίου μεθύσκον πᾶσαν τὴν γῆν· ἀπὸ τοῦ οἴνου αὐτῆς ἐπίοσαν ἔθνη, διὰ τοῦτο ἐσαλεύθησαν. καὶ ἄφνω ἔπεσεν Βαβυλὼν καὶ συνετρίβη, "Babylon was a golden cup [see Rev 17:4] in the hand of the Lord making all the earth intoxicated. The nations drank from her wine; because of this they staggered. Suddenly Babylon fell and was crushed." Since this is the first occurrence of the term "Babylon" and the Babylon theme does not occur again (with the exception of 16:19) until 17:1–19:10 (where the name occurs four times, 17:5; 18:2, 10, 21), Rev 14:8 appears to be a redactional insertion whose purpose it is to anticipate the extensive section on the judgment of Babylon-Rome in 17:1–19:10; 16:19 functions in the same way and is also redactional (Bergmeier, *ANRW* II, 25/5:3906).

9a καὶ ἄλλος ἄγγελος τρίτος ἠκολούθησεν αὐτοῖς λέγων ἐν φωνῇ μεγάλῃ· εἴ τις προσκυνεῖ τὸ θηρίον καὶ τὴν εἰκόνα αὐτοῦ, "Another angel, a third one, followed them, proclaiming with a loud voice, 'If anyone worships the beast and his cultic image.'" The extended clause introduced with "If anyone" constitutes the protasis of a first-class conditional sentence in which the condition is assumed as real (the apodosis is introduced with καί in v 10). The protasis has two verbs, προσκυνεῖ, "worship," and λαμβάνει, "receive [a brand]," both in the present tense. This recalls the narrative in 13:15–18 in which the themes of worshiping the beast and his image and receiving his brand on the right hand or forehead (v 16) are first mentioned. The theme of worshiping the beast has already been mentioned in the narrative of 13:4, 8, 12, while the theme of worshiping the *image* of the beast was mentioned in 13:15. Both themes are repeated in v 11bc, forming a chiasm with v 9b. They are also repeated several times in later passages:

16:2	τοὺς ἀνθρώπους τοὺς ἔχοντας τὸ χάραγμα τοῦ θηρίου people who have the brand of the beast
	καὶ τοὺς προσκυνοῦντας τῇ εἰκόνι αὐτοῦ. and who worship his image.
19:20	τοὺς λαβόντας τὸ χάραγμα τοῦ θηρίου those who received the brand of the beast
	καὶ τοὺς προσκυνοῦντας τῇ εἰκόνι αὐτοῦ and who worshiped his cultic image.
20:4	οἵτινες οὐ προσεκύνησαν τὸ θηρίον οὐδὲ τὴν εἰκόνα αὐτοῦ who had not worshiped the beast nor his image
	καὶ οὐκ ἔλαβεν τὸ χάραγμα ἐπὶ τὸ μέτωπον καὶ ἐπὶ τὴν χεῖρα αὐτῶν. and they have not received his brand on their foreheads and on their hands.

9b καὶ λαμβάνει χάραγμα ἐπὶ τοῦ μετώπου αὐτοῦ ἢ ἐπὶ τὴν χεῖρα αὐτοῦ, "and receives a brand on his forehead or upon his hand." It is peculiar that χάραγμα, "brand," is anarthrous, for the term first occurs in 13:16, where it is appropriately anarthrous, but it has an anaphoric article when next used in 13:17. After this anarthrous occurrence in 14:9c, the other four uses of the term are arthrous as expected (14:11; 16:2; 19:20; 20:4). This may suggest that this section (at least vv 9–11) was composed without chap. 13 in view.

10a καὶ αὐτὸς πίεται ἐκ τοῦ οἴνου τοῦ θυμοῦ τοῦ θεοῦ τοῦ κεκρασμένου ἀκράτου ἐν τῷ ποτηρίῳ τῆς ὀργῆς αὐτοῦ, "then he too will drink the wine, which is the fury of God poured unmixed into the cup, which is his anger." The καί, "then," introduces the apodosis of a conditional sentence (cf. Ign. *Smyrn.* 4:2), while the protasis is expressed in v 9. The metaphor of the "cup of wrath" is found with some frequency in the OT: Pss 11:6; 75:9; Isa 51:17, 22; Jer 49:12; 51:7; Lam 4:21; Ezek 23:31–33; Hab 2:15–16; Obad 16; Zech 12:2 (Ringgren, *SEÅ* 17 [1953] 19–30; A. T. Hanson, *Wrath,* 27–36; Brongers, *OTS* 15 [1969] 177–92; McKane, *VT* 3 [1980] 474–92). The common element in these OT passages is that Yahweh is presented as compelling his enemies to drink a cup resulting in their drunkenness, which is considered a judgment (Holladay, *Jeremiah 1,* 673).

Here the αὐτός, "himself," is emphatic (all eleven occurrences of καὶ αὐτός in Revelation are emphatic or intensive; see 3:20; 6:11; 14:17; 17:11; 18:6; 19:12, 15[2x]; 21:3, 7; Mussies, *Morphology,* 169–70). The unstressed use of καὶ αὐτός does not occur in Revelation, an absence that is strange since the phrase is a Septuagintism used to translate the Hebrew וְהוּא *wĕhûʾ* and occurs more than twenty times in Luke (Fitzmyer, *Luke* 1:120–21).

That the wine is ἄκρατος, "unmixed," emphasizes the potency of the mixture, since Greeks customarily diluted wine with water in a special vessel called a κρατήρ, "crater," "mixing bowl," with equal parts of water and wine or three parts water to two parts wine (Blümner, *Greeks,* 209–10) or even one part wine to three parts water (Seltman, *Wine,* 91). Applied to wine, the adjective ἄκρατος means "pure," "unmixed," "undiluted," and hence "extremely strong" (Herodotus 1.207; Xenophon *Anab.* 4.5.27; Theocritus *Idylls* 2.152; 3 Macc 5:2); the adjective ἄμικτος is used in the same way (Plutarch *De garrul.* 6.504e). The phrase ἄκρατος ὀργή, "untempered rage," occurs in several ancient writers (Aeschylus *Prom.* 678; Aristotle *Rhet.* 3.3 [1406A.9–10]); Jos. *Ant.* 5.150; 17.148). There are two close parallels in the LXX: Jer 32:15[MT 25:15], Λαβὲ τὸ ποτήριον τοῦ οἴνου τοῦ ἀκράτου τούτου ἐκ χειρός μου καὶ ποτιεῖς πάντα τὰ ἔθνη, "Take the unmixed cup of wine from my hand and make all the nations drink," and Ps 74:9, ὅτι ποτήριον ἐν χειρὶ κυρίου οἴνου ἀκράτου πλῆρες κεράσματος, "because the cup poured full of unmixed wine is in the hand of the Lord." In both passages the ἄκρατος οἶνος is a metaphor for severe judgment.

It should also be noted that the term ποτήριον, "cup," can be used as a metaphor for destiny (Isa 51:17, 22; Lam 4:21; Ps 75:8[MT 74:9]; John 18:11; see Ps 11:6[MT 10:6]) and for violent death (*Asc. Isa.* 5:13), either the fact of violent death or violent death as the consequence of divine punishment (Mark 10:38–39 = Matt 20:22–23; Mark 14:36 = Luke 22:42; John 18:11; *Mart. Pol.* 14:2). On the view that "cup" in the Synoptic passages involves divine judgment, see W. Lotz, "Das Sinnbild des Bechers," *NKZ* 28 (1917) 396–407; R. Feldmeier, *Die Krisis des Gottessohnes,* WUNT 2/21 (Tübingen: Mohr-Siebeck, 1987) 176–85.

The phrase τοῦ οἴνου τοῦ θυμοῦ [τῆς ὀργῆς] τοῦ θεοῦ occurs several times in Revelation:

14:10a:	ἐκ [some]	τοῦ οἴνου of wine	τοῦ θυμοῦ of fury		τοῦ θεοῦ of God
14:10b:	τῷ ποτηρίῳ the cup			τῆς ὀργῆς of anger	αὐτοῦ his
14:19:	τὴν ληνὸν the press		τοῦ θυμου of fury		τοῦ θεοῦ of God
15:7:	φιάλας bowls		τοῦ θυμοῦ of fury		τοῦ θεοῦ of God
16:1:	τὰς . . . φιάλας the bowls		τοῦ θυμοῦ of fury		τοῦ θεοῦ of God
16:19:	τὸ ποτήριον the cup	τοῦ οἴνου of wine	τοῦ θυμοῦ of fury	τῆς ὀργῆς of anger	αὐτοῦ his
19:15:	τὴν ληνὸν the press	τοῦ οἴνου of wine	τοῦ θυμοῦ of fury	τῆς ὀργῆς of wrath	τοῦ θεοῦ of God

There is a striking compositional similarity between these statements and two in which θυμός is used with the meaning "intense desire":

14:8:	ἐκ [some]	τοῦ οἴνου of wine	τοῦ θυμοῦ of passion	τῆς πορνείας of immorality	αὐτῆς her
18:3:	ἐκ [some]	τοῦ οἴνου of wine	τοῦ θυμοῦ of passion	τῆς πορνείας of immorality	αὐτῆς her

In classical Greek θυμός is used of the inner emotion of anger, while ὀργή is used for its external expression, though these terms are used interchangeably in the LXX as they are in Revelation (14:10; 16:19; 19:15; see S. H. Travis, *ABD* 6:996). The emphasis on the wrath of God, provoked by wicked behavior, which results in the judgment of the offenders, is a biblical motif found frequently in Revelation (14:10, 19; 15:7; 16:1, 19; 19:15). The passion of anger and the justice of appropriate retaliation was much discussed in Greek thought. A widespread assumption about human anger was that, if justified, the angry person should seek to harm his or her enemy (Pindar *Pyth.* 2.83–85; Euripides *Medea* 807–10; *Ion* 1046–47; Plato *Meno* 71E; Isocrates *Ad Dem.* 26), a sentiment echoed in the OT (Exod 21:24–25; Lev 24:19–20; Deut 19:21). Socrates, if the report in Plato *Critias* 48B is historical, was the first Greek thinker to argue that "we should never return an injustice [οὐδαμῶς δεῖ ἀνταδικεῖν]" and that "we should never return evil for evil [ἀντικακουργεῖν]" (cf. Vlastos, *Socrates,* 179–99). Following this line, the Epicureans regarded anger as an expression of weakness, not in accord with a condition of blessedness for either humans or gods (Nussbaum, *Desire,* 239–79). They were particularly insistent that the gods, who dwell in unperturbed peace and tranquillity, are never angry and do not punish people (Diogenes Laertius 10.76–77; Lucretius *De rerum nat.* 6.71–

79). In the first of his *Kyriai Doxai* or Principal Opinions (Diogenes Laertius 10.139; preserved also in Diogenes Oen. *Frag.* 24 [C. W. Chilton, ed., *Diogenis Oenoandensis fragmenta* [Leipzig: Teubner, 1967]]), Epicurus insists that "a blessed and eternal being has no trouble himself and brings no trouble upon any other being; hence he is exempt from movements of anger and partiality, for every such movement implies weakness." Injunctions against retaliation are reflected in the teaching of Jesus (Matt 5:38–42 = Luke 6:27–31) and elsewhere in the NT (Rom 12:17; 1 Cor 6:7; 1 Pet 2:19–20; 3:9).

10b καὶ βασανισθήσεται ἐν πυρὶ καὶ θείῳ ἐνώπιον ἀγγέλων ἁγίων καὶ ἐνώπιον τοῦ ἀρνίου, "with the result that he will be tormented in fire and sulfur before the holy angels and before the Lamb." The combination of "fire and sulphur" as a means of torment occurs four times in Revelation (14:10; 19:20; 20:10; 21:8), three times in the fixed expression "the lake of fire and sulfur" (19:20; 20:10; 21:8), and twice more in the expression "fire, smoke, and sulphur" (9:17, 18). According to Gen 19:24 (alluded to in Luke 17:29; *1 Clem.* 11:1; *PGM* XXXVI.302), fire and brimstone rained on Sodom (see *Sib. Or.* 3.690–92; Philo *Mos.* 2.56). Sulfur or brimstone is frequently mentioned in the OT in connection with divine punishment (Deut 29:23; Job 18:15; Isa 30:33; 34:9–10), and the phrase "fire and sulfur" is used to indicate divine punishment in Ps 11:6 and Ezek 38:22. In Greek, τὸ θεῖον, "sulfur," may be derived from θεῖος, "divine," perhaps meaning "[divine] incense." Sulfur was found in relatively pure form in volcanic areas, where it could be mined (Jos. *J.W.* 7.189; Ulpian *Digest* 47.2.57.8; 48.19.9.10), and the ancients were aware of the connection between sulfur and volcanic activity. Further, sulfur burns at a low temperature and could be used ritually as an incense or a fumigant (*PGM* VII.490; XXXVI.295–96; Odyssey 22.481, 493; see Parker, *Miasma,* 227–28) or (sometimes combined with pitch and bitumen) as a defensive weapon in siege warfare, horribly effective because it stuck to the body (Herodian 8.4.9–10).

There is no parallel in early Jewish or early Christian eschatological scenarios for the eternal punishment of the wicked *in the presence of* the angels and the Lamb, understood to represent the Messiah (v 10c). The phrase "and before the Lamb" is very probably a gloss added to the text since the Lamb is in effect subordinated to the angels (Spitta, 149; Müller, *Messias,* 166). However, as commentators frequently point out, the notion that the wicked will be forever judged and tormented before the *righteous* occurs in *1 Enoch* 27:2–3 and perhaps 90:26–27. A related view is found in *1 Enoch* 48:9 and 62:12–13, in which the wicked are temporarily tormented before the righteous and then vanish forever; thus it is said in *1 Enoch* 48:9 (tr. Knibb), "so they will burn before the righteous, and sink before the holy, and no trace will be found of them." According to 4 Ezra 7:36, the pit of torment and the place of rest are in close proximity, though it is not explicitly stated that the wicked are tormented *in the presence of* the righteous. In the parable of the rich man and Lazarus (Luke 16:19–31), the rich man, tormented in Hades, could see Lazarus in the bosom of Abraham (v 23).

One might well ask what kind of cosmography is presupposed by this verse. It seems unlikely that Hades, understood as the underground region of the dead, is the place of eternal punishment described here. By the first century A.D., the older conception of Hades or Sheol as a subterranean region had given way to the tendency to locate it in a supraterrestrial region. In Dan 7:10, where the Ancient of Days sits in judgment, it is said that "a stream of fire [נהר די־נור *nĕhar dî nûr* issued and came forth from before him." The setting of judgment and the presence of a "stream of fire" make punishment in the presence of God and his angelic court possible, though that conclusion is not made explicit in Daniel. In Plato *Republica* 10.13 (6:14c–d), the judgment of souls reportedly takes place somewhere between the "gates of heaven" and the "gates of earth," i.e., in a place that is certainly *above* the earth (Culianu, *Psychanodia,* 41). Plutarch has transferred the underground rivers of Plato's Hades to the sky, for in *De genio Socratis* 509d–f, Timarchus saw a sea or lake far above the earth into which two rivers of fire flowed (probably the Pyriphlegeton and the Cocytus; see Plato *Phaedo* 111d; cf. Culianu, *Psychanodia,* 45). The Styx is described as "the path to Hades" and flows up from Hades to a point just below the moon (*De genio Socratis* 591a–c).

The phrase (οἱ) ἄγγελοι (οἱ) ἅγιοι, "holy angels," occurs only here in Revelation, suggesting that the author has used a fixed tradition. The phrase also occurs in Mark 8:38 (= Luke 9:26); Acts 10:22; *1 Clem.* 39:7; Hermas *Vis.* 2.2.7; 3.4.1, 2; *Sim.* 5.5.3, reflecting a phrase found with some frequency in early Jewish literature, particularly in the various component sections of *1 Enoch* (*1 Enoch* 20:2–7; 21:5, 9; 22:3; 23:4; 24:6; 27:2; 32:6; 46:1; 69:5; 71:1, 8, 9; 72:1; 74:2; 93:2; 100:5; 108:5; *Adam and Eve* 7:2; Tob 11:14). This expression may reflect the use of the term ἅγιοι, "holy ones," or קְדֹשִׁים *qĕdōšîm,* for angels in the OT (Zech 14:5; Dan 4:17[MT 4:14], 37; Job 5:1; 15:15), early Jewish literature particularly (Tob 12:15 [MSS B A]; *1 Enoch* 1:9; 8:1; 12:2; *Jub.* 17:11; 31:14; 33:12; *Pss. Sol.* 17:43; 1QS 11:7–8), and early Christian literature (Col 1:12; Eph 1:18; 1 Thess 3:13; 2 Thess 1:10).

11a καὶ ὁ καπνὸς τοῦ βασανισμοῦ αὐτῶν εἰς αἰῶνας αἰώνων ἀναβαίνει, "The smoke of their torment ascends forever." The image here is based on the sight of a conquered city burning in the distance (Josh 8:20; Judg 20:40; Rev 18:9–10, 18). More specifically, there may be an allusion here to Isa 34:10, where it is said of Edom "its smoke shall go up for ever" (see Fekkes, *Isaiah,* 206–8). If so, the Hebrew text is probably in view, for the LXX lacks the Greek phrase "forever" corresponding to the Hebrew לְעוֹלָם *lĕʿōlām.* In 20:10, it is said of the devil, the beast, and the false prophet that "they will be tormented day and night forever." There is a close verbal parallel in 19:3, where the destruction of Babylon is in view: καὶ ὁ καπνὸς αὐτῆς ἀναβαίνει εἰς τοὺς αἰῶνας τῶν αἰώνων, "her smoke ascends foreever," Note that while the phrase εἰς τοὺς αἰῶνας τῶν αἰώνων, "forever," occurs twelve times in Revelation (1:6 [*var. lect.*], 18; 4:9, 10; 5:13; 7:12; 10:6; 11:15; 15:7; 19:3; 20:10; 22:5) and seven times elsewhere in the NT (Gal 1:5; Eph 3:21; Phil 4:20; 1 Tim 1:17; 2 Tim 4:18; Heb 13:21 [*var. lect.*]; 1 Pet 4:11), the anarthrous phrase εἰς αἰῶνας αἰώνων, "forever," occurs only here in the NT.

11b καὶ οὐκ ἔχουσιν ἀνάπαυσιν ἡμέρας καὶ νυκτὸς οἱ προσκυνοῦντες τὸ θηρίον καὶ τὴν εἰκόνα αὐτοῦ, "Those who worship the beast and its cultic image will have no relief day and night." The first six Greek words are virtually identical to 4:8c, καὶ ἀνάπαυσιν οὐκ ἔχουσιν ἡμέρας καὶ νυκτός, "and day and night they do not cease [chanting 'holy, holy, holy']." While Rev 4:8 describes the unceasing liturgy of praise offered to God by the four heavenly cherubim, 14:11 emphasizes the unremitting torment of those who worship the beast. This latter passage has certainly been consciously composed as the antithesis of the former and (together with vv 9–11) is a later insertion, which functions to tie together themes from the main section of the First Edition of Revelation (4:1–22:5). A close parallel is the fate of the devil, the beast, and the false prophet, who will be tormented "day and night forever" according to 20:10. On the hendiadys "day and night" meaning "twenty-four hours" or by extension "unceasingly," see *Comment* on 4:8. The reference to the worship of the beast is an analeptic interpolation referring back to the same motifs in the narrative in 13:4, 8, 12, 15 (see the similar analeptic interpolations in 16:2 and 20:4) and is used here as a link to Rev 13, confirming the proposal that 14:9–11 is a later insertion.

11c καὶ εἴ τις λαμβάνει τὸ χάραγμα τοῦ ὀνόματος αὐτοῦ, "and whoever receives the brand with its name." The brand consists of the number 666; see *Comment* on 13:17–18. τοῦ ὀνόματος, "the name," is a genitive of apposition, corresponding to the phrase τὸ χάραγμα τὸ ὄνομα, "the brand, the name," in 13:17, where τὸ ὄνομα is a nominative of apposition.

12 Ὧδε ἡ ὑπομονὴ τῶν ἁγίων ἐστίν, οἱ τηροῦντες τὰς ἐντολὰς τοῦ θεοῦ καὶ τὴν πίστιν Ἰησοῦ, "This indicates that the perseverance of God's people involves keeping the commandments of God and maintaining faithfulness to Jesus." This verse is grammatically problematic. The author apparently intends to define ἡ ὑπομονή, "perseverance," more specifically through the participial phrase beginning with οἱ τηροῦντες, "keeping"; i.e., "perseverance consists in keeping the commands of God. . . ." Of the modern English versions, the NEB comes closest to construing the verse in this way: "This is where the fortitude of God's people has its place—in keeping God's commands and remaining loyal to Jesus," a translation that was abandoned by the REB. The phrase τηρεῖν τὰς ἐντολάς, "keep the commandments," certainly relates to obedience to the Torah (understood primarily in an ethical sense), an important constituent motif in narratives concerning Jewish martyrdom (where the emphasis, however, is particularly on the ceremonial aspects of the Torah, such as circumcision, dietary laws, and sabbath observance); see *Excursus 12B: The Commandments of God and the Torah.* A verbatim phrase occurs elsewhere in Revelation only in 12:17, which is clearly set in a context of persecution. There, as here, the first phrase is part of a couplet, the second line of which pertains to faith in (or faithfulness to) Jesus (see *Comment* on 12:17). There is a striking parallel to v 12 in 1QpHab 8:1–3:

> Its interpretation pertains to all of the doers of the Law [עוֹשֵׂי הַתּוֹרָה *'ôśê hattôrâ*] in the House of Judah, whom God will rescue from the House of Judgment for their tribulation and their fidelity to the Teacher of Righteousness [וַאֲמָנָתָם בְּמוֹרֵה הַצֶּדֶק *we'ĕmunātām bĕmôrēh haṣṣedek*].

Here the phrase "those who keep the commands of God" is closely paralleled by "the doers of the Law," while "and maintaining faith in Jesus" is parallel to "fidelity to the Teacher of Righteousness." In the NT and early Christian literature, the phrase "keep the commandments" occurs frequently (Matt 19:17; John 14:15, 21; 15:10; 1 John 2:3; 3:22, 24; 5:3; Herm. *Mand.* 7.7.5; 12.3.4; 12.6.3; *Sim.* 5.1.5; 5.3.3; cf. 1 Tim 6:4). The phrase καὶ τὴν πίστιν Ἰησοῦ, "and faithfulness to Jesus," appears to be a gloss added during the revisions made for the Second Edition since πίστις is used in Revelation only in 2:13, 19, in the two ὧδε sayings (which are probably glosses) in 13:10, and here in 14:12. It also appears somewhat awkward in this context for the noun τὴν πίστιν, "faithfulness," to be used as the object of the verb τηρεῖν, "keep," since τηρεῖν must then be understood to have two simultaneous meanings, "obey" with τὰς ἐντολάς, "the commandments," and "remain, maintain" with τὴν πίστιν. The phrase πίστιν τηρεῖν occurs a few times in Josephus with the meaning "to keep a pledge" (*Ant.* 13.207; *J.W.* 6.345), while the equivalent phrase πίστιν φυλάττειν is used more frequently, meaning either "to keep an oath or a pledge" (*Ant.* 1.321; 10.97, 101, 230; 12.8, 396) or "to remain faithful" (*Ant.* 7.43; *Life* 39, 43, 93, 349; *Ps.-Phocylides Sententiae* 13; see Lindsay, *Faith,* 95). There is, however, an example of this usage in 2 Tim 4:7, where the author says (in the persona of Paul), τὴν πίστιν τετήρηκα, "I have kept the faith." The phrase πίστιν τηρεῖν, "to keep faith, to remain loyal," was a common Greek expression (Polybius 6.56.13; 10.37.9; Jos. *J.W.* 2.121 [τηρεῖν . . . τὴν πρὸς ἕνα πίστιν, "remain loyal to one man"]; 6.345; *Ant.* 13.207, 415 [*var. lect.*]; *BMI* 3:587b, lines 5ff. [quoted in MM, 515]; Dittenberger, *OGIS,* 1:339, line 47 [quoted in MM, 515]; see M. Dibelius and H. Conzelmann, *The Pastoral Epistles,* tr. P. Buttolph and A. Yarbro [Philadelphia: Fortress, 1972] 121 n. 18), though never in the LXX. In the Pauline letters it is still debated whether the phrase πίστις Ἰησοῦ Χριστοῦ means "faith in Jesus Christ" or "the faith of Jesus Christ." In the phrase τὴν πίστιν Ἰησοῦ, "Jesus" is probably an objective genitive, so the entire phrase means "(their) faithfulness to Jesus" (Deer, *BT* 38 [1987] 328–30); cf. Rev 2:13. Since πίστιν τηρεῖν was a widespread idiom with this recognized meaning, it is likely that in Rev 14:12 it means "to remain loyal, to be faithful."

13a καὶ ἤκουσα φωνῆς ἐκ τοῦ οὐρανοῦ λεγούσης· γράψον, "Then I heard a voice from heaven saying, 'Write.'" There are several commands to write in Revelation that appear to have the entire composition in view (1:11, 19; 21:5; cf. 10:4), and this is one of them. On the motif of the unidentified voice in Revelation, see *Comment* on 10:4.

13b μακάριοι οἱ νεκροὶ οἱ ἐν κυρίῳ ἀποθνήσκοντες, "How fortunate are the dead who die in the Lord." On the punctuation of this sentence, see *Note* 14:13.d-d. This is one of seven beatitudes found in Revelation (1:3; 14:13; 16:15; 19:9; 20:6; 22:7, 14; see *Form/Structure/Setting* on 1:1–3). This beatitude is formulated in the plural form as are those in 19:9 and 22:14 (and as are the beatitudes in Matt 5:3–12 and Luke 6:20–23). There seems to be no material difference between the singular and plural forms, for the beatitude in 20:6 begins in the singular and concludes in the plural, and the series of five beatitudes in 4Q*525* = 4QBéat 2 ii 1–3 begins and ends with singular formulations that frame three plural formulations (tr. García Martínez, *Dead Sea Scrolls,* 395):

> [Blessed is the one who speaks the truth] with a pure heart,
> and does not slander with his tongue.
> Blessed are those who adhere to his laws,
> and who do not adhere to perverted paths.
> Blessed are those who rejoice in her,
> and do not explore insane paths.
> Blessed are those who search for her with pure hands,
> and do not importune her with a treacherous heart.
> Blessed is the man who attains Wisdom,
> and walks in the law of the Most High.

Though a persecution that has produced a number of martyrs has already occurred in the past (6:9–11; 17:6), this statement is a prophecy of an impending series of martyrdoms. The author regards martyrdom in effect as a victory, just as the death of Jesus was a victory (Rev 3:21; 5:5; cf. John 16:33). Even though the beast is able to "conquer" (νικῆσαι) the saints (13:7), in reality it is they who "conquer" through martyrdom (12:11). In 1 John 2:13; 5:4–5, the Christian also "conquers," though martyrdom is not in view. It is possible to understand the innumerable multitude of "those who come out of the great tribulation" (7:14) as future martyrs. A beatitude in *1 Clem.* 44:5 exhibits some similarities in both form and content to this one:

> Blessed are those presbyters who have traveled on before, who had a perfect and fruitful departure, for they are no longer concerned that anyone remove them from the place established for them.

In this instance, however, death has prevented these presbyters from being expelled from office, unlike the living presbyters at Corinth. The phrase ἐν κυρίῳ, "in the Lord," is a formula found frequently in Paul but elsewhere only in Rev 14:13 and Ign. *Pol.* 8:3. In ancient consolation literature, a favorite *topos* was the view that death is not an evil but rather a blessing, a remedy for evils (Plato *Phaedo* 62a; *Apol.* 40c; Stobaeus 3.120; Cicero *In Cat.* 4.4; Lucretius *De rerum nat.* 3.915ff.; Seneca *Marc.* 19–20; see Moran, *Consolations,* 31–39).

13c ἀπαρτὶ λέγει τὸ πνεῦμα, ἵνα ἀναπαήσονται ἐκ τῶν κόπων αὐτῶν, "Truly, says the Spirit, that they might rest from their labors." In the Nestle-Aland[27] text (which reads ναί, λέγει τὸ πνεῦμα), ναί, "yes," is used as a functional equivalent to ἀμήν, "amen" (both terms are used interchangeably in the following texts: Matt 23:26 = Luke 11:51; 2 Cor 1:20; Rev 1:7; 22:20; *Acts Thom.* 121; see K. Berger, *Amen-Worte,* 6–9); see *Note* 14:13.d-d. On the use of ἀναπαύειν and ἀνάπαυσις and cognates to refer to the rest or repose of the dead, see *Comment* on 6:11. 1 Tim 4:1 is a formal parallel to the first part of this passage: τὸ δὲ πνεῦμα ῥητῶς λέγει, "the Spirit clearly says." A close parallel to the last part of this passage occurs in Heb 4:10, "for whoever enters God's rest [κατάπαυσιν αὐτοῦ] also ceases from his labors [κατέπαυσεν ἀπὸ τῶν ἔργων αὐτοῦ] as God did from his." Similarly, Philo speaks of a "soul which rests [ἀναπαυομένης] in God and toils no more [ἔτι πονουμένης] at any mortal task [ἔργων]" (*Deus immut.* 12).

13d τὰ γὰρ ἔργα αὐτῶν ἀκολουθεῖ μετ' αὐτῶν, "for their works follow after them." *M. ʾAbot* 6:9 states (tr. Danby, *Mishnah*), "Moreover at the time of a man's departure, neither silver nor gold nor precious stones nor pearls go with him, but only [his knowledge of] the Law and good works." "Works" are mentioned frequently in Rev 2–3 (2:2, 19; 3:2, 15). The parenthetical character of 14:13, together with this thematic link with Rev 2–3, suggests that this is an interpolation made during the final revision of the book. Further rabbinic parallels are listed in Str-B, 3:817, and several parallels occur in 4 Ezra: (1) 4 Ezra 7:35 (RSV), "And recompense shall follow, and the reward shall be manifested; righteous deeds shall awake, and unrighteous deeds shall not sleep"; (2) 4 Ezra 7:77 (RSV), "For you have a treasure of works laid up with the Most High; but it will not be shown to you until the last times"; and (3) 4 Ezra 8:33 (RSV), "For the righteous, who have many works laid up with thee, shall receive their reward in consequence of their deeds."

14a καὶ εἶδον, καὶ ἰδοὺ νεφέλη λευκή, "Then I looked, and behold, a white cloud." Vv 14–16 constitute a textual unit with two main problems for the interpreter: Should the "one like a son of man" be identified with Christ or an angel, and does the harvest represent judgment or salvation? (On καὶ εἶδον, see

Comment on 5:1.) In descriptions in Revelation, there is a tendency on the part of the author to describe first that upon which a visionary figure is seated before describing the figure itself (see *Comment* on 4:2). The white color of the cloud could be taken as a positive sign.

14b καὶ ἐπὶ τὴν νεφέλην καθήμενον ὅμοιον υἱὸν ἀνθρώπου, "and upon the cloud was seated one like a son of man." This (along with 1:7, 13) is one of three allusions in Revelation to Dan 7:13, two of which have the phrase ὅμοιον υἱὸν ἀνθρώπου (1:13; 14:14), "son of man," "human being." The phrase ἐπὶ τήν νεφέλην, "*on* the cloud," suggests an allusion to the LXX version of Dan 7:13 (Matt 24:30; 26:64; Irenaeus *Adv. haer.* 3.19.2; 4.33.1, 11; Tertullian *Carn.* 15.1; *Acts Peter* [Latin] 24), whereas the phrase μετὰ τῶν νεφελῶν, "*with* the clouds," in Rev 1:7 suggests familiarity with the Theodotianic version of Daniel (Mark 14:62; Rev 1:7; Justin *Dial.* 31.3; Tertullian *Marc.* 3.7.4; 4.10.12; 4.39.11; *Adv. Iud.* 14.4; Hippolytus *de Ant.* 22, 26, 44; *Comm. in Dan.* 4.11.1; cf. P. Grelot, "Les versions grecques de Daniel," *Bib* 47 [1966] 386–87; Bodenmann, *Naissance,* 46–47). Justin alludes four times to the phrase ἐπάνω [τῶν] νεφελῶν from Dan 7:13, in approximate agreement with the LXX (*1 Apol.* 51.9; *Dial.* 14.8; 31.1; 120.4), and once to μετὰ τῶν νεφελῶν, in agreement with Theodotion (*Dial.* 31.3). The preposition ἐν is used in Mark 13:26 (ἐν νεφέλαις, "with clouds") and Luke 21:27 (ἐν νεφέλῃ, "with a cloud"). The Aramaic phrase in the MT of Dan 7:13 is עם ענני שׁמיא *ʿim ʿănānê šĕmayyāʾ,* "with the clouds of heaven," translated by the LXX as ἐπὶ τῶν νεφελῶν τοῦ οὐρανοῦ, "*upon* the clouds of heaven," in which ἐπί might appear to presuppose the Aramaic preposition על *ʿal,* "upon" (S. P. Jeansonne, *The Old Greek Translation of Daniel 7–12,* CBQMS 19 [Washington, DC: Catholic Biblical Association, 1988] 65), and by Theodotion as μετὰ τῶν νεφελῶν τοῦ οὐρανοῦ, "*with* the clouds of heaven." Some scholars have suggested that the use of the preposition ἐπί, "upon," reveals a theological motivation and could only refer to *God* coming on the clouds (based on Canaanite imagery of Baal riding the cloud-chariot, reflecting the Ugaritic epithet of Baal, *rkb ʿrpt,* "rider of the clouds"; cf. LXX and MT versions of Isa 14:14 and 19:1), while the preposition μετά, "with," refers to the rider as something less than divine (Jeansonne, *Daniel 7–12,* 109–10; Montgomery, *Daniel,* 303). Jeansonne (*Daniel, 7–12,* 112), however, argues that since Dan 7:13 is the only place in the OT where someone other than God rides the clouds, the evidence is too meager to argue that עם *ʿim,* "with," should have been used rather than על *ʿal,* "upon."

The singular term νεφέλη, "cloud," found in Rev 14:4, 6 (cf. 11:12) is unusual in allusions to Dan 7:13, where a plurality of clouds is mentioned. Elsewhere in the NT the singular occurs only in Luke 21:27, though more frequently in patristic allusions (*Acts Peter* [Latin] 24; Irenaeus *Adv. haer.* 3.19.2; 4.33.1, 33; Tertullian *Carn.* 15.1; see Bodenmann, *Naissance,* 45 n. 107). That does not mean that Rev 14:14, 16 is dependent on Luke 21:27 (Vos, *Synoptic Traditions,* 146–47), however, since the "one like a son of man" in Rev 14:14 is presented as *sitting* on a cloud, an image that would be awkward if a plurality of clouds were in view.

In view of the parallel structure and themes of vv 14–16 and 17–20, it appears likely that the author has added the phrases "like a son of man" (v 14b) and "with a golden crown upon his head" (v 14c) to an existing composition.

Clouds are used as transport in a number of ways (see Vermes, *Jesus,* 186–88: "Excursus I: the cloud, a means of heavenly transport"): (1) As a means of transportation from earth to heaven (Rev 11:12; 2 Kgs 2:11; *1 Enoch* 14:8; 39:3; 52:1; 70:2; *2 Enoch* 3:1; *T. Abr.* [Rec. A] 10:1; [Rec. B] 8:3; 10:2; Acts 1:9; *b. Yoma* 4a ["Moses ascended in the cloud"]; *Pesiq. R.* 20.4 [96b]: "the cloud covered Moses and carried him up" [A. Jellinek, *Bet Ha-Midrasch* 1:59]); Ares ascends to heaven ὁμοῦ νεφέεσσιν, "with clouds," in *Iliad* 5.867. (2) As a means of transport from one area of heaven to another (Pss 68:4; 104:3; Isa 19:1; Dan 7:13; *T. Abr.* [Rec. B] 12:1, 9; 4 Ezra 13:3). (3) As a means of transport from heaven to earth, often associated in early Christian sources with the coming of the Son of man (Rev 1:7; 10:1; Mark 13:26 = Matt 24:30 = Luke 21:27; Mark 14:62 = Matt 26:64; *T. Abr.* [Rec. A] 9:8; 15:2). (4) As a mode of enthronement (Rev 14:14–16; Sir 24:4; Vergil *Aeneid* 9.638–39: "cloud-enthroned [*nube sedens*] Apollo"). (5) As a symbol associated with theophanies or angelophanies (Rev 10:1; Exod 14:24; 16:10; 24:16; Lev 16:2; Num 12:5; Deut 1:33; Lam 3:44; 2 Macc 2:8; Mark 9:7 = Matt 17:5 = Luke 9:34–35).

The unusual image of the "one like the son of man" *sitting* on a cloud in this verse may preserve allusions to the earlier combination of Ps 110:1 with Dan 7:13, such as that found in Mark 14:62 (cf. Matt 26:64), καὶ ὄψεσθε τὸν υἱὸν τοῦ ἀνθρώπου [Dan 7:13] ἐκ δεξιῶν καθήμενον τῆς δυνάμεως [Ps 110:1], καὶ ἐρχόμενον μετὰ τῶν νεφελῶν τοῦ οὐρανοῦ [Dan 7:13], "and you will see the Son of man *sitting* at the right hand of the Power and coming with the clouds of heaven." The two participial phrases linked with καί coordinate the "sitting" and "coming" of Jesus as the Son of man and *may* lead to the logical textual development found in Rev 14:14, i.e., one like a son of man seated (i.e., enthroned) upon a cloud. Other passages that similarly reflect combined allusions to Dan 7:13 and Ps 110:1 include Luke 22:69; Acts 7:56; Justin *Dial.* 32.3, 6 (see Lindars, *Apologetic,* 48–49; Bodenmann, *Naissance,* 204–6). In the Parables of Enoch, the Son of man is *seated* on the throne of his glory for judgment in *1 Enoch* 69:27. While the allusion to Dan 7:13 is certain, in the end, the possible allusion either to Ps 110:1 or to Mark 14:62 is extremely doubtful (Yarbro Collins, "'Son of Man,'" 563).

In the phrase ὅμοιον υἱὸν ἀνθρώπου, "as a son of man," the word υἱόν, "son," in the accusative is a solecism (see BDR § 183.4), for it should more properly have been the dative υἱῷ (see *Note* 14.e). As a solecism, this coheres well with the peculiar and erratic Greek style of our author and therefore suggests that he has coined this expression himself, possibly on the basis of the Aramaic phrase כבר אנש *kĕbar ʾĕnāš,* "as a son of man," in the MT of Dan 7:13, in which the prefixed -כְּ *kĕ-*, "as, like," could be translated either by ὡς, "as, like," or by its synonym, the comparative adjective ὅμοιος, "of the same kind, similar." This phrase is also found in 1:13, and in both instances it is an allusion to Dan 7:13. In both the LXX and Theodotion, however, the comparative particle ὡς, "as," is found. It is also significant that both here and in 1:13 the phrase υἱὸς ἀνθρώπου is *anarthrous* (i.e., it does not refer to a figure well known by the audience, presumably the Son of man of the Gospel-sayings traditions) and therefore is an allusion to Dan 7:13. When Justin alludes to the son of man of Dan 7:13 (as opposed to the Son of man of Gospel tradition), he uses the anarthrous phrase υἱὸς ἀνθρώπου (Justin *1 Apol.* 51.9; *Dial.* 31.3; 76.1; 79.2; Borsch, *Son of Man,* 43–44). This is followed by the appearance of three other heavenly beings, each referred to as ἄλλος ἄγγελος, "another angel," in vv 15, 17, and 18. The context suggests that the υἱὸς ἀνθρώπου is a reference not to the exalted Jesus but rather to an angelic being (Kiddle-Ross, 285; Casey, *Son of Man,* 148–49); note that the term בני אדם *bĕnê ʾādām,* "sons of man," is used of an angelic being in Dan 10:16. Holtz (*Christologie,* 16; followed by Rusam, "Formeln," 7) argues unconvincingly that the author has consciously replaced ὁ υἱὸς τοῦ ἀνθρώπου with this phrase. It is clear, at any rate, that the phrase in context (in both 1:13 and 14:14) betrays no awareness of the Son of man traditions of the Gospels but alludes directly to Dan 7:13 (Borsch, *Son of Man,* 238–40).

14c ἔχων ἐπὶ τῆς κεφαλῆς αὐτοῦ στέφανον χρυσοῦν καὶ ἐν τῇ χειρὶ αὐτοῦ δρέπανον ὀξύ, "with a golden wreath upon his head and with a sharp sickle in his hand." While a gold wreath-crown has a variety of connotations (see *Excursus 2C: Ancient Wreath and Crown Imagery*), here it appears to suggest the status and authority of the wearer. The metaphor is too varied to suggest, as many do, that it symbolizes victory. Gold wreaths are mentioned in Revelation only here and in 4:4, 10 (where they are worn by the twenty-four elders), 6:2 (where a gold wreath is worn by the rider on the white horse), and 9:7 (where they are worn by the demonic locust cavalry). The view supported above, that the figure wearing this wreath is an angel, is not contradicted by the fact that he wears a golden wreath, for angels are occasionally depicted as even wearing *diadems,* probably a consequence of conceiving of them as princes (*Apoc. Zeph.* A [Clement of Alex. *Strom.* 5.11.77]; *3 Enoch* 16:1; 17:8; 18:25; 21:4), or *golden wreaths* as here (*Jos. As.* 14:8–9; Kropp, *Koptische Zaubertexte,* vol. 3 § 371, fig. 10; Baus, *Kranz,* 221); see Mach, *Engelglaubens,* 191–208. The figure on the white horse in 19:12 wears "many diadem-crowns," though they are not described as golden. The dragon (12:3) and the beast from the sea (13:1) are described as wearing seven and ten diadem-crowns, respectively. The *Apoc. Pet.* 6 (a text that may date from as early as the first half of the second century A.D.) refers to Christ being crowned by the Father. The tradition that the king Messiah wears the crown of God is extremely late (*Exod. Rab.* 8.1; *Midr. Ps.* 21:1; Braude, *Midrash* 1:204).

Bentzen (*VT* 1 [1951] 216–17) erroneously refers to "*the* sickle" in this verse as though it were a known apocalyptic conception, though in fact δρέπανον here is anarthrous. There are some passages, however, in which δρέπανον *is* articular and could refer to a known apocalyptic notion (e.g., Mark 4:29; *T. Abr.* [Rec. A] 4:11; 8:9, 10; *Vit. Proph.* 3.6–7). That the harvest instrument is a δρέπανον ὀξύ, "*sharp* sickle" (the identical phrase is used to describe the tool used for the grape harvest in v 17), indicates that *judgment* is in view.

15a καὶ ἄλλος ἄγγελος ἐξῆλθεν ἐκ τοῦ ναοῦ κράζων ἐν φωνῇ μεγάλῃ τῷ καθημένῳ ἐπὶ τῆς νεφέλης, "Then another angel came out of the temple, exclaiming with a loud voice to the one seated upon the cloud." On the phrase "another angel," see *Comment* on v 6. The adjective ἄλλος, "another," suggests that the figure just referred to in v 14 as "a son of man" is an *angelic* figure and therefore reflects a Jewish perspective (Bousset [1906] 388; Müller, *Messias,* 197; Coppens, "Fils d'homme angélique," 229; Casey, *Son of Man,* 148–49). According to Bousset, the adjective ἄλλος has been added by the author to his source ([1906] 388–89), but it is hardly likely that the final editor of Revelation would have demoted the Son of man in v 14 to an angel (the logic of Bousset's view). That this angel emerges from the heavenly temple implies the divine authorization of his command to the "one sitting on the cloud" to begin the harvest. It is striking that both here and in v 16, the first figure, described as "one like a human being" or literally "one like a son of man," is not referred to in that way, nor as one who is crowned, but rather as "the one sitting on the cloud." Therefore, of the three characteristics of this figure, only this aspect is emphasized in the narrative. The fact that the second figure commands the first to begin harvesting is a strong reason for not regarding the latter as either the Messiah or the exalted Jesus.

15b πέμψον τὸ δρέπανόν σου καὶ θέρισον, "Use your sickle for harvesting." The phrase πέμψον τὸ δρέπανόν σου, "send your sickle," repeated with some variation in v 18—πέμψον σου τὸ δρέπανον τὸ ὀξύ, "send your sharp sickle"—is an allusion to Joel 3:13(MT 4:13), שִׁלְחוּ מַגָּל *šilḥû maggāl,* "put in the sickle" (an allusion continued in v 15c); LXX Joel 3:13, ἐξαποστείλατε δρέπανα, "send the sickles"; cf. Mark 4:29, ἀποστέλλει τὸ δρέπανον, "he sends the sickle." While it is not immediately evident why the two commands in Joel 4:13 ("Put in the sickle, for the harvest is ripe" and "Go in, tread, for the wine press is full") are transformed into commands from one angelic being to another here in vv 15 and 18, the answer may lie in the traditional Jewish exegesis of this passage found in the *Midr. Ps.* 8.1.73 (tr. Braude, *Midrash* 1:119):

> Scripture says elsewhere: "Put ye in the sickle, for the harvest is ripe. Come tread ye; for the winepress is full, the vats overflow[Joel 4:13]." To whom will God say "Put ye in the sickle . . . tread ye, for the winepress is full"? R. Pineḥas taught in the name of R. Ḥilkiah: God will say this to the angels.

In this midrash, *God* commands *angels* to harvest and to tread the winepress, while in Rev 14:14–20, some angels command other angels to perform tasks that are metaphors for divine judgment. The role of angels as reapers is explicitly stated in the Matthaean interpretation of the parable of the sower in Matt 13:39, οἱ δὲ θερισταὶ ἄγγελοί εἰσιν, "And the reapers are angels" (n.b. that no rabbinic parallels to this verse, apart from the irrelevant citation of *b. B. Meṣ.* 83b, are cited in Str-B, 1:672). In Mark 13:26–27 = Matt 24:30–31, the returning Son of man sends his angels to gather the elect from all parts of the world, and this older logion is probably the source of Matt 13:39. In Jewish tradition, however, there are angels of punishment, as in Rev 9:15 (see *Comment* there), who are agents of God in punishing and destroying humans (*1 Enoch* 53:3; 56:1; 62:11; 63:1; 66:1; *3 Enoch* 31:2; 32:1; 33:1; *b. Šabb.* 55a; 88a; cf. P. S. Alexander in Charlesworth, *OTP* 1:285 nn. 31–32; K. E. Grözinger, "Engel III," *TRE* 9:591; Michl, "Engel II," *RAC* 5:75–76).

The term δρέπανον is used metaphorically in a variety of contexts in which it has an extremely negative meaning, suggesting death, destruction, and judgment. In the LXX version of Zech 5:1–5, the prophet sees a δρέπανον πετόμενον, "flying sickle." Here the sickle is a metaphor for a curse that goes over the face of the whole earth and punishes all thieves and those who swear falsely. Though this is a misreading of the consonantal text (מגלה עפה *miglâ ʿāpâ,* which means "flying scroll," is understood as though it were מגל עפה *maggāl ʿāpâ,* "flying sickle"), it makes perfectly good sense in the context of Zech 5:1–5. The phrase ἡ τοῦ θανάτου δρεπάνη, "the sickle of death," is a phrase found three times in *T. Abr.* [Rec. A] 4:11; 8:9, 10; it is obviously a metaphor for death (cf. Horace *Ep.* 2.2.171–79; Claudian *Eutrop.* 2.141–46; see *Neuer Wettstein,* vol. 2/2, ad loc.). In *Vit. Proph.* 3.6–7, Ezekiel is said to have predicted the coming of τὸν δρέπανον τῆς ἐρημώσεως εἰς πέρας τῆς γῆς, "the sickle of devastation to the end of the earth," clearly a metaphor for universal divine judgment (see Schwemer, "Vitae Prophetarum," 244–47). In a Greco-Jewish sepulchral inscription from Acmonia in Asia Minor (ca. third century A.D.), the author refers to τὸ ἀρᾶς δρέπανον, "the sickle of the curse," as the means whereby those who violate the tomb will be punished, perhaps alluding to Zech 5:1 (*CIJ,* 769; see Trebilco, *Jewish Communities,* 74–76). In dream interpretation the sickle had an extremely negative connotation (Artemidorus *Oneir.* 2.24).

The term δρέπανον can refer to various types of curved knives (Jos. *J.W.* 3.95, 225), including a scythe or sickle (LXX Deut 16:9; 23:25), a pruning knife (LXX Mic 4:3; Joel 3:10[MT 4:10]; Isa 2:4), a vintager's knife, or a scimitar (LSJ, 449). Bentzen (*VT* 1 [1951] 216–17) argues that the curved scimitar was a symbol of royalty, like the crown in Babylonia, Egypt, and Phoenicia, that the Son of man in this verse is being portrayed as a king, and that the LXX reading of Zech 5:1 (discussed above) was based on ancient Near Eastern royal ideology. According to *Vit. Proph.* 22.11, the term can also be used of an axehead. The Hebrew term מגל *maggāl* in Jer 50:16 and Joel 3:13 (MT: 4:13) is more narrow in meaning, but it can include both a scythe or sickle and a vintager's knife (Galling, *BibReal,* 475–76).

15c ὅτι ἦλθεν ἡ ὥρα θερίσαι, ὅτι ἐξηράνθη ὁ θερισμὸς τῆς γῆς, "for the hour to harvest has arrived, because the harvest of the earth is ripe." For the harvest (grain, grape, or olive) as a metaphor for divine judgment, see Isa 17:5; 18:4–5; 24:13; Jer 51:33; Hos 6:11; Joel 3:13 (MT 4:13); Mic 4:12–13; Matt 13:24–30, 36–43; Mark 4:29; 4 Ezra 4:28–32; *2 Apoc. Bar.* 70:20. In Matt 3:11–12 the threshing floor is the image used for the separation of the righteous from the wicked, resulting in the salvation of the former and the damnation of the latter. The grain harvest is also used in a positive sense as a metaphor for the gathering of the elect (Luke 10:2 = Matt 9:37–38 = *Gos. Thom.* 73; Matt 13:30, 43; John 4:35–38) or the reward of the righteous (4 Ezra 4:35). While the grain harvest in 14:14–16 is sometimes interpreted as a reference to the eschatological harvest as a metaphor for the gathering of the elect, this view is without basis.

16 καὶ ἔβαλεν ὁ καθήμενος ἐπὶ τῆς νεφέλης τὸ δρέπανον αὐτοῦ ἐπὶ τὴν γῆν καὶ ἐθερίσθη ἡ γῆ, "The one sitting upon the cloud began to swing his sickle on the earth, and the earth was harvested." This continues the allusion to Joel 3:13 (MT 4:13) begun in v 15. The entire passage in Joel uses the metaphor of the two parallel couplets of the *grape* harvest (the LXX therefore correctly understands קָצִיר *qāṣîr* as τρύγητος), including the gathering in of the clusters of grapes and the treading out of their juice in the winepress. Rev 14:15–16, however, reads Joel 3:13 as if it related to the *grain* harvest, an understanding that may reflect traditional Jewish exegesis of Joel 3:13 (cf. Mark 4:29; *Midr. Ps.* 8.1 [partially quoted below]). Rev 14:15–20, then, deals successively with *two* harvests, the grain harvest (vv 15–16) and the grape harvest (vv 17–20), both derived from a particular way of reading Joel 3:13 (MT 4:13). Bauckham ("Conversion," 283–96) construes the grain harvest in vv 15–16 in a *positive* sense as the conversion of people from the nations of the world and the grape harvest in vv 17–20 in a *negative* sense as the punishment of the unrepentant people from the nations of the world. The metaphor of the grain harvest is abruptly abandoned in v 16 and not developed by referring, for example, to threshing and winnowing, which are frequently used as metaphors for divine judgment (see Jer 51:33; Mic 4:12–13; Hab 3:12; Matt 3:2 [= Luke 3:17]). This is in contrast to the metaphor of the grape harvest in vv 18–20, which ends with the treading of the grapes in the winepress as a clear metaphor of judgment. Apart from the usually negative metaphorical meaning of threshing and winnowing, reaping itself can certainly have a positive meaning (John 4:35–38), but in biblical texts occasionally also a negative significance (Isa 17:4–5; Jer 51:33; Hos 6:11). However, in some rabbinical texts, the tradition of two harvests in Joel 3:13 was understood negatively. This is reflected in *Midr. Ps.* 8.1 (tr. Braude, *Midrash* 1:119–20):

> By "harvest" is meant the fall of Babylon [Jer 51:33] . . . by "grape gathering" is meant the fall of Greece [Zeph 9:13] . . . by "olive picking" is meant the fall of Media [Esth 7:10] . . . by "treading the winepress" is meant the fall of Edom [Isa 63:3].

(Edom, like Babylon, became a frequent symbol in rabbinic Judaism for the Roman empire; see Hadas-Lebel, *Jérusalem,* 460–73; Avemarie, "Edom," 177–208.) The simile of the harvesting of wheat or barley in *Iliad* 11.67–71 is used of the Trojans and Greeks mowing each other down in battle. Macrobius claims that Homer uses the expression *messem hominum,* "a harvest of men," to describe the slaughter of many men.

The description of this first harvest ends abruptly with nothing said about what was done with the grain (i.e., the threshing process), in contrast to the second harvest in vv 17–20, which emphasizes the treading of the grapes that had been gathered. Since threshing is almost always a negative metaphor, its absence makes it possible (though not necessary) to construe this grain harvest as a metaphor referring to the eschatological salvation of those "harvested" (the theme of the eschatological gathering of the elect occurs occasionally in early Christian literature: 1 Thess 4:17; 2 Thess 2:1; Mark 13:27 = Matt 24:31); see *Form/Structure/Setting,* III. Interpreting Rev 14:14–20. These two sections are in this respect literarily asymmetrical. The putting in of the sickle and the harvesting of the earth may be viewed as a single action, in which case the aorist passive ἐθερίσθη, "was harvested," refers to "the one seated on the cloud" who does the harvesting. Or they may be viewed as two separate actions, in which case the subject of ἐθερίσθη remains unidentified (Lohmeyer, 128; Kraft, 198).

Finally, the phrase ἐθερίσθη ἡ γῆ, "the earth was harvested," is obviously a figure of speech for ὁ θερισμὸς τῆς γῆς, "the harvest of the earth" (v 15), which is close to one of the allegorical equations found in the Matthaean explanation of the meaning of one of the features of the parable of the tares (Matt 13:24–30) in Matt 13:38, ὁ δὲ ἀγρός ἐστιν ὁ κόσμος, "and the field is the world." Since another of the allegorical equations specifies that the reapers are angels (Matt 13:39), there appears to be a traditional link between Matt 13:36–43 and Rev 14:14–16.

17 καὶ ἄλλος ἄγγελος ἐξῆλθεν ἐκ τοῦ ναοῦ τοῦ ἐν τῷ οὐρανῷ ἔχων καὶ αὐτὸς δρέπανον ὀξύ, "Then another angel came out of the temple which is in heaven, and he also had a sharp sickle." On the phrase "another angel," see *Comment* on v 6. As in the case of the angel in v 15, the emergence of this angel from the heavenly temple indicates the divine authorization of his mission.

18a καὶ ἄλλος ἄγγελος [ἐξῆλθεν] ἐκ τοῦ θυσιαστηρίου [ὁ] ἔχων ἐξουσίαν ἐπὶ τοῦ πυρός, "Yet another angel emerged from the sanctuary (the one with authority over fire)." (On the phrase "another angel," see *Comment* on v 6.) The term θυσιαστήριον occurs eight times in Revelation and can refer to the heavenly counterparts of the altar of incense (8:3[2x], 5; 9:13) or the altar of burnt offerings (6:9; 9:13; 14:18; 16:7), or by extension it can mean "sanctuary," as it does here, i.e., as a synonym for ναός (see *Comment* on 6:9).

The phrase "the one with authority over fire" serves several literary functions. In general it conforms to the author's tendency to identify various figures with descriptive participial phrases (see Rev 11:7; 17:1, 7, 8, 11; 21:9), and more particularly it serves to distinguish this particular angel from the many other anonymous angels mentioned by the author. The phrase also identifies this angel as one of special importance, because as the angel with authority over fire, he is a divine agent for punishing the enemies of God. According to Jewish tradition, various angels had authority over various aspects of the world, including the four winds (Rev 7:1), the abyss (Rev 9:11), and the waters (Rev 16:5). *Bib. Ant.* 38.3 refers to "Nathaniel, the angel in charge of fire," while according to *T. Abr.* [Rec. A] 13:10, Πυρουὴλ ὁ [ἀρχ]άγγελος ὁ ἐπὶ τὸ πῦρ ἔχων τὴν ἐξουσίαν, "Purouel is the [arch]angel who has authority over fire" (this angel is referred to earlier as "the fiery angel who held the fire" in *T. Abr.* [Rec. A] 12:14) and whose task it is to test the works of people by fire. Similarly CD [MS A] 2:5–6 threatens torment "with fiery flames by all the angels of destruction [בלהבי אש בי כל מלאכי הבל *bělahăbê ʾeš by kol malʾăkê ḥebel*]," i.e., angels whose task it is to torture the wicked. A curse text from Kidrama in Asia Minor includes the phrase ὑπὸ τῶν πυ[ρὸς] ἀνγέλω[ν], "may you suffer at the hands of the angels of fire" (J. and L. Robert, *La Carie* [Paris, 1954] 366, no. 191, frag. A). Similarly, an Aramaic incantation bowl from Tell Khafaje in Iraq (third to seventh centuries A.D.), describes an angelic being who is "the head of the kingdom of fire" (E. M. Cook, "An Aramaic Incantation Bowl from Khafaje," *BASOR* 285 [1992] 79–81). The notion that angels were created out of fire was widespread in early Judaism, based on Ps 104:4, quoted in Heb 1:7 (*Jub.* 2:2; *2 Apoc. Bar.* 21:6; 48:8; *2 Enoch* 39:5; *Apoc. Abr.* 19:6; *Gen. Rab.* 78:1; 1QH 1:10–11; *Hekalot Rabbati* 15:8–16:2; *Masseket Hekalot* 4; *Sepher ha-Razim* 1.9–10 [tr. Morgan, 21]), and the phrase "angel(s) of fire" occurs several times in the *Sepher ha-Razim* (3.23, 28, 57–58; 4.9). In *2 Enoch* 29:2–3 there is a reference to the creation of angels from fire, and consequently both their weapons and their garments are fire.

18b καὶ ἐφώνησεν φωνῇ μεγάλῃ τῷ ἔχοντι τὸ δρέπανον τὸ ὀξὺ λέγων· πέμψον σου τὸ δρέπανον τὸ ὀξὺ καὶ τρύγησον τοὺς βότρυας τῆς ἀμπέλου τῆς γῆς, "and called with a loud voice to the one who had the sharp sickle, 'Use your sharp sickle to gather the grape clusters from the vineyard which is the earth.'" This continues the allusion to Joel 3:13 (MT 4:13), in which the vintage harvest is a metaphor for divine judgment; see also Isa 63:1–6; Lam 1:15 (Fekkes [*Isaiah,* 195–96] argues for an allusion to Isa 63:3 here as well as to Joel 3:13 [MT 4:13] because of the motifs of wrath and blood that occur in Isa 63:2–3 but not in Joel 3:13). The angel who emerged from the heavenly temple in v 17 has just a *single* defining characteristic (in contrast to the figure in v 14, who has three characteristics): he holds a sharp sickle, and he is therefore referred to simply as "the one who had the sharp sickle," even though the figure in v 17 is also described as having a sharp sickle.

19a καὶ ἔβαλεν ὁ ἄγγελος τὸ δρέπανον αὐτοῦ εἰς τὴν γῆν καὶ ἐτρύγησεν τὴν ἄμπελον τῆς γῆς, "Then the angel began to swing his sickle toward the earth and gathered the vintage of the earth." The gathering of the vintage is itself a metaphor for eschatological judgment, while the emphasis on the winepress in v 19b is a second metaphor for judgment (cf. 19:15c). The vintage harvest and the winepress as metaphors for divine judgment are found in Joel 3:13 (MT 4:13), mentioned above.

19b καὶ ἔβαλεν εἰς τὴν ληνὸν τοῦ θυμοῦ τοῦ θεοῦ τὸν μέγαν, "and cast it into the great winepress of the wrath of God." This clause is an allusion to Isa 63:1–6, which depicts the Lord as the divine warrior coming with garments stained with the blood of his enemies, compared with the garments of one who treads grapes in the winepress (see *Comment* on 19:15). The links between the vintage harvest and the final eschatological battle (which become clear in v 20) appear in the *Tg. Isa.* 63:3–4 (tr. Chilton, *Isaiah Targum;* italics indicate additions to the MT):

> *Behold, as grapes trodden in the press, so shall slaughter increase among the armies of the* peoples, *and their* [sic] *will be no strength for them before* me; I will *kill* them in my anger and trample them in my wrath; *I will break the strength of their strong ones before me,* and I *will annihilate* all *their wise ones.* For *the* day of *vengeance is before me,* and *the* year of my *people's salvation* has come.

A similar connection occurs in *Tg. Neb.* Joel 4:13–14 (tr. Cathcart-Gordon, *Targum;* italics indicate additions to the MT):

> Put the *sword into them,* for the *time of their end has arrived; go down* and *tread their warrior dead like grapes that are trodden in* the winepress; *pour out their blood,* for their wickedness is great. *Army* upon *army* in the valley of *judicial* decision; for near is the day *which will come from* the Lord in the valley of *judicial* decision.

The term ληνός, "winepress," occurs in Revelation just here in vv 19–20 and in 19:15.

20a καὶ ἐπατήθη ἡ ληνὸς ἔξωθεν τῆς πόλεως, "The winepress was trodden outside of the city." The identity of the city is not specified, though the presence of the definite article may indicate that the city is Jerusalem (Lohmeyer, 129), and the treading of the grapes may be a metaphor for a final eschatological battle in the vicinity of Jerusalem (Joel 3:2, 12; Zech 14:2–4; 4 Ezra 13:33–35; *2 Apoc. Bar.* 40.1; cf. Rev 19:17–21; 20:7–9). The identity of the one who treads the winepress is also not made clear since the aorist passive verb ἐπατήθη, "was trodden," is extremely vague and may be the *passivum divinum,* i.e., the passive used as a circumlocution for the activity of God. However, in 19:15 it is the rider on the white horse (i.e., the exalted Christ returning with his heavenly armies in judgment) who treads the grapes in the winepress of God's wrath.

It is possible that the reference to "outside" the city may indicate that the principle of *ius talionis* is operative here in that according to Gospel tradition Jesus himself was executed *outside of Jerusalem* (Matt 27:33 = Mark 15:22 = Luke 23:33 = John 19:17; Heb 13:12–13), and thus this judgment constitutes a kind of poetic justice. Of course, winepresses were always found in vineyards of any size, and vineyards were usually located outside the walls of local urban centers, including Jerusalem. Bousset speculated that this passage was a reworked apocalyptic fragment ([1906] 390).

20b καὶ ἐξῆλθεν αἷμα ἐκ τῆς ληνοῦ ἄχρι τῶν χαλινῶν τῶν ἵππων ἀπὸ σταδίων χιλίων ἑξακοσίων, "and blood flowed from the winepress to the height of the bridles of horses for one thousand six hundred stadia." There is a widespread ancient association between blood and wine, for the juice of grapes is frequently referred to as the αἷμα σταφυλῆς, the "blood of the grape," and similar expressions (Gen 49:11; Deut 32:14; Sir 39:26; 50:15; 1 Macc 6:34; *ANET,* 133; Achilles Tatius 2.2.5 [αἷμα βότρυος]; Clement Alex. *Paed.* 2.19.3; 2.29.1; *Strom.* 5.8.48.8), obviously because the juice of red grapes resembled blood (St ephanus, *TGL* 1:972).

Bauckham has shown that this hyperbole, consisting of an extraordinary amount of blood indicating a slaughter of exceptional proportions, is a *topos* frequently found in ancient literature ("Traditions," 40–48). The earliest occurrence of this *topos* is found in *1 Enoch* 100:3 (tr. Knibb, *Enoch*), "And the horse will walk up to its chest in the blood of sinners." A parallel from perhaps the second century A.D. occurs in 4 Ezra (6 Ezra) 15:35b–36, "and there shall be blood from the sword as high as a horse's belly and a man's thigh and a camel's hock." Though there is no evidence of any literary borrowing among these sources, it is striking that they share a common hyperbole for the extent of slaughter, namely, that horses will be wading in three to four feet of blood. Other parallels include *y. Taʿan.* 4.8; *Lam. Rab.* 2.2.4; *b. Giṭ.* 57a; see Bauckham, "Traditions," 40–43; Str-B, 3:817. Josephus historicizes this *topos* by referring to the many Jews killed by Romans when Jerusalem was captured in A.D. 70 (*J.W.* 6.406): the number of corpses "deluged the whole city with blood to such an extent that many fires were extinguished by the gory stream." The inclusion of the mention of the horses' bridles in this apocalyptic hyperbole indicates that the author is alluding to a decisive eschatological battle, perhaps that reflected in 19:11–21 (Charles, 2:26; Yarbro Collins, *Combat Myth,* 37). The mention of the bridles of horses appears to be an allusion to the presence of a victorious heavenly army, as in 19:14 (Charles, 2:26; Bornkamm, *TDNT* 4:256). Bornkamm argues that 14:20 is literarily dependent on 19:11–20 (*TDNT* 4:256).

Explanation

Rev 14 is a particularly complex section consisting of four self-contained units of text (vv 1–5, 6–12, 13, 14–20) framed by the introductory formula "I saw, and behold" (v 1) and by the clear beginning of a new subject in 15:1, "Then I saw another sign." The many parallels with other passages in Revelation suggest that Rev 14 is a pastiche of the author's favorite themes and formulas. The chapter is unified in part by the six references to "another angel" in vv 6–20. As a counterpoint to Rev 13, which describes those who worship the beast and receive his brand, 14:1 introduces the 144,000 who bear the name of the Lamb and his Father on their foreheads (alluding to 7:3–8), and 14:9–11 consigns those who worship the beast and receive his brand to eternal torment.

The first unit of text (vv 1–5) focuses on an eschatological scene centering on the Lamb, representing the Davidic Messiah in the paradoxical role of shepherd and guide (see 7:17), and the 144,000 who have been redeemed from humanity and are gathered on Mount Zion, the location of Jerusalem (an allusion to Ps 2:6). The number 144,000 occurs twice, reminding us of the 144,000 who were sealed in 7:4–8. The mysterious new song sung by the unidentified heavenly choir, intercalated between vv 1 and 4–5, is known only to the 144,000, thus underscoring their special status. The identity of the 144,000 is carefully described in vv 4–5 in three parallel clauses: (1) They have not polluted themselves with women; they are "virgins" or "celibates" (a metaphor for their moral and spiritual purity). (2) They follow the Lamb wherever he goes (the language of discipleship). (3) They have been redeemed from the earth and are servants dedicated to God and to the Lamb, and guile is not in their mouths for they (like other sacrificial victims) are blameless.

The second unit of text (vv 6–12) consists of three parallel angelic speeches and concludes with an exhortation for endurance (v 12), which is based on vv 9–11. The first angelic message is the universal proclamation of the eternal message or gospel of God, an eschatological message that announces the necessity of repentance and conversion in view of the imminent end of the world and the judgment of God. The second angelic message consists of an anticipatory announcement of the fall of Babylon-Rome (v 8), an eschatological event later narrated in Rev 17:1–19:10 and closely similar verbally to 18:3. The third angelic message announces the eternal torment awaiting those who worship the beast and accept his brand on their bodies (vv 9–11). The exhortation to endure persecution is directed to God's people, who keep the commandments of God and are faithful to Jesus.

The third textual unit is the beatitude in v 13, which is introduced by a command to write and which pronounces a blessing on those who are killed for their faith, an allusion to the program of persecution and murder carried out by the beast from the sea against the people of God predicted in the previous chapter (13:7).

The fourth unit (14–20) consists of vv 14–16 and a doublet in vv 17–20. The "one like a son of man" in v 14 (an allusion to Dan 7:13) is an angelic figure, not the Messiah or (more specifically) the exalted Christ, though the same allusion in Rev 1:13 is clearly used of the exalted Christ. Both the grain harvest depicted in vv 14–16 and the grape harvest in vv 17–20 (both dramatized allusions to Joel 3:13) are metaphors representing eschatological judgment carried out by angelic emissaries of God. The explicit mention of the treading of the grapes in the great winepress of God's wrath (v 19), with its reference to the blood high as a horse's bridle, refers to God's climactic victory in the final eschatological battle (see 19:17–21 and 20:7–10).

5. The Seven Bowls (15:1–16:21)

Bibliography

Amiram, D. H. K., Arieh, E., and **Turcotte, T.** "Earthquakes in Israel and Adjacent Areas: Macroseismic Observations since 100 B.C.E." *IEJ* 44 (1994) 260–305. **Aune, D. E.** "A Latinism in Revelation." *JBL* 110 (1991) 691–92. **Betz, H. D.** "On the Problem of the Religio-Historical Understanding of Apocalypticism." *JTC* 6 (1969) 134–56. **Brown, J. P.** "The Ark of the Covenant and the Temple of Janus: The Magico-Military Numen of the State in Jerusalem and Rome." *BZ* 30 (1986) 20–35. **Brox, N.** *Der Hirt des Hermas.* KAV 7. Göttingen: Vandenhoeck & Ruprecht, 1991. **Cérny, L.** *The Day of the Lord and Some Relevant Problems.* Prague: Náskladem Filofické Fakulty University Karlovy, 1948. **Charlesworth, M. P.** "The Virtues of a Roman Emperor." *PBA* 23 (1937) 105–34. **Davies, G. I.** *Megiddo.* Grand Rapids, MI: Eerdmans, 1986. **De Moor, J. C.,** and **Staalduine-Sulman, E. van.** "The Aramaic Song of the Lamb." *JST* 24 (1993) 266–79. **Everson, A. J.** "The Days of Yahweh." *JBL* 93 (1974) 329–37. **Eybers, I. H.** "Shephelah and Armageddon—What Do They Signify?" *Theologia Evangelica* 10 (1977) 7–13. **Ford, J. M.** "The Structure and Meaning of Revelation 16." *ExpTim* 98 (1987) 327–30. **Goldin, J.** *The Song at the Sea.* New Haven, CT: Yale UP, 1971. **Haran, M.** *Temples and Temple-Service in Ancient Israel.* Oxford: Clarendon, 1978. **Hartman, L.** *Prophecy Interpreted: The Formation of Some Jewish Apocalyptic Texts and of the Eschatological Discourse Mark 13 par.* ConBNT 1. Lund: Gleerup, 1966. **Hoffmann, Y.** "The Day of the Lord as a Concept and a Term in the Prophetic Literature." *ZAW* 93 (1981) 37–50. **Jeremias, Joachim.** "Har Magedon (Apc

16:16)." *ZNW* 31 (1932) 73–77. ———. "*Har Magedon* (Apk. 16:16) and Megiddo." *JPOS* 12 (1932) 49–50. **Jørgensen, G.** "Gravhulen på Makpelas mark: Mosebøgerne." In *Sola Scriptura,* ed. K. M. Andersen, E. Hviid, and H. J. Lundager Jensen. Frederiksberg, 1993. 102–15. **LaRondelle, H. K.** "The Biblical Concept of Armageddon." *JETS* 28 (1985) 21–31. ———. "The Etymology of *Har-Magedon* (Rev 16:16)." *AUSS* 27 (1989) 69–73. **Loasby, R. E.** "'Har-Magedon' according to the Hebrew in the Setting of the Seven Last Plagues of Revelation 16." *AUSS* 27 (1989) 129–32. **Michael, J. H.** "Har-Magedon." *JTS* 38 (1937) 168–72. **Müller, H.-P.** "Die Plagen der Apokalypse: Eine formgeschichtliche Untersuchung." *ZNW* 51 (1960) 268–78. **Nielsen, K.** *Incense in Ancient Israel.* Leiden: Brill, 1986. **Rad, G. von.** "The Origin and the Concept of the Day of Yahweh." *JSS* 4 (1959) 97–108. **Schäfer, P.** *Rivalität zwischen Engeln und Menschen: Untersuchungen zur rabbinischen Engelvorstellung.* SJ 8. Berlin; New York: de Gruyter, 1975. **Schieber, A. S.** *The Flavian Eastern Policy.* Ann Arbor, MI: University Microfilms, 1975. **Shea, W. H.** "The Location and Significance of Armageddon in Rev 16:16." *AUSS* 18 (1980) 157–62. **Spiekermann, H.** "Die Irae: Der alttestamentliche Befund und Seine Vorgeschichte." *VT* 39 (1989) 194–208. **Staalduine-Sulman, E. van.** "The Aramaic Song of the Lamb." In *Verse in Ancient Near Eastern Prose,* ed. J. C. de Moor and W. G. E. Watson. Neukirchen: Neukirchener, 1993. 265–92. **Stanley, D. M.** "'Carmenque Christo quasi Deo dicere.'" *CBQ* 20 (1958) 173–91. **Staples, P.** "Rev XVI 4–6 and Its Vindication Formula." *NovT* 14 (1972) 280–93. **Thomas, D. W.** "A Consideration of Some Unusual Ways of Expressing the Superlative in Hebrew." *VT* 3 (1953) 209–24. **Torrance, T. F.** "Liturgie et Apocalypse." *VCaro* 11 (1957) 34. **Torrey, C. C.** "Armageddon (Apoc. 16:16)." *HTR* 31 (1938) 237–48. **Ward-Perkins, J. B.** "The Roman West and the Parthian East." *PBA* 51 (1966) 175–99. **Weiss, M.** "The Origin of the 'Day of the Lord'—Reconsidered." *HUCA* 37 (1966) 29–60. **Yarbro Collins, A.** "The History-of-Religions Approach to Apocalypticism and the 'Angel of the Waters' (Rev 16:4–7)." *CBQ* 39 (1977) 367–81. **Ziegler, K.-H.** *Die Beziehungen zwischen Rom und dem Partherreich.* Wiesbaden: Steiner, 1964.

Translation

1 *Then I saw another* [a]*great and wonderful*[a] *sign in heaven,* [b]*seven angels*[b] *with the seven*
[c]*last plagues, for* [d]*with them the wrath of God was spent.*[d] 2 *Then I saw* [a]*something like*[a] *a*
[b]*sea of glass mingled with fire, and* [c]*those who were victorious*[c] *over the beast, that is,*[d] *over*[e]
its image and over the number [f]*of its name, stood*[g] *near the sea*[f] *of glass with* [h]*kitharas of*
[i]*God.*[h] 3 *They*[a] *sang*[b] *the song of Moses*[c] *the servant of God and the song of the Lamb:*[d]

"Great and wonderful are your deeds,
  [e]*Lord God Almighty;*[e]
Righteous and true are your ways,
  King[f] *of the nations.*[g]
4 *Who,* [a]*Lord,* [b]*does not fear*[b]
  [c]*and glorify*[d] *your name?*
Because you alone [e]*are holy,*[e]
  Because all the nations will come
  [f]*to worship*[f] *before you,*
Because your righteous judgments are evident."[g]

5 *After this I saw the temple, namely,*[a] *the tent of testimony* [b]*in heaven, open,*[c] 6 *and* [a]*the seven*
angels [b]*with the seven plagues emerged from the temple clothed in pure, shining linen*[c] *and*
with golden sashes encircling[d] *their waists.* 7 *Then one*[a] *of the four cherubim*[b] *gave to the seven*
angels [c]*seven golden libation bowls full of the wrath of the God who lives for ever and ever.*
8 *Thereupon the temple was filled with* [a]*smoke from the glory of God and from his power, and*
no one was able to enter the temple until the seven plagues of the seven[b] *angels had been*
accomplished.

16:1 Then I heard a [a]loud voice[a] [b]from the temple[b] telling the seven angels, “Be on your
way[c] to[d] begin pouring out[e] the seven[f] libation bowls containing[g] the wrath of God [h]upon
the earth.”[h] 2 The[a] first one departed[b] and poured out[c] his bowl on the earth, with the result
that[d] a harmful [e]and festering[e] sore afflicted those people who have the brand[f] of the beast
and who worship [g]his image.[g] 3 Then[a] the second one poured out his bowl on the sea, and it
became blood as from a corpse, with the result that[b] every living creature[c] died which[d] was
in the sea. 4 Then the third one poured out his bowl on[a] the rivers and [bc]springs of water,[c] with
the result[d] that they became[e] blood. 5 Then I heard the angel over the waters saying:

> *“Righteous are you, who is and who[a] was, the holy one,*
> *[b]for you have decided to inflict these punishments,[b]*
> 6 *because they[a] poured out the [b]blood [c]of God’s people[c] and the prophets,*
> *and [d]you have given[d] them blood [e]to drink;[e] they are [f]worthy.”*

7 I then heard someone[a] from the altar say:

> *“Yes, Lord God Almighty,*
> *True and just are your judgments.”[b]*

8 The fourth one[a] poured out his bowl upon the sun, and it[b] was permitted[c] to burn people
[d]with fire.[d] 9 People were [a]burned by the intense heat.[a] They reviled the name of God who had
the[b] authority over these plagues, but[c] they did not repent so as to give[d] glory to him.

10 Then the fifth one poured out his libation bowl upon the throne of the beast, so that[a] his
kingdom [b]became darkened.[b] Consequently,[c] people[d] bit their[e] tongues because of the pain,
11 and [a]they reviled[a] the God of heaven because of their sufferings and their sores, yet[b] they[c]
did not [d]repent of[d] their behavior.

12 Then the sixth [a]one poured out his bowl on the great river [b]Euphrates, [c]with the result
that[c] its[d] waters dried up, so that a road was made ready for the kings from the[e] east. 13 Then
I saw three unclean spirits [a]like frogs[a] emerge from the mouth of the dragon and from the
mouth of the beast and from the mouth of the false prophet. 14 For they are[a] spirits, that is,
demons producing signs, who [b]travel[b] to the kings of the whole world to gather them for the[c]
battle on [d]the great day[d] of God the Almighty.

(15 “Indeed, [says Jesus,] I am coming[a] like a thief. [b]How fortunate[b] is the one who watches
and remains fully clothed, lest[c] he go about naked and people[d] see[e] his shameful state.”[f])

16 The [a]demonic spirits[a] gathered[b] them together to [c]the [d]place called [e]Armageddon in
Hebrew.

17 [a]The seventh[a] poured out his libation bowl [b]into the air, and a [c]loud voice came [d]from
the [e]temple, that is, [f]from the throne, saying,[f] “It is finished.” 18 Then there were [a]lightning
and rumbling and thunder,[a] and there was a great earthquake such[b] as has never been since
people have been[c] on the earth, so great[d] was the earthquake. 19 The great city [a]split into[a] three
parts, and [b]the cities of the nations[b] fell. God remembered[c] [d]to give[d] Babylon the great [e]the[f]
cup of[g] wine, that is, his[h] furious wrath,[e] 20 and every island fled,[a] and the mountains
disappeared.[b] 21 Then large hailstones weighing nearly a hundred pounds fell on people from
the sky,[a] so that people reviled God as the result of[b] the plague of hail,[c] because that plague[d]
was so terrible.

Notes

1.a-a. The adjs. μέγα καὶ θαυμαστόν, “great and wonderful,” are separated from the noun phrase they modify, ἄλλο σημεῖον, “another sign,” by the prep. phrase ἐν τῷ οὐρανῷ, “in heaven.” Elsewhere when the author uses ἄλλος together with another adj. to modify a noun, ἄλλος is placed before the noun, while the other adj. follows the noun (6:4; 10:1; 14:8, 9). This particular pattern occurs nowhere else in the NT and just once in the LXX (1 Esdr 2:13). In the LXX when ἄλλος modifies a noun, it is usually in the postposition.

1.b-b. The phrase ἀγγέλους ἑπτά, "the seven angels," is anarthrous because this particular group is mentioned for the first time. The anaphoric article is used when they are mentioned again (15:6, 7, 8; 16:1; 17:1; 21:9).

1.c. τὰς ἐσχάτας is an arthrous adj. modifying the anarthrous substantive πληγάς. This phenomenon occurs only here in Revelation, with the exception of the phrase Βαβυλὼν ἡ μεγάλη, "Babylon the great," which occurs five times (14:8; 16:19; 17:5; 18:2, 21; cf. 18:10), though as a proper name it is anarthrous (Mussies, *Morphology*, 194). In 15:1, πληγάς becomes definite only as an afterthought (BDF § 270.3; BDR § 270.2; cf. Luke 23:49; John 14:27; Acts 7:35; 9:22; 2 Tim 1:13).

1.d-d. Variants: (1) ἐν αὐταῖς ἐτελέσθη] *lectio originalis.* (2) ἐτελέσθη ἐν αὐταῖς] 𝔓[47]; singular reading. (3) ἐν ταύταις ἐτελέσθη] 051 Andreas. τελεῖν here can mean "to complete" (Louw-Nida, § 68.22) or "to end" (Louw-Nida, § 67.67). τελεῖν is used in the sense of "complete, fulfill" (of OT prophecy) in 10:7, while here the intended notion is "to end," which in connection with anger can be translated "to be spent, to be exhausted."

2.a-a. The comparative particle ὡς, "as, like," is used here in a typically apocalyptic sense to emphasize the mysterious nature of what is seen in a vision (see *Comment* on v 2a).

2.b. The term θάλασσα, "sea," occurs twenty-six times in Revelation and is articular in all but three instances (4:6; 14:7; 15:2); cf. BDR § 253.2. Though the presence of the article is optional in prep. phrases, θάλασσα is articular in all twelve instances in which it occurs in prep. phrases in Revelation. In 4:6 and 15:2 the phrase ὡς θάλασσα occurs; cf. ὡς θάλασσα in *T. Jude* 21:6. The absence of the article in 14:7 is textually disputed (cf. *Note* 14:7.d.).

2.c-c. Charles (2:33) and Robertson (*Grammar*, 881) suggest that the present ptcp. τοὺς νικῶντας functions as a pf. (cf. S. Thompson, *Apocalypse*, 76). However, the aspectual character of the pf. is in view here, not the supposedly temporal character. It is unnecessary to attribute any specific temporal significance to such articular substantival ptcps. since they function as nouns and exclude indications of time (Winer, *Grammar*, 444; Porter, *Verbal Aspect*, 293–301). τοὺς νικῶντας might better be translated "victors" here, though the context makes such a translation unidiomatic.

2.d. The καί here is epexegetical or explanatory.

2.e. Variant: omit ἐκ before τῆς εἰκόνος] 𝔓[47].

2.f-f. The reading of 𝔓[47] is peculiar here. The last line of col. 8 verso reads [τος αυτο]υ εστωτασ επι την θαλασ, while (following at least two missing lines) col. 9 recto (as reconstructed) reads: [ονοματος α]του ε[στ]ωτας [επι την θαλασ. It appears that several lines have been repeated through dittography.

2.g. The pf. ptcp. ἑστῶτας here is peculiar since it is part of a sequence of *three* substantival ptcps., and the others are present ptcps.: τοὺς νικῶντας . . . ἑστῶτας . . . ἔχοντας.

2.h-h. The noun phrase κιθάραι τοῦ θεοῦ is somewhat ambiguous (some of the possibilities are mentioned in BAGD, 432; only one possibility is considered in Bauer-Aland, 878): (1) If τοῦ θεοῦ is construed as a gen. of possession, the phrase can be translated "God's kitharas," i.e., "kitharas belonging to God." (2) The phrase can also mean "kitharas for [the praise of] God" (Bauer-Aland, 878). An example of this construction is found in LXX 1 Chr 16:42, which contains the phrase καὶ ὄργανα τῶν ᾠδῶν τοῦ θεοῦ, "instruments of song for God" (cf. RSV, "and instruments of sacred song"; NRSV, "and instruments for sacred song"; REB, "and the instruments used for sacred song"). (3) At one time scholars argued that, in certain passages in the NT, nouns followed by [τοῦ] θεοῦ functioned as Hebraic periphrasis for the superlative (e.g., Col 2:19; 2 Cor 1:12; 1 Thess 4:16; Jas 5:11; cf. Winer, *Grammar*, 309–10, who argues against this view). In Ps 36:7, for example, in the phrase צדקתך כהררי־אל *ṣidqātĕkā kĕharrê-ʾēl*, lit. "your righteousness [is] as the mountains of God," אל *ʾēl* is used to express the superlative height and grandeur of mountains, and the phrase can be construed as "your righteousness is like the lofty mountains" (REB) or "your righteousness is like the marvelous mountains" (P. C. Craigie, *Psalms 1–50*, WBC 19 [Waco, TX: Word, 1983] 289–90; cf. Thomas, *VT* 3 [1953] 210–19, who lists eight passages in the OT in which אלהים *ʾĕlōhîm* or אל *ʾēl* is an epithet used with intensifying or superlative force: Gen 23:6; 30:8; Exod 9:28; 1 Sam 14:15; Jonah 3:3; Pss 36:7; 80:11; Job 1:16). For other possible examples of this use of אל *ʾēl* following a noun in the construct state, see Pss 50:10; 80:11; Isa 14:13 (cf. BDB, 42).

2.i. Variant: κυρίου before τοῦ θεοῦ] א; singular reading. This reading is an interpolation based on the frequently occurring divine name κύριος ὁ θεός (1:8; 4:8; 11:17; 15:3; 16:7; 18:8; 19:6; 21:22; 22:5, 6), one instance of which (15:3) occurs in the immediate context.

3.a. See *Note* 16:2.a.

3.b. ᾄδωσιν] 𝔓[47]; error based on the phonetic confusion of ο = ω (Gignac, *Grammar* 1:275–77). The verb ᾄδουσιν, "they sing," is a 3rd present ind., which I have translated as a past tense; this is another example of the author's practice of beginning a vision narrative with past tenses and then switching to the present ind.; cf. Mussies, *Morphology*, 334. This verb is also cited as an example of a Hebraism in which a ptcp. is continued through the use of a finite verb, in vv 2–3: εἶδον . . . νικῶντας . . . ἑστῶτας . . . ἔχοντας . . . ᾄδουσιν (Schmid, *Studien* 2:243).

3.c. The name Μωϋσέως, "Moses," is anarthrous because it is a gen. forming a word group with the preceding articular noun (cf. Mussies, *Morphology*, 192).

3.d. The redundant ptcp. λέγοντες (masc. nom. pl. ptcp.) is omitted in the translation since it is a Semitism that simply functions to introduce direct discourse, much like ὅτι *recitativum.*

3.e-e. The address κύριε ὁ θεὸς ὁ παντοκράτωρ begins with a vocative, followed by two noms. of apposition that function like vocatives. This formulaic phrase occurs three times in Revelation (11:17; 15:3; 16:7). A similar construction is found in 18:20 (οὐρανὲ καὶ οἱ ἅγιοι καὶ οἱ ἀπόστολοι καὶ οἱ προφῆται), in which the initial vocative, οὐρανέ, is followed by three articular noms. of apposition that function like vocatives. On this construction, cf. *Introduction,* p. clxxvi.

3.f. ὁ βασιλεύς, "king," is an articular nom. that functions as a vocative; this construction occurs eighteen times elsewhere in Revelation (cf. *Note* 4:11.a.). In 15:3, the vocative form βασιλεῦ is weakly attested by א* fam 1611^{1854} Andr d Andr Ø^{94}.

3.g. Variants: (1) ἐθνῶν] A 025 046 051 Andreas Byzantine it$^{gig\ h}$ cop^{bo} arm eth Cyprian Primasius Beatus (*omnium gentium*); Tischendorf, *NT Graece;* Bousset ([1906] 393); Merk, *NT;* Nestle-Aland^{27}; UBSGNT^{4}. (2) αἰώνων] 𝔓^{47} א^{*c} C fam 1006 fam 1611$^{1611\ 2344}$ 1778 2040 Andr Ø^{94} vg syr cop^{sa}. This passage is discussed in some detail in *TCGNT*^{1}, 753–54; *TCGNT*^{2}, 679–80, where it is suggested that the phrase τῷ δὲ βασιλεῖ τῶν αἰώνων, "and to the king of the ages," from 1 Tim 1:17 may have influenced the copyist. This argument is not very convincing, though the phrase "King of the Ages" may have influenced the copyist because of its general currency: Jer 10:10 (מלך עולם *melek ʿôlām*), absent from LXX, though present in Theodotion; Tob 13:7, 11; *Tg. Jer.* 10:7, 10; 1QapGen 2:7 (במלך כול עלמים *bmlk kwl ʿlmym*); Gk. *1 Enoch* 9:4; 12:3; 25:3, 5, 7; cf. 90:5; *T. Reub.* 6:12; *Jos. As.* 16:16. The phrase מלם העילם *melek hāʿôlām,* "king of the universe," is a formula found at the beginning of every rabbinic benediction except the benediction of the Amidah. A number of Jewish scholars argue that this emphasis on the kingship of God was formulated in conscious opposition to emperor worship; cf. E. J. Wiesenberg, "The Liturgical Term *melekh ha-olam,*" *JJS* 15 (1964) 1–56; J. Heinemann, "Once Again *melekh ha-olam,*" *JJS* 15 (1964) 149–54; id., *Prayer in the Talmud: Forms and Patterns* (Berlin; New York: de Gruyter, 1977) 93–95. A variation of the phrase occurs once in the pagan magical papyri (*PGM* XII.247, Αἰώνων βασιλεῦ, "king [voc.] of the ages") and once in a Christian magical papyrus, *PGM* 21.42, dated ca. A.D. 300. For similar phrases, cf. Str-B, 2:320.

4.a. Variant: Add σε before οὐ μή] 𝔓^{47} א fam 1006$^{1006\ 1841}$ fam 1611$^{1854\ 2329}$.

4.b-b. Variant: (1) οὐ μὴ φοβηθῇ] A C 025 046 fam 1611^{1611} Oecumenius^{2053} it$^{gig\ h}$ cop^{bo} arm eth Cyprian. (2) omit μή] א fam^{1006} Andr n^{-2429}. (3) omit οὐ] fam 1611^{1854}. οὐ μή is used here with the aor. subjunctive as an emphatic fut. in a rhetorical question (BDR § 365.4; BDR § 364.4); cf. John 18:11; Luke 18:7. Reading (1) is probably original since the other readings can be explained as alterations of it (*TCGNT*^{1}, 754).

4.c. Variant: insert σε] Andr f$^{051\ 2023}$ h 94 Byzantine.

4.d. Variants: (1) δοξάσει] 𝔓^{47} (δοξήσει) A C 025 046 051 Oecumenius^{2053} fam 1611^{2329} Andreas. (2) δοξάσῃ] א fam 1006$^{1006\ 1841}$ fam 1611^{1611} Oecumenius^{2062} Andr a c^{2069} d e f^{2023} l^{-2080} Byzantine; von Soden, *Text.* (3) δοξάσοι] Andr f^{2056} n^{2065} 2019. (4) θαυμάσῃ] fam 1611^{1854}. Reading (2) is an obvious assimilation of δοξάσει to the previous φοβηθῇ, with which it is parallel (cf. Schmid, *Studien* 2:120, 224).

4.e-e. Variant: εἶ instead of ὅσιος] 𝔓^{47}.

4.f-f. The phrase καὶ προσκυνήσουσιν functions as a final clause and can therefore be translated "that they might worship" (cf. S. Thompson, *Apocalypse*, 99). Several final clauses in Revelation have an identical construction (4:1; 5:10; 9:19; 11:7; 13:7–8; 20:10; cf. S. Thompson, *Apocalypse,* 99).

4.g. Variant: ἐφανερώθη] 𝔓^{47}; scribal correction using 3rd sing. verb with neut. pl. subject.

5.a. τῆς σκηνῆς, "the tent," is translated as a gen. of apposition, with Bousset (1906) 394 (against Charles, 2:37).

5.b. The expected article ὁ (modifying ὁ ναός) before ἐν τῷ οὐρανῷ is missing, and the phrase τῆς σκηνῆς τοῦ μαρτυρίου, between ὁ ναός and ἐν τῷ οὐρανῷ, is problematic because in Revelation a prep. phrase modifying an articular substantive is normally articular; cf. 1:4; 2:24; 5:5; 8:3, 9; 11:16, 19; 14:17; 19:14; 20:8, 13 (see below under *Comment*). Charles (2:37–38), retroverting the clause into Heb., suggests that היכל אהל מועד בשמים *hêkal ʾōhel môʿēd bašāmayim,* "the temple of the tent of witness in heaven," behind the present Gk. text, is a corruption of היכל אלהים שבשמים *hêkal ʾĕlōhîm šebbašāmayim,* "the temple of the God of heaven," i.e., ὁ ναὸς τοῦ θεοῦ ὁ ἐν τῷ οὐρανῷ. Bousset ([1906] 174), however, is probably correct in his view that the article was omitted before ἐν τῷ οὐρανῷ because of its distance from the articular noun ὁ ναός, on which it is dependent.

5.c. The second aor. pass. verb ἠνοίγη, "was opened," or "opened itself," a pass. of divine activity (see *Comment* on 9:3), is an example of Johannine parataxis, for a subordinate ptcp. commonly used in hypotactic sentences would normally be expected here (cf. BDR, § 471; Ljungvik, *Syntax,* 80).

6.a. The definite article used with οἱ ἑπτὰ ἄγγελοι is anaphoric, referring back to the first (anarthrous) mention of this particular group of angels in 15:1.

6.b. Variants: (1) οἱ before ἔχοντες] A C fam 1611$^{1611\ 2329}$ fam 1006$^{911\ 1841}$ Andreas; Tischendorf, *NT Graece;* [WHort]; Bousset ([1906] 394); Merk, *NT;* [UBSGNT^{4}]; [Nestle-Aland^{27}]. (2) omit οἱ] 𝔓^{47} א 025 046 fam 1006$^{1006\ 1854}$ fam 1611^{2344} Oecumenius$^{2053\ 2062}$ Andr a^{1} d f$^{051\ 2031\ 2056}$ i^{-2042} n^{2065} 598 Byzantine. The combinations of A and C for reading (1) and 𝔓^{47}, א, and Oecumenius^{2053} for reading (2) are both very strong. Nevertheless, a consideration of the use of the article in such cases in Revelation suggests that the article was originally *present,* making ἔχοντες a substantival ptcp. This follows the syntactical rule that an adj. following an articular substantive will itself be articular (cf. 8:6; 9:15; 11:4; 14:13; 17:18; 21:9; Bousset [1906] 173–74; Schmid, *Studien* 2:196). There is a striking tendency in א to omit the article repeated before the adj. (cf. 5:6; 8:6; 9:15; 11:4; 17:18).

6.c. Variants: (1) λίνον] 025 051 fam 1006^{1006} fam 1611^{1611} Andreas Byzantine syr$^{ph\ h}$ it$^{c\ dem\ div\ haf}$ vg^{ww} arm Primasius (*linea*); Tyc^{2} (*lino*); Beatus (*linum*). (2) λίθον] A C Oecumenius$^{2053\ 2062}$ 2020^{mg} Andr l$^{1778mg\ 2080}$ vg; WHort, Charles, 2:331. (3) λινοῦν] 𝔓^{47} 046 Andr f$^{2031\ 2056}$ it^{gig} (*lintheamen*); it^{h} (*linteamina*). (4) λινοῦς] א. (5) omit] Cassiodorus cop^{sa} eth. Reading (1) is probably the *lectio originalis* since λίνον (which occurs only here in Revelation) is rarely used with the meaning "linen garment" (Westcott-Hort, *Introduction,* Appendix I, 139, claim that λίνον *never* denotes a fabric or garment made of flax, though several examples of this usage were uncovered later and are mentioned in MM, 376). Yet reading (2) must be considered the *lectio difficilior* since it is difficult to conceive of an angel wearing a stone garment, and it would certainly be easier to change λίθον to λίνον than the reverse. The textual variants for this passage are extremely diverse (Hoskier, *Text,* 2:407–9), and only the more significant have been reproduced above. Ezek 28:13 has been adduced as a parallel in support of reading (2)—πᾶν λίθον χρηστὸν ἐνδέδεσαι, "clothed with every valuable stone"—but it is not really relevant, for the adj. καθαρός in 15:6 is not appropriate with λίθος. While the MS evidence strongly favors reading (2), that reading makes no sense in the context and must be a primitive corruption for the rare λίνον = linen garment (B. Weiss, *Offenbarung,* 98; Charles, 2:38; *TCGNT*^{1}, 751; *TCGNT*^{2}, 680). Charles, suggesting that λίθος represents the mistranslation of a Heb. original, points out that Heb. שֵׁשׁ *šēš* is ambiguous in that it can mean "linen," i.e., βύσσινος (KB^{3}, 4:1534; Gen 41:42; Exod 28:5, 39; Ezek 16:13; Prov 31:22), or "alabaster," λίθος (KB^{4}, 4:1535–35; Esth 1:6; Cant 5:15). Ep Jer 71 has the phrase "the purple and marble [τῆς πορφύρας καὶ τῆς μαρμάρου] that rot upon them," which is nonsense, apparently reflecting the mistaken translation of שֵׁשׁ *šēš* by τῆς μαρμάρου, "marble," rather than by τοῦ βυσσίνου, "fine linen." Nevertheless, the weakness of Charles's proposal lies in the fact that שֵׁשׁ *šēš* is never translated λίθος in the LXX. Reading (3) is either an error resulting from the phonetic similarity of ο = ου (Gignac, *Grammar* 2:211–14) or the substitution of the contracted acc. form of the adj. λίνεος, "of linen," which is spelled λίνεον in its uncontracted form. Reading (4) is the contracted form of the masc. nom. λίνεος. Both readings (3) and (4) indicate scribal difficulties in understanding λίνον as "linen *garment.*" Reading (1) is certainly original, though it was altered to λίθον because of the unusual meaning of λίνον.

6.d. περιεσζωμένοι] 𝔓^{47}; singular reading; spelling error through transposition of the sigma.

7.a. Variant: omit ἕν before ἐκ τῶν τεσσάρων] 𝔓^{47} א* Andreas.

7.b. Variant: omit ζῴων] 𝔓^{47}; singular reading.

7.c. The phrase ἑπτὰ φιάλας χρυσᾶς, "seven golden libation bowls," is anarthrous because the bowls are introduced here for the first time and are apparently unknown to the readers; these bowls, individually and collectively, are mentioned ten more times in Revelation, each time with the anaphoric definite article (16:1, 2, 3, 4, 8, 10, 12, 17; 17:1; 21:9).

8.a. Variant: insert ἐκ τοῦ before καπνοῦ] 𝔓^{47} Byzantine.

8.b. Variants: (1) ἑπτά before ἀγγέλων] 𝔓^{47}. (2) omit ἑπτά] 051 Andreas it^{gig}.

16:1.a-a. Variants: (1) φωνῆς μεγάλης] א 025. (2) μεγάλη φωνή] fam 1611$^{1611\ 2050\ 2329}$. The phrase μεγάλη φωνή in the order adj. + noun occurs only here in Revelation, though ἐν ἰσχυρᾷ φωνῇ does occur in 18:2; the phrase φωνὴ μεγάλη occurs nineteen times in Revelation and provides a motivation for the correction. In Greco-Jewish literature, the phrase φωνὴ μεγάλη is relatively common (*Adam and Eve* 5:2; 29:11; *T. Abr.* [Rec. A] 5:9; 14:13; *Jos. As.* 28:9; *Par. Jer.* 3:2; *3 Apoc. Bar.* 11:3: *Sib. Or.* 3.669; 5.63), though the reverse order does occur (*Par. Jer.* 5:32; 7:15; *T. Job* 3.1).

1.b-b. Variants: (1) ἐκ τοῦ ναοῦ] א A C 025 fam 1611^{2329} vg Primasius Andreas. (2) omit ἐκ τοῦ ναοῦ] 046 94 Byzantine. (3) (ἐν τῷ ναῷ)] arm$^{1\ 2}$. Reading (1) has the strongest support (*TCGNT*^{1}, 754–55; *TCGNT*^{2}, 680).

1.c. Variant: ὑπάγεται] ℵ C Oecumenius^{2062} Andr b^{2059} c$^{(2033)}$ e^{2091} f^{2031} i^{2043} n^{2065} Andr Ø$^{181\ 2038}$ Andr/ Byz 4c Byz^{2022} l^{2256}.

1.d. The phrase that begins the brief speech by the voice from the temple is ὑπάγετε καὶ ἐκχέετε, lit. "depart and pour out," yet the context makes it clear that the coordinate clause introduced by καί functions as a final clause to express purpose. As such, καὶ ἐκχέετε functions as an equivalent to ἵνα with the subjunctive, i.e., ἵνα ἐκχῆτε, "that you may pour out" or "to pour out" (Ljungvik, *Syntax*, 72–76, with many examples from the papyri). This use of καί to introduce a purpose clause can be clearly seen in Matt 5:15, οὐδὲ καίουσιν λύχνον καὶ τιθέασιν αὐτὸν ὑπὸ τὸν μόδιον, ἀλλ' ἐπὶ τὴν λυχνίαν, καὶ λάμπει πᾶσιν τοῖς ἐν τῇ οἰκίᾳ, "Nor do men light a lamp and put it under a bushel, but on a stand, and [i.e., 'so that'] it gives light to all in the house" (RSV), but better translated "People light a lamp not just to put it under a basket but to put it on a stand to give light to everyone in the house." In the Synoptic parallels, Mark 4:21 has ἵνα + subjunctive in both clauses in place of καί + ind., while Luke 8:16 (and the doublet in Luke 11:44) replaces the first clause with a subordinate ptcp. followed by a finite verb but replaces the second clause with ἵνα + subjunctive. καί is omitted before ἐκχέετε by 051 1854 Andr. καί is attested by 025 Andr c d f^{2073} l.

1.e. Variants: (1) ἐκχέετε] A 025 fam 1006 Oecumenius$^{2053\ 2062}$ Andr a^{1} b$^{2059\ 2081}$ e$^{2026\ 2091}$ n^{2065} l$^{1678\ 1778\ 2080}$ Andr Ø^{598}. (2) ἐκχέεται] ℵ C 2329 Andr Ø^{181} Byz 2^{2200} . The two present impers. ὑπάγετε, "depart, leave," and ἐκχέετε, "pour out," both action verbs, are used here in an inceptive or conative way; i.e., the command involves the beginning of an activity since there are seven bowls to be poured out.

1.f. Variant: delete ἑπτά] 051 1854 Andr h cop Beatus.

1.g. In the noun phrase τοῦ θυμοῦ τοῦ θεοῦ, the first articular noun is a gen. of content, while the second can be construed as a subjective gen.

1.h-h. Variant: omit εἰς τὴν γῆν] 𝔓^{47}.

2.a. The conjunction καί, "and," with which this sentence begins is left untranslated since it functions as a discourse marker indicating the beginning of a new sentence.

2.b. Here the author has varied his vocabulary by choosing the aor. ind. form of ἀπέρχεσθαι, "to go away, depart," having just used the present imper. form of ὑπάγειν, "to leave, depart."

2.c. Variant: ἐξεχέην for ἐξέχεεν] 𝔓^{47}; singular reading, possibly an error of the eye that occurred because the next two words end with -ην.

2.d. The clause introduced by the conjunction καί has a cause-and-effect relationship to the previous clause, so that καί here functions as a καί *consecutivum,* permitting the translation "with the result that." Cf. Aejmelaeus, *Parataxis,* 15–18.

2.e-e. Variant: omit κακὸν καί] 𝔓^{47}.

2.f. On this translation, see *Note* 13:16.b.

2.g-g. Variants: (1) προσκυνοῦντας τῇ εἰκόνι αὐτοῦ] A C 025 046 051 Oecumenius$^{2053\ 2062}$ fam 1006 fam 1611$^{1611\ 1854\ 2329}$ Andreas Byzantine. (2) προσκυνοῦντα τὴν εἰκόνα αὐτοῦ] ℵ 𝔓^{43} (only τήν visible); Andr a b c d e^{2091} f^{35} cop. On the use of προσκυνεῖν + dat. or acc., see *Note* 4:10.b.

3.a. A verb meaning "depart" is missing from the description of the action of the second through the seventh angel; the 3rd sing. aor. ind. ἀπῆλθεν in 16:2 applies only to the first angel.

3.b. See *Note* 16:2.d.

3.c. The word ζωῆς, "of life," is a qualitative gen. functioning as an adj. modifying the noun ψυχή, "being." It is a lit. rendering of the Heb. phrase נפש חיה *nepeš ḥayyâ* (LXX Gen 1:20 [ψυχῶν ζωσῶν], 30 [ψυχὴν ζωῆς]). Though the reading ζῶσα (a nom. sing. fem. present adj. ptcp. modifying ψυχή) has strong attestation (𝔓^{47} ℵ 046 051 fam 1611$^{1854\ 2344}$ Oecumenius$^{2053\ 2062}$ Andreas lat syr^{ph} cop TR), ζωῆς, a Hebraism, is the *lectio difficilior* supported by very few but very important MSS: A C fam 1006 fam 1611^{1611}.

3.d. Variant: omit τά before ἐν τῇ θαλάσσῃ] 𝔓^{47}.

4.a. Variant: ἐπί for εἰς] 𝔓^{47} ℵ.

4.b. Variants: (1) ἐπί before τὰς πηγάς] 𝔓^{47}. (2) εἰς before τὰς πηγάς] Byzantine.

4.c-c. τὰς πηγὰς τῶν ὑδάτων, lit. "the springs of waters," is a phrase in which the second articular noun functions as a gen. of apposition, so the entire noun phrase can be translated "the springs, i.e., the waters," or in English simply "the springs." The phrase (in both sing. and pl.) occurs frequently in the LXX (Gen 24:13; Exod 15:27; Lev 11:36; Num 33:9; Josh 15:9; Isa 35:7; 49:10), usually as a translation of עין מים *ʿên mayim* or עינת מים *ʿênōt mayim.* In Revelation the phrase (τὰς) πηγὰς (τῶν) ὑδάτων occurs four times (7:17; 8:10; 14:7; 16:4), while the sing. τῆς πηγῆς τοῦ ὕδατος occurs once in 21:6. The concord that exists between the presence or absence of the article from both nouns suggests LXX influence (cf. Mussies, *Morphology,* 82 n. 1).

4.d. See *Note* 16:3.b.

4.e. Variants: (1) ἐγένοντο] 𝔓^{47} A fam 1006 fam 1611$^{1854\ 2329}$ 1773 2019 Oecumenius$^{2053\ 2062}$ Andr e^{2091}

f$^{2073\ 2254}$ i^{2042} n^{2432} Byz 4^{1719} Byz 5$^{808\ 1893}$ Byz 17$^{469\ 2078\ 2436}$ cop eth syr it^{gig} Primasius; Charles, 2:333 (though on 2:44 he assumes the correctness of ἐγένετο). (2) ἐγένετο] ℵ C 025 046 051 Andreas Beatus; it^{ar} vg arm; Tischendorf, *NT Graece;* WHort; Bousset (1906) 396; Merk, *NT;* Nestle-Aland^{27}; UBSGNT^{4}. Because of the strength and breadth of the MS attestation, reading (1) is probably original. Some argue that reading (1) is a mechanical conformation of the verb to the preceding pl. forms (*TCGNT*^{1}, 755; *TCGNT*^{2}, 681). Reading (2), the *lectio difficilior,* is supported by some impressive, but definitely weaker witnesses. Since the subject of the verb is not expressed, the reader can supply τὰ ὕδατα, "the waters," a neut. nom. pl. that often takes a 3rd sing. verb. That is doubtless the reason for the correction from ἐγένοντο to ἐγένετο, though the previous use of ἐγένετο in v 3 may have also been influential. However, the implied subject of the verb must be οἱ ποταμοὶ καὶ αἱ πηγαὶ τῶν ὑδάτων, "the rivers and springs of water," for which the verb *must* be a 3rd pl. such as ἐγένοντο.

5.a. Variants: (1) ὁ ἦν ὁ ὅσιος] ℵ 051 Andreas cop^{sa}; [WHort]. (2) ὃς ἦν καὶ ὅσιος] 𝔓^{47} fam 1611^{2329} Andr c e. (3) ὁ ἦν καὶ ὁ ὅσιος] fam 1006$^{1006\ 1841}$ Oecumenius$^{2053\ 2062}$. (4) ὁ ἦν ὅσιος] A C fam 1611$^{1611\ 1854}$; Charles, 2:355. This is a variation on the formula ὁ ὢν καὶ ὁ ἦν καὶ ὁ ἐρχόμενος (1:4, 8; 4:8). The first two titles occur in 11:17 and here, where ὁ ὅσιος is also found. On the analogy of 1:8, where ὁ παντοκράτωρ is an asyndetic addition to the three polysyndetic titles, it would appear that ℵ in reading (1) preserves an originally arthrous ὅσιος (Schmid, *Studien* 2:120, 138).

5.b-b. The verbal phrase ὅτι ταῦτα ἔκρινας is difficult to translate. The pronoun ταῦτα, "these things," refers to the preceding three plagues, and an adequate translation should reflect this. The entire phrase ὅτι ταῦτα ἔκρινας has been translated in two main ways: (1) *as a verb clause:* (a) KJV, "because thou hast judged thus"; (b) Charles, 2:435, "in that thou hast judged"; and (c) NRSV, "for you have judged these things"; and (2) *as a noun clause:* (a) RSV, NEB, "in these thy judgments"; NIV, "in these judgments"; and (b) REB, "in these your judgments." Even though many of these translations omit it, the causal force of the ὅτι should nevertheless be retained, because the Gk. text focuses adverbially not on *how* God is righteous (e.g., "in these thy/your judgments") but on *why* God is righteous (i.e., "for you have judged"). The least acceptable translation above is the NRSV, for it is not at all clear what "judged these things" means. Translations that are both idiomatic and retain the force of the Gk. text are these: "you have decided to inflict these punishments" and "you have decreed these judgments."

6.a. The subject of the 3rd pl. aor. ἐξέχεαν, lit. "they poured out," is not immediately evident, suggesting that this is an indefinite 3rd pl., used with a general meaning, i.e., "people poured out," or a pass. meaning, "was poured out" (for other examples of the indefinite 3rd pl. verb in Revelation, see *Note* 2:24.a-a.).

6.b. Variant: αἵματα] ℵ fam 336 2019.

6.c-c. Variant: ἅγιον for ἁγίων] C Andr c^{2033} h Byz 19^{1094}. The phonetic equation of ο = ω undoubtedly produced this error, which construed ἅγιον as an adj. modifying αἷμα (Gignac, *Grammar* 1:275–77).

6.d-d. Variants: (1) δέδωκας] A C fam 1611$^{1611\ 2329}$; WHort; B. Weiss, *Johannes-Apokalypse,* 106; Charles, 2:355; Merk, *NT;* [δ]έδωκας bracketed in Nestle-Aland^{27} and UBSGNT^{4}. (2) ἔδωκας] 𝔓^{47} ℵ 051 Andreas Byzantine; Tischendorf; WHort^{mg}; Bousset (1906) 396; von Soden, *NT Graece;* Charles, 2:355^{mg}. (3) ἔδωκεν] fam 1611^{1854}. Reading (2) is a scribal alteration based on assimilation to the form of ἐξέχεαν (B. Weiss, *Johannes-Apokalypse,* 106; Schmid, *Studien* 2:92, 207).

6.e-e. Variants: (1) πεῖν] A C (πῖν); Tischendorf, *NT Graece;* WHort; B. Weiss, *Johannes-Apokalypse,* 105; Charles, 2:355. (2) πιεῖν] 𝔓^{47} ℵ Andreas Byzantine; Bousset (1906) 396; von Soden, *Text;* Nestle-Aland^{27}; UBSGNT^{4}. (3) ποιεῖν] Andr d^{2051} e^{2057} g^{2071} i$^{2014\ 2043\ 2082}$ n^{2429} Andr Ø^{2038} Byz 3$^{429\ 522}$ Byz 4^{1719} Byz 7^{2024} Byz 11^{368} Byz 16^{69} Andr/Byz 2b^{336} Andr/Byz 3$^{1248\ 1551}$ Andr/Byz 4a^{616} Andr/Byz 4b^{2018}. Reading (1) represents a non-Attic orthography that is first attested in the second century B.C. and occurs frequently in LXX MSS (Thackeray, *Grammar,* 63–64), in which two *i* sounds are contracted into one, so that forms such as the following arose: πιεῖν > π(ε)ῖν; ὑγίεια > ὑγ(ε)ῖα; ταμιεῖον > ταμ(ε)ῖον. These forms are reflected in the earlier uncials, though later the disyllabic Atticistic contractions found their way into many minuscules (Moulton, *Prolegomena,* 44–45; Moulton-Howard, *Accidence,* 89–90; MM, 513). π(ε)ῖν is not a mistaken form as claimed by von Soden (*Text* 1:1377) and B. Weiss (*Johannes-Apokalypse,* 105). The form πιεῖν in reading (2) is attested several times in the NT (Matt 27:34; Mark 10:38; Acts 23:12, 21; Rom 14:21; see *T. Sim.* 3:2; *Jos. As.* 21:21; *Vit. Proph.* 1.2), while πεῖν occurs in John 4:7, 9; 1 Cor 9:4; 10:7 (see *1 Enoch* 102:8). The fact that Atticistic forms have frequently replaced non-Atticistic forms argues for the originality of reading (1).

6.f. Variants: (1) ἄξιοι] A Andreas vg^{CFT}; Beatus. (2) ὅπερ ἄξιοι] ℵ vg^{mss} Byzantine. (3) ἄρα ἄξιοι] fam 1611^{2329}. (4) ἄξιοι γάρ] Oecumenius$^{2053\ 2062}$ it^{gig} (*digni enim sunt*). (5) ὅτι ἄξιοι] 2019 it$^{c\ dem\ diu}$ (*ut digni sunt*); it^{haf} (*ut digni enim sunt*); vg^{II} (*quod digni sunt*); vg^{AGIKOUVW} (*ut digni sunt*); Primasius (*quoniam digni sunt*) cop syr eth. (6) καὶ ἄξιοι γάρ εἰσιν] 792 it^{haf} (*ut digni enim sunt*). Reading (1) is certainly original, for its asyndetic construction encouraged scribes to insert transitional terms, though a similar construction occurs in 14:5 (ἄμωμοί εἰσιν). Note, however, that the phrase ὅτι ἄξιοί εἰσιν occurs in 3:4.

7.a. ἤκουσα τοῦ θυσιαστηρίου λέγοντος can be translated (taking the gen. as the obj. of the verb) "I heard the incense altar saying." Another alternative is to construe the gen. as a partitive gen. functioning as the obj. of the verb, making it necessary to supply an indefinite pronoun such as τινά or τινός, "someone," resulting in the translation "I heard someone from the incense altar saying," which accords with the author's style. While the simple τοῦ θυσιαστηρίου is certainly original (supported by ℵ A C Oecumenius^{2053}), the fact that it could be construed as a partitive gen. obj. of the verb ἤκουσα is confirmed by the few MSS that insert ἐκ before τοῦ θυσιαστηρίου as a correction and by 2019, which supplies φωνὴν ἐκ. Variants: (1) τοῦ θυσιαστηρίου] (lacuna in 𝔓^{47}) ℵ A C 025 051 Oecumenius^{2053} Andreas Andr/Byz 2$^{620\ 628}$ syr cop arm Beatus (*et audivi aram dei dicentem*); it^{gig} (*et audivi alterum dicentem*). (2) ἐκ τοῦ θυσιαστηρίου] 046 fam 1611^{2311} Andr a b c d m$^{2037\ 2046}$. (3) ἄλλου ἐκ τοῦ θυσιαστηρίου] TR. (4) φωνὴν ἐκ τοῦ θυσιαστηρίου] 2019. Reading (1) is the *lectio difficilior* and in addition has the overwhelming support of ℵ A C Oecumenius^{2052}; it is very probably original. The other readings are attempts to remove the ambiguity from τοῦ θυσιαστηρίου.

7.b. Variant: αἱ κρίσις] 𝔓^{47} C; spelling error based on the phonetic similarity of ει and ι (see Gignac, *Grammar* 1:249–51).

8.a. Variant: ἄγγελος before ἐξέχεεν] ℵ 051 fam 1611$^{1854\ 2329\ 2344}$ Andreas cop Primasius Beatus.

8.b. The subject of ἐδόθη could be the sun, but then a period should be inserted after τὸν ἥλιον since it is in the acc. case. Or, it could refer to the fourth angel, in which case a comma can be inserted after τὸν ἥλιον since ὁ τέταρτος is in the nom.

8.c. Variant: omit αὐτῷ] 𝔓^{47} Byz 1^{-1872}. Scribal improvement through elimination of a redundant pronoun.

8.d-d. ἐν πυρί is an instrumental dat.

9.a-a. καῦμα μέγα is a cognate acc. (internal obj.) dependent on ἐκαυματίσθησαν (Winer, *Grammar,* 281; Robertson, *Grammar,* 478; Turner, *Syntax,* 245; BDR § 153.2) and functions more specifically as an adv. acc. of manner. The only other example of a cognate acc. in Revelation is in 17:6.

9.b. Variants: (1) omit τήν before ἐξουσίαν] C fam 1006$^{1006\ 1841}$ fam 1611^{1611} Oecumenius$^{2053\ 2062}$ Andr a c d h i^{-2074} 94 Byzantine TR. (2) τήν before ἐξουσίαν] ℵ A 025 051 209 fam 1611$^{1854\ 2329}$ 2019 Andr b^{2059} d^{-2051} f g$^{205\ 2045}$ i^{2074} l$^{1778\ 2080}$ n^{2065} Andr Ø$^{181\ 598}$ Byz 2^{2076} Byz 17$^{2078\ 2436}$ Byz 19$^{2075\ 2077}$ Andr/Byz 3 Andr/Byz 4$^{2070\ 2305}$. Though the evidence for the omission of τήν is strong (particularly the combination of C and 2053), nevertheless the agreement of ℵ and A is significant and tips the scales in favor of the authenticity of τήν in the original text.

9.c. καί here functions as καί *adversativum* and is therefore translated "but."

9.d. The inf. δοῦναι functions to introduce a consecutive or result clause; the most common form of consecutive clause in the NT is ὥστε + inf.

10.a. καί here functions to introduce a consecutive clause giving the results of the action narrated in the previous clause.

10.b-b. Variants: (1) ἐσκοτωμένη] 𝔓^{47} ℵ* A C Andreas Byzantine. (2) ἐσκοτισμένη] ℵ^{1} 046 Andr d f$^{2031\ 2056}$ i n^{2065}. Reading (1) is an Attic form of the verb σκοτοῦν, while reading (2) is a Hellenistic form from the verb σκοτίζειν. There is evidence that Attic words were changed to more current Hellenistic words; cf. *Note* 12:5.f-f. (ἡρπάσθη). See *Note* 9:2.d-d. (ἐσκοτώθη).

10.c. See *Note* 16:10.a.

10.d. The verb ἐμασῶντο, 3rd pl. impf. ind., uses the 3rd pl. to express an impersonal subject, here translated "people."

10.e. Variant: omit αὐτῶν after τὰς γλώσσας] 𝔓^{47} ; singular reading.

11.a-a. Variant: ἐβλασφημοῦν] 𝔓^{47} Andr l it^{gig} cop^{sa}. The 3rd pl. verb is an indefinite pl. and has the same subject as ἐμασῶντο in v 10.

11.b. καί is used here in an adversative sense and must be translated "but, yet" (Mussies, *Morphology,* 231–32).

11.c. The subject of the verb μετενόησαν, an indefinite pl. referring back to the subject of the verbs ἐβλασφήμησαν in v 11a and ἐμασῶντο in v 10, may be rendered "people."

11.d-d. On the phrase μετανοεῖν ἐκ, see *Note* 2:21.c-c.

12.a. Variant: add ἄγγελος] 051 fam 1611$^{2329\ 2344}$ Andreas it vg syr^{ph} cop^{bo} Primasius Beatus.

12.b. Variants: (1) add τόν] 𝔓^{47} A C fam 1006$^{1006\ 1841}$ fam 1611$^{1611\ 2329}$ Andr a c d e^{2026} i$^{-1685\ -2074}$ 94. (2) omit τόν] ℵ 025 051 fam 1611^{1854} Oecumenius$^{2053\ 2062}$ cop$^{bo\ mss}$.

12.c-c. See *Note* 16:10.a.

12.d. Variant: omit αὐτοῦ] fam 1611^{2344} Andreas cop^{bo}.

12.e. Variant: ἀνατολῶν] A 051 Andreas syr^{ph}.

13.a-a. Variants: (1) ὡς βάτραχοι] A (lacuna in C) Oecumenius^{2053} Andreas. (2) ὡσει βατράχους] 𝔓^{47}

א* 94 2019. (3) ὅμοια βατράχοις] Andr a^{1} b$^{2059\ 2081}$ d e$^{2057\ 2091}$ h$^{2060\ 2286\ 2302}$ Andr Ø$^{181\ 598}$ Andr/Byz 3^{2186} TR. (4) omit] fam 1621^{2344}. πνεύματα, as the obj. of εἶδον, should be an acc. Since the substantive introduced by ὡς should be in the same case as the substantive modified by the ὡς clause (i.e., πνεύματα), the more correct reading would be ὡς βατράχους. Reading (1) either assumes that πνεύματα is in the nom. case and that the clauses following καὶ εἶδον are independent of that verb or that πνεύματα is a solecism. Normally this occurs in Revelation only after καὶ εἶδον καὶ ἰδού (6:2, 5, 8; 7:9; 14:1, 14). There are examples in the LXX of translators abandoning the regular case form of the noun following ὡς, as in Deut 10:3 (ἐλάξευσα τὰς δύο πλάκας τὰς λιθίνας ὡς αἱ πρῶται [for τὰς πρώτας]) and 1 Macc 11:1 (ἤθροισεν δυνάμεις πολλὰς ὡς ἡ ἄμμος ἡ [for τὴν ἄμμον τὴν] παρὰ τὸ χεῖλος τῆς θαλάσσης); see T. Muraoka, "The Use of ΩΣ in the Greek Bible," *NovT* 7 (1964–65) 58. Nevertheless, this reading is the *lectio difficilior,* which probably indicates its originality. Readings (2) and (3) are corrections attempting to solve the solecism.

14.a. πνεύματα, a neut. pl. nom. (v 13), is the subject of the 3rd pl. verb εἰσίν, but n.b. the 3rd sing. verb ἐκπορεύεται. However, it is possible that ἃ ἐπορεύεται refers not to the πνεύματα but to the σημεῖα. In the NT the tendency is to use a 3rd pl. verb when referring to living beings (expressed in the neut. pl.), whereas 3rd sing. verbs tend to be used with inanimate things (when expressed in the neut. pl.); cf. Mussies, *Morphology,* 230–31. However, since the inf. συναγαγεῖν, "to assemble," can only apply to the πνεύματα, ἐκπορεύεται must have πνεύματα rather than σημεῖα as its subject. In Revelation, a *pl.* verb is often used with a pl. neut. subject (e.g., 1:19; 3:2, 4; 5:14; 9:20; 11:18; 15:4; cf. Charles, 1:cvli). However, a sing. verb can also be used with a neut. pl. subject (e.g., 1:19, ἃ μέλλει; 2:27; 4:8; 13:14; 14:13; 18:14; 19:14; cf. Charles, 1:cvli).

14.b-b. Variants: (1) ἃ ἐκπορεύεται] original. (2) ἃ ἐκπορεύονται] א. (3) ἐκπορεύεσθαι] 𝔓^{47} א* 051 fam 1006$^{1006\ 1841}$ Andr.

14.c. Variant: the article τόν is omitted before πόλεμον in 𝔓^{47} A 051 fam 1611^{1854}. The article is certainly original, since it refers to the well-known eschatological battle, and is anaphoric in that sense.

14.d-d. Variant: for τῆς ἡμέρας τῆς μεγάλης read τῆς μεγάλης ἡμέρας] 𝔓^{47}.

15.a. A present-tense verb (here ἔρχομαι) is used in this passage and in others in which the author addresses the readers, frequently in Rev 22 (Mussies, *Morphology,* 333).

15.b-b. On the translation "how fortunate," see *Note* 1:3.b.

15.c. ἵνα μή can be understood in a causal sense; cf. *Note* 14:13.f.

15.d. The verb βλέπωσιν is a 3rd pl. present subjunctive, with the 3rd pl. functioning as an impersonal subject, here translated "people." See *Notes* on 2:24; 10:11; 12:6; 13:16; 18:14; 20:4 (Mussies, *Morphology,* 231–32).

15.e. Variants: (1) βλέπουσιν] 𝔓^{47} 051 fam 1611^{2329} 2351 Andr a^{1} e^{2091} i^{2082} Andr Ø$^{181\ 598}$. (2) βλέπουσι] 209 fam 1611^{1854} 2019 Andreas Byz 12^{2048} Byz 2^{2200} Byz 13^{2058} Byz 18^{256} Andr/Byz 3^{35}. (3) βλέπωσιν] א A Andr e^{2057} f l n 94 1773 Byzantine. (4) βλέπωσι] Oecumenius^{2053} TR. Here, apart from the unimportant presence or absence of the movable -ν, the differences probably originate in the phonetic similarity of ω and ου (see Gignac, *Grammar* 1:275–77). Since there are no instances in the NT of ἵνα + present ind., it is very unlikely that βλέπουσι(ν) is the original reading.

15.f. Louw-Nida, § 25.202.

16.a-a. The subject of the 3rd sing. aor. verb συνήγαγεν is πνεύματα in v 14a, for a neut. pl. verb is frequently made the subject of a 3rd sing. verb form. The connection is somewhat obscured by v 15, which is a redactional addition to the text (see *Comment*).

16.b. Variants: (1) συνήγαγεν] *lectio originalis.* (2) συνήγαγον] א vg^{ms} (*congraegaverunt,* MS I); syr^{ph}. Reading (2) is an obvious correction intended to make it clear that the πνεύματα of v 14 is the subject. συνήγαγεν is a 3rd sing. aor. whose subject is the pl. neut. noun πνεύματα, and therefore the verb has been translated as a pl. in harmony with Eng. usage.

16.c. Variant: omit τόν] א Andr c.

16.d. Variants: (1) ποταμόν] A 1773. (2) πόλεμον] cop^{sa}.

16.e. Variants: (1) Ἁρμαγεδών] A א 051 fam 1006 fam 1611^{2329} Andreas Beatus syr^{ph} arab eth. (2) Μαγε[δ]δών] fam 1611^{1611} Oecumenius$^{2053\ 2062}$ Byzantine vg^{mss} syr^{ph} cop$^{bo\ mss}$. Variants in the spelling of reading (1) are numerous: ἀμαγεδών] Andr a^{1} 1773; ἁρμεγεδών] Andr a^{2186} Andr c; ἁρμαγεδόν] Andr n; ἁρμαγεδώμ] Andr g. The name "Harmagedon" in reading (1) is found only in Rev 16:16. Since reading (2), "Megiddo," refers to a Palestinian town where many battles were fought in the OT (several spellings in Heb. and in Gk., the most common of which are Heb. מְגִדּוֹ *mĕgiddô* and Grk. Μαγεδδώ [Judg 5:19]; Μαγεδδώρ [Josh 17:11 A]; Μαγεδαών [4 Kgdms 9:27 B]; Μαγεδδεί [1 Chr 7:29]; Μαγεδώ [Judg 1:27 B; 4 Kgdms 23:29 B]). The various spellings are discussed in *TCGNT*^{2}, 755; *TCGNT*^{2}, 681. In Zech 12:11, the Heb. מְגִדּוֹן *mĕgiddôn* is translated as ἐν πεδίῳ ἐκκοπτομένου, i.e., "in the plane of what is cut down," presumably understanding the word מגדון *mĕgiddôn* to be derived from the Heb. root גדד *gādad*, "to cut down." The known place name in reading (2) was therefore substituted for the unknown place name of reading (1), which is the *lectio difficilior.*

17.a-a. Variants: (1) ὁ ἕβδομος] A 046 fam 1006 fam 1611[1611] Oecumenius[2053text] Andr l; 94 Byzantine. (2) ὁ ἕβδομος ἄγγελος] ℵ[2] (ὁ ζ´ ἄγγελος); 051 fam 1611[1854 2329 2344] Andreas it vg cop[bo] Primasius Beatus. (3) ὁ ἄγγελος ἕβδομος] syr[ph] arab. (4) ὅτε] ℵ.

17.b. Variants: (1) ἐπί] ℵ A 046 Oecumenius[2053 2062] fam 1006 fam 1611[1611 2050] Andr l; 94. (2) εἰς] 051 fam 1611[1854 2329 2344] Andreas.

17.c. Variants: (1) μεγάλη] 𝔓[47] ℵ fam 1006 fam 1611[-2344] Oecumenius[2053 2062] Byzantine. (2) omit μεγάλη] A fam 1611[2344] Andreas.

17.d. Variants: (1) ἐκ] ℵ A 046 fam 1006 fam 1611 Oecumenius[2053 2062] lat syr. (2) ἀπό] Andr f[051 2023 2073] i Byzantine.

17.e. Variants: (1) ναοῦ] 𝔓[47] A fam 1006[1006] Andr l n. Unfortunately, 0163, which closely agrees with A, is ambiguous at this point, for although the reading [τοῦ ναο]ῦ has been restored at the beginning of POxy 848 (= 0163) by the editors, the letters [οὐρανο]ῦ (if uncontracted) fit the available space just as well. (2) οὐρανοῦ in place of ναοῦ] 051* fam 1611[1854] Andreas it[gig]. (3) τοῦ ναοῦ τοῦ οὐρανοῦ] Andr d f[051c-2023-2073] i Byzantine. See the brief discussion in *TCGNT*[2], 681.

17.f-f. Variant: omit] Andr f[051* 2031 2056].

18.a-a. Variants: (1) ἀστραπαὶ καὶ φωναὶ καὶ βρονταί] A (lacuna in C) 0163 fam 1006 Oecumenius[2053] Andr l[1678]; Tischendorf, *NT Graece;* WHort; B. Weiss, *Johannes-Apokalypse,* 205; Charles, 2:336; Merk, *NT;* Nestle-Aland[27]; UBSGNT[4]. (2) ἀστραπαὶ καὶ βρονταὶ καὶ φωναί] 𝔓[47] 051 2329 Byzantine Andr/Byz syr[h]. (3) βρονταὶ καὶ ἀστραπαὶ καὶ φωναὶ καὶ βρονταί] ℵ* cop[bo]. (4) ἀστραπαὶ καὶ βρονταί] Andr l[1778] fam 1611[2344] syr[ph]. The originality of (1) is made probable by the occurrence in 4:5 and 11:19 of the stereotypical expression ἀστραπαὶ καὶ φωναὶ καὶ βρονταί (Schmid, *Studien* 2:227–28). However, 8:5 has similar elements in the phrase, but the textual evidence indicates that no major group of witnesses has a reading that conforms to the pattern of 4:5, 11:19, and 16:18. βρονταὶ καὶ φωναί constitutes a *hendiadys* (i.e., a single complex idea conveyed through two words connected by a conjunction) for "the rumbling of thunder" (cf. 4:5).

18.b. The correlative pronoun οἷος is followed by the pleonastic correlative pronoun τηλικοῦτος in a pattern similar to the Hebraisms found in 2:7, 17; 6:4; 21:6 (Zerwick, *Greek,* § 202; BDR § 297.1).

18.c. Variants: (1) ἄνθρωπος ἐγένετο] A (lacuna in C) Andr Ø[254]; Tischendorf, *NT Graece;* WHort[marg]; B. Weiss, *Johannes-Apokalypse,* 205; Bousset (1906) 400 (in parentheses); Charles, 2:336. (2) ἄνθρωπος ἐγένοντο] 𝔓[47]. (3) ἄνθρωποι ἐγένοντο] ℵ 051 Oecumenius[2053] Andreas Byzantine TR latt syr; Bousset (1906) 400; Charles, 2:51; Merk, *NT.* The problem in part stems from the fact that ἐγέν- occurs four times in this one verse. Reading (1) seems to explain the origin of the other variants (*TCGNT*[1], 755–56).

18.d. The demonstrative pronoun τηλικοῦτος, "so great, so large," is repeated through the use of the redundant phrase οὕτω μέγας, "so great."

19.a-a. γίνεσθαι εἴς τι is a Hebraism or Septuagintism (Gen 20:12; 1 Kgdms 4:19; Jdt 5:18; 1 Macc 2:11, 43; 3:58; Conybeare-Stock, *Septuagint,* 81) that means "to become something," with the prep. εἰς expressing goal or end condition and used to introduce a predicate, as in 8:11, ἐγένετο . . . εἰς ἄψινθον, "it became bitter" (see BDR § 145.1 n. 2; Turner, *Style,* 70). A close parallel to 16:19 occurs in *Jos. As.* 24:20, γεγόνασιν εἰς τέσσαρας ἀρχάς, "they [2,000 fighting men] split into four detachments." For examples, see Matt 19:5; 21:42; Luke 13:19; John 16:20; Acts 5:36; Rom 5:18; 1 John 5:8; Herm. *Sim.* 9.13.5; *1 Clem.* 11:2; Ign. *Eph.* 11:1; *3 Apoc. Bar.* 4:15; *T. Job* 32.11. In a Christian interpolation in *Vit. Proph.* 10.8b, the statement is made that "This is that Jonah who became a type [γενόμενος εἰς τύπον] of the Lord's resurrection."

19.b-b. Variants: (1) αἱ πολῖς αἱ τῶν ἐθνῶν] 𝔓[47]; singular reading. (2) ἡ πόλις τῶν ἐθνῶν] ℵ*. In reading (1), aside from the itacism in πολῖς (αἱ πολῖς is also found in ℵ[1]), the insertion of the second αἱ is an attempt to improve the Gk. style.

19.c. The verb μιμνήσκεσθαι means not only "to remember" but also to be aware of information and to act appropriately (Louw-Nida, § 29.16). It is possible that ἐμνήσθη means that "Babylon the great *was mentioned* before God," i.e., that a prayer for divine retribution upon Babylon had been heard by God (BAGD, 522). In Acts 10:31 there is a close parallel: "Cornelius, your prayer has been heard [εἰσηκούσθη] and your alms remembered before God [ἐμνήσθησαν ἐνώπιον τοῦ θεοῦ]." Yet here ἐμνήσθησαν is a substitute for ἀνέβησαν εἰς μνημόσυνον ἔμπροσθεν τοῦ θεοῦ, "[Your prayers and your alms] have ascended as a memorial before God." However, since an appeal to God to remember is not found in the text of Rev 18, μιμνήσκεσθαι probably means "remember and respond."

19.d-d. δοῦναι is an explanatory or epexegetical inf. that more closely defines the verb ἐμνήσθη (cf. Votaw, *Infinitive,* 14–15). The variant τοῦ before δοῦναι is found in ℵ and Andr i.

19.e-e. In this concatenation of four gens. (on this syntactical phenomenon, see J. H. Moulton, *Grammar* 3:218; a string of *five* gens. is found in Rev 19:15), τοῦ οἴνου, "wine," is a gen. of content, τοῦ θυμοῦ, "fury," is an appositive or epexegetic gen., τῆς ὀργῆς, "wrath," is a gen. of quality (BDR § 165) or a so-called Hebraic gen. (Zerwick, *Greek,* § 40–41), which intensifies the meaning of θυμός, and αὐτοῦ, "his," is a gen. of poss.

19.f. Variant: omit τό] ℵ fam 1006 fam 1611[1854] Oecumenius[2053comm 2062comm] Andr n Andr/Byz 2b[1918] Andr/Byz 3[1551 2061] Andr/Byz 4c[2070].

19.g. Variant: omit τοῦ] ℵ cop[bo].

19.h. Variant: omit αὐτοῦ] ℵ cop[bo] it[gig].

20.a. φεύγειν here can mean either "to rapidly cease to exist, to quickly disappear" (Louw-Nida, § 13.95) or "become invisible, disappear (Louw-Nida, § 24.6).

20.b. The use of εὑρίσκειν in the pass. with a negative particle can mean "disappear" (BAGD, 324), though this idiom does not appear in Louw-Nida. Here 𝔓[47] is alone in attesting a neut. pl. followed by a sing. verb: ὄρη οὐχ εὑρέθη instead of ὄρη οὐχ εὑρέθησαν. This is certainly a scribal improvement, for the sing. verb tends to be used with neut. pl. subjects with a non-personal meaning (BDR § 133). While the author can use a *pl.* verb following a pl. neut. subject (e.g., 1:19, ἅ εἰσίν; 3:2, 4; 5:14; 9:20; 11:18; 15:4; cf. Charles, 1:cvli), he is inconsistent, for there are several instances in which a sing. verb follows a neut. pl. subject (e.g., 1:19, ἅ μέλλει; 2:27; 4:8; 13:14; 14:13; 18:14; 19:14; cf. Charles, 1:cvli).

21.a. οὐρανός here obviously refers to the sky rather than to the dwelling place of God.

21.b. Here ἐκ + gen. can be understood to convey the idea of reason, cause, or occasion (Robertson, *Grammar,* 599; Louw-Nida, § 89.25).

21.c. τῆς χαλάζης can be either a descriptive gen., i.e., "the hail plague," or an epexegetical gen., i.e., "the plague, that is, the hail storm."

21.d. In the phrase ἡ πληγὴ αὐτῆς, lit. "the plague of it," αὐτῆς probably refers back to τῆς χαλάζης and can be translated "that plague." However, since the fem. noun βαβυλὼν ἡ μεγάλη is mentioned in v 19, αὐτῆς could also refer to it and should then be translated "her [i.e., 'Babylon's'] plague" (cf.18:8, αἱ πληγαὶ αὐτῆς). αὕτη is a correction found in two important minuscule MSS (fam 1006[1006] fam 1611[1611]) and in a few other witnesses (Andr c i Byzantine).

Form/Structure/Setting

I. OUTLINE

5. The seven angels with the seven last plagues (15:1–16:21)
    a. Prologue (15:1–4)
        (1) Superscription (v 1)
            (a) Introductory formula: "Then I saw" (v 1a)
            (b) Summary of vision (v 1a–c)
                [1] Another sign (v 1a)
                    [a] Location of sign: in heaven
                    [b] Qualities of sign
                        {1} Great
                        {2} Wonderful
                [2] The nature of the sign: seven angels (v 1bc)
                    [a] With the seven last plagues
                    [b] With these the wrath of God is spent
        (2) Vision of the heavenly court with a hymn of praise sung by victorious martyrs (vv 2–4)
            (a) Introductory vision formula: "Then I saw" (v 2a)
            (b) Setting of the hymn (v 2a–c)
                [1] A sea of glass mingled with fire (v 2a)

[2] Those who were victorious (v 2bc)
[a] Over the beast (v 2b)
{1} Over its cult statue
{2} Over the number of its name
[b] They stand by the sea of glass (v 2c)
[c] They have the kitharas of God (v 2c)
(c) The hymn title: The song of Moses and the Lamb (v 3a)
(d) Descriptive hymn of praise in "you style" (vv 3b–4)
[1] Praise of God (v 3bc)
[2] Rhetorical question (v 4a)
[3] Reasons for praise (v 4bc)
[a] You alone are holy (v 4b)
[b] All nations will come to worship before you (v 4b)
[c] Your righteous judgments are evident (v 4c)
b. The commission of the seven angels (vv 5–8)
(1) Introductory vision formula: "After this I saw" (v 5a)
(2) The setting in the vision (vv 5b–6)
(a) The temple or the tent of witness (v 5b)
[1] Location: in heaven
[2] Condition: open
(b) Appearance of the angels with the seven plagues (v 6)
[1] They emerge from the temple
[2] They are clothed in pure, shining linen
[3] They have golden sashes around their waists
(3) The commissioning ceremony (vv 7–8)
(a) Distribution of the bowls (v 7)
[1] By one of the four cherubim
[2] Given to the seven angels
[3] Content of bowls: full of the wrath of the eternal God
(b) Divine manifestation (v 8)
[1] The temple is filled with smoke (v 8a)
[a] From the glory of God
[b] From the power of God
[2] No one is able to enter the temple until the seven plagues have been accomplished (v 8b)
c. The seven last plagues (16:1–21)
(1) The commission of the bowl angels (v 1)
(a) Source of command: an unidentified voice (v 1a)
[1] Quality of voice: loud
[2] Location of voice: from the temple
(b) Content of command (v 1b)
[1] Be on your way
[2] Begin pouring out the seven bowls
[a] Content of bowls: the wrath of God
[b] Destination: upon the earth
(2) The bowl angels go forth (vv 2–21)
(a) The first angel with the first bowl (v 2)
[1] Action: poured out on the earth (v 2a)

[2] Result: painful sores afflict those who worship the beast (v 2b)
(b) The second angel with the second bowl (v 3)
[1] Action: poured into the sea (v 3a)
[2] Primary result: sea turned to blood (v 3b)
[3] Secondary result: all sea life dies (v 3b)
(c) The third angel with the third bowl (vv 4–7)
[1] Action: poured into rivers and springs (v 4a)
[2] Primary result: rivers and springs turn to blood (v 4b)
[3] Antiphonal hymns (vv 5–7)
[a] Judgment doxology (vv 5–6)
[b] Affirmative response from the altar (v 7)
(d) The fourth angel with the fourth bowl (vv 8–9)
[1] Action: poured out on the sun (v 8)
[2] Primary result: sun scorches people (v 9a)
[3] Secondary results of those afflicted (v 9bc)
[a] They curse God's name (v 9b)
[b] They do not repent (v 9c)
(e) The fifth angel with the fifth bowl (vv 10–11)
[1] Action: poured out on the throne of the beast (v 10a)
[2] Primary result:
[a] Darkness covers the throne of the beast (v 10a)
[b] Darkness covers the kingdom of the beast (v 10b)
[3] Secondary results:
[a] People bite their tongues in pain (v 10c)
[b] People curse God (v 11a)
[c] People do not repent (v 11b)
(f) The sixth angel and the sixth bowl (vv 12–16)
[1] Action: poured out on the the great river Euphrates (v 12a)
[2] Result:
[a] The river dries up (v 12b)
[b] Preparing the way for the kings from the east (v 12c)
[3] Demonic spirits summon the kings of the world to battle (vv 13–14)
[4] Parenthetical promise of the Parousia and exhortation to faithfulness (v 15)
[5] The armies assemble at Harmagedon (v 16)
(g) The seventh angel with the seventh bowl (vv 17–21)
[1] Action: poured into the air (v 17a)
[2] Commentary: voice from the throne announces "It is finished" (v 17b)
[3] Atmospheric and seismic disturbances (v 18)
[a] Earthquake splits "the great city" into three parts (v 19a)
[b] Cities of the nations fall (v 19b)
[c] Islands and mountains disappear (v 20)
[d] Hundred-pound hailstones fall and people curse God (v 21)

II. Literary Analysis

The narrative of the seven bowls containing the seven last plagues in Rev 15:1–16:21 has a literary character that differs from either the narrative of the opening of the seven seals (6:1–8:1) or that of the seven trumpets (8:2–11:18) in several respects: (1) Once the pouring out of the seven bowl plagues commences in 16:2, there are no extended sections that interrupt or expand the narrative. (2) Stereotypical motifs and formulas occur more frequently in 15:1–16:21 than in the other heptads. (3) There are more verbal links to earlier textual units than in the other heptads, giving the distinct impression that much of 15:1–16:21 was formulated at a relatively late stage in the composition of the entire book.

A new unit of text is introduced in 15:1 with the phrase "Then I saw another great and wonderful sign in heaven." The phrase "then I saw" (καὶ εἶδον) is used thirty-two times in Revelation, sometimes to introduce major textual units (6:1; 8:2; 10:1; 13:1; 14:1; 19:11; 20:1; 21:1) but more frequently to introduce obviously subordinate textual units. The phrase "another sign," however, is the third such sign referred to in Revelation. The first two are mentioned in 12:1, 3. Since the seer could not have seen the seven angels with the seven last plagues until they emerged from the heavenly temple-tabernacle in 15:5–6 and received the seven bowls filled with the wrath of God from one of the cherubim in 15:7 (Wellhausen, *Analyse,* 25), the use of the phrase ἄλλο σημεῖον "another sign," therefore, is a literary device to connect 15:2–16:21 with the previous narrative and functions as a *title* or *superscription* for the entire text unit. Wellhausen (*Analyse,* 25) regards this textual unit as beginning with v 1 and concluding with vv 2–4, with the central portion missing (he speculates that the missing portion may have had essentially the same content as the plagues effected by each of the seven bowls).

The second unit of text, 15:2–4, is introduced with the formula καὶ εἶδον, another indication that 15:1 is a separate textual subunit. 15:2–4 contains a narrative introduction (15:2–3a) and a focal hymnic section in 15:3b–4 and functions as an introductory heavenly throne-room scene (cf. 4:1–5:14; 8:2–5), though neither the throne itself nor the presence of God is specifically mentioned. In form, this hymn is a descriptive hymn of praise (Deichgräber, *Gotteshymnus*, 55). It is introduced as the song of Moses the servant of God and the song of the Lamb (v 3a), though it exhibits no clear literary relationship to either the song of Moses celebrating the victory of the Exodus in Exod 15:1–18 or the song of Moses in Deut 31:30–32:43 (Schüssler Fiorenza, *Revelation*, 135). Another reworking of the song of Moses from Exod 15:1–18 is found in Isa 12:1–6, which consists of two thanksgiving hymns (vv 1–2, 4–6), written to be sung when God brings the exiles back in a new Exodus (Isa 11:11–16). In the first hymn, Isa 12:2 clearly alludes to Exod 15:2, and in the second hymn, Isa 12:5a alludes to Exod 15:1.

The third unit of text is found in 15:5–8, and the importance of this section is indicated by the introductory formula (καὶ) μετὰ ταῦτα εἶδον, "and after these things I saw," which occurs just four times in Revelation and in every instance is used to introduce a major textual unit (4:1; 7:1 [μετὰ τοῦτο εἶδον]; here; 18:1). Since 15:5 appears to be an exception to this rule, it is likely that 15:1–4 was prefixed to a unit of text that narrated the seven bowl plagues. In its present context, 15:5–8 serves as an introduction to the bowl vision of 16:1–21.

The fourth unit of text consists of 16:1–21, a narrative of the pouring out of each of the seven bowls upon the earth and their resultant effects. In 16:1, the bowl angels receive a (divine) commission instructing them to pour out their bowls upon the earth. In the narrative that follows, there is a striking absence of symmetry among the seven subunits of text.

1. The plague unleashed by the *first bowl* (Rev 16:2), which is poured out on the earth (the explicit command of the voice from the temple in v 1), affects only people who had received the brand of the beast and worshiped its image. The motif of worshiping the *image* of the beast is first mentioned in 13:15, while the brand of the beast on the right hand or forehead is first mentioned in 13:16. These two motifs are thereafter combined and mentioned five times (14:9, 11; 16:2; 19:20; 20:4; see *Comment* on 14:9 for fuller discussion).

2. The *second bowl* (16:3) is poured out on the sea, which became blood, causing all sea creatures to die. This is parallel to the effects of the second trumpet, which causes one-third of the sea to become blood, killing one-third of the sea animals and destroying one-third of the ships (8:8–9).

3. The *third bowl* (16:4–7) is poured out on the rivers and springs (τοὺς ποταμοὺς καὶ τὰς πηγὰς τῶν ὑδάτων), causing them to be turned to blood (v 4). While v 4 belongs to the original composition, vv 5–7 have been added (Yarbro Collins, *CBQ* 39 [1977] 372–73); that is, vv 5–7 were either composed expressly for insertion in this particular literary setting or are a fragment from another text. The secondary character of both the introduction to the hymn in v 5a (καὶ ἤκουσα τοῦ ἀγγέλου τῶν ὑδάτων λέγοντος) and the hymn of the angel of the water in vv 5b–7 is suggested by the *allegorical* interpretation of blood, which is used to refer to divine punishment following the pattern of *lex talionis* (i.e., they shed the blood of the prophets, so God gave them blood to drink [vv 5–6]); i.e., the angel functions here as an *angelus interpres,* though the explanation is not given in response to a question by the seer. Another indication of the secondary character of vv 5b–7 is the presence of the divine title "who is and who was," drawn from elsewhere in Revelation (the title "who is and who was" occurs elsewhere only in 11:17; the tripartite title "who is and who was and who is to come" occurs in 1:4, 8; 4:8). The third trumpet (8:10–11) also affected the rivers and the fountains (τῶν ποταμῶν καὶ ἐπὶ τὰς πηγὰς τῶν ὑδάτων), but rather than turn them to blood, it caused them to become bitter and poisonous, and hence unpotable. Charles (2:122) restores this hymn after 19:4, but on somewhat flimsy grounds.

The hymn in 16:5b–6 is in the form of a *Gerichtsdoxologie,* "judgment doxology" (Deichgräber, *Gotteshymnus,* 56; cf. von Rad, *Wisdom,* 196–97, 211–13; id., *OT Theology,* 1:357–59; R. Knierim, *Die Hauptbegriffe für Sünde im Alten Testament* [Gütersloh: Mohn, 1965] 125–26; Betz, *JTC* 6 [1969] 139), which often begins with the phrase δίκαιος εἶ κύριε, "righteous are you, O Lord" (in Hebrew צדיק אתה יהוה *ṣaddîq ʾattâ YHWH*). This form is found occasionally in the LXX (Ps 118:137[MT 119:137]; Jer 12:1; Dan 3:27 [additions to Daniel not in MT]; Esth 4:17n [additions to Esther not in MT]; Tob 3:2) and other early Jewish literature (*Apoc. Moses* 27:5). There are two further examples of the "judgment doxology" in Revelation (16:7b; 19:1–2). Staples, who attempts to refute the contention (which he erroneously attributes to Betz) that a "judgment doxology" is an "apocalyptic pericope," prefers the designation "vindication formula" (apparently ignorant that this term is used in German OT form criticism), for it characteristically occurs in contexts in which the righteousness or justice of God has been questioned. This particular stereotypical introduction, however, occurs infrequently. The *content* of the "judgment doxology," however, is more characteristic than the stereotyped introductory phrase and centers on the affirmation (in both hymns and prayers) that the divine punishments meted out by God are both just and appropriate (2 Chr 12:6; Ezra 9:15; Neh 9:33; Pss 7:11; 9:4; Jer 46:28; 3 Macc 2:3). In this hymn, vv 5b–6 and v 7b belong together (Deichgräber, *Gotteshymnus,* 46), a relationship that Jörns (*Evangelium* , 132) sees as antiphonal.

H. D. Betz has argued that the Hellenistic "elements of the cosmos" (earth, air, fire, water) played a more prominent role in the traditions behind Revelation than they do in the present text of Revelation and that the judgment doxology of vv 5–7 is therefore derived from an older tradition that reflects an interest in the four elements. His discussion is intended to demonstrate that apocalypticism is not a phenomenon found only within early Judaism but is rather an aspect of Jewish and Hellenistic religious syncretism, for Rev 6:4–7 exhibits an affinity to a wide range of Hellenistic religious literature. The Exodus plague tradition, reinterpreted eschatologically in Revelation in the heptads of trumpets (8:7–9:21; 11:15–19) and bowls (16:1–21), for example, was already linked to the four elements in Hellenistic Judaism (Philo *Mos.* 96–146; Betz's reference to Wis 12ff. in this connection is problematic). In particular, in the judgment doxology found in 16:5–7, the "angel of the waters" is a Jewish variant of the Hellenistic view that the waters (as well as the other basic elements of the cosmos) are supernatural beings (Wis 13:2). Betz argues that the closest parallel to Rev 16:5–7 is the Hermetic treatise *Corp. Herm.* 23, "Kore Kosmou" (Nock-Festugière, *Hermès Trismégiste* 4:1–22), where the four elements, polluted by humans killing each other, cry out to God for purification (*Corp. Herm.* 23.54–63). Of the four complaints, the most relevant is that of Water (tr. W. Scott, *Hermetica* 1:489):

> Next, my magnanimous son, Water was given leave to speak and spoke thus: "O Father, self-begotten, and Maker of Nature, that power which generates all things to give thee pleasure, it is high time for thee to give command that my streams be kept pure; for the rivers and the seas are ever washing off the defilement of the slayers, and receiving the corpses of the slain."

The Father of All responds to these complaints by sending Osiris and Isis to help the world by infusing it with that which is divine and by introducing religious ritual on earth. In *Corp. Herm.* 23, as well as in other texts adduced by Betz (e.g., *1 Enoch* 7:6, "Then the earth complained about the lawless ones"; cf. *1 Enoch* 9:2), the real evil in the world is murder and the pollution that it causes.

There are, however, a number of serious weaknesses in the arguments proposed by Betz (the following critique is partly dependent on A. Yarbro Collins, *CBQ* 39 [1977] 367–81): (1) Rather than reflecting an older tradition, Rev 16:5–7 (which really consists of two complementary hymnic pieces, vv 5b–6 and v 7b) appears to have been largely composed by the author at a relatively late stage in the composition of Revelation (for details see *Comments* on vv 5–7). While five of the seven plagues involve *earth* (the first bowl, 16:2), *water* (the second bowl is poured on the sea which turns to blood, 16:3; the third bowl is poured on the rivers and fountains, which also turn to blood, 16:4–7), *fire* (the fourth bowl is poured on the sun, which scorches people with fire, 16:8–9), and *air* (the seventh bowl is poured into the air, resulting in the eschatological consummation, 16:17–21), such a fourfold schema is not evidenced in the present text of Revelation and cannot be reconstructed with any assurance from the presumed sources of Revelation. (2) While the present version of Revelation admittedly exhibits little interest in the traditional four cosmic elements of Hellenism, the view that Rev 16:5–7 *presupposes* such an interest (i.e., the fact that only the element of water is involved constitutes the tip of the iceberg) can only be sustained if the parallels adduced by Betz are convincing (i.e., reveal the rest of the iceberg). (3) Unfortunately, the parallel with *Corp. Herm.* 23.58 is problematic, for there water has been (involuntarily) polluted by the blood and corpses of murdered people and cries out for purification. However, in Rev 16:5–7 the rivers and springs have not been polluted by the shedding of blood; rather they have been turned to blood as an act of divine judgment, though the deadly effects of this judgment have not been elaborated as they were by Philo (*Mos.* 1.98–101) and Josephus (*Ant.* 2.294–95).

4. The *fourth bowl* (16:8–9) was poured on the sun, causing it to scorch people, while the fourth trumpet is only said to darken one-third of the sun, moon, and stars (8:12).

5. The *fifth bowl* (16:10–11) is poured out on the throne of the beast (mentioned earlier only in 13:2, so this reference, like that in 16:2, constitutes another link with Rev 13), plunging his kingdom into darkness (cf. Exod 10:21). This suggests that this unit was composed *after* Rev 13.

6. The *sixth bowl* (16:12–16) causes the Euphrates to be dried up, thus opening the way for an invasion of the kings of the east. With the sixth trumpet (9:13–21), the angels bound at the Euphrates are released, thus causing an enormous army to kill one-third of the human race. The sixth plague is unique in that the *effects* of the pouring out of the sixth bowl are not immediate, though anyone familiar with this particular eschatological scenario would know that this is a prelude for the final eschatological struggle. This plague involves the gathering of a great army, which is briefly mentioned in a redactional passage in 17:14 and further discussed in 19:19–21. That 16:12–16 is "continued" suggests that a textual unit consisting originally of 16:12–16 and 19:19–21 has been interrupted in order to accommodate the extensive section on Babylon, which extends from 16:19b to 19:10, and the introduction of the heavenly warrior in 19:11–16. This is suggested in part by the awkward juxtaposition of two separation motifs in 16:19 (see below under 16:17–21). Further, the evil trinity of the dragon, the beast, and the false prophet is mentioned in v 13 (another reference back to Rev 13), though in 16:13 the beast from the land is first designated the "false prophet." The mention of these three also in part confirms the organic unity of 16:13–14, 16 with 19:19–21, for in 19:20 the beast and the false prophet are cast into the lake of fire. Let us juxtapose these passages, and then compare them with the eschatological attack of the Parthians and Medes upon the Holy Land in *1 Enoch* 56:5–8.

Rev 16:13–14 Then I saw [καὶ εἶδον] three unclean spirits like frogs
from the mouth of the dragon
and from the mouth of the beast
and from the mouth of the false prophet.
For they are spirits, that is, demons, producing signs, who travel to the kings of the whole world to gather [συναγαγεῖν] them for the battle on the great day of God the Almighty.

Rev 16:16	The demonic spirits gathered them together [συνήγαγεν] to the place called Armageddon in Hebrew.
Rev 19:19–21	Then I saw [καὶ εἶδον] the beast and the kings of the earth and their armies assembled [συνηγμένα] to wage war with the one mounted on the steed and with his army. The beast was captured and with him the false prophet who performed signs on his authority, by which he deceived those who received the brand of the beast and who worshiped his cultic image; they were both hurled alive into the lake of fire burning with sulfur. The rest were slain with the sword projecting from the mouth of the one mounted on the steed, and all the birds feasted on their carrion.
1 Enoch 56:5–8	[5]And in those days the angels will gather together, and will throw themselves towards the east upon the Parthians and Medes; they will stir up the kings, so that a disturbing spirit will come upon them, and they will drive them from their thrones; and they will come out like lions from their lairs, and like hungry wolves in the middle of their flocks. [6]And they will go up and trample upon the land of my chosen ones, and the land of my chosen ones will become for them a tramping-ground and a beaten track. [7]But the city of my righteous ones will be a hindrance to their horses, and they will stir up slaughter amongst themselves, and their (own) right hand will be strong against them; and a man will not admit to knowing his neighbour or his brother, nor a son his father or his mother, until through death there are corpses enough, and their punishment—it will not be in vain. [8]And in those days Sheol will open its mouth, and they will sink into it; and their destruction—Sheol will swallow up the sinners before the face of the chosen. (tr. Knibb, *Enoch*)

Actually Rev 16:12–16 consists of *three* textual units: (1) v 12, (2) vv 13–14 and 16 (note that καὶ εἶδον introduces v 13, thereby indicating a new theme or textual unit, that the verb συνάγειν, "to gather," is a catchword linking v 14 with v 16 [and with 19:19], where the mention of the dragon, the beast, and the false prophet appears intrusive, and that "the kings of the entire world" are in tension with "the kings of the east" [mentioned in v 12]), and (3) v 15, an interpolated exhortation (framed by vv 13–14 and 16) that is more in character with 2:1–3:22 and 22:5–21 than with the body of Revelation.

7. The *seventh bowl* (16:17–21) is poured out into the air and causes the destruction of "the great city" (v 19). This unit of text serves as a conclusion to the section on the seven angels with the seven bowls of the wrath of God (15:1–16:21) and at the same time as an introduction to the extensive section on the fall of Babylon (17:1–19:10). This section appears to have been altered in order to serve as an introduction to 17:1–18:24, for in v 19a "the great city" (i.e., Babylon-Rome) is split into three parts, which certainly means its destruction by earthquake, and then immediately after the destruction of the cities of the nations is mentioned, v 19b says that "God remembered great Babylon," as if that city had not been mentioned (and destroyed) in v 19a. Therefore, 16:19b appears to be an interpolation into the seventh bowl plague in 16:17–21 for the purpose of making a transition to the section on Babylon that follows in 17:1–18:24.

There are common to all of the sections of text in Rev 16 a number of features that describe the pouring out of the seven bowls of the wrath of God: (1) a numbered angel pours out his bowl, (2) the devastating effects of the plague are described, and (optionally) (3) the unrepentant human response to the plague is mentioned (vv 9, 11, 21). The third and sixth plagues are distinctive.

III. Stereotypical Features of Rev 16:1–21

There are more stereotypical features evident in the composition of the vision of the seven bowls in 16:1–21 than in any of the two other series of seven plagues narrated in Revelation, the seven seals (6:1–17; 8:1) and the seven trumpets (8:7–9:22; 11:15–19). H.-P. Müller has suggested that the narratives of the outpouring of the seven bowls consist of five motifs:

1. The angels who bring the seven last plagues are empowered (15:5–16:1), i.e., they receive the seven bowls from the four cherubim (15:7), and they are commissioned by an unidentified voice from the heavenly temple (16:1).

2. Each individual vision begins with the stereotypical expression καί [the X (angel)] ἐξέχεεν τὴν φιάλην αὐτοῦ εἰς/ἐπί . . . , "Then [the X (angel)] poured his bowl upon the . . ." (16:2a, 3a, 4a, 8a, 10a, 12a, 17a). The contents of the bowls are poured out seriatim on the earth (16:2a), the sea (v 3a), the rivers and springs (v 4a), the sun (v 8a), the throne of the beast (v 10a), the river Euphrates (v 12a), and the air (v 17a). Only in the case of the first angel is the verb of motion ἀπῆλθεν used (16:2a) to correspond to the command to go (ὑπάγετε in 16:1).

3. The effects of the pouring out of five of the seven bowls is introduced with the stereotyped expression καὶ ἐγένετο, "and [it] happened," "with the result that":

Vision 1 (v 2b):	καὶ ἐγένετο ἕλκος
Vision 2 (v 3b):	καὶ ἐγένετο αἷμα ὡς νεκροῦ
Vision 3 (v 4b):	καὶ ἐγένετο αἷμα
Vision 5 (v 10b):	καὶ ἐγένετο ἡ βασιλεία αὐτοῦ ἐσκοτωμένη
Vision 7 (v 18a):	καὶ ἐγένοντο ἀστραπαὶ καὶ φωναὶ καὶ βρονταί
(v 18b):	καὶ σεισμὸς ἐγένετο μέγας . . .
(v 19a):	καὶ ἐγένετο ἡ πόλις ἡ μεγάλη εἰς τρία μέρη

The formulaic character of καὶ ἐγένετο is revealed in v 19a, where we find the unfelicitous clause καὶ ἐγένετο . . . εἰς τρία μέρη, "and . . . into three parts happened." Variations on this ἐγένετο formula occur in connection with the fifth seal (6:12) and the seventh seal (8:1) and with the first trumpet (8:7b), the second trumpet (8:8c), and the third trumpet (8:11b).

4. Most of the visions then speak of the effects of the plague on those living beings within the affected area (visions 1 and 3 are exceptions):

Vision 2 (v 3b):	καὶ πᾶσα ψυχὴ ζωῆς ἀπέθανεν
Vision 4 (v 9a):	καὶ ἐκαυματίσθησαν οἱ ἄνθρωποι
Vision 5 (v 10c):	καὶ ἐμασῶντο τὰς γλώσσας αὐτῶν
Vision 6 (v 12c):	ἵνα ἑτοιμασθῇ ἡ ὁδὸς τῶν βασιλέων
[Vision 7 (v 19a):	καὶ ἐγένετο ἡ πόλις ἡ μεγάλη εἰς τρία μέρη]

5. In three instances the negative response of people to the plague is mentioned:

Vision 4 (v 9bc):	καὶ ἐβλασφήμησαν . . . καὶ οὐ μετενόησαν
Vision 5 (v 11):	καὶ ἐβλασφήμησαν . . . καὶ οὐ μετενόησαν
Vision 7 (v 21b):	καὶ ἐβλασφήμησαν

Comment

1a καὶ εἶδον ἄλλο σημεῖον ἐν τῷ οὐρανῷ μέγα καὶ θαυμαστόν, "Then I saw another great and wonderful sign in heaven." (On the introductory vision formula καὶ εἶδον, see *Comment* on 5:1.) V 1 functions as a summary or title of 15:2–16:21 (see *Comment* on 1b). The phrase "another sign" designates a *third* heavenly sign, perhaps a constellation, which refers back to the two previous signs or constellations referred to in 12:1 and 12:3 and subsequently interpreted (note the three heavenly signs in *Did.* 16:6 discussed in the *Comment* on 12:1). This is an editorial attempt to link Rev 15–16 more closely to the preceding visions. The coordinated adjectives μέγα καὶ θαυμαστόν, "great and wonderful," are paired in Revelation only here and in 15:3. Deut 28:59 refers to מַכּוֹת גְּדֹלֹת וְנֶאֱמָנוֹת ***makkôt gĕdōlôt*** *wĕneʾĕmānôt,* "plagues great and lasting" (LXX πληγὰς μεγάλας καὶ θαυμαστάς, "plagues great and wonderful"; see Tob 12:22). The Greek version (Syncellus) of *1 Enoch* 8:3 greatly expands the list of angels who taught esoteric sciences, including astrological lore (Black, *Apocalypsis,* 22): "the eighth taught the signs of the sun [τὰ σημεῖα τοῦ ἡλίου]; the twentieth taught the signs of the moon [τὰ σημεῖα τῆς σελήνης]."

1b ἀγγέλους ἑπτὰ ἔχοντας πληγὰς ἑπτὰ τὰς ἐσχάτας, "seven angels with the seven last plagues." The masculine plural accusative noun ἀγγέλους, "angels," is in apposition to ἄλλο σημεῖον, "another sign" (v 1a), which more closely defines it (cf. 12:1, 3, where a similar grammatical phenomenon occurs). This scene might initially appear anachronistic or unconnected with vv 5–8 since the seer could not see the seven angels with the seven last plagues *before* they had emerged from the heavenly temple, described in v 6, and *before* they had received the libation bowls, described in v 7 (Wellhausen, *Analyse,* 25). Some have therefore judged 15:1 to be an interpolation into the text (Charles, 2:29–32). However, it appears likely that this verse is rather a *summary* of the vision reported in 15:2–16:21 and therefore functions as a title or superscription (Bousset [1906] 394–95; Lohse, 86; Beasley-Murray, 233–34), analogous to 17:1–2 (see *Comments* there). This superscription introduces two separate scenes, the first in vv 2–4, introduced with καὶ εἶδον, "then I saw," and the second in vv 5–8, introduced with καὶ μετὰ ταῦτα εἶδον, "after this I saw." The first scene in vv 2–4 appears to be a later insertion, for in content it exhibits no connections with v 1 or with vv 5–8. Yet the reference to the glassy sea in v 2 (see 4:6) indicates that this is a throne-room scene and is placed here by design as part of vv 2–8, which constitute a throne-room scene similar to those that introduce each heptad (see 4:1–5:14, which introduces the seven seals, and 8:1–5, which introduces the seven trumpets). The phrase "seven plagues" is used of the bowl plagues (15:1, 6, 8; 21:9), while the phrase "the seven last plagues" occurs only in 15:1 and 21:9. The description of the plagues as the seven *last* plagues connects them with the earlier series of plagues connected with the seven seals (6:1–17; 8:1) and the seven trumpets (8:1–9:21; 11:15–18), though neither of these series is called "plagues" (with the possible, but unlikely, exception of 9:20). The divine punishments narrated in Revelation are referred to collectively as "plagues" in 22:18, and the fire, smoke, and sulfur associated with the sixth trumpet are called "these three plagues" (9:18).

1c ὅτι ἐν αὐταῖς ἐτελέσθη ὁ θυμὸς τοῦ θεοῦ, "for with them the wrath of God was spent." The aorist passive verb ἐτελέσθη (see 10:7, καὶ ἐτελέσθη τὸ μυστήριον τοῦ θεοῦ, "and the mystery of God was accomplished") is a passive of divine activity indicating that it is God who who concludes history. The term τελεῖν is used of the fulfillment of OT prophecy or of the word of God (Rev 10:7; 17:17; Luke 18:31; 22:37; Acts 13:29). The phrase "the wrath of God" occurs six times in Revelation (14:10, 19; 15:1, 7; 16:1; cf. 19:15). In the OT the phrase אַף יהוה *ʾap YHWH,* "anger of the Lord," occurs about forty times and can be translated (ὁ) θυμὸς (τοῦ) κυρίου or (ἡ) ὀργὴ (τοῦ) κυρίου (Num 16:22; 32:14; 2 Kgs 22:13; 2 Chr 34:21; 36:16; Isa 30:33; 34:2; 51:20), while the term אַף אֱלֹהִים *ʾap ʾĕlōhîm,* "anger of God," occurs just twice (Num 22:22; Ps 78:31). In the Dead Sea Scrolls the phrase אף אל *ʾap ʾēl,* "anger of God," occurs more frequently (1QM 4:1; 6:3; CD 1:21; 3:8; 10:9; 20:16; see *DCH* 1:354). In the OT the anger of the Lord is brought about by Israel's rebellion against the kingship and rule of God and is therefore primarily an inner-Israel phenomenon in which the anger of the Lord is expressed against Israel as both punishment and correction (*TDOT* 1:357; G. A. Herion in *ABD* 6:994). In later writers the wrath of the Lord is transformed into an eschatological event (Isa 26:20; Ezek 7:19; 22:24; Zeph 1:15, 18;2:2–3; *1 Enoch* 62:12; 1QM 3:9; 1QH 15:17; 1QS 4:12). During the post-exilic period the anger of the Lord was at times thought to be directed against other nations, primarily because of their interference with Israel (Isa 13:1–22; Obad 1–14; Nah 1:2; *Jub.* 24:30), but there are other texts in which the wrath of God directed toward the nations appears to be unrelated to their relationship with Israel (Jer 10:25–26; Zeph 3:8). The eschatological wrath of God expressed against the inhabitants of the earth in Revelation presupposes a universal divine law or standard, repeated violations of which are now thought to have caused a final eschatological manifestation of the wrath of God (A. T. Hanson, *Wrath,* 85, 110; Dunn, *Romans* 1:54). In the NT the wrath or anger of God is primarily used in an eschatological sense of the final judgment of God (Luke 3:7 = Matt 3:7; Rom 1:18; 2:5,8; 3:5; 5:9; Col 3:6; Eph 5:6), which can be escaped through faith in Christ (John 3:36; Rom 5:9; 1 Thess 1:10; 5:9). While the wrath or anger of God is obviously an anthropomorphism, the focus of this metaphor is the anticipation that those who violate the laws of God will be punished.

2a καὶ εἶδον ὡς θάλασσαν ὑαλίνην μεμιγμένην πυρί, "Then I saw something like a sea of glass mingled with fire." (On the introductory vision formula καὶ εἶδον, see *Comment* on 5:1.) Vv 2–8 describe a heavenly court scene used to introduce God's punitive action on earth (4:1–5:14; 8:2–5). The comparative particle ὡς is used in a distinctive way typical of apocalyptic visions to emphasize the mysterious and enigmatic character of what is seen (Dan 7:4, 7, 13; 4 Ezra 11:37; 14:39; Volz, *Eschatologie,* 11–12). ὡς is used similarly in Rev 4:6; 5:6; 6:6; 8:8; 9:7; 13:2; 14:2; 19:6. The anarthrous comparative phrase ὡς θάλασσα ὑαλίνη, "like a sea of glass," was mentioned in 4:6 as part of a throne scene (see *Comment* on 4:6). This second use of the same phrase is unaccountably anarthrous, though it is, as one would expect, repeated with the definite article in v 2c. The "sea of glass mingled with fire" combines the motifs of a celestial sea above which the throne of God is set (see *Comment* on 4:6) and the river (or rivers) of fire that flows forth from his throne (Dan 7:10; *1 Enoch* 14:19; 71:2; *3 Enoch* 18:19 [four fiery rivers]; 19:4 [the mention of four fiery rivers that flow from God's throne is an allusion to Gen 2:10–14]; 33:4 [seven rivers of fire]; 36:1–2; 37:1; *Sepher ha-Razim* 7 [tr. Morgan, 81]; for rabbinic references, see P. Alexander in Charlesworth, *OTP* 1:273 n. a2). The phrase "mingled with fire," absent from 4:6, is probably included here to symbolize impending judgment (Lohmeyer, 130). Though this is, of course, a *heavenly* reality, the corresponding cosmic counterpart is the lake of fire (19:20; 20:10, 14[2x], 15; 21:8), which is the place of eternal punishment for unbelievers.

2b καὶ τοὺς νικῶντας ἐκ τοῦ θηρίου καὶ ἐκ τῆς εἰκόνος αὐτοῦ καὶ ἐκ τοῦ ἀριθμοῦ τοῦ ὀνόματος αὐτοῦ, "and those who were victorious over the beast, that is, over its image and over the number of its name." This is probably a redactional addition to an earlier version by the author-editor (Wellhausen, *Analyse,* 25). Outside of Rev 2–3, the term νικᾶν is used of Christians conquering only in 12:11 and 21:7 (both interpolations). The meaning of the verb νικᾶν, "to be victorious," is restricted by the unexpected prepositional phrase ἐκ τοῦ θηρίου, "over the beast," where the simple accusative τὸ θηρίον, "the beast," would be appropriate. This is a very difficult form of expression; the verb νικᾶν + ἐκ does not occur in any other Greek texts. Yet similar expressions are found using the noun νίκη, "victory." Pindar used νίκη this way in *Isthmian Ode* 7.21–22, φέρει γὰρ Ἰσθμοῖ νίκαν παγκρατίου, "At the Isthmus he brought victory *in the pancratium*" (here παγκρατίου is an objective genitive; cf. the use of νίκη with the objective genitive in Aristophanes *Equites* 521 and Plato *Leges* 840C, τῆς τῶν ἡδονῶν νίκης, "victory *over* pleasures"). In another passage in Pindar, νίκη + ἀπό with the genitive is used in *Isthmian Ode* 6.60–61, ἄραντο γὰρ νίκας ἀπὸ παγκρατίου τρεῖς ἀπ' Ἰσθμοῦ, "For they carried off three victories *in the pancratium* from the Isthmus."

The expression νικᾶν + ἐκ in this verse has been construed in three very different ways, (1) as a *constructio praegnans,* (2) as an Aramaism, and (3) as a Latinism (Aune, *JBL* 110 [1991] 691–92). Beckwith's suggestion (674) that the preposition ἐκ is used with the idea of "coming off victorious from" (Thayer, *Lexicon,* 426) is semantically unlikely since he cites no parallels. (1) *As a constructio praegnans.* In understanding the phrase as a *constructio praegnans,* i.e., an elliptical or brachylogical expression, Stuart (2:305) suggests that the idea of σωζόμενοι, "being saved," is implied, a term that would naturally be used with the preposition ἐκ. Turner (*Style,* 260) proposes that a phrase meaning "by separating themselves from" or "and delivered themselves from" be supplied. BDR § 212.3 (accepted by Prigent, 239 n. 4) suggests that τοὺς νικῶντας ἐκ τοῦ θηρίου means τηρήσαντας ἑαυτοὺς ἐκ τοῦ θηρίου, "guarding themselves from the beast." (2) *As an Aramaism.* Torrey (*Apocalypse,* 108–9) argued that the translator of Revelation used νικᾶν here as the standard translation of the Aramaic verb זכא *zĕkāʾ,* which means "pure, clean, innocent," for in the courts of law the "innocent" man is "victorious." The Hebrew verb זכה *zākâ* is used with מן *min* (= ἐκ) with the meaning "innocent of," and Torrey cites a number of passages exhibiting this construction (Num 5:31; Josh 2:17, 20; 2 Sam 3:28; Ps 19:14). The problem, however, is that all these passages have the Hebrew verb נקה *niqqâ,* not זכה *zākâ,* thus considerably weakening his case. Since (according to Torrey) νικᾶν is used to translate זכא *zĕkāʾ* in Rev 15:2, the meaning is "those who *are innocent* of the beast, and of his image, and of the number of his name." According to Torrey, the notion of conquering is completely missing. The chief difficulty with Torrey's imaginative solution to the problem of νικᾶν ἐκ in Rev15:2 is that it does not make sense to say that someone is "*innocent* of the beast," unless it is taken to mean "*undefiled* by the beast," a meaning for which there is no clear parallel. (3) *As a Latinism.* Despite the demurrer of Charles (2:33), this expression is probably best construed as a Latinism, in which the noun *uictoria,* "victory," sometimes used as the predicate with the verb *ferre,* "bear, carry, bring," and the prepositions *de,* "from," or *ex,* "from," with the ablative of the person or thing conquered (*OLD,* 2057), e.g., *uictoriam de Hannibale,* "victory *over Hannibal*" (Livy 21.46.8); *iuvenis . . . ex centurione Latino victoriam tulit,* "the youth won the victory *over the Latin centurion*" (cf. Livy 4.6.5; 5.15.11; 25.39.17; 29.9.5; 38.37.2); Velleius Paterculus 2.10.2, *Eodem tractu temporum et Domitii ex Arvernis et Fabii ex Allobrogibus uictoria fuit nobilis,* "At the same time the noteworthy victory of Domitius *over the Averni* and Fabius *over the Allobroges* took place." Despite the rarity of Latinisms in Revelation, it is possible that the author was familiar with Greek sources that had been translated woodenly from Latin but are now unknown. Had the author omitted the preposition ἐκ, the following articular genitive τοῦ θηρίου could be construed as an objective genitive.

2c ἑστῶτας ἐπὶ τὴν θάλασσαν τὴν ὑαλίνην ἔχοντας κιθάρας τοῦ θεοῦ, "stood near the sea of glass with kitharas of God." In Rev 4:6 it is said that *before* the throne of God was something like a glass or crystal sea, so it is not appropriate to regard the crystal sea as the "floor" of heaven upon which its inhabitants stand (ἑστῶτας ἐπί can be understood as "standing upon" or "standing by"). The song of Moses (see v 3a) was sung near the sea with the accompaniment of musical instruments (Exod 15:8). Note that in *Mek. de-Rabbi Ishmael, Beshallah* 5 (on Exod 15:8; tr. Lauterbach, 1:224), "The sea congealed on both sides and became a sort of glass crystal [כמין בולוס של זכוכית *kmyn bwlws šl zkwkyt*] as it is said: 'The deeps were congealed in the heart of the sea.'"

3a καὶ ᾄδουσιν τὴν ᾠδὴν Μωϋσέως τοῦ δούλου τοῦ θεοῦ καὶ τὴν ᾠδὴν τοῦ ἀρνίου, "They sang the song of Moses, the servant of God, and the song of the Lamb." Moses is frequently referred to as the servant of God, particularly in Jewish tradition (Exod 14:31; Num 12:7; Deut 34:5; Josh 1:1, 15; 8:31; 9:24; 1 Kgs 8:53; 2 Kgs 18:12; 21:8; 2 Chr 24:9; Neh 1:8; Ps 105:26; Mal 4:4[MT 3:22]; Bar 1:20; Jos. *Ant.* 5.39; *1 Clem.* 4:17; 51:5, 8). Does this refer to the Song *about* Moses (objective genitive) or the Song *by* Moses (subjective genitive)? The OT contains three songs *by* Moses, Exod 15:1–18, Deut 31:30–32:43 (cf. Philo *Virt.* 11.72–75), and Ps 90 (the only psalm linked to the name Moses and entitled "A prayer [תפלה *tĕpillâ*] of Moses, the man of God," though למשה *lĕmōšeh* can mean "to/by/for/about Moses" [Craigie, *Psalms 1–50,* 33–35], translated in LXX Ps 89:1 as Προσευχὴ τοῦ Μωυσῆ ἀνθρώπου τοῦ θεοῦ). Josephus refers to the songs in Exod 15:1–18 and Deut 31:30–32:42 as compositions in hexameter (*Ant.* 2.346; 4.303), which may suggest that he was familiar with hymnic compositions based on these biblical texts (see Thackeray, *Josephus,* 90–91). Since the song sung in Rev 15:3b–4 is obviously not that found in Exod 15, some commentators argue that the hymn referred to here is Deut 31:30–32:43 (Beckwith, 677; Ford, 247). However, Exod 15:1–18 is certainly the more appropriate (this was the view of ancient commentators such as Oecumenius *Comm. in Apoc.* 15:3), for it is a song of victory sung after the miraculous crossing of the Red Sea, and the motifs of *sea* and *victory* are explicitly emphasized in v 2. Yet it must be admitted that there is no literary relationship between the song in Rev 15:3b–4 and either Exod 15 or Deut 30–32 (Schüssler Fiorenza, *Revelation,* 135).

The concluding phrase, "and the song of the Lamb," is similarly problematic. If it is parallel to "the song of Moses," it should perhaps mean "the song *by* the Lamb" (subjective genitive), though nowhere else do we learn of a song sung *by* the Lamb. It is more likely, therefore, that this phrase means "the song *about* the Lamb" (objective genitive), an example of which is found in Rev 5:9–12. Since the phrase τὴν ᾠδήν is repeated a second time, it might appear that *two* songs are being described (Zahn, 2:530), yet in the context it seems that the single hymn in vv 3–4 must be intended. It is possible, however, that the doxology in vv 3–4 (n.b. that the original song of Moses ended with a doxology in Exod 15:18) may be the *conclusion* of a song that is not actually sung but only mentioned. At any rate, "the song of the Lamb" is very probably an editorial addition to an earlier form of the text (Wellhausen, *Analyse,* 25), though Charles (2:34–35) argues that the phrase "the song of Moses, the servant of God" is an interpolation that began as a marginal gloss. Note that there are several passages in Revelation in which "Lamb" has been added: (1) "and before the Lamb" (7:9), (2) "and to the Lamb" (7:10), (3) "and the Lamb"(14:4), (4) "and before the Lamb" (14:10), (5) "and the Lamb (21:22), (6) "and the lamp of it the Lamb" (21:23), (7) "and the Lamb" (22:1), (8) "and of the Lamb" (22:3). The insertion of references to the Lamb in these passages is part of the author's task of editorial homogenization, in which themes and motifs belonging to later strata of material are added to earlier material in order to tie the entire composition more closely together.

Rabbinic tradition enumerates ten biblical songs (Goldin, *Song,* 68–72). There is a rabbinic tradition that just as Moses sang a song at the Sea of Reeds, so in the world to come he will sing a "new song" of praise to God (*Qoh. Rab.* 1.9; *Mek.* Exod 15:1). This tradition is also reflected in *Tanḥuma Exod.* 30b (S. Buber, ed., *Midrash Tanḥuma,* 2 vols. [Jerusalem: Eshkol, 1990]): "It is not said, 'Then *šar,*' [i.e., a perfect or past tense, "he sang"] but, 'Then *yāšîr,*' [i.e., an imperfect or future tense, "he will sing"] in the Age to Come—in the Age to Come Israel will recite Shirah to the Lord." De Moor and van Staalduine-Sulman (*JST* 24 [1993] 261–79) claim to have identified an Aramaic acrostic "Song of the Lamb," discovered in fragmentary form in some fragments of the *Tosepta-Targum* to 1 Sam 17:43, which describes David as a messianic lamb conquering Goliath, depicted as an anti-messianic giant bear (= beast), and which may be part of a larger poetic composition. The fragments exploit the ambiguity of the term טליא *ṭalyāʾ,* which can mean either "boy" or "lamb," though David is also called an אימרא *ʾimmĕrāʾ,* "lamb." The waw strophe reads as follows (De Moor and Staalduine-Sulman, *JST* 24 [1993] 269):

> Woe to you lamb [*ʾymrʾ*],
>   you who want to wage battle with a bear!
> But there is no lamb
>   which can stand up against a bear.

Despite the late date of these targumic texts, De Moor and Staalduine-Sulman argue that the composition was written between 100 B.C. and A.D. 100. This proposal is interesting, but the early date of the text is highly questionable, and the parallels to Revelation proposed (*JST* 24 [1993] 272–79) are simply too speculative and far-fetched.

3b λέγοντες· μεγάλα καὶ θαυμαστὰ τὰ ἔργα σου, κύριε ὁ θεὸς ὁ παντοκράτωρ, "Great and wonderful are your deeds, / Lord God Almighty." Vv 3–4 constitute a hymn to God in the form of a descriptive hymn of praise (Westermann, *Praise,* 116–

51; Deichgräber, *Gotteshymnus,* 55), composed of a pastiche of stereotypical hymnic phrases gathered primarily from the Psalms. Westermann describes this hymn type as speech directed toward God that does not rehearse specific instances of deliverance but rather focuses on God's majesty in a summarizing or descriptive manner (Westermann, *Praise,* 118). The particular importance of this hymn is emphasized by the extensive introduction in v 2a and by the explicit mention of the title or titles of the song (which occurs only here in Revelation). However, since the typical introduction to a descriptive hymn of praise is lacking, namely, the call to praise in the imperative, it is appropriate to recognize this as a partial hymn (K. Berger, *Formgeschichte,* 242).

It is possible that ἔργα here means "miracles," in which case it is the only instance in Revelation of the use of ἔργον with this meaning, though it occurs seventeen times in the Fourth Gospel (5:20, 36[2x]; 7:3, 21; 9:3, 4; 10:25, 32[2x], 33, 37, 38; 14:10, 11, 12; 15:24). The song that follows is a pastiche of lyrical fragments. In Tob 12:22, which introduces a hymn of praise, there occurs the phrase τὰ ἔργα τὰ μεγάλα καὶ θαυμαστὰ τοῦ θεοῦ, "the great and wonderful works of God" (LXX see Job 42:3). These epithets are applied to God himself in Theod Dan 9:4, Κύριε ὁ θεὸς ὁ μέγας καὶ θαυμαστός, "Lord, great and wonderful God." The phrase μεγάλα καὶ θαυμαστά, "great and wonderful," occurs as "Baruch's" description of what the angel has shown him in *3 Apoc. Bar.* (Gk. text) 4:1, while in *Ep. Arist.* 155, the phrase is used of the "great and wonderful" things God has done in a combined quotation from Deut 7:18 and 10:21 (though in the latter passage the phrase is τὰ μεγάλα καὶ ἔνδοξα ταῦτα, "great and glorious things," an essentially synonymous phrase; see LXX 2 Chr 2:8; LXX Dan 6:4; Jdt 16:13, κύριε, μέγας εἶ καὶ ἔνδοξος, "Lord, you are great and glorious"). The phrase ἡ καλλονὴ αὐτὴ ἡ μεγάλη καὶ θαυμαστή, "her great and wonderful beauty," occurs in *Jos. As.* 18:11, where the adjectives describe Aseneth's pulchritude. In the Apostolic Fathers, μέγα καὶ θαυμαστόν is used of various special things but never of God himself (*Barn.* 6:4 [altered quotation of Ps 117:22, 24]; *1 Clem.* 26:1; 50:1; 53:3 [altered quotation of LXX Deut 9:14]; *2 Clem.* 5:5). One can conclude that this was a formulaic phrase in Greek (reflecting various Hebrew words) used in contexts of praise and thanksgiving in which a person (primarily God), action, or thing is extolled. See also Ps 111:2 (LXX 110:2), "Great are the works of the Lord," and 139:14 (LXX 138:14), "Wonderful are your works." The meaning of ἔργα, "works, deeds," overlaps with that of ἀρεταί, "virtues," i.e., actions through which the deity manifests his power (Engelmann, *Aretalogy,* 26, line 31). The phrase κύριε ὁ θεὸς ὁ παντοκράτωρ, "Lord God Almighty," occurs in 4:8; 11:17; 16:7; 19:6; 21:22; see *Comment* on 4:8.

3c δίκαιαι καὶ ἀληθιναὶ αἱ ὁδοί σου, ὁ βασιλεὺς τῶν ἐθνῶν, "Righteous and true are your ways, / King of the nations." The phrase "king of the nations," which occurs in Jer 10:7 (missing from the LXX), is significant here since Jer 10:7 is also alluded to in 15:4a. It is significant that this is an allusion to Deut 32:4 (a song of Moses), ἀληθινὰ τὰ ἔργα αὐτοῦ καὶ πᾶσαι αἱ ὁδοὶ αὐτοῦ κρίσεις, "His words are true and all his ways are judgments [just?]," perhaps combined with Ps 145:17 (LXX 144:17), δίκαιος κύριος ἐν πάσαις ταῖς ὁδοῖς αὐτοῦ, "the Lord is righteous in all his ways." The *Res Gestae Divi Augusti* 34.2 makes particular mention of four imperial virtues: *virtus, clementia, iustitia,* and *pietas* (courage, clemency, justice, and piety); see the commentary by P. A. Brunt and J. M. Moore, *Res Gestae Divi Augusti: The Achievements* *of the Divine Augustus* (Oxford: Oxford UP, 1967) 78. The Greek equivalents of these four cardinal virtues are ἀρετή, ἐπιείκεια, δικαιοσύνη, and εὐσέβεια (Danker, *Benefactor,* 279). *Iustitia,* or justice, an important virtue in a ruler, is frequently mentioned in inscriptions but rarely on coins. A statue representing the "Justice of Augustus" was erected in A.D. 13, and thereafter dedications to "the most just of princes" become relatively common. After the overthrow of Domitian, Nerva minted coins announcing his "Justice" and the "Freedom of the Roman People" (Charlesworth, *PBA* 23 [1937] 113).

For ὁ βασιλεὺς τῶν ἐθνῶν, "king of the nations," as a divine title, see Ps 47:8; cf. 1 Chr 16:31; Ps 22:28; LXX Ps 46:3; Pss 96:10; 99:2; cf. Ps 9:7–8 (Nebuchadrezzar is designated "king of all nations" in Dan 4:11, as is Cyrus in Jos. *Ant.* 11.5). Although the term βασιλεύς, "king," was a common Greek translation of the Latin term *imperator,* "emperor," the term never entered the official language of Rome until the Byzantine period (Mason, *Greek Terms,* 120). The earliest known application of the term βασιλεύς is the reference to Augustus in the poetry of Antipater of Thessaly (*Anth. Pal.* 10.25). Cognates of βασιλεύς were used by Plutarch's time (*Amatorius* 25.771), and Josephus spoke of the βασιλεία of Vespasian (*J.W.* 5.409) and used the verb βασιλειᾶν for would-be emperors (*J.W.* 1.5; 4.546). The generic phrase "kings of the nations [βασιλεῖς τῶν ἐθνῶν]" occurs in *Jos. As.* 21.8; *Sib. Or.* 3.663.

4a τίς οὐ μὴ φοβηθῇ, κύριε, καὶ δοξάσει τὸ ὄνομά σου; "Who, Lord, does not fear / and glorify your name?" These two cola exhibit synonymous parallelism (Jörns, *Evangelium,* 130). Rhetorical questions are characteristic in hymns (Exod 15:11; Pss 2:1; 6:3; 8:4; 10:13; 11:3; 13:2; 14:4; 15:1; 22:1; 35:10; 89:6,8; 113:5; 1 Sam 26:15; Isa 40:25; 46:5; Mic 7:18; 1QH 1:25; 3:23–24; 7:28–29; 10:5–6); see *Comment* on 13:4b. This rhetorical question is an allusion to Jer 10:7 (RSV; missing from LXX), "Who would not fear you, / O King of the nations?"

4b ὅτι μόνος ὅσιος ὅτι πάντα τὰ ἔθνη ἥξουσιν καὶ προσκυνήσουσιν ἐνώπιόν σου, "Because you alone are holy, / Because all the nations will come / to worship before you." The adjective μόνος is used in divine predications in later OT writings, early Judaism, and early Christianity to underscore aspects of the uniqueness of God (2 Kgs 19:15, 19; Neh 9:6; Pss 72:18; 83:18; 86:10; 136:4; Isa 2:11, 17; 26:13; 37:16, 20; 1 Esdr 8:25; 4 Ezra 8:7; 2 Macc 1:24–25; 7:37; Mark 2:7; Rom 16:27; 1 Tim 1:17; 6:15–16; Jude 25). Only in Rev 15:4, however, is the predication "you alone are holy" found, and it must therefore be considered a formulation by the author. The divine attribute ὅσιος, "holy," occurs only here and in 16:5 in Revelation. The term ὅσιος is only rarely used of the holiness of God (Deut 32:4; Ps 144:17; *1 Clem.* 56:16; 58:1; see *Comment* on Rev 16:5). There is a likely allusion here and in v 4c to Ps 86:9–10 (LXX 85:9–10):

πάντα τὰ ἔθνη, ὅσα ἐποίησας, ἥξουσιν
All the nations you have made will come

καὶ προσκυνήσουσιν ἐνώπιόν σου, κύριε,
to bow before you, Lord,

καὶ δοξάσουσιν τὸ ὄνομά σου
and honor your name.

ὅτι μέγας εἶ σύ
For you are great

καὶ ποιῶν θαυμάσια,
and do wonderful things.

σὺ εἶ ὁ θεὸς μόνος ὁ μέγας.
You alone are God.

In this parallel, the motif of the pilgrimage of the nations to worship the God of Israel is prominent and is combined with the themes of the uniqueness of God and his performance of wonderful acts (see *Comment* on v 4c). The phrase πάντα τὰ ἔθνη, "all the nations," is a fixed phrase that occurs five times in Revelation (12:5; 14:8; 15:4; 18:3, 23); see *Comment* on 12:5. The theme of the coming of the nations to worship God in Jerusalem occurs frequently in the OT (Isa 2:2–4; 14:1–2; 45:14; 60:1–3; 66:18; Jer 16:19; Zech 8:20–23); see *Comment* on Rev 21:24.

4c ὅτι τὰ δικαιώματά σου ἐφανερώθησαν, "Because your righteous judgments are evident." The phrase τὰ δικαιώματά σου can mean "your righteous ordinances" or "your righteous judgments"(Rom 1:32; 2:26; 8:4), perhaps in the sense of the punishment of the ungodly (1 Kgs 3:28; 2 Chr 6:35; Plato *Leg.* 9.864e; *CIJ,* 361) since δικαίωμα can refer to a just decree or sentence of condemnation (Rom 5:16; Thayer, *Lexicon,* 151; Charles, 2:36–37; BAGD, 198; Prigent, 240; the evidence in Spicq, *TLNT* 1:344 n. 96). The phrase can also mean "your righteous deeds" (Rev 19:8; Bar 2:17 [*GELS,* 115]), referring to the striking manifestations of the sovereignty of God. Since the previous line refers to the pilgrimage of all nations to worship before God, a positive rather than a negative construal of τὰ δικαιώματά σου is appropriate, favoring the translation "righteous actions" (NIV; NEB, "just dealings"; Swete, 196; Bousset [1906] 394; Bratcher-Hatton, *Revelation,* 226) rather than "righteous judgments" (REB, "just decrees"). This contextual argument is strengthened by the likelihood that this verse alludes to Ps 86:9–10 (LXX 85:9–10), where it is said that God is great and does wonderful things. Some prefer the more ambiguous translation "judgments" (RSV; NRSV; Kraft, 200 [*Gerichte*]). Lohmeyer (131–32) blends these two aspects of δικαίωμα when he claims that the term designates "juridical judgment" as well as "righteous action" and concludes that *both* are relevant since the judgment of God is an action of God.

5 καὶ μετὰ ταῦτα εἶδον, καὶ ἠνοίγη ὁ ναὸς τῆς σκηνῆς τοῦ μαρτυρίου ἐν τῷ οὐρανῷ, "After this I saw the temple, namely, the tent of testimony in heaven, open." (On the introductory vision formula καὶ μετὰ ταῦτα εἶδον, see *Comment* on 4:1.) A parallel phrase occurs in 11:19, καὶ ἠνοίγη ὁ ναὸς τοῦ θεοῦ ὁ ἐν τῷ οὐρανῷ, "Then the temple of God in heaven opened," with the difficult phrase τῆς σκηνῆς τοῦ μαρτυρίου, "the tent of testimony," noteworthy by its absence. Temple doors that opened by themselves were considered a prodigy. The doors that connected the porch or vestibule to the holy place or sanctuary in the temple in Jerusalem were large and heavy (Josephus gives two conflicting reports about their size and how many men it took to open them in *Ag. Ap.* 2.119 and *J.W.* 5.202; 6.293) and were reported to have opened by themselves (αὐτομάτως ἠνοιγμένη), interpreted to symbolize either the coming of divine blessings or the impending desolation (*J.W.* 6.293–96).

The term ναός, usually translated "temple," requires some discussion at this point. In the LXX and later Jewish and Christian Greek literature, four different terms were used for the temple in Jerusalem: τὸ ἅγιον (Exod 26:33; Num 3:38; Ezek 45:18; 1 Macc 10:42), τὸ ἱερόν (2 Macc 3:2), ὁ οἶκος (3 Kgdms 7:31; Jos. *J.W.* 4.281; Mark 2:26; Matt 12:4), and τὸ ναός (3 Kgdms 6:5, 17; Jos. *J.W.* 5.207, 209, 211; *Ant.* 15.391; Matt 23:16, 17, 21). These terms can be used interchangeably (*TDNT* 9:882), and there are no discernible ideological reasons for preferring some of these terms over others in particular contexts (Barr, *Semantics,* 282–87). ναός is used in the LXX ca. 120 times, almost always as a translation of הֵיכָל *hêkāl,* which can mean "palace," "temple," or the holy place that occupied the middle area of the Solomonic temple (references in *DCH* 2:541–42). When הֵיכָל *hêkāl* is used of the temple, it normally refers to the sacred building itself, which consisted of three rooms: (1) an innermost shrine called the holy of holies (דְּבִיר *dĕbîr* or קֹדֶשׁ הַקֳּדָשִׁים *qōdeš haqqādāšîm*), a nave called the holy place (קֹדֶשׁ *qōdeš*), and a porch or vestibule called an אוּלָם *ʾûlām.* The porch was separated from the holy place by doors (1 Kgs 6:33–35; Ezek 41:21–25; Jos. *Ag. Ap.* 2.119; *J.W.* 5.202; 6.293). Occasionally the translators of Chronicles used ναός to translate the term אולם *ʾûlām* (1 Chr 28:11; 2 Chr 8:12; 15:8; 29:7, 17), referring to the "porch" or "vestibule" of the temple of Solomon (references in *DCH* 1:152–53), but ναός is *never* used as a term for the *dĕbîr* or most holy place (and therefore the comments of Bratcher-Hatton, *Revelation,* 227, are quite wrong). This is in contrast to classical and Hellenistic Greek usage in which ναός was used for the sanctuary within a temple in which the cult statue of the god was placed (Herodotus 1.183; 6.16), while τὸ ἱερόν was the term used for the temple as a whole.

In Revelation, the term ναός is used to mean four different things: (1) the temple in Jerusalem, consisting of a three-room building, which the author may have used secondarily to refer to the heavenly temple (11:1–2); (2) the temple as a metaphor for the people of God (3:12); (3) the heavenly temple (7:15; 11:19[2x]; 15:5, 6, 8[2x]; 16:1, 17); and (4) the presence of God as a temple in the New Jerusalem (21:22[2x]).

Though Bousset ([1906] 394) and Lohmeyer (129) are among those who suggest that the OT Hebrew phrase משכן אהל מועד *miškan ʾōhel môʿēd,* literally, "the tabernacle of the tent of meeting" (Exod 40:2, 6, 29; n.b. that the LXX does not translate משכן *miškān*), lies behind ὁ ναὸς τῆς σκηνῆς τοῦ μαρτυρίου, this is simply not plausible, for משכן *miškān* is never translated ναός in the LXX, and מועד *môʿēd* means "meeting," not "testimony." However, the Hebrew phrases אֹהֶל הָעֵדֻת *ʾōhel haʿēdut,* "tent of testimony," and אֹהֶל מוֹעֵד *ʿōhel môʿēd,* "tent of meeting," are frequently translated in the LXX as ἡ σκηνὴ τοῦ μαρτυρίου, "tent of testimony." The corresponding Hebrew phrase should rather be מִקְדַּשׁ אֹהֶל הָעֵדוּת *miqdaš ʾōhel hāʿēdût,* "sanctuary of the tent of testimony," which occurs in the OT only in the form אֶת־הַמִּשְׁכָּן לְאֹהֶל הָעֵדֻת *ʾet-hammiškān lĕʾōhel hāʿēdut,* "[the cloud covered] the tabernacle, the tent of testimony" (Num 9:15). The LXX version of Num 9:15 reflects this difficult concatenation: τὴν σκηνήν, τὸν οἶκον τοῦ μαρτυρίου, "the tent, the house of testimony," though *Tg. Neof.* Num 9:15 and *Tg. Ps.-J.* Num 9:15 read simply "the tent of testimony." In the phrase ὁ ναὸς τῆς σκηνῆς τοῦ μαρτυρίου, "the temple, namely, the tent of witness," the first genitive, τῆς σκηνῆς, "the tent," is probably an appositive genitive (Bousset [1906] 394; Beckwith, 678; NIV), while the second, τοῦ μαρτυρίου, "of witness," is a descriptive genitive. Charles thought the phrase so difficult that he considered τῆς σκηνῆς τοῦ μαρτυρίου to be a later addition to the text (2:38). Eichhorn (2:170) tried to solve the problem by translating the entire clause *aperiebatur templum illud coeleste, in quo arca foederis* [should not Eichhorn have used *testimonii?*] *reposita erat,* "the heavenly temple was opened in which the ark of covenant was located." The same solution appears in TEV: "After this I saw the temple in heaven open, with the Covenant Tent in it." The unusual juxtaposition of "temple" and "tent of meeting" is also found in the reconstructed text of 4QMMT 32–35 (tr. García Martínez, *Dead Sea Scolls,* 77), "And we think that the temple [is the place of the tent of meeting, and Je]rusalem is the camp." In the OT the term tabernacle (Hebrew משכן *miškān*) is used for the temple (Pss 26:8; 46:4[MT 5]; 74:7 [it is interesting that in this passage משכן *miškān,* "tabernacle," and מקדש *miqdāš,* "sanctuary, temple," are used as synonyms]; 84:2; 132:5, 7). The heavenly tabernacle (ἡ σκηνή) is mentioned twice in Hebrews (8:2; 9:11), and also in 4Q*403* 1 ii 10 and 4Q*405* 20–21–22 ii 7. In the OT the pattern of the tabernacle is revealed by God to Moses, suggesting its heavenly preexistence (Exod 25:9, 40; 26:30; 27:8). The opening of the heavenly temple (see 11:19) functions as an introduction to the judgments of the seven bowls. Similarly, the opening of heavenly gates precedes judgment in 3 Macc 6:18–19 (tr. M. Hadas, *Maccabees*):

> Then the greatly glorious, almighty, and true God, making His countenance manifest, opened the gates of heaven, from which two glorified angels of terrible aspect descended . . . [T]hey confronted the forces of their [the Jews'] adversaries, and filled them with confusion and terror, and bound them with immovable fetters.

In Rome the *templum Iani,* "Temple of Janus" (actually a gateway rather than a temple), was opened as both a prelude to and a declaration of war (Vergil *Aeneid* 1.294; Servius on *Aeneid* 1.294; Macrobius *Saturnalia* 1.9.17–18; Livy 1.19.2–4; Varro *De lingua Latina* 5.165; Horace *Ep.* 2.1.255; Ovid *Fasti* 1.121–24). Augustus closed the doors of the temple of Janus three times, the first time in January 29 B.C., at the end of the civil war, inaugurating a new era of the *pax Romana,* the "Roman peace," a second time in 25 B.C., and yet a third time, though the specific date of that closing is unknown (*Res Gestae Divi Augusti* 13).

6a καὶ ἐξῆλθον οἱ ἑπτὰ ἄγγελοι [οἱ] ἔχοντες τὰς ἑπτὰ πληγὰς ἐκ τοῦ ναοῦ, "and the seven angels with the seven plagues emerged from the temple." Though it is said that the seven angels already *have* the plagues (which are not presented in any symbolic or metaphorical way), it is striking that nothing has yet been said about the seven libation bowls, which they will use to pour out, or unleash, the seven plagues upon the earth.

6b ἐνδεδυμένοι λίνον καθαρὸν λαμπρόν, "clothed in pure, shining linen." The term λίνον, "linen," occurs only here in Revelation, where it is used of a sacral garment. Elsewhere in Revelation the adjective βύσσινος, "made of fine linen" (from βύσσος, a loanword from the Semitic languages; see בוץ *bûṣ* in 2 Chr 2:14[LXX 2:13]; 3:14), occurs five times (18:12, 16; 19:8[2x], 14). Linen garments are worn by priests (Lev 16:4, 23; 1 Sam 2:8). The term בד *bad* or בדים *baddîm* is used of "linen garments" worn by angels (Ezek 9:2, 3, 11; 10:2, 6, 7; Dan 10:5; 12:6, 7). Josephus, in rewriting the section of the Pentateuch dealing with the priests' garments, mentions the "girdle" (ζώνη) of the high priest (*Ant.* 3.153–54, 185). According to the Priestly writer, the basic priestly wardrobe consisted of a coat, breeches, girdle, and turban, all of linen (Lev 16:4, 10). In *Jos. As.* 3:6, the garments of Aseneth are described as a linen robe interwoven with violet and gold and a golden girdle (along with golden shoes, jewelry, a tiara, and a veil). The priest of Isis in the Hellenistic period wore linen robes (Plutarch *De Iside* 352C).

6c καὶ περιεζωσμένοι περὶ τὰ στήθη ζώνας χρυσᾶς, "and with golden sashes encircling their waists." Cf. 1:13b, where the exalted Christ is described as having "a golden sash encircling his chest." The color gold is a frequent symbol of divine or heavenly realities.

7a καὶ ἓν ἐκ τῶν τεσσάρων ζῴων ἔδωκεν τοῖς ἑπτὰ ἀγγέλοις ἑπτὰ φιάλας χρυσᾶς, "Then one of the four cherubim gave to the seven angels seven golden libation bowls." This action (ἔδωκεν) constitutes, at least in part, the commissioning and empowerment of the angels; a similar motif precedes the seven seals (6:6–14) and the seven trumpets (8:2, ἐδόθησαν). The author frequently uses individual figures from groups of heavenly courtiers as influential actors in the continuing eschatological saga (5:5; 7:13; 17:1; 21:9). The word φιάλη, usually translated "bowl" (Louw-Nida, § 6.124), must be understood as a *cultic utensil* and should therefore be translated "bowl used in offerings" (BAGD, 858) or *Opferschale* (Bauer-Aland, 1711). These libation bowls are mentioned twelve times in Revelation (5:8; 15:7; 16:1, 2, 3, 4, 8, 10, 12, 17; 17:1; 21:9). The cultic use of φιάλαι is attested for Greek religion (Diodorus 4.49.8), where it was used primarily to pour libations of wine. The term is also used in connection with revelatory magic ceremonies, where visions are reflected on the surface of the liquid contained in the bowl (*PGM* IV.224, 3210; LXII.44, 48). The equivalent Latin term is *patera,* meaning a shallow, broad dish used in libation offerings (*OLD,* 1308; see Varro *De lingua Latina* 5.122 [LCL tr.]: "it is this kind of cup that the magistrate uses in sacrificing to the gods, when he gives wine to the god"). Vergil *Georgics* 2.192 mentions offering wine from golden pateras (*qualem pateris libamus et auro*). The Pentateuch mentions "libation vessels" (מזרקות *mizrāqôt;* מזרק *mizrāq* is always translated φιάλη in the LXX; since מזרק *mizrāq* is from the verb זרק *zāraq,* meaning "to toss, splash," it means a container from which something is thrown or splashed) in Exod 27:3; 38:3; Num 4:14. Aramaic letters from Jewish officials concerned with the temple at Elephantine reported that their temple was destroyed and the "libation vessels of gold and silver" (ומזרקיא זי זהבא וזי כספא *wmzrqy' zy zhb' wzy ksp'*) were stolen (Cowley, *Aramaic Papyri,* no. 30, line 12; no. 31, line 11). These were used as containers for flour mixed with oil (Num 7:13, 19, 25, 31), wine (Zech 9:15), and perhaps blood. In Exod 24:6, 8; 29:16, 20; 2 Kgs 16:13, 15, the verb זרק *zāraq* is used, though no vessel is specified (see Haran, *Temples,* 216 n. 13). It is probable that animal sacrifices were generally accompanied by libations of wine (Hos 9:4; see Gen 35:14; 2 Kgs 16:13; *T. Levi* 18:30 [MS *e* only, printed in de Jonge, *Testaments,* 46–48]; see T. H. Gaster, *IDB* 4:156). *Adam and Eve* 2:2 refers to angels gathered before the Father, "some with censers in their hands, and others with harps and bowls and trumpets" (τινὲς ἔχοντες θυμιατήρια ἐν χερσὶν αὐτῶν ἄλλοι δὲ κιθάρας καὶ φιάλας καὶ σάλπιγγας). Again in *Adam and Eve* 33:4, "I saw golden censers [θυμιατήρια χρυσᾶ] and three bowls [τρεῖς φιάλας], and behold all the angels with frankincense [λίβανον] and censers [θυμιατήρια] came with haste to the altar of incense [θυσιαστήριον] and blew on it." These references indicate that the angels are thought of as heavenly priests possessing cultic instruments and utensils such as harps, libation bowls, censers, and trumpets. *Ep. Arist.* 33 (see Jos. *Ant.* 12.40) mentions Ptolemy's gift of fifty talents of gold and seventy talents of silver for the fabrication of "mixing bowls, bowls, a table, and libation bowls of gold" (κρατήρων τε καὶ φιαλῶν καὶ τραπέζης καὶ σπονδείων χρυσίου). *Ep. Arist.* 42 reports that twenty gold and thirty silver bowls were constructed, while a description of the "golden bowls" (χρυσᾶς φιάλας) is found in *Ep. Arist.* 79 (see Jos. *Ant.* 12.82).

7b γεμούσας τοῦ θυμοῦ τοῦ θεοῦ τοῦ ζῶντος εἰς τοὺς αἰῶνας τῶν αἰώνων, "full of the wrath of the God who lives forever and ever." This is very probably an interpretive gloss or parenthetical explanation inserted by the author. On the phrase "the God who lives for ever and ever," see *Comment* on 4:9.

8a καὶ ἐγεμίσθη ὁ ναὸς καπνοῦ ἐκ τῆς δόξης τοῦ θεοῦ καὶ ἐκ τῆς δυνάμεως αὐτοῦ, "Thereupon the temple was filled with smoke from the glory of God and from his power." Here "filled with smoke" is parallel to "fill with the wrath of God" (v 7b), which serves to interpret the metaphorical meaning of "smoke." Here "smoke" is a theophanic image based on the combination of the metaphorical significance of smoke in the Sinai tradition with the meaning of the cloud of incense smoke that filled the holy place during the time when incense was burned on the altar of incense in front of the *dĕbîr* (holy of holies), as in Lev 16:2 (the Priestly writer): "I will appear in the cloud upon the mercy seat" (see Lev 16:12–13; *m. Yoma* 5). The motif of the cloud or smoke as a *theophany of Yahweh,* or as a reaction to such a theophany, sometimes accompanied by the quaking of the earth, is found in Exod 19:18; Pss 18:7–9; 104:32; Isa 6:4. In Isa 6:4, in the theophany that was part of the narrative of Isaiah's prophetic call, "the foundations of the thresholds shook at the voice of him who called, and the house was filled with smoke [LXX ὁ οἶκος ἐπλήσθη καπνοῦ]," though the suggestion that more of Isa 6 is present thematically both in this context and in that of Rev 4:8 is overdrawn (see Fekkes, *Isaiah,* 146–47). There is a close association between the glory of Yahweh (כבוד יהוה *kĕbôd YHWH*) and the cloud of smoke in Isa 6:1–4 (clearly a cultic context). According to Exod 24:16 (part of the Sinai pericope), "The glory of the Lord settled on Mount Sinai, and the cloud covered it six days." Clouds and thick darkness surround Yahweh, according to Ps 97:2, and Ps 97:8 suggests that this is not at Sinai but at Mount Zion. According to 1 Kgs 8:10–12 (RSV),

> And when the priests came out of the holy place, a cloud filled the house of the Lord, so that the priests could not stand to minister because of the cloud; for the glory of the Lord filled the house of the Lord. Then Solomon said, "The Lord has set the sun in the heavens, but has said that he would dwell in thick darkness."

All of these passages (see Nielsen, *Incense,* 81–84) suggest a close connection between the theophanic cloud of smoke and the temple in Jerusalem. In Rev 8:4 the smoke of the incense burned by the angel goes up before God. Here in 15:8 (following the logic of the narrative), the smoke that fills the heavenly temple would be that produced by the incense burned by the angels on the golden altar of incense. The revelation at Sinai was accompanied by the theophanic phenomena of thunder, lightning, the sound of the shofar or ram's horn trumpet, and a heavy cloud covering the mountain (Exod 19:16). In Exod 19:18, the emphasis is on the heavy smoke, "because the Lord descended upon it in fire," and upon the quaking of the mountain. According to Exod 34:5, "the Lord descended in the cloud." The Sinai pericope appears to have been shaped by projecting the incense cloud of the temple back into the period of the wilderness wandering (Nielsen, *Incense,* 85). This notion is related to the tradition that Yahweh was thought present in the pillar of cloud; see Exod 40:34–35, a passage that was undoubtedly shaped by the later burning of incense in the temple in Jerusalem:

> Then the cloud covered the tent of meeting [τὴν σκηνὴν τοῦ μαρτυρίου], and the glory of the Lord filled the tabernacle [καὶ δόξης κυρίου ἐπλήσθη ἡ σκηνή]. And Moses was not able to enter the tent of meeting [καὶ οὐκ ἠδυνάσθη Μωυσῆς εἰσελθεῖν εἰς τὴν σκηνὴν τοῦ μαρτυρίου], because the cloud abode upon it, and the glory of the Lord filled the tabernacle. (RSV)

It is clear that Rev 15:5–8 alludes to both Exod 40:34–35 and 1 Kgs 8:10–12.

It should be noted in passing that smoke also functions in Revelation as a metaphor for the presence of Satan. According to Rev 9:2, the smoke from the abyss "went up" (ἀνέβη καπνός), in language identical with the description of the rising of the smoke produced by burning incense in Rev 8:4, ἀνέβη ὁ καπνὸς τῶν θυμιαμάτων, "the smoke of the incense went up." This is not limited to Revelation, for smoke as a metaphor for Satan is reflected in *Apoc. Sedr.* 5:4–5 (Charlesworth, *OTP* 1:610), "Who can fight against an invisible spirit? He enters the hearts of men like smoke [ὡς καπνός] and teaches them all kinds of sin."

The phrase "the glory of God" or "the glory of the Lord" occurs frequently in the OT, often as a circumlocution referring to the presence of God in the various ways in which he chooses to reveal himself (Exod 16:7, 10; 24:16–17; Isa 35:2): (1) on Mount Sinai (Exod 24:16–17), (2) in the tabernacle (Exod 40:34–35; Lev 9:6, 23; Num 14:10; 16:19, 42; 20:6), (3) in the temple (1 Kgs 8:11; 2 Chr 5:14; 7:1–3; Ezek 10:4, 18; 11:23; 43:4; 44:4), and (4) as a way of referring to God's presence in prophetic visions (Ezek 1:28; 3:12, 23; 10:4; Acts 7:55).

8b καὶ οὐδεὶς ἐδύνατο εἰσελθεῖν εἰς τὸν ναὸν ἄχρι τελεσθῶσιν αἱ ἑπτὰ πληγαὶ τῶν ἑπτὰ ἀγγέλων, "and no one was able to enter the temple until the seven plagues of the seven angels had been completed." The aorist passive of τελεῖν, "complete," which occurs both here and in v 1b, forms an inclusio for vv 1–8, a unit that constitutes an introductory heavenly court scene of the kind used in Revelation as a prelude to God's action on earth (4:1–5:14; 8:2–5). This is an allusion to the common features of an anecdote, narrated in three versions in the OT, that relates that the glory of God so filled the house of God that Moses or the priests were unable to enter. The first narrative pertains to the erection and furnishing of the tabernacle of the tent of meeting in Exod 40:16–38. When these tasks were completed, it is said that a cloud covered the tent of meeting (Exod 40:34–35).

A very similar account is narrated in two versions in connection with the much more elaborate story of the dedication of the temple of Solomon in Jerusalem (1 Kgs 8:1–66 = 2 Chr 5:1–7:10). The dedication of Solomon's temple focused on the procession that brought the ark into the holy of holies. When this task was completed, an anecdote very similar to the one in Exod 40:34–35 is narrated in 1 Kgs 8:10–11 (quoted in *Comment* on v 8a). The parallel account in 2 Chr 5:11–14 is very similar, though greatly expanded by additional material in vv 12–13. However, when the Chronicler concludes the great dedicatory prayer of king Solomon (2 Chr 6:12–42), he inserts a variant of the account in 2 Chr 5:11–14:

> When Solomon had ended his prayer, fire came down from heaven and consumed the burnt offering and the sacrifices, and the glory of the Lord filled the temple. And the priests could not enter the house of the Lord, because the glory of the Lord filled the Lord's house. (2 Chr 7:1–2, RSV)

These brief narratives of the inability of certain people to enter the house of God because the cloud and the glory of God (Exod 40:34–35; 1 Kgs 8:10–11), or the glory of God alone (2 Chr 7:1–2), filled the sanctuary occurs in just four OT passages, and in each passage the event has a very positive connotation. The allusion to these passages in Rev 15:8, however, is primarily negative since it deals with the infliction of plagues on the people of the world. In part this negative use of anecdotes in the OT with positive connotations is signaled by the substitution of "smoke" for "cloud" in v 8a, for unlike "cloud," "smoke" is used as a metaphor for divine judgment (Deut 29:20; 2 Sam 22:9 = Ps 18:8; Isa 9:18–21; 34:10; 65:5–6; see *Comment* on 15:8a). But why does the author insist that no one can enter the heavenly temple until the seven bowl plagues have been dispensed? The most widely held view among commentators is that God is temporarily unapproachable because his presence has become a presence of wrath and judgment (Bousset [1906] 395; Behm, 89; Lohmeyer, 132; Lohse, 90; Roloff [ET] 185). A second view, which emphasizes the OT parallels discussed above (Exod 40:34–35; 1 Kgs 8:10–11 = 2 Chr 5:11–14; 2 Chr 7:1–2), argues that God is temporarily unapproachable because of the full manifestation of his majesty and power (Beckwith, 679; Beasley-Murray, 238). A third view is that, since the time of final judgment has now arrived, it is too late for an angelic mediator (as in 5:8 and 8:3) to present prayers of intercession to God to save the world (Charles, 2:40; Mounce, 290). The weakness of this view is that the prayers presented to God by the angel in 8:3 are probably intended to be understood as prayers asking for divine vengeance as in 6:10–11.

The motif of the impossibility or even the danger of approaching God when he manifests his presence in a particularly powerful manner is also integral to the story of Israel at Sinai. According to Exod 19:9, 16, God's presence was manifest in a thick cloud, and no one could touch the mountain under penalty of death (19:12–13). The theophanic function of the cloud in a cultic context is found in Lev 16:2, where Aaron is forbidden to enter the holiest of holies when God appears in a cloud upon the mercy seat.

16:1a καὶ ἤκουσα μεγάλης φωνῆς ἐκ τοῦ ναοῦ λεγούσης τοῖς ἑπτὰ ἀγγέλοις, "Then I heard a loud voice from the temple telling the seven angels." This may be an allusion to Isa 66:6, where the phrase "a voice from the temple" occurs, though the notion is extremely general. Only here and in v 17 is the unidentified voice said to come "from the temple," and the presumption is that it is the voice of God. An unidentified voice from the temple in Jerusalem reportedly said "We are departing from here," anticipating its destruction by the Romans (Jos. *J.W.* 6.299–300; Tacitus *Hist.* 5.13.1; John Malalas *Chron.* 10.26; see Kuhn, *Offenbarungsstimmen,* 176–84; cf. Jos. *Ant.* 13.282–83). (On the motif of the unidentified voice in Revelation, see *Comment* on 10:4.) Though the phrase φωνὴ μεγάλη, "loud voice," occurs twenty times in Revelation (1:10; 5:2, 12; 6:10; 7:2, 10; 8:13; 10:3; 11:12, 15 [the plural form φωναὶ μεγάλαι occurs only here]; 12:10; 14:7, 9, 15, 18; 16:1, 17; 19:1, 17; 21:3), this is the only use in which the adjective precedes the noun. φωνὴ μεγάλη occurs forty-eight times in the LXX, usually in the dative form φωνῇ μεγάλῃ, three times in the accusative (LXX Gen 27:34; 1 Esdr 3:11; Sir 50:16), and once in the nominative (LXX Esth 1:1). In four additional instances the adjective is placed before the noun as here, in the phrase μεγάλῃ τῇ φωνῇ (1 Esdr 5:64; 9:10; Prov 2:3; 26:25; see Rev 16:1). Though φωνὴ μεγάλη also occurs seven times in the Greek texts and fragments of the pseudepigrapha (*Adam and Eve* 5:2; 29:11; *T. Abr.* [Rec. A] 5:9; *Par. Jer.* 2:2; *2 Apoc. Bar.* 11:3; *Sib. Or.* 3.669; 5.63), the adjective always follows the noun, reflecting the Semitic pattern. The avoidance of the explicit mention of the name of God as the one speaking is a device frequently found in Revelation (6:6; 9:13; 16:17; 18:4; 19:5).

1b ὑπάγετε καὶ ἐκχέετε τὰς ἑπτὰ φιάλας τοῦ θυμοῦ τοῦ θεοῦ εἰς τὴν γῆν, "Be on your way to begin pouring out the seven libation bowls containing the wrath of God upon the earth." The verb ἐκχεῖν, "to pour out," is often used with cultic significance for the pouring out of libations, though it does not belong to technical religious vocabulary. It overlaps in meaning with σπένδειν, which specifically means "to pour out a libation," a term used only twice in the NT, both times figuratively (Phil 2:17; 2 Tim 4:6). Libations of oil and wine were part of the Israelite temple ritual (see Jos. *Ant.* 3.234, where the verb σπένδειν is used), and in Sir 50:15, in praising the priest Simon son of Onias, he describes how he "reached out his hand to the cup and poured a libation [ἔσπεισεν] of the blood of the grape; he poured it out [ἐξέχεεν] at the foot of the altar." Here σπένδειν and ἐκχεῖν are used with largely overlapping meanings. ἐκχεῖν is also used in the LXX for the pouring out of libations of water (1 Kgdms 7:6; 2 Kgdms 23:16) or for pouring out a libation of wine, i.e., a drink offering (Isa 57:6). ἐκχεῖν is frequently used of "shedding" blood, i.e., committing murder (LXX Jer 7:6). On libations in the ancient world, see O. Michel, *TDNT* 7:528–36; H. D. Betz, "Libations," *EncRel* 8:537–40; K. Hanell, "Trankopfer, Spenden, Libationen," *RE* vol. 6 (1937).

The use of the term ἐκχεῖν in connection with φιάλαι, "libation bowls," is clearly based on cultic practices, but its meaning has been extended figuratively to refer to the pouring out of the wrath of God. Precedent for this is found in LXX Jer 7:20, Ἰδοὺ ὀργὴ καὶ θυμός μου χεῖται [*var. lect.* ἐκχεῖται] ἐπὶ τὸν τόπον τοῦτον, "Behold, my wrath and anger will be poured out upon this place." Similarly, we read in LXX Jer 10:25, ἔκχεον τὸν θυμόν σου ἐπὶ ἔθνη, "Pour out your wrath upon the nations," and in LXX Jer 14:16, καὶ ἐκχεῶ ἐπ' αὐτοὺς τὰ κακὰ αὐτῶν, "and I will pour out upon them their own evils." These texts indicate that Jeremiah is using the language of *ius talionis;* i.e., those who "shed" (i.e., "pour out") blood will have the wrath of God and their own evil deeds "poured out" on them. LXX Lam 2:4 uses the same metaphor for divine judgment: ἐξέχεεν ὡς πῦρ τὸν θυμὸν αὐτοῦ, "He has poured out his wrath like fire." Similarly, LXX Lam 4:11 says ἐξέχεεν θυμὸν ὀργῆς αὐτοῦ, "He poured out his furious anger." The same imagery is found in LXX Ezekiel. The phrase ἐκχεῖν τὸν θυμὸν/τὴν ὀργὴν ἐπί, "to pour out wrath/anger upon," is found in Ezek 7:8; 9:8; 14:19; 20:8, 13, 21; 21:36[MT 21:31]; 22:22; 30:15; 39:29.

2a καὶ ἀπῆλθεν ὁ πρῶτος καὶ ἐξέχεεν τὴν φιάλην αὐτοῦ εἰς τὴν γῆν, "The first one departed and poured out his bowl upon the earth." Only the first angel is actually said to pour out his bowl on the earth, which is in keeping with the explicit command of the voice from the temple in v 1.

2b καὶ ἐγένετο ἕλκος κακὸν καὶ πονηρὸν ἐπὶ τοὺς ἀνθρώπους τοὺς ἔχοντας τὸ χάραγμα τοῦ θηρίου καὶ τοὺς προσκυνοῦντας τῇ εἰκόνι αὐτοῦ, "with the result that a harmful and festering sore afflicted those people who have the brand of the beast and who worship his image." This plague of festering sores resembles the sixth plague of boils narrated in Exod 9:8–12. While Wellhausen (*Analyse,* 26) regarded τοὺς ἀνθρώπους as a redactional expansion, it appears rather that the substantival participial phrases "who have the brand of the beast" and "who worship his image" constitute an analeptic interpolation (like 14:11 and 20:4), referring back to the same motifs in the narrative in 13:4, 8, 12, 15 (see also *Comment* on 20:4).

3a καὶ ὁ δεύτερος ἐξέχεεν τὴν φιάλην αὐτοῦ εἰς τὴν θάλασσαν, "Then the second one poured out his bowl on the sea." There is a distant parallel in a Coptic magical papyrus (London Ms. Or. 6796[4].6796; Kropp, *Zaubertexte* 2:57–58): "I am Jesus Christ, I have taken a cup [Coptic *apot,* which can also mean "chalice"] of water in my hand. . . . I have poured out my cup of water into the sea [*thalassa*]. It split in the middle" (n.b. that the Sahidic version of the NT uses the Greek loanword φιάλη consistently throughout Rev 16).

3b καὶ ἐγένετο αἷμα ὡς νεκροῦ, καὶ πᾶσα ψυχὴ ζωῆς ἀπέθανεν τὰ ἐν τῇ θαλάσσῃ, "and it became blood as from a corpse, with the result that every living creature died which was in the sea." In the ancient world, blood was paradoxically both a source of pollution and the means of purification (Parker, *Miasma,* 370–74). The pollution of the sea with blood is reminiscent of the first plague in Exod 7:14–24 (see Pss 78:44; 105:29), in which the Nile was turned to blood, which made the water unpotable and caused the fish to die. Other references to waters polluted by blood are found in Isa 15:9 and 2 Macc 12:16.

4 Καὶ ὁ τρίτος ἐξέχεεν τὴν φιάλην αὐτοῦ εἰς τοὺς ποταμοὺς καὶ τὰς πηγὰς τῶν ὑδάτων, καὶ ἐγένετο αἷμα, "Then the third one poured out his bowl on the rivers and springs of water, with the result that they became blood." This is an allusion to the first plague of the Exodus in which the rivers, canals, ponds, and pools of water in Egypt all turned to blood (Exod 7:14–19; see Pss 78:44; 105:29). In Ezekiel *Exagoge* 133–34, the plague affects the rivers, the springs, and the pools (πρῶτον μὲν αἷμα ποτάμιον ῥυήσεται πηγαί τε πᾶσαι καὶ ὑδάτων συστήματα). While the transformation of water into blood in Rev 16:4 (as in 8:9 and 16:3) is an act of divine punishment, there are a number of texts that describe bodies of water, particularly rivers, as filled with the blood of the slain. In *Apoc. Elijah* (P. Chester Beatty 2018) 5–7 (tr. Pietersma, *Elijah*), "Blood will flow from Qus to Memphis. The river of Egypt will turn into blood so that no one can drink it for three days." Similarly, in the *Asclepius* 3.24b (tr. W. Scott, *Hermetica* 1:341), "To thee, most holy Nile, I cry, to thee I foretell that which shall be; swollen with torrents of blood, thou wilt rise to the level of thy banks, and thy sacred waves will be not only stained but utterly fouled with gore." *Sib. Or.* 4.61 predicts that a great battle between the Medes and Persians will be preceded by the Euphrates flooded with blood. This reference is in accord with the ancient Roman conception of prodigies (unusual occurrences in nature understood as messages or warnings from the gods), one common type of which was a river turned to blood (Cicero *De div.* 1.43.97; 2.27.58; see *Excursus 6A: Ancient Prodigies and the Plagues of Revelation*).

5a καὶ ἤκουσα τοῦ ἀγγέλου τῶν ὑδάτων, "Then I heard the angel over the waters." This assumes a cosmos in which the various material elements are presided over by, or are personified by, particular angelic beings (*1 Enoch* 60:12–22 [which mentions the spirits or angels of the sea, hoarfrost, hail, snow, mist, dew, and rain]; 69:22; 75:3; *2 Enoch* 4–6; 19:1–4; *Jub.* 2:2; 1QH 1:8–13; Str-B, 3:818–20; *1 Enoch* 61:10 mentions angels of the water). In rabbinic literature the term, שר העולם *śar haʿôlām,* "prince of the world," refers to an angelic prince who is in charge of various aspects of creation (Str-B, 2:552). Various lesser angelic figures who are guardians of various aspects of the cosmos are mentioned in Revelation: Rev 7:1–2 refers to angels who control the four winds (see *b. Git.* 31b; Schäfer, *Rivalität,* 57), while Rev 14:18 (and *Apoc. Abr.* [Rec. A] 13:10) refers to the angel who has authority over fire (see *Comment* on 14:18); in rabbinic literature Gabriel was known as the prince of fire (*Cant. Rab.* 3.11 § 1; Schäfer, *Rivalität,* 57). *1 Enoch* 66:2 refers to angels or powers who were in charge of the waters, and *Sepher ha-Razim* 4.10 speaks of "the angels of water." Rabbinic literature mentions Ridja as the angel in charge of water and particularly rain (*b. Taʿan.* 25b; *b. T. Yom* 20b; Schäfer, *Rivalität,* 58). The medieval cabbalistic work in Hebrew, the *Clasicula Salomonis,* mentions a number of angels in charge of various elements, including Taliahad, the angel of the water (S. L. M. Mathers, *The Key of Solomon the King* [London, 1888] 74). *PGM* XIII.169–70, 481–84 (a parallel) speaks of a god who appeared and "was placed in authority over the abyss, for without him moisture neither increases nor decreases." *PGM* XXXV.7–10, part of a magical recipe heavily influenced by Judaism, mentions several supernatural beings in authority over various aspects of the cosmos: "I invoke you, who is in charge of the showers, Telze; I invoke you, Edanoth, who is in charge of the sea; I invoke you, Saesechel, who is in charge of the dragons; I invoke you, Tabium, who is in charge of the rivers."

5b δίκαιος εἶ, ὁ ὢν καὶ ὁ ἦν, ὁ ὅσιος, ὅτι ταῦτα ἔκρινας, "Righteous are you, who is and who was, the holy one, for you have decided to inflict these punishments." Rev 16:5–6 has been described as a "judgment doxology" (Deichgräber, *Gotteshymnus,* 45, 56; Betz, "Apocalypticism," 139; Yarbro Collins, *CBQ* 39 [1977] 368–70; K. Berger, *Formgeschichte,* 238), i.e., a brief hymnic passage that provides general or specific justification for the judgment of God. Staples argues for the designation "vindication formula," which he insists is non-apocalyptic, though he struggles with Dan 9:14 (*NovT* 14 [1972] 280–93), while Yarbro Collins prefers the designation "eschatological vindication formula," which she considers a subgenre of the judgment doxology (*CBQ* 39 [1977] 369). The so-called judgment doxology has been briefly discussed, though not analyzed, by von Rad and is normally thought to include the confession of sin that contrasts with the affirmation of the justice of God in punishing sin (*OT Theology* 1:357–58; *Wisdom,* 196, 211–13), a feature clearly missing from Rev 16:5–6. An early example of this form is the prayer of Achan in Josh 7:19–21, while I suggest Pr Azar 4 as a late example:

> For thou art just in all that thou hast done to us,
>   and all thy works are true and thy ways right,
>   and all thy judgments are truth.
> Thou hast executed true judgments in all that thou hast brought upon us
>   and upon Jerusalem, the holy city of our father,
>   for in truth and justice thou hast brought all this upon us because of our sins.

However, the "judgment doxology" is not really a literary genre; rather it is a theological motif used in a variety of hymnic and prayer contexts in the OT. It is not without significance that formal analyses of types of songs and prayers in the OT (e.g., Gunkel, Mowinckel, Weiser) have not found it necessary to include this generic category. From a more formal perspective, Jörns (*Evangelium,* 135) categorizes this hymn, following Westermann (*Praise,* 81–101), as a *declarative hymn of praise* (*ein berichtende Lobpreis*), which contains three recurring features: (1) God has acted; let him be praised! (2) Praise is a direct response to the act that has just occurred. (3) Praise is expressed joyously. The "judgment doxology" is in fact a more specific form of the *declarative hymn of praise,* in which the focal issue is the justice of God's punitive actions. In OT hymns the glorification of Yahweh as judge occurs more frequently than the celebration of Yahweh as creator or king (Weiser, *Psalms,* 64). There are a number of prayers and hymns to God in the OT and early Jewish literature affirming that he dispenses judgment properly and never in an arbitrary or undeserved manner (Neh 9:33; Dan 9:14; Tob 3:2; 3 Macc 2:3). The initial predication δίκαιος εἶ, "you are righteous," introducing prayers or hymns to God in the "you style," occurs in the LXX (Tob 3:2; Esth 4:17; Pss 118:37; 119:137; Jer 12:1 [צדיק אתה יהוה *ṣaddîq ʾattâ YHWH,* translated δίκαιος εἶ, κύριε]). There are two close parallels to Rev 16:7 in early Jewish literature, the first in the *du-Stil,* "thou style," the second in the *er-Stil,* "he style": (1) *Apoc. Moses* 27:7 (within the context of a judgment doxology pronounced by angels), δίκαιος εἶ κύριε καὶ εὐθύτητας κρίνεις, "You are just, O Lord, and you judge rightly"; (2) *T. Job* 43:13, δίκαιός ἐστιν ὁ κύριος, ἀληθινὰ αὐτοῦ τὰ κρίματα, "Righteous is the Lord, true are his judgments." The predication is followed by the address. The two divine titles ὁ ὤν and ὁ ἦν also occur in 11:17 (preceded by ὁ παντοκράτωρ) and as part of the tripartite formula ὁ ὤν καὶ ὁ ἦν καὶ ὁ ἐρχόμενος, "who is and who was and who is coming," in 1:4, 8; 4:8. ὁ ὤν and ὁ ἦν belong together and have been inserted between δίκαιος and ὅσιος, which also constitute a complementary pair of divine attributes. While צדיק *ṣaddîq* or δίκαιος is a relatively frequent attribute of God in Israelite, early Jewish, and early Christian literature (Exod 9:27; Deut 32:4; Josh 7:19–21; 2 Chr 12:6; Ezra 9:15; Neh 9:8, 33; Jer 11:20; 12:1; Pss 7:11; 116:5; 119:137; 145:17; Tob 3:2; Esth 4:17; Dan 9:14; 3 Macc 2:3; *Adam and Eve* 27:5; *Pss. Sol.* 2:18; Jos. *J.W.* 7.323; John 17:25; Rom 3:26), ὅσιος (which also occurs in 15:4 as a divine attribute) occurs very rarely as a divine attribute (it is often used in the plural of the righteous), though the titles δίκαιος and ὅσιος are paired in Deut 32:4 and *Pss. Sol.* 10:5; see *1 Clem.* 14:1 (these paired terms are used in the singular [*T. Abr.* (Rec. A) 9:2] and plural of the righteous in early Jewish literature; see *1 Enoch* 25:4; 104:12). Elsewhere in Revelation the title ὁ ὅσιος occurs *only* in 15:4. There is a great deal of inscriptional evidence from Asia Minor (primarily from Phrygia and Lydia) concerning a cult of Hosios and Dikaios (Holiness and Justice), often associated with other deities such as Men, the Rider God, Zeus Bronton, and Apollo; see A. R. R. Sheppard, "Pagan Cults of Angels in Roman Asia Minor," *Talanta* 12–13 (1980–81) 77–100. A corpus of all relevant inscriptions that mention Hosios and Dikaios can be found in M. Ricl, "Die Götter Hosios und Dikaios in Mäonien und Phrygien," *Epigraphica Anatolica* 18 (1991) 1–70; 19 (1992) 71–103, and there is a succinct summary of the major contours of the Hosios and Dikaios cult by R. A. Kearsley in *New Docs* 6:206–9; see also Mitchell, *Anatolia* 2:25–26. The phrase ταῦτα ἔκρινας, "you have decided to inflict these punishments" (see *Note* 16:5.b–b.), refers to the wrath of God previously mentioned in 15:1, 7.

6a ὅτι αἷμα ἁγίων καὶ προφητῶν ἐξέχεαν, "because they poured out the blood of God's people and the prophets." On "God's people" (literally "holy ones") as Christians, see *Comment* on 5:8.

The rejection of prophets by killing them is a theme found in the OT, early Judaism, and the NT (1 Kgs 19:10, 14; 2 Chr 36:16; Ezra 9:11; Neh 9:26; *Jub.* 1:12; Jos. *Ant.* 9.265; 10.37; Matt 5:11–12 = Luke 6:22–23; Matt 23:34 = Luke 11:49; Matt 23:37–39; Luke 13:34–35; Acts 7:52; Rom 11:3; 1 Thess 2:15; Justin *Dial.* 16:4; *Asc. Isa.* 5.1–14); see Aune, *Prophecy,* 157–59; O. H. Steck, *Israel und das gewaltsame Geschick der Propheten* (Neukirchen: Neukirchener, 1967); O. Michel, *Prophet und Märtyrer* (Gütersloh: Mohn, 1932); H. J.

Schoeps, "Die jüdischen Prophetenmorde," in *Aus frühchristlichen Zeit* (Tübingen: Mohr-Siebeck, 1950) 126–43; H. A. Fischel, "Martyr and Prophet," *JQR* 37 (1946–47) 265–80, 363–86.

This motif of the death of saints and prophets is repeated in 17:6, where the great prostitute is said to be "drunk with the blood of the saints and the blood of the witnesses to Jesus." As in 17:6 and 18:24 (see *Comments* on those verses), all or part of vv 6–7 appears to be a redactional addition to link an earlier text to the motif of martyrdom, which was important for the final editor. The term "prophets" is used of envoys of God who are also heroes of the faith (Luke 10:24; Matt 13:17; John 8:52; Heb 11:32–38; Jas 5:10; see J. Barton, *Oracles of God* [New York: Oxford UP, 1988] 96–98). The phrase αἷμα ἐκχεῖν, found only here in Revelation, can be literally translated "to shed blood" or "to pour out blood" (Hebrew שפך דם *šāpak dām*) and means "to murder" (Gen 9:6; Deut 19:10; Jer 7:6; *1 Enoch* 9:1; *T. Levi* 16:3; *T. Zeb.* 2:2; *Pss. Sol.* 8:20; *Sib. Or.* 3.311, 320; *Vit. Proph.* 23.1; Aeschylus *Eum.* 653; cf. Schwemer, "Vita Prophetarum" 2:287). This meaning is clearly expressed in *Sib. Or.* 3.311–12 (tr. Collins in Charlesworth, *OTP* 1:369):

> Then you will be filled with blood, as you yourself formerly poured out [ἐξέχεας] the blood of good men and righteous men, whose blood even now cries out to high heaven.

Betz (*JTC* 6 [1969] 139–54) adduces a number of ancient texts in which the four elements (earth, air, fire, water) cry out to God for purification from the pollution of bloodshed. In *1 Enoch* 7:6, the earth complains of the lawless ones, and in *1 Enoch* 9:1 it becomes clear that the complaint is based on the blood that has been shed on the earth (passages that clearly reflect Hellenistic presuppositions). The same motif from a pagan context occurs in *Corp. Herm.* 23.54–70, which includes a complaint from Water (58; tr. W. Scott, *Hermetica* 1:489):

> Next, my magnanimous son, Water was given leave to speak, and spoke thus: "O Father, self-begotten, and Maker of Nature, that power which generates all things to give thee pleasure, it is high time for thee to give command that my streams be kept pure; for the rivers and seas are ever washing off the defilement of the slayers, and receiving the corpses of the slain.

6b καὶ αἷμα αὐτοῖς δέδωκας πιεῖν, ἄξιοί εἰσιν, "and you have given them blood to drink; they are worthy." The chief exegetical problem here is to identify the αὐτοῖς, "to them." Should they be identified with the unidentified third-person plural subject of ἐξέχεαν, "they poured out" (i.e., the murderers), or with "the holy ones and prophets"? The phrase "to give someone blood to drink" can mean "to die" (Isa 49:26 [NRSV], "I will make your oppressors eat their own flesh, and they shall be drunk with their own blood as with wine"), in which case this phrase expresses the principle of *lex talionis*. But it more frequently means "to kill" (Rev 17:6; Num 23:24; 2 Sam 23:17; 1 Chr 11:19; Jer 46:10; Ezek 39:17–19; Zech 9:15; *1 Enoch* 7:5; Aeschylus *Cho.* 577–78; Sophocles *Electra* 1417–21; Sophocles *Oed. Col.* 622; *PGM* IV.2594–95, 2656–57). According to Charles, the meaning of this clause (which he renders "drink each other's blood") is that God will cause internecine war between Rome and her allies, yet the Johannine editor, he claims, did not understand this but took the clause to mean that as Rome shed the blood of

Christians, so it will be forced to drink actual blood (2:123). Such internecine conflict is clear in *1 Enoch* 7:5, but that is not what is said here in v 6. Despite the parallels adduced above, it seems inappropriate to construe this clause to mean that God allows the saints and prophets to die. If this were so, the αὐτοῖς would refer to the prophets and saints. However, it seems more appropriate to construe the αὐτοῖς to refer to those responsible for the deaths of the prophets and saints. This group could be "those people who have the brand of the beast and who worship his cultic statue" (v 2); see Jörns, *Evangelium,* 134. Clearly, "giving them blood to drink" refers to the fact that the rivers and the springs have been turned to blood, and that the inhabitants of the earth are being punished by literally being forced to drink blood as repayment for the blood that they have shed. Of course, people cannot drink blood, and therefore the symbolic interpretation proposed in the hymn seems secondary. The adjective ἄξιοι, "worthy," is used ironically in comparison with its use in 3:4. The symbolic interpretation of the turning of the rivers and springs of the earth into blood suggests that the hymn in vv 5–6 has been inserted into an existing narrative. Charles (2:120–24) thought that 16:5–7 was displaced and thought it appropriate to insert it after 19:4.

7a καὶ ἤκουσα τοῦ θυσιαστηρίου λέγοντος, "Then I heard someone from the altar say." Here it is not a question of the personified altar that cries out, as in 9:13 (a view reflected in several modern translations including the RSV, "And I heard the altar cry"; the NRSV, "Then I heard the altar respond"; and the NIV, "And I heard the altar respond" [Charles, 2:123–24]), for the object of ἤκουσα, "I heard," is the partitive genitive τοῦ θυσιαστηρίου, "[someone] from the altar." Within the narrative context of the final version of Revelation, the voice may perhaps belong to one of the martyrs under the altar in 6:10, whose request for vengeance has not yet been answered (Bousset [1906] 396). On the use of θυσιαστήριον in Revelation, see *Comment* on 6:9.

7b ναί, κύριε ὁ θεὸς ὁ παντοκράτωρ, ἀληθιναὶ καὶ δίκαιαι αἱ κρίσεις σου, "Yes, Lord God Almighty, / true and just are your judgments." The term ναί means "yes" and is used here to mark the emphatic affirmation of the judgment doxology in vv 5–6 (Louw-Nida, § 69.1); as such, it functions in hymnic contexts as part of antiphonic style. ναί, a synonym of ἀμήν, "amen," is used in affirmative responses four times in Revelation (1:7; 14:13; 16:7; 20:22). The expression ναί, κύριε is found in Matt 9:28; 15:27 in responses to Jesus, and it also occurs in some magical texts (e.g., Daniel and Maltomini, *Supplementum Magicum* I.42, line 35 [commentary], II.57, line 14 [commentary]). This is a brief judgment doxology paired as a response to that found in vv 5b–6 (Deichgräber, *Gotteshymnus,* 45, 56; K. Berger, *Formgeschichte,* 238). On the divine title κύριε ὁ θεὸς ὁ παντοκράτωρ, which occurs five times in Revelation (4:8; 11:17; 15:3; 16:7; 21:22), see *Comment* on 4:8. The phrase ἀληθιναὶ καὶ δίκαιαι αἱ κρίσεις σου, "true and just are your judgments," occurs again verbatim in 19:2. The attributes δίκαιος and ἀληθινός are paired three times in Revelation but are never predicated directly of God (as they are in Jos. *J.W.* 7.323; *Ant.* 11.55); rather they occur in the plural of God's ὁδοί, "ways" (15:3), or his κρίσεις, "judgments" (16:7; 19:2). An emphasis on God as a righteous judge is found in LXX Ps 7:12[MT 7:11], ὁ θεὸς κριτὴς δίκαιος, "God is a righteous judge"; 2 Macc 12:6, τὸν δίκαιον κριτὴν θεόν, "God the righteous judge"; and 2 Tim 4:8; ὁ κύριος . . . ὁ δίκαιος κριτής, "the Lord . . . the righteous judge"; see also *1 Clem.* 27:1; 60:1.

8a καὶ ὁ τέταρτος ἐξέχεεν τὴν φιάλην αὐτοῦ ἐπὶ τὸν ἥλιον, καὶ ἐδόθη αὐτῷ καυματίσαι τοὺς ἀνθρώπους ἐν πυρί, "The fourth one poured out his bowl upon the sun, and it was permitted to burn people with fire." This (like v 17) appears to contradict the divine command given in v 1, where the seven bowl angels were commanded to go and pour the contents of their bowls upon the *earth.* However, note the earth, water, fire, air schema in *Comment* on v 17. The blessings enjoyed by the victorious martyrs, according to 7:16, include the promise that the sun will not strike them and the assurance that they will not be affected by scorching heat (an allusion to Isa 49:10). A myth of the near destruction of the earth by a fiery sun is preserved in Ovid *Metam.* 1.749–79, 2.1–366 (see also Lucian *Dial. Deorum* 25). Phaethon, the son of Helios (Sun) and Clymene, received a promise from his father, Helius, that he could have whatever he wanted. He rashly chose, against his father's advice, to drive the chariot of the sun during one of its daily journeys between sunrise and sunset. His inexperience caused the horses to run wild and take the chariot off its normal course, coming too close to the earth and burning the mountains, forests, meadows, and cities of the earth. The scorching heat blackened the skin of the Ethiopians, turned fertile Libya into a desert (2.235–38), and dried up the Nile (2.254–56). It is striking that this is the only classical myth that narrates the scorching of the earth by the sun.

9a καὶ ἐκαυματίσθησαν οἱ ἄνθρωποι καῦμα μέγα, "People were burned with the intense heat." This is an example of the Hebrew infinitive absolute (see 17:6; 18:6; Turner, *Style,* 152).

9b καὶ ἐβλασφήμησαν τὸ ὄνομα τοῦ θεοῦ τοῦ ἔχοντος τὴν ἐξουσίαν ἐπὶ τὰς πληγὰς ταύτας, "They reviled the name of God who had authority over these plagues." The response of blaspheming or reviling the name of God on the part of people who have been affected by divine retribution occurs only here and in vv 11 and 21 and forms a distinctive motif in Revelation found only in 16:1–21 (though the beast is said to revile God and his dwelling in 13:6). The reviling or blaspheming of the name of God implicitly involves breaking the third commandment, which warns against the wrongful use of the name of God (Exod 20:7 = Deut 5:11; cf. Reicke, *Die zehn Worte,* 54–56) and is a sin punishable by death (Lev 24:16). This response is repeated in varied language as the human reaction to the seventh bowl.

9c καὶ οὐ μετενόησαν δοῦναι αὐτῷ δόξαν, "but they did not repent so as to give glory to him." The fourth plague produces a negative reaction on the part of the people of the world; i.e., they do not repent and (therefore) are not converted. The two phrases βλασφημεῖν τὸ ὄνομα τοῦ θεοῦ, "to blaspheme the name of God" (v 19b), and διδόναι δόξαν τῷ θεῷ, "to give glory to God," are antithetical and occur together in early Jewish literature (*T. Job* 16.4). This emphasis on the failure to repent is part of the Exodus motif in which Pharaoh's response to the plagues inflicted on Egypt through Moses is to harden his heart (Exod 7:13, 22; 8:15, 19, 32; 9:7, 12, 34–35; 10:1, 20; 11:9–10; 14:4). The motif of repentance is used in the context of the divine punishment in connection with the sixth trumpet (9:20–21), as well as the fifth (16:9) and sixth (16:11) bowls.

10a καὶ ὁ πέμπτος ἐξέχεεν τὴν φιάλην αὐτοῦ ἐπὶ τὸν θρόνον τοῦ θηρίου, "Then the fifth one poured out his libation bowl upon the throne of the beast." The throne of the beast is mentioned only in Rev 13:2, where it is said that the dragon gave his throne to the beast along with great authority. Many commentators think that "the throne of the beast" refers to Rome (Swete, 204; Bousset [1906] 397; Charles, 2:45; Behm, 89; Lohse, 92; Mounce, 297).

10b καὶ ἐγένετο ἡ βασιλεία αὐτοῦ ἐσκοτωμένη, "so that his kingdom became darkened." This plague calls to mind the ninth plague of the Exodus tradition in which thick darkness covered the land of Egypt for three days (Exod 10:21–29; cf. Wis 17:1–18:4), as well as the fourth trumpet plague (8:12) in which the light of the sun, moon, and stars was partially obliterated (a typical apocalyptic event; cf. Isa 13:10; Joel 2:10; 3:15; Amos 8:9; Hab 3:11; *Sib. Or.* 5.344–49; *Bib. Ant.* 19:13; *T. Moses* 10:5; Mark 13:24 = Matt 24:29; Acts 2:20 [Joel 2:10]). The crucifixion of Jesus was reportedly followed by a miraculous eclipse of the sun (Mark 15:33 = Matt 27:45 = Luke 23:44), to be understood as a sign (*TDNT* 7:439). Darkness is a symbol of judgment (1 Sam 2:9; Amos 5:20 [the day of Yahweh will be darkness and not light]; Joel 2:2; Zeph 1:15), ignorance and wickedness (Ps 82:5; Prov 2:13; Eccl 2:14; 4 Ezra 14:20), death (Ps 143:3), and the underworld as a place of punishment (*Jub.* 5:14; *1 Enoch* 17:6; *2 Enoch* 7:1; *Pss. Sol.* 14:9; *Bib. Ant.* 16:3; 51:1; Matt 8:12; 22:13; 25:30; Jude 13 = 2 Pet 2:17). Satan is called a מלאך חושך *malʾak ḥôšek*, "angel of darkness" (1QS 3:20–21). Darkness resulting from disturbances of the sun, moon, and stars became part of the apocalyptic scenario of the last days (Isa 13:10; Joel 2:10; 3:15; Amos 8:9; Hab 3:11; *Sib. Or.* 5.344–49; *Bib. Ant.* 19:13; *T. Moses* 10:5; Mark 13:24 = Matt 24:29; Acts 2:20 [Joel 2:10]; Rev 8:12; 9:2).

10c καὶ ἐμασῶντο τὰς γλώσσας αὐτῶν ἐκ τοῦ πόνου, "Consequently, people bit their tongues because of the pain." It is not immediately evident why the plague of darkness should inflict pain on people who are part of the kingdom of the beast. Charles saw this as a reference to the first woe, i.e., the fifth trumpet plague, in 9:1–12, for there the smoke from the abyss darkened the sun and the air (9:2), and people were tormented by hordes of demonic locusts. Charles assumed that several clauses in which the causes of the darkness and the suffering of humanity were narrated have dropped out of the text here (2:45; cf. Behm, 89; Lohmeyer, 135). Swete thought that the pain was the result of the previous plagues, particularly the fourth plague narrated in vv 8–9 (204; see also Kraft, 207; Sweet, 246).

11a καὶ ἐβλασφήμησαν τὸν θεὸν τοῦ οὐρανοῦ ἐκ τῶν πόνων αὐτῶν καὶ ἐκ τῶν ἑλκῶν αὐτῶν, "and they reviled the God of heaven because of their sufferings and their sores." Vv 10c and 11a exhibit synonymous parallelism. There is an inconsistency in the text in that there is no evident connection between darkness and the experience of pain and sores.

11b καὶ οὐ μετενόησαν ἐκ τῶν ἔργων αὐτῶν, "yet they did not repent of their behavior." On the motif of repentance, see *Comment* on 16:9.

12a καὶ ὁ ἕκτος ἐξέχεεν τὴν φιάλην αὐτοῦ ἐπὶ τὸν ποταμὸν τὸν μέγαν τὸν Εὐφράτην, "Then the sixth one poured out his bowl on the great river Euphrates." The Euphrates is mentioned in connection with both the sixth trumpet (9:14) and the sixth bowl. The river Euphrates, the largest river in southwest Asia, has been mentioned in connection with the sixth trumpet (9:14), which causes the four angels bound at the Euphrates to be liberated, thereby unleashing a demonic army that kills one-third of humanity (9:15–19). The Euphrates, sometimes called "the river" (Deut 11:24) and "the great river" (Gen 15:18; Deut 1:7; Josh 1:4), was one of the great natural boundaries in the ancient world (Exod 23:31; Deut 1:7; Josh 24:2; 1 Kgs 4:21; 2 Kgs 24:7; 1 Macc 3:32). The sixth libation bowl introduces a unit of text consisting of vv 12–16, composed of three units of text: (1) v 12, (2) vv 13–14 and 16, and (3) v 15 (framed by the interrupted text unit in vv 13–14 and 16).

12b καὶ ἐξηράνθη τὸ ὕδωρ αὐτοῦ, "with the result that its waters dried up." As the largest river in the southwest Asia, the Euphrates was *never* known to dry up, unlike most of the rivers in the Near East. The drying up of the river Euphrates to allow the kings of the east to cross over it is the typological antithesis of the Exodus from Egypt, in which the Israelites under Moses crossed the Reed Sea, and the later crossing of the Jordan under Joshua. The drying up of rivers is one of the responses of nature to the coming of God (Isa 50:2; Hos 13:15; Nah 1:4; see Jörg Jeremias, *Theophanie,* 90–97); it is also a miracle attributed to Ezekiel in *Vit. Proph.* 3.7 (see Schwemer, "Vitae Prophetarum," 242–48). The drying up of the Sea of Reeds (Exod 14:21; cf. Isa 11:15; Jer 51:36 [LXX 28:36]) and the drying up of the Jordan River (Josh 3:17) function as miraculous means enabling the passage of victorious armies.

12c ἵνα ἑτοιμασθῇ ἡ ὁδὸς τῶν βασιλέων τῶν ἀπὸ ἀνατολῆς ἡλίου, "so that a road was made ready for the kings from the east." In the OT hostile nations are sometimes used by God as instruments for inflicting punishments on Israel (Isa 10:5; Jer 50:25; Lam 3:1). In the OT prophecies are sometimes made that enemies of Israel will come from a particular direction of the compass, either the north (Jer 1:15; 4:6; 6:22) or the east (Isa 41:2; 46:11; Dan 11:44). The phrase "kings of the east" suggests that the east is not unified but is ruled by a coalition of kings, perhaps even more specifically by vassal kings subject to Rome. *T. Moses* 3:1 mentions a king from the east who will come and burn the city and temple, referring to Nebuchadrezzar. *1 Enoch* 56:5 mentions angels who assemble toward the east to incite the kings of the Parthians and Medes to invade Palestine and attack Jerusalem. In the view of many commentators, the phrase "the kings of the east" refers to the Parthian kings led by Nero *redivivus* (Bousset [1906] 397). One variant of the Nero *redivivus* myth included the belief that Nero would return from the east leading a vast Parthian army (see *Excursus 13A: The Nero* Redux *or* Redivivus *Legend*). The Euphrates is specifically mentioned as the river past which the "great king" (i.e., Nero *redivivus*) flees (*Sib. Or.* 4.120) and the river he will cross with an enormous army (*Sib. Or.* 4.139). It is worth noting that while there were many dynastic kingdoms in the Near East during the reign of Augustus, by the early second century all those west of the Euphrates had disappeared.

Excursus 16A: Rome and Parthia

Bibliography

Charlesworth, M. P. "The Fear of the Orient in the Roman Empire." *Cambridge Historical Journal* 2 (1926) 9–16. **Colledge, M. A. R.** *The Parthians.* New York: Praeger, 1967. **Dabrowa, E.** *La politique de l'État Parthe à l'égard de Rome—d'Artaban II à Vologèse I (ca 11–ca 79 de n. e.) et les facteurs qui la conditionnaient.* Krakow: Uniwersytet Jagiellonski, 1983. **Debecq, J.** "Les Parthes et Rome." *Latomus* 10 (1951) 459–69. **Debevoise, N. C.** *A Political History of Parthia.* Chicago: University of Chicago, 1938. **Ensslin, W.** "Die weltgeschichtliche Bedeutung der Kämpfe zwischen Rom und Persien." *Neue Jahrbücher für deutsche Wissenschaft* 4 (1928) 399–415. **Frye, R. N.** *The History of Ancient Iran.* Munich: Beck, 1984. **Ghirshman, R.** *Iran: Parthians and Sassanians.* London: Thames and Hudson, 1962. **Schieber, A. D.** *The Flavian Eastern Policy.* Ann Arbor, MI: University Microfilms, 1976. **Ward Perkins, J. B.** "The Roman West and the Parthian East." *PBA* 51 (1965) 175–99. **Ziegler, K.-H.** *Die Beziehungen zwischen Rom und dem Partherreich.* Wiesbaden: Steiner, 1964.

The phrase "the kings of the east" in Rev 16:12 appears to be an ambiguous expression, though it reflects the ancient cliché of the conflict between the East and the West first formulated by Herodotus and Aeschylus in their views of the Persian invasion of Greece early in the fifth century B.C. Rev 16:12 has often been construed as a reference to the Parthians, and other references to the Parthians have sometimes been suggested in 9:13–19 and 17:10–12 (Wellhausen, *Analyse,* 26). Alexander's short-lived attempt to join East and West became a reality on a smaller scale under the Seleucid empire. With the rise in power of Rome, however, the ancient rivalry between East and West was revitalized, with various kingdoms taking on the role of the East: Pontus, Armenia, Arsacid Parthia, and then Sassanid Persia.

The Parthians themselves have left few written records, and references to Parthia and Parthians in Western writers are generally hostile. The Parthian kings were usually insecure on their thrones because of rivalries within their royal households as well as shifting loyalties among the Parthian aristocrats who often controlled their own regions with royal autonomy. The Arsacid dynasty began 247 B.C. and continued until A.D. 224, when it was replaced by the Sassanid dynasty (A.D. 224–636). The tension between Rome and Parthia was largely over land, particularly that which was strategically located (see Frye, "Wars with Rome," in *Iran,* 233–44). The most intensely disputed areas were Armenia and the land between the Tigris and the Euphrates. The Parthians invaded Babylonia in 141 B.C., and the first known contact between Parthia and Rome occurred in 92 B.C. when an envoy of the Parthian king Mithridates II Eupator (ca. 124/3–87 B.C.) met L. Cornelius Sulla on the west bank of the Euphrates and asked for the *amicitia* of Rome (Ziegler, *Beziehungen,* 20–24), which lasted until 70/69 B.C. Then Tigranes of Armenia aided Mithridates of Pontus in his war against Rome, and both requested help from the Parthian king Phraates III (70–58 B.C.), who chose to remain neutral even though Rome invaded Armenia and established φιλία τε καὶ συμμαχία, "friendship and alliance." Perhaps a *foedus,* i.e., a "formal treaty," was established between Armenia and the Roman general Lucullus (Dio 36.3.2–3; Ziegler, *Beziehungen,* 24–28). In 67 B.C. Syria became a Roman province, later a "province of Caesar" or imperial province, as a result of the victories of Pompey. In 66 B.C. Pompey replaced Lucullus in the war against Mithridates of Pontus and apparently concluded a *foedus* with Phraates III since the Parthians thereafter invaded Armenia, implying that the Euphrates was the boundary between the Roman and Parthian spheres of influence (Dio 36.45.2–3; Ziegler, *Beziehungen,* 28–32), though the Armenian king Tigranes was soon forced to become a client of Pompey (i.e., an *amicus et socius populi Romani;* see Rev 17:12–13). When Pompey insulted Phraates by calling him only "king" rather than "king of kings" in his letters (Plutarch *Pompey* 38.2; Dio 37.6.1), Phraates forbad the Romans to cross the Euphrates and then successfully invaded Armenia.

A series of events produced tension between Rome and Parthia. In 55 B.C. M. Licinius Crassus became governor of Syria and boasted that he could conquer Parthia (the desire to imitate the feat of Alexander providing motivation). Crassus crossed the Euphrates in 53 B.C. but was decisively defeated at Carrhae by mounted archers and ἡ καταφράκτος ἵππος, "kataphracts" (i.e., heavily armored cavalry; Polybius 30.25.9), perhaps the most disastrous Roman defeat since Cannae (Plutarch *Crassus* 23–28). Julius Caesar made plans for a campaign of revenge against Parthia through Armenia, a plan that remained unrealized because of his death in 44 B.C. (Debevois, *Parthia,* 106–7). Antony too had designs on Parthia (Plutarch *Antony* 25.2), and his abortive attack on Palmyra may have provoked the Parthian invasion of 40 B.C. (Appian *Bell. Civ.* 5.9), actually the last successfully mounted Parthian invasion (but one that would live in Roman memory as an ever-present possibility). By 34 B.C. Antony had taken over Armenia, attempting to make it a Roman province, and after some delay began an invasion of Parthia in 33 B.C., though it was aborted because of the threat of Octavian. After Octavian's decisive victory over Antony at Actium in 31 B.C., he chose to reaffirm the Euphrates as the frontier between the Roman and Parthian spheres of interest, though many Romans favored the conquest of Parthia (Vergil *Aeneid* 7.606; Horaces *Odes* 1.12.53). Augustus, however, installed a client king in Armenia (*Res Gestae* 27.2) and settled for a diplomatic victory by the return of Roman standards captured at Carrhae (*Res Gestae* 29.2). Following Actium, the control of Seleucia or Zeugma ("bridge"), the main crossing point for the Euphrates, passed into the hands of the Romans, and the Euphrates became the main symbolic boundary between Rome and Parthia (Strabo 16.1.28; Velleius 2.101; Millar, *Near East,* 33). After years of tension, Gaius Caesar met Phraates V (2 B.C.–A.D. 4) on an island in the Euphrates in A.D. 1 and agreed on mutual spheres of influence; the Parthians dropped claims on Armenia, and Phraates allowed his four half brothers, sons of Phraates IV, to remain in Rome as hostages (Velleius Paterculus 2.101; Dio 55.10a.4; Ziegler, *Beziehungen,* 54–55). This provided the Romans with a coterie of Arsacid princes who lived and had children in Rome and who could serve as client kings if and when the need arose. Following the death of the Parthian king Orodes III in A.D. 6/7, the Parthians asked Augustus to send one of the sons of Phraates IV to Parthia as king. This king was removed by another, Arsacid Artabanus III (A.D. 12–38), who was hostile to Rome. Artabanus invaded Armenia in 35 B.C., and the Romans countered by sending L. Vitellius as governor of Syria, who promptly invaded Mesopotamia and crowned a client Parthian king at Ctesiphon, the capital. Artabanus soon regained his throne, however. Tiberius continued the Augustan policy of maintaining peace with Parthia and control of Armenia, though it fell again into Parthian control during the reign of Gaius (A.D. 37–54). Artabanus III had a summit conference with the Roman governor at the Euphrates (Suetonius *Gaius* 14.2), thereby establishing parity between the two empires. Throughout the reigns of Tiberius, Gaius, and Claudius, there were internal struggles for the Parthian throne. During the reign of Nero, a running war with Parthia began and ended with a settlement made in Rhandeia in A.D. 63, in which it was agreed that the king of Armenia would be an Arsacid (thus satisfying Parthia), though that king would either be crowned or approved by Rome; the Arsacid Tirdates was thus installed on the throne of Armenia (Schieber, *Policy,* 36–51; Ziegler, *Beziehungen,* 67–78; R. Syme, *Tacitus* [Oxford: Clarendon, 1958] 1:237). The actions of the Roman governor Corbulo in the East (Schieber, *Policy,* 42–51), together with the popularity of Nero in Parthia (Suetonius *Nero* 57; Ziegler, *Beziehungen,* 77–78), guaranteed that the possibility of a Parthian invasion was remote, at least during Nero's lifetime (he died in A.D. 68). The Euphrates continued to be the frontier between Rome and Parthia from the battle of Mount Gindarus (the defeat of Antony in 36 B.C.) to the invasion of Parthia by Trajan. One legion, X Fretensis, had been stationed in Zeugma in the 60s and joined Vespasian in A.D. 66/67 for his campaign to suppress the Jewish revolt. This legion was replaced by the IV Scythica (Jos. *J.W.* 7.17; Millar, *Near East,* 75).

The irrational Roman fear of the Parthians was *not* shared by Palestinian Jews, who rather hoped that the Parthian king, Vologaeses I (A.D. 51/2–79/80), would come to their aid against the Romans (Jos. *J.W.* 2.389), but this hope did not materialize. In A.D. 71, after the conquest of Jerusalem, Titus visited Lebanon and Syria and met at Zeugma the envoys of King Vologaeses, who presented Titus with a golden crown congratulating him on his victory over the Jews (Jos. *J.W.* 7.105–6). King Vologaeses of Parthia requested help from Vespasian against the Alani, a request rejected by Vespasian though supported by Domitian (Suetonius *Dom.* 2.2). During the Roman civil war of 69, Vologaeses offered Vespasian forty thousand Parthian cavalry, but this offer was refused (Tacitus *Hist.* 4.51). With the loss of Armenia, Vespasian attempted to secure the borders with Parthia by reorganizing the border provinces, by building new roads, and by stationing two additional legions in Cappadocia. Between 71 and 73, Armenia Minor and Commagene were annexed by Rome (Schieber, *Policy,* 130–33).

When King Osroes removed the Roman vassal King Axidares from the throne ca. A.D. 110, Trajan set out in 113 with the probable intention of annexing Armenia, which he in fact achieved in 114. Trajan moved south into Mesopotamia and in 115 crossed the

Tigris and occupied Ctesiphon, the capital of Parthia. After quelling a revolt, he installed Parthamaspates as a client king on the throne of Parthia.

13 Καὶ εἶδον ἐκ τοῦ στόματος τοῦ δράκοντος καὶ ἐκ τοῦ στόματος τοῦ θηρίου καὶ ἐκ τοῦ στόματος τοῦ ψευδοπροφήτου πνεύματα τρία ἀκάθαρτα ὡς βάτραχοι, "Then I saw three unclean spirits like frogs emerge from the mouth of the dragon and from the mouth of the beast and from the mouth of the false prophet." (On καὶ εἶδον, see *Comment* on 5:1.) This sentence lacks a main verb (the verb one must supply is "emerge"), though it is clearly implied that an unclean spirit resembling a frog emerged from each of the three figures. These three figures are all mentioned in Rev 13, though the beast from the land of 13:11–17 is here designated the false prophet. There is an interesting connection between 1 John 4:1–3 and Revelation; in 1 John 4:1, "false prophets" are referred to, while in 4:3 that which false prophets say is called "the spirit of antichrist." Since Rev 13:11–18 is based on traditions of the eschatological antagonist, i.e., the Antichrist, this characterization suggests how the label "false prophet" arose as an alias of the eschatological antagonist in Rev 16:13; 19:20; 20:10. The beast and the false prophet are again mentioned in 19:20 (the context of this passage, 19:11–21, was originally a continuation of 16:12–16) and 20:10. The term ψευδοπροφήτης, "false prophet," occurs several times in the NT of OT figures (Luke 6:26), of opponents or heretics (Matt 7:15; Acts 13:6; 1 John 4:1; cf. Herm. *Mand.* 11.1–2, 4, 7; *Did.* 11:5–10; 16:3), and (as here) of eschatological figures (Mark 13:22 = Matt 24:11; 2 Pet 2:1). There is a traditional connection between evil spirits and the mouth or nostrils as a passageway for entering or leaving a person. According to Josephus (*Ant.* 8.46–49), the Jewish exorcist Eleazar drew demons out of the nostrils of the afflicted individual (see Ps.-Plutarch *De fluv.* 16; Eitrem, *Demonology,* 48). In *Gk. Apoc. Ezra* 6:3–15, angels try unsuccessfully to take the soul of Ezra, first by threatening to cast it forth from his mouth (6:5) and then by threatening to bring it forth through his nostrils (6:7). These conceptions reflect a belief in the way in which the breath of life, the soul (*psyche*), was breathed into the nostrils of the first man (see Gen 2:7). They also reflect the association of the *psyche* with breath, for, in early Greek thought, *psyche* was thought to leave the body from the mouth at death (*Iliad* 9.409). In an Egyptian instructional text from a Heracleopolitan king to his son Merikare from the early Middle Kingdom, he states that "he [Re] gave the breath of life to their noses, for they are likenesses of Him which issued from His flesh" (L. H. Lesko, "Egyptian Religion," *EncRel* 5:41). In Hermas's vision of the beast, fiery locusts are said to come out (ἐξεπορεύοντο; the same term used in Rev 16:14b) of its mouth (*Vis.* 4.1.6); see Brox, *Hirt,* 168.

14a εἰσὶν γὰρ πνεύματα δαιμονίων ποιοῦντα σημεῖα, "For they are spirits, that is, demons, producing signs." On the idiom ποιεῖν σημεῖα, "producing signs," see *Comment* on 13:13. The chief interpretive problem with this explanatory phrase is that as the text stands it is not the dragon, the beast, and the false prophet who go out to assemble the kings of the world for battle, but the demons that proceed from their mouths (this leads to the problem of the subject of συνήγαγεν, "gathered," in v 16; it could be the demons or the unholy trinity of the dragon, beast, and false prophet). Because of these problems, Charles (2:47–48) regards the entire clause ὡς βάτραχοι . . . σημεῖα as a marginal gloss later incorporated into the text. There is a parallel in 1 Kgs 22:19–23, where the prophet Micaiah ben Imlah overhears a conversation in the heavenly court in which a spirit volunteers to be a "lying spirit" speaking through prophets to entice Ahab to go to war and so die (cf. Jer 20:7–10; Ezek 14:9).

In the phrase πνεύματα δαιμονίων, "spirits of demons," the plural genitive δαιμονίων (an adjective used as a substantive) can be either a descriptive genitive, so that the noun phrase should be translated "demonic spirits" (unlikely because they have already been characterized as πνεύματα ἀκάθαρτα, "unclean spirits," in v 13), or a genitive of apposition in which spirits = demons, so that the phrase can be translated "spirits, that is, demons." Since δαιμόνιον is primarily a Hellenistic term, the phrase would then serve to clarify the meaning of a more ambiguous Semitic term πνεῦμα by providing a Greek equivalent. Josephus does this in *Ant.* 6.211 when he says that David "drove out the evil spirit and the demons [τοῦ πονηροῦ πνεύματος καὶ τῶν δαιμονίων]" that afflicted Saul. Elsewhere Josephus (*J.W.* 7.185) finds it necessary to define δαιμόνια as πονηρῶν ἐστιν ἀνθρώπων πνεύματα, "spirits of wicked men" (a major way in which *daimons* were understood in the Greco-Roman world; cf. Plutarch *De def. orac.* 415B–C). This phrase, which exhibits an "abundance of style" (Eitrem, *Demonology,* 38 n. 5), is less awkward than the similar phrase in Luke 4:33, πνεῦμα δαιμονίου ἀκαθάρτου, in which the two genitives are probably appositional, i.e., "a spirit, that is, an unclean demon" (cf. Fitzmyer, *Luke* 1:544–45, who also suggests [less probably] that the πνεῦμα may be the man's spirit afflicted by an "unclean demon"). A similar phrase, τὰ πνεύματα τῶν δαιμόνων, "the spirits of the daimons," occurs in *PGM* XV.15–16, where the plural genitive is similarly appositional. The phrase δαιμόνιον πνεύμα, "demonic spirit" (in which δαιμόνιον functions as an adjective), also occurs in magical texts (*PGM* IV.3038–39, 3065–66, 3075, a Jewish text also published in Deissmann, *Light,* 251–60; Denis, *Fragmenta,* 236–38; line 1 of the lead tablet from Hadrumetum written by a Hellenistic Jew and published with commentary in Deissmann, *Bible Studies,* 273–300). Yet in *PGM* IV.3081 these terms are used to refer to different types of supernatural beings: "every spirit and daimon [πνεῦμα καὶ δαιμόνιον] will be subject to you" (cf. *PGM* XII.261). This may, however, reflect the magician's attempt to be inclusive.

14b ἃ ἐκπορεύεται ἐπὶ τοὺς βασιλεῖς τῆς οἰκουμένης ὅλης, "who travel to the kings of the whole world." Since the verb ἐκπορεύεσθαι means "to move out of an enclosed or well-defined two or three dimensional area" (Louw-Nida, § 15.40), it refers to the emergence of the demons *from the mouths* of the dragon, the beast, and the false prophet (Acts 19:12 refers to the evil spirits that "came out" [ἐκπορεύεσθαι] of people; see Matt 17:21). ἐκπορεύεσθαι is particularly associated with that which emerges from the mouth (Matt 4:4; Mark 7:15, 19, 20, 21, 23 = Matt 15:11, 18; Luke 4:22; Eph 4:29; Herm. *Mand.* 3.1), such as the demons "emerging" from the mouths of this unholy trinity, and this image has a counterpart in the sword "emerging" (ἐκπορεύεται) from the mouth of the heavenly warrior in 19:15 (see 1:16). The phrase "the kings of the entire world" is in tension with "the kings of the east" mentioned in v 12c since there is no clear reason why *two* groups of kings should be involved, nor is it clear what the relationship between the two groups might be. This suggests that vv 13–14 constitute a later interpolation that exhibits the theme of kings hostile to God and his people. The "kings of the whole world" are often identified with the ten kings in 17:12–14, 16–17 (Beckwith, 683; Bousset [1906] 397), though in my view the battle motif in 17:14 is an interpolation. In 1QM, the

War Scroll, it is clear that the adversaries of the "sons of light" in the eschatological battle are "all nations" (כול הגויים *kôl haggôyîm*, 15:1; 16:1; see P. R. Davies, *1QM*, 79), also called "all the nations of wickedness" (כול גוי רשעה *kôl gôy riš'â*, 1QM 15:2), yet the fact that the primary adversary is the "king of the Kittim" (מלך הכתיים *melek hakkittiyyîm*, 15:2) suggests that some kind of coalition is assumed. It is clear in 1QM 2:10–14 that the sons of light systematically make war on many of the traditional eastern enemies of Israel, which are identified by the biblical names for their founders: Aram-Naharaim, Lud, Aram, Uz, Hul, Togal, Mesha, Arpachsad, Assyria, Persia, Elam, Ishmael, Ketura, Ham, Japhet.

14c συναγαγεῖν αὐτοὺς εἰς τὸν πόλεμον τῆς ἡμέρας τῆς μεγάλης τοῦ θεοῦ τοῦ παντοκράτορος, "to assemble them for battle on the great day of God the Almighty." The term συνάγειν, "to gather together," is repeated in v 16, thematically linking vv 13–14 with 16 (συνάγειν occurs again in a similar context in 19:19). The gathering of the nations hostile to the people of God for the final eschatological struggle is also found in 16:16; 19:17, 19; 20:8 and in a number of OT and early Jewish texts (Ezek 38–39; Joel 3:2; Zech 14:2; Ps 2:1–2; 4 Ezra 13:34–35; *1 Enoch* 56:7; 90:16–19; *2 Apoc. Bar.* 70:7–10; *Sib. Or.* 3.663–68; *T. Joseph* 19; LXX Esth 11:5–8; 1QM 1:10–11; 15:2–3). That πόλεμον, "batte," is articular suggests that a well-known battle is in view, i.e., the great messianic battle of the end time. Hartman has labeled this theme "the tumult and assault of the heathen," which consists of the heathens attacking each other or Israel (*Prophecy Interpreted*, 77–101). This theme is found in many apocalyptic passages (Ezek 38–39; Zech 12:1–9; *1 Enoch* 90:13–19; 99:4; *Jub.* 23:23). 1QM 1:10 mentions the יום יעוד *yôm yā'ûd*, the "appointed day," for the battle in which the sons of darkness will be destroyed. Jdt 16:17 pronounces woe on the nations that fight Israel and concludes "The Lord Almighty will take vengeance on them in the day of judgment." While it is difficult to determine if this is eschatology or history (C. A. Moore, *Judith*, 251; Enslin-Zeitlin, *Judith*, 174–75), the phrase "day of judgment" means the day on which God defeats the enemies of his people, presumably in battle. In the eschatological battle anticipated in Ezek 38–39, many nations are assembled for battle against the people of God (38:1–6).

15a Ἰδοὺ ἔρχομαι ὡς κλέπτης, "(Indeed, [says Jesus] I am coming like a thief." This is clearly an intrusive comment unrelated to what precedes or follows, and though the speaker is not identified, it is clear that it is the exalted Jesus. The metaphor of Jesus coming like a thief occurs in 3:3 (see *Comment* there). V 15 is therefore an interpolation derived from 3:3, which has a parenetic character and belongs to the Second Edition of Revelation, i.e., to the framework in 1:3–14; 2:1–3:22; 22:5–21.

15b μακάριος ὁ γρηγορῶν καὶ τηρῶν τὰ ἱμάτια αὐτοῦ, "How fortunate is the one who watches and remains fully clothed." This is the third of seven beatitudes or makarisms in Revelation (1:3; 14:13; here; 19:9; 20:6; 22:7, 14; see *Form/Structure/Setting* on 1:1–3). The motif of watchfulness in expectation of the sudden eschatological consummation occurs elsewhere in Revelation only in 3:2–3, where it is combined with the threat that Jesus will come as a thief in the event that Christians fail to be watchful. See *Comment* on 3:2–3. There is a close similarity with *Gos. Thom.* 103, which is also in the form of a beatitude and which also emphasizes the motif of vigilance (tr. B. Layton, *The Gnostic Scriptures* [Garden City: Doubleday, 1987] 397):

> Jesus said, "Blessed is the man who recognizes [which] district the brigands are going to enter, so as to arise, gather (the forces of) his domain, and arm himself before they enter.

Only here in Revelation is the verb τηρῶν, "keeping," used metaphorically with "garments." The importance of having appropriate garments (cf. 3:4) is underscored in the *Acta Alexandrinorum* 7.101–7 (Musurillo, *Acts*, 42), where the emperor is accused of condemning a man to death who sat in the theater without wearing a white festal garment (οὐκ ἐν λευκαῖς ἐσθῆσιν).

15c ἵνα μὴ γυμνὸς περιπατῇ καὶ βλέπωσιν τὴν ἀσχημοσύνην αὐτοῦ, "lest he go about naked and people see his shameful state.)" This suggests that the sudden and unexpected coming of Christ brings both salvation and judgment; salvation for those who are prepared, judgment for those who are not. In the OT and early Judaism, the notions of "nakedness" and "shame" were closely associated (Gen 9:20–24; Isa 20:4; 47:3; Hos 2:10; 1 Cor 12:23; *Apoc. Moses* 20). See *Tg. Ps.-J.* Gen 3:10 (tr. Maher), where Adam reportedly says "I was afraid, for I was naked, *because I neglected the commandment you gave me,* and I hid myself *for shame*" (italicized words not in MT). The Hebrew term עֶרְוָה *ʿerwâ,* "nakedness, genitalia," is translated eight times in the LXX with the Greek term αἰσχύνη, "shame, disgrace" (Isa 20:4; 47:3; Ezek 16:36, 38; 22:10; 23:10, 18, 29), suggesting that in Rev 16:15 αἰσχύνη also means "nakedness." The same idiom occurs in *Apoc. Moses* 20:4, where Adam says "I looked for leaves in my area to hide my shame [ὅπως καλύψω τὴν αἰχύνην μου]." According to Israelite protology, nakedness had not always been associated with shame, as Gen 2:25 makes clear: "The man and his wife were both naked, and were not ashamed" (RSV). The notions of "nakedness" and "shame" are also linked in Rev 3:18 in the phrase ἡ αἰσχύνη τῆς γυμνότητός σου, "the shame of your nakedness" (the specific terms αἰσχύνη and γυμνότης occur only there in Revelation). Rev 16:15 may, then, be an allusion to the tradition of "Adam's coat" (based on Gen 3:7, 10–11), a magical garment guaranteeing invincibility, which was venerated by his descendants and was eventually buried in the Cave of Machpelah, where it was preserved for twenty generations (*Gen. Rab.* 63.13; Ginzberg, *Legends* 1:177; 2:139; 5:199, 276–77; Jørgensen, "Gravhulen," 102–15). One facet is reflected in the poetic mythological variant of the Adam tradition in Ezek 28:13, where the garment is described as a series of precious stones similar to those worn on the garments of high priests (Ginzberg, *Legends* 1:332; 5:104). Adam and Eve lost their celestial "garments of light" (עור *ʿôr,* "skin," in Gen 3:21, explained as though it were written אור *ʾôr,* "light") when expelled from Eden (Irenaeus *Haer.* 3.23.5; Tertullian *De pudicitia* 9; *De resurrectione* 7; Ginzberg, *Legends* 1:79; 5:42, 97, 103–4). Another strand of this tradition (linked exegetically in *Jub.* 3:26 to Gen 3:7, 9–10) is also reflected in *Jub.* 3:30, where the term "shame" is a metaphor for nakedness (Charlesworth, *OTP* 2:60):

> But from all the beasts and all the cattle he [God] granted to Adam alone that he might cover his shame. Therefore it is commanded in the heavenly tablets to all who will know the judgment of the Law that they should cover their shame and they should not be uncovered as the gentiles are uncovered.

Nakedness is associated with shame, together with hunger, as divine punishments in 4Q*166* = 4QHosea Pesher[a] 2:12–13 (tr. García Martínez, *Dead Sea Scrolls,* 192), "he has punished them with hunger and with nakedness so they will be shame [*sic*] and disgrace in the eyes of the nations on whom they relied." There was a different attitude toward the body in the Greek world, though public nudity was always relatively unusual; nudity was considered shameful in some contexts, but not in others, e.g., athletics, battle (*Odysseus* 22.1; F. Pfister, "Nacktheit," PW 16/2:1541–49; *Kleine Pauly* 3:1556–57). The first naked man presented in Greek literature is Odysseus, and he expresses shame at his nakedness in the presence of young women (*Odyssey* 6.127–29, 221–22; Pfister, PW 16/2:1545). Odysseus threatens to beat and strip Thersites and so shame him (*Iliad* 2.261–62), and dead enemy warriors were stripped as a final form of humiliation (*Iliad* 11.99–100; 22.510). The Romans, in contrast, tended to disapprove of Greek forms of public nudity (Cicero *Tusc. disp.* 4.70). In comparing Greek and Roman statuary, Pliny observes that Greek statues of prominent males are characteristically nude, while Roman statues are clothed (*Hist. nat.* 34.18).

16a καὶ συνήγαγεν αὐτοὺς εἰς τὸν τόπον τὸν καλούμενον Ἑβραϊστὶ Ἁρμαγεδών, "The spirits gathered them together to the place called Armageddon in Hebrew." The place name "Armageddon" occurs only here, where it represents the mythical apocalyptic-world mountain where the forces hostile to God, assembled by demonic spirits, will gather for final battle against God and his people (other versions of this myth are preserved in Rev 19:19; 20:9; 4 Ezra 13:34–35; *1 Enoch* 56:7; *Sib. Or.* 3.663–68; see Joel 3:2; Zech 14:2). In the Gog and Magog oracle in Ezek 38–39, the place where the enemy from the north assembles and is defeated is called simply "the mountains of Israel" (38:8; 39:2, 4, 17), in agreement with the mention of Harmagedon, but in contrast to Rev 19:19 (where no gathering place is mentioned) and Rev 20:9 (where the enemy surrounds "the beloved city"). The name "Harmagedon" has never been satisfactorily explained (Charles, 2:50–51; Joachim Jeremias, *TDNT* 1:468; KB³, 515–16). The most common explanation of the name is that *har* (הר *hâr*) is the Hebrew word for "mountain(s), hill(s)," while *magedon* refers to the biblical town of "Megiddo," with the entire construction meaning "mountain(s) of Megiddo." Megiddo was an ancient city located on a plain in the southwest portion of the Valley of Jezreel or Esdraelon, the site of several significant ancient battles, including the Battle of Megiddo, part of the campaign of Thutmose III against a coalition of Canaanite petty kings in 1468 B.C., the campaign of Merneptah in 1220 B.C., the battle led by Deborah and Barak against a Canaanite coalition (Judg 4:6–16; 5:19), the victory of Gideon over the Midianites (Judg 7), the defeat of Saul by the Philistines (1 Sam 29:1; 31:1–7), the campaign of Shishak in 924 B.C., and the clash between Josiah and Pharaoh Neco in 609 B.C. in which Josiah was killed (2 Kgs 23:29–30; 2 Chr 35:22–24). During the reign of Solomon, Megiddo (along with Hazor and Gezer) was rebuilt as a central fortress city (Jos. *Ant.* 8.151). During the reign of the Assyrian king Tiglath-Pileser III, an Assyrian governor apparently resided at Megiddo, which was used as the name of a newly created province. During Roman times the site of Megiddo became a permanent Roman camp called *Legio* or Λεγεὼν ἐν τῷ μεγάλῳ πεδίῳ, "Legio in the great plain" (Eusebius *Onomasticon* [ed. E. Klostermann] 14.31; 28.26; 58.1; 70.10; 90.12; 100.10; 108.6, 13; 110.21; 116.21; 140.1). The Valley of Jezreel, through which the Kishon River threads in a northeasterly direction to the Bay of Acco, was (and still is) the breadbasket of lower Galilee (Isa 28:1), providing a natural route for the invasion of Palestine. The "Way of the Sea" (Isa 9:1 [MT 8:23]), later called the *Via*

Maris, ran along the coast north from Egypt and through the Valley of Jezreel to Megiddo across the volcanic causeway north of Mount Tabor, where it then split into two routes, one northwest to Acco on the coast and the other to Hazor and thence to Damascus. Another proposal is that that Ἁρμαγεδών is derived from ער מגדון *ʿir mĕgiddôn,* "city of Megiddo." This mention of the Hebrew name for the place may be classified grammatically as a parenthetical remark in the form of a relative clause that does not interrupt the structure of the sentence (G. Rudberg, "Parentesen i Nya Testamentet," *SEÅ* 5 [1940] 136; BDR § 465; BDF § 465). Other examples of such parentheses in Revelation are found in 9:11; 20:8. This verse is one small indication that the author knew Hebrew (see 11:11). Loasby, following F. Hommel (*NKZ* 1 [1890] 407–8), construes the Hebrew underlying Ἁρμαγεδών to be הר מועד *har môʿēd,* "mountain of assembly" (Hebrew ע is often transliterated with the Greek γ), referring to Mount Zion from where the Messiah will destroy the ungodly. This term, used in Isa 14:13, appears to mean "mountain [where the gods] assemble" (J. D. W. Watts, *Isaiah 1–33,* WBC 24 [Waco, TX: Word, 1985] 207). Both Oecumenius (Hoskier, *Oecumenius,* 180) and Andreas of Caesarea (Schmid, *Studien,* 1/1:175) claim that Ἁρμαγεδών means διακοπή or διακοπτομένη, i.e., "cutting" or "cut through," because it is the place where the hostile enemies of God will attempt to "cut through" and conquer. This interpretation is probably derived from the LXX translation in Zech 12:11, ἐν πεδίῳ ἐκκοπτομένου (*var. lect.* ἐν πεδίῳ μαγεδδών; Ziegler, *Duodecim prophetae,* 320), "in the plain of that which is cut down," reflecting the LXX translators' view that מְגִדּוֹן *mĕgiddôn* in Zech 12:11 was derived from the Hebrew root גדד *gdd,* "to cut down."

17a καὶ ὁ ἕβδομος ἐξέχεεν τὴν φιάλην αὐτοῦ ἐπὶ τὸν ἀέρα, "The seventh poured out his libation bowl into the air." In 16:1, the bowl angels are commanded to pour out their libation bowls upon the *earth.* While this plague is not closely related to the others, it does result in the affliction of the four elements, considered basic from the time of the Greek natural philosophers (e.g., Empedocles, frags. B96, B98, B107, B115 in H. Diels and W. Kranz, *Die Fragmente der Vorsokratiker,* 6th ed. [Zürich; Hildesheim: Weidmann, 1951]): (1) *earth* (v 2), (2) *water* (sea, v 3; rivers and springs, v 4; the Euphrates, v 12), (3) *fire* (sun, v 8), and (4) *air* (v 17); the throne of the beast (v 10) is obviously missing from this schema.

17b καὶ ἐξῆλθεν φωνὴ μεγάλη ἐκ τοῦ ναοῦ ἀπὸ τοῦ θρόνου λέγουσα· γέγονεν, "and a loud voice came from the temple, that is, from the throne, saying, 'It is finished.'" This may be an allusion to the phrase "a voice from the temple" in Isa 66:6 (see Rev 16:1). This reiterates the summary in Rev 15:1, which concludes by saying that with these seven bowls the wrath of God is finished. However, if the wrath of God has ended, it remains unclear why Babylon is the focus of 17:1–18:24. The perfect tense of γέγονεν, "it is finished," suggests a contrast with the previous use of aorist tenses and points to the climactic end of the series of plagues that God has inflicted on the world (Lambrecht, "Structuration," in *L'Apocalypse,* ed. J. Lambrecht, 94 n. 45).

18 καὶ ἐγένοντο ἀστραπαὶ καὶ φωναὶ καὶ βρονταὶ καὶ σεισμὸς ἐγένετο μέγας, οἷος οὐκ ἐγένετο ἀφ᾽ οὗ ἄνθρωπος ἐγένετο ἐπὶ τῆς γῆς τηλικοῦτος σεισμὸς οὕτω μέγας, "Then there were lightning and rumbling and thunder, and there was a great earthquake such as has never been since people have been on the earth, so great was the earthquake." (On the significance of the four lists of atmospheric and seismic phenomena [4:5; 8:5; 11:19; 16:18–21], see *Comment* on 4:5; on the earthquake motif, see *Comment* on 8:5). V 18b alludes to Dan 12:1 and is closer to Theod Dan 12:1 (itself an allusion to Jer 30:7) than to the LXX or the MT: θλίψις οἵα οὐ γέγονεν ἀφ' οὗ γεγένηται ἔθνος ἐπὶ τῆς γῆς ἕως τοῦ καιροῦ ἐκείνου, "tribulation, such as had not occurred since a nation had appeared on the earth until that time." A prophecy that Babylon-Rome will be flattened by an earthquake is found in *Sib. Or.* 5.38–39. A very similar list of atmospheric and seismic phenomena in a context of divine punishment is found in *Sib. Or.* 3.689–92 (tr. Collins in Charlesworth, *OTP* 1: 377):

> God will judge all men by war and sword
> and fire and torrential rain. There will also
> be brimstone from heaven and stone and much
> grievous hail.

This may in turn be dependent on analogous lists like that in Isa 29:5b–6:

> And in an instant, suddenly,
> you will be visited by the Lord of hosts
> with thunder and with earthquake and great noise,
> with whirlwind and tempest, and the flame of a devouring fire. (RSV)

Another such list is found in Isa 30:30:

> And the Lord will cause his majestic voice to be heard and the descending blow of his arm to be seen, in furious anger and a flame of devouring fire, with a cloudburst and tempest and hailstones. (RSV)

The singularity and intensity of this occurrence is underlined by claiming that it is unique in the history of the world, or that an event of such magnitude had never before occurred, a *topos* that occurs in Israelite, early Jewish, Greco-Roman, and early Christian literature (Exod 9:18, 24 [for Egyptian parallels to the phrase "since the founding of Egypt," see C. Couroyer, "Un égyptianisme biblique: 'Depuis la fondation de l'Égypte' (Exode, IX,18)," *RB* 67 (1960) 42–48]; Joel 2:2; Jer 30:7; Dan 12:1; *T. Moses* 8:1 ["And there will come upon them punishment and wrath such as has never happened to them (*ira quae talis non fuit in illis*) from the creation till that time"]; 1QM 1:12; 4QD^b frag. 3 iv 1–2; 1 Macc 9:27; Jos. *J.W.* 1.12; 5.442; 6.429; Herodotus 6.109; Thucydides 1.21; Mark 13:19 = Matt 24:21 [allusion to Dan 12:1]).

19a καὶ ἐγένετο ἡ πόλις ἡ μεγάλη εἰς τρία μέρη, "The great city fell into three parts." The identification of "the great city" is problematic (see *Comment* on 11:8). A number of earlier commentators identify this city as Jerusalem (B. Weiss, *Johannes-Apokalypse;* Schlatter, *Apokalypse;* J. Weiss-Heitmüller, 301; Lohmeyer), though others understand it to be Babylon-Rome (Bousset [1906] 400; Charles, 2:52; Zahn; Behm; Hadorn, 166–67; Wikenhauser, 124). Supporting the view that the city must be Jerusalem is the fact that only in v 19c does the text say that "God remembered great Babylon," implying that the city in v 19a must be a different city. "The great city" should probably be understood as Babylon-Rome, however, for the fact that the city was split into three parts by the earthquake does not mean that it had yet been adequately punished. Further, Babylon-Rome is certainly referred to as "the great city" in Rev 17:18; 18:10(2x), 16, 18, 19, 21 (ἡ μεγαλὴ πόλις). The phrase is used once of Jerusalem (11:8), but the context here cannot refer to Jerusalem. Charles (2:52) regards this clause as an interpolation, although he does not provide adequate justification. There is evidence for historical earthquakes in Jerusalem in A.D. 30, 33, and 48, though they were all relatively slight (Amiran et al., *IEJ* 44 [1994] 260–305).

19b καὶ αἱ πόλεις τῶν ἐθνῶν ἔπεσαν, "and the cities of the nations fell." The "fall" of the cities of the nations means that they were also destroyed in the great earthquake narrated in v 18, which must therefore be understood as affecting the entire inhabited world. The term πίπτειν, "fall," is the same term used for the "fall," i.e., the destruction of Babylon, in 14:8; 18:2 (Isa 21:9; Jer 28:8). This phrase provides some support for those who regard the great city in v 19a as Jerusalem, since it is implicitly contrasted here in the phrase the "cities of the nations."

19c καὶ Βαβυλὼν ἡ μεγάλη ἐμνήσθη ἐνώπιον τοῦ θεοῦ δοῦναι αὐτῇ τὸ ποτήριον τοῦ οἴνου τοῦ θυμοῦ τῆς ὀργῆς αὐτοῦ, "God remembered to give Babylon the great the cup of wine, that is, his furious wrath." (On the title "Babylon the Great," see *Comment* on 14:8.) The verb μιμνῄσκεσθαι, "to remember," occurs only here in Revelation (though a parallel that uses the verb μνημονεύειν occurs in 18:5, "God remembered her [Babylon's] crimes"). In the OT, God is the subject of the verb זכר *zākar* more than fifty times (*TDOT* 4:69–72), and it is also a relatively common form of expression throughout ancient Near Eastern literature. The motif of remembering is also important in the context of ancient Greek prayer and votive offerings (Versnel, "Prayer," 59–60). Divine justice is often intimately linked with the motive of divine remembrance, for the ancient Israelite and early Jewish view of God is that he does not let those who do good go unrewarded, nor does he allow those who do evil go unpunished. God's "punitive remembrance," somewhat surprisingly, is mentioned with relative infrequency in the OT and early Judaism (Hos 7:2; 8:13; 9:9; Jer 14:10; Sir 49:9). In prayer, God can be asked to remember past wickedness and to punish the perpetrators (Ps 137:7; Neh 6:14; 13:29; 1 Macc 7:38; 2 Macc 8:4; see *Comment* on 6:9–11). On the redundant phrase "the fury of his wrath" or "his furious wrath," see the similar expression "the fury of his great wrath" in 4Q*375* = 4QApocryphon of Moses B 1:3.

20 Καὶ πᾶσα νῆσος ἔφυγεν καὶ ὄρη οὐχ εὑρέθησαν, "and every island fled, and the mountains disappeared." The motif of the disappearance of mountains is often connected in the OT and early Judaism with a theophany or the eschatological judgment, conceptions that tend to merge (Ps 97:5; Isa 40:4; 42:15; 45:2; 54:10; Ezek 38:20; 4 Ezra 15:42), though more frequently the seismic phenomenon of the quaking of mountains is mentioned (Pss 18:7; 46:2, 3; Isa 5:25; 64:1, 3; Sir 43:16). The use of εὑρίσκειν in the passive with a negative particle can mean "disappear" (BAGD, 324; this idiom does not appear in Louw-Nida). οὐχ εὑρέθησαν, "disappeared," is a Hebraism or Septuagintalism (LXX Isa 35:9; LXX Theod Dan 11:19; *Pss. Sol.* 14:19) that occurs a few times in the NT (2 Pet 3:10 [εὑρεθήσεται is emended to οὐχ εὑρεθήσεται by several scholars; see discussion in Bauckham, *Jude*, 316–21]; Rev 18:21).

21a καὶ χάλαζα μεγάλη ὡς ταλαντιαία καταβαίνει ἐκ τοῦ οὐρανοῦ ἐπὶ τοὺς ἀνθρώπους, "Then large hailstones weighing nearly a hundred pounds fell on people from the sky." The seventh plague in Exod 9:13–35 consisted of thunder, hail, and lightning, with "heavy hail, such as had never been in all the land of Egypt since it became a nation" (Exod 9:24 [RSV]; cf. Ps 105:32–33; Jos. *Ant.* 2.305). Hail is sometimes mentioned as a divine means of punishment: Josh 10:11 narrates the punitive miracle of huge hailstones, which the Lord "threw down" from heaven on the Amorites and killed large numbers of them (see Isa 28:17; Ezek 38:22; Hag 2:17; Job 38:22–23; Ps 78:47; *Sib. Or.* 3.691). If people are struck by such heavy objects, death appears inevitable, though that does not seem to be the result envisaged here (see *Comment* on v 21b). While hailstorms were not considered unusual in northern Mediterranean countries (Ovid *Metam.* 5.158), unusual hail was regarded by the Romans as a prodigy indicating a disruption in relations with the gods requiring diagnosis and reparation; E. S. McCartney, "Greek and Roman Weatherlore of Hail," *Classical World* 28. See *Excursus 6A: Ancient Prodigies and the Plagues of Revelation.* Diodorus Siculus (19.45.2; Wettstein, *Novum Testamentum* 2:819) reports that there was a great rainstorm in Rhodes during which "hail of incredible size" (χαλάζης ἀπίστου τὸ μέγεθος) weighing as much as one mina (= one English pound) fell, causing houses to collapse from the weight, resulting in many deaths. The addition of hail to the four lists of atmospheric and seismic disturbances in Revelation (4:5; 8:5; 11:19; 16:18–21) occurs only in the two lists in 11:19 and 16:18–21:

Rev 11:19c:	καὶ ἐγένοντο ἀστραπαὶ καὶ φωναὶ καὶ βρονταὶ καὶ σεισμὸς καὶ χάλαζα μεγάλη, "and there was lightning and rumbling and thunder and an earthquake *and great hail.*"
Rev 16:18–21:	καὶ ἐγένοντο ἀστραπαὶ καὶ φωναὶ καὶ βρονταὶ καὶ σεισμὸς ἐγένετο μέγας . . . καὶ χάλαζα μεγάλη, "Then there was lightning and rumblings and thunder and there was a great earthquake . . . *and great hail.*"

21b καὶ ἐβλασφήμησαν οἱ ἄνθρωποι τὸν θεὸν ἐκ τῆς πληγῆς τῆς χαλάζης, ὅτι μεγάλη ἐστὶν ἡ πληγὴ αὐτῆς σφόδρα, "so that people reviled God as the result of the plague of hail, because that plague was so terrible." This is a repetition in slightly varied language of the human response to the fourth plague in v 9 and the fifth plague in v 11. It is clear that the phrase τὸ ὄνομα τοῦ θεοῦ in v 9 is equivalent to ὁ θέος here in v 21. Since such an unusual occurrence as the falling of gigantic hailstones would be regarded by ancients as a prodigy (i.e., a symbolic revelation) of the anger of the gods (see *Comment* on v 21a), it is remarkable that their response is so negative.

Explanation

The narrative of the seven bowl plagues in 15:1–16:21 is the last of the three series of seven plagues in Revelation, though unlike the seven seals and the seven trumpets (each of which inserts what appear to be digressions between the sixth and seventh plagues), the seven bowl plagues are narrated sequentially in 16:2–21 without any interruption. The opening statement in v 1 in which the author reports sighting "another sign" in heaven (cf. 12:1, 3), perhaps a constellation, which consists of seven angels with the seven last plagues, serves as a title or introduction to 15:2–16:21.

The next textual unit (vv 2–8) is a heavenly throne-room scene that serves to introduce the narrative of seven bowl plagues, just as previous throne-room scenes were placed before the narratives of the seven seals (4:1–5:14) and the seven trumpets (8:2–5), indicating the divine origin of these eschatological punishments. While neither the presence of the throne nor the presence of God is directly mentioned, the hymn of descriptive praise in vv 3–4 is sung to God by the heavenly company of martyrs who had not worshiped the beast. Although this hymn is called the song of Moses the servant of God and the song of the Lamb, it bears no close resemblance to the two biblical songs attributed to Moses in Exod 15:1–18 and Exod 32:1–43.

After this, John saw the seven angels emerge from the heavenly tabernacle (the heavenly model for the portable sanctuary used by Israel before the building of Solomon's temple; see Exod 25–27; Heb 8:2–5). They are given seven bowls or cups filled with the wrath of God (v 7), a judgment metaphor from the OT (Isa. 51:17–23).

The seven bowl plagues are enumerated in Rev 16:2–21: (1) The plague of sores or boils (v 2; the sixth plague of Exod 9:9) affects those who had received the brand of the beast and worshiped its image (continuing these motifs first mentioned in 13:15–16 and reiterated in 14:9–11). (2) The sea becomes blood, killing all sea creatures (v 3), parallel to the effects of the second trumpet plague in 8:8–9 and reminiscent of the first plague of Exod 7:20–21. (3) The rivers and wells become blood (v 4), also reminiscent of the first plague of Exod 7:20–21. This bowl plague is accompanied by a "judgment doxology" sung by a mysterious angel of the water, emphasizing the justice of God in avenging the death of his prophets and saints (vv 5–7). (4) The sun scorches people (vv 8–9; partially resembles the fire from heaven of the seventh plague of Exod 9:22–24). (5) The throne of the beast (already mentioned in 13:2) and its kingdom are covered with darkness (v 10), reminiscent of the ninth plague of Exod 10:21. (6) The Euphrates dries up (an unheard of and therefore miraculous event, probably modeled on the Exodus story) to make possible an invasion by the kings of the east (v 12), perhaps an allusion to the Parthian menace. The unholy trinity of the dragon, the beast, and the false prophet is identified as the cause of this rebellion against God (vv 13–14). This plague is similar to the sixth trumpet plague (9:13–21), where the release of the angels bound at the Euphrates made it possible for an enormous army (see 17:14; 19:19–21) to kill one-third of the human race. (7) The seventh bowl (16:17–21) causes the destruction of "the great city" (v 19), i.e., Babylon-Rome. This unit of text concludes the narrative of the seven bowl plagues and also serves to introduce the extensive section on the fall of Babylon (17:1–19:10).

The pouring out of the seventh bowl represents the climax to which the three heptads of seals, trumpets, and libation bowls have been leading, the last of the plagues sent by God to afflict humanity (15:1). For with the pouring out of the seventh bowl, God himself (identified as "a voice from the throne") proclaims "It is done!" (16:17). As part of this final plague "God remembered great Babylon" (v 19), which suggests that the punishment of Babylon treated in 17:1–19:10 must be included as an aftereffect of the seventh plague. The author has used a transitional passage in 16:7–20, linking the series of seven bowls to the imminent destruction of Babylon.